DIRECTORY OF FOREIGN FIRMS OPERATING IN THE UNITED STATES

9th Edition

Edited by Uniworld Business Publications, Inc.

Uniworld Business Publications, Inc.
257 Central Park West
New York, NY 10024
Tel: (212)496-2448 Fax: (212)769-0413
www.uniworldbp.com
uniworldbp@aol.com

First Edition	1969
Second Edition	1972
Third Edition	1975
Fourth Edition	1978
Fifth Edition	1986
Sixth Edition	1989
Seventh Edition	1992
Eighth Edition	1995
Ninth Edition	1998

Copyright © 1998 by
Uniworld Business Publications, Inc.

Published by
Uniworld Business Publications, Inc.
257 Central Park West
New York. NY 10024

ISBN: 0-8360-0042-0

Library of Congress Catalog Card Number: 85-051906

Printed in the United States of America

Table Of Contents

PART ONE
FOREIGN FIRMS OPERATING IN THE UNITED STATES   1
(Grouped by Country)

(continued)

PART TWO

PART THREE

PART FOUR

Introduction

This is the 9th Edition of **DIRECTORY OF FOREIGN FIRMS OPERATING IN THE UNITED STATES.** First published in 1969, it has been an authoritative and valuable source of information for corporations, agencies, organizations, institutions, and individuals involved in many forms of international commerce or investment. The current edition contains over 2,000 foreign firms in 69 countries and more than 4,000 businesses in the US which they own, wholly, or in part. Only the American headquarters and selected locations of each branch, subsidiary or affiliate are listed.

The 1980's brought intense foreign investment and acquisition activity to the United States. It grew dramatically in 1983 and reached a peak in 1989 with $69 billion annual foreign capital inflow. There followed a period of significant annual decrease to a low of $11.5 billion in 1992. However, the annual inflow accelerated, nearly doubling in 1993 to $22.5 billion, and doubling again in 1994 to $47 billion. For the two years since our 8th Edition, direct foreign investment has surged to $69.4 billion in 1995, and set an all time high of $78.8 billion in 1996, as reported by the Bureau of Economics Analysis of the US Department of Commerce. Cumulative foreign direct investment in the United States had exceeded $496 billion by the end of 1994; and, based on the Bureau's revised 1996 data had reached $630 billion by year end 1996. By comparison, the total US cumulative direct investment abroad reached $796.5 billion in 1996.

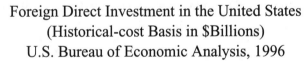

Foreign Direct Investment in the United States
(Historical-cost Basis in $Billions)
U.S. Bureau of Economic Analysis, 1996

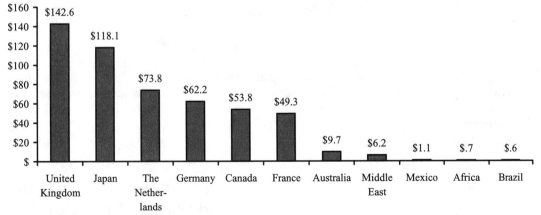

SOURCE AND ACCURACY OF LISTINGS

Firms in the 8th Edition were sent a print-out of their listing which they were asked to update. It was stated that if we did not receive a response, and there was no evidence that the firm had gone out of business, the previous entry would be carried forward to this edition. The primary sources of information for all entries were questionnaires mailed to the corporations and/or annual reports provided by them. Direct telephone and telefax contact were used extensively for verification and clarification. Overseas companies in the 8th Edition which no longer have a US subsidiary were deleted, as were US firms whose ownership by foreign firms had ceased; also many new listings were added.

The aim of this Directory is to provide accurate, up-to-date listings, but the Editor and Publisher cannot guarantee that the information received from a company or other source is correct. Also, as extensive as this Directory may be, it does not claim to be all-inclusive. It contains only what has been disclosed to us. In addition, the designations and listings are not to be considered definitive as to legal status or the relationship between the foreign and American firms. Some US companies included here are technically owned by other US companies which, in turn, are owned by non-US firms. "Foreign-owned," therefore, refers to the ultimate owner. Also, no assumptions should be made if the percentage of ownership is not specified. Neither the direct nor indirect nature of ownership nor the degree of participation is of primary importance to the purpose of this directory.

In a compilation of this scope inaccuracies are inevitable. It would be appreciated if the reader would inform the Publisher of inaccuracies so corrections can be made in the next edition.

ACKNOWLEDGMENTS

We thank, most sincerely, the many company representatives who cooperated generously in providing information for this directory, and those who assisted in its preparation; Associate Editor Lynn Sherwood, Associate Publisher Debra Lipian, Computer Consultant David Bornstein, Assistant Research Editor Uri Toch, and research interns, Joshua Shimkin and Gabriella Bass.

Barbara D. Fiorito, Editor
Uniworld Business Publications, Inc.

Key to Abbreviations

The following abbreviations have been used in the Directory

A/C	Air Conditioning	Equip	Equipment
Access	Accessories	Exch	Exchange
Adv	Advertising	Exec	Executive
Affil	Affiliate(d)	Exp	Export(er)
Agcy	Agent/Agency	Explor	Exploration
Agric	Agriculture	Fax	Facsimile
Arch	Architect(ural)	Fin	Financial/Finance
Assur	Assurance	Fl	Floor
Auto	Automotive	For	Foreign
Aux	Auxiliary	Furn	Furniture
Bldg	Building	Fwdg	Forwarding
Bus	Business	Gds	Goods
CEO	Chief Executive Officer	Gen	General
COO	Chief Operating Officer	Gov	Governor
Chem	Chemical	Hdwe	Hardware
Chrm	Chairman	Hos	Hospital
Cir	Circulation	Hydr	Hydraulic(s)
Com	Components	Imp	Import(er)
Coml	Commercial	Ind	Industrial/Industry
Commun	Communications	Inf	Information
Conslt	Consultant/Consulting	Ins	Insurance
Constr	Construction	Inspec	Inspect(ion)
Cont	Controller	Instru	Instrument
Cor	Corporate	Intl	International
Cust	Customer	Invest	Investment
Dept.	Department	JV	Joint Venture
Devel	Development	Lab	Laboratory
Diag	Diagnostic	Liq	Liquid
Dir	Director	Mach	Machine(ry)
Dist	District	Maint	Maintenance
Distr	Distributor/Distribution	Mat	Material
Divers	Diversified	Mdse	Merchandise
Dom	Domestic	Mdsng	Merchandising
Econ	Economist	Meas	Measurement
Educ	Education(al)	Med	Medical
Elec	Electrical	Mfg	Manufacturing
Electr	Electronic	Mfr.	Manufacture(r)
Emp	Employee(s)	Mgmt	Management
Engr	Engineer(ing)	Mng	Managing
Envi	Environmental	Mgr	Manager

(continued)

Mkt	Market	Rel	Relations
N/A	Not Available	Rep	Representative
Nat	Natural	Ret	Retail(er)
Oper	Operation	Rfg	Refining
Orgn	Organization(al)	Ry	Railway
Pass	Passenger	Sci	Scientific
Petrol	Petroleum	Serv	Service
Pharm	Pharmaceutical	Spec	Special(ty)/Specialized
Plt	Plant	Sta	Station
Prdt	Product(s)	Subs	Subsidiary
Pres	President	Super	Supervision
Prin	Principal	Svce	Service(s)
Print	Printing	Sys	System
Proc	Process(ing)	TV	Television
Prod	Production	Tech	Technical/Technology
Prog	Programming	Tel	Telephone
Ptnr	Partner	Telecom	Telecommunications
Ptrn	Partner	Temp	Temperature
Pub	Publishing	Tlx	Telex
Pubi	Publisher	Trans	Transmission
R&D	Research & Development	Transp	Transport(ation)
Recre	Recreation(al)	VP	Vice President
Refrig	Refrigeration	Whl	Wholesale(r)
Reins	Reinsurance	Whse	Warehouse

Notes on Alphabetizing

Alphabetizing in this directory is by computer sort which places numerals before letters; and among names, places blanks, hyphens and ampersands before letters. Thus, 3D Co. precedes A Z Co., which precedes A-Z Co., which precedes A&Z Co., which precedes Abiz Co.

Names such as The Jones Corp., Charles Jones Inc., and L. M. Jones & Co. are alphabetized conventionally: all will be found under J.

Names which consist of initials only (e.g., LFM Co.) are in strict alphabetical order: Lewis Corp., LFM Co., Lintz Inc.

While the custom in most countries is to place company designations (Co., Inc., etc.) at the end of the firm's name, that is not always the case. For example, Finland's "Oy" and Sweden's "AB" sometimes appear at the end and sometimes at the beginning of the company's name; in this directory they have been disregarded in alphabetizing. The reader is advised to check more than one location when looking for a firm whose listing might be affected by the company designation.

Company Designations

Abbreviation	Term	Country
AB	Aktiebolag	Sweden
AG	Aktiengesellschaft	Austria, Germany, Switzerland
AS	Anonim Sirketi	Turkey
A/S	Aktieselskab	Denmark
	Aksjeselskap	Norway
BV	Beslotene Vennootschap	Netherlands
CA	Compania Anonima	Venezuela
CIE	Compagnie	Belgium, France
CO	Company	Canada, England, U.S.
CORP	Corporation	England, U.S.
GMBH	Gesellschaft mit beschrankter Haftung	Austria, Germany
INC	Incorporated	Canada, England, U.S.
KG	Kommanditgesellschaft	Germany
KK	Kabushiki Kaisha	Japan
LTD	Limited	Canada, England, U.S.
MIJ	Maatschappij	Netherlands
NV	Naamloze Vennoostchap	Belgium, Netherlands
OY	Osakeyhtio	Finland
P/L	Proprietary Limited	Australia
PLC	Public Limited Company	England, Scotland
PT	Perusahaan Terbatas	Indonesia
SA	Sociedad Anonima	Argentina, Brazil, Colombia Spain, Venezuela
	Societe Anonyme	Belgium, France, Switzerland
SPA, SpA	Societa per Azioni	Italy
SPRL	Societe de Personnes a Responsabilite Limitee	Belgium
SRL	Societa a Responsabilita Limitata	Italy

FOREIGN FIRMS OPERATING IN THE UNITED STATES

(Grouped by country)

Part One groups foreign firms by country. Within each country, the foreign firms are listed alphabetically noted by a bullet. Indented are the American firm(s) owned by or affiliated with the foreign firm.

Argentina

- **AEROLINEAS ARGENTINAS**
Torre Bouchard 547, 1106 Buenos Aires, Argentina
CEO: Manuel Moran, Pres.   Tel: 54-1-317-3000   Emp: N/A
Bus: *Commercial air transport services.*   Fax:54-1-317 3581

> **AEROLINEAS ARGENTINAS**
> 630 Fifth Avenue, Suite 1661, New York, NY   10111
> CEO: Arturo Muzzio, Mgr.   Tel: (212) 698-2077   Emp: 15
> Bus: *International commercial air transport*   Fax:(212) 698-2067   %FO: 100
> *services.*

> **AEROLINEAS ARGENTINAS**
> 6100 Blue Lagoon Drive, #210, Miami, FL   33126
> CEO: Marcelo Moscheni, Reg. Mgr.   Tel: (305) 261-0100   Emp: 35
> Bus: *International commercial air transport*   Fax:(305) 264-9116   %FO: 100
> *services.*

- **ALLENDE & BREA**
Maipú 1300, 10th Fl, 1006 Buenos Aires, Argentina
CEO: Enrique Garrido, Mng. Ptnr.   Tel: 54-1-313-9191   Emp: 100
Bus: *International law firm.*   Fax:54-1-313-9010

> **ALLENDE & BREA**
> 10 Rockefeller Plaza, Ste. 1001, New York, NY   10020
> CEO: C. Alsaro, Mng. Ptnr.   Tel: (212) 698-2230   Emp: N/A
> Bus: *International law firm.*   Fax:(212) 489-7317   %FO: 100

- **BANCO DE GALICIA Y BUENOS AIRES**
General Juan D. Peron 407, 2 Piso, 1038 Buenos Aires, Argentina
CEO: E. Escasany, Pres. & CEO   Tel: 54-1-329-6000   Emp: N/A
Bus: *General banking services.*   Fax:54-1-329-6313

> **BANCO DE GALICIA Y BUENOS AIRES**
> 300 Park Avenue, 20th Fl., New York, NY   10022
> CEO: Hector E. Arzeno, SVP   Tel: (212) 906-3700   Emp: N/A
> Bus: *General banking services.*   Fax:(212) 906-3777   %FO: 100

• BANCO DE LA NACION ARGENTINA
Bartolmoe Mitre 326, 1036 Buenos Aires, Argentina
CEO: Roque Maccarone, Pres.   Tel: 54-1-347-6000   Emp: 400
Bus: *Commercial banking services.*   Fax:54-1-347-8097

BANCO DE LA NACION ARGENTINA
777 Brickell Avenue, Miami, FL   33131
CEO: Arturo Almada   Tel: (305) 371-7500   Emp: N/A
Bus: *Commercial banking services.*   Fax:(305) 374-7805   %FO: 100

BANCO DE LA NACION ARGENTINA
299 Park Avenue - 2nd Fl., New York, NY   10171
CEO: Jorge del Rio, SVP   Tel: (212) 303-0600   Emp: N/A
Bus: *Commercial banking services.*   Fax:(212)303-0805   %FO: 100

• BANCO DE LA PROVINCIA DE BUENOS AIRES
San Martin 137, Buenos Aires, Argentina
CEO: Ernesto Bruggia, Asst. Gen .Mgr.   Tel: 54-1-331-4011   Emp: 13730
Bus: *General banking services.*   Fax:54-1-331-8375

BANCO DE LA PROVINCIA DE BUENOS AIRES
609 Fifth Avenue, 3rd Fl., New York, NY   10017
CEO: Regulo Riviera, VP   Tel: (212) 292-5400   Emp: 37
Bus: *Commercial & investment banking, trade*   Fax:(212) 688-6827   %FO: 100
     finance.

• BANCO FRANCÉS DEL RÍO DE LA PLANTA SA
Reconquista 199, P.O. Box 3196, 1003 Buenos Aires, Argentina
CEO: Luis Roque Otero Monsegur, Chrm.   Tel: 54-1-346-4000   Emp: N/A
Bus: *General commercial banking services.*   Fax:54-1-346-4320

BANCO FRANCÉS
660 Madison Avenue, New York, NY   10022
CEO: Carolos Bianchetti, SVP   Tel: (212) 371-0111   Emp: N/A
Bus: *International commercial banking services.*   Fax:(212) 371-0922   %FO: 100

• BANCO RIO DE LA PLATA SA
Bartolome Mitre 480, Buenos Aires 1036, Argentina
CEO: Marcelo Pestarino, Gen.Mgr.   Tel: 54-1-340-1000   Emp: 2500
Bus: *International banking services.*   Fax:54-1-331-9833

BANCO RIO DE LA PLATA SA
650 Fifth Ave., 29th Fl., New York, NY   10019
CEO: Thomas J. Charters, Mgr.   Tel: (212) 974-6800   Emp: 25
Bus: *International banking services.*   Fax:(212) 974-6828   %FO: 100

● **BANCO ROBERTS**
25 de Mayo 258, 1002 Buenos Aires,Argentina

CEO: Jorge A. Heinze, Chrm.	Tel: 54-1-331-0061 Emp: N/A
Bus: *Commercial banking services.*	Fax:54-1-331-3960

>   **BANCO ROBERTS**
>   156 West 56th Street, New York, NY   10019

CEO: Gabriel Castelli, Fin. & Intl.	Tel: (212) 974-1188 Emp: 15
Bus: *Commercial banking services.*	Fax:(212) 586-7581 %FO: 100

● **INDUSTRIAS METALURGICAS PESCARMONA SAIC y F**
Carril Rodriguez Pena 2451Godoy Cruz 5503, Argentina

CEO: Enrique M. Pescarmona, Pres.	Tel: 54-61-316127 Emp: 1100
Bus: *Mfr. turbines, generators, gates & valves, cranes, pressure vessels.*	Fax:54-61-316124

>   **IMPSA INTERNATIONAL INC.**
>   Manor Oak II, #536, 1910 Cochran Rd., Pittsburgh, PA   15220

CEO: Gerald L. Katz, Pres.	Tel: (412) 344-7003 Emp: 10
Bus: *Sales/purchasing/service turbines, generators, gates & valves, cranes, pressure vessels.*	Fax:(412) 344-7009 %FO: 100

● **YPF SOCIEDAD ANÓNIMA**
Avenida Presidente Roque Sáenz Peña 777, Piso 8, 1364 Buenos Aires, Argentina

CEO: Nells León, Pres.	Tel: 54-1-329-2126 Emp: 9350
Bus: *Integrated oil & gas company.*	Fax:54-1-329-2113

>   **YPF- USA INC.**
>   5 Greenway Plaza, Suite 250, Houston, TX   77046

CEO: Mateo Juan, VP	Tel: (713) 977-4481 Emp: N/A
Bus: *Integrated oil & gas company.*	Fax:(713) 621-4803 %FO: 100

Australia

- **ACSIS NURSING MANAGEMENT SERVICES**
161 Walker Street, North Sydney, NSW 2060, Australia
CEO: Tessa Qua, Mgr.   Tel: 6129-956-7533   Emp: N/A
Bus: *Employment agencies and management services.*   Fax:6129-956-7833

   NURSING MANAGEMENT SERVICES, INC.
   3423 Piedmont Road, Ste. 500, Atlanta, GA   30305
   CEO: Efrom Barsam, Pres.   Tel: (770) 956-0500   Emp: N/A
   Bus: *Employment agencies.*   Fax:(770) 956-1894   %FO: 100

- **AMCOR LTD.**
Southgate Tower East, 40 City Road, South Melbourne, VIC 3205 Australia
CEO: Don MacFarlane, Dir.   Tel: 61-3-9694-9000   Emp: N/A
Bus: *Mfr./sales paper and wood products, packaging.*   Fax:61-3-9686-2924

   McKINLEY PAPER COMPANY
   10501 Montgomery, NE, Ste.300, Albuquerque, NM   87111
   CEO: Anthony P. Joyce, VP   Tel: (505) 271-7500   Emp: N/A
   Bus: *Mfr./sale paper and wood pulp, packaging*   Fax:(505) 271-7510   %FO: 100
   products.

- **AUSTRALIA & NEW ZEALAND BANKING GROUP LTD.**
55 Collins Street, Melbourne, VIC 3000, Australia
CEO: Don Mercer, Pres.   Tel: 61-3-9273-555   Emp: N/A
Bus: *International banking services.*   Fax:61-3-9273-4909

   AUSTRALIA & NEW ZEALAND BANKING GROUP LTD.
   1177 Avenue of the Americas, 6th Fl., New York, NY   10036
   CEO: Roy Marsden, Pres.   Tel: (212) 801-9800   Emp: N/A
   Bus: *International banking services.*   Fax:(212) 801-9859   %FO: 100

- **AUSTRALIAN BROADCASTING CORP.**
700 Harris Street, Ultimo, NSW 2007, Australia
CEO: Brian Johns, Dir.   Tel: 61-2-9339-1500   Emp: 4000+
Bus: *TV & radio broadcasting.*   Fax:61-2-9333-5305

   AUSTRALIAN BROADCASTING CORP.
   630 Fifth Avenue, #2260, New York, NY   10111
   CEO: Maggie M. Jones, Mgr.   Tel: (212) 332-2540   Emp: N/A
   Bus: *TV & radio broadcasting*   Fax:(212) 332-2546   %FO: 100

- **AUSTRALIAN CONSOLIDATED PRESS**
  54 Park Street, Sydney, NSW 2000, Australia
  CEO: Kerry Packer, Chrm.   Tel: 61-2-9282-8000   Emp: N/A
  Bus: *Magazine publishing; sports & leisure facilities.*   Fax:61-2-9267-2111

    AUSTRALIAN CONSOLIDATED PRESS LTD.
    110 Green Street, #803, New York, NY   10012
    CEO: Lesa Tinker, Bureau Chief   Tel: (212) 966-5300   Emp: N/A
    Bus: *Newsgathering services.*   Fax:(212) 966-1118   %FO: 100

- **AUSTRALIAN MEAT & LIVESTOCK CORP.**
  Box 4129, GPO, Sydney, NSW 2001, Australia
  CEO: Dr. Bruce Standen, Dir.   Tel: 61-2-9267-6620   Emp: N/A
  Bus: *Processing/distribution meat products.*   Fax:61-2-9260-3111

    AUSTRALIAN MEAT & LIVESTOCK CORP
    750 Lexington Ave., 17th fl, New York, NY   10022
    CEO: Frances Cassidy, CEO   Tel: (212) 486-2405   Emp: N/A
    Bus: *Processing/distribution meat products.*   Fax:(212) 355-1471   %FO: 100

- **AUTOMOTIVE COMPONENTS LTD.**
  Level 8 St. Kilda Road, Melbourne, Victoria 3004, Australia
  CEO: Ivan D. James, Pres.   Tel: 61-3-9285-4000   Emp: 1250
  Bus: *Mfr. engine bearings, gaskets.*   Fax:61-3-9866-4300

    ACL AUTOMOTIVE AMERICA INC
    2488 Tuckerstone Pkwy, Tucker, GA   30084
    CEO: Tim Vehlenwald, Pres.   Tel: (770) 491-3935   Emp: 30
    Bus: *Distribution engine bearings & gaskets.*   Fax:(770) 939-8249   %FO: 100

- **BORAL LIMITED**
  Level 39, 50 Bridge Street, GPO Box 910, Sydney, NSW 2001, Australia
  CEO: Anthony R. Berg, Mng. Dir.   Tel: 61-2-232-6300   Emp: N/A
  Bus: *Mfr./distributor building & construction materials*   Fax:61-2-233-6605
  (bricks, timber, tiles); and energy
  marketing/exploration.

    BORAL INDUSTRIES, INC.
    2859 Paces Ferry Road, Suite 1520, Atlanta, GA   30339
    CEO: Timothy C. Tuff, Pres & CEO   Tel: (770) 801-8700   Emp: N/A
    Bus: *Mfr./distributor building & construction*   Fax:(770) 801-9922   %FO: 100
    materials.

● **THE BROKEN HILL PROPRIETARY CO LTD.**
BHP Tower, Bourke Place, 600 Bourke Street, - 40th Fl., Melbourne, VIC 3000, Australia
CEO: John B. Prescott, Mng. .Dir.   Tel: 61-3-9609-3333   Emp: 60000
Bus: *Petroleum, steel, minerals.*   Fax:61-3-9609-3575

BHP BUILDING PRODUCTS (USA)
2110 Enterprise Boulevard, West Sacramento, CA   95691-3491
CEO: Jeffrey Friedman, Gen.Mgr.   Tel: (916) 372-0933   Emp: N/A
Bus: *Mfr. steel building materials, pipeline systems*   Fax:(916) 372-5442   %FO: 100
   for energy production industry, etc.

BHP COATED STEEL CORP.
222 West Kalama River Road, Kalama, WA   98625
CEO: Richard Weshsler, Pres.   Tel: (360) 673-8200   Emp: N/A
Bus: *Steel production.*   Fax:(360) 673-8250   %FO: 100

BHP COPPER
550 California Street, San Francisco, CA   94104
CEO: J.E.Lewis, EVP/Gen.Mgr.   Tel: (415) 981-1515   Emp: N/A
Bus: *Copper mining & processing.*   Fax:(415) 774-2026   %FO: 100

BHP ENGINEERING AMERICAS INC.
Suite 500, 4 Oak Pl., 1360 Post Oak Blvd., Houston, TX   77056-3020
CEO: Warwick Aldham, Tech. Mgr.   Tel: (713) 961-8534   Emp: N/A
Bus: *Engineering, project management, and systems*   Fax:(713) 961-8557   %FO: 100
   consulting services.

BHP HOLDINGS NORTH AMERICA INC.
550 California Street, San Francisco, CA   94104
CEO: J. Riemersma, VP/Gen.Mgr.   Tel: (415) 774-2030   Emp: N/A
Bus: *Holding company North America: minerals,*   Fax:(415) 981-4746   %FO: 100
   petroleum, steel fabricating.

BHP INSURANCE
550 California Street, San Francisco, CA   94104
CEO: Stephen M. Honeychurch, Mgr.   Tel: (415) 981-1515   Emp: N/A
Bus: *Risk management and insurance consulting*   Fax:(415) 774-2010   %FO: 100
   services.

BHP PETROLEUM (AMERICA) INC.
BHP Tower, 1360 Post Oak Blvd., Ste 500, Houston, TX   77056-3020
CEO: E.A. Blair, Pres.   Tel: (713) 961-8500   Emp: N/A
Bus: *Exploration & production, oil & gas.*   Fax:(713) 961-8400   %FO: 100

BHP STEEL BUILDING PRODUCTS
2141 Milwaukee Way, Tacoma, WA   98421
CEO: Jeff Friedman, Pres.   Tel: (206) 383-4955   Emp: 80
Bus: *Mfr./distributor steel products.*   Fax:(206) 272-0791   %FO: 100

BHP WORLD MINERALS
550 California Street, San Francisco, CA 94104

CEO: T.R. Winterer, EVP & Gen.Mgr.   Tel: (415) 981-1515   Emp: N/A

Bus: *Minerals/mining: steam coal mines. U.S.*   Fax:(415) 774-2090   %FO: 100
operations; AZ, CO, UT, VA, WI.

BHP HAWAII
733 Bishop Street, Honolulu, HI 96813

CEO: H.G.M.Neal, Pres.& Gen.Mgr.   Tel: (808) 547-3111   Emp: N/A

Bus: *Petroleum refining & retailing services.*   Fax:(808) 547-3145   %FO: 100

THE BROKEN HILL PROPRIETARY CO. LTD
1155 Connecticut Avenue, Ste. 1120, Washington, DC 20036

CEO: R.T.Collins, VP & Sr.Rep.   Tel: (202) 463-1514   Emp: N/A

Bus: *Holding company: minerals, petroleum, steel*   Fax:(202) 463-8557   %FO: 100
fabricating.

● **CASINOS AUSTRIA INTERNATIONAL LTD.**
Level 31, Waterford Place, One Eagle Street, Brisbane 4000 QLD, Australia

CEO: Alexander Tucek, Pres.   Tel: 61-7-3370-3100   Emp: 1250

Bus: *Casino operations.*   Fax:61-7-3370-3111

CASINOS AUSTRIA MARITIME
4651 Sheridan Street, Suite 303, Hollywood, FL 33021

CEO: Alexander Tucek, Pres.   Tel: (954) 964-4131   Emp: 60

Bus: *Casino operations.*   Fax:(954) 964-4246   %FO: 100

● **COMMONWEALTH BANKING CORP**
Level 6, 48 Martin Place, Box 2719 GPO, Sydney, NSW 2001, Australia

CEO: D.V. Murray, Mng. Dir.   Tel: 61-2-227-7111   Emp: N/A

Bus: *General banking, investment and life insurance*   Fax:61-2-227-3650
services.

COMMONWEALTH BANK OF AUSTRALIA
599 Lexington Avenue, 17th Fl., New York, NY 10022

CEO: Ian Phillips, EVP   Tel: (212) 848-9200   Emp: N/A

Bus: *International banking services.*   Fax:(212) 336-7725   %FO: 100

● **CSR LIMITED**
Level 24, One O'Connell Street, Sydney, NSW 2000, Australia

CEO: G.V. Kells, Mng. Dir.   Tel: 61-2-9235-8000   Emp: N/A

Bus: *Mfr./distribution building and construction*   Fax:61-2-9235-8044
materials; real estate and sugar industry
investments.

BEADEX MANUFACTURING CO., LTD.
401 C Street, NW, Auburn, WA 98001

CEO: Jim Richie, Pres.   Tel: (253) 931-6600   Emp: N/A

Bus: *Mfr. building & construction materials.*   Fax:(253) 931-0601   %FO: 100

CSR AMERICA INC.
Resurgens Plaza, 945 East Paces Ferry Road, Suite 2110, Atlanta, GA 30326
CEO: David Clarke | Tel: (404) 237-8811 | Emp: N/A
Bus: *Building & construction materials.* | Fax:(404) 237-9237 | %FO: 100

CSR INC,
7150 Pollock Drive, Las Vegas, NV 89119
CEO: Ennis B. Jordan, Pres. | Tel: (702) 260-9900 | Emp: N/A
Bus: *Building materials, holding company.* | Fax:(702) 260-9903 | %FO: 100

CSR RINKER INC.
1501 Belvedere Road, West Palm Beach, FL 33406
CEO: Willaim Snyder | Tel: (407) 833-5555 | Emp: N/A
Bus: *Build & Construction materials company.* | Fax:(407) 655-6876 | %FO: 100

HYDRO CONDUIT CORP.
16701 Greenpoint Park Drive, Suite 350, Houston, TX 07060
CEO: Adrian Driver, Pres, | Tel: (281) 872-3500 | Emp: N/A
Bus: *Mfr. building & construction materials.* | Fax:(281) 872-5709 | %FO: 100

● JOHN FAIRFAX LTD.
201 Sussex Street, Box 506, GPO, Sydney, NSW 2000, Australia
CEO: Bob Muscat, Pres. | Tel: 61-2-9282-2822 | Emp: 3000
Bus: *Publishing.* | Fax:61-2-9282-1640

JOHN FAIRFAX (US) LTD
1500 Broadway, New York, NY 10036
CEO: Jean Shelley, Pres. | Tel: (212) 398-9494 | Emp: 5
Bus: *Newspapers, magazines.* | Fax:(212) 819-1745 | %FO: 100

● GOODMAN FIELDER, LTD.
45-47 Green Street, Botney, NSW 2019, Australia
CEO: Barry Weir, CEO | Tel: 61-2-9384-5135 | Emp: 24000
Bus: *Baking, milling, consumer foods, poultry, special ingredients.* | Fax:61-2-9384-5153

GERMANTOWN INTERNATIONAL LTD.
505 Parkway, Broomall, PA 19008
CEO: Barry Weir, Pres. | Tel: (610) 544-8400 | Emp: 65
Bus: *Mfr. food stabilizers and emulsifiers.* | Fax:(610) 544-4490 | %FO: 100

● **LEINER DAVIS GELATIN**
15 Holt Road, Taren Point, New South Wales 2229, Australia
CEO: Ian Glasson, Mng. Dir.   Tel: 61-2-9384-5175   Emp: N/A
Bus: *Mfr. gelatin.*   Fax:61-2-9384-5151

   DYNAGEL, INC.
   Plummer Street & Wentworth Avenue, Calumet City, IL   60409
   CEO: George Riesenfeld, Pres.   Tel: (708) 891-8400   Emp: N/A
   Bus: *Mfr. gelatin. (JV with Deutsche Gelatine*   Fax:(708) 891-8432   %FO: JV
      FabrikenStoess AG, Germany)

● **JOHN LYSAGHT (AUSTRALIA) LTD.**
50 Young Street, Sydney, NSW 2001, Australia
CEO: Ron McNeilly, CEO   Tel: 61-2-3609-3333   Emp: N/A
Bus: *Manufacturer of steel products.*   Fax:N/A

   PHB BUILDING PRODUCTS, INC.
   2141 Milwaukee Way, Tacoma, WA   98401
   CEO: Steve Staulding, Mgr.   Tel: (206) 383-4955   Emp: N/A
   Bus: *Plant; steel products.*   Fax:(206) 272-0791   %FO: 100

   PHB BUILDING PRODUCTS, INC.
   2110 Enterprise Blvd., Sacramento, CA   95691
   CEO: Jeff Friedman, Pres.   Tel: (916) 372-0933   Emp: N/A
   Bus: *Distribution/sales steel products.*   Fax:(916) 372-5442   %FO: 100

● **NATIONAL AUSTRALIA BANK LIMITED**
500 Bourke Street, GPO Box 84A, Melbourne, Victoria, 3001, Australia
CEO: R. Prowse, Chrm.   Tel: 61-3-9641-3500   Emp: N/A
Bus: *International banking, investment and insurance*   Fax:61-3-9641-4916
  services.

   NATIONAL AUSTRALIA BANK LTD.
   200 Park Avenue, 34th Fl., New York, NY   10166
   CEO: Geoff Cullen, EVP   Tel: (212) 916-9500   Emp: N/A
   Bus: *International banking, investment and*   Fax:(212) 983-1969   %FO: 100
      insurance services.

● **THE NEWS CORP LTD.**
2 Holt Street, Sydney, NSW 2010, Australia
CEO: K. Rupert Murdoch, CEO   Tel: 61-2-288-3000   Emp: 27250
Bus: *Publishing, broadcasting, filmed entertainment.*   Fax:61-2-228-3292

   FOX BROADCASTING COMPANY
   10201 West Pico Blvd., Los Angeles, CA   90035
   CEO: Peter Chernin, Chrm.   Tel: (213) 277-2211   Emp: N/A
   Bus: *Program services.*   Fax:(213) 203-2735   %FO: 100

FOX TELEVISION STATIONS INC.
10201 West Pico Blvd., Los Angeles, CA   90035
CEO: Chase Carey, Chrm.   Tel: (213) 277-2211   Emp: N/A
Bus: *Owns & operates TV stations.*   Fax:(213) 203-2735   %FO: 100

HARPER COLLINS PUBLISHING COMPANY
10 East 53rd Street, New York, NY   10022
CEO: Anthea Disney, Pres.   Tel: (212) 207-7000   Emp: 3200
Bus: *Publishing.*   Fax:(212) 207-7552   %FO: 100

KESMAI CORP.
230 Court Square, Charlotteville, VA   22902
CEO: John Taylor, Pres.   Tel: (804) 963-8500   Emp: N/A
Bus: *Design/mfr./sale multi-player on-line software,* Fax:(804) 963-8801   %FO: 100
   games.

NEWS AMERICA PUBLISHING INC.
1211 Ave. of the Americas, New York, NY   10036
CEO: K. Rupert Murdoch, Chrm.   Tel: (212) 852-7000   Emp: N/A
Bus: *Newspaper & magazine publishing. (The New*   Fax:(212) 852-7145   %FO: 100
   York Post, Soap Opera News & TV Guide.)

TWENTIETH CENTURY-FOX FILM CORP.
10201 West Pico Blvd., Los Angeles, CA   90035
CEO: Peter Chernin, Chrm.   Tel: (213) 277-2211   Emp: N/A
Bus: *Motion pictures, TV, music publishing, resorts.* Fax:(213) 203-2735   %FO: 100

ZONDERVAN PUBLISHING (DIV OF HARPER COLLINS)
5300 Patterson Avenue SE, Grand Rapids, MI   49530
CEO: Bruce E. Ryskamp, Pres.   Tel: (616) 699-6900   Emp: N/A
Bus: *Publisher; religious (Christian) materials.*   Fax:(616) 698-3255   %FO: 100

● **NORTH LTD.**
North House, 476 St. Kilda Road, Melbourne VIC 3004, Australia
CEO: Campbell McCheyne Anderson, Mng.Dir. & CEO   Tel: 61-3-9207-5111   Emp: 3852
Bus: *Diversified resources company; mining, (copper-* Fax:61-3-9250-1600
   gold, iron ore, uranium, zinc) forestry, and mfr.
   centrifugal slurry pumps and process.

HAZELTON PUMPS, INC.
225 North Cedar Street, Hazelton, PA   18201-0488
CEO: Peter Haentjens, Pres.   Tel: (717) 455-7711   Emp: N/A
Bus: *Mfr. centrifugal slurry pumps, process*   Fax:(717) 459-2586   %FO: 100
   equipment and valves

NORTH MINING INC.
Suite 1200, 475 17th Street, Denver, CO   80202-4022
CEO: N/A   Tel: (303) 297-1440   Emp: N/A
Bus: *Mining, exploration*   Fax:(303) 297-1556   %FO: 100

WARMAN INTL INC.
2701 S. Stoughton Road, Madison, WI   53716-3315
CEO: Mick Von Bergen, Pres.   Tel: (608) 221-2261   Emp: 150
Bus: *Mfr. centrifugal slurry pumps, process*   Fax:(608) 221-5807   %FO: 100
      equipment and valves.

• **PACIFIC DUNLOP LIMITED**
Level 41, 101 Collins Street, Melbourne Victoria 3000, Australia
CEO: Phillip Gay, Pres.   Tel: 61-3-9270-7270   Emp: 40671
Bus: *Consumer, automotive, healthcare, industrial and*   Fax:61-3-9270-7300
      electrical groups.

   GNB TECHNOLOGIES
   Center Point Curve, P.O Box 641000, Mendota Heights, MN   55164
   CEO: Thomas Uhlemann, VP & Mgr.   Tel: (612) 681-5000   Emp: 150
   Bus: *Mfr./sales/distribution of batteries.*   Fax:(612) 681-5487   %FO: 100

   PACIFIC DUNLOP HOLDINGS INC.
   6121 Lakeside Drive, Suite 200, Reno, NV   89511
   CEO: Michael McGetrick, VP & Finance   Tel: (702) 824-4600   Emp: N/A
   Bus: *Diversified mfr./sales/service; consumer,*   Fax:(702) 824-4626   %FO: 100
      automotive, healthcare, industrial & electrical
      groups.

• **PIONEER INTERNATIONAL, LTD.**
Level 46, Governor Phillip Tower, 1 Farrer Place, Sydney, NSW 2000, Australia
CEO: Dr. J.M. Schubert, Dir.   Tel: 61-2-9323-4000   Emp: 10000
Bus: *Production/sale concrete, sand and gravel products.*   Fax:61-2-9323-4009

   AGGREGATE HAULERS INC
   800 Gessner, Houston, TX   77024
   CEO: M.O. Ogier, Pres.   Tel: (713) 468-6868   Emp: N/A
   Bus: *Trucking services.*   Fax:(713) 468-8742   %FO: 100

   G&S TOWING CO INC
   400 Industrial Boulevard, New Kensington, PA   15068
   CEO: Dave Clement, Pres.   Tel: (412) 335-7400   Emp: 60
   Bus: *Marine towing service.*   Fax:(412) 335-6745   %FO: 100

   PIONEER CONCRETE OF AMERICA INC.
   800 Gessner, Suite 1100, Houston, TX   77024
   CEO: M.O. Ogier, Pres.   Tel: (713) 468-6868   Emp: 2600
   Bus: *Mfr./supplier ready mixed concrete.*   Fax:(713) 468-8724   %FO: 100

   PIONEER CONCRETE OF TEXAS INC.
   10715 Galveston Road, Houston, TX   77034
   CEO: M. O. Ogier, Pres.   Tel: (281) 481-3570   Emp: N/A
   Bus: *Mfr./supplier ready mixed concrete.*   Fax:(281) 922-9404   %FO: 100

PIONEER ROOFING TILE INC.
10650 Poplar Avenue, Fontana, CA   92337
CEO: D.G. Rowe, Pres.   Tel: (909) 350-4238   Emp: 150
Bus: *Mfr. concrete roofing tiles.*   Fax:(909) 350-2298   %FO: 100

● **QANTAS AIRWAYS LTD.**
Qantas Centre, Level 9, Bldg. A, 203 Coward Street, Mascot, NSW 2000, Australia
CEO: James A. Strong, Mng. Dir.   Tel: 61-2-9691-3636   Emp: 30000
Bus: *Commercial airline & hotel operators.*   Fax:61-2-9691-3339

    QANTAS AIRWAYS LTD.
    841 Apollo Street, Suite 400, El Segundo, CA   90245
    CEO: Wally Mariani, Reg. Gen. Mgr.   Tel: (310) 726-1400   Emp: N/A
    Bus: *Air transportation.*   Fax:(310) 726-1401   %FO: 100

● **RENISON GOLDFIELDS CONSOLIDATED LTD.**
1 Alfred Street, Circular Quay, NSW 2000, Australia
CEO: Max Roberts, Chrm.   Tel: 61-2-2520-5120   Emp: N/A
Bus: *Industrial sand, metal ores supplier.*   Fax:61-2-9934-8555

    ASSOCIATED MINERALS USA INC.
    1223 Warner Road, Green Cove Springs, FL   32043
    CEO: Graeme Sloan, Mgr.   Tel: (904) 284-9832   Emp: N/A
    Bus: *Non-metallic mineral services.*   Fax:(904) 284-4006   %FO: 100

● **SAVAGE RESOURCES LTD.**
Level 15, 1 Alfred Street, Sydney, NSW 2000, Australia
CEO: John G. Gaskell, Int. Mng. Dir.   Tel: 61-2-9373-7700   Emp: 900
Bus: *Non-ferrous mining.*   Fax:61-2-9373-7799

    SAVAGE ZINC INC.
    1800 Zinc Plant Road, P O Box 1104, Clarksville, TN   37041-1104
    CEO: David Rice, Pres.   Tel: (615) 552-4200   Emp: 650
    Bus: *Zinc mining & refining.*   Fax:(615) 552-0471   %FO: 100

● **TELSTRA CORP. LTD.**
242 Exhibition Street, Melbourne, Vic 3000, Australia
CEO: William Franklin Blount, CEO   Tel: 61-3-9634-8686   Emp: 75000
Bus: *Telecommunications services.*   Fax:61-3-9634-8826

    TELSTRA INC.
    50 Francisco Street, Suite 105, San Francisco, CA   94133
    CEO: Gregg Dunfield, VP   Tel: (415) 788-5951   Emp: 14
    Bus: *Telecommunications services. Offices in NY,*   Fax:(415) 788-5902   %FO: 100
        TX, CT, IL, NJ, VA.

● **TNT LIMITED**
TNT Plaza, Tower One, Lawson Square, 5th Level, Redfern, NSW 2016, Australia
CEO: David A. Mortimer, Mng. Dir.　　　　　Tel: 61-2-699-2222　　Emp: N/A
Bus: *International transport services.*　　　　Fax:61-2-699-9238

　　TNT LOGISTICS CORP.
　　1306 Concourse Drive, Suite 401, Linthicum, MD　21090-1032
　　CEO: Brian P. Flood. VP　　　　　　　Tel: (410) 859-3313　　Emp: N/A
　　Bus: *International transport services.*　　Fax:(410) 859-8844　　%FO: 100

● **J.B. WERE & SON INC.**
101 Collins Street, 16th Floor, Melbourne, Victoria 3000, Australia
CEO: Bruce Teele, Pres.　　　　　　　　Tel: 61-3-9679-1111　　Emp: N/A
Bus: *Financial services: securities.*　　　Fax:61-3-9679-1493

　　J.B. WERE & SON INC.
　　101 East 52nd Street, 34th Floor, New York, NY　10022
　　CEO: Ian Ward-Ambler　　　　　　　Tel: (212) 355-6611　　Emp: N/A
　　Bus: *Financial services; securities.*　　Fax:(212) 824-4501　　%FO: 100

● **WESTPAC BANKING CORP**
60 Martin Place, Sydney, NSW 2000, Australia
CEO: Robert L. Joss, Mgn Dir. & CEO　　　Tel: 61-2-9226-3311　　Emp: 33832
Bus: *International banking services.*　　　Fax:61-2-9226-4128

　　WESTPAC BANKING CORP
　　575 Fifth Avenue, 39th Floor, New York, NY　10017-2422
　　CEO: James J. Tate, Sup.& Ctry Mgr.　　Tel: (212) 551-1800　　Emp: 445
　　Bus: *General international banking services.*　　Fax:(212) 818-2800　　%FO: 100

Austria

• AUSTRIAN AIRLINES AG
Fontanastrassa 1, A-1107 Vienna, Austria
CEO: Dr. Bammer Herbert, Pres.   Tel: 43-1-683511   Emp: 3200
Bus: *Commercial air transport services.*   Fax:43-1-685505

AUSTRIAN AIRLINES
17-20 Whitestone Expwy, Whitestone, NY   11357
CEO: Jorgen Jensen, Gen. Mgr.   Tel: (718) 670-8600   Emp: 70
Bus: *Air transportation services.*   Fax:(718) 670-8619   %FO: 100

• BANK AUSTRIA AG
Vodere Zollamtstrasse 13, A-1030 Vienna, Austria
CEO: Gerhard Randa, Chrm. & CEO   Tel: 43-1-71191-0   Emp: 8700
Bus: *Commercial banking services.*   Fax:43-1-71191-3230

BANK AUSTRIA AG - Chicago Office
70 West Madison, Suite 5320, Chicago, IL   60602
CEO: Martin E. Rahe, Representative   Tel: (312) 263-6803   Emp: 5
Bus: *International banking services.*   Fax:(312) 263-7138   %FO: 100

BANK AUSTRIA AMERICA INC.
565 Fifth Avenue, New York, NY   10017
CEO: Heinrich P Schmitz, Gen'l Mgr   Tel: (212) 880-1000   Emp: 80
Bus: *US headquarters. International banking*   Fax:(212) 880-1110   %FO: 100
services.

BANK AUSTRIA FINANCE INC
565 Fifth Avenue, New York, NY   10017
CEO: Heinrich P Schmitz, Pres.   Tel: (212) 880-1000   Emp: N/A
Bus: *Single purpose commercial paper.*   Fax:(212) 880-1160   %FO: 100

BANK AUSTRIA SECURITIES INC
565 Fifth Ave., New York, NY   10017
CEO: Sarkis Poriadjian, Pres.   Tel: (212) 880-1021   Emp: 5
Bus: *Discount broker/dealer.*   Fax:(212) 880-1030   %FO: 100

LB CAPITAL INC.
565 Fifth Avenue, New York, NY   10017
CEO: Heinrich P Schmitz, Pres.   Tel: (212) 880-1000   Emp: N/A
Bus: *Merchant banking.*   Fax:(212) 880-1160   %FO: 100

RNC CAPITAL GROUP INC.
11601 Wilshire Blvd., Los Angeles, CA   90025
CEO: Dan Genter, Pres.   Tel: (310) 477-6543   Emp: 53
Bus: *Asset management holding company.*   Fax:(310) 479-6406   %FO: 100

● **BERNDORF BAND G.m.b.H.**
Leobersdprfer Str. 26, Berndorf A-2560, Austria
CEO: Rupert Harreither, Mng.Dir.　　　　Tel: 43-2672-800　　　Emp: 300
Bus: *Production of stainless, carbon, etc. conveyor*　Fax:43-2672-84176
　　belting.

　　BERNDORF INTERNATIONAL CONVEYOR BELTS, INC.
　　820 Estes Avenue, Schaumburg, IL　60193
　　CEO: Dietmar Mueller, Pres.　　　　Tel: (847) 891-8450　　Emp: 32
　　Bus: *Mfr./distributor of conveyor systems and*　Fax:(847) 891-7563　%FO: 100
　　　　related equipment.

● **CERHA, HEMPEL & SPIEGELFELD**
Parkring 2, A-101o Vienna, Austria
CEO: A. Junius, Mng. Dir.　　　　　Tel: 43-1-514-350　　Emp: N/A
Bus: *Legal services.*　　　　　　　Fax:43-1-514-3535

　　GRUNDER GROUP
　　152 West 57th Street, New York, NY　10019
　　CEO: A. Junius, Mng. Dir.　　　　Tel: (212) 582-2828　　Emp: N/A
　　Bus: *Law firm.*　　　　　　　Fax:(212) 582-2424　%FO: 100

● **CREDITANSTALT-BANKVEREIN**
Schottengasse 6, A-1010 Vienna, Austria
CEO: Guido Schmidt-Chiari, Chrm.　　Tel: 43-1-53131-4306　Emp: N/A
Bus: *General banking services.*　　　Fax:43-1-53131-44268

　　CREDITANSTALT INTERNATIONAL ADVISERS INC.
　　245 Park Avenue, 32nd Fl., New York, NY　10167
　　CEO: Geoffrey Hoguet, Pres.　　　Tel: (212) 856-1003　　Emp: N/A
　　Bus: *Investment advisory services.*　Fax:(212) 856-1444　%FO: 100

　　CREDITANSTALT-BANKVEREIN -SAN FRANCISCO BRANCH
　　4 Embarcadero Center, Suite 630,, San Francisco, CA　94111
　　CEO: Jack Bertges, Pres.　　　　Tel: (415) 788-1371　　Emp: N/A
　　Bus: *International banking services.*　Fax:(415) 781-0622　%FO: 100

　　CREDITANSTALT-BANKVEREIN
　　2 Arvinia Drive, Atlanta, GA　30346
　　CEO: B. Biringer, Mgr.　　　　Tel: (770) 390-1850　　Emp: N/A
　　Bus: *International banking services.*　Fax:(770) 390-1851　%FO: 100

　　CREDITANSTALT-BANKVEREIN
　　2 Greenwich Plaza, Greenwich, CT　06830-6353
　　CEO: Dennis C. O'Dowd, CEO　　　Tel: (203) 861-6464　　Emp: N/A
　　Bus: *International banking services.*　Fax:(203) 861-1414　%FO: 100

- **ELIN ENERGIEVERSORGUNGS GMBH**
Penzingerstrasse 76, A-1140 Vienna, Austria
CEO: Roland Scharb, CEO   Tel: 43-1-89100   Emp: 5000
Bus: *Mfr. motors, transformers, generators, switchgear,*   Fax:43-1-894-6370
and power plants.

    AMERICAN ELIN CORP.
    405 Lexington Avenue, New York, NY   10174
    CEO: Walter Paminger, Pres   Tel: (212) 808-4470   Emp: 10
    Bus: *Sale/service motors, power transformers,*   Fax:(212) 808-4473   %FO: 92
    hydropower generators.

- **EMCO MAIER GMBH**
Friedman Maier Strasse 9, P.O. Box 131, A-5400 Hallein, Austria
CEO: E. Maier, Pres.   Tel: 43-6245-891 311   Emp: N/A
Bus: *Mfr. industrial machinery.*   Fax:43-6245-869 65

    EMCO MAIER CORPORATION
    2757 Scioto Parkway, Columbus, OH   43026
    CEO: E. Maier, Pres.   Tel: (614) 771-5991   Emp: N/A
    Bus: *Mfr./ distribution industrial machinery.*   Fax:(614) 771-5990   %FO: 100

- **GIROCREDIT BANK**
Schubertring 5, A-1011 Vienna, Austria
CEO: Ferdinand Lacina, Chmn.   Tel: 43-1-71194-8620   Emp: 2500
Bus: *Commercial banking services.*   Fax:43-1-71194-8655

    GIROCREDIT BANK
    65 East 55th St, Park Avenue Towers, New York, NY   10022
    CEO: Hans Krikava, Gen.Mgr..   Tel: (212) 644-0660   Emp: 40
    Bus: *Banking services.*   Fax:(212) 421-2719   %FO: 100

- **KOHLBRAT & BUNZ GmbH**
LoretostraBe 4-8, Radstadt A-5550, Austria
CEO: Christine Dzionara, Pres.   Tel: 43-6452-7193-0   Emp: 22
Bus: *Distributor of forestry products.*   Fax:43-6452-7193-13

    KOHLBRAT & BUNZ CORPORATION
    122 Summerville Drive, Suite 101, Mooresville, NC   28115-7864
    CEO: Michael J. Koledin, Pres.   Tel: (704) 663-0170   Emp: 20
    Bus: *Mfr. of fighting position overhead cover,*   Fax:(704) 663-0264   %FO: 100
    UT2000 Universal transport sled and
    backpack, pre-hospital emergency care
    products.

● **MAIER & COMPANY**
Postfach 131, A-5400 Hallein, Austria
CEO: E. Maier, Pres.   Tel: 43-6-2452581   Emp: 1000
Bus: *Mfr. machine tools.*   Fax:45-6-2456965

    EMCO MAIER CORP.
    7523 Greystone, West Hills, CA   91304
    CEO: Rodger Pinner, Gen. Mgr.   Tel: (818) 703-7982   Emp: N/A
    Bus: *Distributor machine tools.*   Fax:(818) 703-7982   %FO: 100

    EMCO MAIER CORP.
    2757 Scioto Pkwy, Columbus, OH   43026
    CEO: Rodger Pinney, VP & Gen.Mgr.   Tel: (614) 771-5991   Emp: 46
    Bus: *Distributor machine tools.*   Fax:(614) 771-5990   %FO: 100

● **ÖSTERREICHISCHE INDUSTRIEHOLDING AG**
Katgasse 1, Postfach 99, A-1015 Vienna, Austria
CEO: Karl Hollweger, Chrm.   Tel: 43-1-71114   Emp: N/A
Bus: *Engineering services; mfr. electronic equipment &*   Fax:43-1-71114245
    steel.

    VOEST-ALPINE INTERNATIONAL CORP.
    60 East 42nd Street, New York, NY   10165
    CEO: Gerhard Nussbaumer, Pres.   Tel: (212) 922-2000   Emp: N/A
    Bus: *Engineering services; mfr. electronic*   Fax:(212) 922-3810   %FO: JV
        equipment & steel.

● **JOHANN ROHRER GmbH**
A-8712 Niklasdorf, Proleb 167, Leoben, Austria
CEO: Johann Rohrer, Pres.   Tel: 43-3842-82727   Emp: 65
Bus: *Cleaning crude oil tank storage.*   Fax:43-3842082815

    ROHRER INTERNATIONAL, INC.
    4525 Brittmoore Road, Houston, TX   77041
    CEO: George Abadjian, VP Operations   Tel: (713) 937-1465   Emp: 5
    Bus: *Oil tank cleaning..*   Fax:(713) 937-9258   %FO: 100

● **SEZ AG**
Draubodenweg 29, Villach A-9500, Austria
CEO: Egon Putzi, Pres. & CEO   Tel: 43-42-422040   Emp: 250
Bus: *Chemical spin etch systems for semiconductor*   Fax:43-42-4220421
    wafers.

    SEZ AMERICA, INC.
    4824 South 40th Street, Phoenix, AZ   85040
    CEO: Donald P. Baumann, EVP & GM   Tel: (602) 437-5050   Emp: 50
    Bus: *Chemical spin etch systems for semiconductor*   Fax:(602) 437-4949   %FO: 100
        wafers.

● **UNITEK MASCHINEN GmbH**
Universumstrasse 33, Vienna A-1200, Austria
CEO: K. Streitenberger, Mng. Dir.　　　　　　Tel: 43-1-332-5510　　　Emp: 35
Bus: *Fixed center crossheads and color change systems*　Fax:43-1-332-5515
for wire extrusion.

　　　UNITEK NORTH AMERICA, INC.
　　　1185 South Main Street, Cheshire, CT　06410
　　　CEO: Thomas J. Siedlarz, Pres.　　　　　Tel: (203) 250-9858　　　Emp: 3
　　　Bus: *Fixed center crossheads and color change*　Fax:(203) 272-4398　　%FO: 100
　　　systems for wire extrusion.

● **WINTERSTEIGER**
Dimmelstrasse 9, Ried 4910, Austria
CEO: Peter Kuchnor, CEO　　　　　　　　Tel: 43-7752-919　　　Emp: 300
Bus: *Ski tuning machines, agricultural machines,*　Fax:43-7752-919-55
woodworking machines.

　　　WINTERSTEIGER
　　　217 Wright Brothers Drive, Salt Lake City, UT　84116
　　　CEO: Fritz Hoeckner, CEO　　　　　　　Tel: (801) 355-6550　　　Emp: 25
　　　Bus: *Ski tuning machines, agricultural machines,*　Fax:(801) 355-6541　　%FO: 100
　　　woodworking machines.

● **WITTMANN KUNSTSTOFFGERÄTE GMBH**
Lichtblaustrasse 10, Vienna A-1220, Austria
CEO: Dr. Werner Wittmann, Pres.　　　　　Tel: 43-1-250-390　　　Emp: 260
Bus: *Mfr. of water flow regulators, temperature*　Fax:43-1-259-7170
controllers and automation systems for plastic
industry.

　　　WITTMANN KUNSTSTOFFGERÄTE INC.
　　　175 Industrial Lane, Torrington, CT　06790
　　　CEO: Michael Wittmann, Pres.　　　　　Tel: (860) 496-9603　　　Emp: N/A
　　　Bus: *Mfr. of water flow regulators, temperature*　Fax:(860) 482-2069　　%FO: 100
　　　controllers and automation systems for plastic
　　　industry.

● **ZUMTOBEL A.G.**
Hochsterstrasse 8, Dornbirn A-6850, Austria
CEO: Juerg Zumtobel, Chrm.　　　　　　　Tel: 43-5572-390　　　Emp: N/A
Bus: *Mfr. lighting fixtures.*　　　　　　　Fax:43-5572-20721

　　　ZUMTOBEL STAFF LIGHTING, INC.
　　　141 Lanza Avenue, Garfield, NJ　07026
　　　CEO: Wolfgang Egger, EVP　　　　　　Tel: (201) 340-8900　　　Emp: 100
　　　Bus: *Mfr. lighting fixtures.*　　　　　Fax:(201) 340-9898　　%FO: 100

ZUMTOBEL STAFF LIGHTING, INC.

300 Route 9W North, PO Box 1020, Highland, NY   12528

CEO: Karl Lamprecht, EVP	Tel: (914) 691-6262	Emp: 100
Bus: *Mfr. lighting fixtures.*	Fax: (914) 691-6289	%FO: 100

Bahrain

- **ARAB BANKING CORPORATION**
P.O. Box 5698, ABC Tower, Diplomatic Area, Manama, Bahrain
CEO: Ghaze M. Abdul-Jawad, Chrm.   Tel: 973-532-235   Emp: N/A
Bus: *International banking services.*   Fax:973-533-062

  ARAB BANKING CORPORATION
  277 Park Avenue, New York, NY   10172-3299
  CEO: Geoffrey Milton, Gen. Mgr.   Tel: (212) 583-4720   Emp: N/A
  Bus: *International banking services.*   Fax:(212) 583-0921   %FO: 100

- **GULF AIR COMPANY GSC**
Gulf Air Headquarters, Manama, Bahrain
CEO: Salim Bin Abdulla al Ghazali, Chrm.   Tel: 973-322200   Emp: 4402
Bus: *Commercial air transport services.*   Fax:973-338980

  GULF AIR COMPANY GSC
  104 South Central Avenue, Valley Stream, NY   11580
  CEO: F. Salehgjee, Pres.   Tel: (516) 568-0860   Emp: 8
  Bus: *Commercial air transport services.*   Fax:(516) 553-2824   %FO: 100

- **GULF INVESTMENT CORPORATION**
Al-Dowali Building, Three Palace Avenue, P.O.Box 1017, Manama, Bahrain
CEO: Dr. Abdullah I. LeKuwaiz, Dir.   Tel: 973-552663   Emp: N/A
Bus: *Banking services.*   Fax:N/A

  GULF INVESTMENT CORPORATION
  380 Madison Avenue, New York, NY   10017
  CEO: Issa N. Baconi, SVP   Tel: (212) 922-2300   Emp: N/A
  Bus: *International banking services.*   Fax:(212) 922-2309   %FO: 100

Belgium

- **BANQUE BRUSSELS LAMBERT**
24 ave. Marnix, B-1050 Brussels, Belgium
CEO: Michel Tilmant, Pres.   Tel: 32-2-517-2111   Emp: N/A
Bus: *General banking services.*   Fax:32-2-5173663

  BANK BRUSSELS LAMBERT
  630 Fifth Avenue, 6th Floor, New York, NY   10111-0020
  CEO: Jean-Louis Recoussine, Gen. Mgr.   Tel: (212) 632-5300   Emp: 100
  Bus: *International banking services.*   Fax:(212) 632-5308   %FO: 100

- **BARCO INDUSTRIES, NV.**
President Kennedy Park 35, B-8500 Kortrijk, Belgium
CEO: Hugo Van Damme, Pres.   Tel: 32-56-262611   Emp: 2700
Bus: *Integrated systems for textile industry, graphic*   Fax:32-56-262690
   displays, broadcast monitors.

  BARCO INC.
  4420 Taggert Creek Road, Charlotte, NC   28208
  CEO: Denny Claeys, VP   Tel: (704) 392-9371   Emp: 30
  Bus: *Automation division.*   Fax:(704) 399-5588   %FO: 100

- **NV BEKAERT SA**
President Kennedy Park 18, B-8500 Kortrijk, Belgium
CEO: Raphel Decaluwe   Tel: 32-56-230-511   Emp: N/A
Bus: *Mfr. steel wire & cord, wire-related products,*   Fax:32-56-230543
   conductive fibers.

  BEKAERT CORP.
  3200 W Market St., #303, Akron, OH   44333
  CEO: Henri Velge, Pres.   Tel: (330) 867-3325   Emp: N/A
  Bus: *Mfr. steel wire & wire products.*   Fax:(330) 867-3328   %FO: 100

  BEKAERT CORP.
  1395 South Marietta Parkway, Bldg. 500, Marietta, GA   30067
  CEO: Henri Velge, Pres.   Tel: (770) 421-8520   Emp: N/A
  Bus: *Mfr. steel wire & wire products.*   Fax:(770) 421-8521   %FO: 100

- **BELGACOM**
Blvd E Jacqmain 166, B-1210 Brussels, Belgium
CEO: John Goossens, Pres.   Tel: 32-2-202-8080   Emp: 26000
Bus: *Telecommunications services.*   Fax:N/A

    BELGACOM NORTH AMERICA
    320 Post Road West, Suite 250, Westport, CT 06880-4748
    CEO: Susan Mirbach, Pres.   Tel: (203) 221-5250   Emp: 14
    Bus: *Telecommunications services, branch office.*   Fax:(203) 222-8401   %FO: 100

- **BROWNING SA**
Parc Indust des Hauts-Sarts, 3ieme Ave., B-4040 Herstal, Belgium
CEO: Jacques Gentgen, Pres.   Tel: 32-42-405-211   Emp: N/A
Bus: *Hunting, shooting & fishing products.*   Fax:32-42-405212

    BROWNING
    One Browning Place, Morgan, UT 84050-9326
    CEO: Don W. Gobel, Pres.   Tel: (801) 876-2711   Emp: N/A
    Bus: *Distributor hunting, fishing & shooting*   Fax:(801) 876-3331   %FO: 100
        products.

- **CBR GROUP**
Brussels, Belgium
CEO: Donald Fallon, Pres.   Tel: 32-2-678-3211   Emp: N/A
Bus: *Supplies construction products and engineering*   Fax:N/A
    services.

    CBR CEMENT CORPORATION
    7660 Imperial Way, Allentown, PA 18195
    CEO: Richard Kline, CEO   Tel: (610) 366-4600   Emp: N/A
    Bus: *Supplies construction products and*   Fax:(610) 366-4684   %FO: 100
        engineering services. Formerly Lehigh
        Portland Cement.

- **DE BANDT, VAN HECKE & LAGAE**
Rue Brederode 13, B-1000 Brussels, Belgium
CEO: N/A   Tel: 32-2-238-1062   Emp: N/A
Bus: *General European and international law practice.*   Fax:(32-2) 216-4717

    DE BANDT, VAN HECKE & LAGAE
    712 Fifth Avenue, New York, NY 10019
    CEO: Vincent Macq   Tel: (212) 801-3420   Emp: 3
    Bus: *International law firm.*   Fax:(212) 801-3425   %FO: 100

● **DELHAIZE FRERES ET CIE - LE LION SA**
Rue Osseghem 53, B-1080 Brussels, Belgium
CEO: Gui de Vaucleroy, Mng.Dir.   Tel: 32-2-4122-111   Emp: N/A
Bus: *General merchandise and food retailers.*   Fax:32-2-4122-2194

   CUB FOODS
   420 Thornton Road, Suite 103, Lithia Springs, GA   30057
   CEO: Preston Slayden, Pres.   Tel: (770) 732-6800   Emp: N/A
   Bus: *Supermarket chain.*   Fax:(770) 732-6818   %FO: 100

   DELHAIZE AMERICA
   950 East Paces Ferry, Suite 2160, Atlanta, GA   30326
   CEO: Linda Allen, Mgr.   Tel: (440) 365-8435   Emp: N/A
   Bus: *Holding company.*   Fax:(440) 365-8358   %FO: 100

   FOOD LION INC.
   P O Box 1330, Executive Dr. 2110,, Salisbury, NC   28145-1330
   CEO: Tom E. Smith, Pres.   Tel: (704) 633-8250   Emp: 48360
   Bus: *Supermarket chain.*   Fax:(704) 636-4940   %FO: 51

● **ELECTRAFINA**
24 ave. Marnix, B-100 Brissels, Belgium
CEO: Baron Frere, Pres.   Tel: 32-2-547-2352   Emp: N/A
Bus: *Industrial/energy products/services holding*   Fax:32-2-547-2352
    company.

   AMERICAN COMETRA INC.
   500 Throckmorton Street, Fort Worth, TX   76102
   CEO: Mark W. Young   Tel: (817) 877-1585   Emp: N/A
   Bus: *Industrial/energy products/services.*   Fax:(817) 877-4464   %FO: 100

   ROCKLAND PIPELINE COMPANY
   500 Throckmorton Street, Fort Worth, TX   76102
   CEO: Mark W. Young   Tel: (817) 336-3602   Emp: N/A
   Bus: *Industrial/energy products/services.*   Fax:(817) 877-4464   %FO: 100

● **FONDERIES MAGOTTEAUX SA**
B-4601 Vaux Sous, Chevremont, Belgium
CEO: Walter Mersch   Tel: 32-43-617-550   Emp: N/A
Bus: *Mfr. white iron grinding media, iron & steel*   Fax:32-43-617617
    castings.

   AMERICAN MAGOTTEAUX CORP
   2409 21st Avenue, SPO Box 120915, Nashville, TN   37212
   CEO: Jack Mattan, Pres.   Tel: (615) 385-3055   Emp: N/A
   Bus: *Grinding media, iron & steel castings*   Fax:(615) 297-6743   %FO: 100

WOLLASTON ALLOYS INC
205 Wood Road, Braintree, MA   02184

CEO: David Bernardi, Pres.　　　　　　　Tel: (781) 848-3333　　　Emp: N/A

Bus: *Stainless steel valves & pumps, defense*　Fax:(781) 848-3993　　%FO: 100
　　　castings.

• FORTIS AG
Emile Jacqmainlaan 53, B-1000 Brussels, Belgium

CEO: Maurice Lippens, Joint Chrm.　　　　Tel: 32-2-220-8111　　　Emp: 33000

Bus: *Insurance, banking, financial services (see joint*　Fax:32-2-220-8150
　　　parent: FORTIS AMEV, NETHERLANDS)

AMERICAN SECURITY GROUP
3290 Northside Parkway, N.W., Atlanta, GA   30327

CEO: Jeffrey W. Williams, Pres.　　　　　Tel: (404) 261-9000　　　Emp: N/A

Bus: *Insurance underwriters, specialty insurance*　Fax:(404) 264-2443　　%FO: 100
　　　related products.

FIRST FORTIS LIFE INSURANCE CO
220 Salina Meadow Pkwy, #255, Syracuse, NY   13212

CEO: Zafar Rashid, Pres.　　　　　　　　Tel: (315) 453-2340　　　Emp: N/A

Bus: *Life, disability, medical & dental group*　Fax:(315) 453-2340　　%FO: 100
　　　insurance.

FORTIS SALES
501 West Michigan, Milwaukee, WI   53201-2989

CEO: Benjamin Cutler, CEO　　　　　　　Tel: (414) 271-3011　　　Emp: N/A

Bus: *Financial services.*　　　　　　　Fax:(414) 271-0879　　%FO: 100

FORTIS ADVISERS INC
One Chase Manhattan Plaza, New York, NY   10005

CEO: Gary N. Yalen, Pres.　　　　　　　Tel: (212) 859-7000　　　Emp: N/A

Bus: *Financial asset management.*　　　Fax:(212) 859-7010　　%FO: 100

FORTIS BENEFITS INSURANCE CO.
2323 Grand Boulevard, Kansas City, MO   64108

CEO: Robert B. Pollock, Pres.　　　　　Tel: (816) 474-2345　　　Emp: N/A

Bus: *Insurance services.*　　　　　　Fax:(816) 881-8646　　%FO: 100

FORTIS FINANCIAL GROUP
500 Bielenberg Drive, Woodbury, MN   55125

CEO: Dean C. Kopperud, Pres.　　　　　Tel: (612) 738-4000　　　Emp: N/A

Bus: *Financial services; mutual funds, insurance &*　Fax:(612) 738-5534　　%FO: 100
　　　annuities.

FORTIS INC.
One Chase Manhattan Plaza, New York, NY   10005

CEO: Allen R. Freedman, Pres.　　　　　Tel: (212) 859-7000　　　Emp: 6040

Bus: *Financial services holding company.*　Fax:(212) 859-7071　　%FO: 100

FORTIS REAL ESTATE
One Chase Manhattan Plaza, New York, NY   10005
CEO: Gary N. Yalen, Pres.   Tel: (212) 859-7000   Emp: N/A
Bus: *Real estate asset management services.*   Fax:(212) 859-7010   %FO: 100

TIME INSURANCE CO.
515 West Wells, Milwaukee, WI   53201
CEO: Thomas Keller, Pres.   Tel: (414) 271-3011   Emp: N/A
Bus: *Life & individual & small group medical*   Fax:(414) 224-0472   %FO: 100
    insurance.

UNITED FAMILY LIFE INSURANCE CO.
230 John Wesley Dobbs Avenue, Atlanta, GA   30303
CEO: Alan W.Feagin, Pres.   Tel: (404) 659-3300   Emp: N/A
Bus: *Insurance: small life & pre-need products.*   Fax:(404) 524-4945   %FO: 100

● **GENERALE BANQUE**
CEO: Ferdinand Chaffart, Chrm.   Tel: 32-2-565-2111   Emp: 9000
Bus: *General banking services.*   Fax:32-2-565-4222

GENERALE BANK
520 Madison Avenue, 3rd Floor, New York, NY   10022
CEO: Johan Beckers, CEO   Tel: (212) 418-8700   Emp: 60
Bus: *International banking services.*   Fax:(212) 838-7492   %FO: 100

● **GIB GROUP**
Avenues des Olympiades 20, B-1140 Brussels, Belgium
CEO: N/A   Tel: N/A   Emp: N/A
Bus: *Retail operations: supermarkets, food service,*   Fax:N/A
    renovators "do-it-yourself," specialty retailers.

SCOTTY'S INC.
5300 North Recker Highway, Winter Haven, FL   33882
CEO: Thomas Morris   Tel: (941) 299-1111   Emp: N/A
Bus: *Renovators "do-it-yourself," specialty retailers.*   Fax:(941) 299-4196   %FO: 100

● **INTERBREW S.A**
Vaartstraat 94, B-3000 Leuven, Belgium
CEO: Paul De Keersmaeker, Chrm.   Tel: 32-16-247-111   Emp: 13237
Bus: *Brews beers; bottles soft drinks, juices, & water;*   Fax:32-16-247407
    operates restaurants.(U.S. Brands; Rolling Rock,
    Labatt, & Tecate).

INTERBREW AMERICAS
23 Old Kings Highway, Darien, CT   06820
CEO: Hugo Powell, COO   Tel: (203) 656-1876   Emp: N/A
Bus: *Brews beers; bottles soft drinks, juices, &*   Fax:(203) 656-0838   %FO: 100
    water; operates restaurants.(U.S. Brands;
    Rolling Rock, Labatt, & Tecate.)

LABATT USA
23 Old Kings Highway, Darien, CT   06820
CEO: Thane A. Pressman, Pres.   Tel: (203) 656-1876   Emp: N/A
Bus: *Brews beers; bottles soft drinks, juices, &*   Fax:(203) 656-0838   %FO: 100
   water; operates restaurants.(U.S. Brands;
   Rolling Rock, Labatt, & Tecate.)

● **KREDIETBANK NV**
Arenbergstraat 7, B-1000 Brussels, Belgium
CEO: Marcel Cockaerts, Pres   Tel: 32-2-546-4111   Emp: 9600
Bus: *General banking services.*   Fax:32-2-5464209

   KREDIETBANK NV
   550 South Hope Street, Ste. 1775, Los Angeles, CA   90071
   CEO: Thomas Jackson, Reg.Mgr.   Tel: (213) 624-0401   Emp: 6
   Bus: *International banking services.*   Fax:(213) 629-6801   %FO: 100

   KREDIETBANK NV
   Two Midtown Plaza, 1349 Peachtree St., #1440, Atlanta, GA   30309
   CEO: Michael Sawicki, Reg. Mgr.   Tel: (404) 876-2556   Emp: 6
   Bus: *International banking services.*   Fax:(404) 876-3212   %FO: 100

   KREDIETBANK NV
   125 West 55th Street, New York, NY   10019
   CEO: Pierre Koningst, SVP & Gen.Mgr.   Tel: (212) 541-0600   Emp: 114
   Bus: *International banking services.*   Fax:(212) 956-5580   %FO: 100

● **OILFIN SA**
283 Ave Louise, B-1050 Brussels, Belgium
CEO: Jacques Focquet, Pres.   Tel: 32-2-640-7430   Emp: 30
Bus: *Trades in tubular products for oil & gas industry.*   Fax:32-2-617-7297

   SOCONORD CORP.
   2200 Post Oak Blvd, Suite 712, Houston, TX   77056
   CEO: Luke Vollemaere, Pres.   Tel: (713) 871-1262   Emp: 5
   Bus: *Sale tubular products for oil & gas industry.*   Fax:(713) 871-0328   %FO: 75

● **PETROFINA SA**
Rue de l' Industrie 52, B-1040 Brussels, Belgium
CEO: François Cornélis, Mng. Dir.   Tel: 32-2-288-9111   Emp: 13700
Bus: *Oil, gas and chemicals producing conglomerate.*   Fax:32-2-288-3445

   FINA INC.
   Fina Plaza, 8350 N. Central Expressway, Dallas, TX   75206
   CEO: Ronald W. Haddock, Pres.   Tel: (214) 750-2400   Emp: 3500
   Bus: *Prod/mfr./marketing petroleum, mfr.*   Fax:(214) 750-2773   %FO: 86
      petrochemicals & plastics, retail convenience
      stores.

● **PICANOL NV**
Polenlaan 3/7, B-8900 Ieper, Belgium
CEO: Patrick Steverlynck, Pres.　　　　Tel: 32-57-222-111　　Emp: N/A
Bus: *Mfr./sale weaving machine & parts, technical*　Fax:32-57-222001
service for installation & training.

　PICANOL OF AMERICA INC
　Ketron Court, P O Box 5519, Greenville, SC　29606
　CEO: James C. Thomas　　　　Tel: (864) 288-5475　　Emp: 50
　Bus: *Sale weaving machine & parts, technical*　Fax:(864) 297-5081　%FO: 100
　service for installation & training.

● **POWERFIN SA**
Place du Trone 1, B-1000 Brussels, Belgium
CEO: Philippe Bodson, Chrm.　　　　Tel: 32-2-510-7184　　Emp: 34000
Bus: *Electric power production, gas & electric*　Fax:32-2-510-7133
distribution, communications, technical services,
real estate, & engineering.

　AMERICAN TRACTEBEL CORP
　1177 West Loop S., Ste. 900, Houston, TX　77027-9006
　CEO: Philippe van Marcke, EVP　　　　Tel: (713) 552-2223　　Emp: 215
　Bus: *Independent power production.*　　Fax:(713) 552-2364　%FO: 100

● **SABENA BELGIAN WORLD AIRLINES**
ave. E. Mounierlaan 2, B-1200 Brussels, Belgium
CEO: Paul Reutlinger, CEO　　　　Tel: 32-2-723-3111　　Emp: N/A
Bus: *International air transport services.*　Fax:32-2-723-8399

　SABENA BELGIAN WORLD AIRLINES
　1155 Northern Blvd, Manhasset, NY　11030-3017
　CEO: J.L. Lindekens, VP　　　　Tel: (516) 562-9200　　Emp: N/A
　Bus: *International air transport.*　　Fax:　　%FO: 100

● **SOCIETE EUROPEENE DES DERIVES DU MANGANESE (SEDEMA)**
Ave. de la Renaissance 12, B-1040 Brussels, Belgium
CEO: Francis DePauw, Pres.　　　　Tel: 322-627-5311　　Emp: N/A
Bus: *Produces manganese chemicals & metal derivatives,*　Fax:322-627-5390
copper chemicals, etc.

　CHEMETALA, INC.
　711 Pittman Road, Baltimore, MD　21226
　CEO: Francis DePauw, Pres.　　　　Tel: (410) 789-8800　　Emp: N/A
　Bus: *Manganese chemicals & metal derivatives,*　Fax:(410) 636-7134　%FO: 100
　copper chemicals, etc.

• SOLVAY SA
rue du Prince Albert 33, B-1050 Brussels, Belgium

CEO: Baron Daniel Janssen, Chrm.   Tel: 32-2-509-6111   Emp: 36000

Bus: *Chemicals, plastics, human & health products.*   Fax:32-2-509-6617

D&S PLASTICS INTL
1201 AvenueH East, Grand Prairie, TX   75050

CEO: Joseph Grulich, Pres.   Tel: (972) 988-4200   Emp: 300

Bus: *Mfr. thermoplastic polyolefins for auto*   Fax:(972) 988-4238   %FO: JV
industry.

HEDWIN CORP
1600 Roland Heights Avenue, Baltimore, MD   21211

CEO: David Rubley, Pres   Tel: (410) 467-8209   Emp: N/A

Bus: *Mfr./distributor plastic containers, automotive*   Fax:(410) 467-1761   %FO: 100
parts, film.

SOLVAY AMERICA INC.
3333 Richmond Avenue, Houston, TX   77098

CEO: M Whitson Sadler, Pres   Tel: (713) 525-6000   Emp: N/A

Bus: *Holding company. U.S. headquarters.*   Fax:(713) 525-7887   %FO: 100

SOLVAY AUTOMOTIVE INC.
2565 West Maple Road, Troy, MI   48084

CEO: Norman Johnston, Pres.   Tel: (248) 435-3300   Emp: 516

Bus: *Mfr. gas tanks & plastic parts for auto*   Fax:(248) 435-3957   %FO: 100
industry; design, test, mfr. blow-molded plastic
components.

SOLVAY INDUSTRIAL FILMS INC.
1207 East Lincoln Way, Laporte, IN   46350

CEO: F.W. Young, Pres.   Tel: (219) 324-6886   Emp: N/A

Bus: *Mfr./distribution high-clarity polypropylene*   Fax:(219) 324-8696   %FO: 100
film.

SOLVAY INTEROX
PO Box 27328, Houston, TX   77227

CEO: Foster E Brown, Pres   Tel: (713) 525-6500   Emp: N/A

Bus: *Mfr./distribution peroxygen chemicals.*   Fax:(713) 524-9032   %FO: 100

SOLVAY MINERALS INC.
3333 Richmond Avenue, Houston, TX   77098-3009

CEO: Richard Hogan, Pres.   Tel: (713) 525-6100   Emp: N/A

Bus: *Producer of soda ash & caustic soda.*   Fax:(713) 525-7804   %FO: 100

SOLVAY PERFORMANCE CHEMICALS
41 W Putnam Avenue, Greenwich, CT   06830

CEO: J. Anspach, Pres.   Tel: (203) 629-7900   Emp: N/A

Bus: *Distributor, chemicals.*   Fax:(203) 629-9074   %FO: 100

SOLVAY PHARMACEUTICALS INC.
901 Sawyer Road, Marietta, GA   30062
CEO: D.A. Dodd, Pres.   Tel: (770) 578-9000   Emp: N/A
Bus: *Mfr./distributor, pharmaceuticals.*   Fax:(770) 578-5597   %FO: 100

SOLVAY POLYMERS INC
PO Box 27328, Houston, TX   77227-7328
CEO: David G Birney, Pres.   Tel: (713) 525-4000   Emp: N/A
Bus: *Mfr./distributor, plastics.*   Fax:(713) 522-2435   %FO: 100

SOLVAY SPECIALTY CHEMICALS, INC.
30 Two Bridges Roadd, Fairfield, NJ   07006-1530
CEO: Jean-Louis Anspach, Pres   Tel: (201) 882-7900   Emp: 133
Bus: *Mfr./distribution semiconductor gases, safety-*   Fax:(201) 882-7967   %FO: 100
     related products.

WALL TRENDS INC.
17 Mileed Way, Avenel, NJ   07001
CEO: Donald C. Choate, Pres.   Tel: (908) 382-8600   Emp: N/A
Bus: *Distributor, wall coverings.*   Fax:(908) 382-6885   %FO: 100

● **ZEYEN BEGHIN FEIDER**
67, Rue Ermesinde, L-1469 Luxembourg, Luxembourg
CEO: Marc Feider, Mng. Ptnr.   Tel: 352-468-946   Emp: N/A
Bus: *International law firm.*   Fax:352-468-947

   ZEYEN BEGHIN FEIDER
   Swiss Bank Tower, 10 East 50th St., New York, NY 10022
   CEO: Robert Abendroth, Mng. Prtn.   Tel: (212) 759-9000   Emp: N/A
   Bus: *International law firm.*   Fax:(212) 759-9018   %FO: 100

Bermuda

- **THE BANK OF BERMUDA LTD.**
6 Front Street, Hamilton HM-DX, Bermuda
CEO: Charles Vaughan-Johnson   Tel: (809) 295-4000   Emp: 1800
Bus: *International commercial banking & trust services.*   Fax:(809) 295-7093

   BANK OF BERMUDA (NEW YORK) LTD
   570 Lexington Avenue, 25th Fl., New York, NY   10022
   CEO: Robert M. Hill, Chrm.   Tel: (212) 980-4500   Emp: 42
   Bus: *International banking & trust services.*   Fax:(212) 980-5079   %FO: 100

- **BERMUDA DEPARTMENT OF TOURISM**
PO Box 465, HM 465, Hamilton, Bermuda HMBX
CEO: Gary Phillips, Dir.   Tel: 441-292-0023   Emp: N/A
Bus: *Tourism and travel.*   Fax:441-292-7537

   BERMUDA DEPARTMENT OF TOURISM
   310 Madison Avenue, New York, NY   10017
   CEO: Toby Dillas, Dir.   Tel: (212) 818-9800   Emp: N/A
   Bus: *Tourism and travel.*   Fax:(212) 983-5289   %FO: 100

- **JARDINE MATHESON HOLDINGS LTD.(Legal home of Hong Kong based operating Co.)**
Jardine House, 33-35 Reid Street, Hamilton, Bermuda
CEO: Alasdair G. Morrison, Mng. Dir.   Tel: 441-292-0515   Emp: 200000
Bus: *Active in engineering/construction, financial*   Fax:441-292-4072
    services, marketing & distribution, real estate,
    transportation services, food service.

   THEO H. DAVIES & CO LTD.
   841 Bishop Street, Honolulu, HI   96813
   CEO: Martin J. Jaskot, Pres.   Tel: (808) 532-6500   Emp: N/A
   Bus: *Active in engineering/construction, financial*   Fax:(808) 532-6544   %FO: 100
    services, marketing & distribution, real estate,
    transportation services, food service.

- **TYCO INTERNATIONAL, LTD.**
Cedar House, 41 Cedar Avenue, Hamilton HM 12, Bermuda
CEO: L. Dennis Kozlowski, Chrm./CEO   Tel: (441) 292-2033   Emp: N/A
Bus: *Home and office security systems.*   Fax:to NH office

   ADT SECURITY SERVICES, INC.
   290 A Veterans Blvd., Rutherford, NJ   07070
   CEO: Art Stromstedt, Mgr.   Tel: (201) 804-8600   Emp: N/A
   Bus: *Home and office security systems.*   Fax:(201) 842-8265   %FO: 100

ADT SECURITY SERVICES, INC.
431 N. Washington Street, Wichita, KS   67202
CEO: Mark Simmons, Mgr.   Tel: (316) 267-0048   Emp: N/A
Bus: *Home and office security systems.*   Fax:(316) 267-5329   %FO: 100

ADT SECURITY SERVICES, INC.
1750 Clintmore Road, PO Box 5035, Boco Raton, FL   33431
CEO: Michael Snyder, Pres.   Tel: (561) 988-3600   Emp: N/A
Bus: *Home and office security systems.*   Fax:(561) 241-1923   %FO: 100

TYCO INTERNATIONAL LTD.
1 Tyco Park, Exeter, NH   03833
CEO: L. Dennis Kozlowski, Chrm. & CEO   Tel: (603) 778-9700   Emp: N/A
Bus: *Home and office security systems.*   Fax:(603) 778-7330   %FO: 100

Bolivia

- **BANCO ECONOMICO SA**
  La Paz, Bolivia
  CEO: Pedro Yovhio Ferreira, Pres.   Tel: 591-3-361177   Emp: N/A
  Bus: *Commercial banking services.*   Fax:591-3-361184

    BANCO ECONOMICO SA
    630 Rockefeller Plaza, New York, NY   10111
    CEO: G. Pessoa, Pres.   Tel: (212) 758-3700   Emp: N/A
    Bus: *International commercial banking services.*   Fax:(212) 332-5005   %FO: 100

Brazil

● **AGC OPTOSYSTEMS INDÚSTRIA E COMÉRCIO LTDA.**
Rua Panaçu, 54, São Paulo, SP 04264-080, Brazil
CEO: Jonah Trunk, Pres. Tel: 55-11-272-1544 Emp: 45
Bus: *Optical instruments, lenses and communications* Fax:55-11-274-3997
equipment.

AGC OPTOSYSTEMS, LTD.
1025 South Semoran Boulevard, Suite 1093, Winter Park, FL 32792
CEO: Jonah Trunk, Pres. Tel: (407) 679-7780 Emp: N/A
Bus: *Optical instruments, lenses; communications* Fax:(407) 677-1472 %FO: 100
equipment.

● **ALTUS SISTEMAS DE INFORMÁTICA SA**
Avenida São Paulo, 555, Porto Alegre, RS 90230-161 Brazil
CEO: Ricardo Felizzola, Chrm. Tel: 55-51-337-3633 Emp: 150
Bus: *Electronic components; relays & industrial controls.* Fax:55-51-337-3632

ALTUS AUTOMATION INC.
9050 Pines Blvd., Suite 210, Pembroke Pines, FL 33024
CEO: Joni Girardi, Sales Tel: (954) 450-0480 Emp: N/A
Bus: *Electronics, computers, relays & Industrial* Fax:(954) 438-1995 %FO: 100
controls.

● **ARACRUZ CELULOSE SA**
Rua Lauro Muller, 116, 21o./22o. andares, Rio de Janeiro, RJ 22299-900 Brazil
CEO: Luiz Kaufmann, Pres. Tel: 55-21-545-8111 Emp: 3100
Bus: *Pulp mills, forestry services.* Fax:55-21-295-7943

ARACRUZ CORPORATION
140 Winchime Court, Raleigh, NC 27615
CEO: Colin Bilton, Sales Mgr. Tel: (919) 847-9437 Emp: 5
Bus: *Paper & pulp mills; forestry services.* Fax:(919) 847-9265 %FO: 100

● **ARBI PARTICIPAÇÕES, S.A..**
Av. Almirante Borroso, 52, 11o. andar, Rio de Janeiro, RJ 20031-000 Brazil
CEO: Daniel Birmann, Pres. Tel: 55-21-212-8282 Emp: 1200
Bus: *Investment advisor services.* Fax:55-21-220-5232

ARBI TRANSNATIONAL, INC.
601 California Street, Suite 615, San Francisco, CA 94108
CEO: Terry Vogt, Mng. Dir. Tel: (415) 989-2884 Emp: 6
Bus: *Investment advisory.* Fax:(415) 989-2904 %FO: 100

• **ARTEX S.A.**
Rua Proresso 150, Blumenau, SC 89026-900 Brazil
CEO: Jose Bucci, Mng. Dir.   Tel: 55-47-324-1833   Emp: 5000
Bus: *Household furnishings.*   Fax:55-47-324-2212

    KMC MARKETING & SALES
    25 Lakeside Drive, Ramsey, NJ   07446
    CEO: Keith Callanan, Pres.   Tel: (201) 760-9756   Emp: N/A
    Bus: *Household furnishings.*   Fax:(201) 760-0889   %FO: JV

• **BANCO BANDEIRANTES S.A.**
Rua Boa Vista, 162, 7o.andar, São Paulo, SP 01014-902 Brazil
CEO: Gilberto de Andrade Faria, Pres.   Tel: 55-11-233-7155   Emp: 4900
Bus: *Commercial banking services.*   Fax:55-11-233-7329

    BANCO BANDEIRANTES S.A.
    280 Park Avenue, 38th Fl., New York, NY   10017
    CEO: Roberto L. Paladini, Exec. Dir.   Tel: (212) 972-7455   Emp: 6
    Bus: *Commercial banking services.*   Fax:(212) 949-9158   %FO: 100

• **BANCO BANORTE S.A.**
Rua Jose Bonifacio, 944, Torre, Recife, PE 50710-900 Brazil
CEO: Jorge Amorim Baptista da Silva   Tel: 55-81-412-8671   Emp: 3500
Bus: *Commercial banking services.*   Fax:55-81-227-3251

    BANCO BANORTE, S.A.
    201 South Biscayne Blvd., Ste. 3150, Miami, FL   33131
    CEO: Robert Potter, Mgr.   Tel: (305) 577-0472   Emp: 2
    Bus: *Commercial banking.*   Fax:(305) 577-0474   %FO: 100

• **BANCO BMC S.A.**
Av. Paulista, 302, São Paulo, SP 01310-000 Brazil
CEO: Francisco Jaime Noguieira Pinheiro Fihlo, Chrm..   Tel: 55-11-283-7811   Emp: 674
Bus: *Commercial banking services.*   Fax:55-11-284-5753

    PINEBANK
    1001 S. Bayshore Drive, Lobby Level, Miami, FL   33131
    CEO: Francisco Jaime Noguieira Pinheiro Fihlo,   Tel: (305) 539-3400   Emp: 32
        Chmn..
    Bus: *Commercial banking.*   Fax:(305) 358-3433   %FO: 100

- **BANCO BOAVISTA S.A.**
  Praça Pio X, 118, 12 andar, Rio de Janeiro, RJ 20091-040 Brazil
  CEO: Linneo Eduardo de Paula Machado, Pres.   Tel: 55-21-211-1711   Emp: 2200
  Bus: *Commercial banking services.*   Fax:55-21-253-1579

  - **BANCO BOAVISTA S.A.**
    100 S.E. 2nd. Street, Suite 2330, Miami, FL   33131
    CEO: Antonio Castello Branco, E.V.P. Int'l   Tel: (305) 530-9057   Emp: 3
    Bus: *Representative office.*   Fax:(305) 530-1357   %FO: 100

- **BANCO BOZANO, SIMONSEN S.A.**
  Av. Rio Branco, 138, 16o. andar, Rio de Janeiro, RJ 20057-900 Brazil
  CEO: Paulo V. Ferraz, Pres.   Tel: 55-21-271-8000   Emp: 350
  Bus: *Banking services.*   Fax:55-21-271-8053

  - **BANCO BOZANO, SIMONSEN S.A.**
    590 Fifth Avenue, 2nd Fl., New York, NY   10036-4702
    CEO: Alvaro Lopes da Silva Neto, Rep.   Tel: (212) 869-3690   Emp: 3
    Bus: *Representative office.*   Fax:(212) 869-3867   %FO: 100

- **BANCO BRADESCO SA**
  Av. Ipiranga 282, 10 andar, CEP 01046-010, Sao Paulo, SP, Brazil
  CEO: Lázaro de Mello Brandão, Chrm.   Tel: 55-11-235-9566   Emp: 63,549
  Bus: *Commercial banking services.*   Fax:55-11-256-8442

  - **BANCO BRADESCO SA**
    450 Park Ave. - 32nd Fl., New York, NY   10022
    CEO: Karl Heinz Kern, Mgr.   Tel: (212) 688-9855   Emp: 30
    Bus: *International commercial banking services.*   Fax:(212) 754-4032   %FO: 100

- **BANCO DA BAHIA INVESTIMENTOS S.A.**
  Praça Pio X, 98, 7o.andar, Rio de Janeiro, RJ 20091-040 Brazil
  CEO: Pedro Henrique Mariani Bitencourt, Pres.   Tel: 55-21-211-8448   Emp: 250
  Bus: *Investment banking.*   Fax:55-21-263-9527

  - **BAHIA SECURITIES, INC.**
    375 Park Avenue, Suite 3302, New York, NY   10152
    CEO: Bruno Mariani, Pres.   Tel: (212) 319-5959   Emp: 3
    Bus: *Investment banking.*   Fax:(212) 319-1317   %FO: 100

- **BANCO DE CRÉDITO NACIONAL S.A.**
  Av. Andromeda s/n, Alphaville, Barueri, SP 06473-900 Brazil
  CEO: Arlindo Conde, Chrm.   Tel: 55-11-244-1879   Emp: 7300
  Bus: *Commercial banking.*   Fax:55-11-244-1014

  - **BANCO DE CRÉDITO NACIONAL S.A.**
    499 Park Avenue, 10th Fl., New York, NY   10022
    CEO: Celso V. Barison, Gen'l Mgr.   Tel: (212) 980-8383   Emp: 28
    Bus: *Commercial banking.*   Fax:(212)755-0626   %FO: 100

- **BANCO DE INVESTIMENTOS GARANTIA S/A**
Rua Jorge Coelho, 16,13o.andar, São Paulo, SP 01451-020 Brazil
CEO: Fernando Antionio Botelho Prada, Dir.   Tel: 55-11-821-6900   Emp: 300
Bus: *Security brokers, dealers & flotation services.*   Fax:55-11-821-6913

> **GARANTIA INC.**
> 126 East 56th Street, 18th Fl., New York, NY   10022
> CEO: George Ehrensperger, Ptr.   Tel: (212) 223-1699   Emp: 16
> Bus: *Security brokers, dealers & flotation services.*   Fax:(212) 223-4701   %FO: 100

- **BANCO DO BRASIL**
Ed. Sede III, Bloco C, 24 and SBS, Quadro 4 Lote 32, 70089-900 Brasilia, DF Brazil
CEO: Paulo César Ximenes Alves Ferreira, Pres.   Tel: 55-61-310-3400   Emp: 91000
Bus: *Commercial banking services.*   Fax:55-61-310-2563

> **B.B. LEASING SERVICES, LLC**
> 530 Fifth Avenue, 19th Fl., New York, NY   10036
> CEO: Jose Tadeu Antunes de Paiva, Exec. Dir.   Tel: (212) 764-9560   Emp: 10
> Bus: *Business credit institution.*   Fax:(212) 764-9566   %FO: 100

> **BANCO DO BRASIL**
> 550 Fifth Avenue, New York, NY   10036
> CEO: Wolney Ferreira, Gen.Mgr.   Tel: (212) 626-7000   Emp: 210
> Bus: *Savings institution.*   Fax:(212) 626-7045   %FO: 100

> **BANCO DO BRASIL**
> 2020 K Street NW - Suite 450, Washington, DC   20006
> CEO: Paulo de Tarso Mederios,   Tel: (202) 857-0320   Emp: 100
> Bus: *International commercial banking services.*   Fax:(202) 872-8649   %FO: 100

> **BANCO DO BRASIL**
> 811 Wilshire Boulevard, Los Angeles, CA   90017-2624
> CEO: A de Azevedo Bomfim, Gen.Mgr.   Tel: (213) 688-2996   Emp: 21
> Bus: *International commercial banking services.*   Fax:(213) 688-2994   %FO: 100

- **BANCO DO ESTADO DE SÃO PAULO SA**
Pc. Antonio Prado 06 São Paulo, SP, 01010-010 Brazil
CEO: Antonio Carlos Feitosa, Pres.   Tel: 55-11-249-1033   Emp: 33900
Bus: *State commercial bank.*   Fax:55-11-239-2414

> **BANCO DO ESTADO DE SÃO PAULO SA**
> #2 South Biscayne Blvd., Suite 3700, Miami, FL   33131
> CEO: Eliseu Lima, Gen.Mgr.   Tel: (305) 358-9167   Emp: 40
> Bus: *International commercial banking services.*   Fax:(305) 381-6967   %FO: 100

> **BANCO DO ESTADO DE SÃO PAULO SA**
> 399 Park Avenue - 39th Fl., New York, NY   10022
> CEO: Maria A. Martins Boni, Gen.Mgr.   Tel: (212) 715-2800   Emp: 52
> Bus: *International commercial banking services.*   Fax:(212) 371-1034   %FO: 100

● **BANCO DO ESTADO DO PARANÁ SA**
Rua Maximo João Kopp 274, Santa Candida/Cambio, 82630-900 Curitiba, Brazil
CEO: Aldo Almeido Jr., Director   Tel: 55-41-351-7591   Emp: 12000
Bus: *State Commercial Bank.*   Fax:55-41-351-7239

    BANCO DO ESTADO DO PARANA SA
    125 W 55th St., #900, New York, NY 10019-2532
    CEO: Valdir Perin, Gen.Mgr.   Tel: (212) 956-0011   Emp: 10
    Bus: *International commercial banking services.*   Fax:(212) 956-0506   %FO: 100

● **BANCO DO ESTADO DO RIO GRANDE DO SUL SA**
Rua Capitão Montanha, 177 Porto Alegre, RS 90018-900 Brazil
CEO: Ricardo Russowsky, Pres.   Tel: 55-51-215-2887   Emp: 10000
Bus: *State commercial bank.*   Fax:55-51-228-6473

    BANRISUL
    500 Fifth Ave., #2310, New York, NY 10110
    CEO: Carlos R. Becker, Gen.Mgr.   Tel: (212) 827-0390   Emp: 4
    Bus: *Banking services.*   Fax:(212) 869-0844   %FO: 100

● **BANCO FATOR**
Praia de Botafogo, 228, 1o.andar, Rio de Janeiro, RJ 22250-040 Brazil
CEO: Francisco Pierotti, Dir.   Tel: 55-21-553-7000   Emp: 140
Bus: *Investment banks.*   Fax:55-21-553-5834

    FATOR INVESTMENT RESEARCH
    5 River Road, Suite 29, Wilton, CT 06897
    CEO: Marcus Regueira, Mng. Ptr.   Tel: (203) 761-9855   Emp: 3
    Bus: *Investment advice.*   Fax:(203) 761-9351   %FO: 10O

    FATOR SECURITIES L.L.C
    5 River Road, Suite 29, Wilton, CT 06897
    CEO: Marcelo Cabral, Mng. Ptr.   Tel: (203) 761-9855   Emp: 5
    Bus: *Business services.*   Fax:(203) 761-9351   %FO: 100

● **BANCO FIBRA S.A (Sub. of Grupo Vicunha)**
Rua Jorge Coelho, 16, 7o.andar, São Paulo, SP 01451-020 Brazil
CEO: Benjamin Steinbruch, Pres.   Tel: 55-11-827-6700   Emp: 450
Bus: *Security brokers, dealers and flotation services.*   Fax:55-11-827-6891

    FIBRA SECURITIES INC.
    300 Park Avenue, 17th Floor, New York, NY 10022
    CEO: Yukio Aoki, Mng. Dir.   Tel: (212) 572-6390   Emp: 8
    Bus: *Security brokers, dealers, & flotation services.*   Fax:(212) 572-6458   %FO: 100

● **BANCO ICATU S.A.**
Av. Presidente Wilson, 231, 9o.andar, Rio de Janeiro, RJ 20030-021 Brazil
CEO: José Luiz Osório, Dir.   Tel: 55-21-217-1300   Emp: 320
Bus: *Investment banking.*   Fax:55-21-240-4133

    ICATU INVESTMENT CORP.
    527 Madison Avenue, Suite 2500, New York, NY   10022
    CEO: Alden Brewster, Pres.   Tel: (212)479-1100   Emp: 8
    Bus: *Investment banking.*   Fax:(212)479-1111   %FO: 100

    ICATU SECURITIES INC.
    527 Madison Avenue, Suite 2500, New York, NY   10022-4304
    CEO: Sergio Cunha, Principal   Tel: (212) 478-6600   Emp: 4
    Bus: *Investment banking, securities brokers, dealers*   Fax:(212) 478-6633   %FO: 100
       & flotation services.

● **BANCO INDUSVAL S.A**
Rua Boavista 356, 7o.andar, São Paulo, SP 01014 Brazil
CEO: Luiz Ribeiro, Pres.   Tel: 55-11-225-6888   Emp: 178
Bus: *Security brokers, dealers & flotation services.*   Fax:55-11-225-0815

    INDUSVAL USA CORPORATION
    300 Park Avenue, Suite 1716, New York, NY   10022
    CEO: George Lee Rexing, EVP   Tel: (212) 572-6365   Emp: 4
    Bus: *Broker, dealer & Investment advisory.*   Fax:(212) 572-6456   %FO: 100

● **BANCO ITAÚ S.A.**
Rua Boavista, 176, São Paulo, SP 01092-900 Brazil
CEO: Olavo Egydio Setubal, Chrm.   Tel: 55-11-237-3000   Emp: 37000
Bus: *Investment and commercial banking.*   Fax:55-11-277-1044

    BANCO ITAÚ S.A., NEW YORK BRANCH
    540 Madison Avenue, 24th fl., New York, NY   10022
    CEO: Almir Vignoto, Gen. Mgr.   Tel: (212) 486-1380   Emp: 24
    Bus: *International banking services.*   Fax:(212) 888-9342   %FO: 100

● **BANCO MERCANTIL DE SÃO PAULO S.A**
Av. Paulista, 1450, São Paulo, SP 01310-100 Brazil
CEO: Gastão E. Zidigal, Pres.   Tel: 55-11-252-2121   Emp: 6700
Bus: *Commercial banking services.*   Fax:55-11-284-3312

    BANCO MERCANTIL DE SÃO PAULO S.A
    450 Park Avenue, 14th Floor, New York, NY   10022
    CEO: Irones Oliveira Paula, Gen'l Mgr.   Tel: (212) 888-0030   Emp: 7
    Bus: *International banking services.*   Fax:(212) 888-4631   %FO: 100

● **BANCO PACTUAL S.A.**
Av. Rebublica do Chile, 230, 29o.andar, Rio de Janeiro, RJ 20031-170 Brazil
CEO: Luis Cesar Fernandes, Pres.   Tel: 55-21-272-1100   Emp: 280
Bus: *Investment banking & investment advisory services.*   Fax: 55-21-533-1661

> **PACTUAL CAPITAL CORPORATION**
> 527 Madison Avenue, 14th Fl., New York, NY   10022
> CEO: Thomas W. Keesee III, Mng. Dir.   Tel: (212) 702-4100   Emp: 10
> Bus: *Investment banking.*   Fax: (212) 702-4110   %FO: 100

● **BANCO REAL SA**
Av. Paulista 1374, 01310-916 Sao Paulo, Brazil
CEO: Paulo Guilherme M. Lobato Ribeiro, Pres.   Tel: 55-11-251-9655   Emp: 15000
Bus: *National commercial bank.*   Fax: 55-11-251-9222

> **BANCO REAL INTL INC**
> 200 W Adams St., #1610, Chicago, IL   60606
> CEO: Thomas P Campbell, Gen.Mgr.   Tel: (312) 853-3421   Emp: 5
> Bus: *International banking services.*   Fax: (312) 853-3424   %FO: 100

> **BANCO REAL SA**
> 1800 K Street, NW, Suite 301, Washington, DC   20006
> CEO: Henrique Campos, Gen.Mgr.   Tel: (202) 452-6870   Emp: 6
> Bus: *International banking services.*   Fax: (202) 452-6873   %FO: 100

> **BANCO REAL SA**
> South Biscayne Blvd., Suite 1870, Miami, FL   33131
> CEO: Vincente Timiraos, Gen.Mgr.   Tel: (305) 358-2433   Emp: 25
> Bus: *International banking services.*   Fax: (305) 375-8214   %FO: 100

> **BANCO REAL SA**
> 680 Fifth Ave., 6th Fl., New York, NY   10019
> CEO: Humberto M de Carvalho, Reg. Dir.   Tel: (212) 489-0100   Emp: 50
> Bus: *International banking services.*   Fax: (212) 307-5627   %FO: 100

● **BFII, SUDAMERIS**
Av. Paulista, 1000. 7o. andar, São Paulo, SP 01310-912 Brazil
CEO: Giovanni Urizio, Dir. & Superindente   Tel: 55-11-283-9633   Emp: 3800
Bus: *Investment banking services.*   Fax: 55-11-289-1239

> **BANK SUDAMERIS-MIAMI**
> 701 Brickell Avenue, 9th Fl., Miami, FL   33131
> CEO: Hubert de la Felda, SVP & Mgr.   Tel: (305) 372-2200   Emp: 58
> Bus: *Investment banking.*   Fax: (305) 374-1137   %FO: 100

- **BM & F - BOLSA DE MERCADORIAS E FUTUROS**
Praça Antonio Prado, 48, São Paulo, SP 01010-901 Brazil
CEO: Dorival Rodrigues Alves   Tel: 55-11-232-5454   Emp: 288
Bus: *Commodities, futures, and options exchanges.*   Fax:55-11-239-3531

    AIM BRAZIL CORPORATION
    450 Park Avenue, Suite. 2101, New York, NY 10022-2605
    CEO: Luiz F. Forbes, Pres.   Tel: (212) 750-4197   Emp: 3
    Bus: *International financial advisory firm.*   Fax:(212) 750-4198   %FO: 100

- **BRAZMEDIA INTERNACIONAL PUBLICIDADE E EDIÇÕES LTDA.**
Alameda Gabriel Monteiro da Silva, 366, São Paulo, SP 01442-900 Brazil
CEO: Les Bilyk, Pres.   Tel: 55-11-853-4133   Emp: 17
Bus: *Advertising agency.*   Fax:55-11-852-6485

    THE N. DEFILIPPES CORPORATION
    310 Madison Ave., Suite 1012, New York, NY 10017-6009
    CEO: Del Stella, Pres.   Tel: (212) 697-6868   Emp: 10
    Bus: *Advertising agency.*   Fax:(212) 697-6770   %FO: 100

- **COMPANHIA CACIQUE DE CAFÉ SOLÚVEL**
Avenida das Nações Inidas, 10989, 10o ao 11o. andares, São Paulo, SP 04578-000 Brazil
CEO: Sérgio Coimbra, Pres.   Tel: 55-11-829-8233   Emp: 2000
Bus: *Mfr. roasted coffee.*   Fax:55-11-829-7278

    BRASTRADE (Brazilian Trading Co., Inc.)
    120 Wall Street, Suite 1801, New York, NY 10005
    CEO: Sérgio C. Pereria, Pres.   Tel: (212) 363-2575   Emp: 11
    Bus: *Coffee brokers & dealers.*   Fax:(212) 514-6119   %FO: 100

- **CONSTRUTORA ANDRADE GUTIÉRREZ SA**
Rua dos Pampas, 484, Belo Horizonte, MG 34010-900 Brazil
CEO: Ildeu Olintho de Freitas, Int'l Dir.   Tel: 55-31-290-6933   Emp: 9500
Bus: *Metal mining services; heavy construction.*   Fax:55-31-290-6104

    ANDRADE GUTIÉRREZ OF AMERICA
    1200 19th Street, N.W., Suite 606, Washington, DC 20036
    CEO: Henrique A. Trinckquel   Tel: (202) 293-0330   Emp: N/A
    Bus: *Metal mining services; heavy construction.*   Fax:(202) 293-8108   %FO: 100

- **CSPR ALLIOTT BRASIL AUDITORES E CONSULTORE**
Av. Faria Lima , 1476, cjto. 61/62, São Paulo, SP 04012 Brazil
CEO: Nelmir Pereira Rosas, Chrm.   Tel: 55-11-813-8188   Emp: 23
Bus: *Accounting, auditing and bookkeeping services.*   Fax:55-11-813-8153

    RD HUNTER & COMPANY
    1 Mack Center Drive, Paramus, NJ 07652
    CEO: Lawrence Cinquegrama, Mgr.   Tel: (201) 261-4030   Emp: 75
    Bus: *Accounting/auditing services.*   Fax:(201) 261-8588   %FO: 100

● DURATEX
Avenida Paulista 1938, CEP 01310-200 São Paulo, Brazil
CEO: Paulo Setubal, Pres.   Tel: 55-11-3179-7834   Emp: N/A
Bus: *Mfr./sale hardboard & particleboard.*   Fax:55-11-3179-7707

DURATEX NORTH AMERICA, INC.
1208 Eastchester Drive, Suite 202, High Point, NC   27265
CEO: Gary Wikstrom, Gen.Mgr.   Tel: (910) 885-1500   Emp: N/A
Bus: *Mfr./sale hardboard & particleboard.*   Fax:(910) 885-1501   %FO: 100

● EMBRAER, EMPRESA BRASILEIRA DE AERONAUTICA S.A.
Caixa Postal 343, São José dos Campos, SP 12227-901 Brasil
CEO: Mauricio Botelho, Pres.   Tel: 55-123-25-1000   Emp: 3800
Bus: *Aircraft, engines & parts.*   Fax:55-123-25-1090

EMBRAER AIRCRAFT CORPORATION
276 SW 34th Street, Ft. Lauderdale, FL   33315
CEO: Sam Hill, Pres.   Tel: (954) 359-3700   Emp: 76
Bus: *Aircraft engines & parts.*   Fax:(954) 359-8170   %FO: 100

● EMPRESA DE NAVEGAÇÁO ALIANÇA S.A.
Av. Pasteur, 110, Rio de Janeiro, RJ 22290 Brazil
CEO: Carlos Eduardo Fischer, Chrm.   Tel: 55-21-546-1122   Emp: 500
Bus: *Transportation, freight, deep sea.*   Fax:55-21-546-1161

EMPRESA DE NAVEGAÇÁO ALIANÇA
50 Cragwood Road, South Plainfield, NJ   07080
CEO: Lucio Pimenta, Gen'l Mgr   Tel: (908) 668-5480   Emp: 531
Bus: *Transportation, freight, deep sea.*   Fax:(908) 668-5380   %FO: 100

● EUCATEX S.A. INDÚSTRIA
Av. Francisco Matarazzo, 584, São Paulo, SP 05032-900 Brazil
CEO: Roberto Maluf, Pres.   Tel: 55-11-823-2266   Emp: 4764
Bus: *Forest products.*   Fax:55-11-823-2452

EUCATEX TRADING S.A. EXPORTAÇÃO E IMPORTAÇÃO
780 Third Avenue, Suite 1601, New York, NY   10017
CEO: William F. Monck, Pres.   Tel: (212) 750-8610   Emp: 5000
Bus: *Wood products; hardwood veneer & plywood.*   Fax:(212) 750-7897   %FO: 100

● FERMER INTERNATIONAL FINANCE CORPORATION
Av. Nove de Julho, 3147, 4o. andar São Paulo, SP 01407-000 Brazil
CEO: Ricardo de Carvalho Loueiro, Pres.   Tel: 55-11-884-7766   Emp: 8
Bus: *Investment advisory services.*   Fax:55-11-884-7372

FERMER INTERNATIONAL FINANCE CORPORATION
35 Chittenden Avenue, Crestwood, NY   10707
CEO: Ricardo de Carvalho Loureiro   Tel: (914) 793-0744   Emp: 8
Bus: *Investment advisory.*   Fax:(914) 799-1804   %FO: 100

- **GAFISA PARTICIPAÇÕES S.A.**
  Av. Brigadeiro Faria Lima, 2100, 22o.andar, São Paulo, SP 01452-002 Brazil
  CEO: Carlos Moasyr Gomes de Alemeida, Chrm. Tel: 55-11-817-9000 Emp: 2853
  Bus: *Real estate services.* Fax: 55-11-814-0881

    GAFISA (USA) INC.
    16 East 52nd Street, 9th Fl., New York, NY 10022
    CEO: Raul Leite Luna, Pres. Tel: (212) 888-5155 Emp: 15
    Bus: *Real estate agents & managers.* Fax: (212) 888-5470 %FO: 100

- **GAZETA MERCANTIL S.A.**
  Rua Engenheiro Francisco Pitta de Brito, 125 São Paulo, SP 04753-080 Brazil
  CEO: Luis Fernando Ferreira Levy, Pres. Tel: 55-11-547-3090 Emp: 500
  Bus: *Books, periodicals & newspapers.* Fax: 55-11-547-3011

    GAZETA MERCANTIL
    450 Lexington Avenue, GCS- POBox 994,, New York, NY 10163
    CEO: Getúlio Bittencourt Tel: (800) 952-4541 Emp: 2
    Bus: *Books, periodicals & newspapers.* Fax: (914) 738-5439 %FO: 100

- **HANSA AGÊNCIA DE COMÉRCIO IMPORTAÇÃO E EXPORTAÇÃO LTDA.**
  Rua Paraiba, 846, Aatiradores joinville, SC 89203-530 Brazil
  CEO: Carlo Kadur, Pres. Tel: 55-474-33-5266 Emp: 11
  Bus: *Transportation services.* Fax: 55-474-33-0757

    HANSA USA CORPORATION
    2654 NW 112 Avenue, Miami, FL 33172
    CEO: Marcos Kadur, Pres. Tel: (305) 594-4000 Emp: 10
    Bus: *Transportation, freight & cargo services.* Fax: (305) 594-4100 %FO: 100

- **INSTITUTO DE RESEGUROS DO BRASIL**
  Av. Marechal Câmera, 171, Rio de Janeiro, RJ 20023--900 Brazil
  CEO: Demosthenes Madureira de Pinho, Pres. Tel: 55-21-272-0200 Emp: 600
  Bus: *Insurance agency, brokerage & service.* Fax: 55-21-240-9370

    UA HOLDING CORPORATION
    83 Maiden Lane, 6th Fl., New York, NY 10038
    CEO: Ms. Kathleen Wodzinski, Acting Pres. Tel: (212) 514-7400 Emp: 5
    Bus: *Reinsurance services.* Fax: (212) 363-4803 %FO: 100

● IOCHPE-MAXION S.A.
Av. das Nações Unidas, 1789, 8o. ao 10o. andares, São Paulo, SP 04795-100 Brazil
CEO: Ivoncy Brochmann Ioschpe, Chrm.   Tel: 55-11-514-7700   Emp: 9500
Bus: *Motor vehicles, car bodies, parts & accessories.*   Fax: 55-11-514-7717

IOCHPE-MAXION USA Inc.
9100 S. Dadeland Blvd., Ste 1101, Miami, FL   33156
CEO: Salamon Iochpe, Pres.   Tel: (305) 670-8030   Emp: 14
Bus: *Motor vehicles: car bodies, parts &*   Fax: (305) 670-9966   %FO: 100
accessories.

● JÚLIO BOGORICIN IMÓVEIS
Av. Brasil, 876, São Paulo, SP Brazil
CEO: Júlio Bogoricin, Pres.   Tel: 55-11-833-0244   Emp: 1600
Bus: *Real estate managers & agents.*   Fax: 55-11-881-5011

JÚLIO BOGORICIN REAL ESTATE CORP.
485 Madison Avenue, Suite 1306, New York, NY   10022
CEO: Julio Bogoricin, Pres.   Tel: (212) 888-7755   Emp: 3
Bus: *Real estate brokers & managers.*   Fax: (212) 755-4286   %FO: 100

● MANAGER COMUNICAÇÃO LTDA.
Av. Brigadeiro Faria Lima, 1698, 4o. andar, São Paulo, SP 01452 Brazil
CEO: Gilberto L. Pierro, Pres.   Tel: 55-11-816-4688   Emp: 48
Bus: *Public relations & advertising services.*   Fax: 55-11-814-0132

MANAGER WORLDWIDE CORPORATE
80 SW 8th Street, Suite 2000, Miami, FL   33130
CEO: Gilberto L. Pierro II, Pres.   Tel: (305) 577-4454   Emp: 56
Bus: *Public relations services.*   Fax: (305) 577-0105   %FO: 100

● MANGELS INDUSTRIAL S.A.
Av. Robert Kennedy, 925, São Bernardo do Campo, SP 09860-000 Brazil
CEO: Roberto Mangels, Chrm.   Tel: 55-11-541-8699   Emp: 1700
Bus: *Motor vehicle parts & accessories.*   Fax: 55-11-247-0155

POSITRADE CORPORATION
405 North Smith Avenue, Corona, CA   91720
CEO: Edson Andrade, Pres.   Tel: (909) 737-2117   Emp: 16
Bus: *Motor vehicles: parts & accessories.*   Fax: (909) 737-0292   %FO: 100

• **MAPPIN LOJAS DE DEPARTAMENTOS S.A.**
Praca Ramos de Azevedo, 131, 9o. andar, Sao Paulo, SP 01037-000 Brazil
CEO: Carlos Antonio Rocca, Pres.   Tel: 55-11-214-4411   Emp: 7200
Bus: *Retail department stores.*   Fax:55-11-605-7470

    MAPPIN STORES COMPANY
    1480 NW 79th Avenue, Miami, FL 33126
    CEO: Decio Ortiz, Pres.   Tel: (305) 591-3309   Emp: 24
    Bus: *Retail department stores.*   Fax:(305) 592-6108   %FO: 100

• **COMPANHIA MARITIMA NACIONAL**
Rua São Bento, 8 8o. andar, Rio de Janeiro, RJ 20090-010 Brazil
CEO: Pedro Henrique Garcia, Dir.   Tel: 55-21-272-2400   Emp: 150
Bus: *Transportation, freight, deep sea.*   Fax:55-21-263-0036

    NATIONAL LINE (Comp. Marítima Nacional)
    99 Wood Avenue South, Suite 307, Iselin, NJ 08830
    CEO: Thomas M. Lloyd Jr., Gen'l Mgr.   Tel: (908) 494-2150   Emp: 4
    Bus: *International freight transportation services.*   Fax:(908) 494-2272   %FO: 150

• **METAL LEVE S/A INDÚSTRIA E COMÉRCIO**
Rua Brasílio Luz, 535, Santo Amaro, SP 04746-901 Brazil
CEO: José E. Mindlin, Chrm.   Tel: 55-11-545-0711   Emp: 4415
Bus: *Motor vehicle parts & accessories.*   Fax:55-11-521*8762

    METAL LEVE INC.
    560 Avis Drive, Ann Arbor, MI 48108
    CEO: Duraid Mahrus, Mgr   Tel: (313) 930-1590   Emp: 25
    Bus: *Motor vehicle parts & accessories.*   Fax:(313) 930-1792   %FO: 100

    METAL LEVE INC.
    500 Prosperity Drive, Orangeburg, SC 29115
    CEO: Davlio Giovanetti, Mgr.   Tel: (803) 534-0040   Emp: 200
    Bus: *Mfr. motor vehicles parts & accessories.*   Fax:(803) 534-3331   %FO: 100

    METAL LEVE INC.
    990 Jefferson Road, Sumter, SC 29153
    CEO: Paulo Dellanoce, Mgr.   Tel: (803) 469-4722   Emp: 250
    Bus: *Mfr. motor vehicles parts & accessories.*   Fax:(803) 469-4727   %FO: 100

• **NORONHA ADVOGADOS**
Av. Brig. Faria Lima, 2100, 3o. andar, Sao Paulo, SP 01452-919 Brazil
CEO: Durval de Noronha Goyos Jr., Sr. Ptnr.   Tel: 55-11-816-6609   Emp: 90
Bus: *Legal services.*   Fax:55-11-212-2495

    NORONHA ADVOGADOS
    1211 Brickell Avenue, Suite 1040, Maimi, FL 33131
    CEO: Durval de Noronha Goyos, Jr., Sr. Ptnr.   Tel: (305) 372-0844   Emp: 2
    Bus: *Legal services.*   Fax:(305) 372-1792   %FO: 100

● **PETROBRÁS - PETRÓLEO BRASILEIRO S.A.**
Av. República do Chile, 65, Rio de Janeiro, RJ 20132-900 Brazil

CEO: Joel Mendes Rennó, Pres.	Tel: 55-21-534-2040	Emp: 46200
Bus: *Petroleum, oil & gas product-drilling & refining services; natural health products.*	Fax:55-21-533-2614	

    PETROBRÁS (NY) - PETRÓLEO BRASILEIRO S.A.
    1330 Avenue of the Americas, 16th Fl., New York, NY   10019

CEO: Carlos Serzadello Correa, Gen'l Mgr	Tel: (212) 974-0777	Emp: 15
Bus: *Petroleum, oil & gas production -drilling & refining services; natural health products.*	Fax:(212) 974-1169	%FO: 100

    PETROBRÁS (HOUSTON) - PETRÓLEO BRASILEIRO S.A.
    10777 Westheimer Road
    Ste. 625, Houston, TX   77042

CEO: Luiz Reis, Gen'l Mgr.	Tel: (713) 781-9798	Emp: 50
Bus: *Petroleum, oil & gas production -drilling & refining services; natural health products.*	Fax:(713) 781-9790	%FO: 100

● **PREVIPLAN CONSULTORIA E PLANEJAMENTO S/C LTDA.**
Rua Ramos Batista, 152, 5o. andar, Itaim Bibi, Sao Paulo, SP 04552 Brazil

CEO: Wadico Bucchi, Pres.	Tel: 55-11-829-9711	Emp: 40
Bus: *Investment advisory services.*	Fax:55-11-820-2382	

    PREVIPLAN INVESTMENTS, INC.
    5850 Lakehurst Drive, Suite 150-25, Orlando, FL   32819

CEO: Wadico Bucchi, Pre.	Tel: (407) 248-3414	Emp: 5
Bus: *Investment advisory services.*	Fax:(407) 248-3415	%FO: 100

● **SÃO PAULO ALPARGATAS S.A.**
Rua Urussuí, 300, São Paulo, SP 04542-903 Brazil

CEO: Diego J. Bush, Chrm.	Tel: 55-11-827-7322	Emp: 17175
Bus: *Mfr. textiles.*	Fax:55-11-820-8866	

    EXPASA FLORIDA, INC.
    8284 14th Street, N.W., Miami, FL   33126

CEO: Nelson Ortega, Pres.	Tel: (305) 594-4353	Emp: 15
Bus: *Export/import textiles.*	Fax:(305) 592-1733	%FO: 100

● **SMAR EQUIPAMENTOS INDUSTRIAS LTDA.**
Av. Doutor Antionio Furlan Jr., 1028, Sertãozinho, SP 14160-000 Brazil

CEO: Edmundo Corini, Pres.	Tel: 55-16-642-3466	Emp: 730
Bus: *Ind. measurement instruments, display & control, and machinery.*	Fax:55-16-642-3661	

    SMAR INTERNATIONAL CORPORATION
    7240 Brittmoore, Suite 110, Houston, TX   77041

CEO: Paulo Garrone, Gen'l Mgr	Tel: (713) 849-2021	Emp: 25
Bus: *Ind. measurement instruments, display & control machinery*	Fax:(713) 849-2022	%FO: 100

- **SOLA S.A. INDÚSTRIAS ALIMENTICIAS**
Rua Stet de Setembro, 111, sala 2102, Centro Rio de Janeiro, RJ 20159-900 Brazil
CEO: Carlo Sola, Chrm.   Tel: 55-21-232-8080   Emp: 2000
Bus: *Meat products.*   Fax:55-21-221-9463

    RBI COMPANY, INC.
    358 Lawton Avenue, Cliffside Park, NJ   07010
    CEO: Reinaldo Barbosa, Pres.   Tel: (201) 941-2020   Emp: 4
    Bus: *Import/export canned meats.*   Fax:(201) 941-5319   %FO: 100

- **TRANSBRASIL LINHAS AEREAS**
Rua Galeao Pantaleao Telles 40, Jardim Aeroporto, Sao Paulo, SP 04355-040 Brazil
CEO: Omar Fontana, Pres.   Tel: 55-11-532-4600   Emp: 4700
Bus: *International air transport services.* Fax:55-11-543-8048

    TRANSBRASIL AIRLINES INC.
    5757 Blue Lagoon Drive, Suite 400, Miami, FL   33126
    CEO: Marise Barbosa, Mgr.   Tel: (305) 591-8322   Emp: 151
    Bus: *International air transport services.* Fax:(305) 477-9509   %FO: 100

    TRANSBRASIL AIRLINES INC.
    500 Fifth Avenue, Suite 1710, New York, NY   10110
    CEO: Lincoln Delbone, Genl Mgr   Tel: (212) 944-7374   Emp: 20
    Bus: *International air transport services.* Fax:(212) 944-7458   %FO: 100

- **TRISTÃO COMERCIAL E PARTICIPAÇÕES S.A.**
Av. Nossa Senhora dos Navegantes, 675, 8o. andar, Enseada do Suá, Vitória,   ES 29056-900
Brazil
CEO: Sérgio Dominguez Sotelino, Pres.   Tel: 55-27-325-4000   Emp: 24
Bus: *Mfr. roasted coffee.*   Fax:55-27-325-2739

    TRISTÃO TRADING, INC.
    116 John Street, Suite 2401, New York, NY   10038
    CEO: Paul J. Fisher, Pres.   Tel: (212) 285-8120   Emp: 8
    Bus: *Roasted coffee, trading.*   Fax:(212) 964-1735   %FO: 100

- **UNIBANCO (União de Bancos Brasileiros S.A)**
Av. Eusãébio Matoso, 891, 4o. andar, São Paulo, SP 05423-180 Brasil
CEO: Roberto Ronder Bornhausen, Chrm.   Tel: 55-11-867-4322   Emp: 17025
Bus: *Commercial banking.*   Fax:55-11-815-5084

    UNIBANCO - União de Bancos Brasileiros S. A.
    701 Brickell Avenue, Suite 2080, Miami, FL   33131
    CEO: Marcos Rodrigues Pereira, Mgr.   Tel: (305) 372-0100   Emp: 15
    Bus: *Commercial banking.*   Fax:(305) 374-5652   %FO: 100

UNIBANCO - New York Agency (União de Bancos Brasileiros S.A)
555 Madison Avenue, 19th Fl., New York, NY   10022-3393

CEO: Edson F. da Silva, Dir.	Tel: (212) 207-9416	Emp: 27
Bus: *Commercial banking.*	Fax:(212) 754-4872	%FO: 100

● **COMPANHIA VALE DO RIO DOCE**
Av. Graça Aranha, 26, Rio de Janeiro, RJ 20005-900 Brazil

CEO: Francisco Jose Schettino, Pres.	Tel: 55-21-272-4477	Emp: 17000
Bus: *Metal mining & non-metallic mineral services; import/export & consulting services.*	Fax:55-21-262-8026	

RIO DOCE AMERICA, INC.
114 West 47th Street, 22nd Fl., New York, NY   10036

CEO: Mario R.M. Pierry, Pres.	Tel: (212) 626-9800	Emp: 32
Bus: *Metals & wood pulp, export/import services.*	Fax:(212) 391-1000	%FO: 100

● **VARIG BRAZILIAN AIRLINES SA**
Av. Almiranti Silvio de Noronha 365, Rio de Janeiro, RJ 20021-010 Brazil

CEO: Fernando Pinto, Chrm. & Pres.	Tel: 55-21-272-5310	Emp: 18000
Bus: *International commercial air transport services.*	Fax:55-21-272-5720	

VARIG BRAZILIAN AIRLINES
380 Madison Avenue, New York, NY   10017

CEO: Carlos Muzzio, Gen.Mgr.	Tel: (212) 850-8200	Emp: 360
Bus: *Commercial air transport.*	Fax:(212) 850-8201	%FO: 100

● **VOTORANTIM**
Rua Gomes de Carvalho. 1356, 7o. andar, São Paulo, SP 04547-005 Brazil

CEO: José Ermírio de Moraes, Chrm.	Tel: 55-11-829-9622	Emp: 50000
Bus: *Paper mfr., chemicals & allied products.*	Fax:55-11-820-0330	

VOTORANTIM INTERNATIONAL NORTH AMERICA, INC.
111 Continental Dr., Ste. 111, Newark, DE   19713

CEO: Eduardo Scabbia, Mng. Dir.	Tel: (302) 454-8300	Emp: 6
Bus: *Import/export commodity sales office.*	Fax:(302) 454-8309	%FO: 100

● **WEG S.A.**
Rua Joinville, 3300, Jaraguá do Sul, SC 89256-900 Brazil

CEO: Eggon João da Silva, CEO	Tel: 55-473-72-4000	Emp: 7000
Bus: *Mfr./sales electric motors.*	Fax:55-473-72-4010	

WEG ELECTRIC MOTORS CORPORATION
252 Ginbert Drive, Viriginia Beach, VA   23452

CEO: Marco Marino, Gen'l Mgr.	Tel: (800) 343-9996	Emp: N/A
Bus: *Mfr./sales electric motors.*	Fax:(757) 340-3530	%FO: 100

WEG ELECTRIC MOTORS CORPORATION
2200 Commercial Blvd., Ste. 101, Ft. Lauderdale, FL   33309

CEO: Celso V. Siebert, Pres.	Tel: (954) 486-2483	Emp: N/A
Bus: *Mfr./sales electric motors.*	Fax:(954) 735-6677	%FO: 100

Canada

- **ABITIBI-CONSOLIDATED INC.**
800 Rene Levesque Blvd. Quest, Montreal, Quebec, Canada H3B 1YR9
CEO: James Doughan, Pres.   Tel: (514) 875-2160   Emp: N/A
Bus: *Mfr. newsprint, specialty papers, paperboard;*   Fax:(514) 875-6284
timberland management.

   ABITIBI CONSOLIDATED
   4 Manhattanville Road, Purchase, NY   01577-2126
   CEO: Don Martin, Pres.   Tel: (914) 696-6900   Emp: N/A
   Bus: *US headquarters, sales.*   Fax:(914) 696-6980   %FO: 100

   ALABAMA RIVER NEWSPRINT COMPANY
   PO Box 10, Perdue Hill, AL   36470
   CEO: T. Thorsteinson, Pres.   Tel: (334) 575-2800   Emp: N/A
   Bus: *Production of newsprint.*   Fax:(334) 743-6427   %FO: JV

   AP SUPPORT SERVICES
   1491 Meridan Drive, Buffalo, NY   14150
   CEO: Rory O'Connor, Pres.   Tel: (716) 564-2777   Emp: N/A
   Bus: *Sales/service support.*   Fax:(716) 564-3033   %FO: 100

   AUGUSTA NEWSPRINT COMPANY
   P O Box 1647, Augusta, GA   30913
   CEO: Bob Collez, Pres.   Tel: (706) 798-3440   Emp: N/A
   Bus: *Production of newsprint*   Fax:(706) 793-4149   %FO: JV

   AZERTY INC.
   13 Centre Drive, Orchard Park, NY   14127
   CEO: Jane Todd, Pres.   Tel: (716) 662-0200   Emp: N/A
   Bus: *Sales/service office products.*   Fax:(716) 662-7616   %FO: 100

   POSITIVE ID WHOLESALE, INC.
   1000 Young Street, Suite 320, Torowanda, NY   14150
   CEO: Bill Dueger, Pres.   Tel: (716) 692-2008   Emp: N/A
   Bus: *Bar coating equipment.*   Fax:(716) 692-3863   %FO: 100

- **ACRES INC.**
480 University Ave, Toronto, ON, Canada M5G 1V2
CEO: O. Sigvaldafon, Pres.   Tel: (416) 595-2000   Emp: N/A
Bus: *Engineering services.*   Fax:(416) 595-2004

   ACRES CORPORATION
   140 John James Audubon Pkwy, Amherst, NY   14228
   CEO: Jeff Argauer, Pres.   Tel: (716) 689-3737   Emp: N/A
   Bus: *Engineering services.*   Fax:(716) 689-3749   %FO: 100

• AGRA EARTH & ENVIRONMENTAL LTD.
221 18th Street SE, Calgary, AB, Canada T2E 6J5

CEO: W. A. Slusarchuk, CEO	Tel: (403) 248-4331	Emp: 200
Bus: *Consulting services: geotechnical, environmental, water resources.*	Fax:(403) 248-2188	

AGRA EARTH & ENVIRONMENTAL INC
11335 NE 122nd Way, Ste.100, Kirkland, WA   98034

CEO: Jim Dransfield, Pres.	Tel: (206) 820-4669	Emp: 150
Bus: *Consulting services: geotechnical, environmental, water resources.*	Fax:(206) 821-3914	%FO: 100

• AIR CANADA
Air Canada Centre, P O Box 14000, 7373 Cote Vertu West, St-Laurent, PQ, Canada H4Y 1H4

CEO: R. Lamar Durrett, Pres.	Tel: (514) 422-5000	Emp: N/A
Bus: *Commercial air transport services.*	Fax:(514) 422-5799	

AIR CANADA
1133 Ave. of the Americas, New York, NY   10036

CEO: Lamar Durrett, Pres.	Tel: (212) 869-8840	Emp: N/A
Bus: *International commercial air transport services.*	Fax:(212) 960-3000	%FO: 100

AIR CANADA
4890 West Kennedy Blvd., Tampa, FL   33609

CEO: Bruce Deitch, Gen. Mgr.	Tel: (800) 776-3000	Emp: N/A
Bus: *International commercial air transport services.*	Fax:(212) 960-3000	%FO: 100

• ALBERTA NATURAL GAS CO., LTD.
Suite 2900, 240 Fourth Ave South, Calgary, AB, Canada T2P 4L7

CEO: Dr. N. E. Wagner, Chmn. & CEO	Tel: (403) 691-7777	Emp: 136
Bus: *Specialty chemicals & natural gas liquids, magnesium; operates gas pipelines; property development.*	Fax:(403) 691-7401	

ANGUS CHEMICAL COMPANY
1500 E. Lake Cook Road, Buffalo Grove, IL   60089

CEO: G.W. Granzow, CEO	Tel: (847) 215-8600	Emp: 500
Bus: *Production/marketing nitroparaffins, specialty chemicals, erythromycin.*	Fax:(847) 808-3703	%FO: 100

● **ALCAN ALUMINUM LTD.**
1188 Sherbrooke Street West, Montreal, PQ, Canada H3A 3G2
CEO: Jacques Bougie, Pres.   Tel: (514) 848-8000   Emp: 39000
Bus: *Mfr./sale aluminum products.*   Fax:(514) 848-8115

    ALCAN ALUMINUM CORP.
    6060 Parkland Blvd., Mayfield Heights, OH   44124
    CEO: Dick Evans, Pres.   Tel: (216) 423-6600   Emp: N/A
    Bus: *Aluminum plate, foil products, electronic*   Fax:(216) 423-6667   %FO: 100
        equipment, agricultural products.

● **AMERICAN BARRICK RESOURCES CORP.**
Royal Bank Plaza, South Tower, P O Box 119, Toronto, ON, Canada M5J 2J3
CEO: Robert M. Smith, Pres. & CEO   Tel: (416) 861-9911   Emp: 2000
Bus: *Gold mining.*   Fax:(416) 861-2492

    BARRICK GOLDSTRIKE MINE
    PO Box 29,
    790 Commercial Blvd., Elko, NV   89801
    CEO: Don Prahl, VP & Gen.Mgr.   Tel: (702) 738-8381   Emp: N/A
    Bus: *Mining*   Fax:(702) 738-6543   %FO: 100

    BARRICK MERCER GOLD MINE
    PO Box 838, Tooele, UT   84074
    CEO: Clayton Landa, VP & Gen.Mgr.   Tel: (801) 268-4447   Emp: N/A
    Bus: *Mining*   Fax:(801) 266-4296   %FO: 100

● **ANACHEMIA LTD.**
PO Box 147, Lachin, PQ, Canada H8S 4A7
CEO: J.K.Kudrnac, Pres.   Tel: (514) 489-5711   Emp: N/A
Bus: *Mfr. chemicals, etc.*   Fax:(514) 363-5281

    ANACHEMIA CANADA INC.
    3 Lincoln Boulevard, Rouses Point, NY   12979
    CEO: I. K. Kudrnac, Pres.   Tel: (518) 297-4444   Emp: N/A
    Bus: *Mfr. chemicals, lab chemicals/solvents, etc.*   Fax:(518) 297-2960   %FO: 100

● **ARMSTRONG LTD.**
23 Bertrand Avenue, Scarborough, ON, Canada M1L 2P3
CEO: Charles Armstrong, Pres.   Tel: (416) 755-2291   Emp: 200
Bus: *Mfr. pumps, pumping equipment.*   Fax:(416) 759-9101

    ARMSTRONG PUMPS INC.
    93 East Avenue, North Tonawanda, NY   14120
    CEO: Michael Scharring, Mng. Dir.   Tel: (716) 693-8813   Emp: 100
    Bus: *Mfr. pumps, pumping equipment.*   Fax:(716) 693-8970   %FO: 100

● **BANISTER FOUNDATION LTD.**
3660 Midland Avenue, Scarborogh, ON, Canada MIV 4V3
CEO: Norm Harrison, Pres.   Tel: 416-754-8735   Emp: 370
Bus: *Construction services.*   Fax:416-754-8736

FRONTIER CONSTRUCTION COMPANY, INC.
19217-36 Avenue West, Suite 200, Lynnwood, WA 98036-5707
CEO: Jim Dougan, Pres.   Tel: (206) 774-2945   Emp: 15
Bus: *Construction services.*   Fax:(206) 771-8094   %FO: 98

● **BANK OF MONTREAL**
P.O. Box 6002, Place d' Armes, Montreal, PQ Canada H2Y 3S8
CEO: Matthew W. Barrett, Chrm.   Tel: (514) 877-7110   Emp: 33468
Bus: *Commercial banking services.*   Fax:(514) 877-7525

BANK OF MONTREAL
430 Park Avenue, New York, NY   10022
CEO: Sanjiv Tandon, SVP   Tel: (212) 758-6300   Emp: N/A
Bus: *Commercial banking services.*   Fax:(212) 702-1193   %FO: 100

BANK OF MONTREAL TRUST COMPANY
77 Water Street - 4th Fl., New York, NY   10005
CEO: Mark McLaughlin, VP   Tel: (212) 701-7650   Emp: N/A
Bus: *Commercial banking services.*   Fax:(212) 701-7684   %FO: 100

HARRIS BANK INT'L CORP.
430 Park Avenue, New York, NY   10022
CEO: Gerald R. Daly, VP & Gen.Mgr.   Tel: (212) 715-2600   Emp: N/A
Bus: *International banking services.*   Fax:(212) 758-9847   %FO: 100

HARRIS BANKCORP INC.
111 West Monroe Street, Chicago, IL   60603
CEO: Alan G. McNally, Chrm.   Tel: (312) 461-2121   Emp: N/A
Bus: *Commercial banking services.*   Fax:(312) 461-7385   %FO: 100

HARRIS INVESTMENT MANAGEMENT CORP
190 South LaSalle Street, Chicago, IL   60690-0755
CEO: Donald G.M. Coxe, Chrm.   Tel: (312) 461-5365   Emp: N/A
Bus: *Investment management services.*   Fax:(312) 765-8160   %FO: 100

HARRIS TRUST AND SAVINGS BANK
111 West Monroe Street, Chicago, IL   60603
CEO: Charles H. Davis, EVP   Tel: (312) 461-2121   Emp: N/A
Bus: *Commercial banking services.*   Fax:(312) 461-7385   %FO: 100

NESBITT THOMPSON SECURITIES, INC.
430 Park Avenue, New York, NY   10022
CEO: John D. Mills, EVP   Tel: (212) 702-1200   Emp: N/A
Bus: *Investment management services.*   Fax:(212) 702-1922   %FO: 100

- **THE BANK OF NOVA SCOTIA**
44 King Street West, Toronto, ON, Canada M5H 1H1
CEO: Peter C. Godsoe, Chrm. &CEO   Tel: (416) 866-6161   Emp: 30766
Bus: *General banking services.*   Fax:(416) 866-3750

  THE BANK OF NOVA SCOTIA TRUST CO OF NEW YORK
  One Liberty Plaza, 23rd fL., New York, NY   10006
  CEO: Barry R. F. Luter, EVP   Tel: (212) 225-6500   Emp: 300
  Bus: *Commercial banking services.*   Fax:(212) 225-5436   %FO: 100

  SCOTIA CAPITAL MARKETS (USA) INC.
  One Liberty Plaza -23rd Fl., New York, NY   10006
  CEO: Ted Price, CEO   Tel: (212) 225-6500   Emp: N/A
  Bus: *Investment banking, securities brokerage and* Fax:(212) 225-6767   %FO: 100
       underwriting.

- **BARRICK GOLD CORPORATION**
Royal Bank Plaza, 200 Bay Street, PO Box 119, Toronto, Ontario M5J 2J3, Canada
CEO: John Carrington, Pres. & COO   Tel: (416) 861-9911   Emp: N/A
Bus: *Gold mining.*   Fax:(416) 861-2492

  BARRICK GOLDSTRIKE MINES, INC.
  801 Pennsylvania Avenue, NW, Ste. 730, Washington, DC   20004
  CEO: Michael Brown, VP   Tel: (202) 638-0026   Emp: N/A
  Bus: *U.S. representative office.*   Fax:(202) 638-7787   %FO: 100

- **BENTALL DEVELOPMENT COMPANY INC.**
3100 Three Bentall Centre, P O Box 49001, Vancouver, BC, Canada V7X 1B1
CEO: Robert G. Bentall, Pres.   Tel: 604 661-5000   Emp: 150
Bus: *Real estate development services.*   Fax:604 661-5055

  BENTALL DEVELOPMENT INC.
  1551 N. Tustin Avenue, #650, Santa Ana, CA   92701
  CEO: Karen Winter, Pres.   Tel: (714) 543-5050   Emp: N/A
  Bus: *Real estate development services.*   Fax:(714) 749-1132   %FO: 100

- **BOMBARDIER INC.**
800 René-Lévesque Blvd., Montréal, PQ, Canada H3N 1Y8
CEO: Laurent Beaudoin, Chrm.   Tel: (514) 861-9481   Emp: 40000
Bus: *Civil aerospace; mfr. diesel electric locomotives,* Fax:(514) 861-7053
     engines; water, snow craft; defense systems, & lease
     financing.

  AUBURN TECHNOLOGY, INC.
  100 Orchard Street, Auburn, NY   13021
  CEO: William Lynch, VP & Gen.Mgr.   Tel: (315) 255-7800   Emp: N/A
  Bus: *Mfr./sales aircraft equipment & diesel engines.* Fax:(315) 253-9175 %FO: 100

BOMBARDIER CAPITAL
1600 Mountain View Drive, Colchester, VT   05446
CEO: Pierre-Andre Roy, Pres.　　　　　　　Tel: (802) 654-8100　　Emp: N/A
Bus: *Financing and leasing services.*　　　Fax:(802) 654-8421　　%FO: 100

LEARJET INC.
One Learjet Way, Wichita, KS   67277
CEO: Mac Beaston, Pres.　　　　　　　　　Tel: (316) 946-2000　　Emp: N/A
Bus: *Mfr. commercial executive aircraft.*　Fax:(316) 946-2220　　%FO: 100

UTDC CORP.
380 North Woodward, Suite 212, Birmingham, MI   48009
CEO: Robert Furniss, Pres.　　　　　　　　Tel: (810) 642-6600　　Emp: N/A
Bus: *Design/mfr./service ground transport systems.*　Fax:(810) 642-6951　　%FO: 100

● **BRICKFIELD HOMES LTD.**
181 Bay Street, #420, P O Box 763, Toronto, ON Canada M5J 2T3
CEO: Bill Pringle, Pres. & CEO　　　　　　Tel: (416) 369-8200　　Emp: N/A
Bus: *Real estate development.*　　　　　　Fax:(416) 369-0973

BRICKFIELD HOMES INC.
8521 Leesburg Pike, Vienna, VA   22180
CEO: Gerard M. Armstrong, Pres.　　　　　Tel: (703) 356-9090　　Emp: N/A
Bus: *Real estate development.*　　　　　　Fax:(703) 442-4820　　%FO: 100

COSCAN WATERWAYS INC.
20803 Biscayne Boulevard, Aventura, FL   33180
CEO: James E. MacKenzie, Pres.　　　　　Tel: (305) 935-0255　　Emp: N/A
Bus: *Real estate development.*　　　　　　Fax:(305) 932-9870　　%FO: 100

● **BROOKFIELD COMMERCIAL PROPERTIES, LTD.**
Bay Wellilngton Twr., 181 Bay Street, Ste. 4300, PO Box 739, Toronto, Ontario M5J 2T3, Canada
CEO: David Arthur, Pres.　　　　　　　　　Tel: (416) 369-2300　　Emp:
Bus: *Develop commercial and retail real estate.*　Fax:(416) 369-3201

BROOKFIELD LEPAGE MANAGEMENT, INC.
370 Seventeenth Street, Denver, CO   80202
CEO: Mr. Tracy Wilkes, Pres.　　　　　　　Tel: (303) 595-7000　　Emp: N/A
Bus: *Develop commercial and retail real estate.*　Fax:(303) 595-7003　　%FO: 100

BROOKFIELD MANAGEMENT SERVICES, INC.
4340 Multifoods Tower, 33 South Street, Minneapolis, MN   55402
CEO: Harold R. Brandt, Sr. VP　　　　　　Tel: (612) 372-1500　　Emp: 177
Bus: *Develop commercial and retail real estate.*　Fax:(612) 372-1510　　%FO: 100

- **BROOKFIELD HOMES**
Toronto, Ontario, Canada
CEO: William Pringle, Pres.   Tel: 416-369-8200   Emp: N/A
Bus: *Real estate development services.*   Fax:416-369-0973

    COSCAN CORPORATION
    8521 Leesburg Pike, Vienna, VA   22180
    CEO: Gerarld M. Armstrong, Pres.   Tel: (703) 356-9090   Emp: N/A
    Bus: *Real estate development services.*   Fax:(703) 442-4828   %FO: 100

- **CAE INC.**
Royal Bank Plaza #3060, P O Box 30, Toronto, ON, Canada M5J 2J1
CEO: John E. Caldwell, Pres. & CEO   Tel: (416) 865-0070   Emp: 8800
Bus: *Mfr. flight simulators, training services, rail*   Fax:(416) 865-0337
equipment service, forest product machinery &
equipment.

    CAE VANGUARD INC.
    3500 W 80th St., #125, Minneapolis, MN   55431
    CEO: Glen Frederick, Pres.   Tel: (612) 896-3915   Emp: 300
    Bus: *Mfr./service railroad equipment.*   Fax:(612) 896-3913   %FO: 100

- **CANADIAN IMPERIAL BANK OF COMMERCE (CIBC)**
Commerce Court, 25 King Street, Toronto, ON Canada M5L 1A2
CEO: A. L. Flood, Chrm.   Tel: (416) 980-2210   Emp: 41606
Bus: *General banking services.*   Fax:(416) 980-5026

    C.I.B.C. WOOD GUNDY
    425 Lexington Avenue, New York, NY   10017
    CEO: Michael S. Rulle, Pres.   Tel: (212) 856-4000   Emp: 300
    Bus: *Commercial & investment banking, securities*   Fax:(212) 885-4936   %FO: 100
    brokerage & asset management services.

    CANADIAN IMPERIAL HOLDINGS, INC.
    425 Lexington Avenue, New York, NY   10017
    CEO: Matthew Singleton, Pres.   Tel: (212) 856-4000   Emp: 50
    Bus: *Commercial & investment banking, securities*   Fax:(212) 885-4936   %FO: 100
    brokerage & asset management services.

● **CANADIAN MARCONI COMPANY**
600 Dr. Frederica Philipps, St.Laurent, Montreal PQ, Canada H4N 2S9
CEO: John H. Simons, Pres. & CEO   Tel: (514) 748-3148   Emp: 3200
Bus: *Design/mfr. hi-tech electrical systems & components*   Fax:(514) 748-3100
for communication & navigation.

    CINCINNATI ELECTRONICS CORP.
    7500 Innovation Way, Mason, OH   45040
    CEO: James Wimmers, Pres.   Tel: (513) 573-6100   Emp: 800
    Bus: *Mfr. communications systems & equipment,*   Fax:(513) 733-6855   %FO: 100
    space & military electronic systems, contract
    prod, envimetrology service

    CMC ELECTRONICS INC.
    1 Madison Street, East Rutherford, NJ   07073-1687
    CEO: Ervin Spinner, Pres.   Tel: (201) 777-1662   Emp: N/A
    Bus: *Full service to commercial airlines for*   Fax:(201) 389-3091   %FO: 100
    avionics.

● **CANADIAN NATIONAL RAILWAYS**
935 de la Gauchetiére Street West, Montreal, PQ Canada H3B 2M9
CEO: R. E. Lawless, Pres.   Tel: (514) 399-5430   Emp: 50800
Bus: *Railway & intermodal transportation,*   Fax:(514) 399-5586
telecommunications.

    CANADIAN NATIONAL RAILWAYS
    2800 Livernois Avenue, Troy, MI   48083
    CEO: Anthony Rossi, Mng. Dir.   Tel: (248) 740-6000   Emp: N/A
    Bus: *Holding company.*   Fax:(248) 740-6276   %FO: 100

● **CANADIAN PACIFIC LTD.**
910 Peel Street, P O Box 6042, Station Centre-Ville Montreal, PQ Canada H3C 3E4
CEO: David P. O'Brien, Chrm.   Tel: (514) 395-5151   Emp: 36100
Bus: *Transportation, waste services, energy, real estate,*   Fax:(514) 395-5511
hotels, telecommunications.

    CANADIAN PACIFIC RAILWAY
    800 Soo Line Bldg., 105 South Fifth Street, Minneapolis, MN   55402
    CEO: Edwin V.Dodge, Pres. & CEO   Tel: (612) 347-8000   Emp: 4500
    Bus: *Transportation & real estate services.*   Fax:(612) 347-8000   %FO: 100

    LAIDLAW TRANSIT CORPORATION.
    35 Troy Lane, Lincoln Park, NJ   07035
    CEO: Laura Stoddart, Genl Mgr.   Tel: (201) 696-1441   Emp: N/A
    Bus: *Educational transport services.*   Fax:(201) 696-8883   %FO: 100

    LAIDLAW WASTE SYSTEMS, INC.
    8101 Beachcraft Avenue, Gaithersburg, MD   20879
    CEO: Martha A. Gibbons, Dir.   Tel: (301) 840-0300   Emp: N/A
    Bus: *Solid waste management.*   Fax:(301) 840-0388   %FO: 100

NYCO MINERALS INC.
124 Mountainview Drive, Willsboro, NY   12996-0368

CEO: J.J. Moroney, Pres. & CEO	Tel: (518) 963-4262	Emp: 140
Bus: *Produce industrial minerals.*	Fax:(518) 963-4187	%FO: 100

UNITED DOMINION INDUSTRIES LTD.
2300 One First Union Center, 301 S. College St., Charlotte, NC   28202-6039

CEO: N/A	Tel: (704) 347-6800	Emp: N/A
Bus: *US sub. of Canadia Pacific Ltd.*	Fax:(704) 347-6940	%FO: 100
Transportation, waste services, energy, real		
estate, hotels, telecommunications.		

● **CANADIAN TECHNICAL TAPE LTD.**
455 Cote Vertu, Montreal, PQ Canada H4N 1E8

CEO: Leonard Cohen, Pres.	Tel: (514) 334-1510	Emp: 600
Bus: *Mfr. pressure sensitive tape.*	Fax:(514) 745-0764	

CANTECH INDUSTRIES INC.
2222 Eddie Williams Drive, Johnson City, TN   37601

CEO: Thomas Butler, Mgr.	Tel: (423) 928-8331	Emp: 60
Bus: *Mfr. pressure sensitive tapes.*	Fax:(423) 928-0311	%FO: 100

● **CANFOR CORPORATION**
2900-1055 Dunsmuir Street, Bentall Postal Sta., Vancouver, BC, Canada V7X 1B5

CEO: P.J.G.Bentley, Chrm.	Tel: (604) 661-5241	Emp: 4530
Bus: *Mfr. pulp, paper, wood products.*	Fax:(604) 661-5235	

CANFOR (USA) CORP.
240 West Taylor Avenue, Meridian, ID   83642

CEO: George Layton, Mng. Dir.	Tel: (208) 888-2456	Emp: 134
Bus: *Mfr. pulp, paper, wood products.*	Fax:(208) 888-7428	%FO: 100

CANFOR (USA) CORP.
4395 Curtis Road, Bellingham, WA   98225

CEO: George Layton, Mng. Dir.	Tel: (360) 647-2434	Emp: N/A
Bus: *Mfr. pulp, paper, wood products.*	Fax:(360) 647-2437	%FO: 100

● **CCL INDUSTRIES INC.**
105 Gordon Baker Rd, Willowdale, ON, Canada M2H 3P8

CEO: Wayne McLesch, Pres.	Tel: (416) 756-8500	Emp: 6000
Bus: *Mfr. cleaning & sanitation products, paints, toilet*	Fax:(416) 391-5558	
preparations.		

ADVANCED MONOBLOC CORP.
One Llodio Drve, Hermitage, PA   16148

CEO: Rami Younes, Pres	Tel: (412) 981-4420	Emp: 130
Bus: *Mfr. aluminum cans.*	Fax:(412) 342-1116	%FO: 100

CCL LABEL, INC.
500 Park Blvd., Suite 776, Itasca, IL   60143
CEO: William Carley, VP   Tel: (630) 773-8888   Emp: N/A
Bus: *Mfr. labels.*   Fax:(630) 773-8004   %FO: 100

● **CINEPLEX ODEON CORP.**
1303 Yonge Street, Toronto, ON Canada M4T 2Y9
CEO: Allen Karp, Pres. & CEO   Tel: (416) 323-6600   Emp: 8000
Bus: *Exhibit motion pictures through company-operated*   Fax:(416) 323-6677
    theater circuit; distribution motion pictures.

   CINEPLEX ODEON INC.
   1925 Century Park East, #300, Los Angeles, CA   90067
   CEO: Allen Karp, Pres. & CEO   Tel: (310) 551-2500   Emp: N/A
   Bus: *Exhibit motion pictures through company-*   Fax:(310) 203-9698   %FO: 100
       operated theater circuit; distribute motion
       pictures.

   CINEPLEX ODEON INC.
   241 East 34th Street, New York, NY   10016
   CEO: Ken Naccari, Pres.   Tel: (212) 679-2000   Emp: N/A
   Bus: *Exhibit motion pictures through company-*   Fax:(212) 679-4954   %FO: 100
       operated theater circuit; distribute motion
       pictures.

● **CO-STEEL INC.**
Scotia Plaza, 40 Kings Street West, Ste. 5010, Toronto, Canada N5H 3Y2
CEO: Lou Hutchinson, Mng. Dir.   Tel: 416-366-4500   Emp: 2440
Bus: *Mfr. steel rod, bar & structural shapes.*   Fax:416-366-4616

   CO-STEEL RARITAN INC.
   225 Elm Street, Perth Amboy, NJ   08862
   CEO: George Mischenko, Gen. Mgr.   Tel: (732) 442-1600   Emp: 485
   Bus: *Mfr. steel rod, bar & structural shapes.*   Fax:(732) 442-3957   %FO: 100

● **COGNOS INC.**
3755 Riverside Drive, PO Box 9707, Ottawa, ON, Canada K1G 3U9
CEO: R. Zambonini, Pres.   Tel: (613) 738-1440   Emp: 1000
Bus: *Development/marketing computer software.*   Fax:(613) 738-0002

   COGNOS CORP.
   67 South Bedford Street, Suite.1005, Burlington, MA   01803-5164
   CEO: Terry Hall, SVP   Tel: (617) 229-6600   Emp: 205
   Bus: *Marketing/sale computer software.*   Fax:(617) 229-9844   %FO: 100

- **COMINCO LTD.**
200 Burrard Street, Suite 500, Vancouver, BC Canada V6C 3L7
CEO: D.A. Thompson, Pres.   Tel: (604) 682-0611   Emp: 8407
Bus: *Mining, smelting, refining mineral exploration .*   Fax:(604) 685-3019

   COMINCO AMERICAN INC.
   601 West Riverside Avenue, Spokane, WA   99201
   CEO: W.J. Robertson, Pres.   Tel: (604) 682-0611   Emp: N/A
   Bus: *Base metal mining.*   Fax:(604) 685-3019   %FO: 100

- **COMPAS ELECTRONICS LTD.**
1245 California Avenue, Brockville, ON, Canada K6V 5Y6
CEO: Bob Corson, Pres.   Tel: (613) 342-5041   Emp: 480
Bus: *Electronic assembly, mfr. surface mounts.*   Fax:(613) 342-1774

   COMPAS ELECTRONICS INC.
   100 Chimney Point Drive, Ogdensburg, NY   13669
   CEO: Bob Corson, Pres.   Tel: (315) 393-3573   Emp: 330
   Bus: *Electronic assembly, mfr. surface mounts.*   Fax:(315) 393-7638   %FO: 100

- **CONFEDERATION LIFE INSURANCE CO.**
321 Bloor St E, Toronto, ON, Canada M4W 1H1
CEO: Patrick D. Burns, Chmn. & Pres   Tel: (416) 228-7600   Emp: 4500
Bus: *Insurance & financial services.*   Fax:(416) 228-7650

   CONFEDERATION LIFE INSURANCE AND ANNUITY CO.
   260 Interstate North, Atlanta, GA   30339
   CEO: Kip Sickington, Mgr.   Tel: (800) 233-4634   Emp: N/A
   Bus: *Insurance services.*   Fax:(770) 850-8664   %FO: 100

- **CONNAUGHT LABORATORIES LTD.**
1755 Steeks Ave West, Willowdale, ON, Canada M2R 3T4
CEO: R. Chase, Pres.   Tel: (416) 667-2701   Emp: N/A
Bus: *Biological products for healthcare*   Fax:(416) 667-0313

   CONNAUGHT LABORATORIES INC
   PO Box 187, Route 611, Swiftwater, PA   18370
   CEO: David J. Williams, Pres.   Tel: (717) 839-7187   Emp: N/A
   Bus: *Mfr. biological products for health care.*   Fax:(717) 839-7235   %FO: 100

● **CONSUMERS GAS CO LTD.**
P.O. Box 650, Scarborough, Ontario, Canada M1K 5E3
CEO: Ronald D. Munkley, Pres.   Tel: (416) 492-5000   Emp: 3500
Bus: *Natural gas distribution, utility.*   Fax:(416) 498-2904

    ST. LAWRENCE GAS COMPANY, INC.
    33 Stearns Street, Massena, NY   13662
    CEO: F. D. Rewbotham, Pres.   Tel: (315) 769-3516   Emp: 50
    Bus: *Utility, natural gas distribution.* Fax:(315) 764-9226   %FO: 100

● **CORNUCOPIA RESOURCES LTD.**
355 Burrand Street, #520, Vancouver, BC, Canada V6C 2G8
CEO: Andrew F.B. Milligan, Pres.   Tel: (604) 687-0619   Emp: N/A
Bus: *Gold mining.*   Fax:(604) 681-4170

    MINERAL RIDGE RESOURCES INC.
    PO Box 67, 200 Mica Way, Silver Peak, NV   89047
    CEO: Andrew F.B. Milligan, Pres.   Tel: (702) 937-2266   Emp: 56
    Bus: *Gold mining.*   Fax:(702) 937-2202   %FO: 100

● **CROWN LIFE INSURANCE COMPANY**
1901 Scarth Street, Regina, SK, S4P 4L4, Canada
CEO: Brian A. Johnson, Pres.   Tel: (306) 751-6000   Emp: 1400
Bus: *Insurance, healthcare & financial services.* Fax:(306) 751-6001

    CROWN LIFE INSURANCE COMPANY
    201 North Union Street, Suite 140, Alexandria, VA   22314
    CEO: Eugene S. Koster, V.P.   Tel: (703) 684-4100   Emp: N/A
    Bus: *Insurance, healthcare & financial services.* Fax:(703) 739-6999   %FO: 100

    UNITED HEALTH INC.
    105 West Michigan Street, Milwaukee, WI   53203
    CEO: Guy W. Smith, Pres.   Tel: (414) 271-9696   Emp: N/A
    Bus: *Nursing center care, retirement homes,* Fax:(414) 347-4321   %FO: 100
        pharmaceutical services.

    US ADMINISTRATORS INC.
    3540 Wilshire Blvd., Los Angeles, CA   99010
    CEO: Geoffrey T. Wood, Pres.   Tel: (213) 383-1100   Emp: N/A
    Bus: *Administration, quality assurance, healthcare* Fax:(213) 738-0386   %FO: 100
        cost management.

● **CUTTING INTL LTD.**
30 Constellation Court Rexdale, ON Canada M9W 1K1
CEO: Jerry Bryant, Pres.   Tel: (416) 675-7077   Emp: N/A
Bus: *Paper roll products.*   Fax:(416) 675-7088

    CUTTING CORP.
    4940 Hampden Lane, Bethesda, MD   20814
    CEO: James Cutting, Pres.   Tel: (301) 654-2887   Emp: N/A
    Bus: *Tape reproductions, studio recordings.*   Fax:(301) 657-9057   %FO: 100

    CUTTING USA INC
    7768 Zionsville Road #400, Indianapolis, IN   46268
    CEO: G A Maynard, Pres.   Tel: (317) 288-6400   Emp: N/A
    Bus: *Mfr. paper products, commercial printing.* Fax:(317) 228-6401   %FO: 100

● **DENTECH PRODUCTS LTD.**
2120 Paramount Crescent, Clearbrook, BC, Canada V2S 4N5
CEO: Kent Fletcher, Pres.   Tel: (604) 852-6911   Emp: 52
Bus: *Mfr. dental equipment.*   Fax:(604) 852-4823

    DENTECH CORP.
    529 West Front Street, Sumas, WA   98295
    CEO: Kent Fletcher, Pres.   Tel: (206) 988-7911   Emp: 45
    Bus: *Assembly/sale dental equipment.*   Fax:(206) 988-7906   %FO: JV

● **DERLAN INDUSTRIES LTD.**
95 King Street, Toronto, ON, Canada M5C 1G4
CEO: Dermot Coughlin, Pres. & CEO   Tel: (416) 364-5852   Emp: 3800
Bus: *Holding company.*   Fax:(416) 362-5334

    K&M ELECTRONICS INC.
    11 Interstate Drive, West Springfield, MA   01089
    CEO: John Marriott, Pres.   Tel: (413) 781-1350   Emp: 500
    Bus: *Mfr. power supplies, lighting fixtures.*   Fax:(413) 737-0608   %FO: 100

● **DEVTEK CORPORATON**
100 Allatate Parkway, Suite 500, Markham, Ontario, L3R 6H3, Canada
CEO: James Renner, Pres.   Tel: 905-477-6861   Emp: N/A
Bus: *Mfr. automobile and industrial parts.*   Fax:905-477-0481

    ACD TRIDON NORTH AMERICA, INC.
    8100 Tridon Drive, Smyrna, TN   37167
    CEO: Michael Hottinger, Pres.   Tel: (615) 459-5800   Emp: N/A
    Bus: *Mfr./distribute automobile and industrial parts.* Fax:(615) 355-1104   %FO: 100

● **DOFASCO, INC.**
PO Box 2460, Hamilton, Ontario L8N 3J5, Canada
CEO: Charles H. Hantho, Chrm.   Tel: 905-544-3761   Emp: N/A
Bus: *Mfr. steel and steel products.*   Fax:905-545-3236

    DOFASCO, U.S.A., INC.
    26877 Northwest Hwy, Ste.104, Southfield, MI   48034-8431
    CEO: David Black, Gen.Mgr.   Tel: (248) 357-3090   Emp: N/A
    Bus: *Mfr./sale steel and steel products.*   Fax:(248) 357-9888   %FO: 100

    GALLATIN STEEL COMPANY
    Route One, Ghent, KY   41045
    CEO: John Holditch, Pres.   Tel: (606) 567-3100   Emp: N/A
    Bus: *Mfr./sale steel and steel products.*   Fax:(606) 567-3169   %FO: JV

● **DOMINION TEXTILE INC.**
1950 Sherbrooke Street W, Montreal PQ, Canada H3H 1E7
CEO: John A. Boland III, Pres.   Tel: (514) 989-6000   Emp: 6200
Bus: *Mfr. denim, nonwovens, industrial fabrics, technical*   Fax:(514) 989-6331
    fabrics, workwear and careerwear apparel.

    DOMINION TEXTILE (USA) INC.
    120 West 45th Street, New York, NY   10036
    CEO: John A. Boland III, Pres. & CEO   Tel: (212) 687-2424   Emp: 3200
    Bus: *Mfr. nonwoven fabrics, denim.*   Fax:(212) 687-8855   %FO: 100

    POLY-BOND, INC.
    1020 Shenandoah Village Drive, Waynesboro, VA   22980
    CEO: Alex J .Hay, Pres.   Tel: (540) 946-9250   Emp: 210
    Bus: *Mfr./sale/distribution non-wovens.*   Fax:(540) 946-9261   %FO: 100

    SWIFT DENIM, INC.
    Concourse Pkwy., Ste. 2300, Atlanta, GA   30328-5350
    CEO: John Heldrich, Pres. & CEO   Tel: (770) 901-6300   Emp: N/A
    Bus: *Mfr./sale and distribution of denim.*   Fax:(770) 901-6309   %FO: 100

    SWIFT DENIM, INC.
    233 12th Street, Columbus, GA   31902
    CEO: Greg Rowell, Mgr.   Tel: (706) 324-3623   Emp: 2900
    Bus: *Mfr./sale and distribution of denim.*   Fax:(706) 571-8452   %FO: 100

● **DOREL INDUSTRIES INC.**
4750 Des Grandes Prairies, Montreal, PQ, Canada H1R 1A3
CEO: Leo Schwartz, Pres.   Tel: (514) 523-5701   Emp: 1800
Bus: *Mfr. general household furniture.*   Fax:(514) 523-5701

    COSCO INC.
    2525 State Street, Columbus, IN   47201
    CEO: Nick Costides, Pres.   Tel: (812) 372-0141   Emp: 1100
    Bus: *Mfr. juvenile furniture & vehicles, padded*   Fax:(812) 372-0911   %FO: 100
        seats.

● **ELECTROHOME LTD.**
809 Wellington St N, Kitchener, ON, Canada N2G 4J6
CEO: J. A. Pollock, Pres.   Tel: (519) 744-7111   Emp: 800
Bus: *Mfr. electronics and provides broadcasting services.*   Fax:(519) 749-3131

    ELECTROHOME (USA) INC.
    700 Ensminger Road, Tonawanda, NY   14150
    CEO: J. A. Pollock, Pres   Tel: (716) 874-3630   Emp: 16
    Bus: *Mfr./marketing electronics.*   Fax:(716) 874-4309   %FO: 100

● **EMCO LTD.**
620 Richmond Street, P.O. Box 5252, London, ON Canada N6A 4L6
CEO: Douglas Speers, Pres.   Tel: (519) 645-3900   Emp: N/A
Bus: *Mfr. fluid handling systems & equipment.*   Fax:(519) 645-2465

    MASCO CORP.
    21001 Vanborn Road, Taylor, MI   48180
    CEO: Richard Manoogian   Tel: (313) 274-7400   Emp: N/A
    Bus: *Mfr. fluid handling systems & equipment.*   Fax:(313) 274-6134   %FO: 100

    METCRAFT INC
    13910 Kessler Drive, Grandview, MO   64030
    CEO: Jim Forgie, Pres.   Tel: (816) 761-3250   Emp: 60
    Bus: *Stainless steel fabrication for institutional,*   Fax:(816) 761-0544   %FO: 100
        commercial markets.

● **ENDEAN IMPORT/EXPORT LIMITED**
41 Mutual Street, Toronto, ON, Canada M5B 2A7
CEO: Diaa Gabbani, Pres.   Tel: (416) 365-7011   Emp: 110
Bus: *Grain, feedstuffs and protein meals.*   Fax:(416) 365-1552

    ENDEAN IMPORT/EXPORT USA LTD.
    205-2700 Broening Hwy, Baltimore, MD   21222
    CEO: Maryanne Stroud, Pres.   Tel: (410) 284-7288   Emp: N/A
    Bus: *Grain, feedstuffs and protein meals.* Fax:(410) 284-2321   %FO: 100

● **EXTENDICARE, INC.**
120 Bloor Street East, Toronto, ON, Canada M4W 1B8
CEO: H. Michael Burns, Pres.   Tel: (905) 470-4000   Emp: N/A
Bus: *Operators of skilled nursing homes, rehab centers,*   Fax:(905) 470-5588
retail pharmacies and medical equipment.

    EXTENDICARE HEALTH SERVICES, INC.
    105 West Michigan Street, Milwaukee, WI   53203
    CEO: J. Wesley Carter, Chrm.   Tel: (414) 271-9696   Emp: 2800
    Bus: *Nursing care centers, retirement centers and*   Fax:(414) 347-4321   %FO: 100
    pharmaceutical services.

● **FALCONBRIDGE, INC.**
95 Wellington Street West, Ste. 1200, Toronto, Ontario M5J 2V4, Canada
CEO: Oyvind Hushovd, Pres.   Tel: (416) 956-5700   Emp: N/A
Bus: *Nickel mining company.*   Fax:(416) 956-5757

    FALCONBRIDGE US, INC.
    4955 Steubenville Pike, Ste. 245, Pittsburgh, PA   15205
    CEO: James Moore, Pres.   Tel: (412) 787-0220   Emp: N/A
    Bus: *Nickel mining.*   Fax:(412) 787-0287   %FO: 100

● **FISHERY PRODUCTS INTERNATIONAL LTD.**
PO Box 550 St. Johns, NF Canada A1C 5L1
CEO: Victor L .Young, CEO   Tel: (709) 570-0000   Emp: N/A
Bus: *Supplies frozen seafood products.*   Fax:(709) 570-0209

    FISHERY PRODUCTS INTERNATIONAL CLOUSTIN, INC.
    18 Electronics Avenue, Danvers, MA   01923
    CEO: John D. Cummings, Pres.   Tel: (508) 777-2660   Emp: N/A
    Bus: *Supplies frozen seafood products.*   Fax:(508) 777-7458   %FO: 100

● **GEAC COMPUTER CORP. LTD.**
11 Allstate Pkwy, Markham, ON, Canada L3R 9TB
CEO: William Nelson, Pres.   Tel: (905) 475-0525   Emp: 900
Bus: *Automation systems for divers industry & services.*   Fax:(905) 475-3847

    GEAC COMPUTERS, INC.
    1807 Park 270 Drive, St. Louis, MO   63146
    CEO: Brian McGibbon, Gen.Mgr.   Tel: (314) 878-4210   Emp: 20
    Bus: *Sale/service retail banking software.*   Fax:(314) 878-6783   %FO: 100

- **GROUPE TRANSCONTINENTAL GTC LTEE**
375 Lebeau, Montreal, PQ, Canada H4N 1S2
CEO: Remi Marcoux, Chrm.   Tel: (514) 337-8560   Emp: 3300
Bus: *Commercial printing, graphic design, periodicals.*   Fax:(514) 339-5230

    TRANSCONTINENTAL PRINTING, INC.
    678 Yellow Spring-Fairfield, Fairborn, OH   45324
    CEO: Ralph Pontillo, Pres.   Tel: (937) 879-5678   Emp: 240
    Bus: *Commercial offset printing products &*   Fax:(937) 878-5283   %FO: 100
      services.

- **HARLEQUIN ENTERPRISES LTD.**
225 Duncan Mill Rd, Don Mills, ON Canada M3B 3K9
CEO: S. J. Campbell, Pres.   Tel: (416) 445-5860   Emp: 1200
Bus: *Publishing.*   Fax:(416) 445-8655

    HARLEQUIN BOOKS
    300 East 42nd Street, 6th Fl., New York, NY   10017
    CEO: Horst Bausch, Editor-in-Chief   Tel: (212) 682-6080   Emp: N/A
    Bus: *Publishing company.*   Fax:(212) 682-4539   %FO: 100

    HARLEQUIN BOOKS DISTRIBUTION CENTRE
    3010 Walden Avenue, Depew, NY   14043
    CEO: Jim Broihier, VP   Tel: (716) 684-1800   Emp: N/A
    Bus: *Book distribution.*   Fax:(716) 684-5066   %FO: 100

- **HELMITIN CANADA, INC.**
99 Shorecliffe Road, Toronto, Ontario, Canada M8Z SK7
CEO: Ernie Leiner, Pres.   Tel: (416) 239-3105   Emp: N/A
Bus: *Mfr. adhesives.*   Fax:(416) 239-6487

    AMERICAN HELMITIN CORPORATION
    11110 Airport Road, Olive Branch, TN   38654
    CEO: Larry Droski, VP & Mgr.   Tel: (601) 895-4565   Emp: N/A
    Bus: *Sales/distribution of adhesives.*   Fax:(601) 895-4583   %FO: 100

- **HOLLINGER INC.**
10 Toronto Street, Toronto, ON M5C 2B7 Canada
CEO: Conrad M. Black, Chrm.   Tel: 416-363-8721   Emp: 8700
Bus: *International newspaper publishing.*   Fax:416-364-0832

    HOLLINGER INTERNATIONAL INC.
    401 N. Wabash Avenue, Chicago, IL   60611
    CEO: F. David Radler, Pres.   Tel: (312) 321-2299   Emp: N/A
    Bus: *Newspaper publishing.*   Fax:(312) 321-0629   %FO: 100

● **HURON TECH OF CANADA LTD.**
P O Box 1145 Kingston, ON, Canada K7L 4Y5
CEO: Dennis Dong, Mgr.   Tel: (613) 546-2651   Emp: N/A
Bus: *Electrolytic equipment.*   Fax:(613) 545-1761

    HURON TECH OF CANADA, INC.
    PO Box 189, Delco, NC   28436
    CEO: Warren Bailey, Pres. & CEO   Tel: (910) 655-3845   Emp: N/A
    Bus: *Sodium chlorate electrolytic equipment.*   Fax:(910) 655-3892   %FO: 100

    HURON TECH OF CANADA, INC.
    6860 Philips Industrial Blvd., Jacksonville, FL   32256
    CEO: Allen Eckloss, Pres.   Tel: (904) 262-6999   Emp: N/A
    Bus: *US headquarters office.*   Fax:(904) 262-6990   %FO: 100

● **INCO LTD.**
145 King Street West, Suite 1500, Toronto, ON, Canada M5H 4B7
CEO: Michael D. Sopko, Chrm.   Tel: (416) 361-7511   Emp: 16000
Bus: *Mines/processes nickel, copper, precious metals,*   Fax:(416) 361-7782
    cobalt.

    DON CASTERS INCO ENGINEERED PRODUCTS LTD.
    Pond Meadow Road, Ivoryton, CT   06442
    CEO: M. D. Sopko, Pres.   Tel: (860) 767-0161   Emp: N/A
    Bus: *Gas & steam turbine blades.*   Fax:(860) 767-2518   %FO: 100

    INCO ALLOYS INTERNATIONAL INC.
    3200 Riverside Drive, Huntington, WV   25705
    CEO: Francis J. Petro, Pres.   Tel: (304) 526-5100   Emp: 1750
    Bus: *Mfr. high nickel alloys.*   Fax:(304) 526-3959   %FO: 100

    INCO UNITED STATES INC.
    One New York Plaza, New York, NY   10004
    CEO: Richard L. Guido, Pres.   Tel: (212) 612-5500   Emp: 100
    Bus: *Adm. services, metals, alloys, engineered*   Fax:(212) 612-5688   %FO: 100
      products.

    INCO UNITED STATES INC.
    1225 I Street, NW, Suite 500, Washington, DC   20005
    CEO: Kenneth J. Money, EVP   Tel: (202) 682-4715   Emp: N/A
    Bus: *Metals, alloys, engineered products.*   Fax:(202) 787-1550   %FO: 100

- **INDUSTRIAL-ALLIANCE LIFE INSURANCE CO.**
1080 St Louis Road, Sillery, PQ, Canada G1K 7M3
CEO: Raymond Garneau, Pres. & CEO   Tel: (418) 684-5000   Emp: 1300
Bus: *Life insurance services.*   Fax:(418) 684-5294

> **NORTH WEST LIFE OF AMERICA**
> 3350 Airport Drive, Ste. 700, Bellingham, WA   98225
> CEO: John Gill, Pres.   Tel: (360) 715-8936   Emp: 20
> Bus: *Insurance services.*   Fax:(360) 715-8953   %FO: 99

- **INNOPAC INC.**
1055 W Hastings Street, Vancouver, BC, Canada V6E 2H2
CEO: Martin Fabi, Pres.   Tel: (604) 688-6764   Emp: 2000
Bus: *Mfr. plastic products, signs & advertising specs, industrial machinery.*   Fax:(604) 687-2601

> **CONTINENTAL EXTRUSION CORPORATION**
> 11 Cliffside Drive, Cedar Grove, NJ   07009
> CEO: Ronald Basso, VP & Gen.Mgr.   Tel: (201) 239-4030   Emp: 130
> Bus: *Mfr. plastic bags.*   Fax:(201) 239-9220   %FO: 100

- **INTER-CITY PRODUCTS CORP**
20 Queen St. W, 35th Fl., Toronto, ON, Canada M5H 3R3
CEO: Robert Graham   Tel: (416) 955-4665   Emp: N/A
Bus: *Air conditioning, industrial products.*   Fax:(416) 955-9789

> **THOMPSON PIPE & STEEL CO**
> PO Box 2852, Denver, CO   80201
> CEO: Tim Phillips, Pres.   Tel: (303) 290-9490   Emp: 200
> Bus: *Mfr. welded steel pipe for water transmission, domestic propane tank cylinders.*   Fax:(303) 290-0662   %FO: 100

- **IPL ENERGY, INC.**
2900 Canada Trust Tower, 421 7th Avenue SW, Calgary, AB, Canada T2P 4K9
CEO: Brian F. MacNeill, Pres.   Tel: (403) 231-3900   Emp: 2000
Bus: *Crude petrol pipelines.*   Fax:(403) 2313920

> **LAKEHEAD PIPELINE COMPANY**
> 21 West Superior Street, Duluth, MN   55802
> CEO: Stephen J. Wuori, Pres.   Tel: (218) 725-0100   Emp: 360
> Bus: *Crude petrol pipelines.*   Fax:(218) 725-0109   %FO: 100

● **IPSCO, INC.**
Armour Road, PO Box 1670, Regina, SK, Canada S4P 3C7
CEO: Roger Phillips, Pres. & CEO   Tel: (306) 924-7700   Emp: 1000
Bus: *Mfr. steel & pipe.*   Fax:(306) 924-7413

> **IPSCO STEEL, INC.**
> 2011 7th Avenue, PO Box 180, Camanche, IA   52730
> CEO: Neil Percival, Pres.   Tel: (319) 242-0000   Emp: N/A
> Bus: *Steel mill operators.*   Fax:(319) 242-9408   %FO: 100

> **PAPER CAL STEEL COMPANY**
> Hwy 280 at 36, St. Paul, MN   55164
> CEO: David Sutherland, Pres.   Tel: (612) 631-9031   Emp: 40
> Bus: *Steel service center.*   Fax:(612) 631-9670   %FO: 100

● **IVACO Inc.**
Place Mercantile, 770 rue Sherbrooke ouest - 20th Fl., Montreal, PQ Canada H3A 1G1
CEO: Paul Ivanier, Pres. & CEO   Tel: (514) 288-4545   Emp: 12000
Bus: *Mfr./fabrication of steel & other diversified*   Fax:(514) 284-9414
        products.

> **AMERCORD INC.**
> Industrial Park, P.O. Box 458, Lumber City, GA   31549
> CEO: N/A   Tel: (912) 363-4371   Emp: N/A
> Bus: *Mfr. steel cord. tire bead wire, amd armor*   Fax:(912) 363-4991   %FO: 100
>   *wire for fobre optic cables.*

> **ATLANTIC STEEL INDUSTRIES, INC.**
> 1300 Mecaslin Street, N.W., Atlanta, GA   30318
> CEO: J. Webb, Pres.   Tel: (404) 897-4500   Emp: 1200
> Bus: *Hot rolled merchant and specialty quality bars*   Fax:(404) 897-4623   %FO: 100
>   *and wire rod.*

> **CANRON CONSTRUCTION CORP. - Eastern Division**
> P.O.Box 421, Shaw Road, Conklin, NY   13748
> CEO: N/A   Tel: (607) 723-4862   Emp: N/A
> Bus: *Mfr. structural steel, erection and construction*   Fax:(607) 723-4882   %FO: 100
>   *services.*

> **IVACO STEEL MILLS LTD.**
> 920 Providence Road - Suite 305, Towson, MD   21286
> CEO: P. Ivanier, Pres.   Tel: (410) 823-7696   Emp: 10
> Bus: *Mfr. wire rods & wire products*   Fax:(410) 823-3081   %FO: 100

> **LACLEDE STEEL COMPANY**
> One Metropolitan Square, 211 N. Broadway, St. Louis, MO 63102
> CEO: John B. McKinney, Pres.   Tel: (314) 425-1400   Emp: 1900
> Bus: *US headquaters. Mfr. billets, bars, pipe, wire*   Fax:(314) 425-1561   %FO: 51
>   *rods & wire products.*

SIVACO / NATIONAL WIRE GROUP
Overlook III, Suite 1900. 2859 Paces Ferry Road, Atlanta, GA   30339

CEO: N/A	Tel: (770) 431-5100	Emp: N/A
Bus: *Corporate headquaters. SNW*	Fax:(770) 431-5102	%FO: 100

SIVACO / NATIONAL WIRE OF FLORIDA
1314 - 31st Street, Tampa, FL   33605

CEO: N/A	Tel: (813) 248-4135	Emp: N/A
Bus: *Mfr. wire and welded wire fabric.*	Fax:(813) 248-3057	%FO: 100

SIVACO NEW YORK, INC.
3937 River Road, Tonawanda, NY   14151-0646

CEO: N/A	Tel: (716) 874-5681	Emp: N/A
Bus: *Mfr. wire porducts and wire rod processing.*	Fax:(716) 874-4440	%FO: 100

SNW Georgia
24 Herring Road, Newnan, GA   30265

CEO: G. Seling, Pres.	Tel: (770) 253-6333	Emp: 1400
Bus: *Mfr. wire & wire products.*	Fax:(770) 253-3550	%FO: 100

● JANNOCK LTD.
Scotia Plaza, #5205, 40 King St W, Toronto, ON, Canada M5H 3Y2

CEO: R. Jay Atkinson, Pres. & CEO	Tel: (416) 364-8586	Emp: 5000
Bus: *Clay bricks, steel fabrication, tubing, vinyl siding.*	Fax:(416) 364-9342	

JANNOCK INC.
Foster Plaza Seven, 661 Andersen Dr., Pittsburgh, PA   15220

CEO: Michael A. Risso, Pres.	Tel: (412) 928-5740	Emp: 2000
Bus: *Mfr. clay bricks, steel fabrications, tubing, vinyl siding, windows & fences.*	Fax:(412) 928-5745	%FO: 100

● KAUFEL GROUP LTD.
1811 Blvd Hymus, Pointe Claire, PQ, Canada H9P 1J5

CEO: Bruce Kaufman, Pres.	Tel: (514) 685-2270	Emp: 1280
Bus: *Lighting equipment, plastic products.*	Fax:(514) 685-0378	

LIGHTALARMS ELECTRONICS CORP
1170 Atlantic Avenue, Baldwin, NY   11510

CEO: Michael Kaufman, Pres.	Tel: (516) 379-1000	Emp: 150
Bus: *Mfr. emergency lighting equipment.*	Fax:(516) 379-1698	%FO: 100

● KILBORN ENGINEERING LTD.
2200 Lakeshore Blvd. W, Toronto, ON, Canada M8V 1A4

CEO: Ted Bassett, Pres.	Tel: (416) 252-5311	Emp: 1000
Bus: *Engineering, consult & management services.*	Fax:(416) 231-5356	

KILBORN INC.
5775 DTC Boulevard, Greenwood Valley, CO   80111

CEO: Mike Krossey, Mgr.	Tel: (303) 689-9144	Emp: N/A
Bus: *Consulting engineering services.*	Fax:(303) 689-9148	%FO: 100

- **LABATT BREWERIES OF CANADA**

Labatt House, BCE Place, Suite 200, 181 Bay Street, Toronto M5J 2T3, Canada

CEO: Don Kitchen, Pres.	Tel: 416-361-5050	Emp: N/A
Bus: *Mfr./distributor beers, and interests in sports, broadcasting and entertainment industry.*	Fax:416-865-6084	

LABATT USA, INC.

101 Merritt 7, PO Box 5075, Norwalk, CT 06856-5075

CEO: Thane A. Pressman, Pres. & CEO	Tel: (203) 750-6600	Emp: N/A
Bus: *Brewery/importer/marketer of beer.*	Fax:(203) 750-6699	%FO: JV

LABTROBE BREWING CO.

119 Jefferson Street, Labtrobe, PA 15650

CEO: Philip Hall, Mgr.	Tel: (412) 537-5545	Emp: 40
Bus: *Brewery; Rolling Rock, Carlsberg, and other specialty beers.*	Fax:(412) 537-4035	%FO: 100

- **LAIDLAW INC.**

3221 North Service Road, Burlington, ON, Canada L7N 3G2

CEO: John Grainger, Pres.	Tel: (905) 275-1615	Emp: N/A
Bus: *Holding company: ambulances, passengers services and food services.*	Fax:(905) 332-2022	

GALLAGHER ENTERPRISES INC.

241 Bridge Road, Rt. 1, Salisbury, MA 01952

CEO: David C. Gallagher, CEO	Tel: (508) 462-1266	Emp: N/A
Bus: *Furniture stores, refinishing.*	Fax:(508) 462-0799	%FO: 100

LAIDLAW TRANSIT CORP.

35 Troy Lane, Lincoln Park, NJ 07035

CEO: Laura Stoddart, Mgr.	Tel: (201) 696-1441	Emp: N/A
Bus: *School bus operators.*	Fax:(201) 696-8883	%FO: 100

SC FOOD SERVICE (USA), INC.

816 South Military Trail, Deerfield Beach, FL 33442

CEO: R. Berlind, Pres.	Tel: (954) 481-9555	Emp: N/A
Bus: *Food industry; operates Manchu-Wok restaurants in food courts.*	Fax:(954) 481-9670	%FO: 100

- **LUMONICS INC.**

105 Schneider Road, Kanata, ON, Canada K2K 1Y3

CEO: Robert J. Atkinson, Chrm.	Tel: (613) 592-1460	Emp: 800
Bus: *Develop/mfr. lasers & laser systems.*	Fax:(613) 592-7706	

LUMONICS CORP.

130 Lombard Street, Oxnard, CA 93031-9010

CEO: J. Scaroni, Gen.Mgr..	Tel: (805) 485-5559	Emp: 150
Bus: *Mfr. lasers & laser-based advanced manufacturing systems.*	Fax:(805) 485-3310	%FO: 100

LUMONICS CORP.
6690 Shady Oak Road, Eden Prairie, MN   55344
CEO: Jeff Haley, Gen.Mgr..   Tel: (612) 941-9530   Emp: 75
Bus: *Mfr. lasers & laser-based advanced*   Fax:(612) 941-7611   %FO: 100
    manufacturing systems.

LUMONICS CORP.
19776 Haggerty Road, Livonia, MI   48152-1016
CEO: Earle Braley, Gen.Mgr.   Tel: (313) 592-0101   Emp: 100
Bus: *North American service organization.*   Fax:(313) 592-0045   %FO: 100

● **MACLEAN HUNTER PUBLISHING LTD. (Sub. of Rogers Communications Inc.)**
777 Bay Street, Toronto, ON, Canada M5W 1A7
CEO: John H. Tory, Pres.   Tel: (416) 596-5000   Emp: 12000
Bus: *Pub consumer magazine & business pubs,*   Fax:(416) 593-3175
    newspapers, cable TV, radio & television, printing,
    book distribution, radio paging, trade shows.

    ROGERS M&N COMPANY
    30 East 33rd Street, 4th Floor, New York, NY   10018
    CEO: Robert Webster, Pres.   Tel: (212) 629-8229   Emp: N/A
    Bus: *Medical education publication/ Rogers US*   Fax:(212) 629-8559   %FO: 100
        holding company.

● **MACMILLAN BLOEDEL LTD.**
925 West Georgia Street, Vancouver, BC, Canada V6C 3L2
CEO: Robert B. Findlay, Pres.   Tel: (604) 661-8000   Emp: 12886
Bus: *Forest products: pulp, paper, building materials,*   Fax:(604) 661-8377
    engineered wood, containerboard & packaging.

    AMERICAN CEMWOOD
    3615 Pacific Blvd., SW, Albany, OR   97321
    CEO: Bradley D. Kirkbirde, Pres. & CEO   Tel: (541) 928-6397   Emp: N/A
    Bus: *Forest products.*   Fax:(541) 928-8110   %FO: 100

    FIBRES INTL INC.
    PO Box 1691, Bellevue, WA   98009
    CEO: John W. Matheson, Pres   Tel: (206) 455-9811   Emp: N/A
    Bus: *Scrap & waste material.*   Fax:(206) 454-4252   %FO: 51

    MACMILLAN BLOEDEL INC.
    PO Box 336, Montgomery, AL   36769
    CEO: Jim Emerson, Pres.   Tel: (334) 963-4391   Emp: N/A
    Bus: *Mfr. linerboard, corrugating medium, lumber,*   Fax:(334) 963-4391   %FO: 100
        plywood.

MACMILLAN BLOEDEL PACKAGING INC.
4001 Carmichael Road, Ste.300, Montgomery, AL 36106-3635

CEO: Frederick V. Ernst, Pres.	Tel: (334) 213-6100	Emp: N/A
Bus: *Mfr./sales linerboard, corrugating medium, lumber, plywood.*	Fax:(334) 213-6199	%FO: 100

MACMILLAN BLOEDEL PAPER SALES
3500 188th Street, SW, Lynnwood, WA 98037

CEO: Richard Harris, Pres.	Tel: (206) 672-3344	Emp: N/A
Bus: *Printing paper.*	Fax:(206) 672-2799	%FO: 100

● **MAGELLAN AEROSPACE CORPORATION**
55 York Street, #1450, Toronto, ON, Canada M5J 1R7

CEO: Richard Neill, Pres.	Tel: (416) 365-0565	Emp: 700
Bus: *Mfr. aircraft components, communications hardware.*	Fax:(416) 365-2131	

AERONCA INC.
1712 Germantown Road, Middletown, OH 45042

CEO: James Stine, EVP & Gen.Mgr.	Tel: (513) 422-2751	Emp: 330
Bus: *Aircraft/aerospace parts and assemblies.*	Fax:(513) 422-0812	%FO: 100

● **MAGNA INTL INC.**
36 Apple Creed Blvd., Markham, ON, Canada L3R 4Y4

CEO: Don Walker, Pres.	Tel: (905) 477-7766	Emp: 17000
Bus: *Holding company.*	Fax:(905) 475-0776	

EAGLE BEND MFG INC.
1000 Yarnell Industrial Pkwy, Clinton, TN 37716

CEO: Adam Seipl, Gen. Mgr.	Tel: (423) 457-3800	Emp: 180
Bus: *Motor vehicle parts & accessories.*	Fax:(423) 457-0140	%FO: 100

NASCOTE INDUSTRIES INC.
Enterprise Avenue, Nashville, IL 62263

CEO: Karl Poehlmann, Pres	Tel: (615) 327-4381	Emp: 500
Bus: *Mfr. motor vehicle bumpers.*	Fax:(615) 327-3566	%FO: 100

WEBASTO SUNROOFS INC
2700 Product Drive, Rochester Hills, MI 48309

CEO: Fred Olson, Mgr.	Tel: (248) 853-2270	Emp: 800
Bus: *Mfr. motor vehicle sun roofs.*	Fax:(248) 853-2279	%FO: 100

- **MANULIFE FINANCIAL (THE MANUFACTURERS LIFE INSURANCE CO)**
200 Bloor Street East, Toronto, ON, Canada M4W 1E5
CEO: Dominic D'Alessandro, Pres.　　　　　Tel: (416) 926-0100　　Emp: 3500
Bus: *Insurance services.*　　　　　　　　　Fax:(416) 926-5410

　　THE MANUFACTURERS LIFE INS. CO. OF AMERICA
　　500 N. Woodward Ave, #250, Bloomfield Hills, MI　48304
　　CEO: John Richardson, SVP, US Operations　　Tel: (248) 644-1444　　Emp: N/A
　　Bus: *Life insurance services..*　　　　　　Fax:(248) 644-5639　　%FO: 100

　　MANULIFE FINANCIAL
　　116 Huntington Avenue, Boston, MA　02116
　　CEO: John Richardson, SVP US Operations　　Tel: (617) 854-4300　　Emp: N/A
　　Bus: *Mutual funds/annuities. (FORMERLY N.A.*　Fax:(617) 854-4306　　%FO: 100
　　　　SECURITY LIFE)

- **McCAIN FOODS, LTD.**
Florenceville, NB, Canada E0J 1K0
CEO: Howard Mann, Pres.　　　　　　　　　Tel: (506) 392-5541　　Emp: 12500
Bus: *Food processing, storage and transport.*　Fax:(506) 392-8156

　　McCAIN FOODS, INC.
　　2905 Butterfield Road, Oak Brook, IL　60523-1102
　　CEO: David L. Beré, Pres. & CEO　　　　Tel: (630) 472-0420　　Emp: 1885
　　Bus: *Mfr. potato & vegetable specialties, pizza*　Fax:(630) 472-0451　　%FO: 100
　　　　products.

　　McCAIN CITRUS, INC.
　　2905 Butterfield Road, Oak Brook, IL　60523-1102
　　CEO: Peter O. Reijula, Pres. & CEO　　　Tel: (630) 472-0440　　Emp: N/A
　　Bus: *Mfr. juice products.*　　　　　　　Fax:(630) 472-0161　　%FO: 100

　　ORE-IDA FOODS, INC.
　　220 West Parkcenter Blvd., Boise, ID　83706
　　CEO: Richard Wamhoff, Pres. & CEO　　　Tel: (208) 383-6100　　Emp: N/A
　　Bus: *Mfr./distribute potato products, commercial*　Fax:(208) 383-6570　　%FO: J/V
　　　　and retail.

- **MONARCH INDUSTRIES LTD.**
PO Box 429, 889 Erin Street, Winnipeg, MB, Canada R3C 3E4
CEO: Gene D. Dunn, Pres. & CEO　　　　　Tel: (204) 786-7921　　Emp: 375
Bus: *Mfr. centrifugal pumps, concrete mixers, hydraulic*　Fax:(204) 889-9120
　　cylinders, water systems, self priming pumps.

　　MONARCH INDUSTRIES INC.
　　P.O. Box 20476, Minneapolis, MN　55420
　　CEO: Gene D. Dunn, Pres. & CEO　　　　Tel: (612) 884-0226　　Emp: N/A
　　Bus: *Distribute centrifugal pumps, concrete mixers,*　Fax:(612) 889-9120　　%FO: 100
　　　　hydraulic cylinders, water systems, self
　　　　priming pumps.

● MONENCO/AGRA INC.
2010 Winston Park Drive, Oakville, ON, Canada L6H 6A3

CEO: Bob Van Adel, Pres.	Tel: (905) 829-5400	Emp: N/A
Bus: *Multi-disciplinary engineering & technology.*	Fax:(905) 829-5401	

BAYMONT INC.
14100 58th Street North, Clearwater, FL 34620

CEO: Bob Van Adel, Pres.	Tel: (813) 539-1661	Emp: 300
Bus: *Data conversion services for automated mapping.*	Fax:(813) 539-1749	%FO: 100

● MOORE CORP. LTD.
One First Canadian Plaza, Toronto, ON, Canada M5X 1G5

CEO: Reto Braun, Pres.	Tel: (416) 364-2600	Emp: 18771
Bus: *Mfr. business forms & systems, information management services.*	Fax:(416) 364-1667	

MOORE BUSINESS FORMS & SYSTEMS INC.
275 Field Drive, Lake Forest, IL 60045

CEO: George Gilmore, Jr., Pres.	Tel: (847) 615-6000	Emp: 13000
Bus: *Mfr. business forms & systems, information management services.*	Fax:(847) 615-7300	%FO: 100

MOORE BUSINESS SOLUTIONS DIRECT, INC.
One Hawthorne Pl., 175 Hawthorne Pkwy. Ste. 245, Vernon Hills, IL 60061

CEO: Sieg Buck, VP & Gen.Mgr.	Tel: (603) 742-8455	Emp: N/A
Bus: *Information management services.*	Fax:(603) 742-8320	%FO: 100

MOORE DOCUMENTATION AUTOMATION SYSTEMS, INC.
279 Locust Street, Dover, NH 03820-1229

CEO: Reto Braun, Pres.	Tel: (847) 615-6000	Emp: N/A
Bus: *Mfr. business forms & systems, information management services.*	Fax:(847) 615-7750	%FO: 100

REDIFORM, INC.
555 Airline Drive, Coppell, TX 75019

CEO: John Newfang, VP & Gen.Mgr.	Tel: (972) 393-8080	Emp: N/A
Bus: *Mfr. business forms & systems, information management services.*	Fax:(972) 393-5685	%FO: 100

● NATIONAL BANK OF CANADA
600 Rue de la Gauchetiere W., Montreal, PQ, H3B 4L2 Canada

CEO: Leon Courville, Pres.	Tel: (514) 394-4000	Emp: 11992
Bus: *General banking services.*	Fax:(514) 394-8434	

NATIONAL BANK , FSB
Oakwood Plaza - 4031 Oakwood Blvd., Hollywood, FL 33020

CEO: Raymond Gelinas, Pres.	Tel: (954) 272-1515	Emp: N/A
Bus: *Commercial banking.*	Fax:(954) 923-3347	%FO: 100

NATIONAL BANK OF CANADA - Agency
725 South Figueroa Street, Los Angeles, CA   90017
CEO: N/A   Tel: (213) 629-3300   Emp: N/A
Bus: *Commercial banking services.*   Fax: %FO: 100

NATIONAL BANK OF CANADA - Chicago Branch
225 West Washington Street, #1100, Chicago, IL   60606
CEO: N/A   Tel: (312) 263-1616   Emp: N/A
Bus: *Commercial banking services.*   Fax: %FO: 100

NATIONAL BANK OF CANADA
125 West 55th Street, 23rd Fl., New York, NY   10019
CEO: Roger P. Smock, Sr. VP   Tel: (212) 632-8500   Emp: N/A
Bus: *Commercial banking.*   Fax:(212) 632-8545   %FO: 100

NATIONAL CANADA CORPORATION
125 West 55th Street, New York, NY   10019
CEO: Declan Meagher, Pres.   Tel: (212) 632-8580   Emp: N/A
Bus: *Real estate.*   Fax:(212) 632-8785   %FO: 100

NATIONAL CANADA FINANCE CORP.
125 West 55th Street, New York, NY   10019
CEO: John M Richter, Pres   Tel: (212) 632-8521   Emp: 65
Bus: *Corporate lending.*   Fax:(212) 632-8545   %FO: 100

NATIONAL CANADIAN BUSINESS CORP.
125 West 55th Street, New York, NY   10019
CEO: Frank P. Johnston, Pres.   Tel: (212) 632-8698   Emp: N/A
Bus: *Financial services.*   Fax:(212) 632-8564   %FO: 100

● **NEWBRIDGE NETWORKS CORP.**
600 March Road, Kanata, Ottawa ON K2K 2E6 Canada
CEO: Terry Mattherws, CEO   Tel: (416) 599-3600   Emp: N/A
Bus: *Mfr./service communications equipment.*   Fax:(416) 591-3680

NEWBRIDGE NETWORKS INC.
593 Herndon Parkway, Herndon, VA   20170
CEO: Michael Pascoe   Tel: (703) 834-3600   Emp: N/A
Bus: *US headquarters. Mfr./service*   Fax:(703) 471-7080   %FO: 100
     communications equipment.

●**NORANDA FOREST**
P.O. Box 7, Suite 4500, Toronto Dominion Centre, Toronto, ON M5K Iai, Cananda
CEO: K. Linn Macdonald, Pres.   Tel: (416) 982-7444   Emp: 10177
Bus: *Pulp, paper and lumber products. Sub of Noranda*   Fax:(416) 982-7423
    Inc.

    FRASER PAPER, LTD.
    9 West Broad Street, Stamford, CT   06904
    CEO: John Wasserlein, Pres.   Tel: (203) 705-2800   Emp: 10
    Bus: *Mfr./sales paper products.*   Fax:(203) 705-2801   %FO: 100

    FRASER PAPER, LTD.
    25 Bridge Street, Madawaska, ME   04756-1298
    CEO: Bert Martin, Gen. Mgr.   Tel: (207) 728-3321   Emp: 3710
    Bus: *Mfr./sales paper products.*   Fax:(207) 728-8726   %FO: 100

●**NORANDA INC.**
181 Bay Street, #4100, P O Box 755, BCE Place, Toronto, ON, Canada M5J 2T3
CEO: David W. Kerr, Chrm.   Tel: (416) 982-7111   Emp: 33000
Bus: *Processes natural resources.*   Fax:(416) 982-7021

    NORANDA ALUMINUM, INC.
    1000 Corporate Center Drive, Suite 300, Franklin, TN   37067
    CEO: Elzie Borders, Pres.   Tel: (615) 771-5700   Emp: 1200
    Bus: *Primary aluminum, aluminum sheet & foil.* Fax:(615) 771-5703   %FO: 100

    NORANDA EXPLORATION INC.
    1101 West Grant Road, Suite 202, Tuscon, AZ   85705
    CEO: Cort E. Hogge, Sr. Geologist   Tel: (520) 792-2504   Emp: N/A
    Bus: *Exploration/mining metals, non-metal*   Fax:(520) 792-3725   %FO: 100
        minerals.

    NORANDA SALES INC.
    30100 Chagrin Blvd, #207, Cleveland, OH   44124
    CEO: Ed Hawks, Pres.   Tel: (216) 292-1720   Emp: N/A
    Bus: *Sales natural resources & products.*   Fax:(216) 292-1756   %FO: 100

●**NORBORD INDUSTRIES, INC.**
CEO: Paul Tindell, CEO   Tel: (416) 365-0700   Emp: N/A
Bus: *Mfr. wood products.*   Fax:(416) 365-3292

    NORTHWOOD PANELBOARD COMPANY
    RR 1, P.O. Box 2650, Solway, MN   56678
    CEO: Bruce Grebe, VP   Tel: (218) 751-2023   Emp: 141
    Bus: *Mfr. wood products.*   Fax:(218) 751-2075   %FO: 100

- **NORCEN ENERGY RESOURCES LTD.**
Box 2595 Station M, Calgary, AB, Canada T2P 4V4
CEO: Grant Billing, Pres.   Tel: (403) 947-4000   Emp: 3249
Bus: *Oil & gas exploration products.*   Fax:(403) 231-0187

   NORCEN EXPLORER INC./NORCEN OFFSHORE PROPERTIES INC
   200 W. Lake Park Blvd., Houston, TX   77079-2653
   CEO: Byron F Dyer, Pres   Tel: (713) 558-6611   Emp: 40
   Bus: *Oil & gas exploration/products.*   Fax:(713) 558-2549   %FO: 100

- **NORTEL (NORTHERN TELECOM) LTD.**
8200 Dixie Road, Ste. 100, Brampton, ON, Canada L6T 5P6
CEO: John Roth, Pres.   Tel: 905-863-0000   Emp: 63715
Bus: *Telecommunications services.*   Fax:905-863-8408

   NORTEL COMMUNICATIONS
   330 Madison Avenue, New York, NY   10017
   CEO: Leonard Satterfield, VP   Tel: (212) 856-7300   Emp: N/A
   Bus: *Telecommunications*   Fax:(212) 856-7550   %FO: 100

   NORTHERN TELECOM INC.
   2221 Lakeside Blvd., Richardson, TX   75082
   CEO: Richard P. Faletti, Pres.   Tel: (972) 684-1000   Emp: 6000
   Bus: *Telecommunications services.*   Fax:(972) 684-3733   %FO: 100

   NORTHERN TELECOM INC.
   4001 East Chapel Hill - Nelson Hwy, Research Triangle Park, NC   27709
   CEO: John Roth, Pres.   Tel: (800) 466-7835   Emp: 2000
   Bus: *Telecommunications services.*   Fax:(800) 896-8944   %FO: 100

   NORTHERN TELECOM INC.
   200 Athens Way, Nashville, TN   37220
   CEO: R. Merrills, Pres.   Tel: (615) 734-4000   Emp: N/A
   Bus: *Telecommunications services.*   Fax:(615) 734-5190   %FO: 100

   NORTHERN TELECOM INC.
   225 West 34th Street, New York, NY   10012
   CEO: George Fishetti, Pres.   Tel: (212) 629-4591   Emp: N/A
   Bus: *Telecommunications services.*   Fax:(212) 239-0537   %FO: 100

- **NORTH AMERICAN LIFE ASSURANCE CO.**
5650 Yonge Street, North York, ON, Canada M2M 4G4
CEO: W.E. Bradford, Deputy Chrm.   Tel: (416) 229-4515   Emp: 1150
Bus: *Life insurance and financial services.*   Fax:(416) 229-6594

   NORTH AMERICAN SECURITY LIFE
   116 Huntington Ave, Boston, MA   02116
   CEO: Jim Boyle, Pres.   Tel: (617) 266-6004   Emp: 138
   Bus: *Mutual funds, annuities*   Fax:(617) 375-5723   %FO: 100

● **NOVA CORP. OF ALBERTA**
P. O. Box 2535, Station M, Calgary, AB, Canada 2P 2N6
CEO: J. E. Newall, Pres.   Tel: (403) 290-6000   Emp: 6500
Bus: *Produces/markets/distributes natural gas, energy*   Fax:(403) 290-6379
     services & petrochemicals.

     NATURAL GAS CLEARINGHOUSE CORP. (NGC)
     1000 Louisiana Street, Houston, TX   77002
     CEO: C.L. Watson, Ores.   Tel: (713) 507-6400   Emp: N/A
     Bus: *Natural gas services.*   Fax:(703) 507-6813   %FO: 36.5

● **NOVATEL COMMUNICATIONS LTD**
6732 8th St. NE, Calgary, AB, Canada T2E 8M4
CEO: Pascal Spothelfer, CEO   Tel: (403) 295-4500   Emp: 300
Bus: *Design/mfr. global positioning systems, wireless*   Fax:(403) 295-0230
     access & personal communications products.

     JRC/NOVATEL COMMUNICATIONS, INC.
     4000 Sandshell Drive, Ft Worth, TX   76137
     CEO: Pascal Spothelfer, Pres.   Tel: (817) 847-2100   Emp: 5
     Bus: *Sales wireless access products*   Fax:(817) 847-2174   %FO: 100

● **ONTARIO DIE COMPANY INTERNATIONAL**
119 Roger Street, Waterloo, Ontario N2J 3Z6, Canada
CEO: Martin Levine, Chrm.   Tel: 519-576-8950   Emp: N/A
Bus: *Mfr. die cuts and machinery leasing.*   Fax:519-579-3670

     ONTARIO DIE COMPANY OF AMERICA
     PO Box 610397, Port Huron, MI   48601
     CEO: Mike Geffros, EVP   Tel: (810) 987-5060   Emp: N/A
     Bus: *Mfr./sales die cuts and machinery leasing.*   Fax:(810) 987-3688   %FO: 100

● **OSLER, HOSKIN & HARCOURT**
1 First Canadian Place, P.O. 50, Toronto, Ontario M5X 1B8, Canada
CEO: John Stevens, Mng.Ptnr.   Tel: (416) 362-2111   Emp: N/A
Bus: *International law firm. Barristers & Solicitors;*   Fax:(416) 862-6666
     Patent & Trade-Mark Agents.

     Osler, Hoskin & Harcourt
     280 Park Avenue, Suite 30W, New York, NY   10017
     CEO: John Stevens, Managing Partner   Tel: 212-867-5800   Emp: N/A
     Bus: *International law firm.*   Fax:212-867-5802   %FO: 100

● **JIM PATTISON GROUP**
1600-1055 West Hastings Street, Vancouver BC V6E 2H2, Canada
CEO: Jim Pattioson, CEO   Tel: (604) 688-6764   Emp: N/A
Bus: *Mfr. flexible packaging.*   Fax:(604) 687-2601

> **JIM PATTISON GROUP - STROUT PLASTICS DIVISION**
> 9611 James Avenue, Bloomington, MN   55431
> CEO: Thomas S. Everett, VP & Gen.Mgr.   Tel: (612) 881-8673   Emp: 180
> Bus: *Mfr. flexible packaging.*   Fax:(612) 881-9697   %FO: 100

● **PERMA FLEX INC.**
6015 Kestrel Road, Mississauga, ON, Canada L5T 1S8
CEO: M. Berwick, VP & Gen.Mgr.   Tel: (905) 670-0670   Emp: N/A
Bus: *Mfr. rollers & roller coverings.*   Fax:(905) 670-3299

> **PERMA FLEX NORTH AMERICA INC.**
> 56 West Main Street, #211, Newark, DE   19702
> CEO: L. Bakker, Pres.   Tel: (302) 731-5022   Emp: N/A
> Bus: *Rollers & roller coverings.*   Fax:(302) 731-0483   %FO: 100

● **PHARMASCIENCE INC.**
8400 Darnley Road, Montreal, PQ, Canada H4T 1M4
CEO: Morris Goodman, Chrm.   Tel: (514) 340-1114   Emp: 100
Bus: *Pharmaceuticals, surgical supplies.*   Fax:(514) 342-7764

> **AMD-RITMED INC.**
> 175 Rano Street, Buffalo, NY   14207
> CEO: Gloria Heuget, Gen. Mgr.   Tel: (716) 871-9164   Emp: 28
> Bus: *Mfr. disposable O/R supplies.*   Fax:(716) 871-3415   %FO: 100

● **PLACER DOME INC.**
PO Box 49330, Bentall Postal Station, Vancouver, BC, Canada V7X 1P1
CEO: John W. Willson, Pres.   Tel: (604) 682-7082   Emp: 6230
Bus: *Mineral exploration, development & production.*   Fax:(604) 682-7092

> **PLACER DOME US ,INC.**
> One California Street, #2500, San Francisco, CA   94111-5472
> CEO: Jay K. Taylor, Pres.   Tel: (415) 986-0740   Emp: 950
> Bus: *Mineral exploration, development and* Fax:(415) 397-0747   %FO: 100
>   *production.*

- **ARNOLD PORTIGAL INVESTMENTS, INC.**
1700 Corydon Avenue, #204, Winnipeg, MB, Canada R3N 0K1

CEO: Arnold A. Portigal, CEO	Tel: (204) 488-6737	Emp: N/A
Bus: *Commercial mortgage lending and real estate.*	Fax:(204) 488-6747	

GENEVIEVE HOLDINGS OF ARIZONA LTD
2111 E. Highlands Ave., Ste. 225, Phoenix, AZ 85016-4733

CEO: Arnold A.Portigal, Pres.	Tel: (602) 381-0177	Emp: 7
Bus: *Commercial mortgage lending, real estate.*	Fax:(602) 381-0260	%FO: 100

- **POWER CORPORATION OF CANADA LTD.**
759 Victoria Square, Montreal, PQ, Canada H2Y 2K4

CEO: Paul Desmarais, Jr., Chrm./CEO	Tel: (514) 286-7400	Emp: N/A
Bus: *Holding company.*	Fax:(514) 286-7424	

THE GREAT-WEST LIFE ASSURANCE COMPANY
8505-8515 East Orchard Road, Englewood, CO 80111

CEO: William T. McCallum, EVP	Tel: (303) 889-3000	Emp: N/A
Bus: *Life & health insurance and annuities.*	Fax:(303) 689-5220	%FO: 99

- **PREVOST CAR INC.**
35 Blvd Gagnon, Ste Claire, PQ, Canada G0R 2V0

CEO: Georges Bourelle, Pres.	Tel: (418) 883-3391	Emp: 800
Bus: *Mfr. intercity coaches & special purpose vehicles.*	Fax:(418) 883-4157	

PREVOST CAR INC.
862 Valley Brook Avenue, Lyndhurst, NJ 07071

CEO: Joseph Craig, VP & Gen.Mgr.	Tel: (201) 933-3900	Emp: 33
Bus: *Sales/service intercity coaches & special purpose vehicles*	Fax:(201) 933-2785	%FO: 100

- **PROVIGO INC.**
1611 Cremazie Blvd East, Montreal, PQ, Canada H2M 2R9

CEO: Pierre Michaud, Chrm.	Tel: (514) 383-3000	Emp: 16000
Bus: *Marketing/distribution in food & convenience sectors.*	Fax:(514) 383-2964	

BAY AREA FOODS
PO Box 3668, Danville, CA 94526

CEO: Mark Sellers, Pres.	Tel: (510) 648-7010	Emp: 2000
Bus: *Supplier wholesale/retail food & related services/products.*	Fax:(510) 648-7030	%FO: 100

- **PWA CORPORATION**
Scotia Center #2800, 700 2nd Street SW, Calgary, AB, Canada T2P 2W2
CEO: Rhys Eton, Pres.   Tel: (403) 294-2000   Emp: 15000
Bus: *Air transportation, equipment rental and leasing.*   Fax:(403) 294-6299

    CANADIAN AIRLINES INTL.
    595 Madison Avenue, 23rd Fl., New York, NY 10022-1907
    CEO: Donald Pluto, Mgr.   Tel: (212) 759-1326   Emp: N/A
    Bus: *Commercial air transport.*   Fax:(212) 759-1326   %FO: 100

- **QUEBECOR PRINTING INC.**
612 St. Jacques Street, Montreal, PQ, Canada H3C 4M8
CEO: Jean Neveu, Chrm.   Tel: (514) 954-0101   Emp: 28900
Bus: *Commercial printing services.*   Fax:(514) 954-1426

    QUEBECOR PRINTING (USA) CORP.
    125 High Street, Boston, MA 02110
    CEO: James A. Dawson, Pres.   Tel: (617) 346-7300   Emp: 16000
    Bus: *Commercial printing services.*   Fax:(617) 346-7361   %FO: 100

- **RAYCO ELECTRONOC SYSTEMS LTD.**
1370 Chemin Filteau, St. Nicolas, Quebec G7A 2K1, Canada
CEO: Normand Hinse, Pres. & CEO   Tel: 418-831-6137   Emp: 100
Bus: *Supply crane safety systems.*   Fax:418-831-0856

    WYLIE SYSTEMS INC
    5877 South Garnett Road, Tulsa, OK 74146
    CEO: Normand Hinse, Pres. & CEO   Tel: (918) 252-1957   Emp: 5
    Bus: *Distribution/service crane safety systems.* Fax:(918) 252-2048   %FO: 100

- **RBC DOMINION SECURITIES**
130 Adelaide Street West, Toronto, ON, Canada M5H 1T8
CEO: Charles M. Winograd, Pres.   Tel: (416) 860-3400   Emp: 2000
Bus: *Investment broker.*   Fax:(416) 365-5500

    RBC DOMINION SECURITIES, INC.
    Financial Square, 24th Floor, New York, NY 10005-3532
    CEO: Gordon Rigchie, Pres.   Tel: (212) 361-2700   Emp: N/A
    Bus: *Investment broker.*   Fax:(212) 361-4506   %FO: 100

- **RECOCHEM INC.**
850 Montee de Liesse, Montreal, PQ, Canada H4T 1P4
CEO: Eva Kuchar, VP   Tel: (514) 341-3550   Emp: 450
Bus: *Mfr. chemicals.*   Fax:(514) 341-6553

    RECOCHEM (USA)
    640 Pleasant Street, Norwood, MA 02062
    CEO: Bert White, VP   Tel: (617) 762-4843   Emp: N/A
    Bus: *Mfr./sales chemicals.*   Fax:(617) 762-7743   %FO: 100

● **REPAP ENTERPRISES CORP.**
1250 Rene Levesque Blvd., Suite 3800, Montreal, PQ, Canada H3B 4W8

CEO: George S. Petty, CEO | Tel: (514) 846-1316 | Emp: N/A
Bus: *Mfr. coated papers.* | Fax:514-846-1313

    REPAP WISCONSIN INC.
    433 North Main Street, Kimberly, WI   54136

    CEO: George S. Petty, CEO | Tel: (414) 788-3511 | Emp: 1200
    Bus: *Mfr./sales coated papers.* | Fax:(414) 788-5368 | %FO: 100

● **RIO ALGOM LTD.**
120 Adelaide Street West, Toronto, ON, Canada M5H 1W5

CEO: C. A .Macaulay, Pres. | Tel: (416) 367-4000 | Emp: 3500
Bus: *Mining, metals distributor.* | Fax:(416) 365-6870

    POTASH CO OF AMERICA, INC.
    1120 Boston Post Road, Darien, CT   06820

    CEO: R. G. Connochie, Pres. | Tel: (203) 655-4420 | Emp: 506
    Bus: *Marketing potash.* | Fax:(203) 655-4523 | %FO: 100

    RIO ALGOM MINING CORP.
    6305 Waterford Blvd. #325, Oklahoma City, OK   73118

    CEO: Robert P. Luke, Pres. | Tel: (405) 848-1190 | Emp: 100
    Bus: *Uranium mining.* | Fax:(405) 848-1208 | %FO: 100

● **ROYAL BANK OF CANADA**
P O Box 6001, One Place Villek Marie, Montreal, PQ, Canada H3C 3A9

CEO: John E. Cleghorn, Chrm. | Tel: 514- 874-2110 | Emp: 48200
Bus: *General banking services.* | Fax:514-874-7197

    ROYAL BANK OF CANADA
    One Financial Square Bldg., 23rd Fl., New York, NY   10005-3531

    CEO: David L. Robertson, SVP | Tel: (212) 428-6200 | Emp: N/A
    Bus: *Commercial banking services.* | Fax:(212) 968-1293 | %FO: 100

● **SANDWELL INC.**
Park Pl, 666 Burrard Street, Vancouver BC , Canada V6C 2X8

CEO: Alan Pyatt, Pres. & CEO | Tel: (604) 684-0055 | Emp: 1700
Bus: *Engineering, plan, design, project & construction* | Fax:(604) 684-7533
    management.

    SANDWELL INC.
    2690 Cumberland Pkwy., Atlanta, GA   30339

    CEO: Jon Ferguson, VP & Gen.Mgr. | Tel: (770) 433-9336 | Emp: 350
    Bus: *Engineering, planning, design, project &* | Fax:(770) 433-9518 | %FO: 100
    construction management

- **SCI-TEC INSTRUMENTS, INC.**
  1526 Fletcher Road, Saskatoon, Saskatchewan S7M 5M1, Canada
  CEO: Robert Berman, Pres.   Tel: (306) 934-0101   Emp: N/A
  Bus: *Mfr. instruments for scientific research.*   Fax:(306) 978-2339

  > **SCI-TEC INSTRUMENTS USA, INC.**
  > 390 Central Avenue, Bohemia, NY   11716
  > CEO: Bill Irwin, Gen. Mgr.   Tel: (516) 589-2065   Emp: N/A
  > Bus: *Mfr. instruments for scientific research.*   Fax:(516) 589-2068   %FO: 100

- **SCOTIAMCLEOD INC.**
  P O Box 433, Commercial Union Tower, Toronto, ON, Canada M5K 1M2
  CEO: Gordon Cheesbrough, Pres. & COO   Tel: (416) 863-7411   Emp: 2000
  Bus: *Investment broker/dealer.*   Fax:(416) 862-3001

  > **SCOTIA CAPITAL MORTGAGE**
  > 165 Broadway, 25th Fl, New York, NY   10006
  > CEO: Ted Price, Pres.   Tel: (212) 225-6500   Emp: 65
  > Bus: *Investment dealer.*   Fax:(212) 225-6527   %FO: 100

- **THE SEAGRAM COMPANY LTD.**
  1430 Peel Street, Montreal PQ, Canada H3A 1S9
  CEO: Edgar M. Bronfman Jr., Pres.   Tel: (514) 849-5271   Emp: 30000
  Bus: *Mfr. and distributes distilled spirits, wines &*   Fax:(514) 987-5224
       beverages; produces and distributes entertainment
       product, theme parks.

  > **MCA Inc.**
  > 100 University City, Universal City, CA   91608
  > CEO: Frank J. Biondi, Jr.   Tel: (818) 777-1000   Emp: N/A
  > Bus: *Entertainment, media production and services;*   Fax:(818) 733-7402   %FO: 100
  >   *film, video & music production & distribution.*

  > **JOSEPH E. SEAGRAM & SONS INC.**
  > 375 Park Avenue, New York, NY   10152-0192
  > CEO: Edgar Bronfman Jr, Pres.   Tel: (212) 572-7000   Emp: N/A
  > Bus: *Distilled spirits & wines*   Fax:(212) 838-5052   %FO: 100

  > **SEAGRAM AMERICAS**
  > 800 Third Avenue, New York, NY   10152-0192
  > CEO: Fernando Kfouri, EVP   Tel: (212) 572-7000   Emp: N/A
  > Bus: *Distribution distilled spirits, wines and*   Fax:(212) 572-7058   %FO: 100
  >   *beverages.*

  > **SEAGRAM CHATEAU & ESTATE WINES COMPANY**
  > 2600 Campus Drive, Ste.160, San Mateo, CA   94403
  > CEO: Samuel Bronfman II, Pres.   Tel: (415) 378-3800   Emp: N/A
  > Bus: *Mfr. & distribution wines and spirits.*   Fax:(415) 378-3820   %FO: 100

THE SEAGRAM CLASSICS WINE COMPANY
2600 Campus Drive, Ste.160, San Mateo, CA   94403

CEO: Samuel Bronfman II, Pres.	Tel: (415) 378-3800	Emp: N/A
Bus: *Mfr. and distribution wine.*	Fax:(415) 378-3820	%FO: 100

SEAGRAM LATIN AMERICA
Two Alahambra Plaza - Suite 807, Coral Gables, FL   33134

CEO: Fernando Kfouri, Pres.	Tel: (305) 567-3260	Emp: N/A
Bus: *Distribution distilled spirits, wines and beverages.*	Fax:(305) 441-0979	%FO: 100

The SEAGRAM SPIRITS & WINE GROUP
375 Park Avenue, 5th Fl., New York, NY   10152

CEO: Edgar M. Bronfman, Jr. CEO	Tel: (212) 572-7000	Emp: N/A
Bus: *US Headquarters; distilled spirits and wines.*	Fax:(212) 572-1022	%FO: 100

TROPICANA DOLE BEVERAGES WORLDWIDE
1001 13th Avenue East, Bradenton, FL   34208

CEO: Gary M. Rodkin, Pres.	Tel: (941) 747-4461	Emp: N/A
Bus: *Mfr. and distribute beverages.*	Fax:(941) 746-5896	%FO: 100

UNIVERSAL STUDIOS, INC.
100 Univesity City, Universal City, CA   91608

CEO: Frank J. Biondi, Jr. Chmn.	Tel: (818) 777-1000	Emp: N/A
Bus: *Production and distribution entertainment product; theme parks.*	Fax:(818) 733-7402	%FO: 100

● **SICO INC.**
2505 de la Metropole Street, Longueuil, PQ, Canada J4G 1E5

CEO: Jean-Paul Lortie, Chrm. & CEO	Tel: (514) 527-5111	Emp: 1000
Bus: *Paint, coatings, sealants, concrete admixtures.*	Fax:(514) 646-7699	

　NU-BRITE CHEMICAL COMPANY, INC.
　24 Plain Street, Braintree, MA   02184

CEO: Elaine Arend, Mgr.	Tel: (617) 387-5000	Emp: N/A
Bus: *Mfr. paint, industry coatings.*	Fax:(617) 794-0809	%FO: 100

● **SINCLAIR TECHNOLOGIES LTD.**
85 Mary Street, Aurora, ON, Canada L4G 3G9

CEO: Douglas Jones, Pres.	Tel: 905) 727-0165	Emp: 170
Bus: *Mfr. antennas & filters for radio communication systems.*	Fax:905) 727-0861	

　SINCLAIR TECHNOLOGIES INC.
　55 Oriskany Drive, Tonawanda, NY   14150

CEO: Douglas Jones, Pres	Tel: (716) 874-3682	Emp: 65
Bus: *Mfr. antennas & filters for radio communication systems.*	Fax:(716) 874-4007	%FO: 100

• **SLATER INDUSTRIES INC**
4100 Yonge Street, Willowdale, ON, Canada M2P 2B5
CEO: B. Swirsky, Pres.   Tel: (416) 733-4400   Emp: 2100
Bus: *Steel products & special steel, hardware for electric*   Fax:(416) 733-4429
transmission.

    SLATER STEEL INC.
    2400 Taylor Street West, PO Box 630, Fort Wayne, IN   46801
    CEO: Hank Winters, Pres.   Tel: (219) 434-2800   Emp: 721
    Bus: *Mfr. stainless & special alloy steel.*   Fax:(219) 434-2801   %FO: 100

• **SOBEYS STORES LTD.**
115 King Street, Stellarton, NS, Canada B0K 1S0
CEO: William M. Sobey, Chrm.   Tel: (902) 752-8371   Emp: N/A
Bus: *Retail groceries.*   Fax:(902) 928-1101

    HANNAFORD BROS COMPANY
    145 Pleasant Hill Road, Scarborough, ME   04074
    CEO: Hugh Farrington, Pres.   Tel: (207) 883-2911   Emp: N/A
    Bus: *Wholesale food distribution, supermarkets &*   Fax:(207) 885-2276   %FO: 26
    drug stores

• **SODARCAN INC.**
1140 de Maisonneuve Blvd, Montreal, PQ, Canada H3A 1M8
CEO: Gerald Parizeau, Pres.   Tel: (514) 288-0100   Emp: 1300
Bus: *Insurance services.*   Fax:(514) 288-0840

    AINON BEP INTL CORPORATION
    10 Exchange Place Center, Jersey City, NJ   07302
    CEO: Robert W. Bailey, Pres.   Tel: (201) 332-1020   Emp: N/A
    Bus: *Reinsurance services.*   Fax:(201) 332-5673   %FO: 100

• **SOUTHAM INC.**
1450 Don Mills Rd, Don Mills, ON, Canada M3B 2X7
CEO: Don Babick, Pres. & COO   Tel: (416) 442-2900   Emp: 8164
Bus: *Newspaper printing & pub, trade magazine pub,*   Fax:(416) 442-2077
information services (electronic & print).

    AMERICAN TRUCKER
    7355 N. Woodland Drive, PO Box 603, Indianapolis, IN   46206
    CEO: Jim Bellin, Pres.   Tel: (317) 297-5500   Emp: N/A
    Bus: *Trade publication.*   Fax:(317) 299-1312   %FO: 100

• ST MARY'S ENTERPRISES INC.
2200 Yonge Street, Toronto, ON, Canada M4S 2C6
CEO: M. Eugene Wrinkle, Pres.   Tel: (416) 484-4411   Emp: N/A
Bus: *Cement, concrete products.*   Fax:(416) 484-5260

ST. MARY'S CEMENT - BLUE CIRCLE CANADA, INC.
9333 Dearborn Street, Detroit, MI   48209
CEO: M. E. Wrinkle, Pres. & CEO   Tel: (313) 842-4600   Emp: N/A
Bus: *Cement, concrete products.*   Fax:(313) 849-4555   %FO: 100

ST. LAWRENCE CEMENT, INC.
1945 Graham Boulevard, Mount-Royal, PQ, Canada H3R 1H1
CEO: Bernard Kueng, Pres.   Tel: (514) 340-1881   Emp: 3000
Bus: *Cement, concrete, aggregates, construction services.*   Fax:(514) 342-8154

INDEPENDENT CEMENT CORPORATION
3 Columbia Circle, Albany, NY   12203
CEO: Dennis W. Skidmore, Pres.   Tel: (518) 452-3001   Emp: 23
Bus: *Mfr./distribution cement.*   Fax:(518) 452-3045   %FO: 100

STELCO, INC.
Stelco Tower, 100 King West, PO Box 2030, Hamilton, ON, Canada L8N 3T1
CEO: James C. Alfano, Pres.   Tel: 905-528-2511   Emp: 16000
Bus: *Blast furnaces and steel mills.*   Fax:905-577-4493

CHIMHOLD COAL COMPANY, INC.
32601 Highway 194 East, Jamboree, KY   41536
CEO: Brian Warry, Pres.   Tel: (606) 456-3432   Emp: 260
Bus: *Coal production.*   Fax:(606) 456-8565   %FO: 100

SUN LIFE ASSURANCE COMPANY OF CANADA
150 King Street West, Toronto, ON, Canada M5H 1J9
CEO: John R. Gardner, Pres.   Tel: (416) 979-9966   Emp: 5300
Bus: *Insurance, pensions, mutual funds.*   Fax:(416) 585-9546

SUN LIFE OF CANADA
1 Sun Life Executive Park, Wellesley Hills, MA   02181
CEO: Donald Stewart, Pres.   Tel: (617) 237-6030   Emp: N/A
Bus: *Ins, pensions, mutual funds*   Fax:(617) 237-6309   %FO: 100

TECSYN INTL INC.
One St. Paul Street - Suite 602, St. Catherine, ON L2M 7L2 Canada
CEO: Zoltan D. Simo, Pres. & CEO   Tel: (905) 687-8811   Emp: 580
Bus: *Holding company.*   Fax:(905) 687-6917

POLI-TWINE WESTERN INC.
PO Box 160430 Freeport Center Bldg. A-16-A, Clearfield, UT   84016-0430
CEO: Wayne Corbett, Pres.   Tel: (801) 773-8756   Emp: 75
Bus: *Mfr. baler, tomato & industrial twines.*   Fax:(801) 773-8664   %FO: 100

POLYTECH NETTING IND INC.
631 East Big Beaver Road Ste .207, Troy, MI   48083
CEO: William P. Schroers, Pres.   Tel: (248) 680-9020   Emp: 500
Bus: *Mfr. auto convenience & restraint nets.*   Fax:(248) 680-9024   %FO: 100

TECSYN PMP INC.
4950 Gilmer Drive, Huntsville, AL   35805
CEO: Wayne Corbett, Pres.   Tel: (205) 722-9092   Emp: 7
Bus: *Mfr. pressed powdered metal products.*   Fax:(205) 722-7939   %FO: 100

● **TELEGLOBE INC.**
1000 de la Gauchtière Street West, 24th Fl., Montreal, PQ, Canada H3B 4X5
CEO: Charles Sirois, CEO   Tel: 514-868-8124   Emp: 1620
Bus: *International telecommunications services and*   Fax:514-868-7234
products.

    ISI SYSTEMS, INC.
Two Tech Drive, Andover, MA   01810
CEO: Simon N. Garneau, Pres.   Tel: (508) 682-5500   Emp: 300
Bus: *International telecommunications services and*   Fax:(508) 686-0130   %FO: 100
products.

● **THE THOMSON CORP.**
P.O.Box 24, Toronto-Dominion Tower,#2706, Toronto, ON, Canada M5K 1A1
CEO: Kenneth R. Thomson, CEO   Tel: (416) 360-8700   Emp: 48000
Bus: *Publishing, newspapers, information services,*   Fax:(416) 360-8812
leisure travel.

    FAUKNER & GRAY
11 Penn Plaza, New York, NY   10001
CEO: John Love, Pres.   Tel: (212) 967-7000   Emp: 100
Bus: *Book publishers.*   Fax:(212) 967-7155   %FO: 100

THOMSON CORPORATION PUBLISHING INTERNATIONAL INC.
Metro Center, One Station Place, 8th Fl., Stamford, CT   06902
CEO: J.Gordon Paul, CEO   Tel: (203) 969-8700   Emp: N/A
Bus: *Publishing, newspapers, information services.*   Fax:(203) 977-8354   %FO: 100

THOMSON FINANCIAL & PROFESSIONAL PUBLISHING GROUP
22 Pittsburgh Street, Boston, MA   02210
CEO: Andrew G. Mills, CEO   Tel: (617) 345-2000   Emp: 16000
Bus: *Regulatory & financial information services.*   Fax:(617) 772-5007   %FO: 100

THOMSON HOLDINGS INC.
Metro Center, One Station Place, 8th Fl., Stamford, CT   06902
CEO: J.Gordon Paul, CEO   Tel: (203) 969-8700   Emp: N/A
Bus: *U.S. headquarters. Holding company.*   Fax:(203) 977-8354   %FO: 100

THOMSON INFORMATION PUBLISHING INTERNATIONAL
Metro Center, One Station Place, 8th Fl., Stamford, CT 06902

CEO: J.Gordon Paul, CEO	Tel: (203) 969-8700	Emp: 8000
Bus: *Information services & publishing.*	Fax:(203) 977-8354	%FO: 100

THOMSON NEWSPAPERS INC.
Metro Center, One Station Place, 8th Fl., Stamford, CT 06902

CEO: Richard J. Harrington, Pres.	Tel: (203) 425-2500	Emp: 6000
Bus: *Newspaper publishing.*	Fax:(203) 425-2516	%FO: 100

WARREN GORHAM & LAMONT
375 Hudson Street, New York, NY 10014

CEO: Evan Manzies, Pres.	Tel: (212) 367-6300	Emp: 100
Bus: *Book publishers.*	Fax:(212) 367-6305	%FO: 100

TOROMONT INDUSTRIES LTD.
65 Villiers Street, Toronto, ON, Canada M5A 3S1

CEO: Robert Ogilvie, Chrm.	Tel: (416) 465-3518	Emp: 11000
Bus: *Mfr. refrigeration & heating equipment, electro-metalurgical products.*	Fax:(416) 465-8255	

TOROMONT INDUSTRIES/AEROTECH, INC.
395 West 1100 North, North Salt Lake, UT 84054

CEO: Jerry Quest, Pres.	Tel: (801) 292-0493	Emp: 100
Bus: *Refrigeration equipment.*	Fax:(801) 292-9908	%FO: 100

TORONTO-DOMINION BANK
55 King St. W, Box 1, Toronto, ON, Canada M5K 1A2

CEO: Richard M. Thomson, Chrm.	Tel: (416) 982-8222	Emp: 21710
Bus: *Banking, financial services.*	Fax:(416) 944-5718	

TORONTO-DOMINION BANK TRUST CO
31 West 52nd Street, New York, NY 10019-6101

CEO: Michael Mueller, Sr.VP	Tel: (212) 468-0600	Emp: N/A
Bus: *Commercial banking & trust services.*	Fax:(212)426-9285	%FO: 100

TORONTO-DOMINION HOLDINGS (USA) INC.
909 Fannin Street, Houston, TX 77010

CEO: Carole Clause, Assoc. VP	Tel: (713) 653-8200	Emp: N/A
Bus: *Bank holding company.*	Fax:(713) 951-9921	%FO: 100

WATERHOUSE SECURITIES INC.
100 Wall Street, 28th Fl., New York, NY 10005

CEO: Larry Waterhouse, Pres.	Tel: (212) 344-7500	Emp: N/A
Bus: *Securities brokerage and investment services.*	Fax:(212) 509-8122	%FO: 100

● **TRANSCANADA PIPELINES LTD.**
P O Box 1000, Station M, Calgary, AB, Canada T2P 4K5

CEO: George W. Watson   Tel: (403) 267-6100   Emp: 1700
Bus: *Nat gas marketing & transmission, electric power*   Fax:(403) 267-8993
generation.

   GREAT LAKES GAS TRANSMISSION COMPANY
   One Woodard Avenue, Suite 1600, Detroit, MI   48226

   CEO: Derek E. Henwood, Pres.   Tel: (313) 596-4400   Emp: N/A
   Bus: *Natural gas transmission.*   Fax:(313) 596-4612   %FO: 100

   IROQUOIS GAS TRANSMISSION SYSTEM
   One Corporate Drive, Suite 606, Shelton, CT   06484-6211

   CEO: Craig R. Frew, Pres.   Tel: (203) 926-7200   Emp: 282
   Bus: *Natural gas transmission.*   Fax:(203) 929-9501   %FO: 50

● **TRIDON LTD.**
1150 Corporate Drive, PO Box 5029, Burlington L7R 482, Canada

CEO: D.M. Green, Chrm. & CEO   Tel: ((905) 3321007   Emp: N/A
Bus: *Mfr./distribution auto & industrial parts.*   Fax:(800) 563-1464

   TRIDON INC.
   P O Box 1600, Nashville, TN   37202

   CEO: Paul Davidson, Pres   Tel: (615) 459-5800   Emp: N/A
   Bus: *Mfr. of hose clamps & distribution auto &*   Fax:(615) 355-0879   %FO: 100
   industry parts

● **TRIZEC CORP. LTD.**
1700 Bankers Hall, 855 Second St SW, Calgary, AB, Canada T2P 4J7

CEO: Bill L'Heureux, Pres.   Tel: (403) 269-8241   Emp: 7000
Bus: *Development, own & manage commercial income*   Fax:(403) 265-7301
property.

   TRIZEC HAHN INC.
   4350 La Jolla Village Drive, San Diego, CA   92122-1233

   CEO: Lee Wagman, Pres.   Tel: (619) 546-1001   Emp: 1900
   Bus: *Real estate develop/management*   Fax:(619) 546-3413   %FO: 100

   TRIZEC HAHN INC.
   15760 Ventura Blvd, Encino, CA   91436-3095

   CEO: Robert Forrest, Sr VP   Tel: (818) 783-0660   Emp: 300
   Bus: *Real estate development & management* Fax:(818) 783-2108   %FO: 100

• UNICAN SECURITY SYSTEMS, LTD.

7301 Decarie Blvd, Montreal, PQ Canada H4P 2G7

CEO: Peter Blaikie, Pres.   Tel: (514) 735-5411   Emp: 1500

Bus: *Mfr. key blanks & duplicating equipment, locks &*   Fax:(514) 735-0428
    electronic access systems, die cast products,
    furniture hardware

ILCO UNICAN CORP.

400 Jeffreys Road, Rocky Mount, NC 27801

CEO: Don Wright, EVP   Tel: (919) 446-3321   Emp: 500

Bus: *Mfr. keys, key mach, locks, locksmith supplies.*   Fax:(919) 446-4702   %FO: 100

• VELAN INC.

2125 Ward Ave., Montreal, PQ, Canada H4M 1T6

CEO: A. K. Velan, Pres.   Tel: (514) 748-7743   Emp: N/A

Bus: *Mfr. forged & cast pressure valves.*   Fax:(514) 748-8635

VELAN-VALVE CORPORATION

Griswold Industrial Park, Avenue "C", Williston, VT 05495

CEO: Michael A Parsons, Mgr   Tel: (802) 863-2561   Emp: N/A

Bus: *Steel gates, cast valves*   Fax:(802) 862-4014   %FO: 100

• WESTERN POTTERY COMPANY, INC.

1740 One Bentall Centre, 505 Burrard Street, Vancouver, BC, Canada V7X 1M6

CEO: David C. Pegg, Pres.   Tel: (604) 688-2464   Emp: N/A

Bus: *Mfr. sanitaryware, vitreous china.*   Fax:(604) 688-0097

WESTERN POTTERY COMPANY, INC.

15129 Garfield Avenue, Paramount, CA 90723-4019

CEO: Richard A.Coury, VP & Gen.Mgr.   Tel: (562) 529-6560   Emp: 88

Bus: *Mfr. sanitaryware, vitreous china.*   Fax:(562) 630-5040   %FO: 100

• GEORGE WESTON LTD.

22 St. Clair Avenue East, Ste. 1901, Toronto, ON Canada M4T 2S7

CEO: W. Galen Weston, Chrm.   Tel: (416) 922-2500   Emp: 76650

Bus: *Bakery & confectionery product, groceries, pulp &*   Fax:(416) 922-4395
    paper, fisheries.

E. B. EDDY PAPER INC.

1700 Washington Avenue
PO Box 5003, Port Huron, MI 48060-5003

CEO: E. F. Boswell, Pres.   Tel: (810) 982-0191   Emp: N/A

Bus: *Mfr. fine paper.*   Fax:(810) 982-7124   %FO: 100

INTERBAKE FOODS INC.

2821 Emerywood Parkway, Ste. 210, Richmond, VA 23294-3727

CEO: Raymond A. Baxter, Pres.   Tel: (804) 755-7107   Emp: N/A

Bus: *Mfr./distribution cookies & crackers.*   Fax:(804) 755-7173   %FO: 100

MAPLEHURST BAKERIES INC.
50 Maplehurst Drive, Brownsburg, IN   46112
CEO: E.F.Riswick, Pres.   Tel: (317) 858-9000   Emp: N/A
Bus: *Mfr./distribution cookies, pies, pastries.*   Fax:(317) 858-9009   %FO: 100

STROEHMANN BAKERIES, INC.
255 Business Center Drive, Horsham, PA   19044
CEO: G. Prince, Pres.   Tel: (215) 672-8010   Emp: N/A
Bus: *Mfr./distribution bread, rolls, cake.*   Fax:(215) 672-6988   %FO: 100

Chile

• BANCO DE CHILE
Ahumada 251, Santiago, Chile
CEO: S. Schulin-Zeuthen, CEO   Tel: 56-2-637-2111   Emp: 4000
Bus: *Commercial banking services.*   Fax:56-2-637-2103

    BANCO DE CHILE - New York Branch
    124 E 55th Street, New York, NY 10022
    CEO: Hernan Donoso, Gen.Mgr.   Tel: (212) 758-0909   Emp: 33
    Bus: *General banking services.*   Fax:(212) 593-9770   %FO: 100

    BANCO DE CHILE - Miami Agency
    200 South Biscayne Boulevard, Miami, FL 33131-5307
    CEO: Matias Herrera, Gen. Mgr.   Tel: (305) 373-0041   Emp: 10
    Bus: *International banking services.*   Fax:(305) 373-6465   %FO: 100

• BANCO DE SANTIAGO
Bandera 172, Santiago, Chile
CEO: Julio Barriga, Chrm.   Tel: 56-2-672-8072   Emp: 4000
Bus: *Commercial banking services.*   Fax:56-2-698-7948

    BANCO DE SANTIAGO
    375 Park Avenue, Suite 2605, New York, NY 10152
    CEO: Carlos Singer, Rep.   Tel: (212) 826-0550   Emp: 2
    Bus: *Commercial banking services.*   Fax:(212) 826-1218   %FO: 100

BANCO SUD AMERICANO
Morande 226, Santiago, Chile
CEO: Jose Borda, CEO   Tel: 56-2-692-6000   Emp: N/A
Bus: *Commercial banking services.*   Fax:56-2-698-6008

    BANCO SUD AMERICANO
    1 World Trade Center, Ste 8947, New York, NY 10048
    CEO: John N. Myers, Sr. Rep.   Tel: (212) 938-5896   Emp: 2
    Bus: *International banking services.*   Fax:(212) 938-5985   %FO: 100

CHILE FAST
Manquelhue Norte 444, Apoquindo 5856, Las Condes, Santiago, Chile
CEO: Ana Maria Carey, Admin.   Tel: 56-2-201-0450   Emp: N/A
Bus: *Tourism, cargo transport.*   Fax:56-2-240-0450

    INTER-HEMISPHERE TOURS
    82 Wall Street, #1009, New York, NY 10005
    CEO: Cecilia Carey, Owner & Mgr   Tel: (212) 344-4690   Emp: 2
    Bus: *Tourism, cargo.*   Fax:(212) 344-0004   %FO: JV

● **CODELCO-CHILE**
Huerfanos 1270, Santiago, Chile
CEO: Marcos Lima, Pres.   Tel: 56-2 6903067   Emp: 24000
Bus: *Mining copper & by-products*   Fax:56-2 6903059

    CODELCO (USA) INC.
    177 Broad Street, 14th Fl., Stamford, CT   06901
    CEO: J. Pablo Bunster, Pres.   Tel: (203) 425-4321   Emp: 5
    Bus: *Marketing/sale copper & by-products.*   Fax:(203) 425-4322   %FO: 100

● **EMPRESA NACIONAL DEL PETROLEO (ENAP)**
Ahumada 341, Santiago, Chile
CEO: Alvaro García Alamos   Tel: 56-2-280-3000   Emp: 3000
Bus: *Oil & gas production and refineries.*   Fax:56-2-638-0164

    EMPRESA NACIONAL DEL PETROLEO (ENAP)
    One World Trade Center, New York, NY   10048
    CEO: Danilo Martic, Representative   Tel: (212) 938-0557   Emp: 2
    Bus: *Petroleum industry, representative office,* Fax:(212) 938-0559   %FO: 100
        procurement coordination.

● **LADECO CHILEAN AIRLINES**
Avenida 107, Santiago, Chile
CEO: Jose Ibanez Santa Maria, Chrm.   Tel: 56-2-216-355   Emp: 1200
Bus: *Commercial air transport services.*   Fax:56-2-687-2817

    LADECO CHILEAN AIRLINES
    9500 S Dadeland Blvd, #510, Miami, FL   33156
    CEO: Eduardo Gallardo, Pres   Tel: (305) 670-3066   Emp: N/A
    Bus: *Commercial air transport services.*   Fax:(305) 636-3777   %FO: 100

● **LAN CHILE AIRLINES**
Estado 10, Santiago, Chile
CEO: E. Cueto, Pres.   Tel: 56-2-639-4411   Emp: N/A
Bus: *International commercial air transport.*   Fax:56-2-638-1729

    LAN CHILE AIRLINES
    630 Fifth Avenue, Suite 809, New York, NY   10111
    CEO: Rolando Damas, Reg.Sales Mgr.   Tel: (212) 582-3250   Emp: N/A
    Bus: *International commercial air transport.*   Fax:(212) 582-6863   %FO: 100

    LAN CHILE AIRLINES
    1960 East Grand Avenue, Ste. 522, El Segundo, CA 90245
    CEO: Buddy Lander, Reg. Sales Mgr.   Tel: (310) 416-9061   Emp: N/A
    Bus: *International commercial air transport.*   Fax:(310) 416-9864   %FO: 100

    LAN CHILE AIRLINES
    9700 S. Dixie Hwy, PH, Miami, FL   33156
    CEO: Alex DeGunter, VP   Tel: (305) 670-1961   Emp: N/A
    Bus: *International commercial air transport.*   Fax:(305) 670-9553   %FO: 100

LAN CHILE AIRLINES
PO Box 1207, Lake Geneva, WI   53147
CEO: Jackie Huml, Mgr.   Tel: (414) 249-0900   Emp: N/A
Bus: *International commercial air transport.*   Fax:(414) 249-0616   %FO: 100

SOCIEDAD QUIMICA Y MINERA DE CHILE
Miraflores 222, Piso 11, Santiago, Chile
CEO: Julio Ponce, Chrm.   Tel: 56-2-632-6888   Emp: 4000
Bus: *Mfr. industrial products and fertilizers.*   Fax:56-2-633-4223

   CHILEAN NITRATE CORP
   150 Boush St., Norfolk, VA   23510
   CEO: Guillermo Farias, Pres.   Tel: (757) 640-7270   Emp: 25
   Bus: *Distributor industrial products and fertilizers.* Fax:(757) 640-7271   %FO: 100

   SQM IODINE CORPORATION, USA
   150 Boush St., Norfolk, VA   23510
   CEO: Sebastian Rios, Pres.   Tel: (757) 640-7273   Emp: 3
   Bus: *Distributor industrial iodine.*   Fax:(757) 640-7271   %FO: 100

China

- **AIR CHINA**
Jing Xin Building, No. 2 (a), Beijing , China
CEO: Mr. Hong, Pres.   Tel: 86-1-466-3586   Emp: 14000
Bus: *Commercial air transport services.*   Fax:86-1-466-3587

    AIR CHINA INTERNATIONAL INC.
    540 California Street, San Francisco, CA   94104
    CEO: Mr. Chen, Mgr.   Tel: (415) 392-2156   Emp: N/A
    Bus: *Commercial air transport services.*   Fax:(415) 392-2156   %FO: 100

    AIR CHINA INTERNATIONAL INC.
    45 East 49th Street, New York, NY   10017
    CEO: Mr. Hong, Pres.   Tel: (212) 371-9898   Emp: N/A
    Bus: *Commercial air transport services.*   Fax:(212) 935-7951   %FO: 100

- **BANK OF CHINA**
410 Fuchengmen Nei Dajie, Beijing 100818, China
CEO: Xuebing Wang, Chrm. & Pres.   Tel: 86-10-6601-6688   Emp: 214000
Bus: *Commercial banking services.*   Fax:86-10-6601-6869

    BANK OF CHINA
    410 Madison Avenue, New York, NY   10017
    CEO: Zhicheng Zhu, Gen.Mgr.   Tel: (212) 935-3101   Emp: 280
    Bus: *International banking services.*   Fax:(212) 593-1831   %FO: 100

    BANK OF CHINA
    444 South Flower Street, 39th Fl., Los Angeles, CA   90071
    CEO: Gianhua Gao, Gen. Mgr.   Tel: (213) 688-9700   Emp: 100
    Bus: *International banking services.*   Fax:(213) 688-0198   %FO: 100

- **BANK OF COMMUNICATIONS**
Shanghai, China
CEO: Quchange Pan, Pres.   Tel: 86-21-6275-1234   Emp: N/A
Bus: *Commercial banking services.*   Fax:86-21-6275-6784

    BANK OF COMMUNICATIONS
    55 Broadway, 31/32 Fls., New York, NY   10006-3008
    CEO: S.Z. Shen, Gen. Mgr.   Tel: (212) 376-8030   Emp: N/A
    Bus: *Commercial banking services.*   Fax:(212) 376-8089   %FO: 100

● **CHINA NATIONAL CHEMICAL IMPORT & EXPORT CORPORATION**
A2 Fuxingmenwai Dajie, Beijing, China 100046
CEO: N/A   Tel: 86-1-6856-9972   Emp: N/A
Bus: *Mfr./import/export chemicals and specialty chemical* Fax:86-1-6856-9967
products.

   SC POLYMERS, INC.
   2000 Post Oak Blvd., Suite 2450, Houston, TX   77056
   CEO: C. Jinxueyan, Mgr.   Tel: (713) 623-6127   Emp: N/A
   Bus: *Mfr./import/export chemicals and specialty*   Fax:(713) 623-6128   %FO: 100
   chemical products.

   SINO-CHEM AMERICA HOLDING, INC
   One World Trade Center, New York, NY   10048
   CEO: Hongwei Yang, Mgr.   Tel: (212) 488-8060   Emp: 6
   Bus: *US headquarters. Mfr./import/export*   Fax:(212) 488-1140   %FO: 100
   chemicals and specialty chemical products.

   SINO-CHEM USA, INC.
   2 World Trade Center, New York, NY   10048
   CEO: Chanman Ngok, Mgr.   Tel: (212) 432-2100   Emp: 10
   Bus: *Mfr./import/export chemicals and specialty*   Fax:(212) 432-9179   %FO: 100
   chemical products.

   US AGROCHEMICAL CORP.
   3225 State Road, 630 West, Ft. Mcadc, FL   33841
   CEO: Alex Song Yu, Mgr.   Tel: (941) 285-8121   Emp: N/A
   Bus: *Mfr./import/export chemicals and specialty*   Fax:(941) 285-7984   %FO: 100
   chemical products.

● **CHINA NATIONAL FOREIGN TRADE TRANSPORTATION CORP**
Jiuling Bldg #21, Xisanhuanbei Road, Beijing, China
CEO: N/A   Tel: 86-1-840-2503   Emp: N/A
Bus: *Freight forwarding services.*   Fax:86-1-840-5228

   CHINA INTEROCEAN TRANSPORT INC.
   223 Lawrence Avenue, South San Francisco, CA   94080
   CEO: S. Y. Chen, Gen. Mgr.   Tel: (415) 588-7685   Emp: N/A
   Bus: *Freight forwarding services.*   Fax:(415) 588-3157   %FO: 100

● **SHANGHAI PETROCHEMICAL COMPANY LIMITED**
Jinshanwei, Shanghai 2000540, China
CEO: Wu Yixin, Pres.   Tel: 86-21-794-3143   Emp: 38000
Bus: *Petrochemicals*   Fax:86-21-794-0050

   CHINA PETROCHEMICAL CORP. (Sinopec)
   1 World Trade Center, Suite 4655, New York, NY   10048
   CEO: Q. Kang, Pres.   Tel: (212) 321-9460   Emp: N/A
   Bus: *US representative office.*   Fax:(212) 321-9467   %FO: 100

Colombia

• BANCO CAFETERO (A.K.A. BANCAFE)
Calle 28 #13A-15, Apartado Aereo 240332, Bogota, Colombia
CEO: Gilberto Gomez, Pres.   Tel: 57-1-284-6800   Emp: 6900
Bus: *International banking services.*   Fax:57-1-286-8893

BANCO CAFETERO INTL CORP. (A.K.A. BANCAFE INTL)
801 Brickell Avenue, PH-1, Miami, FL   33131
CEO: Alfredo Quintero, Pres.   Tel: (305) 372-9909   Emp: 46
Bus: *International banking services.*   Fax:(305) 372-1797   %FO: 100

• BANCO COLPATRIA SA
Carretera 7 #24-89, Bogota, Colombia
CEO: Santiago Perdonp, Pres.   Tel: 57-1-334-0600   Emp: 480
Bus: *International banking services.*   Fax:N/A

BANCO COLPATRIA F. A.
801 Brickell Avenue, Suite 2360, Miami, FL   33131
CEO: Ernesto Cordovez, Gen.Mgr.   Tel: (305) 374-4026   Emp: 5
Bus: *International banking services.*   Fax:(305) 372-0605   %FO: 100

• BANCO DE BOGOTA
Calle 36 #7-47, Bogota, Colombia
CEO: Alejandro Figueroa, Gen. Mgr.   Tel: 57-1-288-1188   Emp: N/A
Bus: *International banking services.*   Fax:N/A

BANCO DE BOGOTA INTERNATIONAL CORP.
800 Brickell Avenue, Miami, FL   33131
CEO: Alfonso Garcia, Mgr.   Tel: (305) 371-4201   Emp: 10
Bus: *International banking services. Sub of Banco*   Fax:(305) 372-9947   %FO: 100
de Bogota.

FIRST BANK OF THE AMERICAS
375 Park Avenue, 23rd Floor, New York, NY   10152
CEO: Herman Salazar, Mgr.   Tel: (212) 826-0250   Emp: 50+
Bus: *International banking services.*   Fax:(212) 715-4313   %FO: 100

• BANCO GANADERO, S.A.
Carrera 9, No. 72-21, Bogota, Colombia
CEO: Jose Maria Ayala, Pres.   Tel: 571-312-4666   Emp: N/A
Bus: *International banking services.*   Fax:N/A

BANCO GANADERO, S.A.
1150 South Miami Avenue, Miami, FL   33130
CEO: Manuel R. Manotas, EVP & Gen. Mgr.   Tel: (305) 374-3955   Emp: N/A
Bus: *International banking services.*   Fax:(305) 374-7710   %FO: 100

Cyprus

• **CYPRUS AIRWAYS LTD.**
21 Alkeou Street, Nicosia, Cyprus
CEO: Vasillis G. Rologis, Chrm.   Tel: 35-72-443054 Emp: 2017
Bus: *Commercial air transport services.* Fax:35-72-443167

 CYPRUS AIRWAYS LTD.
 71 West 35th Street, New York, NY 10016-3813
 CEO: Vasillis G. Rologis, Chrm.   Tel: (212) 714-2190 Emp: N/A
 Bus: *Commercial air transport services.* Fax:(212) 714-2543 %FO: 100

• **CYPRUS TOURISM ORGANIZATION**
PO Box 4535, Nicosia, Cyprus
CEO: Kostas Papageorgious, Marketing Dir. Tel: 35-72-337715 Emp: N/A
Bus: *Tourism and travel.*   Fax:35-72-331644

 CYPRUS TOURISM ORGANIZATION
 13 East 40 Street, New York, NY 10016
 CEO: Neophytos Christolou, Dir.   Tel: (212) 663-5280 Emp: N/A
 Bus: *Tourism and travel.*   Fax:(212) 663-5282 %FO: 100

Czech Republic

● **CENTROTEX PRAHA LTD.**
Praha 4, 19061, Czech Republic
CEO: M. Cervencl, Pres.   Tel: 420-2-6115-1111   Emp: N/A
Bus: *Trading company.*   Fax: N/A

   CENTROTEX USA, INC.
   990 Avenue of the Americas, New York, NY   10018
   CEO: Miroslav Tvaruzek, Pres.   Tel: (212) 947-8094   Emp: 2
   Bus: *Trading company; import/export of textiles.*   Fax:(212) 947-8228   %FO: 100

● **CZECH AIRLINES LTD.**
Letiste Ruzyne, Prague 16000, Czech Republic
CEO: Antonin Jakubse, Pres.   Tel: 42-23-341540   Emp: 4300
Bus: *Commercial air transport services.*   Fax:42-23-162774

   CZECH AIRLINES LTD.
   1350 Avenue of the Americas, New York, NY   10036
   CEO: Jiri Hrdina, Mgr.   Tel: (212) 765-6022   Emp: N/A
   Bus: *Commercial air transport services.*   Fax:(212) 765-6108   %FO: 100

● **STROJEXPORT TRADE s.r.o, PRAHA**
U Demartinky 1, Phaha 5, 150 00, Czech Republic
CEO: Krel Tumlir, Pres.   Tel: 420-2-573-11940   Emp: 28
Bus: *Reconstruction of heating, power plants,*   Fax:420-2-573-11972
import/export, client consulting, financing.

   STROJEXPORT TRADE, INC.
   1501 East Hallandale Beach Blvd., Hallandale, FL   33009
   CEO: Karel Tumlir, Pres.   Tel: (954) 927-3453   Emp: 4
   Bus: *Import/export.*   Fax:(954) 927-3453   %FO: 100

Denmark

● **BRUEL & KJAER INTERNATIONAL**
Q850, Naerum Hove Gade 18, Naerum, DK-2850 Copenhagen, Denmark
CEO: Viggo Kjaer, Mgn .Dir.   Tel: 45-4580-0500   Emp: N/A
Bus: *Mfr. electrotechnical products.*   Fax:45-4580-1405

SPECTRIS TECHNOLOGIES
2364 Park Central Boulevard, Decatur, GA   30035
CEO: Ralph Genesi, Pres.   Tel: (770) 981-9311   Emp: N/A
Bus: *Sound, vibration and data analysis*   Fax:(770) 987-8704   %FO: 100
    instrumentation.

● **CHR HANSEN GROUP A/S**
10-12 Bøge Allé, PO Box 407, DK-2970 Hørsholm, Denmark
CEO: Eric Sorensen, Pres.   Tel: 45-45-767676   Emp: 1600
Bus: *Supplies ingredients; food industry, pharmaceuticals* Fax:45-45-765576
    and diagnostics for specific allergy disease
    treatment.

ALK LABORATORIES INC. sub of ALK-ABELLÓ
1700 Royston Lane, Round Rock, TX   78664
CEO: Brien J. DeBari, Pres.   Tel: (512) 251-0037   Emp: N/A
Bus: *Mfr./distribution allergy treatment products.*   Fax:(512) 251-8450   %FO: 100

ALK LABORATORIES INC., RESEARCH CENTER sub of ALK-ABELLÓ
27 Village Lane, Wallingford, CT   06492
CEO: Brien J. DeBari, Pres.   Tel: (203) 949-2727   Emp: N/A
Bus: *Mfr./distribution allergy treatment products.*   Fax:(203) 949-2718   %FO: 100

ALK LABORATORIES INC.
2840 8th Street, Berkeley, CA   94710
CEO: Brien J. DeBari, Pres.   Tel: (510) 843-6846   Emp: N/A
Bus: *Mfr./distribution allergy treatment products.*   Fax:(510) 843-1304   %FO: 100
    Sub of ALK-ABELLÓ

CHR HANSEN INC. BIOSYSTEMS
9015 West Maple Street, Milwaukee, WI   53214-4298
CEO: Leif Nøgaard, Pres.   Tel: (414) 476-3630   Emp: N/A
Bus: *Mfr. supplies for dairy and agricultural*   Fax:(414) 259-9399   %FO: 100
    industry.

DIVERSITECH, INC.
2411 N.W. 41st Street, Gainsville, FL   32606-6662
CEO: Jim Bacus, Pres.   Tel: (352) 377-7071   Emp: N/A
Bus: *Mfr./sales production ingredients for dairy and*   Fax:(352) 377-7073   %FO: 100
    food industry.

VESPA LABORATORIES INC. sub of ALK-ABELLÓ
R D NBR #1, Spring Mills, PA   16875
CEO: Miles Guralnick, Pres.   Tel: (814) 422-8165   Emp: N/A
Bus: *Research/mfr./mktg. insect venom therapies.*   Fax:(814) 422-8424   %FO: 100

● **CR SYSTEMS A/S**
Lautrupvang 1B, DK-2750 Ballerup, Denmark
CEO: Soren Sorensen, Pres.   Tel: 45-44-661144   Emp: N/A
Bus: *Data communications software.*   Fax:45-44-42651388

    CR SYSTEMS CORP.
    100 Hartsfield Centre Pkwy, Atlanta, GA   30354
    CEO: Klaus Akselsen, Gen. Mgr.   Tel: (404) 767-8230   Emp: N/A
    Bus: *Data communications software.*   Fax:(404) 767-1372   %FO: 100

● **CRISPLANT A/S**
Pedersens Vej 10, DK-8200, Årthus, Denmark
CEO: M. Petersen, Pres.   Tel: 45-86-78-4411   Emp: N/A
Bus: *Manufactures automated high-speed sortation*   Fax:45-86-78-4432
    systems.

    CRISPLANT, INC.
    7495 New Technology Way, Frederick, MD   21703
    CEO: D. James Smallwood, Pres.   Tel: (301) 663-8710   Emp: 90
    Bus: *Sales/distribution/service automated high-*   Fax:(301) 662-0449   %FO: 100
        speed sortation systems.

● **L DAEHNFELDT A/S**
P O Box 185, DK-5100 Odense C, Denmark
CEO: Povl B. Jorgensen, Dir.   Tel: 45-66-170606   Emp: N/A
Bus: *Seed production and sales.*   Fax:45-66-170479

    DAEHNFELDT INC.
    P.O. Box 947, Albany, OR   97321
    CEO: Henry C. Hayes, Pres.   Tel: (541) 928-5868   Emp: 18
    Bus: *Seed production and sales.*   Fax:(541) 928-5581   %FO: 100

● **DANFOSS A/S**
DK-6430 Nordborg, Denmark
CEO: Jørge M. Clausen, Pres.   Tel: 45-7488-2222   Emp: 17000
Bus: *Refrigeration controls, heating & water controls,*   Fax:45-7488-0949
    and motion controls.

    DANFOSS AUTOMATIC CONTROLS
    1775-G MacLeod Drive, Lawrenceville, GA   30243
    CEO: Michael S. Beuke, V.P. Operations   Tel: (770) 339-9492   Emp: 60
    Bus: *Mfr. refrigerant compressors and condensing*   Fax:(770) 339-9612   %FO: 100
        units.

DANFOSS AUTOMATIC CONTROLS

794-1 Corporate Drive, Baltimore, MD   21236

CEO: Robert W. Wilkins, Pres.   Tel: (410) 931-8250   Emp: 142

Bus: *Refrigerant flow controls, industrial controls*   Fax:(410) 931-8256   %FO: 100
& compressors, refrigeration compressors,
condensing units, electronic products.

DANFOSS ELECTRONIC DRIVES

2995 Eastrock Drive, Rockford, IL   61109

CEO: Erhardt Jessen, Pres.   Tel: (815) 398-2770   Emp: 135

Bus: *Mfr. AC electronic frequency converters.*   Fax:(815) 398-2869   %FO: 100

DANFOSS FLUID POWER

8635 Washington Avenue, Racine, WI   53406-3773

CEO: Ronald G. Wickline, Pres.   Tel: (414) 884-7400   Emp: 600

Bus: *Mfr. hydraulic integrated circuits, motors,*   Fax:(414) 884-7470   %FO: 100
pumps, power units, and manual & electrically
operated valves.

DANFOSS VIDEK USA

2200 Brighton, Henriette Town Line Road, Rochester, NY   14623-2706

CEO: Wes M. Perdue, Pres.   Tel: (716) 292-6210   Emp: 21

Bus: *Vision product for the optimizing of production*   Fax:(716) 292-5884   %FO: 100
processes.

FLOMATIC CORPORATION

145 Murray Street, Glens Falls, NY   12801

CEO: Bo Andersson, Pres.   Tel: (518) 761-9797   Emp: 50

Bus: *Mfr./sale check valves, foot valves, back flow*   Fax:(518) 761-9798   %FO: 100
preventers, control valves.

GRAHAM - DIV OF DANFOSS INC.

Box 23880/8800, West Bradley Road, Milwaukee, WI   53223-0880

CEO: Erhardt Jessen, Pres.   Tel: (414) 355-8800   Emp: 130

Bus: *Mfr. of DC electronic frequency converters.*   Fax:(414) 355-6117   %FO: 100

• DANISCO A/S

PO Box 17, DK-1001 Copenhagen K, Denmark

CEO: Alf Dutch-Pedersen, CEO   Tel: 45-31-951700   Emp: 12000

Bus: *Food & beverages, sugar, food ingredients &*   Fax:45-31-543650
packaging.

DANISCO INGREDIENTS USA, INC.

200 New Century Parkway, New Century, KS   66031

CEO: Robert H. Mayer, Pres.   Tel: (913) 764-8100   Emp: 240

Bus: *Mfr./sale food ingredients.*   Fax:(913) 764-5407   %FO: 100

● **DANTEC MEDICAL A/S**
Tonsbakker 16-18, DK-2740 Skovlunde, Denmark
CEO: Eric Jensen, Pres.   Tel: 45-44-923132   Emp: N/A
Bus: *Medical diagnostic equipment in neurological &*   Fax:45-42-846346
urological fields.

    DANTEC MEDICAL INC.
    3 Pearl Court, Allendale, NJ   07401-1610
    CEO: Alan J. Schaefer, Pres. & CEO   Tel: (201) 236-6330   Emp: 25
    Bus: *Sales/service medical diagnostic equipment.*   Fax:(201) 236-6348   %FO: 100

● **DEN DANSKE BANK**
2-12 Holmens Kanal, DK-1092 Copenhagen, Denmark
CEO: Peter Staarup, CEO   Tel: 45-33-440000   Emp: N/A
Bus: *General commercial banking services.*   Fax:45-33-185873

    DEN DANSKE BANK
    280 Park Avenue, New York, NY   10017
    CEO: James M. Stewart, Gen. Mgr.   Tel: (212) 984-8400   Emp: 65
    Bus: *International commercial banking services.*   Fax:(212) 370-9239   %FO: 100

● **DFDS A/S**
Sankt Annae Plads 30, DK-1295 Copenhagen, Denmark
CEO: Bo-Lennart Thorbjornsson, CEO   Tel: 45-33-423342   Emp: 5000
Bus: *Travel & transport services.*   Fax:45-33-154993

    DFDS SEAWAYS (USA) INC.
    6555 NW 9th Ave., #207, Ft Lauderdale, FL   33309
    CEO: L. Michael Zacchilli, Pres.   Tel: (954) 491-7909   Emp: 5
    Bus: *Marketing/reservations travel & transport.*   Fax:(305) 491-7958   %FO: 100

● **ENKOTEC A/S**
Danmarksvej 37, DK-8660 Skanderborg, Denmark
CEO: Svend-Helge Sorensen, Pres.   Tel: 45-86-524444   Emp: 60
Bus: *Mfr. rotary forming nail machines & cold forgers.* Fax:45-86-524199

    ENKOTEC CO INC
    31200 Solon Road, #16, Solon, OH   44139
    CEO: Jan Sorige, Pres.   Tel: (216) 349-2800   Emp: 7
    Bus: *Sale/service rotary forming nail machines, and*   Fax:(216) 349-3575   %FO: 100
    cold formers.

• EPOKE A/S
Vejenvej 50, Askov Postbox 230, DK-6600 Vejen , Denmark

CEO: Thyge Hvass Rasmussen, Pres.	Tel: 45-75-360700	Emp: 400
Bus: *Spreaders, de-icing & anti-icing equipment.*	Fax:45-75-363867	

EPOKE INC.
1099 Atlantic Drive, Unit #2, West Chicago, IL   60185

CEO: Torben Zerlang, Pres.	Tel: (630) 231-4622	Emp: 4
Bus: *Spreaders, de-icing & anti-icing equipment.*	Fax:(630) 231-4794	%FO: 100

• FISKER & NIELSEN, A/S
Sognevej, No. 25, Brondby 2605, Denmark

CEO: Ole Jakobsen, Chrm.	Tel: 45-4323-8100	Emp: N/A
Bus: *Mfr. floor maintenance equipment.*	Fax:45-4343-7700	

ADVANCE MACHINE, INC.
14600 21st Avenue North, Plymouth, MN   55447

CEO: Jack Cooney, Pres.	Tel: (612) 473-2235	Emp: 600
Bus: *Sales/distribution of floor maintenance equipment.*	Fax:(612) 473-1764	%FO: 100

• FLS INDUSTRIES A/S
Vigersleve Alle 77, DK-2500 Valby, Copenhagen, Denmark

CEO: Jens Münter, Chrm. & CEO	Tel: 45-36-181800	Emp: N/A
Bus: *Engineering, building materials, real estate, aerospace services.*	Fax:45-36-304441	

DAN TRANSPORT CORP USA
1210 Corbin Street, Elizabeth, NJ   07201

CEO: Jorgen Moller, Pres.	Tel: (908) 353-0800	Emp: N/A
Bus: *International freight forwarding.*	Fax:(908) 353-8717	%FO: 100

F.L.S. MILJO AIRPOL INC.
3 Century Drive, Parsippany, NJ   07608

CEO: P. Lausen, Pres.	Tel: (201) 288-7070	Emp: N/A
Bus: *Design/install pollution control equipment.*	Fax: 201) 288-6441	%FO: 100

FULLER COMPANY
2040 Avenue C, Bethlehem, PA   18017

CEO: Kai Lyngsie, Pres.	Tel: (610) 264-6011	Emp: 1163
Bus: *Supplier custom equipment, systems, products & processes for cement, pulp, paper, mining, and chemical industry.*	Fax:(610) 264-6170	%FO: 100

● **FOSS ELECTRIC A/S**
Slangerupgade 69, DK-3400 Hillerod, Denmark
CEO: Peter Foss, CEO   Tel: 45-42-263366   Emp: 700
Bus: *Electronic equipment, measure control devices.*   Fax:45-42-269322

    FOSS FOOD TECHNOLOGY CORP
    10355 West 70th Street, Hopkins, MN   55344
    CEO: Brendan Martin, Pres.   Tel: (612) 941-8870   Emp: 45
    Bus: *Sale/service analytical instruments for dairy,*   Fax:(612) 941-6533   %FO: 100
        food & feed industry.

● **GREAT NORDIC A/S**
Mårkaervej 2A, Postbox 224, DK-2630 Taastrup, Denmark
CEO: Ole Nyvold, Chrm.   Tel: 45-4371-4100   Emp: 2500
Bus: *Mfr. hearing healthcare products and services.*   Fax:45-4371-4104

    GN DANAVOX, INC.
    5600 Rowland Road, Ste. 250, Minnetonka, MN   55343
    CEO: Tim Pawlak, Pres.   Tel: (612) 930-0416   Emp: 140
    Bus: *Sales/distribution of hearing instruments.*   Fax:(612) 930-0516   %FO: 100

● **HALDOR TOPSOE A/S**
Nymollevej 55, DK-2800 Lyngby, Denmark
CEO: Giorgio Girola, Mng. Dir.   Tel: 45-45-272000   Emp: 1000
Bus: *Engineering/licensing, chemical process*   Fax:45-45-272999
    development, mfr./research/sale catalyst.

    HALDOR TOPSOE INC.
    17629 El Camino Real, Houston, TX   77058
    CEO: Alex Barlowen, EVP   Tel: (281) 228-5000   Emp: 150
    Bus: *Engineering/licensing, chemical process*   Fax:(281) 228-5019   %FO: 100
        development, mfr./research/sale catalyst.

● **HARDI INTERNATIONAL A/S**
Helgeshoj Alle 38, DK-2630 Taastrup, Denmark
CEO: Jorgen Hartvig Jensen, Pres.   Tel: 45-43-711900   Emp: 750
Bus: *Mfr. agricultural sprayers.*   Fax:45-43-713355

    HARDI, INC.
    1500 West 76th Street, Davenport, IA   52806-1356
    CEO: Tom Kinzenbaw, Pres.   Tel: (319) 386-1730   Emp: 40
    Bus: *Mfr./distribution agricultural sprayers.*   Fax:(319) 386-1710   %FO: 100

● **INTERNATIONAL SERVICE SYSTEM A/S**
Kongevejen 195, DK-2840 Holte, Denmark
CEO: Waldemar Schmidt, Pres.   Tel: 45-4541-0811   Emp: N/A
Bus: *Supplies cleaning and security services.*   Fax:45-4541-0888

    ISS INTERNATIONAL SERVICE SYSTEM
    Two Concourse Parkway, Suite 270, Atlanta, GA   30328
    CEO: Martin O'Halloran, Pres.   Tel: (770) 512-7333   Emp: N/A
    Bus: *Supplies cleaning and security services.*   Fax:(770) 668-9121   %FO: 100

● **KEW INDUSTRI A/S**
Industrikvarteret, DK-9560 Handund, Denmark
CEO: Erik Holst, Pres.   Tel: 45-9- 572111   Emp: 600
Bus: *Mfr. high pressure cleaners & related cleaning*   Fax:45-9-572739
    equipment.

    KEW CLEANING SYSTEMS INC.
    130 E. St. Charles Road, #B, Carol Stream, IL   60188
    CEO: Torben Zerlang, Pres.   Tel: (630) 690-3000   Emp: 13
    Bus: *Mfr./distribution high pressure cleaners,*   Fax:(630) 690-2789   %FO: 100
    related equipment, waste water treatment
    systems.

    KEW CLEANING SYSTEMS INC.
    1500 North Belcher Road, Clearwater, FL   34625
    CEO: Chuck Katz, Sales Mgr.   Tel: (800) 237-5918   Emp: N/A
    Bus: *Mfr./distribution high pressure cleaners,*   Fax:(800) 405-9092   %FO: 100
    related equipment, waste water treatment
    systems.

● **KOSAN CRISPLANT A/S**
Pedersens Vej 10, DK-8200 Aarhus, Denmark
CEO: Mogens Petersen, Mgn. Dir.   Tel: 45-86-784411   Emp: 800
Bus: *Mfr. automated high-speed sortation system.*   Fax:45-86-784432

    KOSAN CRISPLANT USA INC
    7495 New Technology Way, Frederick, MD   21703
    CEO: D. James Smallwood, Pres. & CEO   Tel: (301) 663-8710   Emp: 21
    Bus: *Sales/service automated high speed sortation*   Fax:(301) 662-0449   %FO: 100
    systems.

● **I. KRUGER ENGINEERING A/S**
Gladsaxevej 363, DK-2860 Soborg, Denmark
CEO: Ole Rendback, Pres.   Tel: 45-39-690222   Emp: N/A
Bus: *Wastewater treatment systems.*   Fax:45-39-692392

  I KRUGER INC
  401 Harrison Oaks Blvd, #100, Cary, NC   27513
  CEO: Finn M. Nielsen, Pres.   Tel: (919) 677-8310   Emp: 19
  Bus: *Sale/distribution wastewater treatment*   Fax:(919) 677-0082   %FO: 100
   equipment & technology.

● **LABOTEK A/S**
PO Box 100, DK-3600 Frederikssund, Denmark
CEO: Jan Fussing, CEO   Tel: 45-42-288411   Emp: 100
Bus: *Auxiliary plastic processing equipment.*   Fax:45-42-289030

  LABOTEK INC.
  1170-F University Avenue, Rochester, NY   14607
  CEO: Philip Green, Pres.   Tel: (716) 244-4840   Emp: 3
  Bus: *Sale of plastic processing equipment.*   Fax:(716) 244-1690   %FO: 100

● **J. LAURITZEN A/S**
Sankt Annae Plads 28, P O Box 2147, DK-1291 Copenhagen, Denmark
CEO: Claus Ipsen, Pres.   Tel: 45-33-111222   Emp: 1075
Bus: *Shipowner & operator.*   Fax:45-33-118513

  J. LAURITZEN (USA) INC.
  645 Madison Avenue, Suite 610, New York, NY   10022-1010
  CEO: Peter B. Koken, Pres.   Tel: (212) 688-6660   Emp: 20
  Bus: *Shipowner & operator.*   Fax:(212) 688-8244   %FO: 100

  SABROE REFRIGERATION INC.
  4401 23rd Avenue West, Seattle, WA   98199
  CEO: Nils Rutlan, Pres.   Tel: (206) 285-0904   Emp: N/A
  Bus: *Mfr. marine refrigeration.*   Fax:(206) 285-0965   %FO: 100

● **MAN B&W DIESEL A/S**
Center Syd, Stamholmen 161, DK-2650 Copenhagen, Denmark
CEO: Gerrit Korte, Mgn. Dir.   Tel: 45-33-851100   Emp: 3000
Bus: *Mfr. marine diesel engines & propulsion systems.*   Fax:45-33-851030

  MAN B&W DIESEL INC.
  17 State Street, 18th Fl., New York, NY   10004
  CEO: Claus Windelev, Pres   Tel: (212) 269-0980   Emp: N/A
  Bus: *Mfr./sale diesel engines.*   Fax:(212) 363-2469   %FO: 100

● **NILAN A/S**
Nilanvej 2, P O Box 10, DK-8722 Hedensted, Denmark
CEO: Torben Andersen, Pres.   Tel: 45-75-892222   Emp: N/A
Bus: *Mfr. air exchange equipment.*   Fax:45-75-890394

    NILAN AMERICA INC
    275 Cottage Street, Athol, MA   01331
    CEO: Richard E. Paul, Pres.   Tel: (508) 249-8664   Emp: N/A
    Bus: *Distribution/service air exchange equipment.*   Fax:(508) 249-7762   %FO: 100

● **NIRO ATOMIZER A/S**
305 Gladsaxevej, DK-2860 Soeborg, Denmark
CEO: Klaus Bro, Pres.   Tel: 45-39-545454   Emp: 300
Bus: *Mfr. industrial drying agglomeration equipment.*   Fax:45-39-545800

    NIRO INC.
    9165 Rumsey Road, Columbia, MD   21045
    CEO: Steve Kaplan, Pres.   Tel: (410) 997-8700   Emp: 170
    Bus: *Mfr./sale industrial drying agglomeration*   Fax:(410) 997-5021   %FO: 100
        equipment, consulting, industrial testing
        facilities.

● **NORDFAB INTL OVERSEAS A/S**
Industrigade 13, DK-9550 Mariager, Denmark
CEO: J. B. Sorensen, Pres.   Tel: 45-98-583422   Emp: 150
Bus: *Mfr. air pollution control systems.*   Fax:N/A

    NORDFAB SYSTEMS INC
    102 Transit Avenue, PO Box 429, Thomasville, NC   27360
    CEO: Niels Pedersen, Pres.   Tel: (910) 889-9187   Emp: 45
    Bus: *Mfr./distribution/service air pollution control*   Fax:(910) 884-0017   %FO: 100
        systems.

● **NOVO NORDISK A/S**
Novo Allé, DK-2880 Bagsvaerd, Denmark
CEO: Mads Øvlisen, Pres.   Tel: 45-4444-8888   Emp: 13400
Bus: *Pharmaceuticals company: leader in diabetes care,*   Fax:45-4449-0555
    mfr./markets pharmaceutical products.

    NOVO NORDISK BIOCHEM North America, INC.
    77 Perry Chapel Road, Franklinton, NC   27525
    CEO: Lee Yarbrough, Pres.   Tel: (919) 494-2014   Emp: N/A
    Bus: *Biotechnology R&D.*   Fax:(919) 494-3461   %FO: 100

    NOVO NORDISK BIOTECH, INC.
    1497 Drew Avenue, Davis, CA   95616
    CEO: Pamela G Marrone, Pres.   Tel: (916) 757-8100   Emp: 35
    Bus: *Biopesticide R&D.*   Fax:(916) 758-0317   %FO: 100

NOVO NORDISK OF NORTH AMERICA, INC.
405 Lexington Avenue, Suite 6400, New York, NY   10017
CEO: Henrik Aagaard, Pres.   Tel: (212) 867-0123   Emp: 12
Bus: *North American operations headquarters.*   Fax:(212) 867-0298   %FO: 100

NOVO NORDISK PHARMACEUTICAL IND., INC.
3612 Powhatan Road, Clayton, NC   27520
CEO: John Pratt, Gen. Mgr.   Tel: (919) 550-2200   Emp: N/A
Bus: *Mfr./sales pharmaceuticals.*   Fax:(919) 553-4057   %FO: 100

NOVO NORDISK PHARMACEUTICALS, INC. , LARON DIV
1776 North Pine Island Road, #108, Plantation, FL   33322
CEO: N/A   Tel: (954) 424-0006   Emp: N/A
Bus: *Mfr./sales pharmaceuticals.*   Fax:(954) 424-0074   %FO: 100

NOVO NORDISK PHARMACEUTICALS, INC.
100 Overlook Center, #200, Princeton, NJ   08540-7810
CEO: C. Henk Bleeker, Pres.   Tel: (609) 987-5800   Emp: N/A
Bus: *Pharmaceutical sales.*   Fax:(609) 921-8082   %FO: 100

ZYMOGENETICS INC.
1201 Easte Lake Avenue East, Seattle, WA   98105-3702
CEO: Bruce L A Carter, Pres.   Tel: (206) 442-6600   Emp: 100
Bus: *Biotechnology R&D.*   Fax:(206) 442-6608   %FO: 100

● **OLICOM A/S**
Nybrovej 114, DK-2800 Lyngby, Denmark
CEO: Lars Stig Nielsen, Pres.   Tel: 45-45-270-000   Emp: 250
Bus: *Complete networking services.*   Fax:45-45-270-101

OLICOM USA INC.
900 East Park Blvd, #250, Plano, TX   75074
CEO: Michael Camp, Pres.   Tel: (972) 423-7560   Emp: 80
Bus: *Complete networking solutions.*   Fax:(972) 423-7261   %FO: 100

● **ORTOFON DK**
Telegafvej 5, DK-2750 Ballerup, Denmark
CEO: Anna Rohmann, Pres.   Tel: 45-44-681033   Emp: 100
Bus: *Mfr. phonograph cartridges.*   Fax:45-44-680970

ORTOFON INC.
63 Mall Drive, Commack, NY   11725
CEO: Anna Rohmann, Pres.   Tel: (516) 543-6950   Emp: N/A
Bus: *Phonograph cartridges*   Fax:(516) 543-6915   %FO: 100

● **PHASE ONE - DENMARK**
Roskildevej 39, DK-2000 Frederiksberg, Denmark

CEO: Carston Steenberg, Pres.	Tel: 45-36-460111	Emp: N/A
Bus: *Mfr. digital camera equipment.*	Fax:45-36-460222	

PHASE ONE - USA
24 Woodbine Avenue, Suite 15, Northport, NY   11768

CEO:Carston Steenberg, Pres.	Tel: (888) 742-7366	Emp: 18
Bus: *Sales/service digital camera equipment.*	Fax:(516) 757-2217	%FO: 100

● **RADIOMETER A/S**
Emdrupvej 72, DK-2400 Copenhagen, Denmark

CEO: Johann Schroder, Pres.	Tel: 45-38-273827	Emp: N/A
Bus: *Electronic instruments for science, medicine & industry.*	Fax:45-38-272727	

RADIOMETER AMERICA INC.
810 Sharon Drive, Westlake, OH   44145

CEO: W. Richard Keller, Pres.	Tel: (216) 871-8900	Emp: N/A
Bus: *Mfr./sale electronic instruments for science, medicine & industry.*	Fax:(216) 871-8117	%FO: 100

● **SABROE REFRIGERATION A/S**
Christian Den x's vej 201, PO Box 1810, DK 8270, HOJ BJERG, Denmark

CEO: N/A	Tel: 45-88-271-260	Emp: N/A
Bus: *Mfr. refrigeration and heating equipment systems.*	Fax:N/A	

SABROE REFIRGERATION
3580 Progress Drive, Bensalem, PA   19020

CEO: B. Grinneby, Pres.	Tel: (215) 638-7330	Emp: N/A
Bus: *Sales/distribution of refrigeration equipment and heating pumps.*	Fax:(215) 638-9212	%FO: 100

● **SCANVIEW A/S**
Meterbuen 6, DK-2740 Skovlunde, Denmark

CEO: Ib Drachmann-Hansen, Pres.	Tel: 45-44-536100	Emp: 90
Bus: *Mfr. desktop drum scanners & software, image setters.*	Fax:45-44-536108	

SCANVIEW INC.
330 Hatch Dr, Ste. A, Foster City, CA   94404

CEO: Bo Larsson, Pres.	Tel: (415) 378-6360	Emp: 9
Bus: *Sale/service desktop drum scanners & software, image setters.*	Fax:(415) 378-6368	%FO: 100

- **SCHUR INTERNATIONAL A/S**
J.W. Schurs Vej, DK-8700 Horsens, Denmark
CEO: Leif Sorensen, Pres.   Tel: 45-76-272727   Emp: N/A
Bus: *Mfr. packaging products.*   Fax:45-76-272700

  SCHURPACK, INC.
  2313 Lower Lake Road, St. Joseph, MO 64504
  CEO: Leif Sorensen, Pres.   Tel: (816) 238-1703   Emp: N/A
  Bus: *Mfr./distributor packaging products.*   Fax:(816) 238-7102   %FO: 100

- **SOPHUS BERENDSEN A/S**
1 Klausdalsbrovej, DK-2860 Soborg, Denmark
CEO: Hans K. Werdelin, Pres.   Tel: 45-3969-8500   Emp: N/A
Bus: *Provides healthcare, pest control, laundry & textile*   Fax:45-3969-7300
services; distribution, industrial parts;
hydraulics/electronics.

  BERENDSEN FLUID POWER INC.
  1700 Mid-Continent Tower, 401 S. Boston, Tulsa, OK 74103-3781
  CEO: Ian Hill, Pres.   Tel: (918) 592-3781   Emp: N/A
  Bus: *Distribution, industrial parts;*   Fax:(918) 592-7051   %FO: 100
  hydraulics/electronics.

- **SUPERFOS A/S**
3O Frydenlundsvej, DK-2950 Vedbaek, Denmark
CEO: Poul Andreassen, Chrm.   Tel: 45-42-893111   Emp: N/A
Bus: *Operates construction services, packaging &*   Fax:45-42-660405
chemical facilities.

  SUPERFOS PACKAGING, INC.
  11301 Superfos Drive, Cumberland, MD 21502
  CEO: James Mason, Pres.   Tel: (301) 759-3145   Emp: N/A
  Bus: *Provides packaging products & services.*   Fax:(301) 459-4905   %FO: 100

- **TELECOM DANMARK A/S**
Kannikegade 16, DK-8000 Århus, Denmark
CEO: Hans Wurtzen, CEO   Tel: 45-89-337777   Emp: 1700
Bus: *Telecommunications services.*   Fax:45-89-529341

  TELE DENMARK USA INC.
  50 Main Street, Ste. 1275, White Plains, NY 10606-1920
  CEO: Richard Pape, Pres.   Tel: (914) 289-0100   Emp: N/A
  Bus: *Telecommunications & data communications*   Fax:(914) 289-0105   %FO: 100
  services.

● **ALFRED THOMSEN A/S**
Vajenvej 50, DK-6600 Vejen, Denmark
CEO: Elisabeth Rudolph, Chrm.   Tel: 45-75-360700   Emp: 300
Bus: *Mfr. spreaders & related products, mowers.*   Fax:45-75-363867

   EPOKE INC.
   1099 Atlantic Drive, Suite 2, West Chicago, IL   60185-5102
   CEO: Torben Zerlang, Pres.   Tel: (630) 231-4622   Emp: N/A
   Bus: *Sale/service spreaders, ice & snow control*   Fax:(630) 231-4794   %FO: 100
      equipment.

● **TYTEX A/S**
Industrivej 21, DK-7430 Ikast, Denmark
CEO: Finn Kjaergaard, Pres.   Tel: 45-97-153100   Emp: 300
Bus: *Mfr. textiles.*   Fax:45-97-156294

   TYTEX, INC.
   601 Park East Drive, Woonsocket, RI   02895
   CEO: Peter Aggersbjerg, VP   Tel: (401) 762-4100   Emp: 55
   Bus: *Mfr./sale textiles.*   Fax:(401) 762-4262   %FO: 100

● **UNIBANK A/S**
Torvegade 2, DK-1256 Copenhagen, Denmark
CEO: Thorleif Krarup, Chrm.   Tel: 45-3333-3333   Emp: N/A
Bus: *Commercial banking services.*   Fax:45-3333-6262

   UNIBANK A/S - NEW YORK BRANCH
   13-15 West 54th Street, New York, NY   10019-5404
   CEO: John Mulligan, Treas.   Tel: (212) 603-6900   Emp: 60
   Bus: *International banking services.*   Fax:(212) 603-1685   %FO: 100

   UNIBANK SECURITIES, INC.
   13-15 West 54th Street, New York, NY   10019-5404
   CEO: Peter Caroe, Exec.VP   Tel: (212) 603-6966   Emp: 20
   Bus: *Financial/securities services.*   Fax:(212) 245-1684   %FO: 100

● **VESTAS WIND SYSTEMS A/S**
Smed Hansens Vej 27, DK-6940 Lem, Denmark
CEO: Johannes Poulsen, Mgn. Dir.   Tel: 45-44-443335   Emp: 625
Bus: *Mfr./install/maintenance wind turbines, wind*   Fax:45-97-341484
   turbine projects.

   VESTAS-AMERICAN WIND TECHNOLOGY, INC.
   19020 North Indian Avenue, Suite 4C, North Palm Springs, CA   92258-2010
   CEO: Johannes Poulsen, Pres.   Tel: (619) 329-5400   Emp: 12
   Bus: *Sale/install/maintenance wind turbines & wind*   Fax:(619) 329-5555   %FO: 100
      turbine projects.

● **VIKING LIFE-SAVING EQUIPMENT A/S**
Saedding Ringvej, DK-6710 Esbjerg V, Denmark
CEO: Katty Tornaes, Admin. Dir.   Tel: 45-76-118100   Emp: 500
Bus: *Liferafts, escape systems, survival & protection*   Fax:45-79-118101
      suits, mob rescue boats.

    VIKING LIFE-SAVING EQUIPMENT (AMERICA) INC.
    1625 North Miami Avenue, Miami, FL   33136
    CEO: Poul V. Jensen, Mgn. Dir.   Tel: (305) 374-5115   Emp: 21
    Bus: *Liferafts, marine escape systems, survival &*   Fax:(305) 374-1535   %FO: 100
       protection suits, water-activated lights,
       thermal protective aides.

● **WOLFKING DANMARK A/S**
Industrivej 6, DK-4200 Slagelse, Denmark
CEO: Ole Most, Mgn. Dir.   Tel: 45-58-502-525   Emp: 240
Bus: *Industrial meat processing equipment.*   Fax:45-58-501-031

    WOLFKING INC.
    825 Taylor Road, PO Box 30970, Columbus, OH   43230
    CEO: Jan Erik Kuhlmann, Pres.   Tel: (614) 863-3144   Emp: 30
    Bus: *Industrial meat processing equipment..*   Fax:(614) 863-3296   %FO: 100

Dominican Republic

● **BANCO HIPOTECARIO DOMINICANO**
Winston Curchill Esq., 27 de Febrero, Santo Domingo, Dominican Republic
CEO: Louis M. Achear, Chrm.   Tel: 809-243-3232   Emp: N/A
Bus: *Commercial banking.*   Fax:N/A

    BANCO HIPOTECARIO DOMINICANO
    561 West 181st Street, New York, NY   10033
    CEO: Wilson Ramos, Gen. Mgr.   Tel: (212) 927-6700   Emp: 50
    Bus: *International banking services.*   Fax:(212) 927-7768   %FO: 100

Ecuador

- **SAETA AIRLINES**
Avenida Carlos Julio Arosemena, Km. 2½, Guayaquil, Equador
CEO: Roberto Dum Barreiro, Pres.   Tel: 593-4-200-277   Emp: N/A
Bus: *Commercial air transport.*   Fax:593-4-296-397

    SAETA AIRLINES
    500 Fifth Avenue, Ste. 1421, New York, NY   11010
    CEO: Roberto Dum Barreiro, Pres.   Tel: (212) 302-0004   Emp: N/A
    Bus: *International air transport carrier.*   Fax:(212) 302-4608   %FO: 100

    SAETA AIRLINES
    7200 Corporate Center Drive, Miami, FL   33126
    CEO: Roberto Dum Barreiro, Pres.   Tel: (305) 477-3947   Emp: N/A
    Bus: *International air transport carrier.*   Fax:(305) 593-2746   %FO: 100

Egypt

- **EGYPTAIR**
Cairo International Airport, Cairo, Egypt
CEO: Mohamed Fahim Rayan, Chrm.   Tel: 20-2-245-4400   Emp: 3000
Bus: *Commercial air transport services.*   Fax:20-2-245-9316

    EGYPTAIR
    720 Fifth Avenue, New York, NY   10022
    CEO: Aly Mourad, VP   Tel: (212) 581-5600   Emp: N/A
    Bus: *Commercial air transport services.*   Fax:(212) 586-6599   %FO: 100

England

- **600 GROUP PLC**
  Witan Court, 284 Witan Gates, Milton Keyes, England MK9 1EJ
  CEO: Anthony Sweeten, Gen. Mgr.   Tel: 44-1908-446-1545 Emp: 2500
  Bus: *Holding company: real estate subdivision and* Fax:44-1908-446-1545
    development, building management, optical lenses.

  ### CLAUSING INDUSTRIAL INC.
  1819 North Pitcher Street, Kalamazoo, MI   49007
  CEO: William Nancarrow, Pres.   Tel: (616) 345-7155 Emp: 100+
  Bus: *Mfr. industrial machinery & equipment.* Fax:(616) 345-5945 %FO: 100

  ### COHERENT GELBER GROUP, INC.
  2303 Lindergh, Auburn, CA   95602
  CEO: Robert Gelber, Pres.   Tel: (916) 823-9550 Emp: N/A
  Bus: *Mfr. electro-optical equipment.*   Fax:(916) 889-5353 %FO: 100

- **ACSIS GROUP, PLC.**
  6 Derby Street, London W1Y 7HD, England
  CEO: Ephram Barsaim, Pres.   Tel: 44-181-349-2218 Emp: N/A
  Bus: *Employment agencies and management services.* Fax:44-181-917-2218

  ### NURSING MANAGEMENT SERVICES INC
  3423 Piedmont Road, Ste.500, Atlanta, GA   30305
  CEO: Efrom Barsaim, Mgr.   Tel: (770) 956-0500 Emp: N/A
  Bus: *Employment agencies.*   Fax:(770) 956-1894 %FO: 100

- **ADWEST GROUP PLC**
  Woodley, Reading, Berks RG5 45N, England
  CEO: G.R. Menzies, CEO   Tel: 44-118-969-7171 Emp: 2750
  Bus: *Holding company: industrial instruments, motor* Fax:44-118-969-0121
    vehicle parts, machine tools, plastic products.

  ### ADWEST ABBOTT ELECTRONICS, INC.
  2727 S. La Cienega Blvd, Los Angeles, CA   90034
  CEO: R. Emami, Pres.   Tel: (310) 202-8820 Emp: 90
  Bus: *Mfr. electronic power supplies.*   Fax:(310) 861-1027 %FO: 100

  ### ADWEST CONVERSION SEVICES, INC
  15 Jonathan Drive, Brockton, MA   02402
  CEO: S.W. Forrester, Pres.   Tel: (508) 559-0880 Emp: 200
  Bus: *Mfr. electronic power supplies.*   Fax:(508) 588-1962 %FO: 100

ADWEST MODULAR DEVICES, INC.
4115 Spencer Street, Torrance, CA   90503
CEO: M. Dulion, Pres.   Tel: (310) 542-8561   Emp: 740
Bus: *Mfr. electronic power supplies.*   Fax:(310) 371-6331   %FO: 100

ADWEST WESTERN AUTOMOTIVE, INC.
576 Beck Street, Jonesville, MI   49250
CEO: A. Symonds, Pres.   Tel: (517) 849-9945   Emp: 103
Bus: *Mfr. automotive components.*   Fax:(517) 849-2556   %FO: 100

● **AIM AVIATION LTD.**
16 Carlton Crescent, Southampton, Hampsire SO1 2ES, England
CEO: Jeffrey C. Smith, Pres.   Tel: 44-1-703-335111   Emp: 900
Bus: *Holding company; aircraft parts & equipment, real*   Fax:44-1-703-228733
estate, textile products.

AIM AVIATION AUBURN, INC.
1530 22nd Street NW, Auburn, WA   98001
CEO: John Feutz, Gen. Mgr.   Tel: (253) 804-3355   Emp: N/A
Bus: *Aircraft assemblies & parts.*   Fax:253) 804-3356   %FO: 100

AIM AVIATION INC.
705 SW 7th Avenue, Renton, WA   98055
CEO: Mark Potensky, Pres.   Tel: (206) 235-2750   Emp: 250
Bus: *Aircraft interiors, assemblies & parts.* Fax:(206) 228-0761   %FO: 100

● **ALH SYSTEMS LTD.**
Station Rd, Westbury, Wiltshire BA13 4TN, England
CEO: Robin Thomas, Mng. Dir.   Tel: 44-137-386-4744   Emp: 50
Bus: *Natural gas encapsulation, gas conditioning.*   Fax:44-137-385-8235

ALH SYSTEMS INC.
119 North Lively Boulevard, Elk Grove Village, IL   60007
CEO: Peter S. James, EVP   Tel: (847) 228-1170   Emp: 30
Bus: *Natural gas encapsulation.*   Fax:(847) 228-1171   %FO: 100

● **ALLEN & OVERY**
One New Change, London EC4M 9QQ, England
CEO: William Tudor John   Tel: 44-171-330-3000   Emp: N/A
Bus: *International law firm; one of the largest in the UK.*   Fax:44-171-330-9999

ALLEN & OVERY
Swiss Bank Tower, 10 East 50th St., New York, NY   10022
CEO: David Reid, Dir.   Tel: (212) 754-3340   Emp: N/A
Bus: *International law firm.*   Fax:(212) 754-7903   %FO: 100

- **ALLIED COLLOIDS GROUP PLC**
PO Box 38 Road, Low Moor, Bradford, West Yorkshire, BD12 0JZ England
CEO: Peter Flesher, Mgn Dir.　　　　　　　　　Tel: 44-127-467-1267　　Emp: 1600
Bus: *Specialty chemicals.*　　　　　　　　　　Fax:44-127-460-6499

    ALLIED COLLOIDS, INC.
    2301 Wilroy Road, PO Box 820, Suffolk, VA　23439-0820
    CEO: David Farrar, Pres.　　　　　　　　　Tel: (757) 538-3700　　Emp: 500
    Bus: *Mfr./distribution/sale specialty chemicals.*　　Fax:(757) 539-3989　　%FO: 100

- **ALLIED DOMECQ, PLC.**
24 Portland Place, London W1N 4BB, England
CEO: Tony Hales, CEO　　　　　　　　　　　Tel: 44-171-323-9000　　Emp: 55000
Bus: *International spirits manufacturing and retailing*　Fax:44-171-323-1742
group: wine, spirits, frozen foods & desserts, tea &
coffee.

    ALLIED DOMECQ SPIRITS & WINES
    3000 Town Center, 31st Fl., Southfield, MI　48075-1102
    CEO: Donald M. Coe, Pres.　　　　　　　　Tel: (248) 938-6500　　Emp: 33
    Bus: *Centralized and special sales/marketing*　Fax:(248) 948-8917　　%FO: 100
    services for spirits and wines.

    ALLIED DOMECQ, INC.
    31 Baskin-Robbins Place, Glendale, CA　91201
    CEO: Robert Rosenberg, Pres.　　　　　　　Tel: (818) 956-0031　　Emp: 200+
    Bus: *Mfr. ice cream & dessert products (Baskin*　Fax:(818) 243-7969　　%FO: 100
    Robbins, Dunkin Donuts, Togo's).

    DOMECQ IMPORTERS, INC.
    143 Sound Beach Avenue, Old Greenwich, CT　06870
    CEO: Martin Jones, Pres.　　　　　　　　　Tel: (203) 637-6500　　Emp: 100
    Bus: *Sales and marketing company for distilled*　Fax:(203) 637-6599　　%FO: 100
    spirits.

    HIRAM WALKER, INC.
    3000 Town Center, Suite 3200, Southfield, MI　48075-1102
    CEO: George DiBenedetto, Pres.　　　　　　Tel: (248) 948-6500　　Emp: 235
    Bus: *Sales and marketing company for distilled*　Fax:(248) 948-8891　　%FO: 100
    spirits.

    TETLEY, INC.
    100 Commerce Drive, Shelton, CT　06484
    CEO: Charles McArthy, Pres.　　　　　　　Tel: (203) 929-9200　　Emp: 100+
    Bus: *Mfr. teas, coffee, frozen food products.*　Fax:(203) 925-0512　　%FO: 100

THE WINE ALLIANCE
132 Mill Street, PO Box 948, Hearldsburg, CA   95448

CEO: Jon Moramarco, Pres.	Tel: (707) 433-8268	Emp: 150
Bus: *Sales and marketing company for wine products.*	Fax:(707) 433-3538	%FO: 100

● **AMERSHAM INTL PLC**
Little Chalfont, Bucks HP7 9NA, England

CEO: William M. Castell, CEO	Tel: 44-14-94-542-281	Emp: 3200
Bus: *Radiochemicals, radiopharmaceuticals, devices & sources for radiography.*	Fax:44-14-94-542-266	

    AMERSHAM HOLDINGS
    2636 South Clearbrook Drive, Arlington Heights, IL   60010

CEO: Alan F. Herbert, Pres.	Tel: (708) 593-6300	Emp: 850
Bus: *Mfr./distribution radiochemicals, radiopharmaceuticals; nuclear pharmaceutical services, industrial radiography.*	Fax:(708) 593-8010	%FO: 100

● **APV PLC**
1 Lygon Place, London SW1W 0JR, England

CEO: Clive Strowger, CEO	Tel: 44-171-730-7244	Emp: 12000
Bus: *Process plant and equipment for food and beverage industry. (Sub of SIEBE PLC, acquired June 1997).*	Fax:44-171-730-2660	

    APV & HYDRO SEPARATION, INC.
    395 Fillmore Avenue, Tonawanda, NY   14150

CEO: Mike Sanders, Gen. Mgr.	Tel: (716) 692-3000	Emp: 137
Bus: *Mfr. dryers for chemical and food processing industry. (Division of APV NA, INC.)*	Fax:(716) 879-3335	%FO: 100

    APV BAKER INC.
    3200 Fruit Ridge Avenue, NW, Grand Rapids, MI   49504

CEO: Robert Rander, Pres.	Tel: (616) 784-3111	Emp: N/A
Bus: *Mfr. process packaging equipment for bakery/cereal industry. (Division of APV NA, INC.)*	Fax:(616) 784-0973	%FO: 100

    APV CREPACO INC.
    9525 West Bryn Mawr Avenue, Rosemont, IL   60018

CEO: John Hartzworm, Pres.	Tel: (847) 678-4300	Emp: 1000+
Bus: *Mfr. food, dairy, chemical processing & automation equipment & systems.*	Fax:(847) 678-4407	%FO: 100

    APV HOMOGENIZER, INC.
    500 Research Drive, Wilmington Tech. Pk., Wilmington, MA   01887

CEO: David Duffin, Pres.	Tel: (508) 988-9300	Emp: N/A
Bus: *Mfr. homogenizes & high-pressure pumps.(Division of APV NA, INC.)*	Fax:(508) 988-9111	%FO: 100

- **ARJO WIGGINS APPLETON PLC**
Box 88, Gateway House, Basing View, Basingstoke Hants RG 21 4EE, England
CEO: Daniel Melin, Chrm.   Tel: 44-1256-72-3590   Emp: N/A
Bus: *Mfr./distributes specialty paper products.*   Fax:44-1256-72-3841

    APPLETON PAPERS, INC.
    825 East Wisconsin Avenue, Appleton, WI   54911
    CEO: Richard Curwen, Pres.   Tel: (414) 734-9841   Emp: N/A
    Bus: *Distribution/sale of specialty paper products.*   Fax:(414) 749-8796   %FO: 100

- **B.A.T. INDUSTRIES PLC**
Windsor House, 50 Victoria Street, London SW1H 0NL, England
CEO: Martin F. Broughton, CEO   Tel: 44-171 2227979   Emp: 170000
Bus: *Tobacco products, financial services.*   Fax:44-171 2224269

    BROWN & WILLIAMSON TOBACCO CORP.
    401 South Fourth Street, Louisville, KY   40202
    CEO: Nick G. Brookes, Pres.   Tel: (502) 568-7000   Emp: 6088
    Bus: *Mfr. tobacco products.*   Fax:(502) 568-7107   %FO: 100

    FARMERS GROUP, INC.
    4680 Wilshire Blvd., Los Angeles, CA   90051
    CEO: Martin D. Feinstein, Pres.   Tel: (213) 932-3200   Emp: N/A
    Bus: *Financial services, management & holding*   Fax:(213) 964-8093   %FO: 100
        company. Property & casualty insurance.

    FARMERS LIFE INSURANCE COMPANY
    3003 77th Avenue, SE, Mercer Island, WA   98040
    CEO: Glen. W. Vining, Jr., Pres.   Tel: (206) 232-8400   Emp: N/A
    Bus: *Financial services. Property & casualty*   Fax:(206) 236-6547   %FO: 100
        insurance.

- **BAA PLC**
130 Wilton Road, London SW1V 1LQ, England
CEO: Sir John Egan, CEO   Tel: 44-171-834-9449   Emp: 8000
Bus: *Airport management and operations.*   Fax:44-171-932-6699

    BAA INDIANAPOLIS INC.
    2500 South High School Road, Indianapolis, IN   46241
    CEO: David Roberts, Pres.   Tel: (317) 487-5003   Emp: 199
    Bus: *Airport management and operations.*   Fax:(317) 487-5034   %FO: 100

    BAA PITTSBURGH INC.
    Pittsburgh Intl Airport, PO Box 12318, Pittsburgh, PA   15231-0318
    CEO: Mark Knight, Pres.   Tel: (412) 472-5180   Emp: 8
    Bus: *Airport management and operations.*   Fax:(412) 472-5190   %FO: 100

BAA USA INC.
45240 Business Court, Ste. 225, Sterling, VA   20166
CEO: Michael Bell, Pres.   Tel: (703) 708-7998   Emp: 7
Bus: *Airport management and operations.*   Fax:(703) 708-7991   %FO: 100

DUTY FREE INTERNATIONAL
63 Copps Hill Road, Ridgefield, CT   06877
CEO: Alfred Carfora, CEO   Tel: (203) 431-6057   Emp: 2000
Bus: *Duty free shop operations in international*   Fax:(203) 438-1356   %FO: 100
      airport terminals. (Acquired July 1997, $674
      mil.)

• **J.C.BAMFORD EXCAVATORS LTD.**
Rochester, Straffordshire ST14 5JP, England
CEO: Sir Anthony Bamford, Chrm.   Tel: 44-1889-959-0312   Emp: 1550
Bus: *Mfr. construction & materials handling equipment.*   Fax:44-1889-590-588

JCB INC.
10939 Philadelphia Road, White Marsh, MD   21162
CEO: Dennis R. Slagle, Pres.   Tel: (410) 335-2800   Emp: 115
Bus: *Mfr. construction & materials handling*   Fax:(410) 335-3695   %FO: 100
      equipment.

• **BARCLAYS BANK PLC**
54 Lombard Street, London EC3P 3AH, England
CEO: Andrew Buxton, Group Chrm.   Tel: 44-171-626-1567   Emp: N/A
Bus: *International investment banking and asset*   Fax:44-171-692-4252
      management services.

BARCLAYS - Private Banking
801 Brickell Avenue, Miami, FL   33131
CEO: Marilyn Moll, CEO   Tel: (305) 374-1043   Emp: 500
Bus: *International private banking.*   Fax:(305) 579-2066   %FO: 100

BARCLAYS - Private Banking
12 East 49th Street, 34th Floor, New York, NY   10017
CEO: Mark Fiebert, CEO   Tel: (212) 415-5900   Emp: 87
Bus: *International private banking.*   Fax:(212) 838-2255   %FO: 100

BARCLAYS BANK PLC
801 Brickell Avenue, Miami, FL   33131
CEO: Gonzalo Valdes-Fauli, Mgr.   Tel: (305) 374-1043   Emp: N/A
Bus: *Latin America Regional Office. Securities*   Fax:(305) 579-2066   %FO: 100
      broker/dealer, futures commission agent and
      investment banking.

BARCLAYS BANK PLC
75 Wall Street, New York, NY   10038
CEO: Collum McCarthy, CEO   Tel: (212) 412-4000   Emp: 30
Bus: *international investment banking and asset*   Fax:(212) 412-6955   %FO: 100
management services.

BARCLAYS GLOBAL INVESTORS
45 Fremont Street, San Francisco, CA   94105
CEO: Fred Grauer, CEO   Tel: (415) 597-2000   Emp: 3000
Bus: *International investment banking and asset*   Fax:(415) 597-2010   %FO: 100
management services.

BARCLAYS GROUP NORTH AMERICA
222 Broadway, New York, NY   10038
CEO: Collum Mc Carthy, CEO   Tel: (212) 412-4000   Emp: 1400
Bus: *International investment banking and asset*   Fax:(212) 412-6995   %FO: 100
management services.

BZW INC.
141 West Jackson Street, Chicago, IL   60606
CEO: Collum Mc Carthy, CEO   Tel: (312) 939-6300   Emp: N/A
Bus: *Futures commission agent.*   Fax: %FO: 100

BZW INC.
222 Broadway, New York, NY   10038
CEO: Collum Mc Carthy, CEO   Tel: (212) 412-7173   Emp: 1400
Bus: *Securities broker/dealer, futures commission*   Fax:(212) 412-7300   %FO: 100
agent and investment banking.

● **BASS PLC**
20 N. Audley Street, London W1Y 1WE, England
CEO: Ian Prosser, Chrm. & CEO   Tel: 44-171 4091919   Emp: 84900
Bus: *Brewing & soft drinks, hotels, taverns & leisure*   Fax:44-171 4098503
retailing, travel services.

HOLIDAY INN WORLDWIDE
3 Ravinia Drive, Suite 2900, Atlanta, GA   30346-2149
CEO: Bryan Langton, Chrm. & CEO   Tel: (404) 604-2000   Emp: 10000
Bus: *Hotels & leisure time operations management.*   Fax:(404) 604-2009   %FO: 100

● **BBA GROUP, PLC.**
70 Fleet Street, Fifth Fl., London EC4Y 1EU, England
CEO: Roberto Quarta, Pres.   Tel: 44-171-842-4900   Emp: N/A
Bus: *Mfr. aircraft landing gear/hydraulic actuators,*   Fax:44-171-583-0506
aviation products and heating/melting machinery

AJAX MAGNETHERMIC CORPORATION
1745 Overland Avenue, NE, Warren, OH   44483
CEO: Frank Spalla, Pres.   Tel: (330) 372-8511   Emp: N/A
Bus: *Produces heating and melting machinery.*   Fax:(330) 372-8644   %FO: 100

BBA US HOLDINGS, INC.
401 Edgewater Place, Ste. 670, Wakefield, MA 01880

CEO: Greg Murrer, Pres.	Tel: (617) 246-8900	Emp: N/A
Bus: *U.S. holding company.*	Fax:(617) 245-3227	%FO: 100

OZONE INDUSTRIES, INC.
29 Industrial Park Road, East Lyme, CT 06333

CEO: Frank Robilotto, Pres.	Tel: (860) 739-4926	Emp: N/A
Bus: *Mfr. aircraft landing gear and hydraulic actuators.*	Fax:(860) 691-2321	%FO: 100

TEXSTAR, INC.
802 Avenue J. East, Grand Prairie, TX 75050

CEO: David Rollings, Pres.	Tel: (972) 647-1366	Emp: 65
Bus: *Mfr. auto, aviation and industrial products.*	Fax:(972) 641-2800	%FO: 100

• THE BERISFORD GROUP
One Baker Street, London W1M 1AA, England

CEO: Alan J. Bowkett, Pres.	Tel: 44-171-312-2500	Emp: N/A
Bus: *Mfr. building materials, property, agribusiness and food.*	Fax:44-171-312-2501	

WELBILT CORPORATION
225 High Ridge Road, Stamford, CT 06905

CEO: Marlon Antonini, Chrm.	Tel: (203) 325-8300	Emp: N/A
Bus: *Mfr. building materials, agribusiness, property, and food.*	Fax:(203) 325-9800	%FO: 100

• BERMANS
Trident House, 31/33 Dale Street, Liverpool L2 2NS, England

CEO: Keith Berman, Pres.	Tel: 44-151-236-2107	Emp: N/A
Bus: *Law firm services.*	Fax:44-151-236-2107	

DIBB LUPTON
230 Park Avenue, Ste. 1150, New York, NY 10169

CEO: Keith Berman, Pres.	Tel: (212) 956-7767	Emp: N/A
Bus: *English solicitors and international attorneys.*	Fax:(212) 956-1099	%FO: 100

• BESPAK PLC
North Lynn Industrial Estate, King's Lynn, Norfolk PE30 255, England

CEO: R.H.King, Chrm. & CEO	Tel: 44-1553-369-1000	Emp: 560
Bus: *Pharmaceuticals valve delivery systems, specialty valves, pumps.*	Fax:44-1553-369-1622	

BESPAK INC.
PO Box 5033, Cary, NC 27512

CEO: William Altman, CEO	Tel: (919) 387-0112	Emp: 60
Bus: *Mfr./distribution pharmaceuticals valve delivery systems, specialty valves, pumps.*	Fax:(919) 387-0116	%FO: 100

● **BEVAN FUNNELL, LTD.**
Beach Road, Newhaven, Sussex BN9 OBZ, England
CEO: B. Funnell, Chrm.   Tel: 44-12-7351-3762   Emp: N/A
Bus: *Distributes antique reproductions.*   Fax:44-12-7351-6735

    BEVAN FUNNELL, LTD.
    105 Depot Place, PO Box 1109, High Point, NC   27260
    CEO: Hal McAdams, Gen. Mgr.   Tel: (910) 889-4800   Emp: N/A
    Bus: *Sales/distribution/service of antique*   Fax:(910) 889-7037   %FO: 100
        reproductions.

● **BICC PLC**
Devonshire House, Mayfair Place, London W1X 5FH, England
CEO: Viscount W. Weir, Chrm.   Tel: 44-171 6296622   Emp: 44000
Bus: *Engineering for power, construction and*   Fax:44-171 4090070
communications industries.

    BICC CABLES CORPORATION
    1 Crosfield Avenue, West Nyack, NY   10994-1100
    CEO: Charles Painter, Pres & CEO   Tel: (914) 353-4000   Emp: N/A
    Bus: *Mfr. electric power cables and related*   Fax:(914) 353-4032   %FO: 100
        products.

● **BLUE CIRCLE INDUSTRIES PLC**
84 Eccleston Sq, London SW1V 1PX, England
CEO: J. W. McColgan, Mng. Dir.   Tel: 44-171 828-3456   Emp: N/A
Bus: *Mfr. building materials and home products.*   Fax:44-171 245-8169

    BLUE CIRCLE AMERICA, INC.
    2 Parkway Center, #1200, 1800 Parkway Place, Marietta, GA   30067
    CEO: David Lovett, Pres.   Tel: (770) 423-4700   Emp: N/A
    Bus: *Building materials and home products.*   Fax:(770) 423-4738   %FO: 100

● **THE BOC GROUP INC**
Chertsey Rd, Windlesham, Surrey GU20 6HJ, England
CEO: Richard V. Giordano, Chrm.   Tel: 44-276 477222   Emp: 38434
Bus: *Industrial gases, health care products and services.* Fax:44-276 471333

    THE BOC GASES GROUP INC.
    575 Mountain Avenue, Murray Hill, NJ   07974
    CEO: Richard V. Giordano, Chrm.   Tel: (908) 665-2400   Emp: 9700
    Bus: *Mfr. industrial gases and health care products* Fax:(908) 464-9015   %FO: 100

• THE BODY SHOP INTERNATIONAL PLC
Watersmead, Littlehampton, West Sussex BN17 6LS, England
CEO: Anita Roddick, CEO Tel: 44-1-90-373-1500 Emp: 3670
Bus: *Mfr./retailer health and beauty products.* Fax:44-1-90-372-6250

THE BODY SHOP, INC.
One World Way, Wake Forest, NC 27587
CEO: Steen Kanter, CEO Tel: (919) 554-4900 Emp: 1000+
Bus: *Retailer health and beauty products.* Fax:(919) 554-4361 %FO: 100

• BONEHAM & TURNER LTD.
Nottingham Road, Mansfield, Notts NG1 B4AF, England
CEO: J. Boneham, CEO Tel: 44-1623-327641 Emp: 225
Bus: *Mfr. precision machinery and tools.* Fax:44-1623-27645

BONEHAM METAL PRODUCTS, INC.
356 Nye Avenue, Irvington, NJ 07111
CEO: Doreen Guenther, Mgr. Tel: (201) 371-4477 Emp: 10
Bus: *Import/distribute industrial equipment.* Fax:(201) 399-5193 %FO: 100

• THE BOOTS COMPANY PLC.
One Thane Road, Nottingham NG2 3AA, England
CEO: Jmaes Blyth, Chrm. Tel: 44-1-159-506111 Emp: 78000
Bus: *Mfr. ethical pharmaceuticals.* Fax:44-1-159-687151

ASF - KNOLL BOOTS (Div BASF)
3000 Continental Drive North, Mt. Olive, NJ 07828
CEO: Carter H. Eckert, Pres. Tel: (201) 426-2600 Emp: 900
Bus: *Mfr. ethical pharmaceuticals.* Fax:(201) 426-2852 %FO: 100

• BRAIME PRESSINGS PLC
Hunslett Road, Leeds LS10 13Z, England
CEO: Nicholas Braime, Pres. Tel: 44-1132-457-491 Emp: 300
Bus: *Mfr. seamless pressings.* Fax:N/A

4B ELEVATOR COMPONENTS LTD.
729 Sabrina Drive, East Peoria, IL 61611
CEO: Chris Robinson, Mgr. Tel: (309) 698-5611 Emp: 5
Bus: *Mfr. material handling components.* Fax:(309) 698-5615 %FO: 100

• BRIDON PLC
Warmsworth Hall, Doncester, S Yorkshire, DN4 9JX, England
CEO: Jack Laird, Chrm. Tel: 44-130-234-4010 Emp: N/A
Bus: *Wire, rope & related engineering products.* Fax:44-130-234-1262

BRIDON-AMERICAN CORPORATION
PO Box 6000, Wilkes Barre, PA 18773
CEO: W. Adams, Pres. Tel: (717) 822-3349 Emp: N/A
Bus: *Steel wire rope, synthetic ropes, etc.* Fax:(717) 829-1136 %FO: 100

● **BRINTONS LTD.**
Exchange Street, Kidderminster DY10 1AG, England
CEO: M. A. C. Brinton, Chrm.   Tel: 44-56-2820000   Emp: 2000
Bus: *Mfr. carpets.*   Fax:N/A

    BRINTONS CARPETS (USA) LTD.
    East 210 Rt. 4, Paramus, NJ   07652
    CEO: Stuart Bell, Mgr.   Tel: (201) 368-0080   Emp: N/A
    Bus: *Sale/distribution of carpets.*   Fax:(201) 368-9097   %FO: 100

● **BRITISH AEROSPACE PLC**
Warwick House-POB 87, Farnborough Aerospace Ctr., Farnborough, Hampshire GU14 6YU,
England
CEO: Richard H. Evans, CEO   Tel: 44-1-252 383000   Emp: 42500
Bus: *Design mfr. aerospace products, commercial &* Fax:44-1-252 373232
    military aircraft, artillery, missiles, defense systems.

    BRITISH AEROSPACE HOLDINGS, INC.
    15000 Conference Center Drive, #200, Chantilly, VA   20151
    CEO: Robert L. Kirk, Chrm.   Tel: (703) 802-0080   Emp: 380
    Bus: *Sale & support aerospace products &*   Fax:(703) 227-1515   %FO: 100
        operations.

● **BRITISH AIRWAYS PLC**
Speedbird House, Heathrow Airport, Hounslow, Middlesex TW6 2JA, England
CEO: Robert Ayling, CEO   Tel: 44-181-759-5511   Emp: 55296
Bus: *International air transport services.*   Fax:44-181-562-5557

    BRITISH AIRWAYS (US), INC.
    1850 K Street, NW, Suite 300, Washington, DC   20006
    CEO: Anthony Fortnam, VP   Tel: (202) 331-9524   Emp: N/A
    Bus: *Government affairs representative.*   Fax:(202) 466-3745   %FO: 100

    BRITISH AIRWAYS (US), INC.
    Bulova Corporate Center
    7520 Astoria Blvd., Jackson Heights, NY   11370
    CEO: Barbara Cassani, Gen. Mgr.   Tel: (718) 397-4000   Emp: 5000+
    Bus: *International air transport services.*   Fax:(718) 397-4364   %FO: 100

● **THE BRITISH PETROLEUM CO PLC**
Britannic House, One Finsbury Circus, London EC2M 7BA, England
CEO: John P. Browne, Mng. Dir.   Tel: 44-171-496 4000   Emp: 57000
Bus: *Oil & natural resources, exploration, production &* Fax:44-171-496 5636
    distribution.

    BP AMERICA, INC.
    200 Public Square, Cleveland, OH   44114
    CEO: Steven W. Percy, Chrm.   Tel: (216) 586-4141   Emp: N/A
    Bus: *Oil & natural resources, exploration,*   Fax:(216) 586-5173   %FO: 100
        production & distribution. US headquarters.

BP AMERICA, INC.
1776 I Street NW, Suite 1000, Washington, DC   20006
CEO: Larry D. Burton, VP   Tel: (202) 785-4888   Emp: N/A
Bus: *Government affairs representatives.*   Fax:(202) 457-6597   %FO: 100

BP CHEMICALS INC.
200 Public Square, Cleveland, OH   44114
CEO: R. R. Mesel, Pres.   Tel: (216) 586-4141   Emp: 1118
Bus: *Mfr./sale agricultural, industrial &*   Fax:(216) 586-5173   %FO: 100
   commercial chemicals.

BP EXPLORATION (ALASKA) INC.
900 East Benson Blvd., Anchorage, AK   99508
CEO: J. C. Morgan, Pres.   Tel: (907) 564-5111   Emp: 1295
Bus: *Exploration, production oil & gas.*   Fax:(907) 564-5514   %FO: 100

THE CARBORUMDUM COMPANY
P O Box 156, Niagara Falls, NY   14302
CEO: L. F. Kahl, Pres.   Tel: (716) 278-2000   Emp: 1583
Bus: *Mfr. hi-temp fiber insulation, refractory*   Fax:(716) 278-2900   %FO: 100
   products, resins..

● **BRITISH RAILWAYS BOARD**
Euston House, 24 Eversholt Street, PO Box 100, London NW1 1DZ, England
CEO: J. Welsby, Chrm.   Tel: 44-171-928-5151   Emp: N/A
Bus: *Passenger and freight services.*   Fax:44-171-922-6545

BRITRAIL TRAVEL INTERNATIONAL, INC.
1500 Broadway, New York, NY   10036
CEO: Tim Roebuck, Pres.   Tel: (212) 382-3737   Emp: 30
Bus: *U.S. headquarters office.*   Fax:(212) 575-2542   %FO: 100

● **BRITISH STEEL, PLC**
9 Albert Embankment, London SE1 7SN, England
CEO: Brian S. Moffat, Chrm.   Tel: 44-171-735-7654   Emp: N/A
Bus: *Steel production, rollings, processing and* Fax:44-171-587-1142
   distribution.

BRITISH STEEL, INC.
475 North Martingale Road, Ste. 400, Schaumburg, IL   60173
CEO: Thomas E. Kinley, Pres.   Tel: (847) 619-0400   Emp: N/A
Bus: *Sales/distribution of steel products.*   Fax:(847) 619-0468   %FO: 100

• BRITISH TELECOMMUNICATIONS PLC

BT Centre, 81 Newgate Street, London EC1A 7AJ, England

CEO: Iain Vallance, Chrm.

Bus: *Telecommunications and information systems/services.*

Tel: 44-171-356 5000   Emp: 131000
Fax:44-171-356 5520

BT NORTH AMERICA, INC.

40 East 52nd Street, 14th Fl., New York, NY   10022

CEO: Nick Williams, CEO & Operations

Bus: *Telecommunications, private circuits, video conferencing, financial trading systems.*

Tel: (212) 418-7800   Emp: 100
Fax:(212) 418-7788   %FO: 100

BT NORTH AMERICA, INC.

601 Pennsylvania Avenue, NW, Suite 725, Washington, DC   20004

CEO: James E. Graf, Pres.

Bus: *U.S. headquarters and government affairs representatives.*

Tel: (202) 639-8222   Emp: N/A
Fax:(202) 434-8867   %FO: 100

CONCERT COMMUNICATIONS SERVICES, INC,

11921 Freedom Drive, Reston, VA   20190

CEO: Peter Manning, Pres.

Bus: *Telecommunications services, JV with MCI, Inc. BT plc acquisition of MCI pending as of 9/98.*

Tel: (703) 707-4000   Emp: N/A
Fax:(703) 707-4018   %FO: 100

• BTP PLC.

Hayes Road, Cadishead, Manchester, England

CEO: F. W. Buckley, Chrm.

Bus: *Chemical and engineer production.*

Tel: 44-617-775-3945   Emp: 1625
Fax:N/A

DBI/SALA

PO Box 46, 3965 Pipin Avenue, Red Wing, MN   55066-1837

CEO: Wayne Burow, Pres.

Bus: *Mfr. fall protection equipment.*

Tel: (612) 388-8282   Emp: 40
Fax:(612) 388-5065   %FO: 100

• BTR PLC

Silvertown House, Vincent Square, London SW1P 2PL, England

CEO: Ian C. Strachan, CEO

Bus: *Holding company for industrial manufacturing companies. (Formerly British Tyre & Rubber).*

Tel: 44-171 834 3848   Emp: 125000
Fax:44-171 834 3879

BTR, INC.

Stamford Harbor Park, 333 Ludlow Street, Stamford, CT   06902

CEO: John S. Thompson, Pres.

Bus: *U.S. headquarters for BTR Dunlop - rubber products & tire company, and BTR - industrial manufacturing companies.*

Tel: (203) 352-0000   Emp: 47
Fax:(203) 964-8025   %FO: 100

BTR PAPER GROUP, INC.
60 William Street, Suite 300, Wellesley, MA   02181

CEO: Michael Collins, Pres.	Tel: (617) 237-1980	Emp: N/A
Bus: *Mfr./sale paper & pulp products.*	Fax:(617) 237-1987	%FO: 100

DCE, INC.
11301 Electron Drive, Jeffersontown, KY   40299-3867

CEO: Dale Doyle, Pres.	Tel: (502) 267-0707	Emp: N/A
Bus: *Mfr./distribution industrial dust control equipment & filters..*	Fax:(502) 267-4490	%FO: 100

DUNLOP SLAZENGER CORP.
P.O.Box 3070, Greenville, SC   29602

CEO: William Olson, Pres.	Tel: (803) 241-2200	Emp: N/A
Bus: *Mfr./distribution sports & leisure products.*	Fax:(803) 241-2294	%FO: 100

KEE INDUSTRIAL PRODUCTS, INC.
100 Stradtman Street, Buffalo, NY   14206

CEO: H. K. Burnett, Pres.	Tel: (716) 896-4949	Emp: N/A
Bus: *Mfr. pipe fittings, castors & wheels.*	Fax:(716) 892-1886	%FO: 100

McCANNA, INC.
400 Maple Avenue, Carpentersville, IL   60110

CEO: Rick Giannini, Pres.	Tel: (847) 426-4100	Emp: N/A
Bus: *Mfr. valves.*	Fax:(847) 426-1729	%FO: 100

NORDSTROM VALVES
1511 Jefferson Street, PO Box 501, Sulphur Springs, TX   75482

CEO: Ray LeSage, Pres.	Tel: (903) 885-3151	Emp: N/A
Bus: *Mfr. valves for oil & gas industry.*	Fax:(903) 439-3313	%FO: 100

REXNORD HANSEN, INC.
2045 West Hunting Park Avenue, Philadelphia, PA   19140

CEO: Robert Wallis, Pres.	Tel: (215) 255-6000	Emp: N/A
Bus: *Mfr. speed reducers & parts.*	Fax:(215) 227-9463	%FO: 100

SCHLEGEL NORTH AMERICA
1555 Jefferson Road, Rochester, NY   14692

CEO: Wayne Bowser, Dir. Mktg.	Tel: (716) 427-7200	Emp: N/A
Bus: *Mfr./distribution sealing systems.*	Fax:(716) 427-9993	%FO: 100

TILCON, INC.
Black Rock Avenue, P.O.Box 1357, New Britain, CT   06050

CEO: Al Paolini, Pres.	Tel: (203) 223-3651	Emp: N/A
Bus: *Road surfacing materials, sand, gravel, concrete.*	Fax:(203) 225-1865	%FO: 100

● **BUNZL PLC**
Stoke House, Stoke Green, Slough, Berks SL2 4JN, England
CEO: Anthony Habgood, CEO   Tel: 44-753 693693   Emp: N/A
Bus: *Mfr. plastic products, marketing/distribute building*   Fax:44-753 694694
     materials, paper & plastic disposables.

   BUNZL DISTRIBUTION USA INC.
   701 Emerson Road, St. Louis, MO   63141
   CEO: Paul Lorenzini, Pres.   Tel: (314) 997-5959   Emp: N/A
   Bus: *distribution paper & plastic products, building*   Fax:(314) 997-0247   %FO: 100
        materials

   BUNZL PLASTICS INC.
   27 Distribution Way, South Brunswick, NJ   08852
   CEO: Rob Thomas, Reg. Mgr.   Tel: (908) 821-7000   Emp: N/A
   Bus: *Distributor packaging supplies for food*   Fax:(908) 821-3150   %FO: 100
        industry.

● **BURMAH CASTROL PLC**
Pipers Way, Swindon, Wilts SN3 1RE, England
CEO: Lawrence M. Urquhart, Chrm.   Tel: 44-1793-351-1521 Emp: 25000
Bus: *Lubricants, chemicals, fuels, LNG transport, energy*   Fax:44-1793-351-3506
     investment.

   CASTROL INC.
   1500 Valley Road, Wayne, NJ   07470
   CEO: Thomas Crane Jr., Pres. & CEO   Tel: (201) 633-2200   Emp: 1600
   Bus: *Mfr. industrial and auto lubricants.*   Fax:(201) 633-9867   %FO: 100

● **CABLE & WIRELESS PLC**
124 Theobalds Road, London WC1X 8RX, England
CEO: Richard Brown, CEO   Tel: 44-171-350 4000   Emp: 39500
Bus: *Global telecommunications services and products.*   Fax:44-171-315 5000

   CABLE & WIRELESS COMMUNICATIONS, INC.
   8219 Leesburg Pike, Vienna, VA   22182-2625
   CEO: C. Alan Peyser, Pres.   Tel: (703) 790-5300   Emp: N/A
   Bus: *Telecommunications services & equipment.*   Fax:(703) 905-7099   %FO: 100

   CABLE & WIRELESS COMMUNICATIONS, INC.
   777 Third Avenue, New York, NY   10017
   CEO: Tom McDonnell, VP   Tel: (212) 407-2049   Emp: N/A
   Bus: *Investor relations representatives.*   Fax:(212) 593-9069   %FO: 100

● **CADBURY SCHWEPPES PLC**
25 Berkeley Square, London W1X 6HT, England
CEO: N. Dominic Cadbury, Chrm.   Tel: 44-171 409 1313   Emp: 42000
Bus: *Mfr./franchiser confectionery products and soft*   Fax: 44-171 830 5200
drinks.

    DR. PEPPER/SEVEN-UP, INC.
    8144 Walnut Hill Lane, Dallas, TX   75231-4372
    CEO: Todd Stitzer, Pres.   Tel: (214) 360-7000   Emp: 2700
    Bus: *Mfr. fruit drinks, franchise soft drinks*   Fax: (214) 360-7981   %FO: 100

● **CALDER WILKINSON LTD.**
Station Road, Sowerby Bridge, West Yorkshire HX6 3LA, England
CEO: John Reed, Sales Mgr.   Tel: 44-142-283 1861   Emp: N/A
Bus: *Mfr. woodworking equipment.*   Fax: 44-142-283 9785

    E & R System Technik, Inc.
    85 St. George Road, Springfirld, MA   01104
    CEO: Robert G. Weithofer, Pres.   Tel: (413) 827-7600   Emp: 10
    Bus: *Import/distribution specialty woodworking*   Fax: (413) 827-0696   %FO: 100
    machinery & vacuum coaters.

● **CAMAS, PLC.**
Solihall, West Midlands, London B91 2AA, England
CEO: N/A   Tel: 44-121-711-1717   Emp: N/A
Bus: *Mfr. building materials.*   Fax: 44-121-711-1504

    CAMAS KOST BROTHERS, INC.
    1515 First Avenue North, PO Box 499, Moorhead, MN   56560
    CEO: Robert N. Stabo, VP   Tel: (218) 236-9640   Emp: 100
    Bus: *Sales/distribution of building materials and*   Fax: (218) 236-5660   %FO: 100
    fibre mesh produces.

    CAMAS SHIELY, INC.
    2915 Water Road, Ste. 103, Eagan, MN   55121
    CEO: Jonathan Wilmshurst, VP   Tel: (612) 686-7100   Emp: 245
    Bus: *Mfr. concrete masonry units.*   Fax: (612) 686-6969   %FO: 100

    CAMAS, INC.
    3605 South Teeler, Lakewood, CO   80235
    CEO: Mike Hayes, Pres.   Tel: (303) 987-2300   Emp: N/A
    Bus: *Sales/distribution of building materials.*   Fax: (303) 987-9039   %FO: 100

● **CARADON, INC.**
Caradon House, 24 Queens, Waybridge, Surrey KT13 9UX, England
CEO: N. Brayshaw, CEO   Tel: 44-1932-850-850   Emp: N/A
Bus: *Manufactures aluminum doors and windows.*   Fax:N/A

   BETTER-BILT SMYRNA, INC.
   704 Twelfth Avenue, Smyrna, TN   37167
   CEO: David Goodwill, Pres.   Tel: (615) 459-4161   Emp: N/A
   Bus: *Sales/distribution of aluminum doors and*   Fax:(615) 459-0959   %FO: 100
      windows.

   CARADON PEACHTREE, INC.
   4350 Peachtree Industrial Blvd., Norcross, GA   30071
   CEO: Roy Messing, Pres.   Tel: (770) 497-2000   Emp: N/A
   Bus: *Sales/distribution of aluminum doors and*   Fax:(770) 497-2562   %FO: 100
      windows.

   CARADON, INC.
   33 Riverside Avenue, Westport, CT   06880
   CEO: Roy Messing, Pres.   Tel: (203) 341-3000   Emp: N/A
   Bus: *U.S. headquarters office.*   Fax:(203) 226-8588   %FO: 100

● **CARLTON COMMUNICATIONS PLC**
15 St. George Street, Hanover Square, London WIR 9DE, England
CEO: Michael P. Green, Chrm. & CEO   Tel: 44-171-663-6363   Emp: N/A
Bus: *Video systems mfr., media, television & feature film*   Fax:44-171-663-6300
production.

   TECHNICOLOR INC.
   4050 Lankershim Blvd., North Hollywood, CA   91608
   CEO: Ron Jarvis, Pres.   Tel: (818) 769-8500   Emp: N/A
   Bus: *Video, television and feature film production*   Fax:(818) 769-1027   %FO: 100

● **CAZENOVE & CO.**
12 Tokenhouse Yard, London EC2R 7AN, England
CEO: Mark A. Loveday, Sr. Ptnr.   Tel: 44-171-588-2828   Emp: 900
Bus: *Securities broker/dealer, money management, and*   Fax:44-171-606-9205
investment banking.

   CAZENOVE & CO.
   1177 Avenue of the Americas, 39th Fl., New York, NY   10036
   CEO: Anthony F.W. Talbot, Pres.   Tel: (212) 376-1225   Emp: 32
   Bus: *Securities broker/dealer, money management,*   Fax:(212) 376-6160   %FO: 100
      and investment banking.

• CHELSFIELD PLC
67 Brook Street, London W1Y 1YE, England

CEO: Bernerd Elliot, Pres.   Tel: 44-171-493-3977   Emp: N/A

Bus: *Real estate (see joint parent: PENINSULAR &*   Fax:44-171-493-1444
ORIENTAL STEAM NAVIGATION CO, England).

LAING PROPERTIES INC.
5901-B Peachtree Dunwoody Road, Atlanta, GA   30328

CEO: Ned S. Holmes, Pres.   Tel: (770) 551-3400   Emp: 352

Bus: *Investment/development/management of real*   Fax:(770) 551-3494   %FO: JV
estate.

• CHLORIDE GROUP LTD.
130 Wilton Rd, London SW1V 1LQ, England

CEO: Keith Hotchkins, Pres.   Tel: 44-171-834-5500   Emp: 7800

Bus: *Mfr. batteries, lighting fixtures, non-electric*   Fax:44-171-630-0563
transformers.

CHLORIDE ELECTRO NETWORKS
1 Technology Place, Caledonia, NY   14423

CEO: Keither Yeates, Pres.   Tel: (716) 538-4421   Emp: N/A

Bus: *Mfr. batteries*   Fax:(716) 538-6017   %FO: 100

CHLORIDE SYSTEMS INC.
126 Chloride Road, Burgaw, NC   28425

CEO: Pat Hutchins, Pres.   Tel: (910) 259-1000   Emp: N/A

Bus: *Mfr. power supplies.*   Fax:(910) 259-1146   %FO: 100

C & J CLARK LTD.
40 High Street, Somerset BA16 0YA, England

CEO: J. D. Clothier, Mng. Dir.   Tel: 44-1-458-43131   Emp: N/A

Bus: *Manufacture & sale of shoes and shoe components.*   Fax:44-1-458-46496

THE CLARK COMPANIES
520 South Broad Street, Kennett Square, PA   19348

CEO: Kim Jones, Gen. Mgr.   Tel: (215) 444-6550   Emp: N/A

Bus: *Shoes and shoe components.*   Fax:(215) 692-5471   %FO: 100

THE CLARK COMPANIES
156 Oak Street, Newton Upper Falls, MA   02164

CEO: Robert Infantino, Pres.   Tel: (617) 964-1222   Emp: N/A

Bus: *Shoes and shoe components.*   Fax:(617) 243-4210   %FO: 100

• **CLIFFORD CHANCE**
200 Aldersgate Street, London EC1A 4JJ, England
CEO: Chris Perrin, Mg. Ptnr.   Tel: 44-171- 600 1000   Emp: N/A
Bus: *International law firm.*   Fax:44-171- 600 5555

    CLIFFORD CHANCE
    One New York Plaza, New York, NY   10004
    CEO: Steven Hood, Mng. Ptnr.   Tel: (212) 709-4200   Emp: 90
    Bus: *International law firm.*   Fax:(212) 709-4242   %FO: 100%

• **COMMERCIAL UNION ASSURANCE CO. PLC**
P O Box 420, St. Helen's 1 Undershaft, London EC3P 3DQ, England
CEO: John G.T. Carter, CEO   Tel: 44-171-283-7500   Emp: N/A
Bus: *General insurance underwriters & investment*   Fax:44-171-628-8427
     advisory services.

    COMMERCIAL UNION INSURANCE CO.
    One Beacon Street, Boston, MA   02108
    CEO: Robert C. Gowdy, Pres.   Tel: (617) 725-6000   Emp: N/A
    Bus: *Insurance services.*   Fax:(617) 725-6702   %FO: 100

    COMMERCIAL UNION LIFE INSURANCE COMPANY OF AMERICA
    108 Myrtle Street, North Quincy, MA   02171-1753
    CEO: Raymond Von Dette, Pres.   Tel: (617) 786-2015   Emp: N/A
    Bus: *Life insurance services.*   Fax:(617) 786-2015   %FO: 100

    INTERNATIONAL MARINE UNDERWRITERS
    77 Water Street, New York, NY   10005-4488
    CEO: Raymond F. Marine, Pres.   Tel: (212) 440-6500   Emp: N/A
    Bus: *Insurance services.*   Fax:(212) 440-6689   %FO: 100

• **THE COMPASS GROUP, PLC.**
Cowy Lodge, Guilford Street, Chertsey, Surrey, KT169BA, England
CEO: Francis Mackay, CEO   Tel: 44-193-257-3000   Emp: N/A
Bus: *Provides vending and food services.*   Fax:44-193-256-9956

    CANTEEN CORPORATION
    1091 Pierce Butler Route, St. Paul, MN   55104
    CEO: Victor Klein, Pres.   Tel: (612) 488-0515   Emp: 395
    Bus: *Provides vending and food services.*   Fax:(612) 488-8014   %FO: 100

    THE COMPASS GROUP
    2400 Yorkmont Road, Charlotte, NC   28217
    CEO: Mike Bailey, Pres.   Tel: (704) 329-4000   Emp: 350
    Bus: *US headquarters office; vending and food*   Fax:(704) 329-4259   %FO: 100
     services.

• CONSOLIDATED GOLD FIELDS PLC
31 Charles II Street, London SW1 4AG, England
CEO: Rudolph I. J. Agnew, Chrm.   Tel: 44-171-9306200   Emp: N/A
Bus: *Natural resource group, mining, financial services.*   Fax:44-171-9309677

    AMERICAN AGGREGATES CORPORATION
    6450 Sand Lake Road, Dayton, OH   45414
    CEO: Keith Orrell-Jones, Pres.   Tel: (937) 454-1128   Emp: N/A
    Bus: *Natural resource group, mining, finance.*   Fax:(937) 454-2919   %FO: 100

    ASSOCIATED SAND & GRAVEL CO INC
    PO Box 2037, Everett, WA   98203
    CEO: Tim Shearer, Mgr.   Tel: (206) 355-2111   Emp: N/A
    Bus: *Natural resource group, mining, finance.*   Fax:(206) 348-6378   %FO: 100

COOKSON GROUP PLC
130 Wood Street, London EC2V 6EQ, England
CEO: R. M .Oster, Mng. Dir.   Tel: 44-171-606-4400   Emp: N/A
Bus: *Mfr./process industrial materials.*   Fax:44-171-606-2851

    COOKSON AMERICA INC.
    1 Cookson Place, Providence, RI   02903
    CEO: D.L.Carcieri, Pres.   Tel: (401) 521-1000   Emp: N/A
    Bus: *Mfr. industrial materials.*   Fax:(401) 521-5273   %FO: 100

CORANGE LTD.
36 Dover Street, London W1X 3RB, England
CEO: Max Link, CEO   Tel: 44-171-3551500   Emp: 20000
Bus: *Health care products.*   Fax:44-171-3553040

    BOEHRINGER MANNHEIM CORPORATION
    9115 Hague Road, Indianapolis, IN   46250
    CEO: D. Ware, Pres.   Tel: (317) 845-2000   Emp: 1500
    Bus: *Health care products: diagnostics &*   Fax:(317) 576-7019   %FO: 100
        biochemical.

    DEPUY INC.
    700 Orthopaedic Drive, Warsaw, IN   46581-0988
    CEO: James Lent, Pres.   Tel: (219) 372-7504   Emp: 1000
    Bus: *Mfr./distribution orthopedic, sports medical,*   Fax:(219) 269-4532   %FO: 100
        joint replacement products, environmental
        protection products

● **CORDIANT PLC**
83/89 Whitfield Street, London WiA 4XA, England
CEO: Robert Seelert, CEO   Tel: 44-171-436-4000   Emp: 10200
Bus: *Holding company for international advertising*   Fax:44-171-436-1998
agencies.

BATES WORLDWIDE
The Chrysler Bldg., 405 Lexington Ave., New York, NY   10174
CEO: Michael Bungey, Chrm.   Tel: (212) 297-7000   Emp: 1005
Bus: *Advertising agency.*   Fax:(212) 986-0270   %FO: 100

CLIFF FREEMAN & PARTNERS
375 Hudson Street, New York, NY   10014-3620
CEO: Cliff Freeman, Chrm.   Tel: (212) 463-3200   Emp: 125
Bus: *Advertising agency.*   Fax:(212) 463-3225   %FO: 100

CONILL ADVERTISING, INC.
375 Hudson Street, New York, NY   10014-3620
CEO: Nancy Pendas-Smith, CEO   Tel: (212) 463-2500   Emp: 30
Bus: *Advertising agency.*   Fax:(212) 463-2509   %FO: 100

CORDIANT HOLDINGS (USA), INC.
375 Hudson Street, New York, NY   10014-3620
CEO: Robert Seelert, CEO   Tel: (212) 463-4000   Emp: 2000
Bus: *U.S. headquarters for group of international*   Fax:(212) 463-9855   %FO: 100
advertising agencies.

KLEMTNER A'DVERTISING
375 Hudson Street, New York, NY   10014-3620
CEO: Gavin A. Scotti, Pres.   Tel: (212) 463-3400   Emp: 139
Bus: *Advertising agency.*   Fax:(212) 463-3456   %FO: 100

ROWLAND WORLDWIDE
1675 Broadway, New York, NY   10019
CEO: Martin Franken, Pres.   Tel: (212) 527-8800   Emp: N/A
Bus: *Public relations agency.*   Fax:(212) 527-8912   %FO: 100

SAATCHI & SAATCHI ADVERTISING, INC.
375 Hudson Street, New York, NY   10014-3620
CEO: Edward L. Wax, CEO   Tel: (212) 463-2000   Emp: 1400
Bus: *International advertising agency.*   Fax:(212) 463-9855   %FO: 100

SAATCHI & SAATCHI BUSINESS COMMUNICATIONS, INC.
60 Corporate Woods, Rochester, NY   14623
CEO: Timothy P. Cronin, Pres.   Tel: (716) 272-6100   Emp: 151
Bus: *Advertising agency.*   Fax:(716) 272-6161   %FO: 100

SIEGEL & GALE, INC.
Ten Rockefeller Plaza, 3rd Fl., New York, NY 10020
CEO: Alan Siegel, Chrm.　　　　Tel: (212) 730-0101　Emp: N/A
Bus: *Advertising agency.*　　　Fax:(212) 707-4001　%FO: 100

TEAM ONE ADVERTISING
1960 E. Grand Avenue, Ste. 700, El Segundo, CA 90245
CEO: Scott Gilbert & Tom Cordner, Co-Chrm.　Tel: (310) 615-2000　Emp: 193
Bus: *Advertising agency.*　　　Fax:(310) 322-7565　%FO: 100

ZEINITH MEDIA SERVICE, INC.
299 Hudson Street, New York, NY 10014
CEO: Steve King, CEO　　　　Tel: (212) 859-5100　Emp: N/A
Bus: *Media services agency.*　Fax:(212) 886-8803　%FO: 100

● COURTAULDS PLC
50 George Street, London W1A 2BB, England
CEO: Sipko Huismans, CEO　　Tel: 44-171-6121000　Emp: N/A
Bus: *Coatings & sealants, polymer products, fibers &*　Fax:44-171-6121500
chemicals.

COURTAULDS AEROSPACE INC.
P O Box 1800, Glendale, CA 91209
CEO: Ted Clark, Pres.　　　　Tel: (818) 240-2060　Emp: N/A
Bus: *Mfr. sealants, adhesives & coatings for*　Fax:(818) 240-2060　%FO: 100
aerospace industry.

COURTAULDS COATINGS INC.
PO Box 1439, Louisville, KY 40201
CEO: Thomas Horton, Pres.　　Tel: (502) 588-9200　Emp: N/A
Bus: *Mfr. paints & coatings.*　Fax:(502) 588-9307　%FO: 100

COURTAULDS FIBERS INC.
PO Box 141, Axis, AL 36505
CEO: David Duthie, Pres. & CEO　Tel: (334) 679-2200　Emp: N/A
Bus: *Mfr. cellulose fibers.*　Fax:(334) 679-2452　%FO: 100

COURTAULDS PERFORMANCE FILMS
PO Box 5068, Martinsville, VA 24115
CEO: Ken Vickers, CEO　　　Tel: (540) 629-1711　Emp: N/A
Bus: *Mfr. solar & industrial film.*　Fax:(540) 627-3085　%FO: 100

COURTAULDS US INC.
2 Manhattanville Road, Purchase, NY 10577-2111
CEO: Bob Champagne, Chrm.　Tel: (914) 642-8000\　Emp: N/A
Bus: *Tax and finance division.*　Fax:(914) 694-1941　%FO: 100

KNIGHT ENGINEERING & PLASTICS
1600 East Davis Street, Arlington Heights, IL   60005
CEO: Peter Rickerson, Pres.   Tel: (708) 259-1600   Emp: N/A
Bus: *Mfr. packaging materials.*   Fax:(708) 259-1740   %FO: 100

● **COUTTS & COMPANY**
440 Strand, London WC2R 0QS, England
CEO: David Went   Tel: 44-171-753-1000   Emp: 3800
Bus: *International private banking services.*   Fax:44-171-753-1050

COUTTS BANK (SWITZERLAND) LTD.
65 East 55th Street, 21st Fl., New York, NY   10022
CEO: Douglas Marston, Americas Reg. Head   Tel: (212) 303-2900   Emp: 134
Bus: *International private banking services.*   Fax:(212) 303-2929   %FO: 100

COUTTS (USA) INTERNATIONAL
Penthouse One, 421 North Rodeo Drive, Beverly Hills, CA   90210
CEO: Camilo Patiño, Pres./Gen.Mgr.   Tel: (310) 858-2924   Emp: 19
Bus: *International private banking services.*   Fax:(310) 278-2361   %FO: 100

COUTTS (USA) INTERNATIONAL
701 Brickell Avenue, Suite 300, Miami, FL   33131
CEO: Camilo Patiño, Pres. & Gen.Mgr.   Tel: (305) 789-3700   Emp: 19
Bus: *International private banking services.*   Fax:(305) 789-3724   %FO: 100

COUTTS (USA) INTERNATIONAL
550 West C Street, Suite 2000, San Diego, CA   92101
CEO: Camilo Patiño, Pres. & Gen.Mgr.   Tel: (619) 699-5828   Emp: 94
Bus: *International private banking services.*   Fax:(619) 699-5825   %FO: 100

● **CRODA INTL PLC**
Cowick Hall, Snaith Goole, N.Humberside, DN14 9AA, England
CEO: K. G. G. Hopkins, Gp. Chief Exec.   Tel: 44-1405-586-0551 Emp: N/A
Bus: *Chemical specialties.*   Fax:44-1405-586-1767

CRODA INC.
7 Century Drive, Parsippany, NJ   07054-4698
CEO: Chares Irace, Pres.   Tel: (201) 644-4900   Emp: N/A
Bus: *Chemical specialties*   Fax:(201) 644-9222   %FO: 100

● **DALGETY PLC**
100 George Street, London W1H 5RH, England
CEO: Richard J. Clothier, CEO   Tel: 44-171 4860200   Emp: 15000
Bus: *Agribusiness and food manufacturing and*   Fax:44-171 4930982
      distribution.

THE MARTIN-BROWER COMPANY
333 East Butterfield Road, Ste. 500, Lombard, IL   60148
CEO: Dennis Malchow, Pres.   Tel: (630) 271-8300   Emp: 3300
Bus: *Distributor food/paper products to fast*   Fax:(630) 663-4180   %FO: 100
      food/specialty restaurants.

PIG IMPROVEMENT COMPANY, LTD.
PO Box 348, Franklin, KY   42134
CEO: Jim Anderson, Pres.   Tel: (502) 586-9226   Emp: 500
Bus: *Develops and markets breeding pigs.*   Fax:(502) 586-5958   %FO: 100

● **DE LA RUE PLC**
3-5 Burlington Gardens, London W1A 1DL, England
CEO: J. J. S. Marshall, CEO   Tel: 44-171-836-8383   Emp: 8200
Bus: *Security print & payment systems.*   Fax:44-171-240-4224

DE LA RUE BRANDT, INC.
705 South 12th Street, Watertown, WI   53094
CEO: Edward Opperud, Pres.   Tel: (414) 261-1780   Emp: N/A
Bus: *Mfr. facility for software systems and coin*   Fax:(414) 261-1783   %FO: 100
      products.

DE LA RUE FARADAY
4250 Pleasant Valley Road, Chantilly, VA   22021-1213
CEO: S. L .Schulman, Pres.   Tel: (703) 263-0100   Emp: N/A
Bus: *Payment card processing.*   Fax:(703) 263-0503   %FO: 100

THOMAS DE LA RUE, INC.
100 Powers Court, Dulles, VA   20166
CEO: S. J .Wass, Pres.   Tel: (703) 450-1300   Emp: N/A
Bus: *Marketing services.*   Fax:(703) 502-0210   %FO: 100

DE LA RUE SYSTEMS AMERICAS
PO Box 2028, Cedar Rapids, IA   52406
CEO: Joseph P. Patten, Pres.   Tel: (319) 369-5000   Emp: N/A
Bus: *U.S. headquarters; currency handling and*   Fax:(319) 366-7608   %FO: 100
      security systems.

● **DELTA PLC**
One Kingsway, London WC2B 6XF, England
CEO: J. Scott-Maxwell, CEO   Tel: 44-171-836-3535   Emp: N/A
Bus: *Mfr. engineering and electrical equipment.*   Fax:44-171-836-4511

     ACCURATE FORGING CORPORATION
     201 Pine Street, Bristol, CT   06010
     CEO: Paul Matyszyk, VP   Tel: (860) 582-3169   Emp: N/A
     Bus: *Mfr. brass forgings.*   Fax:(860) 583-3495   %FO: 100

     DELTA AMERICA, INC.
     433 South Main Street, Ste. 117, West Hartford, CT   06110
     CEO: Jon Scott-Maxwell, Pres.   Tel: (860) 561-2244   Emp: N/A
     Bus: *Holding company.*   Fax:(860) 561-2083   %FO: 100

● **DOBSON PARK INDUSTRIES PLC**
Manchester Road, Ince, Wigan WN2 2DX, England
CEO: Alan Kaye   Tel: 44-1942-282-1750   Emp: N/A
Bus: *Mfr. industrial electric, mining equipment, power tools, toy, plastics.*   Fax:44-1942-424-7058

     ELGAR CORPORATION
     9250 Brown Deer Road, San Diego, CA   92121
     CEO: Ken Kilpatrick, Pres.   Tel: (619) 450-0085   Emp: 250
     Bus: *Mfr. power supplies.*   Fax:(619) 458-0267   %FO: 100

● **DRUCK HOLDINGS PLC**
Fir Tree Lane, Groby, Leicester LE6 0FH, England
CEO: John Salmon, Chrm.   Tel: 44-116-231-4314   Emp: 500
Bus: *Mfr. pressure measuring devices.*   Fax:44-116-875-022

     DRUCK INC.
     4 Dunham Drive, New Fairfield, CT   06812
     CEO: Robert P. Knowles, Pres.   Tel: (203) 746-0400   Emp: 53
     Bus: *Mfr./distribution/service pressure measuring devices.*   Fax:(203) 746-2494   %FO: 100

● **ALFRED DUNHILL LTD.**
30 Duke Street, London SW1Y 6DL, England
CEO: Callum Barton, Chrm.   Tel: 44-171-838-8000   Emp: N/A
Bus: *Mfr. clothing, leather goods, jewelry.*   Fax:44-171-838-8333

     ALFRED DUNHILL OF LONDON INC.
     450 Park Avenue, New York, NY   10022
     CEO: David Salz, Pres.   Tel: (212) 888-4000   Emp: N/A
     Bus: *Mfr./retailer clothing, leathergoods, jewelry.*   Fax:(212) 750-8841   %FO: 100

● **EDWARDS HIGH VACUUM INTL**
Manor Royal, Crawley, West Sussex, RH10-2LW, England
CEO: Alan Giles, Pres.   Tel: 44-1293-528-844   Emp: N/A
Bus: *High vacuum equipment and service pumps.*   Fax:N/A

     EDWARDS HIGH VACUUM INC.
     3279 Grand Island Blvd., Grand Island, NY   14072
     CEO: Alan Giles, Pres..   Tel: (716) 773-7552   Emp: N/A
     Bus: *High vacuum equipment & service pumps.*   Fax:(716) 773-3864   %FO: 100

● **EMI GROUP PLC**
4 Tenterden Street, Hanover Square, London W1A 2AY, England
CEO: Sir Colin Southgate, Chrm.   Tel: 44-171-355 4848   Emp: 16800
Bus: *Entertainment, consumer electronics. Recorded*   Fax:44-171-355 1308
     music, music publishing & retail sale of recorded
     music and video.

     CAPITAL-EMI MUSIC, INC.
     1750 North Vine Street, Hollywood, CA   90028-5274
     CEO: Gary Gersh, Pres.   Tel: (213) 462-6252   Emp: N/A
     Bus: *Full service music company.*   Fax:(213) 467-6550   %FO: 100

     EMI GROUP, INC.
     2751 Centerville Road, Suite 205, Wilmington, DE   19808
     CEO: John Skolas, Pres.   Tel: (302) 994-4100   Emp: N/A
     Bus: *U.S. headquarters. Entertainment, consumer*   Fax:(302) 994-4100   %FO: 100
     electronics. Music publisher and retailer.

     EMI MUSIC, INC.
     Carnegie Hall Tower,
     152 West 57th Street, New York, NY   10019
     CEO: James G. Fifield, Pres.   Tel: (212) 261-3000   Emp: N/A
     Bus: *Recorded music.*   Fax:(212) 246-8262   %FO: 100

     HMV, USA
     Stamford Harbor Park, 333 Ludlow Street, Stamford, CT   06902-6987
     CEO: Peter Luckhurt, Pres.   Tel: (203) 969-0105   Emp: N/A
     Bus: *Pre-recorded music & video retailer.*   Fax:(203) 969-0144   %FO: 100

     VIRGIN RECORDS AMERICA, INC.
     338 N. Foothill Road, Beverly Hills, CA   90210
     CEO: P. Quartararo, Pres.   Tel: (310) 278-1181   Emp: N/A
     Bus: *Recorded music, music publishing.*   Fax:(310) 278-2460   %FO: 100

- **ENGLISH CHINA CLAYS PLC**
1015 Arlington Business Park, Theale, Reading, Berks RG7 4SA, England
CEO: A. Teare, CEO   Tel: 44-1734 304010   Emp: 12000
Bus: *Industrial minerals, specialty chemicals.*   Fax:44-1734 309500

    CALGON CORPORATION
    P O Box 1346, Pittsburgh, PA   15230-1346
    CEO: James Heagle, Pres.   Tel: (412) 494-8000   Emp: 1200
    Bus: *Mfr./supply specialty chemicals & related*   Fax:(412) 496-8555   %FO: 100
        services for water/surface treatment, paper
        chemicals, cosmetic ingredient & specialty
        biocide industry

- **EUROTHERM INTERNATIONAL PLC**
Leonardslee, Brighton Road, Horsham RH13 6PP, England
CEO: George Stubds, Chrm.   Tel: 44-403-892-000   Emp: 2800
Bus: *Holding company: industrial instruments, auto*   Fax:44-403-892-011
    controls for environment & appliances.

    EUROTHERM CONTROLS INC.
    11485 Sunset Hills Road, Reston, VA   22090
    CEO: William Perry, Pres.   Tel: (703) 471-4870   Emp: 122
    Bus: *Mfr. industrial temp controls.*   Fax:(703) 787-3436   %FO: 100

    EUROTHERM RECORDERS
    1 Pheasant Run, Newtown, PA   18940
    CEO: Dennis Stoneman, Pres.   Tel: (215) 968-0660   Emp: N/A
    Bus: *Mfr. industrial data loggers.*   Fax:(215) 968-0662   %FO: 100

- **EVODE GROUP PLC**
Common Rd, Stafford, Staffs ST16 3EH, England
CEO: J. P. Moyes, CFO   Tel: 44-582-557755   Emp: 2600
Bus: *Holding company: resins, plastics, paints &*   Fax:44-582-448221
    coverings, plastics.

    GARY CHEMICAL CORPORATION
    PO Box 808, Leominster, MA   01543
    CEO: Robert Gingue, Pres.   Tel: (508) 537-8071   Emp: 140
    Bus: *Mfr. plastics material, synthetic rubber.*   Fax:(508) 840-0015   %FO: 100

- **FAIREY GROUP PLC**
Cranford Lane, Heston, Mid TW9 5NQ, England
CEO: Sir Robin Biggam, Chrm.   Tel: 44-178-447-0470   Emp: 3195
Bus: *Holding company: mfr. filtration, measuring &*   Fax:44-178-443-9519
    sensing equipment, and military control systems.

FAIREY ARLON, INC.
2920 99th Street, Sturtevant, WI   53177
CEO: W,S. Dawson, Pres.   Tel: (414) 886-0888   Emp: N/A
Bus: *Mfr. industrial filtration equipment.*   Fax:(414) 886-6099   %FO: 100

FAIREY HYDRAULICS INC.
6400 West Snowville Road, Cleveland, OH   44141-3248
CEO: Mark S. Carroll, Gen .Mgr.   Tel: (216) 838-1500   Emp: N/A
Bus: *Sale/service military control systems, landing*   Fax:(216) 838-1580   %FO: 100
    gear.

FAIREY INC.
Willow Spring Cir, RD5, York, PA   17402
CEO: J.G. Zacharias, Pres.   Tel: (717) 764-0321   Emp: N/A
Bus: *Holding company: mfr. filtration, measuring &*   Fax:(717) 764-0839   %FO: 100
    sensing equipment, and military control
    systems.

FUSION UV SYSTEMS, INC.
910 Clopper Road, Gaithersburg, MD   20878-1357
CEO: A.D.P. Harbourne, Pres.   Tel: (301) 527-2660   Emp: N/A
Bus: *Ultraviolet light processing technology for*   Fax:(301) 527-2661   %FO: 100
    curing photosensitive inks, coating &
    adhesives in mfr. processes.

IMAGING TECHNOLOGY, INC.
55 Middlesex Turnpike, Bedford, MA   01730
CEO: S. Silver, Pres.   Tel: (617) 275-2700   Emp: N/A
Bus: *Mfr. high speed vision & image processors.*   Fax:(617) 275-9590   %FO: 100

IRCON, INC.
7300 N. Natchez Avenue, Niles, IL   60714
CEO: J.A. Salemi, Pres.   Tel: (847) 967-5151   Emp: N/A
Bus: *Mfr. infrared non-contact temperature*   Fax:(847) 764-7094   %FO: 100
    measuring instruments.

LASERMIKE INC.
8001 Technology Blvd, Dayton, OH   45424
CEO: S. R. Cox, CEO   Tel: (937) 233-9935   Emp: 103
Bus: *Mfr. non-contact dimensional measuring*   Fax:(937) 233-7284   %FO: 100
    equipment.

LUXTRON CORPORATION
2775 Northwestern Pkwy, Santa Clara, CA   95051-0941
CEO: R.J. Goldman, Pres.   Tel: (408) 727-1600   Emp: N/A
Bus: *Mfr. semiconductor process endpoint*   Fax:(408) 727-1677   %FO: 100
    controllers, fibreoptic thermometers & non-
    contact temperature measurement equipment.

MICROSCAN SYSTEMS, INC.
1201 SW 7th Street, Renton, WA   98055
CEO: G. Love, Pres.   Tel: (206) 226-2570   Emp: N/A
Bus: *Mfr. high performance fixed mount bar code*   Fax:(206) 226-8340   %FO: 100
scanning & decoding instruments.

PARTICLE MEASURING SYSTEMS, INC.
5475 Airport Blvd., Boulder, CO   80301
CEO: P. Kelly, Pres.   Tel: (303) 443-7100   Emp: N/A
Bus: *Mfr. on-line laser based particle detection*   Fax:(303) 449-6870   %FO: 100
systems

RED LION CONTROLS INC.
Willow Spring Cir, RD 5, York, PA   17402
CEO: L. E. Goodman, Pres.   Tel: (717) 767-6961   Emp: 150
Bus: *Mfr. digital control, sensing & measuring*   Fax:(717) 764-6587   %FO: 100
devices.

● **FENNER PLC**
Welton Hall, P O Box 3, Brough HU1S 1PQ, England
CEO: Colin Cooke, Chrm.   Tel: 44-482-668-112   Emp: 3900
Bus: *Mfr./distribute fluid power equipment, industrial*   Fax:44-482-667-597
conveyor belting, polymer products and power
transmission.

FENNER DRIVES, INC.
311 W. Stiegel Street, Manheim, PA   17545
CEO: Julian Bigden, Pres. & CEO   Tel: (717) 665-2421   Emp: 350
Bus: *Mfr./sale fluid power equipment and industrial*   Fax:(717) 665-2649   %FO: 100
belting.

FENNER FLUID POWER, INC.
5885 11th Street, Rockford, IL   61109-3699
CEO: Gary Nierhoff, Pres.   Tel: (815) 874-5556   Emp: 200
Bus: *Mfr. ac/dc hydraulic power units, pumps and*   Fax:(815) 874-7853   %FO: 100
motors.

● **FKI PLC**
Cleveland House, St. James's Square, London SW1Y 4LN, England
CEO: Jell Whalley, Chrm.   Tel: 44-422-330267   Emp: N/A
Bus: *Diversifies engineering services.*   Fax:44-422-330084

AMS TECHNOLOGY
PO Box 463, Youngwood, PA   15697
CEO: Wayne C. Minton, VP & Gen.Mgr.   Tel: (412) 925-3950   Emp: N/A
Bus: *Mfr. mining chain, flight bars, cable handlers*   Fax:(412) 925-3790   %FO: 100

• FORWARD TECHNOLOGIES INDUSTRIES, PLC.
2 Pont Street, London, SWIX 9E1, England
CEO: Ken Cobley, CEO   Tel: 44-171-235-9119   Emp: N/A
Bus: *Mfr. plastic assembly equipment, cleaning systems,*   Fax:44-171-235-1509
    and lampmaking equipment.

    FORWARD TECHNOLOGY INDUSTRIES, INC.
    13500 Country Road 6, Plymout, MN   55441
    CEO: Robert Musselman, Pres. & CEO   Tel: (612) 559-1785   Emp: 175
    Bus: *Mfr. plastic assembly equipment, cleaning*   Fax:(612) 559-3929   %FO: 100
        systems, lampmaking equipment.

• FOSECO PLC
285 Long Acre, Nechells, Birmingham B7 5JR, England
CEO: John G. Griffiths, Mng. Dir.   Tel: 44-21-327-1911   Emp: N/A
Bus: *Industrial chemicals, chemical products, abrasive*   Fax:44-21-328-4236
    diamonds.

    FOSECO INC.
    20200 Sheldon Road, PO Box 81227, Cleveland, OH   44181
    CEO: Lee Plutshack, Pres.   Tel: (216) 826-4548   Emp: N/A
    Bus: *Mfr. sleeves & fluxes for foundry industry.*   Fax:(216) 243-7658   %FO: 100

• FRENCH CONNECTION
75-83 Fairfield Road, London E3 2QR, England
CEO: Stephen Marks, Pres.   Tel: 44-181-981-3831   Emp: N/A
Bus: *Mfr. women's clothing; chain stores.*   Fax:N/A

    FRENCH CONNECTION
    184-02 Jamaica Avenue, Hollis, NY   11423
    CEO: Brian Sloan, EVP   Tel: (718) 465-0500   Emp: N/A
    Bus: *U.S. headquarters office; women's clothing*   Fax:(718) 465-0550   %FO: 100
        chain.

    FRENCH CONNECTION
    512 Seventh Avenue, 42nd Fl., New York, NY   10018
    CEO: Stephen Marks, Pres.   Tel: (212) 221-7504   Emp: N/A
    Bus: *Showroom; women's clothing.*   Fax:(212) 302-6839   %FO: 100

• FRESHFIELDS
65 Fleet Street, London EC4Y 1HS, England
CEO: Ian K. Terry, Mg. Ptnr.   Tel: 44-171-936-4000   Emp: N/A
Bus: *International law firm.*   Fax:44-171-832-7001

    FRESHFIELDS
    45 Rockefeller Plaza, Suite 2750, New York, NY   10111
    CEO: Ms. Ailsa Urwin, Mng. Ptnr.   Tel: (212) 765-8685   Emp: 8
    Bus: *International law firm.*   Fax:(212) 977-7199   %FO: 100

● **BEVAN FUNNELL LTD.**
Beach Rd, Newhaven, BN9 0BZ, England
CEO: B. B. Funnell, Chrm.   Tel: 44-1273-513762   Emp: 850
Bus: *Antique reproductions.*   Fax:44-1273-516735

     BEVAN FUNNELL, LTD.
     105 Depot Place, PO Box 1109, High Point, NC   27260
     CEO: DiAnn & Tony Williams, Mgrs.   Tel: (919) 882-4800   Emp: 11
     Bus: *Distribution/service antique reproductions.*   Fax:(919) 889-7037   %FO: 100

● **GARGOUR (UK) LTD.**
5 Cromwell Place, London SW 7, England
CEO: Gilbert Gargour, Pres.   Tel: 44-171-581-5711   Emp: N/A
Bus: *Ceramic floor and wall tile.*   Fax:44-171-584-5740

     MONARCH TILE INC.
     834 Rickwood Road, PO Box 999, Florence, AL   35631
     CEO: Thomas White, Pres.   Tel: (205) 764-6181   Emp: 650
     Bus: *Mfr. ceramic floor and wall tile.*   Fax:(205) 760-8686   %FO: 100

● **GEI INTERNATIONAL PLC**
Aspley Hill, Woburn Sands, Beds MK17 8NW, England
CEO: Michael Hale, Mng. Dir.   Tel: 441-908 281199   Emp: 1700
Bus: *Engineering and special products.*   Fax:441-908 281233

     GEI NORTH AMERICA, INC.
     One Indian Lane East, P.O.Box 242, Towaco, NJ   07082
     CEO: Robert J. Fortier, VP   Tel: (201) 402-7900   Emp: N/A
     Bus: *Sales/service pharmaceutical equipment and*   Fax:(201) 402-7920   %FO: 100
     associated products.

     MATEER-BURT CO., INC.
     436 Devon Park Drive, Wayne, PA   19087
     CEO: Tony Izzi, Pres.   Tel: (610) 293-0100   Emp: 115
     Bus: *Mfr. fillers and labelers.*   Fax:(610) 341-9345   %FO: 100

● **THE GENERAL ELECTRIC CO PLC**
One Stanhope Gate, London W1A 1EH, England
CEO: Rt. Hon. James Prior, Chrm.   Tel: 44-171-493-8484   Emp: 120000
Bus: *Electronics, electric & power generation apparatus*   Fax:44-171-493-1974
& system.

     AMERICAN FAN COMPANY
     2933 Symmes Road, Fairfield, OH   45014
     CEO: Ronald Stoffer, Pres.   Tel: (513) 874-2400   Emp: N/A
     Bus: *Mfr./distribution industrial fans.*   Fax:(513) 870-5577   %FO: 100

BALTEAU STANDARD INC.
8001 Table Rock Road, Medford, OR 97503
CEO: Rick Sawyer, Pres.   Tel: (503) 826-2113   Emp: N/A
Bus: *Instrument transformers (firms marked "JV"*   Fax:(503) 826-8847   %FO: 100
this entry are co-owned by Alcatel Alsthom,
France).

CINCINNATI ELECTRONICS CORPORATION
7500 Innovation Way, Mason, OH 45040-9699
CEO: Dr. James Wimmers, Pres.   Tel: (513) 573-6100   Emp: N/A
Bus: *Design/mfr. aerospace & tactical*   Fax:(513) 573-6290   %FO: 100
communications equipment.

CREDA INC.
5700 West Touhy Avenue, Niles, IL 60648
CEO: Coleen Garcia, Admin. Mgr.   Tel: (847) 647-8024   Emp: N/A
Bus: *North American sales office; mfr. cookers,*   Fax:(847) 647-6917   %FO: 100
washers & dryers, freezers, built-in appliances.

THE CYRIL BATH COMPANY
1610 Airport Road, Monroe, NC 28110
CEO: Joseph Hiteshue, Pres.   Tel: (704) 289-8531   Emp: N/A
Bus: *Hydraulic presses.*   Fax:(704) 289-3932   %FO: JV

DEVELOPMENTAL SCIENCES CORPORATION
PO Box 50000, Ontario, CA 91761
CEO: David Dallob, Pres.   Tel: (909) 947-7600   Emp: N/A
Bus: *Military systems, advanced power structures.*   Fax:(909) 947-1823   %FO: 100

A .B. DICK COMPANY
5700 West Touhy Avenue, Niles, IL 60714-4690
CEO: Gerald McConnell, Pres.   Tel: (312) 763-1900   Emp: N/A
Bus: *Design/mfr./mkt. complete range of equipment*   Fax:(312) 647-6940   %FO: 100
& related supplies & services for
reprographics industry.

ECOLAIR INC.
1550 Lehigh Drive, Easton, PA 18042
CEO: Alfred Brady, Pres. & CEO   Tel: (610) 250-1000   Emp: N/A
Bus: *Condensers & dampers.*   Fax:(610) 250-1005   %FO: JV

EEV INC.
4 Westchester Plaza, Elmsford, NY 10523
CEO: Jacques Collard, Pres. & CEO   Tel: (914) 592-6050   Emp: N/A
Bus: *Mfr. electronic valves, tubes & devices for*   Fax:(914) 682-8922   %FO: 100
broadcasting, communications, industry,
military & medical applications.

EUROPEAN GAS TURBINES INC.
PO Box 219129, Houston, TX   77218
CEO: John Paull, Pres. & CEO   Tel: (281) 492-0222   Emp: N/A
Bus: *Small industry & aeroderivative gas turbines,*   Fax:(281) 492-5607   %FO: JV
    hi-speed diesel engines.

GEC ALSTHOM INTL INC.
4 Skyline Drive, Hawthorne, NY   10532
CEO: Paul J. Jancek, Pres. & CEO   Tel: (914) 347-5155   Emp: N/A
Bus: *Generators, motors, controls, valves, pumps,*   Fax:(914) 347-5432   %FO: JV
    transportation and marine equipment.

GEC MARCONI DYNAMICS, INC.
570 Lyndaro Canyon Road, Westlake Village, CA   91362
CEO: John Smith, Pres.   Tel: (818) 991-0300   Emp: N/A
Bus: *Design/develop/test air-launched guided*   Fax:(818) 991-4668   %FO: 100
    missiles.

GEC MARCONI GPT VIDEO
2795 Northwoods Pkwy., Norcross, GA   30071
CEO: Paul Clark, Pres.   Tel: (770) 263-4781   Emp: N/A
Bus: *Digital video communication systems.*   Fax:(770) 263-4789   %FO: 100

GEC MARCONI HAZELTINE CO, INC.
164 Totowa Road, PO Box 975, Wayne, NJ   07474-0975
CEO: Mark F. Ronald, Pres. & CEO   Tel: (201) 633-6000   Emp: N/A
Bus: *Mfr. information distribution system, network*   Fax:(201) 633-6431   %FO: JV
    command & control systems, guidance &
    control systems.

GEC PLESSEY SEMICONDUCTORS
Sequoia Research Park, 1500 Green Hills Rd, Scotts Valley, CA   95066
CEO: Robert Kromer, Pres.   Tel: (408) 438-2900   Emp: N/A
Bus: *Design/mfr. semiconductor devices,*   Fax:(408) 438-5576   %FO: 100
    components & integrated circuits.

GEC PRECISION CORPORATION
1515 Hwy 81 North, PO Box 70, Wellington, KS   67152
CEO: John T. Stewart III, Pres. & CEO   Tel: (316) 359-5000   Emp: N/A
Bus: *Milling & machinery for industry, tool design,*   Fax:(316) 326-5410   %FO: 100
    fabrication & assembly.

GEC-MARCONI AEROSPACE INC.
110 Algonquin Pkwy., Whippany, NJ   07981-1640
CEO: David Sapio, Pres.   Tel: (201) 428-9898   Emp: N/A
Bus: *Design/develop/mfr./support*   Fax:(201) 884-2277   %FO: 100
    electromechanical systems for commercial &
    military aerospace markets.

GEC-MARCONI AVIONICS INC.
PO Box 81999, Atlanta, GA   30366

CEO: Paul Clark, Pres.   Tel: (770) 448-1947   Emp: N/A
Bus: *Engineering/mfr./integrated logistics support.*   Fax:(770) 449-6128   %FO: 100

GEC-MARCONI DYNAMICS LTD.
1111 Jefferson Davis Hwy., #800, Arlington, VA   22202

CEO: Scott Rettig, Mgr.   Tel: (703) 553-5582   Emp: N/A
Bus: *Design/mfr. missile systems.*   Fax:(703) 553-0274   %FO: 100

GEC-MARCONI PURCHASING
2975 Northwoods Pkwy., PO Box 81388, Norcross, GA   30366

CEO: Paul Clark, Pres.   Tel: (770) 448-2186   Emp: N/A
Bus: *Purchasing point for products & services.*   Fax:(770) 417-4680   %FO: 100

GILBARCO INC.
7300 West Friendly Avenue, PO Box 22087, Greensboro, NC   27420

CEO: W. B. Korb, Pres. & CEO   Tel: (910) 547-5000   Emp: N/A
Bus: *Mfr. service station pumps & control systems.*   Fax:(910) 292-8871   %FO: 100

LEAR ASTRONICS CORPORATION
3400 Airport Avenue, PO Box 442, Santa Monica, CA   90406-0442

CEO: David L. Dallob, Pres. & CEO   Tel: (310) 915-6000   Emp: N/A
Bus: *Defense contractor.*   Fax:(310) 915-8384   %FO: 100

MARCONI COMMUNICATIONS INC.
1861 Wiehle Avenue, Ste. 300, Reston, VA   22091

CEO: Peter Vickers, Pres.   Tel: (703) 736-3300   Emp: N/A
Bus: *Broadcasting stations systems integration.*   Fax:(703) 620-0415   %FO: 100

MARCONI INSTRUMENTS, INC.
13600 Heritage Pkwy., Fort Worth, TX   76177

CEO: James Koehn, Pres.   Tel: (817) 224-9200   Emp: N/A
Bus: *Design/mfr. test & measurement*   Fax:(817) 224-9200   %FO: 100
     instrumentation systems.

MARCONI SYSTEMS TECHNOLOGY
4115 Pleasant Valley Road, #100, Chantilly, VA   22021

CEO: Harry D. F. Eagles, Gen. Mgr.   Tel: (703) 263-1260   Emp: N/A
Bus: *Mktg. computer aided software engineering*   Fax:(703) 263-1533   %FO: 100
     tools.

PICKER INTL INC.
595 Miner Road, Cleveland, OH   44143

CEO: Cary J Nolan, Pres.   Tel: (216) 473-3000   Emp: N/A
Bus: *Mfr. .medical & surgical equipment, supplies*   Fax:(216) 473-4915   %FO: 100
     and accessories.

SCHILLING ROBONICS, INC.
1632 DaVinci Court, Davis, CA   95616
CEO: Tyler Schilling, Pres.   Tel: (916) 753-6718   Emp: N/A
Bus: *Hydraulic equipment.*   Fax:(916) 753-8092   %FO: JV

SIEMENS-STROMBERG CARLSON
900 Broken Sound Pkwy., Boca Raton, FL   33487-3587
CEO: Anton Hasholzner, CEO   Tel: (561) 955-5000   Emp: N/A
Bus: *Design/develop/mfr. systems and equipment*   Fax:(561) 955-6538   %FO: 100
    for network communications   (see joint
    parent: SIEMENS AG, Germany).

VIDEOJET SYSTEMS INTL INC.
1500 Mittel Blvd., Wood Dale, IL   60191-1073
CEO: Henry J. Bode, Pres.   Tel: (630) 860-7300   Emp: N/A
Bus: *Design/engineering/mfr. industrial non-*   Fax:(630) 616-3621   %FO: 100
    contact ink jet coders.

● **GKN, PLC.**
PO Box 4128, Chester Road, Erdington, Birmingham B24 0AW, England
CEO: C.K. Chow, Pres.   Tel: 44-121-377-7766   Emp: N/A
Bus: *Mfr. automotive components.*   Fax:44-121-377-8185

    GKN AUTOMOTIVE, INC.
    3300 University Drive, Auburn Hills, MI   48326
    CEO: Ignacio Martin, CEO   Tel: (248) 377-1200   Emp: N/A
    Bus: *Sales/distribution of automotive components.*   Fax:(248) 377-1370   %FO: 100

● **GLAXO WELLCOME PLC**
Lansdownw House, Berkeley Square, London W1X 6BB, England
CEO: Sir Colin Corness, Chrm.   Tel: 44-171-493-4060   Emp: 65700
Bus: *Research/mfr./market pharmaceuticals.*   Fax:44-171-493-4809

    GLAXO WELLCOME, INC.
    Five Moore Drive, Research Triangle Park, NC   27709
    CEO: Robert A. Ingram, Pres.   Tel: (919) 483-2100   Emp: 4300
    Bus: *Research/mfr./market pharmaceuticals.*   Fax:(919) 483-2412   %FO: 100

    GLAXO WELLCOME, INC.
    1500 K Street, NW, Suite 650, Washington, DC   20005
    CEO: Janie Ann Kinney, VP   Tel: (202) 783-1277   Emp: N/A
    Bus: *Government relations services.*   Fax:(202) 783-1740   %FO: 100

● **GOLD GREENLEES TROTT, PLC.**
82 Dean Street, London, WN5AB, England
CEO: Michael Greenlees, Pres. & CEO   Tel: 44-171-437-0434 Emp: N/A
Bus: *Full service advertising services.*   Fax:44-171-434-3670

 MARTIN/WILLIAMS, INC.
 60 South Sixth Street, Minneapolis, MN 55402
 CEO: David D. Floren, Chrm.   Tel: (612) 340-0800 Emp: 250
 Bus: *Full service advertising services.* Fax:(612) 342-9700 %FO: 100

● **GOLIATH INTERNATIONAL TOOLS LTD.**
Newtown Row, Aston, Birmingham, B6 4NQ, England
CEO: Norman E. Moore, Pres.   Tel: 44-21-359-6621 Emp: 200
Bus: *Mfr. Threading taps & ties.*   Fax:44-21-359-7092

 GOLIATH THREADING TOOLS INC.
 9092 Telegraph Road, Redford, MI 48239
 CEO: Tad C. Wrobel, Gen.Mgr.   Tel: (313) 538-2460 Emp: 4
 Bus: *Distribution threading taps & dies.* Fax:(313) 558-8099 %FO: 100

● **GRAND METROPOLITAN PLC**
8 Henrietta Place, London W1M 9AG, England
CEO: George J. Bull, Chrm.   Tel: 44-171-518-5200 Emp: 80000
Bus: *Food & drink businesses.*   Fax:44-171-518-4600

 BURGER KING CORP.
 17777 Old Cutler Road, Miami, FL 33157
 CEO: James B. Adamson, CEO   Tel: (305) 378-7011 Emp: 31000
 Bus: *Restaurants, fast food outlets.* Fax:(305) 378-7262 %FO: 100

 CARILLON IMPORTERS
 Glenpointe Centre West, Teaneck, NJ 07666-6897
 CEO: Michelle Roux, Pres.   Tel: (201) 836-7799 Emp: 50
 Bus: *Importing/marketing alcoholic beverages.* Fax:(201) 836-3312 %FO: 100

 HAAGEN-DAZS
 Glenpointe Centre East, Teaneck, NJ 07666
 CEO: Michael J. Paxton, Pres.   Tel: (201) 692-0900 Emp: 24OO
 Bus: *Mfr. ice cream & frozen yogurt products.* Fax:(201) 907-6700 %FO: 100

 HEUBLEIN
 450 Columbus Blvd., PO Box 778, Hartford, CT 06142
 CEO: Charles Phillips, Pres.   Tel: (860) 702-4000 Emp: 2600
 Bus: *Mfr./import/distribution wines & spirits.* Fax:(860) 702-4169 %FO: 100

 IDV CORPORATION
 One Parker Plaza, Ft Lee, NJ 07024
 CEO: Pat Parker, Mgr.   Tel: (201) 592-5700 Emp: 165
 Bus: *Importing/marketing cordials, distilled spirits,* Fax:(201) 592-0859 %FO: 100
  non-alcoholic drinks .

PILLSBURY BAKERIES & FOOD SERVICE INC.
Pillsbury Center, Minneapolis, MN   55402

CEO: S. Paul Oliver, Pres.	Tel: (612) 330-4966	Emp: 1200
Bus: *Foodservice for bakery, prepared foods.*	Fax:(612) 330-5200	%FO: 100

THE PILLSBURY CO
Pillsbury Center, Minneapolis, MN   55402

CEO: Paul S. Walsh, CEO	Tel: (612) 330-4966	Emp: 13000
Bus: *Prepared baking mixes, flour, frozen vegetables & pizza, petfood, foodservice & wholesale bakery products, ice cream, frozen yogurt.*	Fax:(612) 330-5200	%FO: 100

● **THE GREAT UNIVERSAL STORES PLC**
Universale House, Devonshire Street, Manchester M60 IXA, England

CEO: Ellen Macsarlane, Mgr.	Tel: 44-171 6364080	Emp: N/A
Bus: *Wearing apparel, catalog shopping, financial & information services, property investment & development*	Fax:44-171 6313641	

BURBERRY'S LTD.
9 East 57th Street, New York, NY   10022

CEO: Victor Barnett, CEO	Tel: (212) 371-5010	Emp: N/A
Bus: *Wearing apparel.*	Fax:(212) 980-5095	%FO: 100

● **GUARDIAN ROYAL EXCHANGE ASSURANCE PLC**
Royal Exchange, London EC3V 3LS, England

CEO: Sidney A. Hopkins, CEO	Tel: 44-171-283-7101	Emp: N/A
Bus: *Insurance services.*	Fax:44-171-621 2599	

GRE CORPORATION
61 Broadway, 33rd Fl., New York, NY   10006

CEO: Victor Yerrill, CEO	Tel: (212) 208-4100	Emp: N/A
Bus: *Insurance.*	Fax:(212) 635-3621	%FO: 100

● **GUINNESS PLC**
39 Portman Square, London W1H 0EE, England

CEO: Anthony Greener, Chrm.	Tel: 44-171 486 0288	Emp: 22000
Bus: *Brew/marketing beers & distillers of whisky, gin and other wines and spirits.*	Fax:44-171 935 5500	

GUINNESS IMPORT CO.
6 Landmark Square, Stamford, CT   06901

CEO: Gary Matthews, Pres.	Tel: (203) 323-3311	Emp: N/A
Bus: *Import/distribution alcoholic beverages.*	Fax:(203) 325-0137	%FO: 100

GUINNESS UNITED DISTILLERS.
1200 G Street, NW, Ste. 800, Washington, DC   20005

CEO: Carolyn L. Panzer, VP	Tel: (202) 434-8994	Emp: N/A
Bus: *Government affairs representative office.*	Fax:(202) 737-2508	%FO: 100

• HALMA PLC

Misbourne Court, Rectory Way, Amersham, Buckinghaamshire HP7 0DE, England

CEO: Steven O'Shay, Chief Exec.　　　　Tel: 44-149-472111　　Emp: N/A

Bus: *Supplies environmental control, fire and gas*　Fax:N/A
detection, safety and security products and services.

AMERICAN TECH MANUFACTURING CORP.

322 Oak Lane, Glenolden, PA　19036

CEO: P. Hammond, Pres.　　　　Tel: (610) 461-4100　　Emp: N/A

Bus: *Mfr. process control equipment for*　Fax:(610) 583-3469　%FO: 100
semiconductor industry.

HALMA HOLDINGS, INC.

3100 East Kemper Road, Cincinnati, OH　45241

CEO: J.C. Conacher, Pres.　　　　Tel: (513) 772-5501　　Emp: N/A

Bus: *U.S. headquarters holding company; firms*　Fax:(513) 772-5507　%FO: 100
supply environmental control, fire & gas
detection, safety and security products &
services.

JANUS ELEVATOR PRODUCTS INC.

125 Ricefield Lane, Happauge, NY　11788

CEO: W. Seymour & M. Byrne, Co-Pres.　Tel: (516) 864-3699　　Emp: N/A

Bus: *Mfr. safety drives for elevators.*　Fax:(516) 864-2631　%FO: 100

•► HANSON PLC

1 Grosvenor Place, London SW1X 7JH, England

CEO: Andrew J.H. Dougal, CEO　　　Tel: 44-171-245-1245　　Emp: 25000

Bus: *Building materials & equipment.*　Fax:44-171-235-3455

CORNERSTONE CONS'T & MATERIALS, INC.

Corp. Pk, 1350 Campus Pkwy #302, Wall Township, NJ　07719

CEO: Craig Sergeant, CEO　　　　Tel: (908) 919-9777　　Emp: N/A

Bus: *Supplier of aggregates, cement and road*　Fax:(908) 919-1149　%FO: 100
materials; construction services.

GROVE WORLDWIDE COMPANY

1565 Buchanan Trail East, Shady Grove, PA　17256-0021

CEO: Robert C Stift, CEO　　　　Tel: (717) 597-8121　　Emp: N/A

Bus: *Mfr. mobile hydraulic & truck mounted*　Fax:(717) 597-4062　%FO: 100
cranes, aerial access equipment.

HANSON NORTH AMERICA

581 Main Street, Woodbridge, NJ　07095

CEO: Peter J. Statile, CFO　　　　Tel: (908) 726-2600　　Emp: N/A

Bus: *Mobile hydraulic and truck mounted cranes;*　Fax:(908) 726-9290　%FO: 100
aerial access equipment.

● **HEATHWAY, LTD.**
Featherstone Road, Wolverton Mill, Milton Keynes MK12 6LA, England
CEO: Charles Glover, Pres.   Tel: 44-1908-222-500   Emp: 70
Bus: *Fiber optic, TV & quartz-working machinery.*   Fax:44-1908-222-564

> **HEATHWAY INC.**
> 4030-C Skyron Drive, Doylestown, PA   18901
> CEO: Robert Halbreiner, Pres.   Tel: (215) 348-2881   Emp: 5
> Bus: *Distributor fiber optic, TV & quartz-working machinery.*   Fax:(215) 348-2309   %FO: 95

● **HILL SAMUEL GROUP PLC**
100 Wood Street, London EC2P 2AJ, England
CEO: Sir Richard Lloyd, Chrm.   Tel: 44-171-628-8011   Emp: 870
Bus: *Merchant banking services.*   Fax:N/A

> **HILL SAMUEL & McCRORY INTL BANKING CORP.**
> 527 Madison Avenue, New York, NY   10022
> CEO: Stephen Aulseberook, Pres.   Tel: (212) 486-7600   Emp: N/A
> Bus: *Financial services.*   Fax:(212) 486-8699   %FO: 100

● **HOPKINSONS HOLDINGS PLC**
Birkby Grange, Birkby Hall Road, Huddersfield, W Yorks, 422 2XB, England
CEO: J.R.S. Russell, Pres.   Tel: 44-1484-454-6821   Emp: N/A
Bus: *Mfr. valves and spare parts service.*   Fax:N/A

> **ATWOOD & MORRILL CO., INC.**
> 285 Canal Street, Salem, MA   01970
> CEO: Robert Genier, Pres.   Tel: (508) 744-5690   Emp: 146
> Bus: *Mfr. valves and spare parts service.*   Fax:(508) 744-5690   %FO: 100

● **HSBC HOLDINGS PLC**
10 Lower Thames Street, London, EC3R 6AE, England
CEO: John R.H. Bond, Group CEO   Tel: 44-171 260 0500   Emp: 104000
Bus: *Banking, trade and financial services and insurance.*   Fax:44-171 260 0501

> **CONCORD LEASING INC.**
> 40 Richards Avenue, Norwalk, CT   06856
> CEO: Matthew Colasanti, Pres. & CEO   Tel: (203) 854-5454   Emp: 258
> Bus: *Equipment financing*   Fax:(203) 866-5409   %FO: 100

> **THE HONGKONG and SHANGHAI BANKING CORP Limited.**
> 140 Broadway, New York, NY   10005
> CEO: John Holsey, Sr. EVP   Tel: (212) 658-5100   Emp: 535
> Bus: *Banking*   Fax:(212) 658-5179   %FO: 100

> **HSBC - WASHINGTON OFFICE**
> 1130 Connecticut Avenue, NW, Washington, DC   20036
> CEO: Les Alperstein, SVP   Tel: (202) 659-3030   Emp: N/A
> Bus: *Commercial banking & securities services.*   Fax:(202) 463-5167   %FO: 100

HSBC AMERICAS, INC.
140 Broadway, New York, NY   10005
CEO: James H Cleave, Pres. & CEO   Tel: (212) 658-5500   Emp: N/A
Bus: *U.S. headquarters. Banking, trade & financial*   Fax:(212) 658-5897   %FO: 100
services, insurance.

HSBC ASSET MANAGEMENT AMERICAS, INC.
250 Park Avenue, 3rd Floor, New York, NY   10177
CEO: Paul Guidone, CEO   Tel: (212) 503-6815   Emp: N/A
Bus: *Investment advisory services.*   Fax:(212) 503-6609   %FO: 100

HSBC EQUATOR BANK
1850 K Street N.W., Washington, DC   20006
CEO: Rush Taylor, VP   Tel: (202) 293-3275   Emp: N/A
Bus: *Commercial banking services.*   Fax:(202) 872-1521   %FO: 100

HSCB EQUATOR BANK
45 Glastonbury Blvd., Glastonbury, CT   06033
CEO: John Kearney, COO   Tel: (860) 633-9999   Emp: N/A
Bus: *Commercial banking services.*   Fax:(860) 633-6799   %FO: 100

HSBC GIBBS LIMITED
190 South Lasalle St., Ste. 1100, Chicago, IL   60603
CEO: David Fried, EVP   Tel: (312) 853-6408   Emp: N/A
Bus: *Commercial banking & securities services.*   Fax:(312) 853-0502   %FO: 100

HSBC JAMES CAPEL
250 Park Avenue, New York, NY   10177
CEO: James O'Donnell, Pres.   Tel: (212) 808-0500   Emp: 110
Bus: *Securities-related activities.*   Fax:(212) 687-1650   %FO: 100

HSBC MARKETS, INC.
140 Broadway, New York, NY   10005
CEO: Herbert Evers, Treas.   Tel: (212) 825-3379   Emp: 580
Bus: *Treasure & capital marketing products.*   Fax:(212) 825-9203   %FO: 100

HSBC SECURITIES INC.
140 Broadway, New York, NY   10005
CEO: James O'Donnell, Pres.   Tel: (212) 825-6780   Emp: N/A
Bus: *Securities broker/dealer.*   Fax:(212) 825-3861   %FO: 100

MARINE MIDLAND BANKS INC
One Marine Midland Center, Buffalo, NY   14203
CEO: James H .Cleave, Pres. & CEO   Tel: (716) 841-2424   Emp: 8700
Bus: *Banking, financial services.*   Fax:(716) 841-5391   %FO: 100

MARINE MIDLAND SECURITIES, INC.
250 Park Avenue, New York, NY   10077
CEO: Todd Tilton, SVP   Tel: (212) 503-6550   Emp: N/A
Bus: *Securities broker/dealer services.*   Fax:(212) 503-6542   %FO: 100

MIDLAND BANK PLC
140 Broadway, New York, NY   10005
CEO: Stewart Gager, Mng. Dir.   Tel: (212) 568-2700   Emp: 138
Bus: *Commercial banking services.*   Fax:(212) 568-1344   %FO: 100

WELLS FARGE HSBC TRADE BANK
525 Market Street, 25th Fl., San Francisco, CA   94105
CEO: David Zuercher, Pres.   Tel: (415) 396-5240   Emp: N/A
Bus: *International trade financing services.*   Fax:(415) 541-0299   %FO: JV

● **IBSTOCK JOHNSEN PLC**
Lutterworth House, Lutterworth, Leicestershire, LE17 4PS, England
CEO: Philip Mengel, CEO   Tel: 44-145-555-3071   Emp: N/A
Bus: *Mfr. brick.*   Fax:44-145-55-3182

   GLEN-GERY CORP.
   1166 Sprin Street, Wyomissing, PA   19610-6001
   CEO: Philip Mcngel, CEO   Tel: (610) 374-4011   Emp: 1200
   Bus: *Mfr. brick, brickwork design & services.*   Fax:(610) 374-1622   %FO: 100

● **IMI PLC**
PO Box 216, Witton, Birmingham B6 7BA, England
CEO: Gary J. Allen, Mng. Dir. & CEO   Tel: 44-121-356-4848   Emp: 20000
Bus: *Holding company. Mfr. building products, liquid*   Fax:44-121-356-3526
dispensers & designs engineering systems.

   CANNON EQUIPMENT COMPANY
   324 West Washington, Cannon Falls, MN   55009
   CEO: R. Rosa, Pres.   Tel: (507) 263-4231   Emp: N/A
   Bus: *Mfr. point of sale & display equipment, mobile*   Fax:(507) 263-4010   %FO: 100
   merchandising carts.

   CONTROL COMPONENTS INC.
   22591 Avenida Empresa, Rancho Sta Margarita, CA   92688
   CEO: S. A. Carson, Pres.   Tel: (714) 858-1877   Emp: N/A
   Bus: *Mfr./sale/service control valves for power, oil,*   Fax:(714) 858-1878   %FO: 100
   gas & petrochemicals industry.

   IMI CORNELIUS INC.
   1 Cornelius Place, Hwy 10 W., Anoka, MN   55303
   CEO: Rick Barklay, Pres.   Tel: (612) 421-6120   Emp: N/A
   Bus: *Mfr. beverage dispensing systems & equipment.*   Fax:(612) 427-4522   %FO: 100

   NORGREN COMPANY
   5400 South Delaware, Littleton, CO   80120-1663
   CEO: Pat Maley & William Wolsky, Co-Pres.   Tel: (303) 794-2611   Emp: N/A
   Bus: *Mfr. pneumatic products.*   Fax:(303) 795-9487   %FO: 100

TILINE, INC.
150 West Queen Avenue SW, PO Box 908, Albany, OR   97321-0336

CEO : Randy Turner, Pres.	Tel: (503) 926-7711	Emp : N/A
Bus: *Mfr. titanium investment castings for aerospace.*	Fax:(503) 967-7786	%FO : 100

TITECH INTL INC.
4000 West Valley Blvd.
PO Box 3060, Pomona, CA   91769-3060

CEO : P. Roybal, Pres.	Tel: (909) 595-7455	Emp : N/A
Bus: *Mfr. titanium rammed graphite & investment castings.*	Fax:(909) 598-3005	%FO : 100

● **IMPERIAL CHEMICAL INDUSTRIES PLC**
Imperial Chemical House, 9 Millbank, London SW1P 3JF, England

CEO : Charles M. Smith, CEO	Tel: 44-171-834-4444	Emp: 65000
Bus: *Mfr. industrial & special chemicals, agrochems seeds, pharmaceuticals, films, paints, explosives, fibers, acrylics.*	Fax:44-171-834-2042	

ICI EXPLOSIVES, INC.
15301 Dallas Parkway, #1200, Dallas, TX   75248

CEO : David Taylor, Pres.	Tel: (972) 387-2400	Emp : N/A
Bus: *Mfr./sale explosives.*	Fax:(972) 392-2940	%FO : 100

ICI ACRYLICS, INC.
7275 Goodlett Farms Pkwy, Cordova, TN   38018

CEO : Ross McMillan, Pres.	Tel: (901) 381-2000	Emp : N/A
Bus: *Mfr./sale acrylics.*	Fax:(901) 381-2444	%FO : 100

ICI AMERICAS, INC.
1300 Connecticut Avenue, Washington, DC   20036

CEO : Joseph J. Martyak, VP	Tel: (202) 862-8300	Emp : N/A
Bus: *Government affairs representative.*	Fax:(202) 862-8303	%FO : 100

ICI AMERICAS, INC.
3411 Silverside Road, Wilmington, DE   19850-5391

CEO : John Danzeisen, Chrm.	Tel: (302) 886-3000	Emp : 19000
Bus: *Mfr. pharmaceuticals, agrochemicals seeds, paints, films, industry & specialty chemicals, advanced materials, polymers, polyurethanes.*	Fax:(302) 887-2972	%FO : 100

NATIONAL STARCH & CHEMICAL CORP.
10 Finderne Avenue, Bridgewater, NJ   08807

CEO : James A. Kennedy, Pres. & CEO	Tel: (908) 685-5000	Emp : 1200
Bus: *Mfr. starches, specialty chemicals and resins. (Acquired from Unilever plc,1997)*	Fax:(908) 685-5005	%FO : 100

● **INDIA IMPORTS OF RHODE ISLAND LTD.**
24 Commerce Road, Brentford, Middlesex, TW8 8LE, England
CEO: Lakhi S. Paintal, Pres.   Tel: N/A   Emp: N/A
Bus: *Mfr. ladies fashion-wear garments, sportswear.*   Fax:N/A

    PHOOL FASHION LTD.
    1411 Broadway, 16th Floor, New York, NY   10018
    CEO:Lakhi S. Paintal, Pres.   Tel: (212) 944-0910   Emp: N/A
    Bus: *Mfr./sale ladies fashion-wear garments,*   Fax:(212) 944-0286   %FO: 100
        sportswear.

● **INVESCO PLC**
11 Devonshire Square, London EC2M 4YR, England
CEO: Michael Benson, CEO Global   Tel: 44-171-6263434   Emp: 2700
Bus: *Institutional and retail investment advisory services,*   Fax:44-171-929-5888
mutual funds distribution.

    AIM MANAGEMENT GROUP, INC.
    11 Greenway Plaza, #100, Houston, TX   77046
    CEO:Charles W. Brady, Chrm. & CEO   Tel: (713) 626-1919   Emp: N/A
    Bus: *Institutional and retail investment advisory*   Fax:(713) 214-7565   %FO: 80
        services, mutual funds distribution.

    AMVESCAP, PLC
    1315 Peachtree Street, Suite 500, Atlanta, GA   30309
    CEO:Charles W. Brady, Chrm. & CEO   Tel: (404) 892-0896   Emp: N/A
    Bus: *Investment management holding company.*   Fax:(404) 724-4270   %FO: 100

    INVESCO CAPITAL MANAGEMENT, INC.
    241 Sevilla Avenue, Suite 905, Coral Gables, FL   33134
    CEO:Edward Mitchell, CEO   Tel: (305) 443-3241   Emp: N/A
    Bus: *Institutional and retail investment advisory*   Fax:(305) 443-6963   %FO: 100
        services.

    INVESCO FUNDS GROUP, INC.
    7800 East Union Avenue, #800, Denver, CO   80237
    CEO:Dan Hesser, CEO   Tel: (303) 930-2700   Emp: N/A
    Bus: *Mutual fund advisory services.*   Fax:(303) 930-6307   %FO: 100

    INVESCO Management & Research, Inc.
    101 Federal Street, Boston, MA   02110
    CEO:Frank Keeler, Pres.   Tel: (617) 345-8200   Emp: N/A
    Bus: *Institutional and retail investment advisory*   Fax:(617) 261-4560   %FO: 100
        services.

    INVESCO NORTH AMERICA
    1315 Peachtree Street, Suite 500, Atlanta, GA   30309
    CEO:Wendell M. Starke, Chief Inv.Off.   Tel: (404) 892-0896   Emp: 2600
    Bus: *Institutional and retail investment advisory*   Fax:(404) 724-4270   %FO: 100
        services.

INVESCO RETIREMENT PLAN ERVICES, INC.
1315 Peachtree Street, Suite 500, Atlanta, GA   30309
CEO: N/A   Tel: (404) 892-0896   Emp: N/A
Bus: *Retirement plan services.*   Fax:(404) 724-4270   %FO: 100

PRIMCO CAPITAL MANAGEMENT, INC.
101 South Fifth Street, #2150, Louisville, KY   40202
CEO: Dennis Donahue, CEO   Tel: (502) 589-2011   Emp: N/A
Bus: *Institutional and retail investment advisory*   Fax:(502) 589-2157   %FO: 100
services.

● **JAEGER HOLDINGS**
57 Broadwick Street, London W1V 1FU, England
CEO: Sir David Alliance, Chrm.   Tel: 44-171-200-4000   Emp: N/A
Bus: *Manufacturer of wholesale/retail wearing apparel.*   Fax:44-171-200-4001

JAEGER SPORTSWEAR LTD.
818 Madison Avenue, New York, NY   10021
CEO: Sid Gibson, Pres.   Tel: (212) 794-0780   Emp: N/A
Bus: *Wholesale/retail wearing apparel.*   Fax:(212) 570-9530   %FO: 100

● **JOHNSON MATTHEY PLC**
New Garden House, 78 Hatton Garden, London EC1N 8JP, England
CEO: David Davies   Tel: 44-171-430-0011   Emp: 7100
Bus: *Advance materials, precious metals technology.*   Fax:44-171-242-6024

JOHNSON MATTHEY INVEST INC.
PO Box 733, Valley Forge, PA   19482-0733
CEO: Chris Clark, COO   Tel: (610) 971-3000   Emp: 1000
Bus: *Mfr. advance materials & precious metals*   Fax:(610) 971-3051   %FO: 100
technology.

● **H & R JOHNSON TILES LTD.**
Highgate Tile Works, Tunstall, Stoke-On-Trent, ST6 4JX, England
CEO: David Dry, Pres.   Tel: 44-178-2575-575   Emp: N/A
Bus: *Mfr. ceramic tile.*   Fax:44-178-2577-377

H & R JOHNSON, INC.
PO Box 2335, Farmingdale, NJ   07727
CEO: Paul McGinty   Tel: (908) 280-7900   Emp: N/A
Bus: *Ceramic tile.*   Fax:(908) 280-7902   %FO: 100

● **KLEINWORT BENSON GROUP PLC**
20 Fenchurch Street, London EC3P 3DB, England
CEO: Lord Rockley, Chrm.   Tel: 44-171-623-8000   Emp: 2500
Bus: *International financial services. (See Dresdner*   Fax:44-171-623-4069
      Bank).

    FENCHURCH CAPITAL MGMT LTD.
    311 South Wacker Drive, #4825, Chicago, IL   60606
    CEO: Marcus Hutchins, Pres.   Tel: (312) 922-1717   Emp: 23
    Bus: *Commodity fund management.*   Fax:(312) 554-7707   %FO: 100

    KLEINWORT BENSON NA INC.
    200 Park Avenue, New York, NY   10166
    CEO: Ulrik Trampe, Pres.   Tel: (212) 983-4000   Emp: 60
    Bus: *Marketing securities to institutional clients,*   Fax:(212) 983-5798   %FO: 100
        marketing making, corporate finance.

● **LADBROKE GROUP PLC**
Maple Court, Central Park, Reeds Crescent, Watford, Hertfordshire WD1 1HZ, England
CEO: Peter M. George, Vice Chrm., & Mg, Dir.   Tel: 44-171-856-8000   Emp: 69000
Bus: *Leisure industry, gaming, real estate, hotels, retail.*   Fax:44-171-436-1300

    HILTON INTERNATIONAL COMPANY
    1 Wall Street, New York, NY   10005
    CEO: David W. Jarvis, CEO   Tel: (212) 820-1700   Emp: N/A
    Bus: *Hotels.*   Fax:(212) 809-7595   %FO: 100

    LONDON & LEEDS DEVELOPMENT CORP.
    82 Beaver Street, New York, NY   10022
    CEO: Howard Friedman, Pres.   Tel: (212) 344-4030   Emp: N/A
    Bus: *Commercial real estate develop*   Fax:(212) 344-5166   %FO: 100

    PACIFIC RACING ASSOCATION
    1100 Eastshore Hwy., Albany, CA   94710
    CEO: David J. Goodwill, Pres.   Tel: (510) 559-7300   Emp: 600
    Bus: *Horses, racing, restaurants.*   Fax:(510) 559-7300   %FO: 100

    WASHINGTON TROTTING ASSN
    Race Trace Road, PO Box 499, Meadow Lands, PA   15347
    CEO: Peter George, Pres.   Tel: (412) 225-9300   Emp: N/A
    Bus: *Harness horse racing.*   Fax:(412) 225-0298   %FO: 100

● **JOHN LAING PLC**
Page Street, Mill Hill, London NW7 2ER, England
CEO: J. Martin Laing, CEO   Tel: 44-171-906-5600   Emp: 10500
Bus: *Construction, industrial engineering and trading.*   Fax:44-171-906-5073

    JOHN LAING HOMES INC.
    8618 Westwood Center Drive, Vienna, VA   22181
    CEO: Steve Baldwin, Pres.   Tel: (703) 827-4141   Emp: 30
    Bus: *Home building company.*   Fax:(703) 827-4149   %FO: 100

● **LAND INSTRUMENTS INTL LTD. (Land Infrared Division)**
Stubley Lane, Dronfield S18 6DJ, England
CEO: Tony Duncan, Mng. Dir.   Tel: 44-1246-417-691   Emp: 230
Bus: *Mfr. infrared temperature measuring instruments*   Fax:44-1246-410-585
    and devices.

    LAND INFRARED
    2525 Pearl Buck Road, Bristol, PA   19007
    CEO: Richard Parello, Pres.   Tel: (215) 781-0700   Emp: 25
    Bus: *Sale/distribution infrared temperature*   Fax:(215) 781-0723   %FO: 100
      measuring instruments & devices.

● **LAPORTE PLC**
Nations House, 103 Wigmore Street, London W1H 9AB England
CEO: Jim Leng, CEO   Tel: 44-171-399-2400   Emp: N/A
Bus: *Mfr./distributor chemicals.*   Fax:44-171-399-2401

    LAPORTE, INC.
    22 Chambers Street, Princeton, NJ   08542
    CEO: Michael J. Kenny   Tel: (609) 430-1199   Emp: 47
    Bus: *Mfr./distributor chemicals.*   Fax:(609) 430-1524   %FO: 100

● **LEGAL & GENERAL GROUP, PLC.**
Bucklersbury House, 3 Queen Victoria Street, London EC4N-8EL, England
CEO: Christopher Harding, Chrm.   Tel: 44-171-528-6200   Emp: N/A
Bus: *Life insurance.*   Fax:N/A

    LEGAL & GENERAL AMERICAN, INC.
    1701 Research Blvd., Rockville, MD   20850
    CEO: David Lenaburg, Pres.   Tel: (301) 279-4800   Emp: N/A
    Bus: *Life insurance.*   Fax:(301) 294-6986   %FO: 100

● **LINKLATERS & PAINES**
Barrington House, 59-67 Gresham Street, London, EC2V 7JA, England
CEO: Charles P. Jones, Mng. Dir.   Tel: 44-171-606-7080   Emp: N/A
Bus: *International law firm; one of the world's largest.*   Fax:44-171-606-5113

> **LINKLATERS & PAINES**
> 885 Third Avenue, Suite 2600, New York, NY   10022
> CEO: David Barnard, Mng. Dir.   Tel: (212) 751-1000   Emp: 40
> Bus: *International law firm.*   Fax:(212) 751-9335   %FO: 100

● **LISTER-PETTER, LTD.**
P O Box 1, Dursley, Glos G11 4HS, England
CEO: R. Terry Sharpe, Mng. Dir.   Tel: 44-1453-544-141   Emp: 1500
Bus: *Mfr. diesel & marine engines and generators.*   Fax:44-1453-546-732

> **LISTER-PETTER INC.**
> 555 East 56 Highway, Olathe, KS   66061
> CEO: Phil Cantrill, Pres.   Tel: (913) 764-3512   Emp: 60
> Bus: *Mfr./distribution diesel, marine & natural gas*   Fax:(913) 764-5493   %FO: 100
> *engines, generators.*

● **LLOYD'S OF LONDON**
One Lime Street, London EC3M 7HA, England
CEO: Ron Sandler, CEO   Tel: 44-171-623-7100   Emp: 2042
Bus: *Insurance market services.*   Fax:44-171-626-2389

> **LLOYD'S AMERICA LIMITED**
> 712 Fifth Avenue, New York, NY   10019
> CEO: Peter Lane, Mng. Dir.   Tel: (212) 632-0500   Emp: N/A
> Bus: *North America representative office.*   Fax:(212) 632-0505   %FO: 100

● **LLOYDS TSB GROUP PLC**
71 Lombard Street, London EC3P 3BS, England
CEO: Peter Ellwood, CEO   Tel: 44-171-626 1500   Emp: 82506
Bus: *Financial services group. Commercial banking*   Fax:44-171-356 1369
services.

> **LLOYDS BANK PLC**
> 575 Fifth Avenue, New York, NY   10017
> CEO: Annabelle Reid, VP & Mgr.   Tel: (212) 930-5000   Emp: N/A
> Bus: *International commercial banking services.*   Fax:(212) 930-5098   %FO: 100

> **LLOYDS BANK PLC**
> One Biscayne Tower, #3200, Miami, FL   33131
> CEO: John Alexander, SVP & Mgr.   Tel: (305) 579-8900   Emp: N/A
> Bus: *International commercial banking services.*   Fax:(305) 371-8607   %FO: 100

LLOYDS BANK PLC
One Seaport Plaza,
99 Water Street, 9th Fl., New York, NY   10038
CEO: Peter J Phillips, EVP & Gen. Mgr.   Tel: (212) 607-4300   Emp: 123
Bus: *International commercial banking services.*   Fax:(212) 607-5410   %FO: 100

● **LOGICA PLC**
Stephenson House, 75 Hampstead Road, London NW1 2PL, England
CEO: Martin Read, Mng. Dir.   Tel: 44-171-637-9111   Emp: 4800
Bus: *Systems integration, consulting and software*   Fax:44-171-468-7006
development.

    LOGICA, INC.
    32 Hartwell Avenue, Lexington, MA   02173
    CEO: Jim Yates, CEO   Tel: (617) 476-8000   Emp: 400
    Bus: *Systems integration, consulting and software*   Fax:(617) 476-8010   %FO: 100
    development.

● **LOVELL WHITE DURRANT**
65 Holborn Viaduct, London EC1A 2DY. England
CEO: Andrew Walker, Mg. Ptrn.   Tel: 44-171 236 0066   Emp: N/A
Bus: *International law firm.*   Fax:44-171 248 4212

    LOVELL WHITE DURRANT
    527 Madison Avenue, 10th Floor, New York, NY   10022
    CEO: Philip Gershung, Mng. Ptrn.   Tel: (212) 758-3773   Emp: N/A
    Bus: *International law firm.*   Fax:(212) 486-0367   %FO: 100%

● **LUCAS INDUSTRIES PLC**
Brueton House, New Road, Solihull, West Midlands B91 3TX, England
CEO: Anthony Gill, Chrm.   Tel: 44-121 -627-6000   Emp: N/A
Bus: *Advanced technology systems, components and*   Fax:44-121-627-4363
services to aerospace, automotive and other markets

    LUCAS AEROSPACE AIRCRAFT SYSTEMS
    145 S. State College Blvd., #280, Brea, CA   92621
    CEO: Saleem Naber, Mng. Dir   Tel: (714) 671-7600   Emp: N/A
    Bus: *Design/mfr./support aerospace aircraft*   Fax:(714) 671-4593   %FO: 100
    systems & equipment.

    LUCAS AEROSPACE ELECTRO PRODUCTS
    610 Neptune Avenue, Brea, CA   92622
    CEO: Tom Schlessinger, Pres.   Tel: (714) 671-4500   Emp: N/A
    Bus: *Aerospace motors/controls.*   Fax:(714) 671-4503   %FO: 100

    LUCAS AEROSPACE POWER TRANSMISSION CORP.
    211 Seward Avenue, Utica, NY   13503
    CEO: Frank Robilotto, Mgr.   Tel: (315) 793-1200   Emp: N/A
    Bus: *Mfr. aircraft power transmission shafting,*   Fax:(315) 793-1209   %FO: 100
    couplings, pumps, pivots, de-icers, etc.

LUCAS ASSEMBLY & TEST SYSTEMS
12841 Start Road, Livonia, MI   48150-1588
CEO: David Watkins, Pres.   Tel: (313) 522-1900   Emp: N/A
Bus: *Mfr. assembly & test stands.*   Fax:(313) 458-1323   %FO: 100

LUCAS CONTROL SYSTEMS PRODUCTS
1000 Lucas Way, Hampton, VA   23666
CEO: John Berkenkamp, Pres.   Tel: (804) 766-1500   Emp: N/A
Bus: *Mfr. man-machine interface products*   Fax:(804) 766-3979   %FO: 100

LUCAS NOVASENSOR INC.
1055 Mission Court, Fremont, CA   94539
CEO: John Pendergrass, Pres.   Tel: (510) 490-9100   Emp: N/A
Bus: *Mfr. mini & micro silicon devices & structures*   Fax:(510) 770-0645   %FO: 100

LUCAS ZETA INC.
2811 Orchard Pkwy., San Jose, CA   95134
CEO: Norman D. Steckline, Pres.   Tel: (408) 434-3600   Emp: N/A
Bus: *Microwave products, communication, intercept*   Fax:(408) 433-0205   %FO: 100
     & direction finding systems, radio monitoring
     systems, high power RF products

• MACMILLAN LTD.
25 Eccleston Place, London SW1W 9WF, England
CEO: N. B. Shaw, Chrm.   Tel: 44-171-881-8000   Emp: 1900
Bus: *Publishing conglomerate.*   Fax:44-171-881-8001

GROVES DICTIONARIES, INC.
345 Park Avenue South, New York, NY   10010-1707
CEO: Janice Kuta, Pres.   Tel: (212) 689-9200   Emp: N/A
Bus: *Book publishing.*   Fax:(212) 689-9711   %FO: 100

NATURE PUBLISHING
345 Park Avenue South, New York, NY   10010-1707
CEO: Mary Waltham, Pres.   Tel: (212) 726-9200   Emp: N/A
Bus: *Publishing.*   Fax:(212) 696-9006   %FO: 100

ST. MARTIN'S PRESS, INC.
175 Fifth Avenue, New York, NY   10010
CEO: John Sargent, Pres.   Tel: (212) 674-5151   Emp: 500
Bus: *Book publishing*   Fax:(212) 420-9314   %FO: 100

● **MARKS AND SPENCER PLC**

Michael House, 37-67 Baker Street, London W1A 1DN, England

CEO: Sir Richard Greenbury, Chrm. Tel: 44-171-935-4422 Emp: 65500

Bus: *Retail stores, internationally markets clothing, food* Fax:44-171-487-2679
  stuffs and household goods.

 BROOKS BROTHERS

 346 Madison Avenue, New York, NY 10017

 CEO: Joseph Gromek, Chrm. Tel: (212) 682-8800 Emp: N/A

 Bus: *Retail clothing.* Fax:(212) 309-7372 %FO: 100

 KING SUPERMARKETS, INC.

 Two Dedrick Place, West Caldwell, NJ 07006

 CEO: James Meister, Pres. Tel: (201) 575-3320 Emp: N/A

 Bus: *Chain store; retail foods.* Fax:(201) 575-7629 %FO: 100

 MARKS AND SPENCER U.S. HOLDINGS, INC.

 346 Madison Avenue, New York, NY 10017

 CEO: Chris Littmoden, Exec.Dir. Tel: (212) 697-3886 Emp: N/A

 Bus: *U.S. headquarters, holding company. Retails* Fax:(212) 697-3857 %FO: 100
  clothing, food stuffs and household goods.

● **MARLEY PLC**

Seven Oakhill Road, Seven Oaks, Kent TN13 1NQ, England

CEO: David Trapnell, CEO Tel: 44-732-455255 Emp: N/A

Bus: *Mfr. construction materials; concrete & clay roofing* Fax:44-732-740694
 products, cement blocks, flooring materials,
 drainage products, automotive components,
 furniture & home furnishings and financial services.

 GENERAL SHALE PRODUCTS CORP.

 3211 Roan Street, Johnson City, TN 37601

 CEO: Richard L. Green, Pres. & CEO Tel: (423) 282-4661 Emp: N/A

 Bus: *Mfr./distribution construction materials; brick.* Fax:(423) 926-9432 %FO: 100

 MARLEY MOULDINGS

 Rural Rt. 4, PO Box 610, Marion, VA 24354

 CEO: Larry Davis, Pres. Tel: (540) 783-8161 Emp: N/A

 Bus: *Mfr./distribution construction materials;* Fax:(540) 783-3292 %FO: 100
  moldings.

 SYROCO, INC.

 83 Pine Street, Peabody, MA 01960

 CEO: John Fravel, Pres. Tel: (508) 536-7444 Emp: N/A

 Bus: *Mfr./distribution home furnishings.* Fax:(508) 536-2007 %FO: 100

● **MC KECHNIE, PLC.**
Leighswood Road, Aldridge, Waisall, West Midland W59 8DS, England
CEO: Vanni Treves, Chrm.   Tel: 44-19-2274-3887   Emp: N/A
Bus: *Mfr. plastic components.*   Fax:44-19-2251-1045

    MC KECHNIE PLASTIC COMPONENTS, N.A.
    Highway 93, PO Box 2369, Easley, SC   29641
    CEO:Randy Herman, Pres.   Tel: (864) 859-7548   Emp: N/A
    Bus: *Sales/distribution of plastic components.*   Fax:(864) 859-8687   %FO: 100

    MC KECHNIE PLASTIC COMPONENTS, N.A.
    7309 West 27th Street, Minneapolis, MN   55426
    CEO:Brian Evanson, Pres.   Tel: (612) 929-3312   Emp: 280
    Bus: *Sales/distribution of plastic components.*   Fax:(612) 929-8404   %FO: 100

● **MEPC PLC**
12 St James Sq, London SW1Y 4LB, England
CEO: Christopher Benson, Chrm.   Tel: 44-171-911-5300   Emp: 2500
Bus: *Commercial real estate.*   Fax:44-171-839-2340

    MEPC AMERICAN PROPERTIES
    15303 Dallas Pkwy, #400, Dallas, TX   75248
    CEO:David S. Gruber, Pres.   Tel: (972) 980-5000   Emp: 100
    Bus: *Develop/manage commercial real estate.*   Fax:(972) 980-5092   %FO: 100

● **METAL BULLETIN PLC**
Park House, Park Torrace, Worcester Park KT4 7HY, England
CEO: T. J. Tarring, Mng. Dir.   Tel: 44-171-330-4311   Emp: 150
Bus: *Publish magazine; conference organization service.*   Fax:44-171-337-8943

    METAL BULLETIN, INC.
    220 Fifth Avenue, New York, NY   10001
    CEO:Greg Newton, Pres.   Tel: (212) 213-6202   Emp: 10
    Bus: *Publish magazine; conference organization   Fax:(212) 213-6273   %FO: 100
    service.*

● **MEYER INTERNATIONAL, PLC.**
Aldwych House, 81 Aldwych, London WC2B 4HQ, England
CEO: Alan Peterson, CEO   Tel: 44-171-839-7766   Emp: N/A
Bus: *Mfr. building materials.*   Fax:44-171-839-5520

    MEYER LAMINATES, INC.
    1264 La Quinta Drive, Ste.4A, Orlando, FL   32809
    CEO:Rocky Johnson, Pres.   Tel: (407) 857-6353   Emp: N/A
    Bus: *Mfr./distribute building materials.*   Fax:(407) 857-1376   %FO: 100

    MEYER LAMINATES, INC.
    330 Patton Drive, SW, Atlanta, GA   30336
    CEO:Bob Sweat, Pres.   Tel: (404) 699-3900   Emp: 50+
    Bus: *Mfr./distribute building materials.*   Fax:(404) 699-3914   %FO: 100

MEYER USA, INC.
1900 Australian Avenue, Riviera Beach, FL   33404
CEO: H.R. Fedden, CEO   Tel: (561) 842-4281   Emp: N/A
Bus: *Mfr./distribute building materials.*   Fax:(561) 842-4477   %FO: 100

● **MICRO FOCUS LTD.**
26 West Street, Newbury, Berkshire RG13 1JT, England
CEO: J. Michael Gullard, Chrm.   Tel: 44-171-532646   Emp: 250
Bus: *Development and market software products.*   Fax:N/A

   MICRO FOCUS INC.
   2465 East Bayshore Road, Palo Alto, CA   94303
   CEO: Nancy Rolden, Pres.   Tel: (415) 938-3700   Emp: 100
   Bus: *Development and marketing software products.*   Fax:(415) 856-6134   %FO: 100

● **MITCHELL GRIEVE LTD.**
Wolsey Rd, Coalville, Leices LE6 4ES, England
CEO: Byron Head, Chrm.   Tel: 44-1530-510565   Emp: 600
Bus: *Mfr. knitting needles and elements.*   Fax:44-1530-510458

   MITCHELL GRIEVE (USA) INC.
   9600 F Southern Pine Blvd, Charlotte, NC   28273
   CEO: Ian Tyson, Pres.   Tel: (704) 525-0325   Emp: 5
   Bus: *Distribute needles and elements for knitting*   Fax:(704) 525-9471   %FO: 100
        and hosiery industries, dental scalpels and
        blades.

● **MORGAN GRENFELL & CO LTD.**
23 Great Winchester Street, London EC2P 2AX, England
CEO: G. W. Mackworth-Young, Chrm.   Tel: 44-171-545-8000   Emp: N/A
Bus: *International merchant banking.*   Fax:44-171-971-7455

   LAWRENCE MORGAN GRENFELL INC.
   1290 Avenue of the Americas, New York, NY   10019
   CEO: Martin Wade, Pres.   Tel: (212) 468-5000   Emp: N/A
   Bus: *Investment banking services.*   Fax:(212) 469-4133   %FO: JV

● **MUIRHEAD VACTIC COMPONENTS PLC**
Oakfield Road, SE 20, Beckenham, Kent BR3 4BE, England
CEO: Peter E.Gough, Pres.   Tel: 44-181-659-9090   Emp: N/A
Bus: *Precision electric and electric-mechanical*   Fax:44-181-659-9906
     engineering.

   MUIRHEAD INC.
   871 Mountain Avenue, Springfield, NJ   07081
   CEO: George Sinclair, Pres.   Tel: (973) 376-1222   Emp: N/A
   Bus: *Precision electric and electric-mechanical*   Fax:(973) 376-0939   %FO: 100
        engineering.

• NATIONAL FREIGHT CONSORTIUM PLC (NFC)
66 Chiltern Street, London W1M 1PR, England
CEO: Sir Christopher Bland, Chrm.   Tel: 44-171-317-0123   Emp: 29000
Bus: *Global transportation and logistics services.*   Fax: 44-171-224-2385

ALLIED VAN LINES, INC.
PO Box 4403, Chicago, IL   60680
CEO: David Buth, Pres.   Tel: (312) 717-3000   Emp: 750
Bus: *Commercial transport services.*   Fax: (312) 717-3000   %FO: 100

ALLIED VAN LINES, INC.
215 West Diehl Road, Naperville, IL   60563
CEO: Michael Fergus, Pres.   Tel: (630) 717-3000   Emp: N/A
Bus: *Transport services.*   Fax: (630) 717-3606   %FO: 100

EXEL LOGISTICS, INC.
501 West Shrock Road, Westerville, OH   43081
CEO: Bruce Edwards, Pres.   Tel: (614) 890-1730   Emp: 300
Bus: *Logistics consulting.*   Fax: (614) 898-7436   %FO: 100

MERCHANTS HOME DELIVERY SERVICE, INC.
2400 Latigo Avenue, Oxnard, CA   93030
CEO: James Allyn, Pres.   Tel: (805) 485-7979   Emp: 80
Bus: *Furniture delivery services.*   Fax: (805) 988-6387   %FO: 100

NFC INTERNATIONAL HOLDINGS (USA) INC.
215 West Diehl Road, Naperville, IL   60563
CEO: Robert D. Lake, CEO, N.A.   Tel: (630) 717-4897   Emp: N/A
Bus: *US headquarters. International transport*   Fax: (630) 717-3615   %FO: 100
    services.

• NATIONAL WESTMINSTER BANK PLC
41 Lothbury, London EC2P 2BP, England
CEO: Derek Wanless, CEO   Tel: 44-171-726-1000   Emp: 104000
Bus: *Investment banking, institutional securities and*   Fax: 44-171-726 1035
    options brokerage, lease financing.

GLEACHER NATWEST, INC.
660 Madison Avenue, New York, NY   10021
CEO: Eric Gleacher, Chrm.   Tel: (212) 418-4220   Emp: N/A
Bus: *Merchant banking & investment advisory*   Fax: (212) 935-4839   %FO: 100
    services.

GREENWICH CAPITAL MARKETS
600 Steamboat Road, Greenwich, CT   06830
CEO: G.F.Holloway & K.R. Kruger, Co-Pres.   Tel: (203) 625-2700   Emp: N/A
Bus: *Securities broker/dealer & investment advisory*   Fax: (203) 629-8743   %FO: 100
    services.

NATWEST MARKETS, INC.
175 Water Street, New York, NY   10038
CEO: Michael V.F. Allsop, Reg. Mng. Dir.   Tel: (212) 602-4800   Emp: 8500
Bus: *Investment & corporate banking services.*   Fax:(212) 602-4278   %FO: 100

NATWEST SECURITIES CORP.
175 Water Street, New York, NY   10036
CEO: Ralph Reynolds, Pres.   Tel: (212) 602-4800   Emp: N/A
Bus: *Securities broker/dealer & investment advisory* Fax:(212) 602-4278   %FO: 100
    services.

● **NEOTRONICS LTD.**
Parsonage Rd, Bishop's Stortford, Takeley CM22 6PU, England
CEO: Paul Johnson, CEO   Tel: 44-1279-870182   Emp: 400
Bus: *Mfr. portable and fixed gas detection, fuel efficiency,* Fax:44-1279-870377
    pressure, velocity and emergency resuscitation
    equipment.

NEOTRONICS OF NORTH AMERICA, INC.
4331 Thurmond Tanner Road, Flowery Branch, GA   30542
CEO: Kevin D. York, Gen. Mgr.   Tel: (770) 967-2196   Emp: 30
Bus: *Mfr./sale/service of portable and fixed gas*   Fax:(770) 967-1854   %FO: 100
    detection, fuel efficiency, pressure, velocity
    and emergency resuscitation equipment.

● **NORTHERN ENGINEERING IND PLC**
NEI House, Regent Centre, Newcastle upon Tyne, NE3 3SB, England
CEO: Terry Harrison, Chrm.   Tel: 44-121-454-3531   Emp: 22000
Bus: *Mfr. power station equipment, gears, boilers, etc.* Fax:44-121-455-8607

BELLISS & MORCOM (USA) INC.
1275 West Roosevelt Road, #125, West Chicago, IL   60185
CEO: Robert O'Brien, Pres.   Tel: (630) 231-9544   Emp: N/A
Bus: *Sales/service of industrial air and gas*   Fax:(630) 231-9018   %FO: 100
    compressors

● **OXFORD INSTRUMENTS, MEDICAL SYSTEMS DIVISON**
One Kimber Road, Abingdon OX14 1BZ, England
CEO: Jack M. Frost, Mng. Dir.   Tel: 44-235-533433   Emp: N/A
Bus: *Mfr.. patient monitoring systems.*   Fax:44-235-534465

OXFORD MEDICAL INSTRUMENTS INC.
11526 53rd Street North, Clearwater, FL   34620
CEO: Mike Dadswell, Pres.   Tel: (813) 573-4500   Emp: 40
Bus: *Distribution of patient monitoring systems.*   Fax:(813) 572-6836   %FO: 100

● **P&O CRUISES LTD.**
77 New Oxford Street, London WC1A 1PP, England
CEO: Tim Harris, Chrm.   Tel: 44-171-831-1234   Emp: N/A
Bus: *Passenger cruises.*   Fax:44-171-265-3018

     PRINCESS CRUISES
     10100 Santa Monica Blvd., Los Angeles, CA   90067-4189
     CEO: Peter Ratcliffe, Pres.   Tel: (310) 553-1770   Emp: 600
     Bus: *Passenger cruises*   Fax:(310) 557-8469   %FO: 100

● **P.E. INTERNATIONAL PLC**
Lincoln House, Wellington Crescent, Fradley Park, Lichfield, Staffordshire, England
CEO: Malcolm Coster, CEO   Tel: 44-1543-444222   Emp: 500
Bus: *Management consulting services to public and*   Fax:44-1543-418059
     private sectors.

     P.E. HANDLEY WALKER INC.
     6000 Freedom Square Drive, Cleveland, OH   44141
     CEO: R.I. Garrington, Pres.   Tel: (216) 524-2200   Emp: 25
     Bus: *Management consultants services to public*   Fax:(216) 524-1488   %FO: 100
     and private sectors.

● **PEARSON PLC**
Three Burlington Gardens, London W1X 1LE, England
CEO: Marjorie Scardino, CEO   Tel: 44-171-411-2000   Emp: 19400
Bus: *Newspapers & book publishing, visitor attractions,*   Fax:44-171-828-3342
     TV, investment banking.

     ADDISON-WESLEY PUBLISHING CO.
     Jacob Way, Reading, MA   01867
     CEO: J. Larry Jones, Pres.   Tel: (617) 944-3700   Emp: 500
     Bus: *Book publishing.*   Fax:(617) 944-9338   %FO: 100

     PEARSON, INC.
     30 Rockefeller Center, 50th Floor, New York, NY   10112-5095
     CEO: David M. Velt, Pres.   Tel: (212) 713-1919   Emp: N/A
     Bus: *US Headquarters. Newspapers & book*   Fax:(212) 713-1919   %FO: 100
     publishing, visitor attractions, TV, investment
     banking.

     PENGUIN BOOKS USA INC
     375 Hudson Street, New York, NY   10014
     CEO: Michael Jacobs, Pres.   Tel: (212) 366-2000   Emp: 180
     Bus: *Book publishing.*   Fax:(212) 366-2666   %FO: 100

     PUTNAM GROUP INC.
     200 Madison Avenue, New York, NY   10014
     CEO: Phyllis Grann, Pres.   Tel: (212) 366-2000   Emp: N/A
     Bus: *Book publishing.*   Fax:(212) 366-2606   %FO: 100

● **THE PENINSULAR & ORIENTAL STEAM NAVIGATION CO.**
79 Pall Mall, London SW1Y 5EJ, England
CEO: Sir Bruce D. Mac Phall, CEO　　　　　　　Tel: 44-171-930-4343　　Emp: 67000
Bus: *Real estate investment & development, ocean*　Fax:44-171-930-8572
　　 passenger/cargo shipping, construction services.
　　 (JV:CHELSFIELD PLC, UK).

　　BOVIS INC.
　　200 Park Avenue, 9th Floor, New York, NY　10166
　　CEO: Luther Crochrane, Pres.　　　　　　Tel: (212) 592-6800　　Emp: N/A
　　Bus: *Real estate development and construction.*　Fax:(212) 592-6988　%FO: 100

　　LAING PROPERTIES INC.
　　5901-B Peachtree Dunwoody Rd, Atlanta, GA　30328
　　CEO: Ned S. Holmes, Pres.　　　　　　　Tel: (770) 551-3400　　Emp: 352
　　Bus: *Invest, develop, manage real estate.*　Fax:(770) 551-3494　%FO: 100

　　LEHER MCGOVERN BOVIS, INC.
　　200 Park Avenue, 9th Floor, New York, NY　10166
　　CEO: Luther Cochrane, Pres.　　　　　　Tel: (212) 592-6700　　Emp: N/A
　　Bus: *Real estate development and construction.*　Fax:(212) 592-6988　%FO: JV

　　MCDEVITT STREET BOVIS, INC.
　　2400 Yorkmont Road, Charlotte, NC　28217
　　CEO: John Nicolay, EVP　　　　　　　　Tel: (704) 357-1919　　Emp: N/A
　　Bus: *Real estate development, engineering, and*　Fax:(704) 357-2854　%FO: JV
　　　　 construction services.

　　PRINCESS CRUISES
　　10100 Santa Monica Blvd., Los Angeles, CA　90067-4189
　　CEO: Peter G. Ratcliffe, Pres.　　　　　Tel: (310) 553-1770　　Emp: N/A
　　Bus: *International cruise shipping.*　　Fax:(310) 227-6175　%FO: 100

　　SCHAL BOVIS INC.
　　200 West Hubbard Street, Chicago, IL　60610
　　CEO: Jeffrey Arfsten, Pres.　　　　　　Tel: (312) 245-1000　　Emp: N/A
　　Bus: *Real estate development, engineering, and*　Fax:(312) 245-1379　%FO: JV
　　　　 construction services.

● **PILKINGTON BROTHERS PLC**
Prescot Rd, St. Helen's, Merseyside, WA1 D3T, England
CEO: Antony R. Pilkington, Chrm.　　　　　Tel: 44-174-428882　　Emp: N/A
Bus: *Mfr. glass, specialty glass products.*　　Fax:44-174-4692660

　　LIBBEY-OWENS-FORD COMPANY
　　PO Box　0799, Toledo, OH　43697-0799
　　CEO: Mark Schwabero & Steve Kalosis, Co-Pres.　Tel: (419) 247-3731　　Emp: N/A
　　Bus: *Mfr. glass, specialty glass products*　Fax:(419) 247-3821　%FO: 100

● **PRUDENTIAL CORP. PLC**
142 Holborn Bars, London EC1N 2NH, England
CEO: Michael G. Newmatch, Pres.   Tel: 44-171-405-9222   Emp: 35000
Bus: *Insurance and financial services.*   Fax:44-171-548-3725

     JACKSON NATIONAL LIFE INSURANCE CO.
     5901 Executive Drive, Lansing, MI   48911
     CEO: Robert P. Saltzman, Pres.   Tel: (517) 394-3400   Emp: 1300
     Bus: *Life insurance and annuities.*   Fax:(517) 394-7107   %FO: 100

● **RACAL ELECTRONICS PLC**
Western Road, Bracknell, Berkshire RG12 1RG, England
CEO: Sir Ernest Harrison, Chrm.   Tel: 44-1344-481222   Emp: 13000
Bus: *Diversified mfr. electronics; communications,*   Fax:44-1344-54119
     industrial, defense, health systems and equipment.

     EFI CORPORATION
     5357 Randall Place, Freemont, CA   94538
     CEO: R. Berrisford, Dir. Opers.   Tel: (510) 353-9900   Emp: N/A
     Bus: *Mfr. safety equipment.*   Fax:(510) 353-9939   %FO: 100

     RACAL ANTENNAS, INC.
     501 Tradeway, Mineral Wells, TX   76067
     CEO: Anthony Martin, VP   Tel: (940) 325-2341   Emp: N/A
     Bus: *Base station antennas.*   Fax:(940) 325-4377   %FO: 100

     RACAL AVIONICS INC.
     8851 Monard Drive, Silver Spring, MD   20910-1878
     CEO: S. Kemp, Gen. Mgr.   Tel: (301) 495-6695   Emp: N/A
     Bus: *Avionics equipment.*   Fax:(301) 585-7578   %FO: 100

     RACAL COMMUNICATIONS INC.
     5 Research Place, Rockville, MD   20850
     CEO: Mark Lipp, Pres.   Tel: (301) 948-4420   Emp: N/A
     Bus: *Mfr. tactical radios.*   Fax:(301) 948-6015   %FO: 100

     THE RACAL CORPORATION
     1601 N. Harrison Pkwy., Sunrise, FL   33323-2899
     CEO: Edward Bleckner Jr., Chrm.   Tel: (954) 846-1601   Emp: N/A
     Bus: *Holding company, U.S. headquarters.*   Fax:(954) 846-3030   %FO: 100
     diversified mfr. electronics; communications,
     industrial, defense, health systems &
     equipment.

     THE RACAL CORPORATION
     11 Penn Plaza, New York, NY   10001
     CEO: Edward W. Cheatham, VP   Tel: (212) 268-0918   Emp: N/A
     Bus: *Corporate communications center.*   Fax:(212) 563-9087   %FO: 100

RACAL HEALTH & SAFETY INC.
7305 Executive Way, Frederick, MD 21701
CEO: P. Cooper, Mng. Dir.   Tel: (301) 695-8200   Emp: N/A
Bus: *Health & safety equipment.*   Fax:(301) 695-4413   %FO: 100

RACAL INSTRUMENTS INC.
4 Goodyear Street, Irvine, CA 92718-2002
CEO: Gordon W. Taylor, Pres.   Tel: (714) 859-8999   Emp: N/A
Bus: *Test/measuring instruments.*   Fax:(714) 859-7139   %FO: 100

RACAL PELAGOS CORPORATION
5434 Ruffin Road, San Diego, CA 92123
CEO: Randall J. Ashley, SVP   Tel: (619) 292-8922   Emp: N/A
Bus: *Survey services.*   Fax:(619) 292-5308   %FO: 100

RACAL RECORDERS INC.
15375 Barranca Pkwy, Irvine, CA 92718
CEO: John Cummings, VP & Gen.Mgr.   Tel: (714) 727-3444   Emp: N/A
Bus: *Voice & data recorders.*   Fax:(714) 727-1774   %FO: 100

RACAL-NCS, INC.
3624 Westchase Drive, Houston, TX 77042
CEO: Anthony Harrison, Pres.   Tel: (713) 784-4482   Emp: N/A
Bus: *Marine & survey services.*   Fax:(713) 784-8162   %FO: 100

• RANK ORGANISATION PLC
6 Connaught Place, London W2 2EZ, England
CEO: Andrew Teare, CEO   Tel: 44-171-706-1111   Emp: 37500
Bus: *Diversified leisure, entertainment, holiday,*   Fax:44-171-262-9866
recreation and industrial group.

DELUXE LABORATORIES, INC.
1377 North Serrano Avenue, Hollywood, CA 90027
CEO: Cyril Drabinsky, Pres.   Tel: (213) 462-6171   Emp: N/A
Bus: *Research/mfr./processing film and video.*   Fax:(213) 466-1647   %FO: 100

DELUXE LABORATORIES, INC.
1377 North Serrano Avenue, Hollywood, CA 90027
CEO: Cyril Drabinsky, Pres.   Tel: (213) 462-6171   Emp: N/A
Bus: *Research/mfr. processing film and video*   Fax:(213) 466-1647   %FO: 100

HARD ROCK CAFÉ INTERNATIONAL, INC.
5401 South Kirkman Road, Ste 200, Orlando, FL 32819
CEO: James Berk, Pres.   Tel: (407) 351-6000   Emp: 3000+
Bus: *Chain of theme restaurants.*   Fax:(407) 352-2596   %FO: 100

HARD ROCK CAFÉ INTERNATIONAL, INC.
5401 South Kirkman Road, Ste. 200, Orlando, FL 32819
CEO: James Berk, Pres.   Tel: (407) 351-6000   Emp: 3000+
Bus: *Chain of theme restaurants*   Fax:(407) 352-2596   %FO: 100

RANK AMERICA, INC.
5 Concouse Pkwy, Suite 2400, Atlanta, GA   30328-5350

CEO: John H. Watson, EVP	Tel: (770) 392-9029	Emp: N/A
Bus: *U.S. headquarters of diversified leisure, entertainment, holiday, recreation & industrial group.*	Fax: (770) 392-0585	%FO: 100

RANK AMERICA, INC.
5 Concourse Pkwy., Ste. 2400, Atlanta, GA   30328

CEO: John H. Watson, Pres.	Tel: (770) 392-9029	Emp: N/A
Bus: *U.S. headquarters of diversified leisure, entertainment, holiday, recreation and industrial group.*	Fax: (770) 392-0585	%FO: 100

RANK TAYLOR HOBSON, INC.
2100 Golf Road, Ste. 350, Rolling Meadows, IL   60008

CEO: Roger Morton, Sr. VP & Gen.Mgr.	Tel: (847) 290-8090	Emp: 33
Bus: *Sale/service & engineering customization precision instruments to measure surface, roundness & optical features.*	Fax: (847) 290-1430	%FO: 100

RANK VIDEO SERVICES AMERICA, INC.
540 Lake Cook Road, Ste. 200, Deerfield, IL   60015

CEO: David Cuyler, Pres. & CEO	Tel: (847) 291-1150	Emp: N/A
Bus: *Sales/service and engineering customization precision instrument to measure surface, roundness and optical features.*	Fax: (847) 480-6077	%FO: 100

RANK VIDEO SERVICES AMERICA, INC.
540 Lake Cook Road #200, Deerfield, IL   60015

CEO: David Cuyler, Pres.	Tel: (847) 291-1150	Emp: N/A
Bus: *Sale/service & engineering customization precision instruments to measure surface, roundness & optical features.*	Fax: (847) 480-6077	%FO: 100

RESORTS USA, INC.
Route 209, Bushkill, PA   18324

CEO: Daniel Howells, Pres.	Tel: (717) 588-6661	Emp: N/A
Bus: *Leisure time industry.*	Fax: (717) 588-2787	%FO: 100

RESORTS USA, INC.
Route 209, Bushkill, PA   18324

CEO: Daniel Howells, Pres.	Tel: (871) 758-8666	Emp: N/A
Bus: *Leisure time industry*	Fax: (717) 588-2787	%FO: 100

● **READICUT INTL PLC**
PO Box 15, Clifton Mills, Brighouse, West Yorkshire HD6 4ET, England
CEO: Clive Shaw, Mng. Dir.   Tel: 44-484-721233   Emp: 4500
Bus: *Industrial products and services; carpets, fibers,*   Fax:44-484-716135
home and automobile textile.

REGAL RUGS INC.
819 Buckeye Street, North Vernon, IN   47265
CEO: R. Andrew Smithson, Pres. & CEO   Tel: (812) 346-3601   Emp: 300
Bus: *Mfr. fashion bath and area rugs.*   Fax:(812) 346-7112   %FO: 100

● **RECKITT & COLMAN PLC**
Burlington Lane, London W4 2RW, England
CEO: Vernon L. Sankey, CEO   Tel: 44-181-994-6464   Emp: 19000
Bus: *Mfr./marketing branded/generic food, wine,*   Fax:44-181-994-8920
pharmaceuticals, household & leisure products.

RECKITT & COLMAN, INC.
1655 Valley Road, P O Box 943, Wayne, NJ   07474
CEO: Joseph Healy, Pres.   Tel: (201) 633-3600   Emp: N/A
Bus: *Mfr./marketing branded/generic food, wine,*   Fax:(201) 573-5858   %FO: 100
pharmaceuticals, household & leisure
products.

● **REDLAND PLC**
Redland House, Reigate, Surrey R2 0SJ, England
CEO: Robert Napier, CEO   Tel: 44-173-724-2488   Emp: N/A
Bus: *Mfr. construction materials globally; roofing tiles,*   Fax:44-173-722-1938
clay bricks, and aggregate materials.

MONIER LIFETILE, INC.
Jamboree Center , One Park Plaza, #900, Irvine, CA   92714
CEO: Don Henshaw, Pres.   Tel: (714) 756-1605   Emp: N/A
Bus: *Mfr./distributor construction materials;*   Fax:(714) 756-2401   %FO: JV
roofing tiles, clay bricks, and aggregate
materials.

REDLAND GENSTAR STONE PRODUCTS COMPANY
300 East Joppa Road, Ste. 200, Towson, MD   21286
CEO: Donald Bowman, Pres.   Tel: (410) 847-3300   Emp: N/A
Bus: *Mfr./distributor construction materials;*   Fax:(410) 847-3308   %FO: 100
roofing tiles, clay bricks, and aggregate
materials.

WESTERN MOBILE, INC.
1400 West 64th Street, Denver, CO   80221
CEO: Patrick H. Walker, Pres. & CEO   Tel: (303) 657-4000   Emp: 1800
Bus: *Mfr./distributor construction materials;*   Fax:(303) 657-4407   %FO: 100
roofing tiles, clay bricks, and aggregate
materials.

• REED ELSEVIERPLC

Reed House, 6 Chesterfield Gardens, London W1A 1EJ, England

CEO: Nigel Stapleton, Chrm.   Tel: 44-171-499-4020   Emp: 30500

Bus: *Publishing holding company. JV of Reed Int'l plc,*   Fax:44-171-491-8212
London,(50%) ; Elsevier NV, Amsterdam,(50%).
Information products.

CAHNERS PUBLISHING COMPANY

275 Washington Street, Newton, MA   02158

CEO: Bruce Barnet, Chrm.   Tel: (617) 964-3030   Emp: N/A

Bus: *Publishing.*   Fax:(617) 558-4700   %FO: 100

CONGRESSIONAL INFORMATION SERVICE

4520 East-West Hwy, Bethesda, MD   20814

CEO: Paul Massa, Pres.   Tel: (301) 654-1550   Emp: N/A

Bus: *Publishing services.*   Fax:(301) 654-4033   %FO: 100

ELSEVIER SCIENCE INC.

655 Avenue of the Americas, New York, NY   10010

CEO: Russell White, Pres.   Tel: (212) 989-5800   Emp: N/A

Bus: *Publisher of science & medical journals.* Fax:(212) 633-3990   %FO: 100

EXCERPTA MEDICA INC.

105 Raider Blvd., Belle Mead, NJ   08502

CEO: Kevin Connolly, Pres.   Tel: (908) 874-8550   Emp: N/A

Bus: *Publishing.*   Fax:(908) 874-6545   %FO: 100

GORDON PUBLICATIONS INC., CAHNERS PUBLISHING

301 Gibraltar Drive, PO Box 650, Morris Plains, NJ   07950

CEO: David Exola, Sr. V.P.   Tel: (201) 292-5100   Emp: N/A

Bus: *Publishing.*   Fax:(201) 605-1220   %FO: 100

GREENWOOD PUBLISHING GROUP INC.

88 Post Road West, PO Box 5007, Westport, CT   06881

CEO: Robert Hagelstein, Pres.   Tel: (203) 226-3571   Emp: N/A

Bus: *Publishing*   Fax:(203) 222-1502   %FO: 100

LEXIS NEXIS

9393 Springboro Pike, Miamisburg, OH   45342

CEO: Ira Siegel, Pres.   Tel: (937) 865-7000   Emp: N/A

Bus: *On-line information service; reference*   Fax:(937) 865-1555   %FO: 100
information & databases.

REED ELSEVIER TRAVEL GROUP INC.

500 Plaza Drive, Secaucus, NJ   07096

CEO: Kathy Misonas, CEO   Tel: (201) 902-2000   Emp: N/A

Bus: *Travel related publishing & services.*   Fax:(201) 319-1726   %FO: 100

REED ELSEVIER, INC.
275 Washington Street, Newton, MA   02158
CEO: Bruce A. Barnet, Pres.	Tel: (617) 964-3030	Emp: N/A
Bus: *Publishing.*	Fax:(617) 558-4667	%FO: 100

REED ELSEVIER, INC.
200 Park Avenue, New York, NY   10166
CEO: Nigel Stapleton, Co. Chrm.	Tel: (212) 309-8136	Emp: N/A
Bus: *U.S. headquarters for publishing holding company. JV of Reed Int'l plc, London,(50%) ; Elsevier NV, Amsterdam,(50%).*	Fax:(212) 309-7818	%FO: 100

REED EXHIBITION CO.
383 Main Avenue, Norwalk, CT   06851
CEO: Pat Dolson, Pres.	Tel: (203) 840-4800	Emp: N/A
Bus: *Exhibition/conference organization*	Fax:(203) 840-9400	%FO: 100

SPRINGHOUSE CORPORATION
1111 Bethlehem Pike, Springhouse, PA   19477
CEO: Kevin Hurley, Pres.	Tel: (215) 646-8700	Emp: N/A
Bus: *Publishing.*	Fax:(215) 628-3080	%FO: 100

● **RENOLD PLC**
Wythenshawe, Manchester M22 5WL, England
CEO: David Cotteril, Grp.Mng.Dir.	Tel: 44-161-437778	Emp: 2000
Bus: *Transmission chain, gears, couplings, machine tools.*	Fax:44-161-4375221	

RENOLD AJAX, INC.
100 Bourne Street, PO Box A, Westfield, NY   14787
CEO: Tom Murrer, Pres.	Tel: (716) 326-3121	Emp: 130
Bus: *Mfr. rolling mill spindles, coupling, gears, vibrators, material handling vibratory equipment.*	Fax:(716) 326-6121	%FO: 100

● **RENTOKIL GROUP TLC**
Rentokil UK Felcourt, E. Grinsteadt, West Sussex RH19 21Y, England
CEO: Alan Ross Jones, Pres.	Tel: 44-134-283-3022	Emp: 70000
Bus: *Transportation, electronic & leisure, industry & construction service.*	Fax:44-134-283-5176	

DSI TRANSPORTS, INC.
15600 JFK Boulevard, Ste. 200, Houston, TX   77267
CEO: Philip Abraira, Pres.	Tel: (281) 985-0000	Emp: N/A
Bus: *Tank truck transportation company.*	Fax:(281) 590-1117	%FO: 100

RENTOKIL INITIAL
17 Executive Park South, Ste. 600, Atlanta, GA   30329
CEO: Clive Thompson, Pres.	Tel: (404) 321-6067	Emp: N/A
Bus: *Rental/staffing and resort management.*	Fax:(404) 248-1782	%FO: 100

RENTOKIL, INC.
3750 West Deerfield Road, Riverwoods, IL   60015
CEO: Terry Anderson, Pres.   Tel: (847) 634-4250   Emp: N/A
Bus: *Plants and pest control specialists.*   Fax:(847) 634-6820   %FO: 100

TALENT TREE STAFFING SERVICES, INC.
9703 Richmond Avenue, Houston, TX   77042
CEO: William Sadler, Pres.   Tel: (713) 789-1818   Emp: N/A
Bus: *Personnel staffing.*   Fax:(713) 974-6507   %FO: 100

● **REUTERS HOLDINGS PLC**
85 Fleet Street, London EC4P 4AJ, England
CEO: Peter J.D. Job, CEO   Tel: 44-171-250-1122   Emp: 14500
Bus: *Produces and distributes news and financial*   Fax:44-171-510-5896
     information and photographs globally.

     REUTERS AMERICA, INC.
     1700 Broadway, New York, NY   10019
     CEO: Andre Villeneuve, Pres.   Tel: (212) 603-3300   Emp: N/A
     Bus: *U.S. headquarters. Produces and distributes*   Fax:(212) 247-0346   %FO: 100
       news and financial information and
       photographs globally.

● **REXAM PLC**
114, Knightsbridge, London SW1X 7NN, England
CEO: J. Lancaster, Chrm.   Tel: 44-171-584-7070   Emp: 26000
Bus: *Holding company: print, packaging, building*   Fax:44-171-581-1149
     materials.

     MITEK, INC.
     14515 N. Outer Forty Road, Ste. 300, Chesterfield, MO   63017
     CEO: Gene Tombs, Pres.   Tel: (314) 434-1200   Emp: N/A
     Bus: *Mfr. metal connector plates & builders*   Fax:(314) 434-5334   %FO: 100
       hardware.

     REXAM CLOSURES, INC.
     3245 Kansas Road, Evansville, IN   47711
     CEO: Clauf Nilstoft, Pres.   Tel: (812) 867-6671   Emp: N/A
     Bus: *Mfr. child-resistant, dispensing & standard*   Fax:(812) 867-7802   %FO: 100
       screw closures.

     REXAM COSMETIC PACKAGING, INC.
     129 Industrial Lane, Torrington, CT   06790
     CEO: Tom Faath, Pres.   Tel: (860) 482-4314   Emp: N/A
     Bus: *Mfr. cosmetic packaging, compacts, powder*   Fax:(860) 496-9849   %FO: 100
       boxes, deodorant sticks.

REXAM CUSTOM, INC.
700 Crestdale Street, PO Box 368, Matthews, NC 28106
CEO: Wayne Moore, Pres.   Tel: (704) 847-9171   Emp: N/A
Bus: *Custom coating & laminating.*   Fax:(704) 845-4307   %FO: 100

REXAM DSI, INC.
One Canal Street, South Hadley, MA   01075
CEO: Anthony Maclaurin, Pres.   Tel: (413) 533-0699   Emp: N/A
Bus: *Mfr. decorative covering materials.*   Fax:(413) 535-2458   %FO: 100

REXAM EXTRUSIONS, INC.
3555 Moser Street, Oshkosh, WI   54901
CEO: Ron Johnson, Pres.   Tel: (414) 236-2888   Emp: N/A
Bus: *Mfr. cast extrusion film & sheet.*   Fax:(414) 236-2882   %FO: 100

REXAM GRAPHICS, INC.
28 Gaylord Street, South Hadley, MA   01075
CEO: Robert Champigny, Pres.   Tel: (413) 536-7800   Emp: N/A
Bus: *Mfr. precision coated imaging films & papers.*   Fax:(413) 536-6226   %FO: 100

REXAM MEDICAL PACKAGING, INC.
4101 Lien Road, PO Box 7730, Madison, WI   53707-7730
CEO: Ron Johnson, Pres.   Tel: (608) 249-0404   Emp: 60
Bus: *Coating, printing, conversion of paper &*   Fax:(608) 249-4175   %FO: 100
    plastic films for flexible medical packaging.

REXAM MEDICAL PACKAGING, INC.
8235 220th Street West, PO Box 1089, Lakeville, MN   55044-9013
CEO: David Timmons, Pres.   Tel: (612) 469-5461   Emp: N/A
Bus: *Mfr. blown extrusion film, protection*   Fax:(612) 469-5337   %FO: 100
    packaging.

REXAM MEDICAL PACKAGING, INC.
1919 Butterfield Road, Mundelein, IL   60060-9735
CEO: Robert Gluskin, Pres.   Tel: (847) 362-9000   Emp: N/A
Bus: *Mfr. blown film, surgical drapes, adhesive*   Fax:(847) 918-4660   %FO: 100
    materials, sterilizable medical pouches & bags.

REXAM METALLISIN, INC.
915 Harger Road, Suite 310, Oak Brook, IL   60521
CEO: Dan Napralla, Pres.   Tel: (630) 586-0200   Emp: N/A
Bus: *Mfr. metalized & coated films & papers.*   Fax:(630) 586-0208   %FO: 100

REXAM MULOX USA, INC.
7592 Northeast Industrial Blvd., Macon, GA   31297
CEO: Peter Gaymon, Pres.   Tel: (912) 784-9040   Emp: N/A
Bus: *Mfr. flexible intermediate bulk containers.*   Fax:(912) 788-3920   %FO: 100

REXAM PERFORMANCE PRODUCTS, INC.
P.O.Box 800, Lancaster, SC   29720
CEO: Wayne Moore, Pres.   Tel: (803) 285-9401   Emp: N/A
Bus: *Mfr. coated & laminated films, foil, fabric &*   Fax:(803) 285-4631   %FO: 100
      paper.

REXAM RELEASE, INC.
5001 West 66th Street, Bedford Park, IL   60638
CEO: Mike Durkin, Mgr.   Tel: (708) 458-0777   Emp: N/A
Bus: *Mfr. silicone-coated release films & papers.*   Fax:(708) 458-4907   %FO: 100

REXHAM INC
4201 Congress Street, #340, Charlotte, NC   28209
CEO: Frank Brown, Pres.   Tel: (704) 551-1500   Emp: N/A
Bus: *Corporate headquarters.*   Fax:(704) 551-1570   %FO: 100

● **ROLLS-ROYCE PLC**
65 Buckingham Gate, London SW1E 6AT, England
CEO: John E.V. Rose, CEO   Tel: 44-171-222-9020   Emp: 43500
Bus: *Develops/mfr. turbine engines for aerospace, marine*   Fax:44-171-227-9178
      and industrial power uses.

    ROLLS-ROYCE, INC.
    11911 Freedom Drive, Reston, VA   20190
    CEO: John W. Sandford, Pres.   Tel: (703) 834-1700   Emp: N/A
    Bus: *U.S. headquarters. Develops/mfr. turbine*   Fax:(703) 709-6086   %FO: 100
          engines for aerospace, marine and industrial
          power uses.

● **ROYAL & SUN ALLIANCE GLOBAL**
Leadenhall Court, One Leadenhall Street, London, Engalnd 3V 1PP
CEO: Tel: 44-171-337-2345   Emp: 40000
Bus: *Insurance services.*   Fax:44-171-337-5764

    ROYAL & SUN ALLIANCE GLOBAL
    88 Pine Street, New York, NY   10005
    CEO: Charles J. Bird, CEO   Tel: (212) 510-1100   Emp: 5000
    Bus: *Insurance services.*   Fax:(212) 510-1111   %FO: 100

● **ROYAL INSURANCE PLC**
One Corn Hill, London EC3V 3QR, England
CEO: Richard Gamble, CEO   Tel: 44-171-283-4300   Emp: 40000
Bus: *Insurance services. Sub of Royal & Sun Alliance*   Fax:44-171-283-5282
      Global.

    ROYAL INSURANCE COMPANY OF AMERICA, INC.
    9300 Arrowpoint Road, Charlotte, NC   28217
    CEO: Robert Mendelsohn, Pres.   Tel: (704) 522-2000   Emp: 5000
    Bus: *Insurance services.*   Fax:(704) 522-3200   %FO: 100

• THE RTZ CORPORATION, PLC.

6 St. James's Square, London SW1Y 4LD, England
CEO: Robert P. Wilson, CEO   Tel: 44-171-930-2399   Emp: 45000
Bus: *Natural resources; metals & mining activities. Sub*   Fax:44-171-930-3249
     along with Australian CRA Ltd. of RTZ-CRA, to be
     renamed Rio Tinto.

KENNECOTT ENERGY COMPANY

Box 3009
505 S. Gillette Avenue, Gillette, WY   82717
CEO: Greg H. Boyce, Pres.   Tel: (307) 587-6000   Emp: 54
Bus: *Coal mining.*   Fax:(307) 687-6036   %FO: 100

KENNECOTT EXPLORATION COMPANY

224 North 2200 West, Salt Lake City, UT   84116
CEO: Bill Orchow, Pres.   Tel: (801) 238-2400   Emp: 822
Bus: *Mining/refining precious and base metals.*   Fax:(801) 322-7349   %FO: 100

KENNECOTT UTAH COPPER CORP.

8315 West 3595 South, Magna, UT   84044
CEO: Bruce D. Farmer, Pres.   Tel: (801) 252-3000   Emp: 2200
Bus: *Mining/refining base & precious metals.*   Fax:(801) 252-3303   %FO: 100

LUZENAC AMERICA, INC.

9000 East Nichols Street
Ste. 200, Englewood, CO   80112
CEO: Thomas Kwasizur, Pres.   Tel: (303) 643-0400   Emp: 50
Bus: *Industrial minerals.*   Fax:(303) 643-0446   %FO: 100

U. S. BORAX, INC.

P.O. Box 926, 26877 Tourney Road, Valencia, CA   91380
CEO: I. L. White-Thomson, Pres.   Tel: (805) 251-5400   Emp: 200
Bus: *Mining/refining borates.*   Fax:(805) 287-5495   %FO: 100

SAATCHI & SAATCHI CO PLC

80 Charlotte Street, London W1A 1AQ, England
CEO: Alan Bishop, CEO   Tel: 44-171-636-5060   Emp: N/A
Bus: *Advertising agency.*   Fax:44-171-631-0312

BACKER SPIELVOGEL BATES INC.

405 Lexington Avenue, New York, NY   10174
CEO: Carl Spielvogel, Chrm.   Tel: (212) 297-7000   Emp: 5000
Bus: *Advertising agency.*   Fax:(212) 986-0270   %FO: 100

SAATCHI & SAATCHI HOLDINGS USA

375 Hudson Street, New York, NY   10014
CEO: Kevin Roberts, CEO   Tel: (212) 463-2000   Emp: 400
Bus: *Advertising agencies.*   Fax:(212) 463-2000   %FO: 100

● **J. SAINSBURY PLC**
Stamford House, Stamford Street, London SE1 9LL, England
CEO: David Sainsbury, Chrm.   Tel: 44-171-921-6000   Emp: 160000
Bus: *Retail food distribution, pig production, home*   Fax:44-171-921-6132
improvement centers.

    GIANT FOOD, INC.
    6300 Sherroff Road, Landover, MD   20785
    CEO: Peter Manos, Pres.   Tel: (301) 341-4100   Emp: N/A
    Bus: *Owner/operator supermarket chain; retailer.*   Fax:(301) 341-4582   %FO: 100

    SHAW'S SUPERMARKETS, INC.
    140 Laurel Street, Bridgewater, MA   02333
    CEO: Philip L. Francis, Pres.   Tel: (508) 378-7211   Emp: 20000
    Bus: *Owner/operator supermarket chain; retailer.*   Fax:(508) 378-7680   %FO: 100

● **SAUDI INTERNATIONAL BANK**
99 Bishops Gate, London EC2M 3TB, England
CEO: Peter de Roos, Dir.   Tel: 44-171-638-2323   Emp: N/A
Bus: *Commercial banking services.*   Fax:44-171-628-8633

    SAUDI INTERNATIONAL BANK
    520 Madison Avenue, New York, NY   10022
    CEO: Phillip Murray, Gen. Mgr.   Tel: (212) 355-6530   Emp: N/A
    Bus: *International banking services.*   Fax:(212) 702-1045   %FO: 100

● **SCHEDULING TECH GROUP LTD.**
The Hounslow Centre, Lampton Toad, Hounslow, Middlesex TW3 1JB, England
CEO: G. D. Rowett, CEO   Tel: 44-181-572-3111   Emp: N/A
Bus: *Manufacturer of software.*   Fax:44-181-577-5605

    SCHEDULING TECHNOLOGY, INC.
    100 Medway Road, Milford, MA   01757-2915
    CEO: Tap H. Luke, CEO   Tel: (508) 478-7063   Emp: N/A
    Bus: *Software distributor.*   Fax:(508) 634-0379   %FO: 100

● **SCHRODERS PLC**
120 Cheapside, London EC2V 6DS, England
CEO: George W. Mallinckrodt, Chrm.   Tel: 44-171-382-6000   Emp: N/A
Bus: *Financial services.*   Fax:44-171-382-6965

    SCHRODERS INC.
    787 Seventh Avenue, New York, NY   10019
    CEO: Ash Williams, Pres.   Tel: (212) 841-3800   Emp: N/A
    Bus: *Financial services*   Fax:(212) 582-1460   %FO: 100

●SEDGWIK NOBLE LOWNDES
Norfolk House, Wellesley Rd, Croydon CR9 3EB, England
CEO: Alistair M. Hunter, Mng. Dir.- Global Div.   Tel: 44-171-686 2466   Emp: 1850
Bus: *Employee benefits consultants, and actuaries.*   Fax:44-171-681 1458

> **SEDGWIK NOBLE LOWNDES**
> 525 W. Monroe Street, #2405, Chicago, IL   60606
> CEO: Alistair M. Hunter, Mng. Dir.- Global Div.   Tel: (312) 648-1919   Emp: 35
> Bus: *Employee benefits, consultants & actuaries.*   Fax:(312) 648-0936   %FO: 100

●SEVERN TRENT, PLC.
2297 Coventry Road, Sheldon, Birmingham B26 3PU, England
CEO: Victor Cocker, CEO   Tel: 44-121-722-4000   Emp: N/A
Bus: *Provides water and waste management services.*   Fax:44-121-722-6150

> **SEVERN TRENT SYSTEMS, INC.**
> 20405 Highway 249, Suite 600, Houston, TX   77070
> CEO: Jim Oliver, Pres.   Tel: (280) 320-7100   Emp: 80
> Bus: *Provides water and waste management*   Fax:(280) 321-7111   %FO: 100
> *services.*

> **SEVERN TRENT US, INC.**
> 2980 Advance Lane, Colmar, PA   18915
> CEO: Kenneth Kelly, Pres.   Tel: (215) 997-6530   Emp: 2
> Bus: *Provides water and waste management*   Fax:(215) 997-6533   %FO: 100
> *services.*

> **ST ENVIRONMENT SERVICES**
> 16337 Park Row, Houston, TX   77084
> CEO: Rennie T. Quinn, Pres.   Tel: (281) 578-4200   Emp: 200
> Bus: *Provides water and waste management*   Fax:(281) 398-3550   %FO: 100
> *services.*

SHELL CHEMICAL
Shell Centre, London SE17NA, England
CEO: J. Sloane, CEO   Tel: 44-171-934-1234   Emp: N/A
Bus: *Gas/chemical company.*   Fax:44-171-934-7169

> **SHELL OIL COMPANY**
> One Shell Plaza, Houston, TX   77002
> CEO: J. Sloane, Pres.   Tel: (713) 241-6161   Emp: N/A
> Bus: *Oil and gas; JV with Royal Dutch, The*   Fax:(713) 241-4044   %FO: JV
> *Netherlands.*

• THE SHELL TRANSPORT & TRADING CO PLC
Shell Centre,Waterloo, London SE1 7NA, England
CEO: Philip J. Carroll, CEO   Tel: 44-171-934-1234   Emp: N/A
Bus: *Holding company: exploration & prod*   Fax:44-171-934-8060
    oil/gas/minerals; chemicals, metals (see joint
    parent: ROYAL DUTCH PETROLEUM CO.
    Netherlands)

SHELL OIL COMPANY
One Shell Plaza, 900 Louisiana Street, Houston, TX   77002
CEO: Philip J. Carroll, Pres. & CEO   Tel: (713) 241-6161   Emp: 22000
Bus: *Exploration/prod oil, gas, chemicals and*   Fax:(713) 241-4044   %FO: 100
    related products (Royal Dutch/Shell Group).

• SIEBE PLC
Saxon House, 2-4 Victoria Street, Windsor, Berkshire, SL4 1EN, England
CEO: Barrie Stephens, Chrm.   Tel: 44-753-855411   Emp: N/A
Bus: *Holding company; engineering services.*   Fax:44-753-840638

THE FOXBORO COMPANY
Bristol Park, Foxboro, MA   02035
CEO: George W Sarney, Pres.   Tel: (508) 543-8750   Emp: N/A
Bus: *Mfr. industrial automation system.*   Fax:(508) 543-6750   %FO: 100

RANCO, INC,
PO Box 248, Dublin, OH   43017
CEO: John W Reid, Pres.   Tel: (614) 873-9200   Emp: N/A
Bus: *Mfr. controls, relays, etc., for refrigeration, air*   Fax:(614) 873-9290   %FO: 100
    conditioning & automotive industry.

ROBERTSHAW CONTROLS COMPANY
2809 Emerywood Pkwy, Richmond, VA   23261
CEO: B. A. Henderson, Pres.   Tel: (804) 756-6500   Emp: N/A
Bus: *Mfr./wholesale control system & products for*   Fax:(804) 756-6563   %FO: 100
    home & industry.

SIEBE ENVIRONMENTAL CONTROLS
1354 Clifford Avenue, Loves Park, IL   61111
CEO: R. Armbrust, Pres.   Tel: (815) 637-3000   Emp: N/A
Bus: *Mfr. environmental & power controls.*   Fax:(815) 637-5305   %FO: 100

SIEBE NORTH, INC.
4090 Azalea Drive, Charleston, SC   29415
CEO: J.R. Schmidt, Pres.   Tel: (803) 554-0660   Emp: N/A
Bus: *Mfr. safety & life support equipment.*   Fax:(803) 744-2857   %FO: 100

● SIMMONS & SIMMONS
21 Wilson Street, London EC2M 2TX, England
CEO: William J. Knight, MNg. Ptr. Tel: 44-171-628-2020 Emp: N/A
Bus: *Full service, international law firm.* Fax: 44-171-628-2070

SIMMONS & SIMMONS
115 East 57th Street, New York, NY 10022
CEO: Alistard S. Bird, CEO Tel: (212) 688-6620 Emp: N/A
Bus: *Full service, international law firm.* Fax: (212) 355-3594 %FO: 100%

● SIMON ENGINEERING PLC
Simon House, 6 Eaton Gate, London SW1W 9BJ, England
CEO: M.C.S. Dixson, CEO Tel: 44-171-730-0777 Emp: 4000
Bus: *Access equipment, process engineer & bulk storage* Fax: 44-171-881-2200
for liquids, solids & gases

SIMON AERIALS INC.
10600 West Brown Deer Road, Milwaukee, WI 53224
CEO: M.D. O'Toole, Pres. Tel: (414) 355-0802 Emp: 190
Bus: *Mfr./sale/service self-propelled booms,* Fax: (414) 355-0832 %FO: 100
scissors lifts, trailer-mounted lifts, aircraft de-
icers.

SIMON LADDER TOWERS INC.
64 Cocalico Creek Road, Ephrata, PA 17522
CEO: S. Gerber, Pres. Tel: (717) 859-1176 Emp: 370
Bus: *Mfr./sale/service telescoping ladders &* Fax: (717) 859-2774 %FO: 100
platforms for fire-fighting operations.

SIMON U S HOLDINGS INC.
8044 Montgomery Rd, #270, Cincinnati, OH 45236
CEO: T. J. Redburn, Pres. Tel: (513) 792-2300 Emp: N/A
Bus: *Holding company.* Fax: (513) 792-2312 %FO: 100

SIMON-TELELECT INC.
600 Oakwood Road, P O Box 1150, Watertown, SD 57201
CEO: Ken Mikesell, Pres. Tel: (605) 882-4000 Emp: 545
Bus: *Mfr./sale/service digger derricks, telescopic &* Fax: (605) 882-1842 %FO: 100
insulated truck-mounted platforms.

SLAUGHTER AND MAY
35 Basinghall Street, London EC2V 5DB, England
CEO: Giles Henderson, MNg. Ptnr. Tel: 44-171-600-1200 Emp: N/A
Bus: *International law firm.* Fax: 44-171-726-0038

SLAUGHTER AND MAY
126 East 56th Street, New York, NY 10022-3613
CEO: P.A.S. Grindrod, CEO Tel: (212) 888-1112 Emp: N/A
Bus: *International law firm.* Fax: (212) 888-1170 %FO: 100

● **SMITH & NEPHEW, INC.**
2 Temple Place, Victoria Embankment, London WC2R-3BP, England
CEO: Chril J. O'Donnell, CEO   Tel: 44-171-836-7922   Emp: 12000
Bus: *Develop/mfr./marketing healthcare products; tissue*   Fax:44-171-240-7088
     repair.

     SMITH & NEPHEW, INC. - Wound Mgmt. Div.
     11775 Starkey Road, Largo, FL   33773
     CEO: Ron Sparks, Pres.   Tel: (813) 392-1261   Emp: N/A
     Bus: *Develop/mfr./marketing healthcare products;*   Fax:(813) 399-3498   %FO: 100
       wound care products.

     SMITH & NEPHEW, INC. - Rehabilitation Div.
     N104 W13400 Donges Bay Road, Germantown, WI   53022
     CEO: John Clark, Pres.   Tel: (414) 251-7840   Emp: 325
     Bus: *Develop/mfr./marketing healthcare products;*   Fax:(414) 251-7758   %FO: 100
       physical rehabilitation products.

     SMITH & NEPHEW, INC. - Endoscopy Div.
     160 Dascomb Road, Andover, MA   01810
     CEO: Crispin Simon, Pres.   Tel: (508) 749-1000   Emp: N/A
     Bus: *Develop/mfr./marketing healthcare products;*   Fax:(508) 749-1212   %FO: 100
       endoscopy products.

     SMITH & NEPHEW, INC. - Casting Div.
     2500 Distribution Street, Charlotte, NC   28203
     CEO: Bruce Parker, Pres.   Tel: (704) 331-0600   Emp: N/A
     Bus: *Develop/mfr./marketing healthcare products;*   Fax:(704) 358-4558   %FO: 100
       casting products.

     SMITH & NEPHEW, INC. - DonJoy Div.
     2777 Loker Avenue West, Carlsbad, CA   92008
     CEO: Les Cross, Pres.   Tel: (760) 438-9091   Emp: N/A
     Bus: *Develop/mfr./marketing healthcare products.*   Fax:(760) 438-3210   %FO: 100

     SMITH & NEPHEW, INC. - ENT Div.
     2925 Appling Road, Bartlett, TN   38134
     CEO: Jerry Dowdy, SVP & Gen. Mgr.   Tel: (901) 373-0200   Emp: N/A
     Bus: *Develop/mfr./marketing healthcare products;*   Fax:(901) 373-0220   %FO: 100
       ENT.

     SMITH & NEPHEW, INC.
     1450 Brooks Road, Memphis, TN   38116
     CEO: Jack R. Blair, Pres.   Tel: (901) 396-2121   Emp: N/A
     Bus: *North America Headquarters.*   Fax:(901) 348-6151   %FO: 100
       Develop/mfr./marketing healthcare products;
       tissue repair.

SMITH & NEPHEW, INC. - Orthopedic Div,
1450 Brooks Road, Memphis, TN   38116
CEO: Larry W. Papasan, Pres.   Tel: (901) 396-2121   Emp: N/A
Bus: *Develop/mfr./marketing healthcare products;*   Fax:(901) 348-6151   %FO: 100
    bone, joints.

SMITH & NEPHEW, INC. - Healthcare Div.
1450 Brooks Road, Memphis, TN   38116
CEO: Brian Splan, Pres.   Tel: (901) 396-2121   Emp: N/A
Bus: *Develop/mfr./marketing healthcare products;*   Fax:(901) 348-6151   %FO: 100
    tissue repair.

● **SMITHKLINE BEECHAM**
One New Horizon Ct, Brentford, Middlesex TW8 9EP, England
CEO: Jan Leschly, CEO   Tel: 44-181 975 2000   Emp: 52000
Bus: *Development/mfr./marketing human & animal*   Fax:44-181 975 2764
    health care products, over-counter medicines;
    clinical lab testing services; healthcare services.

    SMITHKLINE BEECHAM
    1020 19th Street, NW, Suite 420, Washington, DC   20036
    CEO: Burt E. Rosen, VP & Dir.   Tel: (202) 452-8490   Emp: N/A
    Bus: *U.S. governments affairs representative office.*   Fax:(202) 452-8489   %FO: 100

    SMITHKLINE BEECHAM
    One Franklin Plaza. P.O.Box 7929, Philadelphia, PA   19101
    CEO: Jan Leschly, CEO   Tel: (215) 751-4000   Emp: 22000
    Bus: *Develop /mfr./marketing human & animal*   Fax:(215) 751-3400   %FO: 100
        health care products, over-counter medicines;
        clinical lab testing services; healthcare
        services.

● **SMITHS INDUSTRIES PLC**
765 Finchley Road, London NW11 8DS, England
CEO: Keith Butler-Wheelhouse, CEO   Tel: 44-181 458-3232   Emp: 12000
Bus: *Mfr. aerospace electronics, medical system,*   Fax:44-181 458-4380
    specialized industrial products.

    DURA-VENT
    1177 Markley Drive, Plymouth, IN   46563
    CEO: Barbara Dunbar, Mgr.   Tel: (219) 936-2432   Emp: 36
    Bus: *Mfr. industrial ducting.*   Fax:(219) 936-2505   %FO: 100

    FLEXIBLE TECHNOLOGIES INC.
    Carwellyn Road, PO Box 888, Abbeville, SC   29620
    CEO: N/A   Tel: (864) 459-5441   Emp: 470
    Bus: *Mfr. ducting & hosing.*   Fax:(864) 459-8282   %FO: 100

HYPERTRONICS CORP.
16 Brent Drive, Hudson, MA   01749
CEO: Richard T. Downey, Pres.   Tel: (508) 568-0451   Emp: 145
Bus: *Mfr. electronic connectors.*   Fax:(508) 568-0680   %FO: 100

ICORE INTL INC.
180 North Wolfe Road, Sunnyvale, CA   94086
CEO: Ian Humphries, Pres.   Tel: (408) 732-5400   Emp: 50
Bus: *Mfr. conduit.*   Fax:(408) 720-8507   %FO: 100

INTERTECH RESOURCES
5100 Tice Street, Ft. Myers, FL   33905
CEO: John MacNeil, Pres.   Tel: (813) 694-2104   Emp: 400
Bus: *Mfr. medical devices.*   Fax:(813) 693-6869   %FO: 100

LELAND ELECTROSYSTEMS, INC.
740 East National Road, Vandalia, OH   45377
CEO: John MacNeil, Pres.   Tel: (937) 898-5881   Emp: 300
Bus: *Mfr. avionics.*   Fax:(937) 898-5819   %FO: 100

RESPIRATORY SUPPORT PRDTS INC
2552 McGaw Avenue, Irvine, CA   92714
CEO: Anthony Baron, Pres.   Tel: (714) 756-2250   Emp: 136
Bus: *Mfr. medical systems.*   Fax:(714) 660-8611   %FO: 100

SIMS DELTEC INC.
1265 Grey Fox Road, St. Paul, MN   55112
CEO: James Stitt, Pres.   Tel: (612) 633-2556   Emp: 600
Bus: *Mfr. medical systems.*   Fax:(612) 639-2530   %FO: 100

SIMS INDUSTRIES Medical Systems Inc.
Kit Street, Keene, NH   03431
CEO: Jeffrey Spielman, Pres.   Tel: (603) 352-3812   Emp: 800
Bus: *Mfr. medical devices.*   Fax:(603) 352-3703   %FO: 100

SIMS LEVEL 1
160 Weymouth Street, Rockland, MA   02184
CEO: John Hertig, Pres.   Tel: (617) 878-8011   Emp: 222
Bus: *Mfr. medical equipment.*   Fax:(617) 878-8201   %FO: 100

SMITHS INDUSTRIES AEROSPACE & DEFENSE SYSTEMS INC
1225 Jefferson Davis Hwy, #1100, Arlington, VA   22202
CEO: George Donovan, VP   Tel: (703) 416-9400   Emp: N/A
Bus: *Mfr./marketing/service avionics.*   Fax:(703) 416-9404   %FO: 100

SMITHS INDUSTRIES INC
435 Devon Park Drive, #101, Wayne, PA   19087
CEO: Walter Orme, VP   Tel: (610) 964-0501   Emp: N/A
Bus: *Holding company.*   Fax:(610) 964-1445   %FO: 100

TIMES MICROWAVE SYSTEMS
358 Hall Avenue, PO Box 5039, Wallingford, CT   06492-5039
CEO: Peter Paige, Pres.   Tel: (203) 949-8400   Emp: 117
Bus: *Mfr. microwave cable.*   Fax:(203) 949-8423   %FO: 100

TUTCO INC.
500 Gould Drive, Cookeville, TN   38501
CEO: Michael Mahoney, Pres.   Tel: (615) 432-4141   Emp: 430
Bus: *Mfr. heating elements.*   Fax:(615) 432-4140   %FO: 100

SPIRAX SARCO LTD.
Charlton House, Cheltenham, Glouc, GL53 8ER, England
CEO: Chris Tappin, Chrm.   Tel: 44-124-252-1361   Emp: N/A
Bus: *Mfr. temperature controls, steam traps, pressure* Fax:44-124-257-3342
reduction, pipeline aux.

SPIRAX SARCO INC.
1951 Glenwood Street, SW, Allentown, PA   18103
CEO: Anthony Mauriello, Pres.   Tel: (610) 797-5830   Emp: 300
Bus: *Mfr. temp control, steam traps, pressure*   Fax:(610) 433-1346   %FO: 100
reduction, pipeline auxiliary.

STAMFORD GROUP LTD.
Bayley Street, Staly Bridge, Cheshire SK15 1QP, England
CEO: John Nugent, Chrm.   Tel: 44-1963-303-6051 Emp: N/A
Bus: *Mfr. clamps and tubing.*   Fax:44-161-330-5576

OPTO INC.
65 East Palatine Road, Prospect Heights, IL   60070
CEO: Graham Wood, Pres.   Tel: (847) 541-6786   Emp: N/A
Bus: *Sale clamps, tubing & display fixtures.*   Fax:(847) 541-8160   %FO: 100

STANDARD CHARTERED, PLC
1 Aldermanbury Square, London EC2V 7SB, England
CEO: Patrick J. Gillam, Chrm.   Tel: 44-171-280-7500   Emp: N/A
Bus: *International banking.*   Fax:44-171-280-7191

STANDARD CHARTERED, PLC.
701 Brickell Avenue, Suite 1700, Miami, FL   33131
CEO: Mark North, EVP   Tel: (305) 539-7000   Emp: 40
Bus: *International banking.*   Fax:(305) 539-7774   %FO: 100

STANDARD CHARTERED, PLC.
707 Wilshire Boulevard, Los Angeles, CA   90012
CEO: Paul Johnson, Gen. Mgr.   Tel: (213) 614-2822   Emp: 200
Bus: *International banking.*   Fax:(213) 614-3430   %FO: 100

STANDARD CHARTERED, PLC.
7 World Trade Center, 26th Fl., New York, NY   10048
CEO: Robert McDonald, Pres.   Tel: (212) 667-0700   Emp: N/A
Bus: *International banking.*   Fax:(212) 667-0535   %FO: 100

● **STAVELEY INDUSTRIES, PLC.**
Staveley House, 11 Dingwall Road, Croydon, CR9 3AB, England
CEO: Roy Hitchens, CEO   Tel: 44-181-688-4404   Emp: N/A
Bus: *Mfr. electrical weighing equipment.*   Fax:44-181-760-0563

   WEIGH-TRONIX, INC.
   1000 Armstrong Drive
   PO Box 1000, Fairmont, MN   56031
   CEO: John McCann, Pres.   Tel: (507) 238-4461   Emp: 416
   Bus: *Sales/distribution of electrical weighing* Fax:(507) 238-2373   %FO: 100
      equipment.

● **STOLT-NIELSEN SA**
Aldwych House, 71-91 Aldwych, London WC2B 4HN, England
CEO: Jacob Stolt-Nielsen, Jr., Chrm.   Tel: 44-171-611-8960   Emp: 6700
Bus: *International transport, storage & distribution* Fax:44-171-611-8965
   specialty bulk liquids, subsea contracting &
   aquaculture

   STOLT PARCEL TANKERS INC.
   8 Sound Shore Drive, PO Box 2300, Greenwich, CT   06836
   CEO: Samuel Cooperman, Pres.   Tel: (203) 625-9400   Emp: 500
   Bus: *International transport of specialty bulk* Fax:(203) 661-7695   %FO: 100
      liquids.

   STOLTHAVEN (HOUSTON) INC.
   15602 Jacintoport Blvd., Houston, TX   77015
   CEO: Jacob B. Stolt-Neilsen, Pres.   Tel: (713) 457-1080   Emp: 300
   Bus: *Parcel tanker operations, tank container sales* Fax:(713) 457-4945   %FO: 100
      & operations, barge/rail sales & operations,
      terminal sales & operations.

● **STRACHAN HENSHAW MACHINERY**
Deep Pit Road, Speedwell, Bristol BS5 7UZ, England
CEO: Robert Smallcombe, Pres.   Tel: 44-117-951-7272   Emp: 350
Bus: *Mfr. printing and sheeting equipment.*   Fax:44-117-952-2401

   STRACHAN HENSHAW MACHINERY, INC.
   492 Bonnie Lane, Elk Grove Village, IL   60007
   CEO: Stephen A. Barker, Pres.   Tel: (847) 956-6727   Emp: 13
   Bus: *Sale printing & sheeting equipment*   Fax:(847) 956-7045   %FO: 100

● **SYSTEMS UNION LIMITED**
Mytchett Place, Mychett Place Road, Mytcheet, Camberley, Surrey GU16 6DQ, England
CEO: John Pemberton, CEO   Tel: 44-1252-378837   Emp: 500
Bus: *Supply/service of accounting software.*   Fax:44-1252-371559

    SYSTEMS UNION LIMITED
    150 Spear Street, Suite 1750, San Francisco, CA   94105
    CEO: Dinesh Wadhawan, Mgr.   Tel: (415) 247-7989   Emp: 15
    Bus: *Supply/service of accounting software.*   Fax:(415) 247-7986   %FO: 100

    SYSTEMS UNION LIMITED
    10 Bank Street, White Plains, NY   10606
    CEO: Larry Helft, CEO   Tel: (914) 948-7770   Emp: 60
    Bus: *Supply/service of accounting software.*   Fax:(914) 948-7399   %FO: 100

● **T & N PLC**
Manchester International Office, Centre Styal Road, Manchester M22 5TN, England
CEO: Colin F.N. Hope, Chrm. & CEO   Tel: 44-161-955-5200   Emp: N/A
Bus: *Mfr./distributor automotive, petrochemicals, power*   Fax:44-161-955-5208
    generation, aerospace, electrical & construction
    industry materials and components.

    AE CLEVITE, INC.
    325 East Eisenhower Parkway Ste. 202, Ann Arbor, MI   48108
    CEO: J. Washbish, Pres.   Tel: (313) 663-6400   Emp: 150
    Bus: *Sub of T & N INDUSTRIES INC.*   Fax:(313) 663-0868   %FO: 100
        Mfg./supplier of engine parts.

    AE GOETZE NORTH AMERICA, INC.
    3605 West Cleveland Road, South Bend, IN   46628
    CEO: Richard Monagle, Opers. Mgr.   Tel: (219) 272-5900   Emp: 350
    Bus: *Sub of T & N INDUSTRIES INC. Mfg./supplier*   Fax:(219) 272-5918   %FO: 100
        of pistons.

    BENTLEY-HARRIS MANUFACTURING CO.
    241 Welsh Pool Road, Exton, PA   19341
    CEO: Ronald Quell, Pres.   Tel: (610) 363-2600   Emp: 300
    Bus: *Sub of T & N INDUSTRIES INC. Mfg./supplier*   Fax:(610) 524-9086   %FO: 100
        braided electrical sleeves, automotive hose
        coverings.

    BRICO METALS, INC.
    5800 Wolf Creek Pike, Dayton, OH   45426
    CEO: Ben James, Pres.   Tel: (937) 837-2671   Emp: 150
    Bus: *Sub of T & N INDUSTRIES INC. Mfg./supplier*   Fax:(937) 854-1345   %FO: 100
        powdered metal parts for automotive industry.

FERODO AMERICA, INC.
One Grizzly Lane, Smithville, TN   37166
CEO: Brian Lindsay, Pres.   Tel: (615) 597-6700   Emp: 500
Bus: *Sub.of T&N INDUSTRIES INC. Mfg./supplier*   Fax:(615) 597-5243   %FO: 100
  brakes and brake parts to the automotive
  industry.

GLACIER DAIDO AMERICA, LLC
1215 Greenwood Street, Bellefontaine, OH   43311
CEO: Jerry Butler, Opers. Mgr.   Tel: (937) 592-2447   Emp: 350
Bus: *Sub.of T&N INDUSTRIES INC. Mfg./supplier*   Fax:(937) 593-8874   %FO: 100
  engine bearingss to the automotive industry.

McCORD PAYEN, INC.
1500 Freeman Avenue, Athens, AL   35613
CEO: Ronald Comer, Pres.   Tel: (205) 233-0140   Emp: N/A
Bus: *Sub.of T&N INDUSTRIES INC. Supplies*   Fax:(205) 233-0578   %FO: 100
  components to industrial users.

T & N INDUSTRIES, INC.
777 Eisenhower Parkway Ste. 600, Ann Arbor, MI   48108
CEO: William Pichan, Pres.   Tel: (313) 663-6749   Emp: 26
Bus: *US headquarters. Mfr./distributor automotive,*   Fax:(313) 663-7165   %FO: 100
  petrochemicals, power generation, aerospace,
  electrical and construction industry materials
  and components.

● **TARMAC PLC**
Hilton Hall, Essington, Wolverhampton WV11 2BQ, England
CEO: John D. Lovering, GRP.CEO   Tel: 44-90-230-7407   Emp: N/A
Bus: *Mfr. construction materials.*   Fax:44-90-230-7408

  TARMAC AMERICA INC.
  1151 Azalea Garden Road, Norfolk, VA   23502
  CEO: John D.Carr, EVP & CEO   Tel: (757) 858-6500   Emp: N/A
  Bus: *Mfr. construction materials.*   Fax:(757) 855-2919   %FO: 100

● **TATE & LYLE PLC**
Sugar Quay, Lower Thames Street, London EC3R 6DQ, England
CEO: Neil M. Shaw, Chrm.   Tel: 44-171-626 6525   Emp: 17000
Bus: *Sugar refining, bulk liquid storage, agriculture*   Fax:44-171-623 5213
  consulting.

  DOMINO SUGAR CORP.
  1114 Ave. of the Americas, New York, NY   10036
  CEO: Edward Makin, Pres.   Tel: (212) 789-9700   Emp: N/A
  Bus: *Mfr. refined cane sugar.*   Fax:(212) 789-9746   %FO: 100

PM AG PRODUCTS, INC.

17475 Jovanna Street, Holmwood, IL   60430

CEO: Michael A. Reed, Pres.	Tel: (708) 206-2030	Emp: N/A
Bus: *Mfr. molasses & animal feeds.*	Fax:(708) 206-1340	%FO: 100

A .E. STALEY MFG CO.

2200 E. Eldorado Street, Decatur, IL   62525

CEO: Loren Luppes, Pres.	Tel: (217) 423-4411	Emp: N/A
Bus: *Mfr. refined corn products.*	Fax:(217) 421-2216	%FO: 85

TATE & LYLE, INC.

1402 Foulk Road, #102, Wilmington, DE   19803

CEO: Murray D. McEwen, Chrm.	Tel: (302) 478-4773	Emp: N/A
Bus: *Holding company.*	Fax:(302) 478-6915	%FO: 100

VIGORTONE AG PRODUCTS

5264 Council Street, NE, Cedar Rapids, IA   52406

CEO: R.L .Coffey, Pres.	Tel: (319) 393-3310	Emp: N/A
Bus: *Mfr. special animal feeds.*	Fax:(319) 393-6388	%FO: 100

THE WESTERN SUGAR CO.

1700 Broadway, #1600, Denver, CO   80290

CEO: Thomas F. Chandler, Pres.	Tel: (303) 830-3939	Emp: N/A
Bus: *Mfr. beet sugar.*	Fax:(303) 830-3940	%FO: 100

• TAYLOR WOODROW PLC

Four Dunraven Street, London W1Y 3FG, England

CEO: Colin J. Parsons, Chrm.	Tel: 44-171-629-1201	Emp: 9000
Bus: *Property development, housing & general construction, & trading activities.*	Fax:44-171-493-1066	

MONARCH COMMUNITIES OF CALIFORNIA

30251 Gloden Lantern, Laguna Niguel, CA   92677

CEO: Gordon Craig, Pres.	Tel: (714) 363-7010	Emp: N/A
Bus: *Property development, housing & general construction.*	Fax:(714) 363-9360	%FO: 100

MONARCH DEVEL OF TEXAS, INC.

623 Lakeshore Drive, Sugar Land, TX   77478

CEO: Jeffrey Anderson, Pres.	Tel: (281) 242-4004	Emp: N/A
Bus: *Property development, housing & general construction.*	Fax:(281) 242-6968	%FO: 100

MONARCH DEVELOPMENT OF GEORGIA, INC.

712 Malvern Blvd., Stone Mountain, GA   30087

CEO: George Gourley, Pres.	Tel: (770) 879-8212	Emp: N/A
Bus: *Property development, housing & general construction.*	Fax:(770) 879-7842	%FO: 100

MONARCH HOMES OF FLORIDA, INC.
7129 South Beneva Road, Sarasota, FL   34238-2150

CEO: John Peshkin, Pres.   Tel: (941) 927-0999   Emp: N/A

Bus: *Property development, housing & general*   Fax:(941) 925-4856   %FO: 100
construction.

TAYLOR WOODROW CONSTRUCTION CORP.
100 First Stamford Place, Stamford, CT   06902

CEO: Dennis MacDaio, Pres.   Tel: (203) 975-0928   Emp: N/A

Bus: *U.S. holding company; property development,* Fax:(203) 975-0930   %FO: 100
housing & general construction.

TAYLOR WOODROW HOMES CALIFORNIA LTD.
24461 Ridge Route Drive, Laguna Hills, CA   92653-1686

CEO: Richard Pope, Pres.   Tel: (714) 581-2626   Emp: N/A

Bus: *Property development, housing & general*   Fax:(714) 581-2727   %FO: 100
construction.

TAYLOR WOODROW HOMES NEVADA LTD
6655 West Sahara, Suite 110, Las Vegas, NV   89102

CEO: N/A   Tel: (702) 255-7137   Emp: N/A

Bus: *Property development, housing & general*   Fax: %FO: 100
construction.

● TI GROUP PLC
Lambourn Court, Abingdon, Oxon OX14 1UH, England

CEO: Sir Christopher Lewinton, Chrm.   Tel: 44-123-555-5570   Emp: 22000

Bus: *Specialized engineering group.*   Fax:44-123-555-5818

BUNDY NORTH AMERICA
12345 E. Nine Mile Road, Warren, MI   48090-2001

CEO: William J. Laule, CEO   Tel: (810) 758-4511   Emp: N/A

Bus: *Mfr. fluid carrying systems.*   Fax:(810) 758-1131   %FO: 100

JOHN CRANE NORTH AMERICA, INC,
6400 West Oakton Street, Morton Grove, IL   60053

CEO: John W. Potter, CEO   Tel: (847) 967-2400   Emp: N/A

Bus: *Engineered sealing systems, polymer products.* Fax:(847) 967-3700   %FO: 100

DOWTY AEROSPACE
1700 Business Center Drive, Duarte, CA   91010-0259

CEO: Peter Wright Mng. Dir.   Tel: (818) 359-9211   Emp: N/A

Bus: *Mfr. aircraft landing gear systems, propeller* Fax:(818) 357-1095   %FO: 100
systems, engine rings, hydraulic & actuation
systems; repair & overhaul services.

KING FIFTH WHEEL

P.O.Box 68, Crestwood Ind. Park, Mountaintop, PA 18707-0068

CEO: Mark Celusniak, Pres.	Tel: (717) 474-6371	Emp: N/A
Bus: *Mfr. aircraft landing gear systems, propeller systems, engine rings, hydraulic & actuation systems; repair & overhaul services.*	Fax:(717) 474-9901	%FO: 100

MILLER FREEMAN PSN INC.

460 Park Avenue South, 9th Fl., New York, NY 10016

CEO: Paul Gallo, Pres.	Tel: (212) 378-0400	Emp: N/A
Bus: *Trade magazine publishing.*	Fax:(212) 378-2160	%FO: 100

TI GROUP, INC.

375 Park Avenue, New York, NY 10152-0222

CEO: James H. Katzoff, Pres.	Tel: (212) 319-3101	Emp: N/A
Bus: *Holding company.*	Fax:(212) 319-3199	%FO: 100

TI GROUP, INC.

2001 Jefferson Davis Highway, #607-A, Arlington, VA 22202

CEO: Alan Fenwick, VP	Tel: (703) 418-6087	Emp: N/A
Bus: *Government relations representative office.*	Fax:(703) 418-0946	%FO: 100

UNITED ADVERTISING PUBLICATIONS INC.

15400 Knoll Trail, Ste. 400, Dallas, TX 75248

CEO: Nigel Donaldson, Pres.	Tel: (972) 701-0244	Emp: N/A
Bus: *Real estate publications.*	Fax:(972) 991-9543	%FO: 100

► TOMKINS PLC

East Putney House, 84 Upper Richmond Road, London SW15 2ST, England

CEO: Gregory F. Hutchings, CEO	Tel: 44-181-871-4544	Emp: 54496
Bus: *Industrial management services. Mfr. garden/leisure products, food, baking, milling products, industrial products and handguns.*	Fax:44-181-877-9700	

AIR SYSTEM COMPONENTS

9990 Security Row, Richardson, TX 75081

CEO: Terry O'Halloran, Pres.	Tel: (972) 907-0791	Emp: N/A
Bus: *Mfr. HVAC components.*	Fax:(972) 918-8880	%FO: 100

ARROWHEAD CONVEYOR

3255 Medalist Drive, Oshkosh, WI 54903

CEO: Philip Florek, VP & Gen. Mgr.	Tel: (920) 235-5562	Emp: 225
Bus: *Mfr. light duty conveyor systems and components.*	Fax:(920) 235-3638	%FO: 100

CARRIAGE HOUSE FRUIT COMPANY

1901 Las Plumas Avenue, San Jose, CA 95133

CEO: Gene Bailen, Pres.	Tel: (408) 928-1100	Emp: N/A
Bus: *Supplies frozen food & fruit products.*	Fax:(408) 729-7698	%FO: 100

DEARBORN MID-WEST
19440 Glendale Avenue, Detroit, MI   48223
CEO: Wes Paisley, Pres.   Tel: (313) 273-2800   Emp: N/A
Bus: *Mfr. heavy duty conveyor equipment, postal*   Fax:(313) 273-5252   %FO: 100
and bulk system conveyors.

DEXTER AXLE
222 Collins Road, Elkhart, IN   46515
CEO: W. Michael Jones, Pres.   Tel: (219) 295-1900   Emp: N/A
Bus: *Mfr. axles and wheels for trailers, motor*   Fax:(219) 295-1069   %FO: 100
homes and recreational vehicles.

GATES RUBBER COMPANY
900 South Broadway, Denver, CO   80217
CEO: John Riess, Pres. & CEO   Tel: (303) 744-1911   Emp: N/A
Bus: *Mfr./distributor auto & industrial rubber*   Fax:(303) 744-4000   %FO: 100
products.

INTERGRATED MATERIAL HANDLING
3255 Medalist Drive, Oshkosh, WI   54903
CEO: Phil Florek, Acting Pres.   Tel: (414) 235-5562   Emp: N/A
Bus: *Mfr. industrial machinery systems.*   Fax:(414) 235-3638   %FO: 100

LASCO BATHWARE
3255 East Miraloma Avenue, Anaheim, CA   92806
CEO: Dave Blenek, Pres.   Tel: (714) 993-1220   Emp: N/A
Bus: *Mfr. fibreglass & acrylic baths & whirlpools.*   Fax:(714) 572-0998   %FO: 100

LASCO FLUID DISTRIBUTION
540 Lasco Street, Brownsville, TN   38012
CEO: Jack McDonald, Pres.   Tel: (901) 772-3180   Emp: N/A
Bus: *Mfr. PVC pipe.*   Fax:(901) 772-0835   %FO: 100

LASCO PANELS
8015 Dixon Drive, Florence, KY   41042
CEO: Jim Amundson, Pres.   Tel: (606) 371-7720   Emp: N/A
Bus: *Mfr. construction fibreglass panels.*   Fax:(606) 371-8466   %FO: 100

LAU INDUSTRIES
4509 Springfield Street, Dayton, OH   45431
CEO: Will Jones, Pres.   Tel: (937) 476-6500   Emp: N/A
Bus: *Mfr. centrifugal fans & propellers.*   Fax:(937) 254-9519   %FO: 100

MALTA WINDOW DIVISION
PO Box 397, Malta, OH   43758
CEO: David Bird, Pres.   Tel: (614) 962-3131   Emp: N/A
Bus: *Mfr. aluminum clad patio doors & wood/vinyl*   Fax:(614) 962-3700   %FO: 100
windows.

MAYFRAN INTERNATIONAL, INC.
650 Beta Drive, Cleveland, OH   44143

CEO: Bruce Terry, Pres.	Tel: (216) 461-4100	Emp: N/A
Bus: *Mfr. industrial machinery; conveyors for waste recovery &. metalworking.*	Fax:(216) 461-5565	%FO: 100

MILLIKEN VALVES COMPANY, INC.
3864 Courtney Street, Suite 100, Bethlehem, PA   18107

CEO: N/A	Tel: (610) 861-3303	Emp: N/A
Bus: *Distributor; valves.*	Fax:(610) 861-8094	%FO: 100

MURRAY INC.
219 Franklin Road, Brentwood, TN   37027

CEO: Ed Shultz, Pres.	Tel: (615) 373-6500	Emp: N/A
Bus: *Mfr. power tool & mowing equipment, snowblowers & bicycles.*	Fax:(615) 373-6771	%FO: 100

PHILIPS PRODUCTS, INC.
3221 Magnum Drive, Elkhart, IN   46516

CEO: W. Michael Jones, Pres.	Tel: (216) 296-0000	Emp: N/A
Bus: *Mfr. aluminum/vinyl doors, windows, hoods, and ventilating devices.*	Fax:(216) 296-0147	%FO: 100

THE RED WING COMPANY
196 Newton Street, Fredonia, NY   14063

CEO: Gene Bailen, Pres.	Tel: (716) 673-1000	Emp: N/A
Bus: *Distributor private label grocery products.*	Fax:(716) 679-7702	%FO: 100

RUSKIN MANUFACTURING
3900 Doctor Greaves Road, Grandview, MO   64030

CEO: Tom Edwards, Pres.	Tel: (816) 761-7476	Emp: N/A
Bus: *Mfr. air, fire and smoke dampers, louvers & fibreglass products.*	Fax:(816) 763-8102	%FO: 100

SMITH & WESSON
2100 Roosevelt Avenue, PO Box 2208, Springfield, MA   01102-2208

CEO: Edward Shultz, Pres.	Tel: (413) 781-8300	Emp: N/A
Bus: *Mfr. handguns, handcuffs & Identi-Kit systems.*	Fax:(413) 734-9023	%FO: 100

TOMKINS INDUSTRIES INC.
4801 Springfield Street, PO Box 943, Dayton, OH   45401-0943

CEO: Anthony J. Reading, Chrm.	Tel: (937) 253-7171	Emp: 60
Bus: *Holding company.*	Fax:(937) 253-9822	%FO: 100

VERSA CORPORATION
North Clark Street, PO Box 152, Mt. Sterling, OH   43143

CEO: Lloyd Dodds, Plant Mgr.	Tel: (614) 869-2738	Emp: 150
Bus: *Mfr. light duty conveyor systems and components.*	Fax:(614) 869-2839	%FO: 100

● **TOOTAL GROUP PLC**
Tootal House, 19/21 Spring Gardens, Manchester M60 2TL, England
CEO: Geoffrey K. Maddrell, CEO　　　　　Tel: 44-161-831-7777　Emp: 14600
Bus: *Mfr./distribution threads, fabrics, clothing,*　Fax:44-161-835-1223
housewares, etc.

　　　THE AMERICAN THREAD COMPANY
　　　8757 Red Oak Blvd., Charlotte, NC　28217
　　　CEO: Richard A .Rinaldi, Pres.　　　　Tel: (704) 523-1000　Emp: N/A
　　　Bus: *Mfr./distribution industrial sewing threads.*　Fax:(704) 529-4905　%FO: 100

● **TRAFALGAR HOUSE PLC**
1 Berkeley Street, London W1A 1BY, England
CEO: Nigel Rich, Chrm.　　　　　　　　Tel: 44-171-499-9020　Emp: 40000
Bus: *Commercial residential property, construction,*　Fax:44-171-493-5484
engineering, passenger/cargo shipping, hotels

　　　JOHN BROWN ENGINEERING & CONSTRUCTION, INC.
　　　7909 Parkwood Circle Drive, Houston, TX　77036
　　　CEO: D. Keith Dodson, Pres. & CEO　　Tel: (713) 988-2002　Emp: 3000
　　　Bus: *Engineering/construction/management/mainten*　Fax:(713) 772-4673　%FO: 100
　　　ance to energy, chemicals, petrochemicals,
　　　pharmaceuticals, refining industry

　　　DAVY INTERNATIONAL
　　　1 Oliver Plaza, Pittsburgh, PA　15222-2604
　　　CEO: John M. Kelman, Pres.　　　　　Tel: (412) 566-4500　Emp: 1600
　　　Bus: *Engineering, construction and equipment*　Fax:　　　　　　　%FO: 100
　　　supply to metals industry.

● **UNILEVER PLC**
Unilever House, London EC4P 4BQ, England
CEO: Niall FitzGerald, Chrm.　　　　　Tel: 44-171-822 5252　Emp: 308000
Bus: *Soaps & detergents, foods, chemicals, personal*　Fax:44-171-822 5511
products (see joint parent: UNILEVER NV,
Netherlands).

　　　CALVIN KLEIN COSMETICS CO.
　　　725 Fifth Avenue, New York, NY　10022
　　　CEO: Paulanne Mancuso, Pres.　　　　Tel: (212) 759-8888　Emp: N/A
　　　Bus: *Mfr. perfumes, cosmetics.*　　　　Fax:(212) 755-8792　%FO: 100

　　　CHESEBROUGH POND'S INC.
　　　33 Benedict Place, Greenwich, CT　06830
　　　CEO: Robert Phillips, Chrm.　　　　　Tel: (203) 661-2000　Emp: N/A
　　　Bus: *Mfr. health & beauty products.*　　Fax:(203) 625-1602　%FO: 100

ELIZABETH ARDEN
1345 Ave. of the Americas, New York, NY   10105
CEO: Peter England, Pres.   Tel: (212) 261-1000   Emp: N/A
Bus: *Mfr. cosmetics, perfumes.*   Fax:(703) 563-3109   %FO: 100

HELENE CURTIS
325 North Wells Street, Chicago, IL   60610
CEO: Ronald J. Gidwitz, Pres.   Tel: (312) 661-0222   Emp: N/A
Bus: *Mfr. cosmetics & fragrances.*   Fax:(312) 836-0125   %FO: 100

LEVER BROTHERS CO.
390 Park Avenue, New York, NY   10022
CEO: John W. Rice, Pres.   Tel: (212) 688-6000   Emp: N/A
Bus: *Mfr. soaps, detergents.*   Fax:(212) 906-4411   %FO: 100

THOMAS J. LIPTON INC.
800 Sylvan Avenue, Englewood Cliffs, NJ   07632
CEO: Richard Goldstein, Pres.   Tel: (201) 567-8000   Emp: N/A
Bus: *Mfr. tea, seasonings, food products.* Fax:(201) 871-8280   %FO: 100

UNILEVER US, INC
390 Park Avenue, New York, NY   10022=4698
CEO: Richard A. Goldstein, Pres.   Tel: (212) 888-1260   Emp: 25000
Bus: *Holding company.*   Fax:(212) 318-3800   %FO: 100

VAN DEN BERGH FOODS CO.
2200 Cabot Drive, Lisle, IL   60532
CEO: John E. Mueller, Pres.   Tel: (630) 505-5300   Emp: N/A
Bus: *Mfr. food products.*   Fax: %FO: 100

● **UNITED BISCUITS (UK) LTD.**
Church Road, West Drayton, Middlesex UB7 7PR, England
CEO: Eric L. Nicoli, Gp. CEO   Tel: 44-189-543-2100   Emp: 39352
Bus: *Mfr. snackfoods.*   Fax:44-189-544-8848

KEEBLER COMPANY
One Hollow Tree Lane, Elmhurst, IL   60126
CEO: Sam Reed, Pres.   Tel: (630) 833-2900   Emp: 10330
Bus: *Mfr. snackfoods, cookies.*   Fax:(630) 530-8773   %FO: 100

● **UNITED NEWSPAPERS PLC**
Ludgate House, 245 Blackfriars Rd, London SE1 9UY, England
CEO: Lord David Stevens, Chrm.   Tel: 44-171-921-5000   Emp: 13053
Bus: *Publishes trade and consumer*   Fax:44-171-921-2728
      magazines/newspapers.

   MILLER FREEMAN INC.
   600 Harrison Street, San Francisco, CA   94107
   CEO: Marshall W. Freeman, Chrm.   Tel: (415) 905-2200   Emp: 1200
   Bus: *Publishes trade & consumer magazines,* Fax:(415) 905-2232   %FO: 100
         newspapers.

   PR NEWSWIRE ASSOC INC.
   810 Seventh Avenue, 35th Floor, New York, NY   10019
   CEO: Ian Capps, Pres.   Tel: (212) 596-1500   Emp: N/A
   Bus: *News gathering/dissemination.*   Fax:(212) 596-1516   %FO: 100

   PSN PUBLICATIONS INC., PRO SOUND NEWS
   460 Park Avenue South, 9th Floor, New York, NY   10016
   CEO: Paul Gallo, Pres.   Tel: (212) 378-0400   Emp: N/A
   Bus: *Trade magazine publishing.*   Fax:(212) 378-2160   %FO: 100

   UNITED ADVERTISING PUBLICATIONS INC.
   15400 Knoll Trail, #400, Dallas, TX   75248
   CEO: Nigel Donaldson, CEO   Tel: (972) 701-0244   Emp: N/A
   Bus: *Real estate publications.*   Fax:(972) 701-0244   %FO: 100

● **VICKERS PLC**
Millbank Tower, Millbank, London SW1P 4RA, England
CEO: Sir Colin Chandler, Dep.Chrm.   Tel: 44-171 828-7777   Emp: 10500
Bus: *Engineering company with a broad products &* Fax:44-171 331-3964
      technologies in automotive, defense, marine
      propulsion & medical industries.

   AIR-SHIELDS VICKERS, INC.
   330 Jacksonville Road, Hatboro, PA   19040
   CEO: Harry Gugnani, Pres.   Tel: (215) 675-5200   Emp: N/A
   Bus: *Mfr. neonatal intensive care equipment.* Fax:(215) 675-0275   %FO: 100

   COSWORTH ENGINEERING, INC.
   41000 Vincenti Court, Novi, MI   48375-1921
   CEO: M. Wetzler, CEO   Tel: (310) 534-1390   Emp: N/A
   Bus: *Supplier to domestic automotive*   Fax:(810) 471-3680   %FO: 100
         manufacturers.

   COSWORTH ENGINEERING, INC.
   3031 Fujita Street, Torrance, CA   90505-4004
   CEO: I. Bisco, VP & Gen. Mgr.   Tel: (310) 534-1390   Emp: N/A
   Bus: *Motor racing support services.*   Fax:(310) 534-2631   %FO: 100

JERED BROWN BROTHERS, INC.
1608 Newcastle Street, Brunswick, GA   31520-6729
CEO: Craig Hooson, Pres.   Tel: (912) 262-2000   Emp: N/A
Bus: *Mfr. marine machinery & equipment.*   Fax:(912) 262-2051   %FO: 100

ROLLS-ROYCE MOTOR CARS, INC. - NORTHERN REGION
140E Ridgewood Avenue, 5th Fl., Paramus, NJ   07652
CEO: Robert R. Wharen, Mng. Dir.   Tel: (201) 967-9100   Emp: N/A
Bus: *Import/distribution/service motor vehicles.*   Fax:(201) 967-2070   %FO: 100

ROLLS-ROYCE MOTOR CARS, INC. - CENTRAL REGION
303 East Army Trail Road, #108, Bloomingdale, IL   60108
CEO: Robert R. Wharen, Mng. Dir.   Tel: (630) 529-5330   Emp: N/A
Bus: *Import/distribution/service motor vehicles.*   Fax:(630) 529-9841   %FO: 100

ROLLS-ROYCE MOTOR CARS, INC. - SOUTHERN REGION
900 N. Federal Highway, #360, Boca Raton, FL   33432
CEO: Gustavo Velazute, Reg. Dir.   Tel: (561) 750-8381   Emp: N/A
Bus: *Import/distribution/service motor vehicles.*   Fax:(561) 750-8421   %FO: 100

ROLLS-ROYCE MOTOR CARS, INC. - WESTERN REGION
5136 Commerce Avenue, Moorpark, CA   93020
CEO: Robert R. Wharen, Mng. Dir.   Tel: (310) 750-8381   Emp: N/A
Bus: *Import/distribution/service motor vehicles.*   Fax:(310) 750-8421   %FO: 100

TECA CORPORATION
140 East Ridgewood Avenue, 5th Fl., Paramus, NJ   07652
CEO: Mike Pattinson, Pres.   Tel: (201) 986-0225   Emp: N/A
Bus: *Mfr. neurodiagnostic equipment.*   Fax:(201) 986-0919   %FO: 100

TRUCAST, INC.
81 Mossoms Way, Newberry, SC   29108
CEO: Chris Pritchard, Pres.   Tel: (803) 276-5353   Emp: N/A
Bus: *Mfr. wheels.*   Fax:(803) 276-6340   %FO: 100

VICKERS AMERICA HOLDINGS, INC.
Mac Ctr III, 140 East Ridgewood Avenue, Paramus, NJ   07652
CEO: D. J. DeAngelis, EVP   Tel: (201) 986-0225   Emp: N/A
Bus: *Holding company for U.S. operations.*   Fax:(201) 986-0919   %FO: 100

● **VIRGIN GROUP LTD.**
120 Campden Hill Road, London W8 7AR, England
CEO: Richard C.N. Branson, Chrm. Tel: 44-171-229 1282 Emp: 10000
Bus: *Holding company: travel, hotels, communications,* Fax:44-171-229 5834
cinemas, radio, retail, financial services &
investments..

VIRGIN ATLANTIC AIRWAYS LTD.
747 Belden Avenue, Norwalk, CT 08650
CEO: David Tait, EVP Tel: (203) 750-2000 Emp: 500+
Bus: *International commercial air transport.* Fax:(203) 750-6490 %FO: 100

VIRGIN ATLANTIC CARGO
1963 Marcus Avenue, Lake Success, NY 11042
CEO: Angelo Pasateri, Pres. Tel: (516) 775-2600 Emp: N/A
Bus: *International commercial air transport.* Fax:(516) 354-3760 %FO: 100

VIRGIN GAMES INC., VIRGIN INTERACTIVE ENTERTAINMENT, INC.
18061 Fitch Avenue, Irvine, CA 92714
CEO: Martin Alper, Pres. Tel: (714) 833-8710 Emp: N/A
Bus: *Design/mfr. interactive video games.* Fax:(714) 833-8717 %FO: 100

VIRGIN RIVER HOTEL CASINO & BINGO
PO Box 1620, Mesquite, NV 89024
CEO: Lex Hall, Mgr. Tel: (702) 346-7777 Emp: N/A
Bus: *Hotel & entertainment services.* Fax:(702) 346-7780 %FO: 100

● **VITALOGRAPH LTD.**
Maids Moreton House, Buckingham MK18 1SW, England
CEO: Bernard Garbe, Pres. Tel: 44-1280-816-868 Emp: N/A
Bus: *Pulmonary function testing equipment* Fax:N/A

VITALOGRAPH MEDICAL INSTRUMENTATION, INC.
8347 Quivira Road, Lenexa, KS 66215
CEO: Bernard Garbe, Pres. Tel: (913) 888-4221 Emp: N/A
Bus: *Pulmonary function testing equipment.* Fax:(913) 888-4259 %FO: 100

● **W.H. SMITH GROUP PLC**
Audrey House, Ely Place, London EC1N 6SN, England
CEO: Bill Cockburn, CEO Tel: 44-171-730 1200 Emp: 36000
Bus: *Retailer; books, music, newspaper & magazines.* Fax:44-171-25- 0195
Chains: WH Smith, Virgin Our Price; Waterstones.

W.H. SMITH GROUP (USA), INC.
3200 Windy Hill Road, #1500 W. Tower, Atlanta, GA 30339
CEO: John Hancock, CEO Tel: (770) 952-0705 Emp: 300
Bus: *U.S. headquarters for retailing operations.* Fax:(770) 618-2788 %FO: 100

THE WALL MUSIC, INC.
2191 Hornig Road, Philadelphia, PA   19116
CEO: John Hancock, CEO   Tel: (215) 676-1250   Emp: 950
Bus: *Music retailer. 170 stores in the US.*   Fax:(215) 676-1251   %FO: 100

WATERSTONE'S, INC.
3200 Windy Hill Road, #1500 W. Tower, Atlanta, GA   30339
CEO: John Hancock, CEO   Tel: (770) 952-0705   Emp: N/A
Bus: *Book retailer. 4 stores in the US>*   Fax:(770) 618-2788   %FO: 100

● **S G WARBURG GROUP PLC**
33 King William Street, London EC4R 9AS, England
CEO: Sir David Scholey, Chrm.   Tel: 44-171-280-2222   Emp: 4000
Bus: *International investment banking, securities and*   Fax:44-171-568-4800
     asset management.

S.G. WARBURG & COMPANY INC.
277 Park Avenue, New York, NY   10072
CEO: H.N.Millward, Mng.Dir.   Tel: (212) 224-7000   Emp: 250
Bus: *Investment banking, security broker and dealer.* Fax:(212) 459-7251   %FO: 100

● **THE WELLCOME FOUNDATION LTD.**
Unicorn House, 160 Euston Rd, P O Box 129, London NW1 2BP, England
CEO: John W. Robb, Chrm. & CEO   Tel: 44-171 3874477   Emp: 15000
Bus: *Pharmaceutical research, development,*   Fax:N/A
     manufacturing and marketing.

BURROUGHS WELLCOME COMPANY
5 Moore Drive, P.O. Box 13398,, Research Tri Pk, NC   27709
CEO: Robert Ingram, Pres.   Tel: (919) 248-2100   Emp: 4800
Bus: *Pharmaceutical research, development,*   Fax:(919) 549-7459   %FO: 100
     manufacturing and marketing

● **WHATMAN REEVE ANGEL PLC**
Springfield Mill, Maidstone, Kent, England
CEO: J .Leigh Pemberton, Mng. Dir.   Tel: 44-18846-269-   Emp: N/A
                                                          2022
Bus: *Lab filtration and chromatography products.*   Fax:44-18846-269-
                                                          1425

WHATMAN INC.
9 Bridewell Place, Clifton, NJ   07014
CEO: Rubin Schevere, Pres.   Tel: (201) 773-5800   Emp: N/A
Bus: *Lab filtration and chromatography products.*   Fax:(201) 472-6949   %FO: 100

- **WIGGIN AND COMPANY**
The Quadrangle, Imperial Square, Cheltenham, GL50 1YX, England
CEO: N/A   Tel: 44-1242-224114   Emp: N/A
Bus: *International law firm.*   Fax:44-1242-224223

  WIGGIN AND COMPANY
  Fox Plaza, Ste. 1730, 2121 Avenue of the Stars, Los Angeles, CA   90067
  CEO: M.W. Turner   Tel: (310) 556-7878   Emp: N/A
  Bus: *International law firm.*   Fax:(310) 556-7882   %FO: 100

- **WILDE SAPTE**
1, Fleet Place, London EC4M 7WS, England
CEO: Steve Blakeley, CEO   Tel: 44-171-246-7000   Emp: 600
Bus: *International law firm.*   Fax:44-171-246-7777

  WILDE SAPTE
  450 Lexington Avenue, 19th Floor, New York, NY   10017
  CEO: Diarmuid Brennan, Resident Ptnr.   Tel: (212) 867-4530   Emp: 600
  Bus: *International law firm.*   Fax:(212) 557-4451   %FO: 100

- **WILLIAMS HOLDINGS PLC**
Pentagon House, Sir Frank Whittle Rd, Derby DE21 4XA, England
CEO: Robert M. Carr, CEO   Tel: 44-332-202020   Emp: 14900
Bus: *Holding company: paints & allied products, aircraft*   Fax:44-332-384402
parts, consumer products., security devices/system,
fire detection systems.

  DETECTOR ELECTRONICS CORP.
  6901 W. 110th Street, Minneapolis, MN   55438
  CEO: Gerald F. Slocum, Pres.   Tel: (612) 941-5665   Emp: 200
  Bus: *Fire & safety devices & systems.*   Fax:(612) 829-8745   %FO: 100

  FENWAL SAFETY SYSTEMS, INC.
  700 Nickerson Road, Marlborough, MA   01752
  CEO: D. E. Bissonnette, CEO   Tel: (508) 481-5800   Emp: N/A
  Bus: *Fire & safety devices & systems.*   Fax:(508) 485-1485   %FO: 100

  FIREYE, INC.
  3 Manchester Road, Derry, NH   03038
  CEO: Robert D. Doenin, Pres.   Tel: (603) 432-4100   Emp: N/A
  Bus: *Fire & safety devices & systems.*   Fax:(603) 432-1570   %FO: 100

  FRAZEE INDUSTRIES, INC.
  6625 Miramar Road, San Diego, CA   92121
  CEO: H. L. Overocker, Pres.   Tel: (619) 276-9500   Emp: 300
  Bus: *Paints, wallcoverings, waterproofing &*   Fax:(619) 452-3568   %FO: 100
  supplies.

KIDDE TECHNOLOGIES, INC.
2500 Airport Drive, Wilson, NC   27893
CEO: J. L. Then, CEO

Tel: (919) 237-7004   Emp: N/A
Bus: *Fire protection technology.*
Fax: (919) 237-9323   %FO: 100

KIDDE-FENWAL, INC.
400 Main Street, Ashland, MA   01721
CEO: Richard H. De Marle, Pres.

Tel: (508) 881-2000   Emp: N/A
Bus: *Fire & safety devices & systems.*
Fax: (508) 881-6729   %FO: 100

KWAL-HOWELLS, INC.
3900 Joliet Street, Denver, CO   80239
CEO: K. P. Child, Pres.

Tel: (303) 371-5600   Emp: N/A
Bus: *Mfr. paint.*
Fax: (303) 373-2709   %FO: 100

MASTERCHEM INDUSTRIES, INC.
3135 Highway M., Antonia, MO   63012
CEO: R.W. Caldwell, Pres.

Tel: (314) 942-2510   Emp: N/A
Bus: *Mfr. paint.*
Fax: (314) 942-3663   %FO: 100

NUTONE, INC.
Madison & Red Banks Road, Cincinnati, OH   45227
CEO: Gregory E. Lawton, Pres.

Tel: (513) 527-5100   Emp: N/A
Bus: *Mfr. built-in household building products.*
Fax: (513) 527-5130   %FO: 100

PARKER PAINT MFG CO., INC.
3003 South Tacoma Way, Tacoma, WA   98409
CEO: Richard LaFond, Pres.

Tel: (253) 473-1122   Emp: N/A
Bus: *Mfr. paint.*
Fax: (253) 474-4655   %FO: 100

WALTER KIDDE AEROSPACE, INC.
2500 Airport Drive, Wilson, NC   27893
CEO: R. J. Eisenhauer, CEO

Tel: (919) 237-7004   Emp: N/A
Bus: *Fire & safety devices & systems.*
Fax: (919) 237-8533   %FO: 100

WALTER KIDDE PORTABLE EQUIPMENT, INC.
1394 S Third Street, Mebane, NC   27302
CEO: G. L. Wannop, Pres.

Tel: (919) 563-5911   Emp: N/A
Bus: *Fire & safety devices & systems.*
Fax: (919) 563-3954   %FO: 100

WILLIAMS HOLDINGS, INC.
700 Nickerson Road, Marlborough, MA   01759
CEO: John F. Hannon, Pres.

Tel: (508) 481-0700   Emp: N/A
Bus: *Holding company; U.S. headquarters.*
Fax: (508) 624-0579   %FO: 100

YALE SECURITY, INC.
1902 Airport Road, Monroe, NC   28110
CEO: Patrick J. McCord, Pres.

Tel: (704) 283-2101   Emp: N/A
Bus: *Mfr. locksets, door closures, exit devices.*
Fax: (704) 289-2875   %FO: 100

- **WINN & COALES INTL**

Denso House, Chapel Rd, London SE27 OTR, England

CEO: David Winn, Chrm./Mng.Dir.   Tel: 44-171-670-7511 Emp: N/A

Bus: *Mfr. tapes, pastes, mastics and protal coatings.* Fax:N/A

  DENSO INC.

  18211 Chisholm Trail, Houston, TX 77060

  CEO: Ken Hickes, Pres.   Tel: (281) 821-3355 Emp: 5

  Bus: *Distribution mastics, pastes, protal coatings,* Fax:(281) 821-0304 %FO: 100
    sea shield systems.

- **WPP GROUP PLC**

27 Farm Street, London W1X 6RD, England

CEO: Martin S. Sorrell, CEO   Tel: 44-171-408-2204 Emp: 20412

Bus: *Media and non-media marketing services group.* Fax:44-171-493-6819

  HILL & KNOWLTON, INC.

  466 Lexington Avenue, New York, NY 10017

  CEO: Howard Paster, Chrm. & CEO   Tel: (212) 885-0300 Emp: 1200

  Bus: *International public relations agency.* Fax:(212) 885-0570 %FO: 100

  J. WALTER THOMPSON CO.

  466 Lexington Avenue, 6th Fl., New York, NY 10017

  CEO: Burt Manning, Chrm.   Tel: (212) 210-7000 Emp: 7000

  Bus: *International advertising agency.* Fax:(212) 210-7078 %FO: 100

  OGILVY & MATHER WORLDWIDE

  309 West 49th Street, 12th Fl., Worldwide Plaza, New York, NY 10019

  CEO: Shelly Lazarus, Chrm.   Tel: (212) 237-4000 Emp: 6000

  Bus: *International advertising agency.* Fax:(212) 237-5123 %FO: 100

  WPP GROUP USA, INC.

  309 West 49th Street, 14th Fl., New York, NY 10019

  CEO: John Zweig, CEO   Tel: (212) 632-2200 Emp: 80

  Bus: *Media & non-media advertising, marketing* Fax:(212) 632-2222 %FO: 100
    services, public relations, market research,
    communications, including: J. Walter
    Thompson Co; Ogilvy & Mather Worldwide;
    Hill & Knowlton; Carl Byoir Associates; Cole
    & Weber; The Futures Group.

- **ZENECA GROUP**

15 Stanhope Gate, London W1Y 5TG, England

CEO: N/A   Tel: 44-171-304-5000   Emp: N/A

Bus: *Mfr. pharmaceutical (cancer drugs) and managed*   Fax:N/A
     healthcare centers.

ZENECA, INC.

PO Box 15438, Wilmington, DE   19850

CEO: A. Keith Willard, Chrm.   Tel: (302) 886-3000   Emp: N/A

Bus: *Sales phamaceutical (cancer drugs) and*   Fax:(302) 886-2972   %FO: 100
     management of cancer centers.

Finland

• A. AHLSTROM CORPORATION

P.O. Box 329, Eteläesplanadi 14, FIN-00101 Helsinki, Finland

CEO: Krister Ahlstrom, Pres.　　　　　　　　　　　Tel: 358-9-503-911　　　Emp: N/A

Bus: *Systems & equipment for pulp & paper industry,*　Fax:358-9-503-9709
industrial automation, specialty papers, packaging,
building materials.

AHLSTROM CAPITAL CORP

10745 Westside Parkway, Alphaetta, GA　30201

CEO: Brain Bezanson, Pres.　　　　　　　　　　　Tel: (770) 640-2500　　Emp: N/A

Bus: *Third party financing services.*　　　　　　　　Fax:(770) 640-2604　　%FO: 100

AHLSTROM DEVELOPMENT CORP

4350 La Jolla Village Drive, San Diego, CA　92122

CEO: Gerald C. Mayers, Pres.　　　　　　　　　　Tel: (619) 550-7020　　Emp: N/A

Bus: *Development services.*　　　　　　　　　　　　Fax:(619) 458-9591　　%FO: 100

AHLSTROM FILTRATION INC

Krystal Bldg., PO Box 1151, Chattanooga, TN　37401-1151

CEO: Edward A Leinss, Pres.　　　　　　　　　　　Tel: (615) 821-4090　　Emp: N/A

Bus: *Mfr. specialty papers.*　　　　　　　　　　　　Fax:(615) 756-0140　　%FO: 100

AHLSTROM INDUSTRIAL HOLDINGS INC

P.O. Box 2179, Glens Falls, NY　12801

CEO: Olli Malkki, Pres.　　　　　　　　　　　　　Tel: (518) 745-2900　　Emp: N/A

Bus: *System & equipment for pulp & paper*　　　　　Fax:(518) 745-2749　　%FO: 100
industry, specialty papers & packaging.

AHLSTROM MACHINERY INC

Ridge Center, Glens Falls, NY　12801-3686

CEO: Vic Biladeau, EVP　　　　　　　　　　　　　Tel: (518) 793-5111　　Emp: N/A

Bus: *Equipment for pulp & paper industry.*　　　　　Fax:(518) 793-1917　　%FO: 100

AHLSTROM PUMPS LLC

155 Ahlstrom Way, Easley, SC　29640

CEO:Dale Libby, Pres.　　　　　　　　　　　　　　Tel:(864) 855-9090　　Emp:N/A

Bus: *Equipment for pulp & paper industry.*　　　　　Fax:(864) 855-9095　　%FO:100

AHLSTROM RECOVERY INC
10745 Westside Parkway, Alphacetta, GA   30201
CEO: Tuomo Ronkko, Pres.   Tel: (770) 640-2500   Emp: N/A
Bus: *Equipment for pulp & paper industry.*   Fax:(770) 670-9454   %FO: 100

AHLSTROM USA INC
P.O. Box 2179, Glens Falls, NY   12801
CEO: Olli Malkki, Pres.   Tel: (518) 745-2900   Emp: N/A
Bus: *Holding company. U.S. headquarters.*   Fax:(518) 745-2749   %FO: 100

AKERLUND & RAUSING N.A., INC.
3450 Corporate Way, Ste. C, Duluth, GA   30136
CEO: Brian Bailey, Pres.   Tel: (770) 623-8235   Emp: 10
Bus: *Equipment for pulp & paper industry.*   Fax:(770) 623-8236   %FO: 100

KAMTECH INC.
11 Pearl Street, Glens Falls, NY   12801
CEO: Robert C. Neapole, Pres.   Tel: (518) 798-6401   Emp: N/A
Bus: *Industrial contractors.*   Fax:(518) 798-6635   %FO: 100

SIBILLE AHLSTROM INC.
One Corporate Pl.#200, 55 Ferncroft Road, Danvers, MA   01923
CEO: Scott McLaughlin, Pres.   Tel: (508) 777-9888   Emp: N/A
Bus: *Equipment for pulp & paper industry.*   Fax:(508) 777-9444   %FO: 100

TITANIUM FABRICATION CORP.
110 Lehigh Dr, Fairfield, NJ   07006-3044
CEO: Robert Catanzariti, Pres.   Tel: (201) 227-5300   Emp: N/A
Bus: *Mfr./sale titanium equipment for industry.*   Fax:(201) 227-6541   %FO: 100

● **AMER GROUP LTD.**
Mäkelänkatu 91, P.O. Box 130, Helsinki FIN-00601, Finland
CEO: Roger Talermo, Pres. & CEO   Tel: 358-9-757-71   Emp: 4667
Bus: *Mfr./marketing sporting goods, tobacco products &*   Fax:358-9-757-7200
     personnel time planning systems.

ATOMIC SKI USA INC.
9 Columbia Drive, Amherst, NH   03031
CEO: Jack Baltz, Pres.   Tel: (603) 880-6143   Emp: 30
Bus: *Marketing ski, snowboarding & skating*   Fax:(603) 880-6099   %FO: 100
     equipment.

WILSON SPORTING GOODS CO.
8700 West Bryn Mawr Ave., Chicago, IL   60631
CEO: Jim Baugh, Pres.   Tel: (773) 714-6400   Emp: 3049
Bus: *Mfr./marketing sporting goods; racquet, golf*   Fax:(773) 714-4565   %FO: 100
     & team sports equipment & apparel.

• DUOPLAN OY
Teollisuuskatu 33, SF-00510 Helsinki, Finland

CEO: Heikki I. Mannisto, Pres.　　　　　　　Tel: 358-9-3933-672　　Emp: 10

Bus: *Consulting engineering services.*　　　　Fax:358-9-3933-696

EKONO INC.
11601 NE 2nd St., Ste.107, Bellevue, WA　98004-6409

CEO: Heikki I. Mannisto, Pres.　　　　　　　Tel: (425) 455-5969　　Emp: 8

Bus: *Consulting engineering to pulp & paper*　　Fax:(425) 455-3091　　%FO: 51
　　　industry.

• FINNAIR
Tietotie 11A, Helsinki-Vantaa Airport, Box 15, 01053 FINNAIR, Finland

CEO: Antti Potila, Pres./CEO　　　　　　　　Tel: 358-9-818-8100　　Emp: 8300

Bus: *Passenger & cargo air transport.*　　　　Fax:358-9-818-4092

FINNAIR
228 East 45th Street, New York, NY　10017

CEO: Bo W. Long, Gen. Mgr.　　　　　　　　Tel: (212) 499-9000　　Emp: 100

Bus: *Passenger & cargo air transport.*　　　　Fax:(212) 499-9039　　%FO: 100

• FISKARS OY AB
Mannerheimintie 14A, SF-00101 Helsinki, Finland

CEO: Reijo Kaukonen, Pres.　　　　　　　　Tel: 358-9-350-9000　　Emp: N/A

Bus: *Mfr. plastic & metal products.*　　　　　Fax:358-9-350-9009

FISKARS MANUFACTURING
636 Science Drive, Madison, WI　53711

CEO: Wayne Fethke, Pres.　　　　　　　　　Tel: (608) 233-1649　　Emp: N/A

Bus: *Mfr. cutlery & scissors.*　　　　　　　Fax:(608) 233-5321　　%FO: 100

GERBER LEDENDARY BLADES
14200 Southwest 72nd Avenue, Portland, OR　97281

CEO: Jim Wehrf　　　　　　　　　　　　　Tel: (503) 639-6161　　Emp: N/A

Bus: *Mfr. cutlery.*　　　　　　　　　　　　Fax:(503) 620-3446　　%FO: 100

• JAAKKO PÖYRY GROUP OY
Jaakonktau 3, P O Box 4, FIN-01621 Vantaa, Finland

CEO: Niilo Pellonmaa, Pres.　　　　　　　　Tel: 358-9-8947-3002　　Emp: 2600

Bus: *Forest industry consulting.*　　　　　　Fax:358-9-878-5855

JAAKKO PÖYRY CONSULTING (NORTH AMERICA), INC.
580 White Plains Road, 3rd Fl., White Plains, NY　10591-5183

CEO: Tapio Korpeinen, Pres.　　　　　　　　Tel: (914) 332-4000　　Emp: 29

Bus: *Forest industry consulting.*　　　　　　Fax:(914) 332-4411　　%FO: 100

JAAKKO PÖYRY FLOUR DANIEL
100 Flour Daniel Drive, Greenville, SC　29607-2762

CEO: Bill Leistner, Pres.　　　　　　　　　Tel: (864) 281-5733　　Emp: N/A

Bus: *Forest industry consulting.*　　　　　　Fax:(864) 676-7630　　%FO: 50

JAAKKO PÖYRY, INC.
5510 Six Forks Road, Raleigh, NC   27609
CEO: Paul Talvio, Pres.   Tel: (919) 847-6842   Emp: 46
Bus: *Forest industry consulting.*   Fax:(919) 847-2902   %FO: 100

● **KEMIRA OY**
Porkkalankatu 3, P O Box 330, SF-00101 Helsinki, Finland
CEO: Heimo Karinen, CEO   Tel: 358-9-132-11   Emp: N/A
Bus: *Mfr. chemicals, paints & pigments, fertilizers,*   Fax:358-9-132-1794
filters, safety equipment, and biotechnology
products.

    KEMIRA PIGMENTS INC.
    P O Box 368, Savannah, GA   31402
    CEO: R. Ojala, Pres.   Tel: (912) 652-1000   Emp: N/A
    Bus: *Paints & pigments.*   Fax:(912) 652-1175   %FO: 100

● **KONE CORPORATION**
PO Box 8, FIN-00331 Helsinki, Finland
CEO: Gerhard Weindt, Pres.   Tel: 358-4751000   Emp:
Bus: *Mfr. elevators, rail-mounted cranes, cargo handling*   Fax:358-4754375
and access equipment.

    MONTGOMERY KONE, INC.
    One Montgomery Court, Moline, IL   61265
    CEO: Heimo Makinen, Pres.   Tel: (309) 764-6771   Emp: 4200
    Bus: *Mfr. hydraulic and traction elevators and*   Fax:(309) 757-1469   %FO: 100
    escalators.

● **KYMMENE CORPORATION**
Mikonkatu 15A, PO Box 1079, FIN-00101 Helsinki, Finland
CEO: H. Piehl, Chrm.   Tel: 358-131-411   Emp: N/A
Bus: *Mfr. paper, pulp and wood-based products.*   Fax:358-653-884

    UPM - KYMMENE, INC.
    9 Rockefeller Plaza, New York, NY   10020
    CEO: Raimo Waltasaari, Pres.   Tel: (212) 246-9373   Emp: N/A
    Bus: *Sales/distribution of printing/writing papers.*   Fax:(212) 765-0869   %FO: 100

● **MERITA BANK LTD.**
Helsinki, Finland
CEO: Vesa Vainio, Chrm.   Tel: 358-0-1651   Emp: N/A
Bus: *International commercial banking services.*   Fax:358-165-53595

    MERITA BANK LTD.
    437 Madison Avenue, New York, NY   10022
    CEO: Theo Mezger, Gen.Mgr.   Tel: (212) 318-9300   Emp: N/A
    Bus: *International banking services.*   Fax:(212) 421-4420   %FO: 100

● **METRA CORPORATION**
John Stenbergin ranta 2, Postilokero 230, FIN-00101 Helsinki, Finland
CEO: Georg Ehrnrooth, Pres. & CEO   Tel: 358-9-70951   Emp: N/A
Bus: *Mfr. diesel engines and security systems.*   Fax:358-9-762278

    ENVIROVAC, INC.
    1260 Turret Drive, Rockford, IL   6115
    CEO: George T. Beatty, Pres.   Tel: (800) 435-6951   Emp: N/A
    Bus: *Mfr. distributor diesel engines and security*   Fax:(815) 654-8306   %FO: 100
        systems.

● **NESTE OY**
Keilaniemi, P.O. Box 20, FIN-02150, Espoo, Finland
CEO: Mauri Hattunen, Chrm.   Tel: 358-9-450-1   Emp: N/A
Bus: *Oil exploration, production & refining,*   Fax:358-9-450-4447
petrochemicals, gas, power systems; engineering &
transport services.

    NESTE HOLDING (USA) INC.
    Five Post Oak Park, Ste. 1230, Houston, TX   77027
    CEO: Mauri Hattunen, Pres.   Tel: (713) 622-7459   Emp: 400
    Bus: *Holding company for Neste Oy U.S. operations.*   Fax:(713) 622-5570   %FO: 100

    NESTE OIL SERVICES, INC.
    3731 East University Drive, Ste. B, Phoenix, AZ   85034
    CEO: N/A   Tel: (602) 437-8068   Emp: N/A
    Bus: *Mfr. sales petrochemicals.*   Fax:(602) 437-5729   %FO: 100

    NESTE PETROLEUM, INC.
    Five Post Oak Park, Ste. 1230, Houston, TX   77027
    CEO: Gerald McKenna, Pres.   Tel: (713) 407-4400   Emp: N/A
    Bus: *Oil exploration, production & refining,*   Fax:(713) 407-4480   %FO: 100
        petrochemicals, gas, power systems;
        engineering & transport services.

    NESTE RESINS CORP.
    1600 Valley River Drive,, Eugene, OR   97401
    CEO: Jorma Rinta, Pres.   Tel: (541) 687-8840   Emp: N/A
    Bus: *Mfr./distribution petrochemicals.*   Fax:(541) 683-1891   %FO: 100

● **NOKIA GROUP**
P.O. Box 226, Keilalandentie 4, Espoo FIN-00045, Finland
CEO: Jorma Ollila, Pres.   Tel: 358-9-18071   Emp: 31700
Bus: *Telecommunications, mobile phones, base stations.*   Fax:358-9-656388

    NOKIA AMERICAS INC.
    2300 Valley View Lane, Ste. 100, Irving, TX   75062
    CEO: Karl-Pekka Wilska, Pres.   Tel: (972) 257-9800   Emp: 3000
    Bus: *Telecommunications equipment, mobile*   Fax:(972) 257-9877   %FO: 100
        phones U.S. headquarters mobile.

NOKIA DESIGN CENTER
23621 Park Sorrento Rd., Suite 101, Calabases, CA   91302

CEO: Frank Nuovo, VP	Tel: (818) 876-6000	Emp: 15
Bus: *Telecommunications equipment, design &* *research.*	Fax:(818) 876-6089	%FO: 100

NOKIA DISPLAY PRODUCTS INC.
1505 Bridgeway Blvd., Suite 128, Sausalito, CA   94965

CEO: Mahyar Mot Raghi, Mgr.	Tel: (415) 331-4244	Emp: N/A
Bus: *Designs, mfr./sales electronics,* *telecommunications equipment.*	Fax:(415) 331-0424	%FO: 100

NOKIA DISPLAY PRODUCTS, INC.
5942-C Six Forks Road, Raliegh, NC   27609

CEO: N/A	Tel: (919) 870-0081	Emp: N/A
Bus: *Designs, mfr./sales electronics,* *telecommunications equipment.*	Fax:(919) 870-9993	%FO: 100

NOKIA MOBILE PHONES, INC.
6200 Courtney Campbell Causeway, Ste. 900, Tampa, FL   33607-3730

CEO: Paul Chellgren, Pres.	Tel: (813) 287-1141	Emp: 100
Bus: *Designs, mfr./sales electronics,* *telecommunications equipment.*	Fax:(813) 287-8321	%FO: 100

NOKIA PAGING, INC.
12345 Starkey Road, Suite 450, Largo, FL   33773

CEO: N/A	Tel: (813) 532-4241	Emp: N/A
Bus: *Sales/service telecommunications equipment,* *paging instruments.*	Fax:(813) 531-4847	%FO: 100

NOKIA PRODUCTS CORPORATION
1801 Penn Street, Suite 3, Melbourne, FL   32901

CEO: Larry M. Paulson, Mng. Dir.	Tel: (407) 952-2100	Emp: N/A
Bus: *Designs, mfr./sales electronics,* *telecommunications equipment.*	Fax:(407) 952-2101	%FO: 100

NOKIA TELECOMMUNICATION, INC.
Seven Village Circle, Suite 100, West Lake, TX   76262

CEO: Jyrki Salo, Pres.	Tel: (817) 491-5800	Emp: N/A
Bus: *Designs, mfr./sales electronics,* *telecommunications equipment.* *Telecommunications U.S. headquarters.*	Fax:(817) 491-5888	%FO: 100

NOKIA TELECOMMUNICATIONS, INC.
1850 K Street, NW, Suite 1175, Washington, DC   20006

CEO: Claudia Cheek, Mgr.	Tel: (202) 887-1798	Emp: N/A
Bus: *Telecommunications, business & industry* *relations.*	Fax:(202) 887-0432	%FO: 100

NOKIA TELECOMMUNICATIONS, INC.
3 Burlington Woods Drive, Burlington, MA 01803
CEO: N/A   Tel: (617) 238-4900   Emp: N/A
Bus: *Telecommunications equipment, ATM systems*   Fax:(617) 238-4949   %FO: 100
R&D.

NOKIA TELECOMMUNICATIONS, INC.
PO Box 155335, Fort Worth, TX 76155
CEO: N/A   Tel: (817) 355-9000   Emp: N/A
Bus: *Telecommunications equipment, base station*   Fax:(817) 355-9067   %FO: 100
systems.

● **OUTOKUMPU OY**
Läsituulentie 7A, P.O. Box 280 FIN 02101 Espoo, Finland
CEO: Jyrki Juusela, Pres.   Tel: 358-9421-1   Emp: N/A
Bus: *Mfr. base metals; stainless steel & copper products:*   Fax:358-9421-3888
technological services.

THE NEUMAYER COMPANY
PO Box 620236, Middleton, WI 53562-0236
CEO: Gunther Felderer, Pres.   Tel: (608) 836-6664   Emp: N/A
Bus: *Mfr. base metals.*   Fax:(608) 836-9266   %FO: 100

THE NIPPERT COMPANY
801 Pittsburgh Drive, Delaware, OH 43015
CEO: Russell Nippert, Pres.   Tel: (614) 363-1981   Emp: N/A
Bus: *Mfr. base metals.*   Fax:(614) 363-3847   %FO: JV

OUTOKUMPU AMERICAN BRASS, INC.
P.O. Box 981, Buffalo, NY 14240-0981
CEO: Warren Bartel. Pres.   Tel: (716) 879-6700   Emp: N/A
Bus: *Mfr. brass products.*   Fax:(716) 879-6735   %FO: 100

OUTOKUMPU COPPER USA, INC.
129 Fairfield Way, Bloomington, IL 60108
CEO: Uls Anvin, Pres.   Tel: (630) 980-8400   Emp: N/A
Bus: *Mfr./sale copper products.*   Fax:(630) 980-8891   %FO: 100

OUTOKUMPU MINTEC USA INC.
109 Inverness Drive East, Englewood, CO 80112
CEO: Kauko Laukkanen, Pres.   Tel: (303) 792-3110   Emp: N/A
Bus: *Marketing base metals; stainless steel &*   Fax:(303) 799-6892   %FO: 100
copper products: technological services.

PRINCETON GAMMA-TECH, INC.
1200 State Road, Princeton, NJ 08540
CEO: John Patterson, Pres.   Tel: (609) 924-7310   Emp: N/A
Bus: *Mfr. high-tech equipment.*   Fax:(609) 924-1729   %FO: 100

VALLEYCAST
PO Box 1714, Appleton, WI   549-1714
CEO: Charles McClay   Tel: (414) 749-3820   Emp: N/A
Bus: *Mfr. base metals; stainless steel & copper*   Fax:(414) 749-3830   %FO: 100
products: technological services. US
management company.

• **PARTEK AB, OY**
Sörnäisten rantatie 23/25, P.O.Box 61, SF-00501 Helsinki, Finland
CEO: Christoffer Taxell, Pres.   Tel: 358-204-554261   Emp: 13000
Bus: *Materials handling, minerals, insulation.*   Fax:358-204-55-4844

CARGOTEC, INC.
307 Broadway, P.O. Box 298, Swanton, OH   43558
CEO: Lennart Brelin, Pres.   Tel: (419) 825-2331   Emp: 60
Bus: *Cargo handling equipment, cranes, forklifts.*   Fax:(419) 826-8439   %FO: 100

KALTEX, INC.
2310 Peachtree Road, Atlanta, GA   30338
CEO: Warwick Johnston, Exec.VP   Tel: (770) 457-8795   Emp: N/A
Bus: *Materials handling, minerals, forest products,*   Fax:(770) 454-7908   %FO: 100
insulation.

OTTAWA TRUCK, INC.
415 East Dundee Street, Ottawa, KS   66067
CEO: Frank Pubbert, Pres.   Tel: (913) 242-2200   Emp: N/A
Bus: *Materials handling, minerals, forest products,*   Fax:(913) 242-6117   %FO: 100
insulation.

PARTEK INSULATION INC
908 SE Partek Drive, Phenix City, AL   36869
CEO: Kaj Westeren, Pres. & CEO   Tel: (205) 291-6300   Emp: 140
Bus: *Mfr. rock wool insulation.*   Fax:(205) 297-0203   %FO: 100

SISU LOGGING USA, INC.
103 North 12th St., PO Box 401, Gladstone, MI   49837-0401
CEO: K. Lannenpaa, Pres.   Tel: (906) 428-4800   Emp: N/A
Bus: *Materials handling, minerals, forest products,*   Fax:(906) 428-3922   %FO: 100
insulation.

SISU TERMINAL SYSTEMS (USA) INC.
2520 Randolph Avenue, Avenel, NJ   07001-2408
CEO: Jari Pirhonen, Pres.   Tel: (908) 396-4160   Emp: N/A
Bus: *Materials handling, minerals, forest products,*   Fax:(908) 815-1809   %FO: 100
insulation.

SISU TERMINAL SYSTEMS (USA) INC.
777 Brickell Avenue, Suite 640, Miami, FL   33121-2803
CEO: K. Holmroos, Pres.   Tel: (305) 379-6200   Emp: N/A
Bus: *Materials handling, minerals, forest products,*   Fax:(305) 379-8822   %FO: 100
    insulation.

SISU USA, INC.
1301 Cherokee Trace, White Oaks, TX   75693
CEO: Mike Godsey, Plant Mgr.   Tel: (903) 759-5490   Emp: N/A
Bus: *Materials handling, minerals, forest products,*   Fax:(903) 297-8166   %FO: 100
    insulation.

● **POSTIPANKKI, LTD.**
Unioninkatu #22, Helsinki 00007, Finland
CEO: Eino Keinänen, CEO   Tel: 358-204-2511   Emp: N/A
Bus: *Commercial banking services.*   Fax:N/A

    POSTIPANKKI, LTD.
    153 East 53rd Street, New York, NY   10022
    CEO: Pekka Vataja, Gen. Mgr.   Tel: (212) 758-8181   Emp: N/A
    Bus: *International banking services.*   Fax:(212) 758-0011   %FO: 100

● **RAUMA OY**
P.O. Box 1220, Fin-00101 Helsinki, Finland
CEO: Heikki Hakala, Pres.   Tel: 358-204-80140   Emp: 9474
Bus: *Mfr. metals and engineering equipment.*   Fax:358-204-80141

    NELES-JAMESBURY, INC.
    640 Lincoln Street, Worcester, MA   01615
    CEO: Thomas Sturiale, CEO   Tel: (508) 852-0200   Emp: 850
    Bus: *Mfr. valves.*   Fax:(508) 852-8172   %FO: 100

    NORDBERG, INC.
    3073 S. Chase Avenue, Milwaukee, WI   53207
    CEO: Thys DeBeers, Pres.   Tel: (414) 769-4300   Emp: 350
    Bus: *Mfr. crushing equipment.*   Fax:(414) 747-1766   %FO: 100

    PEERLESS CORP.
    603 North 3rd Avenue, Paragould, AR   72450
    CEO: Fred Workman, Pres.   Tel: (870) 236-7753   Emp: N/A
    Bus: *Mfr. forest machinery & transportation*   Fax:(870) 236-2230   %FO: 100
        equipment.

    RAUMA USA, INC.
    133 Federal Street, Suite 302, Boston, MA   02110
    CEO: Zachery Tamminen, Pres.   Tel: (617) 369-7850   Emp: N/A
    Bus: *U.S. headquarters, holding company. Mfr./sale* Fax:(617) 369-7877   %FO: 100
        metals & engineering equipment.

SUNDS DIFIBRATOR WOODHANDLING, INC.
104 Inverness Center Place, Ste. 300, Birmingham, AL 35242

CEO: Gerry Albertson, Pres.	Tel: (205) 995-0190	Emp: 30
Bus: *Engineering office for pulp and papermill machinery.*	Fax:(205) 995-0198	%FO: 100

SUNDS DEFIBRATOR, INC.
2900 Courtyards Drive, Norcross, GA 30017

CEO: Hannu Melarti, Pres.	Tel: (770) 263-7863	Emp: N/A
Bus: *Pulp and papermill machinery.*	Fax:(770) 441-9852	%FO: 100

TIMBERJACK CORPORATION
6215 East Fulton Industrial Blvd., Unit E, Atlanta, GA 30336

CEO: Joe Kalinowski, Pres.	Tel: (404) 629-9044	Emp: N/A
Bus: *Sales/distribution of part for forest machinery.*	Fax:(404) 629-9911	%FO: 100

● **SUUNTO OY**
Juvan Teollisuuskatu 8, SF-02920 Espoo, Finland

CEO: Jorma Kallio, Pres.	Tel: 358-9-847033	Emp: 600
Bus: *Marine field compasses, professional instruments.*	Fax:358-9-8438108	

SUUNTO USA
2151 Las Palmas Dr, #G, Carlsbad, CA 92009

CEO: Henri Syvanen, Pres.	Tel: (760) 931-6788	Emp: 18
Bus: *Distribution/sale compasses, professional instruments, camping equipment.*	Fax:(760) 931-9875	%FO: 100

● **TAMROCK CORP.**
P.O. Box 125, Taivalkatu 8, FIN 15101 Lahti, Finland

CEO: Matt Tuominen, Pres.	Tel: 358-205-44161	Emp: N/A
Bus: *Mfr./sales hydraulic demolition hammers & compactors.*	Fax:358-205-44160	

RAMMER INC.
7391 Washington Blvd., Suite 101, Baltimore, MD 21227

CEO: Pekka Heikkila, Pres.	Tel: (410) 796-9047	Emp: 30
Bus: *Mfr./sales hydraulic demolition hammers & compactors.*	Fax:(410) 796-9313	%FO: 100

● **UNION BANK OF FINLAND**
Aleksanterinkatu 30, SF-00100 Helsinki, Finland

CEO: Vesa Vainio, Pres.	Tel: 358-9-01651	Emp: 10000
Bus: *Commercial banking.*	Fax:358-9-165-42838	

MERITA BANK
437 Madison Ave, 21st Fl., New York, NY 10022

CEO: Jorma Laakkonen, Pres.	Tel: (212) 318-9300	Emp: 100
Bus: *Commercial banking.*	Fax:(212) 421-4420	%FO: 100

• **UPM KYMMENE GROUP**
Snellmaninkatu 13, FIN-00170 Helsinki, Finland
CEO: Juha Niemelä, Pres.   Tel: 358-204-15111   Emp: 45000
Bus: *Forest industries-related products.*   Fax:358-204-15110

> **UPM-KYMMENE USA**
> 9 Rockefeller Plaza, 4th Floor, New York, NY   10020
> CEO: Raimo Wattasaari, Pres.   Tel: (212) 246-9373   Emp: 12
> Bus: *Distribution printing & writing papers.*   Fax:(212) 765-0869   %FO: 100

> **WALKISOFT USA INC.**
> 100 UPM Drive, Mount Holly, NC   28120
> CEO: Pekka Helynrauta, Pres.   Tel: (704) 822-6400   Emp: 67
> Bus: *Mfr. airlaid paper.*   Fax:(704) 822-0101   %FO: 100

• **VAISALA OY**
PL 26, SF-00421 Helsinki, Finland
CEO: Pekka Ketonen, Mgn. Dir.   Tel: 358-9-89491   Emp: 700
Bus: *Meteorological instruments.*   Fax:358-9-49227

> **VAISALA, INC.**
> 100 Commerce Way, Woburn, MA   01801-1068
> CEO: Steven H. Chansky, Pres.   Tel: (617) 933-4500   Emp: 80
> Bus: *Mfr. meteorological instruments.*   Fax:(617) 933-8029   %FO: 100

• **VALMET OY**
Panuntie 6, P O Box 27, FIN-00621 Helsinki, Finland
CEO: Matti Sundberg, Pres.   Tel: 358-9-777-051   Emp: 13000
Bus: *Industrial machinery & equipment, measuring &*   Fax:358-9-7770-5580
     control devices.

> **VALMET AUTOMATION (USA) INC.**
> 3100 Medlock Bridge Rd, Suite 250, Norcross, GA   30071
> CEO: Antti Kusima, Pres.   Tel: (770) 446-7818   Emp: 100
> Bus: *Process automation, integration, distribution*   Fax:(770) 446-8794   %FO: 100
>   *& control systems.*

> **VALMET INC., Appleton Division**
> PO Box 2339, Appleton, WI   54913
> CEO: Pekka Haapanen, VP   Tel: (414) 733-7361   Emp: 400
> Bus: *Mfr. paper finishing systems.*   Fax:(414) 733-1048   %FO: 100

> **VALMET INC.**
> 12933 Sam Neely Road., P O Box 7467, Charlotte, NC   28241
> CEO: Juhani Pakkala, Pres.   Tel: (704) 588-5530   Emp: 210
> Bus: *Mfr. paper & board machinery.*   Fax:(704) 587-2320   %FO: 100

VALMET INC., Enerdry Division
2200 Sutherland Ave., Ste B-201, Knoxville, TN   37919
CEO: Marco Marcheggiani, Pres.   Tel: (423) 525-6990   Emp: 52
Bus: *Mfr. air systems.*   Fax:(423) 522-3281   %FO: 100

VALMET INC., Honeycomb Division
P.O. Box 502, Biddeford, ME   04005
CEO: Donald Beaumont, Exec.VP & Gen.Mgr.   Tel: (207) 282-1521   Emp: 180
Bus: *Mfr. air systems.*   Fax:(207) 283-0926   %FO: 100

VALMET INC., Hudson Falls Division
27 Allen Street, Hudson Falls, NY   12839-1958
CEO: Kalevi Puolamaki, Gen.Mgr.   Tel: (518) 747-3381   Emp: 142
Bus: *Equipment servicing.*   Fax:(518) 747-1541   %FO: 100

France

- **ACCOR SA**
  2 rue de la Mare-Neuve, F-91021 Evry Cédex, France
  CEO: Jean-Marc Espalioux, Chrm.   Tel: 33-1-6087-4320   Emp: 120668
  Bus: *Hotel owner/manager, catering; Sofitel, Motel 6;*   Fax:33-1-6077-0458
  retirement homes.

      ACCOR NORTH AMERICA CORP.
      2 Overhill Road, Scarsdale, NY   10583
      CEO: Patrick Bourguignon, Pres.   Tel: (914) 725-5055   Emp: N/A
      Bus: *Hotels & restaurants; Motel 6.*   Fax:(914) 725-5640   %FO: 100

- **AEROSPATIALE SNL**
  37 boulevard de Montmorency, F-75781 Paris Cedex 16, France
  CEO: Yves Michot, Chrm.   Tel: 33-1-4224-2424   Emp: 36000
  Bus: *Design/mfr. aircraft, aircraft engines & parts.*   Fax:33-1-4224-2619

      AEROSPATIALE FINANCE CORP.
      1101 15th Street, N.W., Washington, DC   20005
      CEO: Pierre de Bausset, Pres.   Tel: (202) 785-8210   Emp: N/A
      Bus: *Financial services company.*   Fax:(202) 785-8324   %FO: 100

      AEROSPATIALE, INC.
      1101 15th Street, N.W., Washington, DC   20005
      CEO: Gregory Bradford, Pres.   Tel: (202) 293-0650   Emp: N/A
      Bus: *U.S. headquarters for Aerospatiale SNL.*   Fax:(202) 429-0638   %FO: 100

      AIR AMERICAN SUPPORT INC.
      13850 McLearen Road, Herndon, VA   20171
      CEO: Jean-Daniel Leroy, Pres., Marketing   Tel: (703) 736-1090   Emp: N/A
      Bus: *Services Aerospatiale products & systems.*   Fax:(703) 736-4266   %FO: 100

      AIR MARKETING INC.
      13850 McLearen Road, Herndon, VA   20171
      CEO: Jean-Michel Leonard, Pres.   Tel: (703) 736-1080   Emp: N/A
      Bus: *Marketing/distribution/service Aerospatiale*   Fax:(703) 736-4266   %FO: 100
      products & systems.

      SOCATA AIRCRAFT
      North Perry Airport, 7501 Pembroke Road., Pembroke Pines, FL   33023
      CEO: Bernard Silvie, Pres.   Tel: (954) 964-6877   Emp: N/A
      Bus: *Fixed-wing aircraft sales/service.*   Fax:(952) 964-1668   %FO: 100

● **AIR FRANCE**
45, rue de Paris, F-95747 Roissy CDG Cédex , France
CEO: Christian Blanc, Chrm.   Tel: 33-1-4156-7800   Emp: 55000
Bus: *Airline, catering, maintenance.*   Fax:33-1-4156-8419

   AIR FRANCE
   142 West 57th Street - 18th Fl., New York, NY   10019
   CEO: Robert Iversen, EVP   Tel: (212) 830-4000   Emp: 70
   Bus: *International air transport services.*   Fax:(212) 830-4244   %FO: 100

● **AIRBUS INDUSTRIE**
1 Rond Point Maurice Bellonte, F-31707 Blagnac Cédex, France
CEO: Jean Pierson, Mng. Dir.   Tel: 33-5-6193-3431   Emp: 2182
Bus: *Mfr. aircraft.*   Fax:33-5-6193-4955

   AIRBUS INDUSTRIE OF NORTH AMERICA, INC.
   198 Van Buren Street, Herndon, VA   20170
   CEO: Jonathan M. Schofield, Chrm.   Tel: (703) 834-3400   Emp: N/A
   Bus: *Mfr./sale aircraft.*   Fax:(703) 834-3340   %FO: 100

● **ALCATEL ALSTHOM COMPAGNIE GÉNÉRALE D'ELECTRICITÉ SA**
54, rue La Boétie, F-75008 Paris, France
CEO: Serge Tchuruk, Chrm.   Tel: 33-1-4076-1010   Emp: 191830
Bus: *Industrial conglomerate; telecommunications,*   Fax:33-1-4076-1400
    energy, transportation & communications.

   ALCATEL COMPTECH INC.
   550 Parrott Street, San Jose, CA   95112
   CEO: Jean-Yves Guegan, Chm.   Tel: (408) 947-7000   Emp: N/A
   Bus: *Computer services.*   Fax:(408) 280-7847   %FO: 100

   ALCATEL CONTRACTING (NA) INC.
   2001 Westside Parkway Ste 190, Alpharetta, GA   30201
   CEO: Charles Willingham, Pres.   Tel: (770) 664-7327   Emp: N/A
   Bus: *Computer services.*   Fax:(770) 664-7692   %FO: 100

   ALCATEL DATA NETWORKS INC.
   12502 Sunrise Valley Drive, Reston, VA   22096
   CEO: Jean-Luc Abaziou, Pres.   Tel: (703) 689-6000   Emp: N/A
   Bus: *Telecommunications.*   Fax:(703) 689-5843   %FO: 100

   ALCATEL ENGINEERING & SERVICE CENTER INC.
   6701 Democracy Blvd. #706, Bethesda, MD   20817-1572
   CEO: Philip Benson, Mng. Dir.   Tel: (301) 897-0849   Emp: N/A
   Bus: *Consulting engineers.*   Fax:(301) 897-3758   %FO: 100

ALCATEL ITS INC.
12030 Sunrise Valley Drive, Reston, VA   22091

CEO: Patrice Fyda, Pres.	Tel: (703) 715-1100	Emp: N/A
Bus: *Telecommunications, energy, transportation, communications.*	Fax:(703)715-9004	%FO: 100

ALCATEL NA CABLE SYSTEMS INC. (formerly ALCATEL NA INC.)
39 Second Street, NW, Hickory, NC   28601

CEO: Marvin Edwards, Pres.	Tel: (704) 323-1120	Emp: N/A
Bus: *U.S. headquarters, Alcatel Alstrom Compagnie Générale d'Electricité SA.*	Fax:(704) 328-6339	%FO: 100

ALCATEL NA INC.
39 Second Street, NW, Hickory, NC   28601

CEO: Marvin S. Edwards, Jr.,Chrm.	Tel: (704) 323-1120	Emp: N/A
Bus: *Telecommunications, energy, transportation, communications.*	Fax:(704) 328-6329	%FO: 100

ALCATEL NETWORK SYSTEMS, INC.
1225 North Alma Road, MS 406-410, Richardson, TX   75081-2206

CEO: David Orr, Pres.	Tel: (972) 996-5000	Emp: N/A
Bus: *Telephone communication equipment and systems.*	Fax:(972) 996-7062	%FO: 100

ALCATEL SCANWIRE INC.
739 Roosevelt Road, Ste 301, Glen Ellyn, IL   60137

CEO: J. Pulkinen, Pres.	Tel: (630) 469-1348	Emp: N/A
Bus: *Telephone communication equipment and systems.*	Fax:(630) 469-1374	%FO: 100

ALCATEL TELECOMMUNICATIONS CABLE INC.
2515 Penny Road, Claremont, NC   28610

CEO: C.J. Phillips, Pres.	Tel: (704) 459-9787	Emp: N/A
Bus: *Telecommunications products/systems.*	Fax:(704) 459-9312	%FO: 100

ALCATEL TITN INC.
12030 Sunrise Valley Drive, Reston, VA   22091

CEO: Paul Caizergues, Chrm.	Tel: (703) 715-1148	Emp: N/A
Bus: *Telecommunications, energy, transportation, communications.*	Fax:(703) 758-1416	%FO: 100

ALCATEL USA CORP.
39 Second St., N.W., Hickory, NC   28601

CEO: Serge Tchuruk, Chrm.	Tel: (704) 323-2601	Emp: N/A
Bus: *Telecommunications, energy, transportation, communications.*	Fax:(704) 328-9117	%FO: 100

ALCATEL VACUUM PRODUCTS INC.
67 Sharp Street, Hingham, MA   02043
CEO: Jean-Yves Guegan, Chrm.   Tel: (617) 331-4200   Emp: N/A
Bus: *Mfr. pumps.*   Fax:(617) 331-4230   %FO: 100

ALCATEL WIRE & CABLE INC.
15 Oakland Avenue, Chester, NY   10916
CEO: Gordon Thursfield, Pres.   Tel: (914) 469-2141   Emp: N/A
Bus: *Mfr. wire & cable.*   Fax:(914) 469-9935   %FO: 100

ALTA TECHNOLOGY
2 Enterprise Drive - Suite 303, Shelton, CT   06484
CEO: Pierre Lereboullet, Pres.   Tel: (203) 929-7931   Emp: N/A
Bus: *Telecommunications products & services.*   Fax:(203) 929-8286   %FO: 100

ASPEN TECHNOLOGIES
14701 St. Mary's Lane, Houston, TX   77079
CEO: Douglas C. White, Chrm.   Tel: (713) 621-6900   Emp: N/A
Bus: *Telecommunications service & products.*   Fax:(713) 496-3232   %FO: 100

CEGELEC AUTOMATION INC.
DL Clark Building, 5th Fl.
503 Martindale St., Pitttsburgh, PA   15212
CEO: R.T. Pickering, Pres.   Tel: (412) 967-5999   Emp: N/A
Bus: *Telecommunications service & products.*   Fax:(412) 967-7660   %FO: JV

DELEGATION CEGELEC
c/o Cegelec Automation Inc., 490 Lapp Road, Malvern, PA   19355
CEO: Brian Pope   Tel: (610) 651-7605   Emp: N/A
Bus: *(Firms marked "JV" are co-owned by The*   Fax:(610) 296-2854   %FO: JV
  General Electric Co Plc, England).

ECOLAIR INC.
1550 Lehigh Drive, Easton, PA   18042
CEO: Alfred Brady, Pres   Tel: (610) 250-1000   Emp: N/A
Bus: *Mfr. condensers & dampers.*   Fax:(610) 250-1005   %FO: JV

ECSA Corporation
11120 NE 33rd Place, Bellevue, WA   98004
CEO: Neil Stanton, Chrm.   Tel: (206) 822-6800   Emp: N/A
Bus: *Telecommunications service & products.*   Fax:(206) 889-1700   %FO: 100

EUROPEAN GAS TURBINES INC.
15950 Park Row, Houston, TX   77084
CEO: John Paull, Pres.   Tel: (713) 492-0222   Emp: N/A
Bus: *Mfr. small industry & aeroderivative gas*   Fax:(713) 492-5607   %FO: JV
  turbines, hi-speed diesel engines.

GEC ALSTHOM INC.
4 Skyline Drive, Hawthorne, NY   10532
CEO: Paul J Jancek, Pres.   Tel: (914) 347-5155   Emp: N/A
Bus: *Mfr. generators, motors, controls, valves,*   Fax:(914) 347-5432   %FO: JV
        pumps, transportation & marine equipment.

GEC ALSTHOM CYRIL BATH
1610 Airport Road, Monroe, NC   28110
CEO: Joseph Hiteshue, Pres.   Tel: (704) 289-8531   Emp: N/A
Bus: *Mfr. hydraulic presses.*   Fax:(704)289-3932   %FO: JV

GEC ALSTHOM ELECTRO- MECHANICAL CORP.
One Corporate Drive - Ste 502, Shelton, CT   06484
CEO: Douglas Miller, Mng. Dir.   Tel: (203) 926-2626   Emp: N/A
Bus: *Mfr. low voltage fusegear.*   Fax:(203) 926-1980   %FO: JV

GEC ALSTHOM SCHILLING ROBOTIC SYSTEMS INC.
1632 DaVinci Court, Davis, CA   95616
CEO: Tyler Schilling, Pres.   Tel: (916) 753-6718   Emp: N/A
Bus: *Mfr. hydraulic equipment.*   Fax:(916) 753-8092   %FO: JV

GEC ALSTHOM T & D BALTEAU
West Antelope Road Road 300, Medford, OR   97503
CEO: James E. Moreau, Pres.   Tel: (503) 826-2113   Emp: N/A
Bus: *Mfr. instrument transformers.*   Fax:(503) 826-8847   %FO: JV

GEC ALSTHOM T&D INC.
4 Skyline Drive, Hawthorne, NY   10532
CEO: Paul J. Jancek, Pres.   Tel: (914) 353-6090   Emp: N/A
Bus: *Hi-volt switchgear, transformers, protection &* Fax:(914) 353-6188   %FO: JV
        control equipment.

GEC ALSTHOM TRANSPORTATION Inc.
4 Skyline Drive, Hawthorne, NY   10532
CEO: Paul J. Jancek, Pres.   Tel: (914) 345-5155   Emp: N/A
Bus: *Mfr. transportation equipment.*   Fax:(914) 345-5432   %FO: JV

GEC ALSTROM DIESELS INC.
10801 Kempwood Drive, Ste. 1, Houston, TX   77043
CEO: Tim Gale, Pres.   Tel: (713) 939-0073   Emp: N/A
Bus: *Mfr. engines.*   Fax:(713) 939-0105   %FO: JV

KABELMETAL ELECTRO NORTH AMERICA INC.
39 2nd Street West, Hickory, NC   28601
CEO: Marvin S. Edwards, Jr. Pres.   Tel: (704) 323-2610   Emp: N/A
Bus: *Telecommunications.*   Fax:(704) 328-6339   %FO: 100

NEYRPIC INC.
Two Corporate Drive, Shelton, CT   06484
CEO: Douglas L. Miller, Pres.   Tel: (203) 926-2626   Emp: N/A
Bus: *Mfr. hydro turbines.*   Fax:(203) 929-1980   %FO: JV

RADIO FREQUENCY SYSTEMS INC.
2 Ryan Place, Marlboro, NJ   07746
CEO: Dr. Jurgen W. Luehring, Pres   Tel: (908) 462-1880   Emp: N/A
Bus: *Telecommunications service & products.*   Fax:(908) 306-3518   %FO: 100

SAFT AMERICA INC.
711 Industrial Boulevard, Valdosta, GA   31601
CEO: Frank D. Westfall, Pres.   Tel: (912) 247-2331   Emp: N/A
Bus: *Mfr. batteries.*   Fax:(912) 247-7120   %FO: 100

● **ALDES AERAULIQUE**
20 Blvd. Joliot-Curie, 69200 Venissieux, France
CEO: Bruno Lacroix, CEO   Tel: 33-4-7877-1515   Emp: 500
Bus: *Mfr. ventilation, fire protection equipment & metal*   Fax:33-4-7876-1597
     stamping.

    AMERICAN ALDES VENTILATION CORPORATION
    4537 Northgate Court, Sarasota, FL   34234-2124
    CEO: Dwight R. Shackelford, EVP   Tel: (941) 351-3441   Emp: 6
    Bus: *Distribution ventilation products.*   Fax:(941) 351-3442   %FO: 100

● **ARIANESPACE SA**
blvd de l'Europe, B P 177, F-91006 Evry Cédex, France
CEO: Charles Bigot, Chrm.   Tel: 33-1-60876000   Emp: 320
Bus: *Prod/marketing/sales operations for launch services*   Fax:33-1-60876247
     worldwide.

    ARIANESPACE, INC.
    700 13th Street NW, #230, Washington, DC   20005
    CEO: Douglas A. Heydon, Pres.   Tel: (202) 628-3936   Emp: 6
    Bus: *Satellite launching services.*   Fax:(202) 628-3949   %FO: 100

● **AUCHAN**
18 Residence Flanders, 59170 Croix, France
CEO: Gerard Mulliez, Pres.   Tel: 33-320-2005-0202 Emp: 32000
Bus: *Hypermarket retailing.*   Fax:N/A

    AUCHAN USA, INC.
    8800 W. Sam Houston Pkwy S., Houston, TX   77099
    CEO: Wilfrid d'Audiffrett, Pres.   Tel: (281) 530-9855   Emp: 500
    Bus: *Retail hypermarket.*   Fax:(281) 530-2533   %FO: 100

• **AUDAX INDUSTRIES**
2 rue de Tours, 72500 Chateau du Loir, France
CEO: Dominique de Gelis, CEO   Tel: 33-1-344-0235   Emp: N/A
Bus: *Mfr. loudspeaker components.*   Fax:33-1-344-1202

> **POLYDAX SPEAKER CORPORATION**
> 10 Upton Drive, Wilmington, MA   01887
> CEO: Ralph Nichols, Gen. Mgr.   Tel: (508) 658-0700   Emp: 6
> Bus: *Distribution loudspeaker components.*   Fax:(508) 658-0703   %FO: 100

• **AXA - UAP**
21-23 Avenue Matignon, 75008 France
CEO: Claude Bébéar, Chrm.   Tel: 33-1-4075-5700   Emp: 36625
Bus: *Global financial services; insurance, merchant*   Fax:31-1-4075-4792
banking, securities broker/dealer, investment
advisory services.

> **ALLIANCE CAPITAL MANAGEMENT CORP.**
> 1345 Avenue of the Americas, New York, NY   10105
> CEO: Dave Williams, Chrm.   Tel: (212) 969-1000   Emp: N/A
> Bus: *Investment advisory services.*   Fax:(212) 969-1255   %FO: 36

> **AXA RE US, INC.**
> 17 State Street, New York, NY   10004
> CEO: Robert Lippencott, Pres.   Tel: (212) 493-9300   Emp: N/A
> Bus: *Reinsurance services.*   Fax:(212) 425-2914   %FO: 100

> **DONALDSON, LUFKIN & JENRETTE, INC.**
> 277 Park Avenue, New York, NY   10172
> CEO: John S. Chalsty, Chrm.   Tel: (212) 892-3000   Emp: N/A
> Bus: *Securities broker/dealer, investment banking*   Fax:(212) 892-2520   %FO: 60
> *services. Sub. of the Equitable Companies Inc.*

> **THE EQUITABLE COMPANIES INC.**
> 787 Seventh Avenue, New York, NY   10019
> CEO: Edward D. Miller, Chrm.   Tel: (212) 554-1234   Emp: N/A
> Bus: *Insurance, investment & real estate*   Fax:(212) 554-2320   %FO: 60
> *management services.*

> **EQUITABLE REAL ESTATE INVESTMENT MANAGEMENT, INC.**
> 3414 Peachtree Road, NE, Ste. 1400, Atlanta, GA   30326
> CEO: George R. Puskar, Chrm.   Tel: (404) 239-5000   Emp: N/A
> Bus: *Real estate investment and management*   Fax:(404) 231-4091   %FO: 60
> *services. Sub. of the Equitable Companies Inc.*

- **BANQUE FRANÇAISE DU COMMERCE EXTERIEUR**
21 blvd Haussmann,F-75009 Paris, France
CEO: François Gavois, Pres.   Tel: 33-1-4800-4800   Emp: N/A
Bus: *Commercial banking services.*   Fax:33-1-4800-4151

    BANQUE FRANCAISE DU COMMERCE EXTERIEUR
    645 Fifth Avenue, New York, NY   10022
    CEO: Jean Pierre Masson, Gen.Mgr.   Tel: (212) 872-5000   Emp: 80
    Bus: *Banking services.*   Fax:(212) 872-5045   %FO: 100

- **BANQUE INDOSUEZ**
1 rue d' Astorg, F- 75008 Paris, France
CEO: Gerard Mestrallet, Chrm.   Tel: 33-1-4006-6400   Emp: 16500
Bus: *Financial services company: banking, insurance,*   Fax:33-1-4006-6688
    real estate.

    BANQUE INDOSUEZ
    1211 Ave. of the Americas, New York, NY   10036
    CEO: Bernard Chauvel, Pres.   Tel: (212) 278-2000   Emp: 300
    Bus: *Banking services.*   Fax:(212) 278-2444   %FO: 100

    INDOSUEZ CAPITAL
    1211 Ave of the Americas, New York, NY   10036
    CEO: Les J. Lieberman, Mng. Dir.   Tel: (212) 278-2222   Emp: 50
    Bus: *Investment banking services.*   Fax:(212) 278-2201   %FO: 100

    INDOSUEZ VENTURES
    2180 Sand Hill Road, Suite 450, Menlo Park, CA   94025
    CEO: Nancy Burns, Gen. Ptnr.   Tel: (415) 854-0587   Emp: 30
    Bus: *Merchant banking services.*   Fax:(415) 323-5561   %FO: 100

- **BANQUE NATIONALE DE PARIS**
16 blvd des Italiens, F-75009 Paris, France
CEO: Michel Pebereau, Chrm.   Tel: 33-1-4014-4546   Emp: N/A
Bus: *Commercial & investment banking, and securities &*   Fax:33-1-4244-6940
    asset management services.

    BANEXI INTERNATIONAL
    499 Park Avenue, New York, NY   10022
    CEO: Alain Bankier, Mng. Dir.   Tel: (212) 418-8200   Emp: N/A
    Bus: *Merchant banking & investment advisory*   Fax:(212) 838-7590   %FO: 100
      services.

    BANK OF THE WEST
    180 Montgomery Street, San Francisco, CA   94104
    CEO: Don Mc Grath, CEO   Tel: (415) 765-4800   Emp: N/A
    Bus: *General commercial banking services.*   Fax:(415) 399-9118   %FO: 100

BANQUE NATIONALE DE PARIS
499 Park Avenue, New York, NY   10022
CEO: Pierre Schneider, Gen.Mgr.						Tel: (212) 750-1400		Emp: N/A
Bus: *Commercial & investment banking, and*				Fax:(212) 415-9717		%FO: 100
securities & asset management services.

• BANQUE SUDAMERIS (sub of Banca Commerciale Italiana Group)
4, rue Meyerbeer, Paris 75009, France
CEO: A. Abelli, Chrm. & Pres.						Tel: 33-1-4801-7777		Emp: 6689
Bus: *Commercial banking services.*					Fax:33-1-4246-3213

BANK SUDAMERIS
One William Street, New York, NY   10004
CEO: Robert J. Marcuse, Rep.						Tel: (212) 509-7858		Emp: N/A
Bus: *International commercial banking services.*			Fax:(212) 943-0943		%FO: 100

BANK SUDAMERIS
701 Brickell Avenue, 9th Fl., Miami, FL   33131
CEO: Hubert de la Feld							Tel: (305) 372-2200		Emp: N/A
Bus: *International commercial banking services.*			Fax:(305) 374-1130		%FO: 100

• BANQUE WORMS
1, Place de Degrés, Paris, France
CEO: Jacques-Henri Gougenheim, Chrm.				Tel: 33-1-4907-5050		Emp: N/A
Bus: *International merchant banking services. Subsidiary*		Fax:33-1-4907-5911
of Union Des Assurances de Paris, owned by AXA.

BANQUE WORMS CAPITAL CORP.
450 Park Avenue, New York, NY   10022
CEO: Marc Devaux							Tel: (212) 758-6375		Emp: N/A
Bus: *International merchant banking services.*			Fax:(212) 593-4854		%FO: 100

• BDDP GROUPE
162-164, rue de Billancourt, F-92100 Boulogne, Paris
CEO: Jean-Claude Boulet, Pres.						Tel: 33-1-4909-7010		Emp: 2255
Bus: *International advertising/communications group of*		Fax:33-1-4909-7232
companies.

BASTONI BARNES
1740 Broadway, New York, NY   11758
CEO: Chrintine Bastoni, Mng. Ptnr.					Tel: (212) 484-5943		Emp: 35
Bus: *Advertising agency.*						Fax:(212) 765-3305		%FO: 100

McCRACKEN BROOKS COMMUNICATIONS
8400 Normandale Lake Blvd., Minneapolis, MN   55437
CEO: A. Keith McCracken, Chrm.						Tel: (612) 896-8400		Emp: 45
Bus: *Advertising agency.*						Fax:(612) 896-8477		%FO: 100

WELLS, RICH, GREENE BDDP
9 West 57th Street, New York, NY   10019

CEO: Frank Assumma, Chrm.	Tel: (212) 303-5400	Emp: 465
Bus: *International advertising agency.*	Fax:(212) 303-6400	%FO: 100

● **BENETEAU SA**
Zone Industrielle des Mares, - BP 66, F-85270 Saint-Hilaire-de-Riez, France

CEO: Anette Roux, Pres.	Tel: 33-51-555382	Emp: N/A
Bus: *Builds sailboats & yachts.*	Fax:33-51-558910	

BENETEAU USA, INC.
24 North Market Street, Ste 201, Charleston, SC   29401

CEO: Jean-Francois De Premorel, EVP	Tel: (803) 805-5000	Emp: N/A
Bus: *Builds sailboats & yachts.*	Fax:(805) 805-5010	%FO: 100

● **BESNIER SA**
10-20 rue Adolphe Beck, 53002 Laval, France

CEO: Bernard Decker, Pres. Int'l.	Tel: 33-2-4356-0721	Emp: N/A
Bus: *Produces/distributes dairy products.*	Fax:33-2-4349-1960	

BESNIER USA, INC.
950 Third Avenue, 22nd Fl., New York, NY   10022

CEO: Paul Bensabat, EVP	Tel: (212) 758-6666	Emp: N/A
Bus: *Dairy products.*	Fax:(212) 758-6678	%FO: 100

SORRENTO CHEESE COMPANY, INC.
2375 South Park Avenue, Buffalo, NY   14220-2653

CEO: Paul Bensabat, EVP	Tel: (716) 823-6262	Emp: 1000
Bus: *Dairy products.*	Fax:(716) 823-0448	%FO: 70+

SOCIÉTÉ BIC S.A.
9 rue Petit, F-92110 Clichy, France

CEO: Bruno Bich, CEO	Tel: 33-1-45-195200	Emp: N/A
Bus: *Mfr. writing instruments, shavers, and lighters,*	Fax:33-145-195299	

BIC CORPORATION
500 Bic Drive, Milford, CT   06460

CEO: Raymond Winter, Pres.	Tel: (203) 783-2000	Emp: 1500
Bus: *Mfr./distributor writing instruments, shavers, and lighters.*	Fax:(203) 763-2108	%FO: 100

BOIRON
20 rue de la Liberation, 69110 Ste-Foy-les-Lyon, France

CEO: Christian Boiron, Pres.	Tel: 33-472-324020	Emp: 2200
Bus: *Mfr./distribution homeopathic pharmaceuticals.*	Fax:33-478-596916	

BOIRON BORNEMAN INC.
6 Campus Blvd., Newton Square, PA   19073

CEO: Thierry Boiron, Pres.	Tel: (610) 325-7464	Emp: 64
Bus: *Mfr./distribution homeopathic medicines.*	Fax:(610) 325-7480	%FO: 100

● **COMPAGNIE DES MACHINES BULL**
68, route de Versailles, F-78430 Louveciennes, France
CEO: Jean-Marie Descarpentries, Pres.   Tel: 33-1-3966-6060   Emp: 24000
Bus: *Design/mfr. computer systems & networks.*   Fax:33-1-4696-9092

    BULL CORP. OF AMERICA
    2 Wall Street, Billerica, MA   01821
    CEO: James Quinn, Gen. Mgr.   Tel: (508) 294-5739   Emp: 25
    Bus: *Financial holding company.*   Fax:(508) 294-5736   %FO: 100

    BULL H.N. INFORMATION SYSTEMS
    300 Concord Road, Billerica, MA   01821
    CEO: Donald Zereski, Pres.   Tel: (508) 294-6000   Emp: 20000
    Bus: *Design/mfr. networks & computer systems.*   Fax:(508) 294-5736   %FO: 100

    MICRO CARD TECHNOLOGIES INC
    14070 Proton Road, Dallas, TX   75244
    CEO: A. D'Avezac, Pres.   Tel: (972) 788-4055   Emp: 50
    Bus: *Mfr./distribution smart cards.*   Fax:(972) 239-7138   %FO: 100

    NIPSON
    2 Wall Street, Billerica, MA   01821
    CEO: Raoul Nehme, Pres.   Tel: (508) 294-6000   Emp: 50
    Bus: *Non-impact printers.*   Fax:(214) 239-7138   %FO: 100

● **C.E.P. COMMUNICATION**
20 ave. Hoche, F-75008 aris, France
CEO: Christian Bregou, Chrm.   Tel: 33-1-4495-5600   Emp: N/A
Bus: *Book publishing company.*   Fax:33-1-4495-5656

    LAROUSSE KINGFISHER CHAMBERS INC,
    95 Madison Avenue, New York, NY   10016
    CEO: Dennis Doran, Pres.   Tel: (212) 686-1060   Emp: N/A
    Bus: *Book publishing company.*   Fax:(212) 686-1082   %FO: 100

● **CAISSE CENTRALE DE BANQUES POPULAIRES**
10-12 Avenue Winston Churchill, F-94677 Charente-le-Pont, France
CEO: Jacques Delmas-Maisalet, Chrm.   Tel: 33-1-4039-3000   Emp: N/A
Bus: *General banking services.*   Fax:33-1-4039-4001

    CAISSE CENTRALE DE BANQUES POPULAIRES
    126 East 56th Street, Suite 5N, New York, NY   10022
    CEO: Alain Demoustier, Gen.Mgr..   Tel: (212) 753-6018   Emp: N/A
    Bus: *International banking services.*   Fax:(212) 593-3291   %FO: 100

• CAISSE DES DEPOTS ET CONSIGNATIONS

56 rue de Lille, F-75007 Paris, France

CEO: Philippe Lagayette, Dir. Gen.   Tel: 33-1-4049-5678   Emp: 10000

Bus: *Financial services companies.*   Fax:33-1-4049-6554

CAISSE DES DEPOTS SECURITIES INC.

9 West 57th Street, 36th Fl., New York, NY 10019

CEO: Luc DeClapiers, Pres.   Tel: (212) 891-6250   Emp: 6

Bus: *Brokerage government securities, corporate equities.*   Fax:(212) 527-1426   %FO: 100

CDC CAPITAL INC.

9 West 57th Street, 36th Fl., New York, NY 10019

CEO: Luc de Clapiers, Pres. & CEO   Tel: (212) 891-6100   Emp: 52

Bus: *Fin trading, investment.*   Fax:(212) 891-6295   %FO: 100

CDC INVESTMENT MANAGEMENT CORP.

9 West 57th Street, 36th Fl., New York, NY 10019

CEO: Luc de Clapiers, Pres. & CEO   Tel: (212) 891-6150   Emp: 26

Bus: *Invest management services.*   Fax:(212) 891-6294   %FO: 100

CDC NORTH AMERICA INC.

9 West 57th Street, 36th Fl., New York, NY 10019

CEO: Luc de Clapiers, Pres. & CEO   Tel: (212) 891-6137   Emp: 3

Bus: *Financial services.*   Fax:(212) 891-6118   %FO: 100

CAISSE NATIONALE DE CRÉDIT AGRICOLE

91-93 blvd Pasteur, F-75015 Paris, France

CEO: Lucien Douroux, CEO   Tel: 33-1-4323-5202   Emp: 74400

Bus: *General commercial banking.*   Fax:33-1-4323-4489

CAISSE NATIONALE DE CRÉDIT AGRICOLE

55 East Monroe Street, Chicago, IL 60603

CEO: Bernard Chauvel, Pres., US Operations   Tel: (312) 372-9200   Emp: N/A

Bus: *Commercial banking services.*   Fax:(312) 372-2830   %FO: 100

CRÉDIT AGRICOLE

520 Madison Avenue, New York, NY 10022

CEO: Bernard Chauvel, Pres. & Gen. Mgr.   Tel: (212) 418-2200   Emp: N/A

Bus: *International commercial banking services.*   Fax:(212) 418-2273   %FO: 100

CRÉDIT AGRICOLE FUTURES INC.

227 W. Monroe Street, #4850, Chicago, IL 60605

CEO: Mark Vaughn, COO   Tel: (312) 201-7900   Emp: N/A

Bus: *Futures commission merchant.*   Fax:(312) 201-7927   %FO: 100

CRÉDIT AGRICOLE SECURITIES INC.

520 Madison Avenue, 42nd fl, New York, NY 10022

CEO: Pascal Viornery, CEO   Tel: (212) 593-9320   Emp: N/A

Bus: *Securities dealer/broker.*   Fax:(212) 593-7976   %FO: 100

UI-USA INC.
610 Fifth Avenue, #306, New York, NY   10020
CEO: Philippe Guimard, Mgn. Dir.   Tel: (212) 218-5025   Emp: N/A
Bus: *Investment banking services.*   Fax:(212) 218-5035   %FO: 100

● **CAP GEMINI SA**
Place de l'Etoile-11, rue de Tilsitt, 75017 Paris, France
CEO: Serge Kampf, Exec. Chrm.   Tel: 33-1-4754-5000   Emp: 30000
Bus: *Computer services and management consulting.* Fax:33-1-4227-3211

   CAP GEMINI AMERICA
   1114 Avenue of the Americas, 29th Fl., New York, NY   10036
   CEO: Michael Meyer, Chrm.   Tel: (212) 944-6464   Emp: 3200
   Bus: *Computer services & management consulting.* Fax:(212) 575-9101   %FO: 100

   CAP GEMINI AMERICA
   400 Courtyard Square, 80 Summit St., Akron, OH   44308
   CEO: Jerry Nuzum, Exec.VP   Tel: (330) 342-3900   Emp: N/A
   Bus: *Computer services & management consulting.* Fax:(330) 342-3734   %FO: 100

● **CARREFOUR BV**
6, ave. Raymond Poincaré, 75116 Paris, France
CEO: Daniel Bernard, Chrm.   Tel: 33-1-5370-1900   Emp: 102900
Bus: *International retail, diversified.*   Fax:33-1-5370-8616

   OFFICE DEPOT, INC.
   2200 Old Germantown Road, Delray Beach, FL   33445
   CEO: David I. Fuente, Chmn.   Tel: (561) 265-4001   Emp: N/A
   Bus: *Retail, discount office supplies retailer.* Fax:(561) 265-4001   %FO: 6

   PETSMART INC.
   10000 North 31st Avenue
   Suite C100, Phoenix, AZ   85051
   CEO: Sam Parker, Pres.   Tel: (602) 944-7070   Emp: N/A
   Bus: *Retail supplier of pets and pet supplies.* Fax:(602) 944-9391   %FO: 6

   PRICE/COSTCO INC.
   10809 120th Avenue, NE, Kirkland, WA   98033
   CEO: James Sinegal, Pres.   Tel: (206) 313-8100   Emp: 40000
   Bus: *Wholesale membership product outlet.*   Fax:(206) 313-8103   %FO: 21

● **CEDRAT SA**
Chemin du Pre Carre-Zirst, F-38240 Meylan, France
CEO: Pierre Ribard, Pres.   Tel: 33-476-905045   Emp: 40
Bus: *CAD/CAM element analysis engineering,*   Fax: 33-476-901609
agricultural planification.

   MAGSOFT CORP.
   1223 Peoples Avenue, Troy, NY   12180
   CEO: Sheppard J. Salon, Pres.   Tel: (518) 271-1352   Emp: 6
   Bus: *Engineering CAD/CAM software.*   Fax: (518) 276-6380   %FO: 30

● **CEGELEC**
2 quai Michelet, F-92309 Levallois-Perret, France
CEO: Pierre Bonafe, Chrm.   Tel: 33-1-4149-2000   Emp: N/A
Bus: *Electrical contracting, process control, technical*   Fax: 33-1-4149-2485
assistance.

   ASPENTECH SETPOINT INC.
   14701 St. Mary's Lane, Houston, TX   77079
   CEO: Larry Evans, Pres.   Tel: (281) 584-1000   Emp: N/A
   Bus: *Electrical contracting services.*   Fax: (281) 496-3232   %FO: 100

   CEGELEC AUTOMATION INC.
   301 Alpha Drive, Pittsburgh, PA   15238
   CEO: Ralph T. Pickering, Pres.   Tel: (412) 967-0765   Emp: N/A
   Bus: *Electrical contracting services.*   Fax: (412) 967-7660   %FO: 100

   ESCA INC.
   11120 NE 33rd Place, Bellevue, WA   98004
   CEO: Alain Steven, Pres.   Tel: (425) 822-6800   Emp: N/A
   Bus: *Design/develop computer software for*   Fax: (425) 889-1700   %FO: 100
   electrical industry.

● **CEGOS**
Tour Chenonceaux, 204 Rond Point, Pont de Sevres, 92516 Paris, France
CEO: Pierre Leboullieux, Pres.   Tel: 33-1-4620-6060   Emp: 2000
Bus: *Consulting & training.*   Fax: 33-1-4620-6088

   CEGMARK INTL INC.
   1350 Ave. of the Americas, New York, NY   10019
   CEO: Ronald R. Mullins, Pres.   Tel: (212) 541-7010   Emp: 20
   Bus: *Marketing consulting services.*   Fax: (212) 581-9819   %FO: 49

● **CELLIER GROUPE SA**
14 rue du Maroc, F-73106 Aix les Bains Cedex, France
CEO: Alain Lebre, Gen. Dir.   Tel: 33-4-7935-0565   Emp: 250
Bus: *Equipment & engineer service in paper, lube oil,*   Fax:33-4-7988-3771
paint, fine chemicals & pharmaceuticals industries.

    CELLIER CORP.
    135 Robert T. Paine Drive, Taunton, MA   02780
    CEO: Joe Kulbok, Gen. Mgr.   Tel: (508) 823-6777   Emp: 10
    Bus: *Equipment & engineer service in paper, lube*   Fax:(508) 823-6699   %FO: 100
    oil, paint, fine chemicals & pharmaceuticals
    industries.

● **CHANTIERS BENETEAU SA**
Zone Industrielle des Mares, 85270 St Hilaire de Riez,, France
CEO: Madame Anette Roux, Pres.   Tel: 33-51-555382   Emp: 1103
Bus: *Shipyard services.*   Fax:33-51-805010

    BENETEAU MANUFACTURERS
    P O Drawer 1218, Marion, SC   29571
    CEO: Christian Iscouici, Pres.   Tel: (803) 423-4201   Emp: 125
    Bus: *Mfr. sailboats.*   Fax:(803) 423-4912   %FO: 100

    BENETEAU USA
    8720 Red Oak Blvd, Charlotte, NC   28217
    CEO: Christian Iscouici, Pres.   Tel: (704) 527-8244   Emp: 12
    Bus: *Distribution sailboats.*   Fax:(704) 527-0760   %FO: 100

● **CIMENTS FRANCAIS**
22, Tour Ariane, F92088 Paris La Défense, France
CEO: Yves-Rene Nanot, Chrm.   Tel: 33-1-4291-7627   Emp: N/A
Bus: *Mfr./sale cement and construction materials.*   Fax:33-1-4774-5955

    ESSROC CORP.
    3251 Bath Pike, Nazareth, PA   18064
    CEO: Robert Rayner, Pres.   Tel: (610) 837-6725   Emp: N/A
    Bus: *Cement and construction materials.*   Fax:(610) 837-9614   %FO: 100

● **CIS BIO INTERNATIONAL**
B P 6, 91192 Gif-sur-Yvette, France
CEO: Liliane Sardais, Pres.   Tel: 33-1-6985-7085   Emp: 1100
Bus: *Nuclear medical, clinical lab products, sources &*   Fax:33-1-6985-7071
irradiators.

    CIS-US INC.
    10 DeAngelo Drive, Bedford, MA   01730
    CEO: Charles Panneciere, Chrm.   Tel: (617) 275-7120   Emp: 50
    Bus: *Radiopharmaceuticals: RIA laboratory*   Fax:(617) 275-2634   %FO: 100
    products, radiation therapy equipment.

● **CITEL**
8 ave Jean-Jaures, F-92130 Issy-les-Moulineaus, France
CEO: Francois Guichard, Pres. Tel: 33-1-4123-5023 Emp: 120
Bus: *Mfr. surge & lightning protectors.* Fax:33-1-4123-5009

    CITEL AMERICA INC.
    1111 Parkcentre Blvd., Miami, FL 33169
    CEO: Fabrice Larmier, EVP Tel: (305) 421-0022 Emp: 3
    Bus: *Distributes surge protectors.* Fax:(305) 621-0766 %FO: 100

● **CLUB MÉDITERRANÉE SA**
11, rue de Cambrai, 75957 Paris Cedéx 19, France
CEO: Serge Trigano, Chrm. Tel: 33-1-5335-3553 Emp: 8008
Bus: *Own and operate vacation resorts, hotels, ships,* Fax:33-1-5335-3616
    planes.

    CLUB MED INC.
    40 W 57th Street, New York, NY 10019
    CEO: Andrew Jordan, Pres. Tel: (212) 977-2100 Emp: N/A
    Bus: *Sales and management, vacation hotel, resorts,* Fax:(212) 315-5392 %FO: 100
    cruise ships.

● **CMB PACKAGING SA**
153 rue de Courcelles, 75817 Paris, France
CEO: Jacque Liget, Pres. Tel: 33-1-4415-6800 Emp: N/A
Bus: *Mfr. metal & plastic packaging systems.* Fax:33-1-4053-0303

    RISDON CORPORATION
    1 Risdon Street, Naugatuck, CT 06770
    CEO: Steve Levine, VP Tel: (203) 723-6100 Emp: N/A
    Bus: *Mfr. packaging products.* Fax:(203) 723-6101 %FO: 100

● **COFLEXIP STENA OFFSHORE SA**
23, ave. de Neuilly, F-75116 Paris, France
CEO: Pierre Marie Valentin, Chrm. Tel: 33-1-4067-6000 Emp: 2500
Bus: *Engineering/mfr./offshore installation flexible pipe.* Fax:33-1-4067-6003

    COFLEXIP STENA OFFSHORE INC.
    16661 Jacintoport Blvd., Houston, TX 77015
    CEO: Tom Kazusky, Mgr. Tel: (713) 457-3018 Emp: 50
    Bus: *Engineering/mfr./offshore installation flexible* Fax:(713) 457-1537 %FO: 100
    pipe.

    COFLEXIP STENA OFFSHORE INC.
    7660 Woodway, #390, Houston, TX 77063
    CEO: Ken Hulls, Pres. & CEO Tel: (713) 789-8540 Emp: 50
    Bus: *Engineering/mfr./offshore installation flexible* Fax:(713) 789-7367 %FO: 100
    pipe.

PERRY TRITECH INC.
821 Jupiter Park Drive, Jupiter, FL   33458
CEO: John Jacobson, Gen. Mgr.   Tel: (407) 743-7000   Emp: N/A
Bus: *Engineering/mfr./offshore installation flexible*   Fax:(407) 743-1313   %FO: 100
pipe.

● **COMPAGNIE FINANCIÈRE DE CIC ET DE L'UNION EUROPÉENNE**
4, rue Gaillon, F-75002 Paris, France
CEO: N/A   Tel: 33-1-4266-7000   Emp: N/A
Bus: *General commercial banking services.*   Fax:33-1-4266-7890

   COMPAGNIE FINANCIÈRE DE CIC ET DE L'UNION EUROPÉENNE
   520 Madison Avenue, New York, NY   10022
   CEO: Serge Bellanger, EVP & Gen. Mgr.   Tel: (212) 715-4400   Emp: 100
   Bus: *International commercial banking services.*   Fax:(212) 715-4477   %FO: 100

● **COMPAGNIE FINANCIÈRE SUCRES ET DENRÉES SA**
20/22 rue de la Ville L'Eveque, F-75008 Paris, France
CEO: Serge Varsano, Chrm.   Tel: 33-1-5330-1234   Emp: N/A
Bus: *International sugar trading.*   Fax:33-1-5330-1212

   AMEROP SUGAR CORPORATION
   701 Brickell Avenue, Suite 2200, Miami, FL   33131
   CEO: Stephen A. Hedrei, SVP   Tel: (305) 374-4440   Emp: N/A
   Bus: *International sugar trading.*   Fax:(305) 374-4330   %FO: 100

● **COMPAGNIE GENERALE D'INFORMATIQUE**
34 rue du Chateau des Rentiers, F-75649 Paris Cedex, France
CEO: Christian Nivoix, CEO   Tel: 33-1-4077-2020   Emp: 3950
Bus: *Software sales/consulting services.*   Fax:33-1-4077-2222

   CGI SYSTEMS INC.
   301 Lindenwood Drive, Malverne, PA   19355
   CEO: Joseph Ferrandino, Pres.   Tel: (610) 993-8082   Emp: 400
   Bus: *Information software system consulting &*   Fax:(610) 993-8125   %FO: 100
   services.

● **COMPAGNIE GENERALE DE GEOPHYSIQUE**
1 rue Leon Migaux, F-91341 Massy Cedex, France
CEO: Robert Brunk, Pres.   Tel: 33-1-6447-3000   Emp: 3000
Bus: *Geophysical exploration & data processing services.* Fax:33-1-6447-3970

   CGG AMERICAN SERVICES INC.
   2500 Wilcrest, #200, Houston, TX   77042-2797
   CEO: Jonathan Miller, EVP   Tel: (713) 784-0740   Emp: 125
   Bus: *Geophysical exploration & data processing*   Fax:(713) 266-9754   %FO: 100
   services.

● **COMPAGNIE GENERALE DES MATIERES NUCLEAIRES**
2 rue Paul Dautier, F-78141 Velizy-Villacoublay, France
CEO: Jean Syrota, Chrm.   Tel: 33-1-3926-3000   Emp: N/A
Bus: *Nuclear fuel products & services.*   Fax:33-1-3926-2700

　COGEMA INC.
　7401 Wisconsin Avenue, Bethesda, MD   20814
　CEO: Michael Poissonnet, Pres.   Tel: (301) 986-8585   Emp: N/A
　Bus: *Nuclear fuel products & services.*   Fax:(301) 652-5690   %FO: 100

● **CREDIT COMMERCIAL DE FRANCE**
103 ave des Champs Elysees, 75008 Paris, France
CEO: Charles de Croisset, Chrm.   Tel: 33-1-4070-7040   Emp: 12000
Bus: *General commercial banking.*   Fax:33-1-4720-2372

　CREDIT COMMERCIAL DE FRANCE
　590 Madison Avenue, New York, NY   10022-2526
　CEO: Jean de Courreges, Gen.Mgr.   Tel: (212) 486-3080   Emp: 75
　Bus: *International commercial banking.*   Fax:(212) 832-7469   %FO: 100

CRÉDIT LYONNAIS
19, boulevard des Italiens, 75002 Paris, France
CEO: Jean Peyrelevade, Chrm.   Tel: 33-1-4295-7000   Emp: 59018
Bus: *General commercial banking, asset management,*   Fax:33-1-4295-0095
　　securities trading & insurance services.

　CRÉDIT LYONNAIS - Chicago Branch
　224 West Monroe Street, #3800, Chicago, IL   60606
　CEO: Sandra Horowitz, Mgr.   Tel: (312) 641-0500   Emp: 27
　Bus: *International banking services.*   Fax:(312) 641-0527   %FO: 100

　CRÉDIT LYONNAIS - Boston Branch
　53 State Street, 27th Floor, Boston, MA   02109
　CEO: Silvana Burdick, Mgr.   Tel: (617) 723-2615   Emp: N/A
　Bus: *International banking services.*   Fax:(617) 723-4803   %FO: 100

　CRÉDIT LYONNAIS - New York Branch
　1301 Ave. of the Americas, New York, NY   10019
　CEO: Robert Cohen, CEO   Tel: (212) 261-7000   Emp: 600
　Bus: *International banking services.*   Fax:(212) 459-3170   %FO: 100

　CRÉDIT LYONNAIS - Houston Branch
　1000 Louisiana St., Suite 5360, Houston, TX   77002
　CEO: Michael Azark, Mgr.   Tel: (713) 751-0500   Emp: 25
　Bus: *International banking services.*   Fax:(713) 751-0307   %FO: 100

　CRÉDIT LYONNAIS -Los Angeles Branch
　515 South Flower St., Ste.2200, Los Angeles, CA   90071
　CEO: Diane Scott, Mgr.   Tel: (213) 362-5900   Emp: 15
　Bus: *International banking services.*   Fax:(213) 623-3437   %FO: 100

CRÉDIT LYONNAIS -Miami Branch
601 Brickell Drive, #800, Miami, FL   33131
CEO: Huguette Duewuella, Mgr.   Tel: (305) 374-0900   Emp: 35
Bus: *International banking services.*   Fax:(305) 577-8925   %FO: 100

CRÉDIT LYONNAIS - Atlanta Branch
303 Peachtree St., NE, Atlanta, GA   30308
CEO: David Cowrse, Mgr.   Tel: (404) 524-3700   Emp: N/A
Bus: *International banking services.*   Fax:(404) 584-5249   %FO: 100

CRÉDIT LYONNAIS - Dallas Branch
2200 Ross Avenue, Dallas, TX   75201
CEO: Sam Hill, Mgr.   Tel: (214) 220-2300   Emp: 20
Bus: *International banking services.*   Fax:(214) 220-2323   %FO: 100

CRÉDIT LYONNAIS -San Francisco
Embarcadero 3, Suite 1640, San Francisco, CA   94111
CEO: Edward Leong, Mgr.   Tel: (415) 956-7002   Emp: 6
Bus: *International banking services.*   Fax:(415) 956-7008   %FO: 100

• CRÉDIT NATIONAL
45 rue Saint-Dominique, F-75700 Paris France
CEO: Emmanuel Rodocanachi, Chrm.   Tel: 33-1-4550-9000   Emp: N/A
Bus: *Commercial lending, investment banking, equity and* Fax:33-1-4555-6896
     debt financing, and real estate financing services.

ASSET BACKED MANAGEMENT CORP.
520 Madison Avenue, 34th Floor, New York, NY   10022
CEO: Daniel Lescop, Mng. Dir.   Tel: (212) 835-6080   Emp: 8
Bus: *Commercial lending, investment banking,*   Fax:(212) 832-6088   %FO: 100
     equity and debt financing, and real estate
     financing services.

• CROUZET BRISSANT
111 Cehmin de la Foret BP 59, 26902 Valence, Cedex 9, France
CEO: J. P. Rebault, CEO   Tel: 33-47-544-8844   Emp: N/A
Bus: *Mfr. aircraft relays and controls*   Fax:33-47-555-9803

CROUZET CORPORATION
3237 Commander Drive, Carrollton, TX   76001
CEO: Gerald Vincent, Pres.   Tel: (972) 250-1647   Emp: N/A
Bus: *Mfr. relays and controls.*   Fax:(972) 447-6786   %FO: 100

• GROUPE DANONE SA

7, rue de Téhéran, 75381 Paris Cédéx 8, France
CEO: Franck Riboud, Chrm.　　　　　　　　Tel: 33-1-4435-2020　　Emp: 73823
Bus: *Produce/distribution of dairy, other branded food*　Fax:33-1-4225-6716
　　and beverage products worldwide.

THE DANNON COMPANY

120 White Plains Road, Tarrytown, NY　10591-5536
CEO: Antonio Spagnolo, Pres.　　　　　　Tel: (914) 366-9700　　Emp: 130
Bus: *Produce/distribution of dairy products.*　　Fax:(914) 366-2805　　%FO: 100

LEA & PERRINS INC.

15-01 Pollitt Drive, Fair Lawn, NJ　07410
CEO: Ralph Abrams, Pres.　　　　　　　　Tel: (201) 791-1600　　Emp: 120
Bus: *Mfr. sauces.*　　　　　　　　　　　　Fax:(201) 791-8945　　%FO: 100

• DASSAULT SYSTEMES

9 quai Marcel Dassault,　BP 310, F-92156, Suresnes, France
CEO: Serge Dassault, Chrm.　　　　　　　Tel: 33-1-4099-4099　　Emp: 18000
Bus: *Manufacturer of aircraft.*　　　　　　Fax:33-1-4204-4581

DASSAULT FALCON JET CORPORATION

Teterboro Airport, PO Box 2000, S. Hackensack, NJ　07606
CEO: John Rosanvallon, Pres.　　　　　　Tel: (201) 262-0800　　Emp: 180
Bus: *Aircraft assembly, sales and service.*　Fax:(201) 967-4469　　%FO: 100

DASSAULT SYSTEMES OF AMERICA

1935 North Buena Vista Street, Burbank, CA　91504
CEO: P. Forestier, Pres.　　　　　　　　　Tel: (818) 559-3600　　Emp: N/A
Bus: *Develops cad/cam software for aerospace and*　Fax:(818) 559-3339　　%FO: 100
　　automotive industries.

DAVAL

Immeuble Elysees La Defense, 92072 Paris, France
CEO: Pierre Jacque, Pres.　　　　　　　　Tel: 33-1-4125-8383　　Emp: 140
Bus: *Steel export.*　　　　　　　　　　　Fax:33-1- 4125-8393

FRANCOSTEEL CORPORATION

345 Hudson Street, New York, NY　10014-4502
CEO: Michel Longchampt, Pres.　　　　　Tel: (212) 633-1010　　Emp: 65
Bus: *Import/export/distribution steel products.*　Fax:(212) 633-1398　　%FO: 100

● **DEGRÉMONT SA**
183 ave de 18 Juin 1940, F-92508 Rueil-Malmaison, France
CEO: Olivier Kreiss, Pres.   Tel: 33-1-4625-6048   Emp: N/A
Bus: *Water & wastewater treatment equipment.*   Fax:33-1-4204-1699

    INFILCO DEGREMONT INC.
    2924 Emerywood Parkway, Richmond, VA   23294
    CEO: Yves M. Moyne, Pres.   Tel: (804) 756-7600   Emp: 180
    Bus: *Water & wastewater treatment equipment.* Fax:(804) 759-7643   %FO: 100

● **DOLISOS LDPH**
71, rue Beauborg, F-75003 Paris, France
CEO: Jean-Christophe Gouache, Pres.   Tel: 33-1-4478-1000   Emp: N/A
Bus: *Mfr. homeopathic remedies/veterinary medicines.*   Fax:33-1-4478-1010

    DOLISOS AMERICA, INC.
    3014 Rigel Avenue, Las Vegas, NV   89102
    CEO: William Nicoletti, Pres.   Tel: (702) 871-7153   Emp: N/A
    Bus: *Supplies homeopathic remedies/veterinary*   Fax:(702) 871-9670   %FO: 100
        medicines.

● **DOLLFUS MIEG & CIE**
10 ave Lefru-Rollin, 75579 Paris, France
CEO: Julien Charlier, Pres.   Tel: 33-1-4928-1000   Emp: 1000
Bus: *Mfr. textiles.*   Fax:33-1-4342-5654

    THE DMC CORP
    Port Kearny, Bldg 10, South Kearny, NJ   07032
    CEO: Nicholas F. Wallaert, CEO   Tel: (201) 589-0606   Emp: 40
    Bus: *Distributor embroidery threads.*   Fax:(201) 589-8931   %FO: 100

● **DOSATRON INTL SA**
rue Pascal, B.P. 6, Tresses, F-33370 Bordeaux, France
CEO: John D. Kelly, Pres.   Tel: 33-5-5797-1111   Emp: 120
Bus: *Mfr. hydraulic injectors.*   Fax:33-5-5797-1129

    DOSATRON INTERNATIONAL INC.
    2090 Sunnydale Blvd., Clearwater, FL   34625
    CEO: Eddy Kelly, Pres.   Tel: (813) 443-5404   Emp: 12
    Bus: *Sale/distribution hydraulic injectors.* Fax:(813) 447-0591   %FO: 99

● **LOUIS DREYFUS & CIE**
87 ave de la Grande Armee, F-75782 Paris Cedex 16, France
CEO: Bernard Baldensperger, CEO & Pres.   Tel: 33-1-4066-1111   Emp: N/A
Bus: *Wholesalers of cereals, grains; shipowners.*   Fax:33-1-4066-1612

    LOUIS DREYFUS CORP.
    Ten Westport Road, Wilton, CT   06897
    CEO: William Louis-Dreyfus, Chrm.   Tel: (203) 961-0602   Emp: N/A
    Bus: *Supplier grains, cereals, seeds.*   Fax:(203) 964-8275   %FO: 100

● **EDITIONS QUO VADIS SA**
20-26 rue Caisserie, 13235 Marseille, France
CEO: M. Mallavoy, Pres.   Tel: 33-491-9191-9261 Emp: 250
Bus: *Publishers diaries/appointment books.*   Fax:33-491-9191-8761

    QUO VADIS PUBLICATIONS
    120 Elmview Avenue, Hamburg, NY   14075
    CEO: Richard Lydo, Pres.   Tel: (716) 648-2602   Emp: 40
    Bus: *Publishers diaries/appointment books.*   Fax:(716) 648-2607   %FO: 100

● **ELA MEDICAL SA**
98 rue Maurice Arnoux, 92120 Montrouge, France
CEO: Pierre Franchi, Pres.   Tel: 33-1-4965-5555   Emp: 250
Bus: *Mfr. cardiac pacemakers, medical equipment.*   Fax:33-1-4655-7548

    ELA MEDICAL INC.
    15245 Minnetonka Blvd., Minnetonka, MN   55345-1510
    CEO: Jim Stasik, Pres.   Tel: (612) 519-9400   Emp: 30
    Bus: *Cardiac pacemakers, medical equipment.*   Fax:(888) 352-3299   %FO: 90

● **ÉLECTRICITÉ DE FRANCE (EDF)**
2 rue Louis-Murat, F-75384 Paris, France
CEO: Edmond Alphandery, Chrm.   Tel: 33-1-4042-2222   Emp: N/A
Bus: *Generation/distribution electricity.*   Fax:33-1-4042-6200

    ÉLECTRICITÉ DE FRANCE INTERNATIONAL NORTH AMERICA, INC.
    1730 Rhode Island Avenue, NW, Washington, DC   20036
    CEO: Pierre Boussard, Pres.   Tel: (202) 429-2527   Emp: 10
    Bus: *U.S. headquarters of EDF; an energy*   Fax:(202) 429-2532   %FO: 100
        generator and distributor.

● **SOCIÉTÉ NATIONALE ELF AQUITAINE (SNEA)**
Tour Elf, 92078 Paris Cédex 45, France
CEO: Philippe Jaffré, Chrm.　　　　　　　　　Tel: 33-1-4744-4546　　Emp: 8500
Bus: *Oil & gas, petroleum products chemicals,*　Fax:33-1-4744-6946
　　　pharmaceuticals.

   ELF AQUITAINE INC.
   280 Park Avenue, 36th Floor, New York, NY　10019
   CEO: Philippe Jaffré, Pres.　　　　　　　Tel: (212) 922-3000　　Emp: 62
   Bus: *Holding company for US operations.*　Fax:(212) 922-3001　　%FO: 100

   ELF ATOCHEM North America, Inc.
   2000 Market Street, Philadelphia, PA　19103-3222
   CEO: S S Preston III, Pres.　　　　　　　Tel: (215) 587-7000　　Emp: 7000
   Bus: *Mfr. chemicals, polymers, activated carbons,*　Fax:(215) 587-7591　　%FO: 100
   　　molecular sieves.

   ELF EXPLORATION, INC.
   1000 Louisiana, Suite 3800, Houston, TX　77002-5091
   CEO: G. Fneyrou, Pres.　　　　　　　　Tel: (713) 658-9811　　Emp: N/A
   Bus: *Oil & gas exploration services.*　　Fax:(713) 650-1189　　%FO: 100

   ELF LUBRICANTS North America, Inc.
   5 North Stiles Street, P.O.Box 1063, Linden, NJ　07036-0001
   CEO: Tony Soriano, Pres.　　　　　　　Tel: (908) 862-9300　　Emp: N/A
   Bus: *Marketing petrochemical products.*　Fax:(908) 862-5087　　%FO: 100

   ELF TRADING, INC.
   San Felipe Plaza, 5847 San Felipe, Ste. 2100, Houston, TX　77057-3010
   CEO: Gary Paradise, Exec.VP　　　　　　Tel: (713) 953-8000　　Emp: N/A
   Bus: *Oil & gas trading.*　　　　　　　Fax:(713) 953-1078　　%FO: 100

   FINDLEY ADHESIVES, INC.
   11320 Watertown Plank Road, Milwaukee, WI　53226
   CEO: P. Jaffré, Pres.　　　　　　　　Tel: (414) 774-0115　　Emp: N/A
   Bus: *Mfr. hotmelt adhesives for non-woven*　Fax:(713) 774-0115　　%FO: 100
   　　applications and industrial adhesives.

   SANOFI, INC.
   90 Park Avenue, New York, NY　10016
   CEO: Douglas Doherty, Pres.　　　　　　Tel: (212) 551-4300　　Emp: N/A
   Bus: *Mfr./marketing healthcare, skincare,*　Fax:(212) 551-4900　　%FO: 100
   　　fragrances, clothing & household linen
   　　products.

   TG SODA ASH, INC,
   P O Box 30321, Raleigh, NC　27622
   CEO: Thomas Wright, Pres.　　　　　　Tel: (919) 881-2700　　Emp: N/A
   Bus: *Phosphates, feed products, soda ash, sulfur,*　Fax:(919) 881-2847　　%FO: 100
   　　potash, salt.

● **ELSYDEL**
63 blvd Bessieres, 75017 Paris, France
CEO: Pierre F. Vargioni, Chrm.   Tel: 33-1-4226-8157   Emp: 300
Bus: *Install/maintenance computerized parking control &*   Fax:33-1-4226-1591
  toll road systems.

ASCOM TRINDEL AMERICA CORP.
2831 Peterson Place, Norcross, GA   30071-1812
CEO: Peter Sands, Pres.   Tel: (770) 368-2003   Emp: 50
Bus: *Install/maintenance computerized parking*   Fax:(770) 368-2093   %FO: 100
  control & toll road systems.

● **ETS AMYOT**
1 rue Denis Papin, 25303 Pontarlier, France
CEO: Michel Amyot, Pres.   Tel: 33-381-391396   Emp: 100
Bus: *Mfr. drill chucks & accessories.*   Fax:33-381-396249

LFA INDUSTRIES INC.
9100 W Plainfield Rd, #7, PO Box 95, Brookfield, IL   60513
CEO: Sigmund Travis & Don Travis   Tel: (708) 485-6610   Emp: 8
Bus: *Mfr./distribution drill chucks & accessories.*   Fax:(708) 485-6610   %FO: 50

● **EUROCOPTER SA**
72 blvd de Courcelles, 75017 Paris, France
CEO: Jean-Francois Bigay, Pres.   Tel: 33-1-4934-4102   Emp: 10500
Bus: *Mfr. helicopters.*   Fax:33-1-4267-7082

AMERICAN EUROCOPTER CORP.
2701 Forum Drive, Grand Prairie, TX   75052-7099
CEO: Jean-Francois Bigay, Pres.   Tel: (972) 641-0000   Emp: 300
Bus: *Assembly/sale helicopters.*   Fax:(972) 641-3761   %FO: 100

EUROP ASSISTANCE
23-25 rue Chaptal, 75445 Paris, France
CEO: P. Rovere, CEO   Tel: 33-1-2858585   Emp: N/A
Bus: *Emergency services.*   Fax:33-1-2937605

EUROP ASSISTANCE WORLDWIDE SERVICES
1133 15th St. NW, #400, Washington, DC   20005
CEO: John Shanley, Pres.   Tel: (202) 331-1609   Emp: N/A
Bus: *Travel assistance, travel emergency network.*   Fax:(202) 331-1588   %FO: 100

● **FRAMATOME SA**
Tour Fiat, F-92084 Paris, La Defense, France
CEO: Dominique Vignon, Chrm. & CEO   Tel: 33-1-4796-1414   Emp: 14850
Bus: *Nuclear power engineering services.*   Fax:33-1-4796-3031

    FRAMATOME COGEMA FUELS, INC.
    3315 Old Forest Road, Lynchburg, VA   24506-0935
    CEO: Robert Hoffman, Pres.   Tel: (804) 832-3000   Emp: N/A
    Bus: *Sub of FRAMATOME USA, INC. Nuclear*   Fax:(804) 832-3663   %FO: 51
        power engineering & fuel services.

    FRAMATOME CONNECTORS USA, INC.
    51 Richards Avenue, Norwalk, CT   06856
    CEO: John Mayo, Pres.   Tel: (203) 852-8567   Emp: 1300
    Bus: *Mfr. electronic/electrical connectors &* Fax:(203) 852-8520   %FO: 100
        connection devices.

    FRAMATOME USA, INC.
    1911 North Fort Myer Drive, #705, Rosslyn, VA   22209
    CEO: Richard DeVane, Pres.   Tel: (703) 527-4747   Emp: N/A
    Bus: *US headquarters. Nuclear power engineering* Fax:(703) 527-7973   %FO: 100
        services.

● **FRANCE TELECOM**
6 place d'Alleray, 75740 Paris Cedex 15, France
CEO: Michel Bon, Chrm.   Tel: 33-1-4444-2222   Emp: 167660
Bus: *International telecommunications carrier.*   Fax:33-1-4444-0146

    FRANCE TELECOM NORTH AMERICA INC.
    1270 Avenue of the Americas, 28th Fl,, New York, NY   10020
    CEO: Marie-Monique Steckel, Pres.   Tel: (212) 332-2100   Emp: 30
    Bus: *International telecommunications carrier.* Fax:(212) 245-8605   %FO: 100

    MINITEL USA INC.
    888 Seventh Avenue, New York, NY   10106
    CEO: Hilary Thomas, Pres.   Tel: (212) 399-0080   Emp: 8
    Bus: *Develop joint ventures in videotex industry.* Fax:(212) 399-0129   %FO: 100

● **FROMAGERIES BEL**
4, rue d'Anjou, F-75008 Paris, France
CEO: Bertrand Dufort, Chrm.   Tel: 33-1-4007-7250   Emp: N/A
Bus: *Mfr. dairy products.*   Fax:33-1-4007-7230

    BEL CHEESE USA, INC.
    Polygon Plaza, 2050 Center Avenue, Fort Lee, NJ   07024
    CEO: Patrick Robbe, Pres.   Tel: (201) 592-6601   Emp: N/A
    Bus: *Distributes dairy products.*   Fax:(201) 592-9242   %FO: 100

● **GROSFILLEX SARL**
B.P.2, F-01107 Arbent, France
CEO: Raymond Grosfillex, Pres.　　　　Tel: 33-1-7473-3030　　Emp: 1200
Bus: *Mfr./sales furniture & home products.*　　Fax:N/A

　GROSFILLEX, INC.
　Old West Pennsylvania Avenue, Robesonia, PA　19551
　CEO: Carel Harmsen, CEO　　　　Tel: (610) 693-5835　　Emp: 180
　Bus: *Mfr./sales furniture & home products and*　Fax:(610) 693-5414　　%FO: 100
　　　plastics.

● **GROUPE CASINO**
24 rue de la Montat, 42008 St-Etienne Cedex 2, France
CEO: Georges Plassat, Pres.　　　　Tel: 33-7745-3131　　Emp: N/A
Bus: *Food processing/retailing, restaurants, real estate.*　Fax:33-7721-8515

　CASINO USA INC.
　524 Chapala Street, Santa Barbara, CA　93101
　CEO: Robert Emmons, Pres　　　　Tel: (805) 564-6700　　Emp: N/A
　Bus: *Grocery stores, restaurants, specialty retail*　Fax:(805) 564-6729　　%FO: 100
　　　stores.

　SMART & FINAL
　4700 South Boyle Avenue, Vernon, CA　90058
　CEO: Roger M. Laverty III, Pres.　　　Tel: (213) 589-1054　　Emp: N/A
　Bus: *Grocery store operators.*　　　Fax:(213) 589-4283　　%FO: 51

● **GUERLAIN SA**
125 rue de President Wilson, F-92593 Levallois-Perret Cedex, France
CEO: Jean-Michel Paulhac, Pres.　　　Tel: 33-141-273107　　Emp: N/A
Bus: *Mfr. fragrances and cosmetics.*　　Fax:33-141-273100

　GUERLAIN, INC.
　444 Madison Avenue, New York, NY　10022
　CEO: Patrick Waterfield, Pres.　　　Tel: (212) 751-1870　　Emp: 175
　Bus: *Mfr./distribute fragrances and cosmetics.*　Fax:(212) 593-2909　　%FO: 100

　GUERLAIN, INC.
　1045 Centennial Avenue, Piscataway, NJ　08854
　CEO: Tom Bakcsy, VP　　　　　Tel: (732) 981-2500　　Emp: 100
　Bus: *Mfr./distribute fragrances and cosmetics.*　Fax:(732) 981-2580　　%FO: 100

● **GUIRAUDIE-AUFFEVE SA**
24 rue Georges Picot, 31030 Toulouse, France
CEO: Rene Soum, Pres.   Tel: 33-5-6125-2166   Emp: 7
Bus: *General contractors, specialty concrete systems.*   Fax:33-5-6152-9196

    AMEGA INVESTMENTS CORP.
    8989 North Loop East, Houston, TX   77029
    CEO: James E. Stubbs, Pres.   Tel: (713) 672-8989   Emp: 4
    Bus: *Land development & investments.*   Fax:(713) 675-2461   %FO: 100

● **HARTH & CIE**
30 rue St. Lazare, 75009 Paris, France
CEO: Francois Harth, Pres.   Tel: 33-1-4970-8383   Emp: 35
Bus: *Buying services.*   Fax:33-1-4526-2125

    FRENCH & PACIFIC TRADING CORP.
    13816 Magnolia Avenue, Chino, CA   91710
    CEO: Steven L. Haas, Admin. Dir.   Tel: (909) 902-1320   Emp: 8
    Bus: *Import/export, buying services.*   Fax:(909) 902-1327   %FO: 100

● **HAVAS ADVERTISING**
84 rue de Villers, F-92683 Levallois-Perret Cedex, France
CEO: Alain de Pouzilhac, Chrm.   Tel: 33-1-4134-3434   Emp: 5000
Bus: *International advertising agency. (Sub of Havas SA)*   Fax:33-1-4134-4567

    COHN & WELLS
    909 Montgomery Street, San Francisco, CA   94133
    CEO: Bradley H. Wells, CEO   Tel: (415) 705-6600   Emp: 95
    Bus: *Direct response agency.*   Fax:(415) 705-6648   %FO: 100

    EURO RSCG HOLDINGS
    350 Hudson Street, New York, NY   10014
    CEO: Robert W. Parker, EVP   Tel: (212) 886-2000   Emp: 1319
    Bus: *International communications group of*   Fax:(212) 886-4428   %FO: 100
        companies. Advertising; audiovisual;
        publishing; travel & recreation.

    LALLY, McFARLAND & PANTELLO
    60 Madison Avenue, New York, NY   10010
    CEO: Ronald G. Pantello, Chrm.   Tel: (212) 532-1000   Emp: 114
    Bus: *International advertising agency.*   Fax:(212) 213-0449   %FO: 100

    MESSNER VETERE BERGER McNAMEE SCHMETTERER/EURO RCG
    350 Hudson Street, New York, NY   10014
    CEO: Louise McNamee, Pres.   Tel: (212) 886-4100   Emp: 360
    Bus: *International advertising agency.*   Fax:(212) 886-4415   %FO: 100

ROBERT A. BECKER INC.
350 Hudson Street, New York, NY   10014
CEO: Sander A. Flaum, Chrm.   Tel: (212) 727-7000   Emp: 108
Bus: *Medical advertising agency.*   Fax:(212) 727-7023   %FO: 100

TATHAM EURO RSCG
980 N. Michigan Avenue, Chicago, IL   60611
CEO: Ralph W. Rydholm, CEO   Tel: (312) 337-4400   Emp: 292
Bus: *International advertising agency.*   Fax:(312) 337-8855   %FO: 100

● **IMETAL**
Tour Maine-Montparnasse, 33 ave du Maine, 75755 Paris, France
CEO: Rene Mitieus, Chrm.   Tel: 33-1-4538-4848   Emp: N/A
Bus: *Holding company: building materials, industrial*   Fax:33-1-4538-7478
minerals, international trading services.

COPPERWELD CORPORATION
Four Gateway Center, #2200, Pittsburgh, PA   15222-1211
CEO: John D.Turner, Pres. & CEO   Tel: (412) 263-3200   Emp: 1000
Bus: *Mfr. structural mechanical tubing, bimetallic*   Fax:(412) 263-6995   %FO: 100
rod wire.

● **IMPRIMERIE NORTIER**
16 rue de L'Aqueduc, 75010 Paris, France
CEO: Bertrand Gintz, Pres.   Tel: 33-1-4035-8190   Emp: 185
Bus: *Mfr./printer folding box for fragrances & skin care*   Fax:33-1-4035-9370
industry.

NORTIER INC.
315 West 57th Street, Ste. 300, New York, NY   10019
CEO: Paula J. Hauser-Coburn, Gen.Mgr..   Tel: (212) 582-8365   Emp: 2
Bus: *Sales folding box for fragrances & skin care*   Fax:(212) 582-8158   %FO: 100
industry.

● **JEANTET & ASSOCIES**
87, Avenue Kleber, 75784 Paris Cedex 16, France
CEO: Ferbabd-Charles Jeantet, Mng. Ptnr.   Tel: 33-1-4505-8080   Emp: N/A
Bus: *International law firm.*   Fax:33-1-4704-2041

JEANTET & ASSOCIES
712 Fifth Avenue, 12th Fl., New York, NY   10019
CEO: Yvon Dreano, Mng. Prtn.   Tel: (212) 801-3440   Emp: N/A
Bus: *International law firm.*   Fax:(212) 801-3445   %FO: 100

● **JOUAN SA**
rue Bobby Sands, 44805 St Herblain, France
CEO: Marcel Victorri, Pres.   Tel: 33-2-4016-8025   Emp: 200
Bus: *Mfr. laboratory equipment.*   Fax:33-1-4094-7016

> **JOUAN INC.**
> 100-B Industrial Drive, Winchester, VA   22602
> CEO: Lyle E. Cady Jr, Pres.   Tel: (540) 869-8623   Emp: 110
> Bus: *Mfr. laboratory equipment.*   Fax:(540) 869-8626   %FO: 80

● **L'AIR LIQUIDE**
75, quai d'Orsay, F-75321 Paris Cédex, France
CEO: Gérard Lévy, CEO   Tel: 33-1-4062-5555   Emp: 28000
Bus: *Produces gases; engineering & construction services.*   Fax:33-1-4555-5876

> **AIR LIQUIDE AMERICA CORP.**
> 2700 Post Oak Blvd., Houston, TX   77056-8229
> CEO: Patrick Verschelde, Pres.   Tel: (713) 624-8000   Emp: N/A
> Bus: *Produces gases; engineering & construction services.*   Fax:(713) 624-8794   %FO: 100

> **AIR LIQUIDE AMERICA CORP.**
> 2121 North California Blvd., Walnut Creek, CA   94596-7305
> CEO: Robert D. Cadieux, Pres.   Tel: (510) 977-6500   Emp: 3000
> Bus: *Mfr./distributes industrial gases, technical & related handling equipment.*   Fax:(510) 746-6306   %FO: 100

● **L'OREAL SA**
41, rue Martre, 92117 Clichy, France
CEO: Lindsay Owen-Jones, Chrm.   Tel: 33-1-4756-7000   Emp: 39329
Bus: *Mfr. cosmetics, fragrances, hair care products, fashion publishing.*   Fax:33-1-4756-8002

> **COSMAIR INC**
> 575 Fifth Avenue, New York, NY   10017
> CEO: Guy Peyrelonuge, Pres.   Tel: (212) 818-1500   Emp: 4500
> Bus: *Mfr./sale cosmetics, fragrances, hair care products.*   Fax:(212) 984-4946   %FO: 100

● **LA GARANTIE MUTUELLE DES FONCTIONNAIRES GROUP (GMF)**
76 rue de Prony, F-75857 Paris, France
CEO: Christain Sastre, Pres.   Tel: 33-1-4754-1010   Emp: 11000
Bus: *Insurance services.*   Fax:33-1-4754-1009

> **CIVIL SERVICE EMPLOYEES INSURANCE CO. (CSE)**
> 989 Market Street, San Francisco, CA   94103
> CEO: Pierre Bize, Pres.   Tel: (415) 495-6800   Emp: 340
> Bus: *Provides insurance services.*   Fax:(415) 974-1095   %FO: 100

• LABORATOIRES DOLISOS
71 rue Beauborg, 75003 Paris, France
CEO: J. G. Guillon, Pres.   Tel: 33-1-4478-1109   Emp: N/A
Bus: *Mfr. homeopathic medicines.*   Fax:33-1-4478-1010

DOLISOS AMERICA INC
3014 Rigel Avenue, Las Vegas, NV   89102
CEO: William Nicoletti, Pres.   Tel: (702) 871-7153   Emp: 31
Bus: *Mfr. homeopathic medicines.*   Fax:(702) 871-9670   %FO: 100

• LAFARGE COPPEE
61 rue des Belles Feuilles, 75116 Paris, France
CEO: Bertrand Collomb, Chrm.   Tel: 33-1-4434-1111   Emp: 30000
Bus: *Cement, construction materials, specialty products.*   Fax:33-1-4434-1200

LAFARGE CORPORATION
11130 Sunrise Valley Drive, Ste. 300, Reston, VA   22090
CEO: Michel Rose, CEO   Tel: (703) 264-3600   Emp: 7300
Bus: *Mfr./distribution cement, construction*   Fax:(703) 264-0634   %FO: 53
  materials.

• LAGARDÈRE GROUPE
4 rue de Presbourg, 75116 Paris, France
CEO: Jean-Luc Lagardère, CEO   Tel: 33-1-4069-1600   Emp: 43622
Bus: *Industrial publishing conglomerate; space, defense*   Fax:33-1-4723-0192
  & transportation, communications & media.

CURTIS CIRCULATION COMPANY
2500 McClellan Avenue, Pennsauken, NJ   08109
CEO: Joseph Walsh, Pres. & CEO   Tel: (609) 488-5700   Emp: N/A
Bus: *Magazine distribution.*   Fax:(609) 488-5700   %FO: 100

CURTIS PUBLISHING
730 River Road, New Milford, NJ   07646
CEO: Joseph Walsh, Pres. & CEO   Tel: (201) 634-7499   Emp: N/A
Bus: *Publishing.*   Fax:(201) 634-7498   %FO: 100

FAIRCHILD CONTROLS CORP
20305 Century Blvd, Germantown, MD   20874
CEO: Richard H. Bair, Pres.   Tel: (301) 428-6315   Emp: 70
Bus: *Mfr. aircraft equipment.*   Fax:(301) 428-6622   %FO: 100

GROLIER INC.
Sherman Turnpike, Danbury, CT   06816
CEO: Arnoud Lagardère, CEO   Tel: (203) 797-3500   Emp: N/A
Bus: *Book publishing.*   Fax:(203) 797-3197   %FO: 100

HACHETTE FILIPACCHI PUBLICATIONS INC.
1633 Broadway, New York, NY   10019
CEO: David J. Pecker, Pres.   Tel: (212) 767-6000   Emp: N/A
Bus: *Magazine publishing.*   Fax:(212) 767-5600   %FO: 100

INTECOM
5057 Keller-Spring Road, Ste. 900, Dallas, TX   75248
CEO: George Platt, Pres.   Tel: (972) 447-9000   Emp: N/A
Bus: *Telecommunications systems.*   Fax:(972) 447-8274   %FO: 100

LAGARDÈRE GROUP NORTH AMERICA, INC.
1633 Broadway, New York, NY   10019
CEO: Alain Lemarchand, Pres.   Tel: (212) 767-6753   Emp: N/A
Bus: *US headquarters. Industrial publishing*   Fax:(212) 767-5635   %FO: 100
conglomerate; space, defense &
transportation, communications & media.

• **LAZARD FRÈRES & CIE**
121 blvd Haussmann, F-75382 Paris Cedex 08, France
CEO: Michel David-Weill, Sr. Partner   Tel: 33-1-4413-011   Emp: N/A
Bus: *Investment banking services.*   Fax:33-1-4413-0100

LAZARD FRÈRES ASSET MANAGEMENT
30 Rockefeller Plaza, New York, NY   10020
CEO: Neal J. Howe, SVP   Tel: (212) 632-6419   Emp: 200
Bus: *Investment advisory services.*   Fax:(212) 632-6060   %FO: 100

LAZARD FRÈRES COMPANY
30 Rockefeller Plaza, New York, NY   10020
CEO: Willaim R. Araskog, Mng. Ptnr.   Tel: (212) 632-6000   Emp: 650
Bus: *Investment banking services.*   Fax:(212) 632-6060   %FO: 100

• **LE STUDIO CANAL+**
85-89, quai André Citroën, 75015 Paris Cedёx 15, France
CEO: Pierre Lescure, Chrm.   Tel: 33-1-4425-1000   Emp: 2084
Bus: *International telecommunications, TV entertainment*   Fax:33-1-4720-1358
production, TV station management.

LE STUDIO CANAL SERVICES
301 North Canon Drive, Ste. 228, Beverly Hills, CA 90210
CEO: Richard Garzilli, CEO   Tel: (310) 247-0994   Emp: N/A
Bus: *International telecommunications, TV*   Fax:(310) 247-0998   %FO: 100
entertainment production, TV station
management.

● LEGRAND SA

128 ave du Marechal de Lattre, 87045 Limoges Cedex, France
CEO: F. Grappotte, Pres.   Tel: 33-555-308-806   Emp: 12000
Bus: *Mfr. electric wiring devices.*   Fax:33-555-506-072

PASS & SEYMOUR/LEGRAND

50 Boyd Avenue, PO Box 4822, Syracuse, NY   13221
CEO: William Nuckols, Pres.   Tel: (315) 468-6211   Emp: 500
Bus: *Mfr. electric wiring devices.*   Fax:(315) 463-6296   %FO: 100

● LIPHA SA

34 rue Saint-Romain, F-69008 Lyon, France
CEO: Jean-Noël Treilles, Chrm.   Tel: 33-472-7875-4424 Emp: 2000
Bus: *Pharmaceutical products, rodenticides, legume*   Fax:N/A
inoculants.

LIPHA PHARMACEUTICALS INC.

9 West 57th Steet, New York, NY   10019
CEO: Anita Goodman, Gen. Mgr.   Tel: (212) 223-1280   Emp: N/A
Bus: *Distribution pharmaceutical products.* Fax:(212) 223-1398   %FO: 100

● LTM SA

57 rue Salvador Allende, F-95870 Bezons, France
CEO: Karin Eliescaud, Pres.   Tel: 33-39-96-48-48   Emp: 30
Bus: *Mfr./distribution motion picture & TV lighting*   Fax:33-1-3996-4849
equipment.

LTM CORP OF AMERICA

11646 Pendleton Street, Sun Valley, CA   91352-2501
CEO: Gilles Galerne, Pres.   Tel: (818) 767-1313   Emp: 30
Bus: *Sale/rental motion picture & TV lighting*   Fax:(818) 767-1442   %FO: 100
equipment.

● LVMH MOËT-HENNESSY LOUIS VUITTON SA

30 ave Hoche, 75008 Paris, France
CEO: Bernard J. Arnault, Chrm.   Tel: 33-1-4413-2222   Emp: 19986
Bus: *Holding co. Produces & retails; wines/liquors;*   Fax:33-1-4413-2223
designer clothing; cosmetics/fragrances; shoes,
luggage/leather goods.

DFS GROUP

655 Montgomery Street, 18th Fl., San Francisco, CA   94111
CEO: Myron Ullman, Pres.   Tel: (415) 397-4400   Emp: N/A
Bus: *Duty free retail stores.*   Fax:(415) 397-6958   %FO: 59

DFS GROUP LTD.

525 Market Street, San Francisco, CA   94105-2708
CEO: Tom Stevens, CEO   Tel: (415) 977-2700   Emp:
Bus: *Operators of duty free shops in international*   Fax:(415) 977-2956   %FO:
air terminals.

DOMAINE CHANDON
One California Drive, Yountville, CA   94599

CEO: Bill Newlands, CEO	Tel: (707) 944-8844	Emp: N/A
Bus: *Winery - producer of sparkling wines and restaurateur.*	Fax:(707) 944-1123	%FO: 100

LOUIS VUITTON USA INC.
150 East 57th Street, New York, NY   10022

CEO: Dennis Russell, Pres.	Tel: (212) 371-6111	Emp: N/A
Bus: *Handbags, leather goods, luggage.*	Fax:(212) 759-5591	%FO: 100

LVMH MOËT-HENNESSY LOUIS VUITTON INC.
2 Park Avenue, Suite 1830, New York, NY   10016

CEO: Evan Galbraith, Chrm.	Tel: (212) 340-7480	Emp: N/A
Bus: *US headquarters. Produces & retails; wines/liquors; designer clothing; cosmetics/fragrances; shoes, luggage leather goods.*	Fax:(212) 340-7620	%FO: 100

MOET-HENNESSY US CORP
135 E 57th Street, New York, NY   10022

CEO: Evan Galbraith, Chrm.	Tel: (212) 758-7200	Emp: N/A
Bus: *Holding company: wines & grapes, cosmetics/fragrances.*	Fax:(212) 340-7620	%FO: 100

● **LYONNAISE DES EAUX-DUMEZ**
72 ave de la Liberte, 92022 Nanterre Cedex, France

CEO: Jerome Monod, Pres.	Tel: 33-1-4695-5000	Emp: 43000
Bus: *Water/energy technology, waste management, mortuary services, communications, health care, leisure services, construction.*	Fax:33-1-4695-5000	

AQUA-CHEM INC.
7800 N. 113th Street, PO Box 421, Milwaukee, WI 53201

CEO: Robert W. Agnew, Pres. & CEO	Tel: (414) 359-0600	Emp: 500
Bus: *Mfr. water treatment equipment, boilers, incinerators.*	Fax:(414) 577-2723	%FO: 80

● **MARTIN & MAYNADIER**
198, Avenue Victor Hugo, 7511 Paris, France

CEO: Francois Martin, Mng. Ptnr.	Tel: 33-1-4504-8484	Emp: N/A
Bus: *International law firm.*	Fax:33-1-4504-8722	

MARTIN & MAYNADIER
324 East 51 Street, New York, NY   10022

CEO: Francois Martin, Mng. Ptnr.	Tel: (212) 754-3390	Emp: N/A
Bus: *International law firm.*	Fax:(212) 754-3397	%FO: 100

● **MEG SA**
32-34 rue des Malines, 91000 Lisses-Evry, France
CEO: John Dangelmaier, Pres. Tel: 33-16-989-4793 Emp: 300
Bus: *Mfr. press auxiliary equipment.* Fax:33-16-497-7414

 MEG (US) INC.
 401 Central Avenue, East Rutherford, NJ 07073
 CEO: Donald Dianne, Gen. Mgr. Tel: (201) 939-6600 Emp: 18
 Bus: *Sale/service press auxiliary equipment.* Fax:(201) 939-0135 %FO: 100

● **MERIDIEN GESTION SA**
171 blvd Haussmann, 75008 Paris, France
CEO: Alair Eman, Pres. Tel: 33-1-4068-3131 Emp: N/A
Bus: *Luxury hotels owners & operators.* Fax:33-1-4068-3131

 FORTE AND LE MERIDIEN HOTELS & RESORTS
 420 Lexington Avenue, Ste 1718, New York, NY 10170
 CEO: Fran Brasseux, SVP Tel: (212) 805-5000 Emp: N/A
 Bus: *Luxury hotels owners & operators.* Fax:(212) 805-5047 %FO: 100

 PARKER MERIDIEN HOTELS INC
 119 West 56th Street, New York, NY 10019
 CEO: T. Pipes, Gen. Mgr. Tel: (212) 245-5000 Emp: N/A
 Bus: *Luxury hotels owners & operators.* Fax:(212) 765-1526 %FO: 100

● **MGP FINANCE, SA**
6, rue Piccini, F-75116 Paris, France
CEO: Jean-Francois Croce-Spinelli, CEO Tel: 33-1-7657-6060 Emp: 280
Bus: *Mfr./sale radio protection instrumentation.* Fax:33-1-9059-5518

 MGP INSTRUMENTS, INC.
 5000 Highlands Parkway, Ste. 150, Smyrna, GA 30082
 CEO: Kenneth Rosanski, VP Tel: (770) 432-2744 Emp: 35
 Bus: *Mfr./sale radioprotection instrumentation.* Fax:(770) 432-9179 %FO: 100

● **COMPAGNIE GENERALE DES ETABLISSEMENTS MICHELIN**
12 cours Sablon, F-63040 Clermont-Ferrand 9, France
CEO: François Michelin, Mg. Ptnr. Tel: 33-4-7398-5900 Emp: 115000
Bus: *Mfr. radial tires; publisher, travel related materials.* Fax:33-4-7398-5904

 MICHELIN TIRE CORP., NORTH AMERICA
 One Parkway South, Greenville, SC 29615
 CEO: James Micali, Chrm. Tel: (864) 458-5000 Emp: 26000
 Bus: *Mfr. radial tires; publisher, travel related* Fax:(864) 458-6359 %FO: 100
  materials.

● **NOUVELLES FRONTIERES**
87 blvd de Grenelle, F-75738 Paris, France
CEO: Jacques Maillot, Chrm.   Tel: 33-1-4568-7000   Emp: 3600
Bus: *Travel services, tour operator.*   Fax:33-1-4568-7003

    NOUVELLES FRONTIERES USA INC.
    12 East 33rd Street, New York, NY   10016
    CEO: Jacques Maillot, Pres.   Tel: (212) 779-0600   Emp: 23
    Bus: *Travel services, tour operator.*   Fax:(212) 779-1007   %FO: 100

● **OST SA**
B P 158, rue du Bas Village, 35515 Cesson-Sevigne, France
CEO: Thao Lane, CEO   Tel: 33-299-9932-5050 Emp: 300
Bus: *Mfr. data communications equipment.*   Fax:33-299-9941-7175

    OST INC.
    14225 Sullyfield Circle, Chantilly, VA   22021
    CEO: T. Lane, CEO   Tel: (703) 817-0400   Emp: 9
    Bus: *Engineer support office for sale/service data   Fax:(703) 817-0402   %FO: 100
       communications equipment.*

● **PARFUMS ROCHAS SA**
33 rue Francois 1er, F-75008 Paris, France
CEO: Edda Wendig, Pres.   Tel: 33-1-723-5456   Emp: 645
Bus: *Develop/mfr./marketing perfumes & cosmetics.* Fax:33-1-3074-9539

    PARFUMS ROCHAS INC.
    3217 NW 10th Ter, #301, Fort Lauderdale, FL   33309
    CEO: Thierry Rouquette, Pres.   Tel: (954) 563-9330   Emp: 4
    Bus: *Develop/mfr./marketing perfumes & cosmetics.* Fax:(954) 563-9385   %FO: 100

● **COMPAGNIE FINANCIÈRE DE PARIBAS**
3 rue d'Antin, F-75002 Paris, France
CEO: André Lévy-Lang, CEO   Tel: 33-1-4298-1234   Emp: 5000
Bus: *Diversified financial services group, active in   Fax:33-1-4298-1142
    commercial & merchant banking, investment
    advisory services.*

    BANQUE PARIBAS
    787 Seventh Avenue, New York, NY   10012
    CEO: Alain Louvel, CEO   Tel: (212) 841-2000   Emp: 1000
    Bus: *Commercial & merchant banking and   Fax:(212) 841-2146   %FO: 100
       investment advisory services.*

● **PECHINEY FRANCE**
10 place des Vosges, La Defense 5, F-92400 Courbevoie, France
CEO: Jean Gandois, Chrm. & CEO   Tel: 33-476-4691-4691 Emp: 63300
Bus: *Packaging, aluminum, engineered products,*   Fax:33-476-4691-4646
ferroalloys, carbon products.

AMERICAN NATIONAL CAN COMPANY
8770 West Bryn Mawr Avenue, Chicago, IL   60631
CEO: Jean-Pierre Rodier, CEO   Tel: (773) 399-3000   Emp: 600
Bus: *Mfr. metal, plastic, glass packaging.*   Fax:(773) 399-3322   %FO: 100

CARBONE LORRAINE NA CORPORATION
14 Eastmans Road, Parsippany, NJ   07054
CEO: Michel Coniglio, Pres. & CEO   Tel: (973) 503-0600   Emp: 6
Bus: *Specialty carbon & graphite products.*   Fax:(973) 428-0599   %FO: 100

HOWMET PECHINEY CORPORATION
475 Steamboat Road, Greenwich, CT   06830
CEO: David L Squier, Pres. & CEO   Tel: (203) 661-4600   Emp: 50
Bus: *Precision castings for aerospace & industrial*   Fax:(203) 625-8771   %FO: 100
gas turbine applications.

PECHINEY WORLD TRADE (USA) INC.
475 Steamboat Road, Greenwich, CT   06830
CEO: Bruno Poux-Guillaume, Chrm.   Tel: (203) 622-8300   Emp: N/A
Bus: *International trading, sales agency, metal*   Fax:(203) 655-8669   %FO: 100
distribution.

UGIMAG INC.
405 Elm Street, Valparaiso, IN   46383-3620
CEO: Ferdinand Gallo, Pres.   Tel: (219) 462-3131   Emp: N/A
Bus: *Mfr. permanent magnets.*   Fax:(219) 462-2569   %FO: 100

● **PERNOD RICARD SA**
142 boulevard Haussmann, F-75008 Paris, France
CEO: Patrick Ricard, Chrm.   Tel: 33-1-4076-7778   Emp: N/A
Bus: *Spirits, liquors, wines, soft drinks.*   Fax:33-1-4225-9566

AUSTIN NICHOLS & CO INC.
154 East 46th Street, New York, NY   10017
CEO: Michael Bord, Pres.   Tel: (212) 455-9400   Emp: N/A
Bus: *Distiller & distributor of wines & spirits..*   Fax:(212) 455-9431   %FO: N/A

● **PEUGEOT CITROËN SA**
75 ave de la Grande-Armée, 75116 Paris, France
CEO: Jacques Calvet, Chrm.   Tel: 33-1-4066-5511   Emp: 139900
Bus: *Mfr. automobiles.*   Fax:33-1-4066-5414

     PEUGEOT MOTORS OF AMERICA, INC.
     One Peugeot Plaza, Lyndhurst, NJ   07071
     CEO: Jean-Phillippe Fournier, Pres.   Tel: (201) 935-8400   Emp: 178
     Bus: *Distribution/service automobiles.*   Fax:(201) 935-6425   %FO: 100

● **PORCHER INDUSTRIES**
Badinieres F38300, France
CEO: Robert Porcher, Chrm.   Tel: 33-4-7443-1010   Emp: 2300
Bus: *Mfr. fabrics for technical applications.*   Fax:33-4-7492-1407

     BGF INDUSTRIES, INC.
     3802 Robert Porcher Way, Greensboro, NC   27410
     CEO: Graham Pope, CEO   Tel: (910) 545-0011   Emp: 1150
     Bus: *Glass fabrics for technical applications & non-*   Fax:(910) 545-0233   %FO: 100
          woven fabrics.

● **PROTEX SA**
B P 177, 92305 Levallois Perret Cedex, France
CEO: Robert Moor, Chrm.   Tel: 33-1-4757-7400   Emp: 350
Bus: *Mfr. specialty chemicals.*   Fax:33-1-4757-6928

     SYNTHRON INC.
     305 Amherst Road, Morganton, NC   28655
     CEO: Raymond Pinard, Pres.   Tel: (704) 437-8611   Emp: 20
     Bus: *Mfr. specialty chemicals.*   Fax:(704) 437-4126   %FO: 100

● **PUBLICIS SA**
133 ave des Champs Elysées,F-75008 Paris Cedéx, France
CEO: Maurice Levy, Chrm.   Tel: 33-1-4443-7300   Emp: 6000
Bus: *Advertising & public relations agencies, media*   Fax:33-1-4443-7553
     direct mail services; drugstores.

     PUBLICIS BLOOM INC.
     304 East 45th Street, New York, NY   10017
     CEO: Robert Bloom, Chrm.   Tel: (212) 370-1313   Emp: 100+
     Bus: *Advertising agency.*   Fax:(212) 984-1695   %FO: 100

• RADIALL SA

101 rue Philibert Hoffmann, F- 93116 Rosny-sous-Bois, France

CEO: Yvon Gattaz, Chrm.   Tel: 33-1-4935-3535   Emp: 1500

Bus: *Mfr. coaxial connectors, microwave devices, & fiber*   Fax:33-1-4854-6363
optic connectors.

RADIALL INC.

260 Hathaway Drive, Stratford, CT   06497

CEO: Etienne Lamairesse, Pres.   Tel: (203) 386-1030   Emp: 120

Bus: *Mfr. coaxial connectors, microwave devices, &*   Fax:(203) 375-3808   %FO: 100
fiber optic connectors.

• RENAULT, SA

34, Quai du Pont-du-Jour, 92100 Boulogne-Billancourt Cédex, France

CEO: Louis Schweitzer, Chrm.   Tel: 33-1-4104-5050   Emp: 139950

Bus: *Mfr. Renault & Mack vehicles; cars, trucks, tractors.*   Fax:33-1-4004-5445

MACK TRUCKS INC.

2100 Mack Blvd, P.O.Box M, Allentown, PA   18105-5000

CEO: Michel Gigou, Pres.   Tel: (610) 709-3121   Emp: 5250

Bus: *Mfr./sale Mack trucks.*   Fax:(610) 709-3364   %FO: 100

• RHÔNE-POULENC, SA.

25 quai Paul Doumer, F-92408 Courbevoie Cédex, France

CEO: Jean-René Fourtou, Chrm.   Tel: 33-1-4768-1234   Emp: 82556

Bus: *Mfr. agricultural chemicals.*   Fax:33-1-4768-1911

PASTEUR MERIEUX CONNAUGHT

PO Box 187, Rt. 611, Swiftwater, PA   18370

CEO: David Williams, Pres.   Tel: (717) 839-7187   Emp: 100+

Bus: *Mfr./research of pharmaceutical products.*   Fax:(717) 839-0561   %FO: 100

RHÔNE-POULENC RORER (US), INC.

500 Arcola Road, PO Box 1200, Collegeville, PA   19426-0107

CEO: Timothy Rothwell, Pres.   Tel: (610) 454-8000   Emp: 7500

Bus: *Mfr. pharmaceuticals, medicinals and*   Fax:(610) 454-2121   %FO: JV
botanicals.

RHÔNE-POULENC, INC.

801 Pennsylvania Avenue, NW, Washington, DC   20004

CEO: Mary M. McGrane, Dir.   Tel: (202) 628-0500   Emp: N/A

Bus: *Government relations office.*   Fax:(202) 628-6622   %FO: 100

RHÔNE-POULENC INC.

CN 7500, Prospect Plains Road, Bldg. A, Cranbury, NJ   08512

CEO: David D. Eckert, Pres.   Tel: (609) 860-4000   Emp: 5800

Bus: *Mfr./distribution of chemicals, minerals, resins*   Fax:(609) 860-0464   %FO: 100
and silicones.

- **SAGEM**
  6 ave. d'Rena, 75793 Paris, Cedex 16, France
  CEO: Pierre Raurre, CEO					Tel: 33-1-4770-6363		Emp: 8122
  Bus: *Mfr. navigation, guidance & vehicle control*		Fax:33-1-4720-3946
  equipment, data processing & communications
  systems, industrial equipment.

  SAGEM CORPORATION
  31 South Main Street, PO Box 665, Derry, NH   03038
  CEO: Donald Rondeau, Pres.					Tel: (603) 432-2013		Emp: 14
  Bus: *Mfr./distributor industrial & auto equipment.*		Fax:(603) 432-8987		%FO: 100

- **SAHMM**
  1/7 ave des Guilleraies, 92000 Nanterre, France
  CEO: Alfio Maccarone, Pres.					Tel: 33-3-4451-4751		Emp: 50
  Bus: *Mfr. mobile automobile lifts.*				Fax:33-3-4454-0012

  AMERICAN UNIC CORP.
  225 Industrial Drive, PO Box 3375, College Sta, Fredericksburg, VA   22402
  CEO: Olivier Jacqueau, Pres.					Tel: (540) 898-0720		Emp: 5
  Bus: *Distribution/sale/service mobile auto lifts.*		Fax:(540) 898-2674		%FO: 70

- **COMPAGNIE DE SAINT-GOBAIN**
  Les Miroirs, 18 ave d'Alsace, F-92400 Paris, France
  CEO: Jean-Louis Beffa, Chrm.					Tel: 33-1-4762-3000		Emp: 89852
  Bus: *Holding company: mfr. glass, pipes, paper,*		Fax:33-1-4778-4503
  cardboard, building materials.

  BICRON INC.
  12315 Kinsman Road, Newbury, OH   44065-9677
  CEO: John Crowe, Pres.					Tel: (216) 564-2251		Emp: N/A
  Bus: *Mfr./distribution specialty crystals & process*		Fax:(216) 564-8047		%FO: 100
  systems.

  CERTAINTEED CORP.
  PO Box 860, 750 Swedesford Road, Valley Forge, PA   19482-0101
  CEO: Gian-Paolo Coccini, Pres.					Tel: (610) 341-7000		Emp: 8665
  Bus: *Mfr./distribution asphalt, fiber-glass &*		Fax:(610) 341-7777		%FO: 100
  polyvinyl construction materials, millwork.

  CERTAINTEED CORP.
  3303 East Fourth Avenue, Shakopee, MN   55379
  CEO: Clement C. Carfreu, VP					Tel: (612) 445-6450		Emp: N/A
  Bus: *Mfr. paper pulp, felt & roofing materials.*		Fax:(612) 496-3850		%FO: 100

  CORHART INC.
  600 West Lee Street, PO Box 740009, Louisville, KY   40201-7409
  CEO: Joseph H. Menendez, Pres.					Tel: (502) 778-3311		Emp: N/A
  Bus: *Electrofused refractory products.*				Fax:(502) 775-7300		%FO: 100

FLUID SYSTEMS HI INC.
96-1407 Walhona Place, Pearl City, HI   96782
CEO: Harry M. Imai, Pres.   Tel: (808) 456-5966   Emp: 13
Bus: *Wholesale underground utility equipment.*   Fax:(808) 456-9180   %FO: 100

NORTON ADVANCED CERAMICS
10 Airport Road, East Granby, CT   06026
CEO: Brian McEntire, Gen. Mgr.   Tel: (860) 653-8071   Emp: N/A
Bus: *Design/mfr. advanced ceramic products.*   Fax:(860) 653-6834   %FO: 100

NORTON COMPANY
1 New Bond Street, PO Box 15137, Worcester, MA   01615-0137
CEO: Michel L. Besson, Chrm.   Tel: (508) 795-5000   Emp: 1700
Bus: *Mfr. building materials.*   Fax:(508) 795-5868   %FO: 100

NORTON IGNITERS INC.
47 Powers Street, Milford, NH   03055
CEO: Dennis Alaire, Gen. Mgr.   Tel: (603) 673-7560   Emp: N/A
Bus: *Design/mfr. advanced ceramic products.*   Fax:(603) 673-1028   %FO: 100

NORTON PPL, INC.
150 Dey Road, Wayne, NJ   07470
CEO: Rpbert Ayotte, Pres.   Tel: (973) 696-4700   Emp: 50
Bus: *Mfr./distribution performance plastics.*   Fax:(973) 696-4056   %FO: 100

PRECISION METERS INC.
1110 Astronaut Blvd., Orlando, FL   32821
CEO: Eddie Anderson, Pres.   Tel: (407) 851-4470   Emp: 35
Bus: *Mfr. water meters.*   Fax:(407) 855-1881   %FO: 100

SAINT-GOBAIN INTL GLASSWARE CORPORATION
41 Madison Avenue, New York, NY   10010
CEO: Gerard Quintana, Pres.   Tel: (212) 889-8134   Emp: N/A
Bus: *Mfr. glass products.*   Fax:(212) 685-2628   %FO: 100

● **SAMT-DEVELOPPEMENT**
24 rue de Thann, 68068 Mulhouse, France
CEO: Joseph Schittly, Dir.   Tel: 33-389-321188   Emp: N/A
Bus: *Mfr./sale/service weaving machinery & accessories,*   Fax:33-389-433123
    spare parts.

SACM TEXTILE INC.
120 Lee Joyal Rd/Hwy 29, PO Box Drawer 547, Lyman, SC   29365
CEO: Jean-Paul Heuchel, Pres.   Tel: (864) 877-1886   Emp: N/A
Bus: *Distribute spare parts & accessories for*   Fax:(864) 877-4171   %FO: 100
    weaving machines

● **SANSHA (FRANCE) SARL**
6 rue Coustou, F-75018 Paris, France
CEO: Franck Raoul-Duval, Pres.   Tel: 33-1-4252-5266   Emp: N/A
Bus: *Wholesale & retail ballet shoes.*   Fax:33-1-4255-4536

    SANSHA USA, INC.
    1733 Broadway, New York, NY   10019
    CEO: Franck Raoul-Duval, Pres.   Tel: (212) 246-6212   Emp: N/A
    Bus: *Wholesale & retail ballet shoes.*   Fax:(212) 956-7052   %FO: 100

● **GROUPE SCHNEIDER SA**
64-70, ave. Jean-Baptiste Clement, 92646 Boulogne-Billancourt Cédex, France
CEO: Didier Pineau-Valencienne, Chrm.   Tel: 33-1-4699-7000   Emp: 92700
Bus: *Industrial equipment, electromechanical*   Fax:33-1-4699-7456
engineering, general contracting, engineering &
construction.

    SCHNEIDER AUTOMATION
    One High Street, Noth Andover, MA   01845
    CEO: Paul White, Pres.   Tel: (508) 794-0800   Emp: N/A
    Bus: *Mfr. industrial automation equipment.*   Fax:(508) 975-9574   %FO: 100

    SQUARE D COMPANY
    1415 S. Roselle Road, Palatine, IL   60067
    CEO: Charles W. Denny, Pres. & CEO   Tel: (847) 397-2600   Emp: 16000
    Bus: *Power distribution & electric/electronic*   Fax:(847) 397-8814   %FO: 98
    industry control equipment.

● **SCOR SA**
Immeuble SCOR Cedex 39, F-2074 Paris La Defense Cedex, France
CEO: Jacques Blondeau, Chrm.   Tel: 33-1-4698-7000   Emp: 1164
Bus: *Reinsurance services.*   Fax:33-1-4767-0409

    SCOR U.S. CORP - HARTFORD OFFICE
    One Commercial Plaza, 280 Turnbull St., 21st Fl., Hartford, CT   06103-3599
    CEO: Jerome Karter, Pres.   Tel: (860) 525-2300   Emp: N/A
    Bus: *Property & casualty reinsurance services.*   Fax:(860) 278-9967   %FO: 100

    SCOR U.S. CORP- CHICAGO OFFICE
    300 South Wacker Drive, Chicago, IL   60606-6703
    CEO: Jerome Karter, Pres.   Tel: (312) 663-9393   Emp: N/A
    Bus: *Property & casualty reinsurance services.*   Fax:(212) 663-6611   %FO: 100

    SCOR U.S. CORP - SOUTHWEST OFFICE
    222 West Las Colinas Blvd., Irving, TX   75039-5421
    CEO: Jerome Karter, Pres.   Tel: (972) 401-1066   Emp: N/A
    Bus: *Property & casualty reinsurance services.*   Fax:(972) 869-2311   %FO: 100

SCOR U.S. CORP - SOUTHEAST OFFICE
1401 Brickell Avenue - Ste. 910, Miami, FL   33131-3501

CEO: Jerome Karter, Pres.	Tel: (305) 373-8993	Emp: N/A
Bus: *Property & casualty reinsurance services.*	Fax:(305) 373-8450	%FO: 100

SCOR U.S. CORP -WESTCOAST OFFICE
One Market Pl., Stewart St. Tower, San Francisco, CA   94105-1008

CEO: Jerome Karter, Pres.	Tel: (415) 247-6565	Emp: N/A
Bus: *Property & casualty reinsurance services.*	Fax:(415) 247-6569	%FO: 100

SCOR U.S. CORP/SCOR REINSURANCE CO.
Two World Trade Center, New York, NY   10048-0178

CEO: Jerome Karter, Pres.	Tel: (212) 390-5200	Emp: 258
Bus: *Property & casualty reinsurance services.*	Fax:(212) 390-5415	%FO: 100

● **SCRIPTA, SA**
7 passage Turquetil, F-75011 Paris, France

CEO: Eugene Wayolle, Pres.	Tel: 33-1-4370-2200	Emp: 375
Bus: *Mfr. engraving, copy milling & die sinking machines, cutter grinders & bevelers.*	Fax:33-1-4370-5636	

SCRIPTA MACHINE TOOL CORPORATION
7 Kulick Road, Fairfield, NJ   07004-3307

CEO: Eugene Wayolle, Pres.	Tel: (973) 575-1950	Emp: 5
Bus: *Distribution engraving, copy milling & die sinking mach, cutter grinders & bevelers.*	Fax:(973) 575-0151	%FO: 100

● **SEDIVER SA**
79 ave Francois Arago, 92017 Nanterre Cedex, France

CEO: Georges Kayanakis, Pres.	Tel: 33-1-4614-1516	Emp: 1500
Bus: *Mfr. hi-volt electric insulators for overhead power lines.*	Fax:33-1-4097-9433	

SEDIVER INC.
7801 Park Place Road, PO Box 949, York, SC   29745

CEO: Paul K. Timmons, Pres.	Tel: (803) 684-4208	Emp: 85
Bus: *Mfr. hi-volt electric insulators for overhead power lines.*	Fax:(803) 684-4940	%FO: 100

● **SEFAC EQUIPMENT**
B.P. 15, 42501 Le Chambon Feugerolles, France

CEO: Francois Finet, Pres.	Tel: 33-477-401805	Emp: N/A
Bus: *Mfr. heavy duty lifts & garage equipment.*	Fax:33-477-401804	

SEFAC LIFT & EQUIP CORP.
1516 Bush Street, Baltimore, MD   21046

CEO: Charles Stork, Mgr.	Tel: (410) 539-5616	Emp: 22
Bus: *Distribution/sale maintenance heavy duty lifts & garage equipment*	Fax:(410) 539-8195	%FO: 100

● **SGS- THOMSON MICROELECTRONICS N.V.**
Technoparc de Pays de Gex, B.P. 112, 165, rue Edouard Branly, F-01630 Saint Genis Pouilly, France

CEO: Pasquale Pistorio, Pres.	Tel: 33-4-5040-2640	Emp: 25523
Bus: *French-Italian JV semiconductor company.*	Fax:33-4-5040-2860	

    SGS- THOMSON MICROELECTRONICS, INC.
    1310 Electronics Drive, Carrollton, TX   75006-5039

CEO: Richard Pieranunzi, VP Americas	Tel: (972) 466-6000	Emp: N/A
Bus: *Semiconductor company.*	Fax:(972) 466-8130	%FO: 100

● **SKIS DYNASTAR SA**
B P 3, 74701 Sallanches, France

CEO: Jean Yves Pachoud, Pres.	Tel: 33-1-5058-2930	Emp: 500
Bus: *Mfr. snow skis & poles.*	Fax:33-1-5058-4903	

    SKIS DYNASTAR INC.
    Hercules Drive, PO Box 25, Colchester, VT   05446-0025

CEO: David Provost, Exec.VP	Tel: (802) 655-2400	Emp: 38
Bus: *Snow skis, poles, boots & accessories.*	Fax:(802) 655-4329	%FO: 100

● **SNECMA**
2 blvd Victor, 75015 Paris, France

CEO: M. Bechat, Pres.	Tel: 33-140-608088	Emp: N/A
Bus: *Mfr. aircraft engines & parts.*	Fax:33-140-608147	

    CFM INTL
    PO Box 15667 MD/Y5, Cincinnati, OH   45215

CEO: Francis Avanzi, Pres.	Tel: (513) 552-3300	Emp: N/A
Bus: *Mfr. aircraft engines.*	Fax:(513) 552-3306	%FO: JV

    SNECMA INC.
    PO Box 15667, Mail Drop G-7, Cincinnati, OH   45215

CEO: Jacques Riboni, EVP	Tel: (513) 552-3371	Emp: 67
Bus: *Mfr. aircraft engines.*	Fax:(513) 552-3290	%FO: 100

● **SOCIÉTÉ GÉNÉRALE**
Tour Société Générale, 17 Cours Valmy. F-92972 Paris La Descent, France

CEO: Marc Viénot, Pres.	Tel: 33-1-4214-2000	Emp: 45000
Bus: *General commercial banking.*	Fax:33-1-4214-7555	

    FIMAT FUTURES USA INC
    181 West Madison, #3450, Chicago, IL   60602

CEO: Brian Kaye, Chrm.	Tel: (312) 578-5200	Emp: 41
Bus: *Securities broker/dealer.*	Fax:(312) 578-5299	%FO: 100

    SOCIÉTÉ GÉNÉRALE ASSET MANAGEMENT - SOGEN INTL FUND INC
    1221 Avenue of the Americas, 8th Floor, New York, NY   10020

CEO: Jean-Marie Eveillard, Pres.	Tel: (212) 278-5800	Emp: 10
Bus: *Diversified management investment.*	Fax:(212) 956-4590	%FO: 100

SOCIÉTÉ GÉNÉRALE FINANCIAL CORP

1221 Avenue of the Americas, 8th Floor, New York, NY   10020

CEO: Richard Moskwa, Pres.   Tel: (212) 698-0500   Emp: 34

Bus: *Leasing & financing services.*   Fax:(212) 698-0597   %FO: 100

SOCIÉTÉ GÉNÉRALE SECURITIES CORP.

1221 Avenue of the Americas, 8th Floor, New York, NY   10020

CEO: Curtis Welling, Sr. Mgr. Dir.   Tel: (212) 278-5000   Emp: 45

Bus: *Securities broker/dealer.*   Fax:(212) 278-5474   %FO: 50

SOCIÉTÉ GÉNÉRALE USA

1221 Avenue of the Americas, 8th Floor, New York, NY   10020

CEO: Jean Huet, Pres. & CEO   Tel: (212) 278-6000   Emp: 457

Bus: *International commercial banking services.*   Fax:(212) 278-6789   %FO: 100

● SOCIETE LILLEBONNAISE DE CAOUTCHOUCS

9 rue Louis-Rameau, 95872 Bezons, France

CEO: Jean-Claude Smadja, Pres.   Tel: 33-13-3947-9395   Emp: 250

Bus: *Extruded rubber products.*   Fax:33-13-3947-9395

5 RUBBER CORPORATION

1655 Orr Avenue, Kittanning, PA   16201

CEO: John Mochel, Plant Mgr.   Tel: (412) 545-1790   Emp: 131

Bus: *Plant facility for manufacturing of extruded rubber products.*   Fax:(412) 545-2359   %FO: 100

● SOCLA SA

1 rue Paul Sabatier, B P 300, 71107 Shalon sur Saone, France

CEO: Jaques Chaise, Pres.   Tel: 33-3-8546-3034   Emp: N/A

Bus: *Mfr./wholesale valves.*   Fax:33-3-8597-4269

FLOMATIC CORP.

145 Murray Street, Glens Falls, NY   12801

CEO: Bo Andersson, Pres.   Tel: (518) 761-9797   Emp: 50

Bus: *Mfr./wholesale valves.*   Fax:(518) 761-9798   %FO: 100

● SOMMER ALLIBERT,. SA

2 rue de l'Egalité, F-92748 Nanterre Cedex, France

CEO: Marc Assa, Chrm.   Tel: 33-1-4120-4004   Emp: N/A

Bus: *Design/mfr./market textile/plastic products; consumer goods, auto components, home furnishings, and cosmetics & fragrances.*   Fax:33-1-4120-4704

QUALIPAC PREMINTER, INC.

130 Algonquin Parkway, Whippany, NJ   07981

CEO: Mark Bellard, Pres.   Tel: (201) 503-1199   Emp: N/A

Bus: *Mfr. plastic bottles for fragrance/cosmetic industry.*   Fax:(201) 503-1210   %FO: 100

SAI AUTOMOTIVE FOUNTAIN INN, INC.
101 International Boulevard, Fountain Inn, SC   29044

CEO: Mr. Vogt, Pres.	Tel: (869) 862-1900	Emp: N/A
Bus: *US headquarters. design/mfr./market textile/plastic products; consumer goods, auto components, home furnishings, and cosmetics & fragrances.*	Fax:(869) 862-7700	%FO: 100

• **SOPREMA SA**
14 rue de St Nazaire, B P 121, 67025 Strasbourg, France

CEO: Pierre Bindscheidler, Pres.	Tel: 33-388-8879-9945	Emp: 3535
Bus: *Mfr./sale SBS-modified roofing membranes.*	Fax:33-388-8879-0848	

SOPREMA ROOFING & WATERPROOFING INC
310 Quadral Drive, PO Box 471, Wadsworth, OH   44281-0471

CEO: Gilbert Lorenzo, VP	Tel: (330) 334-0066	Emp: 50
Bus: *Mfr./sale SBS-modified roofing membranes.*	Fax:(330) 334-4289	%FO: 100

• **SOTHYS**
14 rue de L'Hotel de Ville, 19100 Brive, France

CEO: Bernard Mas, Pres.	Tel: 33-1-5517-4500	Emp: 200
Bus: *Skin care products.*	Fax:33-1-5523-3888	

SOTHYS USA INC.
1500 NW 94th Avenue, Miami, FL   33172

CEO: Christian Garces, Pres.	Tel: (305) 594-4222	Emp: 20
Bus: *Skin care products.*	Fax:(305) 592-5785	%FO: 100

• **SPIE-BATIGNOLLES SA**
Parc St. Christophe, 95863 Cergy-Pontoise Cedex, France

CEO: Claude Coppin, Pres.	Tel: 33-1-3424-3000	Emp: N/A
Bus: *Engineering & construction.*	Fax:33-1-3425-3830	

COMSTOCK COMMUNICATIONS, INC.
39 Old Ridgebury Road, PO Box 1127, Danbury, CT   06810

CEO: Robert Robertson, Pres.	Tel: (203) 794-8040	Emp: 1200
Bus: *Electrical contractor.*	Fax:(203) 794-8063	%FO: 100

SPIE GROUP INC.
39 Old Ridgebury Road, PO Box 1127, Danbury, CT   06810

CEO: Robert Robertson, Pres.	Tel: (203) 794-8040	Emp: N/A
Bus: *Holding company.*	Fax:(203) 794-8063	%FO: 100

- **SPOT IMAGE SA**
5 rue des Satellites, F-31030 Toulouse Cedex, France
CEO: Jacques Mouysset, Chrm.   Tel: 33-562-194040   Emp: 200
Bus: *Satellite imagery provider.*   Fax:33-562-194011

   SPOT IMAGE CORP.
   1897 Preston White Drive, Reston, VA   22091-4368
   CEO: Ted Nanz, Pres.   Tel: (703) 715-3100   Emp: 45
   Bus: *Satellite imagery provider.*   Fax:(703) 648-1813   %FO: 100

- **STRAT-X SA**
Tour Pacific, 92977 Paris-la-Défense cedex, France
CEO: James Thorne, Mgn. Dir.   Tel: 33-1-4102-0030   Emp: 21
Bus: *Management development programs, strategic* Fax:33-1-4778-1844
planning, results oriented consulting services.

   STRAT-X INTERNATIONAL
   222 Third Street, Cambridge, MA   02142
   CEO: Scott Imperatore, Mgn. Partner   Tel: (617) 494-8282   Emp: 6
   Bus: *Management development programs, strategic* Fax:(617) 494-1421   %FO: 100
   planning, results oriented consulting services.

- **SYNTHELABO SA**
22 ave Galilee, 92352 Le Plessis-Robinson, France
CEO: Herve Guerin, CEO   Tel: 33-14-4537-5555   Emp: 4900
Bus: *Mfr. pharmaceuticals, pacemakers, urological* Fax:33-14-4630-0144
products.

   SYLAMERICA, INC.
   660 White Plains Rd, #400, Tarrytown, NY   10591
   CEO: George Liney, VP   Tel: (914) 332-0165   Emp: 20
   Bus: *Holding company. Mfr. pharmaceuticals,* Fax:(914) 332-0245   %FO: 100
   pacemakers, urological products.

- **TELEMECANIQUE SA**
7 rue Henri Becquerel, 92508 Rueil-Malmaison, France
CEO: Jean-Louis Andreu, Pres.   Tel: 33-14-4708-8686   Emp: 15000
Bus: *Industrial control products.*   Fax:33-14-4732-9184

   TELEMECANIQUE INC.
   10065 Red Run Blvd, Owings Mills, MD   21117
   CEO: Robert Hendrickson, Pres.   Tel: (410) 581-2000   Emp: 600
   Bus: *Mfr. industrial control products for factory* Fax:(410) 581-2031   %FO: 100
   floor.

● **TF 1, SA**
1, Quai du Point de Jour, F-92100 Boulogne, France
CEO: Patrick Lelay, Pres.   Tel: 33-1-4141-1234   Emp: 2000+
Bus: *Privately owned television network.*   Fax:33-1-4141-1589

   TF 1
   2100 M Street, NW, Washington, DC   20032
   CEO: Ulysse Gosset, Bureau Chief   Tel: (202) 223-3642   Emp: 12
   Bus: *News gathering organization.*   Fax:(202) 223-2196   %FO: 100

● **THIEFFRY ET ASSOCIÉS**
23 Avenue Hoche, 75008 Paris, France
CEO: PatrickThieffry, Mng. Ptnr.   Tel: 33-1-4562-4554   Emp: N/A
Bus: *International law firm.*   Fax:33-1-4225-8007

   THIEFFRY ET ASSOCIÉS
   10 Rockefeller Plaza, Ste. 1001, New York, NY   10020
   CEO: Greg McKenney, Mng. Ptnr.   Tel: (212) 698-4550   Emp: N/A
   Bus: *International law firm.*   Fax:(212) 698-4551   %FO: 100

● **THOMSON-CSF SA**
173 blvd Haussmann, F-75414 Paris Cedex 08, France
CEO: Marcel Roulet, Chrm.   Tel: 33-1-5377-8000   Emp: 96035
Bus: *French government-owned consumer electronics,*   Fax:33-1-5377-8300
    defense system & equipment.

   ALSYS INC.
   11921 Freedom Drive, #600, Reston, VA   22090-9606
   CEO: Benjamin Goodwin, Pres.   Tel: (703) 904-7811   Emp: N/A
   Bus: *Mfr. software.*   Fax:(703) 904-7823   %FO: 100

   AUXILEC INC.
   3920 Park Avenue, Edison, NJ   08820
   CEO: Charles Waroquier, Pres.   Tel: (908) 494-1010   Emp: N/A
   Bus: *Sale/service aeronautical equipment.*   Fax:(908) 494-1421   %FO: 100

   AXYAL CORP.
   4553 Glencoe Avenue, Ste.100, Marina del Ray, CA   90232
   CEO: Philippe Tartavul, Pres. & CEO   Tel: (310) 477-1747   Emp: N/A
   Bus: *Mfr. software.*   Fax:(310) 477-4016   %FO: 100

   BURTEK INC.
   7041 East 15th St., PO Box 1677, Tulsa, OK   74101
   CEO: Patrick Oszczeda, Pres   Tel: (918) 836-4621   Emp: N/A
   Bus: *Mfr. simulation training systems.*   Fax:(918) 831-2301   %FO: 100

CETIA, INC.
58 Charles Street, Cambridge, MA   02141
CEO: Hubert de Lacvivier, Pres.
Bus: *Mfr. computer & data processing systems for air space industry.*

Tel: (617) 494-0987   Emp: N/A
Fax:(617) 494-8786   %FO: 100

COMARK COMMUNICATIONS INC.
104 Feeding Hills Road, Southwick, MA   01007
CEO: Navroze S. Mehta, Pres.
Bus: *Mfr. FM/TV transmitters.*

Tel: (413) 569-0116   Emp: N/A
Fax:(413) 569-0679   %FO: 100

COMWAVE
395 Oakhill Road, Mountaintop, PA   18707
CEO: Steve Koppelman, Pres.
Bus: *Mfr. microwave transmitters & systems.*

Tel: (717) 474-6751   Emp: N/A
Fax:(717) 474-5469   %FO: 100

CROUZET CORPORATION
3237 Commander Drive, Carrollton, TX   75006
CEO: Gerald Vincent, Pres.
Bus: *Mfr. TV transmitters.*

Tel: (972) 250-1647   Emp: N/A
Fax:(972) 250-3865   %FO: 100

IDMATICS INC.
561 Broadway, #10A, New York, NY   10012
CEO: Michel Didier, Pres.
Bus: *Marketing identification systems.*

Tel: (212) 966-3616   Emp: N/A
Fax:(212) 966-3490   %FO: 100

MacKAY RADIO SYSTEMS
2721 Discovery Drive, Raleigh, NC   27604-1851
CEO: William Hamilton, Pres.
Bus: *Mfr. telecommunications equipment & systems.*

Tel: (919) 874-1840   Emp: N/A
Fax:(919) 887-0302   %FO: 100

MUST SOFTWARE INTL.
101 Merritt Seven, Norwalk, CT   06856
CEO: Jean-Luc Badault, Pres.
Bus: *Mfr. software; database management.*

Tel: (203) 845-5000   Emp: N/A
Fax:(203) 845-5252   %FO: 100

SEXTANT AVIONIQUE
Beacon Center, 1924 North West 84th Avenue, Miami, FL   33126
CEO: Willy Moses, Pres.
Bus: *Military & commercial aviation systems and equipment supplier.*

Tel: (305) 597-6300   Emp: N/A
Fax:(305) 597-6363   %FO: 100

SYSECA, INC.
4553 Glencoe Avenue, Marina Del Ray, CA   90292-7901
CEO: Philippe Tartavull, Pres.
Bus: *Mfr. transportation systems.*

Tel: (310) 301-9040   Emp: N/A
Fax:(310) 301-3350   %FO: 100

THOMCAST, INC.
Route 309/Advance Lane, Colmar, PA   18915
CEO: John White, Pres.   Tel: (215) 997-7992   Emp: N/A
Bus: *Design/sale transmitter equipment.*   Fax:(215) 997-7994   %FO: 100

THOMSON COMPONENTS & TUBES.
40 G Commerce Way -P O Box 540, Totowa, NJ   07511
CEO: Ernest L. Stern, CEO   Tel: (201) 812-9000   Emp: N/A
Bus: *Marketing cathode ray tubes.*   Fax:(201) 812-9050   %FO: 100

THOMSON CONSUMER ELECTRONICS INC.
10330 N. Meridian Street, Indianapolis, IN   46290
CEO: James Meyer, Pres.   Tel: (317) 587-3000   Emp: N/A
Bus: *Mfr./distribution consumer electronic products.* Fax:(317) 587-6703   %FO: 100

THOMSON CORP. OF AMERICA
99 Canal Center Plaza, #450, Alexandria, VA   22314
CEO: Daniel O'Brien, Pres.   Tel: (703) 838-9685   Emp: N/A
Bus: *Holding company.*   Fax:(703) 838-1686   %FO: 100

THOMSON PASSIVE COMPONENTS CORP.
9350 Eton Avenue, Chatsworth, CA   91311
CEO: Peter O'Brien, Gen. Mgr.   Tel: (818) 407-4950   Emp: N/A
Bus: *Marketing passive components.*   Fax:(818) 407-4949   %FO: 100

THOMSON-CSF INC.
99 Canal Center Plaza, #450, Alexandria, VA   22314
CEO: Benjamin Sandzer-Bell, Pres.   Tel: (703) 838-9685   Emp: N/A
Bus: *Thomson-CSF, US headquarters. Marketing*   Fax:(703) 838-1686   %FO: 100
    electronics.

WILCOX ELECTRIC CO.
2001 NE 46th Street, Kansas City, MO   64116
CEO: William Marberg, Pres.   Tel: (816) 453-2600   Emp: N/A
Bus: *Mfr. navigation aids, landing systems, air*   Fax:(816) 459-4364   %FO: 100
    traffic control equipment..

● **TOTAL COMPAGNIE FRANCAISE DES PETROLES**
Tour TOTAL, 24, Cours Michelet, La Défense 10, 92800 Puteaux, France
CEO: Thierry Desmarest, Chrm.   Tel: 33-1-4135-5229   Emp: 53000
Bus: *Exploration, development & production of crude oil* Fax:33-1-4135-5220
    and gas.

TOTAL ENERGY RESOURCES INC
P O Box 4326, Houston, TX   77210-4326
CEO: Jean-Claude Gabaix, Pres.   Tel: (713) 739-3000   Emp: N/A
Bus: *Energy industry holding company.*   Fax:(713) 739-3160   %FO: 100

TOTAL MINATOME CORP
P O Box 4326, Houston, TX 77210-4326
CEO: Jean-Claude Gabaix, Pres. Tel: (713) 739-3000 Emp: 324
Bus: *Exploration/production oil & gas.* Fax:(713) 739-3160 %FO: 100

TOTAL PETROLEUM (NA) LTD.
900 19th Street, Denver, CO 80202
CEO: C. Gary Jones, Pres. Tel: (303) 291-2000 Emp: 4700
Bus: *Exploration, refining, production, marketing* Fax:(303) 291-2113 %FO: 100
  petroleum & petroleum products.

● **UGINE, SA**
Immeuble Pacific 13, Cours Balmy TSA 30003, S-92070, La Desense 7 Cedex, Paris, France
CEO: Guy Dollé, Chrm. Tel: 33-1-4125-6576 Emp: N/A
Bus: *Mfr.. stainless steel.* Fax:33-1-4125-6702

 J&L SPECIALTY STEEL, INC.
 One PPG Place, 18th Fl., Pittsburgh, PA   15222
 CEO: Claude F. Kronk, CEO Tel: (412) 338-1600 Emp: 1300
 Bus: *Mfr. stainless steel.* Fax:(412) 338-1614 %FO: 53.6

● **VALEO SA**
43 rue Bayen, F-75848 Paris Cedex 17, France
CEO: Noël Goutard, Chrm. & CEO Tel: 33-1-3069-6000 Emp: 29300
Bus: *Mfr. automotive components.* Fax:33-1-3069-6094

 VALEO INC.
 4100 North Atlantic Blvd., Auburn Hills, MI   48326
 CEO: Edward K. Planchon, VP, North America Tel: (248) 209-8253 Emp: 2500
 Bus: *US headquarters, holding company. Mfr.* Fax:(248) 209-8280 %FO: 100
  automotive components.

 VALEO CLUTCHES & TRANSMISSIONS
 37564 Amrhein, Livonia, MI   48150
 CEO: Skip Nydham, Dir. Tel: (313) 432-7304 Emp: 200
 Bus: *Mfr. automotive components.* Fax:(313) 591-7623 %FO: 100

 VALEO ELECTRICAL SYSTEMS, INC.
 4100 North Atlantic Blvd., Auburn Hills, MI   48326
 CEO: Sam Papazian, Sales Dir. Tel: (248) 209-8447 Emp: N/A
 Bus: *Mfr. automotive components.* Fax:(248) 209-8284 %FO: 100

 VALEO ELECTRONICS, INC.
 4100 North Atlantic Blvd., Auburn Hills, MI   48326
 CEO: Eric Fortems, Dir. Tel: (248) 209-8253 Emp: N/A
 Bus: *Mfr. automotive components.* Fax:(248) 209-8280 %FO: 100

VALEO ENGINE COOLING AND CLIMATE CONTROL CORP.
4100 North Atlantic Blvd., Auburn Hills, MI   48326
CEO: Arthur Connelly, Mng. Dir.   Tel: (248) 209-8332   Emp: N/A
Bus: *Mfr. automotive components.*   Fax:(248) 209-8287   %FO: 100

VALEO FRICTION MATERIALS, INC.
37584 Amrheim, Livonia, MI   48150
CEO: Earl Bloom, Mng.Dir.   Tel: (313) 432-7389   Emp: N/A
Bus: *Mfr. automotive components.*   Fax:(313) 591-7626   %FO: 100

VALEO SECURITY SYSTEMS, INC.
4100 North Atlantic Blvd., Auburn Hills, MI   48326
CEO: John Cooper, Mgr.   Tel: (248) 209-8253   Emp: N/A
Bus: *Mfr. automotive components.*   Fax:(248) 209-8280   %FO: 100

VALEO WIPER SYSTEMS & ELECTRIC MOTORS, INC.
37584 Amrheim, Livonia, MI   48326
CEO: Jerry Dittrich, Mng. Dir..   Tel: (313) 432-7372   Emp: N/A
Bus: *Mfr. automotive components.*   Fax:(313) 591-0351   %FO: 100

● **VERRERIE CRISTALLERIE D'ARQUES, J G DURAND & CIE**
Av. Charles de Gaulle, 62510 Arques, France
CEO: J. G. Durand, Chrm.   Tel: 33-321-2193-0000 Emp: 14000
Bus: *Mfr. lead crystal & glass dinner, stem, bar,*   Fax:33-321-2138-0623
     cook/serve & giftware.

    DURAND INTL & DURAND GLASS MFG CO
    Wade Boulevard, Millville, NJ   08332
    CEO: Jean-Rene Gougelet, CEO   Tel: (609) 825-5620   Emp: 850
    Bus: *Mfr./distribution lead crystal & glassware.*   Fax:(609) 696-3442   %FO: 100

● **VERRERIES BROSSE ET CIE**
39 blvd Bourdon, 75004 Paris, France
CEO: Rene Barre, Pres.   Tel: 33-1-4272-7977   Emp: 85
Bus: *Distribution cosmetic & pharmaceuticals glassware.* Fax:33-1-4272-9088

    BROSSE USA, INC.
    150 E 58th Street, New York, NY   10155
    CEO: Catherine Barre, Pres.   Tel: (212) 832-1622   Emp: 8
    Bus: *Mfr. /distribution glass containers for*   Fax:(212) 838-1995   %FO: 100
         cosmetic/fragrance industry.

● **VILMORIN & CIE (DIV. OF LIMAGRAIN)**
BP 1 Chappes, 63720 Ennezat, France
CEO: Alain Catala, CEO   Tel: 33-473-63-4000   Emp: 3000
Bus: *Mfr./sale seeds.*   Fax:33-473-63-4044

    HARRIS MORAN, INC.
    PO Box 4938, Modesto, CA   95352
    CEO: Phil Ashcraft, Pres.   Tel: (209) 579-7333   Emp: 170
    Bus: *Mfr./sale seeds.*   Fax:(209) 527-5312   %FO: 100

● **ZODIAC SA**
48 Blvd Gallieni, 92130 Issy les Moulineaux, France
CEO: Jean-Louis Gerondeau, Pres.   Tel: 33-1-4123-2323   Emp: 2787
Bus: *Leisure marine inflatable products, aerospace safety* Fax:33-1-4648-7524
    products.

    ZODIAC OF NORTH AMERICA INC.
    540 Thompson Creek Road, PO Box 400, Stevensville, MD   21666
    CEO: Jean-Jacques Marie, Pres.   Tel: (410) 643-4141   Emp: 26
    Bus: *Distribute leisure marine inflatable products,* Fax:(341) 043-4491   %FO: 100
    aerospace safety products.

Germany

- **ACLA-WERKE GMBH**
Frankfurter Str 142-190, 51065 Cologne, Germany
CEO: Gerhard Kieffer, CEO — Tel: 49-221-697121 — Emp: 600
Bus: *Mfr. polyurethane molded parts* — Fax:49-221-699980

> **ACLA USA INC.**
> 109 Thomson Park Drive, Cranberry Township, PA 16066
> CEO: Andrew P. McIntyre, Pres. — Tel: (412) 776-0099 — Emp: 5
> Bus: *Sale/distribution polyurethane molded parts.* — Fax:(412) 776-0477 — %FO: 100

- **ACO SEVERIN AHLMANN GMBH**
Postfach 320, AM Ahlmannkai, Rendsburg D-24755, Germany
CEO: Hans-Julius Ahlmann, Chrm. — Tel: 49-4331-3540 — Emp: 1000
Bus: *Polymer concrete trench drain systems, building products.* — Fax:49-4331-354130

> **ACO POLYMER PRODUCTS**
> PO Box 245,12080 Ravenna Rd., Chardon, OH   44024
> CEO: Maarten Fleurke, Pres. — Tel: (216) 285-7000 — Emp: 45
> Bus: *Polymer concrete trench drain systems, building products.* — Fax:(216) 285-7005 — %FO: 100

- **ADIDAS AG**
Adi-Dassler-Str.1-2, D-91074 Herzogenaurach, Germany
CEO: Robert Louis-Dreyfus, CEO — Tel: 49-9132-84-0 — Emp: 6900
Bus: *Mfr. footwear, sporting & athletic clothing & equipment.* — Fax:49-9132-84-2241

> **ADIDAS AMERICA, INC.**
> 9605 S.W. Nimbus Avenue, Beaverton, OR   97008
> CEO: Steven E. Wynne, Pres. — Tel: (503) 972-2300 — Emp: 800
> Bus: *Athletic clothing, shoes.* — Fax:(503) 797-4935 — %FO: 100

- **AEG AG**
Theodor-Stern-Kai 1, 60596 Frankfurt/Main, Germany
CEO: Ernst Georg Stoeckl, Chrm. — Tel: 49-69-600-5496 — Emp: 59000
Bus: *Equipment & products for rail systems, microelectronics, diesel engines, automation & energy system technology. (Sub of Daimler-Benz AG),* — Fax:49-69-600-4630

> **AEG PHOTOCONDUCTOR CORPORATION**
> 27 Kiesland Court, Hamilton, OH   45015
> CEO: Manfred Richard Wagner, Pres — Tel: (513) 874-4939 — Emp: 27
> Bus: *Mfr. photo-receptor drums.* — Fax:(513) 874-5082 — %FO: 100

● **AERZENER MASCHINENFABRIK GMBH**
Postfach 77,-D 31855 Aerzen, Germany
CEO: M. Heller, Pres.   Tel: 49-5154-810   Emp: N/A
Bus: *Mfr. blowers & compressors.*   Fax:49-5154-81191

    AERZEN USA CORPORATION
    645 Sands Court, Coatsville, PA   19320
    CEO: Pierre Noack, Pres.   Tel: (610) 380-0244   Emp: 17
    Bus: *Mfr. blowers and compressors.*   Fax:(610) 363-7251   %FO: 100

● **ALFRED KARCHER GMBH & CO.**
Alfred-KarcherStrasse 28-40, Winnenden 71349, Germany
CEO: Johannes Karcher, Pres.   Tel: 49-7195-142-369   Emp: N/A
Bus: *Manufacturer of cleaning equipment*   Fax:49-7195-142-704

    AMERICAN KLEANER MANUFACTURING COMPANY
    9000 Rochester Avenue, Rancho Cucamonga, CA   91730
    CEO: S. B. Wishek, V.P.   Tel: (909) 481-4331   Emp: 150
    Bus: *High pressure washers.*   Fax:(909) 431-4330   %FO: 100

● **ALLIANZ AG**
Koeniginstrasse 28, D-80802 Munich, Germany
CEO: Dr. Henning Schulte-Noell   Tel: 49-89-38-000   Emp: 69,000
Bus: *All insurance lines; represented in 55 countries*   Fax:49-89-34-9941
     worldwide.

    ALLIANZ OF AMERICA CORPORATION
    55 Greens Farms Road, P.O. Box 5160, Westport, CT   06881-5160
    CEO: David P. Marks, CIO   Tel: (203) 221-8500   Emp: N/A
    Bus: *Insurance - all lines.*   Fax:(203) 221-8529   %FO: 100

    ALLIANZ INSURANCE COMPANY
    3400 Riverside Drive, Suite 300, Burbank, CA   91505-4669
    CEO: Dr. Wolfgang Schlink, Chrm.   Tel: (818) 972-8000   Emp: N/A
    Bus: *Insurance - all lines.*   Fax:(818) 972-8466   %FO: 100

    ALLIANZ LIFE INSURANCE COMPANY OF NORTH AMERICA
    1750 Hennepin Avenue, Minneapolis, MN   55403-2195
    CEO: Lowell C. Anderson, Chmn. & Pres.   Tel: (612) 347-6500   Emp: N/A
    Bus: *Insurance - all lines.*   Fax:(612) 347-6657   %FO: 100

    ALLIANZ UNDERWRITERS INSURANCE COMPANY
    3400 Riverside Drive, Suite 300, Burbank, CA   91505-4669
    CEO: Dr. Wolfgang Schlink, Chmn. & Pres.   Tel: (818) 972-8000   Emp: N/A
    Bus: *Insurance underwriting services.*   Fax:(818) 972-8466   %FO: 100

    FIREMAN'S FUND INSURANCE COMPANY
    777 San Marin Drive, Novato, CA   94998
    CEO: Joe L. Stinnette, Jr., Pres.   Tel: (415) 899-2000   Emp: 10000
    Bus: *Property/casualty insurance.*   Fax:(415) 899-3600   %FO: 100

FIREMAN'S FUND INSURANCE
1101 Connecticut Avenue. NW, Washington, DC   20036
CEO: Peter Larkin, VP   Tel: (202) 785-3575   Emp: N/A
Bus: *Government affairs Washington office.*   Fax:(202) 785-3023   %FO: 100

JEFFERSON INSURANCE COMPANY OF NEW YORK
Newport Tower, 525 Washington Boulevard, Jersey City, NJ   07310-1693
CEO: Claus Cardinal, Pres.   Tel: (201) 222-8666   Emp: N/A
Bus: *Insurance - all lines.*   Fax:(201) 222-9161   %FO: 100

MONTICELLO INSURANCE COMPANY
Newport Tower, 525 Washington Boulevard, Jersey City, NJ   07310-1693
CEO: Claus Cardinal, Pres.   Tel: (201) 222-8666   Emp: N/A
Bus: *Insurance - all lines.*   Fax:(201) 222-9161   %FO: 100

● **AUTOKUEHLER GmbH**
Hohler Weg 31, 34369 Hofgeismar, Germany
CEO: Dirk Pietzoker, Chrm. & Pres.   Tel: 49-5671-8830   Emp: 1400
Bus: *Mfr. heat exchangers.*   Fax:49-5671-3582

  AKG O.A., INC.
  7315 Oakwood Street Ext., Mebane, NC   27302
  CEO: Heinrich Kuehne, VP   Tel: (919) 563-4286   Emp: 80
  Bus: *Mfr./distribution heat exchangers.*   Fax:(919) 563-6060   %FO: 100

● **AZO GMBH & COMPANY**
Postfach 1120, 74701 Osterburken, Germany
CEO: Rainer Zimmermann, CEO   Tel: 49-6291-8920   Emp: 767
Bus: *Ingredient automation systems.*   Fax:49-6291-8928

  AZO INC.
  4445 Malone Road, Memphis, TN   38118
  CEO: Bob Moore, Pres.   Tel: (901) 794-9480   Emp: 93
  Bus: *Mfr. ingredient automation systems.*   Fax:(901) 794-9934   %FO: JV

● **BABCOCK TEXTILMASCHINEN GMBH**
Postfach 3148, 20209 Seevetal 3-Maschen,   bei Hamburg, Germany
CEO: Peter Boden, Pres.   Tel: 49-40-4105- 8110   Emp: 800
Bus: *Mfr. textile machinery.*   Fax:49-40-4105-8112

  TEXTILE MACHINERY, INC.
  PO Box 240212, Charlotte, NC   28224
  CEO: Gerhard Kuhn, Pres.   Tel: (704) 588-2780   Emp: 45
  Bus: *Mfr. textile machinery.*   Fax:(704) 588-2651   %FO: 100

● **BARMAG AG**

Leverkuserstrasse 65, D-42897 Remscheid-Lennep, Germany

CEO: Claus Rainer Schulze-Oberlaender, Chrm.   Tel: 49-2191-670   Emp: 3500

Bus: *Mfr. of machinery & equipment for the man made*   Fax: 49-2191-671204
      fiber industry.

    AMERICAN BARMAG CORP.

    1101 Westinghouse Blvd., Charlotte, NC   28241

    CEO: Kay E. Schnaidt, EVP   Tel: (704) 588-0072   Emp: 115

    Bus: *Sales/service of machinery & equipment for*   Fax: (704) 588-2047   %FO: 100
      the man made fiber industry.

● **BASF AG**

Carl-Bosch Strasse, 38, D-67056 Ludwigshafen, Germany

CEO: Dr. Jürgen Strube, Chrm.   Tel: 49-621-600   Emp: 106565

Bus: *Oil & gas, petrochemicals, agricultural, plastics &*   Fax: 49-621-604-2525
      fibers, chemicals, dyestuffs, finishing, & consumer
      products.

    BASF - Agricultural Products

    26 Davis Drive, P.O. Box 13528, Reaserch Triangle Park, NC   27709

    CEO: Hans-Juergen Loose, Gp. VP   Tel: (919) 547-2010   Emp: N/A

    Bus: *Mfr./sales agricultural chemicals.*   Fax: (919) 405-2244   %FO: 100

    BASF Corp.

    3000 Continental Drive - North, Mount Olive, NJ   07828

    CEO: J. Dieter Stein, Pres.   Tel: (201) 426-2600   Emp: 14000

    Bus: *Holding co: chemicals, coatings & colorants,*   Fax: (201) 426-2610   %FO: 100
      consumer product & life science, fiber
      products, polymers, & plastic materials.

    BASF - Industrial Fibers

    4824 Parkway Plaza Blvd., Charlotte, NC   28217

    CEO: Walter Seufert, Grp. VP   Tel: (800) 247-0557   Emp: N/A

    Bus: *Mfr./sales flame resistant fibers.*   Fax: (704) 423-2261   %FO: 100

    BASF - Research & Development

    100 Sand Hill Road, Enka, NC   28728

    CEO: Otto Ilg, VP   Tel: (704) 667-7110   Emp: N/A

    Bus: *US R&D facility.*   Fax: (704) 667-7110   %FO: 100

    BASF - Textile Products

    4824 Parkway Plaza Blvd., Charlotte, NC   28217

    CEO: Walter W. Hubbard, Grp. VP   Tel: (704) 423-2377   Emp: N/A

    Bus: *Mfr./sales nylon textile products.*   Fax: (704) 423-2101   %FO: 100

    BASF Bioresearch Corp.

    100 Research Drive, Worcester, MA   01605

    CEO: Robert Kamen, Pres.   Tel: (508) 849-2500   Emp: N/A

    Bus: *Bioscience research facility.*   Fax: (508) 755-8506   %FO: 100

BASF Carpet Center
475 Reed Road, NW, Dalton, GA   30720
CEO: Walter W. Hubbard, Grp. VP   Tel: (706) 259-1200   Emp: N/A
Bus: *Mfr./sales nylon carpet products.*   Fax:(706) 259-1424   %FO: 100

BASF CORP.
1100 New York Avenue, NW, Washington, DC   20005
CEO: E. Thomas Coleman, Pres.   Tel: (202) 682-9462   Emp: N/A
Bus: *Government affairs representative office.*   Fax:(202) 682-9462   %FO: 100

BASF Magnetics Corp.
9 Oak Park, Bedford, MA   01730
CEO: John Healion, Pres.   Tel: (617) 271-4000   Emp: N/A
Bus: *Mfr./sales audio & video tapes, computer*   Fax:(617) 271-4000   %FO: 100
      diskettes & data cartridges.

BASF- Dispersions
11501 Steele Creek Road, Charlotte, NC   28273
CEO: Klaus E. Loeffler, Grp. VP   Tel: (704) 588-5280   Emp: N/A
Bus: *Mfr./sales dispersion and acrylic polymer*   Fax:(704) 588-7903   %FO: 100
      chemicals.

BASF- Nutrition & Cosmetics
3000 Continental Drive-North, Mount Olive, NJ   07828
CEO: Wilhelm Tell, Grp. VP   Tel: (973) 426-2600   Emp: N/A
Bus: *Mfr./sales vitamins, skin care and fragrance*   Fax:(973) 426-5309   %FO: 100
      products.

KNOLL PHARMACEUTICAL CO.
3000 Continental Drive-North, Mount Olive, NJ   07828
CEO: Carter Eckert, Pres.   Tel: (973) 426-2600   Emp: 950
Bus: *Mfr./sales ethical pharmaceuticals.*   Fax:(973) 426-5718   %FO: 100

● **BATTENFELD MASCHINEN-FABRIKEN GMBH**
Postfach 1164/65, D-58540 Meinerzhagen, Germany
CEO: Helmut Eschwey   Tel: 49-2354 720   Emp: N/A
Bus: *Plastics process machinery.*   Fax:49-2354 72442

BATTENFELD GLOUCESTER ENGINEERING COMPANY INC.
Blackburn Ind. Park, PO Box 900, Gloucester, MA   01930
CEO: H. Wrede, Pres.   Tel: (508) 281-1800   Emp: 500
Bus: *Mfr. plastics process machinery.*   Fax:(508) 283-9206   %FO: 100

• CHRISTIAN BAUER GMBH & CO.

Schorndorffstrasse, 73642 Welzheim/Wuertt, Germany

CEO: Helmut Hutt, Gen Dir.	Tel: 49-7182-121	Emp: 536
Bus: *Mfr. precision disc springs.*	Fax:49-7182-12315	

BAUER SPRINGS INC

Parkway West Ind. Pk. 509 Parkway View Dr., Pittsburgh, PA   15205

CEO: Helmut Hutt, Pres.	Tel: (412) 787-7930	Emp: 4
Bus: *Engineering/distribution disc springs.*	Fax:(412) 787-3882	%FO: 100

• BAYER AG

Bayerwerk, D-51368 Leverkusen, Germany

CEO: Dr. Manfred Schneider, Chrm.	Tel: 49-214-301	Emp: 140000
Bus: *Holding company for healthcare, imaging technologies, agricultural, industrial products, chemicals, polymer industries.*	Fax:49-214-308-1146	

BAYER - AGFA Division

100 Challenger Road, Ridgefield Park, NJ   07660-2199

CEO: A. Rettinghaus, Pres.	Tel: (201) 440-2500	Emp: N/A
Bus: *Photographic, imaging technologies.*	Fax:(201) 440-8869	%FO: 100

BAYER - Agricultural Division

8400 Hawthorne Road, Kansas City, MO   64120-2306

CEO: E. Lansu, Pres.	Tel: (816) 242-2000	Emp: N/A
Bus: *Mfr./sale agricultural products.*	Fax:(816) 242-2526	%FO: 100

BAYER - Automotive Products Center

2401 Walton Boulevard, Auburn Hills, MI   48326-1957

CEO: Dr. Joseph Backes, VP	Tel: (248) 475-7700	Emp: N/A
Bus: *Design/mfr./sale automotive products.*	Fax:(248) 475-7700	%FO: 100

BAYER - Consumer Care Division

36 Columbia Road, P.O.Box 1910, Morristown, NJ   07962-0910

CEO: Gary Balkema, VP	Tel: (201) 254-5000	Emp: N/A
Bus: *Consumer products division.*	Fax:(201) 408-8000	%FO: 100

BAYER CORP. (US)

One Mellon Center, 500 Grant Street, Pittsburgh, PA   15219-2505

CEO: Helge H .Wehmeier, Pres.	Tel: (412) 394-5500	Emp: 23000
Bus: *Headquarters US. Chemicals, healthcare, imaging technologies, agricultural, industrial products, chemicals, polymer industries.*	Fax:(412) 394-5578	%FO: 100

BAYER - Diagnostics Division

511 Benedict Avenue, Tarrytown, NY   10591-5097

CEO: Ralph Callsson, Pres.	Tel: (914) 631-8000	Emp: N/A
Bus: *Healthcare diagnostics division.*	Fax:(914) 524-2132	%FO: 100

BAYER - Industrial Chemicals Division
100 Bayer Road, Pittsburgh, PA   15205-9741
CEO: Mike Foote, Pres.   Tel: (412) 777-2000   Emp: N/A
Bus: *Mfr./sales industrial chemicals.*   Fax:(412) 777-4959   %FO: 100

BAYER - Pharmaceutical Division
400 Morgan Lane, West Haven, CT   06516-4175
CEO: David Ebsworth, Pres.   Tel: (203) 812-2000   Emp: N/A
Bus: *R&D/mfr./sales ethical pharmaceuticals.* Fax:(203) 812-5554   %FO: 100

BAYER - Polymers Division
100 Bayer Road, Pittsburgh, PA   15205-9741
CEO: H. Lee Noble, VP   Tel: (412) 777-2000   Emp: N/A
Bus: *R&D, mfr./sales polymers.*   Fax:(412) 777-2000   %FO: 100

BAYER CORP.- Washington Office
1101 Pennsylvania Avenue, NW, Suite 515, Washington, DC   20004-2514
CEO: Ronald F. Docksai   Tel: (202) 737-8900   Emp: N/A
Bus: *Corporate representative office.*   Fax:(202) 737-8900   %FO: 100

CHEMDESIGN CORP.
99 Development Road, Fitchburg, MA   01420-6000
CEO: Hans-Georg Schmidt, Pres.   Tel: (978) 345-9999   Emp: N/A
Bus: *Chemicals.*   Fax:(978) 392-9769   %FO: 100

DEERFIELD URETHANE INC.
P.O. Box 186, Routes 5 & 10,, South Deerfield, MA   01373-0186
CEO: Maurice Courtney   Tel: (413) 665-7016   Emp: N/A
Bus: *Mfr. polyurethane films.*   Fax:(413) 665-7159   %FO: 100

HAARMANN & REIMER CORP
70 Diamond Road, Springfield, NJ   07081-3119
CEO: Klaus H. Birchstaedt, Pres.   Tel: (201) 467-5600   Emp: 700
Bus: *Mfr. aroma chemicals, flavors, food   Fax:(201) 467-3514   %FO: 100
     ingredients, fragrances.*

RHEIN CHEMIE CORPORATION
1008 Whitehead Road Extension, Trenton, NJ   08638-2495
CEO: Richard A. Basile, Pres.   Tel: (609) 771-9100   Emp: N/A
Bus: *Mfr. chemical additives.*   Fax:(609) 771-0409   %FO: 100

H.C. STARK INC.
45 Industrial Place, Newton, MA   02161-1951
CEO: Lawrence F. McHugh, Pres.   Tel: (617) 630-5800   Emp: N/A
Bus: *Mfr. tantalum & niobium products.*   Fax:(617) 630-4888   %FO: 100

WOLFF WALSRODE
15 West 700 South Frontage Road, Burr Ridge, IL   60521-7544
CEO: Timothy M. McDivit, Pres.   Tel: (630) 789-8440   Emp: N/A
Bus: *Bayer AG, US subsidiary.*   Fax:(630) 789-8489   %FO: 100

• **BAYERISCHE LANDESBANK GIROZENTRALE**
Briennerstrasse 20, 80277 Munich, Germany
CEO: Franz Neubauer, CEO   Tel: 49-89-2171-01   Emp: N/A
Bus: *General commercial banking services.*   Fax:49-89-2171-3578

> **BAYERISCHE LANDESBANK GIROZENTRALE**
> 560 Lexington Ave., New York, NY   10022
> CEO: W. Freudenberger, EVP   Tel: (212) 310-9800   Emp: 112
> Bus: *International commercial banking services.*   Fax:(212) 310-9841   %FO: 100

• **BAYERISCHE MOTOREN WERKE AG (BMW AG)**
BMW Haus, Petuelring 130, D-80788 Munich, Germany
CEO: Bernd Pischetsrieder, Chrm.   Tel: 49-89-3895-5387   Emp: 69653
Bus: *Mfr. motor vehicles, engines.*   Fax:49-89-3595-5858

> **BMW OF NORTH AMERICA, INC.**
> 300 Chestnut Ridge Road, Woodcliff, NJ   07675
> CEO: Helmut Panke, Chrm.   Tel: (201) 307-4000   Emp: 910
> Bus: *Import/distribution automobiles, motorcycles,*   Fax:(201) 307-4095   %FO: 100
>   *parts & service.*

• **BAYERISCHE VEREINSBANK AG**
Kardinal-Faulhaber Strasse 14, 80311 Munich, Germany
CEO: Albrecht Schmidt   Tel: 49-89-2137-80   Emp: N/A
Bus: *General commercial banking services.*   Fax:49-89-2132-6415

> **BAYERISCHE VEREINSBANK- North America**
> 335 Madison Avenue, New York, NY   10017
> CEO: Stephan W. Bub, CEO   Tel: (212) 210-0300   Emp: 220
> Bus: *International commercial banking services.*   Fax:(212) 210-0330   %FO: 100

> **BAYERISCHE VEREINSBANK- Los Angeles Branch**
> 800 Wilshire Blvd., #1600, Los Angeles, CA   90017-2620
> CEO: Christine Taylor, Mgr.   Tel: (213) 629-1821   Emp: 30
> Bus: *International commercial banking services.*   Fax:(213) 622-6341   %FO: 100

> **VEREINSBANK CAPTIAL CORP.**
> 575 Fifth Avenue, 17th Floor, New York, NY   10017
> CEO: Dr. Gregor Medinger, Pres.   Tel: (212) 808-0990   Emp: N/A
> Bus: *International commercial banking services.*   Fax:(212) 808-9106   %FO: 100

● **BECKER GMBH**
Im Stockmaedle 1, 76307 Karlsbad, Germany
CEO: Erich Geiger, CEO   Tel: 49-7248-710   Emp: 900
Bus: *Automotive systems, radio, and sound.*   Fax:49-7248-711347

    BECKER OF NORTH AMERICA INC
    16 Park Way, Upper Saddle River, NJ   07458
    CEO: Horst Becker, VP   Tel: (201) 327-3434   Emp: 24
    Bus: *Sale/service automotive systems, radio &*   Fax:(201) 327-2084   %FO: AFFL
        sound.

● **BEHR GMBH & CO.**
Mauserstrasser 3, Stuttgart D-70449, Germany
CEO: Horst Geidel, Chrm.   Tel: 49-711-896-1   Emp: 9483
Bus: *Engine cooling, air conditioning for automotive*   Fax:49-711-896-4000
industry.

    BEHR AMERICA INC.
    4500 Leeds Avenue, Charlestown, SC   29405
    CEO: Hans-Joachim Lange, Pres.   Tel: (803) 745-4074   Emp: 747
    Bus: *Engine cooling & air conditioning for*   Fax:(803) 745-1698   %FO: 100
        automotive industry.

● **BEIERSDORF AG**
Unnastrasse 48, 20253 Hamburg, Germany
CEO: Dr. Rolf Kunisch, Chrm.   Tel: 49-40-5-690   Emp: N/A
Bus: *Mfr. toiletries, pharmaceuticals, medical products,*   Fax:49-40-5-696143
tapes.

    BDF BEIERSDORF JOBST, INC.
    5825 Carnegie Blvd., Charlotte, NC   28209
    CEO: Robert Grauman, Pres.   Tel: (704) 554-9933   Emp: N/A
    Bus: *U.S. headquarters. Mfr. toiletries,*   Fax:(704) 553-5853   %FO: 100
        pharmaceuticals, medical products, tapes.

    BDF BEIERSDORF, INC.
    BDF Plaza, 360 Martin L. King Dr., S. Norwalk, CT   06856
    CEO: Peter Metzger, Pres.   Tel: (203) 853-8008   Emp: 400
    Bus: *Mfr. toiletries, medical products. Nivea &*   Fax:(203) 853-2570   %FO: 100
        Eucerin brand products.

    BDF TESA CORP.
    5825 Carnegie Blvd., Charlotte, NC   28209
    CEO: Herbert Forker, Pres.   Tel: (704) 554-0707   Emp: 100
    Bus: *Mfr. pressure sensitive tape.*   Fax:(704) 553-5853   %FO: 100

- **BEITEN BURKHARDT MITTL & WEGENER**
Kurfürstenstrasse 72-74 D-10787 Berlin, Germany
CEO: M. Kromarek, Mng. Prtn.   Tel: 49-30-264-710   Emp: N/A
Bus: *International law firm.*   Fax:49-30-264-71123

     BEITEN BURKHARDT MITTL & WEGENER
     215 East 73rd Street, New York, NY   10021
     CEO: Michael Stever, Mng. Prtn.   Tel: (212) 570-2141   Emp: N/A
     Bus: *International law firm.*   Fax:(212) 734-7011   %FO: 100

- **BENTELER AG**
Residenstrasse 1, D-33104 Paderborn, Germany
CEO: Hubertus Benteler, Pres.   Tel: 49-5254-810   Emp: 12000
Bus: *Automotive parts, steel tubing, machine tooling and*   Fax:49-5251-408346
     steel distribution.

     BENTELER AUTOMOTIVE CORP.
     5O Monroe Avenue, NW
     Suite 500, Grand Rapids, MI   49503
     CEO: George Simcox, Pres.   Tel: (616) 247-3936   Emp: 1800
     Bus: *Mfr. of metal fabricated products: chassis,*   Fax:(616) 732-1697   %FO: 100
     front exhaust, impact management, and
     stamping systems.

- **BERGES ANGRIEBSTECHNIK GMBH & CO. FG**
Industriestrasse 13, D-51709 Marienheide , Germany
CEO: Dietmar Sarstedt, CEO   Tel: 49-2264-170   Emp: 60
Bus: *Mfr. variable speed drives and pulleys.*   Fax:49-2264-17123

     BERGES NA INC.
     24035 Research Drive, Farmington Hills, MI   48335
     CEO: William L. Roethel, CEO   Tel: (248) 478-8250   Emp: 4
     Bus: *Importation & sale of variable speed drives &*   Fax:(248) 478-0568   %FO: 100
     pulleys.

- **BERLINER HANDELS-UND FRANKFURTER BANK (BHF BANK)**
Bockenheimer Landstrasse 10, 60323 Frankfurt/Main, Germany
CEO: E. Michael Kruse, Mgn Ptnr.   Tel: 49-69-7180   Emp: 20000
Bus: *Wholesale merchant banking.*   Fax:49-69-718-2296

     BHF BANK
     590 Madison Avenue, New York, NY   10022-2540
     CEO: B. Cook & B. Frankenberger, SR. VP   Tel: (212) 756-5500   Emp: 150
     Bus: *Wholesale merchant banking.*   Fax:(212) 756-5536   %FO: 100

     BHF BANK
     111 Ocean Blvd., Ste. 1325, Long Beach, CA   90832-2186
     CEO: Rex Masten, SVP   Tel: (562) 983-5000   Emp: 35
     Bus: *Wholesale merchant banking.*   Fax:(562) 983-5015   %FO: 100

BHF SECURITIES CORP.
590 Madison Avenue, New York, NY   10022-2540
CEO: Frank J. La Salla, CEO   Tel: (212) 756-2800   Emp: 50
Bus: *Financial broker/dealer services.*   Fax:(212) 746-2746   %FO: 100

• BERTELSMANN AG
Carl-Bertelsmann-Strasse 270, Postfach 111, D-33311 Gütersloh, Germany
CEO: Mark Wössner, Pres.   Tel: 49-52-41-800   Emp: 57996
Bus: *International communications holding company.*   Fax:49-52-41-75166
Publishing & printing. Books, Magazines, music,
computer, TV & radio.

BANTAM DOUBLEDAY DELL PUBLISHING GROUP
1540 Broadway, New York, NY   10036
CEO: Jack Hoeft, Chrm.   Tel: (212) 354-6500   Emp: 1000
Bus: *Publishing.*   Fax:(212) 354-7985   %FO: 100

BERRYVILLE GRAPHICS
Springsbury Road, PO Box 272, Berryville, VA   22611
CEO: Wayne Taylor, Pres. & CEO   Tel: (540) 955-2750   Emp: 750
Bus: *Printing services.*   Fax:(540) 955-2633   %FO: 100

BERTELSMANN, INC.
1540 Broadway, New York, NY   10036
CEO: Hans-Martin Sorge, CEO   Tel: (212) 782-1000   Emp: 60
Bus: *Holding company. International*   Fax:(212) 782-1010   %FO: 100
communications holding company. Publishing
& printing. Books, Magazines, music,
computer, TV & radio.

BERTELSMANN INDUSTRY SERVICES
28210 N Avenue Stanford, Valencia, CA   91355-1111
CEO: Ralf Bierfisher, Pres.& CEO   Tel: (805) 257-0584   Emp: 300
Bus: *Printing services.*   Fax:(805) 257-3867   %FO: 100

BERTELSMANN MUSIC GROUP (BMG)
1540 Broadway, New York, NY   10036
CEO: Michael Dornemann, Chrm.   Tel: (212) 930-4000   Emp: 1500
Bus: *Distributor/marketing music and video.*   Fax:(212) 930-4015   %FO: 100

BROWN PRINTING CO.
2300 Brown Avenue, Waseca, MN   56093
CEO: Dan Nitz, Pres. & CEO   Tel: (507) 835-2410   Emp: 1300
Bus: *Printing services.*   Fax:(507) 835-0420   %FO: 100

DOUBLEDAY DIRECT, INC.
401 Franklin Avenue, Garden City, NY   11530
CEO: Markus Wilhelm, CEO   Tel: (516) 873-4561   Emp: 1000
Bus: *Book club.*   Fax:(516) 873-4774   %FO: 100

DYNAMIC GRAPHIC FINISHING INC.
945 Horsham Road, Horsham, PA   19044
CEO: David Liess, Pres. & CEO   Tel: (215) 441-8880   Emp: 65
Bus: *Specialty printing.*   Fax:(215) 441-4277   %FO: 100

GRUNER & JAHR USA PUBLISHING
375 Lexington Avenue, New York, NY   10017
CEO: John Heins, Pres. & CEO   Tel: (212) 499-2000   Emp: 600
Bus: *Publishing magazines.*   Fax:(212) 499-2237   %FO: 100

OFFSET PAPERBACK MFRS INC.
P.O. Box N, Route 309, Dallas, PA   18612
CEO: Michael Gallagher, Pres. & CEO   Tel: (717) 675-5261   Emp: 700
Bus: *Paperback printing.*   Fax:(717) 675-8714   %FO: 100

SONOPRESS INC.
108 Monticello Road, Weaverville, NC   28787
CEO: Michael Harris, Pres. & CEO   Tel: (704) 658-2000   Emp: 850
Bus: *Mfr. audiocassettes.*   Fax:(704) 658-2008   %FO: 100

● **BHK-HOLZU KUNSTSTOFF KG**
Industriegebiet-West, D-33142 Buren, Germany
CEO: Heinz Kottmann, Chrm   Tel: 49-295-16040   Emp: 500
Bus: *Mfr. vinyl-wrapped drawer components, wall &*   Fax:49-295-17588
ceiling paneling, flooring, decorative moldings.

BHK OF AMERICA INC.
3 Bond Street, Central Valley, NY   10917
CEO: Reiner Kamp, Pres.   Tel: (914) 928-6200   Emp: 100
Bus: *Mfr./sale vinyl-wrapped & wood drawer*   Fax:(914) 928-2287   %FO: 70
components, furniture components.

● **BILFINGER + BERGER**
Carl-Reiss-Platz 1-5, Postfach 100562, 68165 Mannheim, Germany
CEO: Christian Roth, Chrm.   Tel: 49-621-4590   Emp: N/A
Bus: *Construction/engineering services.*   Fax:49-621 459 2366

FRU-CON CONSTRUCTION CORP
15933 Clayton Road, PO Box100, Ballwin, MO   63022-0100
CEO: Bruce A. Frost, Pres.   Tel: (314) 391-6700   Emp: 2000
Bus: *Full-service engineering construction.*   Fax:(314) 391-4513   %FO: 100

FRU-CON DEVELOPMENT CORP
15933 Clayton Road, PO Box 100, Ballwin, MO   63022-0100
CEO: Paul Sauer, Pres.   Tel: (314) 391-6700   Emp: 12
Bus: *Real estate development of retail &*   Fax:(314) 391-4513   %FO: *100
commercial complexes. (Sub. of Fru-con
Construction Corp.)

FRU-CON ENGINEERING INC

15933 Clayton Road, PO Box 100, Ballwin, MO   63022-0100

CEO: Charles E. Wallace, Pres.   Tel: (314) 391-6700   Emp: 400

Bus: *Consulting & design services. (*Sub of Fru-*   Fax:(314) 391-4513   %FO: *100
con Construction Corp.)

FRU-CON TECHNICAL SERVICES INC

15933 Clayton Road, PO Box 100, Ballwin, MO   63022-0100

CEO: Shawn G. Kelly, Pres.   Tel: (314) 391-6700   Emp: 131

Bus: *Full-service technical resource for*   Fax:(314) 391-4513   %FO: *100
construction industry. (*Sub of Fru-con
Construction Corp.)

H.E.SARGENT, INC.

101 Bennoch Raod, Stillwater, ME   04489

CEO: John I. Simpson, Pres.   Tel: (207) 827-4435   Emp: 131

Bus: *Full-service engineering construction.(*Sub of* Fax:(207) 827-6150   %FO: *100
Fru-con Construction Corp.)

• ROBERT BOSCH GMBH

Robert Bosch Platz 1, Postfach 106050, D-70049 Stuttgart, Germany

CEO: Hermann Scholl, Chrm.   Tel: 49-711-8110   Emp: 156600

Bus: *Auto components, communications technology,*   Fax:49-711-8116630
consumer & capital goods.

ASSOCIATED FUEL PUMP SYSTEMS CORP.

1100 Scotts Bridge Rd., PO Box 1326, Anderson, SC   29622

CEO: Rainer Biggemann, Pres.   Tel: (864) 224-0012   Emp: N/A

Bus: *Mfr. auto electric gasoline pumps.*   Fax:(864) 224-2927   %FO: JV

AUTOMOTIVE ELECTRONIC CONTROL SYSTEMS INC. (AUTECS)

Hwy 81 at I-85, Anderson, SC   29621

CEO: Andres Knackstedt, VP   Tel: (864) 224-0012   Emp: N/A

Bus: *Mfr. electronic controls for gas injection*   Fax:(864) 224-2927   %FO: JV
systems & auto transmissions, mass airflow
meters

BAUDETTE WINTER TEST FACILTIY - PROVING GROUNDS

2 Airport Road, Baudette, MN   56623

CEO: Jim Glutting, CEO   Tel: (218) 634-2077   Emp: N/A

Bus: *Testing facilities.*   Fax:(218) 634-3109   %FO: 100

BG AUTOMOTIVE MOTORS INC.

250 East Main Street, Hendersonville, TN   37076

CEO: David Momot, Pres.   Tel: (615) 822-2800   Emp: N/A

Bus: *Mfr. small electric motors.*   Fax:(615) 822-2816   %FO: JV

BOSCH - AIRFLOW RESEARCH & MFG CORP.
7565 Haggerty Road, Belleville, MI   48111
CEO: Tilo Stahl, Pres.   Tel: (810) 397-1660   Emp: N/A
Bus: *Mfr. plastic cooling fan assemblies.*   Fax:(810) 397-0530   %FO: 100

BOSCH AUTOMATION PRODUCTS
816 East Third Street, Buchanan, MI   49107
CEO: Dan A. Kelly, VP & Gen.Mgr.   Tel: (616) 695-0151   Emp: N/A
Bus: *Factory transport modules, robotics.*   Fax:(616) 695-5363   %FO: 100

BOSCH AUTOMOTIVE GROUP
38000 Hills Tech Drive, Farmington Hills, MI   48331-3417
CEO: Helmut Schwarz, Pres.   Tel: (248) 553-9000   Emp: N/A
Bus: *Mfr. original equipment for cars & trucks.*   Fax:(248) 553-1426   %FO: 100

BOSCH AUTOMOTIVE MOTOR SYSTEMS CORP.
101 First Street, Waltham, MA   02154
CEO: C. Kent Greenwald, Dir. Research.   Tel: (617) 890-8282   Emp: N/A
Bus: *Develop /mfr./distribution equipment for cars   Fax:(617) 890-1975   %FO: 100
   & trucks.*

BOSCH AUTOMOTIVE MOTOR SYSTEMS CORP.
38000 Hills Tech Drive, Farmington Hills, MI   48331-3417
CEO: David Robinson, Pres.   Tel: (248) 553-9000   Emp: N/A
Bus: *Develop /mfr./distribution equipment for cars   Fax:(248) 553-1309   %FO: 100
   & trucks.*

BOSCH BRAKING SYSTEMS
401 N. Bendix Drive, South Bend, IN   46634-4001
CEO: Mark Schwabero, Pres.   Tel: (219) 237-2000   Emp: N/A
Bus: *Develop /mfr./sale braking systems.*   Fax:(219) 237-3242   %FO: 100

ROBERT BOSCH CORP.
2800 South 25th Avenue, Broadview, IL   60153
CEO: Gary M. Saunders, EVP & CFO   Tel: (708) 865-5200   Emp: N/A
Bus: *Administrative offices.*   Fax:(708) 865-6430   %FO: 100

BOSCH ENGINEERING SENSOR SYSTEMS
280 Enterprise Court, Bloomfield Hills, MI   48302
CEO: Anthony Corrado, VP   Tel: (248) 745-1500   Emp: N/A
Bus: *Develop /mfr./distribution sensor systems.* Fax:(248) 745-1504   %FO: 100

BOSCH HEAVY DUTY ENGINEERING
2800 South 25th Avenue, Broadview, IL   60153
CEO: David Robinson, EVP   Tel: (708) 865-5200   Emp: N/A
Bus: *Sales engineering services.*   Fax:(708) 865-6430   %FO: 100

BOSCH PACKAGING MACHINERY DIV.
121 Corporate Blvd, South Plainfield, NJ   07080
CEO: Peter Loveland, EVP   Tel: (908) 226-5100   Emp: N/A
Bus: *Mfr. packaging machinery.*   Fax:(908) 226-5191   %FO: 100

BOSCH SALES GROUP
2800 South 25th Avenue, Broadview, IL   60153
CEO: Frederick W. Hohage, Pres.   Tel: (708) 865-5200   Emp: N/A
Bus: *Sales auto aftermarket, mobile communication,* Fax:(708) 865-6430   %FO: 100
    household goods.

BOSCH SURF/TRAN DIVISION
30250 Stephenson Hwy, Madison Heights, MI   48071
CEO: Ronald A .Sonego, Pres.   Tel: (810) 547-8103   Emp: N/A
Bus: *Mfr. metal deburring/finishing system,*   Fax:(810) 547-0206   %FO: 100
    computer controls, servo drives.

BOSCH TELECOM
9201 Gaither Road, Gaithersburg, MD   20877
CEO: Michael Gaertner, Pres.   Tel: (301) 670-9777   Emp: N/A
Bus: *Mfr. network transmission & management*   Fax:(301) 670-3992   %FO: JV
    products.

BOSCH TL SYSTEMS CORP.
8700 Wyoming Avenue North, Brooklyn Park, MN   55445-1840
CEO: Don DeMorett, Pres.   Tel: (612) 424-4700   Emp: N/A
Bus: *Mfr./sales packaging machinery for*   Fax:(612) 493-6711   %FO: 100
    pharmaceuticals.

DIESEL TECHNOLOGY CO.
2300 Burlingame Avenue SW, PO Box 919, Wyoming, MI   49509-0919
CEO: Derek Kaufman, CEO   Tel: (616) 246-2600   Emp: N/A
Bus: *Diesel fuel injectors.*   Fax:(616) 246-2620   %FO: JV

EBS HOME APPLIANCES
120 Bosch Blvd., New Bern, NC   28562
CEO: Wolfgang Roeder, Pres.   Tel: (919) 636-4267   Emp: N/A
Bus: *Mfr. consumer appliances & parts.*   Fax:(919) 636-4433   %FO: 100

ROBERT BOSCH FLUID POWER CORP.
7505 Durand Avenue, Racine, WI   53406
CEO: Mike Hadfield, Pres.   Tel: (414) 554-7100   Emp: N/A
Bus: *Mfr. hydraulic/pneumatic products.*   Fax:(414) 554-7117   %FO: 100

S-B POWER TOOL CO..
4300 W. Peterson Avenue, Chicago, IL   60646-5999
CEO: G. Thomas McKane, Pres.   Tel: (773) 794-6617   Emp: N/A
Bus: *Develop /mfr./distribution power tools.*   Fax:(773) 794-6618   %FO: JV

VERMONT AMERICAN CORP.
101 South Fifth Street, #2300, Louisville, KY   40202
CEO: Timothy P. Shea, Pres.   Tel: (502) 625-2000   Emp: N/A
Bus: *Mfr. cutting tools, hand tools & accessories,*   Fax:(502) 625-2122   %FO: JV
     lawn garden products, closet organizers.

WELDUN INTL INC.
9850 Red Arrow Hwy., Bridgman, MI   49106
CEO: Frank H.W. Schoenwitz, Pres.   Tel: (616) 465-6986   Emp: N/A
Bus: *Mfr. integrated manufacturing systems.*   Fax:(616) 465-3400   %FO: 100

● **GEOBRA BRANDSTATTER GMBH & CO KG**
Brandstatter Strasse 2-10, D-90513 Zirndorf, Germany
CEO: Horst Brandstatter, Owner   Tel: 49-91-1966-6125   Emp: 1800
Bus: *Mfr. toys.*   Fax:49-91-1966-6120

    PLAYMOBIL USA INC.
    11 East Nicholas Court, Dayton, NJ   08810
    CEO: Jonathan Thorpe, Pres.   Tel: (908) 274-0101   Emp: 40
    Bus: *Sale/distribution toys.*   Fax:(908) 274-0110   %FO: 100

● **BRUCKHAUS WESTRICK STEGEMANN**
Friedrichstrasse 95 IHZ, 10117 Berlin, Germany
CEO: G. Krüger, Mng. Ptnr.   Tel: 49-30-202-836   Emp: N/A
Bus: *International law firm.*   Fax:49-30-202-837366

    BRUCKHAUS WESTRICK STEGEMANN
    10 Rockefeller Plaza, Ste. 1416, New York, NY   10020
    CEO: Dr. G. Janke, Mng. Ptnr.   Tel: (212) 218-5050   Emp: N/A
    Bus: *International law firm.*   Fax:(212) 218-5055   %FO: 100

● **BUHLER BEBR NACHFOLGER GMBH**
Anne-Frank-Strasse 33, 90459 Nuremberg, Germany
CEO: Wolfgang Klug, Pres.   Tel: 49-911 45040   Emp: N/A
Bus: *Mfr. sub-fractional motors, gear motors & fans.*   Fax:49-911 454626

    BUEHLER PRODUCTS INC.
    PO Box 33400, Raleigh, NC   37606-3400
    CEO: L. P. LaFreniere, Gen.Mgr.   Tel: (919) 469-8522   Emp: 750
    Bus: *Mfr. sub-fractional motors, gear motors & fans*   Fax:(919) 469-8522   %FO: 49

● **BYK-GULDEN LOMBERG CHEMISCH FABRIK GMBH**
Byk-Gulden-Strasse 1, D-78467 Konstanz, Germany
CEO: Heinz W. Bull, Pres.   Tel: 49-7531-840   Emp: 2500
Bus: *Pharmaceutical products.*   Fax:49-7531-842474

    ALTANA INC.
    60 Baylis Road, Melville, NY   11747
    CEO: George Cole, Pres.   Tel: (516) 454-7677   Emp: 470
    Bus: *Mfr. pharmaceutical products.*   Fax:(516) 454-6389   %FO: 76

- **CHIRON-WERKE GMBH & CO KG**
Talstrasse 23, D-78532 Tuttlingen, Germany
CEO: Hans H. Winkler, Pres.   Tel: 49-74-61 9400   Emp: 650
Bus: *CNC vertical machining centers.*   Fax:49-75-61 3159

  CHIRON AMERICA INC.
  14201-G S Lakes Drive, Charlotte, NC   28273
  CEO: William M. Carr, Pres.   Tel: (704) 587-9526   Emp: 42
  Bus: *CNC vertical machining centers.*   Fax:(704) 587-0485   %FO: 100

- **CHRISTIAN BAUER GMBH & COMPANY**
49 Schorndorfer Strasse, D-73642 Welzheim/Württ, Germany
CEO: Helmut Hutt, Gen. Dir.   Tel: 49-7188-2121   Emp: N/A
Bus: *Mfr. precision disc springs.*   Fax:49-7182-12315

  BAUER SPRINGS, INC.
  Parkway West Industrial Pk., 509 Pkwy View Dr., Pitsburgh, PA   15205
  CEO: Ms. U. Tell, Mgr.   Tel: (412) 787-7930   Emp: N/A
  Bus: *Mfr./distribution precision disc springs.*   Fax:(412) 787-3882 %FO: 100

- **CLAAS OF HARSEWINKEL GERMANY**
Muensterstrasse 33, D-33428 Harsewinkel, Germany
CEO: Helmet Claas, Pres.   Tel: 49-5247-120   Emp: N/A
Bus: *Mfr./assembly harvesting equipment.*   Fax:49-5247-12927

  CLAAS OF AMERICA INC.
  3030 Norcross Drive,PO Box 3008, Columbus, IN   47202-3008
  CEO: Roger Parker, Gen. Mgr.   Tel: (812) 342-4441   Emp: 19
  Bus: *Mfr./assembly harvesting equipment.*   Fax:(812) 342-3525   %FO: 100

- **COLOGNE REINSURANCE**
Postfach 102244, D 50462 Cologne, Germany
CEO: Peter-Lutke-Barnefeld, Pres.   Tel: 49-221-9738-40   Emp: 3000
Bus: *Reinsurance facilities.*   Fax:49-221-9739-611

  COLOGNE LIFE REINSURANCE COMPANY
  30 Oak Street, Stamford, CT   06905
  CEO: Michael Magsig, Chrm. & Pres.   Tel: (203) 356-4900   Emp: 150
  Bus: *Reinsurance facilities.*   Fax:(203) 326-4866   %FO: 100

- **COLONIA VERSICHERUNG AG**
Colonia-Allee 10-20, 51067 Cologne, Germany
CEO: Dr. Hans Jaeger, Pres.   Tel: 49-221 929902   Emp: 5500
Bus: *Insurance services.*   Fax:49-21 96992750

  COLONIA INSURANCE COMPANY
  1 Seaport Plaza, 199 Water Street, New York, NY   10038
  CEO: Claus Dannasch, Pres.   Tel: (212) 412-0500   Emp: 73
  Bus: *Casualty/property insurance*   Fax:(212) 412-0701   %FO: 100

● **COMMERZBANK AG**
Neue Mainzer Strasse 32-36, 60311 Frankfurt/Main, Germany
CEO: Martin Kohlhaussen, Chrm.   Tel: 49-69-13620   Emp: 12000
Bus: *Commercial and investment banking services.*   Fax:49-69-285389

COMMERZBANK - Atlanta Branch
Promenade #2, #3500, 1230 Peachtree Street NE, Atlanta, GA   30309
CEO: Andreas Bremer, Mgr.   Tel: (404) 888-6500   Emp: 20
Bus: *International commercial and investment*   Fax:(404) 888-6539   %FO: 100
     banking services.

COMMERZBANK - New York Branch
2 World Financial Center, 225 Liberty Street, New York, NY   10281-1050
CEO: Hermann Burger, Gen. Mgr.   Tel: (212) 266-7200   Emp: 300
Bus: *International commercial and investment*   Fax:(212) 266-7235   %FO: 100
     banking services.

COMMERZBANK - Los Angeles Branch
633 West 5th Street, Suite 6600, Los Angeles, CA   90017
CEO: Christian Jagenberg, Gen. Mgr.   Tel: (213) 623-8228   Emp: 20
Bus: *International commercial and investment*   Fax:(213) 623-0039   %FO: 100
     banking services.

COMMERZBANK - Chicago Branch
311 South Wacker Drive, #5800, Chicago, IL   60606
CEO: Helmut Toellner, Mgr.   Tel: (312) 426-1000   Emp: 25
Bus: *International commercial and investment*   Fax:(312) 425-1485   %FO: 100
     banking services.

● **CONTACT GMBH ELEKTRISCHE BAUELEMENTE**
Gewerbstrasse 30, D-7000 Stuttgart, Germany
CEO: U. A. Lapp, Pres.   Tel: 49-0711 783803   Emp: N/A
Bus: *Mfr. environmentally protected industrial*   Fax:49-0711 7838366
     connectors, electrical connectors & cable
     harnessing.

CONTACT ELECTRONICS INC.
30 Plymouth Street, Fairfield, NJ   07004
CEO: James W. Riff, EVP   Tel: (201) 575-7660   Emp: 25
Bus: *Distribution industrial and electrical*   Fax:(201) 575-7208   %FO: 100
     connectors & harnessing.

- **CONTINENTAL AG**
  Vahrenwalder Str 9, 30165 Hannover, Germany
  CEO: Hubertus von Gruenberg, Chrm.　　　　Tel: 49-511 93801　　Emp: 53000
  Bus: *Mfr. tires & industrial products.*　　　Fax:49-511 9382766

    CONTINENTAL GENERAL TIRE INC.
    1800 Continental Blvd., Charlotte, NC　28278
    CEO: Bernd Frangenberg, Pres.　　　　　Tel: (704) 583-3900　　Emp: 8000
    Bus: *Mfr. tires.*　　　　　　　　　　　Fax:(704) 583-8698　　%FO: 100

- **DAIMLER-BENZ AG**
  Epplestrasse 225, Postfach 800230, D-70546 Stuttgart, Germany
  CEO: Jürgen E. Schrempp, Chrm.　　　　　Tel: 49-711-179-2287　Emp: 310993
  Bus: *Mfr. cars, trucks, commercial vehicles, aircraft*　Fax:49-711-179-45109
  　　engines, electronics.

    DAIMLER-BENZ NA CORP.
    375 Park Avenue, #3001, New York, NY　10152-3001
    CEO: Timotheus R Pohl, Pres. & CEO　　Tel: (212) 909-9700　　Emp: 15000
    Bus: *Headquarters - North America, holding*　Fax:(212) 826-0356　%FO: 100
    　　company.

    DAIMLER-BENZ WASHINGTON, INC.
    1350 I Street, NW, # 800, Washington, DC　20005-3305
    CEO: Peter-HansKeilbach, Pres.　　　　Tel: (202) 408-4900　　Emp: N/A
    Bus: *Government relations, Washington Office.*　Fax:(202) 408-4891　%FO: 100

    FREIGHTLINER CORP.
    4747 N. Channel Avenue, Portland, OR　97217
    CEO: James L.Hebe, Chrm.　　　　　　Tel: (503) 283-8000　　Emp: 4700
    Bus: *Mfr. diesel trucks.*　　　　　　Fax:(503) 283-8192　%FO: 100

    GETTYS CORP.
    2701 N. Green Bay Road, Racine, WI　53404
    CEO: Wayne O. Kanke, VP　　　　　　Tel: (414) 637-6591　　Emp: 140
    Bus: *Mfr. servo motors, amplifiers.*　　Fax:(414) 637-8400　%FO: 100

    MERCEDES-BENZ ADVANCED DESIGN OF NA INC.
    17742 Cowan Street, Irvine, CA　92714
    CEO: Gerhard Steinle, Pres　　　　　　Tel: (714) 476-8300　　Emp: 12
    Bus: *Advanced design center.*　　　　Fax:(714) 476-2366　%FO: 100

    MERCEDES-BENZ CREDIT CORP.
    201 Merritt 7, # 700, Norwalk, CT　06856
    CEO: Georg Bauer, Pres.　　　　　　　Tel: (203) 847-4500　　Emp: 521
    Bus: *Leasing & financing services.*　　Fax:(203) 847-9245　%FO: 100

MERCEDES-BENZ OF NA INC.
One Mercedes Drive, Montvale, NJ   07645

CEO: Michael Bassermann, Chrm.	Tel: (201) 573-0600	Emp: 1606
Bus: *Sale/distribution cars, parts.*	Fax:(201) 573-0117	%FO: 100

SETRA/KASSBOHRER OF NORTH AMERICA, INC.
P.O.Box1270, Gary, ME   04039-1270

CEO: Christoph van der Osten, Pres.	Tel: (207) 657-2455	Emp: 19
Bus: *Sales/service of luxury motor coaches. Sub of EvoBus GmbH, Div. of Daimler-Benz AG*	Fax:(207) 657-3395	%FO: 100

SILICONIX INC.
2201 Laurelwood Road, Santa Clara, CA   95054

CEO: Richard J. Kulle, Pres. & CEO	Tel: (408) 988-8000	Emp: 1757
Bus: *Mfr. semiconductors.*	Fax:(408) 727-5414	%FO: 80

● **WALTER DE GRUYTER & CO**
Postfach 303421, D-10728 Berlin, Germany

CEO: K-G Cram, Pres.	Tel: 49-30 260050	Emp: 270
Bus: *Publisher; scholarly & scientific books & journals.*	Fax:49-30 26005251	

WALTER DE GRUYTER, INC.
200 Saw Mill River Road, Hawthorne, NY   10532

CEO: Eckart A. Scheffler, VP	Tel: (914) 747-0110	Emp: 18
Bus: *Publisher; scholarly & scientific books & journals.*	Fax:(914) 747-1326	%FO: 100

● **DEGUSSA AG**
Weissfrauenstrasse 9, D-60311 Frankfurt, Germany

CEO: Uwe-Ernst Bufe, CEO	Tel: 49-69 21801	Emp: N/A
Bus: *Precious metals, chemical, pharmaceuticals, colors, plastics.*	Fax:49-69 2183218	

DEGUSSA CORP. - CHEMICAL PIGMENT GROUP
65 Challenger Road, Ridgefield Park, NJ   07660

CEO: Andrew J. Burke, CEO	Tel: (201) 641-6100	Emp: N/A
Bus: *Chemicals, electronics, pigments.*	Fax:(201) 807-3167	%FO: 100

DEGUSSA CORP. - MOBILE PLANT
PO Box 606, Mobile, AL   36601

CEO: Wolfgang Buder, Mgr.	Tel: (334) 443-4000	Emp: N/A
Bus: *Chemicals, electronics.*	Fax:(334) 443-4000	%FO: 100

DEGUSSA CORP. - METAL AND DENTAL GROUP
3900 South Clinton Avenue, So. Plainfield, NJ   07080

CEO: Craig Benson, Mgr.	Tel: (908) 561-1100	Emp: N/A
Bus: *Metal, dental products.*	Fax:(908) 668-7896	%FO: 100

- **DETA AKKUMULATORENWERKE GMBH**
Postfach 180, D-37431 Bad Lauterberg, Germany
CEO: Albrecht Leuschner, Pres.　　　　　　Tel: 49-5524 820　　　Emp: 1200
Bus: *Mfr. starter and traction batteries.*　　Fax:49-5524 82341

　　DETA-DOUGLAS BATTERIES INC.
　　500 Battery Drive, P O Box 12665, Winston-Salem, NC　27117
　　CEO: Herbert von Feilitzsch, Gen. Mgr.　Tel: (910) 650-7267　Emp: 2
　　Bus: *Marketing batteries.*　　　　　　Fax:(910) 650-7272　%FO: JV

- **DEUTSCHE BANK AG**
Taunusanlage 12, D-60262 Frankfurt, Germany
CEO: Rolf-Ernst Breuer　　　　　　　　　Tel: 49-69-910-00　　Emp: 74119
Bus: *Commercial, private, investment and merchant*　Fax:49-69-910-34227
　　banking services.

　　DEUTSCHE BANK AG - NEW YORK BRANCH
　　31 West 52nd Street, New York, NY　10019
　　CEO: W. Carter McClelland, Pres.　　Tel: (212) 474-8000　Emp: 100+
　　Bus: *New York branch of DEUTSCHE BANK AG.*　Fax:(212) 474-8560　%FO: 100

　　DEUTSCHE FINANCIAL SERVICES CORP.
　　655 Maryville Centre Drive, St. Louis, MO　63141
　　CEO: Robert M.Martin, Pres.　　　　Tel: (314) 523-3000　Emp: 100+
　　Bus: *Financial services company.*　　Fax:(314) 523-3888　%FO: 100

　　DEUTSCHE FINANCIAL SERVICES CORP.
　　2333 Waukegan Road, Deerfield, IL　60015
　　CEO: M .G. Zitzmann, Pres.　　　　　Tel: (847) 948-7272　Emp: 200
　　Bus: *Financial services company.*　　Fax:(847) 948-5058　%FO: 100

　　DEUTSCHE MORGAN GRENFELL INC.
　　31 West 52nd Street, New York, NY　10019
　　CEO: W. Carter McClelland, Pres.　　Tel: (212) 469-5000　Emp: 200
　　Bus: *Securities broker/dealer, investment banking &*　Fax:(212) 469-4133　%FO: 100
　　asset management services.

- **DEUTSCHE FIBRIT GMBH**
St. Toeniser Strasse 60, D-47803 Krefeld, Germany
CEO: Jan G Mueller, Pres　　　　　　　Tel: 49-215-18420　　Emp: 1900
Bus: *Mfr. automotive interior trim & instrument panels.*　Fax:49-215-891 9595

　　AMERICAN FIBRIT INC
　　76 Armstrong Road, Battle Creek, MI　49015
　　CEO: C Roger Davisson, Pres.　　　Tel: (616) 968-3000　Emp: 250
　　Bus: *Mfr. automotive interior trim & instrument*　Fax:(616) 968-0198　%FO: 50
　　panels.

● **DEUTSCHE GELATINE FABRIKEN-STOESS AG**
Gammelsbacher Strasse 2, D-69412 Eberbach/Baden, Germany
CEO: Jorg Siebert, Pres.   Tel: 49-6271-8401   Emp: N/A
Bus: *Mfr. gelatin.*   Fax:49-6271-8427

     DYNAGEL INC.
     Plummer Street & Wentworth Avenue, Calumet City, IL   60409
     CEO: George Riesenfeld, Pres.   Tel: (708) 891-8400   Emp: 63
     Bus: *Mfr. gelatin. (JV with Leiner Davis Gelatin,*   Fax:(708) 891-8432   %FO: JV
     Australia).

● **DEUTSCHE GENOSSENSCHAFTSBANK (DG BANK)**
Am Platz der Republik, D-60325 Frankfurt am Main, Germany
CEO: Dr. Bernd Thiemann, Chrm   Tel: 49-69-7447-04   Emp: 5104
Bus: *Commercial banking services.*   Fax:49-68-7447-1685

     DG BANK - New York Branch
     DG BANK Building, 609 Fifth Avenue, New York, NY   10017-1021
     CEO: Hans W. Meyers, SVP, Gen. Mgr.   Tel: (212) 745-1400   Emp: N/A
     Bus: *Commercial banking services.*   Fax:(212) 745-1550   %FO: 100

     DG EUROPEAN SECURITIES
     DG BANK Building, 609 Fifth Avenue, New York, NY   10017-1021
     CEO: ValentinN. Graf Kerssenbrock   Tel: (212) 745-1600   Emp: N/A
     Bus: *Securities broker/dealer.*   Fax:(212) 745-1616   %FO: 100

● **DEUTSCHE LUFTHANSA AG**
Lufthansa Basis, D-60546 Frankfurt/Main, Germany
CEO: Jürgen Weber, Chrm.   Tel: 49-69-696-2200   Emp: 57586
Bus: *International air transport services.*   Fax:49-69-696-6818

     LUFTHANSA USA
     680 Fifth Avenue, 17th Fl., New York, NY   10019
     CEO: Uwe Hinrichs, SVP   Tel: (212) 479-8801   Emp: 2000
     Bus: *International air transport services.*   Fax:(212) 479-0795   %FO: 100

     LUFTHANSA USA - EAST
     1640 Hempstead Turnpike, East Meadow, NY   11554
     CEO: Uwe Hinrichs, SVP   Tel: (516) 296-9200   Emp: 700
     Bus: *International air transport services.*   Fax:(516) 296-9639   %FO: 100

     LUFTHANSA USA - WEST
     5230 Pacific Concourse Dr., Los Angeles, CA   90045
     CEO: Rolf Hoehn, VP   Tel: (310) 297-7300   Emp: 200
     Bus: *International air transport services.*   Fax:(310) 297-7329   %FO: 100

- **DEUTSCHE MESSE AG**
Messegelaende, D-30521 Hannover, Germany
CEO: Klaus E. Goehrman, Chrm. Tel: 49-511 890 Emp: 550
Bus: *Trade fairs operators.* Fax:49-511 8932626

 HANNOVER FAIRS USA INC.
 103 Carnegie Center, #207, Princeton, NJ 08540
 CEO: Joachim Schafer, Pres. Tel: (609) 987-1202 Emp: 17
 Bus: *Trade fairs management & promotion.* Fax:(609) 987-0092 %FO: 100

- **DEUTZ AG**
Deutz-Muelheimer Strasse 147-149, D-51063 Cologne, Germany
CEO: Anton Schneider, CEO Tel: 49-221-8220 Emp: N/A
Bus: *Mfr. diesel engines and industrial plant systems.* Fax:49-221-8222-004

 DEUTZ OF AMERICA CORP.
 3883 Steve Reynolds Boulevard, Norcross, GA 30093
 CEO: Manfred A. Kleindienst, Pres. Tel: (770) 564-7100 Emp: N/A
 Bus: *Mfr. diesel engines and industrial plant* Fax:(770) 564-7272 %FO: 100
  systems.

 DEUTZ CORPORATION
 3883 Steve Reynolds Blvd., Norcross, GA 30093
 CEO: Werner Schmitz, Pres. Tel: (770) 564-7100 Emp: N/A
 Bus: *Mfr. diesel engines and industrial plant* Fax:(770) 564-7272 %FO: 100
  systems.

 SCHMIDT BRETTEN INC.
 380E Central Avenue, Bohemia, NY 11716
 CEO: Constatine Triculis, VP Tel: (516) 589-2112 Emp: N/A
 Bus: *Mfr. industrial plant systems.* Fax:(516) 589-2868 %FO: 100

- **DIA-NIELSEN GMBH**
Postfach 100452, D-52304 Dueren, Germany
CEO: Norbert Klinke, Pres. Tel: 49-2421-59010 Emp: 250
Bus: *Mfr. marking systems for recording instruments.* Fax:49-2421-590179

 DIA NIELSEN USA INC.
 2615 River Road, Unit 1, Cinnaminson, NJ 08077
 CEO: Norbert Klinke, Pres. Tel: (609) 829-9441 Emp: 9
 Bus: *Supplier marking systems for recording* Fax:(609) 829-8814 %FO: 100
  instruments.

● **DICK FRIEDR GMBH**
Postfach 209, 73703 Esslingen an Neckar, Germany
CEO: Wilhem Leuze, CEO   Tel: 49-711 2994157   Emp: 300
Bus: *Mfr. cutlery.*   Fax:49-711 2994157

    FRIEDR DICK CORPORATION
    33 Allen Boulevard, Farmingdale, NY   11735
    CEO: Bill Colwin, Gen. Mgr.   Tel: (516) 454-6955   Emp: 6
    Bus: *Distribution/sale cutlery.*   Fax:(516) 454-6184   %FO: 100

● **DIENES-WERKE**
51491 Overath-Vilerath, Germany
CEO: Bernd Supe Dienes, Pres.   Tel: 49-2206-6050   Emp: 250
Bus: *Slitting tools, compressor valves.* Fax:49-2206-605111

    DIENES CORPORATION
    Spencer Corporate Park, Spencer, MA   01562-2498
    CEO: William Shea, VP & Gen.Mgr.   Tel: (508) 885-6301   Emp: 55
    Bus: *Mfr. slitting tools, replacement parts for*   Fax:(508) 885-3452   %FO: 100
        compressors.

● **DRÄEGERWERK AG**
Moislinger Allee 53/55, D-23542 Luebeck, Germany
CEO: Christian Dräeger, Pres.   Tel: 49-451 882-0   Emp: 4200
Bus: *Aerospace, diving & medical technology equipment*   Fax:49-451 882-2080
manufacturer.

    DRÄEGER SAFETY, INC.
    101 Technology Drive, P O Box 120, Pittsburgh, PA 15230-0128
    CEO: Ron Towns, Pres.   Tel: (412) 787-8383   Emp: 200
    Bus: *Mfr. safety equipment, respiratory protection*   Fax:(412) 787-2207   %FO: 100
        products and gas detection products.

● **DRAISWERKE GMBH**
Speckweg 43-59, 68219 Mannheim, Germany
CEO: Paul Eirich, Pres.   Tel: 49-621 75040   Emp: 310
Bus: *Mixing, wet grinding & dispersion equipment.*   Fax:49-621 7504233

    DRAISWERKE INC.
    40 Whitney Road, Mahwah, NJ   07430
    CEO: Gisbert Schall, Pres   Tel: (201) 847-0600   Emp: 15
    Bus: *Mixing, wet grinding & dispersion equipment.*   Fax:(201) 847-0606   %FO: 20

● **DRESDNER BANK AG**
Juergen Ponto Platz 1, 60301 Frankfurt, Germany
CEO: Juergen Sarrazin, Chrm.   Tel: 49-69 2630   Emp: 42017
Bus: *Commercial & merchant banking, investment*   Fax:49-69 4004
advisory, securities broker/dealer services & foreign
exchange services.

   DRESDNER KLEINWORT BENSON - New York Branch
   75 Wall Street, 27th Floor, New York, NY   10005
   CEO: George Fugelsang, CEO   Tel: (212) 429-2000   Emp: 215
   Bus: *Commercial & merchant banking, investment*   Fax:(212) 429-2467   %FO: 100
   advisory, securities broker/dealer services &
   foreign exchange services.

   DRESDNER KLEINWORT BENSON - Chicago Branch
   190 South Lasalle, 27th Floor, Chicago, IL   60603
   CEO: John H. Schaus, SVP Mgr.   Tel: (312) 444-1900   Emp: 16
   Bus: *Commercial & merchant banking, investment*   Fax:(312) 444-1192   %FO: 100
   advisory, securities broker/dealer services &
   foreign exchange services.

   DRESDNER KLEINWORT BENSON - Boston Branch
   1 Boston Place - 29th Floor, Boston, MA   01208
   CEO: Lisa Ryan, Mgr.   Tel: (617) 723-4600   Emp: 5
   Bus: *Commercial & merchant banking, investment*   Fax:(212) 723-4889   %FO: 100
   advisory, securities broker/dealer services &
   foreign exchange services.

   DRESDNER KLEINWORT BENSON - Los Angeles Branch
   333 S. Grand Avenue, Ste. 1700, Los Angeles, CA 90071
   CEO: John Bland, Gen. Mgr.   Tel: (213) 473-5400   Emp: 13
   Bus: *Commercial & merchant banking, investment*   Fax:(213) 473-5450   %FO: 100
   advisory, securities broker/dealer services &
   foreign exchange services.

● **DRESDNER BANK LATEINAMERIKA AG**
Neverjungfernsteig, D-20354 Hamburg, Germany
CEO: Helmut Frohlich, Chrm.   Tel: 49-40-3595-0   Emp: N/A
Bus: *General banking services. Subsidiary of*   Fax:49-40-3595-3314
DRESDNER BANK AG.

   DRESDNER BANK LATEINAMERIKA AG
   801 Brickell Avenue, Miami, FL   33131
   CEO: Helmut G. Jackel, SVP.   Tel: (305) 373-0000   Emp: 50+
   Bus: *International commercial banking services.*   Fax:(305) 374-6912   %FO: 100

● **DURKOPP ADLER AG**
Postfach 170351, 33703 Bielefeld, Germany
CEO: Dr. Forberich, Pres.   Tel: 49-521-55601   Emp: 1500
Bus: *Mfr. industrial sewing equipment.*   Fax:49-521-55601

    DURKOPP ADLER AMERICA INC.
    3025 Northwoods Pkwy, Norcross, GA   30071
    CEO: John Couch, Pres.   Tel: (770) 446-8162   Emp: 100
    Bus: *Sales/service industrial sewing equipment.*   Fax:(770) 448-1545   %FO: 100

● **EISELE GMBH & CO**
Nuertinger Strasse, 7316 Koengen/Germany
CEO: Ralph Dietrich, Pres.   Tel: 49-7102-800169   Emp: N/A
Bus: *Mfr.. machine tools.*   Fax:49-7102-800171

    EISELE CORPORATION
    1500-C Higgins Road, Elk Grove Village, IL   60007
    CEO: Sidney N. Roth, Pres.   Tel: (847) 364-1335   Emp: 6
    Bus: *Sale/distribution machine tools.*   Fax:(847) 364-1336   %FO: 100

● **ELEKTRO-PHYSIK KOLN GMBH & CO. KG**
Pasteurstrasse 15, 5000 Cologne, Germany
CEO: K. Steingroever, Chrm.   Tel: 49-221 752040   Emp: N/A
Bus: *Mfr. coating thickness testing gauges for quality*   Fax:49-221 7520467
    control & corrosion prevention.

    ELECTRO-PHYSIK USA INC.
    770 West Algonquin Road, Arlington Heights, IL   60005
    CEO: Aivars Friedenfelds, Gen. Mgr.   Tel: (708) 437-6616   Emp: N/A
    Bus: *Distribution/service coating thickness gauges.*   Fax:(708) 437-0053   %FO: 100

● **EURO LLOYD REISEBUERO GMBH**
Neumarkt 35-37, 50667 Cologne, Germany
CEO: Rudolf Aenis, Dir.   Tel: 49-221 2028100   Emp: 900
Bus: *Travel agency.*   Fax:49-221 2028125

    EURO LLOYD TRAVEL INC.
    3384 Peachtree Road, NE, Atlanta, GA   30326
    CEO: Klaus van Keiser, Mgr.   Tel: (404) 231-0704   Emp: N/A
    Bus: *Travel agency.*   Fax:(404) 231-5078   %FO: 100

    EURO LLOYD TRAVEL INC.
    125 State Street, Hackensack, NJ   07601
    CEO: Sophie Sbaschnik, Mgr.   Tel: (201) 489-0711   Emp: N/A
    Bus: *Travel agency.*   Fax:(201) 489-8614   %FO: 100

EURO LLOYD TRAVEL INC.
1910 Fairview Avenue East
Ste. 301, Seattle, WA   98102
CEO: Gloria Shigeno, Mgr.   Tel: (206) 860-0715   Emp: N/A
Bus: *Travel agency.*   Fax:(206) 860-0821   %FO: 100

EURO LLOYD TRAVEL INC.
Haywood Plaza, 30 Orchard Park Drive, Ste. 3, Greenville, SC   29615
CEO: Ursula Rhine, Mgr.   Tel: (864) 627-8001   Emp: N/A
Bus: *Travel agency.*   Fax:(864) 627-8003   %FO: 100

EURO LLOYD TRAVEL INC.
220 Sansome Street, San Francisco, CA   94104
CEO: Richard Keefhaver, Mgr.   Tel: (415) 391-9011   Emp: N/A
Bus: *Travel agency.*   Fax:(415) 391-9378   %FO: 100

EURO LLOYD TRAVEL INC.
Empire State Bldg.,350 5th Ave., New York, NY   10118
CEO: Juergen Weinroth, EVP   Tel: (212) 629-5470   Emp: N/A
Bus: *US headquarters. Travel agency and tour*   Fax:(212) 643-0223   %FO: 100
     operators.

EURO LLOYD TRAVEL INC.
1640 Hempstead Turnpike, East Meadow, NY   11554
CEO: Juergen Weinroth, EVP   Tel: (516) 228-4970   Emp: 80
Bus: *Travel agency.*   Fax:(516) 228-8258   %FO: JV

● **FAG KUGELFISCHER GEORG SCHAFER AG**
Postfach 1260, D-97421 Schweinfurt, Germany
CEO: Peter-Juergen Kreher, Pres.   Tel: 49-9721 910   Emp: 16200
Bus: *Mfr./wholesale anti-friction bearings.*   Fax:49-9721 913435

    FAG BEARINGS CORPORATION
    200 Park Avenue, Danbury, CT   06810
    CEO: Mark Murray, EVP   Tel: (203) 790-5474   Emp: 1600
    Bus: *Mfr./distribution/sale bearings.*   Fax:(203) 830-8105   %FO: 100

● **FELDMUHLE AG**
Fritz-Vomfelde-Platz 4, 4000 Dusseldorf, Germany
CEO: Hartwig Geginat, CEO   Tel: 49-211 5810   Emp: N/A
Bus: *Mfr. paper and paperboard, technical ceramics.*   Fax:49-211 5812555

    STORA-FELDMUHLE NORTH AMERICA
    230 Park Avenue, New York, NY   10168
    CEO: Robert Obernier, Mgn Dir   Tel: (212) 983-3080   Emp: N/A
    Bus: *Distribution paper and paperboard.*   Fax:(212) 983-3084   %FO: 100

• **WILHELM FETTE GMBH**
Grabauer Strasse 24, D-2053 Schwarzenbek, Germany
CEO: Eugene Valerius, Mng. Dir.   Tel: 49-4151 12248   Emp: 1200
Bus: *Mfr. thread rolling tools and gear generating*   Fax:49-4151 12510
      equipment.

    LMT - FETTE INC
    3725-I North 126th Street, Brookfield, WI   53005
    CEO: Robert J. Rubenstahl, Pres.   Tel: (414) 783-7606   Emp: 50
    Bus: *Import/sale/service thread rolling, milling*   Fax:(414) 783-5043   %FO: 100
        cutters, gear generating equipment, carbide
        inserts.

    LMT - FETTE INC.
    883 E. Hampshire Road, Stow, OH   44224
    CEO: Robert J. Rubenstahl, Pres.   Tel: (330) 940-4052   Emp: 17
    Bus: *Mfr./distribution Hob's (gear generating*   Fax:(330) 940-3598   %FO: 100
        tools), HSS End-Mills and indexable milling
        cutter's & insert's; general cutting tools.

• **FIRMA AUGUST BILSTEIN GMBH & CO**
Postfach 1151, 58256 Ennepetal, Germany
CEO: F. Riemenschneider, Pres.   Tel: 49-2333 7920   Emp: 1900
Bus: *Mfr. shock absorbers, window hardware, car jacks.*   Fax:49-2333 792253

    KRUPP BILSTEIN CORPORATION
    8845 Rehco Road, San Diego, CA   92121
    CEO: Reinhard Schomburg, Pres.   Tel: (619) 453-7723   Emp: 60
    Bus: *Assembly/distribute shock absorbers.*   Fax:(619) 453-0770   %FO: 100

• **FLEISSNER GMBH & CO**
Wolfsgartenstrasse 6, 63329 bei Frankfurt/Main, Germany
CEO: Gerold Fleissner, Pres.   Tel: 49-6103 4010   Emp: 800
Bus: *Mfr. fiber, textile, non-woven, finishing equipment*   Fax:49-6103 401440

    FLEISSNER INC.
    12301 Moores Chapel Road, Charlotte, NC   28214
    CEO: Don B. Gillespie, VP   Tel: (704) 394-3376   Emp: 6
    Bus: *Sale fiber, textile, non-woven finishing*   Fax:(704) 393-2637   %FO: 100
        equipment.

● **FLUX GERAETE GMBH**
Postfach 2751, 7000 Stuttgart 1, Germany
CEO: Herbert Hann, Pres.   Tel: 49-7043 10141   Emp: N/A
Bus: *Mfr./distribution drum & container chemical*   Fax:49-7043 10133
       transfer pumps.

    FLUX PUMPS CORP.
    4330 Commerce Circle, Atlanta, GA   30336
    CEO:Michael T. O'Toole, Gen. Mgr.   Tel: (404) 691-6010   Emp: N/A
    Bus: *Mfr./distribution drum & container chemical*   Fax:(404) 691-6314   %FO: 100
           transfer pumps.

● **FOMO SCHAUMSTOFF GMBH & CO KG**
Werkstrasse 6, 4353 Oer Erkenschwick, Germany
CEO: Lothar Miczka, Pres.   Tel: 49-23-686004   Emp: 20
Bus: *Mfr. polyurethane foams.*   Fax:N/A

    FOMO PRODUCTS, INC.
    2775 Barber Road, Norton, OH   44203
    CEO: Stefan Gantenbein, Pres.   Tel: (330) 753-4585   Emp: 32
    Bus: *Mfr. polyurethane foams.*   Fax:(330) 753-5199   %FO: 100

● **FORKARDT GMBH**
Heinrich Hertz Strasse 7, 40699 Erkrath, Germany
CEO: N. Greenwood, Pres.   Tel: 49-211-25060   Emp: 300
Bus: *Mfr. metal-forming machine tools.*   Fax:49-211-250 6221

    BUCK FORKARDT, INC.
    406 Farmington Avenue, Farmington, CT   06032
    CEO:Ralph R .Torning, VP & Gen.Mgr.   Tel: (860) 676-7758   Emp: 9
    Bus: *Distribution/sale/service metal-forming*   Fax:(860) 676-7823   %FO: 100
           machine tools.

● **FRANCOTYP-POSTALIA AG & CO.**
Triftweg 21-26, 16542 Birkenwerder, Germany
CEO: Werner Hesshaus, Pres.   Tel: 49-3303 525799   Emp: N/A
Bus: *Mfr. postage meters, mail & shipping room systems.*   Fax:49-3303 525799

    FRANCOTYP-POSTALIA INC.
    1980 University Lane, Lisle, IL   60532
    CEO:George G. Gelfer, Pres.   Tel: (630) 241-9090   Emp: 50
    Bus: *Distribution postage meters, mailing*   Fax:(630) 241-9091   %FO: 100
           machines, office equipment.

- **FRANKL & KIRCHNER GMBH & CO. KG**
Scheffelstrasse 73, 68723 Schwetzingen, Germany
CEO: Lotte Wiest, Pres. Tel: 49-6-202 2020 Emp: N/A
Bus: *Electronic positioning motors for industrial sewing equipment.* Fax:49-6-202 202115

    EFKA OF AMERICA INC.
    3715 Northcrest Rd, #10, Atlanta, GA   30340
    CEO: J. D. Price, VP Tel: (770) 457-7006 Emp: 12
    Bus: *Sale/service electronic positioning motors for industrial sewing equipment* Fax:(770) 458-3899 %FO: 100

- **FRANZ HERMLE & SOHN**
Bahnhofstrasse 6, 78559 Gosheim, Germany
CEO: Rolf Hermle, Pres. Tel: 49-7426 6010 Emp: 300
Bus: *Mfr. of clocks & clock movements.* Fax:49-7426 601333

    HERMLE BLACK FOREST CLOCKS
    P O Box 670, Amherst, VA   24521
    CEO: Helmut Mangold, Gen.Mgr. Tel: (804) 946-7751 Emp: 50
    Bus: *Mfr. of clocks & clock movements, clock kits, Swiss screw machine parts.* Fax:(804) 946-7747 %FO: 100

- **FREUDENBERG & CO**
Postfach 100363, D-69465 Weinheim, Germany
CEO: Reinhart Freudenberg, Pres. Tel: 49-6201 800 Emp: 26600
Bus: *Mfr. seals, rubber/polymer/foam products, leather.* Fax:49-6201 69300

    ELEFATAN USA, INC.
    P.O.Box 560, Port Washington, WI   53074-9763
    CEO: Mark Kohlenberg, Pres. Tel: (414) 284-4320 Emp: N/A
    Bus: *Mfr. seals, rubber/polymer/foam products, leather.* Fax:(414) 241-4351 %FO: 100

    FREUDENBERG BUILDING SYSTEMS INC.
    94 Glenn Street, Lawrence, MA   01843
    CEO: Volker Seims, Pres. Tel: (508) 689-0530 Emp: N/A
    Bus: *Mfr. rubber flooring.* Fax:(508) 975-0110 %FO: 100

    FREUDENBERG LUTRABOND
    100 West Tenth Street, Wilmington, DE   19801
    CEO: Joseph Day, Pres. Tel: (919) 471-2582 Emp: N/A
    Bus: *Mfr. seals, rubber/polymer/foam products, leather.* Fax:(919) 477-1165 %FO: 100

    FREUDENBERG NONWOVENS
    3440 Industrial Park, Durham, NC   27704
    CEO: Cosmo Camelio, Pres. Tel: (508) 454-0461 Emp: N/A
    Bus: *Technical products division; mfr. nonwoven fabrics.* Fax:(919) 620-3909 %FO: 100

FREUDENBERG NORTH AMERICA, LTD.
Route 104, P.O.Box 2001, Bristol, NH   03222-2001

CEO: Joseph C. Day, Pres.   Tel: (603) 744-2281   Emp: N/A

Bus: *Mfr. seals, rubber/polymer/foam products,*   Fax:(603) 744-8722   %FO: 100
leather.

FREUDENBERG SPUNWEB CO.
PO Box 15910, 3500 Industrial Drive., Durham, NC   27704

CEO: Joseph C. Day, Pres.   Tel: (919) 471-2582   Emp: N/A

Bus: *Mfr. polyester spunbond fabric.*   Fax:(919) 477-1165   %FO: 100

FREUDENBERG VITECH LTD.
221 Jackson Street, Lowell, MA   01852

CEO: Joseph C. Day, Pres.   Tel: (508) 454-0461   Emp: N/A

Bus: *Mfr. seals, rubber/polymer/foam products,*   Fax:(508) 454-0461   %FO: 100
leather.

FREUDENBERG-NOK GENERAL PARTNERSHIP
47690 East Anchor Court, Plymouth, MI   48170

CEO: Joseph C. Day, Pres.   Tel: (313) 451-0020   Emp: N/A

Bus: *Mfr. seals, molded rubber & plastic*   Fax:(313) 451-2245   %FO: 100
components, vibration control systems,
aftermarket rebuild kits.

KLUEBER LUBRICATION NA INC.
54 Wentworth Avenue, Londonderry, NH   03053

CEO: E. Stralucke, Pres.   Tel: (603) 434-7704   Emp: N/A

Bus: *Mfr. industrial lubricants.*   Fax:(603) 434-8046   %FO: 100

SUMMIT INDUSTRIAL PRODUCTS INC.
P.O. Box 131359, 9010 Country Road, Tyler, TX   75707

CEO: Joseph Day, Pres.   Tel: (903) 534-8021   Emp: N/A

Bus: *Mfr. seals, rubber/polymer/foam products,*   Fax:(903) 581-4376   %FO: 100
leather.

● **FUCHS SYSTEMTECHNIK GMBH**
Reithallenstrasse 1, D-77731 Willstatt-Legelshurst, Germany

CEO: Gerhard Fuchs, Pres.   Tel: 49-7852 4100   Emp: N/A

Bus: *Mfr. furnaces (electric arc, ladle, shaft), current*   Fax:49-7852 41141
conducting electrode arms, equipment for steel
industry.

FUCHS SYSTEMS, INC.
812 West Innes Street, PO Box 379, Salisbury, NC   28144

CEO: Manfred Haissig, Pres.   Tel: (704) 633-2141   Emp: 141

Bus: *Mfr. furnaces (electric arc, ladle, shaft),*   Fax:(704) 633-6103   %FO: 100
current conducting electrode arms, equipment
for steel industry.

● **GEORGI GMBH**
Theaterstrasse 77, D-52062 Aachen, Germany
CEO: Manfred Georgi, Pres   Tel: 49-241-477910   Emp: 30
Bus: *Publisher books, magazines, calendars.*   Fax:49-241-4779160

     GEORGI PUBLISHERS
     P O Box 6059, Chelsea, MA   02150-0006
     CEO: Manfred Georgi, Pres.   Tel: (617) 387-7300   Emp: N/A
     Bus: *Distribution art calendars.*   Fax:(617) 387-6379   %FO: 100

● **GERLING-KONZERN VERSICHERUNGS BETEILIGUNGS-AG**
Postfach 100808, 50670 Cologne, Germany
CEO: Rolf Gerling, Chrm   Tel: 49-221 1441   Emp: N/A
Bus: *Insurance holding company.*   Fax:49-221 1443319

     GERLING GLOBAL REINSURANCE CORP.
     717 Fifth Ave, New York, NY   10022
     CEO: Charles Troiano, Pres.   Tel: (212) 754-7500   Emp: N/A
     Bus: *Reinsurance products & services.*   Fax:(212) 826-5645   %FO: 100

● **GIRMES AG**
Johannes-Girmes Strasse 27, D-47929 Grefrath-Oedt, Germany
CEO: D. Klimant, CEO   Tel: 49-2158 301   Emp: 2500
Bus: *Mfr. textiles, textile products.*   Fax:49-2158 30433

     J. L .DE BALL OF AMERICA LTD.
     111 West 40th Street, New York, NY   10018
     CEO: Bill Trienekens, Pres.   Tel: (212) 575-8613   Emp: 6
     Bus: *Marketing/trading textiles.*   Fax:(212) 575-8616   %FO: 100

● **GROB WERKE GMBH & CO KG**
Industriestasse 4, D-87719 Mindelheim, Germany
CEO: Karl Rehm, Pres.   Tel: 49-8261 9960   Emp: 2300
Bus: *Machine tools & assembly equipment.*   Fax:49-8261 996108

     GROB SYSTEMS,INC.
     1070 Navajo Drive, Bluffton, OH   45817
     CEO: Markus Grob, Pres.   Tel: (419) 358-9015   Emp: 100
     Bus: *Mfr. machine tools & assembly equipment.*   Fax:(419) 358-3660   %FO: 100

• **GUNOLD + STICKMA GMBH**
Obernburger Strasse 125, 63811 Stockstadt, Germany
CEO: H. Gunold, Pres.   Tel: 49-60 272008   Emp: 110
Bus: *Distributor machine embroidery supplies, CAD*   Fax:49-60 273243
     computer system, punching services for designs;
     consulting for embroidery industry.

   GUNOLD + STICKMA OF AMERICA, INC.
   1000 Cobb Place Blvd., Bldg. 500, Kennesaw, GA   30144
   CEO: Ole Prior, Pres.   Tel: (770) 421-0300   Emp: 50
   Bus: *Wholesale/distribution machine embroidery*   Fax:(770) 421-0505   %FO: 100
        supplies, CAD computer system, punching
        services for designs, letter & appliqués cutting.

• **HACOBA-TEXTILMASCHINEN GMBH & CO KG**
Postfach 200751, 42207 Wuppertal, Germany
CEO: Guenter Refle, Pres.   Tel: 49-202 709101   Emp: N/A
Bus: *Textile machinery & parts.*   Fax:49-02 7091214

   HACOBA TEXTILE MACHINERY LP
   8601 S Tryon Street, PO Box 410307, Charlotte, NC   28241-0307
   CEO: Paul Ledford, Chrm.   Tel: (704) 588-2493   Emp: 2516
   Bus: *Sale/service textile machines.*   Fax:(704) 588-4798   %FO: 100

• **HAFELE KG**
Postfach 1237, D-72192 Nagold, Germany
CEO: Hans Nock, Pres.   Tel: 49-7452-95328   Emp: 1600
Bus: *Distribution European furniture cabinet hardware.* Fax:49-7452-95402

   HAFELE AMERICA CO.
   3901 Cheyenne Drive, PO Box 4000, Archdale, NC   27263
   CEO: Wolfgang Hafele, Pres.   Tel: (910) 889-2322   Emp: 200
   Bus: *Distribution European furniture cabinet*   Fax:(910) 431-3831   %FO: 100
        hardware.

• **HAMBURG-SUED/COLUMBUS LINE**
Ost-West-Strasse 59-61, 20457 Hamburg, Germany
CEO: Dr. Klaus Meeves - Chrm.   Tel: 49-40 3705-2275   Emp: 10000
Bus: *Steamship line.*   Fax:49-40 3705-2649

   COLUMBUS LINE USA INC.
   Plaza II, Harborside Financial Center, Jersey City, NJ   07311-3984
   CEO: Robert Baack, Pres.   Tel: (201) 432-0900   Emp: 250
   Bus: *Containerized shipping to Australia, New*   Fax:(201) 433-0616   %FO: 100
        Zealand, South America and Eastern
        Mediterranean.

• HANNOVER RUECKVERSICHERUNG AG
Karl-Wiechert-Allee 50, Postfach 610369, 30625 Hannover, Germany
CEO: Michael-Anton Reischel, Chrm.   Tel: 49-511 56040   Emp: 530
Bus: *Reinsurance.*   Fax:49-511 5604188

INSURANCE CORP OF HANNOVER
3435 Wilshire Blvd, Ste. 700, Los Angeles, CA   90010
CEO: John F. Sullivan, Pres. & CEO   Tel: (213) 380-8822   Emp: 58
Bus: *Reinsurance services.*   Fax:(213) 386-2062   %FO: 100

• HAPAG-LLOYD AG
Ballindamm 25, Postfach 102626, D-22559 Hamburg, Germany
CEO: Hans Jacob Kruse, Chrm.   Tel: 49-40 30010   Emp: N/A
Bus: *Freight container shipping, cruise line, travel.*   Fax:49-40 336432

EURO-LLOYD TRAVEL, INC.
1640 Hempstead Turnpike, East Meadow, NY   11554
CEO: Juergen Weinroth, EVP   Tel: (516) 228-4970   Emp: N/A
Bus: *Travel agency.*   Fax:(516) 228-8258   %FO: 100

HAPAG-LLOYD (AMERICA) INC.
399 Hoes Lane, Piscataway, NJ   08854
CEO: Dr. Dehn, Pres.   Tel: (908) 562-1800   Emp: 450
Bus: *Ocean freight forwarding.*   Fax:(908) 885-3730   %FO: 100

• HAPFO MACHINES & TOOLS FOR WOODWORKING
Postfach 100, 83085 Kiefersfelden, Germany
CEO: Gerold Pfohl, Gen Mgr   Tel: 49-8033-7029   Emp: 30
Bus: *Mfr. woodworking lathes & machinery*   Fax:49-8033 7787

E&R SUPPLY COMPANY INC.
1095 Route 100, Unit E, Farmingdale, NY   11735
CEO: Robert Weithofer, Pres.   Tel: (516) 752-3510   Emp: 8
Bus: *Distributor/service woodworking mach &*   Fax:(516) 752-3514   %FO: JV
vacuum coating system.

• HAVER & BOECKER
Carl Haver Platz 3, D-59302 Oelde/Westfalen, Germany
CEO: Reinhold Festge, Mgr.   Tel: 49-25 22300   Emp: 1350
Bus: *Mfr./engineering/sale/service individual packaging*   Fax:49-25 2230403
systems.

HAVER FILLING SYSTEMS INC.
460 Gees Mill Business Court, Conyers, GA   30208
CEO: Thomas Reckersdrees, VP   Tel: (770) 760-1130   Emp: 8
Bus: *Engineering/sale/service individual packaging*   Fax:(770) 760-1181   %FO: 100
systems

● **HEIDELBERGER ZEMENT AG**
Berliner Strasse 6, D-69120 Heidelberg, Germany
CEO: Rolf Hülstrunk, Chrm. & CEO   Tel: 49-6221 4810   Emp: 10500
Bus: *Mfr. cements & construction materials.*   Fax:48-6221 481282

    LEHIGH PORTLAND CEMENT CO.
    7660 Imperial Way, Allentown, PA   18195
    CEO: Richard D. Kline, Pres.   Tel: (610) 366-4600   Emp: 6000
    Bus: *Mfr. cement, aggregates, ready-mix cement.*   Fax:(610) 366-4684   %FO: 100

● **DR. JOHANNES HEIDENHAIN GMBH**
Trauntreut, D-8225, Germany
CEO: Ludwig Wagatha, Chrm.   Tel: 49-8669-1331   Emp: N/A
Bus: *Mfr. optical rotary encoders.*   Fax:49-8669-5061

    RENCO ENCODERS, INC.
    26 Coromar Drive, Goleta, CA   93117
    CEO: Dan Baxter, VP & Gen. Mgr.   Tel: (805) 968-1525   Emp: 85
    Bus: *Mfr. optical rotary encoders.*   Fax:(805) 685-7965   %FO: 100

● **HELLA KG HUECK & CO.**
Rixbecker Strasse 75, D-59552 Lippstadt, Germany
CEO: Juergen Behrend, Chrm. & Pres.   Tel: 49-29-41387549   Emp: 21100
Bus: *Mfr. lamps & lighting equipment, pumps, control*   Fax:49-29-41387040
    modules.

    HELLA INC.
    201 Kelly Drrive, P O Box 2665, Peachtree City, GA   30269
    CEO: Mitch Williams, Pres   Tel: (770) 631-7500   Emp: N/A
    Bus: *Sale/distribution automotive lighting &*   Fax:(404) 631-7575   %FO: 100
    accessories.

    HELLA N.A.
    1101 Vincennes Avenue, Flora, IL   62839
    CEO: Michael J. Buford, Pres. & CEO   Tel: (618) 662-4402   Emp: 313
    Bus: *Mfr. automotive relays & flashers for OEM*   Fax:(618) 662-4720   %FO: 100
    marketing.

    HELLA NORTH AMERICA INC.
    26750 Haggerty Road, Farmington Hills, MI   48331
    CEO: Michael J. Buford, Pres. & CEO   Tel: (248) 553-7047   Emp: 26
    Bus: *Mfr./sale lamps & lighting equipment, vacuum*   Fax:(248) 553-5780   %FO: 100
    & pressure pumps.

    NORTH AMERICAN LIGHTING INC.
    20 Industrial Park, Flora, IL   62839
    CEO: Edward Grenda, Pres   Tel: (618) 662-4483   Emp: N/A
    Bus: *Mfr. automotive lighting.*   Fax:(618) 662-8143   %FO: JV

● **HELM AG**
Nordkanalstrasse 28, 20097 Hamburg, Germany
CEO: Dieter Schnabel, Chrm. & CEO Tel: 49-40-23750 Emp: 1300
Bus: *Trading/distribution, warehousing, service functions* Fax:49-40-2375-1845
of medical, pharmaceuticals, chemicals, plastics,
steel, etc.

HELM FERTILIZER CORP
9950 Princess Palm Avenue, #312, Tampa, FL 33619
CEO: Dale A. Miller, Pres. Tel: (813) 621-8846 Emp: 12
Bus: *Trading/distribution chemicals fertilizers.* Fax:(813) 621-0763 %FO: 100

HELM NEW YORK CHEMICAL CORP
1110 Centennial Avenue, Piscataway, NJ 08855-1333
CEO: Christian Torske, EVP & Gen.Mgr. Tel: (908) 981-1160 Emp: 14
Bus: *Import export/distribution pharmaceuticals,* Fax:(908) 981-0528 %FO: 100
veterinary, raw materials, feed & food
additives, essential oils, aroma chemicals.

● **HELMUT MAUELL GMBH**
Am Rosenhuegel 1-5, D-42553 Velbert, Germany
CEO: Helmut Mauell, CEO Tel: 49-2-053 131 Emp: 550
Bus: *Control & display systems.* Fax:49-2-053 13314

MAUELL CORPORATION
31 Old Cabin Hollow Road, Dillsburg, PA 17019-0339
CEO: F. Ulrich, Pres. Tel: (717) 432-8686 Emp: 25
Bus: *Mosaic display panels.* Fax:(717) 432-8688 %FO: 100

● **HENGELER MUELLER WEITZEL WIRTZ**
Kurfürstendamm 54/55, D-10707 Berlin, Germany
CEO: Dr. Hasselmann, Mng. Ptnr. Tel: 49-30-885-7190 Emp: N/A
Bus: *International law firm.* Fax:49-30-882-7144

HENGELER MUELLER WEITZEL WIRTZ
712 Fifth Avenue, New York, NY 10019
CEO: Dr. Bohlhöff, Mng. Ptnr. Tel: (212) 586-4600 Emp: N/A
Bus: *International law firm.* Fax:(212) 586-4481 %FO: 100

● **HENKEL KGAA**
Henklestrasse 67, D-40191 Dusseldorf 40589, Germany
CEO: Hans-Dietrich Winkhaus, Pres. Tel: 49-211-797-3937 Emp: 41728
Bus: *Branded detergents, personal care products,* Fax:49-211-798-2863
chemical products.

APG DIV HENKEL CORPORATION
300 Brookside Avenue, Ambler, PA 19002
CEO: Gary Granzow, EVP Tel: (215) 628-1000 Emp: N/A
Bus: *Mfr. surfactants.* Fax:(215) 628-1200 %FO: 100

THE CLOROX COMPANY
1221 Broadway Street, Oakland, CA   94612
CEO: G. Craig Sullivan, Pres.   Tel: (510) 271-7000   Emp: N/A
Bus: *Mfr. branded detergents, chemical products.*   Fax:(510) 832-1463   %FO: 28

ECOLAB INC.
Ecolab Center 370, Wabasha Street, St. Paul, MN   55102
CEO: Alan Schuman, Chrm.   Tel: (612) 293-2233   Emp: N/A
Bus: *Mfr. branded detergents, chemical products.*   Fax:(612) 293-2092   %FO: 22

HENKEL CORP.
2200 Renaissance Blvd., Ste 200, Gulph Mills, PA   19406
CEO: Robert Lurcott, Pres.   Tel: (610) 270-8100   Emp: 2500
Bus: *Mfr. specialty chemicals.*   Fax:(610) 270-8291   %FO: 100

HENKEL SURFACE TECHNOLOGIES
32100 Stephenson Hwy, Madison Heights, MI   48071
CEO: James W. Harrison, Pres.   Tel: (810) 583-9310   Emp: N/A
Bus: *Mfr. metal pretreatment chemicals.*   Fax:(810) 583-2976   %FO: 100

LOCTITE CORP.
10 Columbus Blvd., Hartford Square N., Hartford, CT   06106
CEO: David Freeman, Chrm.   Tel: (860) 520-5000   Emp: 1700
Bus: *Mfr. adhesives.*   Fax:(860) 520-5073   %FO: 100

ORGANIC PRDTS DIV HENKEL CORP
300 Brookside Avenue, Ambler, PA   19002
CEO: Howard Gross, EVP   Tel: (215) 628-1000   Emp: N/A
Bus: *Mfr. specialty chemicals for paper, coatings,*   Fax:(215) 628-1200   %FO: 100
       textile, leather, and cosmetics markets.

● **HERBOLD GMBH**
Industriestrasse 33, 74909 Meckesheim, Germany
CEO: Peter Abraham, Pres.   Tel: 49-6226 930   Emp: 250
Bus: *Recycling equipment.*   Fax:49-7261 924 897

HERBOLD GRANULATORS USA, INC.
12C John Road, Sutton, MA   01590
CEO: John Pollock, Pres.   Tel: (508) 865-7355   Emp: N/A
Bus: *Recycling equipment.*   Fax:(508) 865-9975   %FO: 100

• **HERION-WERKE KG**
Stuttgarter Strasse 120, 70736 Fellbach, Germany
CEO: Rolf Kopf, Gen.Mgr.   Tel: 49-711 52090   Emp: 2500
Bus: *Mfr. pneumatics, hydraulics, automatics, pressure &*   Fax:49-711 5209614
temperature devices, electric fluid power products,
process valves.

   HERION USA INC.
   176 Thorn Hill Road, Warrendale, PA   15086
   CEO: Kenneth H. Foster, Pres.   Tel: (412) 776-5577   Emp: 45
   Bus: *Fluid power products, process valves;*   Fax:(412) 776-0310   %FO: 90
   pneumatics, hydraulics, automatics, pressure
   & temperature devices.

• **HERMANN BERSTORFF MASCHINENBAU GMBH**
Am der Breiten Wiese 3, 30625 Hannover, Germany
CEO: N/A   Tel: 49-511 57020   Emp: N/A
Bus: *Mfr. industrial machinery.*   Fax:49-511 561916

   PRECISION ROLL GRINDERS INC.
   6356 Chapmans Road, Wescosville, PA   18106
   CEO: George Manialty, VP & Gen.Mgr.   Tel: (610) 395-6966   Emp: N/A
   Bus: *Mfr. and repair metal roll grinders.*   Fax:(610) 481-9130   %FO: 100

• **HERMANN FINCKH MASCHINENFABRIK GMBH & CO.**
Marktstrasse 185, 72793 Pfullingen, Germany
CEO: Hagen Hutzler, Pres.   Tel: 49-7121 2750   Emp: 200
Bus: *Processing equipment for pulp & paper industry.*   Fax:49-7121 275237

   FINCKH MACHINERY CORPORATION
   2302 Columbia Circle, PO Box 912, Merrimack, NH   03054
   CEO: Maurice Lindsay, VP   Tel: (603) 424-4148   Emp: 4
   Bus: *Sales/service processing equipment for pulp &*   Fax:(603) 429-0540   %FO: 100
   paper industry.

• **DR. ERWIN HETTICH GMBH & CO. / ANTON HETTICH GMBH & CO.**
Vahrenkampstrasse 12-16, D-32278 Kirchlengern, Germany
CEO: Hans-Dieter Jähler, Pres.   Tel: 49-5223-770   Emp: 4000
Bus: *Mfr./distribution furniture fittings and furniture*   Fax:49-5223-771202
accessories.

   HETTICH AMERICA LP
   6225 Shilih Road, Alpharetta, GA   30202
   CEO: Ben Burks, Pres.   Tel: (770) 887-3733   Emp: 70
   Bus: *Mfr./distribution furniture fittings and*   Fax:(770) 887-4479   %FO: 100
   furniture accessories.

• HILLE & MÜLLER
Am Trippelsberg 48, Düsseldorf, D-40589, Germany
CEO: J. M. M. van der Ven, CEO   Tel: 49-211-7950-0   Emp: 1500
Bus: *Plated and plain low-carbon strip steel*   Fax:49-211-7950-305

THOMAS STEEL STRIP CORP.
Delaware Avenue, NW, Warren, OH   44485
CEO: Parry L. Hesselman, Pres.   Tel: (330) 841-6222   Emp: 576
Bus: *Nickel, brass, copper, nickel zinc plated strip*   Fax:(330) 841-6260   %FO: 100
and plain cold roll steel.

• RICHARD HIRSCHMANN GMBH & CO
Postfach 110, 73726 Esslingen, Germany
CEO: A. Klaus Eberhardt, Pres.   Tel: 49-711 31010   Emp: 3000
Bus: *Mfr. mobile antenna systems stationary receiving*   Fax:49-711 3101338
system, telecommunication equipment, connectors.

RICHARD HIRSCHMANN AMERICA INC.
Industrial Row, PO Box 229, Riverdale, NJ   07457
CEO: Steve Schueler, EVP   Tel: (201) 835-5002   Emp: 45
Bus: *Distributor mobile antenna systems,*   Fax:(201) 835-8354   %FO: 100
telecommunication technology, connectors.

• HOECHST AG
Brueningstrasse 50, D-65929 Frankfurt am Main, Germany
CEO: Jürgen Dorman, Chrm.   Tel: 49-69-3050   Emp: 161618
Bus: *Pharmaceuticals, chemicals, fibers, plastics, films,*   Fax:49-69-303665
technological information systems, plant
engineering services.

HOECHST CELANESE CORP.
901 15th Street, NW, Ste. 1000, Washington, DC   20006
CEO: H. Newton Williams, VP   Tel: (202) 296-2890   Emp: N/A
Bus: *Government relations representation.*   Fax:(202) 296-7268   %FO: 100

HOECHST CELANESE CORP.
30 Independence Boulevard, Warren, NJ   07059
CEO: Thomas F. Kennedy, Pres.   Tel: (908) 231-2000   Emp: 23000
Bus: *R&D/mfr./distribution fibers, films, plastics,*   Fax:(908) 231-3225   %FO: 100
dyes, pigments, pharmaceuticals, agricultural
& animal health products, polyethylene
products.

HOECHST MARION ROUSSEL, INC.
10236 Marion Park Drive, Kansas City, MO   64134
CEO: Peter W. Ladell   Tel: (816) 966-4000   Emp: N/A
Bus: *Mfr./sale pharmaceuticals.*   Fax:(816) 966-3152   %FO: 100

• HOERMANN GMBH
Hauptstrasse 45-47, D-85614 Kirchseeon, Germany

CEO: Hans Hoermann, Pres.　　　　　　　Tel: 49-8091 520　　　Emp: N/A

Bus: *High power warning systems, electric engineering,*　Fax:49-8091 52200
swim pools, building facades.

RAYTEK INC.
PO Box 1820, Santa Cruz, CA　95060-1820

CEO: Cliff Warren, Pres.　　　　　　　Tel: (408) 458-1110　　Emp: N/A

Bus: *Thermometers & calibration instruments*　　Fax:(408) 458-1239　%FO: 100

• HOHNER VERTRIEB GMBH
Postfach 1260, 78647 Trossingen, Germany

CEO: Guenter Darazs, Dir.　　　　　　Tel: 49-7425-20460　　Emp: N/A

Bus: *Mfr. musical instruments, amplifiers and accessories.*　Fax:49-7425-20371

HOHNER INC.
P O Box 15035, Richmond, VA　23227-5035

CEO: Horst Mucha, Pres.　　　　　　Tel: (804) 550-2700　　Emp: 40

Bus: *Sale/service musical instruments, amplifiers &*　Fax:(804) 550-2670　%FO: 100
accessories.

• HOLTKAMP GREENHOUSES KG
Blumenstrassa 27, Rees 4, 46459 Haffen, Germany

CEO: Hermann Holtkamp, Jr., VP　　　　Tel: 49-28 57 2991　　Emp: 450

Bus: *Produce African violets.*　　　　　Fax:49-28 57 2442

HOLTKAMP GREENHOUSES INC.
1501 Lischey Avenue, Nashville, TN　37207

CEO: Reinhold Holtkamp Sr, Pres.　　　　Tel: (615) 228-2683　　Emp: 120

Bus: *Produce/wholesale African violets.*　　Fax:(615) 228-5831　%FO: 100

• PHILIPP HOLZMANN AG
Taunusanlage 1, D-60299 Frankfurt, Germany

CEO: Hermann Becker, Chrm.　　　　　Tel: 49-69 2621　　　Emp: N/A

Bus: *Construction services; architecture, engineering,*　Fax:49-69 262433
consulting, property management, real estate
development & financing.

PHILLIP HOLZMANN USA, INC.
6060 J.A.Jones Drive, Charlotte, NC　28287

CEO: Dieter Rathke, Pres.　　　　　　Tel: (704) 553-3000　　Emp: 45000

Bus: *Construction services.*　　　　　Fax:(704) 553-3398　%FO: 100

J. A. JONES INC.
J. A. Jones Drive, Charlotte, NC　28287

CEO: William Garnett, Pres.　　　　　Tel: (704) 553-3036　　Emp: 13

Bus: *Project finance.*　　　　　　　Fax:(704) 553-3037　%FO: 100

J. A. JONES CONSTRUCTION CO
6060 J. A. Jones Drive, Charlotte, NC 28287
CEO: Charles T Davidson, Pres.   Tel: (704) 553-3000   Emp: 1400
Bus: *Construction.*   Fax:(704) 553-3524   %FO: 100

J. A. JONES ENVIRONMENTAL SERVICES
6135 Park South Drive, #104, Charlotte, NC 28287
CEO: Vald Heiberg III, Pres.   Tel: (704) 553-3595   Emp: 100
Bus: *Hazardous waste remediation.*   Fax:(704) 553-3599   %FO: 100

LOCKWOOD GREENE
P O Box 491, Spartanburg, SC 29304
CEO: Donald R. Luger, Pres.   Tel: (864) 578-2000   Emp: 1500
Bus: *Engineering, architecture, consulting.*   Fax:(864) 599-0436   %FO: 80

REGENT PARTNERS
3340 Peachtree Road, Atlanta, GA 30326
CEO: David Allman, Pres.   Tel: (404) 364-1400   Emp: 30
Bus: *Real estate acquisition & development,*   Fax:(404) 364-1420   %FO: 100
      property management.

● **HUGO BOSS AG**
Dieselstrasse 15, D-72555 Metzingen, Germany
CEO: Joachim Vogt, Chrm.   Tel: 49-7123-940   Emp: 2147
Bus: *Mfr./distribution of designer Men's Fashion.* Fax:49-7123-942014

    HUGO BOSS USA, INC.
    645 Fifth Avenue, 21st Floor, New York, NY 10022
    CEO: Andreas Wurz, Pres.   Tel: (212) 940-0600   Emp: 509
    Bus: *Mfr./distribution of designer Men's Fashion.* Fax:(212) 840-0615   %FO: 200

● **HYPO BANK**
Theatinerstrasse 11, D-80333 Munich, Germany
CEO: Dr. Eberhard Martini, Chrm.   Tel: 49-89-92440   Emp: 14123
Bus: *International commercial and investment banking* Fax:49-89-92443188
      and asset management services.

    HYPO BANK
    32 Old Slip, Financial Square, 32nd Fl., New York, NY 10005
    CEO: Kurt Sachs, EVP   Tel: (212) 248-0650   Emp: 100
    Bus: *International commercial and investment* Fax:(212) 440-0798   %FO: 100
          banking and asset management services.

    HYPO SECURITIES
    32 Old Slip, Financial Square, 33nd Fl., New York, NY 10005
    CEO: David I. Hoffman, Mng. Dir.   Tel: (212) 742-9701   Emp: 12
    Bus: *Sub of Hypo Bank. Securities services.* Fax:(212) 742-9712   %FO: 100

● **IBENA TEXTILWERKE BECKMANN GMBH & CO**
Teutonenstrasse 2, 46395 Bocholt, Germany
CEO: Josef A. Beckmann, Pres.   Tel: 49-2871 2870   Emp: N/A
Bus: *Mfr. home & industrial textiles, household*   Fax:49-2871 287309
   furnishings.

  IBENA INC.
  197D Ridgeview Center Drive, Duncan, SC   29334
  CEO: Eckhardt Brose, Mgr.   Tel: (864) 433-0669   Emp: N/A
  Bus: *Distribution fabrics, piece goods.*   Fax:(864) 439-4155   %FO: 100

● **IKA WERKE STAUFEN**
Neumagen Str 27, 79217 Staufen, Germany
CEO: Rene Stiegelmann, CEO   Tel: 49-7633 83198   Emp: 300
Bus: *Mfr. laboratory equipment.*   Fax:49-7633 8310

  IKA-WORKS INC.
  2635 North Chase Pkwy., SE, Wilmington, NC   28405
  CEO: N. Connelly, Pres.   Tel: (910) 452-7059   Emp: 18
  Bus: *Mfr./sale lab/process equipment.*   Fax:(910) 452-7693   %FO: 100

● **INDEX - WERKE GMBH & CO KG HAHN & TESSKY**
Plochinger Str 92, 49632 Esslingen, Germany
CEO: D. Frick/Dr Herrscher, Dirs.   Tel: 49-711 31911   Emp: 1200
Bus: *Mfr. metalworking mach tools, turning automatics.*   Fax:49-711 3191587

  INDEX CORPORATION
  829 Bridgeport Avenue, Shelton, CT   06484
  CEO: Gary G. Sihler, Pres.   Tel: (203) 926-0323   Emp: 30
  Bus: *Sales/service metalworking machine tools,*   Fax:(203) 926-0476   %FO: 100
     turning automatics.

● **INSTITUT DR FORSTER**
Postfach 1564, 72705 Reutlingen, Germany
CEO: Martin Forster, Chrm.   Tel: 49-7121 140281   Emp: 500
Bus: *Mfr. non-destructive testing equipment.*   Fax:49-7121 140357

  FORSTER, INC.
  140 Industry Drive, RIDC Park West, Pittsburgh, PA   15275-1028
  CEO: William J. Kitson Jr., Pres.   Tel: (412) 788-8976   Emp: 50
  Bus: *Mfr./distribution/service non-destructive*   Fax:(412) 788-8984   %FO: 90
     testing equipment.

● **INTEGRAL HYDRAULIK GMBH & CO.**
Marienburger Strasse 28, D- 40667 Meerbusch-Buederick, Germany
CEO: Heinz-Juergen Hillebrand, Mng. Dir.   Tel: 49-2132-9770   Emp: N/A
Bus: *Electron Beam welders, Laser Beam systems,*   Fax:49-2132-977252
Electron Beam job shop services.

   PTR - PRECISION TECHNOLOGIES, INC.
   120 Post Road, Enfield, CT   06082-5625
   CEO: Gottfried Kuesters, Pres.   Tel: (860) 741-2281   Emp: 50
   Bus: *Electron Beam welders, Laser Beam systems,*   Fax:(860) 745-7932   %FO: 100
   Electron Beam job shop services.

● **INTERTRACTOR AG**
Postfach 1580, D-58285 Gevelsberg, Germany
CEO: Dr. F. Böttger, Pres.   Tel: 49-2332 6690   Emp: 700
Bus: *Mfr./distribution undercarriage for crawler-type*   Fax:49-2332 669204
equipment.

   INTERTRACTOR AMERICA CORPORATION
   960 Proctor Drive, Elkhorn, WI   53121
   CEO: John Dincan, Gen.Mgr. & EVP   Tel: (414) 723-6000   Emp: 125
   Bus: *Mfr./distribution undercarriage for crawler-*   Fax:(414) 723-4720   %FO: 100
   type equipment.

● **JAGENBERG AG**
Postfach 101123, 40002 Dusseldorf, Germany
CEO: Hans U. Brauner, Pres.   Tel: 49-2131 9901   Emp: 2000
Bus: *Mfr. machinery for paper mills & paper converting*   Fax:49-2131 2900
industry.

   JAGENBERG INC.
   175 Freshwater Blvd., PO Box 1250, Enfield, CT   06083-1250
   CEO: G.E.Schikorra, Pres. & CEO   Tel: (860) 741-2501   Emp: 200
   Bus: *Mfr./sale machinery for paper mills & paper*   Fax:(860) 741-2508   %FO: 100
   converting industry.

● **M K JUCHHEIM GMBH & CO**
Moltkestrasse 13-31, D-36039 Fulda, Germany
CEO: Bernd Juchheim, Pres.   Tel: 49-661 60030   Emp: 1900
Bus: *Mfr. temperature, pressure & humidity sensors,*   Fax:49-661 6003500
transmitters, controls & recorders.

   JUMO PROCESS CONTROL INC.
   735 Fox Chase, Coatesville, PA   19320
   CEO: Haubold vom Berg, Pres.   Tel: (610) 380-8002   Emp: 10
   Bus: *Sale/service temperature, pressure & humidity*   Fax:(610) 380-8009   %FO: 100
   sensors, transmitters, controls & recorders.

• **KALENBORN KALPROTECT**
Postfach 31, D-53558 Vettelschoss, Germany
CEO: Wolf-Dieter Lehrke, Dir.   Tel: 49-2645 1800   Emp: 220
Bus: *Mfr. abrasion & corrosion-resistant linings &*   Fax:49-2645 1880
    pipelines.

    ABRESIST CORPORATION
    5541 N. State Road 13, PO Box 38, Urbana, IN   46990
    CEO: Joe Accetta, Pres.   Tel: (219) 774-3327   Emp: 35
    Bus: *Mfr./sale/service abrasion & corrosion-*   Fax:(219) 774-8188   %FO: 100
      resistant linings & pipelines.

• **KAMPF GMBH & CO MASCHINENFABRIK**
Meuhlenerstrasse 36-42, 51674 Wiehl, Germany
CEO: H. Merch, CEO   Tel: 49-2262 810   Emp: 550
Bus: *Mfr./sale machines for paper, film & foil converting*   Fax:49-2262 81208
    industry.

    KAMPF MACHINERY CORP. OF AMERICA
    175 Freshwater Blvd., Enfield, CT   06083
    CEO: H. Ulrich Jorgens, Pres.   Tel: (860) 253-9660   Emp: 50
    Bus: *Sale/service machines for paper, film & foil*   Fax:(860) 253-9662   %FO: 100
      converting industry.

• **HEINZ KETTLER METALLWARENFABRIK GMBH & CO**
Hauptstrasse, 59463 Ense-Parsit, Germany
CEO: Heinz Kettler, CEO   Tel: 49-2938 811   Emp: 3500
Bus: *Children's wheel toys, patio furniture, table tennis*   Fax:49-2938 2022
    equipment, exercise equipment, juvenile products.

    KETTLER INTL INC.
    PO Box 2747, Virginia Beach, VA   23450-2747
    CEO: Ludger Busche, CEO   Tel: (757) 427-2400   Emp: 15
    Bus: *Distributor children's wheel toys, patio*   Fax:(757) 427-0183   %FO: 100
      furniture, table tennis equipment, exercise
      equipment, juvenile products.

• **KISTERS MACHINENBAU GMBH**
Boschstrasse 1-3, D-47533 Kleve, Germany
CEO: Jean Marti, Mng. Dir.   Tel: 49-28 215030   Emp: 500
Bus: *Mfr. packaging equipment.*   Fax:49-28 2126110

    KISTERS INC.
    1405 Jamike Drive, Suite 8, Erlanger, KY   41018
    CEO: Andrew Neagle, Pres.   Tel: (606) 283-9501   Emp: 10
    Bus: *Sales, service and spare parts for packaging*   Fax:(606) 283-9509   %FO: 100
      equipment.

● **C. KLINGSPOR GMBH**
Huettenstr 36, D-35708 Haiger, Germany
CEO: Walter Klingspor, Pres.   Tel: 49-2773 8160   Emp: N/A
Bus: *Mfr. coated & bonded abrasives.*   Fax:49-2773 816186

　　　KLINGSPOR ABRASIVES INC.
　　　2555 Tate Blvd., SE, Hickory, NC   28602-1445
　　　CEO:Christoph Klingspor, Pres.   Tel: (704) 322-3030   Emp: 150
　　　Bus: *Mfr. coated & bonded abrasives.*   Fax:(704) 322-6060   %FO: 100

● **KLÖCKNER MERCATOR MASCHINENBAU GmbH**
KlöcknerstraBe 299, 47057 Duisburg, Germany
CEO: Klöckner Werke, Chrm.   Tel: 49-203-396   Emp: N/A
Bus: *Mfr. pharmaceutical and food equipment,*   Fax:49-203-396-3535
　　　print/stationary materials, packaging
　　　materials/equipment.

　　　KLÖCKNER-PENTAPLAST OF AMERICA, INC.
　　　Klöckner Road, PO Box 500, Gordonsville, VA   22942
　　　CEO:Harry J. G. van Beek, Pres.   Tel: (540) 832-3600   Emp: 700
　　　Bus: *Sales/distribution of pharmaceutical and food*   Fax:(540) 832-5656   %FO: 100
　　　　　equipment, print/stationary materials,
　　　　　packaging materials/equipment.

● **KLOCKNER-MOELLER GMBH**
Hein-Moeller Strasse 7-11, D-53105 Bonn, Germany
CEO: Dr. Seidel   Tel: 49-228 6020   Emp: 6700
Bus: *Mfr. electrical power distribution equipment,*   Fax:49-228 602433
　　　Industrial electrical/electronic controls & systems.

　　　KLOCKNER-MOELLER CORPORATION
　　　25 Forge Pkwy, Franklin, MA   02038
　　　CEO:Nick Dudas, Pres.   Tel: (508) 520-7080   Emp: 185
　　　Bus: *Mfr./distribution industrial electrical*   Fax:(508) 520-7084   %FO: 100
　　　　　electronic controls & systems.

● **KLOCKNER-WERKE**
Klockner Strasse 29, D-47057 Duisburg, Germany
CEO: Dr. Heinz-Ludwig Schmitz, Chrm.   Tel: 49-203-396-3300   Emp: 18298
Bus: *Mfr. automotive supplier, rigid films, filming &*   Fax:49-203-396-3535
　　　packaging technology.

　　　MPI INTERNATIONAL, INC.
　　　2129 Austin Avenue, PO Box 1995, Rochester Hills, MI   48309-3668
　　　CEO:Karl A. Pfister, Pres.   Tel: (248) 853-9010   Emp: 750
　　　Bus: *Mfr. fineblanked precision components and* Fax:(248) 853-5107   %FO: 100
　　　　　assemblies.

● **KLOECKNER INDUSTRIE-ANLAGEN GMBH**
Neudorfer Strasse 3-5, 4100 Duisburg, Germany
CEO: Hans-Werner Schenk, Mgn. Dir.   Tel: 49-20318   Emp: N/A
Bus: *General contractor for turnkey industrial plants.*   Fax:N/A

    KLOCKNER INA INDUSTRIAL INSTALLATIONS INC.
    775 Park Avenue, Ste. 320, Huntington, NY 11743
    CEO: Klaus Brosig, VP   Tel: (516) 271-3160   Emp: N/A
    Bus: *General contractor for turnkey industrial*   Fax:(516) 271-3465   %FO: 100
    plants.

● **KLOECKNER STAHL- UND METALLHANDEL GMBH**
Neudorfer Strasse 3-5, Duisburg, D-47057 Germany
CEO: R. Muesers, Chrm.   Tel: 49-203-307-0   Emp: 12000
Bus: *Steel and metals.*   Fax:N/A

    KLOCKNER NAMASCO CORPORATION
    666 Old Counry Road, Garden City, NY 11530
    CEO: R. Strassburger, Pres.   Tel: (516) 237-6900   Emp: 700
    Bus: *Steel and metals trading & warehousing.*   Fax:(516) 222-0332   %FO: 100

● **KLOECKNER-HUMBOLDT-DEUTZ AG**
Nikolaus-August-Otto-Alle 2, D-51057 Cologne, Germany
CEO: Werner Kirchgasser, Chrm.   Tel: 49-221 8220   Emp: 11300
Bus: *Mfr. diesel engines, tractors & agricultural*   Fax:49-221 822 2455
machinery; engineering, supply & install industrial
plants, machine systems & components.

    DEUTZ CORPORATION (acquired by Deutz AG)
    3883 Steve Reynolds Blvd., Norcross, GA 30093
    CEO: Werner A. Schmitz, Pres.   Tel: (770) 564-7100   Emp: 91
    Bus: *Sale/distribution/produce support diesel*   Fax:(770) 564-7272   %FO: 100
    engines.

    HUMBOLDT DECANTER INC
    3883 Steve Reynolds Blvd, Norcross, GA 30093
    CEO: Clement O'Donnell, Pres.   Tel: (770) 564-7300   Emp: 23
    Bus: *Design, construction & product support of*   Fax:(770) 564-7343   %FO: 100
    industry centrifuges.

    HUMBOLDT WEDAG INC
    3883 Steve Reynolds Blvd, Norcross, GA 30093
    CEO: Kenneth M. Hitcho, Pres.   Tel: (770) 564-7300   Emp: 17
    Bus: *Engineering & equipment services for cement*   Fax:(770) 564-7333   %FO: 100
    industry.

KHD DEUTZ OF AMERICA CORP
3883 Steve Reynolds Blvd, Norcross, GA   30518
CEO: Manfred A Kleindienst, Pres. Tel: (770) 564-7100 Emp: 4
Bus: *Treasure, legal, tax services for U.S.* Fax:(770) 564-7272 %FO: 100
operations.

SCHMIDT BRETTEN INC
20475 Woodingham Drive, Detroit, MI   48221
CEO: Constantine Triculis, VP Tel: (313) 863-0150 Emp: 8
Bus: *Design, mfr. & sale thermal processing* Fax:(313) 863-9528 %FO: 100
equipment & systems.

● **KOLBUS GmbH + CO. KG**
Postfach 220, Osnabrücker StraBe 77, 32363 Rahden, Germany
CEO: N/A Tel: 499-5771-710 Emp: N/A
Bus: *Mfr. bookbinding machinery.* Fax:49-5771-5155

KILBUS AMERICA, INC.
25 Whitney Road, Mahwah, NJ   07430
CEO: John B. Sloane, Pres. Tel: (201) 848-8300 Emp: 50
Bus: *Sales/distribution of bookbinding machinery.* Fax:(201) 848-0368 %FO: 100

● **KOMET PRÄZISIONSWERKZENGE ROBERT BREUNING GMBH**
Zeppelinstrasse 3, D-74354 Besigheim, Germany
CEO: Peter Höger, CEO Tel: 49-7143-3731 Emp: 12500
Bus: *Mfr. cutting tools.* Fax:49-7143-373-233

KOMET OF AMERICA, INC.
2050 Mitchell Blvd., Schaumburg, IL   60193
CEO: Rick U.V. Martin, Pres. Tel: (847) 923-8400 Emp: 250
Bus: *Mfr./sales cutting tools.* Fax:(847) 923-0638 %FO: 100

● **KRAUSS-MAFFEI AG**
Krauss-Maffei Str 2, D-80997 Munich, Germany
CEO: Cletus von Pichler, CEO Tel: 49-89 88990 Emp: 4500
Bus: *Mfr. plastics machinery, process equipment,* Fax:49-89-88992206
armored tanks, locomotives, high-speed trains.

KRAUSS-MAFFEI CORP.
7095 Industrial Road, PO Box 6270, Florence, KY   41022-6270
CEO: S. Winter & D. Forthuber, VPs Tel: (606) 283-0200 Emp: 115
Bus: *Mfr./assembly/sale/service plastics machinery,* Fax:(606) 283-0290 %FO: 100
process equipment.

● **H KRIEGHOFF GMBH**
Postfach 2610, Boschstrasse 22, D-89016 Ulm, Germany
CEO: Walter Brass, Pres.　　　　　　　　　　Tel: 49-731-401820　　Emp: 95
Bus: *Mfr. hunting & sporting firearms.*　　　Fax:49-731-4018270

　　KRIEGHOFF INTL, INC.
　　PO Box 549, 7528 Easton Road, Ottsville, PA　18942
　　CEO: Jim Hollingsworth, Pres.　　　　　Tel: (610) 847-5173　　Emp: 13
　　Bus: *Importer/distributor hunting & sporting*　Fax:(610) 847-8691　　%FO: JV
　　　　firearms.

● **KROHNE MESSTECHNIK GMBH & CO KG**
Ludwig-Krohne-Strasse 5, D-47058 Duisburg, Germany
CEO: Michael Dubbick, Pres.　　　　　　　　Tel: 49-203 3011　　Emp: N/A
Bus: *Mfr. electromechanical & electronic flow & liquid*　Fax:49-8/97203 301380
　　level measurement equipment.

　　KROHNE AMERICA INC.
　　7 Dearborn Road, Peabody, MA　01960
　　CEO: Horst Focks, Pres.　　　　　　　　Tel: (508) 535-6060　　Emp: 70
　　Bus: *Mfr. electromechanical & electronic flow &*　Fax:(508) 535-1720　　%FO: 100
　　　　liquid level measurement equipment.

● **KRONE AG**
Beeskowdamm 3-11, D-14167 Berlin, Germany
CEO: Klaus Krone, CEO　　　　　　　　　　Tel: 49-30-84530　　Emp: 3000
Bus: *Mfr. telecommunications equipment.*　　Fax:49-30-8453 1703

　　KRONE, INC.
　　6950 S. Tucson Way, Suite R, Englewood, CO　80112
　　CEO: Klaus Remv, VP & Gen. Mgr.　　　　Tel: (303) 790-2619　　Emp: 130
　　Bus: *Mfr. telecommunications equipment.*　Fax:(303) 790-2117　　%FO: 100

● **KRONES AG**
Hermann Kronseder, Maschinenfabrik, Postfach 1230, D-93068 Neutraubling, Germany
CEO: Hermann Kronseder, Pres.　　　　　　Tel: 49-9401 700　　Emp: N/A
Bus: *Mfr. labeling, bottle-filling & packaging equipment.*　Fax:49-9401 702488

　　KRONES INC.
　　9600 S 58th Street, PO Box 32100, Franklin, WI　53132-0100
　　CEO: Rudi Zeus, CEO　　　　　　　　　Tel: (414) 421-5650　　Emp: N/A
　　Bus: *Labeling, bottle-filling & packaging equipment.*　Fax:(414) 421-2222　　%FO: 100

● **FRIED. KRUPP AG HOESCH-KRUPP**
Altencontenstrasse 100, D-45143 Essen, Germany
CEO: Dr. Gerhard Cromme, Chrm.   Tel: 49-201-1881   Emp: 66352
Bus: *Steel production, processing & trading. Formed in*   Fax:49-201-188-4100
        1991 by Freid. Krupp AG acquiring Hoesch AG.

    HOESCH TUBULAR PRODUCTS CO.
    2600 Spur 55, PO Box 779, Houston, TX   77522
    CEO: Wolfgang Schmidt, Pres.   Tel: (713) 383-2603   Emp: 87
    Bus: *Processing of unfinished pipe.*   Fax:(713) 573-1456   %FO: 100

    KRUPP USA INC.
    180 Interstate North Pkwy., Atlanta, GA   30339-2194
    CEO: Daniel R. Fritz, Pres.   Tel: (770) 955-3660   Emp: 32
    Bus: *Sale/distribution steel, non-ferrous & other*   Fax:(770) 955-8789   %FO: 100
        products.

    ROTEK INC.
    1400 S Chillicothe Road, PO Box 312, Aurora, OH   44202
    CEO: Jurgen F. Eysel, Pres.   Tel: (216) 562-4000   Emp: 245
    Bus: *Develop /mfr. large-diameter bearings, rings,*   Fax:(216) 562-4620   %FO: 100
        etc.

    WERNER & PFLEIDERER CORP.
    663 East Crescent Avenue, Ramsey, NJ   07446
    CEO: Jorg Pfeiffer, Pres.   Tel: (201) 327-6300   Emp: N/A
    Bus: *Steel production, processing & trading.*   Fax:(201) 825-6491   %FO: 100

● **KTR KUPPLUNGSTECHNIK GMBH**
Postfach 1763, 48407 Rheine, Germany
CEO: Rainer Reichert, CEO   Tel: 49-5971 798445   Emp: 350
Bus: *Mfr. mechanical power transmission equipment.*   Fax:49-5971 798450

    KTR CORPORATION
    PO Box 9065, 122 Anchor Road, Michigan City, IN   46360
    CEO: Jerry Elenz, VP   Tel: (219) 872-9100   Emp: 20
    Bus: *Sale mechanical power transmission*   Fax:(219) 872-9150   %FO: 100
        equipment.

● **LANDESBANK HESSEN-THÜRINGEN GIROZENTRALE**
Junghofstrasse 18-26, D-60311 Frankfurt am Main, Germany
CEO: Walter Scharfer, Chrm.   Tel: 49-69-13201   Emp: N/A
Bus: *International commercial banking services*   Fax:49-69-291517

    LANDESBANK HESSEN-THÜRINGEN
    420 Fifth Avenue. 24th Floor, New York, Ny   10018
    CEO: Hans-Christian Ritter, EVP   Tel: (212) 703-5200   Emp: 30
    Bus: *International commercial banking services.*   Fax:(212) 703-5256   %FO: 100

• LANGENSCHEIDT KG
Neusser Str 3, 80807 Munich, Germany

CEO: K. T. Langenscheidt, Pres.   Tel: 49-89-36096   Emp: 900

Bus: *Publishers.*   Fax:49-89-3609-6258

ADC The Map People
6440 General Green Way, Alexandria, VA   22312

CEO: Mark Turcotte, EVP   Tel: (703) 750-0510   Emp: 100

Bus: *Mfr./sale/distribution maps.*   Fax:(703) 750-3092   %FO: 100

AMERICAN MAP CORP.
46-35 54th Road, Maspeth, NY   11378

CEO: Stuart Dolgins, EVP   Tel: (718) 784-0055   Emp: 50

Bus: *Mfr./sale/distribution maps.*   Fax:(718) 784-0640   %FO: 100

ARROW PUBLISHING CO INC.
50 Scotland Blvd, Bridgewater, MA   02324

CEO: Stuart Dolgins, EVP   Tel: (508) 279-1177   Emp: 15

Bus: *Mfr./sale/distribution maps.*   Fax:(508) 279-0073   %FO: 100

CREATIVE SALES CORP.
1350 Michael Drive, Wood Dale, IL   60191

CEO: Stuart Dolgins, EVP   Tel: (630) 350-0770   Emp: 10

Bus: *Publishers.*   Fax:(630) 350-1760   %FO: 100

HAGSTROM MAP CO., INC.
46-35 54th Road, Maspeth, NY   11378

CEO: Stuart Dolgins, EVP   Tel: (718) 784-0055   Emp: 30

Bus: *Mfr./sale/distribution maps.*   Fax:(718) 784-0640   %FO: 100

LANGENSCHEIDT PUBLISHERS INC.
46-35 54th Road, Maspeth, NY   11378

CEO: Stuart Dolgins, EVP   Tel: (718) 784-0055   Emp: 15

Bus: *Publishers.*   Fax:(718) 784-0640   %FO: 100

TRAKKER MAP INC. NATIONWIDE DISTRIBUTORS INC.
12027 SW 117th Court, Miami, FL   33186

CEO: Stuart Dolgins, EVP   Tel: (305) 255-4485   Emp: 20

Bus: *Mfr./sale/distribution maps.*   Fax:(305) 232-5257   %FO: 100

• LECHLER GMBH & CO KG
Ulmerstrasse 128, Postfach 1323, D-72555 Metzingen, Germany

CEO: Walter Lechler, Pres.   Tel: 49-7123-9620   Emp: 200

Bus: *Mfr. industrial nozzles & spray equipment.*   Fax:49-7123-962444

LECHLER INC.
445 Kautz Road, St. Charles, IL   60174-5301

CEO: Ralph Fish, Pres.   Tel: (630) 377-6611   Emp: 60

Bus: *Mfr./distribution industrial nozzles & spray*   Fax:(630) 377-6657   %FO: 100
    equipment.

● **LEHMANN & VOSS & CO**
Alsterufer 19, D-20354 Hamburg, Germany
CEO: Drs. Dirk Thomsen/Erik Thomsen, Mng. Ptrns.   Tel: 49-40 44197 0   Emp: N/A
Bus: *Mfr./distribution specialty chemical.*   Fax:49-40 44197 219

    LEHVOSS CORP OF AMERICA
    700 Canal Street, Stamford, CT   06902
    CEO: Joachim Hogenow, Pres.   Tel: (203) 328-3736   Emp: N/A
    Bus: *Distributor/service sourcing for parent*   Fax:(203) 328-3738   %FO: 100
       company, technology transfer.

● **GEBR LEITZ GMBH & CO**
Leitzstrasse 2, Postfach 1229, D-73443 Oberkochen, Germany
CEO: Dieter Brucklacher, CEO   Tel: 49-7364 210   Emp: 2400
Bus: *Mfr. woodworking tooling.*   Fax:49-7364 21277

    LEITZ TOOLING SYSTEMS INC.
    4301 East Paris Avenue SE, Grand Rapids, MI   49512
    CEO: Terry Jacks, Pres.   Tel: (616) 698 7010   Emp: 70
    Bus: *Mfr./sale/service woodworking tooling.*   Fax:(616) 698-9270   %FO: 100

● **LEYBOLD AG**
Postfach 510760, 50968 Cologne, Germany
CEO: Horst Heidsiek, Chrm.   Tel: 49-221 3471429   Emp: 4000
Bus: *Mfr. HV technical equipment.*   Fax:49-221 3471250

    LEYBOLD INFICON INC.
    2 Technology Place, East Syracuse, NY   13057-9714
    CEO: James L. Brissenden, Pres.   Tel: (315) 434-1100   Emp: 220
    Bus: *Mfr. process control instruments (vacuum).*   Fax:(315) 437-3803   %FO: 100

● **HEINRICH LIEBIG STAHLDUBEL-WERKE GMBH**
Wormser Strasse 23, Postfach 1309, D-64319 Pfungstadt, Germany
CEO: Heinrich Liebig, CEO   Tel: 49-6157 2027   Emp: 200
Bus: *Mfr./sales of concrete expansion undercut anchors,*   Fax:49-6157 2020
   self-undercut anchors & chemical anchors.

    LIEBIG INTERNATIONAL INC.
    1545 Avon Street Ext, Charlottesville, VA   22902
    CEO: Heinrich Liebig, Pres.   Tel: (804) 979-7115   Emp: 4
    Bus: *Sale/service Liebig concrete expansion and*   Fax:(804) 979-7117   %FO: 100
       undercut anchors, self-undercut anchors, and
       chemical anchors.

● **LINDE AG**

Abraham-Lincoln-Strasse 21, D-65189 Weisbaden, Germany

CEO: Gerhard Full, Chrm.   Tel: 49-611-7700   Emp: 30068

Bus: *Holding company. Engineering & Contracting;*   Fax:49-611-770269
Material Handling, Refrigeration, and Industrial
gases.

   LOTEPRO CORP.

   115 Stevens Avenue, Valhalla, NY   10595

   CEO: Dr. Hans Kistenmacher, Pres.   Tel: (914) 747-3500   Emp: 130

   Bus: *Engineering services. Sub of Linde AG,*   Fax:(914) 747-3422   %FO: 100
   Engineering and Contracting Division,
   Hoellriegelskreuth, Germany.

   SALES FLUID PROCESSING CORPORATION

   5 Sentry Pkwy East, Ste. 204, Blue Bell, PA   19422

   CEO: Lewis Zirpoli, Pres.   Tel: (610) 834-0300   Emp: 90+

   Bus: *Pyrolysis, steam reforming and refinery,*   Fax:(610) 834-0473   %FO: 100
   furnaces for the chemical, petrochemical and
   refining industries.

● **LISEGA GMBH**

D-27393 ZEVEN, POB 1357, Germany

CEO: Hans Hardtke, Pres.   Tel: 49-42-81713202   Emp: 450

Bus: *Mfr. equipment, piping supports, hangers.*   Fax:49-42-81713214

   LISEGA GMBH

   375 Lisega Blvd., Newport, TN   37821

   CEO: Stephen M. Lanning, Gen. Mgr.   Tel: (423) 625-2000   Emp: 90

   Bus: *Sale/service equipment, piping supports,*   Fax:(423) 625-9009   %FO: 100
   hangers.

● **EDUARD LOEHLE SEN GMBH**

Stoeckachstrasse 11, 70191 Stuttgart, Germany

CEO: Thomas Pfisterer, Mng. Dir.   Tel: 49-711 282041   Emp: 45

Bus: *International moving, crating, shipping.*   Fax:49-711 2868329

   KNOPF & LOEHLE INC.

   3211 Industry Drive, North Charleston, SC   29418

   CEO: Siegfried J. Zarwel, Pres.   Tel: (803) 760-2501   Emp: 8

   Bus: *International moving, crating, shipping.*   Fax:(803) 760-2503   %FO: JV

●**LOHMANN GMBH & CO., KG**
Irlicher Strasse 55, Postfach 2343, D-56567 Neuwied, Germany
CEO: Dr. Peter Barth, Mng. Dir.   Tel: 49-2631-990   Emp: 3000
Bus: *Mfr. of medical products, nonwovens and pressure-*   Fax:49-2631-966 497
      sensitive adhesive tapes.

    LOHMANN CORPORATION
    3000 Earhart Court, Suite 155, Hebron, KY   41048
    CEO: Steven J. DeJong, Pres.   Tel: (606) 334-4900   Emp: 85
    Bus: *Mfr. of medical products, nonwovens and*   Fax:(606) 344-4903   %FO: 100
        pressure-sensitive adhesive tapes.

●**LTU Luft-Transport-Unternehmen-Sued-GmbH & Co.**
Parsevalstrasse 7a, D-40468 Dusseldorf, Germany
CEO: Dr. Heinz Westin, CEO   Tel: 49-211-941-8888   Emp: 826
Bus: *Commercial air transport services.*   Fax:49-8-99781-2363

    LTU INTERNATIONAL AIRWAYS INC.
    100 North Biscayne Blvd., Suite 500, Miami, FL   33132
    CEO: Peter Freymuth, Gen Mgr.   Tel: (305) 530-2208   Emp: 50
    Bus: *International commercial air transport.*   Fax:(305) 375-0091   %FO: 100

●**LUPOFRESH A&E**
Senefelder Str 10-14, Postfach 130149, 90409 Nurnberg, Germany
CEO: Ernst Krakenberger, Partner   Tel: 49-911 519970   Emp: N/A
Bus: *Hop products.*   Fax:49-911 5199777

    LUPOFRESH INC.
    214 Ivy Street, PO Box 36, Wapato, WA   98951
    CEO: Harald T. Doerge, Pres.   Tel: (509) 877-2194   Emp: N/A
    Bus: *Hop products.*   Fax:(509) 877-4032   %FO: 100

●**MANNESMANN AG**
Mannesmannufer 2, Postfach 103641, D-40027 Dusseldorf, Germany
CEO: Dr. Joachim Funk   Tel: 49-211-820-0   Emp: 122684
Bus: *Industrial machinery, plant construction, automotive* Fax:49-211-820-1846
      assemblies, pumps, instruments, construction
      equipment, & printers.

    APPLIED AUTOMATION
    Pawhuska Road, PO Box 9999, Bartlesville, OK   74005
    CEO: Gary Waugh, Pres.   Tel: (918) 662-7000   Emp: N/A
    Bus: *Mfr. automatic controls.*   Fax:(918) 662-7052   %FO: 100

    ARGO INSTRUMENTS INC.
    212 Fort Collier Road, Winchester, VA   22603
    CEO: David Paayne, Pres.   Tel: (540) 665-0200   Emp: N/A
    Bus: *Distributor/sale/service on-board computers,* Fax:(540) 662-2127   %FO: 100
        taxi meters.

BERSTORFF CORP.
8200 Arrowridge Blvd., Charlotte, NC   28224
CEO: Nelson Hopcus, CEO   Tel: (704) 523-2614   Emp: N/A
Bus: *Process plant & equipment.*   Fax:(704) 523-4353   %FO: 100

DEMAG MATERIAL HANDLING EQUIPMENT
29201 Aurora Road, Cleveland, OH   44139-1895
CEO: Wilbert Persch, CEO   Tel: (216) 248-2400   Emp: N/A
Bus: *Mfr. material handling equipment.*   Fax:(216) 248-3086   %FO: 100

DOOR-OLIVER INC.
612 Wheeler's Farm Road, Milford, CT   06460-8719
CEO: E. Sweeney, CEO   Tel: (203) 876-5400   Emp: N/A
Bus: *Process plant and equipment.*   Fax:(203) 876-5432   %FO: 100

FICHTEL & SACHS INDUSTRIES INC.
909 Crocker Road, Westlake, OH   44145
CEO: Dr. Harald Klotzbach, Pres.   Tel: (216) 871-8269   Emp: N/A
Bus: *Automotive & bicycle products & components.*   Fax:(216) 871-6822   %FO: 100

INDRAMAT DIVISION
2556 Mittel Drive, Wood Dale, IL   60191-1117
CEO: Robert Ricket   Tel: (630) 860-1010   Emp: N/A
Bus: *Mfr. NC drive technology.*   Fax:(630) 530-4631   %FO: 100

KINETICS TECHNOLOGY INTL (FTI)
650 Cienega Avenue, San Dimas, CA   91773
CEO: David J. Baker, Pres.   Tel: (909) 592-4455   Emp: N/A
Bus: *Petrochemical engineering, refinery*   Fax:(909) 592-3399   %FO: 100
     construction.

KRAUSS-MAFFEI
7095 Industrial Road, PO Box 6270, Florence, KY   41042-6270
CEO: Dieter Forthuber, CEO   Tel: (606) 283-0200   Emp: N/A
Bus: *Plastics technology, process plant and*   Fax:(606) 283-0291   %FO: 100
     equipment, transport engineering. Surface
     treatment technology. automation technology
     & defense engineering.

MANNESMANN CAPITAL CORP.
450 Park Avenue, 24th Floor, New York, NY   10022-2669
CEO: Peter Prinz Wittgenstein, Pres.   Tel: (212) 826-0040   Emp: 6000
Bus: *Holding company.*   Fax:(212) 826-0074   %FO: 100

MANNESMANN DEMAG CORP.
Airport Office Pk.Building.5, 345 Rouser Rd., Pittsburgh, PA   15108-4744
CEO: Dr. Ulrich George, Pres.   Tel: (412) 269-5600   Emp: N/A
Bus: *Material handling equipment, construction &*   Fax:(412) 262-4919   %FO: 100
     plastics machinery, compression equipment.

MANNESMANN OILFIELD TUBULARS CORP.
1990 Post Oak Blvd, #1700, Houston, TX   77056
CEO: David Hamrick, Pres.   Tel: (713) 552-4069   Emp: N/A
Bus: *Mfr. oilfield casings & tubing.*   Fax:(713) 960-8631   %FO: 100

MANNESMANN PIPE & STEEL CORP.
1990 Post Oak Blvd, 18th Fl., Houston, TX   77056
CEO: Rudolf Georg, Pres.   Tel: (713) 960-1900   Emp: N/A
Bus: *Mfr. rolled steel products for industry.*   Fax:(713) 960-1063   %FO: 100

NETSTAL MACHINERY, INC.
20 Authority Drive, Fitchburg, MA   01420-6017
CEO: Berry Potter, Pres.   Tel: (508) 772-5100   Emp: N/A
Bus: *Plastics technology services.*   Fax:(508) 345-6153   %FO: 100

RAPISTAN DEMAG CORP.
507 Plymouth Avenue NE, Grand Rapids, MI   49505
CEO: Pete Metros, Pres.   Tel: (616) 451-6200   Emp: N/A
Bus: *Mfr. material-handling equipment.*   Fax:(616) 451-6425   %FO: 100

THE REXROTH CORP. - Headquarters
2315 City Line Road, PO Box 25407, Lehigh Valley, PA   18002-5407
CEO: Alfred J. Krug, Pres.   Tel: (610) 694-8300   Emp: N/A
Bus: *Hydraulic & pneumatic system & equipment.*   Fax:(610) 694-8467   %FO: 100

SACH AUTOMOTIVE OF AMERICA
2107 Crooks Road, Troy, MI   48084-5529
CEO: Robert Crysler, Pres.   Tel: (248) 614-6510   Emp: N/A
Bus: *Distributes auto parts: suspension products.*   Fax:(248) 614-6525   %FO: 100

SACHS BICYCLE COMPONENTS
22445 East La Palma Ave., J, Yorba-Linda, CA   92687
CEO: John Neugent, CEO   Tel: (714) 692-6696   Emp: N/A
Bus: *Bicycle components.*   Fax:(714) 692-2638   %FO: 100

SACHS-BODGE OF AMERICA
909 Crocker Road, Westlake, OH   44145
CEO: John Edwards, Pres.   Tel: (216) 871-4890   Emp: N/A
Bus: *Distributes auto parts: clutches & shock*   Fax:(216) 871-6904   %FO: 100
   absorbers.

STABILUS
92 County Line Road, Colmar, PA   18915
CEO: Thomas Blomquist, Pres.   Tel: (215) 822-1982   Emp: N/A
Bus: *Mfr. industrial machinery; gas springs.*   Fax:(215) 822-7057   %FO: 100

STAR LINEAR SYSTEMS
9432 Southern Pine Blvd., Charlotte, NC   28273
CEO: Dennis Bames, CEO   Tel: (704) 523-2088   Emp: N/A
Bus: *Mfr. linear motion technology.*   Fax:(708) 523-4099   %FO: 100

SWISS PRESTIGE, INC.
P.O.Box 1608, Winchester, VA   22603

CEO: Nancy Fox, CEO	Tel: (540) 665-0300	Emp: N/A
Bus: *Mfr. watches.*	Fax: (540) 665-4130	%FO: 100

TALLY PRINTER CORP.
8301 S. 180th Street, Kent, WA   98032

CEO: Bill Munro, Pres.	Tel: (206) 251-5500	Emp: N/A
Bus: *Mfr. computer printers.*	Fax: (206) 251-5520	%FO: 100

VAN DORN DEMAG CORPORATION
11792 Alameda Drive, Strongville, OH   44136-3000

CEO: William Pryor, Pres.	Tel: (216) 238-8960	Emp: N/A
Bus: *Mfr. injection molding equipment.*	Fax: (216) 238-3047	%FO: 100

VDO NORTH AMERICA CORP.
188 Brooke Road, Winchester, VA   22604

CEO: Ulrich Baur, Pres.	Tel: (540) 665-0100	Emp: N/A
Bus: *Mfr. control/information systems/sensors for auto industry.*	Fax: (510) 662-2515	%FO: 100

VDO NORTH AMERICA LLC
2107 Crooks Road, Troy, MI   48084

CEO: Dr. Ulrich Baur, Pres.	Tel: (248) 614-6681	Emp: N/A
Bus: *Mfr. instruments for passenger cars and commercial vehicles.*	Fax: (248) 614-6680	%FO: 100

● **MASCHINENFABRIK NIEHOFF GMBH & CO KG**
Postfach 1860, 91124 Schwabach, Germany

CEO: Heinz Rockenhaeuser, Pres.	Tel: 49-9122 9770	Emp: 580
Bus: *Mfr. machinery & equipment for non-ferrous wire & cable industry.*	Fax: 49-9122 977155	

NIEHOFF OF AMERICA INC.
One Mallard Court, Swedesboro, NJ   08085

CEO: H. Berghold, Pres.	Tel: (609) 467-4884	Emp: 12
Bus: *Sale/service machinery & equipment for non-ferrous wire & cable industry, distribution machinery & equipment for steel wire & cable industry.*	Fax: (609) 467-0584	%FO: 100

● **MASCHINENFABRIK ODERTAL GMBH**
Promenade 51-55, 37431 Bad Lauterburg, Germany

CEO: Gunter Josal, Pres	Tel: 49-5524 8520	Emp: 75
Bus: *Mfr. engraving & milling systems.*	Fax: 49-5524 85227	

GPI TECHNOLOGY INC.
PO Box 433, Shelton, CT   06484

CEO: F. Frei, Pres.	Tel: (203) 929-2200	Emp: 5
Bus: *Sales/service engraving machines*	Fax: (203) 926-0074	%FO: 100

● **KARL MAYER TEXTILMASCHINENFABRIK GMBH**
Bruhlstrasse 25, D-63179 Obertshausen, Germany
CEO: Ingo, Fritz & Ulrich Mayer, Md. Dirs.   Tel: 49-6104-4020   Emp: 3000
Bus: *Mfr. warp knitting machinery & parts, warping*   Fax:49-6104-43574
     equipment.

    MAYER TEXTILE MACHINE CORP.
    310 Brighton Road, P.O.Box 1240, Clifton, NJ   07012
    CEO: Gerd Rohmert. Pres.   Tel: (973) 773-3350   Emp: 140
    Bus: *Mfr./distribution warp knitting machinery &*   Fax:(973) 473-3463   %FO: 100
        parts, warping equipment.

● **MELITTA BENTZ KG**
Marienstrasse 88, 54310 Minden, Germany
CEO: J, T & S Bentz, Chairmen   Tel: 49-571-40460   Emp: 4588
Bus: *Mfr./marketing coffee & coffee related products;*   Fax:49-571-4046499
    food preparation/preservation products; convenient
    products.

    EUROPEAN COFFEE CLASSICS, INC.
    1401 Berlin Road, Cherry Hill, NJ   08003
    CEO: Jau Overcash, VP   Tel: (609) 428-7202   Emp: N/A
    Bus: *Produces/sell Melitta brand coffee & operates*   Fax:(609) 795-7543   %FO: 100
        Coffee World retail stores.

    MELITTA NORTH AMERICA INC.
    13925 58th Street North, Clearwater, FL   34620
    CEO: H-Helmut Radtke, Pres.   Tel: (813) 535-2111   Emp: 175
    Bus: *US holding company.*   Fax:(813) 535-7376   %FO: 100

    MELITTA USA INC.
    1401 Berlin Road, Cherry Hill, NJ   08003
    CEO: H-Helmut Radtke, Pres.   Tel: (609) 428-7202   Emp: 175
    Bus: *Sale coffee, coffee filters, coffeemakers,*   Fax:(609) 795-7543   %FO: 100
        household accessories.

    PORTA WESTFALICA INC.
    150 Mangrove Bay Office Ctr, 17755 US S 19, Clearwater, FL   34624
    CEO: H-Helmut Radtke, Pres.   Tel: (813) 535-7999   Emp: N/A
    Bus: *Real estate development/management.*   Fax:(813) 531-5964   %FO: 100

● **MEPLA-WERKE LAUTENSCHLAEGER GMBH & CO KG**
Egerlanderstrasse 2, Postfach 1161, 64348 Reinheim, Germany
CEO: Horst Lautenschlaeger, Pres.   Tel: 49-6162-8020   Emp: 1000
Bus: *Mfr. furniture fittings.*   Fax:49-6162 80221

    MEPLA INC.
    909 West Market Center Drive, High Point, NC   27261
    CEO: Hilmar Bott, Pres.   Tel: (910) 410-7000   Emp: 120
    Bus: *Mfr./distribution furniture fittings.*   Fax:(910) 883-6170   %FO: 100

• **MARTIN MERKEL GMBH & CO KG**
Sanitasstr 17-21, D-21107 Hamburg, Germany
CEO: H. Merkel, Pres.   Tel: 49-40 753060   Emp: 1000
Bus: *Mfr. hydraulic seals & braided packing.*   Fax:49-40 75306440

> **MARTIN MERKEL INC.**
> 5375 Naiman Pkwy., Cleveland, OH   44139
> CEO: Jack W. Thomason, CEO   Tel: (216) 248-2660   Emp: 15
> Bus: *Hydraulic seals & braided packing.*   Fax:(216) 248-3142   %FO: 100

• **MERO RAUMSTRUKTUR GMBH & CO**
Max-Mengering Hausen - Strabe 5, Postfach 6169, D-97064 Wurzburg, Germany
CEO: Roland Klose, Mgn.Dir.   Tel: 49-931 6670   Emp: 1000
Bus: *Space frames, special structures, exhibits & displays.*   Fax:49-931 6670 547

> **MERO STRUCTURES INC.**
> N112 W18810 Mequon Road, PO Box 610, Germantown, WI   53022
> CEO: Ian Collins, Pres.   Tel: (414) 255-5561   Emp: 30
> Bus: *Space frames, special structures, exhibits &*   Fax:(414) 255-6932   %FO: 100
> *displays.*

• **MESSE DUSSELDORF**
Stockumer Kirchstrasse 61, D.40474 Dusseldorf, Germany
CEO: Hartmut Krebs, Pres.   Tel: 49-211 4560-01   Emp: 700
Bus: *Trade show organizer.*   Fax:49-211 4560-668

> **DUSSELDORF TRADE SHOWS, INC.**
> 70 West 36th Street, New York, NY   10018
> CEO: Thomas Mitchell, Mgr.   Tel: (212) 356-0400   Emp: 10
> Bus: *Promotes trade show program of Messe*   Fax:(212) 356-0404   %FO: 100
> *Dusseldorf in the USA.*

> **DUSSELDORF TRADE SHOWS, INC.**
> 150 N. Michigan Avenue, #2920, Chicago, IL   60601
> CEO: Wolfgang Marzin, Mng. Dir.   Tel: (312) 781-5180   Emp: 7
> Bus: *Promotes trade show program of Messe*   Fax:(312) 781-5188   %FO: 100
> *Dusseldorf in the USA.*

• **METALLGESELLSCHAFT AG**
Reuterweg 14, D-60271 Frankfurt, Germany
CEO: K. J. Neukirch, Chrm.   Tel: 49-69-1590   Emp: N/A
Bus: *Non-ferrous metals, engineering, chemicals,*   Fax:49-69-159-2125
transportation.

> **THE ORE & CHEMICAL CORP.**
> 520 Madison Avenue, New York, NY   10022
> CEO: Joseph E. Robertson Jr., Pres.   Tel: (212) 715-5200   Emp: N/A
> Bus: *Trading of non-ferrous metals & ores, rubber,*   Fax:(212) 715-2357   %FO: 100
> *chemicals*

• LUCAS MEYER GMBH & COMPANY
Postfach 262665, D-20506 Hamburg, Germany
CEO: Lucas C. Meyer, Pres.   Tel: 49-40-789550   Emp: 100
Bus: *Mfr. lecithin.*   Fax:49-40-789329

    LUCAS MEYER INC.
    765 East Pythian Avenue, Decatur, IL   62526
    CEO: Peter Rohde, Pres.   Tel: (217) 875-3660   Emp: 18
    Bus: *Mfr. lecithin.*   Fax:(217) 877-5046   %FO: 100

• MÜNCHENER RÜCKVERSICHERUNGS-GESELLSCHAFT
Kõniginstrasse 107, D-807091 Munich, Germany
CEO: Dr. Hans-Juergen Schinzler, Chrm.   Tel: 49-89-38910   Emp: N/A
Bus: *Multi-line insurance services. (Munich Reinsurance)*   Fax:49-89-399056

    AMERICAN REINSURANCE COMPANY
    55 College Road East, PO Box 5421, Princeton, NJ   08543
    CEO: Edward J. Noonan, Pres.   Tel: (609) 243-4200   Emp: 1500
    Bus: *Multi-line insurance services.*   Fax:(609) 243-4257   %FO: 100

• GEBR NETZSCH MASCHINENFABRIK GMBH & CO.
Gebrueder-Netzsch-Strasse 19, D-8672 Selb/Bayern, Germany
CEO: Erich Netzsch, Chrm.   Tel: 49-9287 750   Emp: 2400
Bus: *Diversified mfr.*   Fax:49-9287-75208

    NETZSCH INC.
    119 Pickering Way, Exton, PA   19341-1393
    CEO: Hanno W. Spranger, Pres.   Tel: (610) 363-8010   Emp: 123
    Bus: *Mfr./service mach for ceramic industry, filter*   Fax:(610) 363-0971   %FO: 100
        presses, grinding & dispersion equipment,
        pumps.

• NORDDEUTSCHE LANDESBANK GIROZENTRALE HANNOVER
Georgsplatz 1, D-30159 Hannover, Germany
CEO: Manfred Bodin, Chrm.   Tel: 49-511 3610   Emp: 6089
Bus: *Commercial banking services.*   Fax:49-511 3612501

    NORDDEUTSCHE LANDESBANK GIROZENTRALE
    1270 Ave of the Americas, New York, NY   10020
    CEO: Jens A .Westrick, EVP   Tel: (212) 332-8600   Emp: 30
    Bus: *International commercial banking services.*   Fax:(212) 332-8660   %FO: 100

● **OPPENHOFF & RÄDLER**
Rankestrabe 21, D-10789 Berlin, Germany
CEO: T. Verhoven, Mng. Ptnr. Tel: 30-214-96-0 Emp: 240
Bus: *International law firm.* Fax:30-214-96-100

 OPPENHOFF & RÄDLER
 712 Fifth Avenue, 30th Fl., New York, NY 10019
 CEO: T. Verhoven, Mng. Ptnr. Tel: (212) 801-3410 Emp: N/A
 Bus: *International law firm.* Fax:(212) 801-3415 %FO: 100

● **OPTIMA MASCHINENFABRIK**
Steinbeis Weg 20, Postfach 100520, 74523 Schwaebisch Hall, Germany
CEO: Hans Buehler, Pres. & CEO Tel: 49-79 7915060 Emp: 400
Bus: *Design/mfr./sale/service packaging & filling* Fax:49-79 79151835
 machinery

 OPTIMA MACHINERY CORPORATION
 1330 Contract Drive, PO Box 28173, Green Bay, WI 64304-0173
 CEO: Tom Seifert, Mgr. Tel: (414) 339-2222 Emp: 25
 Bus: *Mfr./sale/service packaging machinery.* Fax:(414) 339-2233 %FO: 100

● **PAUL FERD PEDDINGHAUS**
Postfach 1860, 58285 Gevelsberg, Germany
CEO: C. U. Peddinghaus, CEO Tel: 49-2332 720 Emp: 1000
Bus: *Mfr. structural steel & plate fabricating equipment.* Fax:49-2332 72208

 PEDDINGHAUS CORP
 300 North Washington Avenue, Bradley, IL 60915
 CEO: Tom Boyer, Pres. Tel: (815) 937-3800 Emp: 106
 Bus: *Mfr./distributor/service structure steel & plate* Fax:(815) 937-4003 %FO: 100
 fabricating equipment.

● **PEPPERL+FUCHS GMBH**
Koenigsberger Allee 87, D-68307 Mannheim, Germany
CEO: Dieter Bihl, Mng. Dir. Tel: 49-621 7760 Emp: 2500
Bus: *Mfr. proximity sensors & electronic controls.* Fax:49-621 7761000

 PEPPERL+FUCHS INC.
 1600 Enterprise Pkwy, Twinsburg, OH 44087
 CEO: Wolfgang Mueller, Pres. Tel: (216) 425-3555 Emp: 125
 Bus: *Mfr. proximity sensors & electronic controls.* Fax:(216) 425-4607 %FO: 100

● **PERI GMBH**
Rudolf-Diesel-Strasse, 89259 Weissenhorn, Germany
CEO: Artur Schworer, Pres.   Tel: 49-7309 9500   Emp: 1500
Bus: *Concrete formwork & scaffolding.*   Fax:49-7309 950176

    PERI FORMWORK INC.
    2031 Inverness Avenue, Baltimore, MD   21230
    CEO: Harvey Evans, VP   Tel: (410) 646-5010   Emp: 100
    Bus: *Distribution/sale/service concrete formwork &*   Fax:(410) 646-5018   %FO: 100
       scaffolding.

● **CARL AUG PICARD GMBH**
Hasteraue 9, D-42857 Remscheid, Germany
CEO: Walter Picard, CEO   Tel: 49-2191 8930   Emp: 350
Bus: *Precision grinding, wear parts & heat treating.*   Fax:49-2191 893111

    C. A . PICARD INC.
    305 Hill Brady Road, Battle Creek, MI   49015
    CEO: Gunter Schramm, Pres.   Tel: (616) 962-2231   Emp: 50
    Bus: *Tooling for printed circuit board industry.*   Fax:(616) 962-4916   %FO: 100

● **PKL VERPACKUNGSSYSTEME GMBH**
52441 Linnich, Germany
CEO: Klaus Kamin, Pres. & Chrm.   Tel: 49-2462-792-000   Emp: 2250
Bus: *Mfr. aseptic packages & filling systems.*   Fax:49-2462-792-682

    CAMBIBLOC, INC.
    4800 Roberts Road, Columbus, OH   43228
    CEO: Warren C. Tyler, Pres./CEO   Tel: (614) 876-3700   Emp: 202
    Bus: *Mfr. aseptic packages, sale filling systems.*   Fax:(614) 876-8678   %FO: 100

● **THE PREUSSAG GROUP**
Postfach 610209, Karl-Wiechert-Allee 4, D-30602 Hannover, Germany
CEO: Mr. R. Vauth, Chrm.   Tel: 49-511 56600   Emp: 74000
Bus: *Steel & non-ferrous metals, energy, trading &*   Fax:49-511 5661901
    transport, shipbuilding & rolling stock, engineering,
    information technology.

    PB-KBB INC.
    11757 Katy Frwy., Ste. 600, Houston, TX   77079
    CEO: Kermit Allen, Pres.   Tel: (281) 496-5590   Emp: 100
    Bus: *Engineering/design/construction underground*   Fax:(281) 496-5658   %FO: 50
       hydrocarbon storage facilities, terminals,
       pipelines, tank farms.

    PREUSSAGE INTERNATIONAL STEEL CORP.
    PO Box 76946, Atlanta, GA   30358
    CEO: R. Botterbusch, Mgr.   Tel: (770) 257-7937   Emp: N/A
    Bus: *Steel and non-ferrous metals production.*   Fax:(770) 256-2230   %FO: 100

PREUSSAG NORTH AMERICA, INC.
55 Railroad Avenue, Greenwich, CT 06830
CEO: N. Englund, CEO   Tel: (203) 629-4400   Emp: N/A
Bus: *US representative office.*   Fax:(203) 863-0700   %FO: 100

● **PROMINENT DOSIERTECHNIK GMBH**
Im Schuhmachergewann 7, D-69123 Heidelberg, Germany
CEO: Viktor Dulger, Pres.   Tel: 49-6221 8420   Emp: 300
Bus: *Mfr. chemical metering pumps & controls.*   Fax:49-6221 842215

    PROMINENT FLUID CONTROLS INC.
    136 Industry Drive, RIDC Park West, Pittsburgh, PA 15275-1014
    CEO: Sandy Chu, VP & Gen.Mgr.   Tel: (412) 787-2484   Emp: 30
    Bus: *Mfr./distribution/sale/service chemical*   Fax:(412) 787-0704   %FO: 100
        metering pumps and controls.

● **PUNDER, VOLHARD, WEBER & AXSTER**
Katharina-Heinroth-Ufer 1, PO Box 311003, 10640 Berlin, Germany
CEO: Jens-Peter Lachmann, Mng. Ptnr.   Tel: 49-30-254-65800   Emp: N/A
Bus: *International law firm.*   Fax:49-30-254-65900

    PUNDER, VOLHARD, WEBER & AXSTER
    152 W 57th Street, Carnegie Hall Tower, New York, NY 10019
    CEO: A. Junius, Mng. Ptnr.   Tel: (212) 582-2828   Emp: N/A
    Bus: *International law firm.*   Fax:(212) 582-2424   %FO: 100

● **A. RACKE GMBH & CO.**
Postfach 1653, 55386 Bingen, Germany
CEO: Marcus Moller-Racke, Chrm.   Tel: 49 67211881   Emp: N/A
Bus: *Prod/marketing wines & spirits.*   Fax:49 6721188220

    RACKE USA BUENA VISTA CARNEROS WINERY, INC.
    PO Box 182, Sonoma, CA 95476
    CEO: Harry Parsley, Pres. & CEO   Tel: (707) 252-7117   Emp: 80
    Bus: *Production & marketing of wine.*   Fax:(707) 252-0392   %FO: 100

● **RACO ELEKTRO MASCHINEN GMBH**
58332 Schwelm, Germany
CEO: R. Wilke, Pres.   Tel: 49-2336-40090   Emp: N/A
Bus: *Electric actuators & cylinders.*   Fax:49-2336-400910

    RACO INTL INC.
    3350 Industrial Blvd, P O Box 151, Bethel Park, PA 15102
    CEO: R. Wilke, Pres.   Tel: (412) 835-5744   Emp: N/A
    Bus: *Electric actuators & cylinders.*   Fax:(412) 835-0338   %FO: 100

- **REEMTSMA CIGARETTENFABRIKEN GMBH**

Parkstrasse 51, Postfach 520653, D-22596 Hamburg, Germany

CEO: Ludger W. Staby, Chrm.   Tel: 49-40-82200   Emp: N/A

Bus: *Mfr. tobacco products; cigarette and fine tobaccos.*   Fax:4940-82201645

> **WEST PARK TOBACCO USA, INC.**
>
> 7443 Lee David Road, #305, Mechanicsville, VA   23111
>
> CEO: McCluskey Bernie   Tel: (804) 746-5277   Emp: N/A
>
> Bus: *Mfr./distributor tobacco products; cigarette*   Fax:(804) 746-8153   %FO: 100
>   *and fine tobaccos.*

- **REICH SPEZIALMASCHINEN GMBH**

Plochinger Strasse 65, D-72622 Nuertingen, Germany

CEO: Wulf W. Reich, CEO   Tel: 49-7022 7020   Emp: 400

Bus: *Mfr. industrial woodworking machines.*   Fax:49-7022 702101

> **HOLZ-HER US, INC.**
>
> 5120 Westinghouse Blvd, Charlotte, NC   28273
>
> CEO: Kurt Waldthausen, Pres.   Tel: (704) 587-3400   Emp: 51
>
> Bus: *Industrial woodworking machines.*   Fax:(704) 587-3412   %FO: 100

- **REIFENHAUSER GMBH & CO. MASCHINENFABRIK**

Postfach 1664, D-53839 Troisdorf, Germany

CEO: Wolfgang Twardziok, Chrm.   Tel: 49-22-41 4810   Emp: N/A

Bus: *Mfr. plastic extrusion equipment.*   Fax:49-22-41 408778

> **REIFENHAUSER, INC.**
>
> 421 Merrimack Street, Lawrence, MA   01843
>
> CEO: Matthew D. Bangert, Gen.Mgr.   Tel: (508) 686-2700   Emp: 10
>
> Bus: *Sale/service & spare parts distribution plastic*   Fax:(508) 686-4765   %FO: 100
>   *extrusion equipment.*

[Entry deleted in late revision]

● **RENFERT GMBH & CO**
Industrial Area, D-78247 Hilzingen, Germany
CEO: Klaus U. Rieger, Pres.
Bus: *Mfr. dental laboratory equipment.*

Tel: 49-77-31 8208   Emp: 100
Fax:49-77-31 820830

    DENERICA DENTAL CORP.
    313 Oswalt Avenue, Batavia, IL   60510
    CEO: Sergio P. Verdicchio, RDT
    Bus: *Distribution/service dental laboratory
       equipment.*

Tel: (630) 761-0680   Emp: 5
Fax:(630) 761-9663   %FO: 100

● **RITTAL - WERK, GMBH**
Postfach 1420, D-35745 Herborn, Germany
CEO: Friedhelm Loh, CEO
Bus: *Mfr. electric/electronic enclosures.*

Tel: 49-2772-5051   Emp: 3500
Fax:49-2772-505319

    RITTAL CORPORATION
    One Rittal Place, Springfield, OH   45504
    CEO: Hans J. Wagner, Pres.
    Bus: *Mfr. electric/electronic enclosures.*

Tel: (937) 399-0500   Emp: 280
Fax:(937) 390-5599   %FO: 100

● **RIWO DRAHTWERK GMBH**
Busumer Strasse 96-104, D-24768 Rendsburg, Germany
CEO: Hagen Buergel, Mng. Dir.
Bus: *Mfr. high carbon and micro-alloyed fine steelwire.*

Tel: 49-43 314580   Emp: 75
Fax:49-43 31458-415

    RIWO-WIRE, INC.
    14 High Street, Plainville, MA   02762
    CEO: Katie Sanford, CEO
    Bus: *Sale/distribution high carbon and micro-
       alloyed fine steelwire.*

Tel: (508) 695-3500   Emp: 2
Fax:(508) 695-3500   %FO: 100

● **ROEDIGER ANLAGENBAU GMBH**
Kinzigheimer Weg 104, 63450 Hanau/Main, Germany
CEO: Michael Holzmann, Pres.
Bus: *Engineering/design/construct waste water treatment
plants, mfr. related equipment.*

Tel: 49-6181 3090   Emp: 400
Fax:49-6181 309111

    ROEDIGER PITTSBURGH INC.
    3812 Route 8, Allison Park, PA   15101
    CEO: Marcus Roediger, Pres.
    Bus: *Engineering/design/mfr. waste water treatment
       equipment.*

Tel: (412) 487-6010   Emp: 40
Fax:(412) 487-6005   %FO: 100

• **ROSENBERG & LENHART**
Ludwig-Landmann-Strasse 349, D-60487 Frankfurt Main, Germany
CEO: Thomas Lenhart, Pres.   Tel: 49-2549-0   Emp: N/A
Bus: *Export/import furs & raw skins.*   Fax:49-2549-117

    ALASKA BROKERAGE
    345 Seventh Avenue, New York, NY   10001
    CEO: Helmut A. Rothe, VP   Tel: (212) 268-3590   Emp: 3
    Bus: *Export/import furs, raw skins.*   Fax:(212) 736-0047   %FO: 100

• **ROSENTHAL AG**
Wittelsbacher Strasse 43, D-95100 Selb/Bayern, Germany
CEO: Ottmar Küsel, Pres.   Tel: 49-92-87-72300   Emp: N/A
Bus: *Manufacturer of china, crystal and flatware.* Fax:49-92-87-72225

    ROSENTHAL USA LTD.
    355 Michele Place, Carlstadt, NJ   07072
    CEO: Georg Simon, Pres.   Tel: (201) 804-8000   Emp: N/A
    Bus: *Wholesale distributor of imported china,*   Fax:(201) 804-9300   %FO: 100
        crystal and flatware

• **ROTRING-WERKE RIEPE KG**
Kieler Strasse 303, D-22525 Hamburg, Germany
CEO: Karl H. Ditze, Pres.   Tel: 49-40 54960   Emp: N/A
Bus: *Mfr. engraving & drafting supplies.*   Fax:49-40 5403551

    KOH-I-NOOR RAPIDOGRAPH INC.
    100 North Street, PO Box 68, Bloomsbury, NJ   08804-0068
    CEO: Klaus Ziegenblin, Pres.   Tel: (908) 479-4124   Emp: 515
    Bus: *Mfr./distributor drafting & graphic art*   Fax:(908) 479-4285   %FO: 100
        supplies, fine writing instruments.

• **ROVEMA VERPACKUNGSMASCHINEN GMBH**
Industriegebiet 49, D-35463 Fernwald, Germany
CEO: Walter Baur, Pres.   Tel: 49-641 4091   Emp: N/A
Bus: *Mfr. packaging machinery.*   Fax:49-641 409212

    ROVEMA PACKAGING MACHINES, INC.
    650 Old Norcross Place, Lawrenceville, GA   30245
    CEO: Gene Waterfall, Pres.   Tel: (770) 513-9604   Emp: N/A
    Bus: *Sale/service packaging machinery.*   Fax:(770) 513-0814   %FO: 100

• RUETGERSWERKE AG
Mainzer Landstrasse 217, D-60326 Frankfurt/Main, Germany

CEO: Eberhardt von Persall, Pres.	Tel: 49-69 75921	Emp: N/A
Bus: *Mfr. coal tar based intermediates.*	Fax:49-69 7592488	

RUETGERS-NEASE CHEMICAL CO. INC.
201 Struble Road, State College, PA   16801

CEO: Robert J. Hamilton, Pres	Tel: (814) 238-2424	Emp: 200
Bus: *Mfr. detergent intermediates, custom organic synthesis*	Fax:(814) 238-1567	%FO: 100

• RWE AKTIENGESELLSCHAFT
Rellinghauser Strasse, 45128 Essen, Germany

CEO: Dietmar Kuhnt, Chrm.	Tel: 49-201-1200	Emp: 132658
Bus: *Holding company. Production/distribution: power, petroleum, mining, waste management, engineering, & construction services.*	Fax:49-201-12155199	

REP Environmental Processes, Inc.
35 Nagog Park Acton, Acton, MA   01720

CEO: Hans Pirk, Pres.	Tel: (508) 635-9500	Emp: N/A
Bus: *Waste management services.*	Fax:(508) 266-4100	%FO: 100

VISTA CHEMICAL COMPANY
900 Treadneedle, Houston, TX   77079

CEO: William C. Knodel, Pres.	Tel: (281) 588-3000	Emp: N/A
Bus: *Headquarters for US activities of RWE AKTIENGESELLSCHAFT.*	Fax:(281) 588-3236	%FO: 100

• RWTÜV GMBH
Steubenstrasse 53, D-45032 Essen, Germany

CEO: N/A	Tel: 49-201-8250	Emp: 5500
Bus: *Testing & certification services.*	Fax:49-201-825 2517	

TÜV ESSEN, INC.
2099 Gateway Place, San Jose, CA   95110

CEO: John Beekman, Pres.	Tel: (408) 441-7888	Emp: 50
Bus: *Testing & certification services.*	Fax:(408) 441-7111	%FO: 100

• SAP AG
Neurottstrasse 16, D-69190 Walldorf, Germany

CEO: Dietmar Hopp, Chrm.	Tel: 49-62-27-340	Emp: 6857
Bus: *Developer/mfr./distributor/service applications software.*	Fax:49-62-27-341282	

SAP AMERICA INC.
701 Lee Road, Suite 200, Wayne, PA   19087

CEO: Paul Wahl, CEO	Tel: (610) 725-4500	Emp: 500
Bus: *Developer/mfr./distributor/service applications software.*	Fax:(610) 725-4555	%FO: 100

- **CARL SCHENCK AG**
Landwehrstrasse 55, D-64273 Darmstadt, Germany
CEO: Ralf Fassbach, Pres.   Tel: 49-6151 320   Emp: 7000
Bus: *Engineering/mfr./instruments for weighing &*   Fax:49-6151-893686
     balancing machine & system.

  SCHENCK ACCU-RATE INC.
  746 East Milwaukee Street, Whitewater, WI   53190
  CEO: Gary Kuehneman, VP Sales & Mktg   Tel: (414) 473-2441   Emp: 135
  Bus: *Metering & measuring devises.*   Fax:(414) 473-4384   %FO: 100

  SCHENCK PEGASUS CORP.
  2890 John R Road, Troy, MI   48083
  CEO: F. Schuppenies, Pres.   Tel: (248) 689-9000   Emp: N/A
  Bus: *Mfr. materials testing, dynamometer system.* Fax:(248) 689-8978   %FO: 100

  SCHENCK TREBEL
  535 Acorn Street, Deer Park, NY   11729
  CEO: Kay Mayland, Pres.   Tel: (516) 242-4010   Emp: N/A
  Bus: *Holding company.*   Fax:(516) 242-5077   %FO: 100

  SCHENCK TREBEL CORP.
  535 Acorn Street, Deer Park, NY   11729
  CEO: Kay Mayland, Pres.   Tel: (516) 242-4010   Emp: 140
  Bus: *Mfr. industry balancing machine & related*   Fax:(516) 242-5077   %FO: 100
       equipment.

  SCHENCK TURNER INC.
  100 Kay Drive, Lake Orion, MI   48035
  CEO: Dr. Juergen Neugebauer, Pres.   Tel: (810) 377-2100   Emp: N/A
  Bus: *Mfr. automated balancing system.*   Fax:(810) 377-2744   %FO: 100

  SCHENCK WEIGHING SYSTEMS
  208 Passaic Avenue, Fairfield, NJ   07004
  CEO: G. Rebucci, Gen.Mgr.   Tel: (201) 882-4650   Emp: N/A
  Bus: *Mfr. weigh-feeders.*   Fax:(201) 882-3796   %FO: 100

- **SCHERING AG**
Mullerstrasse 178, D-13342 Berlin, Germany
CEO: Giuseppe Vita, Chrm.   Tel: 49-30 4680   Emp: 23300
Bus: *Mfr. pharmaceuticals.*   Fax:49-30 4685305

  BERLEX LABORATORIES, INC.
  300 Fairfield Road, Wayne, NJ   07470
  CEO: Lutz Lingnau, Chrm.   Tel: (201) 694-4100   Emp: N/A
  Bus: *Pharmaceuticals.*   Fax:(201) 694-4100   %FO: 100

SCHERING BERLIN, INC.
110 E Hanover Avenue, Cedar Knolls, NJ   07927-0567

CEO: Lutz Lingnau, Chrm.	Tel: (913) 292-8043	Emp: N/A
Bus: *Holding co: ethical pharmaceuticals, agrochemicals.*	Fax:(913) 267-7721	%FO: 100

• **SCHLEICHER & SCHUELL KG & CO**
Postfach 4, D-37586 Dassel, Germany

CEO: Ulrich Vogelsang, Pres.	Tel: 49-5564 7910	Emp: N/A
Bus: *Paper products.*	Fax:49-5564 72743	

SCHLEICHER & SCHUELL INC.
10 Optical Avenue, Keene, NH   03431

CEO: David Bacon, Pres.	Tel: (603) 352-3810	Emp: 150
Bus: *Mfr. filtration, paper products*	Fax:(603) 352-3627	%FO: 100

• **ADOLF SCHNORR GMBH & CO KG**
Postfach 600162, 71050 Sindelfingen, Germany

CEO: D. Jentsch, Pres.	Tel: 49-7031-3020	Emp: N/A
Bus: *Mfr. disc springs & safety washers.*	Fax:49-70-313-2600	

SCHNORR CORPORATION
56-02 Roosevelt Avenue, Woodside, NY   11377-0428

CEO: Gerhard Schremmer, Pres.	Tel: (718) 426-2683	Emp: N/A
Bus: *Distribution disc springs & safety washers*	Fax:(718) 335-0408	%FO: 100

• **SCHOELLER FINANZ**
48712 Burg Gretesch, Germany

CEO: Michael Gallenkamp, Pres.	Tel: 49-3800	Emp: N/A
Bus: *Holding company.*	Fax:49-3800425	

FELIX SCHOELLER TECHNICAL PAPERS INC.
PO Box 250, Pulaski, NY   13142

CEO: Donald Schnackel, Pres.	Tel: (315) 298-5133	Emp: N/A
Bus: *Photographic base papers & technical paper products*	Fax:(315) 298-4337	%FO: 100

• **SCHOTT GLASWERKE**
Hattenbergstrasse 10, 55122 Mainz, Germany

CEO: Hemlut Fahlbusch, Chrm.	Tel: 49-6131-660	Emp: 17300
Bus: *Mfr. specialty glass.*	Fax:49-6131-662000	

SCHOTT CORPORATION
3 Odell Plaza, Yonkers, NY   10701

CEO: Guy De Coninck, Pres. & CEO	Tel: (914) 968-1400	Emp: 2000
Bus: *Mfr./marketing specialty glass.*	Fax:(914) 968-8585	%FO: 100

- **ALBERT SCHULTE SOEHNE GMBH & CO**
Postfach 1550, Remschneider Strasse 25, D-42929 Wermelskirchen, Germany
CEO: Udo Schmidt, CEO　　　　　　　　　　Tel: 49-21-96 82891　　Emp: 750
Bus: *Mfr. casters & wheels.*　　　　　　　　　Fax:49-21-96 6609

　　　RHOMBUS CASTERS INTL, INC.
　　　385 Highland Drive, Westhampton, NJ   08060
　　　CEO: Ward Worthy, VP & CEO　　　　　Tel: (609) 261-4700　　Emp: 12
　　　Bus: *Sale/service caster & wheels.*　　　Fax:(609) 261-4244　　%FO: 100

- **SCHUMAG AG**
Postfach 1330, D-52014 Aachen, Germany
CEO: Harald Breme, Pres.　　　　　　　　　Tel: 49-2408 120　　　Emp: 1000
Bus: *Sale/service drawing & grinding machines and mfr.*　Fax:49-2408 12256
　　of parts.

　　　SCHUMAG-KIESERLING Machinery, inc.
　　　155 Hudson Avenue, Norwood, NJ   07648-0419
　　　CEO: A. Justus, Pres.　　　　　　　　　Tel: (201) 767-6850　　Emp: 20
　　　Bus: *Sale/service drawing, grinding, bar turning &*　Fax:(201) 767-3341　　%FO: 100
　　　　needle grinding machines and mfr. of parts.

- **SCHUNK WERKSTOFFE GMBH**
Postfach 100951, D-35339 Giessen, Germany
CEO: Dagobert Kotzur, Pres.　　　　　　　　Tel: 49-641 6081　　　Emp: 4600
Bus: *Holding company. Carbon & sintered metal*　Fax:49-641 6081223
　　technology; engineering ceramics.

　　　SCHUNK GRAPHITE TECHNOLOGY, INC.
　　　W146 N9300 Held Drive, Menomonee Falls, WI   53051
　　　CEO: Heinz Volk, Pres.　　　　　　　　Tel: (414) 253-8720　　Emp: 105
　　　Bus: *Mfr. carbon/graphite products for purification*　Fax:(414) 255-1391　　%FO: 100
　　　　& coating.

　　　SCHUNK OF NORTH AMERICA INC
　　　W 146 N 9300 Held Dr, Menomonee Falls, WI   53051
　　　CEO: Heinz Volk, Pres.　　　　　　　　Tel: (414) 253-8720　　Emp: N/A
　　　Bus: *Holding company. Mfr. carbon/graphite*　Fax:(414) 255-1391　　%FO: 100
　　　　products for purification & coating.

- **SCHWARZ PHARMA AG**
Alfred Nobelstrasse, D-40789 Monheim, Germany
CEO: H. Sommer, Dir.　　　　　　　　　　　Tel: 49-2173 480　　　Emp: 1288
Bus: *Mfr./distribution ethical pharmaceutical products.*　Fax:49-173 481608

　　　SCHWARZ PHARMA KREMERS URBAN CO.
　　　5600 W. County Line Road, Mequon, WI   53092
　　　CEO: Klaus Jülicher, Pres.　　　　　　Tel: (414) 354-4300　　Emp: 160
　　　Bus: *Gastrointestinal, cardiovascular &*　　Fax:(414) 354-4309　　%FO: 100
　　　　pharmaceutical products.

● **SEMIKRON INTL GMBH & CO**
Sigmundstrasse 200, D-90431 Nuremberg, Germany
CEO: Peter Martin, Pres.   Tel: 49-911 65590   Emp: N/A
Bus: *Mfr.. power semiconductors.*   Fax:49-911 6559262

    SEMIKRON INTL INC.
    11 Executive Drive, PO Box 66, Hudson, NH   03051
    CEO: Richard Griessel, Pres.   Tel: (603) 883-8102   Emp: N/A
    Bus: *Mfr. power semiconductors*   Fax:(603) 883-8021   %FO: 100

● **SHG - SCHACK GMBH**
Ellenbacher Strasse 10, D-34123 Kassel, Germany
CEO: H. Herrmann, Mng. Dir.   Tel: 49-561-9527-115   Emp: 150
Bus: *Mfr. waste heat recovery equipment; recuperators,*   Fax:49-561-9527-109
    boilers, heat exchangers.

    AMERICAN SCHACK, INC.
    P.O.Box 1395, Wexford, PA   15090-1395
    CEO: C.P. Natarajan, Pres.   Tel: (412) 935-5725   Emp: 35
    Bus: *Distributor/service waste heat recovery*   Fax:(412) 935-6580   %FO: 100
       equipment; recuperates, boilers, heat
       exchangers.

● **SIEMENS AG**
Wittelsbacherplatz 2, D-80333 Munich, Germany
CEO: Heinrich von Pierer, Pres.   Tel: 49-89-234-0000   Emp: 379000
Bus: *Design/development/mfr. electrical & electronic*   Fax:49-89-234-4242
    system for industry.

    ADB
    977 Gahanna Pkwy, PO Box 30829, Columbus, OH   43230-0829
    CEO: Steve Rauch, Pres.   Tel: (614) 861-1304   Emp: N/A
    Bus: *Mfr. airfield lighting products, design/mfr.*   Fax:(614) 864-2069   %FO: 100
       airport automation systems.

    CARDION INC.
    100 Sunnyside Blvd, Woodbury, NY   11797-2925
    CEO: Allen Greenberg, Pres.   Tel: (516) 921-7300   Emp: N/A
    Bus: *Mfr./marketing sir traffic management &*   Fax:(516) 921-7330   %FO: 100
       defense surveillance systems.

    NSW CORPORATION
    530 Gregory Avenue, Roanoke, VA   24016
    CEO: Lawrence E. Ptaschek, Pres.   Tel: (540) 981-0362   Emp: N/A
    Bus: *Plastic packaging and industrial nets,*   Fax:(540) 345-8421   %FO: 100
       filtration covers/sleeves/nets, plastic belts;
       waste water filters.

OSRAM SYLVANIA INC.

100 Endicott Street, Danvers, MA   01923-3623

CEO: Dean Langford, Pres. Tel: (508) 777-1900 Emp: N/A

Bus: *Mfr./marketing lighting products, precision* Fax:(508) 750-2152 %FO: 100
materials & components for consumers &
industry.

SIEMENS CORPORATION

1301 Avenue of the Americas, New York, NY   10019-6022

CEO: Albert Hoser, Pres. Tel: (212) 258-4000 Emp: 33400

Bus: *Holding company: electrical & electronic* Fax:(212) 258-4370 %FO: 100
systems.

SIEMENS AUTOMOTIVE CORP.

2400 Executive Hills Drive, Auburn Hills, MI   48326-2980

CEO: George Perry, Chrm. Tel: (248) 253-1000 Emp: N/A

Bus: *Design/mfr. electronic components & system* Fax:(248) 253-2999 %FO: 100
or automotive industry.

SIEMENS BUSINESS COMMUNICATION SYSTEMS, INC.

4900 Old Ironsides Dr., PO Box 58075, Santa Clara, CA   95052-8075

CEO: Karl Geng, Pres. Tel: (408) 492-2000 Emp: N/A

Bus: *Mfr./marketing/support private* Fax:(408) 492-3430 %FO: 100
telecommunications system.

SIEMENS COMPONENTS, INC.

10950 North Tantau Avenue, Cupertino, CA   95014-0716

CEO: Alex Leupp, Pres Tel: (408) 777-4500 Emp: N/A

Bus: *Design/mfr. hi-tech electronic components.* Fax:(408) 777-4977 %FO: 100

SIEMENS CORP.

701 Pennsylvania Avenue, NW, Washington, DC   20004

CEO: Jermiah L. Murphy, VP Tel: (202) 434-4800 Emp: N/A

Bus: *Government relations Washington office.* Fax:(202) 347-4015 %FO: 100

SIEMENS CORPORATE RESEARCH INC.

755 College Road East, Princeton, NJ   08540-6632

CEO: Thomas Grandke, Pres. Tel: (609) 734-6500 Emp: N/A

Bus: *Exploratory & applied research.* Fax:(609) 734-6565 %FO: 100

SIEMENS TRANSPORTATION SYSTEMS, INC.

186 Wood AvenueSouth, Iselin, NJ   08830

CEO: James Morrison, Pres. Tel: (732) 321-3100 Emp: N/A

Bus: *Products & services related to rail transport &* Fax:(732) 603-7379 %FO: 100
technology.

SIEMENS ENERGY & AUTOMATION INC.

3333 Old Milton Pkwy., Alpharetta, GA   30005

CEO: Thomas Malott, Pres. Tel: (770) 751-2000 Emp: N/A

Bus: *Electric & electronic equipment & systems.* Fax:(404) 751-2001 %FO: 100

SIEMENS MEDICAL SYSTEMS INC.
186 Wood Avenue South, Iselin, NJ   08830-2770
CEO: Thomas McCausland, Pres.   Tel: (908) 321-4500   Emp: N/A
Bus: *Research/mfr./marketing health care products.*   Fax:(908) 494-2250   %FO: 100

SIEMENS NIXDORF INFORMATION SYSTEMS INC. (SNI)
200 Wheeler Road, Burlington, MA   01803-5187
CEO: Edward Blechschmidt, CFO   Tel: (617) 273-0480   Emp: N/A
Bus: *Supplies & integrates computer systems &*   Fax:(617) 221-0231   %FO: 100
     peripherals, R&D.

SIEMENS POWER CORPORATION
155 108th Avenue NE, Bellevue, WA   98004-5901
CEO: Robert Stephenson, Pres.   Tel: (206) 453-4300   Emp: N/A
Bus: *Power generation equipment, nuclear fuel,*   Fax:(206) 453-4446   %FO: 100
     power plant services, photovoltaic modules &
     lasers.

SIEMENS SOLAR INDUSTRIES, LP
4650 Adohr Lane, Camarillo, CA   93012-8508
CEO: G. Oswald, Pres.   Tel: (805) 482-6800   Emp: N/A
Bus: *Supplier of photovoltaic (solar) cells and*   Fax:(805) 388-6395   %FO: 100
     panels.

SIEMENS-STROMBERG CARLSON
900 Broken Sound Pkwy., Boca Raton, FL   33487-3587
CEO: Anton Hasholzner, Pres. & CEO   Tel: (561) 955-5000   Emp: N/A
Bus: *Design/develop/mfr. systems & equipment for* Fax:(561) 955-8014   %FO: 100
     network communications (see joint parent:
     THE GENERAL ELECTRIC CO PLC,
     England)

● **SMS SCHLOEMANN-SIEMAG AG**
Eduard-Schloemann-Strasse 4, D-40237 Duesseldorf, Germany
CEO: Heinrich Weiss, Pres.   Tel: 49-211-8810   Emp: 3300
Bus: *Mfr. rolling mills and casters for the steel industry.*   Fax:49-211-8814902

SMS CAPITAL CORP.
100 Sandusky Street, Pittsburgh, PA   15212
CEO: Herbert Fastert, Pres.   Tel: (412) 231-6800   Emp: 10
Bus: *Holding company. Mfr. rolling mills and*   Fax:(412) 321-7654   %FO: 100
     casters for the steel industry.

SMS GHH, INC.
5700 Corporate Drive, Pittsburgh, PA   15237
CEO: Guenter Schieber, Pres.   Tel: (412) 364-3700   Emp: 40
Bus: *Engineering and sales of equipment for the*   Fax:(412) 364-2329   %FO: *100
     steel industry; electric arc furnaces, ladle
     furnaces, bofs, etc. (Sub of SMS CAPITAL
     CORP.)

● **SOLO KLEINMOTOREN GMBH**
Stuttgarter Strasse 41, D-71069 Sindelfingen, Germany
CEO: Hans Emmerich, Pres.   Tel: 49-7013-3010   Emp: N/A
Bus: *Mfr. chain saws, water pumps, lawnmowers,*   Fax:49-7013-301149
sprayers & trimmers.

     SOLO, INC.
     5100 Chestnut Avenue, PO Box 5030, Newport News, VA 23605
     CEO: James Dunne, Pres.   Tel: (757) 245-4228   Emp: 72
     Bus: *Mfr. chain saws, sprayers & trimmers.*   Fax:(757) 245-0800   %FO: 100

● **SPHERETEX GMBH**
Otto-Hahn Str 11, 40721 Hilden, Germany
CEO: Klaus Koelzer, Pres.   Tel: 49-2103 56081   Emp: 20
Bus: *High-tech core materials for fiberglass sandwich*   Fax:49-2103 54901
laminates.

     SPHERETEX AMERICA INC.
     985 11th Avenue South, Jacksonville Beach, FL 32250
     CEO: Klaus Koelzer, Pres.   Tel: (904) 273-0708   Emp: N/A
     Bus: *Sale/service high-tech core materials.*   Fax:(904) 273-0709   %FO: 100

● **SPRINGER-VERLAG GMBH & CO KG**
Tiergartenstrasse 17, 69121 Heidelberg, Germany
CEO: Claus Michaletz, Chrm.   Tel: 49-62-21-4870   Emp: 12646
Bus: *Publishing science, technical, medical books,*   Fax:49-62-21-487366
journals & electronic media.

     SPRINGER-VERLAG NEW YORK INC.
     175 Fifth Avenue, New York, NY 10010
     CEO: Rüdiger Gebauer, Pres.   Tel: (212) 460-1500   Emp: 250
     Bus: *Science technical books, journals.*   Fax:(212) 473-6272   %FO: 100

● **SRS HOTELS - STEIGENBERGER RESERVATION SERVICE**
Dreieichstrasse 59, D-60594 Frankfurt, Germany
CEO: Steffen Weidemann, Mgn. Dir.   Tel: 49-69-6050-9401   Emp: 100
Bus: *Hotel representation & reservation.*   Fax:49-69 6050-9450

     STEIGENBERGER RESERVATION SERVICE
     152 West 57th Street, New York, NY 10019-3301
     CEO: Edward N. Brill, VP   Tel: (212) 956-0200   Emp: 20
     Bus: *Hotel representation & reservation.*   Fax:(212) 956-2555   %FO: 100

● **STAEDTLER MARS GMBH & CO.**
Moosaeckerstrasse 3, D-90427 Nuernberg, Germany
CEO: Oskar Reutter, Mng. Dir.　　　　Tel: 49-911 93650　　Emp: 3700
Bus: *Mfr. writing & drafting materials.*　　Fax:49-911 9365400

　　　STAEDTLER, INC.
　　　21900 Plummer Street, Chatsworth, CA　91311
　　　CEO: Sal R. Elia, Pres.　　　　Tel: (818) 882-6000　　Emp: 60
　　　Bus: *Mfr. writing & drafting materials.*　Fax:(818) 882-0036　%FO: 100

● **R. STAHL GMBH**
Bergstrasse 2, 74653 Kunzelsau, Germany
CEO: Christina Monk, Coordinator　　　Tel: 49-7940-17326　　Emp: N/A
Bus: *Mfr. electronic switchgear, intrinsic safety interface*　Fax:49-7940 17333
　　systems.

　　　R. STAHL INC.
　　　150 New Boston Street, Woburn, MA　01801
　　　CEO: Winfried Faulring, Gen.Mgr.　　Tel: (617) 933-1844　　Emp: 25
　　　Bus: *Sale intrinsic safety interface systems.*　Fax:(617) 933-7896　%FO: 100

● **ANDREAS STIHL**
Badstrasse 115, D-71336 Waiblingen, Germany
CEO: Hans-Peter Stihl, CEO　　　　Tel: 49-151 260　　Emp: 3000
Bus: *Mfr. chain saws, power tools.*　　Fax:49-7151 261140

　　　STIHL INC.
　　　536 Viking Drive, PO Box 2015, Virginia Beach, VA　23450-2015
　　　CEO: F. J .Whyte, Pres.　　　　Tel: (757) 486-8444　　Emp: 400
　　　Bus: *Mfr. chain saws, power tools*　Fax:(757) 486-2825　%FO: 100

● **SUPFINA GRIESHABER GMBH & CO.**
Greuling Strasse 33, D-42859 Remscheid, Germany
CEO: Werner Nühnen, CEO　　　　Tel: 49-2191-37130　　Emp: 200
Bus: *Mfr. superfinishing machines & attachments.*　Fax:49-2191-371357

　　　SUPFINA MACHINE CO.
　　　33 Plan Way, Bldg 1, Warwick, RI　02887
　　　CEO: Wolfgang Auschner, Pres.　　Tel: (401) 738-4010　　Emp: 35
　　　Bus: *Mfr. superfinishing machines & attachments.*　Fax:(401) 738-4266　%FO: 100

- **TENGELMANN GROUP**
Wissollstrasse 5-43, D-54486 Mulheim/Ruhr, Germany
CEO: Erivan Haub, Chrm.   Tel: 49-208 58060   Emp: N/A
Bus: *Retail food chain.*   Fax:N/A

  GREAT ATLANTIC & PACIFIC TEA COMPANY INC. (A&P)
  2 Paragon Drive, Montvale, NJ   07645
  CEO: James Wood, CEO   Tel: (201) 573-9700   Emp: 90000
  Bus: *Retail food chain.*   Fax:(201) 930-4079   %FO: 53

- **TERROT STRICKMASCHINEN GMBH**
Postfach 501129, D-70341 Stuttgart, Germany
CEO: Werner Bohringer, Pres.   Tel: 49-711 70341   Emp: 420
Bus: *Mfr. large diameter circular knitting machines.*   Fax:49-711 5531111

  TERROT KNITTING MACHINES INC.
  4808 Persimmon Court, Monroe, NC   28110
  CEO: Dieter K. Nestvogel, Secty   Tel: (704) 283-9434   Emp: 5
  Bus: *Sale/service large diameter knitting mach*   Fax:(704) 289-9812   %FO: 100

- **THEODOR GROZ & SOHNE & ERNST BECKERT KG**
Postfach 249, d-72423 Albstadt, Germany
CEO: N/A   Tel: 49-7431 101   Emp: 4500
Bus: *Mfr. industrial knitting & sewing needles, felting &*   Fax:49-7431 10277
     fork needles.

  GROZ-BECKERT USA, INC.
  3480 Lakemont Blvd., Fort Mills, SC   29715
  CEO: Henry Tio, Pres.   Tel: (803) 548-4769   Emp: 48
  Bus: *Distributor/sale/service industry knitting &*   Fax:(803) 548-3544   %FO: 100
       sewing needles, felting & fork needles.

- **THIES GMBH & CO**
Borkener Strasse 155, D-48653 Coesfeld, Germany
CEO: Erich Thies, Pres.   Tel: 49-2541 7331   Emp: 500
Bus: *Mfr. textile dyeing equipment.*   Fax:49-2541 733299

  THIES CORPORATION
  PO Box 2875, Rock Hill, SC   29732-2875
  CEO: Ronald Schrell, Pres.   Tel: (803) 366-4174   Emp: 10
  Bus: *Sale/service textile dyeing equipment*   Fax:(803) 366-8103   %FO: 100

• **THYSSEN AG**
August-Thyssen-Strasse 1, D-40211 Düsseldorf, Germany
CEO: Heinz Kriwet, Chrm.   Tel: 49-211-824-1   Emp: 126987
Bus: *Mfr. industrial materials, systems & components.*   Fax:49-211-824-6000

    THE BUDD COMPANY
    3155 West Big Beaver Road, Troy, MI   48084
    CEO: David P. Williams, Pres.   Tel: (248) 643-3500   Emp: 9600
    Bus: *U.S. headquarters. Mfr. sheet metal stampings,*   Fax:(248) 643-3593   %FO: 100
        assemblies, autobody panels, prototypes &
        products for auto industry.

    CONNELLY SKIS INC.
    20621 52nd West, Lynwood, WA   98036
    CEO: Tom Stevens, Pres.   Tel: (206) 775-5416   Emp: 120
    Bus: *Mfr. water skis.*   Fax:(206) 775-5416   %FO: 100

    MILFORD FABRICATING CO.
    19200 Glendale Avenue, Detroit, MI   48223
    CEO: John Edwards, Pres.   Tel: (313) 272-8400   Emp: 440
    Bus: *Sheet metal work, auto stampings, test*   Fax:(313) 272-8370   %FO: 100
        laboratory.

    PHILLIPS TEMRO INC.
    9700 West 74th Street, Eden Prairie, MN   55344
    CEO: Brian Donaher, Pres.   Tel: (612) 941-9700   Emp: 110
    Bus: *Mfr. cold weather products for autos.*   Fax:(612) 941-2285   %FO: 100

    THYSSEN ELEVATOR COMPANY
    665 Concord Avenue, Cambridge, MA   02138
    CEO: John J. DeMartino, Pres.   Tel: (617) 547-9000   Emp: 180
    Bus: *Mfr./sale/service elevators.*   Fax:(617) 876-3167   %FO: 100

    THYSSEN HANIEL LOGISTICS, INC.
    8010 Roswell Road, Suite 300, Atlanta, GA   30350
    CEO: Gary Elsser, Pres.   Tel: (770) 353-4200   Emp: 270
    Bus: *Logistics, air freight, overseas shipping.*   Fax:(770) 698-0695   %FO: 100

    THYSSEN INC.
    400 Renaissance Center, #1700, Detroit, MI   48243
    CEO: Kenneth J. Graham, Pres.   Tel: (313) 567-5600   Emp: 350
    Bus: *Mfr./process steel.*   Fax:(313) 567-5667   %FO: 100

    THYSSEN SPECIALTY STEELS INC.
    365 Village Drive, Carol Stream, IL   60188-1828
    CEO: Holger Flieth, Pres.   Tel: (630) 682-3900   Emp: 140
    Bus: *Sale specialty steels*   Fax:(630) 682-4587   %FO: 100

TRANSIT AMERICA
1 Red Lion Rd, Philadelphia, PA   19115
CEO: Hans V. Wolff, Chrm.   Tel: (215) 934-3400   Emp: 20
Bus: *Railroad cars.*   Fax:(215) 671-9227   %FO: 100

TRANSLOGIC CORP.
10825 East 47th Avenue, Denver, CO   80239-2913
CEO: John Kennedy, Pres.   Tel: (303) 371-7770   Emp: 280
Bus: *Mfr./sales/service elevators.*   Fax:(303) 371-7870   %FO: 83

WAUPACA FOUNDRY INC.
Tower Road, PO Box 249, Waupaca, WI   54981
CEO: Donald G. Brunner, Chrm.   Tel: (715) 258-6611   Emp: 1550
Bus: *Mfr. gray iron castings*   Fax:(715) 258-6731   %FO: 100

WULFRATH REFRACTORIES INC.
6th & Center Streets, Tarentum, PA   15084
CEO: David Robertson, Pres.   Tel: (412) 224-8800   Emp: 110
Bus: *Sale refractory bricks, compounds & mortars.*   Fax:(412) 224-3353   %FO: 100

● **ALFRED TRONSER GMBH**
Postfach 63, Engelsbrand, Germany
CEO: Alfred Tronser, Pres.   Tel: 49-70827980   Emp: N/A
Bus: *Mfr. capacitors, microwave tuning elements.*   Fax:49-70802798155

  TRONSER, INC.
  2763 Route 20 East, PO Box 315, Cazenovia, NY   13035
  CEO: James Dowd, VP   Tel: (315) 655-9528   Emp: N/A
  Bus: *Mfr. capacitors, microwave tuning elements*   Fax:(315) 655-2149   %FO: 100

● **HANS TRUCK GMBH & CO. KG**
Witzlebenstrasse 7, D-45472 Muelheim/Ruhr, Germany
CEO: Hermann Hermes, Mng. Dir.   Tel: 49-208-49520   Emp: 3000
Bus: *Mfr./sales sensors for automation: inductive,*   Fax:49-208-4952-264
capacitive, ultrasonic, inductive magnetic; flow
controls, auto controls.

  TRUCK, INC.
  3000 Campus Drive, Minneapolis, MN   55441
  CEO: William A. Schneider, Pres.   Tel: (612) 553-7300   Emp: N/A
  Bus: *Mfr./distribution inductive, capacitive,*   Fax:(612) 553-0708   %FO: 90
  ultrasonic, inductive magnetic proximity
  sensors; cordsets, intrinsically safe sensors,
  controls and flow switches, junction boxes and
  bus products.

● **TRUMPF GMBH & CO**
Johann-Maus-Strasse 2, D-71254 Ditzingen, Germany
CEO: Berthold Leibinger, Pres.   Tel: 49-7156 3030   Emp: N/A
Bus: *Mfr. sheetmetal fabricating equipment, punch*   Fax:49-7156 303308
    presses, laser processing centers, portable power
    tools.

    TRUMPF AMERICA INC.
    Farmington Industrial Park, 111 Hyde Road, Farmington, CT   06032
    CEO: Daniel DeChamps, Pres.   Tel: (860) 677-9741   Emp: N/A
    Bus: *Mfr. mach tools*   Fax:(860) 677-0146   %FO: 100

● **TUV RHEINLAND**
Am Grauen Stein, D-51105 Cologne, Germany
CEO: Dr. Bruno O. Braun. CEO   Tel: 49-221-8060   Emp: 6000
Bus: *International product safety testing and certification*   Fax:49-221-806114
    services.

    TUV RHEINLAND OF North America, Inc.
    12 Commerce Road, Newtown, CT   06470
    CEO: Stephan Schmitt, Pres.   Tel: (203) 426-0888   Emp: 125
    Bus: *International product safety testing and*   Fax:(203) 270-8883   %FO: 100
        certification services.

● **UNIVERSAL MASCHINENFABRIK DR RUDOLPH SCHIEBER GMBH & CO**
Postfach 20, 73461 Westhausen, Germany
CEO: Richard Geitner, Pres.   Tel: 49-7363 880   Emp: 1000+
Bus: *Mfr. computerized flat sweater, collar & trimming*   Fax:49-7363 88230
    machines.

    UNIVERSAL KNITTING MACHINES CORP. OF AMERICA
    820 Grand Boulevard, Deer Park, NY   11729
    CEO: Alfred Stojda, EVP   Tel: (516) 242-2323   Emp: 10
    Bus: *Distribution/sale/service knitting machines.*   Fax:(516) 242-2276   %FO: 84

● **VEBA AG**
Bennigsenplatz 1, Postfach 301051, 40410 Dusseldorf, Germany
CEO: Hans Dieter Harig, Chrm.   Tel: 49-211-4579   Emp: 125158
Bus: *Holding company .Electricity*   Fax:49-211-4579-501
    production/distribution sale. (Veba is the parent
    company of Stinnes)

    BRENNTAG INTERNATIONAL CHEMICALS INC.
    4 Neshaminy Interplax, #103, Trevosa, PA   19053
    CEO: J. Hallamore, Pres.   Tel: (215) 245-1511   Emp: 14
    Bus: *Mfr. chemicals & plastics.*   Fax:(215) 245-8412   %FO: 100

CROWN CHEMICAL CORPORATION
1888 Nirvana Ave., PO Box 8899, Chula Vista, CA   92011-6197
CEO: William E. Huttner Jr, CEO   Tel: (619) 421-6601   Emp: 32
Bus: *Distribution chemicals.*   Fax:(619) 421-1127   %FO: 100

CYRO INDUSTRIES
Rockaway 80 Corp. Ctr., 100 Enterprise Dr., 7th Fl., Rockaway, NJ   07866
CEO: Matthew A. Taylor, Pres.   Tel: (201) 442-6000   Emp: 628
Bus: *Prod/distribution methyl methacrylate, mfr.*   Fax:(201) 442-6117   %FO: 50
     acrylic sheet, molding compounds. (JV with
     Rohm, GMBH)

DELTA DISTRIBUTORS INC
610 Fisher Road, Longview, TX   75604
CEO: Kevin Kessing, Pres.   Tel: (214) 759-7151   Emp: 187
Bus: *Distribution chemicals.*   Fax:(214) 759-7548   %FO: 100

EASTECH CHEMICAL CORP.
5700 Tacony Street, Philadelphia, PA   19135
CEO: Lawrence J. Kelly, Pres.   Tel: (215) 537-1000   Emp: N/A
Bus: *Sub. of Stinnes AG.*   Fax:(215) 537-8575   %FO: 100

F&S INTERNATIONAL INC.
605 Third Avenue, New York, NY   10158
CEO: Roger U. Engel, Pres.   Tel: (212) 490-1356   Emp: 45
Bus: *Distribution minerals & specialty metals.*   Fax:(212) 557-8457   %FO: 100

HULS AMERICA, INC.
220 Davidson Avenue, Somerset, NJ   08873-6821
CEO: Dr. Klaus Burzin, Pres   Tel: (908) 560-6811   Emp: 950
Bus: *Mfr./distribution pigment pastes & additives,*   Fax:(908) 560-6958   %FO: 100
     lubricants, specialty & fine chemicals, films,
     silanes & silicones.

INSIGHT ELECTRONICS, INC.
9980 Huennkens Street, San Diego, CA   92121
CEO: Greg Proven Zano, Pres.   Tel: (619) 677-3100   Emp: 241
Bus: *Mfr./distribution electronics.*   Fax:(619) 587-1380   %FO: 100

INTEROIL INC.
200 Schultz Drive, Red Bank, NJ   07701
CEO: Frank Copple, Pres.   Tel: (908) 842-4200   Emp: 14
Bus: *Trade petroleum products.*   Fax:(908) 842-5844   %FO: 100

MEMC ELECTRONIC MATERIALS INC.
501 Pearl Drive, PO Box 8, St. Peters, MO   63376
CEO: Ludger Viefhues, Pres. & CEO   Tel: (314) 279-5000   Emp: 5367
Bus: *Mfr. silicon wafers for semi-conductor*   Fax:(314) 279-5162   %FO: 100
     industry.

MILLER & COMPANY
6400 Shafer Court, S 500, Rosemont, IL   60018
CEO: Gary A. Wickham, Pres.   Tel: (847) 696-2400   Emp: 52
Bus: *Distribution specialty metal & ferro-alloys.*   Fax:(847) 696-2419   %FO: 100

PB&S CHEMICAL COMPANY
Hwy 136 W & Geneva Road, PO Box 20, Henderson, KY   42420
CEO: Thomas M. McFarland, Pres.   Tel: (502) 827-3545   Emp: 452
Bus: *Distribution chemicals.*   Fax:(502) 827-4767   %FO: 100

PRECISION NATIONAL PLATING SERVICES INC.
Six Ackerly Road, PO Box 358, Clarks Summit, PA   18411
CEO: Drew J. Anderson, Pres.   Tel: (717) 587-1191   Emp: 10
Bus: *Reconditioning/plating diesel motor parts,*   Fax:(717) 586-0900   %FO: 100
  distribution crank-shafts.

ROHACRYL INC.
13801 Riverport Drive, Maryland Heights, MO   63043
CEO: Karl-Heinz Nothnagel, Pres.   Tel: (314) 298-4106   Emp: N/A
Bus: *Holding company.*   Fax:(314) 298-4185   %FO: 100

SCHENKER INTERNATIONAL, INC.
150 Albany Avenue, Freeport, NY   11520
CEO: P. Robert Doernte, Pres.   Tel: (516) 377-3000   Emp: 700
Bus: *International freight forwarding & distribution.* Fax:(516) 377-3092   %FO: 100

SOCO CHEMICAL INC.
Pottsville Pike & Huller Lane, PO Box 13786, Reading, PA   19612
CEO: Stephen R. Clark, Pres.   Tel: (610) 926-6100   Emp: 15
Bus: *Mfr. chemicals.*   Fax:(610) 926-0411   %FO: 100

SOCO-LYNCH CHEMICAL CORP.
3270 East Washington Blvd., Los Angeles, CA   90023
CEO: Anthony J. Gerace, Pres.   Tel: (213) 269-0191   Emp: 126
Bus: *Distribution chemicals.*   Fax:(213) 264-9181   %FO: 100

SOUTHCHEM, INC.
2000 East Pettigrew, Durham, NC   27703
CEO: Gil Steadman, Pres.   Tel: (919) 596-0681   Emp: 175
Bus: *Sub of Stinnes AG.*   Fax:(919) 596-6438   %FO: 100

STINNES CORPORATION
120 White Plains Road, Tarrytown, NY   10591
CEO: Hans-Henning Maier, Pres.   Tel: (914) 366-7200   Emp: 23
Bus: *Trading wholesale chemicals, coal, metal &*   Fax:(914) 366-8226   %FO: 100
  petroleum product.

STOCKHAUSEN INC.
2401 Doyle Street, Greensboro, NC   27406
CEO: Peter Wasmer, Pres.   Tel: (910) 333-3500   Emp: 382
Bus: *Production/sale hygiene, textile & fiber*   Fax:(910) 333-3545   %FO: 100
    products for chemical industry, skin care
    products.

TEXTILE CHEMICAL CORP.
Pottsville Pike & Fuller Lane, PO Box 13788, Reading, PA   19612-3788
CEO: William E. Huttner, Sr, Pres.   Tel: (610) 926-4151   Emp: 150
Bus: *Distribution chemicals.*   Fax:(610) 926-4160   %FO: 100

VEBA CORPORATION
605 Third Avenue, 44th Fl., New York, NY   10158
CEO: Heinz-Helmer Putthof, Pres.   Tel: (212) 922-2700   Emp: 15
Bus: *Holding company.*   Fax:(212) 922-2798   %FO: 100

• **VILLEROY & BOCH AG**
Postfach 10120, D-66693 Mcttlach, Germany
CEO: Wendelin Von Boch, Mgn. Dir.   Tel: 49-6864 810   Emp: 11000
Bus: *Mfr. tableware, ceramic tiles, plumbing fixtures.*   Fax:49-6864 814456

    VILLEROY & BOCH TABLEWARE LTD.
    5 Vaughn Drive, Princeton, NJ   08540
    CEO: P. Schaus, Pres.   Tel: (609) 734-7800   Emp: 300
    Bus: *Wholesale china dinnerware, crystal stemware*   Fax:(609) 734-7840   %FO: 100
        & gifts.

• **WILLY VOGEL AG**
Motzener Strasse 35/37, D-12277 Berlin, Germany
CEO: Stefan Schindler, Chrm.   Tel: 49-30 720020   Emp: 843
Bus: *Mfr. lubrication equipment & devices for industry,*   Fax:49-30 72002111
    fluid transfer pumps.

    VOGEL LUBRICATION INC.
    1008 Jefferson Avenue, Newport News, VA   23607
    CEO: Joachim Ahrens, Pres.   Tel: (757) 380-8585   Emp: 65
    Bus: *Sale/service lubrication system & equipment,*   Fax:(757) 380-0709   %FO: 100
        fluid transfer pumps.

• **J M VOITH GMBH**
Sankt Poeltener Str 43, Postfach 1940, D-16928 Heidenheim, Germany
CEO: Dr. Hans P. Schiffer, Pres.   Tel: 49-7321-37-0000   Emp: 13000
Bus: *Hydroelectric turbines, paper machinery, power*   Fax:49-7321-37-7000
transmission engines, propellers and special drives
and machine tools.

    APPLETON MILLS
    PO Box 1899, Appleton, WI   54913
    CEO: Thomas Scheetz, Pres.   Tel: (414) 734-9876   Emp: N/A
    Bus: *Installation of stock preparation equipment.*   Fax:(414) 734-1444   %FO: 100

    VOITH HYDRO INC.
    PO Box 712, York, PA   17405
    CEO: Donald A. Bristow, Pres.   Tel: (717) 792-7000   Emp: 550
    Bus: *Mfr. hydroelectric turbines, digital & electro-*   Fax:(717) 792-7263   %FO: 100
    hydraulic governors.

    VOITH TRANSMISSIONS, INC.
    25 Winship Road, York, PA   17402
    CEO: David M. Calveley, Pres.   Tel: (717) 767-3200   Emp: N/A
    Bus: *Sales/distribution of power transmission*   Fax:(717) 767-3210   %FO: 100
    engines.

    VOITH-SLZER PAPERTECHNIC
    2620 East Glendale Avenue, Appleton, WI   54193
    CEO: Werner Kade, Pres.   Tel: (414) 731-7724   Emp: N/A
    Bus: *Machine and paper technology.*   Fax:(414) 731-0240   %FO: 100

• **VOLKSWAGEN AG**
Berliner Ring 2, D-38436 Wolfsburg, Germany
CEO: Ferdinand Piëch, Chrm.   Tel: 49-53-61-90   Emp: 242420
Bus: *Mfr. automobiles & parts.*   Fax:49-53-61-928282

    VOLKSWAGEN OF AMERICA
    3800 Hamlin Road, Auburn Hills, MI   48326
    CEO: Clive B. Warrilow, Pres.   Tel: (248) 340-5000   Emp: 1143
    Bus: *Import/marketing automobiles.*   Fax:(248) 340-4930   %FO: 100

    VORELCO INC.
    3800 Hamlin Road, Auburn Hills, MI   48326
    CEO: Wm H Devine, Gen.Mgr.   Tel: (248) 340-5000   Emp: 40
    Bus: *Commercial & industrial building operator.*   Fax:(248) 340-5525   %FO: 100

- **VOLLMER WERKE MASCHINENFABRIK GMBH**
Ehinger Str 34, D-88400 Biberach, Germany
CEO: Douglas Downs, Pres.   Tel: 49-7351 5710   Emp: N/A
Bus: *Mfr. saw sharpening machines & systems.*   Fax:49-7351 571130

  VOLLMER OF AMERICA
  1004 Parkway View Drive, Pittsburgh, PA   15205
  CEO: Douglas Downs, Pres.   Tel: (412) 787-2627   Emp: N/A
  Bus: *distribution/service saw sharpening machines*   Fax:(412) 787-9610   %FO: 100
  & systems.

- **WACKER WERKE**
Preussenstrasse 41, D-80809 Munich, Germany
CEO: Dr. Ulrich Wacker   Tel: 49-89-35402   Emp: 3000
Bus: *Mfr. light machinery.*   Fax:49-89-35402390

  WACKER CORPORATION
  N92 W15000 Anthony Avenue, Menomonee Falls, WI   53052
  CEO: Tony Meckel, VP   Tel: (414) 255-0500   Emp: 515
  Bus: *Mfr. light machinery.*   Fax:(414) 255-0550   %FO: 100

- **WAESCHLE MASCHINENFABRIK GMBH**
Niederbregerstrasse 9, D-88250 Weingarten, Germany
CEO: Mr. Wolf, Mng. Dir.   Tel: 49-751 4080   Emp: 500
Bus: *Bulk solids handling conveyor systems.*   Fax:49-750 408200

  WAESCHLE, INC.
  303 Covington Drive, Bloomingdale, IL   60108
  CEO: Heinz Schneider, Pres.   Tel: (630) 539-9100   Emp: 42
  Bus: *Bulk solids handling conveyor systems.*   Fax:(630) 539-9196   %FO: 100

- **JEAN WALTERSCHEID GMBH**
Hauptstrasse 150, 53797 Lohmar, Germany
CEO: M. Arntz, Chrm.   Tel: 49-2246 120   Emp: 1300
Bus: *Mfr. agricultural & auto shafts, driveshafts,*   Fax:49-2246 12501
couplings.

  WALTERSCHEID INC.
  16 West 030 83rd Street, Burr Ridge, IL   60521
  CEO: E. Joel Martin, Pres.   Tel: (630) 887-7022   Emp: 55
  Bus: *Mfr. agricultural driveshafts & overload*   Fax:(630) 887-8386   %FO: 100
  clutches.

• WANDEL & GOLTERMANN

Postfach 45, D-72800 Eningen, Germany
CEO: Frank Goltermann, Pres.   Tel: 49-7121 860   Emp: N/A
Bus: *Electric instruments, telecommunications measuring*   Fax:49-7121 88404
     equipment.

WANDEL & GOLTERMANN

1030 Swabia Court, Research Tri Pk, NC   27709
CEO: G. Chastelete, Pres.   Tel: (919) 941-5730   Emp: N/A
Bus: *Electric instruments, telecommunications*   Fax:(919) 941-5751   %FO: 100
     measuring equipment..

• WEIDMULLER INTERNATIONAL AG

Paderborner Strasse 175, D-38444 Detmold, Germany
CEO: W. Schubl, Pres.   Tel: 49-52-31140   Emp: N/A
Bus: *Mfr. terminal blocks & connectors.*   Fax:49-52-3114-1175

WEIDMULLER INC.

821 Southlake Blvd., Richmond, VA   23236
CEO: W. Schubl, Pres.   Tel: (804) 794-2877   Emp: 50
Bus: *Mfr./sale terminal blocks & connectors.*   Fax:(804) 794-0252   %FO: 100

• WELLA AG

Berliner Allee #65, D-64274 Darnstadt, Germany
CEO: Jorg von Craushaar, Chrm.   Tel: 49--6151-340   Emp: N/A
Bus: *Mfr. hair care products.*   Fax:49-6151-342981

WELLA CORPORATION

12 Mercedes Drive, Montvale, NJ   07645
CEO: Carl Pitsch, Pres.   Tel: (201) 930-1020   Emp: 100
Bus: *Mfr./sale hair care products.*   Fax:(201) 505-5200   %FO: 100

• WERZALIT AG & CO

Gronauer Str 70, D-71720 Oberstenfeld, Germany
CEO: N/A   Tel: 49-7062 500   Emp: 600
Bus: *Molded wood products, veneers.*   Fax:49-7062 50208

WERZALIT OF AMERICA INC.

PO Box 373, Bradford, PA   16701
CEO: Herman Henke, VP & Gen.Mgr.   Tel: (814) 362-3881   Emp: 100
Bus: *Mfr. molded wood parts.*   Fax:(814) 362-4237   %FO: 100

- **WESTDEUTSCHE LANDESBANK GIROZENTRALE**
Herzogstrasse 15, D-40217 Düsseldorf, Germany
CEO: N/A   Tel: 49-211-82601   Emp: 7000
Bus: *Commercial & investment banking services.*   Fax:49-211-8266126

> **WESTDEUTSCHE LANDESBANK GIROZENTRALE**
> 1211 Ave of the Americas, 24th Fl., New York, NY   10036-8701
> CEO: John Paul Garber, Mng. Dir.   Tel: (212) 852-6000   Emp: N/A
> Bus: *International commercial banking services.*   Fax:(212) 921-7655   %FO: 100

- **ERNST WINTER & SOHN**
Osterstrasse 58/2, 22359 Hamburg, Germany
CEO: Hans Robert Meyer, CEO   Tel: 49-40-49070   Emp: N/A
Bus: *Mfr. diamond cutting tools, grinding wheels,*   Fax:49-4- 4905102
sawblades.

> **ERNST WINTER & SOHN**
> 21 Saddleback Cove, P.O.Box 1006, Travelers Rest, SC   29690
> CEO: Paul Garner, Pres.   Tel: (864) 834-4145   Emp: 120
> Bus: *Mfr./sale diamond cutting tools.*   Fax:(864) 834-3730   %FO: 100

- **RICHARD WOLF GMBH**
Pforzheimer Strasse 32, D- 75438 Knittlingen, Germany
CEO: Ms. I. Burkhard, Mng. Dir.   Tel: 49-7043 350   Emp: N/A
Bus: *Mfr.. distribution of surgical instruments.*   Fax:49-7043-930000

> **RICHARD WOLF MEDICAL INSTRUMENT CORP.**
> 353 Corporate Woods Pkwy, Vernon Hills, IL   60061
> CEO: Ms. I. Burkhard, Mng. Dir.   Tel: (847) 913-1113   Emp: 170
> Bus: *Mfr./distribution of surgical instruments.*   Fax:(847) 913-1490   %FO: 100

- **ZAHNRAEDERFABRIK RENK AG**
Goegginger Strasse 73, D-86159 Augsburg, Germany
CEO: N/A   Tel: 49-821 5700249   Emp: 1700
Bus: *Mfr./distribution industrial gears & vehicle*   Fax:49-0821 5700226
transmissions.

> **RENK CORPORATION**
> 304 Tucapau Road, Duncan, SC   29334
> CEO: Klaus Bock, VP   Tel: (864) 433-0069   Emp: 9
> Bus: *Assembly/distribution/service sleeve bearings*   Fax:(864) 433-0636   %FO: 100

- **CARL ZEISS**
  Carl-Zeiss Strasse 4, D-73447 Oberkochen, Germany
  CEO: J .Herrmann, Chrm.   Tel: 49-7364-200   Emp: N/A
  Bus: *Mfr. of precision optical/mechanical, electrical*   Fax:49-7364-6808
       instruments & products.

      CARL ZEISS INC.
      One Zeiss Drive, Thornwood, NY   10594
      CEO: Thomas Miller, Pres.   Tel: (914) 747-1800   Emp: N/A
      Bus: *Imp/distribution/mfr. precision optical,*   Fax:(914) 682-8296   %FO: 100
           mechanical, electric instruments & products.

- **ZF FRIEDRICHSHAFEN AG**
  D-88038 Friedrichshafen, Germany
  CEO: Klaus Peter Bleyer, CEO   Tel: 49-7541-770   Emp: 32000
  Bus: *Mfr. axles, transmission & steering products for*   Fax:49-7541-772158
       on/off highway & marine markets

      ZUA AUTOPARTS INC.
      5750 McEver Road, Oakwood, GA   30566
      CEO: Gary Collar, Pres.   Tel: (770) 967-2000   Emp: 132
      Bus: *Mfr. power steering pumps (see joint parent:*   Fax:(770) 967-0827   %FO: 100
           UNISIA JECS CORP, Japan).

Greece

- **HELLENIC MEDITERRANEAN LINES CO. LTD**
P O Box 57, Piraeus, Greece
CEO: Anthony Yannoulatos, Pres.   Tel: N/A   Emp: 50
Bus: *Cruise & ferry service.*   Fax:N/A

    HELLENIC MEDITERRANEAN LINES
    1 Hallidie Plaza, San Francisco, CA   94102
    CEO: Ralph Hartl, Mgr.   Tel: (415) 989-7434   Emp: 3
    Bus: *Cruise & ferry service.*   Fax:(415) 986-4037   %FO: 100

- **NATIONAL BANK OF GREECE**
86 Eolou, GR-102 32 Athens, Greece
CEO: Theordora Karatzas, Governor   Tel: 301-321-0411   Emp: N/A
Bus: *Commercial banking services.*   Fax:301-321-3119

    ATLANTIC BANK OF NEW YORK
    960 Ave. of the Americas, 14th Fl., New York, NY   10001
    CEO: P. Venetis, Pres.   Tel: (212) 695-5400   Emp: 350
    Bus: *Commercial banking services.* Fax:(212) 267-1612   %FO: 100

    NATIONAL BANK OF GREECE
    168 N. Michigan Avenue, Chicago, IL   60601
    CEO: Vassilios Katsaras, Mgr.   Tel: (312) 641-6600   Emp: 25
    Bus: *Banking services.*   Fax:(312) 263-4195   %FO: 100

- **THE OLAYAN GROUP**
206 Syngrou Av., PO Box 75046 Kalilithea, Athens 17610, Greece
CEO: Aziz D Syriani, Pres.   Tel: 30-1-958-2515   Emp: N/A
Bus: *Holding company. (See Saudi Arabia.)*   Fax:30-1-959-5818

    COMPETROL REAL ESTATE LTD.
    505 Park Avenue, 10th Fl., New York, NY   10022
    CEO: Anthony S. Fusco, VP   Tel: (212) 750-4800   Emp: 10
    Bus: *Real estate investment services.*   Fax:(212) 308-3654   %FO: 100

    OLAYAN AMERICA CORP.
    505 Park Avenue, 10th Fl., New York, NY   10022
    CEO: John O. Wolcott, EVP   Tel: (212) 750-4800   Emp: 15
    Bus: *Business development & advisory services.*   Fax:(212) 308-3654   %FO: 100

● **OLYMPIC AIRWAYS SA**
96 Syngrou, GR-117 41 Athens, Greece

CEO: Jordan Karatzas	Tel: 30-1-926-9111	Emp: 8500
Bus: *Commercial air transport services.*	Fax:30-1-926-7154	

OLYMPIC AIRWAYS
645 Fifth Avenue, New York, NY 10022

CEO: Dimitris Chryssikopoulos, Dir.	Tel: (212) 735-0200	Emp: 103
Bus: *Commercial air transport services.*	Fax:(212) 735-0215	%FO: 100

Guatemala

● **AVIATECA GUATEMALAN AIRLINES**
Avda Hincapie, 12-22 Zone 13, Guatemala City, Guatemala
CEO: N/A   Tel: 50-22-31-82-22   Emp: N/A
Bus: *Commercial air transport services.*   Fax:N/A

> **AVIATECA GUATEMALAN AIRLINES**
> SW Freeway, Houston, TX   77032
> CEO: Juan Brother, Mgr.   Tel: (713) 665-2882   Emp: N/A
> Bus: *International commercial air transport*   Fax:(713) 665-1691   %FO: 100
>   *services.*

> **AVIATECA GUATEMALAN AIRLINES**
> 68824 Veterans Blvd., Ste.100, Metairie, LA   70003
> CEO: Tony Diaz, Mgr.   Tel: (504) 887-7411   Emp: N/A
> Bus: *International commercial air transport*   Fax:(504) 887-7856   %FO: 100
>   *services.*

> **AVIATECA GUATEMALAN AIRLINES**
> 5885 NW 18th Avenue, Miami, FL   33142
> CEO: E. Dela Vega, Mgr.   Tel: (305) 876-0036   Emp: N/A
> Bus: *International commercial air transport*   Fax:(305) 871-2667   %FO: 100
>   *services.*

Guyana

- **GUYANA AIRWAYS CORPORATION**
32 Main Street, Georgetown, Guyana
CEO: F. Kahn, Gen. Mgr.   Tel: 592-2-59492   Emp: N/A
Bus: *Commercial air transport.*   Fax:592-2-60032

    GUYANA AIRWAYS CORPORATION
    883 Flatbush Avenue, Brooklyn, NY   11226
    CEO: William Braithwaite, Mgr.   Tel: (718) 693-8000   Emp: N/A
    Bus: *International commercial air transport.*   Fax:(718) 941-2367   %FO: 100

Hong Kong

● **AIR LINK CORPORATION, LTD.**
23 Bailey Street, Kowloon, Hong Kong
CEO: Daniel Fong, Mdg. Dir.   Tel: 852-764-0233   Emp: 75
Bus: *Air freight forwarding services.*   Fax:N/A

    AIR LINK (USA), INC.
    248-06 Rockaway Blvd., Jamaica, NY   11422
    CEO: James Penson, Pres.   Tel: (718) 949-2888   Emp: 50
    Bus: *Air freight forwarding.*   Fax:(718) 712-2284   %FO: JV

● **THE BANK OF EAST ASIA, LIMITED**
10 Des Voeux Road, Central, Hong Kong
CEO: Dr. David K. P. Li, Pres.   Tel: 852-2842-3200   Emp: N/A
Bus: *Commercial banking services.*   Fax:852-2842-9333

    THE BANK OF EAST ASIA, LIMITED
    600 Wilshire Blvd., Ste. 1550, Los Angeles, CA   90017
    CEO: Victor Li, Mgr.   Tel: (213) 892-1572   Emp: 15
    Bus: *International commercial banking services.*   Fax:(213) 892-1004   %FO: 100

    THE BANK OF EAST ASIA, LIMITED
    202 Canal Street, New York, NY   10013
    CEO: Wahtang Peng, VP & Gen.Mgr.   Tel: (212) 233-8833   Emp: 60
    Bus: *International commercial banking services.*   Fax:(212) 219-8299   %FO: 100

● **CATHAY PACIFIC AIRWAYS (sub of Swire Pacific Ltd.)**
Swire House, 5th Fl., 9 Connaught Road, Central District, Hong Kong
CEO: Peter Dennis Antony, Chrm.   Tel: 852-2747-5210   Emp: 14216
Bus: *Commercial air transport services.*   Fax:852-2810-6563

    CATHAY PACIFIC AIRWAYS
    590 Fifth Avenue, New York, NY   10036
    CEO: Ian Callender, VP   Tel: (212) 819-0210   Emp: 6
    Bus: *Commercial air transport services.*   Fax:(212) 944-6519   %FO: 100

    SWIRE PACIFIC HOLDINGS
    875 South West Temple, Salt Lake City, UT   84101
    CEO: Jack Pelo, Pres.   Tel: (801) 530-5300   Emp: N/A
    Bus: *Bottler/distributor of beverages.*   Fax:(801) 530-5342   %FO: 100

● **CHIAP HUA INDUSTRIES, LTD.**
Whole Bldg, 396 Kwun Tong Road, Kwun Tong, Kowloon, Hong Kong
CEO: Herb Cheng, Pres.   Tel: N/A   Emp: N/A
Bus: *Mfr. clock movements.*   Fax:852-2667-5501

     EQUITY INDUSTRIES CORPORATION
     5721 Bayside Road, Virginia Beach, VA 23455
     CEO: Bruce Thomas, Pres.   Tel: (757) 460-2483   Emp: 16
     Bus: *Distributor clock movements, hands & dials.*   Fax:(757) 464-1144   %FO: 100

● **CHINA PATENT AGENT (HK) LTD.**
22/F. Great Eagle Centre, 23 Harbour Rd, Wanchi, Hong Kong
CEO: Songyu Zheng, Chrm. & Gen. Mgr.   Tel: 852-2828-4688   Emp: 250
Bus: *Intellectual property service; consultants, representatives & other legal services.*   Fax:852-2827-1018

     CHINA PATENT & TRADEMARK AGENT (USA) LTD.
     1 World Trade Center, Suite 2957, New York, NY 10048
     CEO: Yansheng Yu, VP   Tel: (212) 912-1870   Emp: 3
     Bus: *Intellectual property service; consultants, representatives & other legal services.*   Fax:(212) 912-1873   %FO: 100

● **CHINA PEARL COMPANY**
Room 1209, Tower 1, Silvercord, 30 Canton Road, Tsimshatsui Kowloon, Hong Kong
CEO: Anna Lam, Pres.   Tel: 852-2736-0038   Emp: N/A
Bus: *Mfr./distribution ceramics and chinaware.*   Fax:852-2735-3298

     CCA INTERNATIONAL, INC.
     328 Thomas Street, Newark, NJ 07114
     CEO: Hung Lam, Pres.   Tel: (201) 817-8337   Emp: N/A
     Bus: *Distribution/sale ceramics and porcelain dinnerware.*   Fax:(201) 817-8552   %FO: 100

● **CHINESE CERAMIC ARTS F E COMPANY, LTD.**
Tung Ning Bldg #1002-3, 249-253 Des Voeux Road, Central, Hong Kong
CEO: Anna Lam, CEO   Tel: 852-2736-6003   Emp: N/A
Bus: *Ceramics and chinaware.*   Fax:852-2735-3298

     CCA INTL, INC.
     328 Thomas Street, Newark, NJ 07114
     CEO: Hung Lam, VP   Tel: (201) 817-8337   Emp: N/A
     Bus: *China and giftware.*   Fax:(201) 817-8552   %FO: 100

● **EISENBERG & COMPANY (UDI), LTD.**
St. John's Building, 15th Fl., 33 Garden Road 7/F, Central, Hong Kong
CEO: A. Hamburger, Dir.   Tel: N/A   Emp: N/A
Bus: *Import/export services.*   Fax:N/A

    EISENBERG & COMPANY USA AGENCY, INC.
    4 East 39th Street, New York, NY   10016
    CEO: Oded Dimant, Pres.   Tel: (212) 683-9400   Emp: N/A
    Bus: *Import/export services.*   Fax:(212) 683-9417   %FO: 100

● **FIRST NATIONAL TRADING, LTD.**
2/F Block C Startex Ind. Bldg. 14, Tai Yau Street, San Po Kong, Kowloon, Hong Kong
CEO: N/A   Tel: 852-23-222231   Emp: N/A
Bus: *Import/export trading company.*   Fax:N/A

    FIRST NATIONAL TRADING, CO., INC.
    855 Avenue of the Americas, #626, New York, NY   10001
    CEO: Paul Shen, Pres.   Tel: (212) 695-1097   Emp: N/A
    Bus: *Import/export trading company.*   Fax:(212) 695-2867   %FO: 100

● **FLYING CRANE H.K. LTD.**
A2 Hang Fung Ind Bldg., 2G Hok Yuen Street, 2/F, Hunghom, Kowloon, Hong Kong
CEO: N/A   Tel: 852-2766-9668   Emp: N/A
Bus: *Import/export services.*   Fax:N/A

    SENTEX ENTERPRISES INC.
    45 West 36th Street, 7th Fl., New York, NY   10018
    CEO: David Turetzky, Mgr.   Tel: (212) 564-5506   Emp: N/A
    Bus: *Import/export services.*   Fax:(212) 564-5542   %FO: 100

● **C. GORDON & COMPANY, LTD.**
Profit Industrial Bldg, Kwai Fung Crescent, Kwai Chung, Hong Kong
CEO: Gordon Chow, Dir.   Tel: 852-2420-4667   Emp: N/A
Bus: *Export services.*   Fax:852-2480-4667

    C. GORDON & COMPANY, LTD. (USA)
    630 Fifth Avenue, Ste.2215, New York, NY   10020
    CEO: Tom Cunow, Mgr.   Tel: (212) 541-8322   Emp: N/A
    Bus: *Importers.*   Fax:(212) 977-4360   %FO: 100

● **HECNY TRANSPORTATION LTD.**
111 Wai Yip Street, Kwun Tong, Kowloon, Hong Kong
CEO: Charles Lee, Chrm.   Tel: 852-2751-4304   Emp: N/A
Bus: *Freight forwarding.*   Fax:852-2798-7719

    HECNY TRANSPORTATION, LTD.
    147-48 175th Street, Jamaica, NY   11434
    CEO: Jim Georgakis, Mgr.   Tel: (718) 656-5537   Emp: N/A
    Bus: *Freight forwarding.*   Fax:(718) 632-8491   %FO: 100

- **HIRAOKA**

Railroad Plaza, 15th Fl., 37-43 Chatham Road South, Tsim Sha Tsui Kowloon, Hong Kong

CEO: Mr. Hiraoka, Pres.   Tel: N/A   Emp: N/A

Bus: *Mfr. electronic products, computers and fishing*   Fax:852-2723-0511
   equipment

    HIRAOKA NEW YORK, INC.

    79 Madison Avenue, Ste. 1210, New York, NY   10016

    CEO: T. Saski Hiraoka, Pres.   Tel: (212) 686-0492   Emp: N/A

    Bus: *Distributor/service electronic products,*   Fax:(212) 725-9693   %FO: 100
   computers and fishing equipment.

- **HONG KONG CARPET MFG, LTD.**

Hutchinson House, 63 Wohyihop Rd., Regent Ctr., Tower A, Dwai Chunt, Central District, Hong Kong

CEO: Gilbert Lee, Pres.   Tel: 852-2521-6281   Emp: N/A

Bus: *Mfr. carpets.*   Fax:N/A

    WORLD WIDE LOOMS, LTD.

    150 East 55th Street, New York, NY   10022

    CEO: Gilbert Lee, Pres.   Tel: (212) 752-4142   Emp: N/A

    Bus: *Sale/distribution of carpets.*   Fax:(212) 371-2355   %FO: JV

- **HONG KONG TELECOMMUNICATIONS LIMITED**

Hong Kong Telecom Tower, TaiKoo Place, 979 Kings Road, Quarry Bay, Hong Kong

CEO: Linus W.L. Cheung   Tel: 852-2888-2888   Emp: 15000

Bus: *Telecommunciations services. (See Cable &*   Fax:852-2877-2877
   Wireless plc)

    HONG KONG TELECOMMUNICATIONS LIMITED

    777 Third Avenue, New York, NY   10017

    CEO: Thomas Mac Donald, VP   Tel: (212) 593-4813   Emp: N/A

    Bus: *Telecommunciations services.*   Fax:(212) 593-9069   %FO: 100

- **JARDINE MATHESON HOLDINGS LTD.(Sub of Bermuda based parent.)**

Jardine House, Connaught Road, P O Box 70 GPO, Central, Hong Kong

CEO: Alasdair G. Morrison, Mng. Dir.   Tel: 852-843-8388   Emp: 200000

Bus: *Active in engineering/construction, financial*   Fax:852-845-9005
   services, marketing & distribution, real estate,
   transportation services, food service.

    JARDINE INSURANCE BROKERS, INC.

    333 Bush Street, Ste.500, San Francisco, CA   94104-2878

    CEO: David J. Batchelor, Pres. & CEO   Tel: (415) 391-2600   Emp: 1035

    Bus: *Insurance brokerage.*   Fax:(415) 773-4475   %FO: 100

THEO H. DAVIES & CO., LTD
841 Bishop Street, Ste. 2300, Honolulu, HI 96802
CEO: Martin J. Jaskot, Pres.   Tel: (808) 532-6500   Emp: N/A
Bus: *Property development, insurance, freight*   Fax:(808) 532-6544   %FO: 100
   forwarding, investment advisory.

THEO H. DAVIES, EUROMOTORS, LTD.
124 Wiwoole Street, Hilo, HI 96720
CEO: Jim Crowley, Gen. Mgr.   Tel: (808) 961-6087   Emp: N/A
Bus: *Import/sales/service automobiles.*   Fax:(808) 935-4949   %FO: 100

● **THE KA WAH BANK LTD.**
232 Des Voeux Road, Central, Hong Kong
CEO: Song Yihan, Pres. & CEO   Tel: 852-2545-7131   Emp: N/A
Bus: *Commercial banking services.*   Fax: N/A

   THE KA WAH BANK LTD
   11 East Broadway, 2nd. Fl., New York, NY 10038
   CEO: Peter Zhao, Exec. VP & Gen. Mgr.   Tel: (212) 732-8868   Emp: 40+
   Bus: *Commercial banking services.*   Fax:(212) 791-3776   %FO: 100

● **KING FOOK FINANCE COMPANY**
30-32 Des Voeux Road, Central, Hong Kong
CEO: Mr. Yeung, Pres.   Tel: 852-2523-5111   Emp: N/A
Bus: *Export jewelry, arts, crafts and antiques.*   Fax: N/A

   KING FOOK NY COMPANY, LTD.
   675 Fifth Avenue, New York, NY 10022
   CEO: Kin Yeung, EVP   Tel: (212) 355-3636   Emp: N/A
   Bus: *Imp/retail jewelry, arts, crafts and antiques.*   Fax:(212) 688-1081   %FO: 100

● **KYCE ENTERPRISE (HK) LTD.**
Shun Wai Ind Bldg., 15 Yuk Yat Street, Kowloon, Hong Kong
CEO: Yuk Yun-Kit, Dir.   Tel: 852-3764-7255   Emp: N/A
Bus: *Mfr. watches and consumer electronics.*   Fax: 852-3764-1401

   KYCE, INC.
   4801 Metropolitan Avenue, Ridgewood, NY 11385
   CEO: Y. K. Yuk, Pres.   Tel: (718) 383-1799   Emp: N/A
   Bus: *Import watches and consumer electronics.*   Fax:(718) 628-1038   %FO: 100

● **LIU CHONG HING BANK, LTD.**
24 Des Voeux Road, Central, Hong Kong
CEO: Mr. Liu, Pres   Tel: N/A   Emp: N/A
Bus: *Commercial banking services.*   Fax:852-2845-9134

   LIU CHONG HING BANK LTD.
   601 California Street, San Francisco, CA 94108
   CEO: K. Hong Chan, VP & Br. Mgr.   Tel: (415) 433-6404   Emp: N/A
   Bus: *International banking services.*   Fax:(415) 433-0686   %FO: 100

● **ORIENT OVERSEAS CONTAINER LINES, LTD.**
Harbour Centre, 25 Harbour Road, Hong Kong
CEO: T.R. Chang, Pres.   Tel: 852-5833-3888   Emp: N/A
Bus: *International steamship transport, freight*   Fax:852-5833-3777
forwarding.

    OOCL (USA), INC.
    4141 Hacienda Drive, Pleasanton, CA 94588
    CEO: C.L. Ting, Pres.   Tel: (510) 460-4800   Emp: N/A
    Bus: *International steamship transport, freight*   Fax:(510) 468-2870   %FO: 100
    forwarding.

    OOCL (USA), INC.
    88 Pine Street, 8th Fl., New York, NY 10005
    CEO: C.L. Ting, Pres.   Tel: (212) 428-2200   Emp: 60
    Bus: *International steamship transport, freight*   Fax:(212) 428-2297   %FO: 100
    forwarding.

● **THE PENINSULA GROUP**
8/F St. George Building, 2 Ice House Street, Central District, Hong Kong
CEO: Oono Poortier, Pres.   Tel: 852-2840-7488   Emp: N/A
Bus: *Operates hotels, tourism industry.*   Fax:852-2845-5508

    THE PENINSULA GROUP
    333 North Michigan Avenue, Ste.1120, Chicago, IL 60601
    CEO: Hedi Weber, VP, Sales & Marketing   Tel: (312) 263-6069   Emp: N/A
    Bus: *Sales; hotels, tourism industry.*   Fax:(312) 263-3744   %FO: 100

● **PEREGRINE INVESTMENTS HOLDINGS LTD.**
New World Tower, 16-18 Queens Rd, Central, Hong Kong
CEO: Philip Leigh Tose, Chrm   Tel: 852-2825-1888   Emp: 150
Bus: *Banking & investment services, securities*   Fax:852-2845-9411
broker/dealer, and property investments.

    PEREGRINE BROKERAGE INC.
    780 Third Ave, #2601, New York, NY 10017
    CEO: Timothy Voake, Mgr.   Tel: (212) 593-5920   Emp: 50
    Bus: *Securities broker/dealer.*   Fax:(212) 593-5932   %FO: 100

● **SHANGHAI COMMERCIAL BANK LTD.**
12 Queen's Rd, Central, Hong Kong
CEO: John Yan, Gen.Mgr.   Tel: 852-841-5415   Emp: 1000
Bus: *Commercial banking services.*   Fax:852-810-4623

    SHANGHAI COMMERCIAL BANK LTD.
    231 Sansome Street, San Francisco, CA 94104
    CEO: David Kwok, Sr VP & Mgr   Tel: (415) 433-6700   Emp: 26
    Bus: *International commercial banking services.*   Fax:(415) 433-0210   %FO: 100

SHANGHAI COMMERCIAL BANK LTD.
135 William Street, New York, NY   10038
CEO: Daniel Chan, VP & Mgr.   Tel: (212) 619-7070   Emp: 15
Bus: *International commercial banking services.*   Fax:(212) 619-7077   %FO: 100

● **SUN HUNG KAI & CO LTD.**
Admiralty Center, 3/F, 8 Harcourt Rd, Hong Kong
CEO: Tony Fung, Mgn. Dir.   Tel: 852-2822-5678   Emp: N/A
Bus: *Merchant banking, stock brokerage & securities*   Fax:852-2822-5678
services.

   SUN HUNG KAI SECURITIES (US) INC
   1 World Trade Center, Ste. 3915, New York, NY   10048
   CEO: K C Poon, Pres.   Tel: (212) 321-1929   Emp: N/A
   Bus: *Merchant banking, stock brokerage &*   Fax:(212) 321-1940   %FO: 100
      securities services.

● **SUNHAM & COMPANY, LTD.**
14 On Lan Street, Hong Kong
CEO: Mr. Yung, Pres.   Tel: 852-2522-8388   Emp: N/A
Bus: *Mfr. linens.*   Fax:N/A

   SUNHAM & COMPANY
   308 Fifth Avenue, New York, NY   10001
   CEO: Albert Yung, Pres.   Tel: (212) 695-1218   Emp: N/A
   Bus: *Sale/distribution of linens.*   Fax:(212) 947-4793   %FO: 100

● **SWIRE PACIFIC LIMITED**
Rm. 423, Swire House #9, Connaught Road, Central Hong Kong
CEO: H. J. Cony-Beare, Chrm.   Tel: 852-2840-8934   Emp: 37000
Bus: *Holding company; commercial air & sea transport,*   Fax:852-2810-1071
beverages, real estate development & investment,
petroleum exploration , entertainment media, food
distribution, trading & financial services.

   CATHAY PACIFIC AIRLINES LTD.
   300 N. Continental Blvd., El Segundo, CA   90245
   CEO: Ian Callendar, VP   Tel: (310) 615-1113   Emp: N/A
   Bus: *International air transport services. (See*   Fax:(310) 615-0042   %FO: 100
      Cathay Pacific Airlines, Ltd.)

   SWIRE COCA-COLA, USA
   875 South West Temple, Salt Lake City, UT   84101
   CEO: Jack Pelo, Pres.   Tel: (801) 530-5300   Emp: N/A
   Bus: *Bottler/distributor of beverages.*   Fax:(801) 530-5342   %FO: 100

   SWIRE PACIFIC HOLDING, INC.
   875 South West Temple, Salt Lake City, UT   84101
   CEO: Craig Taylor, Pres. & CEO   Tel: (801) 530-5300   Emp: N/A
   Bus: *US headquarters.*   Fax:(801) 530-5342   %FO: 100

● **TAIPING CARPETS, LTD.**
63 Wo Yi Sop Road, Kwai Chung, Central District, Hong Kong
CEO: Gilbert Lee, Pres.   Tel: 852-2521-6281   Emp: N/A
Bus: *Mfr. carpets.*   Fax:N/A

    WORLD WIDE LOOMS, LTD.
    150 East 55th Street, New York, NY   10022
    CEO: Gilbert Lee, Pres.   Tel: (212) 752-4142   Emp: N/A
    Bus: *Import/sale carpets.*   Fax:(212) 371-2355   %FO: JV

● **TEXWOOD, LTD.**
6 How Ming Street, Kowloon, Hong Kong
CEO: S. Tam, Pres.   Tel: 852-2797-7415   Emp: N/A
Bus: *Wearing apparel.*   Fax:N/A

    TEXWOOD, INC. (USA)
    850 Seventh Avenue, New York, NY   10019
    CEO: N/A   Tel: (212) 262-8383   Emp: 10
    Bus: *Textiles and wearing apparel.*   Fax:(212) 262-9787   %FO: 100

● **WING LUNG BANK LTD.**
45 Des Voeux Road, Central Hong Kong
CEO: Michael Po-Ko Wu, Chrm.   Tel: 852-2826-8333   Emp: N/A
Bus: *Commercial banking services.*   Fax:N/A

    WING LUNG BANK LTD.
    445 South Figueroa Street
    Suite 2270, Los Angeles, CA   90070
    CEO: Anthony Yip, VP   Tel: (213) 489-4193   Emp: N/A
    Bus: *International banking services.*   Fax:(213) 489-3545   %FO: 100

● **WING ON COMPANY INTERNATIONAL LTD.**
30th Floor, Wing On House, 71 des Voeux Road, Central Hong Kong
CEO: Karl Kwok, Chrm.   Tel: 852-2523-4091   Emp: 3700
Bus: *Department stores, real estate, and automobile*   Fax:852-2522-3173
    dealeerships.

    DAH CHONG HONG TRADING COMPANY
    362 Fifth Avenue, New York, NY   10001
    CEO: Sha-Wai Lam. Pres.   Tel: (212) 947-6860   Emp: 1300
    Bus: *Import/export trading company.*   Fax:(212) 244-1457   %FO: 100

Hungary

- **NAGY ÉS TRÓCSÁNYI**
Pálya Utca 9, H-1012 Budapest, Hungary
CEO: Peter Nagy, Mng. Ptnr.   Tel: 36-1-212-0444   Emp: N/A
Bus: *International law firm.*   Fax:36-1-212-0443

     NAGY ÉS TRÓCSÁNYI
     1114 Avenue of the Americas, New York, NY   10036
     CEO: Peter Nagy, Mng. Ptnr.   Tel: (212) 626-4206   Emp: N/A
     Bus: *International law firm.*   Fax:(212) 626-4208   %FO: 100

- **RECOGNITA CORP.**
Marvany Str 17, H-1012 Budapest, Hungary
CEO: Akos Reszler, Mgn Dir.   Tel: 36-1-2018925   Emp: 75
Bus: *Optical character recognition software and other*   Fax:36-1-2017607
document imaging applications

     RECOGNITA CORP OF AMERICA
     100 Cooper Court, Los Gatos, CA   94086
     CEO: Robert Teresi, CEO   Tel: (408) 241-5772   Emp: 20
     Bus: *OCR software, document imaging applications.*   Fax:(408) 354-2743   %FO: 100

- **TAURUS RUBBER CO LTD.**
Kerepesi ut 17, H-1087 Budapest, Hungary
CEO: Laszlo Toth, Pres.   Tel: 36-1-210-0900   Emp: 4000
Bus: *Rubber products and services*   Fax:36-1-113-5434

     TAURUS INTL INC.
     409 Mimisink Road, Totowa, NJ   07512
     CEO: Peter Kavacs, Pres.   Tel: (201) 785-3400   Emp: 6
     Bus: *Distribute/sale/service tires (truck,*   Fax:(201) 785-9277   %FO: 100
agricultural)

Iceland

● **ICELANDAIR**
Reykjavik Airport, 101 Reykjavik, Iceland
CEO: Hodur Sigurgestsson, Chrm.   Tel: 354-505-0300   Emp: 1280
Bus: *International passenger air carrier.*   Fax:354-505-0350

    ICELANDAIR
    5950 Symphony Woods Road, Ste. 410, Columbia, MD   21044
    CEO: Gunnar Eklund, Director   Tel: (410) 715-5110   Emp: 120
    Bus: *International passenger air carrier.*   Fax:(410) 715-3547   %FO: 100

● **OZ INTERACTIVE INC.**
Snorrabraut 54, Reykjavik 105, Iceland
CEO: Skuli Mogensen, Pres.   Tel: 354-535-0035   Emp: 70
Bus: *Software company.*   Fax:354-535-0055

    OZ INTERACTIVE INC.
    525 Brannan Street, 4th Fl., San Francisco, CA   94107
    CEO: Garry Hare, COO   Tel: (415) 536-0500   Emp: 20+
    Bus: *Software company.*   Fax:(415) 536-0536   %FO: 100

India

● **AIR-INDIA**
Air-India Bldg Nariman Point, Bombay 400 021, India
CEO: S. R. Gupte, Mgn Dir.　　　　　　　　　　Tel: 91-22-202-4142　　Emp: N/A
Bus: *Commercial air transport services.*　　　　Fax:91-22-283-1210

　　　AIR-INDIA
　　　345 Park Avenue, New York, NY   10154
　　　CEO: S. Ghose, Reg Dir　　　　　　　　　Tel: (212) 407-1300　　Emp: N/A
　　　Bus: *International commercial air transport*　Fax:(212) 838-9533　　%FO: 100
　　　　　services.

● **BANK OF BARODA**
3 Walchand Hirachand, Bombay 400 038, India
CEO: P.N. Shah, Gcn. Mgr.　　　　　　　　　　Tel: 91-22-260341　　Emp: N/A
Bus: *Commercial banking services.*　　　　　　Fax:N/A

　　　BANK OF BARODA
　　　One Park Ave., New York, NY   10016
　　　CEO: G.A.Nayak, Mgr　　　　　　　　　　Tel: (212) 578-4550　　Emp: N/A
　　　Bus: *Banking services.*　　　　　　　　　Fax:(212) 578-4565　　%FO: 100

● **BANK OF INDIA**
Express Towers, Nariman Point, Bombay 400 021, India
CEO: V.H.Ramakrishnan, Mng. Dir.　　　　　　Tel: 91-22-202-3020　　Emp: 54000
Bus: *Commercial banking services.*　　　　　　Fax:91-22-202-2831

　　　BANK OF INDIA
　　　277 Park Avenue, New York, NY   10172
　　　CEO: Mrs. Ranjana Kumar, Sr. VP　　　　　Tel: (212) 753-6100　　Emp: 55
　　　Bus: *International banking services.*　　　　Fax:(212) 980-0052　　%FO: 100

● **BHARAT ELECTRONICS LTD.**
116/2 Race Course Road, Bangalore 560 001, India
CEO: Dr. V. K. Koshy, Chrm.　　　　　　　　　Tel: 91-80-226 7322　　Emp: 19000
Bus: *Mfr. semiconductor devices, communication and*　Fax:91-80-226 8410
　　radar systems.

　　　BHARAT ELECTRONICS LTD.
　　　53 Hilton Avenue, Garden City, NY   11530
　　　CEO: T. R. Prasad, Gen.Mgr.　　　　　　　Tel: (516) 248-4020　　Emp: 10
　　　Bus: *Procurement of electronic components and*　Fax:(516) 741-5894　　%FO: 100
　　　　export to India for in-house use.

● **DCM DATA PRODUCTS**
Vikrant Towers, 4 Rajendra Place, New Delhi 110 008, India
CEO: Hemant Bharat Ram, Exec. Dir.   Tel: 91-11-5719967   Emp: 800
Bus: *Software programming service; mfr. computers and*   Fax:91-11-5755731
     related equipment, software products and service.

     DCM DATA PRODUCTS
     610 One Tandy Center, Fort Worth, TX   76102
     CEO: P. V. Ullal, Resident Mgr.   Tel: (817) 870-2202   Emp: 28
     Bus: *Sales/service software products, board level*   Fax:(817) 336-2416   %FO: 100
          products.

     DCM DATA SYSTEMS
     1200 Quail Street, Suite 280, Newport Beach, CA   92660
     CEO: Knvss Ram, VP   Tel: (714) 724-0802   Emp: 68
     Bus: *Software programming service*   Fax:(714) 724-0803   %FO: 100

● **HMT (INTL) LTD.**
17 Ali Asker Road, Bangalore 560 052, India
CEO: N. Ramanuga, Chrm.   Tel: 91-80-2264163   Emp: 28000
Bus: *Mfr. machine tools, agricultural tractors, watches,*   Fax:91-80-2267053
     bearings, plastics; engineering and non-engineering
     projects.

     HMT (INTL) LTD
     15 Mary Bill Drive, Troy, OH   45373
     CEO: Damaroo Shah, Pres.   Tel: (937) 339-4680   Emp: 5
     Bus: *Sales/service machine tools, tractors, watches,*   Fax:(937) 339-7581   %FO: 100
          bearings.

● **OBEROI GROUP OF HOTELS**
7 Sham Nath Marg, Delhi 110 054, India
CEO: Andred Quinlan, CEO   Tel: 91-11-2525464   Emp: 18000
Bus: *Develop and manage hotel properties.*   Fax:91-11-2929800

     OBEROI GROUP OF HOTELS
     509 Madison Avenue, Ste. 1906, New York, NY   10017
     CEO: Caroline Wilson-Kent, NA Sales Mgr.   Tel: (212) 223-8800   Emp: 4
     Bus: *Develop and manage hotel properties.*   Fax:(212) 223-8500   %FO: 100

● **STATE BANK OF INDIA**
Madam Cama Road, Bombay 400 021, India
CEO: P.G.Kakodkar, Chrm.   Tel: 91-22-202-2426   Emp: 226200
Bus: *Commercial banking services.*   Fax:91-22-204-0073

     STATE BANK OF INDIA
     460 Park Avenue, 2nd Fl., New York, NY   10022
     CEO: D.P. Roy, Pres. & CEO   Tel: (212) 521-3200   Emp: 200+
     Bus: *International banking services.*   Fax:(212) 521-3364   %FO: 100

STATE BANK OF INDIA
39 Broadway, New York, NY   10005
CEO: B. Rao, Pres.   Tel: (212) 785-6633   Emp: 26
Bus: *International banking services.*   Fax:(212) 422-6248   %FO: 100

STATE BANK OF INDIA
707 Wilshire Blvd., Ste.11995, Los Angeles, CA   90017
CEO: Birendra Kumar, Mgr.   Tel: (213) 623-7250   Emp: N/A
Bus: *International banking services.*   Fax:(213) 622-2069   %FO: 100

STATE BANK OF INDIA
2001 Pennsylvania Avenue, NW, Ste 625, Washington, DC   20006
CEO: Remesh Khurana, Rep.   Tel: (202) 223-5579   Emp: N/A
Bus: *International banking services.*   Fax:(202) 785-3739   %FO: 100

STATE BANK OF INDIA
19 South LaSalle Street, Ste. 200, Chicago, IL   60603
CEO: B.L. Pattwardhan, Pres.   Tel: (312) 621-1200   Emp: N/A
Bus: *International banking services.*   Fax:(312) 321-0740   %FO: 100

● **STATE TRADING CORP. OF INDIA LTD.**
Jawawar Vyapar Shawan, Tolstoy Marg, New Delhi 110 001, India
CEO: B. K. Chaturveds, Chrm.   Tel: 91-11-332-3002   Emp: N/A
Bus: *General commodities incl. chemicals, rice, wheat,*   Fax:91-11-332-6459
     tea, coffee, oils, textile/leather/sporting goods &
     medical disposables

STATE TRADING CORP OF INDIA
445 Park Avenue, 18th Floor, New York, NY   10022
CEO: G. Jeyakumar, Mgr.   Tel: (212) 753-0770   Emp: 5000
Bus: *Trading company; organizes all products from*   Fax:(212) 888-6159   %FO: 100
     India

● **TATA SONS LTD.**
Bombay House, 24 Homi Mody Street, Bombay 400 001, India
CEO: Ratan N. Tata, Chrm.   Tel: 91-22-204-9131   Emp: 70000
Bus: *Largest industrial conglomerate: TISCO iron &*   Fax:91-22-204-9522
     steel, TELCO engineering & locomotive, mfr.
     commercial vehicles, computer software, tea
     production, hotels, energy, telecommunications,
     other consumer products.

TATA INC.
101 Park Avenue, New York, NY   10178
CEO: Ashok Mehta, Pres.   Tel: (212) 557-7979   Emp: 10
Bus: *US headquarters, diversified conglomerate,*   Fax:(212) 557-7987   %FO: 100
     ngineeing & locomotive, mfr. commercial
     vehicles, computer software, tea production,
     hotels, (US:Lexington Hotel, NY; Executive
     Plaza, Chicago; Hampshire Hotel, D.C.)

● **VOLTAS LTD.**
19 JN Heredia Marg, Ballard Estate, Bombay 400 001, India
CEO: A. H. Tobaccowala, Chrm.   Tel: 91-22-2618131   Emp: 8500
Bus: *Mfr. divers consumer and industrial products and*   Fax:91-22-2618504
    equipment.

VOLTAS LTD.
101 Park Avenue, 26th Fl., New York, NY   10178
CEO: R.M. Gupte, Mgr.   Tel: (212) 557-8393   Emp: 15
Bus: *Import/export engineering equipment, granite*   Fax:(212) 557-8395   %FO: 100
    products, contracting projects, technology
    transfers

Indonesia

- **BANK BUMI DAYA**
Jalan Imam Bonjol 61, Jakarta Pusat, Indonesia
CEO: I. Prawiranata, Pres.   Tel: 62-21-230-0300   Emp: N/A
Bus: *Commercial banking services.*   Fax:62-21-318-7900

    BANK BUMI DAYA
    350 Park Avenue, 10th Floor, New York, NY 10022
    CEO: Taplan Nainggolan, Gen. Mgr.   Tel: (212) 735-5300   Emp: N/A
    Bus: *International banking services.*   Fax:(212) 371-4122   %FO: 100

- **BANK BUMIPUTRA MALAYSIA BERHAD**
Jalan Melaka, 50913 Kiala Lumpur, Malaysia
CEO: N/A   Tel: 329-81011   Emp: N/A
Bus: *General banking services.*   Fax:329-87135

    BANK BUMIPUTRA MALAYSIA BERHAD
    900 Third Avenue, 11th Floor, New York, NY 10022
    CEO: Abdul Kadir Mahmud, Gen.Mgr.   Tel: (212) 644-1280   Emp: N/A
    Bus: *International banking services.*   Fax:(212) 644-1874   %FO: 100

- **BANK CENTRAL ASIA**
J. L. Jendral, Sudirman Kav 22-23, Jakarta 12920, Indonesia
CEO: N/A   Tel: 21-520-8650   Emp: N/A
Bus: *Commercial banking services.*   Fax:21-571-0928

    BANK CENTRAL ASIA
    641 Lexington Avenue, New York, NY 10022
    CEO: Wee Beng Aw, Gen. Mgr.   Tel: (212) 888-3300   Emp: N/A
    Bus: *International banking services.*   Fax:(212) 223-1333   %FO: 100

    BANK CENTRAL ASIA
    180 Madison Avenue, New York, NY 10022
    CEO: Wee Beng Aw, Gen. Mgr.   Tel: (212) 889-1000   Emp: N/A
    Bus: *International banking services.*   Fax:(212) 223-1333   %FO: 100

- **BANK DANANG NASIONAL INDONESIA**
Jl. M. H. Thamrin 5, P.O. Box 1338, 10340 Jakarta, Indonesia
CEO: Subagyo Karsono, Dir.   Tel: 62-21-230-1107   Emp: N/A
Bus: *General commercial banking services.*   Fax:62-21-230-0330

    BANK DANANG NASIONAL INDONESIA
    45 Broadway, New York, NY 10005
    CEO: N/A   Tel: (212) 809-8600   Emp: N/A
    Bus: *International commercial banking services.*   Fax:(212) 797-1287   %FO: 100

● **PT BANK EKSPOR IMPOR INDONESIA (Persero) JAKARTA**
Jalan Jenderal Gatot subroto Kav, 36-38, Jakarta 12190, Indonesia
CEO: N/A   Tel: 62-21-526-3436   Emp: N/A
Bus: *Commercial banking services.*   Fax:62-21-526-3621

    PT BANK EKSPOR IMPOR INDONESIA (Persero)
    100 Wall Street, 18th Floor, New York, NY   10005
    CEO: James F. Marx, Gen. Mgr.   Tel: (212) 509-6191   Emp: N/A
    Bus: *International banking services.*   Fax:(212) 509-2007   %FO: 100

● **BANK INDONESIA**
Jalan M.H. Thamrin No.2, Jakarta 10010, Indonesia
CEO: J. Soedradjad Djiwandono, Gov.   Tel: 62-21-231-0108   Emp: N/A
Bus: *Government banking activities.*   Fax:62-21-231-0592

    BANK INDONESIA
    One Liberty Plaza, 165 Broadway, 31st Fl., New York, NY   10006
    CEO: Sulastinah Tirtonegoro, Rep.   Tel: (212) 732-1958   Emp: N/A
    Bus: *Government banking activities.*   Fax:(212) 732-4003   %FO: 100

● **BANK NEGARA INDONESIA**
Jalan Lada #1, Jakarta-Kota 10001, Indonesia
CEO: Widigdo Sukarman, Pres.   Tel: 62-21-570-0908   Emp: N/A
Bus: *International banking services.*   Fax:62-21-570-0980

    BANK NEGARA INDONESIA
    One Exchange Pl., 55 Broadway, 26th Fl., New York, NY   10006
    CEO: Dewa Suthapa, Gen.Mgr..   Tel: (212) 943-4750   Emp: N/A
    Bus: *International banking services.*   Fax:(212) 344-5723   %FO: 100

● **PT BANK RAKYAT INDONESIA**
Jl. Jenderai Sudirman 44-46, P.O. Box 1094, 10210 Jakarta, Indonesia
CEO: Bantu Hardjijo, Pres.   Tel: 62-21-251-0244   Emp: N/A
Bus: *Government & commercial banking services.*   Fax:62-21-250-0077

    BANK RAKYAT INDONESIA
    430 Park Avenue, New York, NY   10022
    CEO: C. M. Arief, Mgr.   Tel: (212) 750-0222   Emp: N/A
    Bus: *International commercial banking services.*   Fax:(212) 750-0648   %FO: 100

● **PT DJAKARTA LLOYD**
Sangga Buana Bldg., Jalan Senan Raya No.44, Jakarta 10410, Indonesia
CEO: Dr. H.M. Muntaqa, Pres.   Tel: 62-21-345-6208   Emp: N/A
Bus: *International steamship ocean transport services.*   Fax:62-21-380-2545

    DJAKARTA LLOYD INC.
    50 Broad Street, #815, New York, NY   10004
    CEO: Tomi Ibnu Hasjim, Pres   Tel: (212) 344-0426   Emp: 5
    Bus: *Steamship agents.*   Fax:(212) 363-4176   %FO: 100

• **PT GARUDA INDONESIA**
Jl.Medan Merdeka Selatan No.13, Jakarta, Indonesia
CEO: M. Soepandi, Chrm.   Tel: 62-21-231-1962   Emp: 14026
Bus: *Commercial air transport services.*   Fax:62-21-231-1962

    GARUDA INDONESIA AIRLINE
    317 Madison Avenue, New York, NY   10022
    CEO:M. Soepandi, Chrm.   Tel: (212) 370-0707   Emp: N/A
    Bus: *Commercial air transport services.*   Fax:(212) 949-3299   %FO: 100

• **LIPPO BANK**
Menara Asia 8th Floor, Jalan Diponegoro No. 101, LIPPO Karawaci Tangerang 15810, Indonesia
CEO: N/A   Tel: N/A   Emp: N/A
Bus: *International banking services, investments.*   Fax:N/A

    LIPPO BANK
    711 West College Street, Los Angeles, CA   90012
    CEO:James Per Lee, Pres.   Tel: (213) 625-1888   Emp: 30
    Bus: *International banking services. Main United*   Fax:(213) 680-9725   %FO: 100
        States office, branches in San Francisco,
        Westminster and San Jose, CA

    LIPPO BANK
    1001 Grant Avenue, San Francisci, CA   94133
    CEO:James Per Lee, Pres.   Tel: (415) 982-3572   Emp: 50
    Bus: *International banking services.*   Fax:(415) 986-1919   %FO: 100

Iran

● **BANK MELLI IRAN**
Ferdoesi Avenue, Tehran 11354, Iran
CEO: Asadollah Amirsiani, Chrm.   Tel: 98-21-3231   Emp: 32000
Bus: *Banking services.*   Fax:98-21-302813

    BANK MELLI IRAN
    767 Fifth Avenue, 44th Floor, New York, NY   10153
    CEO: Gholamreza Rahi, Chief Rep.   Tel: (212) 759-4700   Emp: N/A
    Bus: *International banking services.*   Fax:(212) 759-4704   %FO: 100

● **BANK SADERAT IRAN**
Bank Saderat Tower, 43 Somayeh Street, P.O.Box 15745-631, Tehran, Iran
CEO: M.R. Moghaddasi, Chrm. & Mng.Dir.   Tel: 98-21-832699   Emp: 30000
Bus: *Commercial banking services. Government Bank.* Fax:98-21-880-9539

    BANK SADERAT IRAN
    120 East 56th Street, Suite 410, New York, NY   10022
    CEO: Ali Eliassi, Gen. Mgr.   Tel: (212) 753-6400   Emp: 2
    Bus: *International banking services.*   Fax:(212) 223-3726   %FO: 100

● **BANK SEPAH-IRAN**
Iman Khomeini Square, Tehran, Iran
CEO: Abolghasem Djamshidi, Chrm.   Tel: 98-21-311-12718   Emp: N/A
Bus: *Commercial banking services. Government Bank.* Fax:98-21-311-2138

    BANK SEPAH-IRAN
    650 Fifth Avenue, New York, NY   10022
    CEO: H. Kosari, Mgr.   Tel: (212) 974-1777   Emp: N/A
    Bus: *International commercial banking services.* Fax: %FO: 100

Ireland

● **AER LINGUS**
PO Box 180, Dublin Airport, Dublin, Ireland
CEO: Gary McGann, Gp. Chief Exec.   Tel: 353-1-705-2222   Emp: 10000
Bus: *Commercial air transport services.*   Fax:353-1-705-3833

    AER LINGUS
    538 Broad Hollow Road, Melville, NY   11747
    CEO: Jack Foley, Sr VP   Tel: (516) 577-5700   Emp: 350
    Bus: *International air transport services.*   Fax:(516) 752-2045   %FO: 100

● **ALLIED IRISH BANKS, PLC**
PO Box 2748, AIB Intl. Ctr. IFSC Dublin 1, Ireland
CEO: T. P. Mulcahy, CEO   Tel: 353-1-874-0222   Emp: N/A
Bus: *Commercial banking services.*   Fax:353-1-679-7127

    ALLIED IRISH BANKS
    405 Park Avenue, New York, NY   10022
    CEO: Brian M. Leeney, EVP   Tel: (212) 339-8000   Emp: 100
    Bus: *International commercial banking.*   Fax:(212) 339-8008   %FO: 100

    FIRST MARYLAND BANKCORP.
    25 South Charles Street, PO Box 1596, Baltimore, DE   21203
    CEO: Frank P. Bramble, Pres.   Tel: (410) 244-4830   Emp: N/A
    Bus: *Commercial and consumer credit services.*   Fax:(410) 244-4459   %FO: 100

    FIRST MARYLAND LEASE CORP.
    25 South Charles Street, PO Box 1596, Baltimore, MD   21203
    CEO: George Wood, Pres.   Tel: (410) 244-3840   Emp: N/A
    Bus: *Lease financing services.*   Fax:(410) 244-3878   %FO: 100

    FIRST MARYLAND LIFE INSURANCE & MARKETING CO.
    25 South Charles Street, P.O.Box 1596, Baltimore, MD   21203
    CEO: Robert H. Zmijewski, Pres.   Tel: (410) 244-4000   Emp: N/A
    Bus: *Insurance services.*   Fax:(410) 244-3751   %FO: 100

    FIRST MARYLAND MORTGAGE CORP.
    25 South Charles Street, PO Box 1596, Baltimore, MD   21203
    CEO: Robert O'Hara, Pres.   Tel: (410) 787-6003   Emp: N/A
    Bus: *Commercial & consumer mortgage services.*   Fax:(410) 787-6189   %FO: 100

    FIRST MARYLAND NATIONAL BANK
    25 South Charles Street, PO Box 1596, Baltimore, MD   21203
    CEO: Jeremiah E. Casey, Chrm.   Tel: (410) 244-4000   Emp: 2000+
    Bus: *Commercial banking services.*   Fax:(410) 244-4026   %FO: 100

FIRST OMNI BANK, N.A.
Mitchell Street, Millsboro, DE   19966
CEO: Richard H. White, Pres.   Tel: (302) 934-9232   Emp: N/A
Bus: *Commercial banking services.*   Fax:(302) 934-2926   %FO: 100

THE YORK BANK & TRUST COMPANY
107 West Market Street, York, PA   17405-0869
CEO: Susan Keating, Pres.   Tel: (717) 771-0888   Emp: N/A
Bus: *Commercial banking & trust services.* Fax:(717) 843-2047   %FO: 100

● **ARTHUR COX**
41/45 St. Stephen's Green, Dublin 2, Ireland
CEO: Padrig Oriordain, Mng. Ptnr.   Tel: 353-1-676-4661   Emp: N/A
Bus: *International law firm.*   Fax:353-1-676-6905

ARTHUR COX
115 East 57th Street, Ste. 1230, New York, NY   10022
CEO: John Menton, Mng. Ptnr.   Tel: (212) 759-0808   Emp: N/A
Bus: *International law firm.*   Fax:(212) 355-3594   %FO: 100

● **BANK OF IRELAND**
Lower Baggot Street, Dublin 2, Ireland
CEO: Patrick Molloy, Pres.   Tel: 353-1661-6433   Emp: N/A
Bus: *Banking services.*   Fax:353-1661-6869

BANK OF IRELAND
640 Fifth Avenue, New York, NY   10019
CEO: Peter Hooper, CEO   Tel: (212) 397-1700   Emp: N/A
Bus: *International banking services.*   Fax:(212) 397-1700   %FO: 100

BANK OF IRELAND ASSET MANAGEMENT (U.S.)
Two Greenwich Plaza, Greenwich, CT   06830
CEO: Dennis Curran, Pres.   Tel: (203) 869-0111   Emp: N/A
Bus: *Investment advisory services.*   Fax:(203) 869-0268   %FO: 100

● **CRH PLC**
Belgard Castle, Clondalkin, Dublin 22, Ireland
CEO: Donald Godson, CEO   Tel: 353-1-404 1000   Emp: N/A
Bus: *Building materials manufacture and distribution.* Fax:353-1-404 1415

OLDCASTLE, INC.
375 Northridge Road, Suite 350, Atlanta, GA   30350
CEO: Liam O'Mahony, CEO   Tel: (770) 804-3360   Emp: N/A
Bus: *Building materials manufacture and*   Fax:(770) 673-2400   %FO: 100
    distribution.

- **ELAN CORPORATION PLC**
Monksland, Athlone, Westmeath, Ireland
CEO: Donal Gearney, Chrm.   Tel: 353-902-94666   Emp: 800
Bus: *Mfr. and research pharmaceuticals.*   Fax:353-902-92427

> **ELAN PHARMACEUTICAL RESEARCH CORP.**
> 1300 Gould Drive, SW, Gainesville, GA   30504
> CEO: Arlene Ocampo, Pres.   Tel: (770) 534-8239   Emp: 70
> Bus: *Mfr./research pharmaceuticals.*   Fax:(770) 534-8247   %FO: 100

- **JEFFERSON SMURFIT GROUP LTD.**
Beech Hill, Clonskeagh, Dublin 4, Rep of Ireland
CEO: M.W.J. Smurfit, Chrm.   Tel: 353-1-269-6622   Emp: 37000
Bus: *Corrugated paper and board, print, packaging and*   Fax:353-1-269-4481
     newsprint.

> **JEFFERSON SMURFIT CORPORATION**
> 8182 Maryland Avenue, Clayton, MO   63105
> CEO: Michael Smurfit, Pres.   Tel: (314) 746-1100   Emp: 20000
> Bus: *Mfr. paper and paperboard packaging.*   Fax:(314) 746-1259   %FO: 50

> **SEQUOIA PACIFIC SYSTEMS CORPORATION**
> 1030 North Anderson Road, Exeter, CA   93221
> CEO: Derry Hobson, VP, Mgr.   Tel: (209) 592-2191   Emp: 300
> Bus: *Commercial printing services.*   Fax:(209) 592-8380   %FO: 100

- **McCANN FITZGERALD, SOLICITORS**
2 Harbourmaster Place, Custom House Dock, Dublin 1, Ireland
CEO: Ronan Molony, Chrm.   Tel: 353-1-829-0000   Emp: 150
Bus: *International law firm. Dublin, New York, London,*   Fax:353-1-829-0010
     Brussels.

> **McCann FitzGerald**
> 320 Park Avenue, New York, NY   10022
> CEO: Alan J. Daly, Resident Assoc.   Tel: (212) 508-3110   Emp: 3
> Bus: *International law firm. Dublin, New York,*   Fax:(212) 508-3111   %FO: 100
>   *London, Brussels.*

- **WATERFORD WEDGWOOD LTD**
Kilbarry, Waterford, Ireland
CEO: Anthony J.F. O'Reilly, CEO   Tel: 353-513-73311   Emp: 4800
Bus: *Manufacturing and marketing of lead crystal and*   Fax:353-513-78539
     china.

> **WATERFORD WEDGWOOD USA INC**
> 1330 Campus Pkwy., Wall, NJ   07719
> CEO: Christopher J. Mc Gillivary, CEO   Tel: (908) 938-5800   Emp: N/A
> Bus: *Marketing of crystal and china.*   Fax:(908) 938-7108   %FO: 100

Israel

• ADIPAZ, LTD.
20 Pier Koenig Street, Box 10325, Jerusalem 91102, Israel
CEO: J. Shals, Pres.   Tel: 972-2-678-3887   Emp: N/A
Bus: *Mfr. jewelry ropes, chains.*   Fax:972-2-678-3884

ADIPAZ, LTD./COLOSSEUM
17 East 45th Street, Suite 800, New York, NY   10036
CEO: Joseph Kaniel, Sales Mgr.   Tel: (212) 557-0060   Emp: 5
Bus: *Mfr. jewelry ropes, chains.*   Fax:(212) 557-4765   %FO: 100

• ALADDIN SOFTWARE SECURITY INC.
15 Bein Oved Street, Tel Aviv 61110, Israel
CEO: Yanki Margalit, Pres.   Tel: 972-3-636-2222   Emp: N/A
Bus: *Develop/sales/installation/service software for security systems.*   Fax:972-3-537-5796

ALADDIN KNOWLEDGE SECURITY INC.
350 Fifth Avenue, Suite 6614, New York, NY   10118
CEO: Ami Dar, Pres.   Tel: (212) 564-5678   Emp: 18
Bus: *Develop/sales/installation/service software for security systems.*   Fax:(212) 564-3377   %FO: 100

• ALLIANCE TIRES & RUBBER
P.O. Box 48, Hadera 38100, Israel
CEO: A. Esroni, Pres.   Tel: 972-6-624-0520   Emp: N/A
Bus: *Mfr. tires.*   Fax:N/A

ALLIANCE TIRES & RUBBER U.S.A., INC.
56 West 45th Street, Suite 1504, New York, NY   10036
CEO: Leslie Gurland, Gen.Mgr.   Tel: (212) 575-2700   Emp: 10
Bus: *Tire distributor.*   Fax:(212) 706-2733   %FO: 100

• AMERICAN ISRAELI PAPER MILLS LTD.
Industrial Zone, .O.Box 142, Hadera 38101, Israel
CEO: Yaacov Yerushalmi, CEO   Tel: 972-6-634-9349   Emp: 2135
Bus: *Mfr. paper & paper products.*   Fax:972-6-633-9740

AMERICAN ISRAELI PAPER LTD.
Green, Lind & McNulty, 1435 Morris Ave., Union, NJ   07083
CEO: Philip Y. Sardoff, SVP   Tel: (908) 686-7500   Emp: N/A
Bus: *Mfr. paper & paper products.*   Fax:(908) 686-4757   %FO: 100

● **BANK HAPOALIM BM**
50 Rothschild Blvd., Tel Aviv, Israel
CEO: Amiram Sivan, Chrm.   Tel: 972-3-567-3333   Emp: N/A
Bus: *Commercial banking services.*   Fax:972-3-560-7028

> **BANK HAPOALIM**
> 1177 Avenue of the Americas, New York, NY   10036
> CEO: Arie Abend, Reg. Mgr.   Tel: (212) 782-2000   Emp: 200
> Bus: *Commercial banking branch office.*   Fax:(212) 782-2007   %FO: 100

> **BANK HAPOALIM**
> 1515 Market Street, Philadelphia, PA   19102
> CEO: Jonathan Kulka, Mgr.   Tel: (215) 665-2200   Emp: N/A
> Bus: *Commercial banking branch office.*   Fax:(215) 665-3566   %FO: 100

● **BANK LEUMI LE ISRAEL BM**
24-32 Yehuda, Halevi Street, Tel Aviv 65546, Israel
CEO: G. Maor, CEO   Tel: 972-3-514-8111   Emp: N/A
Bus: *Commercial banking services.*   Fax:972-3-566-1812

> **BANK LEUMI LE ISRAEL - Chicago Branch**
> 100 North Lasalle Street, Chicago, IL   60602
> CEO: Dr. Zalman Segal, Pres.   Tel: (312) 781-1800   Emp: 35
> Bus: *International commercial banking.*   Fax:(312) 781-1946   %FO: 100

> **BANK LEUMI LE ISRAEL - Beverly Hills Branch**
> 8383 Wilshire Blvd., Ste. 400, Beverly Hills, CA   90211
> CEO: Dr. Zalman Segal, Pres.   Tel: (213) 966-4700   Emp: 60
> Bus: *International commercial banking.*   Fax:(213) 653-9608   %FO: 100

> **BANK LEUMI LE ISRAEL**
> 579 Fifth Avenue, New York, NY   10173
> CEO: Dr. Zalman Segal, Pres.   Tel: (407) 407-4000   Emp: 50
> Bus: *US agency headquarters; commercial banking* Fax:(212) 407-4455   %FO: 100
>   *services.*

> **BANK LEUMI LE ISRAEL - Miami Branch**
> 800 Brickell, Suite 1400, Miami, FL   33131
> CEO: Dr. Zalman Segal, Pres.   Tel: (305) 376-6500   Emp: 35
> Bus: *International commercial banking.*   Fax:(305) 377-6540   %FO: 100

> **BANK LEUMI TRUST COMPANY OF NY**
> 579 Fifth Avenue, New York, NY   10017
> CEO: Aaron Kacarginsky, Sr.EVP   Tel: (212) 407-4400   Emp: 340
> Bus: *NY Branch banking office.*   Fax:(212) 407-4411   %FO: 100

● **CARMEL WINES**
25 Carmel Street, Rishon Lezion 75100, Israel
CEO: Abrah Ben-Moshe, Chrm.   Tel: N/A   Emp: N/A
Bus: *Winery.*   Fax:9723-966-3129

   CARMEL FOOD U.S.A., INC.
   245 Great Neck Road, Great Neck, NY   11020
   CEO: Stephen Anchin, Pres.   Tel: (516) 466-1888   Emp: 10
   Bus: *Distributor; wine.*   Fax:(516) 466-1114   %FO: 100

● **CUBITAL LTD.**
13 Hasahna Street, Raanana, Israel 42650
CEO: Uta Baron, Pres.   Tel: 972-9-741-6888   Emp:
Bus: *Mfr. rapid prototyping equipment.* Fax:972-9-741-9937

   CUBITAL, INC.
   13075 Allen Drive, Troy, NY   48083
   CEO: Uta Baron, Pres.   Tel: (248) 585-7880   Emp: 85
   Bus: *Customer support office; sales/distribution of*   Fax:(248) 585-7884   %FO: 100
      rapid prototyping equipment.

● **DEAD SEA LABORITORIES, LTD.**
Kibbutz Mitzpe Shalem 90670, Israel
CEO: N/A   Tel: 972-2-945-100   Emp: 150
Bus: *Develop & mfr. cosmetics.*   Fax:972-2-945-122

   AHAVA USA, INC.
   2001 West Main Street, Stamford, CT   06902
   CEO: Brett Goldberg, Gen.Mgr.   Tel: (203) 357-1914   Emp: 40
   Bus: *Develop/mfr./market cosmetics.* Fax:(203) 973-0242   %FO: 100

● **DIVA HIRSCHTAL LTD.**
119 Herzl Street, Tel Aviv 66555, Israel
CEO: N/A   Tel: 972-3-683-9151   Emp: N/A
Bus: *Mfg. sportswear.*   Fax:972-3-682-8649

   DIVA FASHIONS, INC.
   1411 Broadway, 4th Floor, New York, NY   10018
   CEO: Joseph Kaminsky, Gen.Mgr.   Tel: (212) 840-7898   Emp: 13
   Bus: *Mfr./sale sportswear.*   Fax:(212) 575-5035   %FO: 100

● **ECI TELECOM LTD.**
30 Hasivim Street, Petah Tokva, Israel 49517
CEO: N/A   Tel: 972-3-926-6555   Emp: N/A
Bus: *Telecommunications services.*   Fax:972-3-926-6500

> **ECI TELECOM INC**
> 927 Fern Street, Altamonte Springs, FL   32701
> CEO: J.R.Kennedy, Pres.   Tel: (407) 331-5500   Emp: N/A
> Bus: *Telecommunications services.*   Fax:(407) 767-0330   %FO: 100

● **EL AL ISRAEL AIRLINES**
Ben Gurion Airport, Lod 71285, Israel
CEO: Rafael Harlev, Pres. & Gen.Mgr.   Tel: 972-39-716111   Emp: 3417
Bus: *International air transport services.* Fax:972-39-721442

> **EL AL ISRAEL AIRLINES**
> 120 W 45th Street, New York, NY   10036-9998
> CEO: Michael Gat, Gen.Mgr.   Tel: (212) 852-0600   Emp: N/A
> Bus: *International air transport services.* Fax:(212) 852-0641   %FO: 100

● **ELBIT SYSTEMS, LTD.**
Advance Technology Center, Haifa, Israel 31053
CEO: Joseph Ackerman, CEO   Tel: 972-4-831-5315   Emp: N/A
Bus: *Mfr. electronic products.*   Fax:972-4-855-0317

> **ELBIT INC.**
> 16 Esquire Road, No. Bellerica, MA   21862
> CEO: N/A   Tel: (978) 670-5555   Emp: N/A
> Bus: *Mfr. electronic products.*   Fax:(978) 667-1046   %FO: 100

> **ELBIT SYSTEMS, INC.**
> 4020 North McArthur Blvd., Suite 122-329, Irving, TX   75038
> CEO: Neil Morris, Pres.   Tel: (972) 257-3311   Emp: N/A
> Bus: *Mfr. electronic products.*   Fax:(972) 257-9719   %FO: 100

> **ESW, INC.**
> 4700 Marine Creek Pkwy, Fort Worth, TX   76179
> CEO: Tim Taylor, Pres.   Tel: (817) 234-6600   Emp: N/A
> Bus: *Mfr. electronic products.*   Fax:(817) 234-6768   %FO: 100

● **ELSCINT LTD. - Advanced Technology Center**
P.O.Box 550, Haifa 31004, Israel
CEO: Jonathan Adareth, Pres.   Tel: 972-4-831-0492   Emp: N/A
Bus: *Mfr. MRI, CATScan and nuclear medical equipment.* Fax:972-4-855-0552

> **ELSCINT, INC.**
> 505 Main Street, Hackensack, NJ   07601
> CEO: Peter Annand, CEO   Tel: (201) 342-2020   Emp: N/A
> Bus: *Sales/service MRI, CATScan and nuclear* Fax:(201) 342-3782   %FO: 100
>   *medical equipment.*

- **GOTTEX MODELS LTD.**
  62 Anilevitch Street, Tel Aviv 67060, Israel
  CEO: N/A   Tel: 972-3-538-7777   Emp: N/A
  Bus: *Design/mfr. swim and beach wear.*   Fax:972-3-333-412

      GOTTEX OF ISRAEL, INC.
      1400 Broadway, New York, NY   10018
      CEO: Miriam Ruzow, Pres.   Tel: (212) 354-1240   Emp: N/A
      Bus: *Design/mfr./sale swim and beach wear.* Fax:(212) 302-3851   %FO: 100

- **IDE TECHNOLOGIES, LTD.**
  13 Zarchin Road, P.O.Box 591, Raanana 43104, Israel
  CEO: David Waxman, CEO   Tel: 972-9-747-9777   Emp: N/A
  Bus: *Mfr. water desalinization plants.*   Fax:972-9-747-9715

      AMBIENT TECHNOLOGY
      2999 N.E. 191st Street, Suite 407, North Miami Beach, FL   33180
      CEO: Phil Elovle, Pres.   Tel: (305) 937-0610   Emp: N/A
      Bus: *Install/service water desalinization plants.* Fax:(305) 937-2137   %FO: 100

- **ISPRA ISRAEL PRODUCT RESEARCH CO., LTD.**
  16 Galgalei Haplada Street, Herzlia, 46130 Israel
  CEO: Jacob Biali, CEO   Tel: 972-99-555-464   Emp: N/A
  Bus: *Mfr. tear gas, and anti-riot gear.*   Fax:972-99-55-9146

      ADVANCED MATERIALS LABORATORIES
      70-09 Austin Street, Suite 205, Forest Hills, NY   11375
      CEO: Malka Geller, Pres.   Tel: (718) 520-8910   Emp: 5
      Bus: *Sale/distributor tear gas, and anti-riot gear.* Fax:(718) 520-8411   %FO: JV

- **ISRAEL AIRCRAFT INDUSTRIES LTD.**
  Ben Gurion Int'l Airport, Tel Aviv 70100, Israel
  CEO: Moshe Keret, Pres.   Tel: 972-3-935-3237   Emp: 13200
  Bus: *Mfr. business jet aircraft, electronic systems,* Fax:972-3-935-8974
       unmanned space vehicles; upgrade civilian &
       military aircraft.

      IAI INTERNATIONAL, INC.
      50 West 23rd Street, New York, NY   10010
      CEO: David Onn, Pres.   Tel: (212) 620-4404   Emp: 15
      Bus: *Marketing, product support; business jet*   Fax:(212) 620-1799   %FO: 100
           aircraft, electronic systems, unmanned space
           vehicles; upgrade civilian & military aircraft.

      IAI INTERNATIONAL, INC.
      1700 North Moore Street, Arlington, VA   22032
      CEO: Itzhak Sharon, VP   Tel: (703) 875-3723   Emp: N/A
      Bus: *Marketing, product support; business jet*   Fax: %FO: 100
           aircraft, electronic systems, unmanned space
           vehicles; upgrade civilian & military aircraft.

● **ISRAEL DISCOUNT BANK LTD.**
27 Yehuda Halevi Street, Tel Aviv 65546, Israel
CEO: Gideon Lahav, Chrm.   Tel: 972-3 5145555   Emp: 5500
Bus: *Commercial banking services.*   Fax:972-3-5145346

    ISRAEL DISCOUNT BANK OF NY
    511 Fifth Avenue, New York, NY   10017
    CEO: A.Sheer, Pres.   Tel: (212) 551-8500   Emp: 530
    Bus: *Commercial banking services.*   Fax:(212) 370-9623   %FO: 100

    ISRAEL DISCOUNT BANK OF NY
    1350 Broadway, New York, NY   10023
    CEO: Anthony R. Esposito   Tel: (212) 714-5660   Emp: 100
    Bus: *Commercial banking services.*   Fax: %FO: 100

● **KOOR INDUSTRIES LTD.**
4 Kaufman Street, Tel Aviv 68012, Israel
CEO: Benjamin D. Gaon, Pres.   Tel: 972-3-519-5201   Emp: 20600
Bus: *Diversified industries; electronics,*   Fax:972-3-519-5353
telecommunications, agrochemicals, food,
construction, steel, tourism & international trade.

    KOOR 2000, INC.
    1270 Avenue of the Americas, Suite 2307, New York, NY   10020
    CEO: Adina Brenner, Pres.   Tel: (212) 765-5050   Emp: 3
    Bus: *Liaison, corporate development.*   Fax:(212) 765-3375   %FO: 100

● **LASER INDUSTRIES LTD.**
Atidim Industrial Park, P.O.Box 13135, Neve Sherett, Tel Aviv 61131, Israel
CEO: Ben Gibli, Pres.   Tel: 972-3-645-4545   Emp: 350
Bus: *Medical lasers.*   Fax:972-3-645-4500

    SHARPLAN LASERS INC
    One Pearl Court, Allendale, NJ   07401
    CEO: Michael Kochman, Pres.   Tel: (201) 327-1666   Emp: 90
    Bus: *Sales/distribution medical lasers.* Fax:(201) 445-4048   %FO: 100

● **MAGIC SOFTWARE ENTERPRISES LTD.**
5 Haplada Street, Or Yehuda 60218, Israel
CEO: David Assia, CEO   Tel: 972-3-538-9292   Emp: N/A
Bus: *Software applications & development systems &*   Fax:972-3-583-9333
training.

    MCE, INC.
    1200 Main Street, Irvine, CA   92714
    CEO: Mike Hassen, VP   Tel: (714) 250-1718   Emp: 50
    Bus: *Software applications & development systems*   Fax:(714) 250-7404   %FO: 100
    & training.

● **NETAFIM**
Kibutz Hatzerim, M P Hanegev 85420, Israel
CEO: Yigal Stav, Pres.   Tel: 972-7-473111   Emp: 420
Bus: *Mfr./distribution micro-irrigation components.*   Fax:972-7-420038

    NETAFIM USA INC.
    5470 East Home Avenue, Fresno, CA   93727
    CEO: Zvi Sella, Pres.   Tel: (209) 453-6800   Emp: 69
    Bus: *Mfr./distribution micro-irrigation components,*   Fax:(209) 453-6803   %FO: 100
        filters, micro-sprinklers.

● **OPHIR OPTRONICS LTD.**
P. O. Box 45021, Jerusalem 91450, Israel
CEO: Jacov Zerem, Pres.   Tel: 972-2-581-8916   Emp: 70
Bus: *Mfr. laser power energy instrumentation, FLIR & IR*   Fax:972-2-582-2338
    optical components.

    OPHIR OPTRONICS INC.
    200 Corporate Place, #7, Peabody, MA   01960
    CEO: Carl G Burns, Gen.Mgr.   Tel: (508) 535-5777   Emp: N/A
    Bus: *Sale/service laser power energy*   Fax:(508) 535-5999   %FO: 100
        instrumentation.

● **ORBIT ALCHUT**
Hakadar Street, Netania, Israel
CEO: Yossi Herlev, Pres.   Tel: 972-9-860-5777   Emp: 160
Bus: *Mfr. antenna positioners, avionics, tracking systems.*   Fax:972-9-860-5701

    ORBIT ADVANCED TECHNOLOGIES
    506 Prudential Road, Horsham, PA   19044
    CEO: Doug Kremer, VP   Tel: (215) 674-4220   Emp: 19
    Bus: *Sale/service antenna positioners, avionics,*   Fax:(215) 674-1102   %FO: 100
        tracking systems; software development.

● **ORBOTECH LTD.**
P O Box 215, Yavne 70651, Israel
CEO: Yochai Richter, Pres.   Tel: 972-89-423533   Emp: 800
Bus: *Automated optical inspection equipment, CAD/CAM*   Fax:972-89-423897
    systems.

    ORBOTECH INC.
    44 Manning Road, Billerica, MA   01821
    CEO: Moshe Levin, Pres.   Tel: (508) 667-6037   Emp: 180
    Bus: *Mfr./sale automated optical inspection*   Fax:(617) 667-9969   %FO: 100
        equipment, CAD/CAM systems, pre-press
        image setters.

● **ORMAT INDUSTRIES LTD.**
Szydlowski Road, Yavne, Israel
CEO: Lucien Bronicki, Chrm.   Tel: 972-89-43 3777   Emp: 200
Bus: *Mfr. geothermal equipment.*   Fax:972-89-43 9901

    ORMAT SYSTEMS INC.
    980 Greg Street, Sparks, NV   89431
    CEO: Dita Bronicki, Pres.   Tel: (702) 356-9029   Emp: 7
    Bus: *Mfr./sale geothermal equipment.*   Fax:(702) 356-9039   %FO: 100

● **PHARMOS LTD.**
Science Based Industrial Park, Kiryat Weizmann Ehovot 76326, Israel
CEO: Haim Aviv, CEO   Tel: 872-8-940-9679   Emp: N/A
Bus: *Research/development pharmaceuticals.*   Fax:972-8-940-9686

    PHARMOS CORPORATION
    2 Innovation Drive, Alachua, FL   32615
    CEO: Gad Riesenfeld, Pres.   Tel: (904) 462-1210   Emp: 30
    Bus: *Research/development pharmaceuticals.*   Fax:(904) 462-5401   %FO: 100

● **ROBOMATIX LTD.**
9 Hataasiya Street, P.O.Box 2092, Industrial Zone, Raanana 43100, Israel
CEO: Zami Aberman, Pres.   Tel: 972-9-986976   Emp: 90
Bus: *Development/marketing/sale robotics, optics; laser*   Fax:972-9-986980
    cutting welding.

    ROBOMATIC INC.
    46992 Liberty Drive, Wixom, MI   48393-3693
    CEO: Doron Laks, Pres.   Tel: (810) 669-7300   Emp: 50
    Bus: *Develop /marketing/sale robotics, optics; laser*   Fax:(810) 669-7310   %FO: 100
    cutting welding.

● **SCITEX CORPORATION LTD.**
Hamada Street, Industial Park, Herzlia B 46103, Israel
CEO: Yoav Z. Chelouche, Pres.   Tel: 972-9-597-222   Emp: 3600
Bus: *Mfr.. digital information systems.*   Fax:972-9-502-922

    SCITEX AMERICA CORP.
    8 Oak Park Drive, Bedford, MA   01730
    CEO: Shlomo Shamir, Pres.   Tel: (617) 275-5150   Emp: N/A
    Bus: *Mfr./sales digital information systems.*   Fax:(617) 275-3430   %FO: 100

● **TADIRAN LTD.**
29 Hamerkava Street, Holon 58101, Israel
CEO: Isreal Zamir, CEO   Tel: 972-3-557-3200   Emp: N/A
Bus: *Sales/logistics appliances, air conditioning systems,* Fax:972-3-557-3280
and advanced technology.

    ATI, INC.
    575 Lexington Avenue, 21st Floor, New York, NY   10022
    CEO: Israel Adan, Pres.   Tel: (212) 751-3600   Emp: 10
    Bus: *Advanced technology logistics.*   Fax:(212) 751-5181   %FO: 100

    TADIRAN LTD.
    575 Lexington Avenue, New York, NY   10022
    CEO: Israel Adan, Pres.   Tel: (212) 751-3600   Emp: 20
    Bus: *Sale/logistics appliances, airconditioners,* Fax:(212) 751-5181   %FO: 100
    advanced technology.

● **TARO PHARMACEUTICAL INDUSTRIES LTD.**
14 Hakitor Street, Haifa Bay 26110, Israel
CEO: Milky Rubenstein, CEO   Tel: 972-4-723-257   Emp: N/A
Bus: *Research/mfr./sale pharmaceuticals.*   Fax:972-4-472-7165

    TARO PHARMACEUTICAL USA INC.
    5 Skyline Drive, Hawthorne, NY   10532
    CEO: Aaron Levitt, Pres.   Tel: (800) 544-1449   Emp: 25
    Bus: *Research/mfr./sale pharmaceuticals.*   Fax:(914) 345-8278   %FO: 100

● **TELRAD TELECOMMUNICATIONS & ELECTRONIC INDUSTRIES LTDA.**
8 Modeen Street, Lod 71100, Israel
CEO: Oded Koritshoner, CEO   Tel: 972-54-238643   Emp: 2100
Bus: *Mfr. central office switching equipment, key systems,* Fax:972-54-224566
PBXs, ACDs, voice mail systems.

    TELRAD TELECOMMUNICATIONS INC.
    135 Crossways Park Drive, Woodbury, NY   11797
    CEO: Aron Toussia-Cohen, Pres.   Tel: (516) 921-8300   Emp: 90
    Bus: *Mfr./distribution/service business*   Fax:(516) 921-8064   %FO: 100
    telecommunications products, voice mail
    systems, ISDN terminals & devices.

● **TEVA PHARMACEUTICAL IND LTD.**
5 Baze Street, Petach-Tikva 49510, Israel
CEO: Eli Hurwitz, Pres.   Tel: 972-3-926-7255   Emp: N/A
Bus: *Mfr. pharmaceuticals, medical & veterinary supplies.* Fax:972-3-924-6025

    MORGEN-WALKE ASSOCIATES
    380 Madison Avenue, 50th Fl., New York, NY   10168
    CEO: David Walke, Partner   Tel: (212) 850-5600   Emp: N/A
    Bus: *US subsidiary, Mfr./sale pharmaceuticals.*   Fax:(212) 850-5790   %FO: 100

PLANTEX INC.
482 Hudson Terrace, Englewood Cliffs, NJ   07632
CEO: Arik Yaari, Gen.Mgr.   Tel: (201) 567-1010   Emp: 40
Bus: *Mfr. pharmaceutical & raw materials.*   Fax:(201) 567-7994   %FO: 100

TEVA PHARMACEUTICAL USA
650 Cathill Road, Sellersville, PA   18960
CEO: Willaim Fletcher, Pres.   Tel: (215) 256-8400   Emp: N/A
Bus: *Mfr./sale pharmaceuticals,*   Fax:(215) 723-6184   %FO: 100

• **UNITED MIZRAHI BANK LTD.**
13 Rothschild Blvd., Tel Aviv 65121, Israel
CEO: Victor Medina, Mgn Dir.   Tel: 972-3-567-9211   Emp: 3400
Bus: *Commercial banking services.*   Fax:972-3-560-4780

  UMB BANK & TRUST CO
  10 Rockefeller Plaza, 4th Fl., New York, NY   10020
  CEO: Moshe Rosen, Pres   Tel: (212) 332-7400   Emp: 90
  Bus: *Commercial banking services.*   Fax:(212) 307-1364   %FO: 94

  UNITED MIZRAHI BANK LTD. - LA Branch
  611 Wilshire Blvd., Ste. 500-700, Los Angeles, CA   90017
  CEO: Jacob Wintner, SVP & Gen.Mgr.   Tel: (213) 362-2999   Emp: 33
  Bus: *International commercial banking services.* Fax:(213) 488-9783   %FO: 100

  UNITED MIZRAHI BANK LTD. - NY Agency
  1270 Avenue of the Americas, Suite 2303, New York, NY   10020
  CEO: Yaron Globus, Agent.   Tel: (212) 332-7496   Emp: 2
  Bus: *Bank agency.*   Fax:(212) 332-7547   %FO: 100

• **ZIM ISRAEL NAVIGATION CO LTD.**
7-9 Pal Yam Ave, Haifa 31000, Israel
CEO: Dr. Y. Sebba, Pres.   Tel: N/A   Emp: N/A
Bus: *Ship owners & operators.*   Fax:N/A

  ZIM CONTAINER SERVICE
  One World Trade Center - 16th Fl., New York, NY   10048
  CEO: E. Steinbuch, Pres.   Tel: (212) 524-1600   Emp: N/A
  Bus: *Container shipping service.*   Fax:(212) 524-1802   %FO: 100

  ZIM-AMERICAN ISRAEL SHIPPING CO INC.
  1 World Trade Center - 16 th Fl., New York, NY   10048
  CEO: E. Steinbuch, Pres.   Tel: (212) 524-1600   Emp: N/A
  Bus: *Ship owners & operators.*   Fax:(212) 524-1802   %FO: 100

Italy

● **3V SIGMA S.p.A.**
Box 219, Via Tasso 58, I-24121 Bergamo, Italy
CEO: Dr. Antonio Seccomandi, Chrm.   Tel: 39-35-416511   Emp: N/A
Bus: *Mfr. chemicals.*   Fax:39-35-239569

   3V CHEMICAL CORP.
   1500 Harbour Blvd., Weehawken, NJ   07087
   CEO: Giorgio Ferraris, EVP   Tel: (201) 865-3600   Emp: N/A
   Bus: *Mfr./sale chemicals.*   Fax:(201) 865-1892   %FO: 100

● **AGUSTA**
Via G Agusta 520, 21017 Cascina Costa, di Samarato (VA), Italy
CEO: A. Caporaletti, Pres.   Tel: 39-331-229111   Emp: 6000
Bus: *Manufacturer of helicopters.*   Fax:39-331-229605

   AGUSTA AEROSPACE CORP.
   3050 Red Lion Road, Philadelphia, PA   19114
   CEO: Robert J. Budica, Pres.   Tel: (215) 281-1400   Emp: 100
   Bus: *Helicopter marketing, after-sale support.*   Fax:(215) 281-0441   %FO: 100

● **ALITALIA S.p.A.**
Centro Direzionale, Viale Alessandro Marchetti 111, 00148 Rome, Italy
CEO: Renato Riverso, CEO   Tel: 39-6-6562-1   Emp: 18676
Bus: *Commercial air transport services.*   Fax:39-6-6562-5650

   ALITALIA AIRLINES
   666 Fifth Avenue, New York, NY   10103
   CEO: Claudio Spagnoletti, Mgr.   Tel: (212) 903-3300   Emp: 334
   Bus: *International commercial air transport   Fax:(212) 903-3331   %FO: 100
      services.*

● **ANSALDO INDUSTRIAS S.p.A.**
Piazza Carigano 2, Genova, Italy 16128
CEO: B. Musso, Pres./CEO   Tel: 39-10-655-1000   Emp: N/A
Bus: *Engineering services.*   Fax:39-10-655-4132

   ANSALDO NORTH AMERICA, INC.
   1401 Brickell Avenue, Suite 600, Miami, FL   33131
   CEO: Dr. Enrico Giberti, CEO   Tel: (305) 374-8829   Emp: 40
   Bus: *Engineering services, sales representative.*   Fax:(305) 374-8947   %FO: 100

● **ASSICURAZIONI GENERALI, S.p.A.**
Piazza Duca degli Abruzzi 2, Casella Poste 538, I-34132 Trieste, Italy
CEO: Roberto Minato, Pres.   Tel: 39-40-671-1   Emp: N/A
Bus: *General insurance services.*   Fax:39-40-671-600

    ASSICURAZIONI GENERALI Inc.
    One Liberty Plaza, 37th Floor, New York, NY   10006
    CEO: Giorgio Balzer, CEO   Tel: (212) 602-7600   Emp: 60
    Bus: *General insurance services.*   Fax:(212) 587-9537   %FO: 100

● **AUTOBLOK S.p.A.**
Via Duca d'Aosta 24, 10040 Novaretto, Italy
CEO: Walter Bronzino, Sales Director   Tel: 39-963-2020   Emp: 250
Bus: *Mfr. power chucks.*   Fax:39-963-2288

    AUTOBLOK CORP.
    285 Egidi Drive, Wheeling, IL   60090
    CEO: Renato Parodi, Pres.   Tel: (847) 215-0591   Emp: 6
    Bus: *Sale/service power chucks, hydrotating*   Fax:(847) 215-0594   %FO: 100
        cylinders, steady rests.

● **BANCA CARIGE**
Via Cassa di Risparmio 15, 16123 Genoa, Italy
CEO: R. Giovanni Berneschi, Mgn Dir.   Tel: 39-10-579-1   Emp: 3500
Bus: *International banking.*   Fax:39-10 579-2747

    BANCA CARIGE
    375 Park Avenue, New York, NY   10152
    CEO: C. Romairone, Rep.   Tel: (212) 421-6010   Emp: 2
    Bus: *International banking.*   Fax:(212) 759-6785   %FO: 100

● **BANCA COMMERCIALE ITALIANA S.p.A.**
Piazza della Scala 6, I-20121 Milan, Italy
CEO: Enrico Beneduce, Mng. Dir.   Tel: 39-2-8850-1   Emp: N/A
Bus: *International banking.*   Fax:39-2-8850-3026

    BANCA COMMERCIALE ITALIANA
    One William Street, New York, NY   10004
    CEO: Giorgio Angelozzi, Sr.VP   Tel: (212) 607-3500   Emp: 150
    Bus: *International banking*   Fax:(212) 809-2124   %FO: 100

● **BANCA CRT S.p.A.**
Via Nizza 150, 10126 Torino, Italy
CEO: Giorgio Giovando, Gen. Mgr.   Tel: 39-11-662-1   Emp: 5000
Bus: *Banking services.*   Fax:39-11-663-9918

    BANCA CRT, NEW YORK BRANCH
    500 Park Avenue, New York, NY 10022
    CEO: Giorgio Cuccolo, EVP & Mgr.   Tel: (212) 980-0690   Emp: 43
    Bus: *Commercial banking services*   Fax:(212) 980-0809   %FO: 100

    BANCA CRT, LOS ANGELES REPRESENTATIVE OFFICE
    515 South Flower Street, Suite 1690, Los Angeles, CA 90071
    CEO: Robert Ferrol, VP & Representative   Tel: (213) 622-9455   Emp: 2
    Bus: *Commercial banking services*   Fax:(213) 622-9386   %FO: 100

● **BANCA DI ROMA S.p.A.**
Via Marco Minghetti, 00181, Rome, Italy
CEO: Cesare Geronzi, Chrm.   Tel: 39-6-67071   Emp: 14241
Bus: *Commercial banking services.*   Fax:39-6-6781929

    BANCA DI ROMA
    34 East 51st Street, New York, NY 10022
    CEO: Antonio Ciocio, EVP   Tel: (212) 407-1600   Emp: 104
    Bus: *Commercial banking services.*   Fax:(212) 407-1677   %FO: 100

● **BANCA MONTE DEI PASCHI DI SIENA S.p.A.**
Piazza Salimbeni 3, I-53100 Siena, Italy
CEO: Divo Gronchi, CEO   Tel: 39-577-294111   Emp: N/A
Bus: *Commercial banking services.*   Fax:39-577-294131

    BANCA MONTE DEI PASCHI DI SIENA S.p.A.
    245 Park Avenue, 26th Fl., New York, NY 10167
    CEO: Guilio Natalicchi, Gen.Mgr..   Tel: (212) 557-8111   Emp: 33
    Bus: *Wholesale corporate banking; US branch.*   Fax:(212) 227-8039   %FO: 100

● **BANCA NAZIONALE DEL LAVORO**
Via Vittorio Veneto 119, I-00187 Rome, Italy
CEO: Nerio Nesi, Chrm.   Tel: 39-6-47021   Emp: N/A
Bus: *Commercial banking services.*   Fax:39-6-47032-665

    BANCA NAZIONALE DEL LAVORO
    25 West 51st Street, New York, NY 10019
    CEO: Walter Golinelli, Reg. Mgr.   Tel: (212) 581-0710   Emp: 122
    Bus: *International banking services.*   Fax:(212) 246-3192   %FO: 100

- **BANCA NAZONALE DELL'AGRICOLTURA**
Via Salaria 231, I-00199 Rome, Italy
CEO: S. Bonini, Pres.   Tel: 39-6-8588-3202   Emp: N/A
Bus: *Commercial banking services.*   Fax:39-6-8588-3396

  BANCA NAZONALE DELL' AGRICOLTURA
  17 State Street, 21st Floor, New York, NY   10004
  CEO: Giuseppe Magaletti, EVP   Tel: (212) 412-9600   Emp: N/A
  Bus: *Commercial banking services.*   Fax:(212) 412-9609   %FO: 100

- **BANCA POPOLARE DI MILANO**
Piazza F Meda 4, 20121 Milan, Italy
CEO: Francesco Cesarini, Chrm.   Tel: 39-2-7700-1   Emp: 4197
Bus: *Commercial banking services.*   Fax:39-2-7700-2280

  BANCA POPOLARE DI MILANO
  375 Park Avenue, New York, NY   10152
  CEO: Anthony Franco, EVP   Tel: (212) 758-5040   Emp: 27
  Bus: *Commercial banking services.*   Fax:(212) 838-1077   %FO: 100

- **BANCA POPOLARE DI NOVARA**
Via Negroni 12, I-28100, Novara, Italy
CEO: Siro Lombardini, Chrm.   Tel: 39-321-662211   Emp: N/A
Bus: *Commercial Banking services.*   Fax:39-321-662100

  BANCA POPOLARE DI NOVARA
  645 Fifth Avenue, Olympic Tower, 3rd Fl., New York, NY   10022
  CEO: Salvatore Catalano, Rep.   Tel: (212) 755-1300   Emp: 2
  Bus: *Commercial banking services.*   Fax:(212) 486-0458   %FO: 100

- **BANCO AMBROSIANO VENETO**
Piazza Paolo Ferrari, 10, I-20121 Milan, Italy
CEO: Carlo Salvatori, Mng. Dir.   Tel: 39-2-8594-1   Emp: N/A
Bus: *Commercial banking services.*   Fax:39-2-8594-7326

  BANCO AMBROSIANO VENETO
  712 Fifth Avenue, 32nd Floor, New York, NY   10019
  CEO: H.Bradley Bloomer, Representative   Tel: (212) 664-0618   Emp: 2
  Bus: *Commercial banking services.*   Fax:(212) 664-0576   %FO: 100

- **BANCO DI NAPOLI**
Via Toledo 177-178, 80132 Naples, Italy
CEO: Giuseppe Falcone, Chrm.   Tel: 39-81-792-1111   Emp: N/A
Bus: *Commercial banking services.*   Fax:39-81-792-4400

  BANCO DI NAPOLI
  4 East 54th Street, New York, NY   10022
  CEO: Vito Spada, EVP   Tel: (212) 872-2400   Emp: 65
  Bus: *Commercial banking services.*   Fax:(212) 872-2426   %FO: 100

● **BANCO DI SICILIA S.p.A**
Via Generale Magliocco 1, 90141 Palermo, Italy
CEO: Giuseppe Antonio Banfi, Chrm. Tel: 39-91-6081110 Emp: 8523
Bus: *Commercial banking services.* Fax:39-91-6085964

  BANCO DI SICILIA
  250 Park Avenue, 8th Floor, New York, NY 10177
  CEO: Carlo Cracilici, Sr VP & Mgr. Tel: (212) 692-4300 Emp: 34
  Bus: *Commercial banking services.* Fax:(212) 370-5790 %FO: 100

● **BARALAN INTL S.p.A.**
Baralan Bldg, Via Copernico, 20090 Trezzano, Italy
CEO: Dr. Victor Halfon, Mng.Dir. Tel: 39-2-484-4961 Emp: 100
Bus: *Mfr. cosmetic packaging.* Fax:39-2-484-2719

  ARROWPAK INC.
  1016 Burgrove Avenue, Carson, CA 90746
  CEO: James J. Slowey, VP Tel: (213) 636-0211 Emp: 7
  Bus: *Sales/distribution cosmetic packaging.* Fax:(310) 635-1959 %FO: 100

  ARROWPAK INC.
  120-19 89th Avenue, Richmond Hill, NY 11418
  CEO: Gino Nahum, Pres. Tel: (718) 849-1600 Emp: 50
  Bus: *Sales/distribution cosmetic packaging.* Fax:(718) 849-1383 %FO: JV

● **BENETTON GROUP, S.p.A.**
Via Villa Minelli 1, I-31050 Ponzano Veneto, Treviso, Italy
CEO: Luciano Benetton, Chmn./Pres. Tel: 39-422-4491 Emp: N/A
Bus: *Mfr. clothing.* Fax:39-422-449930

  BENETTON USA CORP.
  597 Fifth Avenue, New York, NY 10017
  CEO: Carlo Tunioli, Gen.Mgr. Tel: (212) 593-0290 Emp: N/A
  Bus: *Mfr./sale clothing.* Fax:(212) 371-1438 %FO: 100

● **BIESSE S.p.A.**
Via Toscana 75, 61100 Pesaro, Italy
CEO: Roberto Selci, Pres. Tel: 39-721-4391 Emp: 400
Bus: *Mfr. woodworking equipment for furniture industry.* Fax:39-721-453248

  BIESSE AMERICA INC.
  4110 Meadow Oak Lane, P.O.Box 19849, Charlotte, NC 28219-9849
  CEO: Gianni Cavassa, Pres. Tel: (704) 357-3131 Emp: 45
  Bus: *Distribution/service woodworking equipment.* Fax:(704) 357-3130 %FO: 80

● **BONDIOLI & PAVESI S.p.A.**
Via 23 Aprice 35/A, I-46029 Suzzara, Italy
CEO: Edi Bondioli, Pres.   Tel: 39-376-5141   Emp: N/A
Bus: *Mfr. Drive shafts, gear boxes, hydraulics.*   Fax:39-376-300513

   BONDIOLI & PAVESI INC.
   104 Sycamore Drive, Ashland, VA   23005
   CEO: Franco Laghi, Pres.   Tel: (804) 798-1565   Emp: N/A
   Bus: *Distributor drive shafts, gear boxes, and*   Fax:(804) 550-2837   %FO: 100
      hydraulics

● **CARIPLO-CASSA DI RISPARMIO DELLE PROVINCIE LOMBARDE S.p.A.**
Via Monte de Pietà 8, I-20121, P.O.Box 1784 Milan, Italy
CEO: Dr. Carlo Salvatori, CEO   Tel: 39-2-8866-1   Emp: N/A
Bus: *General banking services.*   Fax:39-2-8866-3240

   CARIPLO BANK - New York Branch
   10 East 53rd Street, 36th Floor, New York, NY   10022
   CEO: Luigi Cuminatti, SVP & Gen.Mgr.   Tel: (212) 832-6622   Emp: 45
   Bus: *International banking services.*   Fax:(212) 527-8777   %FO: 100

   CARIPLO BANK - Chicago Rep. Office
   190 South LaSalle Street, #2890, Chicago, IL   60603
   CEO: Luigi Cuminatti, SVP & Gen.Mgr.   Tel: (312) 444-1500   Emp: 2
   Bus: *International banking services.*   Fax:(312) 444-1500   %FO: 100

   CARIPLO BANK - San Francisco Rep. Office
   One Embarcadero Center, Ste. 2820, San Francisco, CA   94111
   CEO: Joseph Raffetto, Rep.   Tel: (415) 439-6780   Emp: 2
   Bus: *International banking services.*   Fax:(415) 439-6785   %FO: 100

● **CASSA DI RISPARMIO DI FIRENZE**
Via Bufalini 6, 50122 Florence, Italy
CEO: Aureliano Benedetti, Chrm.   Tel: 39-55-26121   Emp: 3500
Bus: *Commercial banking services.*   Fax:39-55-230-2277

   CASSA DI RISPARMIO DI FIRENZE
   375 Park Avenue, New York, NY   10152-0054
   CEO: Paolo G. Palli, US Rep.   Tel: (212) 421-6010   Emp: 3
   Bus: *International banking services.*   Fax:(212) 759-6785   %FO: 100

● **CASSA DI RISPARMIO DI TORINO**
Via XX Settembre 31, 10121 Turin, Italy
CEO: Enrico Filippi, Chrm.   Tel: 39-11-6221   Emp: 5300
Bus: *Commercial banking services.*   Fax:39-11-6639918

   CASSA DI RISPARMIO DI TORINO
   500 Park Avenue, New York, NY   10022
   CEO: Giorgio Cuccolo, Sr. VP & Mgr   Tel: (212) 980-0690   Emp: 41
   Bus: *International banking services.*   Fax:(212) 980-0809   %FO: 100

● **DAVIDE CENCI & MGT SRL**
Via Campo Marzio 4/7, 00186 Rome, Italy
CEO: Paolo Cenci, Pres. Tel: 39-6-699-0681 Emp: 65
Bus: *Design/mfr. wearing apparel.* Fax:39-6-379-5900

    DAVIDE CENCI INC.
    801 Madison Avenue, New York, NY 10021
    CEO: David Cenci, VP Tel: (212) 628-5910 Emp: 13
    Bus: *Retail men's wear.* Fax:(212) 439-1650 %FO: 100

● **COSTA CROCIERE**
Via XII, Ittobre 2, I-16121 Genoa, Italy
CEO: Nicola Costa, Chrm. Tel: 39-10-54831 Emp: 1661
Bus: *Shipping/cruise line.* Fax:39-548-3290

    COSTA CRUISE LINES NV
    80 SW 8th Street, Miami, FL 33130-3097
    CEO: Dino Schibuola, Pres. Tel: (305) 358-7325 Emp: 140
    Bus: *Cruise line.* Fax:(305) 375-0676 %FO: 100

● **CREDITO ITALIANO SPA**
Piazza Cordusio 2, 20123 Milan, Italy
CEO: Lucia Rondelli, CEO Tel: 39-2- 8862-1000 Emp: 14428
Bus: *Commercial banking services.* Fax:39-2-8862-3034

    CREDITO ITALIANO - Los Angeles Agency
    500 South Grand Avenue
    Suite 1600, Los Angeles, CA 90071
    CEO: Riccardo Gallo, VP & Rep. Tel: (213) 622-2787 Emp: 3
    Bus: *International commercial banking.* Fax:(213) 623-3799 %FO: 100

    CREDITO ITALIANO - Chicago Agency
    2 Prudential Pl., 180 N. Stetson St., #1310, Chicago, IL 60601
    CEO: Maurizio Brentegani, VP & Rep. Tel: (312) 946-1111 Emp: 4
    Bus: *International commercial banking.* Fax:(312) 946-1112 %FO: 100

    CREDITO ITALIANO
    375 Park Avenue, New York, NY 10152-0099
    CEO: Carmelo Mazza, Sr.VP & Gen.Mgr. Tel: (212) 546-9600 Emp: 63
    Bus: *International commercial banking.* Fax:(212) 546-9675 %FO: 100

● **DELLE VEDOVE LEVIGATRICI SPA**
Viale Treviso 13A, I-33170 Pordenone, Italy
CEO: Gaetano Delle Vedove, Pres.   Tel: 39-434-572 277   Emp: 45
Bus: *Mfr. woodworking machinery.*   Fax:39-434-572 775

    DELLE VEDOVE USA INC.
    6031 Harris Technology Blvd., Charlotte, NC   28269
    CEO: Vittorio Belluz, Pres   Tel: (704) 598-0020   Emp: 6
    Bus: *Sale/service woodworking equipment &*   Fax:(704) 598-3950   %FO: 70
        abrasives.

● **DOBSON & PINCI**
Via Panama 74, Int. 9, 00198 Rome, Italy
CEO: F. Ferrante, Mng. Ptnr.   Tel: 39-6-841-1611   Emp: N/A
Bus: *International law firm.*   Fax:39-6-841-1145

    DOBSON & PINCI
    342 Madison Avenue, New York, NY   10173
    CEO: F. Ferrante, Mng. Ptnr.   Tel: (212) 308-4440   Emp: N/A
    Bus: *International law firm.*   Fax:(212) 888-3839   %FO: 100

● **ENI SPA**
Piazzale E Mattei 1, 00144 Rome, Italy
CEO: Franco Bernabé, CEO   Tel: 39-6-598-21   Emp: 86,000
Bus: *Energy related product and services.*   Fax:39-6-598-25834

    AGIP PETROLEUM CO. INC.
    2950 North Loop West, Ste. 300, Houston, TX   77092
    CEO: Salvatore Fantini, Pres. & CEO   Tel: (713) 688-6281   Emp: N/A
    Bus: *Oil exploration/products, crude oil trading.* Fax:(713) 688-6091   %FO: 100

    AGIP USA INC.
    110 E 59th Street, New York, NY   10022
    CEO: Giovanni Zinnato, Pres. & CEO   Tel: (212) 339-2100   Emp: 55
    Bus: *Sale/service, purchasing, financial &*   Fax:(212) 339-2191   %FO: 100
        marketing research.

    AMERICAN AGIP CO. INC.
    900 Ellison Avenue, Westbury, NY   11590
    CEO: Franco Antonietti, Pres.   Tel: (516) 683-5460   Emp: N/A
    Bus: *Sale/trading petroleum products.*   Fax:(516) 683-5489   %FO: 100

    ENI REPRESENTATIVE FOR THE AMERICAS
    666 Fifth Avenue, New York, NY   10103
    CEO: Enzo Viscusi, ENI Rep.   Tel: (212) 887-0330   Emp: N/A
    Bus: *Group activity coordination.*   Fax:(212) 246-0009   %FO: 100

ENI WASHINGTON REPRESENTATIVE
1667 K Street NW, Washington, DC   20006
CEO: Claudio Moscato, ENI Rep.　　　　　　　Tel: (202) 466-2444　　Emp: N/A
Bus: *Liaison with multinational institutions.*　Fax:(202) 466-2446　%FO: 100

ENICHEM AMERICA INC.
2000 West Loop S., Ste. 2010, Houston, TX   77027
CEO: Luciano Topi, Pres. & CEO　　　　　　　Tel: (713) 940-0770　　Emp: N/A
Bus: *Chemical sales, R&D.*　　　　　　　　　Fax:(713) 960-1541　%FO: 100

ENICHEM ELASTOMERS AMERICAS INC
2000 West Loop S., Ste. 2010, Houston, TX   77027
CEO: Luciano Topi, Pres.　　　　　　　　　　Tel: (713) 940-0770　　Emp: 40
Bus: *Thermoplastic elastomers.*　　　　　　　Fax:(713) 960-1541　%FO: 100

PIGNONE INC.
666 Fifth Avenue, New York, NY   10103
CEO: Mario Soncini, EVP　　　　　　　　　　Tel: (212) 887-0310　　Emp: N/A
Bus: *Machinery sales.*　　　　　　　　　　　Fax:(212) 246-0009　%FO: 20

PIGNONE TEXTILE MACHINERY
P O Box 3323, Spartanburg, SC   29304
CEO: Harold Merck, EVP　　　　　　　　　　Tel: (864) 814-1505　　Emp: N/A
Bus: *Textile machinery sales.*　　　　　　　Fax:(864) 582-3510　%FO: 20

SAIPEM SPA, INC.
15950 Park Row, Houston, TX   77084
CEO: Stefano Bianchi, Rep.　　　　　　　　　Tel: (281) 552-5700　　Emp: N/A
Bus: *Onshore/offshore drilling and pipelines.*　Fax:(281) 552-5915　%FO: 100

SNAMPROGETTI USA
17629 El Camino Reale, Houston, TX   77058
CEO: Giancarlo Stacchi, Pres.　　　　　　　　Tel: (281) 461-7100　　Emp: N/A
Bus: *Technology sales/service.*　　　　　　　Fax:(281) 461-7210　%FO: 100

SONSUB INC.
15950 Park Row, Houston, TX   77084
CEO: Giovanni Rosa, Pres. & CEO　　　　　　　Tel: (281) 552-5600　　Emp: N/A
Bus: *Sub-sea engineering services.*　　　　　Fax:(281) 552-5910　%FO: 100

● **P. FERRERO & C S.p.A.**
Via Maria Cristina 47, I-10025 Pino Torinese, Italy
CEO: Mr. DeBona, Pres.　　　　　　　　　　Tel: 39-11-8152419　　Emp: N/A
Bus: *Mfr. confectionery products*　　　　　　Fax:39-11-840470

FERRERO USA INC.
600 Cottontail Lane, Somerset, NJ   08873
CEO: Michael F. Gilmore, COO　　　　　　　Tel: (732) 764-9300　　Emp: 154
Bus: *Mfr./repackaging sale confectionery goods.*　Fax:(732) 764-2700　%FO: 100

● **FIAT S.p.A.**
Corso Marconi 10, 10125 Turin, Italy
CEO: Paolo Cantarella   Tel: 39-11-686-1111   Emp: 237,426
Bus: *Diversified industrial conglomerate: autos;*   Fax:39-11-686-3400
commercial, industrial, agricultural & construction
equipment; etc.

ALTEK AUTOMOTIVE CASTINGS, INC.
21624 Melrose, Southfield, MI   48075
CEO: Paolo Maccario, Pres.   Tel: (248) 799-8300   Emp: N/A
Bus: *R&D automotive industry.*   Fax:(248) 799-8322   %FO: 100

COMAU NORTH AMERICA, INC.
4475 Parks Drive, Auburn Hills, MI   48326
CEO: Raimondo Zailo. Pres.   Tel: (248) 377-4700   Emp: N/A
Bus: *Designs/mfr./service automated machining*   Fax:(248) 377-4751   %FO: 100
systems.

FERRARI NORTH AMERICA, INC.
250 Sylvan Avenue, Engelwood Cliffs, NJ   07632
CEO: Gianluigi Longinotti Buitoni, Pres.   Tel: (201) 816-2600   Emp: N/A
Bus: *Sale/service automobiles.*   Fax:(201) 816-2626   %FO: 100

FIAT AUTO R&D U.S.A., INC.
39300 Country Club Drive, Farmington Hills, MI   48331-3473
CEO: Alberto Negro   Tel: (248) 488-5600   Emp: N/A
Bus: *R&D automobiles.*   Fax:(248) 488-5820   %FO: 100

FIAT AVIO, INC.
270 Sylvan Avenue, Englewood Cliffs, NJ   07632
CEO: Piergiorgio Romiti, Pres.   Tel: (201) 816-2720   Emp: 10
Bus: *Design/mfr. airplane engines.*   Fax:(201) 816-2740   %FO: 100

FIAT U.S.A, INC.
1176 "I" Street, NW, Washington, DC   20006
CEO: R. Ascari, Mgr.   Tel: (202) 862-1610   Emp: 3
Bus: *Representative office.*   Fax:(202) 429-2959   %FO: 100

FIAT U.S.A, INC.
375 Park Avenue, Suite 2703, New York, NY   10152
CEO: Franco Fornasari, Pres.   Tel: (212) 355-2600   Emp: 16
Bus: *Diversified industrial conglomerate: autos;*   Fax:(212) 308-2968   %FO: 100
commercial, industrial, agricultural, and
construction equipment; transportation
systems; engineering, chemicals, and financial
services.

FIATALLIS NORTH AMERICA, INC.
245 East North Avenue, Carol Stream, IL   60188
CEO: Lucio Catone   Tel: (630) 260-4000   Emp: N/A
Bus: *Sales/service industrial/construction*   Fax:(630) 462-7514   %FO: 100
    equipment.

MAGNETI MARELLI U.S.A., INC.
2101 Nash Street, Sanford, NC   27331
CEO: Fred Gopal, Pres.   Tel: (919) 776-4111   Emp: N/A
Bus: *Mfr. auto engines.*   Fax:(919) 775-6337   %FO: 100

NEW HOLLAND CREDIT COMPANY
33 South Railroad Avenue, New Holland, PA   17557
CEO: Larry L. Mason, Pres.   Tel: (717) 355-3086   Emp: N/A
Bus: *Finances lease/purchase of industrial*   Fax:(717) 355-3092   %FO: 100
    machinery.

NEW HOLLAND NORTH AMERICA, INC.
P.O. Box 1895, New Holland, PA   17557
CEO: Umberto Quadruno, Chrm.   Tel: (717) 355-1121   Emp: N/A
Bus: *Mfr./sale commercial/industrial equipment.* Fax:(717) 355-3600   %FO: 100

NYLSTAR, INC.
317-H Westgate Drive, Greensboro, NC   27407
CEO: Virgilio Vecchio, Pres.   Tel: (910) 299-2926   Emp: N/A
Bus: *Mfr./marketing textile filaments.*   Fax:(910) 299-3593   %FO: 100

NYLTECH NORTH AMERICA, INC.
333 Sundial Avenue, Manchester, NH   03103
CEO: Carlo Pacchini, Pres.   Tel: (603) 627-5150   Emp: N/A
Bus: *Mfr./marketing nylon.*   Fax:(603) 627-5154   %FO: 100

SORIN BIOMEDICAL, INC.
17600 Gilette Drive, Irvine, CA   19503
CEO: Ezio Garibaldi, Chrm.   Tel: (714) 250-0500   Emp: N/A
Bus: *Mfr./sale medical equipment.*   Fax:(714) 250-1524   %FO: 100

TEKSID ALUMINUM FOUNDRY, INC.
1635 Old Columbia Road, Dickson, TN   37055
CEO: Paolo Maccario, Pres.   Tel: (615) 446-8110   Emp: N/A
Bus: *Mfr. aluminum automotive parts.*   Fax:(615) 446-2460   %FO: 100

TEKSID, INC.
39300 Country Club Drive, Farmington Hills, MI   48331
CEO: Paolo Ivanov, Pres.   Tel: (248) 488-5660   Emp: N/A
Bus: *Aluminum manufacturing equipment &*   Fax:(248) 488-5678   %FO: 100
    systems consulting.

- **FILA HOLDINGS S.p.A.**
  Biella, Italy
  CEO: Dr. Frachey, Pres. & CEO   Tel: 39-153-506368   Emp: N/A
  Bus: *Sports footwear and clothing.*   Fax:39-153-506399

  > **FILA FOOTWEAR U.S.A., INC.**
  > 14114 York Road, Sparks, MD 21150
  > CEO: Jack Steinweis, Pres.   Tel: (410) 773-3000   Emp: N/A
  > Bus: *Mfr./sale sports footwear & clothing.* Fax:(410) 773-4967   %FO: 100

- **CESARE FIORUCCI SPA**
  Santa Palomba, 00040 Rome, Italy
  CEO: Ferrucio Fiorucci, Pres.   Tel: 39-6-9119-3600   Emp: N/A
  Bus: *Mfr. specialty meats.*   Fax:39-6-9119-3639

  > **FIORUCCI FOODS INC**
  > 1800 Ruffin Mill Road, PO Box 39, Colonial Heights, VA 23834
  > CEO: Claudio Colmignoli, Pres.   Tel: (804) 520-7775   Emp: 89
  > Bus: *Mfr. specialty meats.*   Fax:(804) 520-7180   %FO: 80

- **GEORGE FUNARO & ASSOCIATES**
  7, Largo Augusto, Milano 20121, Italy
  CEO: G. Funaro   Tel: 39-2-784267   Emp: 50
  Bus: *Financial consultants.*   Fax:39-2-783652

  > **GEORGE FUNARO & ASSOCIATES**
  > One Penn Plaza, New York, NY 10119
  > CEO: Sheldon Satlin, Pres.   Tel: (212) 947-3333   Emp: 40
  > Bus: *Accounting and financial services.*   Fax:(212) 947-4725   %FO: JV

- **GENNY MODA SPA**
  Via Maggini 126, 60127 Ancona, Italy
  CEO: Donatella Girombelli, Pres.   Tel: 39-71-718717   Emp: 400
  Bus: *Mfr. designer clothing.*   Fax:39-71-712865

  > **GENNY USA**
  > 650 Fifth Avenue, 14th Fl., New York, NY 10017
  > CEO: Emilio Macellari, Pres   Tel: (212) 245-4860   Emp: 23
  > Bus: *Import/sales designer clothing.*   Fax:(212) 969-9396   %FO: 100

- **T. GIULIANI SPA**
  Via del Lavoro 7, Quarto Inferiore, I- 40050 Bologna, Italy
  CEO: Saverio Gellini, Gen. Mgr.   Tel: 39-51-767014   Emp: 60
  Bus: *Mfr. machinery for lock industry, transfer machines,*   Fax:39-51-768060
       bar feeder machinery.

    GIULIANI USA INC.
    One Executive Blvd., Ste. 201, Suffern, NY   10901
    CEO: David Rosbottom, VP   Tel: (914) 357-1224   Emp: 5
    Bus: *Sales/service and spare parts for lock industry*   Fax:(914) 267-2276   %FO: 100
         machinery, transfer and bar feeder machinery.

- **GROVE ITALIA SPA**
  Strada Campoferro 15, 27058 Voghera (PV), Italy
  CEO: Salvatore Ruggeri, Pres.   Tel: 39-3-836911   Emp: 350
  Bus: *Mfr. valves and regulators for oil and gas industry.*   Fax:N/A

    DRESSER ENERGY VALVE CO.
    11100 West Airport Blvd., Stafford, TX   77477
    CEO: George Brightman, Pres.   Tel: (281) 568-2211   Emp: 145
    Bus: *Mfr. valves/regulators for oil and gas industry.*   Fax:(281) 568-6731   %FO: 100

- **GRUPPO GFT**
  Corso Emilia 6, 10152 Torino, Italy
  CEO: Marco Rivetti, Chrm.   Tel: 39-11-23971   Emp: 10000
  Bus: *Mfr./distribute wearing apparel.*   Fax:39-11-2397319

    GFT USA INC.
    650 Fifth Avenue, New York, NY   10019
    CEO: Ronald Frasch, Pres. & CEO   Tel: (212) 265-1488   Emp: N/A
    Bus: *Marketing/distribute wearing apparel.*   Fax:(212) 262-0931   %FO: 100

- **IMI SPA**
  Viale dell'Arte 25, 00144 Rome, Italy
  CEO: Luigi Arcuti, Chrm.   Tel: 39-6-54501   Emp: 1400
  Bus: *Banking and financial services.*   Fax:N/A

    IMI CAPITAL MARKETS USA CORP.
    165 Broadway, New York, NY   10006
    CEO: Daniela Giberti, Mgn.Dir.   Tel: (212) 346-5042   Emp: N/A
    Bus: *Financial services.*   Fax:(212) 346-5075   %FO: 100

    MABON SECURITIES CORP.
    165 Broadway, New York, NY   10006
    CEO: Daniela Giberti, CEO   Tel: (212) 346-5000   Emp: 23
    Bus: *Securities broker/dealer.*   Fax:(212) 346-5074   %FO: 100

● **IMT INTERMATO SRL**
Via Carego 14, 21020 Crosio della Valle, Italy
CEO: C. Caprioli, Pres.   Tel: 39-332-966110   Emp: 85
Bus: *Mfr. equipment for machining alloy aluminum*   Fax:39-332-966033
wheels.

  IMT AMERICA INC
  21818 Lassen St "B", Chatsworth, CA   91311
  CEO: Eli Cohen, Pres.   Tel: (818) 882-8106   Emp: 10
  Bus: *Distribution/consulting.*   Fax:(818) 882-4534   %FO: JV

● **ISTITUTO BANCARIO SAN PAOLO DI TORINO**
Piazza San Carlo 156, 10121 Turin, Italy
CEO: Luigi Maranzana, Mng. Dir.   Tel: 39-11-5551   Emp: 20000
Bus: *International banking services.*   Fax:39-11-551-6650

  SAN PAULO BANK
  444 Flower Street, 45th Floor, Los Angeles, CA   90071
  CEO: Donald Brown, Rep.   Tel: (213) 489-3100   Emp: 3
  Bus: *International banking services.*   Fax:(213) 622-2514   %FO: 100

  SAN PAULO BANK
  245 Park Avenue, New York, NY   10167
  CEO: Giuseppe Cuccurese, EVP   Tel: (212) 692-3000   Emp: 85
  Bus: *International banking services.*   Fax:(212) 599-3046   %FO: 100

● **ISTITUTO PER LA RICOSTRUZIONE INDUSTRIALE S.p.A. (IRI)**
Via Versilia 2, I-00187 Rome, Italy
CEO: Gian Maria Gros Pietro, Chrm. & CEO   Tel: 39-6-47271   Emp: 263000
Bus: *Holding company. Steel, technology,*   Fax:39-6-47272148
telecommunications, transportation, engineering,
electronics, shipbuilding, foodstuffs and finance.

  ISTITUTO PER LA RICOSTRUZIONE INDUSTRIALE S.p.A. (IRI)
  1101 15th Street, NW, Suite 612, Washington, DC   20005
  CEO: Oscar Bartoli, Director   Tel: (202) 223-5804   Emp: 3
  Bus: *US headquarters for holding company. Steel,*   Fax:(202) 331-0560   %FO: 100
  technology, telecommunications, transport,
  engineering, electronics, shipbuilding,
  foodstuffs and finance.

● **ITALDESIGN S.p.A.**
Via A Grandi 11, 10024 Moncalieri, Turin, Italy
CEO: Giorgetto Giugiaro, Chrm.   Tel: 39-11-689-1611   Emp: 750
Bus: *Automotive research and construction.*   Fax:39-11-647-0858

    I.D.C. ITALDESIGN CALIFORNIA, INC.
    6481 Oak Canyon, Irvine, CA   92620
    CEO: Dr. Renato Sconfienza, Pres. & CEO   Tel: (714) 654-0070   Emp: 50
    Bus: *Automotive engineering, models and prototype*   Fax:(714) 654-0077   %FO: 100
       building.

● **ITALIA DI NAVIGAZIONE S.p.A.**
Via de Marini 1, 16149 Genova, Italy
CEO: Eugenio Gallo, CEO   Tel: 39-10-2402100   Emp: N/A
Bus: *Shipping services.*   Fax:39-10-2402445

    ITALIAN LINE
    302 Port Jersey Blvd., Jersey City, NJ   07302
    CEO: Dave Grass, Gen. Mgr.   Tel: (201) 413-0300   Emp: 49
    Bus: *Shipping services.*   Fax:(201) 413-0192   %FO: 100

● **IVECO BV**
Via Puglia 35, 10156 Turin, Italy
CEO: Giancarlo Boschetti, Pres.   Tel: 39-11-6872111   Emp: 32200
Bus: *Manufacturer of industrial vehicles.*   Fax:N/A

    IVECO TRUCKS OF NORTH AMERICA
    343 Progress Drive, Bensalem, PA   19020
    CEO: John J. Sherlock, VP, Gen.Mgr..   Tel: (215) 639-9696   Emp: 20
    Bus: *Distributor of spare parts.*   Fax:(215) 639-0962   %FO: 100

● **LOMBARDINI MOTORI SPA**
Via F.lli Manfredi 6, 42100 Reggio Emilia, Italy
CEO: Dr. Gianni Borghi, Gen Mgr.   Tel: 39-522-3891   Emp: 1300
Bus: *Mfr. industrial diesel engines.*   Fax:39-522-580295

    LOMBARDINI USA INC.
    2150 Boggs Road, Bldg 300, #300, Duluth, GA   30136
    CEO: Jim McPherson, Pres.   Tel: (770) 623-3554   Emp: 20
    Bus: *Distribute industrial diesel engines.*   Fax:(770) 623-8833   %FO: 100

● **LUXOTTICA GROUP, S.p.A.**
Agordo, Belluno 32021, Italy
CEO: Leonardo Del Vecchio, CEO   Tel: 39-437-62641   Emp: 3350
Bus: *Mfr. eyeglass frames, retail eyecare and clothing*   Fax:39-437-63840
stores.

   CAUSAL CORNER GROUP, INC.
   100 Phoenix Avenue, P.O.Box 1700, Enfield, CT   06083-1700
   CEO: Claudio Del Vecchio, Pres.   Tel: (860) 741-0770   Emp: 11000
   Bus: *Retail clothing stores.*   Fax:(860) 745-6554   %FO: 100

   LENSCRAFTERS INC.
   8650 Governors Hill Drive, Cincinnati, OH   43068
   CEO: David M. Browne, Pres.   Tel: (513) 583-6000   Emp: 12800
   Bus: *Eyeglass frames, eyecare retail stores.*   Fax:(513) 583-6388   %FO: 100

   LUXOTTICA GROUP, INC.
   44 Harbor Park Drive, Port Washington, NY   11050
   CEO: Claudio Del Vecchio, Pres.   Tel: (516) 484-3800   Emp: 326
   Bus: *Distribution, eyeglass frames.*   Fax:(516) 484-4481   %FO: 100

● **MANFREDI**
Via dei Carantani 10, 21100 Varese, Italy
CEO: Giulio Manfredi, Pres.   Tel: 39-332-283590   Emp: 110
Bus: *Mfr. jewelry.*   Fax:39-332-241605

   MANFREDI
   737 Madison Avenue, New York, NY   10021
   CEO: Denise Rochette, Mgr.   Tel: (212) 734-8710   Emp: 16
   Bus: *Distributor/sale jewelry.*   Fax:(212) 734-4741   %FO: 100

● **MANUFACTURE ASSOCIATE CASHMERE S.p.A.**
Via Faitinella 6, Capalle, 50010, Italy
CEO: Alfredo Canessa, Pres. & Chrm..   Tel: 39-55-898141   Emp: 250
Bus: *Fully fashioned cashmere and other fine*   Fax:39-55-8969015
yarns/knitwear.

   M.A.C., USA
   745 Fifth Avenue, New York, NY   10151
   CEO: Luigi Leonardi, EVP   Tel: (212) 753-7015   Emp: 25
   Bus: *Fully fashioned cashmere and other fine*   Fax:(212) 583-1140   %FO: 100
   yarns/knitwear.

- **OLIVETTI GROUP**
Via Jervis 77, 10015 Ivrea, Italy
CEO: Roberto Colaninno, Chrm.   Tel: 39-125-522525   Emp: 50,000
Bus: *Mfr. office automation systems date processing*   Fax:39-125-522524
products.

    OLIVETTI NORTH AMERICA
    22425 East Appleway Avenue, Liberty Lake, WA   99019
    CEO: Ted DeMerritt, Pres. & CEO   Tel: (509) 927-5600   Emp: N/A
    Bus: *Mfr./sales/service, financing branch,*   Fax:(509) 927-5754   %FO: 100
    automation systems..

    OLIVETTI USA, INC.
    765 US Highway 202, PO Box 6945, Bridgewater, NJ   08807
    CEO: Salomon Suwalsky, Pres. & CEO   Tel: (908) 526-8200   Emp: N/A
    Bus: *Sales/marketing computers, office machinery,*   Fax:(908) 526-8405   %FO: 100
    products and supplies.

- **OTIM S.p.A.**
Via Porro Lambertenghi, 9, Milano, Italy
CEO: Mario Carniglia, Pres.   Tel: 39-2-69912100   Emp: N/A
Bus: *International freight forwarder.*   Fax:39-2-69912245

    OTIM USA INC.
    476 Broadway, 5th Fl., New York, NY   10013
    CEO: Shyrose Remtulla, Mgr.   Tel: (212) 941-1122   Emp: N/A
    Bus: *International freight forwarder.*   Fax:(212) 941-1919   %FO: 100

- **PELUSO & ASSOCIOTI**
Via Panama 74, Rome, 00198 Italy
CEO: Giovanni Peluso, Partner   Tel: 39-6-884-0881   Emp: 35
Bus: *International law firm.*   Fax:39-6-884-1717

    PELUSO & ASSOCIOTI
    375 Park Avenue, 2nd Floor, New York, NY   10152
    CEO: Giovanni Peluso, Partner   Tel: (212) 980-3368   Emp: 5
    Bus: *International law firm.*   Fax:(212) 980-3378   %FO: JV

- **FABIO PERINI SPA**
Via per Mugnano, I-55100 Lucca, Italy
CEO: Giuseppe Antonini, Pres.   Tel: 39-583-9725   Emp: 450
Bus: *Tissue converting equipment.*   Fax:39-583-972610

    PERINI AMERICA INC.
    3060 South Ridge Road, Green Bay, WI   54304
    CEO: Riccardo Baccelli, Pres.   Tel: (414) 336-5000   Emp: 52
    Bus: *Tissue converting equipment.*   Fax:(414) 337-0363   %FO: 100

● **RINALDO PIAGGIO S.p.A.**
Via Cibrario 4, 16154 Genova, Italy
CEO: Dr. Rinaldo Piaggio, Chrm.   Tel: 39-10-60041   Emp: 2000
Bus: *Mfr. aircraft, aerospace systems and equipment,*   Fax:39-10-603378
communications shelters.

　　PIAGGIO AVIATION INC.
　　1802 West 2nd Street, Wichita, KS 67203
　　CEO: Mat Cammeron, Mgr.   Tel: (316) 262-3636   Emp: 100
　　Bus: *Mfr. aircraft structures, aerospace assemblies,*   Fax:(316) 262-1499   %FO: 100
　　tool design and manufacturing.

● **PIRELLI SPA**
Viale Srca, 222, 20126 Milan, Italy
CEO: Marco Tronchetti Provera, CEO   Tel: 39-2-64421   Emp: N/A
Bus: *Tires, rubber products, plastics. sub of Pirelli*   Fax:39-2-6442-3300
International SA, Basel, Switzerland.

　　PIRELLI ARMSTRONG TIRE CORP.
　　500 Sargent Drive, New Haven, CT 06536
　　CEO: Giovanni Ferrario, Pres.   Tel: (860) 784-2200   Emp: 3300
　　Bus: *Mfr. tires, tubes, rubber products.*   Fax:(860) 784-2408   %FO: 100

　　PIRELLI CABLE CORP.
　　700 Industrial Drive, Lexington, SC 29072
　　CEO: Waltet Allessandrini, Pres.   Tel: (803) 951-4800   Emp: 100 +
　　Bus: *Mfr. tires, tubes, rubber products.*   Fax:(803) 951-1069   %FO: 100

● **RCS EDITORI SPA**
Via A Rizzoli 2, 20132 Milan, Italy
CEO: Giorgio Fattori, Chrm.   Tel: 39-2-22584   Emp: 6900
Bus: *Publishing, printing, bookstores, TV/movie*   Fax:39-2-5065390
production.

　　RCS RIZZOLI CORP.
　　300 Park Ave South, New York, NY 10010
　　CEO: Antonio Polito, Chrm. & Pres.   Tel: (212) 387-3400   Emp: 280
　　Bus: *Publishers; bookstores.*   Fax:(212) 387-3535   %FO: 100

● **RITRAMA, S.p.A**
Via della Guerrina 108, Milan, Italy
CEO: Tomas Rink, CEO   Tel: 39-3-983-9215   Emp: N/A
Bus: *Mfr. graphic art supplies and pressure sensitive film.* Fax:39-3-983-4718

　　RITRAMA DURAMARK COMPANIES, INC.
　　800 Kasota Avenue, SE, Minneapolis, MN 55414
　　CEO: Daryl Hanzal, VP   Tel: (612) 378-2277   Emp: 159
　　Bus: *Sales/distribution of graphic art supplies and*   Fax:(612) 378-9327   %FO: 100
　　pressure sensitive film.

● **SAN PELLEGRINO SPA**
17-23 Via Castelvetro, I-20154 Milan, Italy
CEO: Dr. Paolo Luni, Pres.   Tel: 39-2-319-7275   Emp: 1000
Bus: *Sale/distribution beverages.*   Fax:39-2-319-7294

      SAN PELLEGRINO USA
      780 Third Avenue, #1602, New York, NY   10017
      CEO: William O'Donnell, Pres.   Tel: (212) 888-3328   Emp: 20
      Bus: *Sale/distribution beverages.*   Fax:(212) 888-5459   %FO: 100

● **STARHOTELS**
Viale Belfiore 27, Firenze 50144, Italy
CEO: Ferrucio Fabri, Pres.   Tel: 39-55-36921   Emp: 1000
Bus: *Four-star hotel chain.*   Fax:39-55-36924

      THE MICHELANGELO HOTEL (STARHOTELS)
      152 West 51 Street, New York, NY   10019
      CEO: Elizabeth Fabri, Pres.   Tel: (212) 765-1900   Emp: 100
      Bus: *178 room, 4-star hotel.*   Fax:(212) 581-7618   %FO: 100

● **STUDIO LEGALE BISCONTI**
Via Bissolati, 76, 00187 Rome, Italy
CEO: Giuseppe Bisconti, Mng. Ptnr.   Tel: 39-6-479-881   Emp: N/A
Bus: *International law firm.*   Fax:39-6-487-2070

      STUDIO LEGALE BISCONTI
      730 Fifth Avenue,, New York, NY   10019
      CEO: Andre Bisconti, Mng. Ptnr.   Tel: (212) 956-9400   Emp: N/A
      Bus: *International law firm.*   Fax:(212) 956-9405   %FO: 100

● **TEKMA-KINOMAT S.p.A.**
Via Enrico Fermi 635, 21042 Caronno P (VA), Italy
CEO: N/A   Tel: 39-2-9650-6360   Emp: 50
Bus: *Mfr. coil winding equipment and automation*   Fax:39-2-9645-1173
    systems.

      EPM CORP.
      8866 Kelso Drive, Baltimore, MD   21221
      CEO: Donald Lee, Pres.   Tel: (410) 686-7800   Emp: 40
      Bus: *Mfr. coil winding equipment and automation*   Fax:(410) 686-4662   %FO: 95
          systems.

- **TELECOM ITALIA S.p.A.**
  Via Campa Boario, 00153 Rome, Italy
  CEO: Umberto Chirichigno, CEO   Tel: 39-6-5734-1   Emp: 3500
  Bus: *Telecommunication services.*   Fax:39-6-573-44810

  TELECOM ITALIA, INC.
  499 Park Avenue, 23rd Floor, New York, NY 10022-1240
  CEO:Luca Tamburo, CEO   Tel: (212) 755-5280   Emp: 20
  Bus: *Telecommunications services. Formerly*   Fax:(212) 755-5766   %FO: 100
      ITALCABLE USA INC.

- **UNIFOR S.p.A.**
  Via Isonzo 1, 22078 Turate (Como), Italy
  CEO: Gianfranco Marinelli, Dir. Gen.   Tel: 39-2-9675-0233   Emp: 350
  Bus: *Mfr. contract furniture.*   Fax:39-2-9675-0859

  UNIFOR INC.
  149 Fifth Avenue, 3rd Fl., New York, NY 10010
  CEO:Benjamin A. Pardo, VP   Tel: (212) 673-3434   Emp: 5
  Bus: *Sales office & contract furniture.*   Fax:(212) 673-7317   %FO: 100

- **GIANNI VERSACE**
  Via Manzoni, #39, Milan 20121, Italy
  CEO: Santo Versace, CFO   Tel: 39-2-760931   Emp: N/A
  Bus: *Design/mfr./sale clothing, perfume, and retail*   Fax:
      boutiques.

  PRATO VERDE
  645 Fifth Avenue, New York, NY 10022
  CEO:Giovanni Galbiati, CEO   Tel: (212) 752-8002   Emp: 200
  Bus: *Design/mfr./distribute fashion clothing,*   Fax:(212) 752-6072   %FO: 100
      fragrances and retail boutiques.

- **WAM SPA**
  Via Cavour 338-1, I-41030 Pontemotta-Cavezzo, Italy
  CEO: Warner Marchesini, Pres.   Tel: 39-535-618111   Emp: 850
  Bus: *Mfr. industrial and bulk handling equipment.*   Fax:39-535-618226

  WAM CORPORATION OF AMERICA
  2650 Pleasantdale Road, Suite 15, Atlanta, GA 30340
  CEO:Orlando Bergonzini, Pres.   Tel: (770) 446-3640   Emp: 15
  Bus: *Mfr. dust collectors and screw conveyors;*   Fax:(770) 446-3703   %FO: JV
      distribute industrial and bulk handling
      equipment.

● **ZAMBON GROUP, S.P.A.**
Via Lillo del Duca 10, Bresso/Milano 20091, Italy
CEO: Andrea Zambon, M.D., Pres. & CEO   Tel: 39-266-5241   Emp: 2400
Bus: *Prescription/pharmaceutical products, fine*   Fax:39-266-501492
     chemicals and home health.

ZAMBON CORPORATION
1 Meadowlands Plaza, East Rutherford, NJ   07073
CEO: George Griffiths, Gen. Mgr.   Tel: (201) 896-2200   Emp: 17
Bus: *Prescription and OTC pharmaceutical product*   Fax:(201) 896-2209   %FO: 100
     development and licensing.

Ivory Coast

- **AIR AFRIQUE**
  3 Avenue Joseph Anoma, Abidjan 01, Ivory Coast
  CEO: Yves Roland Billecart, Pres.   Tel: 22-520-3000   Emp: 4209
  Bus: *Commercial air transport services.*   Fax:22-520-3006

  ### AIR AFRIQUE
  1350 Avenue of the Americas, 6th Floor, New York, NY   10019
  CEO: Yves Roland Billecart, Pres.   Tel: (212) 586-5908   Emp: 50+
  Bus: *International commercial air transport*   Fax:(212) 541-7539   %FO: 100
       services.

Japan

● **ACHILLES CORPORATION**
22 Daikyo-machi, Shinjuku-ku, Tokyo 160, Japan
CEO: Sadao Nakajima, Pres.　　　　　　　　Tel: 81-3-3341-5111　　Emp: N/A
Bus: *Manufacture rubber and plastic products.*　　Fax:81-3-3225-4013

　　　ACHILLES USA INC.
　　　1407 80th Street SW, Everett, WA　98203
　　　CEO: Toshihiro Katagiri, Pres.　　　　　　Tel: (206) 353-7000　　Emp: 186
　　　Bus: *Manufacture plastic film and sheeting.*　Fax:(206) 347-5785　　%FO: 100

● **AJINMOTO COMPANY, INC.**
1-15-1 Kyobashi 1-chome, Chuo-ku, Tokyo 104, Japan
CEO: Shunshki Inamori, Pres.　　　　　　　　Tel: 81-3-5250-8111　　Emp: 5590
Bus: *Seasonings, amino acids, oil products and other*　Fax:81-3-5250-8293
　　　foodstuffs and specialty chemicals.

　　　AJINMOTO USA, INC.
　　　500 Frank West Burr Blvd., Teaneck, NJ　07666
　　　CEO: Hiroshi Kurihara, Pres.　　　　　　Tel: (201) 488-1212　　Emp: 140
　　　Bus: *Mfr./distribute MSG, amino acids, frozen*　Fax:(201) 488-6282　　%FO: 100
　　　　　foods, fine chemicals, toiletries.

● **ALASKA PULP COMPANY, LTD.**
3-4-1 Marunouchi, Chiyoda-ku, Tokyo 100, Japan
CEO: Susumo Hayakawa, Pres.　　　　　　　　Tel: 81-3-212-2611　　Emp: 20
Bus: *Sale dissolving pulp.*　　　　　　　　　Fax:81-3-284-0955

　　　ALASKA PULP CORPORATION
　　　4600 Sawmill Creek Road, Sitka, AK　99835
　　　CEO: George S. Ishiyama, Pres.　　　　　Tel: (907) 747-2211　　Emp: 400
　　　Bus: *Mfr. dissolving pulp.*　　　　　　　Fax:(907) 747-5588　　%FO: 85

● **ALL NIPPON AIRWAYS CO., LTD.**
PO Box 106, 3-2-5 Kasumigaseki, Chiyoda-ku, Tokyo 100, Japan
CEO: Seiji Fukatsu, Pres. & CEO　　　　　　Tel: 81-3-3592-3049　　Emp: 22000
Bus: *Commercial air transport services.*　　　Fax:81-3-3592-3039

　　　ALL NIPPON AIRWAYS CO., LTD.
　　　630 Fifth Avenue, Ste. 646, New York, NY　10111
　　　CEO: Yogi Ohashi, Gen.Mgr. & Sr.Dir.　　Tel: (212) 956-8200　　Emp: 50
　　　Bus: *International air transport services; hotels.*　Fax:(212) 969-9022　　%FO: 100

- **APLUS COMPANY, LTD.**
  6-6 Minami Kyuhoji-machi, 3-chome, Chuo-ku, Osaka 541, Japan
  CEO: Eigo Maeda, Pres.   Tel: 81-6-245-7771   Emp: 2400
  Bus: *Consumer credit services.*   Fax:81-6-243-0468

  > **DAISHINPAN (USA) INC.**
  > 455 Market Street, Ste.1210, San Francisco, CA   94105
  > CEO: Katusuyuki Hayashi, Pres.   Tel: (415) 512-8440   Emp: N/A
  > Bus: *Real estate investment.*   Fax:(415) 512-8443   %FO: 100

- **ARAKAWA CHEMICAL INDUSTRIES LTD.**
  1-21 Hiranomachi, Higashi-ku, Osaka 541, Japan
  CEO: Shuhei Ishibe, Pres.   Tel: 81-6 209 8580   Emp: 684
  Bus: *Mfr./supplier rosin ester, absorbents, hydrocarbon*   Fax:81-6-209-8542
  and special resins.

  > **ARAKAWA CHEMICAL USA, INC.**
  > 625 North Michigan Avenue, #1700, Chicago, IL   60611
  > CEO: Mack M. Harashima, Pres.   Tel: (312) 642-1750   Emp: 21
  > Bus: *Distributor/supplier rosin ester, absorbents,*   Fax:(312) 642-0089   %FO: 100
  > *hydrocarbon and special resins.*

- **ASA COMPAMY, LTD.**
  P O Box 324, Higashi, Osaka 540-91, Japan
  CEO: M. Sameh, Pres.   Tel: 81-6-263-0631   Emp: 87
  Bus: *Textiles and general merchandise.*   Fax:81-6-263-1819

  > **ASA-TALA USA, INC.**
  > 141 West 36th Street, New York, NY   10018
  > CEO: Peter Tala, Pres.   Tel: (212) 736-1536   Emp: 35
  > Bus: *Mfr./distribute wearing apparel.*   Fax:(212) 736-2124   %FO: JV

- **ASACA CORP. & SHIBASOKU COMPANY, LTD.**
  6-8 Shinbashi 4-chome, Minato-ku, Tokyo 105, Japan
  CEO: Takashi Shigezaki, Pres.   Tel: 81-3-5401-3811   Emp: N/A
  Bus: *Mfr. audio and video test equipment.*   Fax:81-3-5401-3815

  > **ASACA-SHIBASOKU CORP. OF AMERICA**
  > 426 West Florence Street, Englewood, CA   90301
  > CEO: Mr. Saki, Co-Chair   Tel: (310) 827-7144   Emp: N/A
  > Bus: *Sales/service of audio and video test* Fax:(310) 306-1382   %FO: 100
  > *equipment.*

• ASAHI GLASS COMPANY, LTD.
2-1-2 Marunouchi 2-chome, Chiyoda-ku, Tokyo 100, Japan
CEO: Hiromichi Seya, Pres.　　　　　　　Tel: 81-3-3218-5631　　Emp: 20000
Bus: *Mfr. flat and fabricated glass, chemicals and*　Fax: 81-3-3287-0772
　　ceramics and produces optical lenses.

AA GLASS CORPORATION
3050 East Victoria Street, Compton, CA　90221
CEO: Meiji Hasagawa, Pres.　　　　　　　Tel: (213) 631-1123　　Emp: N/A
Bus: *Distributor auto safety glass parts.*　　Fax: (213) 632-7272　　%FO: 100

AFG INDUSTRIES, INC.
1400 Lincoln Street, PO Box 929, Kingsport, TN　27660
CEO: James W. Bradford, Jr., Pres.& CEO　Tel: (423) 229-7200　　Emp: N/A
Bus: *Mfr. mirrors and double glazing glass.*　Fax: (423) 229-7211　　%FO: 100

AMA GLASS CORPORATION, INC.
970 West 190th Street, Ste. 590, Torrance, CA　90502
CEO: M. Kinoshita, Pres.　　　　　　　　Tel: (310) 327-1414　　Emp: N/A
Bus: *Sale/distribution of flat glass.*　　　Fax: (310) 327-7110　　%FO: 100

AP TECHNOGLASS COMPANY
1465 West Sandusky Avenue, PO Box 819, Bellefontaine, OH　43311
CEO: T. Yamaguchi, Pres.　　　　　　　　Tel: (937) 599-3131　　Emp: N/A
Bus: *Sale/distribution of augo safety glass.*　Fax: (937) 599-3322　　%FO: 100

ASAHI GLASS AMERICA, INC.
2201 Water Ridge Pkwy., Ste. 400, Charlotte, NC　28217
CEO: Osamu Wada, Pres.　　　　　　　　Tel: (704) 357-3631　　Emp: 22
Bus: *U.S. headquarters office.*　　　　　Fax: (704) 357-6328　　%FO: 100

CORNING ASAHI VIDEO PRODUCTS
PO Box P-9, State College, PA　16804
CEO: Roger Ackerman, Pres.　　　　　　Tel: (814) 231-4200　　Emp: N/A
Bus: *Mfr. glass bulbs for televisions.*　　Fax: (814) 231-4255　　%FO: 100

• ASAHI MUTUAL LIFE INSURANCE COMPANY
7-3 Nishi-Shinjuku 1-chome, Shinjuku-ku, Tokyo 163-91, Japan
CEO: Yuzuru Fujita, Pres.　　　　　　　Tel: 81-3-3342 3111　　Emp: 37850
Bus: *Life insurance.*　　　　　　　　　Fax: N/A

ASAHI AMERICA INC.
400 Park Avenue, New York, NY　10022
CEO: Shinji Koma, CEO　　　　　　　　Tel: (212) 752-0202　　Emp: 13
Bus: *Investment research.*　　　　　　Fax: (212) 752-0419　　%FO: 100

● **ASAHI OPTICAL COMPANY, LTD.**
1-11-1 Nagata-cho, Chiyoda-ku, Tokyo 100, Japan
CEO: Tohru Matsumoto, Pres.   Tel: 81-3-960-5151   Emp: N/A
Bus: *Mfr. cameras, binoculars, lenses, photo and video*   Fax:81-3-960-5151
components and accessories.

    PENTAX CORPORATION
    35 Inverness Drive East, Englewood, CO   80112
    CEO: Andy Fukano, Pres.   Tel: (303) 799-8000   Emp: N/A
    Bus: *Sales/distribution of cameras, binoculars,*   Fax:(303) 790-1131   %FO: 100
    lenses, etc.

● **ASICS CORPORATION JAPAN**
1-1 Minatojima-Nakamachi, 7-chome, Chuo-ku, Kobe 650, Japan
CEO: Yoshiyuki Takahashi, Pres. & CEO   Tel: 81-78-303-3333   Emp: 5324
Bus: *Mfr. sporting goods & health related products.*   Fax:81-78-303-2244

    ASICS TIGER CORPORATION
    10540 Talbert Avenue, West Bldg, Fountain Valley, CA   92708
    CEO: Rich Bourne, EVP & Gen.Mgr.   Tel: (714) 962-7654   Emp: 186
    Bus: *Mfr./sale/promotion athletic footwear,*   Fax:(714) 962-6661   %FO: 100
    apparel, accessories & skiwear.

● **ASO PHARMACEUTICAL COMPANY, LTD.**
91 Tsukure, Kikuyo, Kikuchi, Kumamoto 869-11, Japan
CEO: Yakushi Kuki, Pres.   Tel: 81-96-232-2131   Emp: 300
Bus: *Mfr. first aid and health care products.*   Fax:81-96-232-2137

    ASO CORPORATION
    300 Sarasota Center Blvd., Sarasota, FL   34240
    CEO: John D. Macaskill, CEO   Tel: (941) 379-0300   Emp: 40
    Bus: *Mfr. bandages.*   Fax:(941) 378-9040   %FO: 100

● **BANK OF JAPAN**
2-1-1, Hongoku-cho, Nihonbashi, Chuo-ku, CPO 203, 100-91 Tokyo, Japan
CEO: Akira Nagashima, Deputy Governor, Int'l   Tel: 81-3-3279-1111   Emp: 1300
Bus: *Government; central bank.*   Fax:81-3-3245-0538

    BANK OF JAPAN
    1 Chase Manhattan Plaza, New York, NY   10005
    CEO: Naoki Tabata, Mgr.   Tel: (212) 269-6566   Emp: 5
    Bus: *Government; central bank.*   Fax:(212) 269-6127   %FO: 100

• BANK OF TOKYO MITSUBISHI, LTD.
2-7-1 Marunouchi 2-chome, Chiyoda-ku, Tokyo 100, Japan

CEO: T. Takagaki, Pres.   Tel: 81-3-3240-1111   Emp: 30333

Bus: *Wholesale and retail banking.*   Fax:81-3-3240-4197

BANK OF TOKYO MITSUBISHI, LTD.
1251 Avenue of the Americas, New York, NY 10022

CEO: T. Shimura, Mgr.   Tel: (212) 782-4000   Emp: 1300

Bus: *International banking services.*   Fax:(212) 782-6439   %FO: 100

BANK OF TOKYO MITSUBISHI, LTD.
227 West Monroe Street, 23rd Fl., Chicago, IL 60606

CEO: Tokutaro Sekine, Mgr.   Tel: (312) 696-4500   Emp: N/A

Bus: *International banking services.*   Fax:(312) 696-4530   %FO: 100

BANK OF TOYKO MITSUBISHI, LTD.
2100 Ponce de Leon Blvd., Coral Gables, FL 33134

CEO: Yoichirou Udagawa, Mgr.   Tel: (305) 445-2100   Emp: N/A

Bus: *International banking services.*   Fax:(305) 446-1842   %FO: 100

BTM CAPITAL CORPORATION
125 Summer Street, Boston, MA 02110

CEO: Leo Chausse, Pres.   Tel: (617) 573-9000   Emp: N/A

Bus: *Financial services.*   Fax:(617) 345-5688   %FO: 100

BTM LEASING AND FINANCE, INC.
1251 Avenue of the Americas, New York, NY 10020

CEO: Isao Nishiyama, Pres.   Tel: (212) 782-4496   Emp: 18

Bus: *Financial services.*   Fax:(212) 782-4006   %FO: 100

UNION BANK OF CALIFORNIA
350 California Street, San Francisco, CA 94104

CEO: Takahiro Moriguchi, Pres.   Tel: (415) 445-0200   Emp: N/A

Bus: *International banking.*   Fax:(415) 765-2841   %FO: 100

• THE BANK OF YOKOHAMA, LTD.
1-1, Minatomirai 3-chome, Nishi-ku, 220 Yokohama, Japan

CEO: Sadaaki Hirasawa, Pres.   Tel: 81-45-225-1111   Emp: 6000

Bus: *General commercial banking services.*   Fax:81-45-225-1160

BANK OF YOKOHAMA, LTD
One World Trade Center, New York, NY 10048

CEO: Michiro Ashba, EVP & Gen. Mgr.   Tel: (212) 775-1700   Emp: 43

Bus: *International commercial banking services.*   Fax:(212) 938-5450   %FO: 100

- **BRIDGESTONE CORPORATION**
10-1 Kyobashi 1-chome, Chuo-ku, Tokyo 104, Japan
CEO: Yoichiro Kaizaki, Pres.   Tel: 81-3-3567-0111   Emp: 89418
Bus: *Mfr. tires and rubber, industry rubber goods and*   Fax:81-3-3567-5958
     sporting goods.

     BRIDGESTONE CYCLE (USA), INC.
     15021 Wicks Blvd., San Leandro, CA   94577
     CEO: Yuki Kimura, Pres.   Tel: (415) 895-5480   Emp: N/A
     Bus: *Mfr. bicycles.*   Fax:(415) 895-5766   %FO: 100

     BRIDGESTONE SPORTS (USA), INC.
     15320 Industrial Park Blvd., NE, Covington, GA   30209
     CEO: Masanori Nakada, Pres.   Tel: (404) 787-7400   Emp: N/A
     Bus: *Sporting goods.*   Fax:(404) 786-6416   %FO: 100

     BRIDGESTONE/FIRESTONE, INC.
     50 Century Blvd., Nashville, TN   37214-0991
     CEO: Masatoshi Ono, Pres.   Tel: (615) 872-5000   Emp: N/A
     Bus: *Mfr./distribution automotive tires and tubes.*   Fax:(615) 872-1414   %FO: 100

     FIRESTONE BUILDING PRODUCTS CO.
     525 Congressional Blvd, Carmel, IN   46032-5607
     CEO: Paul Mineart, Pres.   Tel: (317) 575-7000   Emp: N/A
     Bus: *Mfr. rubber roofing products.*   Fax:(317) 575-7100   %FO: 100

- **BROTHER INDUSTRIES LTD.**
9-35 Horita-Dori, Mizuho-ku, Nagoya 467, Japan
CEO: Y. Yasui, Pres.   Tel: 81-52-824-2511   Emp: 6000
Bus: *Mfr. typewriters, microwave ovens, facsimile*   Fax:81-52-824-3398
     machines, home & industrial sewing machinery.

     BROTHER INTERNATIONAL CORP.
     200 Cottontail Lane, Somerset, NJ   08875
     CEO: Hiromi Gunji, Pres   Tel: (908) 356-8880   Emp: 600
     Bus: *U.S. headquarters. Sale/marketing parent*   Fax:(908) 356-4085   %FO: 49
     company products.

- **CANON, INC.**
30-2 Shimomaruko 3-chome, Ohta-ku, Tokyo 146, Japan
CEO: Fujio Miturai, Pres.   Tel: 81-3 37582111   Emp: 72300
Bus: *Mfr. office equipment, cameras, video, audio,*   Fax:81-3-5482-5130
     medical & broadcast equipment.

     CANON USA, INC.
     One Canon Plaza, Lake Success, NY   11042
     CEO: Haruo Murase, Pres. & CEO   Tel: (516) 488-6700   Emp: 8200
     Bus: *Mfr./distributor office. equipment, cameras,*   Fax:(516) 328-5069   %FO: 100
     video, audio, medical & broadcast equipment.

● **CASIO COMPUTER COMPANY, LTD.**
Shinjuku-Sumitomo Building, 2-6-1, Nishi-Shinjuku, Shinjuku-ku, Tokyo 163-02, Japan
CEO: Kazuo Kashio, Pres.   Tel: 81-3-3347-4803   Emp: 18800
Bus: *Mfr. electronic consumer products; calculators,*   Fax:81-3-3347-4533
     watches, telecommunications equipment, cameras
     and computers.

    CASIO INC.
    570 Mt. Pleasant Avenue, Dover, NJ   07801
    CEO: John J. Mc Donald, Pres.   Tel: (201) 361-5400   Emp: N/A
    Bus: *Mfr./distribution electronic consumer*   Fax:(201) 361-3819   %FO: 100
       products; calculators, watches,
       telecommunications equipment, cameras and
       computers.

● **THE CHIBA BANK, LTD.**
1-2 Chiba-Minato, Chuo-ku, Chiba 260, Japan
CEO: Takashi Tamaki, Pres.   Tel: 81-43-245-1111   Emp: N/A
Bus: *General commercial banking services.*   Fax:81-43-3242-1735

    THE CHIBA BANK, LTD.
    1133 Avenue of the Americas, New York, NY   10036
    CEO: Masamichi Abe, Gen. Mgr.   Tel: (212) 354-7777   Emp: 18
    Bus: *International commercial banking services.*   Fax:(212) 354-8575   %FO: 100

● **CHORI COMPANY, LTD.**
4-5 Kawaramachi 2-chome, Higashi-ku, Osaka, Japan
CEO: Yuji Kobayashi, Pres.   Tel: N/A   Emp: N/A
Bus: *Textiles, chemical products and machinery.*   Fax:81-6-228-5611

    CHORI AMERICA INC
    One Penn Plaza, Ste. 5440, New York, NY   10118
    CEO: Gonosuke Yonezewa, Pres.   Tel: (212) 563-3264   Emp: N/A
    Bus: *Textiles, chemical products and machinery*   Fax:(212) 736-6392   %FO: 100

● **CHUGAI BOYEKI CO LTD.**
2-15-13 Tsukishima, Chuo-ku, Tokyo 104, Japan
CEO: U. Doi, Pres.   Tel: 81-3 35364500   Emp: N/A
Bus: *International trading, diverse products.*   Fax:81-3 35364780

    CHUGAI BOYEKI (AMERICA) CORP
    500 Fifth Avenue, New York, NY   10110-0197
    CEO: K. Suda, Sr. EVP   Tel: (212) 869-4860   Emp: 80
    Bus: *Distribution chemicals, electronics, CCTV,*   Fax:(212) 391-3817   %FO: 100
       foodstuffs.

- **CHUNICHI-SHIMBUN**
  1-6-1 Sannomaru, Naka-ku, Nagoya, Japan
  CEO: Miichiro Kato, Chrm.   Tel: N/A   Emp: N/A
  Bus: *Daily newspaper publisher.*   Fax:N/A

  > **CHUNICHI-TOKYO SHIMBUN**
  > 1012 National Press Bldg., Washington, DC   20045
  > CEO: Moriyoshi Sase, Bureau Chief   Tel: (202) 783-9479   Emp: 6
  > Bus: *Newspaper publishing, U.S. news gathering.*   Fax:(202) 628-9622   %FO: 100

- **CITIZEN WATCH COMPANY, LTD.**
  PO Box 232, 20F Shinjuku Mitsui Bldg., 2-1-1 Nishi-Shinjuku, Tokyo 16304, Japan
  CEO: Michio Nakajima, Pres.   Tel: 81-3-3342-1231   Emp: N/A
  Bus: *Manufactures wrist-watches, information and*   Fax:81-3-3342-1280
  electronic equipment and industrial equipment and
  instruments.

  > **CITIZEN AMERICA CORPORATION**
  > 2450 Broadway, Ste. 600, Santa Monica, CA   90404
  > CEO: H. Sato, Pres.   Tel: (310) 453-0614   Emp: 35
  > Bus: *Information equipment and service/repair of*   Fax:(310) 453-2824   %FO: 100
  > *watches.*

  > **CITIZEN WATCH COMPANY OF AMERICA**
  > 1200 Wall Street West, Lyndhurst, NJ   07071
  > CEO: Laurence Grunstein, Pres.   Tel: (201) 438-8150   Emp: N/A
  > Bus: *U.S. headquarters office.*   Fax:(201) 438-4161   %FO: 100

  > **MARUBENI CITIZEN-CINCOM, INC.**
  > 90 Boroline Road, Allendale, NJ   07401
  > CEO: Tony Yakamuri, Pres.   Tel: (201) 818-0100   Emp: 25
  > Bus: *Manufactures precision industrial machinery.*   Fax:(201) 818-1877   %FO: 100

- **CLARION COMPANY, LTD.**
  22-3 Shibuya 2-chome, Shibuya-ku, Tokyo 150, Japan
  CEO: I. Ishitsubo, Pres.   Tel: 81-6-400-1121   Emp: 3000
  Bus: *Mfr. mobile electronics.*   Fax:81-6-234-3764

  > **CLARION CORPORATION OF AMERICA**
  > 661 West Redondo Beach Blvd., Gardena, CA   90247
  > CEO: Tadashi Kitajima, Pres.   Tel: (310) 327-9100   Emp: 500
  > Bus: *Mfr./sale/service mobile electronics.*   Fax:(310) 327-1999   %FO: 100

● **DAI NIPPON PRINTING CO LTD.**

1-1 Ichigaya-Kagacho 1-chome, Shijuku-ku, Tokyo 162, Japan

CEO: Yoshitoshi Kitajima, Pres. Tel: 81-3-3266-2121 Emp: 12000

Bus: *Printing services.* Fax:81-3-3235-2594

  DNP AMERICA, INC.
  50 California Street, #777, San Francisco, CA 94111

  CEO: Kohei Tsumori, Gen. Mgr. Tel: (415) 788-1618 Emp: 50

  Bus: *Printing sales.* Fax:(415) 495-4481 %FO: 100

● **THE DAI-ICHI KANGYO BANK LTD.**

1-5 Uchisaiwai-cho 1-chome, Chiyoda-ku, Tokyo 100, Japan

CEO: Katsuhiko Kondo, Pres. Tel: 81-3 3596-1111 Emp: 18100

Bus: *General commercial banking services.* Fax:81-3 3596-2539

  THE CIT GROUP HOLDINGS INC
  650 CIT Drive, Livingston, NJ 07039

  CEO: Albert R. Gamper Jr., Pres. & CEO Tel: (201) 740-5000 Emp: 3000

  Bus: *Corporate finance, factoring, multinational* Fax:(201) 740-5527 %FO: 60
    financing, leasing.

  DAI-ICHI KANGYO BANK - Atlanta
  285 Peachtree Center Avenue, NE, Atlanta, GA 30303

  CEO: T. Mochizuki, Gen. Mgr. Tel: (404) 581-0200 Emp: N/A

  Bus: *International commercial banking services.* Fax:(404) 577-0511 %FO: 100

  DAI-ICHI KANGYO BANK - Chicago
  10 Wacker Drive, Chicago, IL 60606

  CEO: Mikio Nishimura, Gen. Mgr. Tel: (312) 876-8600 Emp: N/A

  Bus: *International commercial banking services.* Fax:(312) 876-2011 %FO: 100

  DAI-ICHI KANGYO BANK - New York
  1 World Trade Center, Suite 4911, New York, NY 10048

  CEO: Yoshiro Aoki, Gen. Mgr. Tel: (212) 466-5200 Emp: 400+

  Bus: *International commercial banking services.* Fax:(212) 524-0579 %FO: 100

  DAI-ICHI KANGYO BANK - San Francisco
  101 California Street, San Francisco, CA 94111

  CEO: Takuo Yoshida, Pres. Tel: (415) 393-1800 Emp: N/A

  Bus: *International commercial banking services.* Fax:(415) 788-7868 %FO: 100

  DAI-ICHI KANGYO BANK OF CALIFORNIA - Los Angeles Agency
  555 West 5th Street, Los Angeles, CA 90013

  CEO: Isao Arihara, Pres. Tel: (213) 612-2700 Emp: 125

  Bus: *International commercial banking services.* Fax:(213) 612-2875 %FO: 100

● **DAIDO STEEL CO INC**
11-18 Nishiki l-chome, Naka-ku, Nagoya 460, Japan
CEO: Toshio Kishida, Pres.　　　　　　　　　　Tel: 81-52-2015111　　Emp: N/A
Bus: *Specialty steel products.*　　　　　　　　　Fax:81-52-2219268

　　　DAIDO STEEL (AMERICA), INC.
　　　2200 E Devon Ave., #314, Des Plaines, IL　60018
　　　CEO: Hiromichi Tsuchiya, Pres　　　　　　　Tel: (847) 699-9066　　Emp: 10
　　　Bus: *Import export steel.*　　　　　　　　　Fax:(847) 699-9067　　%FO: 100

● **DAIDO TSUSHO CO LTD.**
1-6 Kyobashi 1-chome, Chuo-ku, Tokyo 104, Japan
CEO: Koki Ogawa, Pres.　　　　　　　　　　　Tel: 81-3-32732451　　Emp: 100
Bus: *Imp/export power transmission products, electronic*　Fax:81-3-5255-6615
control devices, tools, surveying & measuring
instruments.

　　　DAIDO CORPORATION
　　　615 Pierce St., P O Box 6739, Somerset, NJ　08875-6739
　　　CEO: Keith Omata, Pres.　　　　　　　　　Tel: (908) 805-1900　　Emp: 140
　　　Bus: *Distribution/sale power transmission products,*　Fax:(908) 805-0122　　%FO: 100
　　　power tools, general merchandise.

● **DAIDOH, LTD.**
1-16 Sotokanda 3-chome, Chiyoda-ku, Tokyo 101, Japan
CEO: Yoshiya Hatori, Pres.　　　　　　　　　Tel: 81-3-3257-5014　　Emp: 1300
Bus: *Mfr. worsted fabrics and yarns; men's and women's*　Fax:81-3-3257-5051
apparel.

　　　DAIDO NEW YORK, INC.
　　　119 West 57th Street, New York, NY　10019
　　　CEO: Kenji Aoki, Pres.　　　　　　　　　　Tel: (212) 581-8255　　Emp: 3
　　　Bus: *Import/export textile, apparel and furnishings.*　Fax:(212) 541-5120　　%FO: 100

● **THE DAIEI, INC.**
4-1-1, Minatojima, Nakamachi, Chuo-ku, Kobe 650, Japan
CEO: Isao Nakauchi, CEO　　　　　　　　　　Tel: 81-78-302-5001　　Emp: 19000
Bus: *Retail food and chain store operator.*　　　Fax:81-78-302-5572

　　　DAIEI USA, INC.
　　　801 Kahake Street, Honolulu, HI　96814
　　　CEO: Takashi Ichikawa, CEO　　　　　　　Tel: (808) 973-6600　　Emp: N/A
　　　Bus: *Retail food and chain store operator.*　　Fax:(808) 941-6457　　%FO: 100

● **DAIICHI CHUO KK**
3-5-15 Nihonbashi, Chuo-ku, Tokyo 103, Japan
CEO: Mahiko Sotome, Pres.   Tel: 81-3-278-6800   Emp: 650
Bus: *International and domestic shipping.*   Fax:81-3-278-6831

    DAIICHI CHUO SHIPPING AMERICA, INC.
    450 Lexington Avenue, New York, NY   10017
    CEO: J. Kohashi, Pres.   Tel: (212) 972-6080   Emp: 11
    Bus: *Shipping agents and brokers.*   Fax:(212) 370-0831   %FO: 100

● **DAIKIN INDUSTRIES, LTD.**
Umeda Center Bldg., 4-12 Nakazaki-Nishi 2-chome, Kita-ku Osaka 530, Japan
CEO: Mr. H. Inoue, Chrm.   Tel: 81-6-373-4380   Emp: N/A
Bus: *Mfr. industrial pumps and refrigeration equipment,*   Fax:81-6-373-4380
    air-conditioning systems, medical equipment and
    fluorochemicals.

    DAIKIN U.S. CORPORATION, INC.
    375 Park Avenue, New York, NY   10152
    CEO: Haruo Uemachi, Pres.   Tel: (212) 935-4890   Emp: 25
    Bus: *Mfr. commercial/industrial air conditioning*   Fax:(212) 935-4895   %FO: 100
       systems.

● **DAINIPPON INK & CHEMICALS INC.**
7-20 Nihonbashi 3-chome, Chuo-Ku, Tokyo 103, Japan
CEO: Takemitsu Takahashi, Pres.   Tel: 81-3-3272-4511   Emp: 23867
Bus: *Printing inks, supplies, machinery, chemicals,*   Fax:81-3-3278-8558
    imaging reprographic products, resins, plastics,
    petrochemicals, building materials.

    DIC TRADING USA, INC.
    222 Bridge Plaza South, Fort Lee, NJ   07024
    CEO: Tsuguo Tomiyama, Pres.   Tel: (201) 592-5100   Emp: N/A
    Bus: *Sales of DIC products.*   Fax:(201) 592-8232   %FO: 100

    DYNARIC DIC, INC.
    Glenpointe Ctr. W., 500 F.W.Burr Blvd., Teaneck, NJ   07666
    CEO: Joseph Martinez, Pres.   Tel: (201) 692-7700   Emp: N/A
    Bus: *Mfr. plastic strapping material.*   Fax:(201) 692-7757   %FO: 100

    PREMIER POLYMERS, INC.
    4000 East Hwy 6, Rt. 6
    PO Box 353, Alvin, TX   77511
    CEO: Kazuo Okada, Pres.   Tel: (713) 331-8800   Emp: N/A
    Bus: *Mfr./sale plastic compounds and colorants.*   Fax:(713) 585-2157   %FO: 51.6

    REICHHOLD CHEMICALS, INC.
    2400 Ellis Road, Durham, NC   27703-5543
    CEO: Phillip Ashkettle, Pres. & CEO   Tel: (919) 990-7500   Emp: N/A
    Bus: *Mfr. synthetic resins and adhesives.*   Fax:(919) 990-7711   %FO: 100

SUN CHEMICAL CORPORATION
222 Bridge Plaza South, Fort Lee, NJ   07024
CEO: Edward E. Barr, Chrm. & CEO   Tel: (201) 224-4600   Emp: N/A
Bus: *Mfr./sale printing inks and organic chemicals.*   Fax:(201) 224-4512   %FO: 100

● **DAIO PAPER CORPORATION**
2-60 Kamiya-cho, Iyomishima 799-04, Japan
CEO: Tomatsu Osawa, Pres.   Tel: 81-89- 623-3300   Emp: 3600
Bus: *Mfr. pulp and paper.*   Fax:N/A

    CALIFORNIA WOODFIBER CORPORATION
    1890 Parkway Blvd., PO Box 753, West Sacramento, CA   95691
    CEO: Michihiko Tamaki, Pres.   Tel: (916) 371-3682   Emp: 18
    Bus: *Mfr. woodchips for pulp.*   Fax:(916) 371-5060   %FO: 80

● **DAISHOWA INTL CO LTD.**
2-6-1 Otemachi, Chiyoda-ku, Tokyo 100, Japan
CEO: Yuji Nakano, Pres.   Tel: 81-3 32422211   Emp: 3000
Bus: *Import woodchip.*   Fax:81-3 32450133

    DAISHOWA AMERICA CO., LTD.
    701 5th Avenue, Ste. 7200, Seattle, WA   98104
    CEO: Tadashi Sudao, Pres.   Tel: (206) 623-1772   Emp: 320
    Bus: *Export woodchip, mfr. telephone directory*   Fax:(206) 382-9130   %FO: 100
        paper.

● **DAIWA SECURITIES COMPANY, LTD.**
6-4 Otemachi 2-chome, Chiyoda-ku, Tokyo 100, Japan
CEO: Yoshitoki Chino, Chrm.   Tel: 81-3-243-2111   Emp: 9000
Bus: *Broker, dealer and financial advisor.*   Fax:N/A

    DAIWA SECURITIES AMERICA, INC.
    1 World Financial Sq., 200 Liberty St., 25th Fl., New York, NY   10281
    CEO: Shuichi Komori, Chrm. & CFO   Tel: (212) 945-0100   Emp: 400
    Bus: *Investment banking and securities broker.*   Fax:(212) 945-2510   %FO: 100

● **DENKI KAGAKU KOGYO KK**
4-1 Yuraku-ho 1-chome, Chiyoda-ku, Tokyo 100, Japan
CEO: T. Shinmura, Pres.   Tel: 81-3-3507-5401   Emp: N/A
Bus: *Chemical and cement products.*   Fax:81-3-3507-5759

    DENKA CORPORATION
    780 Third Avenue, New York, NY   10022
    CEO: Tatsuhiro Aoyagi, Pres.   Tel: (212) 688-8700   Emp: 4
    Bus: *Service chemical products.*   Fax:(212) 688-8727   %FO: 100

● **DENSO CORPORATION**
1-1 Showa-cho, Kariya Aichi 448, Japan
CEO: Hiromu Okabe, Pres.   Tel: 81-566-25-5511   Emp: 57000
Bus: *Automotive technology, components and systems.*   Fax:81-566-25-4522

    AMERICAN INDUSTRIAL MANUFACTURING SERVICES, INC.
    41673 Corning Place, Murrieta, CA   92562
    CEO: Kazunori Amano, Pres.   Tel: (909) 698-3379   Emp: 90
    Bus: *Mfr. automotive components.*   Fax:(909) 698-1379   %FO: 100

    ASSOCIATED FUEL PUMP SYSTEMS CORP.
    1100 Scotts Bridge Rd., PO Box 1326, Anderson, SC   29622
    CEO: Reiner Biggemann, Pres.   Tel: (864) 224-0012   Emp: N/A
    Bus: *Mfr./sale fuel pumps.*   Fax:(864) 224-2927   %FO: JV

    DENSO INTERNATIONAL AMERICA, INC.
    24777 Denso Drive
    PO Box 5133, Southfield, MI   48086-5133
    CEO: Akira Kataoka, Chrm.   Tel: (248) 350-7500   Emp: 6000
    Bus: *Automotive technology, components and*   Fax:(248) 350-7772   %FO: 100
        systems.

    DENSO MANUFACTURING MICHIGAN, INC.
    One Denso Road, Battle Creek, MI   49015-1083
    CEO: Koichi Fukaya, Pres.   Tel: (616) 965-3322   Emp: 1600
    Bus: *Mfr./sale heaters, radiators, air conditioners,*   Fax:(616) 965-8399   %FO: 100
        and auto components.

    DENSO MANUFACTURING TENNESSEE, INC.
    1720 Robert C. Jackson Drive, Maryville, TN   37801
    CEO: Kiyohiro Shimotsu, Pres.   Tel: (423) 982-7000   Emp: 1900
    Bus: *Mfr./sales alternators/starters and automotive*   Fax:(423) 981-5250   %FO: 100
        electronic products.

    DENSO SALES CALIFORNIA, INC.
    3900 Via Oro Avenue, Long Beach, CA   90810
    CEO: Kazunori Amano, Pres.   Tel: (562) 834-6352   Emp: 400
    Bus: *Automotive component supplier.*   Fax:(562) 513-7319   %FO: 100

    MICHIGAN AUTOMOTIVE COMPRESSOR, INC.
    2400 North Dearing Road, Parma, MI   49269
    CEO: Akira Imura, Pres.   Tel: (517) 531-5500   Emp: N/A
    Bus: *Mfr./sale compressors & clutches.*   Fax:(517) 531-5680   %FO: JV

    PURODENSO COMPANY
    1410 Highway 70 Bypass, Jackson, TN   38302-1887
    CEO: Shinichi Inagaki, Pres.   Tel: (901) 427-4774   Emp: 330
    Bus: *Mfr./sale oil filters & detergents.*   Fax:(901) 424-4733   %FO: 100

- **DENTSU INC.**
  1-1 Tsukiji l-chome, Chuo-ku, Tokyo 104, Japan
  CEO: Yutaka Narita, Pres.   Tel: 81-3-5551-5111   Emp: 5820
  Bus: *Advertising & communications services.* Fax:81-3-5551-2013

  ### DCA ADVERTISING, INC.
  666 Fifth Avenue, 9th Fl., New York, NY   10036
  CEO: Kazuo Miyakawa, Pres.   Tel: (212) 397-3333   Emp: 70
  Bus: *Advertising & communications services.* Fax:(212) 397-3322   %FO: 100

  ### DENTSU INC.
  120 Broadway, Suite 260, Santa Monica, CA   90401
  CEO: Seiji Ito   Tel: (310) 899-1113   Emp: 4
  Bus: *Advertising & communications services.* Fax:(310) 899-0113   %FO: 100

  ### DENTSU INC.
  1114 Ave. of the Americas, 30th Fl., New York, NY   10036
  CEO: Ted Machida, Pres.   Tel: (212) 869-8318   Emp: 20
  Bus: *Advertising & communications services.* Fax:(212) 719-5028   %FO: 100

  ### LORD, DENTSU & PARTNERS
  810 Seventh Avenue, New York, NY   10019
  CEO: James Hood, CEO   Tel: (212) 408-2100   Emp: 193
  Bus: *Advertising & communications services.* Fax:(212) 957-9512   %FO: 100

- **DIAL SERVICE COMPANY, LTD.**
  1-11-11 Jingumae, Shibuya-ku, Tokyo 150, Japan
  CEO: Yuri Konno, Pres.   Tel: 81-3 3478-1001   Emp: 500
  Bus: *Telephone counseling, information services,*   Fax:81-3 3478-1102
       business support, telemarketing and communication
       services.

  ### DIAL SERVICE INTL INC.
  500 Fifth Ave., Ste.1818, New York, NY   10110
  CEO: Shizuko Afukuda, Mgr.   Tel: (212) 764-7200   Emp: 10
  Bus: *Information service.*   Fax:(212) 764-7207   %FO: 100

- **EAST JAPAN RAILWAY COMPANY**
  1-6-5 Marunouchi, Chiyada-ku, Tokyo, Japan
  CEO: Masatake Matsuda, Pres.   Tel: 81-3-3212-3691   Emp: 80000
  Bus: *National railway system.*   Fax:81-3-3212-0535

  ### EAST JAPAN RAILWAY COMPANY
  1 Rockefeller Plaza, New York, NY   10020
  CEO: A. Kambara, Dir.   Tel: (212) 332-8686   Emp: 5
  Bus: *Information and liaison office for East Japan* Fax:(212) 332-8690   %FO: 100
       Railway Company (non-commercial).

● **EIKI INDUSTRIAL COMPANY, LTD.**
CPO Box 1229, Osaka 530-91, Japan
CEO: Shigya Yagi, Pres.   Tel: 81-6-364-5691   Emp: N/A
Bus: *Film projectors and VCRs.*   Fax: N/A

    EIKI INTERNATIONAL INC.
    26794 Vista Terrace Drive, Lake Forest, CA   92630-8113
    CEO: R. Fujishige, Pres.   Tel: (714) 457-0200   Emp: N/A
    Bus: *Film projectors and VCRs.*   Fax: (714) 457-7878   %FO: 100

● **ELMO COMPANY, LTD.**
6-14 Meizen-cho, Mizuho-ku, Nagoya 467, Japan
CEO: Katsuya Iwata, Pres.   Tel: 81-52 821-3141   Emp: 500
Bus: *Mfr. audio-visual, electronic imaging and CCTV*   Fax: 81-52 811-5243
    products.

    ELMO MANUFACTURING CORPORATION
    70 New Hyde Park Road, New Hyde Park, NY   11040
    CEO: Michael Ogari, Pres.   Tel: (516) 775-3200   Emp: 30
    Bus: *Sale/service audio-visual, electronic imaging*   Fax: (516) 775-3297   %FO: 100
    and CCTV products.

● **THE FUJI BANK LTD.**
5-5 Otemachi 1-chome, Chiyoda-ku, Tokyo 100, Japan
CEO: Yashiro Yamamoto, Pres.   Tel: 81-3 3216-2211   Emp: N/A
Bus: *Commercial banking services.*   Fax: 81-3-3216-2211

    THE FUJI BANK & TRUST CO. - New York Branch
    2 World Trade Center, 79th- 81st Fls., New York, NY   10048
    CEO: Shinji Hirayama, Pres. & CEO   Tel: (212) 898-2000   Emp: 1000
    Bus: *Commercial banking services.*   Fax: (212) 321-9407   %FO: 100

    THE FUJI BANK LTD. - Houston Agency
    One Houston Center, Suite 4100, 1221 McKinney Street, Houston, TX   77010
    CEO: Taizo Ishikawa, Gen. Mgr.   Tel: (713) 759-1800   Emp: N/A
    Bus: *Commercial banking services.*   Fax: (713) 759-0048   %FO: 100

    THE FUJI BANK LTD. - Miami Office
    200 Biscayne Blvd, Suite 3440, Miami, FL   33131
    CEO: Hiroshi Kazama, Chief Rep.   Tel: (305) 374-2226   Emp: N/A
    Bus: *Commercial banking services.*   Fax: (312) 381-8338   %FO: 100

    THE FUJI BANK LTD. - San Francisco Agency
    International Bldg., Ste. 500, 601 California St., San Francisco, CA   94108
    CEO: Kazuo Kamio, Gen. Mgr.   Tel: (415) 362-4740   Emp: N/A
    Bus: *Commercial banking services.*   Fax: (415) 362-4613   %FO: 100

THE FUJI BANK LTD. - Washington Office
1155 Conneticut Avenue, N.W., Suite 601, Washington, DC   20036
CEO: Yukihiko Chayama, Chief Rep.   Tel: (202) 467-6660   Emp: N/A
Bus: *Commercial banking services.*   Fax:(202) 467-5045   %FO: 100

THE FUJI BANK LTD. - Chicago Branch
225 West Wacker Drive
Suite 2000, Chicago, IL   60606
CEO: Takeshi Takahashi, Gen. Mgr.   Tel: (312) 621-0500   Emp: N/A
Bus: *Commercial banking services.*   Fax:(312) 621-0539   %FO: 100

THE FUJI BANK LTD. -Los Angeles Agency
333 South Hope Street, Los Angeles, CA   90071
CEO: Hideo Nakajima, Gen. Mgr.   Tel: (213) 680-9855   Emp: N/A
Bus: *Commercial banking services.*   Fax:(213) 253-4198   %FO: 100

THE FUJI BANK LTD. -Atlanta Agency
Marquis One Tower, Suite 2100, 245 Peachtree Centwe Ave., NE, Atlanta, GA   30303
CEO: Tcrumasa Yamasaki, Gen. Mgr.   Tel: (404) 653-2100   Emp: N/A
Bus: *Commercial banking services.*   Fax:(404) 653-2119   %FO: 100

FUJI SECURITIES, INC.
311 South Wacker Drive, Chicago, IL   60606-6620
CEO: Joseph Guinan, EVP & Mng.Dir   Tel: (312) 294-8700   Emp: 55
Bus: *Securities trading and dealing.*   Fax:(312) 294-8721   %FO: 100

FUJI SECURITIES, INC.
Two World Financial Center, South Tower, New York, NY   10281
CEO: Morton Swinsky, Pres. & CEO   Tel: (212) 528-3100   Emp: 109
Bus: *Securities trading and dealing.*   Fax:(212) 786-3347   %FO: 100

FUJI-WOLFENSOHN INTERNATIONAL
599 Lexington Avenue, 39th Fl., New York, NY   10022
CEO: Glen S. Lewy, CEO   Tel: (212) 223-7250   Emp: N/A
Bus: *Corporate advisory services.*   Fax:(212) 909-8178   %FO: JV

FUJILEASE CORPORATION
2 World Financial Center, S. Tower - 26th Fl., New York, NY   10048
CEO: Morton Swinsky, Pres. & CEO   Tel: (212) 898-2400   Emp: N/A
Bus: *Lease financing services.*   Fax:(212) 321-9649   %FO: 100

HELLER INTERNATIONAL CORP.
500 W. Monroe Street, Chicago, IL   60661
CEO: Richard Almeida, Chrm. & CEO   Tel: (312) 441-7000   Emp: 800
Bus: *Financial services.*   Fax:(312) 441-7499   %FO: 100

• **FUJI ELECTRIC COMPANY, LTD.**
New Yurakucho Bldg., 12-1 Yurakucho 1-chome, Chiyoda-ku, Tokyo, Japan
CEO: Takeshi Nakao, Chrm.   Tel: 81-33-211-1171   Emp: 13800
Bus: *Mfr.. electric and electronic products.*   Fax:81-33-438-0434

    FUJI ELECTRIC CORPORATION OF AMERICA, INC.
    80 Plaza West, Saddle Brook, NJ   07663
    CEO: H. Tawarada, Pres.   Tel: (201) 712-0555   Emp: 30
    Bus: *Sales/mktg. of electric and electronic products.*   Fax:(201) 368-8258   %FO: 100

    FUJI HI-TECH, INC.
    47520 Westinghouse Drive, Fremont, CA   94538
    CEO: Minoru Yamamoto, Pres.   Tel: (510) 651-0811   Emp: N/A
    Bus: *Industrial and consumer electronics.*   Fax:(510) 651-9070   %FO: 100

• **FUJI HEAVY INDUSTRIES LTD.**
Subaru Bldg, 7-2 Nishishinjuku 1-chome, Shinjuku-ku, Tokyo 160, Japan
CEO: Takeshi Tanaka, Pres.   Tel: 81-3-3472111   Emp: 15300
Bus: *Mfr. automobiles, aircraft & parts, engines,*   Fax:81-3-3472338
    machinery, buses & rolling stock.

    SUBARU OF AMERICA
    Subaru Plaza, P O Box 6000, Cherry Hill, NJ   08034-6000
    CEO: Yasuo Fujiki, Chrm. & CEO   Tel: (609) 488-8500   Emp: 656
    Bus: *Sale/marketing/service cars, parts &*   Fax:(609) 488-3274   %FO: 100
    accessories.

    SUBURU-ISUZU AUTOMOTIVE INC
    5500 State Road 38 East, Lafayette, IN   47903
    CEO: Hitoshi Maeda, Pres. & CEO   Tel: (765) 449-1111   Emp: 2500
    Bus: *Mfr. motor vehicles (see joint parent: ISUZU*   Fax:(765) 449-6269   %FO: 51
    MOTORS LTD.)

• **FUJI PHOTO FILM CO., LTD.**
26-30 Nishiazabu 2-chome, Minato-ku, Tokyo 106, Japan
CEO: M. Muneyuki, Pres.   Tel: 81-33-406-2111   Emp: 30000
Bus: *Mfr. photographic, reprographic, micrographic,*   Fax:81-33-406-2173
    audio and visual, x-ray and graphic art supplies.

    FUJI HUNT PHOTO. CHEMICALS, INC.
    Country Club Pl., Bldg. 1F, W. 115 Century Road, Paramus, NJ   07652
    CEO: Bert Aerts, Pres.   Tel: (201) 967-7500   Emp: N/A
    Bus: *Photographic chemicals.*   Fax:(201) 967-9299   %FO: 100

    FUJI MEDICAL SYSTEMS USA, INC.
    Stamford Harbor Park, 333 Ludlow Street, P. O. Box 120035, Stamford, CT   06902
    CEO: M. Okada, Chrm.   Tel: (203) 353-0300   Emp: N/A
    Bus: *Distribution/service x-ray film and equipment.*   Fax:(203) 353-0926   %FO: 100

FUJI PHOTO FILM HAWAII, INC.
1650 Kalakaua Avenue, Honolulu, HI 96826
CEO: Masaomi Kadomoto
Bus: *Distribution photo and magnetic products.*
Tel: (808) 942-9400   Emp: N/A
Fax:(808) 946-7071   %FO: 100

FUJI PHOTO FILM, INC.
211 Pucketts Ferry Road, Greenwood, SC 29649
CEO: Harry Watanabe, Pres.
Bus: *Mfr. photo film.*
Tel: (864) 223-2888   Emp: N/A
Fax:(864) 223-8181   %FO: 100

FUJI PHOTO FILM USA, INC.
555 Taxter Road, Elmsford, NY 10523
CEO: Osamu Inoue, Pres.
Bus: *Marketing/distribution photo and magnetic
     products.*
Tel: (914) 789-8100   Emp: 850
Fax:(914) 789-8514   %FO: 100

FUJIFILM MICRODISKS USA, INC.
35 Crosby Drive, Bedford, MA 01730
CEO: Osamu Inoue, Pres.
Bus: *Mfr. floppy disks.*
Tel: (617) 271-4400   Emp: N/A
Fax:(617) 275-4642   %FO: 100

● **FUJI PHOTO OPTICAL COMPANY, LTD.**
324 Uetaki-machi 1-chome, Omiya 330, Japan
CEO: Masaji Mukasa, Pres.
Bus: *Optical equipment.*
Tel: 81-330-630111   Emp: 1400
Fax:N/A

FUJINON INC.
10 Highpoint Drive, Wayne, NJ 07470
CEO: Shoichi Takada, Pres.
Bus: *Mfr. /distribute optical and medical equipment.*
Tel: (201) 633-5600   Emp: 93
Fax:(201) 633-5216   %FO: 100

● **FUJISAWA PHARMACEUTICAL COMPANY, LTD.**
4-7 Doshomachi, 3 chome, Chuo-ku, Osaka 541, Japan
CEO: Akira Fujiyama, Pres. & CEO
Bus: *Mfr./sale healthcare products.*
Tel: 81-6-206-7925   Emp: N/A
Fax:81-6-202-1141

FUJISAWA USA, INC.
3 Parkway North, Deerfield, IL 60015
CEO: Noboru Maeda, Pres.
Bus: *Healthcare products.*
Tel: (847) 317-8800   Emp: N/A
Fax:(847) 317-7296   %FO: 100

● **FUJITA CORPORATION**
6-15 Sendagaya, 4-chome, Shibuya-ku, Tokyo 151, Japan
CEO: K. Kaizuka, Chrm.
Bus: *Engineering and construction.*
Tel: 81-33-402-1911   Emp: N/A
Fax:81-33-402-9815

FUJITA CORPORATION USA, INC.
101 Wilshire Blvd., Ste. 21, Santa Monica, CA 90401
CEO: Isamu Nishiguchi, Pres.
Bus: *Engineering and construction.*
Tel: (310) 393-0787   Emp: N/A
Fax:(310) 395-8130   %FO: 100

● **FUJITEC COMPANY LTD.**
7-4 Utsubo Honmachi, 1-chome, Nishi-ku, Osaka, Japan
CEO: T. Uchiyama, Pres.　　　　　　　　　　　　Tel: 81-6-441-8521　　Emp: N/A
Bus: *Mfr./installation/service of elevators and escalators.*　Fax:81-6-441-8521

　　FUJITEC AMERICA, INC.
　　401 Fujitec Drive, Lebanon, OH　45036
　　CEO: Takakazu Uchiyama, Pres.　　　　　　Tel: (513) 932-8000　　Emp: 276
　　Bus: *Mfr. /installation/service of elevators,*　Fax:(513) 933-5504　　%FO: 100
　　　　escalators and autowalks.

● **FUJITSU LTD.**
Marunouchi Center Bldg, 16-1 Marunouchi 1-chome, Chiyoda-ku, Tokyo 100, Japan
CEO: Tadashi Sekizawa, Pres.　　　　　　　　　Tel: 81-3-3216-3211　　Emp: 165000
Bus: *Mfr. computer systems, telecommunications*　Fax:81-3-3216-9365
　　equipment, semiconductors, electrical components.

　　AMDAHL CORPORATION
　　1250 East Arques Avenue, Sunnyvale, CA　94086
　　CEO: John C. Lewis, Chrm. & Pres.　　　　Tel: (408) 746-6000　　Emp: 7700
　　Bus: *Mfr. mainframes.*　　　　　　　　Fax:(408) 746-6233　　%FO: 44

　　FUJITSU AMERICA, INC.
　　3055 Orchard Drive, San Jose, CA　95134
　　CEO: Yoshio Honda, Pres.　　　　　　　　Tel: (408) 432-1300　　Emp: 4800
　　Bus: *Corporate administration.*　　　　　Fax:(408) 432-1318　　%FO: 100

　　FUJITSU BUSINESS COMMUNICATION SYSTEMS, INC.
　　3190 Miraloma Avenue, Anaheim, CA　92806
　　CEO: Anthony Carrollo, Pres.　　　　　　　Tel: (714) 630-7721　　Emp: N/A
　　Bus: *Mfr. /sale/maintenance PBX switching systems.*　Fax:(714) 630-2991　　%FO: 100

　　FUJITSU COMPUTER PACKAGING TECHNOLOGIES, INC.
　　3811 Zanker Rd, Bldg 8A, San Jose, CA　95134-1402
　　CEO: Y. Honda, Pres.　　　　　　　　　　Tel: (408) 943-7700　　Emp: N/A
　　Bus: *R&D mainframe computers.*　　　　　Fax:(408) 943-7790　　%FO: 100

　　FUJITSU COMPUTER PRODUCTS OF AMERICA, INC.
　　2904 Orchard Pkwy., San Jose, CA　95134
　　CEO: Larry Sanders, Pres.　　　　　　　　Tel: (408) 432-6333　　Emp: N/A
　　Bus: *R&D/Mfr. /sale electronic equipment.*　Fax:(408) 894-1709　　%FO: 100

　　FUJITSU CUSTOMER SERVICE OF AMERICA, INC.
　　11085 North Torrey Pines Road, La Jolla, CA　92037
　　CEO: Robert Powell, Pres.　　　　　　　　Tel: (619) 457-9900　　Emp: N/A
　　Bus: *Service electronic and telecommunications*　Fax:(619) 457-9968　　%FO: 100
　　　　equipment.

FUJITSU MICROELECTRONICS, INC.
33545 North First Street, San Jose, CA   95134
CEO: M. Ashida, Pres.
Bus: *R&D/Mfr. /sale semiconductors.*
Tel: (408) 922-9000   Emp: N/A
Fax:(408) 432-9044   %FO: 100

FUJITSU NETWORK SWITCHING OF AMERICA, INC.
4403 Bland Road, Somerset Park, Raleigh, NC   27609
CEO: Harry Kanzaki, EVP
Bus: *Sale/maintenance telecommunications equipment.*
Tel: (919) 790-2211   Emp: N/A
Fax:(919) 790-8376   %FO: 100

FUJITSU NETWORK TRANSMISSION SYSTEMS, INC.
2801 Telecom Pkwy., Richardson, TX   75082
CEO: A. Kokimasa, Pres.
Bus: *Mfr. /sale telecommunications equipment.*
Tel: (972) 690-6000   Emp: N/A
Fax:(972) 467-6991   %FO: 100

POQET COMPUTER CORPORATION
5200 Patrick Henry Drive, Santa Clara, CA   95054
CEO: Louis Panetta, Pres.
Bus: *Design/sale portable computers.*
Tel: (408) 982-9500   Emp: N/A
Fax:(408) 496-0575   %FO: 100

● **FUJITSU TEN LTD.**
1-2-28 Goshodori, Hyogo-ku, Kobe 652, Japan
CEO: H. Ishii, Pres.
Bus: *Mfr. car stereos, two-way radios, etc.*
Tel: 81-78-671-5081   Emp: 2200
Fax:81-78-671-5325

FUJITSU TEN CORP OF AMERICA
616 Conrad Harcourt Way, Rushville, IN   46173
CEO: Niel Itomine, Pres.
Bus: *Mfr. car stereos.*
Tel: (765) 938-5555   Emp: 50
Fax:(317) 932-3257   %FO: 100

● **FUKUDA DENSHI CO., LTD.**
3-39-4 Hongo, Bunkyo-ku, Tokyo 113, Japan
CEO: Kotaro Fukuda, Pres.
Bus: *Mfr. medical equipment.*
Tel: 81-3 38152121   Emp: 1500
Fax:81-3 56841577

FUKUDA DENSHI AMERICA CORP
17725 NE 65th Street, Redmond, WA   98052
CEO: Harry Harashima, Pres.
Bus: *Sale/service medical equipment.*
Tel: (206) 881-7737   Emp: 35
Fax:(206) 869-2018   %FO: 100

● **G.C. CORPORATION**
76-1 Hasunuma-cho, Itabashi-ku, Tokyo 174, Japan
CEO: Makoto Nakao, Pres.
Bus: *Mfr. professional dental products.*
Tel: 81-33-3965-1231   Emp: 900
Fax:81-33-3965-1221

G. C. AMERICA, INC.
3737 West 127th Avenue, Chicago, IL   60658
CEO: Dean Porter, Pres.
Bus: *Mfr. professional dental products*
Tel: (708) 597-0900   Emp: 120
Fax:(708) 371-5103   %FO: 100

● **GRAPHTEC CORPORATION**
Mita 43 Mori Bldg, 13-16 Mita 3-chome, Minato-ku, Tokyo 108, Japan
CEO: Shigeo Tajimi, Pres.   Tel: 81-3-453-0511   Emp: 625
Bus: *Analog recorders and digital pen plotters.*   Fax: 81-3-453-7187

    WESTERN GRAPHTEC INC.
    11 Vanderbilt, Irvine, CA   92718
    CEO: K. Minejima, Pres.   Tel: (714) 770-6010   Emp: 65
    Bus: *Mfr./distribute analog recorders and digital*   Fax: (714) 855-0895   %FO: 52
        pen plotters.

● **THE HACHIJUNI BANK LTD.**
178-8 Okada, Nagano 380, Japan
CEO: Minoru Chino, Pres.   Tel: 81-26-3227-1182   Emp: 4015
Bus: *Commercial banking services.*   Fax: 81-3-3277-0146

    THE HACHIJUNI BANK LTD.
    280 Park Avenue, West Bldg., 28th Fl., New York, NY   10022
    CEO: Kazuyoshi Araki, Gen. Mgr.   Tel: (212) 557-1182   Emp: 13
    Bus: *International commercial banking services.*   Fax: (212) 557-8026   %FO: 100

● **HAKUHODO, INC.**
4-1, Shibaura 3-chome, Minato--ku, Tokyo 10, Japan
CEO: Takashi Shoji, Pres.   Tel: 81-3-5446-6161   Emp: 3500
Bus: *Advertising and communications services.*   Fax: 81-3-5446-6166

    HAKUHODO ADVERTISING AMERICA, INC.
    475 Park Avenue South, 18th Floor, New York, NY   10020
    CEO: Koichiro Yabuki, Pres.   Tel: (212) 684-7000   Emp: 25
    Bus: *Advertising agency.*   Fax: (212) 684-2801   %FO: 100

● **HAMADA PRINTING PRESS MFG CO LTD.**
15-28 Mitejima 2-chome, Nishi Yodogawa-ku, Osaka 555, Japan
CEO: Y. Ohira, Pres.   Tel: 81-6-472-6200   Emp: N/A
Bus: *Printing machinery and equipment.*   Fax: 81-6-472-6267

    HAMADA OF AMERICA,INC.
    110 Arovista Circle, Brea, CA   92621
    CEO: Tom Nishimura, Pres.   Tel: (714) 990-1999   Emp: N/A
    Bus: *Sheet-fed offset printing presses.*   Fax: (714) 990-1930   %FO: 100

- **HAMAMATSU PHOTONICS KK**
325 Sunayama-Sho, Hamamatsu 430, Japan
CEO: Teruo Hiruma, Pres.   Tel: 81-53-452-2141   Emp: 1500
Bus: *Photosensitive devices and systems.*   Fax:81-53-452-7889

    HAMAMATSU CORPORATION
    360 Foothill Road, PO Box 6910, Bridgewater, NJ   08807
    CEO: Jay R. Eno, Pres.   Tel: (908) 231-1116   Emp: N/A
    Bus: *Holding company.*   Fax:(908) 231-0405   %FO: 100

- **HARADA INDUSTRY CO LTD.**
17-13 Minami Ohi 4-chome, Shinagawa, Tokyo, Japan
CEO: Jiro Harada, Chrm.   Tel: 81-33-765-4321   Emp: 1800
Bus: *Mfr. auto and communication antennas, electric   Fax:81-33-763-0130
equipment, automotive access, household health
appliances.*

    HARADA INDUSTRY OF AMERICA ,INC.
    28333 Telegraph Road, Ste. 275, Southfield, MI   48034
    CEO: Shoji Nagamura, Pres.   Tel: (248) 356-1000   Emp: 102
    Bus: *Sale auto antennas.*   Fax:(248) 356-1520   %FO: 100

- **HAZAMA CORPORATION**
2-5-8 Kita-Aoyama Minato-ku, Tokyo 107, Japan
CEO: Mikio Matsumoto, Pres.   Tel: 81-3-3405-1111   Emp: 5000
Bus: *General construction contractors.*   Fax:81-3-3405-1548

    HAZAMA CORPORATION
    1045 W Redondo Beach Blvd., Ste. 400, Gardena, CA   90247
    CEO: Kenichi Iwao, Gen. Mgr.   Tel: (310) 352-3070   Emp: 30
    Bus: *Construction/engineering services.*   Fax:(310) 352-3077   %FO: 100

- **HIRANO & ASSOCIATES**
8-12-7 Fukazawa, Setagaya-ku, Tokyo, Japan
CEO: Tetsuyuki Hirano, Pres. & CEO   Tel: 81-3-704-3111   Emp: 80
Bus: *Industrial design and architecture.*   Fax:81-3-704-3200

    HIRANO DESIGN INTL INC.
    875 North Michigan Ave., Ste.3443, Chicago, IL   60611
    CEO: Hiroshi Ariyama, VP   Tel: (312) 335-0090   Emp: 8
    Bus: *Industrial and graphic design and marketing.*   Fax:(312) 335-0093   %FO: 100

● **THE HIROSHIMA BANK LTD.**
3-8 Kamiyaa-cho 1-chome, Naka-ku, Hiroshima, Japan
CEO: Osamu Hashiguchi, Pres.   Tel: 81-3-247-5151   Emp: N/A
Bus: *Commercial banking services.*   Fax:N/A

    THE HIROSHIMA BANK LTD.
    1 Wall Street, 31st Fl., New York, NY   10005
    CEO: Akihiro Fujihara, Pres.   Tel: (212) 509-5151   Emp: 15
    Bus: *Commercial banking services.*   Fax:(212) 809-9191   %FO: 100

● **HITACHI LTD.**
6 Kanda-Surugadai 4-chome, Chiyoda-ku, Tokyo 101, Japan
CEO: Tsutomu Kanai, Pres.   Tel: 81-3-3258-1111   Emp: 330000
Bus: *Information systems and electronics, power and*   Fax:81-3-3258-2375
industrial systems, consumer products and materials.

    HITACHI AMERICA, LTD.
    50 Prospect Avenue, Tarrytown, NY   10591-4698
    CEO: Tsuneo Tanaka, Pres.   Tel: (914) 332-5800   Emp: 1000
    Bus: *Information systems and electronics, power*   Fax:(914) 332-5555   %FO: 100
    and industrial systems, consumer products and
    materials.

● **HITACHI METALS LTD.**
Chiyoda Bldg, 1-2 Marunouchi 2-chome, Chiyoda-ku, Tokyo 100, Japan
CEO: Trtuya Eda, Pres.   Tel: 81-3-3284-4511   Emp: 24500
Bus: *Mfr. custom metal products and specialty steel.*   Fax:81-3-3214-1029

    AAP St. MARY'S CORP.
    1100 McKinley Avenue, St. Mary's, OH   44885
    CEO: Norm Katagiri, CEO   Tel: (419) 394-7840   Emp: 340
    Bus: *Mfg. aluminum wheels for automobiles.*   Fax:(419) 394-4776   %FO: 100

    HI SPECIALTY AMERICA, INC.
    PO Box 442, Arona Road, Irwin, PA   15642
    CEO: David Spehar, Pres.   Tel: (412) 864-2370   Emp: 25
    Bus: *Mfr. of cold-drawn special steel products.*   Fax:(412) 864-0366   %FO: 100

    HITACHI MAGNETICS CORPORATION
    7800 Neff Road, Edmore, MI   48829
    CEO: Kurt Miyairi, Pres.   Tel: (517) 427-5151   Emp: 500
    Bus: *Mfr. magnets.*   Fax:(517) 427-5571   %FO: 100

    HITACHI METALS AMERICA, LTD.
    2400 Westchester Avenue, Purchase, NY   10577
    CEO: Keith Okada, Pres.   Tel: (914) 694-9200   Emp: 2500
    Bus: *Mfr./sale custom metal products, magnetic*   Fax:(914) 694-9279   %FO: 100
    products, specialty steel.

HITACHI METALS NORTH CAROLINA, LTD.
1 Hitachi Metals Drive, China Grove, NC 28023
CEO: N. Hamamota, Pres.   Tel: (704) 485-5280   Emp: N/A
Bus: *Mfr. magnets for automobiles.*   Fax:(704) 855-2750   %FO: 100

WARD MANUFACTURING CORP.
115 Gulick St., P.O. Box 9, Blossburg, PA 16912
CEO: Doyne Chartrau, CEO   Tel: (717) 638-2131   Emp: 1000
Bus: *Mfr. pipe fittings & cast iron parts for automobiles.*   Fax:(717) 638-3410   %FO: 100

● HITACHI SEIKI COMPANY, LTD.
1 Abiko Abiko-shi, Chiba-Ken 100, Japan
CEO: Goro Tejima, Pres.   Tel: 81-3-3184-1111   Emp: 1500
Bus: *Mfr. metal cutting machine tools.*   Fax:N/A

HITACHI SEIKI USA, INC.
250 Brenner Drive, Congers, NY 10920
CEO: Masauki Izuchi, Pres.   Tel: (914) 268-4124   Emp: 100
Bus: *Mfr./distribution/service machine tools.*   Fax:(914) 268-7304   %FO: 100

● HITACHI ZOSEN CORP
3-28 Nishikujo 5-chome, Konohana-ku, Osaka 554, Japan
CEO: Isoh Minami, Pres..   Tel: 81-6 4667500   Emp: 12443
Bus: *Shipbuilding & repair offshore equipment, steel structures, industry machinery, plants, press machines.*   Fax:81-6 4667572

HITACHI ZOSEN USA LTD.
767 Third Avenue, 17th Fl., New York, NY 10017
CEO: Koichiro Anzai, Pres.   Tel: (212) 355-5650   Emp: 20
Bus: *Sales/liaison shipbuilding repair offshore equipment.*   Fax:(212) 308-4937   %FO: 100

● HOCHIKI CORP
10-43 Kamiosaki 2-chome, Shinagawa-ku, Tokyo 141, Japan
CEO: Takayoshi Baba, Pres.   Tel: 81-3 3444-4111   Emp: 1200
Bus: *Mfr./install fire alarms, TV equipment.*   Fax:81-3 3444-4167

A.P.A. TECHNOLOGY, INC.
17662 Georgetown Lane, Huntington Beach, CA 92647
CEO: Yuichiro Yamamoto, Pres.   Tel: (714) 848-7022   Emp: N/A
Bus: *Mfr./distribution fire alarms.*   Fax:(714) 848-8072   %FO: 100

HOCHIKI AMERICA CORP.
5415 Industrial Drive, Huntington Beach, CA 92649
CEO: Isao Hanyu, Pres.   Tel: (714) 898-0795   Emp: 80
Bus: *Mfr./distribution fire alarms.*   Fax:(714) 892-2809   %FO: 100

● **HONDA MOTOR CO LTD.**
1-1 Minami-Aoyama 2-chome, Minato-ku, Tokyo 107, Japan
CEO: Nobuhiko Kawamoto, Pres. & CEO   Tel: 81-3-3423-1111   Emp: 96800
Bus: *Mfr. automobiles, motorcycles & power products.*   Fax: 81-3-3423-8947

   AMERICAN HONDA MOTOR CO., INC.
   1919 Torrance Blvd, Torrance, CA   90501
   CEO: Koichi Amemiya, Pres.   Tel: (310) 783-2000   Emp: 12000
   Bus: *Sale/marketing/import/export cars,*   Fax: (310) 783-3900   %FO: 100
      motorcycles & power equipment.

   HONDA OF AMERICA MFG., INC.
   Honda Parkway, Marysville, OH   43040
   CEO: Takeo Kukui, Pres.   Tel: (513) 642-5000   Emp: N/A
   Bus: *Mfr. automobiles, motorcycles.*   Fax: (513) 644-6543   %FO: 100

   HONDA POWER EQUIPMENT MFG., INC.
   Honda Drive, NC Hwy 119, Swepsonville, NC   27359-9999
   CEO: Koji Tsujita, Pres.   Tel: (919) 578-5300   Emp: N/A
   Bus: *Mfr. power equipment.*   Fax: (919) 229-0768   %FO: 100

   HONDA R&D NORTH AMERICA ,INC.
   1900 Harpers Way, Torrance, CA   90501
   CEO: Takeshi Yamada, Pres.   Tel: (310) 781-5500   Emp: N/A
   Bus: *Design/engineer products.*   Fax: (310) 781-5768   %FO: 100

   HONDA TRADING AMERICA INC.
   700 Van Ness Avenue, Torrance, CA   90501
   CEO: T. Nagai, Pres.   Tel: (310) 781-4065   Emp: N/A
   Bus: *Import/export/marketing services for U.S.*   Fax: %FO: 100
      operations.

● **HONSHU PAPER COMPANY, LTD.**
26-20 Higashi 1-chome, Shibuya-ku, Tokyo 150, Japan
CEO: Yoshinobu Yonezawa, Pres.   Tel: 81-3 54671014   Emp: 6000
Bus: *Mfr. paper.*   Fax: 81-3 54676696

   HONSHU PAPER COMPANY, LTD.
   600 University Street, Ste. 2300, Seattle, WA   98101-4153
   CEO: Haruyoshi Harada, CEO   Tel: (206) 624-5145   Emp: 5
   Bus: *Paper industry liaison.*   Fax: (206) 625-1363   %FO: 100

- **HORIBA LTD.**
Miyanohigashi Kisshoin, Minami-ku, Kyoto 601, Japan
CEO: Masao Horiba, Chrm. Tel: 81-75-3138-1231 Emp: N/A
Bus: *Mfr. analyzer systems.* Fax:81-75-3121-5725

 HORIBA INSTRUMENTS, INC.
 17671 Armstrong Avenue, Irvine, CA 92714
 CEO: Neal Harvey, CEO Tel: (714) 250-4811 Emp: 120
 Bus: *Mfr. analyzer systems.* Fax:(714) 250-0924 %FO: 100

- **HOSOKAWA MICRON CORPORATION**
Midosuji-Hommachi Bldg, 5-7 Mommachi 3-chome, Osaka 541, Japan
CEO: Masuo Hosokawa, Chrm. Tel: 81-6-263-2555 Emp: 2800
Bus: *Powder processing equipment & systems,* Fax:81-6-263-2552
environmental protection, filter media, plastics
processing equipment.

 MENARDI-CRISWELL
 PO Box 160, Trenton, SC 30903
 CEO: Larry Patterson, Pres. Tel: (803) 663-6551 Emp: 400
 Bus: *Mfr. filter media for solid-gas and solid-liquid* Fax:(803) 663-1992 %FO: 100
 separation.

 MICRON POWDER SYSTEMS
 10 Chatham Road, Summit, NJ 07901
 CEO: Gordon Ettie, Pres. Tel: (908) 273-6360 Emp: 150
 Bus: *Mfr. powder processing equipment and* Fax:(908) 273-7432 %FO: 100
 systems.

- **THE HYAKUJUSHI BANK LTD.**
5-1 Kamei-cho, Takamatsu, Kagawa 760, Japan
CEO: Hausaku Aynda, Pres. Tel: 81-878-310114 Emp: 2522
Bus: *Commercial banking services.* Fax:N/A

 THE HYAKUJUSHI BANK, LTD.
 2 Wall Street, 11th Fl., New York, NY 10005
 CEO: Toshihiro Fukunishi, Mgr. Tel: (212) 513-0114 Emp: 16
 Bus: *Commercial banking services.* Fax:(212) 619-0757 %FO: 100

- **IKEGAI CORPORATION**
Nihon Seimei Shimbashi Bldg, 18-16 Shinbashi 1-chome, Minata-ku, Tokyo, Japan
CEO: Shoji Inagawa, Pres. Tel: 81-3-5470-1431 Emp: 800
Bus: *CNC machine tool lathe and machine centers.* Fax:81-3-5470-1430

 IKEGAI AMERICA CORPORATION
 2246 North Palmer, Ste.108, Schaumburg, IL 60173
 CEO: Katsuji V. Takagi, VP Tel: (847) 397-3970 Emp: 10
 Bus: *CNC machine tool related parts and service.* Fax:(847) 397-7535 %FO: 100

● **INDUSTRIAL BANK OF JAPAN LTD.**
3-3 Marunouchi 1-chome, Chiyoda-ku, Tokyo 100, Japan
CEO: Masao Nishimura, Pres.   Tel: 81-3-3214-1111   Emp: 5433
Bus: *Wholesale banking and long-term credit facilities.*   Fax:81-3-3201-7643

   IBJ SCHRODER BANK & TRUST COMPANY
   One State Street, New York, NY   10004
   CEO: Alva O. Way, Chrm.   Tel: (212) 858-2000   Emp: 500
   Bus: *Wholesale banking, corporate & private*   Fax:(212) 425-0542   %FO: 100
        banking, trust and investment advisory services.

   IBJ SCHRODER INTERNATIONAL BANK
   200 South Biscayne Blvd., 26th Fl., Miami, FL   33131-2371
   CEO: John H.B. Harriman, Pres. & CEO   Tel: (305) 377-8000   Emp: N/A
   Bus: *Wholesale banking, corporate & private*   Fax:(305) 371-7209   %FO: 100
        banking, trust and investment advisory services.

   IBJS CAPITAL CORPORATION
   One State Street, New York, NY   10004
   CEO: Lawrence S. Zilavy, Pres. & CEO   Tel: (212) 858-2546   Emp: N/A
   Bus: *Wholesale banking, long-term credit facilities.*   Fax:(212) 858-2768   %FO: 100

   INDUSTRIAL BANK OF JAPAN TRUST COMPANY
   1251 Avenue of the Americas, New York, NY   10020
   CEO: Chiharu Baba, Pres.   Tel: (212) 282-3000   Emp: 500
   Bus: *Wholesale banking, long-term credit facilities.*   Fax:(212) 282-4250   %FO: 100

● **ISETAN COMPANY, LTD.**
14-1 Shinjuku 3, chome, Shinjuku-ku, Tokyo 160, Japan
CEO: Kazumasa Koshiba, Pres.   Tel: 81-3-3352-1111   Emp: N/A
Bus: *Manages/operates department stores.*   Fax:81-3-5273-5321

   ISETAN COMPANY, LTD.
   666 Fifth Avenue, New York, NY   10113
   CEO: Tai Ogata, GenMgr.   Tel: (212) 767-0300   Emp: 6
   Bus: *Manages/operates department stores.*   Fax:(212) 767-0307   %FO: 100

● **ISHIHARA SANGYO KAISHA LTD.**
3-15 Edobori 1-chome, Nishi-ku, Osaka 550, Japan
CEO: T. Akizawa, Pres   Tel: 81-6-444-1452   Emp: 2700
Bus: *Mfr. titanium dioxide, agricultural chemicals and*   Fax:81-6-444-1458
     magnetic materials.

   ISK AMERICAS BIOSCIENCES, INC.
   5966 Heisley Road, Mentor, OH   44060
   CEO: Franklin Barry, Pres.   Tel: (216) 357-4100   Emp: 950
   Bus: *Mfr./sale agricultural and specialty chemicals;*   Fax:(216) 354-9507   %FO: 100
        contract research.

ISK AMERICAS BIOSCIENCES, INC.
1523 Johnson Fery Road, Ste. 250, Marietta, GA   30062

CEO: Neil Butler, Pres.	Tel: (770) 565-3499	Emp: N/A
Bus: *Mfr./sale agricultural and specialty chemicals; contract research.*	Fax:(770) 565-4155	%FO: 100

• ISHIKAWAJIMA-HARIMA HEAVY INDUSTRIES COMPANY, LTD.
2-1-1 Ohtemachi, 2-chome, Chiyoda-ku, Tokyo 100, Japan

CEO: Kosaku Inaba, Pres.	Tel: 81-3-3244-5111	Emp: N/A
Bus: *Shipbuilding and repair, mfr. machinery, diesels, boilers, bridges, etc.*	Fax:81-3-3244-5131	

IHI MARINE TECHNOLOGY, INC.
280 Park Avenue, 30th Fl., New York, NY   10017

CEO: M. Kosaka, Pres.	Tel: (212) 599-8100	Emp: N/A
Bus: *Shipbuilding and repair technical consultants; sale of ship-building material.*	Fax:(212) 599-8111	%FO: 100

• ISUZU MOTORS LTD.
26-1 Minami-oi 6-chome, Shinagawa-ku, Tokyo 140, Japan

CEO: Kazuhira Seki, Pres.	Tel: 81-3 5471-1111	Emp: 14317
Bus: *Mfr. motor vehicles, parts and accessories.*	Fax:81-3-5471-1036	

AMERICAN ISUZU MOTORS, INC.
13181 Crossroads Pkwy North, 4th Fl., City of Industry, CA   91746

CEO: Yoshito Mochizuki, Pres.	Tel: (310) 699-0500	Emp: N/A
Bus: *Sale/service trucks, sport utility vehicles.*	Fax:(310) 692-7135	%FO: 100

ISUZU MOTORS AMERICA, INC.
16323 Shoemaker Avenue, Cerritos, CA   90703

CEO: Y. Kubo, Pres.	Tel: (562) 949-0320	Emp: N/A
Bus: *Distribute light-duty motor vehicles.*	Fax:(562) 404-9046	%FO: 100

SUBURU-ISUZU AUTOMOTIVE, INC.
5500 State Road 38 East, Lafayette, IN   47903

CEO: Maeda Hitoshi, Pres.	Tel: (765) 449-1111	Emp: 1900
Bus: *Mfr. motor vehicles (see joint parent: FUJI HEAVY INDUSTRIES LTD).*	Fax:(765) 449-6269	%FO: 49

• ITO-YOKADA COMPANY, LTD.
4-1-4 Shibakoen, Minato-ku, Tokyo 105, Japan

CEO: Toshifumi Suzuki, Pres.	Tel: 81-3-3459-2111	Emp: N/A
Bus: *Convenience and specialty stores, department stores and supermarkets*	Fax:81-3-3434-8378	

THE SOUTHLAND CORPORATION
2711 North Haskell Avenue, PO Box 711, Dallas, TX   75221

CEO: Clark J. Matthews Jr., Pres.	Tel: (214) 828-7011	Emp: N/A
Bus: *Convenience stores.*	Fax:(214) 828-7848	%FO: 100

●**ITOCHU CORP. (formerly C. Itoh & Co., Ltd.)**
5-1 Kita-Aoyama 2-chome, Minato-ku, Tokyo 107-77, Japan
CEO: Minoru Murofushi, Pres. & CEO Tel: 81-3-3497-7295 Emp: 7200
Bus: *General international trading activities.* Fax:81-3-3497-7296

   ITOCHU INTL INC.
   335 Madison Avenue, New York, NY 10017
   CEO: Shigeji Ono, CEO Tel: (212) 818-8000 Emp: 460
   Bus: *General international trading activities.* Fax:(212) 818-8153 %FO: 100

●**IWATANI INTERNATIONAL CORPORATION**
3-4-8 Hommachi, Chuo-ku, Osaka 541, Japan
CEO: Koji Saitoh, Pres. & CEO Tel: 81-6-267-3431 Emp: N/A
Bus: *Mfr./sales consumer products, agricultural and medical products, industrial gases/materials and construction.* Fax:81-6-267-3350

   IWATANI INTERNATIONAL CORPORATION OF AMERICA
   1701 Golf Road, Ste. 1106, Rolling Meadows, IL 60008
   CEO: Shuji Nakamura, Pres. Tel: (847) 290-0300 Emp: N/A
   Bus: *Sales of consumer products, agricultural/medical products, agricultural/medical products, industrial gases/materials and construction.* Fax:(847) 290-0350 %FO: 100

   IWATANI INTERNATIONAL CORPORATION OF AMERICA
   2050 Center Avenue, Ste. 425, Fort Lee, NJ 07024
   CEO: Sadao Yasumi, Pres. Tel: (201) 585-2442 Emp: N/A
   Bus: *U.S. headquarters operation.* Fax:(201) 585-2369 %FO: 100

   IWATANI INTERNATIONAL CORPORATION OF AMERICA
   1025 West 190th Street, Gardena, CA 90248
   CEO: Yasuo Miyauchi, Pres. Tel: (310) 324-9174 Emp: N/A
   Bus: *Sales of consumer products, agricultural/medical products, industrial gases/materials and construction.* Fax:(310) 324-9177 %FO: 100

●**THE IYO BANK LTD.**
1 Minami-Horibata-cho, Matsuyama 790, Japan
CEO: Gizo Mizuki, Pres. Tel: 81-899 411141 Emp: 3500
Bus: *Commercial banking services.* Fax:81-899 469101

   THE IYO BANK LTD.
   1 World Trade Center, #7923, New York, NY 10048
   CEO: Kazuo Kikuchi, Gen. Mgr. Tel: (212) 466-1400 Emp: N/A
   Bus: *Commercial banking services.* Fax:(212) 432-2583 %FO: 100

- **JAPAN AIRLINES COMPANY, LTD.**
  2-4-11 Higashi Shinagawa, Shinagawa-ku, Tokyo 100, Japan
  CEO: Akira Kondo, Pres.   Tel: 81-3-5460-3121   Emp: 20000
  Bus: *International airline, hotels/catering.*   Fax:81-3-5460-5913

  > **JAPAN AIR LINES (USA) Ltd.**
  > 655 Fifth Avenue, New York, NY   10022
  > CEO: Yukio Ohtani, Sr.VP & Gen.Mgr.   Tel: (212) 310-1318   Emp: 200
  > Bus: *International air transport services.*   Fax:(212) 310-1238   %FO: 100

- **JAPAN AVIATION ELECTRONICS INDUSTRY LTD.**
  21-6 Dogenzaka 1-chome, Shibuya-ku, Tokyo 150, Japan
  CEO: Tatsumi Nagatoshi, Pres.   Tel: 81-3-7802701   Emp: 2700
  Bus: *Mfr. connectors and switches.*   Fax:81-3-7802733

  > **JAE ELECTRONICS INC.**
  > 142 Technology Drive, Ste.100, Irvine, CA   92718-2401
  > CEO: Ken Tsukinari, Pres.   Tel: (714) 753-2600   Emp: N/A
  > Bus: *Distribution/sale switches and connectors.* Fax:(714) 753-2699   %FO: 100

- **THE JAPAN DEVELOPMENT BANK**
  9-1 Otemachi 1-chome, Chiyoda-ku, Tokyo 100, Japan
  CEO: Yoshihiko Yoshino, Governor   Tel: 81-3-3244-1770   Emp: N/A
  Bus: *Government long term credit institution.* Fax:81-3-3245-1938

  > **THE JAPAN DEVELOPMENT BANK**
  > 601 South Figueroa Street
  > Ste. 4450, Los Angeles, CA   90017-5748
  > CEO: Toru Tanigawa, Chief. Rep.   Tel: (213) 362-2980   Emp: 4
  > Bus: *Government long term credit institution.* Fax:(213) 362-2982   %FO: 100

  > **THE JAPAN DEVELOPMENT BANK**
  > 1101 17th Street, NW, #1001, Washington, DC   20036
  > CEO: Yoji Inaba, Chief Rep.   Tel: (202) 331-8696   Emp: 4
  > Bus: *Government long term credit institution.* Fax:(202) 293-3932   %FO: 100

  > **THE JAPAN DEVELOPMENT BANK**
  > 575 Fifth Avenue, 28th Fl., New York, NY   10017
  > CEO: Teruo Hanada, Chief Rep.   Tel: (212) 949-7550   Emp: 4
  > Bus: *Government long term credit institution.* Fax:(212) 949-7558   %FO: 100

● **JAPAN ENERGY CORPORATION**
10-1 Toranomon 2-chome, Minato-ku, Tokyo 105, Japan
CEO: K. Nagashima, Pres.   Tel: 81-3-5573-6136   Emp: N/A
Bus: *Electronic and petroleum refining, oil*   Fax:81-3-5573-6782
    exploration/development, specialty metals,
    pharmaceuticals and biotechnology.

   JAPAN ENERGY USA, INC.
   12 East 49 Street, Ste. 1710, New York, NY   10017
   CEO: T. Miki, Pres.   Tel: (212) 832-7400   Emp: N/A
   Bus: *Electronic and petroleum refining, oil*   Fax:(212) 832-7492   %FO: 100
       exploration/development, specialty metals,
       pharmaceuticals and biotechnology.

● **JAPAN INFORMATION SERVICE LTD.**
17-5 Shibuya 2-chome, Shibuya-ku, Tokyo 150, Japan
CEO: Yoshio Tada, Pres.   Tel: 81-3-406-1651   Emp: 1600
Bus: *Data processing service, computer sale/ lease,*   Fax:81-3-406-3425
    software development/sale.

   JAIS USA, INC.
   80 Pine Street, 10th Fl., New York, NY   10005
   CEO: Masao Shiroyama, Pres.   Tel: (212) 487-2000   Emp: 35
   Bus: *Software development/sale, data*   Fax:(212) 487-2047   %FO: 100
       communications and network servicing.

● **JAPAN RADIO COMPANY, LTD.**
17-22 Akasaka 2-chome, Minato-ku, Tokyo 107, Japan
CEO: N/A   Tel: N/A   Emp: N/A
Bus: *Mfr. marine/land radio and navigation equipment.*   Fax:N/A

   JAPAN RADIO COMPANY, LTD.
   430 Park Avenue, New York, NY   10022
   CEO: N. Takeuchi, Gen.Mgr.   Tel: (212) 355-1180   Emp: 7
   Bus: *Sale marine/land radio and navigation*   Fax:(212) 319-5227   %FO: 100
       equipment.

● **JAPAN STORAGE BATTERY CO LTD.**
1 Inobanba-cho Nishinosho, Kisshoin, Minami-ku, Kyoto 601, Japan
CEO: Shigeru Negishi, Pres.   Tel: 81-75-312-1211   Emp: 2800
Bus: *Mfr. storage batteries, rectifiers and lighting*   Fax:81-75-321-6544
    equipment.

   GS BATTERY (USA) INC.
   17253 Chestnut Street, City of Industry, CA   91748
   CEO: Hiroshi Hatano, Pres.   Tel: (818) 964-8348   Emp: 16
   Bus: *Distribution of batteries and chargers.*   Fax:(818) 810-9438   %FO: 100

• JAPAN TOBACCO INC.
2-2-1 Toranomon, Minato-ku, Tokyo
CEO: Masaru Mizuno, Chrm.　　　Tel: 81-3-3582-3111　　Emp: N/A
Bus: *Mfr. tobacco, salt, food and pharmaceutical*　Fax:81-3-5572-1441
　　　products.

JAPAN TOBACCO INC.
375 Park Avenue, # 1307, New York, NY　10152
CEO: Masakazu Shimizu, Mgn.Dir.　　Tel: (212) 319-8990　　Emp: 4
Bus: *Mfr. tobacco, salt, food and pharmaceutical*　Fax:(212) 319-8993　%FO: 100
　　　products.

JT INTL, INC.
2441 205th Street, Torrance, CA　90501
CEO: Masayuki Hamada, Pres.　　　Tel: (310) 212-6416　　Emp: 9
Bus: *Mfr. tobacco, salt, food and pharmaceutical*　Fax:(310) 533-8027　%FO: 100
　　　products.

• JAPAN TRAVEL BUREAU, INC.
1-6-4 Marunouchi, Chiyoda-ku, Tokyo 100, Japan
CEO: Ryuji Funayama, Pres.　　　Tel: 81-3-2847370　　Emp: 10000
Bus: *Travel services.*　　　　　Fax:81-3-2847390

JAPAN TRAVEL BUREAU INTL INC
Equitable Tower, 787 Seventh Avenue, New York, NY　10019
CEO: M. Matsuga, Pres.　　　　Tel: (212) 246-8030　　Emp: 400
Bus: *Travel services.*　　　　　Fax:(212) 265-7234　%FO: 100

JAPAN TRAVEL BUREAU INTL INC
777 S. Figueroa Street, Ste. 3900, Los Angeles, CA　90017
CEO: Kenji Ito, Pres.　　　　　Tel: (213) 553-6500　　Emp: 410
Bus: *Travel services.*　　　　　Fax:(213) 553-6555　%FO: 100

• JEOL LTD.
3-1-2 Musashino, Akishima, Tokyo 196, Japan
CEO: Takashi Takeuchi, Pres.　　　Tel: 81-3-2543-1111　Emp: 1700
Bus: *Mfr. scientific instruments.*　　Fax:N/A

JEOL USA ,INC.
11 Dearborn Road, Peabody, MA　01960
CEO: K. Yasitake, Pres.　　　　Tel: (508) 535-5900　　Emp: 270
Bus: *Distribute/service scientific instruments.*　Fax:(508) 535-7741　%FO: 100

- **JIJI TSUSHIN**
1-3 Hibiyakoen, Chiyoda-ku, Tokyo 100, Japan
CEO: Kouichi Maeda, Pres.   Tel: 81-3-3591-1111   Emp: 1200
Bus: *News syndicate.*   Fax:N/A

  JIJI PRESS AMERICA, LTD.
  120 West 45th Street, 14th Fl., New York, NY   10036
  CEO: S. Kanashige, Pres.   Tel: (212) 575-5830   Emp: 16
  Bus: *News agency.*   Fax:(212) 764-3951   %FO: 100

- **THE JOYO BANK LTD.**
5-5 Minami-machi 2-chome, Mito 310, Japan
CEO: Toranosuke Nishino, Pres.   Tel: 81-292-312151   Emp: 5200
Bus: *Commercial banking services.*   Fax:81-3-3274-3626

  THE JOYO BANK LTD.
  150 East 52nd Street, 6th Fl., New York, NY   10022-6017
  CEO: Yuhihiko Watanabe, Gen. Mgr.   Tel: (212) 752-2500   Emp: 20
  Bus: *Commercial banking services.*   Fax:(212) 752-6900   %FO: 100

- **THE JUROKU BANK LTD.**
8-26 Kandamachi, Gifu 500, Japan
CEO: Kunihiko Katsuno, Dir.   Tel: 81-58-265-2111   Emp: 3000
Bus: *Commercial banking services.*   Fax:81-58-2661925

  THE JUROKU BANK LTD
  2 World Financial Center, 225 Liberty St., New York, NY   10281
  CEO: Yazuo Fujii, Gen.Mgr.   Tel: (212) 786-1600   Emp: 9
  Bus: *Commercial banking services.*   Fax:(212) 786-1697   %FO: 100

- **JUSCO CO., LTD./ AEON GROUP**
5-1, 1-Chome, Nakase, Mihama-ku, Chiba 261, Japan
CEO: Takuya Okada, Chrm. & CEO   Tel: 81-43-212-6075   Emp: 70000
Bus: *Operate retail stores. Sub of AEON Group, global*   Fax:81-43-212-6813
retail conglomerate.

  JUSCO (U.S.A.), INC.
  520 Madison Avenue, New York, NY   10022
  CEO: Isao T. Tsuruta, Sr. VP   Tel: (212) 821-9100   Emp: 7
  Bus: *Retail holding company.*   Fax:(212) 838-0469   %FO: 100

  TALBOTS, INC.
  175 Beal Street, Hingham, MA   02043
  CEO: Arnold Zetcher, Pres.& CEO   Tel: (617) 749-7600   Emp: 1000+
  Bus: *Operates retail clothing chain stores.*   Fax:(617) 749-0845   %FO: 100

- **JVC LTD.**
12 Moriya-cho 3-Chome, Kanagawa-ku, Yokohama 221, Japan
CEO: Takeo Shuzui, Pres.   Tel: 81-45-450-1561   Emp: N/A
Bus: *Mfr. electronic audio equipment.*   Fax:81-45-450-1574

> **JVC AMERICA, INC.**
> One JVC Road, Tuscaloosa, AL   35405
> CEO: Akira Ochida, Pres.   Tel: (205) 556-7111   Emp: N/A
> Bus: *Mfr. electronic audio equipment.*   Fax:(205) 554-5500   %FO: 100

> **U.S. JVC CORPORATION**
> 41 Slater Drive, Elmwood Park, NJ   07407
> CEO: Akira Ochida, Pres.   Tel: (973) 794-3900   Emp: N/A
> Bus: *Mfr. electronic audio equipment.*   Fax:(973) 523-3601   %FO: 100

- **KAJIMA CORPORATION**
2-7 Moto Akasaka 1-chome, Minato-ku, Tokyo 107, Japan
CEO: Akira Miyazaki, Pres.   Tel: 81-3 3404-3311   Emp: 14242
Bus: *General contracting, architectural and engineering*   Fax:81-3 3470-1444
services.

> **KAJIMA DEVELOPMENT CORP**
> 901 Corporate Center Dr, #201, Monterey Park, CA   91754
> CEO: Shoichi Kajima, Pres. & CEO   Tel: (213) 262-8484   Emp: 38
> Bus: *Real estate investment & development.*   Fax:(213) 262-8893   %FO: 100
> *General contracting, architectural &*
> *engineering services.*

> **KAJIMA U.S.A. INC.**
> 320 Park Avenue, New York, NY   10022-6815
> CEO: Shoichi Kajima, Pres. & CEO   Tel: (212) 355-4571   Emp: 25
> Bus: *Real estate investment & development.*   Fax:(212) 355-4576   %FO: 100
> *General contracting, architectural &*
> *engineering services.*

- **KANEKA CORPORATION**
Asahi-Shimbun Bldg., 2-4, 3-chome Nakanoshima Kita-ku, Osaka 530, Japan
CEO: Takeshi Furuta, Pres.   Tel: 81-6-226-5050   Emp: N/A
Bus: *Mfr. performance polymers, plastic products, food*   Fax:81-6-226-5037
products, electronic equipment, pharmaceuticals
and medical devices.

> **KANEKA AMERICA CORPORATION**
> 65 East 55th Street, New York, NY   10022
> CEO: Yutaka Kishida, Pres.   Tel: (212) 705-4340   Emp: N/A
> Bus: *U.S. headquarters office.*   Fax:(212) 705-4350   %FO: 100

KANEKA TEXAS HIGHTECH MATERIALS,CORPORATION
6161 Underwood Road, Pasedena, TX   77507
CEO: Kimikazu Sugawara, Pres. Tel: (281) 474-7084 Emp: N/A
Bus: *Plant site.* Fax:(281) 474-9307 %FO: 100

● **KANEMATSU-GOSHO LTD.**
Sevans North, 1-2-1 Shibaura, Minato-ku, Tokyo 105-05, Japan
CEO: Masao Yosomiya, Pres. Tel: 81-3-5440-8111 Emp: N/A
Bus: *International trading company.* Fax:81-3-5440-6504

 KANEMATSU (USA) INC
 114 West 47th Street, 23rd Fl., New York, NY   10036
 CEO: Noboru Kinoshita, Pres. Tel: (212) 704-9400 Emp: N/A
 Bus: *International trading company.* Fax:(212) 704-9483 %FO: 100

● **KANKAKU SECURITIES CO., LTD.**
Shibuya City Place, 13-16 Nihonbashi-Kayabacho 1-chome Chuo-ku, Toyko 103, Japan
CEO: N/A Tel: 81-3-5640-7805 Emp: N/A
Bus: *Investment banking and securities broker/dealer* Fax:N/A
  services.

 KANKAKU SECURITIES (AMERICA), LTD.
 1 World Trade Center, #8697, New York, NY   10048
 CEO: Mitsuo Suzuki, Pres. & CEO Tel: (212) 839-7700 Emp: N/A
 Bus: *Investment banking and securities* Fax:(212) 524-0860 %FO: 100
  broker/dealer services.

● **THE KANSAI ELECTRIC POWER COMPANY, INC.**
3-22 Nakanoshima 3-chome, Kita-ku, Osaka 530-70, Japan
CEO: Yoshihisa Akiyama, Pres. & CEO Tel: 81-6-441-8821 Emp: 27000
Bus: *Electric utility.* Fax:81-6-441-8598

 THE KANSAI ELECTRIC POWER CO., INC.
 2001 L Street, NW, Washington, DC   20036
 CEO: Ryoji Kishida, Mgr. Tel: (202) 659-1138 Emp: N/A
 Bus: *Washington Office - electric utility.* Fax:(202) 457-0272 %FO: 100

 THE KANSAI ELECTRIC POWER CO., INC.
 375 Park Avenue, #2607, New York, NY   10152
 CEO: Jogo Ozawa, Gen. Mgr. Tel: (212) 758-3505 Emp: N/A
 Bus: *New York Office - electric utility.* Fax:(212) 832-3253 %FO: 100

- **KAO CORPORATION**
  14-10 Nihonbashi Kayabacho 1-chome, Chuo-ku, Tokya 103, Japan
  CEO: Fumikatsu Tokiwa, Pres.   Tel: 81-3-5630-9157   Emp: N/A
  Bus: *Mfr./sales personal care products,*   Fax:81-3-5630-9347
       detergents/chemical products and information
       technology products.

    THE ANDREW JERGENS COMPANY
    2535 Spring Grove Avenue, Cincinnati, OH   45214
    CEO: William Gentner, Pres.   Tel: (513) 421-1400   Emp: N/A
    Bus: *Mfr. personal care products.*   Fax:(513) 421-1590   %FO: 100

    KAO CORPORATION OF AMERICA
    902 Market Street, Ste. 902, Wilmington, DE   19801
    CEO: Tashio Hoshino, Pres.   Tel: (302) 427-0119   Emp: N/A
    Bus: *Representative office.*   Fax:(302) 658-1192   %FO: 100

    KAO INFOSYSTEMS COMPANY
    40 Grissom Road, Plymouth, MA   02360
    CEO: Peter McGuirk, Pres.   Tel: (508) 747-5520   Emp: N/A
    Bus: *U.S. headquarters office.*   Fax:(508) 747-5521   %FO: 100

- **C.I. KASEI CO., LTD.**
  No. 18-1, 1-Chome, Kyobashi, Chuo-ku, Toyko 104, Japan
  CEO: H. Ishigai, Pres. & CEO   Tel: 81-3-3535-4547   Emp: 1400
  Bus: *Mfr. plastics.*   Fax:81-3-3535-4542

    BONSET AMERICA CORPORATION
    6107 Corporate Park Drive, Brown Summit, NC   27214
    CEO: H. Fukuhara, Pres.& CEO   Tel: (910) 375-0234   Emp: 60
    Bus: *Mfr. plastic shrink film.*   Fax:(910) 375-6129   %FO: 100

- **KAWASAKI HEAVY INDUSTRIES, LTD.**
  1-1 Higashi Kawasaki-cho, 3-chome, Chuo-ku, Kobe 650-91, Japan
  CEO: Hiroshi Ohba, CEO   Tel: 81-78-371-9530   Emp: 24000
  Bus: *Mfr.. heavy machinery: transportation equipment;*   Fax:81-78-371-9568
       aerospace and industrial equipment

    KAWASAKI CONSTRUCTION MACHINERY CORP.
    2140 Barrett Park Drive, # 1010, Kennesaw, GA   30144
    CEO: Mack Kodera, Pres.   Tel: (770) 449-7000   Emp: N/A
    Bus: *Mfr./sale heavy machinery*   Fax:(770) 421-6842   %FO: 100

    KAWASAKI HEAVY INDUSTRIES USA, INC.
    599 Lexington Ave, #2705, New York, NY   10022
    CEO: Takeshi Miyakoshi, Pres   Tel: (212) 759-4950   Emp: 11
    Bus: *Mfr./sale industrial equipment*   Fax:(212) 759-6421   %FO: 100

KAWASAKI MOTOR CORPORATION, U.S.A.
9950 Jeronimo Road, Irvine, CA   92718-2016

CEO: Hiroshi Noda, Pres,	Tel: (714) 770-0400	Emp: N/A
Bus: *Mfr./sale motorcycles*	Fax:(714) 460-5600	%FO: 100

KAWASAKI MOTOR MANUFACTURING CORP.
6600 NW 27th Street, Lincoln, NE   68524

CEO: Takehiko Saeki, Pres.	Tel: (402) 476-6600	Emp: N/A
Bus: *Mfr./sale heavy machinery*	Fax:(402) 476-6672	%FO: 100

KAWASAKI RAIL CAR, INC.
One Larkin Plaza, Yonkers, NY   10701

CEO: Masashi Oka, Pres.	Tel: (914) 376-4700	Emp: N/A
Bus: *Mfr./sale transportation equipment*	Fax:(914) 376-4779	%FO: 100

● KAWASAKI KISEN KAISHA LTD.
Hibiya Central Bldg, 2-9 Nishi Shinbashi 1-chome, Minato-ku, Tokyo 105, Japan

CEO: Isao Shintani, Pres.	Tel: 81-3 3595-5000	Emp: N/A
Bus: *Steamship company; cargo and cruise sea transport.*	Fax:81-3 3595-6111	

INTL TRANSPORTATION SERVICE INC. (ITS)
1281 Pier J Avenue, Long Beach, CA   90802

CEO: Masaaki Fumoto, Pres.	Tel: (310) 435-7781	Emp: N/A
Bus: *Steamship & shipping agency; cargo and cruise sea transport.*	Fax:(310) 499-0460	%FO: 100

K LINE AMERICA, INC.
535 Mountain Avenue, Murray Hill, NJ   07974

CEO: Oscar J. Abello, Pres.	Tel: (908) 582-9000	Emp: 25
Bus: *Steamship & shipping agency; cargo and cruise sea transport.*	Fax:(908) 582-9001	%FO: 100

K LINE INTERNATIONAL (U.S.A.), INC.
Three Park Avenue, 28th Fl., New York, NY   10016

CEO: Nigel J.Hawkins, Pres.	Tel: (212) 447-1947	Emp: 4
Bus: *Steamship & shipping agency; cargo and cruise sea transport.*	Fax:(212) 447-1843	%FO: 100

● KAWASAKI STEEL CORPORATION
Hibiya Kokusai Bldg, 2-2-3 Uchisaiwai-cho, Chiyoda-ku, Tokyo 100, Japan

CEO: Kanji Emoto, Pres.	Tel: 81-3-3597-3111	Emp: 13400
Bus: *Mfr. steel, chemicals, semi-conductors and new materials.*	Fax:81-3-3597-4860	

KAWASAKI STEEL AMERICA, INC.
55 East 52nd Street, New York, NY   10055

CEO: Masatoshi Nakamura, Pres.	Tel: (212) 412-9120	Emp: 14
Bus: *Liaison office; information and technical services for steel customers.*	Fax:(212) 308-9292	%FO: 100

KAWASAKI STEEL AMERICA, INC.
Texas Commerce Tower, 600 Travis Street, Ste. 6375, Houston, TX   77002
CEO: Hidenari Yamada, Gen. Mgr. Tel: (713) 654-0031 Emp: N/A
Bus: *Liaison office; information and technical* Fax:(713) 654-9089 %FO: 100
 services for steel customers.

● **KAWASHO CORPORATION**
2-7-1 Otemachi Chiyoda-ku, Tokyo 100, Japan
CEO: Mitsuru Shiokawa, Pres. Tel: 81-3-5203-5001 Emp: 2000
Bus: *General trading company; heavy machinery and* Fax:81-3-5203-5053
 construction building materials.

AMERICAN SOY PRODUCTS, INC.
1474 North Woodland Drive, Saline, MI   48176
CEO: Ron Roller, Pres. Tel: (313) 429-2310 Emp: N/A
Bus: *General trading company activities.* Fax:(313) 429-2112 %FO: 100

KAWASHO INTL (USA), INC.
One Park Plaza, 400 Kelby Street, Fort Lee, NJ   07024
CEO: Akio Ono, Pres. Tel: (201) 585-8115 Emp: 50
Bus: *General trading company activities.* Fax:(201) 585-9670 %FO: 100

VEST INC.
6023 Alcoa Avenue, Los Angeles, CA   90058
CEO: Koji Yamanishi, Pres. Tel: (213) 581-8823 Emp: N/A
Bus: *General trading company activities.* Fax:(213) 581-3465 %FO: 100

● **KAYABA INDUSTRY COMPANY, LTD.**
PO Box 3, World Trade Center Bldg., Minato-ku, Tokyo 105, Japan
CEO: Takashi Chano, Pres. Tel: 81-3-3435-3580 Emp: N/A
Bus: *Mfr. marine, aircraft, auto, hydraulic and* Fax:81-3-3435-3580
 construction parts and components.

KYB CORPORATION OF AMERICA
901 Oak Creek Drive, Lombard, IL   60148
CEO: Takashi Sanada, Pres. Tel: (630) 620-5555 Emp: 34
Bus: *Import/distribute auto shock absorbers,* Fax:(630) 620-8133 %FO: 100
 industrial hydraulic motors and components.

● **KIKKOMAN CORPORATION**
1-25 Kanda Nishiki-cho, Chiyoda-ku, Tokyo 101, Japan
CEO: Kozaburo Nakano, Pres. Tel: 81-3-3233-5610 Emp: N/A
Bus: *Mfr. soy related sauces, wine and pharmaceuticals.* Fax:81-3-3233-5604

KIKKOMAN CORPORATION
6 Corner Road, PO Box 69, Walworth, WI   53184
CEO: Kazuya Hayashi, Pres. Tel: (414) 275-6181 Emp: 130
Bus: *Mfr. soy and related sauces.* Fax:(414) 275-9452 %FO: 100

● **KINOKUNIYA COMPANY, LTD.**
17-7 Shinjuku 3-chome, Shinjuku-ku, Tokyo 160-09, Japan
CEO: Osamu Matsubara, Pres.   Tel: 81-3 3354-0131   Emp: N/A
Bus: *Books, magazines, printed and electronic*   Fax:81-3-3354-2719
publications.

   KINOKUNIYA BOOKSTORES OF AMERICA CO., LTD.
   1581 Webster Street, San Francisco, CA   94115
   CEO: Tomoshige Okazaki, Pres.   Tel: (415) 567-7625   Emp: 95
   Bus: *Books, magazines, printed and electronic*   Fax:(415) 567-4109   %FO: 100
   publication.

   KINOKUNIYA PUBLICATIONS SERVICE OF NEW YORK CO., LTD.
   Ten West 49th Street, New York, NY   10020
   CEO: Eiichi Ichihashi, VP & Gen. Mgr.   Tel: (212) 765-7766   Emp: N/A
   Bus: *Distribution books and periodicals, related*   Fax:(212) 541-9355   %FO: 100
   services.

   LOS ANGELES KINOKUNIYA BOOKSTORES CO., LTD.
   123 Weller Street, Ste.106, Los Angeles, CA   90012
   CEO: T. Suzuki, Gen. Mgr.   Tel: (213) 687-4480   Emp: N/A
   Bus: *Distribution books and periodicals, related*   Fax:(213) 621-4456   %FO: 100
   services.

● **KINTETSU EXPRESS, INC**
3-6 Ohtemachi 2-chome, Chiyoda-ku, Tokyo, Japan
CEO: Toshio Kumokawa, Pres.   Tel: 81-3-3201-2654   Emp: N/A
Bus: *International air freight forwarding services.*   Fax:N/A

   KINTETSU WORLD EXPRESS (USA), INC.
   66 Powerhouse Road, Roslyn Heights, NY   11577
   CEO: Hirokazu Tsujimoto, Pres. & COO   Tel: (516) 625-8700   Emp: N/A
   Bus: *International air freight forwarding.*   Fax:(516) 625-8724   %FO: 100

● **KIRIN BREWERY COMPANY, LTD.**
10-1-Shinkawa 2-chome, Chuo-ku, Tokyo 104, Japan
CEO: Yasuhiro Sato, Pres.   Tel: 81-3-5540-3466   Emp: 8400
Bus: *Brewery.*   Fax:81-3-5540-3536

   KIRIN USA, INC.
   2400 Broadway, Suite 240, Santa Monica, CA   90404
   CEO: A. Shimazu, Pres.   Tel: (310) 829-2400   Emp: 22
   Bus: *Import/distribution beer.*   Fax:(310) 829-0424   %FO: 100

- **KOBE STEEL LTD.**
Tekko Bldg, 8-2 Marunouchi 1-chome, Chiyoda-ku, Tokyo 100, Japan
CEO: Masahiro Kumamoto, Pres.   Tel: 81-3-3218-7111   Emp: 22000
Bus: *Mfr. aluminum and copper products, steel,*   Fax:81-3-3218-6330
industrial and construction machinery and
welding/cutting tools.

   KOBE STEEL USA INC.
   535 Madison Avenue, New York, NY   10022
   CEO: Masumi Sato, Pres.   Tel: (212) 751-9400   Emp: 60
   Bus: *U.S. headquarters. Liaison & development.*   Fax:(212) 355-5564   %FO: 100

   KOBE STEEL USA, INC.
   1000 Town Center, Southfield, MI   48075
   CEO: Hitoshige Tahegaki, Sr.VP   Tel: (248) 827-7757   Emp: N/A
   Bus: *Mfr. steel and related materials.*   Fax:(248) 827-7759   %FO: 100

   MIDREX DIRECT REDUCTION CORPORATION
   2100 Charlotte Plaza, Charlotte, NC   28244-0001
   CEO: Winston L.Tennies, Pres.   Tel: (704) 373-1600   Emp: 70
   Bus: *Direct reduction of iron ore for steelmaking*   Fax:(704) 373-1611   %FO: 100
   industry.

- **KODAMA, LTD.**
2 Kanda-Sakumacho 3-chome, Chiyoda-ku, Tokyo 101, Japan
CEO: Sotoyuki Kodama, Pres.   Tel: 81-3-38648014   Emp: 450
Bus: *Mfr. pharmaceuticals, chemicals, medical, hospital*   Fax:81-3-38649398
supplies and health care products.

   KOPHARM, INC.
   411 Madrid Avenue, Torrance, CA   90501
   CEO: Toshi Watanabe, Pres.   Tel: (310) 320-8860   Emp: 12
   Bus: *Distributes pharmaceuticals, health and*   Fax:(310) 328-1495   %FO: 100
   beauty products.

- **KODANSHA INTL, LTD.**
2-12-21 Otowa, Bunkyo-ku, Tokyo 112, Japan
CEO: Ms. Sawako Noma, Pres.   Tel: 81-3-3944-6493   Emp: N/A
Bus: *Publishing.*   Fax:N/A

   KODANSHA AMERICA, INC.
   114 Fifth Avenue, 18th Fl., New York, NY   10011
   CEO: Minato Asakawa, EVP   Tel: (212) 727-6460   Emp: 25
   Bus: *Publishing.*   Fax:(212) 727-9177   %FO: 100

● **KOMATSU, LTD.**
3-6 Akasaka 2-chome, Minato-ku, Tokyo 107, Japan
CEO: Satoru Anzaki, Pres.   Tel: 81-3 5561-2616   Emp: 26313
Bus: *Mfr. construction equipment, industrial machines &*   Fax:81-3 3505-9662
presses.

KOMATSU AMERICAN INTL CORPORATION
44 N. Fairway Drive, Vernon Hills, IL   60061-8112
CEO: Norimichi Kitagawa, Pres.   Tel: (847) 970-4100   Emp: 50
Bus: *Distribution heavy equipment.*   Fax:(847) 970-4189   %FO: 100

KOMATSU Cutting Technologies, Inc.
265 Vallarvale Street, Wilmington, MA   01887
CEO: Teruo Mochizuki, Pres.   Tel: (508) 658-1650   Emp: 50
Bus: *Distribution industrial machinery.*   Fax:(508) 658-1655   %FO: 100

● **KONICA CORPORATION**
26-2 Nishishinjuku 1-chome, Shinjuku-ku, Tokyo 163, Japan
CEO: Tomiji Uematsu, Pres. & CEO   Tel: 81-3-3349-5044   Emp: 4400
Bus: *Photographic films, papers, chemicals, photo*   Fax:81-3-3349-5250
equipment, business machines, cameras &
accessories, magnetic products.

KONICA Business Machines USA, Inc.
500 Day Hill Road, Windsor, CT   06095
CEO: Teruo Nakazawa, Pres.   Tel: (860) 683-2222   Emp: N/A
Bus: *Photo copiers and copier consumables,*   Fax:(860) 688-0700   %FO: 100
    facsimile terminals, computer terminal printers.

KONICA FINANCE USA CORPORATION
Pencador Corp Center, 225 Corporate Blvd, #206, Newark, DE   19702-3312
CEO: Y. Shibanuma, Pres.   Tel: (302) 737-9293   Emp: N/A
Bus: *Group financial services.*   Fax:(302) 737-3349   %FO: 100

KONICA IMAGING USA, INC.
71 Charles Street, Glen Cove, NY   11542-9001
CEO: Hideaki Iwama, Pres.   Tel: (516) 674-2500   Emp: N/A
Bus: *Graphic arts equipment, film, paper and*   Fax:(516) 676-4124   %FO: 100
    chemicals.

KONICA MANUFACTURING USA, INC.
6900 Konica Drive, Whitsett, NC   27377
CEO: Robert Harris, Pres.   Tel: (910) 449-8000   Emp: N/A
Bus: *Mfr. photographic color paper.*   Fax:(910) 449-7554   %FO: 100

KONICA MEDICAL CORPORATION
411 Newark Pompton Turnpike, Wayne, NJ   07470

CEO: Wayne Thompson, Pres.   Tel: (201) 633-1500   Emp: N/A

Bus: *Medical film processor, medical imaging*   Fax:(201) 523-7408   %FO: 100
    systems, film and accessories, clinical analysis
    equipment.

KONICA PHOTO SERVICE USA INC.
88 Prestige Park Circle, East Hartford, CT   06108

CEO: Shunpei Iwano, Pres.   Tel: (860) 289-0300   Emp: N/A

Bus: *Photographic color film & paper,*   Fax:(860) 528-9929   %FO: 100
    photofinishing equipment, photo color printing.

KONICA QUALITY PHOTO (EAST) INC.
P O Box 2011, Portland, ME   04104-5008

CEO: Tom Meyer, Mgr.   Tel: (207) 883-7200   Emp: N/A

Bus: *Wholesale photofinishing.*   Fax:(207) 883-7309   %FO: 100

KONICA QUALITY PHOTO (WEST) INC.
18250 South Euclid Avenue, Fountain Valley, CA   92708

CEO: Dan Daniel, Pres.   Tel: (714) 549-0500   Emp: N/A

Bus: *Wholesale photofinishing.*   Fax:(714) 549-9178   %FO: 100

KONICA SUPPLIES MFG USA, INC.
Upper Chesapeake Corp. Center, 1000 Konica Drive, Elkton, MD   21921

CEO: Takashi Hogi, Pres.   Tel: (410) 398-7371   Emp: N/A

Bus: *Mfr. photocopier consumables.*   Fax:(410) 392-4626   %FO: 100

KONICA TECHNOLOGY, INC.
777 North Pastoria Avenue, Sunnyvale, CA   94086

CEO: Chao King, Pres.   Tel: (408) 773-9551   Emp: N/A

Bus: *Research and development.*   Fax:(408) 720-9288   %FO: 100

KONICA USA INC.
440 Sylvan Avenue, Englewood Cliffs, NJ   07632

CEO: Richard Carter, Pres.   Tel: (201) 568-3100   Emp: N/A

Bus: *Photographic color film and paper,*   Fax:(201) 816-9541   %FO: 100
    photofinishing equipment, cameras, video tape.

● KOYO SEIKO COMPANY, LTD.
5-8 Minamisemba 3-chome, Chuo-Ku, Osaka 542, Japan

CEO: Hiroshi Inoue, Pres.   Tel: 81-6 245-6087   Emp: 10000

Bus: *Mfr. ball and roller bearings, auto steering gear,*   Fax:81-6 244-0814
    machine tools, industry furnaces and seals.

KOYO CORP. OF USA - Manufacturing Division
Highway 601, Orangeburg, SC   29115

CEO: Yoshitaka Ikeda, Chrm.   Tel: (803) 536-6200   Emp: 701

Bus: *Mfr. bearings.*   Fax:(803) 534-0599   %FO: 100

KOYO CORP. OF USA - Sales Division
29570 Clemens Road, Westlake, OH   44145
CEO: Yoshitaka Ikeda, Chrm.   Tel: (216) 835-1000   Emp: 115
Bus: *Mfr./distribution anti-friction bearings and*   Fax:(216) 835-9347   %FO: 100
   bearing units.

KOYO MACHINERY USA, INC.
47771 Halyard, Plymouth, MI   48170
CEO: Yasunori Kobayashi, Pres.   Tel: (313) 454-4107   Emp: 5
Bus: *Sale machinery.*   Fax:(313) 454-4265   %FO: 100

TRW KOYO STEERING SYSTEMS COMPANY
55 Excellence Way, Vonore, TN   37885
CEO: K.B. Pendse, Pres.   Tel: (423) 884-9200   Emp: 458
Bus: *Mfr. steering gear.*   Fax:(423) 884-9295   %FO: 100

● **KUBOTA CORPORATION**
2-47 Shikitsuhigashi 1-chome, Naniwa-ku, Osaka 556, Japan
CEO: Kouhei Mitsui, Pres.   Tel: 81-6-648-2111   Emp: 15800
Bus: *Mfr. tractors and farm machinery, ductile iron pipe,*   Fax:81-6-648-3862
   roofing and building materials.

AUBURN CONSOLIDATED INDUSTRIES, INC.
2100 South J Street, Auburn, NE   68305
CEO: John S. Skaggs, Pres.   Tel: (402) 274-4911   Emp: N/A
Bus: *Mfr./distribution tractors and farm machinery,*   Fax:(402) 274-5031   %FO: 100
   ductile iron pipe, roofing and building
   materials.

KUBOTA AMERICAN CORPORATION
320 Park Avenue, 23rd Fl., New York, NY   10022
CEO: Yoji Kojima, Pres.   Tel: (212) 355-2440   Emp: N/A
Bus: *Mfr./distribution tractors and farm machinery,*   Fax:(212) 355-2124   %FO: 100
   ductile iron pipe, roofing and building
   materials.

KUBOTA MFG OF AMERICA CORP.
Gainesville Ind. Park North, 2715 Ramsey Road, Gainesville, GA   30501
CEO: Tetsuro Nomoto, Pres.   Tel: (770) 532-0038   Emp: N/A
Bus: *Mfr./distribution tractors and farm machinery,*   Fax:(770) 532-9057   %FO: 100
   ductile iron pipe, roofing and building
   materials.

KUBOTA TRACTOR CORPORATION
3401 Del Amo Boulevard, Torrance, CA   90509-2992
CEO: Shohei Majima, Pres.   Tel: (310) 370-3370   Emp: N/A
Bus: *Corporate financial and administrative*   Fax:(310) 370-2370   %FO: 100
   services.

- **KUMAGAI GUMI COMPANY, LTD.**
2-1 Tsukudo-cho, Shinjuku-ku, Toyko 162, Japan
CEO: Taichiro Kumagai, Pres.　　　　　　　　　Tel: 81-3-3260-2111　　Emp: N/A
Bus: *General contractor and real estate developer.*　　Fax:81-3-3235-3308

KG LAND NEW YORK CORPORATION
1177 Avenue of the Americas, New York, NY　10036
CEO: Naoyuki Yamauchi, Pres.　　　　　　　　Tel: (212) 391-8500　　Emp: N/A
Bus: *Real estate development.*　　　　　　　　Fax:(212) 891-8550　　%FO: 100

KUMAGAI INTERNATIONAL USA CORP.
1875 South Grand Street, Ste.1000, San Mateo, CA　94402-2670
CEO: Katsumi Hayakawa, Pres.　　　　　　　　Tel: (415) 372-9150　　Emp: N/A
Bus: *U.S. headquarters for general contractor*　　Fax:(415) 372-9084　　%FO: 100
services.

- **KUROI ELECTRIC COMPANY, LTD.**
27 Yawata-cho Nishishichijyo, Shimogyo-ku, Kyoto 600, Japan
CEO: T. Matsuura, Pres.　　　　　　　　　　　Tel: 81-75-3135191　　Emp: 750
Bus: *Mfr. lighting products and electronics.*　　Fax:81-75-3141766

KUROI INTL CORPORATION
497 Pini Road, Watsonville, CA　95076
CEO: Sumio Yonemoto, Pres.　　　　　　　　　Tel: (408) 761-8977　　Emp: 5
Bus: *Mfr. lighting products and agricultural*　　Fax:(408) 761-3043　　%FO: 100
products.

- **KYOCERA CORPORATION**
5-22 Kitainoue-cho, Higashino Yamashina-ku, Kyoto 607, Japan
CEO: Kensuke Itoh, Pres.　　　　　　　　　　　Tel: 81-75 5923851　　Emp: 13200
Bus: *Technical, electronic, consumer ceramic products,*　Fax:81-75 5012194
office and telecommunications equipment and
optical systems.

AVX CORPORATION
801 17th Avenue South, Myrtle Beach, SC　29577
CEO: Benedict Rosen, CEO　　　　　　　　　Tel: (803) 448-9411　　Emp: N/A
Bus: *Mfr./sale electronic components.*　　　　Fax:(803) 448-7139　　%FO: 100

ELCO CORPORATION
24422 Avenida de la Carlota, Laguna Hills, CA　92653
CEO: Norman Schoenfeld, Pres.　　　　　　　Tel: (714) 830-8383　　Emp: 400
Bus: *Mfr./sale electronic connectors.*　　　　Fax:(714) 830-9550　　%FO: 100

KYOCERA ELECTRONICS EQUIP., INC.
100 Randolph Road, P O Box 6700, Somerset, NJ　08875-6700
CEO: Mike Okuno, Pres.　　　　　　　　　　　Tel: (908) 560-3400　　Emp: 50
Bus: *Distribute/service office auto equipment, laser*　Fax:(908) 560-8380　　%FO: 100
printers, computer software.

KYOCERA INDUSTRIAL CERAMICS CORP.
5701 East Fourth Plain Blvd., Vancouver, WA   98661

CEO: Robert Osmun, Pres.	Tel: (206) 696-8950	Emp: 100
Bus: *Markets structural ceramics.*	Fax:(206) 696-9804	%FO: 100

MCKENZIE TECHNOLOGY
44370 Old Warm Springs Blvd, Fremont, CA   94538

CEO: Jeffrey L. Davis, Pres.	Tel: (510) 651-2700	Emp: 120
Bus: *Mfr./sale integrated circuit socket connectors.*	Fax:(510) 651-1020	%FO: 100

● KYODO NEWS
2-2-5 Toranomon, Minato-ku, Tokyo 105, Japan

CEO: Yasuhiko Inukai, Pres.	Tel: 81-3-5573-8000	Emp: 1950
Bus: *News wire service (news media).*	Fax:81-3-5573-8018	

KYODO NEWS AMERICA, INC.
50 Rockefeller Plaza, Ste. 816, New York, NY   10020

CEO: Kunihiko Suzuki, Gen.Mgr.	Tel: (212) 603-6600	Emp: 35
Bus: *Wire service (news Media).*	Fax:(212) 603-6621	%FO: 100

● THE KYOEI MUTUAL FIRE & MARINE INSURANCE COMPANY
18-6 Shimbashi l-chome, Minato-ku, Tokyo, Japan

CEO: H. Suzuki, Pres.	Tel: 81-3-504-2335	Emp: N/A
Bus: *Insurance services.*	Fax:81-3-508-7680	

THE KYOEI MUTUAL FIRE & MARINE INSURANCE COMPANY
420 Lexington Avenue, Ste. 2058, New York, NY   10170

CEO: Yoshiyuki Tanaka	Tel: (212) 490-0710	Emp: N/A
Bus: *Representative office: insurance services.*	Fax:(212) 692-9362	%FO: 100

● THE KYOWA BANK
1-1-2 Otemachi, Chiyoda-ku, Tokyo 100, Japan

CEO: Tetsuo Yamanaka, Chrm.	Tel: 81-3-3287-2111	Emp: 8500
Bus: *International banking and financial services.*	Fax:81-3-3287-2556	

THE KYOWA BANK
1 World Trade Center, #4673, New York, NY   10048

CEO: K. Sakai, Gen. Mgr.	Tel: (212) 432-6400	Emp: 50
Bus: *Commercial banking services.*	Fax:(212) 432-1135	%FO: 100

● THE LONG-TERM CREDIT BANK OF JAPAN, LTD.
2-4 Otemachi 1-chome, Chiyoda-ku, Tokyo 100, Japan

CEO: Katsunobu Onogi, Pres.	Tel: 81-3-5511-5111	Emp: N/A
Bus: *Commercial banking services.*	Fax:81-3-5511-5505	

CAPSTAR PARTNERS, INC.
40 East 52nd Street, New York, NY   10022

CEO: R. Lee Rigney, Pres.	Tel: (212) 339-4200	Emp: N/A
Bus: *Financial services.*	Fax:(212) 339-4225	%FO: 100

THE LONG-TERM CREDIT BANK OF JAPAN LTD. - New York Branch
165 Broadway, New York, NY   10006
CEO: Kosaku Sakai, Gen. Mgr.   Tel: (212) 335-4400   Emp: N/A
Bus: *Commercial banking services.*   Fax:(212) 608-2303   %FO: 100

THE LONG-TERM CREDIT BANK OF JAPAN LTD. - Dallas Office
2200 Ross Ave., Ste. 4700 West, Dallas, TX   75201
CEO: Sadao Muraoka, Chief Rep.   Tel: (214) 969-5352   Emp: N/A
Bus: *Commercial banking services.*   Fax:(214) 969-5357   %FO: 100

THE LONG-TERM CREDIT BANK OF JAPAN LTD. - Atlanta Office
245 Peachtree Center, Ste. 2801, Atlanta, GA   30303
CEO: Kazunori Kameyama, Chief Rep.   Tel: (404) 659-7210   Emp: N/A
Bus: *Commercial banking services.*   Fax:(404) 658-9751   %FO: 100

THE LONG-TERM CREDIT BANK OF JAPAN LTD. - Los Angeles Agency
350 S. Grand Avenue, Los Angeles, CA   90071
CEO: Toru Mitani, Gen.Mgr.   Tel: (213) 629-5777   Emp: N/A
Bus: *Commercial banking services.*   Fax:(213) 626-1067   %FO: 100

THE LONG-TERM CREDIT BANK OF JAPAN LTD. - Chicago Branch
190 S. Lasalle Street, Ste 800, Chicago, IL   60603
CEO: Masabaru Kubara, Gen.Mgr.   Tel: (312) 704-1700   Emp: N/A
Bus: *Commercial banking services.*   Fax:(312) 704-8505   %FO: 100

LTCB TRUST CO
165 Broadway, New York, NY   10006
CEO: Kosaku Sakai, Gen. Mgr.   Tel: (212) 335-4900   Emp: N/A
Bus: *Financial services.*   Fax:(212) 608-3081   %FO: 100

LTCB-MAS Investment Management, Inc.
One Tower Bridge, Ste. 1000, West Conshohocken, PA   19428
CEO: John D. Connolly, Pres.   Tel: (610) 940-5200   Emp: N/A
Bus: *Investment management services.*   Fax:(610) 940-5201   %FO: 100

LTCP Latin America, Inc.
527 Madison Avenue, 26th Fl., New York, NY   10022
CEO: Thomas DeCoene, Pres.   Tel: (212) 750-8880   Emp: N/A
Bus: *Commercial banking services.*   Fax:(212) 750-1758   %FO: 100

PEERS & COMPANY
560 Lexington Avenue, New York, NY   10022
CEO: James A. Martens, Pres.   Tel: (212) 339-8400   Emp: N/A
Bus: *Financial services.*   Fax:(212) 888-6687   %FO: 100

• MAKINO MILLING MACHINE COMPANY, LTD.
3-19 Nakane 2-chome, Meguro-ku, Tokyo 152, Japan
CEO: Jiro Makino, Pres.   Tel: 81-3-3717-1151   Emp: 700
Bus: *Machine centers, mfr. systems, electric machinery,*   Fax:81-3-3724-2815
copy mills, engine lathes.

MAKINO
7680 Innovation Way, Mason, OH   45040-9695
CEO: Don Bowers, Pres.   Tel: (513) 573-7200   Emp: 300
Bus: *Mfr./distribution machine tools and systems.*   Fax:(513) 573-7360   %FO: 100

• MAKITA CORPORATION
11-8 Sumiyoshi-cho 3-chome, Anjo Aichi 446, Japan
CEO: Masahiko Goto, Pres.   Tel: 81-5-6698-1711   Emp: 3000
Bus: *Portable electric power tools and accessories.*   Fax:81-5-6698-6021

MAKITA USA INC.
14930-C Northam Street, La Mirada, CA   90638-5753
CEO: Kenji Karube, Pres.   Tel: (714) 522-8088   Emp: 700
Bus: *Portable electric power tools & accessories.*   Fax:(714) 522-8133   %FO: 100

• MARUBENI CORPORATION
4-2 Ohtemachi 1-chome, Chiyoda-ku, Tokyo 100-88, Japan
CEO: Iwao Toriumi, Pres.   Tel: 81-3-3282-2111   Emp: 7000
Bus: *Import/export metals, machinery, chemicals, textiles,*   Fax:81-3-3282-7456
general merchandise, petroleum, agricultural and
marine products.

MARUBENI AMERICA CORPORATION
450 Lexington Avenue, New York, NY   10017-3984
CEO: Katsuo Koh, Pres. & CEO   Tel: (212) 450-0100   Emp: 400
Bus: *Import/export metals, machinery, chemicals,*   Fax:(212) 450-0710   %FO: 100
textiles, general merchandise, petroleum,
agricultural & marine products.

• MARUICHI STEEL TUBE, LTD.
3-9-10 Kita Horie, Nishi-ku, Osaka 550, Japan
CEO: S. Yoshimura, Pres.   Tel: 81-6-531-5201   Emp: N/A
Bus: *Mfr. steel pipe and tubing.*   Fax:81-6-531-1931

MARUICHI AMERICAN CORPORATION
11529 Greenstone Avenue, Santa Fe Springs, CA   90670
CEO: Riichi Soda, Pres.   Tel: (562) 946-1881   Emp: 83
Bus: *Mfr. steel pipe and tubing.*   Fax:(562) 941-0047   %FO: 38

• MARUKAI CORPORATION KK
18-5 Kyomachibori l-chome, Nishi-ku, Osaka 550, Japan

CEO: Junzo Matsu, Pres   Tel: 81-6-443-0071   Emp: 50
Bus: *Import/export general merchandise.*   Fax:81-6-443-2182

MARUKAI CORPORATION
2310 Kamehameha Hwy., Honolulu, HI   96819

CEO: Richard Matsu, EVP   Tel: (808) 845-5051   Emp: 85
Bus: *Sale/distribution of retail oriental goods.*   Fax:(808) 841-2379   %FO: 100

MARUKAI CORPORATION
1740 West Artesia Blvd., Gardenia, CA   90247

CEO: Matsu Hidejiro, Pres.   Tel: (310) 660-6300   Emp: N/A
Bus: *Sale/distribution of retail oriental goods.*   Fax:(310) 660-6301   %FO: 100

• MATSUSHITA ELECTRIC INDUSTRIAL COMPANY, LTD.
1006 Oaza Kadoma, Kadoma City, Osaka 571, Japan

CEO: Yoichi Morishita, Pres.   Tel: 81-6-9081121   Emp: 373100
Bus: *Mfr. electronic and electric products for consumer,*   Fax:81-6-2825777
business and industry.

AMAC CORP.
6550 Katelle Avenue, Cypress, CA   90630

CEO: N/A   Tel: (714) 373-7979   Emp: N/A
Bus: *Export electronic products.*   Fax: %FO: 100

MATSUSHITA ELECTRIC CORPORATION OF AMERICA
One Panasonic Way, Secaucus, NJ   07094

CEO: Kunio Nakamuro, Pres.   Tel: (201) 348-7000   Emp: 14000
Bus: *Mfr. electronic/electrical products for*   Fax:(201) 348-8378   %FO: 100
consumer, business and industry.

MATSUSHITA ELECTRIC CORP. OF AMERICA
1620 L Street, NW, Suite 1150, Washington, DC   20036

CEO: Mary K. Alexander, Dir.Gov't. Affairs Tel: (202) 223-2575   Emp: N/A
Bus: *Government affairs representative office.*   Fax:(202) 223-2614   %FO: 100

MCA/UNIVERSAL INC.
100 Universal City Plaza, Universal City, CA   91608

CEO: Ron Meyer, Pres.   Tel: (818) 777-1000   Emp: 17000
Bus: *Motion picture, TV production and*   Fax:(818) 866-1440   %FO: 100
distribution, music recording and publishing,
communications, real estate.

PANASONIC COMPANY
One Panasonic Way, Secaucus, NJ   07094

CEO: Yoshinori Kobe, Pres.   Tel: (201) 348-7000   Emp: 1100
Bus: *Mfr./wholesale consumer and industrial*   Fax:(201) 271-3092   %FO: 100
electronic products.

PANASONIC/QUASAR COMPANY
1707 North Randall Road, Elgin, IL   60123
CEO: James Indelak, Gen. Mgr.   Tel: (847) 468-5600   Emp: 150
Bus: *Consumer electronic products.*   Fax:(847) 468-4059   %FO: 100

●**MATSUSHITA ELECTRIC WORKS LTD.**
1048 Kadoma, Osaka 571, Japan
CEO: Kiyosuke Imai, Pres.   Tel: 81-6-9081131   Emp: 18000
Bus: *Mfr. electrical fixtures, equipment, appliances,*   Fax:81-6-9094694
building products, electrical & plastic materials.

MATSUSHITA ELECTRIC WORKS, R&D LABORATORY INC
401 River Oaks Pkwy., San Jose, CA   95134
CEO: Hideki Yamaoto, CEO   Tel: (408) 433-3386   Emp: 10
Bus: *Research & development facility.*   Fax:(408) 433-3387   %FO: 100

●**MATSUZAKAYA CO LTD.**
16-1 Sakae 3-chome, Naka-ku, Nagoya 460, Japan
CEO: Akira Ito, Pres.   Tel: 81- 52-251-1111   Emp: 7000
Bus: *Department stores.*   Fax:N/A

MATSUZAKAYA AMERICA, INC.
460 East Third Street, Los Angeles, CA   90013
CEO: Masami Tanizawa, Pres.   Tel: (213) 626-0133   Emp: 42
Bus: *Department stores.*   Fax:(213) 626-7936   %FO: 100

●**MAZDA MOTOR CORPORATION**
3-1 Shinchi, Fucho-cho Aki-Gun, Hiroshima 730-19, Japan
CEO: Henry D.G. Wallace, Pres.   Tel: 81-82-282-1111   Emp: 26100
Bus: *Mfr. automobiles, machine tools and rock drills.*   Fax:81-82-287-5190

MAZDA MOTOR MFG USA, CORPORATION
7755 Irvine Center Drive, Irvine, CA   97218
CEO: George Toyama, Pres.   Tel: (714) 727-1990   Emp: 3105
Bus: *Mfr. automobiles, machine tools and rock*   Fax:(714) 727-6101   %FO: 100
drills.

●**MEIJI SEIKA KAISHA LTD.**
2-4-16 Kyobashi, Chuo-ku, Tokyo 104, Japan
CEO: Akira Sasai, Pres.   Tel: N/A   Emp: N/A
Bus: *Mfr. foods, confectionery, pharmaceuticals and*   Fax:81-3-3274-4063
machinery.

MEIJI SEIKA (USA), INC.
733 Third Avenue, #1910, New York, NY   10017
CEO: Kenji Saito, Gen.Mgr.   Tel: (212) 557-1580   Emp: N/A
Bus: *Sale/distribution of confections and*   Fax:(212) 557-1583   %FO: 100
pharmaceuticals.

STAUFFER BISCUIT COMPANY, INC.
Belmont & Sixth Avenue, York, PA   17405
CEO: S. Onodero, Pres.   Tel: (717) 843-0711   Emp: N/A
Bus: *Mfr. snack foods, specialty confections.*   Fax:(717) 848-1573   %FO: JV

● **MEIKO TRANS COMPANY, LTD.**
4-6 Irifune 2-chome, Nagoy-City, Aichi Pref 455, Japan
CEO: Kazuo Hattori, Pres.   Tel: 81-661-8111   Emp: 650
Bus: *Wholesale, trucking, stevedoring, freight   Fax:81-661-6125
forwarding, customs house broker and air cargo
agent.*

   MEIKO AMERICA, INC.
2160 East Dominguez Street, Long Beach, CA   90810
CEO: Koichiro Murakami, Pres.   Tel: (310) 549-3371   Emp: N/A
Bus: *Warehousing, trucking, freight forwarding,*   Fax:(310) 834-0383   %FO: 100
customs house broker and air cargo agent.

● **MIKUNI CORPORATION**
13-11 Sotokanda 6-chome, Chiyoda-ku, Tokyo, Japan
CEO: Masaki Ikuta, Pres.   Tel: 81-3-3833-0392   Emp: N/A
Bus: *Mfr. motor vehicle parts.*   Fax:81-3-3836-4210

   MIKUNI AMERICAN CORPORATION
8910 Mikuni Avenue, Northridge, CA   91324
CEO: Masaki Ikuta, Pres.   Tel: (818) 885-1242   Emp: N/A
Bus: *Distribution of motor vehicle parts.*   Fax:(818) 993-7387   %FO: 100

● **MINOLTA CO LTD.**
3-13 Azuchi-machi 2-chome, Chuo-ku, Osaka 541, Japan
CEO: Osamu Kanaya, Pres.   Tel: 81-6-271-2251   Emp: 4820
Bus: *Mfr. office equipment, cameras and lenses, optical Fax:81-6-266-1010
products, radiometric instruments, planetariums.*

   MINOLTA BUSINESS SYSTEMS, INC.
500 Franklin Turnpike, Ramsey, NJ   07446
CEO: Joseph M. Murphy, Pres.   Tel: (201) 825-8600   Emp: N/A
Bus: *Distribution business machines.*   Fax:(201) 825-1069   %FO: 100

   MINOLTA COPIER CORPORATION OF NEW YORK
76 Ninth Avenue, New York, NY   10011
CEO: Joseph Villanella, Pres.   Tel: (212) 924-5010   Emp: N/A
Bus: *Distribution camera copiers.*   Fax:(212) 986-9684   %FO: 100

   MINOLTA CORP. (U.S.A.)
101 Williams Drive, Ramsey, NJ   07446
CEO: Hiroshi Fujii, Pres.   Tel: (201) 825-4000   Emp: 2000
Bus: *Distribution/service office machinery, photo   Fax:(201) 825-7605   %FO: 100
and micrographic equipment.*

• MISUMI CORPORATION
4-43 Toyo 2-chome, Kote-ku, Tokyo 135, Japan
CEO: Hiroshi Taguchi, Chrm. & CEO   Tel: 81-3-647-7116   Emp: 300
Bus: *Mfr. press die, plastic mold and automatic machine*   Fax:81-3-647-7125
   components.

MISUMI USA, INC.
1039 Hawthorn Drive, Itasca, IL   60143
CEO: Nobuo Matsushima, Pres.   Tel: (630) 773-3244   Emp: 10
Bus: *Sale press die, plastic mold and automatic*   Fax:(630) 773-3284   %FO: 100
   machine components.

• MITA INDUSTRIAL COMPANY, LTD.
2-28 Tamatsukuri l-chome, Higashi-ku, Osaka 540, Japan
CEO: Yoshihiro Mita, Pres.   Tel: 81-6-764-3555   Emp: 3500
Bus: *Copiers, laser printers, and related products.*   Fax:N/A

MITA COPYSTAR AMERICA, INC.
225 Sand Road, Fairfield, NJ   07004
CEO: Akihiro Nasu, Pres.   Tel: (201) 808-8444   Emp: 165
Bus: *Distributor copiers, facsimile, laser printers*   Fax:(201) 882-4418   %FO: 100
   and related products.

• MITSUBISHI CABLE INDUSTRIES, LTD.
4-1 Marunouchi 3-chome, Chiyoda-ku, Tokyo 100, Japan
CEO: Hayao Shigenari, Pres.   Tel: 81-3-3216-1551   Emp: 2205
Bus: *Mfr. cables and fiber optics.*   Fax:81-3-3201-2239

MITSUBISHI CABLE AMERICA, INC.
411 Hackensack Avenue, Hackensack, NJ   07610
CEO: H. Shigenari, Pres.   Tel: (201) 343-1818   Emp: 10
Bus: *Sales/service silica and plastic optical fibers,*   Fax:(201) 343-6113   %FO: 100
   opti-electronic products, medical angiograms,
   automatic connectors, special gaskets.

• MITSUBISHI CORP
6-3 Marunouchi 2-chome, Chiyoda-ku, Tokyo 100, Japan
CEO: Minoru Makihara, Pres. & CEO   Tel: 81-3 3210-2121   Emp: 9200
Bus: *Trading company: raw materials, chemicals,*   Fax:81-3 3210-8051
   general merchandise.

MITSUBISHI INTERNATIONAL CORP.
520 Madison Avenue, New York, NY   10022
CEO: Motohiko Numaguchi, Pres. & CEO   Tel: (212) 605-2000   Emp: N/A
Bus: *Import/export; raw materials, chemicals,*   Fax:(212) 605-1863   %FO: 100
   general merchandise.

• **MITSUBISHI HEAVY INDUSTRIES LTD.**
5-1 Marunouchi 2-chome, Chiyoda-ku, Tokyo 100, Japan
CEO: Nobuyuki Masuda, Pres.   Tel: 81-3-3212-3111   Emp: N/A
Bus: *Machinery and plants, aerospace system,*   Fax:81-3-3201-6285
    shipbuilding and steel structures, R&D.

    BELOIT CORPORATION
    One St. Lawrence Avenue, Beloit, WI   53511-6270
    CEO: John McKay, Pres.   Tel: (608) 365-3311   Emp: N/A
    Bus: *Mfr. paper-making machinery.*   Fax:(608) 364-7013   %FO: 100

    CORMETECH, INC.
    5000 International Drive, Durham, NC   27712
    CEO: Fred Mauer, Pres.   Tel: (919) 620-3000   Emp: N/A
    Bus: *Mfr. ceramic catalysts.*   Fax:(919) 620-3001   %FO: 100

    MHI CORRUGATING MACHINERY CO.
    Hunt Valley Bldg 12, 11204 McCormick Road, Hunt Valley, MD   21031-1101
    CEO: Roy Willis, Pres. & CEO   Tel: (410) 584-7990   Emp: N/A
    Bus: *Mfr. corrugating machinery.*   Fax:(410) 584-1252   %FO: 100

    MITSUBISHI CATERPILLAR FORKLIFT AMERICA, INC.
    2011 W. Sam Houston Pkwy. N., Houston, TX   77043-2421
    CEO: Y. Okazaki, Pres.   Tel: (713) 467-1234   Emp: N/A
    Bus: *Mfr. forklifts.*   Fax:(713) 467-3232   %FO: 100

    MITSUBISHI HEAVY INDUSTRIES AMERICAS, INC.
    630 Fifth Avenue, New York, NY   10111
    CEO: Seitaro Ohira, Pres.   Tel: (212) 969-9000   Emp: N/A
    Bus: *Industrial machinery and systems.*   Fax:(212) 262-3301   %FO: 100

    MITSIBISHI LITHOGRAPHIC PRESSES, INC.
    600 Barclay Blvd., Lincolnshire, IL   60069
    CEO: R. Buchanan, Pres.   Tel: (847) 634-9100   Emp: N/A
    Bus: *Sales lithographic presses.*   Fax:(708) 634-9109   %FO: 100

    MITSUBISHI MACHINE TOOL USA, INC.
    907 West Irving Park Road, Itasca, IL   60143-2023
    CEO: Shimpei Amano, Pres.   Tel: (630) 860-4220   Emp: N/A
    Bus: *Mfr. machine tools.*   Fax:(630) 860-4233   %FO: 100

• MITSUBISHI MATERIALS CORPORATION
1-5-1, Marunouchi, Chiyoda-ku, Tokyo 101, Japan

CEO: M. Fujimura, Pres.   Tel: 81-3-5252-5409   Emp: 20000

Bus: *Non-ferrous metals, fabricated metals, electronic*   Fax:81-3-5252-5443
*material, aluminum cans, golden jewelry and semi-
conductors.*

MITSUBISHI SILICON AMERICA - Sales Office
16486 Bernardo Ctr Dr.,Ste.348B, San Diego, CA   92128

CEO: Peter Sandow, Mgr.   Tel: (619) 673-4024   Emp: 2

Bus: *Mfr./sale polished & epitaxial silicon wafers*   Fax:(619) 673-4406   %FO: 100
for semiconductor industry.

MITSUBISHI SILICON AMERICA - Sales Office
17304 N. Preston Road, Ste. 800, Dallas, TX   75252-5645

CEO: Mark McGuire, Mgr.   Tel: (972) 733-6878   Emp: 2

Bus: *Sales office for sale of polished & epitaxial*   Fax:(297) 233-6938   %FO: 100
silicon wafers for semiconductor industry.

MITSUBISHI SILICON AMERICA - Marketing Hdqtrs.
P.O.Box 10445, Palo Alto, CA   94303-0912

CEO: M. Fujimura, Pres.   Tel: (415) 328-7600   Emp: N/A

Bus: *Marketing headquarters: mfr./sale polished*   Fax:(415) 853-5080   %FO: 100
*and epitaxial silicon wafers for semiconductor
industry.*

MITSUBISHI SILICON AMERICA
1351 Tanden Avenue, Salem, OR   97303

CEO: Hibashi Uchida, Pres.   Tel: (503) 371-0041   Emp: 1200

Bus: *Mfr. polished and epitaxial silicon wafers for*   Fax:(503) 361-3409   %FO: 100
semiconductor industry.

• MITSUBISHI RAYON COMPANY, LTD.
3-19 Kyobashi 2-chome, Chuo-ku, Tokyo 104, Japan

CEO: Shuzo Kanazawa, Pres.   Tel: 81-3-3245-8734   Emp: N/A

Bus: *Mfr. synthetic fibers, films, resins, medical devices.*   Fax:81-3-3245-8789

MITSUBISHI RAYON AMERICA, INC.
520 Madison Avenue, New York, NY   10022

CEO: M. Gonda   Tel: (212) 759-5605   Emp: N/A

Bus: *Synthetic, optical & carbon fibers, resins,*   Fax:(212) 355-7994   %FO: 100
medical devices.

- **MITSUBISHI TRUST & BANKING CORPORATION**
4-5 Marunouchi 1-chome, Chiyoda-ku, Tokyo, Japan
CEO: Toyoshi Nakano, CEO   Tel: 81-3-3212-1211   Emp: N/A
Bus: *General banking services.*   Fax:81-3-3211-1267

MITSUBISHI TRUST & BANKING CORP.
520 Madison Avenue, 25th Fl., New York, NY   10022
CEO: Yosuke Serizawa, Dir.& Gen.Mgr.   Tel: (212) 838-7700   Emp: N/A
Bus: *International banking services.*   Fax:(212) 755-2349   %FO: 100

MITSUBISHI TRUST & BANKING CORP.
311 South Wacker Drive, Chicago, IL   60606
CEO: Naoya Nishimura, Gen.Mgr.   Tel: (312) 408-6000   Emp: N/A
Bus: *International banking services.*   Fax:(312) 663-0863   %FO: 100

MITSUBISHI TRUST & BANKING CORP.
801 Sout Figueroa Street, Los Angeles, CA   90017
CEO: Yoshiro Nagamata, Gen.Mgr.   Tel: (213) 488-9003   Emp: N/A
Bus: *International banking services.*   Fax:(213) 687-4631   %FO: 100

- **MITSUBOSHI BELTING, LTD.**
Kobe Harborland Center Bldg, 3-3 Higashi 1-chome, Kawasaki-cho, Chuo-ku, Kobe 650, Japan
CEO: Kinzo Oda, Pres.   Tel: 81-78-360-5701   Emp: 2300
Bus: *Mfr. power transmission & conveyor belts, auto*   Fax:81-78-360-5970
comps, structural foam, waterproofing materials,
tires/tubes, engineering. plastics.

MBL (USA) CORPORATION
601 Dayton Road, Ottawa, IL   61350
CEO: Keiji Murata, Pres.   Tel: (815) 434-1282   Emp: 270
Bus: *Mfr. industrial/auto power transmission belts,*   Fax:(815) 434-2897   %FO: 98
polyurethane precision belts and molded
products.

- **MITSUI & COMPANY, LTD.**
2-1 Otemachi 1-chome, Chiyoda-ku, Tokyo 100, Japan
CEO: Shigeji Ueshima, Pres. & CEO   Tel: 81-3 3285-1111   Emp: 11400
Bus: *General trading company and administrative*   Fax:81-3 3285-9800
services for Mitsui Group.

MITSUI & CO., (USA) INC.
200 Park Avenue, 26th Fl., New York, NY   10166-0130
CEO: Masayoshi Furuhata, Pres. & CEO   Tel: (212) 878-4000   Emp: 750
Bus: *General trading company: export/import,*   Fax:(212) 878-4800   %FO: 100
finance, investment, transportation and
technology transfer.

● **MITSUI MARINE & FIRE INSURANCE CO., LTD.**
3-9 Kanda-Surugadai, Chiyoda-ku, Tokyo 101-11, Japan
CEO: Takeo Inokuchi, Pres.   Tel: 81-3-3259-3111   Emp: 8722
Bus: *Non-life insurance services.*   Fax:81-3-3291-5466

    MITSUI MARINE & FIRE INSURANCE CO. OF AMERICA
    33 Whitehall Street, 26th Fl., New York, NY   10004-2112
    CEO: Akira Tomeda, Pres.   Tel: (212) 480-2550   Emp: 24
    Bus: *Non-life insurance.*   Fax:(212) 480-1127   %FO: 100

● **MITSUI MINING & SMELTING COMPANY, LTD.**
2-1-1 Nihonbashi-Muromachi, Chuo-ku, Tokyo 103, Japan
CEO: Shimpei Miyamura, Pres.   Tel: 81-3-3246-8080   Emp: 3700
Bus: *Non-ferrous metals.*   Fax:81-3-3246-8247

    ADVANCED CRYSTAL TECHNOLOGY INC.
    3100 Stock Creek Blvd., Rockford, TN   37853
    CEO: Tashihiko Saito, Pres.   Tel: (423) 579-1630   Emp: 9
    Bus: *Mfr./sale BGO single crystal.* Fax:(423) 577-2052   %FO: 100

    ALLIED SIGNAL OAK-MITSUI, INC.
    80 First Street, PO Box 99, Hoosick Falls, NY   12090
    CEO: Steve Hochhauser, Pres.   Tel: (518) 686-4961   Emp: 230
    Bus: *Mfr./sale copper foil for print circuit.* Fax:(518) 686-4980   %FO: 49.9

    AMERICAN MOLD TECHNOLOGIES, INC.
    42300 Executive Drive, Harrison Twp, MI   48045-1311
    CEO: Karl Blankenburg, Pres.   Tel: (313) 469-0550   Emp: 35
    Bus: *Mfr./sale plastic dies.*   Fax:(313) 465-9973   %FO: 40

    GECOM CORPORATION
    1025 Barachel Lane, Greensburg, IN   47240
    CEO: Yoshihiko Takebayashi, Pres.   Tel: (812) 663-2270   Emp: 642
    Bus: *Mfr./sale automobile door locks.* Fax:(812) 663-2230   %FO: 100

    MAGNOX, INC.
    4 Magnox Drive, Pulaski, VA   24301
    CEO: Frederic H. Pollard, Pres.   Tel: (540) 980-3500   Emp: 180
    Bus: *Mfr./sale magnetic iron powder.* Fax:(540) 980-3538   %FO: 80

    MESCO USA, INC.
    224 North Broadway, #4, Greensburg, IN   47240
    CEO: Tsutomu Tachimoto, Pres.   Tel: (812) 663-2336   Emp: 5
    Bus: *Engineering services.*   Fax:(812) 663-2360   %FO: 100

    MITSUI MINING & SMELTING CO., (USA) INC.
    461 Fifth Avenue, New York, NY   10017
    CEO: Kingo Nakayama, Pres.   Tel: (212) 679-9300   Emp: N/A
    Bus: *Import/export non-ferrous metals and* Fax:(212) 679-9303   %FO: 100
        products, research and service.

MITSUI/ZCA ZINC POWDERS CO.
300 Frankfort Road, Monaka, PA   15061
CEO: Yoshi Takayanagi, Pres.   Tel: (412) 773-2259   Emp: N/A
Bus: *Mfr./sale zinc powder.*   Fax:(412) 773-2229   %FO: 50

OAK-MITSUI PARTNERSHIP.
29 Battleship Road Extension, PO Box 1709, Camden, SC   29020
CEO: Steve Hochhauser, Pres.   Tel: (803) 425-7900   Emp: 140
Bus: *Mfr./sale copper foil for print circuit.* Fax:(803) 425-7925   %FO: 49.9

POWDERTECK CORPORATION
5103 Evance Avenue, Valparaiso, IN   46383
CEO: Kyozo Hisada, Pres.   Tel: (219) 462-4141   Emp: 61
Bus: *Mfr./sale ferrite powder.*   Fax:(219) 462-0376   %FO: 100

● MITSUI OSK LINES LTD.
1-1 Toranomon 2-chome, Minato-ku, Tokyo 105, Japan
CEO: Masaharu Ikuta, Pres.   Tel: 81-3-3587-7111   Emp: 2100
Bus: *International transport, sea, land and rail carriers,*   Fax:81-3-3587-7705
terminals, cruise ships and resorts, and real estate
development.

AMT FREIGHT, INC.
2500 Logistics Drive, Battle Creek, MI   49015
CEO: Isao Okada, Pres.   Tel: (616) 965-0054   Emp: N/A
Bus: *International freight forwarding services.* Fax:(616) 965-2040   %FO: 100

MITSUI OSK LINES (America) LTD.
Harborside Financial Center, Plaza III, #601, Jersey City, NJ   07311
CEO: Akihiko Teramoto, Pres.   Tel: (201) 200-5200   Emp: 415
Bus: *Marine transportation services.*   Fax:(201) 200-5396   %FO: 100

MITSUI OSK LINES (America) LTD.
2300 Clayton Road, Ste. 1500, Concord, CA   94520
CEO: Raymond Keene, EVP   Tel: (510) 688-2600   Emp: N/A
Bus: *Marine transportation services.*   Fax:(510) 688-2604   %FO: 100

● MITSUI TOATSU CHEMICALS INC
3-2-5 Kasumigaseki, Chiyoda-ku, Tokyo 100, Japan
CEO: Akio Sato, Pres.   Tel: 81-3-3592-4111   Emp: 5600
Bus: *Chemicals, plastic resins, agrochemical, specialty*   Fax:81-3-3592-4267
chemicals.

MITSUI TOATSU CHEMICALS, INC.
2500 Westchester Avenue, Suite 110, Purchase, NY   10577
CEO: K. Yoshida, Pres.   Tel: (914) 253-0777   Emp: N/A
Bus: *Sale chemicals, amino acid & polymers.*   Fax:(914) 253-0790   %FO: 100

● **THE MITSUI TRUST & BANKING CO LTD.**
1-1 Nihonbashi-Muromachi, 2-chome, Chuo-ku, Tokyo 103, Japan
CEO: Keiu Nishida, CEO   Tel: 81-3-3270-9511   Emp: 6030
Bus: *General banking services.*   Fax:81-3-3245-0459

     MITSUI TRUST BANK USA
     1 World Financial Center,
     200 Liberty St., New York, NY   10281
     CEO: Tadahiko Yoshimura, Pres.   Tel: (212) 341-0300   Emp: N/A
     Bus: *International banking services.*   Fax:(212) 945-4170   %FO: 100

● **MITSUKOSHI, LTD.**
1-4-1 Muromachi-Nihonbashi, Chuo-ku, Tokyo 103, Japan
CEO: Yoshiaki Sakakura, Pres.   Tel: 81-3-241-3311   Emp: 12000
Bus: *Department stores.*   Fax:N/A

     MITSUKOSHI USA, INC.
     465 Park Avenue, New York, NY   10022
     CEO: Naga Matsu, Pres.   Tel: (212) 753-5580   Emp: 215
     Bus: *Sale/service restaurants, retail, exporting and*   Fax:(212) 355-7161   %FO: 100
          interior decoration.

● **MIURA CO LTD.**
7 Horie-cho, Matsuyama Ehime 799-26, Japan
CEO: Syozo Shiraishi, Pres.   Tel: 81-899-791-111   Emp: 1600
Bus: *Mfr. steam and hot water boilers and food machines.*   Fax:81-899-782-321

     MIURA BOILER USA, INC.
     600 Northgate Pkwy, #M, Wheeling, IL   60090-3201
     CEO: Masashi Hirose, Pres.   Tel: (847) 465-0001   Emp: 10
     Bus: *Sale/service boilers.*   Fax:(847) 465-0011   %FO: 100

● **MIYACHI TECHNOS CORPORATION**
Koyosha Bldg, 8/F, 5-48-5 Higashinippori, Arakawa-ku, Tokyo 116, Japan
CEO: Keiji Nishizawa, Pres.   Tel: 81-6-891-2211   Emp: 250
Bus: *Mfr. welding controls, power supplies and industrial*   Fax:81-6-891-7887
laser systems.

     UNITEC MIYACHI CORPORATION
     4342 Tuller Road, Dublin, OH   43017
     CEO: John Lantz, Mgr.   Tel: (614) 792-2500   Emp: 6
     Bus: *Sale/service welding controls, power supplies*   Fax:(614) 792-2604   %FO: 100
          and monitors.

- **J. MORITA CORPORATION**
3-33-18 Tarumi-cho, Suita City 564, Japan
CEO: Fukuo Morita, CEO   Tel: 81-6-380-1521   Emp: 950
Bus: *Mfr. of furniture and dental instruments/equipment.*   Fax:81-6-380-0585

    J. MORITA USA, INC.
    14712 Bentley Circle, Tustin, CA   92780
    CEO: Junichi Miyata, Pres.   Tel: (714) 544-2854   Emp: 25
    Bus: *Mfr./distribution of furniture and dental*   Fax:(714) 730-1048   %FO: 100
       instruments/equipment.

- **MURATA MFG COMPANY, LTD.**
26-10 Tenjin 2-chome, Nagaokakyo, Kyoto 617, Japan
CEO: Akira Murata, Pres.   Tel: 81-75-951-9111   Emp: 2700
Bus: *Mfr. electronic components.*   Fax:81-75-954-7720

    MURATA ELECTRONICS NORTH AMERICA, INC.
    2200 Lake Drive SE, Smyrna, GA   30080
    CEO: Fred Chanoki, Pres.   Tel: (770) 436-1300   Emp: 1700
    Bus: *Mfr./sale electronic components.*   Fax:(404) 436-3030   %FO: 100

- **NAKANISHI METAL WORKS COMPANY, LTD.**
3-5 Tenmabashi 3-chome, Kita-ku, Osaka 530, Japan
CEO: Kazuo Nakanishi, Pres.   Tel: 81-6-3514832   Emp: 1120
Bus: *Mfr. bearings and conveyors.*   Fax:81-6-3517822

    NKC OF AMERICA, INC.
    1584 Brooks Road East, Memphis, TN   38116
    CEO: Shigeru Yoneda, Pres.   Tel: (901) 396-5353   Emp: 150
    Bus: *Mfr./design conveyor systems.*   Fax:(901) 396-2339   %FO: 100

- **NAMBA PRESS WORKS COMPANY, LTD.**
8-3-8 Kojima-Ogawa, Kurashiki, Okayama 711, Japan
CEO: Shigezo Namba, Pres.   Tel: 81-86-473-3111   Emp: N/A
Bus: *Original equipment auto seating and related*   Fax:81-86-473-4774
products.

    BLOOMINGTON-NORMAL SEATING COMPANY
    2031 Warehouse Road, Normal, IL   61761
    CEO: Nobuhiro Morimoto, Pres.   Tel: (309) 452-7878   Emp: 150
    Bus: *Mfr. automotive seating systems.*   Fax:(309) 452-2312   %FO: JV

● **NEC CORPORATION**
NEC Building, 7-1 Shiba 5-chome, Minato-ku, Tokyo 108-01, Japan
CEO: Hisashi Kaneko, Pres.   Tel: 81-3-3454-1111   Emp: 152700
Bus: *Communication systems & equipment, computers,*   Fax: 81-3-3798-1510
    industrial electronic systems, electronic devices.

    HNSX SUPERCOMPUTERS, INC.
    305 Foster Street, Littleton, MA   01460
    CEO: K. Kagyama, Pres.   Tel: (508) 742-4690   Emp: N/A
    Bus: *Mktg. supercomputers.*   Fax: (508) 742-4689   %FO: 100

    NEC BUSINESS COMMUNICATIONS SYSTEMS, INC.
    5890 Enterprise Parkway, East Syracuse, NY   13057-1094
    CEO: David Montanaro, Pres.   Tel: (315) 446-2400   Emp: N/A
    Bus: *Mfr. communications systems & equipment.*   Fax: (315) 449-5493   %FO: 100

    NEC ELECTRONICS, INC.
    2880 Scott Blvd., Santa Clara, CA   95050
    CEO: S. Matsue, Pres.   Tel: (408) 588-6000   Emp: N/A
    Bus: *Mfr. ICs & electronic devices.*   Fax: (408) 588-6130   %FO: 100

    NEC FOUNDATION OF AMERICA
    Corporate Center Drive, Melville, NY   11747
    CEO: Dr. Mineo Sugiyama, Pres.   Tel: (516) 753-7021   Emp: N/A
    Bus: *Science/technology education & support*   Fax: (516) 753-7096   %FO: 100
        programs.

    NEC INDUSTRIES, INC.
    10 East 50 Street, New York, NY   10017
    CEO: Ko Suzuki, Sen. VP   Tel: (212) 702-7000   Emp: N/A
    Bus: *Financing for US subsidiaries.*   Fax: (212) 702-7020   %FO: 100

    NEC RESEARCH INSTITUTE, INC.
    4 Independent Way, Princeton, NJ   08540
    CEO: C. William Gear, Pres.   Tel: (609) 520-1555   Emp: N/A
    Bus: *Research & management.*   Fax: (609) 951-2961   %FO: 100

    NEC SYSTEMS LABORATORY, INC.
    110 Rio Robles, San Jose, CA   95134
    CEO: S. Tashiro, Pres.   Tel: (408) 434-7100   Emp: N/A
    Bus: *Marketing research services.*   Fax: (408) 434-7119   %FO: 100

    NEC TECHNOLOGIES, INC.
    1250 N. Arlington Heights Road, Itasca, IL   60143-1248
    CEO: T. Ishii, Pres.   Tel: (630) 775-7900   Emp: N/A
    Bus: *Mfr. computers, related systems.*   Fax: (630) 775-7901   %FO: 100

NEC USA, INC.
Corporate Center Drive, Melville, NY 11747
CEO: Dr. Mineo Sugiyama, Pres.   Tel: (516) 753-7000   Emp: N/A
Bus: *Holding company. Communication systems &*   Fax:(516) 753-7434   %FO: 100
 equipment, computers, industrial electronic
 systems, electronic devices.

NMI CORPORATION
14110 N Dallas Pkwy, #300, Dallas, TX 75240
CEO: Don Scherzer, Pres.   Tel: (972) 233-5021   Emp: N/A
Bus: *Sale mobile phones, paging systems, fax*   Fax:(972) 661-1556   %FO: 100
 equipment.

• NEW JAPAN SECURITIES COMPANY, LTD.
3-11 Kanda Surugadai, Tokyo 101, Japan
CEO: Tadashi Iwase, Pres.   Tel: 81-3-3219-1111   Emp: 4800
Bus: *Securities broker/dealer.*   Fax:81-3-3292-6937

NEW JAPAN SECURITIES INTL, INC.
1 World Trade Center, Ste. 9133, New York, NY 10048
CEO: Kenshiro Oshima, Pres.   Tel: (212) 839-0001   Emp: 30
Bus: *Securities broker/dealer.*   Fax:(212) 938-1580   %FO: 100

• THE NEW OTANI COMPANY, LTD.
4-1 Kioi-cho, Chiyoda-ku, Tokyo, Japan
CEO: Kazuhiko Otani, Pres.   Tel: 81-3-3265-1111   Emp: 1300
Bus: *Hotels management services.*   Fax:81-3-3221-2619

HOTEL KAIMANA, INC.
2863 Kalakaua Avenue, Honolulu, HI 96813
CEO: Steven Boyle, Gen. Mgr.   Tel: (808) 923-1555   Emp: 150
Bus: *Hotels management services.*   Fax:(808) 922-9404   %FO: 100

THE NEW OTANI HOTEL & GARDEN
120 South Los Angeles Street, Los Angeles, CA 90012
CEO: Kenji Yoshimoto, VP & Gen.Mgr.   Tel: (213) 629-1200   Emp: 350
Bus: *Hotels management services.*   Fax:(213) 253-9280   %FO: 100

• NEWLONG MACHINE WORKS, LTD.

14-14 Matsugaya 1-chome, Tait-ku, Tokyo 111, Japan

CEO: Y. Cho, Pres.

Tel: 81-3-3843-6548   Emp: 1500

Bus: *Mfr. automated/semi-automated, heavy-duty bag packaging/closing/filling/making equipment, and printing machines.*

Fax:81-3-3843-6574

AMERICA - NEWLONG, INC.

5310 South Harding Street, Indianapolis, IN   46217

CEO: Gary L. Wells, VP & Gen. Mgr.

Tel: (317) 787-9421   Emp: 17

Bus: *Mfr. automated/semi-automated, heavy-duty bag packaging/closing/filling/making equipment, and printing machines.*

Fax:(317) 786-5225   %FO: 100

• NICHIEI COMPANY, LTD.

33-1 Tsurumi-chu 4-chome, Tsurumi-ku, Yokohama 230, Japan

CEO: Koichiro Hirata, Pres.

Tel: 81-45-521-6161   Emp: 1200

Bus: *Wholesale housing materials, real estate development and importer of lumber.*

Fax:81-45-502-5891

NICHIEI AMERICA CORPORATION

1 Southwest Columbia Street, Ste.1450, Portland, OR   97258-2078

CEO: Terumitsu Takeuchi, Pres.

Tel: (503) 226-3303   Emp: 14

Bus: *Export lumber; real estate development.*

Fax:(503) 226-1138   %FO: 100

• NICHIMEN CORPORATION

1-21, Shiba 4-chome, Minato-ku, Tokyo 108, Japan

CEO: Akira Watari, Pres.

Tel: 81-3-5446-1111   Emp: N/A

Bus: *Wholesale textiles, food, machines, metals and chemicals.*

Fax:81-3-5446-1010

NICHIMEN AMERICA, INC.

1345 Avenue of the Americas, New York, NY   10105

CEO: Akira Hashimoto, Pres.

Tel: (212) 698-5000   Emp: N/A

Bus: *Wholesale textiles, food, machines, metals and chemicals.*

Fax:(212) 698-5200   %FO: 100

• NICHIRO CORPORATION

Shinyurakucho Bldg, 1-12-1 Yurakucho, Chiyoda-ku, Tokyo 100, Japan

CEO: Keinosuke Hisai, Pres.

Tel: 81-3-3240-6210   Emp: N/A

Bus: *Seafood products.*

Fax:81-3-5252-7966

PETER PAN SEAFOODS, INC.

2200 Sixth Avenue, Ste.1000, Seattle, WA   98121

CEO: Barry Collier, Pres.

Tel: (206) 728-6000   Emp: N/A

Bus: *Seafood distributor.*

Fax:(206) 441-9090   %FO: 100

- **NIHON KEIZAI SHIMBUN, INC.**
  1-9-5 Otemachi, Chiyoda-ku, Tokyo 100-66, Japan
  CEO: Takuhiko Tsuruta, Pres   Tel: 81-3-270-0251   Emp: 4400
  Bus: *Newspaper publisher, data bank services,*   Fax:N/A
        broadcasting and exhibitions.

  > **NIHON KEIZAI SHIMBUN AMERICA, INC.**
  > 1325 Avenue of the Americas, Ste. 2500, New York, NY   10019
  > CEO: Y. Ikeda, Pres.   Tel: (212) 261-6200   Emp: N/A
  > Bus: *Newspaper publisher, data bank services and*   Fax:(212) 261-6209   %FO: 100
  >   *research.*

- **NIKKO INTL CAPITAL MGMT COMPANY, LTD.**
  17-9 Hakozaki-cho, Nihonbashi, Chuo-ku, Tokyo 103, Japan
  CEO: Tadao Kobayashi, Pres.   Tel: 81-3-3283-3525   Emp: 150
  Bus: *Money management.*   Fax:81-3-3283-1858

  > **NIKKO CAPITAL MGMT (USA), INC**
  > 489 Fifth Avenue, New York, NY   10017
  > CEO: Shigekazu Kurishima, Pres.   Tel: (212) 599-0300   Emp: 10
  > Bus: *Investment advisors.*   Fax:(212) 599-4640   %FO: 100

- **NIKKO SECURITIES COMPANY LTD.**
  3-1 Marunouchi 3-chome, Chiyoda-ku, Tokyo 100, Japan
  CEO: Kichiro Takao, Pres.   Tel: 81-3-283-2211   Emp: 9740
  Bus: *Investment banking/brokerage.*   Fax:N/A

  > **NIKKO SECURITIES COMPANY INTL, INC.**
  > 200 Liberty Street, New York, NY   10281
  > CEO: Masao Ebina, Pres.   Tel: (212) 416-5400   Emp: 275
  > Bus: *Investment banking/brokerage.*   Fax:(212) 416-5600   %FO: 100

- **NIKON CORPORATION**
  Fuji Bldg, 2-3 Marunouchi 3-chome, Chiyoda-ku, Tokyo 100, Japan
  CEO: Shigeo Ono, Pres.   Tel: 81-3-32145311   Emp: 11000
  Bus: *Industrial equipment, imaging and information,*   Fax:81-3-32015856
        health and medical equipment and services.

  > **NIKON PRECISION, INC.**
  > 1399 Shoreway Road, Belmont, CA   94002-4107
  > CEO: David Huchital, Pres.   Tel: (415) 508-4674   Emp: 280
  > Bus: *Service/support semiconductor and*   Fax:(415) 508-4600   %FO: 100
  >   *manufacturing equipment.*

  > **NIKON, INC.**
  > 1300 Walt Whitman Road, Melville, NY   11747
  > CEO: Hideo Fukuchi, Pres.   Tel: (516) 547-4200   Emp: N/A
  > Bus: *US Corporate headquarters.*   Fax:(516) 547-0299   %FO: 100

- **NINTENDO COMPANY, LTD.**
  60 Fukuine Kamitakamatsu-cho, Higashiyama-ku, Kyoto 605, Japan
  CEO: Hiroshi Yamauchi, Pres.　　　　　　　Tel: 81-75-541-6111　　Emp: 2000
  Bus: *Develop/mfr. video games and video equipment.*　Fax:81-75-531-7996

  　　NINTENDO OF AMERICA, INC.
  　　4820 150th Street, NE, Redmond, WA　98052-9733
  　　CEO: Minoru Arakawa, Pres.　　　　　Tel: (425) 882-2040　　Emp: 850
  　　Bus: *Develop/mfr./distribution video games and*　Fax:(425) 882-3585　%FO: 100
  　　　　video equipment.

- **NIPPON COLUMBIA COMPANY, LTD.**
  14-14 Akasaka 4-chome, Minato-ku, Tokyo 107, Japan
  CEO: Kazuo Mochizuki, Pres.　　　　　　Tel: 81-44-575-7810　　Emp: N/A
  Bus: *Mfr. audio and video products.*　　　Fax:81-44-211-2161

  　　DENON CORPORATION USA, INC.
  　　222 New Road, Parsippany, NJ　07054
  　　CEO: Y. Kashida, Pres.　　　　　　　Tel: (201) 575-7810　　Emp: N/A
  　　Bus: *Distribution/sales audio and video products.*　Fax:(201) 575-2532　%FO: 100

- **THE NIPPON CREDIT BANK, LTD.**
  13-10, Kudan-kita 1-chome, Chiyoda-ku, Tokyo 102, Japan
  CEO: H. Kubota, Chrm.　　　　　　　　Tel: 81-3-3263-1111　　Emp: 2848
  Bus: *Credit banking, financing and investment banking.*　Fax:81-3-3264-7025

  　　EASTBRIDGE CAPITAL, INC.
  　　135 East 57th Street, New York, NY　10022
  　　CEO: Messrs. Bauman and Minerva, Co-Pres.　Tel: (212) 756-7200　　Emp: N/A
  　　Bus: *Financial banking services.*　　　Fax:(212) 756-7270　%FO: 100

  　　THE NIPPON CREDIT BANK LTD.
  　　245 Park Avenue, 30th Fl., New York, NY　10167
  　　CEO: N. Osaki, Gen. Mgr.　　　　　　Tel: (212) 984-1200　　Emp: 273
  　　Bus: *NY branch; financial services.*　　Fax:(212) 490-3895　%FO: 100

  　　NIPPON CREDIT TRUST COMPANY
  　　245 Park Avenue, 25th Fl., New York, NY　10167
  　　CEO: T. Idhil, Pres.　　　　　　　　Tel: (212) 503-1700　　Emp: N/A
  　　Bus: *Financial banking services.*　　　Fax:(212) 983-7684　%FO: 100

- **NIPPON DANTAI LIFE INSURANCE COMPANY**
  1-2-19 Shibuya-ku, Tokyo 15020, Japan
  CEO: Takashi Matsudo, Pres.　　　　　　Tel: 81-3-3407-6211　　Emp: N/A
  Bus: *Life insurance services.*　　　　　Fax:81-3-5466-7147

  　　NIPPON DANTAI LIFE INSURANCE COMPANY
  　　45 Broadway, 10th Fl., New York, NY　10006
  　　CEO: M. Maruyama, Mgr.　　　　　　Tel: (212) 363-9550　　Emp: 5
  　　Bus: *Life insurance.*　　　　　　　Fax:(212) 363-9553　%FO: 100

• **NIPPON EXPRESS COMPANY, LTD.**
12-9, Soto Kanda 3-chome, Chiyoda-ku, Tokyo 101, Japan
CEO: Shoichiro Hamanaka, Pres.   Tel: 81-3-3253-1111   Emp: 48000
Bus: *Leasing, finance, import/export, real estate,*   Fax:81-3-5294-5739
     equipment sales.

    NIPPON EXPRESS TRAVEL USA, INC.
    720 Market Street, 7th Fl., San Francisco, CA   94102
    CEO: Motonori Asada, Pres.   Tel: (415) 421-1822   Emp: N/A
    Bus: *Travel services.*   Fax:(415) 421-1809   %FO: 100

    NIPPON EXPRESS USA, INC.
    590 Madison Avenue, Suite 2401, New York, NY   10022
    CEO: Motonori Asada, Pres.   Tel: (212) 758-6100   Emp: 1000
    Bus: *Freight forwarding, air/ocean cargo,*   Fax:(212) 758-2595   %FO: 80
       household goods moving.

    NITTSU SHOJI CO., LTD.
    590 Madison Avenue, Suite 2401, New York, NY   10022
    CEO: Takeshi Tamagawa, Pres.   Tel: (212) 293-8440   Emp: N/A
    Bus: *Leasing, finance, import/export, real estate,*   Fax:(212) 293-7369   %FO: 100
       equipment sales.

• **NIPPON LIFE INSURANCE COMPANY**
2-2 Chiyoda-ku, Tokyo 100, Japan
CEO: Gentaro Kawase, Pres.   Tel: 81-3-507-1435   Emp: 90000
Bus: *Life insurance.*   Fax:81-3-

    NIPPON LIFE INSURANCE OF AMERICA, INC.
    450 Lexington Avenue, Ste. 3200, New York, NY   10017
    CEO: T. Toyomaru, Pres.   Tel: (212) 682-3000   Emp: 10
    Bus: *Insurance research.*   Fax:(212) 682-3002   %FO: 100

• **NIPPON METAL INDUSTRY COMPANY, LTD.**
2-1-1 Nishishijuku, Shinjuku-ku, Tokyo 160-04, Japan
CEO: Kenzo Inagaki, Pres.   Tel: 81-3-3345-5555   Emp: 1620
Bus: *Mfr. stainless steel.*   Fax:81-3-3344-4790

    NIPPON METAL INDUSTRY USA, INC.
    1270 Avenue of the Americas, New York, NY   10020
    CEO: Ikuya Fujimaki, Pres.   Tel: (212) 586-8310   Emp: 3
    Bus: *Sale stainless steel.*   Fax:(212) 757-2628   %FO: 100

• NIPPON PAINT COMPANY, LTD.

6-8-10 Fukushima, Fukushima-ku, Osaka 553, Japan

CEO: Ryutaro Nakashima, Pres.　　　　　Tel: N/A　　　　Emp: N/A

Bus: *Paint, protective coatings and chemicals.*　　Fax:N/A

NIPPON PAINT AMERICA CORPORATION

44790 South Grimmer Blvd., Fremont, CA　94539

CEO: John Patterson, Pres.　　　　　　Tel: (510) 770-9061　　Emp: 5

Bus: *Printing plates, graphic arts, film and paper.*　Fax:(510) 770-9063　%FO: 100

• NIPPON SANSO CORP

16-7 Nishi-Shinbashi 1-chome, Minato-ku, Tokyo 105, Japan

CEO: Jiro Nozaki, Pres.　　　　　　Tel: 81-3-5032271　　Emp: 1700

Bus: *Mfr. industrial gases and industrial gas equipment.*　Fax:81-3-5482-9138

THE THERMOS COMPANY

7360 Northwest 34th Street, Miami, FL　33122

CEO: Manuel Barberian, Mgr.　　　　　Tel: (305) 715-9071　　Emp: 2

Bus: *Mfr./sales thermos containers, gas grilles, gas-*　Fax:(305) 715-9544　%FO: 100
　　fueled equipment.

THE THERMOS COMPANY

300 North Martingale Road, Ste.200, Schaumburg, IL　60173

CEO: Douglas Blair, Pres.　　　　　Tel: (847) 240-3150　　Emp: N/A

Bus: *Mfr. thermos containers, gas grilles, gas-*　Fax:(847) 240-3160　%FO: 100
　　fueled equipment.

TRI-GAS, INC.

4545 Fuller Drive, #200, Irving, TX　75038

CEO: Jeffrey Ellis, Pres.　　　　　Tel: (972) 650-1700　　Emp: N/A

Bus: *Mfr./distribution specialty and industrial gases.*　Fax:(214) 717-2996　%FO: 100

• NIPPON SHEET GLASS COMPANY, LTD.

5-8-1 Nishihimoto Sagamihara, Knagawa, Japan

CEO: Minoru Matsumura, Pres.　　　　Tel: 81-427-751-570　　Emp: 4000

Bus: *Mfr. flat and safety glass, glass fiber and fiber optic*　Fax:81-427-751-578
　　products.

NSG AMERICA, INC.

27 Worlds Fair Drive, Somerset, NJ　08873

CEO: Yoshiro Yakushi, Pres.　　　　Tel: (908) 469-9650　　Emp: 35

Bus: *Mfr. fiber optic products*　　　Fax:(908) 469-9654　%FO: 100

- **NIPPON SHINPAN COMPANY, LTD.**
33-5 Hongo 3-chome, Bunkyo-ku, Tokyo 113-91, Japan
CEO: Yoji Yamada, CEO   Tel: 81-3-8113111   Emp: 6400
Bus: *Consumer finance, credit card and investment*   Fax:N/A
     services.

    NIPPON SHINPAN USA, INC.
    2222 Kalakaua Ave, Ste.1500, Honolulu, HI   96815
    CEO: Takayuki Fukuda, VP   Tel: (808) 971-9000   Emp: 7
    Bus: *Consumer finance, credit card and investment*   Fax:(808) 971-9007   %FO: 100
      services.

- **NIPPON SODA COMPANY, LTD.**
Shin-Ohtemachi Bldg, 2-2-1 Ohtemachi, Chiyoda-ku, Tokyo 100, Japan
CEO: Susumu Shimomura, Pres.   Tel: 81-3-3245-6054   Emp: 2000
Bus: *Mfr. chemicals.*   Fax:81-3-3245-6238

    NISSO AMERICA, INC.
    220 East 42nd Street, Ste. 3002, New York, NY   10017
    CEO: Shinobu Takashima, EVP   Tel: (212) 490-0350   Emp: 4
    Bus: *Distribution of chemicals.*   Fax:(212) 972-9361   %FO: 100

- **NIPPON STEEL CORPORATION**
6-3 Otemachi 2-chome, Chiyoda-ku, Tokyo 100-71, Japan
CEO: Takashi Imai, Pres.   Tel: 81-3-3242-4111   Emp: 41000
Bus: *Mfr. steel products; engineering and construction*   Fax:81-3-3275-5607
    activities.

    NIPPON STEEL USA, INC.
    10 East 50th Street, New York, NY   10022
    CEO: Hiroshi Suetsugu, Pres.   Tel: (212) 486-7150   Emp: 50
    Bus: *Marketing research, liaison services.*   Fax:(212) 593-3049   %FO: 100

- **NIPPON SUISAN KAISHA, LTD.**
Nippon Building, 2-6-2 Otemachi, Chiyoda-ku, Tokhyo 100, Japan
CEO: Yasuo Kunii, Pres.   Tel: 81-3-3244-7000   Emp: N/A
Bus: *Mfr. various food products.*   Fax:81-3-3244-7085

    DUTCH HARBOR SEAFOODS, LTD.
    15400 Northeast 90th Street, Redmond, WA   98052
    CEO: Richard White, Pres.   Tel: (425) 881-8181   Emp: N/A
    Bus: *Sale/distribution of seafood.*   Fax:(425) 861-5249   %FO: 100

    NIPPON SUISAN USA, INC.
    15400 NE 90th Street, Redmond, WA   98052
    CEO: Kanji Kato, Pres.   Tel: (425) 869-1703   Emp: N/A
    Bus: *US headquarters office.*   Fax:(425) 869-1615   %FO: 100

● **NIPPON TELEGRAPH & TELEPHONE CORP. (NTT)**
19-2, Nishi-Shinjuku 3-chome, Shinjuku-ku,, Tokyo 163-19, Japan
CEO: Jun-ichiro Miyazu, Pres.   Tel: 81-3-5353-5111   Emp: 213000
Bus: *Telecommunication services.*   Fax:81-3-5353-5502

    NTT AMERICA, INC.
    101 Park Avenue, 41st Fl., New York, NY   10178
    CEO: Keisuke Nakasaki, Pres.& CEO   Tel: (212) 661-0810   Emp: 60
    Bus: *Telecommunication products & services R&D.* Fax:(212) 661-1078   %FO: 100

● **NIPPON TRAVEL AGENCY CO., LTD.**
2-20-15 Shimbashi, Minato-ku, Tokyo 105, Japan
CEO: Shoji Teruo, Pres.   Tel: 81-3-3572-9818   Emp: 4200
Bus: *Travel agency.*   Fax:81-3-3289-5466

    NIPPON TRAVEL AGENCY PACIFIC INC.
    515 South Figueroa St., Ste. 1600, Los Angeles, CA   90071
    CEO: Hirofumi Oda, Pres.   Tel: (213) 896-0301   Emp: 280
    Bus: *Travel agency services.*   Fax:(213) 623-9384   %FO: 100

● **NIPPON YUSEN KABUSHIKI KAISHA (YYK Line)**
3-2 Marunouchi 2-chome, Chiyoda-ku, Tokyo 100, Japan
CEO: Kentaro Kawamura, Pres.   Tel: 81-3-3284-5151   Emp: 8000
Bus: *Steamship operator and international transportation.* Fax:81-3-3284-6361

    CRYSTAL CRUISES, INC.
    2121 Avenue of the Stars, Los Angeles, CA   90067
    CEO: Joe Watters, Pres.   Tel: (310) 785-9300   Emp: N/A
    Bus: *Cruise ship tour operator.*   Fax:(310) 785-0011   %FO: 100

    NYK BULKSHIP USA, INC.
    150 East 52nd Street, 9th Fl., New York, NY   10022
    CEO: Hisayoshi Mikawa, Pres.   Tel: (212) 935-2490   Emp: N/A
    Bus: *International marine transport.*   Fax:(212) 935-2498   %FO: 100

    NYK LINE North America, INC.
    200 Plaza Drive, Secaucus, NJ   07096
    CEO: Keitaro Kanamori, Pres.   Tel: (201) 330-3000   Emp: 500
    Bus: *International marine transport.*   Fax:(201) 867-9059   %FO: 100

● **NIPPON ZEON COMPANY, LTD.**
2-6-1 Marunouchi, Chiyoda-ku, Tokyo 100, Japan
CEO: Katsuhiko Nakano, Pres.   Tel: 81-3-3216-0543   Emp: N/A
Bus: *Mfr. synthetic rubber, latex, PVC, medical*   Fax:81-3-3216-1790
equipment.

    NIPPON ZEON OF AMERICA, INC.
    50 Main Street, White Plains, NY   10606
    CEO: Masato Matsuo, Pres.   Tel: (914) 683-8500   Emp: 8
    Bus: *Wholesale synthetic rubber, medical*   Fax:(914) 683-8546   %FO: 100
    equipment, licensing, research.

    ZEON AMERICA, INC.
    4111 Bells Lane, Louisville, KY   40211
    CEO: Seiichi Okada, Pres.   Tel: (502) 775-2043   Emp: 5
    Bus: *R & D chemicals, specialty chemicals,*   Fax:(502) 775-2055   %FO: 100
    equipment. and consumer products; flavors &
    fragrances.

● **NISHI NIPPON RAILROAD**
Central Bldg, 1-5 Kyobashi 1-chome, Chuo-ku, Tokyo 104, Japan
CEO: Yoshio Nogami, Pres.   Tel: 81-3-274-4341   Emp: 3000
Bus: *Air freight forwarding and customs.*   Fax:81-3-273-1687

    NNR AIRCARGO SERVICE (USA), INC.
    450 East Devon, Ste. 260, Itasca, IL   60143
    CEO: M. Kitakoga, Pres.   Tel: (630) 773-1490   Emp: 2
    Bus: *Freight forwarding and customs house broker.*   Fax:(630) 773-1442   %FO: 100

● **NISHIMOTO TRADING COMPANY, LTD.**
2-11 Kaigandori 3-chome, Chuo-ku, Kobe 650, Japan
CEO: Tatszo Susaki, Pres.   Tel: 81-78-360-3832   Emp: 50
Bus: *Supplies fresh fruits and vegetables, foodstuffs.*   Fax:81-78-360-3923

    NISHIMOTO TRADING COMPANY OF AMERICA, LTD.
    2747 South Malt Avenue, Los Angeles, CA   90040
    CEO: Richard T. Hashii, Pres.   Tel: (213) 889-4100   Emp: 55
    Bus: *Sale foodstuffs, fresh fruits and vegetables.*   Fax:(213) 888-1601   %FO: 100

● **NISSAN MOTOR COMPANY, LTD.**
17-1 Ginza 6-chome, Chuo-ku, Tokyo 104-23, Japan
CEO: Yoshikazu Hanawa, Pres.   Tel: 81-3-3543-5523   Emp: 140000
Bus: *Mfr. cars, trucks, diesel & marine engines,*   Fax:81-3-3546-2669
industrial machinery & vehicles, boats.

    NISSAN CAPITAL OF AMERICA, INC.
    399 Park Avenue, 18th Fl., New York, NY   10022
    CEO: Minoru Nakamura, Pres.   Tel: (212) 572-9100   Emp: N/A
    Bus: *Financial services.*   Fax:(212) 750-6982   %FO: 100

NISSAN DESIGN INTERNATIONAL
9800 Campus Point Drive, San Diego, CA   92121
CEO: Gerald Hirshberg, Pres.   Tel: (619) 457-4400   Emp: N/A
Bus: *Vehicle design.*   Fax:(619) 450-3332   %FO: 100

NISSAN FORKLIFT CORPORATION, NA
240 North Prospect Street, Marengo, IL   60152
CEO: Mark Akabori, Pres.   Tel: (815) 568-0061   Emp: N/A
Bus: *Production/import/sale forklifts.*   Fax:(815) 568-0179   %FO: 100

NISSAN MOTOR ACCEPTANCE CORP.
990 West 190th Street, Torrance, CA   90502-1019
CEO: Yoichiro Nagashima, Pres.   Tel: (310) 719-8000   Emp: N/A
Bus: *Financial services.*   Fax:(310) 719-8016   %FO: 100

NISSAN MOTOR CORP IN HAWAII, LTD.
2880 Kilihau Street, Honolulu, HI   96819
CEO: Dwane Brenneman, Pres. & CEO   Tel: (808) 836-0888   Emp: N/A
Bus: *Distribute automotive vehicles.*   Fax:(808) 839-0400   %FO: 100

NISSAN MOTOR MFG CORPORATION, USA
983 Nissan Drive, Smyrna, TN   37167
CEO: Jerry L. Benefield, Pres. & CEO   Tel: (615) 459-1400   Emp: N/A
Bus: *Mfr. cars and light trucks.*   Fax:(615) 459-1554   %FO: 100

NISSAN NORTH AMERICA, INC.
990 West 190th Street, Torrance, CA   90502
CEO: Minoru Nakamura, Pres.   Tel: (310) 768-3700   Emp: N/A
Bus: *U.S. corporate headquarters.*   Fax:(310) 327-2272   %FO: 100

NISSAN TEXTILE MACHINERY CORPORATION
8300 Arrowridge Blvd., Charlotte, NC   28273-5679
CEO: Naohiro Kusakabe, Pres.   Tel: (704) 527-5400   Emp: N/A
Bus: *Import/sale textile machinery.*   Fax:(704) 527-3743   %FO: 100

● **NISSEI SANGYO COMPANY, LTD.**
24614 Nishi-Shimbashi, 1-chome, Minato-ku, Tokyo 105, Japan
CEO: T. Ishikawa, Pres.   Tel: 81-3-3504-7111   Emp: N/A
Bus: *Marketing of scientific instruments.*   Fax:81-3-3504-7123

NISSEI SANGYO AMERICA, LTD.
2850 East Golf Road, Ste. 200, Rolling Meadows, IL   60008
CEO: A. Nozaki, Pres.   Tel: (847) 981-8989   Emp: 115
Bus: *Sale electronics and scientific instruments.*   Fax:(784) 364-9052   %FO: 100

- **NISSHIN SPINNING COMPANY, LTD.**
3 Yokoyama-cho Nihonbashi, Chuo-ku, Tokyo, Japan
CEO: T. Tanabe, Pres.   Tel: 81-3-665-8833   Emp: N/A
Bus: *Mfr. yarns and fabrics.*   Fax:81-3-665-8875

    NISSHIN SPINNING COMPANY, LTD.
    1345 Avenue of the Americas, New York, NY   10105
    CEO: S. Koma, Pres.   Tel: (212) 698-5000   Emp: N/A
    Bus: *Mfr./sale of yarns and fabrics.*   Fax:(212) 698-5050   %FO: 100

- **NISSHO IWAI CORPORATION**
2-4-5 Akasaka, Minato-ku, Tokyo 107, Japan
CEO: Masatake Kusamichi, Pres.   Tel: 81-3-3588-2111   Emp: 5500
Bus: *Import/export/trading; industrial development.*   Fax:81-3-3588-4136

    NISSHO IWAI AMERICAN CORPORATION
    1211 Avenue of the Americas, 44th Fl., New York, NY   10036
    CEO: Akira Yokouchi, Pres.   Tel: (212) 704-6500   Emp: 500
    Bus: *Sales/distribution of general commodities and*   Fax:(212) 704-6543   %FO: 100
        food.

- **NISSIN CORPORATION**
5 Sanban-cho, Chiyoda-ku, Tokyo 102, Japan
CEO: H. Tsutsui, Pres.   Tel: 81-3-3238-6607   Emp: 1700
Bus: *Total transportation service.*   Fax:81-3-3238-6638

    NISSIN CUSTOMS SERVICE, INC.
    1580 West Carson Street, Long Beach, CA   90810
    CEO: Bennett Johnson, Pres.   Tel: (310) 816-5706   Emp: N/A
    Bus: *Custom house broker.*   Fax:(310) 816-5716   %FO: 100

    NISSIN INTL TRANSPORT USA, INC.
    1580 West Carson Street, Long Beach, CA   90810
    CEO: Tadakuni Shimoto, Pres.   Tel: (310) 816-5725   Emp: 300
    Bus: *Transportation services.*   Fax:(310) 816-5769   %FO: 100

- **NITTA CORPORATION**
8-12 Hommachi 1-chome, Chuo-ku, Osaka 541, Japan
CEO: Seiichi Nitta, Pres.   Tel: 81-6-266-1921   Emp: 1550
Bus: *Industrial belting, construction materials, conveyor*   Fax:81-6-266-1777
    systems, air filtration products, hoses & tubes,
    farming and forestry.

    NITTA CORPORATION OF AMERICA
    4475 River Green Pkwy, PO Box 1180, Duluth, GA   30136-1180
    CEO: Edward Sullivan, Pres.   Tel: (770) 497-0212   Emp: 55
    Bus: *Mfr./distribute industrial flat belting.*   Fax:(770) 623-1398   %FO: 100

●**NITTETSU SHOJI COMPANY, LTD.**
1-5-7 Kameido Koto-ku, Tokyo 136, Japan
CEO: Kazuhiko Fukuda, Pres.　　　　　　　　Tel: 81-3-5627-2900　　Emp: 1200
Bus: *Trading company: raw materials, steel products,*　Fax:N/A
　　building materials, machinery, non-ferrous metals
　　and construction.

　　NITTETSU SHOJI AMERICA, INC.
　　725 S. Figueroa Street, Ste.1860, Los Angeles, CA　90017
　　CEO: Osamu Maeda, Pres.　　　　　　　　Tel: (213) 485-9072　　Emp: N/A
　　Bus: *Import/export, metal trading, raw materials,*　Fax:(213) 688-7579　　%FO: 100
　　　　steel and aluminum.

●**NITTO BOSEKI COMPANY, LTD.**
1-2-1 Hamacho Nihonbashi, Chuo-ku, Tokyo 103, Japan
CEO: Atsuhiko Sagara, Pres.　　　　　　　　Tel: 81-3-865-6613　　Emp: 5000
Bus: *Textiles, fibers, building materials and specialty*　Fax:N/A
　　chemicals.

　　INTL IMMUNOLOGY CORPORATION
　　25549 Adams Avenue, Murrieta, CA　92562
　　CEO: Katsuhiro Katayama, Pres.　　　　　　Tel: (909) 677-5629　　Emp: 36
　　Bus: *Mfr./sale biological bulk material for*　　Fax:(714) 677-6752　　%FO: 100
　　　　diagnostics industry.

●**NITTO DENKO CORPORATION**
1-1-2 Shimohozumi, Ibarak 567, Japan
CEO: Goro Kamai, Pres.　　　　　　　　　　Tel: 81-726-222-981　　Emp: 6000
Bus: *Mfr. industrial and electric materials.*　　Fax:81-726-261-505

　　NITTO DENKO AMERICA, INC.
　　55 Nicholson Lane, San Jose, CA　94583
　　CEO: Dave Date, Pres.　　　　　　　　　Tel: (408) 432-5400　　Emp: 40
　　Bus: *Distribute electric materials.*　　　　Fax:(408) 432-5480　　%FO: 100

●**NKK CORPORATION**
1-1-2 Marunouchi, Chiyoda-ku, Tokyo 100, Japan
CEO: Shunkichi Miyoshi, Pres.　　　　　　　Tel: 81-3-3212-7111　　Emp: 28000
Bus: *Steel product, shipbuilding, engineering, heavy*　Fax:81-3-3214-8401
　　industrial equipment, new material.

　　INTL LIGHT METALS CORPORATION
　　19200 South Western Avenue, Torrance, CA　90509
　　CEO: Gene Gambill, Pres.　　　　　　　　Tel: (310) 618-3000　　Emp: 1300
　　Bus: *Mfr. aluminum/titanium alloy products.*　Fax:(310) 618-3239　　%FO: 40

　　NATIONAL STEEL CORPORATION
　　4100 Edison Lakes Parkway, Mishawaka, IN　46545-3440
　　CEO: Osamu Sawaragi, Chrm.　　　　　　　Tel: (219) 273-7000　　Emp: 12000
　　Bus: *Mfr. sheet flat rolled steel products.*　　Fax:(219) 273-7867　　%FO: 70

NKK AMERICA, INC.
450 Park Avenue, New York, NY   10022

CEO: Fujio Ono, Pres.   Tel: (212) 826-6250   Emp: 19

Bus: *Marketing research.*   Fax:(212) 826-6358   %FO: 100

• THE NOMURA SECURITIES CO., LTD.
1-9-1 Nihonbashi, Chuo-ku, Tokyo 103, Japan

CEO: Hodeo Sakamaki, Pres.   Tel: 81-3-3211-1811   Emp: 16200

Bus: *International securities broker/dealer, investment*   Fax:81-3-3278-0420
banking and asset management services.

NOMURA SECURITIES INTERNATIONAL INC. (US)
Two World Trade Center, Bldg. B, New York, NY   10281-1198

CEO: Michael A. Berman, Pres.   Tel: (212) 667-9300   Emp: N/A

Bus: *International securities broker/dealer,*   Fax:(212) 667-1058   %FO: 100
investment banking and asset management
services.

• NOMURA TRADING COMPANY, LTD.
15 Bingo-machi l-chome, Chuo-ku, Osaka 541, Japan

CEO: Hiroshi Ikeda, CEO   Tel: 81-6-268-8111   Emp: 600

Bus: *Import/export general merchandise.*   Fax:81-6-268-8133

NOMURA (AMERICA) CORPORATION
60 East 42nd Street, New York, NY   10165

CEO: Masami Ikeuchi, Pres. & CEO   Tel: (212) 867-6684   Emp: 20

Bus: *Import/export general merchandise.*   Fax:(212) 697-3202   %FO: 100

• NORITSU KOKI COMPANY, LTD.
579-1 Umeharaa, Wakayamashi 640, Japan

CEO: Kanichi Nishimoto, Pres.   Tel: 81-734-540-345   Emp: 1700

Bus: *Mfr. photo finishing equipment.*   Fax:81-734-540-330

NORITSU AMERICA CORPORATION
6900 Noritsu Avenue, Buena Park, CA   90620

CEO: Osame Miki, Pres.   Tel: (714) 521-9040   Emp: 290

Bus: *Sales/service of photo finishing equipment*   Fax:(714) 670-2049   %FO: 100

• NOZAKI & COMPANY, LT.D
2-6 Nihonbashi-Bakurocho, 2-chome, Chuo-ku, Tokyo 103-91, Japan

CEO: H. Kozu, Pres.   Tel: 81-3-5641-4304   Emp: N/A

Bus: *Import/export canned foods, hides, meat, shoes and*   Fax:81-3-5641-4381
aerospace equipment.

NOZAKI AMERICA, INC.
1325 Avenue of the Americas,
26th Floor, New York, NY   10019

CEO: Koshiro Shimizu, Pres.   Tel: (212) 424-1500   Emp: N/A

Bus: *Import/distribute general merchandise.*   Fax:(212) 775-0590   %FO: 100

● **NSK, LTD.**
Nissei Bldg.,1-6-3 Ohsaki 1-chome, Shinagawa-ku, Tokyo 141, Japan
CEO: Toshio Arata, Chrm. Tel: 81-3 -3779-7120 Emp: N/A
Bus: *Mfr. motion technology products.* Fax:81-3-3779-7433

NSK CORPORATION
3861 Research Park Drive, Ann Arbor, MI 48106
CEO: Larry McPherson, Pres. Tel: (313) 761-9500 Emp: N/A
Bus: *Mfr. anti-friction bearings and related products* Fax:(313) 761-9510 %FO: 100

● **NTN CORPORATION**
3-17 Kyomachibori 1-chome, Osaka 550, Japan
CEO: Toyoaki Ito, Pres. Tel: 81-6-443-5001 Emp: 8000
Bus: *Mfr. bearings, joints and precision processing equipment.* Fax:81-3-445-8581

AMERICAN NTN BEARING MFG CORP.
9515 Winona Avenue, Schiller Park, IL 60176
CEO: M. Sanami, Pres. Tel: (847) 671-5450 Emp: 457
Bus: *Mfr. bearings, wheel units.* Fax:(847) 681-5298 %FO: 100

NTN BEARING CORP OF AMERICA
1600 East Bishop Court, PO Box 7604, Mt. Prospect, IL 60056-7604
CEO: George Hammond, Pres. Tel: (847) 298-7500 Emp: 298
Bus: *Engineering/sale anti-friction bearings & constant velocity joints.* Fax:(847) 699-9745 %FO: 100

NTN DRIVESHAFT INC.
8251 South International Drive, Columbus, IN 47201
CEO: K. Sakano, Pres. Tel: (812) 342-7000 Emp: 458
Bus: *Mfr. constant velocity joints.* Fax:(812) 342-1155 %FO: 100

NTN TECHNICAL CENTER
3980 Research Park Drive, Ann Arbor, MI 48104
CEO: N. Kashino, Pres. Tel: (313) 761-3610 Emp: 27
Bus: *R&D services.* Fax:(313) 761-3632 %FO: 100

NTN-BOWER CORPORATION
31780 Telegraph Road, Bingham Farms, MI 48025-3468
CEO: S. Yamamori, Pres. Tel: (810) 645-8800 Emp: 1117
Bus: *Mfr. roller bearings.* Fax:(810) 645-8870 %FO: 100

● **OBAYASHI CORPORATION**
2-3 Kanda Tsukasa-cho, Chiyoda-ku, Tokyo 101, Japan
CEO: Yoshiro Obayashi, Chrm. & CEO   Tel: 81-3-3292-1111   Emp: 12700
Bus: *General building contractor.*   Fax:81-3-3219-9340

    OC AMERICA CONSTRUCTION, INC.
    420 East Third Street, Ste. 600, Los Angeles, CA   90013
    CEO: Yoshitaka Hara, Pres.   Tel: (213) 687-8700   Emp: 48
    Bus: *General building contractor.*   Fax:(213) 687-3700   %FO: 100

● **OJI PAPER COMPANY, LTD.**
7-5 Ginza, 4-chome, Chuo-ku, Tokyo 104, Japan
CEO: Masahiko Ohkuni, Pres.   Tel: 81-3-3563-1111   Emp: N/A
Bus: *Mfr. paper, paperboard, pulp and converted*   Fax:81-3-3563-1130
     products.

    KANZAKI SPECIALTY PAPERS
    16306 Bloomfield Avenue, Cerritos, CA   90703
    CEO: Masatsune Ogura, Pres.   Tel: (562) 924-2438   Emp: N/A
    Bus: *Sales/distribution of paper products.*   Fax:(562) 402-5379   %FO: 100

    OJI PAPER COMPANY, LTD.
    600 University Square, Seattle, WA   98101
    CEO: Shiro Takhata, Gen. Mgr.   Tel: (206) 622-2820   Emp: N/A
    Bus: *Woodchip purchasing.*   Fax:(206) 292-9798   %FO: 100

● **OKAMOTO INDUSTRIES INC**
27-12 Hongo 3-chome, Bunkyo-ku, Tokyo, Japan
CEO: Takehiko Okamoto, Pres.   Tel: 81-3-817-4261   Emp: 1800
Bus: *Mfr. quality rubber and plastic products.*   Fax:81-3-814-0894

    OKAMOTO USA, INC
    18 King Street, Stratford, CT   06497
    CEO: Hisayuki Naito, VP   Tel: (203) 378-0003   Emp: 8
    Bus: *Sale/distribution of quality plastic products*   Fax:(203) 375-2040   %FO: 100
     and latex rubber prophylactics.

● **OKAMOTO MACHINE TOOL WORKS LTD.**
2-7-3 Minowa-cho, Kohoku-ku, Yokohama 223, Japan
CEO: Taizo Hosoda, Pres.   Tel: 81-45-562-3113   Emp: 550
Bus: *Mfr./sale of grinding machines.*   Fax:81-45-562-3122

    OKAMOTO CORPORATION
    1500 Busch Parkway, Buffalo Grove, IL   60089
    CEO: J. Asakawa, VP & Gen.Mgr.   Tel: (847) 520-7700   Emp: 35
    Bus: *Mfr./sale/service of grinding machines.*   Fax:(847) 520-7980   %FO: 100

● **OKAYA & COMPANY, LTD.**
5-1 Marunouchi 1-chome, Tokyo 100, Japan
CEO: Tokuichi Okaya, Pres.   Tel: 81-3-3214-8721   Emp: 950+
Bus: *Wholesale iron and steel products, machinery,*   Fax:81-3-3214-8709
    electrical products.

    OKAYA USA, INC.
    Parker Plaza, 16th Fl., 400 Kelby Street, Fort Lee, NJ   07024
    CEO: Minoru Ito, Pres.   Tel: (201) 224-6000   Emp: 41
    Bus: *Import/export and domestic sales of industrial*   Fax:(201) 224-8144   %FO: 100
        goods, iron & steel products.

● **OKI ELECTRIC INDUSTRY COMPANY, LTD.**
7-12, Toranomon 1-chme, Minato-ku, Tokyo 105, Japan
CEO: Shiko Sawamura, Pres.   Tel: 81-3-3501-3111   Emp: 22000
Bus: *Mfr./distribution telecommunications and*   Fax:81-3-3581-5522
    information processing systems and equipment.

    OKI ADVANCED PRODUCTS
    500 Nickerson Road, Marlborough, MA   01752
    CEO: Steve Holford, Pres.   Tel: (508) 624-7000   Emp: N/A
    Bus: *R & D for advances electronics.*   Fax:(508) 480-9635   %FO: 100

    OKI AMERICA, INC.
    3 University Plaza, Hackensack, NJ   07601
    CEO: Hiroshi Yamazaki, CEO   Tel: (201) 646-0011   Emp: 500
    Bus: *Mfr./distribution/service telecommunications*   Fax:(201) 646-9229   %FO: 100
        and information processing systems and
        equipment.

    OKI BUSINESS DIGITAL, INC.
    533 Fellowship Road, Mount Laurel, NJ   08054
    CEO: Kanichi Masuda, Pres.   Tel: (609) 778-3486   Emp: N/A
    Bus: *Mfr./distribution/service electronic publishing.*   Fax:(609) 778-1681   %FO: 100

    OKI SEMICONDUCTOR GROUP
    785 North Mary Avenue, Sunnyvale, CA   94086
    CEO: Hosao Baba, Pres.   Tel: (408) 720-1900   Emp: N/A
    Bus: *R & D, mfr./sales integrated circuits,*   Fax:(408) 720-1918   %FO: 100
        semiconductor products, and advanced
        electronics.

    OKI TELECOM, INC.
    437 Old Peachtree Road, Suwanee, GA   30174
    CEO: Takenori Hanasaki, Pres.   Tel: (770) 995-9800   Emp: N/A
    Bus: *Mfr./distribution/service cellular/cordless*   Fax:(770) 822-0702   %FO: 100
        phone systems.

● **OLYMPUS OPTICAL COMPANY, LTD.**
Monolith, 3-1 Nishi-Shinjuku 2-chome, Shinjuku-ku, Tokyo 163, Japan
CEO: Masatashi Kishimoto, Pres.   Tel: 81-3-3340-2111   Emp: 10000
Bus: *Mfr. opto-electronic products, R&D consumer and*   Fax:N/A
medical products.

　　OLYMPUS AMERICA, INC.
　　Two Corporate Center Drive, Melville, NY   11747-3157
　　CEO: Sidney Braginski, Pres. & CEO   Tel: (516) 844-5000   Emp: 1600
　　Bus: *Distribution consumer and scientific products.*   Fax:(516) 844-5265   %FO: 100

● **ORIENTAL MOTOR CO., LTD.**
6-16-17 Ueno, Taito-ku, Tokyo 110, Japan
CEO: M. Wakabayashi, Pres.   Tel: 81-3-3835-0684   Emp: 2500
Bus: *Mfr./sales small electric motors, drivers and fans.*   Fax:81-3-3835-1890

　　ORIENTAL MOTOR USA CORPORATION
　　2580 West 237th Street, Torrance, CA   90505
　　CEO: M. Tatsuya, Pres.   Tel: (310) 325-0040   Emp: 60
　　Bus: *Assembly/sale/distribute small motors, fans*   Fax:(310) 515-2879   %FO: 100
　　and drives.

● **OSAKA GAS COMPANY, LTD.**
1-2 Hiranomachi 4-chome, Chuo-ku, Osaka 541, Japan
CEO: S. Ryoki, Pres.   Tel: 81-6-202-2221   Emp: N/A
Bus: *Produce/distribute gas.*   Fax:81-6-202-4637

　　OSAKA GAS COMPANY, LTD.
　　375 Park Avenue, Ste. 2109, New York, NY   10152
　　CEO: R. Sakurai, Mgr.   Tel: (212) 980-1666   Emp: N/A
　　Bus: *U.S. representative office.*   Fax:(212) 832-0946   %FO: 100

● **OTSUKA PHARMACEUTICAL COMPANY, LTD.**
31 Otedori 3-chome, Hagashi-ku, Osaka, Japan
CEO: Akihiko Otsuka, Pres.   Tel: 81-6-943-7722   Emp: 4000
Bus: *Pharmaceuticals and chemicals.*   Fax:N/A

　　OTSUKA ELECTRONICS, INC.
　　2555 Midpoint Drive, Ft. Collins, CO   80525
　　CEO: John Heinrich, Pres.   Tel: (303) 484-0428   Emp: 50
　　Bus: *Research/mfr. clinical MRI and imaging*   Fax:(303) 484-0487   %FO: 81
　　systems.

● **PENTEL COMPANY, LTD.**
7-2 Nihonbashi Koamicho, Chuo-ku, Tokyo 103, Japan
CEO: Yukio Horie, Pres.   Tel: 81-3-3667-3331   Emp: 1400
Bus: *Mfr. pens, mechanical pencils, industrial machines*   Fax:N/A
and computers.

     PENTEL OF AMERICA, LTD.
     2805 Columbia Street, Torrance, CA 90509
     CEO: M. Osada, Gen. Mgr.   Tel: (310) 320-3831   Emp: 200
     Bus: *Pens, pencils and art materials.*   Fax:(310) 533-0697   %FO: 100

● **PILOT PEN COMPANY, LTD.**
5 Kyobashi 2-chome, Chuo-ku, Tokyo 104, Japan
CEO: S. Kambe, Pres.   Tel: 81-3-548-78181   Emp: N/A
Bus: *Mfr. writing instruments.*   Fax:N/A

     PILOT PEN CORPORATION OF AMERICA
     60 Commerce Drive, Trumbull, CT 06611
     CEO: Ronald G. Shaw, Pres.   Tel: (203) 377-8800   Emp: 240
     Bus: *Sales/distribution of writing instruments*   Fax:(203) 377-4024   %FO: 100

● **PIONEER ELECTRONICS CORPORATION**
4-1 Meguro 1-chome, Meguro-ku, Tokyo 153, Japan
CEO: Kaneo Ito, CEO   Tel: 81-3-3494-1111   Emp: 19500
Bus: *Mfr.. electronics, video, music, telecommunications*   Fax:81-3-3495-4428
products, consumer electronics.

     PIONEER ELECTRONICS (USA), INC.
     2265 East 220th Street
     PO Box 1760, Long Beach, CA 90810
     CEO: Akira Nijima, Pres.   Tel: (562) 835-6177   Emp: N/A
     Bus: *Mfr. car stereos and home electronics.*   Fax:(562) 952-2402   %FO: 100

● **RHEON AUTOMATIC MACHINERY COMPANY, LTD.**
2-3 Nozawa-machi, P O Box 50, Utsunomiya 320, Japan
CEO: T. Hayashi, Pres.   Tel: 81-286-665-1111   Emp: N/A
Bus: *Mfr. food processing equipment.*   Fax:N/A

     RHEON USA, INC.
     13400 Reese Blvd., Huntersville, NC 28078-7925
     CEO: K. Kamiyama, Gen. Mgr.   Tel: (704) 875-9191   Emp: N/A
     Bus: *Mfr./sale food processing equipment.*   Fax:(704) 875-9595   %FO: 100

● **RICOH COMPANY, LTD.**
15-5 Minami-Aoyama 1-chome, Minato-ku, Tokyo 107, Japan
CEO: Masamitsu Sakurai, Pres.   Tel: 81-3-3479-3111   Emp: 50000
Bus: *Mfr. copiers, facsimiles, cameras, scanners, printers*   Fax:81-3-3402-1578
   and optical storage devices.

   RICOH CORPORATION
   5 Dedrick Place, West Caldwell, NJ 07006
   CEO: Hisao Yuasa, Chrm.   Tel: (201) 882-2000   Emp: 3850
   Bus: *Mfr./sale/service copiers, facsimiles, cameras,*   Fax:(201) 808-7555   %FO: 100
    scanners, printers, optical storage devices.

   RICOH ELECTRONICS, INC.
   One Ricoh Sq., 1100 Valencia Ave., Tustin, CA 92680
   CEO: Takehido Kaneko, Pres.   Tel: (714) 259-1310   Emp: N/A
   Bus: *Mfr./sale/service copiers, facsimiles, cameras,*   Fax:(714) 259-9342   %FO: 100
    scanners, printers, optical storage devices.

● **RINGER HUT COMPANY, LTD.**
Nomura Bldg., 8-5-1 Nishi-Shinjuku, Shinjuku-ku, Tokyo 160, Japan
CEO: Shoji Yonehama, Chrm.   Tel: 81-3-5839-8700   Emp: 7000
Bus: *Restaurant chain.*   Fax:81-3-5839-8765

   RINGER HUT USA CORPORATION
   631 Giguere Court, San Jose, CA 95133
   CEO: Mr. Hideyuki Yamashita   Tel: (408) 259-3101   Emp: 60
   Bus: *Restaurant chain and food production.*   Fax:(408) 259-3297   %FO: 100

● **ROHM COMPANY, LTD.**
21 Saiin Mizosaki-cho, Ukyo-ku, Kyoto 615, Japan
CEO: Ken Sato, Pres.   Tel: 81-75-311-2121   Emp: 12887
Bus: *Mfr. diverse electronic components.*   Fax:81-75-315-0172

   EXAR CORPORATION
   2222 Qume Drive, San Jose, CA 95161-9007
   CEO: Nob Hata, Pres.   Tel: (408) 434-6400   Emp: 65
   Bus: *Mfr./sale diverse electronic components.*   Fax:(408) 943-8245   %FO: 100

   ROHM CORP. - ELECTRONICS DIVISION
   3034 Owen Drive, Nashville, TN 37013
   CEO: Tak Watanabe, Pres.   Tel: (615) 641-2020   Emp: 100
   Bus: *Mktg./sale electronic components.*   Fax:(615) 641-2022   %FO: 100

   ROHM USA EXEL MICROELECTRONICS, INC.
   2150 Commerce Drive, San Jose, CA 95131
   CEO: Kozo Sato, CEO   Tel: (408) 432-0500   Emp: 125
   Bus: *Electric components.*   Fax:(408) 434-6444   %FO: 100

XETEL CORPORATION
2525 Brockton Drive, Austin, TX   78758
CEO: Angelo DeCaro, Pres.   Tel: (512) 834-2266   Emp: 80
Bus: *Design/assemble electronic circuit boards.*   Fax:(512) 834-9250   %FO: 100

• S&B SHOKUHIN COMPANY, LTD.
18-6 Kabuto-cho, Nihonbashi, Chuo-ku, Tokyo, Japan
CEO: Masaru Yamasaki, Pres.   Tel: 81-3-6680551   Emp: N/A
Bus: *Mfr./import/export food products.*   Fax:N/A

S&B INTERNATIONAL CORPORATION
21515 Hawthorne Blvd., Torrance, CA   90503
CEO: Hideki Morimoto, Gen. Mgr.   Tel: (213) 772-3114   Emp: N/A
Bus: *Mfr. food products, import/export.*   Fax:(310) 543-2168   %FO: 100

• SAITAMA BANK LTD.
1-3-1 Kyobashi, Chuo-ku, Tokyo, Japan
CEO: Shigetaka Ijichi, Pres.   Tel: 81-3-2766611   Emp: N/A
Bus: *Commercial banking services.*   Fax:N/A

SAITAMA BANK LTD
2 World Financial Center, 225 Liberty St., 35th Fl., New York, NY   10281
CEO: Sadao Honda, Pres   Tel: (212) 571-5020   Emp: N/A
Bus: *International banking*   Fax:(212) 571-5054   %FO: 100

• THE SAKURA BANK LTD.
3-1 Kudan Minami 1-chome, Chiyoda-ku, Tokyo 100-91, Japan
CEO: Ken-ichi Suematsu, Chrm.   Tel: 81-3-3230-3111   Emp: 20261
Bus: *General banking services.*   Fax:81-3-3821-1084

MANUFACTURERS BANK - Corporate Headquarters
515 South Figueroa Street, Los Angeles, CA   90071
CEO: Masato Kaneko, Chrm. & CEO   Tel: (213) 489-6200   Emp: 400
Bus: *Corporate Headquarters. International*   Fax:(213) 489-6254   %FO: 100
    commercial banking services.

THE SAKURA BANK LTD. - Houston Agency
1100 Louisiana, Suite 2900, Houston, TX   77002
CEO: Akira Hara, Gen.Mgr.   Tel: (713) 754-7200   Emp: N/A
Bus: *International commercial banking services.*   Fax:(713) 659-1404   %FO: 100

THE SAKURA BANK LTD. - Atlanta Branch
245 Peachtree St., Suite 2703, Atlanta, GA   30303
CEO: Tetsuhide Kokido, Gen.Mgr.   Tel: (404) 521-3111   Emp: N/A
Bus: *International commercial banking services.*   Fax:(404) 521-1133   %FO: 100

THE SAKURA BANK LTD. - Chicago Branch
227 West Monroe Street, Suite 4700, Chicago, IL   60606
CEO: Akikazu Hiraoka, Gen.Mgr.   Tel: (312) 782-3144   Emp: N/A
Bus: *International commercial banking services.*   Fax:(312) 332-5345   %FO: 100

THE SAKURA BANK LTD. - Los Angeles Agency
515 South Figueroa Street, Los Angeles, CA 90071
CEO: Daijiro Tsuchiya, Gen. Mgr   Tel: (213) 680-2900   Emp: N/A
Bus: *International commercial banking services.*   Fax:(213) 622-9359   %FO: 100

THE SAKURA BANK LTD. - Seattle Branch
1420 Fifth Avenue, Ste. 2000, Seattle, WA 98101
CEO: Yasuo Miyazaki, Gen.Mgr.   Tel: (206) 224-3541   Emp: N/A
Bus: *International commercial banking services.*   Fax:(206) 382-0770   %FO: 100

THE SAKURA BANK LTD. - Detroit Office
3000 Town Center, Suite 1920, Southfield, MI 48075
CEO: Masahi Hagiwara, Gen.Mgr.   Tel: (248) 355-2525   Emp: N/A
Bus: *International commercial banking services.*   Fax:(248) 355-9717   %FO: 100

THE SAKURA BANK LTD. - San Francisco Agency
345 California Street, Ste. 1100, San Francisco, CA 94104
CEO: Ken-ichi Sato, Gen.Mgr.   Tel: (415) 765-0888   Emp: N/A
Bus: *International commercial banking services.*   Fax:(415) 765-0860   %FO: 100

THE SAKURA BANK LTD. - New York Branch
277 Park Avenue, 8th Fl., New York, NY 10172-0098
CEO: Takashi Fujishima, Gen.Mgr.   Tel: (212) 756-6000   Emp: 440
Bus: *International commercial banking services.*   Fax:(212) 644-9956   %FO: 100

THE SAKURA BANK LTD. - Lexington Office
771 Corporate Drive, 4th Fl., Lexington, KY 40503
CEO: Takatoshi Fujishima, Gen. Mgr.   Tel: (606) 223-8531   Emp: N/A
Bus: *International commercial banking services.*   Fax:(606) 223-5465   %FO: 100

SAKURA DELLSHER INC.
10 South Wacker Drive, 32nd.Fl., Chicago, IL 60606
CEO: Leo Melamed, Chrm. & CEO   Tel: (312) 930-0001   Emp: 85
Bus: *Future commission merchant.*   Fax:(312) 930-4513   %FO: 60

THE SAKURA GLOBAL CAPITAL
65 East 55th Street, Park Ave. Tower, New York, NY 10022
CEO: Takashi Ueno, Pres. & CEO   Tel: (212) 486-8282   Emp: 90
Bus: *Swaps, options market making.*   Fax:(212) 355-4271   %FO: 100

SAKURA SECURITIES (USA) INC.
277 Park Avenue, New York, NY 10172-0121
CEO: Katsumi Matsuzawa, Pres.   Tel: (212) 756-6700   Emp: 8
Bus: *Securities broker.*   Fax:(212) 644-5317   %FO: 100

SAKURA TRUST COMPANY
350 Park Avenue, New York, NY 10022
CEO: Katsumi Matsuzawa, Pres.   Tel: (212) 756-6650   Emp: 27
Bus: *Trust/investment management.*   Fax:(212) 644-5628   %FO: 100

●**SANDEN INTL CORPORATION**
1-31-7 Taito, Taito-ku, Tokyo 110, Japan
CEO: Masayoshi Ushikubo, Pres.　　　　　Tel: 81-3-3835-1321　　Emp: 3200
Bus: *Mfr. auto A/C systems, kerosene heaters,*　Fax:81-3-3835-3169
　　　compressors and components, vending machines
　　　and refrigerated showcases.

　　　SANDEN INTL (USA), INC.
　　　601 South Sanden Blvd., Wylie, TX　75098-4999
　　　CEO: Seishi Kimura, Pres.　　　　　Tel: (972) 442-8400　　Emp: 510
　　　Bus: *Mfr./distribute mobile A/C compressors and*　Fax:(972) 442-8650　%FO: 100
　　　　　components.

●**THE SANKO STEAMSHIP CO., LTD.**
12-1 Yuraku-cho 1-chome, Chiyoda-ku, Tokyo, Japan
CEO: S. Kawai, Pres.　　　　　　　　　Tel: N/A　　　　　　Emp: N/A
Bus: *Ship owners.*　　　　　　　　　　Fax:81-3-3284-1991

　　　SANKO KISEN (USA) CORPORATION
　　　5 River Road, Cos Cob, CT　06807
　　　CEO: Clifford Jagoe, Pres.　　　　　Tel: (203) 625-5584　　Emp: 13
　　　Bus: *Shipowner representation.*　　　Fax:(203) 625-7633　%FO: 100

●**SANRIO COMPANY, LTD.**
1-6-1 Osaki Shinagawa-ku, Tokyo, Japan
CEO: Shintaro Tsuji, Pres.　　　　　　Tel: 81-3-3779-8111　Emp: N/A
Bus: *Mfr./distribute character merchandise for children.*　Fax:81-3-3779-8054

　　　SANRIO, INC.
　　　570 Eccles Avenue, South San Francisco, CA　94080
　　　CEO: Kunihiko Tsuji, Pres.　　　　Tel: (415) 952-2880　　Emp: N/A
　　　Bus: *Sales/distribution of children's gifts and*　Fax:(415) 872-2513　%FO: 100
　　　　　accessories.

●**SANWA BANK, LTD.**
1-1 Otemachi 1-chome, Chiyoda-ku, Tokyo 100, Japan
CEO: Naotaka Saeki, Pres.　　　　　　Tel: 81-6-206-8111　Emp: N/A
Bus: *Commercial banking services.*　　Fax:81-3-3215-1776

　　　SANWA BANK CALIFORNIA
　　　444 Market Street, San Francisco, CA　94104
　　　CEO: Tamio Takakura, CEO　　　　Tel: (415) 597-5000　　Emp: 2800
　　　Bus: *Commercial banking services.*　　Fax:(415) 597-5490　%FO: 100

　　　SANWA BANK LTD. - New York Branch
　　　50 East 52nd Street, New York, NY　10055
　　　CEO: Isao Matsuura, Gen. Mgr.　　Tel: (212) 339-6300　　Emp: N/A
　　　Bus: *Commercial banking services.*　　Fax:(212) 754-1851　%FO: 100

SANWA BUSINESS CREDIT CORP.
One South Wacker Drive, Chicago, IL　60606
CEO: Susumu Tsuchida, Chrm.　　　　　　　Tel: (312) 782-8080　　　Emp: N/A
Bus: *Commercial credit services.*　　　　　　Fax:(312) 782-7046　　　%FO: 100

● **SANYEI CORPORATION**
1-2 Kotobuki 4-chome, Taito-ku, Tokyo 111, Japan
CEO: I. Hori, Pres.　　　　　　　　　　　　Tel: 81-3-38473500　　　Emp: 300
Bus: *Imp/export general merchandise.*　　　　Fax:81-3-3842-4906

　　　SANYEI AMERICA CORPORATION
　　　300 Harmon Meadow Blvd., Secaucus, NJ　07094
　　　CEO: Y. Kawai, Pres.　　　　　　　　　Tel: (201) 864-4848　　　Emp: 8
　　　Bus: *Import/export general merchandise.*　Fax:(201) 864-5770　　　%FO: 100

● **SANYO ELECTRIC COMPANY, LTD.**
5-5 Keihan-Hondori 2-chome, Moriguchi City, Osaka 570, Japan
CEO: Yasuaki Takano, Pres.　　　　　　　　Tel: 81-6-991-1181　　　Emp: 56600
Bus: *Mfr.. audio and video equipment, Commercial and*　Fax:81-6-991-6566
　　　consumer electric appliances, semiconductors,
　　　batteries, and components.

　　　SANYO MANUFACTURING CORPORATION
　　　3333 Sanyo Road, Forrest City, AR　72335
　　　CEO: N. Nakamura, Pres.　　　　　　　Tel: (870) 633-5030　　　Emp: N/A
　　　Bus: *Manufacturing operation; subsidiary of Sanyo*　Fax:(870) 633-0650　　　%FO: 100
　　　　　Electric Co., Ltd.

　　　SANYO NORTH AMERICA CORPORATION
　　　2055 Sanyo Avenue, San Diego, CA　92173
　　　CEO: Motoharu Iue, Pres.　　　　　　　Tel: (619) 661-1134　　　Emp: N/A
　　　Bus: *Mfr./distribution/service audio and video*　Fax:(619) 661-6795　　　%FO: 100
　　　　　equipment. Commercial and consumer electric
　　　　　appliances, semiconductors, batteries, and
　　　　　components.

● **SANYO SPECIAL STEEL COMPANY, LTD.**
3007 Nakashima, Shikama-ku, Himeji 672, Japan
CEO: Seiro Hiwatashi, CEO　　　　　　　　Tel: 81-792-380-001　　　Emp: 3200
Bus: *Mfr. specialty steel.*　　　　　　　　　Fax:N/A

　　　SANYO SPECIAL STEEL COMPANY, LTD.
　　　445 Park Avenue, Ste. 2104, New York, NY　10022
　　　CEO: H. Sakuma, Pres.　　　　　　　　Tel: (212) 935-9033　　　Emp: N/A
　　　Bus: *Mfr. specialty steel.*　　　　　　　Fax:(212) 980-8838　　　%FO: 100

• **SANYO TRADING COMPANY, LTD.**
11 Kandanishiki-cho 2-chome, Chiyoda-ku, Tokyo 101, Japan
CEO: Yoji Oki, Pres.   Tel: 81-3-3233-5700   Emp: 296
Bus: *Import/export rubber, agricultural & chemicals,*   Fax:81-3-3233-5777
   automotive parts, machinery & materials,
   agricultural & marine products & lumber.

  SANYO CORPORATION OF AMERICA
  529 Fifth Avenue, 17th Fl., New York, NY   10017-4608
  CEO: Toru Ohta, Pres.   Tel: (212) 808-4860   Emp: 16
  Bus: *Sale industrial chemicals, plastics and*   Fax:(212) 808-4878   %FO: 100
   machinery.

• **SAPPORO BREWERIES, LTD.**
20-1 Ebisu 4-chome, Shibuyaku, Tokyo 150, Japan
CEO: Iwao Nishiyama, Chrm.   Tel: 81-3-5423-2111   Emp: 4000
Bus: *Mfr. beer & wine and imports soft drinks & spirits.*   Fax:81-3-5423-2057

  SAPPORO USA, INC.
  666 Third Avenue, 18th Fl., New York, NY   10017
  CEO: Yasuyuki Shimauchi, Pres.   Tel: (212) 922-9165   Emp: 30
  Bus: *Import/distribution of beer and production of*   Fax:(212) 922-9576   %FO: 100
   wine.

  SAPPORO USA, INC.
  601 Gateway Blvd., San Francisco, CA   94080
  CEO: Masatiko Yazawa, Pres.   Tel: (415) 583-3222   Emp: N/A
  Bus: *Import/distribution of beer and production of*   Fax:(415) 583-3317   %FO: 100
   wine.

• **SEGA ENTERPRISES, LTD.**
2-12 Haneda 1-chome, Ohta-ku, Tokyo 144, Japan
CEO: Hayao Nakayama, Pres.   Tel: 81-3-5736-7034   Emp: 3800
Bus: *Develop/mfr. video games and equipment.*   Fax:81-3-5736-7058
  Entertainment facilities.

  SEGA OF AMERICA, INC.
  255 Shoreline Drive, Ste. 200, Redwood City, CA   94065
  CEO: Shoichiro Irimajiri, Pres.   Tel: (415) 508-2800   Emp: N/A
  Bus: *Sale/service video games and equipment*   Fax:(415) 802-3622   %FO: 100
   systems.

- **SEIKO CORPORATION**
6-21 Kyobashi 2-chome, Chuo-ku, Tokyo 0104, Japan
CEO: Reijiro Hattori, Chrm.   Tel: 81-3-3563-2111   Emp: 8000
Bus: *Mfr./ sales of clocks/watches, eyeglass lenses/frames*   Fax:81-3-5250-7065
and golf clubs.

   SEIKO CORPORATION OF AMERICA, INC.
   1111 MacArthur Blvd., Mahwah, NJ   07430
   CEO: Takashi Wakuyama, Pres.   Tel: (201) 529-5730   Emp: N/A
   Bus: *Sales of clocks/watches and golf clubs.*   Fax:(201) 529-2736   %FO: 100

   SEIKO OPTICAL PRODUCTS, INC.
   575 Corporate Drive, Mahmah, NJ   07430
   CEO: Akira Isaka, Pres.   Tel: (201) 529-9099   Emp: N/A
   Bus: *Sales of eyeglass lenses and frames.*   Fax:(201) 529-9019   %FO: 100

- **SEIKO EPSON CORPORATION**
3-5 Owa 3-chome, Suwa-Shi, Nagaro-Ken 392, Japan
CEO: Hideaki Yasukawa, Pres.   Tel: 81-2-6652-3131   Emp: N/A
Bus: *Mfr. printer mechanisms, liquid crystal displays,*   Fax:N/A
printers, computers and disk drives.

   EPSON AMERICA, INC.
   20770 Madrona Ave., PO Box 2842, Torrance, CA   90509-2842
   CEO: Norio Niwa, Pres.   Tel: (310) 782-0770   Emp: N/A
   Bus: *Sales desktop and portable computers,*   Fax:(310) 782-5179   %FO: 100
   printers, scanners and related equipment.

- **SEINO COSMO EXPRESS COMPANY, LTD.**
12-9 Nihonbashi Nakasu, Chuo-ku, Tokyo 103, Japan
CEO: Keisuke Ohnishi, Pres.   Tel: 81-3 36641101   Emp: 200
Bus: *International freight forwarding, moving, trade*   Fax:81-3 36675515
consulting and customs brokers.

   SEINO AMERICA, INC.
   8728 Aviation Blvd., Inglewood, CA   90301
   CEO: Norizumi Suma, Pres.   Tel: (310) 215-0500   Emp: 120
   Bus: *International freight forwarding, moving,*   Fax:(310) 337-0073   %FO: 99
   trade consulting and customs brokers.

● **SEINO TRANSPORTATION COMPANY, LTD.**
1 Taguchi-cho, Ogaki-shi, Gifu Pref, Japan
CEO: Yoshikazu Taguchi, Pres.   Tel: 81-584-811111   Emp: 15000
Bus: *Trucking, moving, air and sea transportation,*   Fax:81-584-753366
warehousing and distribution.

   SEINO AMERICA, INC.
   8728 Aviation Blvd., Inglewood, CA   90301
   CEO: Norizumi Suma, Pres.   Tel: (310) 215-0500   Emp: 120
   Bus: *International freight forwarding, moving,*   Fax:(310) 337-0073   %FO: 99
   trade consulting and customs broker.

● **SEKISUI CHEMICAL COMPANY, LTD.**
4-4 Nishitenma 2-chome, Kita-ku, Osaka 530, Japan
CEO: Susumu Nishizawa, Pres.   Tel: 81-6-365-4122   Emp: 6000
Bus: *Molded plastic products and residential housing.*   Fax:81-6-365-4370

   SEKISUI AMERICA CORPORATION
   666 Fifth Avenue, 12th Fl., New York, NY   10103
   CEO: H. Yamasaki, Pres.   Tel: (212) 489-3500   Emp: 500
   Bus: *Manufacture and marketing of plastic products.* Fax:(212) 489-5100   %FO: 100

● **SHARP CORPORATION**
22-22-Nagaike-cho, Abeno-ku, Osaka 545, Japan
CEO: Haruo Tsuji, Pres.   Tel: 81-6-621-1221   Emp: 44800
Bus: *Mfr. .video and audio systems, appliances, office*   Fax:81-6-628-1653
and information equipment and electronic
components.

   SHARP ELECTRONICS CORPORATION
   Sharp Plaza, Mahwah, NJ   07430-2135
   CEO: Toshiaka Urushisako, Pres.   Tel: (201) 529-8200   Emp: N/A
   Bus: *Mfr./sale/service video and audio systems,*   Fax:(201) 529-8425   %FO: 100
   appliances, office and information equipment
   and electronic components.

● **SHIMIZU CONSTRUCTION COMPANY, LTD.**
16-1 Kyobashi 2-chome, Chuo-ku, Tokyo 104, Japan
CEO: Teruzo Yoshino, Pres.   Tel: 81-3-5441-4111   Emp: 14000
Bus: *General contractor.*   Fax:81-3-5441-0070

   SHIMIZU AMERICA CORPORATION
   461 Fifth Avenue, 3rd Fl., New York, NY   10017
   CEO: Akio Ishi, Pres.   Tel: (212) 251-0050   Emp: N/A
   Bus: *General contractor, engineer and design.*   Fax:(212) 251-1052   %FO: 100

- **SHIN-ETSU CHEMICAL COMPANY, LTD.**
  Asahi-Tokai Bldg., 6-1-2-chome, Otemachi, Chiyoda-ku, Tokyo 100, Japan
  CEO: C. Kanagawa, Pres. & CEO   Tel: 81-3-3246-5111   Emp: N/A
  Bus: *Mfr. specialty chemicals and high-tech materials.*   Fax:81-3-3246-5366

  > **HERAEUS SHIN-ETSU AMERICA, INC.**
  > 4600 NW Pacific Rim Blvd., Camas, WA 98607
  > CEO: Dr. K. Kemmochi, Pres.   Tel: (360) 834-4004   Emp: N/A
  > Bus: *Mfr./sales/marketing of high-purity quartz*   Fax:(360) 834-3115   %FO: 100
  >   *glass crucibles.*

  > **SHIN-ETSU SILICONES OF AMERICA, INC.**
  > 1150 Damer Drive, Akron, OH   44305
  > CEO: Mr. Shibata, Pres.   Tel: (330) 630-9860   Emp: N/A
  > Bus: *Mfr./sales/marketing of silicone rubber*   Fax:(330) 630-9855   %FO: 100
  >   *compounds.*

  > **SHINCOR SILICONES, INC.**
  > 1030 Evans Avenue, Akron, OH   44305
  > CEO: Mr. Kitani, Mgr.   Tel: (330) 630-9460   Emp: N/A
  > Bus: *Mfr./sales/marketing of fluoro-silicone and*   Fax:(330) 630-2857   %FO: 100
  >   *silicone rubber.*

- **SHINTOA KOEKI KAISHA, LTD.**
  3-3-1 Marunouchi, Chiyoda-ku, Tokyo 100, Japan
  CEO: Akira Horie, Pres.   Tel: 81-3-3286-0211   Emp: 600
  Bus: *Trading company.*   Fax:81-3-3213-2420

  > **SHINTOA INTL, INC.**
  > 333 South Hope Street, Ste. 2603, Los Angeles, CA 90071
  > CEO: Yoshiyasu Tsutsui, Pres.   Tel: (213) 687-0633   Emp: 21
  > Bus: *Trading company.*   Fax:(213) 586-0755   %FO: 100

- **SHINWA KAIUN KAISHA, LTD.**
  Nittetsu ND Tower, No.5-7. 1-chome, Kameido, Koto-ku, Tokyo 136, Japan
  CEO: Akira Tanikawa, Pres.   Tel: 81-3-5627-7534   Emp: 1200
  Bus: *Shipping operator and tramp chartering and*   Fax:81-3-5627-2200
       shipping agent.

  > **SHINWA USA, INC.**
  > 300 Harmon Meadow Blvd., Secaucus, NJ   07094
  > CEO: Toshiaki Morishima, Pres.   Tel: (201) 348-2101   Emp: 8
  > Bus: *Marine transport operations, tramp chartering*   Fax:(201) 319-0305   %FO: 100
  >   *and shipping agency.*

● **SHINYEI KAISHA**
113-1 Shigashi-cho, Chuo-ku, Kobe 650-01, Japan
CEO: Yoshiaki Fujioka, Pres.   Tel: 81-78-392-6810   Emp: 700
Bus: *Trading: textiles, silk, electronics, agricultural &*   Fax:81-78-392-0707
     marine products; mfr. electronics.

    SHINYEI CORP OF AMERICA
    342 Madison Avenue, New York, NY   10173
    CEO: K. Ikeda, Pres.   Tel: (212) 682-4610   Emp: 10
    Bus: *Import/export electric appliances, foodstuff,*   Fax:(212) 286-8426   %FO: 100
         fish, ball bearings and fasteners.

● **SHISEIDO COMPANY LTD.**
7-5-5, Ginza, Chuo-ku, Tokyo 104-10, Japan
CEO: Yoshiharu Fukuhara, Pres.   Tel: 81-3-3572-5111   Emp: 22300
Bus: *Mfr./market cosmetics and healthcare products.*   Fax:81-3-3574-8380

    SHISEIDO COSMETICS (AMERICA) LTD.
    900 Third Avenue, 15th Floor, New York, NY   10022
    CEO: Takashi Yamaguchi, CEO   Tel: (212) 805-2300   Emp: 41
    Bus: *Mfr./marketing cosmetics and healthcare*   Fax:(212) 688-0109   %FO: 100
         products.

● **THE SHOKO CHUKIN BANK**
10-17 Yaesu 2-chome, Chuo-ku, Tokyo 104, Japan
CEO: Yukiharu Kodama, Pres.   Tel: 81-3-3172-6111   Emp: 6000
Bus: *Commercial banking services.*   Fax:81-3-3274-1257

    THE SHOKO CHUKIN BANK
    666 Fifth Avenue, New York, NY   10019
    CEO: Tamotsu Abe, Gen.Mgr.   Tel: (212) 581-2800   Emp: 20
    Bus: *Commercial banking.*   Fax:(212) 581-4850   %FO: 100

● **SHOWA DENKO KK**
1-13-9 Shiba Daimon, Minato-ku, Toyko 105, Japan
CEO: Makoto Murata, Pres.   Tel: 81-3-5470-3443   Emp: 6000
Bus: *Chemicals and petrochemicals and ceramic*   Fax:81-3-3431-6579
     materials.

    SHOWA DENKO AMERICA, INC.
    280 Park Avenue, 27th Fl., West Bldg., New York, NY   10017
    CEO: Haruo Fukiyama, Pres.   Tel: (212) 687-0773   Emp: 15
    Bus: *Sale/distribution of chemicals.*   Fax:(212) 573-9007   %FO: 100

- **SMC**
16-4, Shimbashi 1-chome, Minato-ku, Tokyo 105, Japan
CEO: Y. Takada, Pres.   Tel: 81-3-502-2740   Emp: 4000
Bus: *Mfr. pneumatic components for automation.*   Fax:81-3-525-17240

> **SMC PNEUMATICS, INC.**
> 3011 North Franklin Road, Indianapolis, IN   46226
> CEO: Dave Robinson, Gen. Mgr.   Tel: (317) 899-4440   Emp: 300
> Bus: *Mfr. pneumatic components for automation.*   Fax:(317) 899-3102   %FO: 100

- **SOC CORPORATION**
Mita-Nitto-Daibiru Bldg, 3-11-36 Mita, Minato-ku, Tokyo 108, Japan
CEO: H. Arikawa, Pres. & CEO   Tel: 81-3-3452-9081   Emp: 1920
Bus: *Mfr. electronic fuses and fuse holders.*   Fax:81-3-5476-7278

> **SAN-O INDUSTRIAL CORPORATION**
> 91-3 Colin Drive, Holbrook, NY   11741
> CEO: Neil Sato, Pres.   Tel: (516) 472-6666   Emp: 38
> Bus: *Mfr./sale electronic fuses and fuse holders.*   Fax:(516) 472-6777   %FO: 95

- **SOFTBANK CORPORATION**
24-1 Nihonbashi Hakozaki-cho, Chuo-ku, Tokyo 103, Japan
CEO: Masayoshi Son, Pres. & CEO   Tel: 81-3-5642-8000   Emp: 4375
Bus: *Retailer; computer software and network products.* Fax:81-3-5641-3401
*Publisher of hi-tech magazines and invests in
technology globally.*

> **SOFTBANK HOLDINGS, INC.**
> Ten Langley Road, Suite 403, Newton Center, MA   02159
> CEO: Ronald Fisher, Vice Chrm.   Tel: (617) 928-9300   Emp: N/A
> Bus: *U.S. headquarters. Retailer; computer*   Fax:(617) 928-9301   %FO: 100
> *software and network products. Publisher of hi-
> tech magazines and invests in technology
> globally.*

- **SONY CORPORATION**
7-35 Kitashinagawa 6-chome, Shinagawa-ku, Tokyo 141, Japan
CEO: Norio Ohga, Chrm. & CEO   Tel: 81-3-5448-2111   Emp: 151000
Bus: *Mfr. audio, video, TV equipment, computer*   Fax:81-3-5448-2244
*peripherals, electronic communications;
entertainment product.*

> **ETAK, INC.**
> 1430 O'Brien Drive, Menlo Park, CA   94025
> CEO: Hirohto Kawada, Pres. & CEO   Tel: (415) 328-3825   Emp: N/A
> Bus: *Develops/publishes digital map data for*   Fax:(415) 328-3148   %FO: 100
> *mobile navigation systems and travel guides.*

MATERIALS RESEARCH CORP.

2120 West Guadelupe Road, Gilbert, AZ   85233

CEO: Dr. Robert Foster, Pres. & CEO

Bus: *Mfr. equipment and high purity materials for semiconductor & magnetic thin-film industries.*

Tel: (602) 437-9035
Fax:(602) 507-9364

Emp: N/A
%FO: 100

SONY CINEMA PRODUCTS CORPORATION

10202 West Washington Blvd., Culver City, CA   90232

CEO: John A. Scarcella, Pres. & CEO

Bus: *Mfr./distribution/sale motion picture digital and analog sound systems to theatrical filmmakers, distributors and exhibitors.*

Tel: (310) 280-5777
Fax:(310) 280-2024

Emp: N/A
%FO: 100

SONY COMPUTER ENTERTAINMENT AMERICA

919 East Hillsdale Blvd., Foster City, CA   94404

CEO: Shigeo Maruyama, Chrm. & CEO

Bus: *Marketing/distribution entertainment computer hardware and licensing activities.*

Tel: (415) 655-8000
Fax:(415) 655-8001

Emp: N/A
%FO: 100

SONY CORP OF AMERICA

550 Madison Avenue, New York, NJ   10022

CEO: Ted Kawai, Deputy Pres.

Bus: *U.S. headquarters for electronics and hardware-related products for global entertainment units.*

Tel: (212) 833-6800
Fax:(212) 833-6924

Emp: 23000
%FO: 100

SONY ELECTRONICS, INC.

One Sony Drive, Park Ridge, NJ   07656-8003

CEO: Carl Yankowski, Pres. & CEO

Bus: *Mfr./distribution consumer/commercial audio & video equipment, televisions, telecommunications, computer and peripheral products, semiconductors and other electronic components.*

Tel: (201) 930-1000
Fax:(201) 358-4060

Emp: N/A
%FO: 100

SONY INTERACTIVE STUDIOS OF AMERICA

919 East Hillsdale Blvd., Foster City, CA   94404

CEO: Kelly Flock, Pres.

Bus: *Develop/produce entertainment computers and multimedia software.*

Tel: (415) 655-8000
Fax:(415) 655-8001

Emp: N/A
%FO: 100

SONY MUSIC ENTERTAINMENT INC.

550 Madison Avenue, New York, NY   10022

CEO: Thomas D. Mottola, Pres. & CEO

Bus: *Mfr. recorded music and video.*

Tel: (212) 833-8000
Fax:(212) 833-7458

Emp: N/A
%FO: 100

SONY ONLINE VENTURES
550 Madison Avenue, 5th Fl., New York, NY   10022

CEO: Mitchell Cannold, Pres.   Tel: (212) 833-6800   Emp: N/A
Bus: *Mfr./sale online entertainment, programming*   Fax:(212) 833-6461   %FO: 100
and shopping.

SONY PICTURES ENTERTAINMENT
10202 West Washington Blvd, Culver City, CA   90232

CEO: John Calley, Pres. & CEO   Tel: (310) 280-8000   Emp: 3000
Bus: *Production/distribution motion pictures &*   Fax:(310) 204-1300   %FO: 100
television, home video, studio operations, new
entertainment technologies, & licensed
merchandise.

SONY RETAIL ENTERTAINMENT
711 Fifth Avenue, 12th Fl., New York, NY   10022

CEO: Stanley "Mickey" Steinberg, Chrm.   Tel: (212) 833-8828   Emp: N/A
Bus: *Operate/develop theatrical exhibition sites,*   Fax:(212) 833-8311   %FO: 100
location-based entertainment centers and
retail stores.

SONY TRANS COM INC.
1833 Alton Ave., PO Box 19713, Irvine, CA   92713

CEO: Douglas Cline, Pres. & CEO   Tel: (714) 252-0600   Emp: N/A
Bus: *Mfr. airborne audio/visual entertainment*   Fax:(714) 252-0721   %FO: 100
systems, distribution/service audio/visual
programs.

SW NETWORKS
1370 Avenue of the Americas, New York, NY   10019

CEO: Daniel Forth, Pres. & CEO   Tel: (212) 833-6800   Emp: N/A
Bus: *Mfr./distribute music & entertainment*   Fax:(212) 421-1674   %FO: 100
programming for radio broadcast.

● SPC ELECTRONICS CORPORATION
2-1-3 Shibasaki Chofu-shi, Tokyo 182, Japan

CEO: M. Kuzuhara, Gen.Mgr.   Tel: 81-3-4248-18518   Emp: 1000
Bus: *Satellite/terrestrial comm. systems, service. &*   Fax:81-3-4248-19696
maintenance industrial equipment, R&D microwave
& millimeter wave energy systems.

SPC ELECTRONICS AMERICA, INC.
105 Technology Pkwy., Norcross, GA   30092

CEO: Shigeru Tagawa, Pres.   Tel: (770) 446-8626   Emp: 16
Bus: *R&D, service communication units and systems*   Fax:(770) 441-2380   %FO: 100

• **STAR MFG COMPANY, LTD.**
194 Nakayoshida, Shizuoka 422-91, Japan
CEO: S. Sato, Pres.　　　　　　　　　　Tel: 81-542-6311　　　Emp: N/A
Bus: *Mfr. computer printers, printer mechanisms, audio*　Fax:N/A
　　　devices and watch parts.

　　STAR MICRONICS, INC.
　　70-D Ethel Road West, Piscataway, NJ　08854
　　CEO: M. Yamaguchi, Pres.　　　　　　Tel: (908) 572-5550　　Emp: N/A
　　Bus: *Computer printers, printer mechanisms and*　Fax:(908) 572-5693　%FO: 100
　　　　OEM audio devices.

• **SUGINO MACHINE, LTD.**
2410 Hongo, Totama Prefect, Uozo 937, Japan
CEO: Kenji Sugino, Chrm.　　　　　　　Tel: 81-24-5111　　　Emp: 750
Bus: *Mfr. machine tools and jet pumps.*　　Fax:81-24-5051

　　SUGINO CORPORATION
　　1700 North Penny Lane, Schaumburg, IL　60173
　　CEO: Steve Sugino, EVP　　　　　　　Tel: (847) 397-9401　　Emp: 30
　　Bus: *Machine tools, pumps and cutting systems.*　Fax:(847) 397-9490　%FO: 100

• **SUMITOMO BAKELITE COMPANY, LTD.**
Tennoz Parkside Bldg., 5-8 Higashi-Shinagawa, 2-chome, Shinagawa-ku, Tokyo 140, Japan
CEO: Naoto Enda, Pres.　　　　　　　　Tel: 81-3-5462-4111　Emp: N/A
Bus: *Mfr. chemical and plastic products.*　Fax:81-3-5462-4873

　　SUMITOMO PLASTICS AMERICA INC.
　　900 Lafayette Street, Ste. 510, Santa Clara, CA　95050-4967
　　CEO: Yoshiaki Suzuki, Pres.　　　　　Tel: (408) 243-8402　　Emp: N/A
　　Bus: *Mfr./sale chemical and plastic products.*　Fax:(408) 243-8405　%FO: 100

• **SUMITOMO BANK, LTD.**
3-2 Marunouchi 1-chome, Chiyoda-ku, Toyko,　Japan
CEO: Toshio Morikawa, Pres.　　　　　Tel: 81-3-3282-5111　Emp: N/A
Bus: *Commercial banking services.*　　Fax:81-3-3287-1640

　　CENTRAL PACIFIC BANK
　　220 South King Street, Honolulu, HI　96813
　　CEO: Yoshiharu Satoh, Pres.　　　　　Tel: (808) 544-0500　　Emp: N/A
　　Bus: *International commercial banking services.*　Fax:(808) 521-3944　%FO: 100

　　SUMITOMO BANK　LEASING & FINANCE, INC.
　　277 Park Avenue, New York, NY　10172-0002
　　CEO: William M. Ginn, Pres.　　　　　Tel: (212) 224-5200　　Emp: N/A
　　Bus: *Commercial financial services.*　　Fax:(212) 224-5222　%FO: 100

SUMITOMO BANK LTD.
277 Park Avenue, New York, NY   10172-0002
CEO: Akira Kondoh, Pres.   Tel: (212) 224-4000   Emp: N/A
Bus: *International commercial banking services.*   Fax:(212) 593-9514   %FO: 100

SUMITOMO BANK OF CALIFORNIA
320 California Street, San Francisco, CA   94104
CEO: Tsuneo Onda, Pres.   Tel: (415) 445-8000   Emp: N/A
Bus: *International commercial banking services.*   Fax:(415) 445-3952   %FO: 100

● **SUMITOMO CHEMICAL COMPANY, LTD.**
27-1, Shinkawa, 2-chome, Chuo-ku, Tokyo 104, Japan
CEO: Akio Kosai, Pres.   Tel: 81-3-5543-5152   Emp: 8000
Bus: *Industrial chemical, fertilizers, fine chemicals,*   Fax:81-3-5543-5901
   agrochemicals, and pharmaceuticals.

SUMITOMO CHEMICAL AMERICA INC
345 Park Avenue, New York, NY   10154
CEO: Susumu Yoshida, Pres.   Tel: (212) 572-8200   Emp: 27
Bus: *Distribution/sale/service specialty chemicals.*   Fax:(212) 572-8234   %FO: 100

● **SUMITOMO CONSTRUCTION COMPANY, LT.D**
13-4 Araki-cho, Shinjuku-ku, Tokyo 160, Japan
CEO: Shinsaku Sammoto, Pres.   Tel: 81-3-353-5111   Emp: 3200
Bus: *Construction, engineering, design.*   Fax:81-3-353-5559

SUMITOMO CONSTRUCTION AMERICA INC
4510 E Pacific Coast Hwy, Long Beach, CA   90804
CEO: Shinzo Matsuno, Pres.   Tel: (310) 498-7241   Emp: 80
Bus: *Construction, engineering, design*   Fax:(310) 985-0692   %FO: 100

● **SUMITOMO CORPORATION**
2-2 Hitotsubashi 1-chome, Chiyoda-ku, Tokyo 100-91, Japan
CEO: Kenji Miyahara, Pres.   Tel: 81-3 32175082   Emp: 9200
Bus: *Worldwide trading group; administrative services.*   Fax:81-3 32175128

SUMITOMO CORPORATION OF AMERICA
345 Park Avenue, New York, NY   10154-0042
CEO: Tsuneo Iwasaki, Pres. & CEO   Tel: (212) 207-0700   Emp: 500
Bus: *Trading and investment services.*   Fax:(212) 207-0456   %FO: 100

SUMITRONICS INC.
2900 Patrick Henry Drive, Santa Clara, CA   95054
CEO: Yoji Sakamoto, Pres.   Tel: (408) 980-0811   Emp: 35
Bus: *Import/export electronics products.*   Fax:(408) 980-1409   %FO: 100

● **SUMITOMO ELECTRIC INDUSTRIES, INC.**
5-33 Kitahama 4-chome, Chuo-ku, Osaka 541, Japan
CEO: Tetsuro Kawakami, Pres.   Tel: 81-6-220-4141   Emp: 15000
Bus: *Mfr. electrical wire and cable, telecommunications*   Fax:81-6-2223380
     cable, specialty steel wire and automotive parts.

   ENGINEERED SINTERED COMPONENTS INC.
   250 Old Murdock Road, Troutman, NC   28168
   CEO: Brian Mahoney, Pres.   Tel: (704) 528-7500   Emp: 114
   Bus: *Mfr. sintered alloy products.*   Fax:(704) 528-7529   %FO: JV

   JUDD WIRE INC.
   55 Turnpike Road, Turners Falls, MA   01376
   CEO: S. Miyauchi, CEO   Tel: (413) 863-4357   Emp: 205
   Bus: *Mfr. electronics wire.*   Fax:(413) 863-2305   %FO: 100

   LITESPEC INC.
   76 Alexander Drive, P.O.Box 13667, Research Tri Pk, NC   27709
   CEO: S. Nishikawa, CEO   Tel: (919) 541-8400   Emp: 138
   Bus: *Mfr. optical fiber.*   Fax:(919) 541-8476   %FO: 49

   LUCAS SUMITOMO BRAKES INC.
   1650 Kingsview Drive, Lebanon, OH   45036
   CEO: Osamu Niwa, Pres.   Tel: (513) 932-7878   Emp: N/A
   Bus: *Mfr. automotive front disc brake calipers.*   Fax:(513) 932-7975   %FO: 100

   O&S CALIFORNIA INC.
   335 H Street, Ste.206, Chula Vista, CA   92010
   CEO: T .Ono, Pres.   Tel: (619) 585-0386   Emp: 266
   Bus: *Mfr. wire harness for electrical appliances.*   Fax:(619) 585-0388   %FO: 30

   SPD MAGNET WIRE CO.
   909 Industrial Drive, Edmonton, KY   42129
   CEO: R. Klauer, CEO   Tel: (502) 432-2233   Emp: 37
   Bus: *Mfr. magnet wire.*   Fax:(502) 432-2838   %FO: JV

   SUMIDEN WIRE PRODUCTS CORP
   1412 El Pinal Drive, Stockton, CA   95205
   CEO: T. Kamise, CEO   Tel: (209) 466-8924   Emp: 78
   Bus: *Mfr. specialty steel wire*   Fax:(209) 941-2990   %FO: 80

   SUMITOMO ELECTRIC CARBINE INC.
   901 N. Business Center Drive, Mt Prospect, IL   60056
   CEO: T. Asai, Pres.   Tel: (847) 635-0044   Emp: 54
   Bus: *Sale powdered metal products.*   Fax:(847) 635-7866   %FO: 100

SUMITOMO ELECTRIC FIBER OPTICS CORP.
78 Alexander Dr, P O Box 13445, Research Tri Pk, NC   27709

CEO: T. Nagao, Pres.	Tel: (919) 541-8100	Emp: 288
Bus: *U.S. headquarters. Mfr. optical fiber cable, connectors & data link.*	Fax:(919) 541-8220	%FO: 100

SUMITOMO ELECTRIC INTERCONNECT PRODUCTS INC.
2930 Patrick Henry Drive, Santa Clara, CA   95054

CEO: Y. Yamamoto, Pres.	Tel: (408) 980-1655	Emp: 20
Bus: *Sale heat shrinkable tape.*	Fax:(408) 980-1699	%FO: 100

SUMITOMO ELECTRIC USA, INC.
65 East 55th Street, 16th Fl., New York, NY   10022

CEO: Satoshi Otohata, Pres.	Tel: (212) 308-6444	Emp: N/A
Bus: *Sale semiconducting material, new material, optical fiber cable.*	Fax:(212) 308-6575	%FO: 100

SUMITOMO ELECTRIC WIRING SYSTEMS INC.
755 Rochester Street, Morgantown, KY   42262

CEO: M. Moriya, Pres.	Tel: (502) 526-5655	Emp: 1900
Bus: *Mfr. auto wire harness & parts.*	Fax:(502) 526-6986	%FO: 60

● **SUMITOMO HEAVY INDUSTRIES, LTD.**
9-11Kitashinagawa 5-chome, Shinagawa-ku, Tokhyo 141, Japan

CEO: Mitoshi Ozawa, Pres.	Tel: 81-3-5488-8059	Emp: 10000
Bus: *Ships, iron & steel mfr. mach, chemical process equipment & plants, logistics & handling system, gear reducers, plastic molding mach*	Fax:81-3-5488-8056	

SHI PLASTICS MACHINERY INC. OF AMERICA
1256 Oakbrook Drive, #D, Norcross, GA   30093

CEO: Koji Shintani, Pres.	Tel: (770) 447-5430	Emp: 20
Bus: *Sale plastics injection molding machines.*	Fax:(770) 441-9168	%FO: 100

SUMITOMO HEAVY INDUSTRIES (USA) INC.
65 East 55th Street, Ste. 2303, New York, NY   10022

CEO: Kohei Takase, Pres.	Tel: (212) 223-1863	Emp: 12
Bus: *Mktg. research.*	Fax:(212) 223-0399	%FO: 100

SUMITOMO MACHINERY CORP. OF AMERICA
4200 Holland Blvd., Chesapeake, VA   23323

CEO: William M. Lechler, Pres.	Tel: (804) 485-3355	Emp: 300
Bus: *Mfr. power transmissions, variators, gear speed reducers.*	Fax:(804) 487-3291	%FO: 100

• **SUMITOMO MARINE & FIRE INSURANCE COMPANY, LTD.**
2-27-2 Shinkawa, Chuo-ku, Tokyo 104, Japan
CEO: Takashi Onoda, Pres.　　　　　　Tel: 81-3-3297-1111　　Emp: 8000
Bus: *Property and casualty insurance.*　Fax:81-3-3297-6930

　　　SUMITOMO MARINE & FIRE INSURANCE CO., LTD.
　　　1 World Trade Center, Ste. 9035, New York, NY　10048
　　　CEO: Ryohei Arima, Dir.　　　　　　Tel: (212) 488-0600　　Emp: 150
　　　Bus: *Property & casualty insurance services.*　Fax:(212) 775-1248　%FO: 100

• **SUMITOMO METAL INDUSTRIES, LTD.**
5-33 Kitahama 4-chome, Chuoi-ku 541, Osaka, Japan
CEO: Yasuo Shigu, Chrm.　　　　　　Tel: 81-6-220-5111　　Emp: N/A
Bus: *Mfr. steel product; steel mill technology.*　Fax:81-6-223-0305

　　　SUMITOMO METAL USA CORP.
　　　420 Lexington Avenue, New York, NY　10170
　　　CEO: Kenzo Makino, Pres.　　　　　　Tel: (212) 949-4760　　Emp: N/A
　　　Bus: *Mfr. steel product; steel mill technology.*　Fax:(212) 490-3949　%FO: 100

　　　SUMITOMO METAL USA CORP.
　　　8750 West Bryn Mawr Ave., Ste. 1000, Chicago, IL　60631-3508
　　　CEO: Masahiro Takoya, Pres.　　　　　Tel: (773) 714-8130　　Emp: N/A
　　　Bus: *Mfr. steel product; steel mill technology.*　Fax:(773) 714-8183　%FO: 100

• **SUMITOMO RUBBER INDUSTRIES LTD.**
1-1 Tsutsui-cho 1-chome, Chuo-ku, Kobe 651, Japan
CEO: Tasuku Yokoi, Chrm.　　　　　　Tel: 81-78-265-3000　　Emp: N/A
Bus: *Mfr. tires.*　　　　　　　　　　Fax:81-78-265-3111

　　　DUNLOP TIRE CORP.
　　　200 John James Audubon Pkwy, West Amherst, NY　14228
　　　CEO: P.D. Campbell, Pres. & CEO　　Tel: (716) 639-5200　　Emp: 3300
　　　Bus: *Mfr. tires.*　　　　　　　　Fax:(716) 639-5515　%FO: JV

• **THE SUMITOMO TRUST & BANKING CO., LTD.**
4-4 Marunouchi 1-chome, Chiyoda-ku, Tokyo 100, Japan
CEO: Osamu Sakurai, Pres.　　　　　　Tel: 81-3-3286-1111　　Emp: 6200
Bus: *Commercial banking.*　　　　　　Fax:81-3-3286-8787

　　　SUMITOMO TRUST & BANKING CO., USA
　　　527 Madison Avenue, New York, NY　10022
　　　CEO: Takashi Inoue, Pres.　　　　　Tel: (212) 326-0600　　Emp: 50
　　　Bus: *Commercial banking.*　　　　Fax:(212) 644-3025　%FO: 100

● **SUNTORY, LTD.**
1-40 Dojimahama 2-chome, Kita-ku, Osaka 0530, Japan
CEO: Shimichiro Torii, Pres.   Tel: 81-6-346-1131   Emp: N/A
Bus: *Wine, liquors, malt beverages and specialty foods.*   Fax:N/A

    SUNTORY INTL CORPORATION
    1211 Avenue of the Americas, New York, NY   10036-8872
    CEO: Y. Tamari, Pres.   Tel: (212) 596-1001   Emp: N/A
    Bus: *Wines, liquors, malt beverages and bottled*   Fax:(212) 398-0268   %FO: 100
        water.

● **SUZUKI MOTOR CORPORATION**
300 Takatsuka-cho, Hamamaysu, Shizuoka Pref. 432-91, Japan
CEO: Osamu Suzuki, Pres. & CEO   Tel: 81-53-440-2061   Emp: 14650
Bus: *Mfr./sale automobiles and motorcycles.*   Fax:81-53-445-0040

    AMERICAN SUZUKI MOTOR CORPORATION
    3251 East Imperial Hwy, Brea, CA   92621-6722
    CEO: Masao Nagura, Pres.   Tel: (714) 996-7040   Emp: N/A
    Bus: *Mfr./sale automobiles and motorcycles.*   Fax:(714) 524-2512   %FO: 100

● **TABUCHI ELECTRIC COMPANY, LTD.**
12-22 Mitejima 1-chome, Nishiyodogawa-ku, Osaka 555, Japan
CEO: Teruhisa Tabuchi, Pres.   Tel: 81-6-64721951   Emp: N/A
Bus: *Mfr. electronic components.*   Fax:N/A

    TABUCHI ELECTRIC CO. OF AMERICA
    65 Germantown Court, Ste. 107, Cordova, TN   38018
    CEO: Setsuhiro Kobashi, Pres.   Tel: (901) 757-2300   Emp: 19
    Bus: *Mfr./sale electronic components.*   Fax:(901) 757-1001   %FO: 100

● **TAKAGI CHOKUKU COMPANY, LTD.**
1525 Nakanoshima, Wakayama City, Japan
CEO: T. Takagi, Pres.   Tel: 81-235205   Emp: N/A
Bus: *Engraving for textiles and other industries.*   Fax:N/A

    TKG INTL CORPORATION
    2630 Weaver Road, Macon, GA   31201
    CEO: M. Takahira, Pres.   Tel: (912) 738-9700   Emp: 50
    Bus: *Engraved screens for textile and printing*   Fax:(912) 738-0307   %FO: 100

● **TAKARA SHUZO COMPANY, LTD.**
Nissei Bldg, Shijo-Higashinotoin, Shimogyo-ku, Kyoto 600, Japan
CEO: A. Omiya, Pres.   Tel: 81-75-241-5110   Emp: 2000
Bus: *Mfr./import wines and liquors.*   Fax:81-75-211-6385

    TAKARA SAKE USA, INC.
    708 Addison Street, Berkeley, CA   94710
    CEO: Takeo Abe, Pres.   Tel: (510) 540-8250   Emp: N/A
    Bus: *Mfr. sake and wines.*   Fax:(510) 486-8758   %FO: 100

● **TAKASHIMAYA COMPANY, LIMITED**
CEO: Tatsuro Tanaka, Pres.   Tel: 81-6-631-1101   Emp: N/A
Bus: *Department store and restaurant owner/operator,*   Fax:81-6-631-9850
direct marketing and design consulting services.

    TAKASHIMAYA ENTERPRISES, INC.
    401 Old Country Road, Carle Place, NY   11514
    CEO: Yuji Okitsu, Pres.   Tel: (516) 997-4770   Emp: N/A
    Bus: *US headquarters. Department store and*   Fax:(516) 997-4772   %FO: 100
    restaurant owner/operator, direct marketing
    and design consulting services.

    TAKASHIMAYA NEW YORK, INC.
    693 Fifth Avenue, New York, NY   10022
    CEO: Yuji Okitsu, Pres.   Tel: (212) 350-0592   Emp: N/A
    Bus: *Department store and restaurant*   Fax:(212) 350-0192   %FO: 100
    owner/operator, direct marketing and design
    consulting services.

    TAKASHIMAYA CALIFORNIA, INC.
    1250 Sixth Street, Suite 102, Santa Monica, CA   90401
    CEO: Hisao Anamoto, Pres.   Tel: (310) 458-6082   Emp: N/A
    Bus: *Department store and restaurant*   Fax:(310) 458-7329   %FO: 100
    owner/operator, direct marketing and design
    consulting services.

    Y.T.PACIFIC ENTERPRISES, INC.
    930 Hauoli Street, Honolulu, HI   96826
    CEO: M. Yamaguci   Tel: (808) 955-4566   Emp: N/A
    Bus: *Department store and restaurant*   Fax: %FO: 100
    owner/operator, direct marketing and design
    consulting services.

● **TAKATA CORPORATION**
25 Mori Bldg, 4-30 Roppongi 1-chome, Minato-ku, Tokyo 106, Japan
CEO: J. Takada, Pres.   Tel: 81-3-582-3222   Emp: 6000
Bus: *Mfr. industrial hose, lubricants, seat belts and air*   Fax:81-3-505-3022
      bags.

      TAKATA FABRICATION CORPORATION
      2500 Takata Drive, Auburn Hills, MI   48326
      CEO: Dan Hess, Pres.   Tel: (824) 873-8040   Emp: N/A
      Bus: *Mfr./distribution seat belts.*   Fax:(248) 373-2897   %FO: JV

● **TAKEDA CHEMICAL INDUSTRIES, LTD.**
1,1 Doshomachi 4-chome, Chuo-ku, Osaka 541, Japan
CEO: Kunio Takeda, Pres.   Tel: 81-6-204-2111   Emp: 15210
Bus: *Mfr. pharmaceuticals, bulk vitamins, agricultural &*   Fax:81-6-204-2880
      environmental products, agricultural chemicals.

      TAKEDA AMERICA, INC.
      400 Park Avenue, New York, NY   10022
      CEO: Shotaro Suita, Pres.   Tel: (212) 421-6950   Emp: N/A
      Bus: *U.S. headquarters.*   Fax:(212) 355-5243   %FO: 100

      TAKEDA CHEMICAL PRODUCTS USA, INC.
      101 Takeda Drive, Wilmington, NC   28402
      CEO: Kazuo Ogino   Tel: (910) 762-8666   Emp: 160
      Bus: *Mfr. ascorbic acid, thiamin.*   Fax:(910) 762-6846   %FO: 100

      TAKEDA USA, INC.
      8 Corporate Drive, Orangeburg, NY   10962-2614
      CEO: Yoshihisa Takeda, Pres.   Tel: (914) 365-2080   Emp: 50
      Bus: *Sale/distribution bulk vitamins, flavor*   Fax:(914) 365-2786   %FO: 100
          enhancers, functional ingredients for farm &
          food industries.

      TAP HOLDINGS INC.
      2355 Waukegan Road, Deerfield, IL   60015
      CEO: Yasuchika Hasegawa, Pres.   Tel: (847) 317-5712   Emp: 850
      Bus: *Mfr. pharmaceuticals.*   Fax:(847) 317-5797   %FO: 50

● **TAKENAKA CORPORATION**
21-1 Ginza 8-chome, Chuo-ku, Tokyo 104, Japan
CEO: Tohichi Takenaka, Pres.   Tel: 81-3-3542-7100   Emp: 11200
Bus: *Planners, architects, engineers and builders.*   Fax:81-3-3545-0584

      TAKENAKA (USA) CORPORATION
      801 S. Figueroa Street, Ste. 1070, Los Angeles, CA   90017
      CEO: Norio Nakada, Pres.   Tel: (213) 489-8900   Emp: 90
      Bus: *Planners, architects, engineers and general*   Fax:(213) 489-8996   %FO: 100
          construction.

● **TAKEUCHI MFG COMPANY, LTD.**
205-3 Uadaira, Sakaki-machi, Hanishina-gun, Nagano 389-07, Japan
CEO: Akio Takeuchi, Pres.　　　　　　　　Tel: 81-262-882331　　　Emp: 350
Bus: *Mfr. compact excavators.*　　　　　　Fax:N/A

　　　　TAKEUCHI MFG (USA), LTD.
　　　　2711 Peachtree Square, Atlanta, GA　30360
　　　　CEO: W. Scott Rogers, EVP　　　　　Tel: (770) 451-5500　　　Emp: 11
　　　　Bus: *Distribute and service compact excavators.*　Fax:(770) 451-4544　%FO: 100

● **TAKISAWA MACHINE TOOL COMPANY, LTD.**
983 Natsukawa, Okayama 701-01, Japan
CEO: Tadayoshi Takisawa, Pres.　　　　　Tel: 81-86-291500　　　Emp: N/A
Bus: *Mfr. machine tools.*　　　　　　　　Fax:N/A

　　　　TAKISAWA USA, INC.
　　　　701 Corporate Woods Pkwy, Vernon Hills, IL　60661
　　　　CEO: T. Todoroki, Pres.　　　　　　Tel: (847) 913-0045　　　Emp: N/A
　　　　Bus: *Sale machine tools.*　　　　　Fax:(847) 913-0114　　%FO: 100

● **TAMRON COMPANY, LTD.**
17-11 Takinogawa 7-chome, Kita-ku, Tokyo, Japan
CEO: Takeyuki Arai, CEO　　　　　　　　Tel: 81-3 39160131　　　Emp: 1200
Bus: *Mfr. photo/video lenses, optical components,*　Fax:81-3 39161860
　　　Broncia medium format cameras.

　　　　TAMRON INDUSTRIES, INC.
　　　　125 Schmitt Blvd., Farmingdale, NY　11735
　　　　CEO: Hisaaki Hagashima, Pres.　　　Tel: (516) 694-8700　　　Emp: 20
　　　　Bus: *Distribution photo & CCTV lenses, optical*　Fax:(800) 767-5551　%FO: 100
　　　　　　components.

● **TDK CORPORATION**
1-13-1 Nihonbashi, Chuo-ku, Tokyo 103, Japan
CEO: Hiroshi Sato, Pres.　　　　　　　　Tel: 81-3-3278-5111　　　Emp: 25000
Bus: *Mfr. electronic materials and components,*　Fax:81-3-3278-5330
　　　recording media.

　　　　DISCOM, INC.
　　　　334 Littleton Road, Westford, MA　01886
　　　　CEO: Toru Watanabe, Pres.　　　　　Tel: (508) 692-6000　　　Emp: 80
　　　　Bus: *Mfr./sale deflection yokes & high voltage*　Fax:(508) 692-8489　%FO: 100
　　　　　　power supply.

　　　　SAKI MAGNETICS, INC.
　　　　26600 Agoura Road, Calabasas, CA　91302
　　　　CEO: Richard Drake, Pres.　　　　　Tel: (818) 880-4054　　　Emp: 40
　　　　Bus: *Mfr./sale industry magnetic recording heads.*　Fax:(818) 880-6242　%FO: 100

SILICON SYSTEMS INC.
14351 Myford Road, Tustin, CA   92680
CEO: Rick Goerner, Pres.   Tel: (714) 731-7110   Emp: 2000
Bus: *Design/mfr. integrated circuits.*   Fax:(714) 731-6901   %FO: 100

TDK COMPONENTS USA, INC.
1 TDK Blvd., Highway 74 South, Peachtree City, GA   30269
CEO: N. Nakamura, Pres.   Tel: (770) 631-0410   Emp: 90
Bus: *Mfr. multiple layer ceramic capacitors.*   Fax:(770) 631-0425   %FO: 100

TDK CORP. OF AMERICA
1600 Feehanville Drive, Mount Prospect, IL   60056
CEO: Mitsukuni Baba, Pres.   Tel: (847) 803-6100   Emp: 200
Bus: *Sale electronic materials & components.*   Fax:(847) 803-6296   %FO: 100

TDK CORPORATION
5900 North Harrison Street, Shawnee, OK   74801
CEO: Isao Matsumara, Pres.   Tel: (405) 275-2100   Emp: 960
Bus: *Mfr. hard & soft ceramic magnetic materials.* Fax:(405) 878-0574   %FO: 100

TDK ELECTRONICS CORPORATION
12 Harbor Park Drive, Port Washington, NY   11050
CEO: Kenjiro Kihara, Pres.   Tel: (516) 625-0100   Emp: 150
Bus: *Sale magnetic recording media.*   Fax:(516) 625-0653   %FO: 100

TDK USA CORPORATION
12 Harbor Park Drive, Port Washington, NY   11050
CEO: Kenjiro Kihara, Pres.   Tel: (516) 625-0100   Emp: 25
Bus: *Holding company.*   Fax:(516) 625-2923   %FO: 100

● **TEIJIN SEIKI COMPANY, LTD.**
9-1 Edobori 1-chome, Nishi-ku, Osaka 550, Japan
CEO: Yakitaka Tobari, Pres.   Tel: 81-6 4486005   Emp: 1700
Bus: *Mfr. aircraft parts, textile & industrial machinery.*   Fax:81-6 4482004

   TEIJIN AMERICA, INC.
   10 East 50th Street, New York, NY   10022
   CEO: Dr. Yoshimichi Hase, Pres.   Tel: (212) 308-8744   Emp: N/A
   Bus: *US headquarters office.*   Fax:(212) 308-8902   %FO: 100

   TEIJIN SEIKI AMERICA, INC.
   17770 NE 78th Place, Redmond, WA   98052-4960
   CEO: Masami Okamoto, Pres.   Tel: (206) 455-5757   Emp: 29
   Bus: *Mfr. aircraft parts, spare sales, repair/overhaul* Fax:(206) 455-1333   %FO: 100

● **TEIJIN SHOJI COMPANY, LTD.**
6-21 Minami-Honmachi 1-chome, Chuo-ku, Osaka 541, Japan
CEO: Y. Okamoto, Pres.   Tel: N/A   Emp: N/A
Bus: *Export textiles, raw materials and machinery.*   Fax:81-62-668-230

    TEIJIN SHOJI USA, INC.
    42 West 39th Street, New York, NY   10018
    CEO: Y. Yokochi, Pres.   Tel: (212) 840-6900   Emp: 20
    Bus: *Import/export textiles, yarns, fibers,*   Fax:(212) 719-9656   %FO: 100
        sleep/sportswear and machinery.

● **TOA MEDICAL ELECTRONICS COMPANY, LTD.**
CPO Box 1002, Kobe, Japan
CEO: Reizo Hashimoto, Pres.   Tel: 81-78-424-1171   Emp: N/A
Bus: *Clinical lab and hematology instruments.*   Fax:N/A

    TOA MEDICAL ELECTRONICS USA, INC.
    10716 Reagan Street, Los Alamitos, CA   90720
    CEO: Katsuo Uhara, Pres.   Tel: (562) 799-4001   Emp: N/A
    Bus: *Clinical lab & hematology instruments.*   Fax:(562) 799-9702   %FO: 100

● **THE TOKAI BANK, LTD.**
21-24 Nishiki 3-chome, Naka-ku, Nagoya 460, Japan
CEO: Satora Nishigaki, Pres.   Tel: 81-52- 2111111   Emp: 37000
Bus: *Commercial banking services.*   Fax:N/A

    THE TOKAI BANK LTD
    55 East 52nd Street, 11th Fl., New York, NY   10055
    CEO: Takashi Inouchi, Dir. & Gen.Mgr.   Tel: (212) 339-1200   Emp: N/A
    Bus: *Commercial banking services.*   Fax:(212) 754-2153   %FO: 100

    TOKAI BANK OF CALIFORNIA
    534 West Sixth Street, Los Angeles, CA   90014
    CEO: Hirohisa Aoki, Pres.   Tel: (213) 972-0200   Emp: N/A
    Bus: *Commercial banking services.*   Fax:(213) 972-0325   %FO: 100

    TOKAI CREDIT CORP.
    1111 South Arroyo Pkwy., Ste. 500, Pasadena, CA   91105
    CEO: Hideki Kasahara, Pres.   Tel: (818) 441-7200   Emp: N/A
    Bus: *Commercial finance.*   Fax:(818) 441-7299   %FO: 100

    TOKAI FINANCIAL SERVICES INC.
    1055 Westlakes Drive, Berwyn, PA   19312
    CEO: Abraham Bernstein, CEO   Tel: (215) 651-5000   Emp: N/A
    Bus: *Leasing services.*   Fax:(215) 651-5140   %FO: 100

    TOKAI SECURITIES INC.
    55 East 52nd Street, New York, NY   10055
    CEO: Kazumi Sato, Pres.   Tel: (212) 339-1111   Emp: N/A
    Bus: *Securities broker/dealer.*   Fax:(212) 223-2414   %FO: 100

TOKAI TRUST COMPANY OF NY
55 East 52nd Street, New York, NY   10055
CEO: Kazumi Sato, Pres.   Tel: (212) 339-1390 Emp: N/A
Bus: *Trust and investment management services.* Fax:(212) 754-2089 %FO: 100

● **TOKINA OPTICAL COMPANY, LTD.**
192 Nozuta-machi, Machida-shi, Tokyo 194-01, Japan
CEO: T. Yamanaka, Pres.   Tel: 81-3-42735-3611 Emp: 500
Bus: *Mfr. photographic & CCTV lenses and security* Fax:N/A
cameras.

 TOKINA OPTICAL CORPORATION
 1512 Kona Drive, Compton, CA   90220
 CEO: Yusu Suga, Pres.   Tel: (213) 537-9380 Emp: 25
 Bus: *Sales/distribution of photographic & CCTV* Fax:(213) 604-9618 %FO: 100
 lenses and security cameras.

● **THE TOKIO MARINE & FIRE INSURANCE CO., LTD**
2-1 Marunouchi 1-chome, Chiyoda-ku, Tokyo, Japan
CEO: Shunji Kono, Chrm.   Tel: 81-3-3212-6211 Emp: 14000
Bus: *Property, casualty & ocean marine insurance.* Fax:81-3-5223-3100

 TOKIO MARINE MANAGEMENT
 101 Park Avenue, New York, NY   10178-0095
 CEO: Masaharu Nakamura, Chrm. & Pres. Tel: (212) 297-6600 Emp: N/A
 Bus: *Property, casualty & ocean marine insurance.* Fax:(212) 297-6898 %FO: 100

● **TOKYO AIRCRAFT INSTRUMENT COMPANY, LTD.**
35-1 Izumi-honcho 1-chome, Komae-shi, Tokyo 201, Japan
CEO: A. Wada, Pres.   Tel: 81-3-489-1191 Emp: 800
Bus: *Mfr. aircraft instruments, business machines and* Fax:81-3-488-5521
industrial equipment.

 UNITED INSTRUMENTS, INC.
 3625 Comotara Avenue, Wichita, KS   67226
 CEO: T. Hanamura, Pres.   Tel: (316) 636-9203 Emp: 21
 Bus: *Mfr. aircraft instruments.*   Fax:(316) 636-9243 %FO: 100

● **TOKYO ELECTRIC POWER COMPANY, INC.**
1-3 Uchisaiwai-cho 1-chome, Chiyoda-ku, Tokyo 100, Japan
CEO: Hiroshi Araki, Pres.   Tel: 81-3 35018111 Emp: 43500
Bus: *Electric power generation & distribution.* Fax:81-3 35914609

 TOKYO ELECTRIC POWER CO., INC.
 1901 L Street NW, # 720, Washington, DC   20036
 CEO: Shuya Shibasaki, Gen.Mgr.   Tel: (202) 457-0790 Emp: N/A
 Bus: *Electric power generation & distribution.* Fax:(202) 457-0810 %FO: 100

- **TOKYO SEIMITSU COMPANY, LTD.**
  9-7-1 Shimorenjaku, Mitaka-shi, Tokyo 181, Japan
  CEO: Hideo Ohtsubo, Pres.   Tel: 81-3-4224-81019   Emp: N/A
  Bus: *Mfr. precision measuring & semi-conductor*   Fax:81-3-4224-97315
      machinery.

      TOKYO SEIMITSU AMERICA, INC.
      39205 Country Club Drive, C-22, Farmington Hills, MI 48331
      CEO: Michiaki Koda, Pres.   Tel: (248) 489-5500   Emp: 10
      Bus: *Sales and service of measuring instruments.*   Fax:(248) 489-5503   %FO: 100

- **TOKYU CORPORATION**
  26-20 Sakuragaoka-cho, Shibuya-ku, Tokyo 150, Japan
  CEO: Jiro Yokota, Pres.   Tel: 81-3-3477-6180   Emp: 7130
  Bus: *Transportation, development, hotels & recreation,*   Fax:81-3-3464-6505
      retail distribution.

      MAUNA LANI RESORT INC.
      P O Box 4959, Kohala Coast, HI 96743
      CEO: Kenneth F. Brown, Chrm.   Tel: (808) 885-6677   Emp: 265
      Bus: *Resort land development.*   Fax:(808) 885-6375   %FO: 99

      SHIROKIYA, INC.
      1450 Ala Moana Blvd., Honolulu, HI 96814
      CEO: Koji Sawa, Pres.   Tel: (808) 347-3777   Emp: N/A
      Bus: *Retail sales.*   Fax:(808) 943-0483   %FO: 100

      VITA USA, INC.
      2222 Kalakaua Avenue, Honolulu, HI 96815
      CEO: T. Okai, Gen. Mgr.   Tel: (808) 922-2315   Emp: N/A
      Bus: *Travel agency.*   Fax:(808) 945-3942   %FO: 100

- **TOMEN CORPORATION**
  6-7 Kawaramachi 1-chome, Chuo-ku, Osaka 541, Japan
  CEO: Yasuo Matsukawa, Pres.   Tel: 81-6-208-2211   Emp: 3000
  Bus: *General trading company.*   Fax:81-6-208-2222

      TOMEN AMERICA INC.
      1285 Avenue of the Americas, New York, NY 10019-6028
      CEO: Hajime Kawamura, Pres.   Tel: (212) 397-4600   Emp: 353
      Bus: *General trading company.*   Fax:(212) 397-5797   %FO: 100

● **TOPPAN PRINTING COMPANY, LTD.**
1 Kanda Izumi-cho, Chiyoda-ku, Tokyo 101, Japan
CEO: Hiromichi Fujita, Pres.   Tel: 81-3-3835-5741   Emp: 26000
Bus: *Printing, publishing, packaging, semi-conductors,*   Fax: 81-3-3835-0674
interior decorating materials, securities.

    TOPPAN ELECTRONICS USA, INC.
    3032 Bunker Hill Lane, Ste. 108, Santa Clara, CA   95054
    CEO: K. Fujita, Pres.   Tel: (408) 982-0944   Emp: N/A
    Bus: *Sales/distribution precision electronic*   Fax: (408) 982-0953   %FO: 100
    components/packaging.

    TOPPAN PRINTING COMPANY OF AMERICA, INC.
    666 Fifth Avenue, 7th Fl., New York, NY   10103
    CEO: Roy Ariga, Pres.   Tel: (212) 489-7740   Emp: 180
    Bus: *Full service commercial printing.*   Fax: (212) 969-9349   %FO: 100

● **TORAY INDUSTRIES INC.**
2-2-1 Nihonbashi Muromachi, Chuo-ku, Tokyo 103, Japan
CEO: Yoshikazu Ito, Chrm.   Tel: 81-3-3245-5111   Emp: 32913
Bus: *Mfr. fibers, plastics & chemicals.*   Fax: 81-3-3245-5555

    MONITOR PERFORMANCE PLASTICS CO.
    100 East Big Beaver, Ste. 310, Troy, MI   48083-1210
    CEO: Tony Oshima, Pres.   Tel: (248) 740-2757   Emp: N/A
    Bus: *Mfr. nylon resin compounds.*   Fax: (248) 740-1150   %FO: JV

    TORAY CAPITAL (AMERICA), INC.
    600 Third Avenue, 5th Fl., New York, NY   10016
    CEO: Akira Uchida, Pres.   Tel: (212) 697-8150   Emp: N/A
    Bus: *Financial services.*   Fax: (212) 972-4279   %FO: 100

    TORAY COMPOSITE (AMERICA), INC.
    19002 50th Avenue East, Tacoma, WA   98446
    CEO: Shizuo Watanbe, Pres.   Tel: (206) 846-1777   Emp: N/A
    Bus: *Mfr. carbon fiber prepreg products.*   Fax: (206) 846-3897   %FO: 100

    TORAY INDUSTRIES (AMERICA), INC.
    600 Third Avenue, 5th Fl., New York, NY   10016
    CEO: Akio Takaya, Pres.   Tel: (212) 697-8150   Emp: 20
    Bus: *Liaison office, U.S. headquarters.*   Fax: (212) 972-4279   %FO: 100

    TORAY MARKETING & SALES (AMERICA), INC.
    600 Third Avenue, 5th Fl., New York, NY   10016
    CEO: Masayochi Kamiura, Pres.   Tel: (212) 697-8150   Emp: 40
    Bus: *Trading, import/export.*   Fax: (212) 972-4279   %FO: 100

TORAY PLASTICS (AMERICA), INC.
50 Belver Avenue, North Kingstown, RI   02852

CEO: Yoshio Kageyama, Pres.	Tel: (401) 294-4500	Emp: N/A
Bus: *Mfr. polypropylene and polyester films.*	Fax:(401) 294-2154	%FO: 100

• TOSHIBA CORPORATION
1-1 Shibaura 1-chome, Minato-ku, Tokyo 105-01, Japan

CEO: Taizo Nishimura, Pres. & CEO	Tel: 81-3-3457-4511	Emp: 189000
Bus: *Mfr. information & communications systems, information media & consumer products, power systems & industrial equipment, electronic components.*	Fax:81-3-3456-1631	

TOSHIBA AMERICA CONSUMER PRODUCTS, INC.
82 Totowa Road, Wayne, NJ   07470

CEO: Toshihide Yasui, Pres.	Tel: (201) 628-8000	Emp: N/A
Bus: *Mfr./sale consumer products.*	Fax:(201) 628-1875	%FO: 100

TOSHIBA AMERICA ELECTRONIC COMPONENTS, INC.
9775 Toledo Way, Irvine, CA   92718

CEO: Robert Brown, Pres.	Tel: (714) 455-2000	Emp: N/A
Bus: *Mfr./sale electronic components.*	Fax:(714) 859-3963	%FO: 100

TOSHIBA AMERICA, INC.
1251 Ave of the Americas, 41st Fl., New York, NY   10020

CEO: Takeshi Okatomi, CEO	Tel: (212) 596-0600	Emp: N/A
Bus: *Holding company. U.S. headquarters.*	Fax:(212) 593-3875	%FO: 100

TOSHIBA AMERICA INFORMATION SYSTEMS, INC.
9740 Irvine Blvd, Irvine, CA   92718

CEO: Shunki Yatsunami, Pres.	Tel: (714) 583-3000	Emp: N/A
Bus: *Mfr./sale of information and communication equipment.*	Fax:(714) 587-6424	%FO: 100

TOSHIBA AMERICA MEDICAL SYSTEMS, INC.
2441 Michelle Drive, Tustin, CA   92681-2068

CEO: Hasamichi Katsurada, Pres.	Tel: (714) 730-5000	Emp: N/A
Bus: *Mfr./sale medical equipment.*	Fax:(714) 505-3076	%FO: 100

TOSHIBA INTERNATIONAL CORP.
13131 West Little York Road, PO Box 40906, Houston, TX   77041

CEO: Teruyuki Sugizaki, Pres.	Tel: (713) 466-0277	Emp: N/A
Bus: *Mfr./sale heavy electrical apparatus.*	Fax:(713) 896-5226	%FO: 100

- **TOSHIBA MACHINE COMPANY, LTD.**
  2-11 Ginza 4-chome, Chuo-ku, Tokyo 104, Japan
  CEO: Sadao Okano, Pres.   Tel: 81-3-3567-0864   Emp: 2920
  Bus: *Mfr. machine tools, plastic machinery, die casting,*   Fax:81-3-3562-5220
       printing press, etc.

  TOSHIBA MACHINE CO. OF AMERICA
  755 Greenleaf Avenue, Elk Grove Village, IL   60007
  CEO: Takanori Yamada, Pres.   Tel: (847) 593-1616   Emp: 95
  Bus: *Import/distribution machine tools, print & die-*   Fax:(847) 593-0897   %FO: 100
       cast machinery, injection molding.

- **TOSHOKU, LTD.**
  4-3 Nihonbashi Muromachi, 2-chome, Chuo-ku, Tokyo 103, Japan
  CEO: Tetsuya Sato, Pres.   Tel: 81-3-3245-2211   Emp: 550
  Bus: *Trade, shipping, insurance, real estate & leasing.*   Fax:81-3-3245-2201

  TOSHOKU AMERICA, INC.
  780 Third Avenue, New York, NY   10017
  CEO: T. Hirano, Pres.   Tel: (212) 759-0300   Emp: 100
  Bus: *Imp/export agricultural commodities and*   Fax:(212) 759-0724   %FO: 100
       seafood products; real estate development and
       restaurants.

- **TOSOH CORPORATION**
  1-7-7 Akasaka, Minato-ku, Tokyo 746, Japan
  CEO: M. Tashiro, Pres.   Tel: 81-3-585-6707   Emp: N/A
  Bus: *Mfr./process chemicals, metals and raw materials.*   Fax:N/A

  TOSOH USA, INC.
  1100 Circle 75 Pkwy, Ste. 600, Atlanta, GA   30339
  CEO: Yoshikazu Horiko, Pres.   Tel: (404) 956-1100   Emp: N/A
  Bus: *Mfr. industrial chemicals & chemical*   Fax:(404) 956-7368   %FO: 100
       intermediates.

- **TOYO SUISAN KAISHA, LTD.**
  13-40 Kohnan 2-chome, Minato-ku, Tokyo 108, Japan
  CEO: Kazuo Mori, Pres.   Tel: 81-3-3458-5090   Emp: 1890
  Bus: *Produce/sale instant noodles, processed foods;*   Fax:N/A
       refrigerated wholesale.

  MARUCHAN, INC.
  15800 Luguna Canyon Road, Irvine, CA   92618
  CEO: Kazuo Mori, Pres.   Tel: (714) 789-2300   Emp: 200
  Bus: *Mfr./sale instant noodles.*   Fax:(714) 789-2350   %FO: 100

● **TOYODA MACHINE WORKS**
1 Asi-hamachi 1-chome, Kariya City, Aichi Prefect, Japan
CEO: T. Onishi, Pres.   Tel: 81-566-255-170   Emp: 4500
Bus: *Mfr./sale machine tools & auto parts.*   Fax:81-566-255-470

    TOYODA MACHINERY USA, INC.
    316 West University Drive, Arlington Heights, IL 60004
    CEO: Jack K. Sakane, Pres.   Tel: (847) 253-0340   Emp: 400
    Bus: *Mfr./distribute horizontal/vertical machining*   Fax:(847) 577-4680   %FO: 100
        centers, grinders, machining cells & systems.

● **TOYOSHIMA SPECIAL STEEL COMPANY, LTD.**
1-6 Sumiyoshi 1-chome, Ikeda 563, Japan
CEO: Susumu Tanabe, Pres.   Tel: 81-7612021   Emp: N/A
Bus: *Springs, fork arms, earthmover equipment and auto*   Fax:N/A
    spare parts.

    TOYOSHIMA INDIANA, INC.
    735 St. Paul Street, Indianapolis, IN 46203
    CEO: Toshi Osanai, Pres.   Tel: (317) 638-3511   Emp: 126
    Bus: *Mfr./distribute springs for trucks and*   Fax:(317) 631-7729   %FO: 100
        automobiles.

● **TOYOTA MOTOR CORPORATION**
1 Toyota-cho, Toyota City, Aichi Prefecture 471-71, Japan
CEO: Hiroshi Okuda, Pres., Chrm.   Tel: 81-565-282121   Emp: 147000
Bus: *Mfr. motor vehicles, prefab housing,*   Fax:81-565-235800
    telecommunications products.

    CALTY DESIGN RESEARCH, INC.
    2810 Jamboree Road, Newport Beach, CA 92660
    CEO: K. Morohoshi, EVP   Tel: (714) 759-1701   Emp: N/A
    Bus: *Automotive design research.*   Fax:(714) 759-0377   %FO: 60

    NEW UNITED MOTOR MFG., INC,
    45500 Fremont Blvd, Fremont, CA 94538
    CEO: I. Itoh, Pres.   Tel: (510) 498-5648   Emp: 2600
    Bus: *Mfr. automobiles.*   Fax:(510) 770-4010   %FO: 50

    TOYOTA MOTOR CORPORATE SERVICES OF NA INC.
    9 West 57th Street, New York, NY 10019
    CEO: T. Nagaya, Pres.   Tel: (212) 223-0303   Emp: N/A
    Bus: *Imp./sale motor vehicles.*   Fax:(212) 759-7670   %FO: 100

    TOYOTA MOTOR MFG. INDIANA, INC.
    20 Nothwest Third Street, Evansville, IN 47713
    CEO: S. Okamoto, Pres.   Tel: (812) 433-5400   Emp: 250
    Bus: *Mfr. pick-up trucks.*   Fax:(812) 433-5450   %FO: 100

TOYOTA MOTOR MFG, INC.
1001 Cherry Blossom Way, Georgetown, KY   40324
CEO: M. Kitano, Pres.   Tel: (502) 868-2000   Emp: N/A
Bus: *Mfr./sale automobiles and parts.*   Fax:(502) 868-2008   %FO: 100

TOYOTA MOTOR SALES USA, INC.
19001 South Western Avenue, Torrance, CA   90509
CEO: Y. Ishizaka, Pres.   Tel: (310) 618-4000   Emp: 3200
Bus: *Mktg./distribution motor vehicles.*   Fax:(310) 618-7802   %FO: 100

TOYOTA TECHNICAL CENTER USA INC.
1410 Woodridge, Ann Arbor, MI   48105
CEO: M. Masaki, Pres.   Tel: (313) 995-2600   Emp: 346
Bus: *Automobile testing, research and information*   Fax:(313) 995-5139   %FO: 100
gathering.

• TOYOTA TSUSHO CORPORATION
7-23 Meieki 4-chome, Nakamura-ku, Nagoya 450, Japan
CEO: Keiji Nogami, Pres.   Tel: 81-52 5845000   Emp: 2000
Bus: *Iron & steel, non-ferrous metals, machinery,*   Fax:81-52 5845037
vehicles, energy, textiles, gen. merchandise,
chemicals, insurance services & products.

TOYOTA TSUSHO AMERICA, INC
437 Madison Avenue, New York, NY   10022
CEO: Senji Fujita, Pres.   Tel: (212) 418-0100   Emp: 250
Bus: *Import/export and domestic trading.*   Fax:(212) 752-3914   %FO: 100

• TSUBAKIMOTO CHAIN COMPANY
4-1 Terauchi 2-chome, Toyonaka-Shi, Osaka 560, Japan
CEO: Tomoichi Urabe, Chrm.   Tel: 81-6-862-2329   Emp: 3000
Bus: *Mfr. chain and power transmission products and*   Fax:81-6-862-8516
material handling systems.

TSUBAKI CONVEYOR OF AMERICA, INC.
138 Davis Street, PO Box 710, Portland, TN   37148-0710
CEO: Akio Yaguchi, Pres.   Tel: (615) 325-9221   Emp: 130
Bus: *Mfr. material handling systems.*   Fax:(615) 325-2442   %FO: 100

• TSUKAMOTO SOGYO COMPANY, LTD.
4-2-15 Ginza, Chuo-ku, Tokyo, Japan
CEO: Seishiro Tsukamoto, Pres.   Tel: 81-3-535-3211   Emp: N/A
Bus: *Steel and iron product trading.*   Fax:N/A

MONTECITO COUNTRY CLUB
P O Box 1170, Santa Barbara, CA   93102
CEO: Seishiro Tsukamoto, Pres.   Tel: (805) 969-3216   Emp: N/A
Bus: *Golf and country club.*   Fax:(805) 565-3906   %FO: 100

● **TSUMURA & COMPANY**
12-7 Nibancho, Chiyoda-ku, Tokyo 102, Japan
CEO: Hachizaemon Kazama, Pres.　　Tel: 81-3-3221-0001　Emp: 2478
Bus: *Mfr. pharmaceutical products, bath additives,*　Fax:81-3-3221-5282
toiletries, and cosmetics.

　TSUMURA INTERNATIONAL INC.
　300 Lighting Way, Secaucus, NJ 07096-1578
　CEO: Dennis M. Newnham, Pres. & CEO　　Tel: (201) 223-9000　Emp: 500
　Bus: *Mfr. fragrances, children's toiletries, luxury*　Fax:(201) 223-8280　%FO: 100
　bath products, home fragrances.

　TSUMURA INTERNATIONAL INC.
　1000 Valley Park Drive, Shakopee, MN 55379
　CEO: Koji Okada, Vice Chrm.　　Tel: (612) 496-4700　Emp: N/A
　Bus: *Mfr. fragrances, children's toiletries, luxury*　Fax:(612) 496-4703　%FO: 100
　bath products, home fragrances.

● **UBE INDUSTRIES LTD.**
UBE Building, 3-11, Higashi-shinagawa, 2-chome, Shinagawa-ku, Tokyo, Japan
CEO: Maomi Nagahiro, Pres.　　Tel: 81-3-5460-3311　Emp: 6025
Bus: *Petrochemicals, chemicals, cement, construction*　Fax:81-3-5460-3388
materials and machinery, coal, and plant
engineering services.

　UBE INDUSTRIES (AMERICA) INC.
　666 Fifth Avenue, New York, NY 10103
　CEO: Nobuyuki Takahashi, Pres.　　Tel: (212) 765-5865　Emp: 12
　Bus: *Export of UBE Group products and import of*　Fax:(212) 765-5263　%FO: 100
　raw materials to Japan.

● **UCHIDA MANUFACTURING COMPANY, LTD.**
7-7 Higashi Shinbo, Sanjyo City, Niigata Prefect 955, Japan
CEO: Tsutomu Uchida, Pres.　　Tel: 81-632-2111　Emp: 2400
Bus: *Mfr. kerosene heaters, A/C, humidifiers, machine*　Fax:81-66892
tools.

　CORONA USA CORPORATION
　2050 Center Ave., #450, Fort Lee, NJ 07024
　CEO: J. Kataoka, Pres　　Tel: (201) 592-0123　Emp: 10
　Bus: *Import mfr. kerosene heaters, humidifiers, A/C.*　Fax:(201) 592-8848　%FO: 100

　UCHIDA OF AMERICA CORPORATION
　3535 Del Amo Blvd., Torrance, CA 90503
　CEO: A. Fugisawa, Pres.　　Tel: (310) 793-2200　Emp: N/A
　Bus: *US representative office.*　Fax:(310) 793-2210　%FO: 100

- **UNISIA JECS CORPORATION**
  1360 Onna, Atsugi-shi, Kanagawa-ken 243, Japan
  CEO: Hiro Yoshii, Pres.   Tel: 81-462 258050   Emp: 8000
  Bus: *Automotive component supplier.*   Fax:81-462 213326

  > **ZUA AUTOPARTS, INC.**
  > 5750 McEver Road, Oakwood, GA   30566
  > CEO: Gary Collar, Pres.   Tel: (770) 967-2000   Emp: 132
  > Bus: *Mfr. power steering pumps (see joint parent:*   Fax:(770) 967-0827   %FO: 100
  >   *ZF FRIEDRICHSHAVEN AG, Germany).*

- **UNITIKA LTD.**
  4-68 Kitakyutaro-machi, Higashi-ku, Osaka, Japan
  CEO: Masaaki Katsu, Pres.   Tel: 81-6-281-5225   Emp: N/A
  Bus: *Mfr. fibers, textiles, plastics.*   Fax:81-6-281-5834

  > **UNITIKA AMERICA CORP.**
  > 666 Fifth Avenue, 14th Fl., New York, NY   10036
  > CEO: Fumio Ohama, Pres.   Tel: (212) 765-3760   Emp: N/A
  > Bus: *Export/import textiles, fibers, plastics.*   Fax:(212) 765-3771   %FO: 100

- **M. WATANABE & COMPANY, LTD.**
  2-16 Nihonbashi-Muromachi, 4-chome, Chuo-ku, Tokyo 103, Japan
  CEO: Masaki Kusuhara, Pres.   Tel: 81-3-3241-9162   Emp: N/A
  Bus: *Mfr. steel and brass tubing.*   Fax:N/A

  > **WACOM CORPORATION**
  > 146 Red School House Road, Spring Valley, NY   10977
  > CEO: Hisao Takahashi, Pres.   Tel: (914) 735-1302   Emp: N/A
  > Bus: *Wholesale non-metallic minerals.*   Fax:(914) 735-3940   %FO: 100

- **YAMAHA CORP**
  10-1 Nakazawa-cho, Hamamatsu, Shizuoka-Pref 430, Japan
  CEO: Seisuke Ueshima, Pres.   Tel: 81-53-460-2850   Emp: 9900
  Bus: *Mfr. musical instruments, audio products, household*   Fax:81-53-456-1107
      & sporting goods, metal products, furniture &
      recreational equipment.

  > **YAMAHA CORP OF AMERICA**
  > 6600 Orangethorpe Avenue, Buena Park, CA   90620
  > CEO: Noriyuki Egawa, Pres.   Tel: (714) 522-9011   Emp: 425
  > Bus: *Distribution musical instruments & products;*   Fax:(714) 522-9350   %FO: 100
  >   *pianos, organs & computer chips.*

  > **YAMAHA ELECTRONICS CORP. USA**
  > 6600 Orangethorpe Avenue, Buena Park, CA   90620-1396
  > CEO: Kenji Iida, Pres.   Tel: (714) 522-9105   Emp: 37
  > Bus: *Distribution home audio equipment..*   Fax:(714) 670-0108   %FO: 100

YAMAHA MUSIC MANUFACTURING INC.
100 Yamaha Park, Thomaston, GA   30286

CEO: Yoshi Ishikawa, Pres.	Tel: (404) 647-9601 Emp: 195
Bus: *Mfr. pianos & organs.*	Fax:(404) 647-8936 %FO: 100

YAMAHA MUSICAL PRODUCTS
PO Box 7271, Grand Rapids, MI   49512

CEO: Kenji Sone, EVP	Tel: (616) 940-4900 Emp: 190
Bus: *Mfr. musical instruments.*	Fax:(616) 949-7721 %FO: 100

YAMAHA SYSTEMS TECHNOLOGY
100 Century Centre Ct., Ste. 800, San Jose, CA   95112

CEO: Tokumasa Ishimoto, Pres.	Tel: (408) 467-2300 Emp: N/A
Bus: *Mfr. CDR & computer chips.*	Fax:(408) 437-9741 %FO: 100

• YAMAICHI SECURITIES COMPANY, LTD.
4-1 Yaesu 2-chome, Chuo-ku, Tokyo 101, Japan

CEO: Shoji Saotome, Chrm.	Tel: 81-3-5541-1111 Emp: N/A
Bus: *Securities trading, broker/dealer, investment research and management services.*	Fax:81-3-3552-6366

YAMAICHI ASSET MANAGEMENT
2 World Trade Center, #9800, New York, NY   10048

CEO: Mitsuru Ueda, Pres.	Tel: (212) 466-6830 Emp: 50
Bus: *Investment management services.*	Fax:(212) 839-0772 %FO: 100

YAMAICHI FINANCIAL SERVICES INC
2 World Trade Center, #9800, New York, NY   10048

CEO: Ryosuke Matsushima, SVP	Tel: (212) 524-8341 Emp: 50
Bus: *Financial services.*	Fax:(212) 524-7359 %FO: 100

YAMAICHI INTL (AMERICA) INC
2 World Trade Center, #9650, New York, NY   10048

CEO: Shuzo Kobayashi, Chrm.	Tel: (212) 524-1200 Emp: 256
Bus: *Securities trading, broker/dealer, investment research and management services.*	Fax:(212) 390-8815 %FO: 100

• YAMAKA SHOTEN LTD.
Izumi-Cho, Toki-Shi, Gifu Pref, Japan

CEO: Kosuke Kato, Pres.	Tel: 81-61-5725-43111 Emp: 700
Bus: *Mfr. dinnerware.*	Fax:N/A

INTERNATIONAL CHINA COMPANY, INC.
131 Seaview Drive, Secaucus, NJ   07094

CEO: Kenichi Kato, Pres.	Tel: (201) 864-9641 Emp: 50
Bus: *Wholesale/distribute dinnerware.*	Fax:(201) 864-4579 %FO: 100

● **YAMAMOTOYAMA CO LTD.**
5-2 Nihonbashi 2-chome, Chuo-ku, Tokyo 103, Japan
CEO: Kahei Yamamoto, Pres.   Tel: 81-3 3278-4479   Emp: 800
Bus: *Tea and dried seaweed.*   Fax:81-3 3278-0704

    YAMAMOTO OF ORIENT INC.
    122 Voyager Street, Pomona, CA   91768
    CEO: Hisayuki Nakagawa, Pres.   Tel: (909) 594-7356   Emp: 100
    Bus: *Tea, dried seaweed, real estate investments.*   Fax:(909) 595-5849   %FO: 100

● **YAMATO TRANSPORT CO.MPANY, LTD.**
16-10 Ginza 2-chome, Chuo-ku, Tokyo 104, Japan
CEO: Koji Miyauchi, Pres.   Tel: 81-3-3541-3411   Emp: 61775
Bus: *Door-to-door parcel delivery services, moving &*   Fax:81-3-35423887
freight forwarding services.

    YAMATO CUSTOMS BROKERS USA INC
    147-39 175th St, #218, Jamaica, NY   11434
    CEO: Makoto Sato, Pres.   Tel: (718) 917-7972   Emp: N/A
    Bus: *Customs brokers.*   Fax:(718) 656-6534   %FO: 100

    YAMATO CUSTOMS BROKERS USA, INC.
    920 North Dillon Drive, Wood Dale, IL   60191
    CEO: Yoshifumi Hirai, Pres.   Tel: (630) 595-8114   Emp: N/A
    Bus: *Custom brokers. U.S. headquarters.*   Fax:(630) 595-9532   %FO: 100

    YAMATO TRANSPORT USA, INC.
    19-26 Hazen Street, Flushing, NY   11370
    CEO: Makoto Sato, Pres   Tel: (718) 204-8800   Emp: 240
    Bus: *Moving & freight forwarding.*   Fax:(718) 204-8381   %FO: 100

● **YAMAZAKI BAKING CO., LTD.**
2-4- Iwamoto-cho 3-chome, Chiyoda-ku, Tokyo 101, Japan
CEO: Nobuhiro Iijima, Pres.   Tel: 81-3-3864-3111   Emp: 20000
Bus: *Wholesale and retail bakery products.*   Fax:81-3-3864-3109

    VIE DE FRANCE YAMAZAKI, INC.
    2070 Chain Bridge Road, Suite 500, Vienna, VA   22182-2536
    CEO: Chisato Hashimoto, Pres.   Tel: (703) 442-9205   Emp: 1000+
    Bus: *Wholesale Baked goods & bakery, café*   Fax:(703) 821-2695   %FO: 100
    restaurant operations.

• **YOKOHAMA RUBBER COMPANY**
36-11 Shimbashi 5-chome, Minato-ku, Tokyo 105, Japan
CEO: Kazuo Motoyama, Pres.   Tel: 81-3-5400-4531   Emp: 10814
Bus: *Mfr. automotive/aerospace/industrial rubber*   Fax:81-3-5400-4570
products.

    YOKOHAMA TIRE CORPORATION
    601 South Acadia, Fullerton, CA   92631
    CEO: Yasuo Tominaga, Pres.   Tel: (714) 870-3800   Emp: 1200
    Bus: *Wholesale tires.*   Fax:(714) 870-3899   %FO: 100

• **YUASA CORPORATION**
12-11 Higashi Shimbashi 2-chome, Minato-ku, Tokyo 105, Japan
CEO: Teruhisa Yuasa, Pres.   Tel: 81-3-5742-7801   Emp: 10000
Bus: *Mfr. batteries.*   Fax:81-3-5742-7835

    YUASA-EXIDE INC.
    2366 Bernville Road, Reading, PA   19605-9457
    CEO: P. Michael Ehlerman, CEO   Tel: (610) 208-1991   Emp: 2500
    Bus: *Mfr./distribute batteries.*   Fax:(610) 208-1807   %FO: 86.5

• **YUASA TRADING COMPANY, LTD.**
13-10 Nihonbashi-Oden Macho, Chuo-ku, Tokyo 103, Japan
CEO: Juichiro Yokoyama, Pres.   Tel: 81-3-265-4411   Emp: 450
Bus: *Import and export of general merchandise.*   Fax:81-3-263-4820

    YUASA TRADING COMPANY (AMERICA) INC.
    150 East 52nd Street, New York, NY   10022
    CEO: Shugi Innove, Pres.   Tel: (212) 751-3800   Emp: 13
    Bus: *Import/sales/distribution of general*   Fax:(212) 751-3831   %FO: 100
    merchandise.

• **ZERIA PHARMACEUTICAL COMPANY, LTD.**
10-11 Nihonbashi Kobuma-cho, Chuo-Ku, Tokyo 103, Japan
CEO: Sachiaki Ibe, Pres.   Tel: 81-3-3663-2351   Emp: 1550
Bus: *Mfr. pharmaceuticals.*   Fax:81-3-3663-4503

    ZERIA USA, INC.
    278 South Healy Avenue, Scarsdale, NY   10583
    CEO: Elio R. Loo, Dir.   Tel: (914) 285-9085   Emp: 2
    Bus: *Sales/distribution of pharmaceuticals.*   Fax:(914) 285-9085   %FO: 100

Jordan

- **ARAB BANK, PLC.**
  P.O. Box 950545, Amman, Jordan
  CEO: Abbul Majeed-Shoman, Pres.   Tel: 962-6-638161   Emp: N/A
  Bus: *Commercial banking services.*   Fax:N/A

  ARAB BANK PLC
  520 Madison Avenue, 2nd Floor, New York, NY   10022
  CEO: Nofal S. Barbar, EVP   Tel: (212) 715-9700   Emp: N/A
  Bus: *Commercial banking services.*   Fax:(212) 593-4632   %FO: 100

- **ROYAL JORDANIAN AIRLINES**
  Housing Bank Complex, Amman 11193, Jordan
  CEO: Basel Jardaneh, Chrm. & CEO   Tel: 962-6-672872   Emp: 5249
  Bus: *Commercial air transport services.*   Fax:962-6-672527

  ROYAL JORDANIAN AIRLINES
  JFK International Airport Bldg., Jamaica, NY   11430
  CEO: Basel Jardaneh, Pres.   Tel: (718) 656-6030   Emp: N/A
  Bus: *International commercial air transport services.*   Fax:(718) 244-1821   %FO: 100

  ROYAL JORDANIAN AIRLINES
  535 Fifth Avenue, New York, NY   10017
  CEO: Taha Abutaha, Reg. Dir.   Tel: (212) 949-0060   Emp: N/A
  Bus: *International commercial air transport services.*   Fax:(212) 949-0488   %FO: 100

Korea

- **ANAM GROUP**
280-8, Sungsudong 2-ka, Seoul, Korea
CEO: Joojin Kim, CEO   Tel: 82-2-460-5114   Emp: 7629
Bus: *Assembly of semiconductor devices.*   Fax:82-2-465-2067

    AMKOR ELECTRONICS INC
    Goshen Corporate Park,1345 Enterprise Drive, Westchester, PA   19380
    CEO:John Boruch, Pres.   Tel: (610) 431-9600   Emp: 50
    Bus: *Sale/distribution of semiconductor devices.*   Fax:(610) 431-5881   %FO: 100

- **ASIANA AIRLINES**
10-1, 2-Ka, Hoehyun-Dong, Chung-Gu, Seoul, Korea
CEO: Sam Koo Park, Pres.   Tel: 82-2-774-4000   Emp: 49
Bus: *Air transport services.*   Fax:82-2-758-8009

    ASIANA AIRLINES
    3530 Wilshire Blvd., Ste. 145, Los Angeles, CA   90010
    CEO:K. S. Park, VP   Tel: (213) 365-4500   Emp: N/A
    Bus: *International air transport services.*   Fax:(213) 365-9630   %FO: 100

    ASIANA AIRLINES
    88 Kearny Street, Ste. 1450, San Francisco, CA   94108
    CEO:I. S. Park, CEO   Tel: (415) 249-4200   Emp: 18
    Bus: *International air transport services.*   Fax:(415) 986-0653   %FO: 100

    ASIANA AIRLINES
    1800 Century Blvd., Ste. 575, Marietta, GA   30345
    CEO:S. Kim, Mgr.   Tel: (404) 634-0018   Emp: N/A
    Bus: *International air transport services.*   Fax:(404) 634-0706   %FO: 100

    ASIANA AIRLINES
    540 Madison Avenue, 14th Fl., New York, Ny   10022
    CEO:J. Lee, Mgr.   Tel: (212) 318-9200   Emp: 100
    Bus: *International air transport services.*   Fax:(212) 317-1212   %FO: 100

- **AUK CORPORATION**
802-12 Sinheung-Dong, Iri-Si, Chunbuk, Korea
CEO: Ki Jung Lee, Pres.   Tel: 653-835-7111   Emp: N/A
Bus: *Mfr. transistors.*   Fax:653-835-2681

    AUK AMERICA
    2101 East Broadway Road, Suite #7, Tempe, AZ   28282
    CEO:M. K. Hong, CEO   Tel: (602) 966-3558   Emp: N/A
    Bus: *Transistors.*   Fax:(602) 966-6998   %FO: 100

● **AURORA TRADING CORPORATION**
Aurora Bldg., 385-10, Kil-Dong, Kangdong-Gu, Seoul, Korea
CEO: Heui-Yul Noh, Pres.   Tel: 82-2-483-7731   Emp: N/A
Bus: *Develops and manufactures plush toys (stuffed*   Fax:82-2-484-9228
animals).

    A&A PLUSH, INC.
    1611 Kona Drive, Compton, CA   90220
    CEO: Kwang-Sik Im, Pres.   Tel: (310) 631-0700   Emp: 36
    Bus: *Develops and manufactures plush toys (stuffed* Fax:(310) 631-0865   %FO: 100
    animals).

● **THE BANK OF KOREA**
110 Namdaemoon-ro, 3-Ga, Joong-ku, Seoul 100-794, Korea
CEO: Kyung-Shik Lee, Governor   Tel: 82-2-759-4114   Emp: N/A
Bus: *Central banking; regulatory agency of the*   Fax:82-2-759-4060
commercial banks; sets the nation's monetary policy.

    THE BANK OF KOREA
    780 Third Ave., 23rd Fl., New York, NY   10017
    CEO: Jae-Joon Park, Chief Rep.   Tel: (212) 759-5121   Emp: N/A
    Bus: *Central banking, economic research.*   Fax:(212) 758-6563   %FO: 100

● **BANK OF SEOUL**
10-1 2-Ka, Namdaemoon-ro, Chung-ku, Seoul 100-746, Korea
CEO: H. H. Sohn, Pres.   Tel: 82-2-774-0428   Emp: 10000
Bus: *Commercial banking services.*   Fax:82-2-756-6389

    BANK OF SEOUL
    280 Park Avenue, 24th Fl., West Bldg., New York, NY   10017
    CEO: Keum S. Moon, Gen.Mgr.   Tel: (212) 687-6160   Emp: 30
    Bus: *International banking services.*   Fax:(212) 818-1721   %FO: 100

● **BYUCKSAN ENGINEERING & CONSTRUCTION CO.**
13-25, Yoido-Dong, Youngdeungpo-Ku, Seoul, Korea
CEO: H. Kim, Pres.   Tel: 82-2-767-5100   Emp: N/A
Bus: *Construction and real estate development.*   Fax:82-2-780-1217

    BACCO, INC.
    3303 Wilshire Blvd., Ste. 300, Los Angeles, CA   90010
    CEO: Joon H. Lee, Mgr.   Tel: (213) 386-6979   Emp: N/A
    Bus: *Construction and real estate development.*   Fax:(213) 386-6828   %FO: 100

● **CHEIL COMMUNICATIONS, INC.**
50 Ulchi-Ro, 1st Street, Chung-Gu, Seoul, Korea
CEO: K. Yoon, Pres.   Tel: 82-2-724-0250   Emp: N/A
Bus: *Worldwide advertising agency.*   Fax:82-2-724-0190

    CHEIL COMMUNICATIONS America, Inc.
    105 Challenger Road, Ridgefield Park, NJ   07660
    CEO: S. Chung, Pres.   Tel: (201) 229-6050   Emp: 30
    Bus: *Advertising & marketing services.*   Fax:(201) 229-6058   %FO: 100

● **CHO YANG SHIPPING CO., LTD.**
85-3 Cheong-Ahm Bldg., Seosomoon-Dong, Chung-Gu, Seoul, Korea
CEO: J. I. Park, Pres.   Tel: 82-2-3708-6000   Emp: N/A
Bus: *International shipping & transportation.* Fax:82-2-37086900

    CHO YANG (AMERICA), INC.
    301 Route 17 North, 16th Fl., Rutherford, NJ   07070
    CEO: S. Bae, Pres.   Tel: (201) 896-2700   Emp: 100
    Bus: *International shipping & transportation.* Fax:(201) 896-6760   %FO: 100

● **CHO-HUNG BANK, LTD.**
14, 1-Ga Namdaemoon-Ro, Chung-Gu, Seoul, Korea
CEO: C. H.M. Woo, CEO   Tel: 82-2-733-2000   Emp: N/A
Bus: *Commercial banking services.*   Fax:82-2-732-0835

    CHO HUNG BANK
    601 California St., Ste. 1502, San Francisco, CA   94108
    CEO: Yeo J. Yun, Mgr.   Tel: (415) 788-7850   Emp: 20
    Bus: *International commercial banking services.* Fax:(415) 788-3412   %FO: 100

    CHO HUNG BANK
    10 S. Wacker Drive, Ste. 1850, Chicago, IL   60606
    CEO: J. R. Lee, Mgr.   Tel: (312) 993-2700   Emp: 15
    Bus: *International commercial banking services.* Fax:(312) 993-2710   %FO: 100

    CHO-HUNG BANK LTD
    320 Park Avenue, New York, NY   10021
    CEO: Soo-Young Cho, Mgr.   Tel: (212) 935-3500   Emp: 40
    Bus: *International commercial banking services.* Fax:(212) 355-2231   %FO: 100

    CHO-HUNG BANK OF NY
    241 Fifth Avenue, New York, NY   10016
    CEO: Won Moon Sang, Mgr.   Tel: (212) 679-7900   Emp: 30
    Bus: *International commercial banking services.* Fax:(212) 447-9069   %FO: 100

• **COMMERCIAL BANK OF KOREA LTD.**
111-1, 2-Ga, Namdaemoon-Ro, Chung-Ku, 100-092 Seoul, Korea
CEO: S. H. Kim, Pres.   Tel: 82-2-775-0050   Emp: N/A
Bus: *Commercial banking services.*   Fax:82-2-7549203

    COMMERCIAL BANK OF KOREA
    230 W. Monroe St., Ste. 1400, Chicago, IL   60606
    CEO:H, Jung, Mgr.   Tel: (312) 580-0020   Emp: 15
    Bus: *Banking services.*   Fax:(312) 580-1983   %FO: 100

    COMMERCIAL BANK OF KOREA
    245 Park Avenue, New York, NY   10167
    CEO: Young Suk Kim, Gen.Mgr..   Tel: (212) 949-1900   Emp: 25
    Bus: *Banking services.*   Fax:(212) 490-7146   %FO: 100

    KOREA COMMERCIAL BANK OF NEW YORK
    1250 Broadway, New York, NY   10001
    CEO:Lsrk Bok Choi, Pres.   Tel: (212) 244-1500   Emp: 25
    Bus: *International commercial banking services.* Fax:(212) 736-5929   %FO: 100

• **COSCO MUSIC SYSTEMS CO., LTD.**
64 Jangsi-Dong, Chongro-Gu, Seoul, Korea
CEO: K. J. Park   Tel: 82-2-278-5333   Emp: N/A
Bus: *Consumer electronic goods, karaoke software and*   Fax:82-2-267-8723
data development.

    COSCO MUSIC SYSTEMS, INC.
    10240 North 31st Avenue, Phoenix, AZ   85051
    CEO:Mr. T. H. Kim, Mgr.   Tel: (602) 906-0100   Emp: N/A
    Bus: *Consumer electronic goods, karaoke software* Fax:(602) 906-0000   %FO: 100
    and data development.

• **DADA CORP.**
Dada Bldg., 769-9 Yeoksam-Dong, Kangnam-Gu, Seoul, Korea
CEO: B. Park, Pres.   Tel: 82-2-538-4271   Emp: N/A
Bus: *Mfr. stuffed toys and hats.*   Fax:82-2-538-0113

    INKO HEADWEAR, INC.
    12350 S. W. 132nd Court, Ste. 210, Miami, FL   33186
    CEO: S. B. Park, Pres.   Tel: (305) 234-9644   Emp: 5
    Bus: *Hats and stuffed toys.*   Fax:(305) 234-9258   %FO: 100

● **DAERIM CORPORATION**
482-2, Bangbae-Dong, Seocho-Gu, Seoul, Korea
CEO: C. Oh, Pres.   Tel: 82-2-3470-6000   Emp: N/A
Bus: *Trade and manufacturing fishery.*   Fax:82-2-523-8900

    ALASKA TRAWL FISHERIES, INC.
    100 Second Avenue South, Ste. 200, Edmonds, WA 98020
    CEO:C. Oh, Pres.   Tel: (206) 771-6164   Emp: 75
    Bus: *Exporter of fish.*   Fax:(206) 771-4653   %FO: 100

● **DAEWOO ELECTRO COMPONENTS**
543 Dangjung-Dong, Kunpo-Si, Dyunggi-Do, Korea
CEO: D.C. Seo, Pres.   Tel: 82-2-7686077   Emp: N/A
Bus: *Fly-back transformers.*   Fax:82-2-7686096

    DAEWOO ELECTRO COMPONENTS, YUMA
    1595 First Avenue, Suite B, Yuma, AZ   85364
    CEO:Kyoung-Duek Kim, Manager   Tel: (520) 539-7265   Emp: N/A
    Bus: *Fly-back transformers.*   Fax:(520) 539-7265   %FO: 100

● **DAEWOO HEAVY INDUSTRIES, LTD.**
1 Aju-Dong, Kuje-Si, Kungnam, Korea
CEO: Young G. Shin, Pres.   Tel: 558-680-2114   Emp: N/A
Bus: *Research & development for auto and heavy*   Fax:558-680-4030
    machinery industries.

    SUTEX CORP.
    14 Brent Drive, Hudson, MA   01749
    CEO:H. S. Shin, Mgr.   Tel: (508) 562-4461   Emp: 8
    Bus: *R&D company specializing in sheet metal*   Fax:(508) 562-9385   %FO: 100
    supplies for auto industry and heavy
    machinery.

● **DAEWOO INTERNATIONAL CORP.**
541 Namdaemun-ro 5-Ga, Chung-Gu, Seoul, Korea
CEO: B. H. Kang, Pres.   Tel: 82-2-759-2114   Emp: N/A
Bus: *Aerospace, electronics/auto parts, textile.*   Fax:82-2-609-2233

    DAEWOO CORPORATION
    1055 West Victoria Street, Compton, CA   90220
    CEO:T. S. Park, Manager   Tel: (310) 884-5800   Emp: 23
    Bus: *Electronics/auto parts, aerospace, textile.*   Fax:(310) 669-2020   %FO: 10

    DAEWOO INT'L CORP. MIAMI
    5200 Blue Lagoon Drive, Ste. 770, Miami, FL   33126
    CEO:H. Choi, Manager   Tel: (305) 267-0091   Emp: 2
    Bus: *Electronic products; heavy machinery.*   Fax:(305) 267-0016   %FO: 100

DAEWOO INTERNATIONAL (America) CORP.
85 Challenger Road, Ridgefield Park, NJ   07660
CEO: S. Kim, Pres.   Tel: (201) 229-4500   Emp: 150
Bus: *Importing/exporting trading services; sale of*   Fax:(201) 440-2244   %FO: 100
       industrial & consumer products.

DAEWOO INTERNATIONAL CORP.
3206-3206 North Kennicott Road, Arlington Heights, IL   60004
CEO: Y. H. Park, Pres.   Tel: (847) 590-9800   Emp: 5
Bus: *Auto parts, electronics, textiles.*   Fax:(847) 590-9814   %FO: 100

DAEWOO INTERNATIONAL CORP.
2120 Hutton Drive, Ste. 800, Carrollton, TX   75006
CEO: Y. Kim, Mgr.   Tel: (972) 481-1616   Emp: 3
Bus: *Clothing garments, footware; electronics.*   Fax:(214) 481-1620   %FO: 100

DAEWOO INTERNATIONAL CORP.
2855 Coolidge Highway, Troy, MI   48084
CEO: II. M. Yeom, Mgr.   Tel: (248) 649-0003   Emp: 6
Bus: *Auto parts.*   Fax:(248) 649-0130   %FO: 100

● **DAI YANG METAL**
94-121 Youngdeunpo-Dong, Youngdeungpo-Gu, Seoul, Korea
CEO: S. T. Kang, Pres.   Tel: 82-2-6756751   Emp: N/A
Bus: *Manufacture of stainless steel tubes*   Fax:82-2-6784061

    OCEAN METAL CORP.
    227 North Sunset Avenue, City of Industry, CA   91744
    CEO: H. B. Choi, Manager   Tel: (818) 333-0160   Emp: 12
    Bus: *Sales of stainless steel tubes/coils.*   Fax:(818) 336-1702   %FO: 100

● **DONGKUK STEEL MILL CO., LTD.**
50 Suha-Dong, Chung-Gu, Seoul, Korea
CEO: S. D. Chang, Pres.   Tel: 82-2-317-1052   Emp: N/A
Bus: *Galvanized coil and sheet, steel scrap, slab, plate,*   Fax:82-2-317-1391
       pipe and tubing.

    DONGKUK INT'L INC.
    19750 Magellan Drive, Torrance, CA   90502
    CEO: Joo Pyo Chae, Manager   Tel: (310) 523-9595   Emp: N/A
    Bus: *Galvanized Coil and sheet/steel scrap, slab,*   Fax:(310) 523-9599   %FO: 100
       plate, pipe, and tubing.

    DONGKUK INTERNATIONAL
    460 Bergen Blvd.., Palisades Park, NJ   07650
    CEO: M. H. Chung, Pres.   Tel: (201) 592-8600   Emp: 35
    Bus: *Steel importing & exporting.*   Fax:(201) 592-8795   %FO: 100

● **THE EXPORT-IMPORT BANK OF KOREA**
16-1 Yoido-Dong, Youngdeungpo-Ku, Seoul 150-606, Korea
CEO: Heon-Sang Moon, Pres.　　　　　　　　Tel: 82-2-784-1021　　Emp: 600
Bus: *Commercial banking services.*　　　　　Fax:82-2-784-1030

　　　THE EXPORT-IMPORT BANK OF KOREA
　　　460 Park Avenue, 20th Fl., New York, NY　10022
　　　CEO: Mr. Rhee, Manager　　　　　　　　Tel: (212) 355-7280　　Emp: 5
　　　Bus: *Banking research & liaison.*　　　　Fax:(212) 308-6106　　%FO: 100

● **GOLDSTAR CO., LTD.**
20 Yoido-Dong, Young dungpo-Gu, Seoul 150-721, Korea
CEO: Hun Jo Lee, Vice Chrm.　　　　　　　Tel: 82-2-787-1114　　Emp: 40000
Bus: *Mfr. consumer electronics.*　　　　　　Fax:82-2-787-690

　　　GOLDSTAR USA INC
　　　1000 Sylvan Ave, Englewood Cliffs, NJ　07632
　　　CEO: Pyung Won Suh, Pres　　　　　　　Tel: (201) 816-2000　　Emp: 125
　　　Bus: *Mfr./sale/service consumer electronics.*　Fax:(201) 816-0636　　%FO: 100

● **HAITAI INTERNATIONAL, INC.**
C.P.O. Box 4488, Seoul, Korea
CEO: Mr. C. W. Yoo, Pres.　　　　　　　　Tel: 82-2-3270-1600　　Emp: 85
Bus: *Wholesaler/exporter of frozen concentrated orange*　Fax:82-2-3701-7573
　　　juice (Sunkist), wheat, beans, livestock.

　　　HAI TAI AMERICA, INC.
　　　7227 Telegraph Road, Montebello, CA　90640
　　　CEO: T. K. Min, Pres.　　　　　　　　Tel: (213) 724-7337　　Emp: N/A
　　　Bus: *Grocery Goods, agricultural products, fresh*　Fax:(213) 724-7373　　%FO: 100
　　　　fruits and fruit juices, grains and confectionery
　　　　goods.

● **HANIL BANK LTD.**
130 2-Ga Namdaemoon-Ro, Chung-Gu, Seoul, Korea
CEO: Kwan Woo Lee, Pres.　　　　　　　Tel: 82-2-259-6114　　Emp: N/A
Bus: *Commercial banking services.*　　　　Fax:N/A

　　　HANIL BANK LTD
　　　399 Park Avenue, New York, NY　10022
　　　CEO: Yong S. Kang, Manager　　　　　Tel: (212) 355-6440　　Emp: 12
　　　Bus: *Banking services.*　　　　　　　Fax:(212) 644-0282　　%FO: 100

　　　HANIL SECURITIES COMPANY
　　　One World Trade Center, New York, NY　10048
　　　CEO: N/A　　　　　　　　　　　　　Tel: (212) 912-0787　　Emp: N/A
　　　Bus: *Securities broker/dealer services.*　Fax:　　　　　　　　%FO: 100

● **HANIL SYNTHETIC FIBER IND. CO., LTD.**
191, 2-Ga, Hanggang-Ro, Yongsan-Gu, Seoul, Korea
CEO: Yong Ku Kim, Pres.   Tel: 82-2-791-1041   Emp: N/A
Bus: *Yarns & piece goods.*   Fax:82-2-791-1122

    HANIL TRADING CORP.
    501 Seventh Avenue, Ste. 1500, New York, NY   10018
    CEO: K. I. Hwang, Manager   Tel: (212) 869-1600   Emp: 5
    Bus: *Sweaters, shirts, fabrics, yarns*   Fax:(212) 869-1065   %FO: 100

● **HANJIN ENGINEERING & CONSTRUCTION CO., LTD.**
546-1 Kuui-Dong, Swangjin-Gu, CPO Box 2034, Seoul, Korea
CEO: Y. J. Kim, Manager   Tel: 82-2-450-8114   Emp: N/A
Bus: *General contracting, home building & developing;*   Fax:82-2-454-1154
      inflight catering

    HACOR, INC.
    11220 Hindry Avenue, Los Angeles, CA   90045
    CEO: N/A   Tel: (310) 645-9011   Emp: 140
    Bus: *General contracting, home building &*   Fax:(310) 645-9110   %FO: 100%
      developing; inflight catering.

● **HANJIN SHIPPING COMPANY, LTD.**
Hanjin Shipping Bldg., 25-11, Yoido Dong, Youngdeungpo-Ku, Yoido, S. Korea
CEO: Sooho Cho, Pres.   Tel: 82-2-3770-6114   Emp: 4000
Bus: *Containerized international shipping and cargo*   Fax:82-2-3770-6746
     transport.

    HANJIN SHIPPING COMPANY, LTD.
    444 West Ocean Blvd., Long Beach, CA   90807
    CEO: D. S. Park, Mgr.   Tel: (562) 499-4500   Emp: 400
    Bus: *Containerized shipping.*   Fax:(562) 491-0128   %FO: 100

    HANJIN SHIPPING COMPANY, LTD.
    80 Route 4 East, Ste. 490, Paramus, NJ   07652
    CEO: H. T. Hwang, Exec. V.P.   Tel: (201) 291-4600   Emp: 430
    Bus: *Cargo transport, containerized systems.*   Fax:(201) 291-9393   %FO: 100

    HANJIN SHIPPING COMPANY, LTD.
    2015 Spring Road, Ste. 650, Oak Brook, IL   60521
    CEO: T. H. Ahn, Mgr.   Tel: (630) 472-1051   Emp: 50
    Bus: *Import/export services.*   Fax:(630) 472-0073   %FO: 100

    HANJIN SHIPPING COMPANY, LTD.
    2000 Powers Ferry Road, Ste. 405, Marietta, GA   30067
    CEO: E. S. Kwon, Mgr.   Tel: (770) 952-0233   Emp: 45
    Bus: *Marine transportation.*   Fax:(770) 952-0118   %FO: 100

HANJIN SHIPPING COMPANY, LTD.
150 Wood Road, Ste. 306, Braintree, MA   02184
CEO: Young Kim, Mgr.   Tel: (617) 849-3130   Emp: 5
Bus: *Ocean shipping.*   Fax:(617) 849-1539   %FO: 100

● **HANWHA MACHINERY CO., LTD.**
#1 Changgyo-Dong, Chung-Gu, Seoul, Korea
CEO: J. B. Song, Pres   Tel: 82-2-729-3423   Emp: N/A
Bus: *Automotive heavy equipment products, i.e..,*   Fax:82-2-729-3420
cylindrical rollers, pins and dowels.

    UNIVERSAL BEARINGS, INC.
    431 North Birkey Drive, Bremen, IN   46506
    CEO: Mr. W. Yang, Pres.   Tel: (219) 546-2261   Emp: 150
    Bus: *Automotive heavy equipment products, i.e.,*   Fax:(219) 546-5085   %FO: 100
    cylindrical rollers, pins and dowels.

● **HUNG CHANG PRODUCTS CO., LTD.**
Hongje Bldg, 301-2 Hongje-dong, Seodaemun-ku, Seoul, Korea
CEO: Chung Soo Sohn, Pres.   Tel: 82-2-395-8601   Emp: 1200
Bus: *Mfr. electronic testing instruments & components,*   Fax:82-2-395-5381
telecommunications equipment..

    HC ELECTRONICS AMERICA INC.
    154 Veterans Dr, Northvale, NJ   07647
    CEO: Sin Gon Kim, Pres   Tel: (201) 784-8400   Emp: 13
    Bus: *Distribution/sale, electronic testing*   Fax:(201) 784-8548   %FO: 100
    instruments.

● **HYOSUNG LTD.**
21-1, Seosomun-Dong, Chung-Gu, Seoul, Korea
CEO: Moo Hyun Won, Pres.   Tel: 82-2-771-1100   Emp: N/A
Bus: *Tires, steel products, electronics, fabrics/yarns, and*   Fax:82-2-754-9983
musical instruments.

    HYOSUNG AMERICA, INC.
    One Penn Plaza, Suite 2220, New York, NY   10119
    CEO: Mr. Y. Park, Pres   Tel: (212) 736-7100   Emp: 33
    Bus: *Agricultural products, chemicals, electronics,*   Fax:(212) 563-1323   %FO: 100%
    textiles and garments.

    HYOSUNG AMERICA, INC.
    18000 Studebaker Road, Ste. 550, Cerritos, CA   90703
    CEO: Y. H. Suk, Manager   Tel: (562) 809-5050   Emp: 47
    Bus: *Steel products, electronics, fabrics/yarns,*   Fax:(562) 809-5251   %FO: 100
    musical instruments.

- **HYUNDAI ELECTRONICS INDUSTRIES CO., LTD.**
  San 136-1, Ami-Ri, Bubal-Eub, Ichon-Gun, Dyonggi-Do 467-860, Korea
  CEO: M. H. Chung, Pres.   Tel: 82-336-741-0661   Emp: 465
  Bus: *Mfr. electronic devices.*   Fax:82-336-7410737

  > **HYUNDAI ELECTRONICS AMERICA**
  > 3101 North First Street, San Jose, CA   95134
  > CEO: Young H. Kim, Pres.   Tel: (408) 232-8000   Emp: 500
  > Bus: *Sale, marketing and distribution of electronic*   Fax:(408) 232-8101   %FO: 100
  >   *devices.*

- **HYUNDAI MERCHANT MARINE CO., LTD.**
  96 Mukyo-Dong, Chung-Gu, Seoul, Korea
  CEO: S. Y. Park, Pres.   Tel: 82-2-311-5114   Emp: N/A
  Bus: *Marine transportation services.*   Fax:82-2-775-8788

  > **HYUNDAI AMERICA SHIPPING AGENCY**
  > 353 Sacramento Street, San Francisco, CA   94111
  > CEO: Y. S. Im, Mgr.   Tel: (415) 956-3233   Emp: 25
  > Bus: *Marine transportation.*   Fax:(415) 362-5433   %FO: 100

- **HYUNDAI MOTOR CO., INC**
  140-2 Kye-Dong, Chongro-Gu, Seoul, Korea
  CEO: Byung Jae Park, Pres.   Tel: 82-2-746-1114   Emp: 40000
  Bus: *Mfr./sale/service automobiles.*   Fax:82-2-741-0470

  > **HYUNDAI CORP. U.S.A**
  > 300 Sylvan Avenue, englewood Cliffs, NJ   07632
  > CEO: D.S. Han, Pres.   Tel: (201) 816-4000   Emp: N/A
  > Bus: *U.S. headquarters; administrative and trading*   Fax:(201) 816-4036   %FO: 100
  >   *operations.*

  > **HYUNDAI MOTOR AMERICA**
  > 10550 Talbert Avenue, Fountain Valley, CA   92728
  > CEO: M.H. Chun, Pres.   Tel: (714) 965-3000   Emp: N/A
  > Bus: *US headquarters. Mfr./sale automobiles and*   Fax:(714) 965-3816   %FO: 100
  >   *parts.*

  > **HYUNDAI MOTOR AMERICA**
  > 700 North Enterprise Street, Aurora, IL   60504
  > CEO: Yoo I. Lee, Pres.   Tel: (630) 820-3100   Emp: N/A
  > Bus: *Mfr./sale automobiles and parts.*   Fax:(630) 820-7110   %FO: 100

  > **HYUNDAI MOTOR AMERICA**
  > 5075 Venture Drive, Ann Arbor, MI   48108
  > CEO: Mr. O. Ch. Rhee, Mgr.   Tel: (313) 332-4120   Emp: 4
  > Bus: *Mfr./sale automobiles and parts.*   Fax:(313) 332-3711   %FO: 100

HYUNDAI MOTOR AMERICA
1100 Cranbury, South River Road, Jamesburg, NJ 08831
CEO: Kwang Hyun Kim, Pres.   Tel: (609) 395-7000   Emp: 40
Bus: *Mfr./sale automobiles and parts.*   Fax: (609) 395-8602   %FO: 100

HYUNDAI MOTOR AMERICA
240 Thornton Road, Lithia Springs, GA 30057
CEO: K. M. Chang, Manager   Tel: (770) 739-9400   Emp: 30
Bus: *Mfr./sale automobiles and parts.*   Fax: (770) 944-0610   %FO: 100

● **HYUNDAI PRECISION INDUSTRY CO.**
140-2 Kye-Dong, Chongro-Gu, Seoul, Korea
CEO: C. J. Yoo, Pres.   Tel: 82-2-746-1114   Emp: N/A
Bus: *Shipping containers/trailers.*   Fax: 82-2-746-4244

HYUNDAI PRECISION & INDUSTRY CO.
7314 19-Mile Road, Sterling Heights, MI 48314
CEO: J. Lee, Mgr.   Tel: (810) 254-5600   Emp: 6
Bus: *Mfr. industrial materials.*   Fax: (810) 254-5603   %FO: 100

HYUNDAI PRECISION AMERICA, INC.
8880 Rio San Diego, Ste. 600, San Diego, CA 92108
CEO: T. Y. Chung, Pres.   Tel: (619) 574-1500   Emp: 90
Bus: *Manufactures shipping containers/trailers.* Fax: (619) 542-0301   %FO: 100

HYUNDAI PRECISION INDUSTRY CO.
300 Sylvan Avenue, Englewood Cliffs, NJ 07632
CEO: H. Chung, Mgr.   Tel: (201) 816-4000   Emp: 2
Bus: *Container manufacturer.*   Fax: (201) 816-4089   %FO: 100

● **HYUP JIN ENTERPRISES CO LTD.**
470-1 Garibong-Dong, Guro-Gu, Seoul 150-020, Korea
CEO: G. S. Kim, Pres.   Tel: 82-2-869-1921   Emp: 3500
Bus: *Manufacturer of clothing/hunting garments.* Fax: 82-2-863-9049

SAM JIN TRADING INC
701 Palisades Avenue, 2nd Fl., Englewood Cliffs, NJ 07632
CEO: Sang C. Lee, Mgr.   Tel: (201) 461-8181   Emp: N/A
Bus: *Importer of clothing/hunting garments* Fax: (201) 461-6761   %FO: 100

● **INDUSTRIAL BANK OF KOREA**
50, Ulchiro 2-Ga, Chung-Gu, Seoul, Korea
CEO: Seung K. Kim, Pres.   Tel: 82-2-729-6114   Emp: N/A
Bus: *Commercial banking services.*   Fax: 82-2-729-7205

INDUSTRIAL BANK OF KOREA
16 West 32nd Street, New York, NY 10001
CEO: J. H. Lee, Manager   Tel: (212) 268-6363   Emp: 34
Bus: *Commercial banking services.*   Fax: (212) 268-1090   %FO: 100

- **JAMES KOREA CO., LTD.**
227-5 Nowon 3 Ga, Buk-Gu, Taegu, Korea
CEO: K. N. Kim, Pres.   Tel: 82-53-351-9027   Emp: N/A
Bus: *Optical frames & sunglasses; mobile amusement*   Fax:82-53-351-2813
products & inflatable fun houses.

    JAMES EYEWEAR CORP.
    4805 N. W. 79th Avenue, Miami, FL 33166
    CEO: K. N. Kim, Pres.   Tel: (305) 477-6336   Emp: 5
    Bus: *Optical frames & sunglasses; mobile*   Fax:(305) 477-9336   %FO: 100
        amusement products & inflatable fun houses.

- **JINDO CORPORATION**
371-62 Kansan-Dong, Keumchon-Gu, Seoul, Korea
CEO: Young-Jim Kim, Pres.   Tel: 82-2-850-8350   Emp: N/A
Bus: *Shipping containers; fur and leather goods.*   Fax:82-2-864-7678

    JINDO AMERICA, INC.
    165 Chubb Avenue, Lyndhurst, NJ 07071
    CEO: H.S.Ahn, Pres.   Tel: (201) 507-5200   Emp: N/A
    Bus: *Shipping containers; fur and leather goods.*   Fax:(201) 507-5299   %FO: 100

- **KANGWON INDUSTRIES LTD.**
6, 2-Ka, Shinmoon-ro, Chongro-ku, Seoul, Korea
CEO: Do Won Chung, Pres.   Tel: 82-2-730-7111   Emp: 6500
Bus: *Mfr. iron & steel products, coal mining, concrete*   Fax:82-2-739-1104
products, aggregates processor.

    SAMPYO AMERICA CORPORATION
    1 Bridge Plaza North, Suite 125, Fort Lee, NJ 07024
    CEO: J.W. Choi, Manager   Tel: (201) 944-3980   Emp: N/A
    Bus: *Sale/distribution of iron, steel & concrete*   Fax:(201) 944-3617   %FO: 100
        products.

- **KIA MOTORS CORPORATION**
15-21 Yoido-Dong, Youngdeungo-G, Seoul, Korea
CEO: Young-Kwi Kim, Pres.   Tel: 82-2-788-1114   Emp: N/A
Bus: *Automotive company.*   Fax:82-2-788-1888

    KIA MOTOR AMERICA, INC.
    2 Cromwell, PO Box 52410, Irvine, CA 92619
    CEO: Hong-Rae Park, Pres.   Tel: (714) 470-7000   Emp: 170
    Bus: *Automotive company.*   Fax:(714) 470-2800   %FO: 100

• KOLON INTERNATIONAL CORP.

Kolon Bldg., 45 Mookyo Dong, Chung-Gu, Seoul 100-170, Korea

CEO: O-Sang Kwon, Pres.	Tel: 82-2-311-8114	Emp: 2500
Bus: *General international trading.*	Fax:82-2-3117988	

KOLON AMERICA INC

Empire State Bldg., 350 Fifth Ave., Ste. 5211, New York, NY 10118

CEO: Chul Hol Yoo, Pres	Tel: (212) 736-0120	Emp: 15
Bus: *Trade company - importing and exporting.*	Fax:(212) 736-0933	%FO: 100

KOLON CALIFORNIA CORPORATION

17211 South Valley View Ave., Cerritos, CA 90703

CEO: M. H. Yoo, Pres.	Tel: (562) 802-9007	Emp: 40
Bus: *International trading.*	Fax:(562) 802-1425	%FO: 100

KOLON SCEN'A INC.

3 Sperry Road, Fairfield, NJ 07004

CEO: C. Y. Lee, Pres.	Tel: (973) 575-2550	Emp: 15
Bus: *Video tape, polyester & nylon films.*	Fax:(973) 575-1332	%FO: 100

• KORAM BANK

1 Kong Pyung Dong, Chongro-ku, Seoul, Korea

CEO: N/A	Tel: N/A	Emp: N/A
Bus: *Commercial banking services.*	Fax:N/A	

KORAM BANK

40 East 52nd Street, New York, NY 10022

CEO: Yong Soo Ahn, Mgr.	Tel: (212) 888-8858	Emp: N/A
Bus: *International banking services.*	Fax:(212) 888-9852	%FO: 100

• KOREA COMMERCIAL BANK OF NY

111-1, 2-Ka Namdaemoon-ro, Chung-ku, Seoul, Korea

CEO: J. Chung, Pres.	Tel: 82-2-775-0050	Emp: N/A
Bus: *Commercial banking services.*	Fax:82-2-754-7773	

KOREA COMMERCIAL BANK OF NY

1250 Broadway, New York, NY 10001

CEO: L.B. Choi, Pres.	Tel: (212) 244-1500	Emp: N/A
Bus: *International commercial banking services.*	Fax:(212) 736-5929	%FO: 100

• KOREA DATA SYSTEM CO., LTD.

170, Gongdan-Dong, Kumi-Si, Kyungbuk-Do, Korea

CEO: J. Koh, Pres.	Tel: 82-546-461-3121	Emp: N/A
Bus: *Personal computer monitors*	Fax:82-546-461-8720	

KDS USA

12300 Edison Way, Garden Grove, CA 92841

CEO: Jong-Wug Kim	Tel: (714) 379-5599	Emp: 50
Bus: *PC Monitors.*	Fax:(714) 379-5595	%FO: 100

- **THE KOREA DEVELOPMENT BANK**
10-2 Kwanchol-Dong, Chongno-gu, Seoul 110-748, Korea
CEO: Shi Hyung Kim, Pres.   Tel: 82-2-398-6114   Emp: 2700
Bus: *Commercial banking services.*   Fax:82-2-733-4768

> **KOREA ASSOCIATED SECURITIES, INC.**
> 1 World Trade Center, Ste. 8121, New York, NY   10048
> CEO: Kyou Won Oh, Pres.   Tel: (212) 775-0730   Emp: N/A
> Bus: *Securities broker/dealer.*   Fax:(212) 432-7111   %FO: 89.42

> **THE KOREA DEVELOPMENT BANK**
> 320 Park Avenue, Suite 31, New York, NY   10022
> CEO: Yong Y. Won, President   Tel: (212) 688-7686   Emp: 6
> Bus: *International commercial banking services.*   Fax:(212) 421-5028   %FO: 100

- **KOREA ELECTRIC POWER CORPORATION**
167 Samsung-Dong, Kangnam-Gu, Seoul, Korea
CEO: Chong-Hun Rieh, Pres.   Tel: 82-2-550-3114   Emp: N/A
Bus: *Nuclear power plant equipment.*   Fax:82-2-550-5981

> **KOREA ELECTRIC POWER CORP.**
> 270 Sylvan Avenue, Englewood Cliffs, NJ   07632
> CEO: J. Choo, Manager   Tel: (201) 894-8855   Emp: 20
> Bus: *Expediting power plant construction*   Fax:(201) 894-8977   %FO: 100
>   *equipment; inspection and shipping.*

- **KOREA EXCHANGE BANK**
181 2-Ga Ulchiro Chung-Gu, Seoul, 100-793, Korea
CEO: M. S. Chang, Pres.   Tel: 82-2-729-8000   Emp: N/A
Bus: *International commercial banking service.*   Fax:82-2-775-9814

> **CALIFORNIA KOREA BANK**
> 3530 Wilshire Blvd., Ste. 1800, Los Angeles, CA   90010
> CEO: Chang Woo Lee, Pres.   Tel: (213) 385-0909   Emp: N/A
> Bus: *Commercial banking services.*   Fax:(213) 386-6869   %FO: 100

> **KOREA EXCHANGE BANK**
> 600 University Street, Seattle, WA   98101
> CEO: Y, Huh, Mgr.   Tel: (206) 622-7821   Emp: 30
> Bus: *International commercial banking services.*   Fax:(206) 343-5874   %FO: 100

> **KOREA EXCHANGE BANK**
> 181 West Madison St., Ste. 2100, Chicago, IL   60602
> CEO: H. Lee, Mgr.   Tel: (312) 372-7890   Emp: 30
> Bus: *International commercial banking services.*   Fax:(312) 372-7839   %FO: 100

> **KOREA EXCHANGE BANK**
> 800 Brickell Avenue, 7th Fl., Miami, FL   33131
> CEO: Kwan Keun Yoo, Gen. Mgr.   Tel: (305) 530-0077   Emp: 18
> Bus: *International commercial banking services.*   Fax:(305) 539-8502   %FO: 100

KOREA EXCHANGE BANK
460 Park Avenue, 14th Fl., New York, NY   10022
CEO: Jaeboo Kim, General Mgr. Tel: (212) 838-4949 Emp: 80
Bus: *International commercial banking services.* Fax:(212) 752-8551 %FO: 100

KOREA EXCHANGE BANK
49 West 33rd Street, New York, NY   1110001
CEO: Lee Jong Hoon, Mgr. Tel: (212) 736-6575 Emp: 25
Bus: *International commercial banking services.* Fax:(212) 736-8655 %FO: 100

KOREA EXCHANGE BANK
136-40 39th Avenue, Flushing, NY   11354
CEO: Choong Goo Cho, Gen. Mgr. Tel: (718) 463-3000 Emp: 22
Bus: *International commercial banking services.* Fax:(718) 767-3762 %FO: 100

● **THE KOREA EXPRESS CO.,LTD.**
58-12 Seosomun-Dong, Chung Gu, Seoul, Korea
CEO: Y. H. Kim, Pres. Tel: 82-2-753-2141 Emp: 6500
Bus: *Air/sea international freight forwarding services.* Fax:82-2-753-3751

   KOREA EXPRESS USA INC
   901 Castle Road, Secaucus, NJ   07094
   CEO: Sang K. Kim, Pres. Tel: (201) 863-7505 Emp: 70
   Bus: *Air/sea international freight forwarding.* Fax:(201) 863-5036 %FO: 100

   KOREA EXPRESS USA, INC.
   709 East Walnut Street, Carson, CA   90746
   CEO: Joong Ku Lee, Manager Tel: (310) 532-3333 Emp: 20
   Bus: *Air and sea international freight forwarding* Fax:(310) 532-9350 %FO: 100

   KOREA EXPRESS USA, INC. SAN FRANCISCO
   451 Eccles Avenue, South San Francisco, CA   94080
   CEO: Jung-Soo Kim, Manager Tel: (415) 583-2440 Emp: 10
   Bus: *Air and sea international freight forwarding* Fax:(415) 583-4403 %FO: 100

● **KOREA FIRST BANK**
#100 Konpyung-Dong, Chang-gu, Seoul, 110-702, Korea
CEO: K. S. Sheen, Pres. Tel: 82-2-733-0070 Emp: N/A
Bus: *Commercial banking services.* Fax:82-2-720-1301

   KOREA FIRST BANK
   205 North Michigan Avenue, Chicago, IL   60601
   CEO: Jae Chang Kim, Gen. Mgr. Tel: (312) 819-2525 Emp: 20
   Bus: *Commercial banking services.* Fax:(312) 819-2535 %FO: 100

   KOREA FIRST BANK
   29 West 30th Street, New York, NY   10001
   CEO: Jae Gwan Song, Gen. Mgr. Tel: (212) 279-2790 Emp: 25
   Bus: *Commercial banking services.* Fax:(212) 564-3278 %FO: 100

KOREA FIRST BANK
410 Park Avenue, 8th Fl., New York, NY   10022
CEO: H. S. Chung, Pres.   Tel: (212) 593-2525   Emp: 25
Bus: *Commercial banking services.*   Fax:(212) 319-0255   %FO: 100

• KOREA LONG TERM CREDIT BANK
15-22 Yoido-Dong, Youngdeungpo-Gu, Seoul 150-757, Korea
CEO: Kwang Hyun Kim, Pres. & CEO   Tel: 82-2-782-0111   Emp: 1,200
Bus: *Domestic and international banking.*   Fax:82-2-786-3479

KOREA LONG TERM CREDIT BANK
565 Fifth Avenue, 24th Fl., New York, NY   10017
CEO: Kang M. Lee, Gen. Mgr.   Tel: (212) 697-6100   Emp: 11
Bus: *Trade finance, loans & securities investments.*   Fax:(212) 697-1456   %FO: 100

• KOREAN AIR
41-3 Seosomun-Dong, Chung-Gu, C.P.O.Box 864,Seoul, 100-110, Korea
CEO: Y. H. Cho, Pres.   Tel: 82-2-751-7114   Emp: 10000
Bus: *International passenger & cargo air transport*   Fax:82-2-484-5757

KOREAN AIR LINES
230 North Michigan Avenue, Chicago, IL   60601
CEO: Byung K. Jun, Mgr.   Tel: (312) 558-9306   Emp: 45
Bus: *International air carrier.*   Fax:(312) 368-4423   %FO: 100

KOREAN AIR LINES
8700 N. Stemmons, Ste. 110, Dallas, TX   75247
CEO: S. Lee, Mgr.   Tel: (214) 637-2444   Emp: 20
Bus: *International air carrier.*   Fax:(214) 905-6014   %FO: 100

KOREAN AIR LINES
1154 15th Street, N.W., Washington, DC   20005
CEO: Y. Moon, Mgr.   Tel: (202) 785-3644   Emp: 20
Bus: *International air carrier.*   Fax:(202) 785-3762   %FO: 100

KOREAN AIR LINES
251 Post Street, Ste. 500, San Francisco, CA   94108
CEO: Moon H. Son, Manager   Tel: (415) 433-4290   Emp: 42
Bus: *International passenger & cargo air transport.*   Fax:(415) 956-1712   %FO: 100

KOREAN AIR LINES
609 Fifth Avenue, New York, NY   10017
CEO: H. Kim, Mgr.   Tel: (212) 326-5000   Emp: 50
Bus: *International air carrier.*   Fax:(212) 326-5090   %FO: 100

KOREAN AIR (CARGO SALES OFFICE)
Bldg. #260, JFK International Airport, Jamaica, NY   11430
CEO: Chung Oh, Pres.   Tel: (718) 632-5554   Emp: 40
Bus: *Air transportation service.*   Fax:(718) 632-5595   %FO: 100

KOREAN AIR (PASSENGER SALES)
1813 Wilshire Blvd., Los Angeles, CA   90057

CEO: J. J. Choi, Manager

Tel: (213) 484-5700   Emp: 75

Bus: *Service, passenger sales.*

Fax:(213) 484-5757   %FO: 100

• KOREAN CARGO CONSOLIDATORS, INC.
Rm. 202, 382-1 Dangsan-Dong, 6-Ga, Youngdeungpo-Gu, Seoul, Korea

CEO: Jung Sik Suh, Pres.

Tel: 82-2-632-2691   Emp: N/A

Bus: *Freight forwarder services.*

Fax:82-2-632-2695

KCC TRANSPORT SYSTEMS
15151 South Main Street, Gardena, CA   90247

CEO: Arthur Lee, Manager

Tel: (310) 323-3500   Emp: 55

Bus: *Freight forwarder.*

Fax:(310) 323-2249   %FO: 100

• KOREANA HOTEL CO., LTD.
61-1-Ga, Tapyung-Ro, Chung-Gu, Seoul, Korea

CEO: Yong H. Bang, Pres.

Tel: 82-2-730-9911   Emp: N/A

Bus: *Hotel and restaurant service*

Fax:82-2-734-0665

RADISSON WILSHIRE PLAZA HOTEL
3515 Wilshire Boulevard, Los Angeles, CA   90010

CEO: Young S. Kim, Pres.

Tel: (213) 381-7411   Emp: 200

Bus: *Hotel and restaurant service.*

Fax:(213) 386-7379   %FO: 100

• KUMHO TIRE COMPANY, LTD.
Asiana Bldg. 10-1, 2-Ga, Hoehyun-Dong, Chung-Gu, Seoul, 100-052, Korea

CEO: I. Nam, Pres.

Tel: 82-2-758-1114   Emp: N/A

Bus: *Passenger, truck, and bus tires*

Fax:82-2-758-1515

KUMHO TIRE USA, INC.
14605 Miller Avenue, Fontana, CA   92336

CEO: Jong G. Kahng, Pres.

Tel: (909) 428-3300   Emp: 48

Bus: *Passenger car, truck and bus tires.*

Fax:(909) 428-3989   %FO: 100

• KUNYOUNG CO., LTD.
13-6 Yoido-Dong, Youngdeungpo-Gu, Seoul, Korea

CEO: Mr. K. S. Ahn, Pres.

Tel: 82-2-369-7207   Emp: N/A

Bus: *Real estate development/investment; active wear clothing*

Fax:82-2-369-7444

K. YOUNG, INC.
3701 Wilshire Blvd, Ste. 1050, Los Angeles, CA   90010

CEO: S. H. Uhm, Pres.

Tel: (213) 385-8797   Emp: 40

Bus: *Real estate development/investment; active wear clothing.*

Fax:(213) 385-5138   %FO: 100

- **KYUNG DONG INDUSTRIAL CO., LTD.**
570-10 Gajwa-Dong, Seo-Gu, Inchon, 404-250, Korea
CEO: Y.J. Choy, Pres.   Tel: 82-32-5708-580   Emp: 2500
Bus: *Manufacturer of stainless steel flatware/cookware,*   Fax:82-32-577-0081
     non-stick aluminum skillets.

    ESTIA CORP
    350 Gotham Pkwy., Carlstadt, NJ   07072
    CEO: Yang W. Kim, Pres.   Tel: (201) 939-7077   Emp: 10
    Bus: *Distribution/sale of stainless steel*   Fax:(201) 939-4925   %FO: 100
         flatware/cookware, non-stick aluminum skillets.

- **LG ELECTRONICS**
20 Youido-Dong, Young dungpo-Gu, Seoul, 150-721, Korea
CEO: John Koo, Pres.   Tel: 82-2-3777-5114   Emp: 35,000
Bus: *Manufacture/sell home electronics, home*   Fax:82-2-3777-3400
     appliances, computer office automation and
     magnetics.

    LG ELECTRONICS
    2021 Archibald Avenue, Ontario, CA   91761
    CEO: Y. Chang, Manager   Tel: (909) 930-2300   Emp: N/A
    Bus: *Electronic products.*   Fax:(909) 947-9899   %FO: 100

    LG ELECTRONICS ALABAMA, INC.
    201 James Record Road, Huntsville, AL   35824
    CEO: Kevin J. Kim, Pres.   Tel: (205) 772-0628   Emp: 185
    Bus: *Manufacturer of consumer electronic products.*   Fax:(205) 772-0623   %FO: 100

    LG ELECTRONICS U.S.A., INC.
    1000 Sylvan Avenue, Englewood Cliffs, NJ   07632
    CEO: Johnny Koo, Pres.   Tel: (201) 816-2000   Emp: 105
    Bus: *Home appliance, monitor, CD-ROM and multi-*   Fax:(201) 816-0636   %FO: 100
         media sales.

    LG ELECTRONICS, INC.
    6133 North River Road, Ste. 1100, Rosemont, IL   60018
    CEO: J. Lim, Mgr.   Tel: (847) 692-4500   Emp: 30
    Bus: *Electronic products.*   Fax:(847) 692-4501   %FO: 100

    LG ELECTRONICS, MIAMI
    5255 N. W. 87th Avenue, Miami, FL   33178
    CEO: C. Choi, Manager   Tel: (305) 477-1882   Emp: 5
    Bus: *Sale of electronic products.*   Fax:(305) 471-0715   %FO: 100

    ZENITH ELECTRONICS CORPORATION
    1000 Milwaukee Avenue, Glenview, IL   60025-2493
    CEO: Peter S. Willmott, Pres.   Tel: (847) 391-7000   Emp: N/A
    Bus: *Mfr./marketing/distribution video products.*   Fax:(847) 391-7523   %FO: 100

● **LG INFORMATION & COMMUNCIATIONS, LTD.**
20 Yoido-Dong, Youngdeungp-Gu, Seoul, Korea
CEO: Jang H. Chung, Pres.   Tel: 82-2-3777-2753   Emp: N/A
Bus: *Wireless communication devices*   Fax: N/A

    LG INFORMATION & COMMUNCIATIONS, LTD.
    1000 Sylvan Avenue, Englewood Cliffs, NJ   07632
    CEO: B. Choi, Mgr.   Tel: (201) 816-2072   Emp: 2
    Bus: *Wireless communication devices.*   Fax: (201) 816-2073   %FO: 100

    LG INFORMATION & COMMUNCIATIONS, LTD.
    9725 Sexinton Road, Ste.140, San Diego, CA   92121
    CEO: E. Y. Yu, Manager   Tel: (619) 622-9922   Emp: 40
    Bus: *Wireless communication devices.*   Fax: (619) 623-9922   %FO: 100

● **LG INTERNATIONAL**
LG Twin Towers, 20 Yoido-Dong, Youngdungpo-Gu, Seoul, 150-721, Korea
CEO: Su-Whan Park, Pres.   Tel: 82-2-3773-1114   Emp: 150,000
Bus: *Chemicals & energy, electronics, machinery &*   Fax: 82-2-3773-2200
    metals, trade & services, finance and public
    services/sports & other fields

    LG INTERNATIONAL AMERICA
    1000 Sylvan Avenue, Englewood Cliffs, NJ   07632
    CEO: Cha Keuk (Charles) Koo, Pres. & CEO   Tel: (201) 816-2000   Emp: 1200
    Bus: *Chemicals & Energy, Electronics, Machinery*   Fax: (201) 816-0604   %FO: 100
        & Metals, Trade & Services, Finance, and
        Public Services/Sports & Other Fields.

    LG INTERNATIONAL, INC.
    13013 East 166th Street, Cerriotos, CA   90703
    CEO: Y. K. Jin, Pres.   Tel: (562) 483-8000   Emp: 35
    Bus: *Import/export; general trading.*   Fax: (562) 483-8080   %FO: 100

● **LG SEMICON LTD.**
1 Hyangjeong-Dong, Chungju-Si, Chungbuk, Korea
CEO: Chung-Hwan Mun, Pres.   Tel: 82-431-270-3114   Emp: N/A
Bus: *Sales of computer memory products*   Fax: N/A

    LG SEMICON AMERICA, INC.
    3003 North First Street, San Jose, CA   95134
    CEO: Yu Sig Kang, Pres.   Tel: (408) 432-5000   Emp: 50
    Bus: *Sales of computer memory products.*   Fax: (408) 432-6067   %FO: 100

• PACIFIC CORPORATION
181 Hangang-Ro, 2-Ga, Yongsan-Gu, Seoul, Korea
CEO: Neung-Hee Lee, Pres   Tel: 82-2-709-5114   Emp: N/A
Bus: *Cosmetics, toiletries, and hair care products*   Fax:82-2-709-6029

PACIFIC CORPORATION OF AMERICA
145 West Commercial Avenue, Moonachie, NJ   07074
CEO: J. Lee, Mgr.   Tel: (201) 507-4900   Emp: 15
Bus: *Cosmetics, toiletries and hair care products.*   Fax:(201) 507-1758   %FO: 100

PACIFIC COSMETICS, INC.
2610 West Olympic Blvd., Los Angeles, CA   90006
CEO: Hong Jin Lee, Manager   Tel: (213) 737-3333   Emp: 23
Bus: *Cosmetics, toiletries and hair care products.*   Fax:(213) 737-2022   %FO: 100

• POHANG IRON & STEEL CO., LTD
1 Koedong-Dong, Kyongsangbuk-Do, Pohang City 790-600, Korea
CEO: Mal Soo Cho, Pres.   Tel: 82-562-220-0114   Emp: 22622
Bus: *Manufacturer of steel products.*   Fax:82-562-220-4499

POHANG IRON & STEEL CO., LTD
1800 K Street, NW, Washington, DC   20006
CEO: Syon-Yong Shin, Chief Rep.   Tel: (202) 785-5643   Emp: N/A
Bus: *Manufacturer of steel products (cold rolled,*   Fax:(202) 785-5647   %FO: 100
    galvanized sheet, tin plate)

POHANG IRON & STEEL CO., LTD
2530 Arnold Drive, Martinez, CA   94553
CEO: Hoon-Kop Oh, Gen. Mgr.   Tel: (510) 228-9720   Emp: N/A
Bus: *Manufacturer of steel products (cold rolled,*   Fax:(510) 228-9729   %FO: 100
    galvanized sheet, tin plate)

POHANG STEEL AMERICA CO. LTD.
300 Tice Blvd., Woodcliff Lake, NJ   07430
CEO: Ha-Young Aum, Pres.   Tel: (201) 782-9200   Emp: 17
Bus: *Steel sales, investment development, holding*   Fax:(201) 782-9210   %FO: 100
    company.

USS/POSCO INDUSTRIES
900 Loveridge Road, Pittsburg, CA   94565
CEO: John D. Ewing, Pres.   Tel: (510) 439-6300   Emp: N/A
Bus: *Manufacturer of steel products (cold rolled,*   Fax:(201) 782-9210   %FO: 50
    galvanized sheet, tin plate).

● **POONGSAN CO., LTD.**
60-1, 3-Ga, Chungmoo-Ro, Chung-Gu, Seoul, Korea
CEO: H. Chung, Pres.   Tel: 82-2-273-3021   Emp: N/A
Bus: *Copper and metal materials.*   Fax:82-2-273-3835

     PMX INDUSTRIES, INC.
     5300 Willow Creek Drive, Cedar Rapids, IA   52404
     CEO: C. Yoo, Mgr.   Tel: (319) 368-7700   Emp: 260
     Bus: *Copper and metal materials.*   Fax:(319) 368-7701   %FO: 100

● **PUSAN BANK**
25-2, 4-ka Chungand-dove, Chung-ku, Pusan, Korea
CEO: N/A   Tel: N/A   Emp: N/A
Bus: *Commercial banking services.*   Fax:N/A

     PUSAN BANK
     505 Park Avenue, 8th Floor, New York, NY   10022
     CEO: Sung Pyo Hong, Chief Rep.   Tel: (212) 355-2005   Emp: N/A
     Bus: *International banking services.*   Fax:(212) 371-6955   %FO: 100

● **SAMJIN TRADING CO., LTD.**
1140-36, Jegi-Dong, Dongdaimoon-Gu, Seoul, Korea
CEO: C. H. Kang, Pres.   Tel: 82-2-961-5501   Emp: N/A
Bus: *Oriental food, Ramen noodles, canned foods, gift*   Fax:82-2-961-5110
     and kitchenware

     SAMJIN AMERICA, INC.
     49-01 Maspeth Avenue, Maspeth, NY   11378
     CEO: S. Jung, Mgr.   Tel: (718) 894-8383   Emp: 15
     Bus: *Importer of Korean food and gift products.*   Fax:(718) 894-8183   %FO: 100

     SAMJIN AMERICA, INC.
     3345 East Slauson Avenue, Vernon, CA   90058
     CEO: S. K. Lee, Manager   Tel: (213) 622-5111   Emp: 16
     Bus: *Oriental food, Ramen noodles, canned food,*   Fax:(213) 622-5285   %FO: 100
     gift and kitchenware.

● **SAMMI STEEL CO., LTD.**
1004 Daechi 3-Dong, Kangnam-Gu, Seoul, Korea
CEO: Bong Kyu Lee, Pres.   Tel: 82-2-222-4114   Emp: N/A
Bus: *Stainless steel sheet & coil, pipe and wire rods.*   Fax:82-2-563-1291

     SAMMI AL TECH, INC.
     19191 South Vermont Ave., Ste. 590, Torrance, CA   90502
     CEO: K. K. Pyun, Pres.   Tel: (310) 515-1155   Emp: 35
     Bus: *Stainless steel sheet & coil, pipe and wire rods.*   Fax:(310) 633-1333   %FO: 100

- **SAMSUNG CORPORATION**
#250, 2-Ga, Taipyung-ro, Chung-Gu, Seoul, Korea
CEO: C. Shin, Pres.   Tel: 82-2-751-2114   Emp: 2000
Bus: *Imp/export general merchandise.*   Fax:82-2-751-2246

> **SAMSUNG AMERICA INC**
> 105 Challenger Rd, Ridgefield Park, NJ   07660-0511
> CEO: Man Soo Lee, Manager   Tel: (201) 229-5000   Emp: N/A
> Bus: *Imp/export general merchandise*   Fax:(201) 229-5080   %FO: 100

> **SAMSUNG AMERICA, INC.**
> 14251 East Firestone Blvd., La Mirada, CA   90638
> CEO: Nam Yun Cho, Pres.   Tel: (310) 802-2211   Emp: 80
> Bus: *Import/export general merchandise*   Fax:(310) 802-3011   %FO: 100

> **SAMSUNG AMERICA, INC.**
> 2700 NW 87th Avenue, Miami, FL   33172
> CEO: Yunhong Hong, Manager   Tel: (305) 477-6550   Emp: N/A
> Bus: *Latin American headquarters office for*   Fax:(305) 471-9666   %FO: 100
> *products*

> **SAMSUNG AMERICA, INC.**
> 3255-4 Scott Blvd., Ste. 101, Santa Clara, CA   95054
> CEO: S. H. Shin, Manager   Tel: (408) 970-8844   Emp: N/A
> Bus: *Semi-conducting equipment and spare parts*   Fax:(408) 970-9534   %FO: 100

- **SAMSUNG DISPLAY DEVICES CO., LTD.**
2-250, Taepyung-Ro, Chung-Gu, Seoul, Korea
CEO: K. P. Park, Pres.   Tel: 82-2-727-3720   Emp: N/A
Bus: *Computer monitors*   Fax:82-2-727-3219

> **SAMTRON DISPLAY, INC.**
> 18600 Broadwick Street, Rancho Dominquez, CA   90220
> CEO: K. W. Park, Pres.   Tel: (310) 537-7000   Emp: 9000
> Bus: *Mfr.distributor computer monitors.*   Fax:(310) 537-1033   %FO: 100

- **SAMSUNG ELECTRONICS CO., LTD.**
250-2-Ga. Taepyung-Ro, Chung-Gu, Seoul, Korea
CEO: Kwang-Ho Kim, Pres.   Tel: 82-2-727-7114   Emp: N/A
Bus: *Computer memory discs, LCD panels, micro*   Fax:82-2-727-7985
products

> **SAMSUNG ELECTRONICS - LATIN AMERICA HQTRS**
> 8240 N.W. 52nd Terrace, Ste. 418, Miami, FL   33166
> CEO: B. Jung, Manager   Tel:(305) 594-2758   Emp:15
> Bus: *Electronics; camcorders, air-conditioners,* Fax:(305) 594-2143   %FO:100
> *washing machines, refrigerators.*

SAMSUNG SEMICONDUCTOR, INC.
3655 North First Street, San Jose, CA   95234

CEO: Young Rha, Pres.	Tel: (408) 954-7000	Emp: 480
Bus: *Computer memory discs, LCD panels, micro products.*	Fax:(408) 954-7875	%FO: 100

SAMSUNG TELECOMMUNICATIONS AMERICA, INC.
1350 East Newport Center Drive, Ste. 110, Deerfield Beach, FL   33442

CEO: H. Shin, Manager	Tel: (305) 426-4100	Emp: 50
Bus: *Sales & marketing of electronic products.*	Fax:(305) 426-5599	%FO: 100

● SAMSUNG HEAVY INDUSTRIES CO., LTD.
290-15 Daechi-Dong, Kangnam-Gu, Seoul, Korea

CEO: D. W. Lee, Pres.	Tel: 82-2-3458-6323	Emp: N/A
Bus: *Construction equipment.*	Fax:82-2-3458-6362	

SAMSUNG CONSTRUCTION EQUIPMENT AMERICA CORP.
5521 Meadowbrook Court, Rolling Meadows, IL   60008

CEO: C. Chun, Pres.	Tel: (847) 582-1000	Emp: 48
Bus: *Wheel loaders and excavators.*	Fax:(847) 806-9155	%FO: 100

● SEAH STEEL CORPORATION
40-153, Hangang-Ro, 3-Ga, Youngsan-Gu, Seoul, Korea

CEO: W. H. Lee, Pres.	Tel: 82-2-797-1881	Emp: N/A
Bus: *Iron and steel products*	Fax:82-2-797-2462	

PUSAN PIPE AMERICA
9615 South Norwalk Blvd., Ste. B, Santa Fe Springs, CA   90670

CEO: B. J. Lee, Mgr.	Tel: (562) 629-0600	Emp: 13
Bus: *Iron and steel products.*	Fax:(562) 629-9295	%FO: 100

● SEOULBANK
10-1 Namdaemun-no 2-ga Chung-gu, C.P.O. Box 276, Seoul 100-746, Korea

CEO: N/A	Tel: 82-2-771-6000	Emp: N/A
Bus: *Commercial banking services.*	Fax:82-2-756-6389	

SEOULBANK
280 Park Avenue, West Bldg., 24th Fl., New York, NY   10017

CEO: Gil H. Chung, Gen. Mgr.	Tel: (212) 687-6160	Emp: N/A
Bus: *International banking services.*	Fax:(212) 818-1721	%FO: 100

● SHIN MYUNG ELECTRIC MFG. CO., LTD.
Banwoul Industrial Zone 98-IL, 835-4 Wonsie-Dong, Ansan-Si, Dyunggi-Do, Korea

CEO: H. M. Kim, Pres.	Tel: 82-345-495-4978	Emp: N/A
Bus: *Electric motors.*	Fax:82-345-495-4971	

SHIN MYUNG ELECTRIC MFG. CO., LTD.
16607 Valley View Avenue, Cerritos, CA   90703

CEO: H. M. Kim, Manager	Tel: (562) 404-4489	Emp: 300
Bus: *Electric motors.*	Fax:(562) 404-6321	%FO: 100

- **SKC LTD.**
199-15, 2-Ga, Ulchi-Ro, Chung-Gu, Seoul, Korea
CEO: Yong K. Chang, Pres.   Tel: 82-2-3708-5151   Emp: N/A
Bus: *Film and microfilm*   Fax:82-2-752-9088

    SKC AMERICA INC.
    307 North Pastoria Avenue, Sunnyvale, CA   94086
    CEO:Dal J. Yoo, Mgr.   Tel: (408) 739-4170   Emp: N/A
    Bus: *Film and microfilm.*   Fax:(408) 730-9778   %FO: 100

- **SKM LTD.**
216 1-Ga, Kwanghee-Dong, Chung-Gu, Seoul, Korea
CEO: J. W. Chey, Pres.   Tel: 82-2-279-1611   Emp: N/A
Bus: *Professional & consumer audio tapes*   Fax:82-2-275-2144

    SKMA, INC.
    4041 Via Oro Avenue, Long Beach, CA   90810
    CEO:W. K. Lee, Pres.   Tel: (310) 830-6000   Emp: 20
    Bus: *Professional & consumer audio tapes.*   Fax:(310) 830-0646   %FO: 100

- **SSANGYONG CORPORATION**
24-1, 2-Ga, Jeo-Dong, Chung Gu, Seoul 100-748, Korea
CEO: Chong-Won Ahn, Pres.   Tel: 82-2-270-8114   Emp: 1100
Bus: *General trading company.*   Fax:82-2-273-0981

    SSANGYONG (USA) INC.
    115 West Century Road, Paramus, NJ   07652
    CEO:Young Woo Chung, Pres.   Tel: (201) 261-9400   Emp: 40
    Bus: *import/export, general trading company.* Fax:(201) 262-9120   %FO: 100

    SSANGYONG SHIPPING
    601 16th Street, Carlstadt, NJ   07072
    CEO:H. E. Kang, Manager   Tel: (201) 939-1220   Emp: 5
    Bus: *Military cargo freight forwarders*   Fax:(201) 939-2616   %FO: 100

    SSANGYONG SHIPPING
    12101 Western Avenue, Garden Grove, CA   92841
    CEO:Y. S. Choi, Manager   Tel: (714) 901-2138   Emp: 12
    Bus: *Military cargo freight forwarders*   Fax:(714) 379-9701   %FO: 100

- **STC CORPORATION**
32, 2-Ga, Moonrae-Dong, Yungdeungpo-Gu, Seoul, Korea
CEO: J. J. Choi, Pres.   Tel: 82-2-675-0621   Emp: N/A
Bus: *Mfr. packing/masking tape.*   Fax:82-2-675-1595

    AMERICAN TAPE CO.
    300 Lighting Way, Secaucus, NJ   07094
    CEO:I. Choi, Pres.   Tel: (201) 866-7178   Emp: N/A
    Bus: *Sales/distribution of pressure-sensitive tape.* Fax:(201) 866-0178 %FO: 100

STC CORPORATION
317 Kendal Avenue, Marysville, MI   48040
CEO: I.J. Choi, Mgr.   Tel: (810) 364-9000   Emp: N/A
Bus: *Sales/distribution of packing/masking tape.*   Fax:(810) 364-9477   %FO: 100

● **SUNKYONG LTD.**
Sunkyong Bldg., 36-1, 2 Ga, Ulchi-Ro, Chung-Gu, Seoul, Korea
CEO: Syng Jeung Kim, Pres. & CEO   Tel: 82-2-758-2114   Emp: 2000
Bus: *Information & communications; domestic bus;*   Fax:82-2-754-9414
global mktg., bus development; organizing &
financing and natural resources development.

   SUNKYONG AMERICA, INC.
   1025 North Hilltop Drive, Itasca, IL   60143
   CEO: J. K. Choi, Manager   Tel: (630) 250-0061   Emp: 4
   Bus: *Import/export of all products.*   Fax:(630) 250-9317   %FO: 100

   SUNKYONG AMERICA, INC.
   71106 South Avalon Blvd., Carson, CA   90746
   CEO: J. C. Park, Manager   Tel: (310) 527-0400   Emp: 30
   Bus: *Import/export of all products.*   Fax:(310) 527-0410   %FO: 100

   SUNKYONG AMERICA, INC.
   110 East 55 Street, New York, NY   10022
   CEO: James M. Demitrieus, Pres. & CEO   Tel: (212) 906-8000   Emp: 252
   Bus: *Global marketing and project organizing*   Fax:(212) 906-8250   %FO: 100

● **TAE YEUN ELECTRONICS CO., LTD.**
Kasas-Dong, Keumchun-Gu, Seoul, Korea
CEO: S. Y. Cho, Pres.   Tel: 82-2-864-2073   Emp: N/A
Bus: *Manufacturer of walkie-talkies.*   Fax:N/A

   TEKK INC.
   226 Northwest Parkway, Kansas City, MO   64150
   CEO: S. Cho, Mgr.   Tel: (816) 746-1098   Emp: 20
   Bus: *Manufacturer of walkie-talkies.*   Fax:(816) 746-1093   %FO: 100

● **TONG IL INDUSTRIES, CO.**
62 B Sungsu Industrial Zone, Dalsu-Gu, Taegu, Korea
CEO: Jong M. Kim, Pres.   Tel: 82-53-583-3690   Emp: N/A
Bus: *Manufacturer of polyethylene foam*   Fax:82-53-583-3698

   TOILON CORP.
   600 South Etiwanda Avenue, Ontario, CA   91761
   CEO: P. Chang, Manager   Tel: (909) 390-6644   Emp: 20
   Bus: *Manufacturer of polyethylene foam.*   Fax:(909) 390-6641   %FO: 100

• **TRIGEM COMPUTER, INC.**
45-2 Yoido-Dong, Youngdeungpo-Gu, Seoul, Korea
CEO: J. S. Lee, Pres.　　　　　　　　　　　Tel: 82-2-3774-3000　　Emp: N/A
Bus: *Manufacturing and trading*　　　　　　Fax:82-2-786-7554

> **TRIGEM AMERICA CORP.**
> 48400 Fremont Blvd., Fremont, CA　94538
> CEO: H. S. Muk, Manager　　　　　　　　Tel: (510) 770-8787　　Emp: 80
> Bus: *Manufacturing and trading..*　　　　　Fax:(510) 770-9928　　%FO: 100

• **UNION STEEL MFG. CO., LTD.**
223 Naeja-Dong,Congro-Gu, Seoul 110-053, Korea
CEO: C. W. Lee, Pres.　　　　　　　　　　　Tel: 82-2-732-4111　　Emp: 2000
Bus: *Flat rolled galvanized steel sheets, steel pipes &*　Fax:82-2-732-3263
tubes.

> **UNION STEEL AMERICA, INC.**
> 460 Bergen Blvd., Palisades Park, NJ　07650
> CEO: M. S. Lee, Manager　　　　　　　　Tel: (201) 947-7373　　Emp: 11
> Bus: *Sale of flat rolled galvanized steel sheets, steel*　Fax:(201) 947-3999　　%FO: 100
> *pipes & tubes.*

• **YUKONG LTD.**
26-4, Yoido-Dong, Youngdeung-Po, Seoul, Korea
CEO: H. D. Kim, Pres.　　　　　　　　　　　Tel: 82-2-788-5114　　Emp: N/A
Bus: *Petrochemicals and petroleum.*　　　　Fax:82-2-788-7001

> **YUKONG LTD.**
> 110 East 55 Street, 14th Fl., New York, NY　10022
> CEO: J. Kim, Mgr.　　　　　　　　　　　　Tel: (212) 906-8140　　Emp: 15
> Bus: *Manufacturer of petroleum and*　　　Fax:(212) 906-8149　　%FO: 100
> *petrochemicals.*

> **YUKONG LTD.**
> 1300 Post Oak Blvd., Ste 780, Houston, TX　77056
> CEO: K. Son, Mgr.　　　　　　　　　　　　Tel: (713) 871-1178　　Emp: 8
> Bus: *Manufacturer of petroleum and*　　　Fax:(713) 871-8050　　%FO: 100
> *petrochemicals.*

Kuwait

● **COMMERCIAL BANK OF KUWAIT**
Box 2861, Safat 13029, Kuwait
CEO: David Berry, GenMgr.   Tel: 96-5-241-1001   Emp: N/A
Bus: *Commercial banking services.*   Fax:N/A

    COMMERCIAL BANK OF KUWAIT
    350 Park Avenue, 19th Fl., New York, NY   10022-6022
    CEO: John W. Speiser, Mgr.   Tel: (212) 207-2420   Emp: N/A
    Bus: *International banking services.*   Fax:(212) 935-6563   %FO: 100

● **KUWAIT AIRWAYS CORP.**
International Airport Building, Safat 13004, Kuwait
CEO: Ahmed Al Mishari, Chrm.   Tel: 96-5-434-5555   Emp: 5250
Bus: *Commercial air transport services.*   Fax:96-5-431-4726

    KUWAIT AIRWAYS CORP.
    430 Park Avenue, New York, Ny   10022
    CEO: Ahmed Al Mishari, Chrm.   Tel: (212) 308-5707   Emp: N/A
    Bus: *International air transport.*   Fax:(212) 308-0524   %FO: 100

● **KUWAIT PETROLEUM CORP**
Box 9282, Ahmadi 61003, Kuwait
CEO: Ali Ahmed Al-Baghi, Chrm.   Tel: 96-5-398-5011   Emp: 15000
Bus: *Integrated petroleum company.*   Fax:96-5-398-1030

    SANTA FE INTERNATIONAL CORP.
    5420 LBJ Freeway, #1100, Dallas, TX   75240
    CEO: Sted Garber, Pres.   Tel: (972) 701-7300   Emp: N/A
    Bus: *Oil drilling services.*   Fax:(972) 701-7777   %FO: 100

● **THE NATIONAL BANK OF KUWAIT S.A.K.**
Box 95, Safat 13001, Kuwait
CEO: N/A   Tel: 96-5-242-2011   Emp: N/A
Bus: *Commercial banking services.*   Fax:96-5-2429442

    THE NATIONAL BANK OF KUWAIT S.A.K.
    299 Park Avenue, 17th Floor, New York, NY   10171
    CEO: George Nasra, Gen. Mgr.   Tel: (212) 303-9800   Emp: N/A
    Bus: *International banking services.*   Fax:(212) 319-8269   %FO: 100

● **THE UNITED BANK OF KUWAIT PLC**
PO Box 2616, Safat 17027, Kuwait
CEO: N/A   Tel: 965-243-7981   Emp: N/A
Bus: *General banking services.*   Fax:965-243-7973

    THE UNITED BANK OF KUWAIT PLC
    126 East 56th Street, New York, NY   10022
    CEO: Abdulkader Steven Thomas, Gen.Mgr.   Tel: (212) 906-8500   Emp: N/A
    Bus: *International banking services.*   Fax:(212) 319-4762   %FO: 100

Lebanon

● **BANK AUDI, SAL**
Charles Malek Avenue, St. Nicolas Area, PO Box 11-2560, Beirut, Lebanon
CEO: George Audi, Chrm.　　　　　　　　　　Tel: 961-1-200-250　　　Emp: N/A
Bus: *Commercial banking.*　　　　　　　　　Fax:961-1-200-955

　　　BANK AUDI
　　　200 South Biscayne Blvd., Miami, FL　33131
　　　CEO: Nabil Achkar, Mgr.　　　　　　　　Tel: (305) 373-1300　　Emp: 5
　　　Bus: *International commercial banking.*　　Fax:(305) 373-1303　　%FO: 100

　　　BANK AUDI
　　　19 East 54 Street, New York, NY　10021
　　　CEO: Larry Ayoub, Mgr.　　　　　　　　Tel: (212) 833-1000　　Emp: 60
　　　Bus: *International commercial banking.*　　Fax:(212) 833-1033　　%FO: 100

● **MIDDLE EAST AIRLINES (MEA)**
PO Box 206, Beirut International Airport, Beirut, Lebanon
CEO: Khaled M. Salaam, Chm. & Pres.　　　　Tel: 961-1-822860　　　Emp: N/A
Bus: *Commercial air transport services.*　　　Fax:961-1-629260

　　　MIDDLE EAST AIRLINES
　　　800 Wilcrest Drive, Suite 116, Houston, TX　77042
　　　CEO: Omar Yamout, Rep.　　　　　　　　Tel: (713) 781-3330　　Emp: 3
　　　Bus: *International air transport.*　　　　　Fax:(713) 781-3374　　%FO: 100

　　　MIDDLE EAST AIRLINES
　　　Airport Center, Suite 810,
　　　9841 Airport Blvd., Los Angeles, CA　90045
　　　CEO: Habib Badaro, Dist. Sales Mgr.　　　Tel: (310) 338-9124　　Emp: 3
　　　Bus: *International air transport.*　　　　　Fax:(310) 338-9148　　%FO: 100

　　　MIDDLE EAST AIRLINES
　　　918 16th St. NW, Suite 301, Washington, DC　20006
　　　CEO: Elie Ghostine, Dist. Sales Mgr.　　　Tel: (202) 429-6868　　Emp: 3
　　　Bus: *International air transport.*　　　　　Fax:(202) 223-5959　　%FO: 100

　　　MIDDLE EAST AIRLINES
　　　680 Fifth Avenue, New York, NY　10019
　　　CEO: Emile Mazzawi, Gen. Mgr.　　　　　Tel: (212) 664-7300　　Emp: 18
　　　Bus: *International air transport.*　　　　　Fax:(212) 664-7301　　%FO: 100

　　　MIDDLE EAST AIRLINES
　　　Statler Bldg., 20 Park Plaza, Suite 610, Boston, MA　02116
　　　CEO: Ms. Nina Salaam, Dist. Sales Mgr.　　Tel: (617) 482-7590　　Emp: 3
　　　Bus: *International air transport.*　　　　　Fax:(617) 482-7692　　%FO: 100

Luxembourg

● **ARBED S.A.**
19, Avenue de la Liberté, L-2930 Grand Duchy of Luxembourg, Luxembourg
CEO: Joseph Kinsch, Chrm. & Pres.   Tel: 352-4792-1   Emp: 39500
Bus: *Mfr.. iron and steel.*   Fax:352-4792-2675

    ARBED AMERICAS INC.
    825 Third Avenue, New York, NY   10022
    CEO: Fred Lamesch, CEO   Tel: (212) 940-8000   Emp: N/A
    Bus: *Trading company.*   Fax:(212) 355-2159   %FO: 100

    COLL-TEC INC.
    2100 18th Avenue North, Bessemer, AL   35020
    CEO: David Clutter, Pres.   Tel: (205) 425-5100   Emp: N/A
    Bus: *Trading company*   Fax:(205) 425-7343   %FO: 100

    CONSIDAR INC.
    825 Third Avenue, 35th Fl., New York, NY   10022
    CEO: Mark Kristoff, Pres.   Tel: (212) 940-8070   Emp: N/A
    Bus: *Trading company.*   Fax:(212) 980-1555   %FO: 100

    J&F STEEL CORP.
    3360 West 43 Street, Chicago, IL   60632
    CEO: Jack Schoettert, Pres.   Tel: (312) 927-4600   Emp: N/A
    Bus: *Steel processing and trading.*   Fax:(312) 927-4461   %FO: 100

    SKYLINE STEEL CORP.
    8 Woodhollow Road, Parsippany, NJ   07054
    CEO: David Clutter, VP   Tel: (201) 428-6100   Emp: N/A
    Bus: *Trading company.*   Fax:(201) 428-7399   %FO: 100

    TRADE ARBED INC.
    825 Third Avenue, New York, NY   10022
    CEO: Robert Bortz, Pres.   Tel: (212) 940-8000   Emp: N/A
    Bus: *Marketing of rolled steel products*   Fax:(212) 355-2159   %FO: 100

    TREFILARBED ARKANSAS INC.
    5100 Industrial Drive South, Pine Bluff, AR   71602
    CEO: Edouard Feipel, Pres.   Tel: (501) 247-2444   Emp: N/A
    Bus: *Mfr. of steelcord and reinforcing wire for*   Fax:(501) 247-1622   %FO: 100
        tire/hose industry.

    TREFILARBED INC.
    825 Third Avenue, New York, NY   10022
    CEO: Alfred H. D. Haiblen, Pres.   Tel: (212) 940-3500   Emp: N/A
    Bus: *Marketing of wire products.*   Fax:(212) 355-2159   %FO: 100

● BANQUE ET CAISSE D'EPARGNE DE L'ETAT, LUXEMBOURG
1 & 2, pl de Metz L-2954 Luxembourg, Luxembourg
CEO: Victor Rod, Chrm.   Tel: 352-4015-1   Emp: N/A
Bus: *Government; state and savings bank services.*   Fax:352-4015-2099

BANQUE ET CAISSE D'EPARGNE DE L'ETAT, LUXEMBOURG
712 Fifth Avenue, New York, NY   10022
CEO: Egide Thein, Rep.   Tel: (212) 245-7100   Emp: 2
Bus: *International banking; representative office.*   Fax:(212) 245-7373   %FO: 100

● BANQUE INTERNATIONALE A LUXEMBOURG SA
69, route d' Esch, L-2953 Luxembourg, Luxembourg
CEO: André Roelants, Chrm.   Tel: 352-4590-1   Emp: 2100
Bus: *Commercial banking services.*   Fax:352-4590-2010

BANQUE INTERNATIONALE A LUXEMBOURG SA
405 Lexington Avenue, 54th Fl., New York, NY   10174-5499
CEO: Barbara V. Weidlich, Reg. Rep.   Tel: (212) 972-6219   Emp: 1
Bus: *Banking; representative office*   Fax:(212) 972-6522   %FO: 100

● IMI INVESTMENTS S.A.
8 Avenue de la Liberté, Luxembourg, L-1930, G.D. of Luxembourg
CEO: Luigi Arcuti, Chairman   Tel: 352-4045751   Emp: 140
Bus: *Financial services company.*   Fax:352-290463

IMI FUNDING CORP. (USA)
165 Broadway, New York, NY   10006
CEO: Andrea Rivano, Chairman   Tel: (212) 346-5042   Emp: N/A
Bus: *Financial services.*   Fax:(212) 346-5075   %FO: 100

● MINORCO SA
9 Rue Ste Zithe, L-2763 Luxembourg, Luxembourg
CEO: H. R. Slack, Pres.   Tel: 352-4041101   Emp: N/A
Bus: *Holding company: trading, banking, mining,*   Fax:352-40411020
    industrial operations.

ENGELHARD CORPORATION
101 Wood Avenue, Iselin, NJ   08830
CEO: Orrin Smith, CEO   Tel: (732) 205-5000   Emp: 8300
Bus: *Mfr. specialty chemicals and engineering*   Fax:(732) 321-1161   %FO: 30
    materials for industry; precious metals
    management.

Malaysia

● **BANK NEGARA MALAYSIA**
Jalan Dato'Onn, (P.O. Box 10922), 50929 Kuala Lumpur, Malaysia
CEO: Ahmed Mohd Don, Governor   Tel: 60-3-298-8044   Emp: N/A
Bus: *Government, Central Bank.*   Fax:60-3-291-2990

> **BANK NEGARA MALAYSIA**
> 900 Third Avenue, New York, NY   10022
> CEO: Mazidah Malik, Mgr.   Tel: (212) 888-9220   Emp: N/A
> Bus: *Government & banking services.*   Fax:(212) 755-4561   %FO: 100

● **MALAYAN BANKING BERHAD**
92 Jalan Bandar, P O Box 12010, Kuala Lumpur, Malaysia
CEO: Amirsham Aziz, Mng. Dir.   Tel: 60-3-230-8833   Emp: N/A
Bus: *Commercial banking services*   Fax:60-3-230-2600

> **MALAYAN BANKING BERHAD**
> 400 Park Ave, 9th fl, New York, NY   10022
> CEO: Baharudin Abd Majid, Gen.Mgr..   Tel: (212) 303-1300   Emp: 30
> Bus: *International banking services.*   Fax:(212) 308-0109   %FO: 100

● **MALAYSIA AIRLINES**
MAS Bldg, 33/F, Jalan Sultan Ismail, 50250 Kuala Lumpur, Malaysia
CEO: Tajudin Ramli, Mgn Dir.   Tel: 60-3-2610555   Emp: 19800
Bus: *International commercial air transport.*   Fax:60-3-2613472

> **MALAYSIA AIRLINES SYSTEMS**
> 100 North Sepulveda Blvd., El Segundo, CA   90245
> CEO: Ahmad Fuaad Dahlan, VP Americas   Tel: (310) 535-9288   Emp: 100
> Bus: *International commercial air transport.*   Fax:(310) 535-9088   %FO: 100

> **MALAYSIA AIRLINES SYSTEMS**
> 140 East 45th Street, New York, NY   10170
> CEO: Fred Siems, Sales Mgr.   Tel: (212) 697-8994   Emp: 100
> Bus: *International commercial air transport.*   Fax:(212) 867-0325   %FO: 100

- **OYL INDUSTRIES, BHD.**

PO Box 7072, Seksyen 16, 40702 Shah Alam Selangor, Malaysia

CEO: Tun Dato' Haji Omar Yoke Lin Ong, Chrm.   Tel: 60-3-559-4922   Emp: N/A

Bus: *Investment holding company with subsidiary companies engaged in mfr./mktg./distri./service of heating, ventilation and air conditioning systems and products.*   Fax:60-3-550-3730

McQUAY INTERNATIONAL

13600 Industrial Park Blvd., Minneapolis, MN   55441

CEO: Gerry Boehrs, Pres.   Tel: (612) 553-5330   Emp: N/A

Bus: *Sales/distribution of heating, ventilation and air conditioning systems and products.*   Fax:(612) 553-5008   %FO: 100

- **SIME DARBY BERHAD**

Wisma Sime Darby, 21st Fl., Jalan Raja Laut 50350 Kuala Lumpur, Malaysia

CEO: Tun Ismail bin Mohamed Ali, Chrm.   Tel: 60-3-291-4122   Emp: N/A

Bus: *Holding co. for agriculture, commodities, mfr.; industrial equipment, motor vehicles; real estate, financial services & energy.*   Fax:60-3-298-7398

SANDESTIN RESORTS, INC.

9300 Highway 98W, Destin, FL   32541

CEO: James Rester, Pres.   Tel: (904) 267-8000   Emp: N/A

Bus: *Hotel/tour management.*   Fax:(904) 267-8197   %FO: 100

SIME HEALTH LIMITED

1200 Sixth Avenue South, Seattle, WA   98134

CEO: Chee Keong Chow, VP   Tel: (206) 622-7390   Emp: N/A

Bus: *Health services management company.*   Fax:(206) 622-9872   %FO: 100

Mexico

- **AEROMEXICO**
Paseo de la Reforma 445, 06500 Mexico DF, Mexico
CEO: Alfonso Pasquel, Dir.Gen.   Tel: 52-5-133-4000   Emp: N/A
Bus: *Commercial air transport carrier.*   Fax:52-5-133-4617

     AEROMEXICO
     13405 NW Freeway, Ste. 111, Houston, TX   77040
     CEO:Paul Obermueller, SVP Oper.   Tel: (713) 744-8400   Emp: 300
     Bus: *International commercial air transport carrier.*   Fax:(713) 460-3334   %FO: 100

- **BANCA SERFIN S.A.**
Perferico Sur 3395, Col. Rincon del Pedregal ,14120 Mexico DF , Mexico
CEO: Adolfo Lagos Espinoza, Pres.   Tel: 52-5-257-8000   Emp: N/A
Bus: *Banking services.*   Fax:52-5-257-8222

     BANCA SERFIN S.A.
     399 Park Avenue, 37th Fl., New York, NY   10022
     CEO:M. Garcia, Reg. Dir.   Tel: (212) 572-0600   Emp: N/A
     Bus: *Commercial banking services.*   Fax:(212) 572-0680   %FO: 100

- **BANCO INTERNACIONAL, S.A.**
Paseo de la Reforma 156, Mexico DF, CP 06600 Mexico
CEO: Antonio del Valle, CEO   Tel: 52-5-721-2222   Emp: 13000
Bus: *International banking services.*   Fax:52-5-721-2993

     BANCO INTERNACIONAL, S.A.
     437 Madison Avenue, 17th Fl., New York, NY   10022
     CEO:Carlos Martinez, EVP   Tel: (212) 758-2660   Emp: 30
     Bus: *International banking services.*   Fax:(212) 758-7552   %FO: 100

- **BANCO INVERLAT S.A.**
Plaza Inverlat, CP 11560, Mexico DF, Mexico
CEO: Timothy Hayward   Tel: 52-5-229-2929   Emp: 10000
Bus: *International banking services.*   Fax:52-5-229-2823

     BANCO INVERLAT, S.A.
     1177 Avenue of the Americas, 42nd Fl., New York, NY   10036
     CEO:Alan Harrison, Gen.Mgr.   Tel: (212) 403-3900   Emp: 25
     Bus: *International banking services.*   Fax:(212) 403-3970   %FO: 100

• BANCO MEXICANO S.A.
Paseo de la Reforma, #213, 06500 Mexico DF, Mexico
CEO: Federico Zorrilla, Gen. Dir.   Tel: 52-5-629-3000   Emp: N/A
Bus: *International banking services.*   Fax:52-5-629-3070

BANCO MEXICANO S.A.
235 Fifth Avenue, New York, NY   10016
CEO: Juan Igancio Cerdé, Gen.Mgr.   Tel: (212) 951-8000   Emp: 38
Bus: *International banking services.*   Fax:(212) 951-2085   %FO: 100

• BANCO NACIONAL DE MEXICO S.A. (BANAMEX)
Isabel la Catolica 44, Mexico DF, CP 06089 Mexico
CEO: Roberto Del Cueto, Pres. Int'l   Tel: 52-5-225-5500   Emp: 33000
Bus: *International banking services.*   Fax:52-5-225-5044

BANCO NACIONAL DE MEXICO
767 Fifth Avenue, 8th Fl., New York, NY   10153
CEO: Raul A. Anaya, Gen. Mgr.   Tel: (212) 751-5090   Emp: 60
Bus: *International banking services.*   Fax:(212) 303-1489   %FO: 100

BANCO NACIONAL DE MEXICO
2029 Century Park East, 42nd Fl., Los Angeles, CA   90017
CEO: Douglas Turley, Mgr.   Tel: (310) 203-3492   Emp: N/A
Bus: *International banking services.*   Fax:(310) 203-3495   %FO: 100

BANCO NACIONAL DE MEXICO
1000 Louisiana Street, Suite 6920, Houston, TX   77002
CEO: Jorge Raull, Mgr.   Tel: (713) 651-9091   Emp: N/A
Bus: *International banking services.*   Fax:(713) 659-2241   %FO: 100

CALIFORNIA COMMERCE BANK
2029 Century Park East, 42nd Fl., Los Angeles, CA   90017
CEO: Salvador Villar, Mgr.   Tel: (310) 203-3401   Emp: N/A
Bus: *International banking services.*   Fax:(310) 203-3587   %FO: 100

• BRYAN, GONZALEZ VARGAS Y GONZALEZ BAZ, S.C.
Temistocles 10, Piso 3, Colonia Polanco, Mexico DF, CP 11560 Mexico
CEO: Eduardo Ramos Gomez, Res. Ptnr.   Tel: 52-5-282-1155   Emp: N/A
Bus: *International law firm; Mexican and Latin American*   Fax:52-5-282-0513
Law.

BRYAN, GONZALEZ VARGAS Y GONZALEZ BAZ, S.C.
161 North Clark Street, Chicago, IL   60601
CEO: Eduardo Ramos Gomez, Res. Ptnr.   Tel: (312) 558-9900   Emp: N/A
Bus: *International law firm; Mexican and Latin*   Fax:(312) 558-9901   %FO: 100
American Law.

BRYAN, GONZALEZ VARGAS Y GONZALEZ BAZ, S.C.
405 Lexington Avenue, New York, NY   10174

CEO: Eduardo Ramos Gomez, Res. Ptnr.　　Tel: (212) 682-1555　　Emp: N/A
Bus: *International law firm; Mexican and Latin*　Fax:(212) 682-3241　　%FO: 100
　　American Law.

● **BURSAMEX CASA DE BOLSA S.A. DE CV**
205 Vias Pascal, Colonia Los Morales, Polanco, Mexico DF, CP 11510 Mexico

CEO: N/A　　　　　　　　　　　　　　　Tel: 52-5-282-6000　　Emp: N/A
Bus: *Securities broker/dealers.*　　　　　Fax:N/A

　　BURSAMEX, INC.
　　565 Fifth Avenue, New York, NY   10017

　　CEO: Eduardo Garza, Gen. Principle　　Tel: (212) 922-3900　　Emp: N/A
　　Bus: *Securities broker/dealers.*　　　Fax:(212) 867-1960　　%FO: 100

● **CEMEX (Cementos Mexicanos)**
Av Constitucion #444 Pte, 64000 Monterrey, Nuevo Leon, Mexico

CEO: Lorenzo H. Zambrano, Pres.　　　Tel: 52-8-452000　　　Emp: 14415
Bus: *Cement & concrete.*　　　　　　　Fax:52-8-452043

　　CEMEX
　　One River Way, Suite 2200, Houston, TX   77056

　　CEO: Ignacio Murguia, Pres.　　　　Tel: (713) 881-1000　　Emp: N/A
　　Bus: *Mfr./distribution cement & concrete.*　Fax:(713) 881-1012　　%FO: 100

　　CEMEX
　　590 Madison Avenue, 41st Fl., New York, NY   10022

　　CEO: Lorenzo Zambrano, Pres.　　　Tel: (212) 317-6000　　Emp: N/A
　　Bus: *Mfr./distribution cement & concrete.*　Fax:(212) 317-6047　　%FO: 100

　　SUNBELT CORP.
　　One River Way, Suite 2200, Houston, TX   77056

　　CEO: Jeff Smith, Pres.　　　　　　　Tel: (713) 881-1000　　Emp: 1111
　　Bus: *Mfr./distribution cement & concrete.*　Fax:(713) 881-1012　　%FO: 100

● **GRUPO FINANCIERO BANCOMER, S.A. de C.V.**
Centro Bancomer, Av. Universidad 1200, Mexico DF, CP 03339, Mexico

CEO: Marcos Garay Velasco, Mg Dir Int'l　Tel: 52-5-621-3434　　Emp: N/A
Bus: *International banking services.*　　Fax:52-5-621-4740

　　BANCOMER S.A.
　　115 East 54th Street, New York, NY   10022

　　CEO: Bartolo Lopez, Sr. VP　　　　　Tel: (212) 759-7600　　Emp: N/A
　　Bus: *International banking services.*　Fax:(212) 750-9228　　%FO: 100

　　BANCOMER S.A.
　　444 South Flower St., Ste.100, Los Angeles, CA   90071

　　CEO: Javier de Leon, Sr. VP　　　　Tel: (213) 489-7245　　Emp: N/A
　　Bus: *International banking services.*　Fax:(213) 622-8519　　%FO: 100

BANCOMER TRANSFER SERVICES, INC.
444 South Flower St., Ste. 100, Los Angeles, CA   90071
CEO: Moises Jaimes, Sr.VP   Tel: (213) 488-3330   Emp: N/A
Bus: *Securities services.*   Fax:(213) 489-9864   %FO: 100

BANCOMES SECURITIES INTERNATIONAL
115 East 54th Street. 3rd Fl., New York, NY   10022
CEO: Pablo Girault, Mgr.   Tel: (212) 759-7600   Emp: N/A
Bus: *Financial/securities services.*   Fax:(212) 230-0355   %FO: 100

● **GRUPO FINANCIERO PROBURSA SA**
Montes Urales 620, 01060 Mexico DF, Mexico
CEO: Jose Madariaga, Chrm.   Tel: 52-5-660-1111   Emp: 5000
Bus: *Financial services.*   Fax:52-5-660-1335

PROBURSA INTL INC
280 Park Ave, 39th Fl W, New York, NY   10017
CEO: Gregorio Merino, Pres   Tel: (212) 949-8855   Emp: 30
Bus: *Securities broker/dealer.*   Fax:(212) 949-8988   %FO: 100

● **GRUPO NACIONAL PROVINCIAL, S.A.**
Cerro de Las Torres 395, Col. Campestere Churubusco, Mexico D.F., CP-04200 Mexico
CEO: Clemente Cabello, Pres   Tel: 52-5-227-3999   Emp: 5000
Bus: *Multi-line insurance.*   Fax:52-5-227-3154

LA PROV CORPORATION
80 Broad Street, 33th Fl., New York, NY   10004
CEO: Marcelo Hernandez Sr., VP   Tel: (212) 785-7616   Emp: 4
Bus: *Insurance services.*   Fax:(212) 785-4381   %FO: 100

● **MEXICANA DE AVIACIÓN SA DE CV**
Xola 535, Colonia del Valle, Mexico DF, CP-03100 Mexico
CEO: Fernando Flores, Dir. Gen.   Tel: 52-5-448-3000   Emp: 6422
Bus: *International commercial air transport services.*   Fax:N/A

MEXICANA AIRLINES
9841 Airport Boulevard, Suite 200, Los Angeles, CA   90045
CEO: Carlos De Uriarte, VP   Tel: (310) 646-0401   Emp: 599
Bus: *Air transport services.*   Fax:(310) 646-0400   %FO: 100

MEXICANA AIRLINES
500 Fifth Avenue, Suite 1717, New York, NY   10110
CEO: Paul Romero, Reg.Mgr.   Tel: (212) 840-2344   Emp: 500
Bus: *Air transport services.*   Fax:(212) 768-3867   %FO: 100

● **NACIONAL FINANCIERA SNC MEXICO**
Av Insurgentes Sur 1971, Col.Guadalupe Inn, 01020 Mexico DF, Mexico
CEO: Gilberto Borja, CEO						Tel: 52-5-325-6700			Emp: N/A
Bus: *Investment & general financial services.*			Fax:52-5-661-8418

    NAFINSA SECURITIES INC.
    21 East 63rd Street, New York, NY	10021-7226
    CEO: Jose Oliveres, Pres.					Tel: (212) 821-0300		Emp: 13
    Bus: *Securities broker/dealer, investment*		Fax:(212) 325-0330		%FO: 100
       management services.

● **SEGUROS COMERCIAL AMERICA**
Insurgente Sur 3900, 14000 Mexico D.F., Mexico
CEO: Fernando Vazquez, Sr.VP					Tel: 52-5-727-2500			Emp: 3000
Bus: *Insurance services.*						Fax:52-5-727-2119

    SEGUROS COMERCIAL AMERICA
    2 World Financial Center, 225 Liberty St., 35th Fl., New York, NY	10281-1008
    CEO: Josefina Garza-Zavaleta, VP				Tel: (212) 786-3295		Emp: N/A
    Bus: *Insurance products & services.*			Fax:(212) 786-1996		%FO: 100

● **GRUPO FINANCIERO SERFIN S.A.**
Prolongacion Paseo de la Reforma #500, Lomas de Santa Fe, Mexico D.F., CP 01219 Mexico
CEO: Adolfo Lagos							Tel: 52-5-257-8000			Emp: 16600
Bus: *Financial services; commercial & investment*		Fax:52-5-257-8566
   banking.

    BANCA SERFIN SA, New York Agency
    399 Park Ave., 37th Fl., New York, NY	10022
    CEO: Alejandro Garcia, Reg. Mgr.				Tel: (212) 572-0617		Emp: 34
    Bus: *Commercial banking.*					Fax:(212) 421-5128		%FO: 100

● **TAESA AIRLINES**
Av. Generale Zona Hangars C-27, Mexico DF, CP 15620 Mexico
CEO: Alberto Abeb, CEO						Tel: 52-5-227-0727			Emp: N/A
Bus: *Air transport services.*					Fax:52-5-227-0768

    TAESA AIRLINES
    500 Fifth Avenue, Suite 420, New York, NY	10110
    CEO: Rafael Montero, Sales Mgr.				Tel: (212) 398-1360		Emp: N/A
    Bus: *Air transport services.*				Fax:(212) 398-6962		%FO: 100

● **TRANSMISIONES Y EQUIPOS - MECANICOS SA DE CV**

Av 5 de Febrero 2115, 76120 Queretaro, Mexico

CEO: Gustavo Olvera, Dir. Gen.   Tel: 52-42-170717   Emp: 1600

Bus: *Mfr. manual transmissions, gears, shafts,*   Fax:52-42-170345
      synchronizers.

    DSA of America

    23382 Commerce Drive, Farmington Hills, MI   48335

    CEO: Lee Davis, VP. & Mgn Dir   Tel: (248) 471-3200   Emp: 29

    Bus: *Sale/distribution automotive manual*   Fax:(248) 471-3722   %FO: 100
      transmissions, gears, shafts, synchronizers.

● **VECTOR CASA DE BOLSA S.A. de C.V.**

Av Roble 565, Colina Valle del Compestre, 66265 Garza Garcia, Mexico

CEO: Pedro Aspe, CEO   Tel: 52-8-3183500   Emp: 350

Bus: *Securities broker/dealer.*   Fax:N/A

    VECTORMEX INC

    535 Madison Avenue, 2nd Fl., New York, NY   10022-4212

    CEO: Sergio Sanchez, Chrm & Pres.   Tel: (212) 407-5500   Emp: 25

    Bus: *Securities broker/dealer.*   Fax:(212) 407-5555   %FO: 100

Morocco

- **ROYAL AIR MAROC**
  Sieje, Casa-Ansa, Casablanca, Morocco
  CEO: Pres. Hassad   Tel: 21-2-231-1122   Emp: N/A
  Bus: *Commercial air transport services.*   Fax:21-2-236-0520

  ROYAL AIR MAROC
  55 East 59th Street, New York, NY 10019
  CEO: Pres. Hassad   Tel: (212) 750-5115   Emp: N/A
  Bus: *Commercial air transport services.*   Fax:(212) 754-4215   %FO: 100

Netherlands

- **ABN AMRO BANK N.V.**
Foppingadreef 22, P O Box 283, 1102 BS, Amsterdam, Netherlands
CEO: P. J. Kalff, Chrm.   Tel: 31-20-628-9898   Emp: 60000
Bus: *Banking, financial services.*   Fax:31-20-628-6184

    ABN AMRO BANK N.V.
    One Union Square, Ste. 2323, Seattle, WA   98101
    CEO: Christian Sievers, Sr. V. P.   Tel: (206) 587-2330   Emp: N/A
    Bus: *International/domestic banking services.*   Fax:(206) 682-5641   %FO: 100

    ABN AMRO BANK N.V.
    101 California Street, Ste. 4550, San Francisco, CA   94111
    CEO: Clayton Jackson, Sr. VP   Tel: (415) 984-3700   Emp: N/A
    Bus: *International/domestic banking services.*   Fax:(415) 362-3524   %FO: 100

    ABN AMRO BANK N.V.
    One Post Office Square, 39th Fl., Boston, MA   02109
    CEO: Carol A. Levine, Sr. VP   Tel: (617) 988-7900   Emp: N/A
    Bus: *International/domestic banking services.*   Fax:(617) 988-7910   %FO: 100

    ABN AMRO BANK N.V.
    500 Park Avenue, New York, NY   10022
    CEO: Thomas Flemming, Sr. VP   Tel: (212) 446-4320   Emp: N/A
    Bus: *International/domestic banking services.*   Fax:(212) 980-9425   %FO: 100

    ABN AMRO BANK N.V.
    One Ravinia Drive, Ste. 1200, Atlanta, GA   30346
    CEO: W. P. Fischer, Sr. VP   Tel: (770) 396-0056   Emp: N/A
    Bus: *International/domestic banking services.*   Fax:(770) 395-9188   %FO: 100

    ABN AMRO SECURITIES, INC.
    335 Madison Avenue, 14th Fl., New York, NY   10017
    CEO: David Woods, Pres. & CEO   Tel: (212) 808-5300   Emp: N/A
    Bus: *Investment advisory services.*   Fax:(212) 808-5528   %FO: 100

    EUROPEAN AMERICAN BANK
    E.A.B. Plaza, Uniondale, NY   11555
    CEO: Harrison S. Tempest, CEO   Tel: (516) 296-5000   Emp: N/A
    Bus: *Banking, financial services*   Fax:(516) 296-6034   %FO: 100

    LASALLE NATIONAL BANK
    135 South LaSalle Street, Chicago, IL   60603
    CEO: Robert K. Wilmouth, Chrm.   Tel: (312) 443-2000   Emp: N/A
    Bus: *Banking, financial services*   Fax:(312) 904-2346   %FO: 100

● **ADEMAR B.V**
Waalstraat 26, Rotterdam 3087 BP, Netherlands
CEO: R. Derksen, Pres.   Tel: 31-10-429-9600   Emp: N/A
Bus: *Transportation and freight forwarding.*   Fax:31-10-495-2444

> **ADEMAR U.S.A.**
> 11712 Concord Hambden Road, Concord, OH   44077
> CEO: Patricia Slover, Mgr.   Tel: (216) 352-9418   Emp: N/A
> Bus: *Transportation and forwarding.*   Fax:(216) 942-2526   %FO: 100

● **ADVANCED SEMICONDUCTOR MATERIALS N.V.**
Jan Steenlaan 9, 3730 AC, Bilthoven, Netherlands
CEO: Arthur H. del Prado, Pres. & CEO   Tel: 31-30-279-8411   Emp: 2250
Bus: *Research, development, Mfr.., marketing and*   Fax:31-30-279-8443
servicing of equipment/materials used to produce
semiconductor devices

> **ASM AMERICA INC.**
> 3411 East Harbour Drive, Phoenix, AZ   85034
> CEO: Daniel Queyssac, Pres.   Tel: (602) 437-1405   Emp: 300
> Bus: *Manufacture/sales/distribution of semi-*   Fax:(602) 437-1403   %FO: 100
> *conductor devices.*

● **AEGON N.V.**
50 Mariahoeveplein, The Hague, NL-2501 CE, The Netherlands
CEO: K. J. Storm, Chrm.   Tel: 31-70-344-3210   Emp: 25000
Bus: *Insurance & financial services.*   Fax:31-70-347-5238

> **AEGON USA INVESTMENT MANAGEMENT, INC.**
> 4333 Edgewter Road, NE, Cedar Rapids, IA   52499-0010
> CEO: Partick Falconio, Pres.   Tel: (319) 398-8660   Emp: N/A
> Bus: *Investment advisory services.*   Fax:(319) 369-2218   %FO: 100

> **AEGON USA, INC.**
> 1111 North Charles Street, Baltimore, MD   21201
> CEO: Donald J. Shepard, Chrm. & Pres.   Tel: (410) 576-4571   Emp: 10000
> Bus: *Insurance & financial services.*   Fax:(410) 347-8686   %FO: 100

> **DIVERSIFIED INVESTMENT ADVISORS, INC.**
> Four Mahattanville Road, Purchase, NY   10577
> CEO: Tom A. Schlossberg, Pres.   Tel: (914) 697-8000   Emp: N/A
> Bus: *Investment advisory services.*   Fax:(914) 697-3743   %FO: 100

> **MONUMENTAL CORP.**
> 1111 North Charles Street, Baltimore, MD   21201
> CEO: Leslie B. Disharoon, CEO   Tel: (410) 685-2900   Emp: 1600
> Bus: *Insurance services.*   Fax:(410) 347-8686   %FO: 100

NATIONAL OLD LINE INSURANCE CO.
501 Wood Lane, Little Rock, AR   72201
CEO: L. Barrt, Pres.   Tel: (501) 372-5000   Emp: N/A
Bus: *Insurance services.*   Fax:(501) 371-4111   %FO: 100

● **AKZO NOBEL N.V.**
P O Box 9300, 76 Velperweg, 6824 BM, Arnhem, Netherlands
CEO: C.J.A. van Lede, Chrm.   Tel: 31-26-366-4433   Emp: 65000
Bus: *Mfr. chemicals, man-made fibers, salt, coatings,*   Fax:31-26-366-3250
    pharmaceuticals.

AKZO INDUSTRIAL FIBERS GROUP
801 F. Blacklawn Road, Conyers, GA   30207
CEO: Lowell D Bivens, Mgr.   Tel: (404) 929-0781   Emp: N/A
Bus: *Mfr./sale industrial fibers.*   Fax:(404) 929-8138   %FO: 100

AKZO NOBEL COATINGS INC.
30 Brush Street, Pontiac, MI   48053
CEO: James Hinsch, Mgr.   Tel: (810) 334-7010   Emp: N/A
Bus: *Mfr./sales, distribution of outdoor*   Fax:(810) 334-6140   %FO: 100
    coatings/paints.

AKZO NOBEL CORP. RESEARCH AMERICA, INC.
7 Livingstone Avenue, Dobbs Ferry, NY   10522
CEO: Kelly B. Triplett, Mgr.   Tel: (914) 674-5000   Emp: N/A
Bus: *Research laboratory.*   Fax:(914) 693-2029   %FO: 100

AKZO NOBEL DREELAND, INC.
1600 Broadway, Ste. 2050, Denver, CO   80202
CEO: Harry R.G. Steeghs, Pres.   Tel: (303) 832-6226   Emp: N/A
Bus: *Sales/distribution of industrial chemicals for*   Fax:(303) 832-5566   %FO: 100
    oil well mining/drilling.

AKZO NOBEL INDUSTRIAL SYSTEMS COMPANY
P O Box 7249, Asheville, NC   28802
CEO: P. L. Skoglund Jr., Gen.Mgr.   Tel: (704) 665-5000   Emp: N/A
Bus: *Mfr./sales/distribution yarns & fibers.*   Fax:(704) 665-5005   %FO: 100

AKZO NOBEL SALT CO
Abington Executive Park, P O Box 352, Clarks Summit, PA   18411-0352
CEO: Alan B Graf, Pres.   Tel: (717) 587-5131   Emp: N/A
Bus: *Mfr. industrial, road & consumer salt products.*   Fax:(717) 586-7426   %FO: 100

AKZO NOBEL, INC.
300 S. Riverside Plaza, Chicago, IL   60606
CEO: P. P. Kluit, Pres.   Tel: (312) 906-7500   Emp: N/A
Bus: *Mfr. salt/basic chemicals, pharmaceuticals &*   Fax:(312) 906-7545   %FO: 100
    coatings, plastics.

AKZO NOBEL/SIKKENS WOODFINISHES
1845 Maxwell Street, Troy, MI 48084
CEO: Richard M. Gray, Executive V.P.   Tel: (248) 334-7010   Emp: N/A
Bus: *Mfr./sales of wood finishes for interior/exterior* Fax:(248) 253-7797   %FO: 100
surfaces.

DIOSYNTH INC.
2745 North Elston Avenue, 3rd Fl., Chicago, IL 60647
CEO: Kees R. Nederveen, Pres.   Tel: (312) 235-7500   Emp: N/A
Bus: *Mfr./sales/distribution of pharmaceuticals raw*   Fax:(312) 235-7504   %FO: 100
materials.

FORTAFIL FIBERS INC
Roane Country Industrial Park, Rockwood, TN 37854
CEO: Roger Prescott, V.P.   Tel: (615) 354-4120   Emp: N/A
Bus: *Manufacturer of carbon fibers.*   Fax:(615) 354-4327   %FO: 100

INTERVET AMERICA INC
405 State Street, Millsboro, DE 19966
CEO: John Hofland, V.P.   Tel: (302) 934-8051   Emp: N/A
Bus: *Mfr./sales/distribution of veterinary*   Fax:(302) 934-8591   %FO: 100
vaccines/medicines & veterinary products.

ORGANON INC.
375 Mt. Pleasant Avenue, West Orange, NJ 07052
CEO: Brian Haigh, Pres.   Tel: (201) 235-4800   Emp: N/A
Bus: *Mfr./sales/distribution of ethical*   Fax:(201) 325-4589   %FO: 100
pharmaceuticals.

ORGANON TEKNIKA CORP.
100 Akzo Avenue, Treyburn, NC 27704
CEO: Robert Timmins, Pres.   Tel: (919) 620-2000   Emp: N/A
Bus: *Healthcare research and*   Fax:(919) 620-2107   %FO: 100
mfr./sales/distribution of artificial kidneys.

ROSEMONT PHARMACEUTICALS INC.
301 South Cherokee, Denver, CO 80223
CEO: Arthur Pelletier, Pres.   Tel: (303) 773-7207   Emp: N/A
Bus: *Mfr./distribution of generic prescriptions*   Fax:(303) 698-1005   %FO: 100

● AMMERAAL INTERNATIONAL BEHEER B.V.
Handelstraat 1, 1704 AC, Heerhugowaard, Netherlands
CEO: I. A. Roberti. CEO   Tel: 31-72-575-1212   Emp: N/A
Bus: *Manufacturer of industrial conveyor belting.*   Fax:31-72-574-3364

AMMERAAL, INC.
30720 Three Mile Road NW, Grand Rapids, MI 49504
CEO: C. H. Stoepler, CEO   Tel: (616) 791-0162   Emp: N/A
Bus: *Mfr./sales/distribution of plastic, rubber &*   Fax:(616) 791-1067   %FO: 100
synthetic conveyor belting

● **ANKER GROEP B.V.**
Vasteland 4, 3000 BK, Rotterdam, Netherlands
CEO: K. Zubli, Mng.Dir.   Tel: 31-10-452-9566   Emp: N/A
Bus: *Sales and export of coal.*   Fax:31-10-452-9073

ANKER ENERGY CORPORTION
2708 Cranberry Square, Morgantown, WV   26505
CEO: John J. Faltis, Pres.   Tel: (304) 594-1616   Emp: N/A
Bus: *Coal mining.*   Fax:(304) 594-3695   %FO: 100

JULIANA MINING CO. INC.
Route 2, Cowen, WV   26206
CEO: Ken James, Pres.   Tel: (304) 226-5383   Emp: N/A
Bus: *Coal mining and preparation.*   Fax:(304) 226-5381   %FO: 100

MARINE COAL SALES CO.
645 West Carmel Drive, Ste. 190, Carmel, IN   46032
CEO: George Yarborough, Mgr.   Tel: (317) 844-6628   Emp: N/A
Bus: *Tank storage for liquid bulk products.*   Fax:(317) 844-6628   %FO: 100

PATRIOT MINING COMPANY
PO Box 4360, Star City, WV   26504
CEO: Bruce Sparks, Mgr.   Tel: (304) 983-8710   Emp: N/A
Bus: *Coal mining and preparation.*   Fax:(304) 983-8714   %FO: 100

PHILIPPI DEVELOPMENT, INC.
Route 3, Box 146, Philippi, WV   26416
CEO: Gary McCauley, Pres.   Tel: (304) 457-1895   Emp: N/A
Bus: *Coal mining and preparation.*   Fax:(304) 457-1005   %FO: 100

VANTRANS, INC.
2708 Cranberry Square, Morgantown, WV   26505
CEO: Bruce Parks, V.P.   Tel: (304) 594-1616   Emp: N/A
Bus: *Sales and export of coal.*   Fax:(304) 594-3695   %FO: 100

● **BALLAST NEDAM GROEP B.V.**
Laan van Kronenburg 2, 1183 AS, Amstelveen, Netherlands
CEO: Martin J.F. Weck, Chrm.   Tel: 31-20-545-9111   Emp: N/A
Bus: *Engineering, construction, dredging, excavation,*   Fax:31-20-647-3000
ship-building, project management.

BALLAST NEDAM CONSTRUCTION, INC.
Picasso Tower, 2800 Biscayne, # 730, Miami, FL   33137
CEO: Ger Van Der Schaaf, Gen.Mgr.   Tel: (305) 576-6617   Emp: N/A
Bus: *Construction and dredging equipment services.*   Fax:(305) 576-6890   %FO: 100

NATCO, INC.
2122 York Road, Oakbrook, IL   60521
CEO: Bill Pagendarm, V.P.   Tel: (630) 574-3000   Emp: N/A
Bus: *Construction and dredging equipment services.*   Fax:(630) 574-3472   %FO: 100

• **BCD HOLDINGS N.V.**
Utrechtseweg 67, 3704 HB, Zeist, Netherlands
CEO: M. J. Bruna, Mgr.   Tel: 31-30-695-8404   Emp: N/A
Bus: *Commercial mortgage banking, travel and leisure.*   Fax:31-30-695-9771

> **BCD HOLDINGS N.V.**
> 2060 Mount Paran Road, Ste. 207, Atlanta, GA   30327
> CEO:John A. Fenterner van Vissingen, Chrm.   Tel: (404) 264-1000   Emp: N/A
> Bus: *Holding company*   Fax:(404) 364-0477   %FO: 100

> **GRAY LINE OF ATLANTA**
> 2541 Camp Creek Parkway, College Park, GA   30337
> CEO:Frederick D. Clemente, Pres.   Tel: (404) 767-0594   Emp: N/A
> Bus: *Sightseeing tours/motor coaches, shuttle buses.*   Fax:(404) 765-1399   %FO: 100

> **NORO-REALTY ADVISORS**
> 2060 Mount Paran Road, Ste. 1000, Atlanta, GA   30327
> CEO:Michael R. Raffety, Pres.   Tel: (404) 262-9400   Emp: N/A
> Bus: *Real estate fund management.*   Fax:(404) 233-4964   %FO: 100

> **PARK ' N FLY INC.**
> 2060 Mount Paran Road, Atlanta, GA   30327
> CEO:Frederick D. Clemente, Pres.   Tel: (404) 264-1000   Emp: N/A
> Bus: *Off-airport parking facilities and shuttle*   Fax:(404) 354-0477   %FO: 100
> *services.*

> **PRIMARY CAPITAL ADVISORS, L.C.**
> 2060 Mount Paran Road, Ste. 101, Atlanta, GA   30327
> CEO: William B. Pendleton, Pres.   Tel: (404) 365-9300   Emp: N/A
> Bus: *Commercial mortgage banking.*   Fax:(404) 266-1448   %FO: 100

> **WORLD TRAVEL PARTNERS GROUP INC.**
> 1055 Lenox Park Boulevard, Atlanta, GA   30319
> CEO:Jack C. Alexander, Pres.   Tel: (404) 841-6600   Emp: N/A
> Bus: *Corporate, group, and event travel.*   Fax:(404) 814-2983   %FO: 100

• **BLYDENSTEIN-WILLINK N.V.**
Amarilstraat 30, 7554 TV, Hengelo, Netherlands
CEO: Ad VerKuyten, Mng.Dir.   Tel: 31-74-243-9900   Emp: N/A
Bus: *Window coverings and textile products.*   Fax:31-74-243-9966

> **VEROSOL USA**
> 215 Beecham Drive, Pittsburgh, PA   15205
> CEO:Leonard Siegel, Mgr.   Tel: (412) 922-4300   Emp: 150
> Bus: *Manufacturer of window shades.*   Fax:(412) 922-5556   %FO: 100

● **BORSTLAP B.V.**
Zevenheuvelenweg 44, 5048 AN, Tilburg, Netherlands
CEO: J. M. A. Borstlap, Mng.Dir.   Tel: 31-13-462-8628   Emp: N/A
Bus: *Metric fasteners.*   Fax:31-13-42-8340

    FABORY METRIC FASTENERS
    824 East Fair Play Boulevard, Fair Play, SC   29643
    CEO: Jim Cohen, Pres & CEO   Tel: (315) 431-6100   Emp: N/A
    Bus: *Sale of fasteners.*   Fax:(315) 422-3116   %FO: 100

    METRIC FASTERNERS CORP.
    2240 29th Street SE, Grand Rapids, MI   49508
    CEO: Leo A. DeJong, Pres.   Tel: (616) 247-4777   Emp: N/A
    Bus: *Import/sales/distribution of metric fasteners*   Fax:(616) 247-0408   %FO: 100
       and hardware.

    METRIC FASTERNERS CORP.
    110 Golden Ring Road, Ste. 105, Baltimore, MD   21221
    CEO: John T. Van Kints, Mgr.   Tel: (410) 780-0311   Emp: N/A
    Bus: *Import/sales/distribution of metric fasteners*   Fax:(410) 780-0384   %FO: 100
       and hardware.

    METRIC FASTERNERS CORP.
    6095 Rickenbacker Road, Los Angeles, CA   90040
    CEO: Mimi Micu, Mgr.   Tel: (213) 726-9944   Emp: N/A
    Bus: *Import/sales/distribution of metric fasteners*   Fax:(213) 726-6718   %FO: 100
       and hardware.

● **BSO/ORIGIN TECHNOLOGY IN BUSINESS**
Euclideslaan 2, 3584 BN, Utrecht, Netherlands
CEO: E. J. Wintzen, Pres.   Tel: 31-30-258-6800   Emp: N/A
Bus: *Software manufacturer.*   Fax:31-30-258-6754

    ORIGIN TECHNOLOGIES IN BUS. INC.
    430 Mountain Avenue, Murray Hill, NJ   07974
    CEO: Peter Lablans, Dir.   Tel: (908) 508-1700   Emp: N/A
    Bus: *Software supplier.*   Fax:(908) 508-0882   %FO: 100

    ORIGIN TECHNOLOGIES IN BUS. INC.
    3001 North Rocky Point Road, Ste. 430, Tampa, FL   33607
    CEO: Steve Blackstone, Mng. Dir.   Tel: (813) 281-0354   Emp: N/A
    Bus: *Software supplier.*   Fax:(814) 281-2105   %FO: 100

    ORIGIN TECHNOLOGIES IN BUS. INC.
    14951 Dallas Parkway, Ste. 300, Dallas, TX   75240
    CEO: Ken Craig, Mng. Dir.   Tel: (214) 770-0062   Emp: N/A
    Bus: *Software supplier.*   Fax:(214) 770-0066   %FO: 100

ORIGIN TECHNOLOGIES IN BUS. INC.
6250 River Road, Ste. 8005, Rosemont, IL   60018
CEO: Pam Farrell, Mng. Dir.   Tel: (847) 318-9800   Emp: N/A
Bus: *Software supplier.*   Fax:(847) 318-9800   %FO: 100

[Entry deleted in late revision]

● **CEBECO-HANDELSRAAD**
Blaak 31, Postbus 182, NL-3000 AD Rotterdam, Netherlands
CEO: H. de Boon, Pres.   Tel: 31-10-454 4911   Emp: N/A
Bus: *Wholesale, agricultural products; mfr., agricultural*   Fax:31-10-411 3889
    machinery and food products.

   CEBECO INC.
   14074 Arndt Road, NE, Aurora, OR   97002
   CEO: Don Egger, Pres.   Tel: (503) 678-1850   Emp: N/A
   Bus: *Wholesale, agricultural products, flowers,*   Fax:(503) 678-1116   %FO: 100
       mfr. agricultural machinery and food products.

   INTERNATIONAL SEEDS, INC.
   820 West First Street, Halsey, OR   97348
   CEO: Rich Underwood, Pres.   Tel: (541) 369-2251   Emp: 3 5
   Bus: *Wholesale, agricultural products; mfr.,*   Fax:(541) 369-2640   %FO: 100
       agricultural machinery and food products.

● **CENTRALE SUIKERMAATSCHAPPIJ N.V.**
Nienoord 13, 1112 XE, Amsterdam, Netherlands
CEO: J. A. J. Vink, Pres.   Tel: 31-20-590-6911   Emp: N/A
Bus: *Manufacturer of specialty food products.*   Fax:31-20-695-1942

   AMERICAN INGREDIENTS COMPANY
   3947 Broadway, Kansas City, MO   64114
   CEO: Jerry L. Cosner, Pres.   Tel: (816) 561-9050   Emp: N/A
   Bus: *Manufacturer of food ingredients.*   Fax:(816) 561-1478   %FO: 100

HENRY & HENRY, INC.
3765 Walden Avenue, Lancaster, NY   14086
CEO: Richard Dahlin, Pres.   Tel: (716) 685-4000   Emp: N/A
Bus: *Production/sales of bakery ingredients.*   Fax:(716) 685-0160   %FO: 100

PURAC AMERICA, INC.
111 Barclay Boulevard, Lincolnshire, IL   60069
CEO: Gerrit Vreeman, Pres.   Tel: (847) 634-6330   Emp: N/A
Bus: *Import/sales/distribution of lactic*   Fax:(847) 634-1992   %FO: 100
    acid/derivatives.

QA PRODUCTS, INC.
1301 Mark Street, Oak Grove Village, IL   60007
CEO: John Tritt, Pres.   Tel: (630) 595-2390   Emp: N/A
Bus: *Specialty decorations for bakery/ice cream* Fax:(630) 595-1960   %FO: 100
    industries.

WESTCO PRODUCTS, INC.
7351 Crider Avenue, Pico Rivera, CA   90660
CEO: Ronald L. Ziegler, Pres.   Tel: (310) 949-1054   Emp: N/A
Bus: *Mfr. of prepared flour mixes/doughs.*   Fax:(310) 949-1257   %FO: 100

● **COOP VERKOOP & PRODUCTIEV-ERENIGING**
Benedon Oosterdiep 27, 9640 AA Groningen, Netherlands
CEO: Arend Brouwer, Chrm.   Tel: 31-50-876-9111   Emp: N/A
Bus: *Corn milling, starches and derivations.*   Fax:N/A

    AVEBE AMERICA INC.
    4 Independence Way, Princeton, NJ   08540
    CEO: Fred Caper, Pres.   Tel: (609) 520-1400   Emp: N/A
    Bus: *Starches/chemicals.*   Fax:(609) 520-1473   %FO: 100

● **DE BRAUW BLACKSTONE WESTBROEK**
7th Fl., Strawinskylaan 3115, 1077 ZX Amsterdam, The Netherlands
CEO: Berend J. H. Crans, Mng. Ptnr.   Tel: 31-20-548-1481   Emp: N/A
Bus: *International law firm.*   Fax:31-20-548-1485

    DE BRAUW BLACKSTONE WESTBROEK
    712 Fifth Avenue, 30th Fl., New York, NY   10019
    CEO: Ms. Kaarina Zimmer, Mng. Ptnr.   Tel: (212) 801-3430   Emp: N/A
    Bus: *International law firm.*   Fax:(212) 801-3435   %FO: 100

● **DELFT INSTRUMENTS N.V.**
Postbus 103, 2600 AC, Delft, Netherlands
CEO: E. Van Hooft, Pres.   Tel: 31-15-260-1200   Emp: N/A
Bus: *Import/export of electronic equipment.*   Fax:31-15-260-1274

ENRAF INC.
500 Century Plaza Drive, Ste. 120, Houston, TX   77073
CEO: W. Oglesby, Pres.   Tel: (713) 443-4291   Emp: N/A
Bus: *Sales/service of tank gauge systems.*   Fax:(713) 443-6776   %FO: 100

ENRAF-NONIUS COMPANY
390 Central Avenue, Bohemia, NY   11716
CEO: Graheme J. Williams, Pres.   Tel: (516) 589-2885   Emp: N/A
Bus: *Import/export, sales/service of electronic*   Fax:(516) 589-2068   %FO: 100
equipment.

OLDELFT CORPORATION OF AMERICA
7080 Columbia Gateway Drive, Columbia, MD   21046
CEO: Vincent Cusack, Pres.   Tel: (410) 312-4100   Emp: N/A
Bus: *Sales/distribution, sales/service of radiation*   Fax:(410) 312-4195   %FO: 100
therapy equipment.

● **DELI UNIVERSAL**
Wijnhaven 65, 3011 WJ, Roterdam, Netherlands
CEO: D. G. Cohen ter Vaert, CEO   Tel: 31-10-420-1700   Emp: N/A
Bus: *Import, sales/distribution of coffee, dried nuts and*   Fax:31-10-411-7694
fruits, sunflower/birdseed, and agricultural
commodities.

BERNS & KOPPSTEIN/IMPERIAL COMMODITIES CORP.
17 Battery Place, 21st Fl., New York, NY   10004
CEO: A. Smaligo, V. P.   Tel: (212) 837-9400   Emp: N/A
Bus: *Trade in canned meat/fish.*   Fax:(212) 797-3528   %FO: 100

CMI INC.
726 Highland Park, Clute, TX   77531
CEO: M. Boez, Pres.   Tel: (409) 265-0655   Emp: N/A
Bus: *Construction and piping for chemical*   Fax:(409) 265-5354   %FO: 100
companies.

GRANT RUBBER/IMPERIAL COMMODITIES CO.
17 Battery Place, 21st Fl., New York, NY   10006
CEO: Warren Heilbron, Pres.   Tel: (212) 837-9400   Emp: N/A
Bus: *Import/export agricultural commodities.*   Fax:(212) 344-0520   %FO: 100

IMPERIAL COMMODITIES CORP./COFFEE DIV.
17 Battery Place, 21st Fl., New York, NY   10004
CEO: Joseph Colaciello, Sr. V.P.   Tel: (212) 837-9400   Emp: N/A
Bus: *Coffee trader.*   Fax:(212) 514-6435   %FO: 100

RED RIVER FOODS
PO Box 13328, Richmond, VA   23225
CEO: James Phipts, Pres.   Tel: (804) 320-1800   Emp: N/A
Bus: *Import/export, sales/distribution of dried nuts*   Fax:(804) 320-1896   %FO: 100
    and fruits

RED RIVER COMMODITIES INC.
PO Box 3022, Fargo, ND   58108
CEO: Robert H. Willey, Jr., Pres.   Tel: (701) 282-2600   Emp: N/A
Bus: *Mfr./sales/distribution/warehousing of*   Fax:(701) 282-5325   %FO: 100
    processors of sunflower and bird seed

● **DRAKA HOLDING B.V.**
Rhijnspoorplein 22, 1018 TX, Amsterdam, Netherlands
CEO: S. J. Van Kesteren, Managing Director   Tel: 31-20-568-9865   Emp: N/A
Bus: *Manufacturer of wire & cable.*   Fax:31-20-663-1666

    BIW CABLE SYSTEMS, INC.
    22 Joseph E. Warner Blvd., North Dighton, MA   02764
    CEO: Dimitri Maistrellis, Gen. Mgr.   Tel: (508) 822-5444   Emp: N/A
    Bus: *Mfr. industrial & specialty cables.*   Fax:(508) 822-1944   %FO: 100

    BIW CONNECTOR SYSTEMS, INC.
    500 Tesconi Circle, Santa Rosa, CA   95401
    CEO: John Hathaway, General Mgr.   Tel: (707) 523-2300   Emp: N/A
    Bus: *Mfr. connectors.*   Fax:(707) 523-3567   %FO: 100

    CHROMATIC TECHNOLOGIES INC
    9 Forge Park, Franklin, MA   02038
    CEO: Gleason Gallagher, General Mgr.   Tel: (508) 541-7100   Emp: N/A
    Bus: *Mfr. fiber optic cables.*   Fax:(508) 541-8122   %FO: 100

    DRAKA USA CORPORATION
    9 Forge Park, Franklin, MA   02038
    CEO: Garo Artinian, Pres. & CEO   Tel: (508) 520-1200   Emp: N/A
    Bus: *Mfr. industrial cables.*   Fax:(508) 541-6862   %FO: 100

    HELIX / HITEMP CABLES, INC.
    9 Forge Park, Franklin, MA   02038
    CEO: W. Dungan, Gen. Mgr.   Tel: (508) 541-7100   Emp: N/A
    Bus: *Mfr. communications & electric cables.*   Fax:(508) 541-8122   %FO: 100

● **DSM N.V.**
Het Overloon 1, 6411 TE, Heerlen, Netherlands
CEO: S. D. DeBree, Chrm.   Tel: 31-45-578-8111   Emp: N/A
Bus: *Manufacture of chemicals, hydrocarbons,*   Fax:31-45-571-9753
synthetic/crude rubber, and printing resins

    DSM CHEMICALS NORTH AMERICA
    PO Box 2451, Augusta, GA   30901
    CEO: William Price, Pres.   Tel: (706) 849-6600   Emp: N/A
    Bus: *Manufacture of chemicals.*   Fax:(706) 849-6999   %FO: 100

    DSM CHEMICALS SERVICES USA, INC.
    PO Box 2451, Augusta, GA   30901
    CEO: W. C. Moye, Manager   Tel: (706) 849-6525   Emp: N/A
    Bus: *Mfr. chemicals.*   Fax:(706) 896-9999   %FO: 100

    DSM COPOLYMER
    Scenic Highway, Baton Rouge, LA   70821
    CEO: Pieter Harten, Pres.   Tel: (504) 355-5655   Emp: N/A
    Bus: *Synthetic/crude rubber.*   Fax:(504) 267-3633   %FO: 100

    DSM ENGINEERING PLASTICS, INC.
    PO Box 3333, Evansville, IL   47732
    CEO: Robert Hartmayer, Pres.   Tel: (812) 424-3831   Emp: N/A
    Bus: *Compounder of reinforced thermoplastics and*   Fax:(812) 435-7709   %FO: 100
    additives.

    DSM FINE CHEMICALS USA, INC.
    217 Route 46 West, Saddle Brook, NJ   07663
    CEO: Richard Morford, Pres.   Tel: (201) 845-4404   Emp: N/A
    Bus: *Powder coating/printing resins.* Fax:(201) 845-4406   %FO: 100

● **ELSAG BAILEY PROCESS AUTOMATION NV**
20 Welplaathoek, 3197 KP Rotterdam, Netherlands
CEO: Vincenzo Canatelli, Managing Director   Tel: 31-10-416-9696   Emp: 4500
Bus: *Process automation systems..*   Fax:31-10-416-9423

    ELSAG BAILEY INC.
    29801 Euclid Avenue, Wickliffe, OH   44092
    CEO: Gene T. Yon, Pres. & CEO   Tel: (216) 585-8500   Emp: 1900
    Bus: *Mfr. process automation equipment/related*   Fax:(216) 585-8756   %FO: 100
    services.

● **ERIKS HOLDING N.V.**
Voormeer 33, 1813 SB, Alkmaar, Netherlands
CEO: A. A. Van Dusseldorp, Pres. Tel: 31-72-514-1217 Emp: N/A
Bus: *Technical components.* Fax:31-72-514-1115

    ERIKS CORPORATION
    443 North Main Street, PO Box 220, Grafton, OH 44044
    CEO: Nicolas Storm, CFO Tel: (216) 926-3681 Emp: N/A
    Bus: *Technical components and systems.* Fax:(216) 926-3519 %FO: 100

    MONTCLAIR ENTERPRISES, INC.
    PO Box 155399, Ft. Worth, TX 76155
    CEO: Shun Courtney, Manager Tel: (817) 267-8837 Emp: N/A
    Bus: *Airline industry materials* Fax:(817) 571-4700 %FO: 100

    NORTHWEST SEALS INC.
    14600 Interuban Avenue, South, Seattle, WA 98168
    CEO: Vicky Lavesseur, V.P. Tel: (206) 342-9660 Emp: N/A
    Bus: *Sealing elements.* Fax:(206) 243-4718 %FO: 100

    ROBERT E. HOOSE, INC.
    PO Box 59, 3087T, Miami, FL 33159
    CEO: R. E. Hoose, Pres. Tel: (305) 871-4055 Emp: N/A
    Bus: *Sale of aircraft maintenance parts.* Fax:(305) 871-1285 %FO: 100

● **FGH BANK N.V.**
Leidseveer 50, 3511, Utrecht, Netherlands
CEO: R. J. Kahlmann, Pres. Tel: 31-30-232-3911 Emp: N/A
Bus: *Real estate financing.* Fax:31-30-233-4572

    FGH REALTY CREDIT CORP.
    292 Madison Avenue, 5th Fl., New York, NY 10017
    CEO: Ralph Miles, CEO Tel: (212) 251-0101 Emp: n/a
    Bus: *Real estate financing.* Fax:(212) 251-0149 %FO: 100

    FGH USA INC.
    292 Madison Avenue, 5th Fl., New York, NY 10017
    CEO: G. Austin Mooney, Pres. Tel: (212) 251-0101 Emp: n/a
    Bus: *Service of real estate financing.* Fax:(212) 251-0149 %FO: 100

● **FOKKER KON. NED. VLIEGTUIGENFABRIEK**
Hoogoorddreef 15, 1100 AE, Amsterdam, Netherlands
CEO: B. J. A. van Schaik, Chrm. Tel: 31-20-605-6666 Emp: 10000
Bus: *Manufacture and sale of aircraft parts.* Fax:31-20-605-7022

    FOKKER SERVICES, INC.
    5169 Southridge Parkway, Ste. 100, Atlanta, GA 30349
    CEO: Henk Kleef, Managing Director Tel: (770) 991-4609 Emp: 23
    Bus: *Mfr. /sales, distribution and service of aircraft* Fax:(770) 991-4608 %FO: 100
        parts.

- **FORTIS INTERNATIONAL N.V.**
  Archimedeslaan 6, 3584 BA, Utrecht, Netherlands
  CEO: J. L. M. Bartelds, Joint Chairman   Tel: 31-30-257-6576   Emp: 33,000
  Bus: *Insurance, banking, and financial services (see joint*   Fax:31-30-257-7835
       parent: FORTIS AG, BELGIUM).

  ### AMERICAN SECURITY GROUP
  3290 Northside Parkway, NW, Atlanta, GA   30327
  CEO: Jeffrey W. Williams, Pres.   Tel: (404) 261-9000   Emp: N/A
  Bus: *Insurance underwriters, specialty insurance*   Fax:(404) 264-2443   %FO: 100
       related products.

  ### FIRST FORTIS LIFE INSURANCE COMPANY
  220 Salina Meadows Parkway, Ste. 255, Syracuse, NY   13220
  CEO: Zafar Rashid, Pres.   Tel: (315) 453-2340   Emp: N/A
  Bus: *Life, disability, medical and dental group*   Fax:(315) 453-2343   %FO: 100
       insurance.

  ### FORTIS ADVISERS, INC.
  1 Chase Manhattan Plaza, 41st Fl., New York, NY   10005
  CEO: Gary N. Yalen, Pres.   Tel: (212) 859-7000   Emp: N/A
  Bus: *Financial asset management.*   Fax:(212) 859-7010   %FO: 100

  ### FORTIS HEALTHCARE
  501 West Michigan, Milwaukee, WI   53201
  CEO: T. M. Keller, Pres.   Tel: (414) 271-3011   Emp: N/A
  Bus: *Health insurance services.*   Fax:(414) 224-0472   %FO: 100

  ### FORTIS INC.
  1 Chase Manhattan Plaza, 41st Fl., New York, NY   10005
  CEO: Allen R. Freedman, CEO   Tel: (212) 859-7000   Emp: 6040
  Bus: *Investments, venture capital services.*   Fax:(212) 859-7111   %FO: 100

  ### FORTIS SALES
  501 Wesi Michigan, Milwaukee, WI   53201-2989
  CEO: Benjamin Cutler, CEO   Tel: (414) 271-3011   Emp: N/A
  Bus: *Financial services.*   Fax:(414) 271-0879   %FO: 100

  ### UNITED FAMILY LIFE INSURANCE COMPANY
  230 John Wesley Dobbs Avenue, N.E., Atlanta, GA   30303
  CEO: Alan W. Feagin, Pres.   Tel: (404) 659-3300   Emp: N/A
  Bus: *Pre-need funeral insurance.*   Fax:(404) 524-4945   %FO: 100

● **GRASSO'S KON. MACHINEFABRIEKEN N.V.**
Parallelweg 27, NL-5201 AG, Hertogenbosch, Netherlands
CEO: J. Bond, Pres.   Tel: 31-73-620-3911   Emp: 1400
Bus: *Holding company; mfr./sales refrigerator equipment.* Fax:31-73-621-0310

    GRASSO INC.
    4250 24th Avenue West, Seattle, WA   98199
    CEO: Lara Matthilsen, Gen.Mgr.   Tel: (206) 213-0040   Emp: N/A
    Bus: *Mfr./sale refrigerator equipment.*   Fax:(206) 213-0045   %FO: 100

    GRASSO INC.
    PO Box 4799, 1101 N. Governor Street, Evansville, IN   47724
    CEO: Robert M. Bonger, Pres. & CEO   Tel: (812) 465-6600   Emp: 40
    Bus: *Mfr./sale refrigerator equipment.*   Fax:(812) 465-6610   %FO: 100

● **HAGEMEYER N.V.**
Rijksweg 69, 1411 GE, Naarden, Netherlands
CEO: Andrew H. Land, Chrm.   Tel: 31-35-695-7611   Emp: 20000
Bus: *Gourmet and specialty foods, indoor plants,*   Fax:31-35-694-4396
     ceramics and decorative articles.

    GOURMET SPECIALTIES INC.
    21001 Cabot Blvd., Hayward, CA   94545
    CEO: Tim Birds, CEO   Tel: (510) 887-7322   Emp: N/A
    Bus: *Distribution of specialty foods.*   Fax:(510) 887-4203   %FO: 100

    HAGEMEYER N.V.
    80 Park West Plaza One, 2nd Fl., Saddle Brook, NJ   07662
    CEO: Michael Corke, Pres. & CEO   Tel: (201) 843-3588   Emp: 50
    Bus: *Holding company.*   Fax:(201) 368-3370   %FO: 100

    HAGEMEYER N.V.
    10825 Watson Road, St. Louis, MO   63127
    CEO: Richard P. Procter, Pres.   Tel: (314) 821-9080   Emp: N/A
    Bus: *Holding company.*   Fax:(314) 821-9183   %FO: 100

    LIBERTY RICHTER, INC.
    400 Lyster Avenue, Saddle Brook, NJ   07663
    CEO: Larry La Pare, Pres.   Tel: (201) 843-8900   Emp: N/A
    Bus: *Distributor of diversified foods.*   Fax:(201) 368-3575   %FO: 100

    NEW HOLLAND FLORAL, INC.
    350 S. White Horse Pike, Waterford Works, NJ   08089
    CEO: D. Roos, Pres.   Tel: (609) 767-9400   Emp: N/A
    Bus: *Distributor of indoor plants and ceramics.* Fax:(609) 767-9051   %FO: 100

    POLYFLAME AMERICA
    69 Jefferson Street, Stamford, CT   06904
    CEO: Emile De Neree, Pres.   Tel: (203) 358-8100   Emp: N/A
    Bus: *Mfr./sales/distribution of novelty items.* Fax:(203) 358-8366   %FO: 100

- **HEINEKEN N.V.**
Tweede Weteringsplantsoen 21, 1017 ZD, Amsterdam, Netherlands
CEO: S. W. Lubsen, Pres.   Tel: 31-20-523-9500   Emp: N/A
Bus: *Heineken, Buckler and Amstel light beers.*   Fax:31-20-693-2959

    HEINEKEN U.S.A., INC.
    50 Main Street, West White Plains, NY   10606
    CEO: Michael Foley, Pres.   Tel: (914) 681-4100   Emp: N/A
    Bus: *Import/sales/distribution of Heineken, Buckler,*   Fax:(914) 681-1900   %FO: 100
    and Amstel light beers.

    HEINEKEN U.S.A., INC.
    3158 River Road, Ste. 127, Des Plaines, IL   60018
    CEO: Robert E. Kenney, Director   Tel: (847) 297-4448   Emp: N/A
    Bus: *Central regional office for Heineken, Buckler,*   Fax:(847) 297-6239   %FO: 100
    and Amstel light beers.

- **HOLMATRO INDUSTRIAL EQUIPMENT B.V.**
Zalmweg 30, 4941VX, Raamsdonksveer, Netherlands
CEO: J. Meyers, Pres.   Tel: 31-16-258-9200   Emp: N/A
Bus: *Industrial and rescue equipment.*   Fax:31-16-252-2482

    HOLMATRO INC.
    1110 Benfield Boulevard, Millersville, MD   21108
    CEO: William G. Swayne, Marketing Mgr.   Tel: (410) 987-6633   Emp: n/a
    Bus: *Mfr./sale/distribution/service and warehousing*   Fax:(410) 987-1638   %FO: 100
    of industrial and rescue equipment.

- **HUNTER DOUGLAS N.V.**
Piekstraat 2, 3071 EL, Rotterdam, Netherlands
CEO: Ralph Sonnenberg, Pres.   Tel: 31-10-486-9911   Emp: 9770
Bus: *Mfr./sale/distribute window covering, architectural*   Fax:31-10-484-7910
products, metals trading, precision machinery.

    HUNTER DOUGLAS ARCHITECTURAL PRODUCTS
    11455 Lakefield Drive, Duluth, GA   30155
    CEO: David Slosberg, Pres.   Tel: (770) 476-8803   Emp: N/A
    Bus: *Mfr./sales/distribution & warehousing of*   Fax:(770) 623-3638   %FO: 100
    architectural products.

    HUNTER DOUGLAS INC.
    2 Parkway & Route 17 South, Upper Saddle River, NJ   07458
    CEO: Gerard Fuchs, Chrm.   Tel: (201) 327-8200   Emp: 3355
    Bus: *Mfr./sale/distribute window covering,*   Fax:(201) 327-5644   %FO: 100
    architectural products.

HUNTER DOUGLAS METALS INC.
915 West 175th Street, Homewood, IL 60430

CEO: R. Sfura, Mgr.	Tel: (708) 799-0800	Emp: N/A
Bus: *Aluminum scrap & primary/secondary aluminum.*	Fax:(708) 799-2787	%FO: 100

• **INDIVERS N.V.**
Gebouw 72, 1117 AA, Schiphol, Netherlands

CEO: E. W. M. Twaalfhoven, Pres.	Tel: 31-20-601-5141	Emp: N/A
Bus: *Specialized honeycomb fabrication and turbine repair.*	Fax:31-20-601-5667	

ELDIM INC.
55 Sixth Road, Woburn, MA 01801

CEO: Felix Twaalfhoven, Manager	Tel: (617) 932-6363	Emp: N/A
Bus: *Specialized honeycomb fabrication*	Fax:(617) 932-1905	%FO: 100

INTERTURBINE DALLAS - CASING DIVISION
2800 Avenue E. East, Arlington, TX 76011

CEO: Jeff Wood, Manager	Tel: (817) 640-0895	Emp: N/A
Bus: *Specialized repair services to the flying turbine industry*	Fax:(817) 649-5896	%FO: 100

INTERTURBINE DALLAS AIRFOIL DIVISION
1177 Great Parkway, Grand Prairie, TX 75050

CEO: Steve Zorko, V.P.	Tel: (972) 647-7800	Emp: N/A
Bus: *Specialized repair services to the flying turbine industry.*	Fax:(972) 647-3024	%FO: 100

INTERTURBINE GROUP OF COMPANIES HEADQUARTERS
1170 111th Street, Grand Prairie, TX 75050

CEO: Gordon Walsh, Pres.	Tel: (972) 647-7800	Emp: N/A
Bus: *Turbine repairs.*	Fax:(972) 660-6868	%FO: 100

INTERTURBINE LOS ANGELES
515 West Apra Street, Compton, CA 90220

CEO: Charley Walters, General Mgr.	Tel: (310) 604-8093	Emp: N/A
Bus: *Specialized repair services to the flying turbine industry.*	Fax:(310) 604-9959	%FO: 100

• **ING GROUP**
De Amsterdam Poort, NL-1102 MG, Amsterdam Zuidoost, Netherlands

CEO: A. G. Jacobs, Chrm.	Tel: 31-20-5639111	Emp: 50000
Bus: *Commercial and investment banking and insurance services.*	Fax:31-20-5635700	

BARING ASSET MANAGEMENT
353 Sacramento Street, Ste. 618, San Francisco, CA 94111

CEO: A.L. Janis, Gen. Mgr.	Tel: (415) 834-1500	Emp: N/A
Bus: *Asset management services.*	Fax:(415) 834-1722	%FO: 100

BARING ASSET MANAGEMENT
125 High Street, Suite 2700, Boston, MA   02110-2713

CEO: Phillip Bullen, Gen. Mgr.	Tel: (617) 951-0052	Emp: N/A
Bus: *Asset management services.*	Fax: (617) 330-7481	%FO: 100

BARING ASSET MANAGEMENT HOLDINGS
700 13TH Street, Ste. 950, Washington, DC   20005

CEO: M.H. Joaquin, Gen. Mgr.	Tel: (202) 434-4549	Emp: N/A
Bus: *Asset management services.*	Fax: (202) 434-4574	%FO: 100

BARING BROTHERS
135 East 57th Street, New York, NY   10022-2101

CEO: M.D.G. Ross, Gen. Mgr.	Tel: (212) 906-8655	Emp: N/A
Bus: *Investment banking and asset management services.*	Fax: (212) 906-8613	%FO: 100

BARING HOUSTON & SAUNDERS
135 East 57th Street, New York, NY   10022-2101

CEO: Richard Saunders, Gen. Mgr.	Tel: (212) 409-7003	Emp: N/A
Bus: *Investment banking and asset management services.*	Fax: (212) 409-7466	%FO: 100

BARING VENTURE PARTNERS
P.O. Box 12491, St. Louis, MO   63132

CEO: N. Klein, Gen. Mgr.	Tel: (314) 933-0007	Emp: N/A
Bus: *Investment banking and asset management services.*	Fax: (314) 993-0464	%FO: 100

INDIANA INSURANCE COMPANY
350 East 96th Street, Indianapolis, IN   46240

CEO: Joseph Yeager, Pres.	Tel: (317) 581-6400	Emp: N/A
Bus: *Property & casualty insurance*	Fax: (317) 581-6405	%FO: 100

ING (U.S.) SECURITIES FUTURES & OPTIONS
233 South Wacker Drive, #5200, Chicago, IL   60606

CEO: N/A	Tel: (312) 496-7000	Emp: N/A
Bus: *Securities broker/dealer trading services.*	Fax: (312) 496-7150	%FO: 100

ING BARING (U.S.) SECURITIES
667 Madison Avenue, New York, NY   10021

CEO: Lanc C. Grijns, Chrm.	Tel: (212) 350-7700	Emp: N/A
Bus: *Securities broker/dealer & investment management services.*	Fax: (212) 371-5967	%FO: 100

ING BARING (U.S.) SECURITIES
456 Montgomery Street, San Francisco, CA   94104

CEO: J. Guasco, Gen. Mgr.	Tel: (415) 788-8870	Emp: N/A
Bus: *Securities broker/dealer & investment management services.*	Fax: (415) 788-8890	%FO: 100

ING BARINGS - Los Angeles Office
330 South Grand Ave., Ste. 3300, Los Angeles, CA   90071
CEO: Mark Vidergauz, Mng. Dir.   Tel: (213) 617-9100   Emp: N/A
Bus: *Financial & investment banking services*   Fax:(213) 687-7324   %FO: 100

ING BARINGS
135 East 57th Street, New York, NY   10022-2102
CEO: Fernando Gentil, Chrm.   Tel: (212) 446-1500   Emp: 350
Bus: *Financial & investment banking services*   Fax:(212) 644-0428   %FO: 100

ING BARINGS
300 Galleria Pkwy NW, Ste. 950, Atlanta, GA   30339
CEO: James W. Latimer, Mgr.   Tel: (770) 956-9200   Emp: N/A
Bus: *Insurance & financial services.*   Fax:(770) 951-1005   %FO: 100

ING CAPITAL ADVISERS
135 East 57th Street, 16th Floor, New York, NY   10022-2101
CEO: Michael Mc Adams, CIO   Tel: (212) 409-0580   Emp: N/A
Bus: *Investment advisory services.*   Fax:(212) 753-7247   %FO: 100

ING INVESTMENT MANAGEMENT
300 Galleria Pkwy NW, #1200, Atlanta, GA   30339
CEO: Thomas J. Balachowski, Pres. & CEO   Tel: (770) 850-4800   Emp: 70
Bus: *Asset management services.*   Fax:(770) 850-4801   %FO: 100

ING NORTH AMERICA INSURANCE CORP.
5780 Power Ferry Road, N.W., Atlanta, GA   30327
CEO: Y. Brouilette, Mgr.   Tel: (770) 980-3300   Emp: N/A
Bus: *Insurance services.*   Fax:(770) 980-3301   %FO: 100

ING REAL ESTATE INVESTORS
11100 Santa Monica Blvd., Ste.500, Los Angeles, CA   90025
CEO: Robert Mc Sween, Mng. Dir.   Tel: (310) 966-2000   Emp: N/A
Bus: *Property asset advisors.*   Fax:(310) 966-2061   %FO: 100

LIFE OF GEORGIA
5780 Powers Ferry Road, N.W., Atlanta, GA   30327
CEO: James C. Brooks, Pres.   Tel: (770) 980-5100   Emp: N/A
Bus: *Life insurance services.*   Fax:(770) 980-5800   %FO: 100

THE NETHERLANDS INSURANCE COs
62 Maple Avenue, Keene, NH   03431
CEO: R. L. Jean, CEO   Tel: (603) 352-3221   Emp: 1950
Bus: *Property & casualty insurance.*   Fax:(603) 352-3802   %FO: 100

PEERLESS INSURANCE CO.
62 Maple Avenue, Keene, NH   03431
CEO: R. L. Jean, CEO   Tel: (603) 352-3221   Emp: N/A
Bus: *Property & casualty insurance.*   Fax:(603) 358-6824   %FO: 100

PEERLESS INSURANCE COMPANY
5062 Brittonfeld Pkwy, East Syracuse, NY   13057

CEO: Mike Christiansen, VP	Tel: (315) 431-6100	Emp: 150
Bus: *Property & casualty insurance.*	Fax:(315) 431-6102	%FO: 100

SECURITY LIFE OF DENVER INSURANCE COMPANY
1290 Broadway, Denver, CO   80203

CEO: S.M. Christopher, Pres.	Tel: (303) 860-1290	Emp: N/A
Bus: *Life insurance*	Fax:(303) 860-2260	%FO: 100

SOUTHLAND LIFE INSURANCE COMPANY
5780 Powers Ferry Road, N.W., Atlanta, GA   30327

CEO: J. D. Thompson, Pres.	Tel: (770) 980-5390	Emp: N/A
Bus: *Life insurance*	Fax:(770) 980-5800	%FO: 100

● **KLM NEDERLAND N.V.**
Amsterdamseweg 55, NL-1182 GP, Schiphol, Amstelveen, Netherlands

CEO: Pieter Bouw, Pres.	Tel: 31-20-649-9123	Emp: N/A
Bus: *International commercial air transport services.*	Fax:31-20-648-8069	

KLM-ROYAL DUTCH AIRLINES
PO Box 60277 AMF, Houston, TX   77205

CEO: Eric Jones, Mgr.	Tel: (713) 821-6642	Emp: N/A
Bus: *International commercial air transport services.*	Fax:(713) 821-1251	%FO: 100

KLM-ROYAL DUTCH AIRLINES
Box 66357 AMF, O'Hare Intl Airport, Chicago, IL   60666

CEO: Michael Gerbino, Mgr.	Tel: (312) 686-6047	Emp: N/A
Bus: *International commercial air transport services.*	Fax:(312) 601-8701	%FO: 100

KLM-ROYAL DUTCH AIRLINES
9841 Airport Boulelvard, Los Angeles, CA   90045

CEO: Paul T. Hanrath, Mgr.	Tel: (310) 646-4004	Emp: N/A
Bus: *International commercial air transport services.*	Fax:(310) 649-0665	%FO: 100

KLM-ROYAL DUTCH AIRLINES
565 Taxter Road, Elmsford, NY   10523

CEO: David Downes, General Manager	Tel: (914) 784-2000	Emp: 1100
Bus: *International commercial air transport services.*	Fax:(914) 784-2413	%FO: 100

KLM-ROYAL DUTCH AIRLINES
Los Angeles International Airport, Los Angeles, CA   90045

CEO: Anton W. Adema, Mgr.	Tel: (310) 646-1080	Emp: N/A
Bus: *International commercial air transport services.*	Fax:(310) 646-7058	%FO: 100

KLM-ROYAL DUTCH AIRLINES
3500 Interloop Road, North Cargo Bldg., Atlanta, GA 30320
CEO: William Blackwelder, Mgr. Tel: (404) 762-3030 Emp: N/A
Bus: *International commercial air transport* Fax:(404) 767-5612 %FO: 100
services.

● **KON. NED. PETROLEIUM MIJ SHELL**
30 Carel van Bylandtlaan, 2596 HR, 's Gravenhage, The Hague, Netherlands
CEO: C. A. J. Herkstroter, Chrm. Tel: 31-70-377-9111 Emp: N/A
Bus: *Holding company: exploration prod oil, gas &* Fax:31-70-377-3115
minerals; chemicals, metals (see joint parent:
SHELL TRANSPORT & TRADING CO, England).

ARGUS REALTY SERVICES, INC.
450 Lexington Avenue, Ste. 1970, New York, NY 10017
CEO: Johannes Van Poppel, Pres. Tel: (212) 916-3940 Emp: N/A
Bus: *Investment management service.* Fax:(212) 808-4585 %FO: 100

BILLITON METALS, INC.
120 West 45 Street, 34th Fl., New York, NY 10036
CEO: George Karpakus, Pres. Tel: (212) 391-1343 Emp: N/A
Bus: *Holding company.* Fax:(212) 764-5142 %FO: 100

MASSEY COAL COMPANY
PO Box 23261, Richmond, VA 23261
CEO: Don Blankenschap, Pres. Tel: (804) 788-1800 Emp: N/A
Bus: *Coal mining.* Fax:(804) 788-1870 %FO: 100

SHELL CHEMICAL COMPANY
PO Box 2463, Houston, TX 77252
CEO: Jeroen van der Veer, Pres. & CEO Tel: (713) 241-4028 Emp: N/A
Bus: *Mfr./sales/distribution/research of oil,* Fax:(713) 241-6902 %FO: 100
petroleum, coal and chemical products.

SHELL CREDIT INC.
PO Box 2463, Houston, TX 77252
CEO: Larry Adams, Mgr. Tel: (713) 241-6161 Emp: N/A
Bus: *Credit card service center.* Fax:(713) 241-4040 %FO: 100

SHELL OIL COMPANY
One Shell Plaza, 900 Louisiana St., Houston, TX 77002
CEO: Philip J. Carroll, Pres. & CEO Tel: (713) 241-4300 Emp: 22000
Bus: *Exploration prod oil & gas, chemicals &* Fax:(713) 241-6781 %FO: 100
related products.(Royal Dutch/Shell Group).

SHELL OIL COMPANY
701 Poydras Street, New Orleans, LA 70160
CEO: R. A. Pattarozzi, Gen. Mgr. Tel: (504) 588-6161 Emp: N/A
Bus: *Oil, petroleum, coal and chemical products.* Fax:(504) 588-4567 %FO: 100

SHELL OIL COMPANY
1401 Eyestreet 1030, Washington, DC   20005
CEO: S. Ward, V. P.   Tel: (202) 466-1410   Emp: N/A
Bus: *Oil, petroleum, coal and chemical products.*   Fax:(202) 466-1498   %FO: 100

SHELL PIPE LINE CORPORATION
777 Walker Street, Ste. 1500, Houston, TX   77002
CEO: G. M. Rootes, Pres.   Tel: (713) 241-3527   Emp: N/A
Bus: *Pipeline operators.*   Fax:(713) 241-5716   %FO: 100

● N.V. KONINKLIJKE BIJENKORF BEHEER
Postbus 12035, 1100 AA, Amsterdam Zuid-Oost, Netherlands
CEO: T. S. Henseleijn, Chrm.   Tel: 31-20-563-0100   Emp: N/A
Bus: *Toy chain-store retailer.*   Fax:31-20-691-1733

FAO SCHWARZ
767 Fifth Avenue, New York, NY   10153
CEO: John Eyler, Chrm.   Tel: (212) 644-9410   Emp: 150
Bus: *Toy store chain..*   Fax:(212) 644-2485   %FO: 100

● N.V. KONINKLIJKE KNP BT
Paalbergweg 2, 1105AG, Amsterdam, Netherlands
CEO: R. Van Oordt, Chrm.   Tel: 31-20-567-2672   Emp: N/A
Bus: *Mfr. graphic paper, distribute business mach &* Fax:31-20-567-2567
graphic systems, mfr. packaging, distribute
paper/office products.

BT BUSCHART OFFICE PRODUCTS, INC.
1834 Walton Road, St. Louis, MO   63114
CEO: Richard Dubin, Pres.   Tel: (314) 426-7222   Emp: N/A
Bus: *Distribution of office products.*   Fax:(314) 426-3026   %FO: 100

BT CURRY OFFICE PRODUCTS, INC.
79 North Industrial Park, Pittsburgh, PA   15225
CEO: John R. Kennedy, Pres.   Tel: (412) 741-6494   Emp: N/A
Bus: *Distribution of office products.*   Fax:(412) 741-9351   %FO: 100

BT FAR WEST OFFICE SYSTEMS, INC.
5105 SE 25th Avenue, Portland, OR   97202
CEO: Dick Matza, Pres.   Tel: (503) 239-4404   Emp: N/A
Bus: *Distribution of office products.*   Fax:(503) 731-6200   %FO: 100

BT GINNS OFFICE PRODUCTS, INC.
93-01 Logo Drive West, Springdale, MD   20774
CEO: Paul Christians, Pres.   Tel: (301) 808-7136   Emp: N/A
Bus: *Distribution of office products.*   Fax:(301) 499-6009   %FO: 100

BT KIELTY & DAYTON
23125 Bernart, Hayward, CA 94545
CEO: Rudolf A. J. Huyzer, CEO   Tel: (510) 732-9100   Emp: N/A
Bus: *Holding company of U.S. interests*   Fax:(510) 293-6280   %FO: 100

BT OFFICE PRODUCTS INTERNATIONAL, INC.
Riverwalk, Ste. 590, 2150 East Lake Cook Road, Buffalo Grove, IL 60089
CEO: Rudolph A. J. Huyzer, Pres. & CEO   Tel: (847) 793-7500   Emp: N/A
Bus: *Office products.*   Fax:(847) 808-3001   %FO: 70

BT OFFICE PRODUCTS, INC.
1834 Walton Road, St. Louis, MO 63114
CEO: Richard Dubin, CEO   Tel: (314) 567-9933   Emp: N/A
Bus: *Office equipmen.t*   Fax:(314) 426-2773   %FO: 100

BT PARAMOUNT STATIONERS, INC.
7340 Alondra Blvd., Paramount, CA 90723
CEO: Charles Stadell, Pres.   Tel: (310) 634-5862   Emp: N/A
Bus: *Distribution of office products.*   Fax:(310) 634-3845   %FO: 100

BT PUBLIX OFFICE PRODUCTS, INC.
700 West Chicago Avenue, Chicago, IL 60610
CEO: David Kirshner, Pres.   Tel: (312) 226-1000   Emp: N/A
Bus: *Sales/distribution of commercial office*   Fax:(312) 226-7725   %FO: 100
    supplies, printing and computer supplies.

BT REDWOOD OFFICE PRODUCTS, INC.
1195 Hamiton Court, Menlo Park, CA 94025
CEO: Dana Parsons, Pres.   Tel: (415) 321-0870   Emp: N/A
Bus: *Distribution of office products.*   Fax:(415) 322-4230   %FO: 100

BT ROSS OFFICE SYSTEMS SUPPLY, INC.
1018 North Ward Street, Tampa, Fl 33607
CEO: David Visger, Pres.   Tel: (813) 289-0130   Emp: N/A
Bus: *Distributor of office products.*   Fax:(800) 289-1792   %FO: 100

BT SUMMIT OFFICE PRODUCTS, INC.
303 West 10th Street, 4th Fl., New York, NY 10014
CEO: Peter Guala, Pres.   Tel: (212) 242-5300   Emp: N/A
Bus: *Distributor office. supplies.*   Fax:(212) 242-3854   %FO: 70

EMF CORPORATION
15110 N.E. 95th Street, Redmond, WA 98052
CEO: David Isett, Pres.   Tel: (206) 883-0045   Emp: N/A
Bus: *Mfr./ sales/distr. of specialized packaging*   Fax:(206) 883-7222   %FO: 100
    equipment.

TENNECO PACKAGING AVI
18 Peck Avenue, Glens Falls, NY   12801

CEO: Christopher Angus, V.P.   Tel: (518) 793-2524   Emp: 100

Bus: *Manufacture & distribution of protective*   Fax:(518) 793-3312   %FO: n/a
packaging material

VAN DAM MACHINE CORPORATION
20 Andrews Drive, West Paterson, NJ   07424

CEO: Tony Hooimeijer, Pres.   Tel: (201) 785-4444   Emp: 35

Bus: *Mfr./sales/distribution printing equipment*   Fax:(201) 785-1167   %FO: 100

• KONINKLIJKE NEDLLOYD GROEP N.V.
Postbus 487, 3000 AL, Rotterdam, Netherlands

CEO: L. J. M. Berndsen, Chrm.   Tel: 31-10-400-7111   Emp: N/A

Bus: *International shipping and transport services*   Fax:31-10-404-6075

DAMCO MARITIME CORPORATION
2400 Elmburst Road, Elk Grove Village, IL   60007

CEO: Keith Smith   Tel: (847) 766-7855   Emp: N/A

Bus: *Customs house brokerage.*   Fax:(847) 766-0161   %FO: 100

DAMCO MARITIME CORPORATION
1 Intercontinental Way, Peabody, MA   01960

CEO: Dick Den Hartog, Pres.   Tel: (508) 535-1170   Emp: N/A

Bus: *Sales/distribution of frozen pastries.*   Fax:(508) 535-7028   %FO: 100

MAMMOET TRANSPORT USA INC.
20525 F. M. 521, Rosharon, TX   77583

CEO: P. Haugaard, Pres.   Tel: (281) 369-3900   Emp: N/A

Bus: *Heavy transport operations.*   Fax:(281) 369-3822   %FO: 100

MAMMOET WESTERN INC.
1419 Potrero Avenue, South El Monte, CA   91733

CEO: Albert A. Slikker, Pres.   Tel: (818) 442-5542   Emp: N/A

Bus: *Heavy transport operations.*   Fax:(818) 442-0841   %FO: 100

NEDLLOYD LINES
400 North Sam Houston East Ste. 325, Houston, TX   77060

CEO: Harold J. Hilliard, V.P.   Tel: (213) 437-3900   Emp: N/A

Bus: *Ocean transportation services.*   Fax:(213) 495-1717   %FO: 100

NEDLLOYD LINES
2655 LeJeune Road, Ste. 703, Coral Gables, FL   33134

CEO: M. Messchaert, Mgr.   Tel: (305) 441-9140   Emp: N/A

Bus: *International shipping agency.*   Fax:(305) 441-2984   %FO: 100

NEDLLOYD LINES
650 California Street, 2nd Fl., San Francisco, CA   94108

CEO: Mark Cornwell, General Mgr.   Tel: (415) 393-9100   Emp: N/A

Bus: *International shipping agency.*   Fax:(415) 397-9252   %FO: 100

NEDLLOYD LINES

4975 LaCrosse Road, Ste. 258, North Charleston, SC   29418

CEO: Harold Tillman, V.P.   Tel: (803) 566-7400   Emp: N/A

Bus: *Ocean transportation services.*   Fax:(803) 747-8238   %FO: 100

NEDLLOYD LINES

1 Green Briar Point, Ste. 285, Chesapeake, VA   23320

CEO: Steve Crouch, Mgr.   Tel: (804) 420-4200   Emp: N/A

Bus: *Steamship line.*   Fax:(804) 399-7887   %FO: 100

NEDLLOYD LINES U.S.A. CORP.

2100 River Edge Parkway, Ste. 300, Atlanta, GA   30328

CEO: James I. Newsome, Pres.   Tel: (770) 951-3600   Emp: N/A

Bus: *Ocean transportation services.*   Fax:(770) 980-4012   %FO: 100

• **KONINKLIJKE TEN CATE N.V.**

Egbert Gorterstraat 3, 7607 GB, Almelo, Netherlands

CEO: F. H. Schreve, Chrm.   Tel: 31-54-654-4911   Emp: N/A

Bus: *Manufacture of industrial/agricultural/erosion*   Fax:31-54-651-4145
    control fabrics, fire hoses, geotextiles.

    NATIONAL FIRE HOSE CORP.

    516 East Oak Street, Compton, CA   90224

    CEO: Eric Iwatshsenko, Mgr.   Tel: (213) 537-5211   Emp: N/A

    Bus: *Manufacture/sales of fire hoses.*   Fax:(213) 604-0881   %FO: 100

    NICOLON BAYCOR CORPORATION

    PO Box 460, Cornelia, GA   30531

    CEO: Monte Thomas, Mgr.   Tel: (770) 778-9794   Emp: N/A

    Bus: *Geotextiles.*   Fax:(770) 778-2048   %FO: 100

    NICOLON CORP/ROYAL TEN CATE USA, INC.

    3500 Parkway Lane, Ste. 500, Norcross, GA   30092

    CEO: Edward V. Baich, Pres. & CEO   Tel: (770) 447-6272   Emp: N/A

    Bus: *Manufacture of industrial/agricultural/erosion*   Fax:(770) 242-3828   %FO: 100
        control fabrics.

    ROYAL TEN CATE (USA) INC.

    3500 Parkway Lane, Ste. 500, Norcross, GA   30092

    CEO: Edward V. Baich, Pres.   Tel: (770) 447-6272   Emp: N/A

    Bus: *U.S. holding company*   Fax:(770) 447-6272   %FO: 100

    TEN CATE AEROSPACE, INC.

    5101 Blue Mound Road, Fort Worth, TX   76106

    CEO: Tom McKlezey, Pres.   Tel: (817) 625-4106   Emp: N/A

    Bus: *Polyacrylate windows for*   Fax:(817) 625-9150   %FO: 100
        airplanes/helicopters.

WEATHERSHADE CORPORATION
3000 West Orange Avenue, Apopka, FL   32703

CEO: Gary S. Gale, Pres. & CEO	Tel: (407) 621-4253	Emp: N/A
Bus: *Fabric weathershades.*	Fax:(407) 621-2500	%FO: 100

• LEASE PLAN HOLDING N.V.
Wisselweg 31, 1314 CB Almere, Netherlands

CEO: Anton C. Goudsmit, Pres.	Tel: 31-36-539-3911	Emp: N/A
Bus: *Corporate fleet leasing and management.*	Fax:31-36-539-4700	

LEASE PLAN INTERNATIONAL
180 Interstate North Pkwy., Ste. 400, Atlanta, GA   30339

CEO: Donald F. Kreft, Pres.	Tel: (770) 933-9090	Emp: 65
Bus: *Sale/service corporate fleet leasing & equipment.*	Fax:(770) 933-9091	%FO: 100

• LOEFF CLAEYS VERBEKE
15 Apollalaan, PO Box 75088, 1070 AB Amsterdam, Netherlands

CEO: C. Adriaansens, Mng. Ptnr.	Tel: 31-20-574-1200	Emp: N/A
Bus: *International law firm.*	Fax:31-20-671-8775	

LOEFF CLAEYS VERBEKE
10 East 50th Street, 23rd Fl., New York, NY   10022

CEO: Robert Abendroth, Mng. Ptrn.	Tel: (212) 759-9000	Emp: 11
Bus: *International law firm.*	Fax:(212) 759-9018	%FO: 100

• LOYENS & VOLKMAARS
Groen Van Prinstererlaan 114, 1181 TW Amstelvgeen, PO Box 71170, 1008 BD Amsterdam, Netherlands

CEO: R. T. Van Der Meer, Mng. Ptnr.	Tel: 31-20-6564-600	Emp: 600
Bus: *International law firm.*	Fax:31-20-6435-396	

LOYENS & VOLKMAARS
712 Fifth Avenue, New York, NY   10019

CEO: Martin Van Der Martin Weijden, Mng. Ptnr.	Tel: (212) 489-0620	Emp: N/A
Bus: *International law firm.*	Fax:(212) 489-0710	%FO: 100

• MARTINAIR HOLLAND N.V.
PO Box 7507, 1118 ZD, Schiphol Airport, Amsterdam, Netherlands

CEO: J. Martin Schroder, Pres.	Tel: 31-20-601-1212	Emp: 1185
Bus: *Passenger and cargo airline.*	Fax:31-20-601-0123	

MARTINAIR SERVICES
11001 Aviation Blvd., Ste. 221, Los Angeles, CA   90045

CEO: Karen L. Olsen, Sales Mgr.	Tel: (310) 645-2570	Emp: N/A
Bus: *International passenger/cargo air transportation.*	Fax:(310) 645-2852	%FO: 100

MARTINAIR SERVICES N.A.
5550 Glades Road, #600, Boca Raton, FL   33431

CEO: Richard Saylor, V.P., Sales	Tel: (561) 391-6165	Emp: 75
Bus: *Airline sales/marketing & service.*	Fax:(561) 391-2188	%FO: 100

MARTINAIR SERVICES, N.A.
7700 Edgewater Drive, Ste. 703, Oakland, CA   94621

CEO: Kathryn Horn, Sales Mgr.	Tel: (510) 568-9441	Emp: N/A
Bus: *International passenger/cargo air transportation.*	Fax:(510) 568-9443	%FO: 100

● **MEMOREX TELEX N.V.**
Hoogarddreef 9, 1100 BA, Amsterdam, Netherlands

CEO: K. Van der Steeg, Managing Director	Tel: 31-20-697-4331	Emp: 13000
Bus: *Mfr./distribution/service plug-compatible computer equipment, disk, tape storage devices, terminals, workstations, printers.*	Fax:31-20-564-8320	

MEMOREX TELEX CORP
545 East John Carpenter Fwy. Ste. 6, Irving, TX   75062

CEO: David Faulkner, CFO	Tel: (972) 444-3500	Emp: 9500
Bus: *Mfr./distribution/service of computer equipment & supplies.*	Fax:(972) 444-3595	%FO: 100

● **NAUTA DUTILH**
Prises Irenestraat 59, NL-1077 WV Amsterdam, The Netherlands

CEO: J. W. Sodderland, Ptnr.	Tel: 31-20-541-4646	Emp: N/A
Bus: *International law firm.*	Fax:31-20-661-2827	

NAUTA DUTILH
101 Park Avenue, New ork, NY   10178

CEO: Robert Norbruis, Mng. Ptnr.	Tel: (212) 218-2990	Emp: N/A
Bus: *International law firm.*	Fax:(212) 218-2999	%FO: 100

● **NUCLETRON**
Waar Dgelder 1, NL-3905 TH Veenendaal, Netherlands.

CEO: Hans Haarman, CEO	Tel: 31-318-533132	Emp: N/A
Bus: *Mfr. medical, industrial and defense imaging and optical instruments.*	Fax:31-318-550485	

ODELFT CORP. OF AMERICA
7080 Columbia Gateway Drive, Columbia, MD   21046

CEO: Thomas Maher, Pres.	Tel: (410) 312-4100	Emp: N/A
Bus: *Mfr./distributor medical, industrial and defense imaging and optical instruments.*	Fax:(410) 312-4199	%FO: 100

• **OCÉ NEDERLAND B.V.**
St. Urbanusweg 43, 5914 CA, Venlo, Netherlands
CEO: E. C. De la Houssaye, Mgr.   Tel: 31-77-359-2222   Emp: N/A
Bus: *Reprographics, copiers, printers, office automation.*   Fax:31-77-3544700

    ARKWRIGHT INC.
    538 Main Street, Fiskeville, RI   02823
    CEO: Frank van Oudenhoven, Pres.   Tel: (401) 821-1000   Emp: N/A
    Bus: *Sales/service office automation equipment.*   Fax:(401) 826-3926   %FO: 100

    OCÉ- OFFICE SYSTEMS, INC.
    One Penn Plaza, 33rd Fl., New York, NY   10119
    CEO: Wayne Frahn, Regional Sales Dir.   Tel: (212) 868-1818   Emp: N/A
    Bus: *Sales/service of copier systems.*   Fax:(212) 564-6604   %FO: 100

    OCÉ- OFFICE SYSTEMS, INC.
    2 Park Plaza, Ste. 200, Irvine, CA   92714
    CEO: Michael Liess, Regional Director   Tel: (714) 223-2742   Emp: N/A
    Bus: *Sales/service of reprographic equipment.*   Fax:(714) 476-2295   %FO: 100

    OCÉ- OFFICE SYSTEMS, INC.
    2300 Clarendon Blvd., Ste. 1200, Arlington, VA 22201
    CEO: Marcel Scherrenberg, Sales Exec.   Tel: (703) 522-3741   Emp: N/A
    Bus: *Sales/distribution, service/warehousing of* Fax:(703) 528-6854   %FO: 100
        paper copier systems.

    OCÉ - USA INC.
    5450 North Cumberland Avenue, Chicago, IL   60656
    CEO: Jan Dix, Pres.   Tel: (773) 714-8500   Emp: N/A
    Bus: *Manufacturer of mid/high volume copiers.*   Fax:(773) 714-0542   %FO: 100

• **PAKHOED HOLDING NV**
Blaak 333, 3011 GB Rotterdam, Postbus 863, 3000 AW, Rotterdam, Netherlands
CEO: N.J. Westdijk, Chrm.   Tel: 31-10-400-2911   Emp: 5200
Bus: *Tank storage, transport/distribution petrochemical* Fax:31-10-413-9829
    and chemical products.

    VAN WATERS & ROGERS INC.
    PO Box 34325, Seattle, WA   98124
    CEO: Paul H. Hough, Pres. & CEO   Tel: (206) 889-3400   Emp: 2700
    Bus: *Distribution of chemicals.*   Fax:(206) 889-4100   %FO: 100

• **PHILIPS ELECTRONICS N.V.**
Groenewoudseweg 1, NL-5600 MD Eindhoven, Netherlands
CEO: Jan D. Timmer, Pres.   Tel: 31-40-278-6022   Emp: 250000
Bus: *Mfr. consumer electronic, lighting components,*   Fax:31-40-278-5486
    appliances, professional system, communications &
    information system, medical imaging equipment.

   ADVANCE TRANSFORMER COMPANY
   10275 West Higgins Road, Rosemont, IL   60018
   CEO: Jack Briody, Pres.   Tel: (847) 390-5000   Emp: 300
   Bus: *Mfr./sales/distribution of professional light*   Fax:(847) 390-5109   %FO: 100
     systems.

   BTS BROADCAST TELEVISION SYSTEMS INC.
   94 West Cochran Street, Simi Valley, CA   93065
   CEO: Jeff Rosica, Pres.   Tel: (310) 966-2700   Emp: 25
   Bus: *Mfr./sale professional TV systems for*   Fax:(310) 966-2765   %FO: 100
     broadcast, production & post-production, &
     corporate applications.

   NORELCO CONSUMER PRODUCTS COMPANY
   1010 Washington Blvd., Stamford, CT   06901
   CEO: Patrick J. Dinley, Pres.   Tel: (203) 973-0200   Emp: 120
   Bus: *Mfr. razors, kitchen & travel appliances.*   Fax:(203) 975-1812   %FO: 100

   PHILIPS AUTOMOTIVE ELECTRONICS
   PO Box 868, Cheshire, CT   06410
   CEO: Ron Marsiglio, Pres.   Tel: (203) 271-6000   Emp: N/A
   Bus: *Mfr. circuit breakers, motor products.*   Fax:(203) 271-6522   %FO: 100

   PHILIPS BROADBAND NETWORKS, INC.
   100 Fairgrounds Drive, Manlius, NY   13104
   CEO: Dieter Brauer, Pres.   Tel: (315) 682-9105   Emp: 150
   Bus: *Mfr. distribution equipment for cable TV &*   Fax:(315) 682-9006   %FO: 100
     business information networks.

   PHILIPS BUSINESS SYSTEMS
   365 Crossways Park Drive, Woodbury, NY   11797-2590
   CEO: Carl Sahora, Pres.   Tel: (516) 921-9310   Emp: N/A
   Bus: *Sales/distribution/service of dictation &*   Fax:(516) 921-9319   %FO: 100
     transcription equipment.

   PHILIPS COMPONENTS DISCRETE PRODUCTS DIVISION
   6071 St. Andrews Road, Columbia, SC   29212
   CEO: William Cvirko, General Manager   Tel: (803) 772-2500   Emp: N/A
   Bus: *Mfr. imaging devices, tubes, solid state*   Fax:(803) 772-2445   %FO: 100
     components.

PHILIPS CONSUMER ELECTRONICS COMPANY
PO Box 14810, One Phillips Drive, Knoxville, TN   37914-1810

CEO: Robert Minkhorst, Pres.	Tel: (423) 521-4316	Emp: N/A
Bus: *Mfr. home & portable audio & video systems & components*	Fax:(423) 521-4308	%FO: 100

PHILIPS DISPLAY COMPONENTS COMPANY
1600 Huron Pkwy., Ann Arbor, MI   48106

CEO: Iva Wilson, Pres.	Tel: (313) 996-9400	Emp: N/A
Bus: *Mfr./sales of color TV tubes, data display tubes.*	Fax:(313) 761-2886	%FO: 100

PHILIPS ELECTRONIC INSTRUMENTS CO.
85 McKee Drive, Mahwah, NJ   07430

CEO: Bill Enser, Pres. & CEO	Tel: (201) 529-3800	Emp: N/A
Bus: *Mfr. X-ray & electron optics, analytical products.*	Fax:(210) 529-2252	%FO: 100

PHILIPS ELECTRONICS NORTH AMERICA CORP.
100 East 42nd Street, New York, NY   10017

CEO: Michael P. Moakley, Pres. & CEO	Tel: (212) 850-5000	Emp: 200
Bus: *Holding company.*	Fax:(212) 850-7304	%FO: 100

PHILIPS LIGHTING COMPANY
2701 West Roosevelt Road, Little Rock, AR   72204

CEO: Thomas B. Moore, Mgr.	Tel: (501) 370-7121	Emp: N/A
Bus: *Manufacturer of lighting products.*	Fax:(501) 370-7127	%FO: 100

PHILIPS LMS
4425 Arrows West Drive, Colorado Springs, CO   80907

CEO: Charles Johnston, Pres.	Tel: (719) 593-7900	Emp: N/A
Bus: *Mfr. magnetic tape drives, optical data storage products.*	Fax:(719) 599-8713	%FO: 100

PHILIPS MEDICAL SYSTEMS NA
710 Bridgeport Avenue, Shelton, CT   06484

CEO: Michael Moakley, Pres.	Tel: (203) 926-7674	Emp: N/A
Bus: *Sale/service of medical diagnostic imaging & radiotherapy equipment.*	Fax:(203) 929-6099	%FO: 100

PHILIPS RESEARCH
345 Scarborough Road, Briarcliff Manor, NY   10510

CEO: P. Bingham, Pres.	Tel: (914) 945-6000	Emp: N/A
Bus: *Electronics R&D.*	Fax:(914) 945-6375	%FO: 100

PHILIPS SEMICONDUCTORS
PO Box 3409, 811 East Arques, Sunnyvale, CA   94088-3409

CEO: Jim Dykes, Pres.	Tel: (408) 991-2000	Emp: N/A
Bus: *Design/mfr./distribution integrated circuits*	Fax:(408) 991-3581	%FO: 100

● **PIE MEDICAL N.V.**
Philipsweg 1, 6227 AJ Maastricht, Netherlands
CEO: Bas Alberts, Pres.   Tel: 31-43-361-2121   Emp: 200
Bus: *Mfr. diagnostic ultrasound systems.*   Fax:31-43-4361-6711

    PIE MEDICAL USA
    6401 Congress Avenue, Boca Raton, FL   33487
    CEO: Kip Speyer, Pres.   Tel: (800) 448-4450   Emp: 10
    Bus: *Sale/marketing/service of diagnostic, ultra-*   Fax:(407) 997-1645   %FO: 100
        sound scanners and medical electronic
        equipment.

● **POLYGRAM B.V.**
Gerrit v.d. Veenlaan 4, 3743 DN, Baarn, Amsterdam
CEO: T. Roos, Pres.   Tel: 31-35-541-9911   Emp: 12500
Bus: *Music and record company.*   Fax:31-35-624-6126

    POLYGRAM HOLDINGS, INC.
    825 Eighth Avenue, New York, NY   10019
    CEO: Eric Kronfeld, Pres. & CEO   Tel: (212) 333-8000   Emp: N/A
    Bus: *Record production and management company.*   Fax:(212) 603-7935   %FO: 100

    POLYGRAM RECORDS, INC.
    11150 Santa Monica Blvd., 11th Fl., Los Angeles, CA   90025
    CEO: Elease Dickerson, Administrative Coordinator   Tel: (310) 996-7200   Emp: N/A
    Bus: *Sales/distribution of music/records.*   Fax:(310) 477-7622   %FO: 100

    POLYGRAM RECORDS, INC.
    9999 East 121st Street, Fishers, IN   46038
    CEO: Steven Margeotes, V.P.   Tel: (317) 594-0404   Emp: N/A
    Bus: *Record warehouse.*   Fax:(317) 595-5305   %FO: 100

● **RABOBANK NEDERLAND**
Croeselaan 18, 3521 CB Utrecht, Netherlands
CEO: H.H.F. Wijffels, Chrm.   Tel: 31-30-909111   Emp: 37000
Bus: *Banking and financial services.*   Fax:31-30-902672

    RABOBANK NEDERLAND
    245 Park Avenue, 37th Fl., New York, NY   10167
    CEO: Dennis J. Ziengs, Mgr.   Tel: (212) 916-7800   Emp: 330
    Bus: *Banking and financial services.*   Fax:(212) 818-0233   %FO: 100

● **RODAMCO N.V.**
Coolsingel 120, Postbus 973, NL-3011 A6 Rotterdam, Netherlands

CEO: Pieter Korteweg, Pres.   Tel: 31-1-224-1224   Emp: N/A
Bus: *Real estate development banking & investment*   Fax:31-1-411-5288
services.

RODAMCO NORTH AMERICA
950 East Paces Freey Raod, Ste. 2275, Atlanta, GA   30326

CEO: Karen Heiser, Mgr.   Tel: (404) 266-1002   Emp: N/A
Bus: *Real estate development banking & investment*   Fax:(404) 239-6097   %FO: 100
services.

● **ROYAL AHOLD N.V.**
Albert Heijnweg 1, P O Box 33, 1500 EA Zaandam, Netherlands

CEO: Cees H. van der Hoeven, Pres.   Tel: 31-75-659-9111   Emp: 107000
Bus: *Retail foodstuffs & consumer goods, food*   Fax:31-75-650-8350
production, processing & retailing.

AHOLD USA, INC.
950 East Paces Ferry Road, N.E, Ste. 2575, Atlanta, GA   30326

CEO: Robert Zwartendijk, Pres.   Tel: (404) 262-6050   Emp: N/A
Bus: *Holding company for Ahold's U.S. interests.*   Fax:(404) 262-6051   %FO: 100

BI-LO
5901 Shallowford Road, Chattanooga, TN   37421

CEO: Marshall J. Collins, Pres.   Tel: (615) 892-8029   Emp: N/A
Bus: *Retail food chain*   Fax:(615) 892-3825   %FO: 100

FIRST NATIONAL SUPERMARKETS INC.
17000 Rockside Road, Maple Heights, OH   44137

CEO: Richard Bogomolny, Pres.   Tel: (216) 587-7100   Emp: N/A
Bus: *Retail food chain.*   Fax:(216) 475-4354   %FO: 100

GIANT FOOD STORES INC.
US 11, North Shady Lane, Carlisle, PA   17013

CEO: Tony Schiano, Pres.   Tel: (717) 249-4000   Emp: N/A
Bus: *Retail food chain.*   Fax:(717) 249-5871   %FO: 100

STOP & SHOP COMPANIES
1385 Hancock Street, Quincy, MA   02169

CEO: Richard G. Tobin, Pres.   Tel: (617) 380-8000   Emp: N/A
Bus: *Retail food chain*   Fax: %FO: 100

TOPS MARKETS
6363 Main Street, Williamsville, NY   14221

CEO: Larry P. Castellani, Pres.   Tel: (716) 635-5000   Emp: N/A
Bus: *Retail food chain*   Fax:(716) 635-5102   %FO: 100

● **ROYAL BOLS WESSANEN N.V.**
Prof. E. M. Meijerslaan 2, 1183 AV Amstelveen, Netherlands
CEO: A. M. Zondervan, Chrm.   Tel: 31-20-574-9547   Emp: N/A
Bus: *Global manufacturing & marketing of food &*   Fax:31-20-645-9160
     beverages.

    A.M. AXELROD FOODS, INC.
    100 Thomas Street, Paterson, NJ   07533
    CEO: David Coyne, Pres.   Tel: (201) 684-0600   Emp: N/A
    Bus: *Sales and distribution of dairy products.*   Fax:(201) 684-0943   %FO: 100

    AMERICAN BEVERAGE CORP
    1 Daily Way, Verona, PA   15147
    CEO: D. Bober, CEO   Tel: (412) 828-9020   Emp: N/A
    Bus: *Production of fruit juices/drinks.*   Fax:(412) 828-5449   %FO: 100

    AMERICAN NATURAL SNACKS INC.
    PO Box 1067, St.. Augustine, FL   32085
    CEO: Casey Rysdam, Pres.   Tel: (904) 825-2056   Emp: N/A
    Bus: *Sales and distribution of health food.*   Fax:(904) 825-2013   %FO: 100

    BOLS INT'L., B.V.
    300 Frank W. Burr Blvd., Teaneck, NJ   07666
    CEO: Dennis McCrone, CEO   Tel: (201) 928-0488   Emp: N/A
    Bus: *Sales/marketing of Bols Liqueurs, Bolskaya*   Fax:(201) 928-0196   %FO: 100
     vodka.

    BOLS WESSANEN USA
    1750 Tree Blvd., St.. Augustine, FL   32086
    CEO: Richard A. Thorne, Pres.   Tel: (904) 825-2001   Emp: N/A
    Bus: *U.S. Headquarters Royal Bolls Wessanen, NV.*   Fax:(904) 825-2230   %FO: 100

    CEDARBURG DAIRY
    PO Box 287, Cedarburg, WI   53012
    CEO: Jim Green, Pres.   Tel: (414) 377-5040   Emp: N/A
    Bus: *Manufacturer of dairy products.*   Fax:(414) 377-9532   %FO: 100

    CROWLEY FOODS INC.
    PO Box 549, Binghamton, NY   13902
    CEO: Robert W. Allen, Pres.   Tel: (607) 779-3289   Emp: N/A
    Bus: *Mfr./sales/distribution of dairy products.*   Fax:(607) 779-3439   %FO: 100

    CROWLEY FROZEN DESERTS, INC.
    PO Box 7007, Lancester, PA   17604
    CEO: Bruce White, Sr. V.P.   Tel: (717) 843-9891   Emp: N/A
    Bus: *Mfr./sales/distribution of dairy products.*   Fax:(717) 399-8584   %FO: 100

FRANKLIN FOODS, INC.
1925 West First Street, Duluth, MN   55816
CEO: Herbert Hacks, Mgr.   Tel: (218) 727-6651   Emp: N/A
Bus: *Sales/distribution of fluid milk bottling.*   Fax:(218) 727-4427   %FO: 100

HELUVA GOOD CHEESE, INC.
6551 Pratt Road, Sodus, NY   14551
CEO: John Boyle, V.P.   Tel: (315) 483-6971   Emp: N/A
Bus: *Distribution of cheese products.*   Fax:(315) 483-9927   %FO: 100

HI-PROFIT DISTRIBUTORS
9505 El Dorado Avenue, Sun Valley, CA   91352
CEO: James Searcie, Pres.   Tel: (818) 768-2330   Emp: N/A
Bus: *Distribution of health foods.*   Fax:(818) 768-9316   %FO: 100

JOHN E. CAIN COMPANY
PO Box 347, Ayer, MA   01432
CEO: Jay M. Hellman, Pres.   Tel: (508) 772-0300   Emp: N/A
Bus: *Mfr./sales/distribution of mayonnaise, salad*   Fax:(508) 772-9876   %FO: 100
dressing, pickles & relishes.

MARIGOLD FOODS INC.
2929 University Avenue, S.E., Minneapolis, MN   55414
CEO: Dwight Holcombe, Pres.   Tel: (612) 331-3775   Emp: N/A
Bus: *Mfr./sales/distribution of milk and dairy*   Fax:(612) 378-8389   %FO: 100
products.

REAL VEAL INC.
America Street, North 8155, Ixonia, WI   53036
CEO: Robert Groenevelt, Pres.   Tel: (414) 567-8989   Emp: N/A
Bus: *Mfr./sales/distribution and warehousing of*   Fax:(414) 567-1041   %FO: 100
specialty feeds.

• ROYAL DUTCH SHELL GROUP
30 Carel van Bylandtlaan, 2596 HR The Hague, Netherlands
CEO: Cornelius A. J. Herkströter, CEO   Tel: 31-70-377-3395   Emp: N/A
Bus: *Oil and natural gas exploration and production.*   Fax:31-70-377-4848

SHELL OIL COMPANY
One Shell Plaza, Houston, TX   77002
CEO: Philip Carroll, Pres.   Tel: (713) 241-6161   Emp: N/A
Bus: *Global oil/gas company; JV with UK.*   Fax:(713) 241-4044   %FO: JV

- **ROYAL NEDLLOYD GROUP N.V.**
  Boompjes 40, 3000 AL Rotterdam, Netherlands
  CEO: H. Rootliep, Chrm.   Tel: 31-10-400-6111   Emp: 23000
  Bus: *Transport, forwarding, storage & distribution ;*   Fax:N/A
        energy exploration & prod.

      P & O NEDLLOYD LINES USA CORP.
      2100 River Edge Pkwy, #300, Atlanta, GA   30328
      CEO: L. Cutrona, V.P.   Tel: (770) 951-3600   Emp: 65
      Bus: *Ocean cargo transport.*   Fax:(770) 980-9409   %FO: 100

- **ROYAL PTT NEDERLAND N.V.**
  Postbus 15000, 9700 CD Groningen, Netherlands
  CEO: Wim Dik, Chrm.   Tel: 31-50-822822   Emp: 90000
  Bus: *Supplies telecommunications services.*   Fax:N/A

      KPN US INC.
      1270 Ave of the Americas, New York, NY   10020
      CEO: Jan Sander, Pres. & CEO   Tel: (212) 246-1818   Emp: 15
      Bus: *Voice/data communications.*   Fax:(212) 246-1905   %FO: 100

- **SAIT- RADIO HOLLAND B.V.**
  Jan Rebelstraat 20, 1069 CC, Amsterdam, Netherlands
  CEO: V. Van Overbeek, Mng.Dir.   Tel: 31-20-667-8100   Emp: N/A
  Bus: *Marine electronic communication for commercial*   Fax:31-20-667-8113
        shipping.

      SAIT RHG NORFOLK/ RH DEFENSE SYSTEMS, INC.
      2703 Avenger Drive, Virginia Beach, VA   23452
      CEO: K. Ravenna, CEO   Tel: (757) 431-2926   Emp: N/A
      Bus: *Sales/service of marine and industrial*   Fax:(757) 431-3676   %FO: 100
        electronics/communication and nautical
        instruments.

      SAIT-RHG
      5233 Interstate 37, Ste. A-1, Corpus Christi, TX   78408
      CEO: Arland Shooks, Manager   Tel: (512) 888-3528   Emp: N/A
      Bus: *Electronic communication equipment for*   Fax:(512) 883-5285   %FO: 100
        commercial shipping.

      SAIT-RHG
      1965 East Srping Street, Long Beach, CA   90806
      CEO: Peter Peterson, Manager   Tel: (310) 595-0039   Emp: N/A
      Bus: *Sales/service of marine/industrial electronics,*   Fax:(310) 988-0236   %FO: 100
        communication and nautical instruments.

SAIT-RHG
910 NE Minni Ha Street, Ste. 3, Vancouver, WA   98665

CEO: Mark Richard, Manager	Tel: (206) 737-0519	Emp: N/A
Bus: *Sales/service of marine/industrial electronics, communication and nautical instruments.*	Fax:(206) 737-0543	%FO: 100

SAIT-RHG
894 Gulf Freeway, Houston, TX   77017

CEO: J. Plenter, General Manager	Tel: (713) 943-3325	Emp: N/A
Bus: *Head office for U.S. interests in electronic communication equipment for commercial shipping.*	Fax:(713) 587-9392	%FO: 100

SAIT-RHG
3007 Green Street, Hollywood, FL   33020

CEO: Mark Mitchell, Manager	Tel: (954) 920-8400	Emp: N/A
Bus: *Service of marine electronic communication for commercial shipping.*	Fax:(954) 920-8450	%FO: 100

SAIT-RHG
1965 East Spring Street, Long Beach, CA   90806

CEO: Bill Herrel, Manager	Tel: (310) 595-0039	Emp: N/A
Bus: *Sales/distribution/service of marine electronic communications equipment for shipping industry.*	Fax:(310) 988-0236	%FO: 100

● SIBBE SIMONT MONAHAN DUHOT
Strawinskylaan 2001, PO Box 75640, 1070 AP Amsterdam, The Netherlands

CEO: Hans M. Van Veggel, Mng. Ptnr.	Tel: 31-20-546-0606	Emp: N/A
Bus: *International law firm.*	Fax:31-20-546-0123	

SIBBE SIMONT MONAHAN DUHOT
335 Madison Avenue, New York, NY   10017

CEO: T. H. Van Engelen, Mng. Ptnr.	Tel: (212) 972-4000	Emp: N/A
Bus: *International law firm.*	Fax:(212) 972-4929	%FO: 100

● STORK N.V.
Amersfoortsestraatweg 7, 1412 KA, Naarden, Netherlands

CEO: J. C. M. Hovers, Chrm.	Tel: 31-35-695-7411	Emp: N/A
Bus: *Machinery and parts for food processing equipment, and mktg. of machines for beverage/food/dairy/pharmaceutical industries.*	Fax:31-35-694-1184	

INSTROMET ULTRASONIC TECHNOLOGY, INC.
3731 Briarpark Drive, Ste. 100, Houston, TX   77042

CEO: Shelby Morley, Manager	Tel: (713) 977-3591	Emp: N/A
Bus: *Flow measuring systems.*	Fax:(713) 977-0810	%FO: 100

STORK
PO Box 1258, Gainesville, GA   30503
CEO: Frits Verbakel, Exec. V.P.   Tel: (770) 532-7887   Emp: N/A
Bus: *Sales/distribution/service of machinery for*   Fax:(770) 536-0841   %FO: 100
       meat processing industry

STORK CELLRAMIC, INC.
8399 North 87th Street, Milwaukee, WI   53224
CEO: Frank Van Den Berge, Operations Mgr.   Tel: (414) 357-0260   Emp: N/A
Bus: *Thermal spray coatings and anilox rolls.*   Fax:(414) 357-0267   %FO: 100

STORK FOOD MACHINERY INC.
3525 West Peterson Avenue, Ste. T-19, Chicago, IL   60659
CEO: Herbert J. Miller, General Mgr.   Tel: (312) 583-1455   Emp: N/A
Bus: *Sales/distribution/service of machinery for*   Fax:(312) 583-8155   %FO: 100
       beverage/food/dairy/pharmaceutical industries.

STOCK LATINO AMERICA
Airport Parkway, Gainesville, GA   30503
CEO: Frank Nicoletti, Manager of Sales   Tel: (770) 532-7041   Emp: N/A
Bus: *After sales service*   Fax:(770) 536-0585   %FO: 100

STORK SCREENS AMERICA INC.
3201 North Interstate 85, Charlotte, NC   28213
CEO: Bart Vogel, Exec. V.P.   Tel: (704) 598-7171   Emp: N/A
Bus: *Sale of seamless rotary screens for the textile*   Fax:(704) 596-0858   %FO: 100
       printing industry.

STORK VECO INTERNATIONAL
3 Loomis Street, Bedford, MA   01730
CEO: William E. McHugh, Pres.   Tel: (617) 275-3292   Emp: N/A
Bus: *Sales/distribution of perforated products*   Fax:(617) 275-4798   %FO: 100

STORK X-CEL, INC.
PO Box 217125, Charlotte, NC   28221
CEO: Jim Cuff, General Mgr.   Tel: (704) 598-6393   Emp: N/A
Bus: *Wall covering/coating and graphics.*   Fax:(704) 598-6693   %FO: 100

● **UNILEVER N.V.**
Weena 455, NL-3013 DK Rotterdam, Netherlands
CEO: Morris Tabaksblat, Chrm.   Tel: 31-10-464-5911   Emp: 308000
Bus: *Soaps and detergents, foods, chemicals, personal*   Fax:31-10-464-4798
       products (see joint parent: UNILEVER PLC,
       England).

CALVIN KLEIN COSMETICS CO.
725 Fifth Avenue, New York, NY   10022
CEO: Kim Dehing, Pres.   Tel: (212) 759-8888   Emp: N/A
Bus: *Manufacturer of perfumes.*   Fax:(212) 755-8792   %FO: 100

CHESEBROUGH POND'S INC.
33 Benedict Place, Greenwich, CT 06830
CEO: Robert M. Phillips, Chrm.   Tel: (203) 661-2000   Emp: N/A
Bus: *Manufacturer of health & beauty products.*   Fax:(203) 625-1602   %FO: 100

DIVERSEY CORPORATION
12025 Tech Center Drive, Livonia, MI 48150
CEO: Arwin Huges, Pres.   Tel: (313) 458-5000   Emp: N/A
Bus: *Mfr. specialty chemicals.*   Fax:(313) 414-3364   %FO: 100

ELIZABETH ARDEN
4411 Plantation Road, N.E., Roanoke, VA 24012
CEO: George Flynn, Pres.   Tel: (540) 563-3000   Emp: N/A
Bus: *Mfr. cosmetics, perfumes.*   Fax:(540) 563-3109   %FO: 100

HELENE CURTIS
325 North Wells Street, Chicago, IL 60610
CEO: Ronald J. Gidwitz, Pres.   Tel: (312) 661-0222   Emp: N/A
Bus: *Mfr. cosmetics, perfumes.*   Fax:(312) 836-0125   %FO: 100

THOMAS J. LIPTON INC.
800 Sylvan Avenue, Englewood Cliffs, NJ 07632
CEO: Blaine Hess, Pres.   Tel: (201) 567-8000   Emp: N/A
Bus: *Manufacturer of tea products.*   Fax:(201) 871-8280   %FO: 100

UNILEVER UNITED STATES INC.
390 Park Avenue, New York, NY 10022
CEO: Richard A. Goldstein, Pres.   Tel: (212) 688-6000   Emp: N/A
Bus: *Manufacturer of soaps, detergents.*   Fax:(212) 318-3800   %FO: 100

● **VAN LEEUWEN BUIZENHANDEL B.V.**
Lindtsedijk 20, 336 LE, Zwinjndrecht, Netherlands
CEO: B. van Dam, Chrm.   Tel: 31-78-625-2525   Emp: N/A
Bus: *Distribution of carbon steel, weld fittings, flanges &*   Fax:31-78-619-4444
pipe.

VAN LEEUWEN PIPE AND TUBE CORP.
15333 Hempstead Road, PO Box 40904, Houston, TX 77240
CEO: Roland Balkenende, Pres.   Tel: (713) 466-9966   Emp: 220
Bus: *Distribution of pipe, fittings, flanges, and*   Fax:(713) 466-7423   %FO: 100
valves.

● **VAN MELLE N.V.**
Zoete Inval 20, 4800 DA Breda, Netherlands
CEO: Izaak L .G. Van Melle, Pres. Tel: 31-76-527-5000 Emp: 1700
Bus: *Mfr. confectionery, biscuits, health foods.* Fax:31-76-522-8560

 VAN MELLE USA INC.
 One Van Melle Lane, PO Box 18190, Erlanger, KY   41018
 CEO: Marius van Melle, Pres. Tel: (606) 283-1234 Emp: 100
 Bus: *Mfr./import candy.* Fax:(606) 283-1316 %FO: 100

● **VERO SALES B.V.**
Nieuwe Hemweg 6b, 1013 BG, Amsterdam, Netherlands
CEO: R. J. M. Van Veldhoven, Pres. Tel: 31-20-681-2593 Emp: N/A
Bus: *International market research services.* Fax:31-20-682-0644

 VERO SALES INC.
 770 North Halsted Street, Ste.100, Chicago, IL   60622
 CEO: Ron Van Velthoven, Pres. Tel: (312) 491-0341 Emp: N/A
 Bus: *International market research services.* Fax:(312) 491-0537 %FO: 100

● **VETUS DENOUDEN NV**
Fokkerstraat 571, NL-3125 BD Schiedam, Netherlands
CEO: W.H.den Ouden, Pres. Tel: 31-10-437700 Emp: N/A
Bus: *Mfr. marine equipment parts and accessories.* Fax:31-10-4152623

 VETUS DENOUDEN, INC.
 7170 Standard Drive, Dorsey, MD   21076
 CEO: Leo J. van Hemert, Pres. Tel: (410) 712-0740 Emp: N/A
 Bus: *Mfr. marine equipment parts and accessories.* Fax:(410) 712-0985 %FO: 100

● **VITESSE B.V.**
Van Riemsdijkweg 12, 3088 HC ,Rotterdam, Netherlands
CEO: Cees Weima, Pres. Tel: 31-10-428-6666 Emp: 250
Bus: *Warehousing & distribution.* Fax:31-10-428-6657

 VITESSE AMERICA INC.
 333 North Michigan Avenue, Ste. 1816, Chicago, IL   60601
 CEO: Herbert Wennink, Dir. Tel: (312) 641-2805 Emp: 3
 Bus: *European warehousing & distribution.* Fax:(312) 641-6733 %FO: 100

- **VNU INTERNATIONAL BV**
Ceylonpoort 5-25, NL-2037 AA Haarlem, Netherlands
CEO: J.L. Brentjens, Chrm.   Tel: 31-23-546-3463   Emp: N/A
Bus: *Publishes/distributes magazines. newspapers,*   Fax:31-23-546-338
educational & business information services.

BELDEN ASSOCIATES
3102 Oak Lawn Avenue, Dallas, TX   75219
CEO: Deanne Termini, Pres.   Tel: (214) 522-8630   Emp: 20
Bus: *Provides full service market research services.* Fax:(214) 522-0926   %FO: 100

BILL COMMUNICATIONS
355 Park Avenue South, New York, NY   10010
CEO: John Wickersham, Pres. & CEO   Tel: (212) 592-6200   Emp: N/A
Bus: *Provides communications services.*   Fax:(212) 592-6209   %FO: 100

BPI COMMUNICATIONS, INC.
1515 Broadway, New York, NY   10036
CEO: John J. Babcock, Jr., Pres. & CEO   Tel: (212) 536-6520   Emp: 900
Bus: *Communications industry magazine*   Fax:(212) 536-5243   %FO: 100
publishers; Ad Week, Media Week, et.al.

CLARITAS, INC.
1525 Wilson Blvd., Suite 1000, Arlington, VA   22209
CEO: Nancy Deck, Pres.   Tel: (703) 812-2700   Emp: 150
Bus: *Provides target marketing services.*   Fax:(703) 812-2701   %FO: 100

COMPETITIVE MEDIA REPORTING
11 West 42nd Street, New York, NY   10036
CEO: Jeffrey Hale, Pres.   Tel: (212) 789-3680   Emp: 75
Bus: *Provides media & marketing consulting*   Fax:(212) 789-3640   %FO: 100
services.

INTERACTIVE MARKET SYSTEMS, INC.
11 West 42nd Street, New York, NY   10036
CEO: Charles Hunt, EVP & Gen.Mgr.   Tel: (212) 789-3600   Emp: 55
Bus: *Provides media & marketing consulting*   Fax:(212) 789-3636   %FO: 100
services.

LAKEWOOD PUBLICATIONS, INC.
50 South Ninth Street, Minneapolis, MN   55402
CEO: James P. Secord, Pres. & CEO   Tel: (612) 333-0471   Emp: N/A
Bus: *Publishers of business book & magazines.*   Fax:(612) 340-4757   %FO: 100

MARKETING RESOURCES PLUS
555 Twin Dolphin Drive, Pacific Dolphin Pl., Redwood City, CA   94065
CEO: Bev Andal, Pres.   Tel: (415) 595-1800   Emp: 52
Bus: *Develop/market software to advertising*   Fax:(415) 595-3410   %FO: 100
agencies.

PERQ RESEARCH CORPORATION
372 Danbury Road, Wilton, CT   06897

CEO: Charles Hunt, Gen.Mgr.

Bus: *Provides media & marketing consulting services.*

Tel: (203) 834-9983   Emp: 20
Fax:(203) 834-9989   %FO: 100

THE SACHS GROUP
1800 Sherman Avenue, Evanston, IL   60201

CEO: Michael Sachs, Chrm.

Bus: *Provides media & marketing consulting services.*

Tel: (847) 475-7526   Emp: 115
Fax:(847) 475-7830   %FO: 100

SCARBOROGH RESEARCH
11 West 42nd Street, New York, NY   10036

CEO: Robert Cohen, Pres.

Bus: *Provides media & marketing consulting services.*

Tel: (212) 789-3560   Emp: 36
Fax:(212) 789-3577   %FO: 100

SPECTRA
333 West Wacker Drive, Chicago, IL   60607

CEO: John Larkin, Pres.

Bus: *Provides media & marketing consulting services.*

Tel: (312) 263-0606   Emp: 40
Fax:(312) 263-7022   %FO: 100

SRDS
1700 West Higgins Road, Des Plaines, IL   60018

CEO: Christopher Lehman, Pres. & CEO

Bus: *Provides media & marketing consulting services.*

Tel: (847) 375-5000   Emp: 131
Fax:(847) 375-5005   %FO: 100

TRADE DIMENSIONS
263 Tresser Blvd., One Stamford Pl., Stamford, CT   06901

CEO: Harold Clark, Pres. & CEO

Bus: *Provides trade consulting services.*

Tel: (203) 977-7600   Emp: 35
Fax:(203) 977-7645   %FO: 100

VIDEO MONITORING SERVICES
330 West 42nd Street, New York, NY   10036

CEO: Robert Cohen, Pres. & CEO

Bus: *Provides video monitoring services.*

Tel: (212) 736-2010   Emp: 300
Fax:(212) 629-0650   %FO: 100

VNU MARKETING INFORMATION SERVICES, INC.
11 West 42nd Street, New York, NY   10036

CEO: Martin Feely, CEO

Bus: *Provides media & marketing consulting services.*

Tel: (212) 789-3502   Emp: 25
Fax:(212) 789-3650   %FO: 100

VNU USA, INC.
1515 Broadway, New York, NY   10036
CEO: Gerald S. Hobbs, Pres.   Tel: (212) 536-6700   Emp: N/A
Bus: *US headquarters. Publishes/distributes*   Fax:(212) 536-5243   %FO: 100
    magazines. newspapers, educational &
    business information services.

● **W. H. DEN OUDEN N.V.**
Fokkerstraat 571, 3125 Schiedam, Netherlands
CEO: W. H. den Ouden, Pres.   Tel: 31-10-437-7700   Emp: 200
Bus: *Marine parts & accessories.*   Fax:31-10-415-2634

  VETUS DENOUDEN INC
  P O Box 8712, Baltimore, MD   21240
  CEO: Leo J van Hemert, Pres.   Tel: (410) 712-0740   Emp: 5
  Bus: *Marine parts & accessories*   Fax:(410) 712-0985   %FO: 100

● **WAVEREN & ZONEN B.V.**
Pastoorslaan 30, 2182 BX, Hillegom, Netherlands
CEO: B. Bakker, Managing Director   Tel: 31-25-251-6141   Emp: N/A
Bus: *Flowerbulbs/perennials.*   Fax:31-25-252-3638

  VAN WAVEREN INC.
  PO Box 12389, Norfolk, VA   23541
  CEO: Chris Verdegaal, Executive V.P.   Tel: (757) 858-5335   Emp: N/A
  Bus: *Import and sales of flowerbulbs/perennials.* Fax:(757) 855-6496   %FO: 100

● **WERELDHAVE N.V**
23 Nassaulaan Postbus 85660, NL-2508 CJ The Hague, Netherlands
CEO: R.L.M. de Ruijter, Chrm.   Tel: 31-70-346-9325   Emp: N/A
Bus: *Real estate investment company.*   Fax:31-70-363-8990

  WEST WORLD HOLDING INC.
  Four Manhattanville Road, 40th Fl., Purchase, NY   10577
  CEO: Charles O.W. Schouten, Pres.   Tel: (914) 694-5900   Emp: N/A
  Bus: *Real estate investment company.*   Fax:(914) 694-4642   %FO: 100

● **WOLTERS KLUWER N.V.**
Stadhouderskade 1, 1054 ES, Amsterdam, Netherlands
CEO: C. J. Brakel, Chrm.   Tel: 31-20-607-0400   Emp: 8089
Bus: *Legal, medical, science, educational, professional &*   Fax:31-20-6070490
    trade publishing.

  ASPEN PUBLISHERS INC.
  200 Orchard Ridge Road, Gaithersburg, MD   20878
  CEO: John Marozsan, Pres.   Tel: (301) 251-5000   Emp: N/A
  Bus: *Publishing*   Fax:(301) 251-5212   %FO: 100

FACTS AND COMPARISONS
111 West Port Plaza, Ste. 423, St. Louis, MO   63146

CEO: Sue Sewester, Pres.	Tel: (314) 878-2515	Emp: N/A
Bus: *Medical publications.*	Fax:(314) 878-5563	%FO: 100

KLUWER ACADEMIC PUBLISHERS
101 Philip Drive, Norwell, MA   02061

CEO: J. K. Smith, CEO	Tel: (617) 871-6600	Emp: 65
Bus: *Scholarly, science, technical and medical publishing.*	Fax:(617) 871-6528	%FO: 100

LIPPINCOTT, J.B.
27 East Washington Square, Philadelphia, PA   19106

CEO: M. Rogers, CEO	Tel: (215) 238-4200	Emp: N/A
Bus: *Medical publisher.*	Fax:(215) 238-4202	%FO: 100

WOLTERS KLUWER U.S. CORP.
161 North Clark Street, Chicago, IL   60601

CEO: Peter Van Wel	Tel: (312) 425-7000	Emp: N/A
Bus: *Publishing.*	Fax:(312) 425-0232	%FO: 100

● **ZUREL & CO B.V.**
Lakenblekerstraat 49, 1431 BB, Aalsmeer, Netherlands

CEO: R. F. Zurel, Pres.	Tel: 31-29-733-3333	Emp: N/A
Bus: *Import/export cut flowers.*	Fax:31-29-733-3318	

ZUREL USA, INC.
253 West Merrick Road, Valley Stream, NY   11580

CEO: Dennis J. Schlosser, Executive V.P.	Tel: (516) 561-5176	Emp: N/A
Bus: *Import/export cut flowers.*	Fax:(516) 561-5495	%FO: 100

ZUREL USA, INC.
174 Touhy Court, Des Plaines, IL   60018

CEO: David J. Laird, Manager	Tel: (847) 296-8181	Emp: N/A
Bus: *Import/export of cut flowers.*	Fax:(847) 296-0312	%FO: 100

New Zealand

- **AIR NEW ZEALAND**
  Private Bag 92007, Auckland, New Zealand
  CEO: Jim McCrea, Mgn. Dir.   Tel: 64-9-366-2400 Emp: N/A
  Bus: *Commercial air transport services.*   Fax:N/A

    AIR NEW ZEALAND LTD.
    1960 East Grand Avenue, Ste. 900, El Segundo, CA 90245
    CEO: Norm Thompson, Reg. Gen.Mgr. Tel: (310) 648-7000 Emp: N/A
    Bus: *International commercial air transport* Fax:(310) 648-7017 %FO: 100
      services.

- **BANK OF NEW ZEALAND**
  BNZ Centre, 1 Willis Street, Wellington, New Zealand
  CEO: R. B. McCay, CEO   Tel: 64-4 746999   Emp: 9000
  Bus: *Commercial banking services.*   Fax:N/A

    NEW ZEALAND BANKING GROUP
    1177 Avenue of the Americas, New York, NY 1010036
    CEO: J.A. Nalepa, EVP   Tel: (212) 801-9900 Emp: 30
    Bus: *Commercial banking services.* Fax:(212) 972-8674 %FO: 100

- **BRIERLEY INVESTMENTS**
  Level 6, CML Building, 22-24 Victoria Street, Wellington, New Zealand
  CEO: Robert H. Matthew, Chrm.   Tel: 64-4-473 8199 Emp: N/A
  Bus: *Investment management services.* Fax:64-4-473 1631

    ASSOCIATED HOSTS, INC.
    18801 Ventura Blvd., Suite 200, Tarzana, CA 91356
    CEO: Mark Rouleau, CEO   Tel: (818) 345-9910 Emp: N/A
    Bus: *Investment management services.* Fax:(818) 881-6150 %FO: 100

    MOLOKAI RANCH LTD.
    55 Merchant Street, Ste. 2000, Honolulu, HI 96813
    CEO: James Mozley, Pres.   Tel: (808) 531-0158 Emp: N/A
    Bus: *Investment management services.* Fax:(808) 521-2279 %FO: 100

- **CARTER HOLT HARVEY LIMITED**
640 Great South Road, Mankau City, Auckland, New Zealand
CEO: Peter Stichbury, Pres. Tel: 64-9-262 0991 Emp: N/A
Bus: *Mfr. forest, wood, pulp products.* Fax:64-9-262 0956

 CARTER HOLT HARVEY ROOFING INC.
 1230 Railroad Street, Corona, CA 91720
 CEO: John Miller, Gen. Mgr. Tel: (909) 272-8180 Emp: N/A
 Bus: *Mfr. forest, wood, pulp products; roofing* Fax:(909) 272-4476 %FO: 100
  materials.

- **FLETCHER CHALLENGE LTD.**
Fletcher Challenge House, 810 Great South Rd, Penrose, New Zealand
CEO: H. A .Fletcher, CEO Tel: 64-9-525-9000 Emp: N/A
Bus: *Pulp & paper, building industries, energy.* Fax:64-9-525-0559

 BLANDIN PAPER COMPANY
 115 Southwest First Street, Grand Rapids, MN 57744
 CEO: Doug Johnston, Pres. Tel: (218) 327-6200 Emp: 1100
 Bus: *Mfr. lightweight coated paper.* Fax:(218) 327-6212 %FO: 100

 DINWIDDIE CONSTRUCTION COMPANY LTD
 275 Battery Street, #300, San Francisco, CA 94111-3330
 CEO: Greg Cosko, Pres. Tel: (415) 986-2718 Emp: N/A
 Bus: *Construction services.* Fax:(415) 956-5669 %FO: 100

 FLETCHER PACIFIC CONSTRUCTION
 Ocean View Ctr. Ste.400, 707 Richards St., Honolulu, HI 96813
 CEO: Dennis Watts, Pres. Tel: (808) 533-5000 Emp: N/A
 Bus: *Construction services.* Fax:(808) 533-5320 %FO: 100

- **NEW ZEALAND LAMB CO (NA) LTD.**
5th Floor Seabridge House, 110 Featherstone Street, Wellington, New Zealand
CEO: Graham Valentine, Pres. Tel: 64-4-472-0236 Emp: N/A
Bus: *Produces/markets fresh meats.* Fax:64-4-801-9994

 NEW ZEALAND LAMB COMPANY
 106 Corporate Park Drive, Suite 113, White Plains, NY 10604
 CEO: Richard G. Lawrence, VP Tel: (914) 253-6904 Emp: N/A
 Bus: *Wholesale lamb, venison, beef, goat.* Fax:(914) 253-8155 %FO: 100

Nigeria

- **UNITED BANK FOR AFRICA, PLC.**
UBA House 57, Marina, PMB 12002 Lagos, Nigeria
CEO: N/A
Bus: *Commercial banking services.*

Tel: 234-264-4722   Emp: N/A
Fax:N/A

UNITED BANK FOR AFRICA, PLC
535 Madison Avenue, 16th Floor, New York, NY   10022
CEO: George H. Denniston Jr., Gen. Mgr.
Bus: *International commercial banking services.*

Tel: (212) 308-7222   Emp: N/A
Fax:(212) 688-0870   %FO: 100

Norway

- **AKER MARITIME, ASA.**
Fjordalleen 16, N-0115, Oslo, Norway
CEO: Sverre Skogen, Pres. — Tel: 47-22-947400 — Emp: 12000
Bus: *Engineering, procurement, construction &* — Fax:47-22-946655
installation of offshore drilling & production
systems.

  AKER GULF MARINE, INC.
  P.O.Box C-FM 1069 South, Ingleside, TX   78362-1302
  CEO: Myron Rodrigue, Pres. — Tel: (512) 776-7551 — Emp: N/A
  Bus: *Engineering, procurement, construction* — Fax:(512) 775-7245 — %FO: 51
  services & installation of offshore drilling &
  production systems.

  AKER MARITIME US, INC.
  11757 Katy Freeway, Ste. 500, Houston, TX   77079-1725
  CEO: Svein Eggen, Pres. — Tel: (281) 588-7500 — Emp: N/A
  Bus: *US representative; engineering, procurement,* — Fax:(281) 588-7599 — %FO: 100
  construction & installation of offshore drilling
  & production systems.

  SPARS INTERNATIONAL, INC.
  11757 Katy Frwy., Ste. 500, Houston, TX   77079
  CEO: Robert M. Harrell, Pres. — Tel: (281) 679-4900 — Emp: 50
  Bus: *JV with Deep Oil Technology; markets oil* — Fax:(281) 679-4910 — %FO: 50
  drilling platform.

- **ANDERS WILHELMSEN & COMPANY**
Storgaten 2, Oslo, Norway
CEO: Arne Wilhelmsen, Pres. — Tel: 47-67-582658 — Emp: N/A
Bus: *Shipping services.* — Fax:47-67-586887

  ROYAL CARIBBEAN CRUISES LTD.
  1050 Caribbean Cruises Ltd., Miami, FL   33132
  CEO: Richard D. Fain, Chrm. — Tel: (305) 539-6000 — Emp: 1642
  Bus: *Cruise shipping line.* — Fax:(305) 374-7354 — %FO: 39

● **BERGEN DIESEL AS**
P O Box 924, 5001 Bergen, Norway
CEO: Morten Ulstein, Mgn.Dir.   Tel: 47-55-190000   Emp: 350
Bus: *Mfr. diesel engines, deck machinery for marine*   Fax:47-55-109405
industry.

    BERGEN DIESEL INC.
    2701 Delaware Avenue, Kenner, LA   70062
    CEO: N. Moerkeseth, Pres.   Tel: (504) 464-4561   Emp: 4
    Bus: *Sale/service diesel engines and deck*   Fax:(504) 464-4565   %FO: 100
    machinery.

● **CHRISTIANIA BANK OG KREDITKASSE ASA**
Middelthunsgaten 17, N-0368 Oslo, Norway
CEO: Borger A. Lenth, Pres.   Tel: 47-22-485000   Emp: N/A
Bus: *Banking services.*   Fax:47-22-484600

    CHRISTIANIA BANK NEW YORK
    11 West 42nd Street, 7th Fl., New York, NY   10036
    CEO: Tore Nag, Exec.VP   Tel: (212) 827-4800   Emp: 50
    Bus: *Commercial banking services.*   Fax:(212) 827-4888   %FO: 100

● **CORROCEAN, INC. (USA)**
N-7005, Trondheim, Norway
CEO: Roe Strohman, Mgr.   Tel: 47-73-825000   Emp: 150
Bus: *Corrosion monitoring equipment.*   Fax:47-73-825050

    CORROCEAN, INC.
    7700 San Felipe, Suite 360, Houston, TX   77063
    CEO: Magne Ostby, Pres.   Tel: (713) 266-0941   Emp: 7
    Bus: *Corrosion monitoring equipment.*   Fax:(713) 266-0172   %FO: 50

● **DEN NORSKE BANK ASA**
Strandon 21, Oslo 2, Norway 0250
CEO: Kristian Ramjor, Pres.   Tel: 47-22-481050   Emp: 5000
Bus: *Banking services.*   Fax:47-22-481870

    DEN NORSKE BANK ASA
    3 Allen Center, Suite 4890, 333 Clay St., Houston, TX   77002
    CEO: Haakon Sandborg, SVP   Tel: (713) 844-9250   Emp: N/A
    Bus: *Commercial banking services.*   Fax:(713) 757-1167   %FO: 100

    DEN NORSKE BANK ASA
    200 Park Avenue, 31st Floor, New York, NY   10166-0396
    CEO: Tony Samuelsen, Exec.VP & Gen. Mgr.   Tel: (212) 681-3800   Emp: 54
    Bus: *Commercial banking services.*   Fax:(212) 681-3900   %FO: 100

● **DEN NORSKE CREDITBANK**
Kirkegaten 21, Oslo, Norway
CEO: Kristian Rambjor, Pres.   Tel: 47-2-248-1050   Emp: 5000
Bus: *Banking services.*   Fax:47-2-248-1870

DNC AMERICA BANKING CORP.
200 Park Avenue, New York, NY   10166
CEO: Tony Samuelsen, Gen. Mgr.   Tel: (212) 681-3800   Emp: 120
Bus: *Commercial banking services.*   Fax:(212) 681-3900   %FO: 100

● **DET NORSKE VERITAS A/S**
Veritasveien 1, P O Box 300, N-1322 Hovik, Norway
CEO: Sven Ullring, Chrm.   Tel: 47-67-579900   Emp: 4000
Bus: *Quality assurance services, ship classification &*   Fax:47-67-579911
inspection.

AVITAS ENGINEERING, INC.
815 NW 57th Avenue, Suite 203, Miami, FL   33126
CEO: Lauren B. Nelson, Pres.   Tel: (305) 267-7332   Emp: 6
Bus: *Engineer/consultant, aircraft-FAA regulations.*   Fax:(305) 267-7365   %FO: 100

DET NORSKE VERITAS (AVITAS), INC.
1835 Alexander Bell Drive, Reston, VA   22091
CEO: John Vitale, Pres.   Tel: (703) 476-2300   Emp: 13
Bus: *Quality assurance services, ship classification*   Fax:(703) 860-5855   %FO: 100
& inspection.

DET NORSKE VERITAS CLASSIFICATION, INC.
110 Pine Street, Suite 725, Long Beach, CA   90802
CEO: Knur Mhre, Stn. Mgr.   Tel: (562) 435-1908   Emp: 2
Bus: *Quality assurance services, ship classification*   Fax:(562) 432-3727   %FO: 100
& inspection.

DET NORSKE VERITAS CLASSIFICATION, INC.
1350 Treat Blvd. Suite 110, Walnut Creek, CA   94596
CEO: Chris Foong, Dist. Mgr.   Tel: (510) 939-1045   Emp: N/A
Bus: *Quality assurance services, ship classification*   Fax:(510) 939-1095   %FO: 100
& inspection.

DET NORSKE VERITAS CLASSIFICATION, INC.
1001 North America Way, Suite 201, Miami, FL   33132-2093
CEO: Bjørn Nystad, Dist. Mgr.   Tel: (305) 358-0156   Emp: N/A
Bus: *Quality assurance services, ship classification*   Fax:(305) 358-3918   %FO: 100
& inspection.

DET NORSKE VERITAS CLASSIFICATION, INC.
707 AAA 3445 N. Causeway Blvd., Metairie, LA   70002
CEO: Derek Wilkinson, Mgr.   Tel: (504) 835-7334   Emp: 5
Bus: *Quality assurance services, ship classification*   Fax:(504) 835-1735   %FO: 100
& inspection.

DET NORSKE VERITAS CLASSIFICATION, INC.
14450 NE 29th Place, Ste. 217, Bellevue, WA   98007

CEO: Olaf R. Hatlen, Dist. Mgr.	Tel: (206) 861-7977	Emp: 8
Bus: *Quality assurance services, ship classification & inspection.*	Fax:(206) 861-0423	%FO: 100

DET NORSKE VERITAS CLASSIFICATION, INC.
502 Oak Crest Lane, Wallingford, PA   19086

CEO: S. Subhas, Mgr.	Tel: (610) 892-9852	Emp: 4
Bus: *Quality assurance services, ship classification & inspection.*	Fax:(610) 892-9842	%FO: 100

DET NORSKE VERITAS INC., DIVISION AMERICAS
70 Grand Avenue, River Edge, NJ   07661

CEO: Helge Dag Tangen	Tel: (201) 343-0800	Emp: 500
Bus: *Ship classification, certification & advisory services.*	Fax:(201) 343-4061	%FO: 100

DET NORSKE VERITAS INDUSTRY, DIVISION AMERICAS
16340 Park Ten Place, Ste. 100, Houston, TX   77084-5143

CEO: Kåre Kristoffersen, Gen. Mgr.	Tel: (281) 579-9003	Emp: N/A
Bus: *Quality assurance services, ship classification & inspection.*	Fax:(281) 579-1360	%FO: 100

DNV LOSS CONTROL, INC.
3805 Crestwood Park, Deluth, GA   30136

CEO: Ray Davies, Mgr.	Tel: (770) 279-0001	Emp: N/A
Bus: *Fuel quality testing & consulting.*	Fax:(770) 279-0282	%FO: 100

DNV PETROLEUM SERVICES, INC.
111 Galway Place, Teaneck, NJ   07666

CEO: William P. Cullen, Gen. Mgr.	Tel: (201) 833-1990	Emp: N/A
Bus: *Fuel quality testing & consulting.*	Fax:(201) 833-4559	%FO: 100

• DRESSER - RAND A/S
P.O. Box 1010 North 3601, Kongsberg, Norway

CEO: T. Diseth, Gen. Mgr.	Tel: 47-3-737-070	Emp: N/A
Bus: *Mfr. motors & generators.*	Fax:	

DRESSER - RAND COMPANY
800 Central Avenue, Minneapolis, MN   55413

CEO: George Johnson, Gen. Mgr.	Tel: (612) 378-8000	Emp: 330
Bus: *Mfr. motors & generators.*	Fax:(612) 378-8050	%FO: 100

● **ELKEM A/S**
Nydalsveien 28, P O Box 4282, 0401 Torshov, Norway
CEO: Ole Enger, Pres.   Tel: 47-22-450100   Emp: N/A
Bus: *Products for steel industry, metallurgical*   Fax:47-22-450155
      technology, ceramics.

     ELKEM METALS CO.
     Airport Office Pk., Bldg.2, 400 Rouser Road, Moon Township, PA   115108
     CEO: Anthony C. LaRusso, Pres.   Tel: (412) 299-7200   Emp: N/A
     Bus: *Sales, distribution steel products.*   Fax:(412) 299-7225   %FO: 100

     ELKEM METALS CO.
     Route 7 South, River View Road, Marietta, OH   45750
     CEO: Russell D. Craig, Plt. Mgr.   Tel: (614) 374-1000   Emp: N/A
     Bus: *Sales, distribution steel products.*   Fax:(614) 374-1386   %FO: 100

     ELKEM-AMERICAN CARBIDE CO.
     2700 Lake Road East, Astabula, OH   44004
     CEO: Steve M. Dopuch, Pres.   Tel: (216) 993-2300   Emp: N/A
     Bus: *Sales, distribution steel products.*   Fax:(216) 993-2379   %FO: 100

● **LEIF HOEGH & CO A/S**
Wergelandsveien 7, P O Box 2596 - Solli, Oslo 2, Norway
CEO: John Smaadal, Pres.   Tel: 47-22-869700   Emp: N/A
Bus: *Ship owners and operators.*   Fax:47-22-201408

     HOEGH LINES (US) INC.
     95 Christopher Columbus Dr, Jersey City, NJ   07302
     CEO: Donald Rupert, Pres.   Tel: (201) 433-4600   Emp: N/A
     Bus: *Ship owners & operators.*   Fax:(201) 433-5195   %FO: 100

● **JAC JACOBSEN A/S**
Enebakkveien 177, Oslo 6, Norway
CEO: Alv I. Karlsen, Pres. & CEO   Tel: 47-22-673893   Emp: N/A
Bus: *Mfr. of functional lighting for home, commerce and*   Fax:N/A
      industry.

     LUXO LAMP CORP.
     Monument Park, PO 951, Port Chester, NY   10573
     CEO: Robert N. Haidinger, Pres.   Tel: (914) 937-4433   Emp: N/A
     Bus: *Mfr. lighting equipment.*   Fax:(914) 937-7016   %FO: 100

● **LAERDAL A/S**
PO Box 377, 4001 Stavanger, Norway
CEO: Tore Laerdal, Pres.   Tel: 47-51-511700   Emp: 700
Bus: *Emergency medical equipment and training.*   Fax:47-51-523557

> **LAERDAL MEDICAL CORP.**
> 167 Myers Corrners Road, Wappinger Falls, NY   12590
> CEO: Clive Patrickson, Pres.   Tel: (914) 297-7770   Emp: 200
> Bus: *Medical training equipment.*   Fax:(914) 297-1137   %FO: 100

● **LAI BERG HOLDING A/S**
Lilleakervelen 31, P O Box 20, Lilleaker, 0216 Oslo, Norway
CEO: Nick Berg, CEO   Tel: 47-22-731-1820   Emp: N/A
Bus: *Holding company. Mfr. refrigeration products.*   Fax:47-22-731-1828

> **VIRGINIA KMP CORP.**
> 4100 Platinum Way, Dallas, TX   75237
> CEO: Finn Jordskogen, Pres.   Tel: (214) 330-7731   Emp: 100
> Bus: *Mfr. refrigeration products.*   Fax:(214) 337-8854   %FO: 100

● **MUNCK AUTECH A/S**
PO Box 3151, 5000 Bergen, Norway
CEO: Mag Nygren, Pres.   Tel: 47-55-595300   Emp: N/A
Bus: *Mfr. cranes, hoists.*   Fax:47-55-595301

> **MUNCK AUTECH INC.**
> 161 Enterprise Drive, PO Box 3135, Newport News, VA   23603-3135
> CEO: Mag Nygren, Pres   Tel: (757) 887-8080   Emp: 48
> Bus: *Mfr. material handling systems.*   Fax:(757) 887-5588   %FO: 100

● **O MUSTAD & SON A/S**
P O Box 40N, 2801 Gjovik, Norway
CEO: Mikal Rotnes, Mgn. Dir.   Tel: 47-61-137700   Emp: N/A
Bus: *Mfr. fish hooks.*   Fax:47-61-137951

> **O MUSTAD & SON (USA) INC**
> PO Box 838 - 253 Grant Avenue, Auburn, NY   13021
> CEO: Arne H.Forsberg, Pres.   Tel: (315) 253-2793   Emp: 45
> Bus: *Distributor fish hooks, fishing tackle.* Fax:(315) 253-0157   %FO: 100

● **NCL HOLDING ASA**
Munkedamsveien 45C, P.O.Box 1811 Vika, N-0123 Oslo, Norway
CEO: Geir Aune, CEO   Tel: 47-22-830310   Emp: 4690
Bus: *Holding company, passenger shipping, cruise line.*   Fax:47-22-830418

> **NORWEGIAN CRUISE LINE**
> 7665 Corporate Center Drive, Miami, FL   33126
> CEO: Hans E. Golteus, Pres.   Tel: (305) 436-4000   Emp: 700
> Bus: *Cruise line, travel industry.*   Fax:(305) 436-4120   %FO: 100

• **NORGES BANK**
Bankplassen 2, P.O. Box 1179, Sentrum 0107 Oslo, Norway
CEO: Kjell Storvik, Governor   Tel: 47-22-316000   Emp: 1500
Bus: *Banking services.*   Fax:47-22-413105

    NORGES BANK/New York
    17 State Street, 11th Floor, New York, NY   10004
    CEO: Ole Christian Frøseth, Director   Tel: (212) 269-8050   Emp: 4
    Bus: *Commercial banking services.*   Fax:(212) 269-7150   %FO: 100

• **NORSK HYDRO A/S**
Bygdoy Alle 2, 0240 Oslo, Norway
CEO: Egil Myklebust, Pres.   Tel: 47-22-432100   Emp: 32455
Bus: *Mfr. mineral fertilizers, industrial gas, chemicals,*   Fax:47-22-432725
    aluminum, magnesium; oil and gas exploration,
    production, refining, mktg.

    NORSK HYDRO USA INC
    800 Third Avenue, 31st Fl., New York, NY   10022-7671
    CEO: N/A   Tel: (212) 688-6606   Emp: 1214
    Bus: *Mfr./marketing fertilizers, industrial*   Fax:(212) 750-1252   %FO: 100
        chemicals, ammonia, aluminum products,
        magnesium

• **OFOTENS OG VESTERAALANS DAMPSKIBSSELSKAB AS**
Post Office Box 43, N-8501 Narvik, Norway
CEO: Jens Smkaar, Pres.   Tel: 47-76-151422   Emp: N/A
Bus: *International passenger and cargo shipping*   Fax:47-76-152469
    services. (JV with TROMS FYLKES
    DAMPSKIBSSELSKAP AS).

    BERGEN LINE INC.
    405 Park Avenue, New York, NY   10022
    CEO: Rosalyn Gershell, Pres.   Tel: (212) 319-1300   Emp: N/A
    Bus: *International passenger and cargo shipping*   Fax:(212) 319-1390   %FO: JV
        services.

• **OLSEN A/S**
Oslo, Norway
CEO: Fred Olsen, Pres.   Tel: 47-22-649000   Emp: N/A
Bus: *Mfr. watches.*   Fax: to US office

    TIMEX GROUP
    PO Box 2126, Waterbury, CT   06720
    CEO: Michael Jacoby, Pres.   Tel: (203) 573-5000   Emp: N/A
    Bus: *Mfr./sale watches.*   Fax:(203) 573-5139   %FO: 100

● **ORKLA, A.S.**
PO Box 218, N-1501 Moss, Norway
CEO: Jens P. Heyerdahl, Pres.   Tel: 47-69-249-9000   Emp: N/A
Bus: *Mfr. chemicals and brand-name consumer products,* Fax:47-69-249-9290
including food/beverage, candy/biscuits, outerwear
and footwear, and cosmetics.

   HELLY HANSEN US, INC.
   PO Box 97031, Redmond, WA   98073
   CEO: Gordon McFadden, Pres.   Tel: (206) 883-8823   Emp: 50
   Bus: *Mfr. of wholesale outerwear.*   Fax:(206) 882-4932   %FO: 100

● **PRONOVA BIOPOLYMER A.S.**
Tomtegt 36, PO Box 494, Drammen, N-3002 Norway
CEO: Steineer Faanes, Pres.   Tel: 47-32-837300   Emp: 300
Bus: *Mfr. chemicals.*   Fax:47-32-833488

   PRONOVA BIOPOLYMER
   135 Commerce Way, Ste. 201, Portsmouth, NH   03801
   CEO: Sandra Platt, Mgr.   Tel: (603) 433-1231   Emp: 10
   Bus: *Mfr. alginates.*   Fax:(603) 433-1348   %FO: 100

● **STATOIL, DEN NORSKE STATS OLJESELSKAP A/S**
Stavanger, Norway
CEO: Harald Norvik, Pres.   Tel: 47-51-808080   Emp: N/A
Bus: *Exploration, production, refining & marketing oil &* Fax:47-51-807042
gas, petrochemical products.

   STATOIL NORTH AMERICA INC.
   225 High Ridge Road, Stamford, CT   06905
   CEO: Sigurd Jansen, Pres.   Tel: (203) 978-6900   Emp: N/A
   Bus: *exploration, production, refining & marketing* Fax:(203) 978-6952   %FO: 100
   oil & gas, petrochemical products.

● **TFDS**
PO Box 548, 9001 Tromso, Norway
CEO: Bjorn Bettum, Mgn .Dir.   Tel: 47-77-648200   Emp: 5087
Bus: *Shipping, transportation, travel and tourism services.* Fax:47-77-648180

   TFDS
   405 Park Avenue, New York, NY   10022
   CEO: Rosalyn Gershell, Pres.   Tel: (212) 319-1300   Emp: 10
   Bus: *Ticketing office for passenger ferries, cruise* Fax:(212) 319-1390   %FO: 100
   ships and tour packages.

- **TROMS FYLKES DAMPSKIBSSELSKAP AS**
P.O. Box 548, N-9001 Tromso, Norway
CEO: Bjorn Kaldhol, Pres.   Tel: 47-73-515120   Emp: N/A
Bus: *International passenger and cargo shipping*   Fax:47-73-515146
   services. (JV with OFOTENS OG VESTERAALANS
   DAMPSKIBSSELSKAB AS.).

   BERGEN LINE INC.
   405 Park Avenue, New York, NY   10022
   CEO: Rosalyn Gershell, Pres.   Tel: (212) 319-1300   Emp: N/A
   Bus: *International passenger and cargo shipping*   Fax:(212) 319-1390   %FO: JV
      services.

- **ULSTEIN INTERNATIONAL AS**
N-6065 Ulsteinvik, Norway
CEO: Steinar Kulen, Mng. Dir.   Tel: 47-70014040   Emp: N/A
Bus: *Mfr. diesel engines.*   Fax:N/A

   ULSTEIN USA, INC.
   200 James Drive West, St. Rose, LA   70087
   CEO: Dagfinn Vattoey, Mgr.   Tel: (504) 464-4561   Emp: N/A
   Bus: *Mfr. diesel engines.*   Fax: %FO: 100

   ULSTEIN USA, INC.
   100 UPM Drive, Mt. Holly, NC   28120
   CEO: Nils Moerkeseth, Pres.   Tel: (206) 281-7388   Emp: N/A
   Bus: *Mfr. diesel engines.*   Fax: %FO: 100

- **PETTER YRAN & BJORN STORBRAATEN ARKITEKTEE A/S**
Frognerstranda 2, N-0271 Oslo, Norway
CEO: Petter Yarn, CEO   Tel: 47-22-557650   Emp: 35
Bus: *Architectural/design services to cruise, ferry and*   Fax:47-22-434361
   private yacht industry.

   P. YRAN & B. STORBRAATEN ARCHITECTS INC.
   1001 North America Way, Ste.115, Miami, FL   33132
   CEO: Bjorn Naerstad, Pres.   Tel:(305) 375-8147   Emp:N/A
   Bus: *Architectural/design services to cruise, ferry*   Fax:(305) 375-0562   %FO:JV
      and private yacht industry.

Pakistan

● **HABIB BANK LTD.**
MA Jinnah Road, Karachi 21, Pakistan
CEO: N/A   Tel: N/A   Emp: N/A
Bus: *General banking services.*   Fax:92-21-241-4191

    HABIB BANK LTD.
    44 Wall Street, 10th Floor, New York, NY   10005
    CEO: Shafeeq H. Jafri, SVP   Tel: (212) 422-9720   Emp: 53
    Bus: *International banking services.*   Fax:(212) 248-8506   %FO: 100

● **NATIONAL BANK OF PAKISTAN**
1-1 Chundrigar, Karachi, Pakistan
CEO: Abu Saeed Islahi, Chrm. & Pres.   Tel: 92-21-241-1974   Emp: N/A
Bus: *Commercial banking services.*   Fax:N/A

    NATIONAL BANK OF PAKISTAN
    One United Nations Plaza, New York, NY   10017
    CEO: Shafiq Ahmed, Mgr.   Tel: (212) 758-8900   Emp: 7
    Bus: *International banking services.*   Fax:(212) 355-6211   %FO: 100

    NATIONAL BANK OF PAKISTAN
    100 Wall Street, 21st Street, New York, NY   10268
    CEO: Nabi Sher Khan, Gen.Mgr.   Tel: (212) 344-8822   Emp: 40
    Bus: *International banking services.*   Fax:(212) 344-8826   %FO: 100

● **PAKISTAN INTERNATIONAL AIRWAYS**
c/o UK Headquarters, 1-15 King Street, London W6 9HR, England
CEO: Arif A.K. Abbasi, Mng.Dir.   Tel: 44-181-741-8066   Emp: 20000
Bus: *International commercial air transport.* Fax:44-181-741-9376

    PAKISTAN INTERNATIONAL AIRWAYS
    521 Fifth Avenue, New York, NY   10017
    CEO: N/A   Tel: (212) 370-9150   Emp: 50+
    Bus: *International commercial air transport.* Fax:(212) 808-4669   %FO: 100

● **UNITED BANK**
1-1 Chundrigar Road, Karachi, Pakistan
CEO: N/A   Tel: N/A   Emp: N/A
Bus: *Commercial banking services.*   Fax:N/A

    UNITED BANK
    30 Wall Street, 10th Fl., New York, NY   10005
    CEO: Masoodur-Rahman Khan, SVP   Tel: (212) 294-3127   Emp: N/A
    Bus: *International banking services.*   Fax:(212) 968-0057   %FO: 100

Panama

- **BANCO LATINOAMERICANO DE EXPORTACIONES SA**
P O Box 6-1497, El Dorado, Panama
CEO: Jose Castaneda, CEO   Tel: 507-263-6766   Emp: N/A
Bus: *International banking services.*   Fax:507-269-6333

    BANCO LATINOAMERICANO DE EXPORTACIONES (BLADEX)
    750 Lexington Avenue, 26th Fl., New York, NY   10022
    CEO: Peter P. Miller, Gen.Mgr.   Tel: (212) 754-2600   Emp: 8
    Bus: *International banking services.*   Fax:(212) 754-2606   %FO: 100

- **MCDERMOTT INTL INC**
all correspondence:, P O Box 61961, New Orleans, LA   70161, USA
CEO: R C Howson, Chrm. & CEO   Tel: N/A   Emp: 30,000
Bus: *Energy services.*   Fax:N/A

    MCDERMOTT INC
    PO Box 60035, New Orleans, LA   70160
    CEO: R E Howson, Chrm. & CEO   Tel: (504) 587-5400   Emp: 17000
    Bus: *Energy services.*   Fax:(504) 587-6158   %FO: 100

Paraguay

- **TAM MERCOSUR AIRLINES**
Hanger Arpa/TAM, Silvio Pettirosi Intl Airport, Asución, Paraguay
CEO: Miguel Candia, Pres.   Tel: 595-21-646000   Emp: N/A
Bus: *Commercial air transport.*   Fax:595-21-645401

  TAM MERCOSUR AIRLINES
  7205 NW 19th Street, Ste. 400, Miami, FL   33126
  CEO: J. Bratkowski, Pres.   Tel: (305) 406-2826   Emp: N/A
  Bus: *International commercial air transport.* Fax:(305) 477-2847   %FO: 100

Peru

● **BANCO DE CREDITO DEL PERU**
Calle Centenario 156, Urbanizacion Laderas de Melgarejo, La Molina, Lima, Peru
CEO: Raimundo Morales, GenMgr.   Tel: 51-1-437-3838   Emp: 5000
Bus: *International banking services.*   Fax:51-1-349-0638

    BANCO DE CREDITO DEL PERU
    410 Park Avenue, 6th Floor, New York, NY   10022
    CEO: Alfredo Montero, Gen. Mgr.   Tel: (212) 644-6644   Emp: 11
    Bus: *International banking services.*   Fax:(212) 826-9852   %FO: 100

Philippines

- **BANK OF THE PHILIPPINE ISLANDS**
BPI Building, Ayala Avenue, Makati Metro Manila, Philippines
CEO: Jaime Zobelbeayala, Chrm.   Tel: N/A   Emp: N/A
Bus: *Commercial banking services.*   Fax:63-2-813-4066

  ### BANK OF THE PHILIPPINE ISLANDS
  7 East 53rd Street, New York, NY   10022
  CEO: Marlene Alindogan, Gen.Mgr.   Tel: (212) 644-6700   Emp: N/A
  Bus: *Commercial banking services.*   Fax:(212) 752-5969   %FO: 100

- **METROPOLITAN BANK & TRUST COMPANY**
Se. Gil Puyat Avenue, Makati, Metro Manila, Philippines
CEO: Melna Madlangbayan, Mgr.   Tel: N/A   Emp: N/A
Bus: *Commercial banking services.*   Fax:63-2-813-4066

  ### METROPOLITAN BANK & TRUST COMPANY
  10 East 53rd Street, New York, NY   10022
  CEO: Alfred V. Madrid, VP & Gen. Mgr.   Tel: (212) 832-0855   Emp: N/A
  Bus: *International commercial banking services.*   Fax:(212) 832-0993   %FO: 100

- **PHILIPPINE AIRLINES (PAL)**
Allied Bank Center 6754, Aalo Avenue, Makati Metro, Manila, Philippines
CEO: Jose Garcia, Pres.   Tel: 632-818-0111   Emp: 14000
Bus: *Commercial air transport carrier.*   Fax:632-817-2083

  ### PHILIPPINE AIRLINES
  447 Sutter Street, San Francisco, CA   94018
  CEO: Alberto Lim, Deputy Mgr.   Tel: (415) 391-0270   Emp: N/A
  Bus: *International airline carrier.*   Fax:(415) 433-6733   %FO: 100

  ### PHILIPPINE AIRLINES
  5959 W. Century Blvd., Ste. 600, Los Angeles, CA   90045
  CEO: A. Ingles, District Sales Mgr.   Tel: (310) 338-9000   Emp: N/A
  Bus: *International airline carrier.*   Fax:(310) 338-7194   %FO: 100

  ### PHILIPPINE AIRLINES
  745 Fort Street Mall, Ste. 902, Honolulu, HI   96183
  CEO: O. Bouffard, District Sales Mgr.   Tel: (808) 536-1928   Emp: N/A
  Bus: *International airline carrier.*   Fax:(808) 536-0978   %FO: 100

- **PHILIPPINE NATIONAL BANK**
Philippine National Bank Financial Center, Roxas Blvd., Pasai City, Manila, Philippines
CEO: Peter Favila, Pres.   Tel: 63-2-891-6040   Emp: N/A
Bus: *Commercial banking services.*   Fax: N/A

    PHILIPPINE NATIONAL BANK
    546 Fifth Avenue, 8th Floor, New York, NY   10036
    CEO: Raul G. De Asis, SVP & Gen.Mgr.   Tel: (212) 790-9600   Emp: N/A
    Bus: *International banking services.*   Fax: (212) 382-2238   %FO: 100

Poland

● **BANK HANDLOWY W WARSZAWIE S.A.**
Ul. Chalubinskiego 8, P.O. Box 129, PL-00-950 Warsaw, Poland
CEO: Cezary Stypulkowski, Pres.   Tel: 48-22-6903-000   Emp: N/A
Bus: *Commercial banking services.*   Fax:N/A

    BANK HANDLOWY W WARSZAWIE S.A.
    405 Park Avenue, Suite 1101, New York, NY   10022
    CEO: Eugeniusz Szewczyk, Chief Rep.   Tel: (212) 371-8390   Emp: N/A
    Bus: *International banking services.*   Fax:(212) 371-8391   %FO: 100

● **BANK POLSKA KASA OPIEKI**
Ul. Grzybowska 53/57, P O Box 108, 00-950 Warsaw, Poland
CEO: Andrzej Dorosz, Pres.   Tel: 48-22-656-0000   Emp: N/A
Bus: *Banking services.*   Fax:48-22-656-0004

    BANK POLSKA KASA OPIEKI
    470 Park Ave. South, New York, NY   10016
    CEO: Alfred Blee, Gen.Mgr.   Tel: (212) 251-1200   Emp: N/A
    Bus: *Commercial banking services.*   Fax:(212) 679-5910   %FO: 100

● **MELEX VECHICLE PRODUCTION PLANT CO., LTD.**
3 Wojska Polskiego Street, PL-39-300 Mielec, Poland
CEO: Mark Garlewicz, Pres.   Tel: 48-196-88-7824   Emp: N/A
Bus: *Mfr. golf cars and specialty vehicles.*   Fax:48-196-88-7945

    MELEX PRODUCTS INTERNATIONAL, INC.
    3900 Business Highway 70 West, PO Box 1355, Smithfield, NC   27577
    CEO: Scott Mallory, CFO   Tel: (919) 938-3800   Emp: N/A
    Bus: *Mfr./sale golf cars & specialty vehicles.*   Fax:(919) 938-3850   %FO: 100

● **PEZETEL FOREIGN TRADE ENTERPRISE, LTD.**
Aleja Stanow Zjedneczonych 61, Box 88, 04-028 Warsaw, Poland
CEO: Andrzej Jesimak, Pres.   Tel: 48-22-133-295   Emp: 60
Bus: *Import/export trading company.*   Fax:48-22-133-356

    MELEX PRODUCTS INTERNATINAL, INC.
    PO Box 1355, Smithfield, NC   27572
    CEO: Scott Mallory, VP   Tel: (919) 938-3800   Emp: 24
    Bus: *Golf carts and parts.*   Fax:(919) 438-2852   %FO: 73

• **PHILIPPS LIGHTING POLAND**
Browarna 6, Warsaw, 00-311 Poland
CEO: Mrs. Barczau, Mgr.   Tel: 48-22-635-9021   Emp: N/A
Bus: *Light bulbs; mirror, motor car, fluorescent, sodium,*   Fax:48-22-635-6855
lamps. Polish folk art, toys, Christmas tree
ornaments.

    AMCECO INTERNATIONAL CORPORATION
    1314 Long Street, Ste. 110, High Point, NC   27262
    CEO: Stanislaw Czernk, Pres.   Tel: (910) 887-8647   Emp: N/A
    Bus: *Light bulbs; mirror, motor car, fluorescent,*   Fax:(910) 887-5797   %FO: 100%
    sodium, lamps. Polish folk art, toys, Christmas
    tree ornaments.

• **POLSKIE LINIE LOTNICZE LOT SA**
39 Ul. 17 Stycznia, Warsaw 00697, Poland
CEO: Jan Litwinski, Pres.   Tel: 48-26-66111   Emp: 4359
Bus: *International commercial air transport services.*   Fax:48-24-66409

    LOT POLISH AIRLINES
    500 5th Avenue, New York, NY   10036
    CEO: Marek Sidor, Dir.   Tel: (212) 852-0244   Emp: 100+
    Bus: *International commercial air transport*   Fax:(212) 302-0191   %FO: 100
    services.

Portugal

- **BANCO ESPIRITO SANTO E COMERICAL DE LISBOA**
Avenida da Leberdade 195, P-1022 Lisbon, Portugal
CEO: Falgado Ricardo — Tel: 351-1-315-8331 — Emp: N/A
Bus: *General commercial banking services.* — Fax: 351-1-350-8972

    BANCO ESPIRITO SANTO E COMERICAL DE LISBOA
    555 Madison Avenue, 7th Floor, New York, NY 10022
    CEO: Joaquim Guarnecho, Gen. Mgr. — Tel: (212) 418-0320 — Emp: N/A
    Bus: *Commercial banking services.* — Fax: (212) 758-4025 — %FO: 100

- **BANCO PORTUGUES DO ATLANTICO**
Rua do Ouro, 1140, Lisbon, Portugal
CEO: Dr. Silva Pereira, CEO — Tel: 351--323-1100 — Emp: N/A
Bus: *General commercial banking.* — Fax: 351-1-342-1307

    BANCO PORTUGUES DO ATLANTICO
    Two Wall Street, New York, NY 10005
    CEO: Pedro J. Bello, Gen. Mgr. — Tel: (212) 306-7800 — Emp: N/A
    Bus: *International banking services.* — Fax: (212) 766-8047 — %FO: 100

- **BANCO TOTTA & ACORES**
Rua Do Ouro 88, 1100 Lisbon, Portugal
CEO: Luis Champalimaud, CEO — Tel: 351-1-321-1500 — Emp: N/A
Bus: *International banking services.* — Fax: 351-1-321-2092

    BANCO TOTTA & ACORES
    590 Fifth Avenue, 8th Floor, New York, NY 10036
    CEO: Herculano de Sousa — Tel: (212) 302-6870 — Emp: N/A
    Bus: *International banking services.* — Fax: (212) 302-7369 — %FO: 100

- **TRANSPORTES AEROS PORTUGUESES SA (TAP)**
Apartado 50194, 1704 Lisbon, Portugal
CEO: Manuel Ferreira Lima, Chrm. — Tel: 351-1-841-5000 — Emp: 7448
Bus: *International commercial air transport services.* — Fax: 351-1-841-5095

    TAP AIR PORTUGAL
    399 Market Street, Newark, NJ 07105
    CEO: Rui Monteiro Cruz, Gen. Mgr. — Tel: (201) 344-4490 — Emp: N/A
    Bus: *International commercial air transport services.* — Fax: (201) 344-7344 — %FO: 100

Romania

- **COMPANIA DE TRANSPORTURI AERIENE ROMANE SA**
16 Km Bucharest, Romania
CEO: Nicolae Brutan, Gen. Mgr.   Tel: 40-12-120138   Emp: 3300
Bus: *Commercial air transport services.*   Fax:40-13-125686

    TAROM ROMANIAN AIR TRANSPORT CO.
    342 Madison Avenue, New York, NY   10022
    CEO: Andrian Sidarov, Mgr.   Tel: (212) 687-6013   Emp: N/A
    Bus: *International commercial air transport*   Fax:(212) 661-6056   %FO: 100
    services.

Russia

● **BANK FOR FOREIGN ECONOMIC AFFAIRS OF USSR (BFEA)**
3/5 Kopjevsky Lane, Moscow 103009, Russia
CEO: Andrei L. Kostin, Chrm.　　　　　　　　　Tel: N/A　　　　　　Emp: 3500
Bus: *Commercial banking services.*　　　　　　Fax: N/A

　　　BANK FOR FOREIGN ECONOMIC AFFAIRS OF USSR (BFEA)
　　　527 Madison Ave., New York, NY　10022
　　　CEO: Sergei Zotov, EVP　　　　　　　　　Tel: (212) 421-8660　Emp: 2
　　　Bus: *International banking services.*　　　Fax: (212) 421-8677　%FO: 100

● **DUN & BRADSTREET NORD**
19 Bol Shaya Mcrskaya Ulitsa, 4th Fl, St. Petersburg 191186, Russia
CEO: Tate Ulsaker, Mgr.　　　　　　　　　　　Tel: 7-812-278-9264　Emp: 200
Bus: *Investment banking.*　　　　　　　　　　Fax: 7-812-278-9265

　　　PALMS & COMPANY OF RUSSIA, INC.
　　　515 Lake Street South, Kirkland, Seattle, WA　98033
　　　CEO: Dr. Pyotr Joannevich Van de Waal-Palms,　Tel: (425) 828-6774　Emp: 200
　　　　　Gen. Dir.
　　　Bus: *Investment banking; import/export.*　　Fax: (425) 527-5528　%FO: 100

● **ITAR-TASS (RUSSIAN NEWS AGENCY)**
10 Tverskoy Boulevard, Moscow 103009, Russia
CEO: Vitary Ignatenko, Director General　　　　Tel: 7-95-229-64-03　Emp: 3500
Bus: *News and photo wires.*　　　　　　　　　Fax: 7-95-229-64-03

　　　ITAR-TASS USA, INC.
　　　50 Rockefeller Plaza, New York, NY　10020
　　　CEO: Michael Koleshichenko, Pres.　　　　Tel: (212) 664-0977　Emp: 15
　　　Bus: *News wires, photos, advertising, PR,*　Fax: (212) 245-4035　%FO: 100
　　　　　consulting.

● **VAO INTOURIST**
13 Mokhovaya Street, 103009 Moscow, Russia
CEO: Alexander P. Zaitsev, Pres.　　　　　　　Tel: 7-95-292-3786　Emp: 1125
Bus: *International tourism and investment operations.*　Fax: 7-95-292-2300

　　　INTOURIST/RAHIM ASSOCIATES, INC.
　　　12 South Dixie Hwy, Ste. 201, Lake Worth, FL　33460
　　　CEO: Alexey N. Mesiatsev, Pres.　　　　　Tel: (561) 585-5305　Emp: 10
　　　Bus: *International tourism and investment*　Fax: (561) 582-1353　%FO: JV
　　　　　operations.

Saudi Arabia

• ALIREZA GROUP
P.O.Box 90, Al-Khobar 31952, Saudi Arabia

CEO: Teymour Alireza, Pres.   Tel: 966-3-857-0234   Emp: N/A

Bus: *Diversified manufacturing and trading company;*   Fax:966-3-857-2846
construction, transportation, healthcare,
engineering, energy etc.

REZAYAT AMERICA INC.
11000 Richmond Avenue
Ste. 580, Houston, TX   77042

CEO: Barry Switzer, Pres.   Tel: (713) 782-0090   Emp: N/A

Bus: *U.S. headquarters for Alireza Group,*   Fax:(713) 782-7395   %FO: 100
diversified manufacturing & trading holding
company.

• THE NATIONAL SHIPPING COMPANY OF SAUDI ARABIA
Al-Akariya Building, Sitteen Street, Malaz P.O.Box 8931, Riyadh 11492, Saudi Arabia

CEO: Abdulla Al-Shuraim, Chief Engineer   Tel: 966-1-478-5454   Emp: N/A

Bus: *International shipping/cargo services.*   Fax:966-1-477-7478

NSCSA (America) INC.
World Trade Ctr, 401 Pratt St., 26th Fl., Baltimore, MD   21202

CEO: Fahad Al- Megren, Pres.   Tel: (410) 625-7000   Emp: N/A

Bus: *International shipping/cargo services.*   Fax:(410) 625-7050   %FO: 100

• THE OLAYAN GROUP
P.O. Box 8772, Riyadh 11492, Saudi Arabia

CEO: Aziz D Syriani, Pres.   Tel: 966-1-477-8740   Emp: N/A

Bus: *Holding company. (See Greece)*   Fax:966-1-478-0988

COMPETROL REAL ESTATE LTD
505 Park Avenue, 10th Fl., New York, NY   10022

CEO: Anthony S. Fucso, VP   Tel: (212) 750-4800   Emp: 10

Bus: *Real estate investment.*   Fax:(212) 308-3654   %FO: 100

OLAYAN AMERICA CORP.
505 Park Avenue, 10th Fl., New York, NY   10022

CEO: John O. Wolcott, EVP   Tel: Emp: 15

Bus: *Business development & advisory services.*   Fax: %FO: 100

• **RIYAD BANK**
King Abdul Aziz Rd, P O Box 22622, Riyadh 11416, Saudi Arabia
CEO: Omran M. Al-Omran, CEO   Tel: 966-1-4013030   Emp: 4300
Bus: *General banking services.*   Fax:966-1-404 2707

    RIYAD BANK
    700 Louisiana, #4770, Houston, TX   77002
    CEO: Samir A. Haddad, Sr.VP   Tel: (713) 224-8071   Emp: 14
    Bus: *International trade & project financing*   Fax:(713) 224-8072   %FO: 100
        services.

• **SAUDI ARABIAN AIRLINES**
Al Khaledyyah District, Jeddah 21231, Sauda Arabia
CEO: Sultan Bin Abdulaziz, Chrm.   Tel: 966-2-686-0000   Emp: 23924
Bus: *International commercial air transport services.*   Fax:966-2-686-4594

    SAUDI ARABIAN AIRLINES
    725 Fifth Avenue, New York, NY   10022
    CEO: Talal Mohsen, Gen.Mgr.   Tel: (212) 751-7000   Emp: N/A
    Bus: *International commercial air transport*   Fax:(212) 751-7270   %FO: 100
        services. Air transport services.

    SAUDI ARABIAN AIRLINES
    2600 Virginia Avenue, N.W., Suite 403, Washington, DC   20037
    CEO: Talal Mohsen, Gen.Mgr.   Tel: (202) 333-3800   Emp: N/A
    Bus: *International commercial air transport*   Fax:(20) 233-3380   %FO: 100
        services.

• **SAUDI ARABIAN OIL COMPANY**
Central Mail Room T-51, Dhahran 31311, Saudi Arabia
CEO: Ali I Naimi, Pres.   Tel: 966-872-0155   Emp: 44700
Bus: *Oil exploration, transportation & refining.*   Fax:966-873-8190

    ARAMCO SERVICES CO.
    9009 West Loop South, Houston, TX   77096
    CEO: Mustafa Jarili, Pres.   Tel: (713) 432-4000   Emp: 1000
    Bus: *Oil industry service/support.*   Fax:(713) 432-8566   %FO: 100

• **SAUDI BASIC INDUSTRIES CORPORATION**
P.O. Box 5101, Riyadh 11422, Saudi Arabia
CEO: Ibrahim A. Salamah, Vice Chrm.   Tel: 966-1-401-2033   Emp: 600
Bus: *Mfr./marketing chemicals, plastics, fertilizers &*   Fax:966-1-401-2045
    steels.

    SABIC AMERICAS, INC.
    2500 City West Blvd., Suite 650, Houston, TX   77042
    CEO: Abdullah Al-Dabibi - Dep. Gen.Mgr.   Tel: (281) 549-4999   Emp: 38
    Bus: *Research/development, procurement &*   Fax:(281) 549-4994   %FO: 100
        recruitment petrochemical/fertilizer/steel
        industries.

SABIC AMERICAS, INC.
One Station Place - Metro Center, Stamford, CT   06902
CEO: Mohammad Al-Deghaithar, Gen.Mgr.   Tel: (203) 353-5350   Emp: 38
Bus: *Marketing chemicals & fertilizers.*   Fax:(203) 353-5353   %FO: 100

Scotland

● **BANK OF SCOTLAND**
P.O. Box 5, The Mound, Edinburgh EH1 1YZ, Scotland
CEO: J. Robin Browning, Gen.Mgr.   Tel: 44-131-442-7777   Emp: N/A
Bus: *General banking services.*   Fax:44-131-243-5437

   BANK OF SCOTLAND
   1750 Two Allen Center, 1220 Smith Street, Houston, TX   77002
   CEO: Rex McSwain, SVP   Tel: (713) 651-1870   Emp: 10
   Bus: *International banking services.*   Fax:(713) 651-9714   %FO: 100

   BANK OF SCOTLAND
   Home Savings of America Tower, 660 Figueroa Suite 1760, Los Angeles, CA   90017
   CEO: Allan Jackson, SVP   Tel: (213) 629-3057   Emp: 5
   Bus: *International banking services.*   Fax:(213) 489-3594   %FO: 100

   BANK OF SCOTLAND
   Suite 3525, 181 West Madison Street, Chicago, IL   60602
   CEO: Jinn Halley, SVP   Tel: (312) 263-4054   Emp: 6
   Bus: *International banking services.*   Fax:(312) 263-1143   %FO: 100

   BANK OF SCOTLAND
   565 Fifth Avenue, 5th Fl., New York, NY   10017
   CEO: William Hendry, EVP   Tel: (212) 450-0800   Emp: 87
   Bus: *International banking services.*   Fax:(212) 557-9460   %FO: 100

   BANK OF SCOTLAND
   The Haskell Bldg., 111 Riverside, Jacksonville, FL   32202
   CEO: Hugh Van Seaton, SVP   Tel: (904) 353-7766   Emp: 6
   Bus: *International banking services.*   Fax:(904) 353-7833   %FO: 100

   BoS (Boston), Inc.
   One Post Office Sq., Suite 3750, Boston, MA   02109
   CEO: Bill Boland, SVP   Tel: (617) 426-0033   Emp: 2
   Bus: *International banking services.*   Fax:(617) 426-1353   %FO: 100

● **COATS VIYELLA PLC**
Pacific House, 70 Wellington Road, Glascow, Scotland, G26UB
CEO: Sir David Alliance, Chrm.   Tel: 44-141-225-6655   Emp: N/A
Bus: *Textiles and precision engineering products.*   Fax:44-141-225-6600

   COATS & CLARK, INC.
   30 Patewood Drive, Ste. 351, Greenville, SC   29615
   CEO: Michael Pratt, Pres.   Tel: (864) 234-0331   Emp: 65
   Bus: *Manufacturer of threads.*   Fax:(864) 234-0103   %FO: 100

COATS NORTH AMERICA, INC.
Two Lake Point Plaza, 4135 South Stream Drive, Charlotte, NC   28217
CEO: Thomas Smith, Pres.   Tel: (704) 329-5800   Emp: 180
Bus: *U.S. holding company.*   Fax:(704) 329-5820   %FO: 100

JAEGER SPORTSWEAR, LTD.
818 Madison Avenue, New York, NY   10021
CEO: Sidney J. Gibson, CFO   Tel: (212) 794-0780   Emp: 30
Bus: *Fashion retailer.*   Fax:(212) 570-9530   %FO: 100

● **GENERAL ACCIDENT FIRE & LIFE ASSURANCE CORP. PLC**
Pithealis, Perth PH2 0NH, Scotland
CEO: W. Nelson Robertson, CEO   Tel: 44-738-621202   Emp: N/A
Bus: *Insurance & financial services.*   Fax:44-738-621843

GENERAL ACCIDENT INSURANCE GROUP
436 Walnut Street, Philadelphia, PA   19106
CEO: Walter E. Farnam, Chrm   Tel: (215) 625-1000   Emp: N/A
Bus: *Insurance & financial services.*   Fax:(215) 625-1930   %FO: 100

● **WILLIAM GRANT & SONS LTD.**
206-208 West George Street, Glasglow G2 2PE, Scotland
CEO: David Grant, Pres.   Tel: N/A   Emp: N/A
Bus: *Distillery/exporter liquor.*   Fax:N/A

WILLIAM GRANT & SON INC
130 Fieldcrest Ave, Edison, NJ   08837
CEO: Derek Anderson, Pres.   Tel: (732) 225-9000   Emp: N/A
Bus: *Distillery/importer liquor.*   Fax:(732) 225-0950   %FO: 100

● **HOWDEN SIROCCO GROUP LTD.**
195 Scotland Street, Glasgow G5 8PJ, Scotland
CEO: N/A   Tel: 44-141-885-2245   Emp: 3849
Bus: *Holding company.*   Fax:44-141-885-2892

HOWDEN GROUP AMERICA
61 Spitbrook Road, Ste. 307, Nashua, NH   03060
CEO: Tom Zacaroti, Pres.   Tel: (603) 888-6909   Emp: 200
Bus: *Mfr. industry fans, blowers, fluid drives*   Fax:(603) 888-6451   %FO: 100

● **THE ROYAL BANK OF SCOTLAND PLC**
42 St. .Andrew Square, Edinburgh EH2 2YE, Scotland
CEO: Dr. George Mathewson, CEO   Tel: 44-131-556-8555   Emp: N/A
Bus: *Financial services company; banking, insurance,*   Fax:44-131-557-6565
investment advisory services.

   CITIZENS FINANCIAL GROUP, INC.
   One Citizens Plaza, Providence, RI   02903-4089
   CEO: Lawrence K. Fish, Chrm.   Tel: (401) 456-7000   Emp: N/A
   Bus: *Financial services company; banking,*   Fax:(401) 455-5715   %FO: 100
   insurance, investment advisory services.
   Holding company.

   CITIZENS FINANCIAL SERVICES CORP.
   One Citizens Plaza, Providence, RI   02903-4089
   CEO: Lawrence K. Fish, Chrm.   Tel: (401) 456-7000   Emp: N/A
   Bus: *Financial services company; banking,*   Fax:(401) 455-5715   %FO: 100
   insurance, investment advisory services.

   CITIZENS LEASING CORP., INC.
   One Citizens Plaza, Providence, RI   02903-4089
   CEO: Myles Gibert, Pres.   Tel: (401) 456-7000   Emp: N/A
   Bus: *Lease financing subsidiary of the ROYAL*   Fax:(401) 455-5715   %FO: 100
   BANK OF SCOTLAND PLC.

   CITIZENS MORTGAGE CORP., INC.
   900 Circle 75 Parkway, Atlanta, GA   30339
   CEO: Mark Thompson, Pres.   Tel: (770) 984-6809   Emp: N/A
   Bus: *Mortgage financing subsidiary of the ROYAL*   Fax:(770) 984-6865   %FO: 100
   BANK OF SCOTLAND PLC.

   CITIZENS SAVINGS BANK
   One Citizens Plaza, Providence, RI   02903-4089
   CEO: Lawrence K. Fish, Chrm.   Tel: (401) 456-7000   Emp: N/A
   Bus: *Savings bank subsidiary of the ROYAL BANK*   Fax:(401) 455-5715   %FO: 100
   OF SCOTLAND PLC.

   CITIZENS TRUST COMPANY
   One Citizens Plaza, Providence, RI   02903-4089
   CEO: Lawrence K. Fish, Chrm.   Tel: (401) 456-7000   Emp: N/A
   Bus: *Trust banking services subsidiary of the*   Fax:(401) 455-5715   %FO: 100
   ROYAL BANK OF SCOTLAND PLC.

   ROYAL BANK OF SCOTLAND
   88 Pine Street, 26th Floor, New York, NY   10005
   CEO: G.F. Stoddart, Pres.   Tel: (212) 269-1700   Emp: N/A
   Bus: *Financial services company; banking,*   Fax:(212) 269-8929   %FO: 100
   insurance, investment advisory services.

● **SCOTTISH & NEWCASTLE, PLC.**
Abbey Brewery, Holyrood Road, Edinburgh, Scotland EH8 8YS
CEO: Richard Keith, Pres.   Tel: 44-131-556-2591   Emp: N/A
Bus: *Mfr./distribution beer; McEwans, Youngers,*   Fax:44-131-558-1165
 Newcastle, Courage & Theakston.

    SCOTTISH & NEWCASTLE IMPORTERS
    444 De Haro Street, Ste. 209, San Francisco, CA   94107
    CEO: Kevin Moodie, Mgr.   Tel: (415) 255-4555   Emp: N/A
    Bus: *Importer/distributor beer.*   Fax:(415) 255-5907   %FO: 100

● **WEIR GROUP PLC.**
149 Newland Road, Catheart, Glasgow G44 4EX, Scotland
CEO: Lord Weir, Chrm.   Tel: 44-141-632-7111   Emp: N/A
Bus: *Valve manufacturer.*   Fax:44-141-632-2221

    ATWOOD & MORRILL CO., INC.
    285 Canal Street, Salem, MA   01970
    CEO: Robert Genier, Pres.   Tel: (508) 744-5690   Emp: 175
    Bus: *Mfr. valves and spare parts service.*   Fax:(508) 741-3626   %FO: 100

Singapore

- **THE DEVELOPMENT BANK OF SINGAPORE**
  6 Shenton Way, Singapore 0106
  CEO: Ngiam Tong Dow, Chrm.   Tel: 65-2201111   Emp: 3500
  Bus: *Commercial banking services.*   Fax:65-2211306

      THE DEVELOPMENT BANK OF SINGAPORE
      420 Fifth Avenue, New York, NY   10018
      CEO: Wil Kim Long, Gen.Mgr.   Tel: (212) 997-7500   Emp: 25
      Bus: *Government banking institution.*   Fax:(212) 997-5713   %FO: 100

- **OVERSEA-CHINESE BANKING CORP. LTD.**
  65 Chulia Street, OCBC Centre, Singapore 0104
  CEO: Seng Wee Lee, Chrm.   Tel: 65-535-7222   Emp: N/A
  Bus: *Commercial banking services.*   Fax:65-533-7955

      OVERSEA-CHINESE BANKING CORP LTD.
      2 World Financial Center, 225 Liberty St., New York, NY   10281
      CEO: James Lee, Gen.Mgr.   Tel: (212) 587-0101   Emp: 18
      Bus: *International commercial banking services.*   Fax:(212) 587-8235   %FO: 100

- **OVERSEAS UNION BANK LTD.**
  OUB Centre, 1 Raffles Pl, Singapore 0104
  CEO: Peter Seah Lim Huat, Pres   Tel: 65-533-9161   Emp: N/A
  Bus: *Commercial banking services.*   Fax:65-533-2293

      INTERNATIONAL BANK OF SINGAPORE LLC
      55 Montgomery Street, Ste. 600, San Francisco, CA   94111
      CEO: Ian Chong, VP   Tel: (415) 788-2121   Emp: N/A
      Bus: *International banking services.*   Fax:(415) 788-1457   %FO: 100

      OVERSEAS UNION BANK LTD
      1 World Trade Center, #3955, New York, NY   10048
      CEO: George Lim Phoon Seng, VP   Tel: (212) 432-9482   Emp: 17
      Bus: *International banking services.*   Fax:(212) 432-9297   %FO: 100

      OVERSEAS UNION BANK, LTD.
      777 S. Figueroa Street, Ste. 3988, Los Angeles, CA   90017
      CEO: Chen Hoong, VP   Tel: (213) 624-3187   Emp: N/A
      Bus: *International banking services.*   Fax:(213) 623-6407   %FO: 100

● **SINGAPORE AIRLINES LTD.**
Airline House, 25 Airline Road, Singapore 1781
CEO: S. Dhanabalan, Chrm.   Tel: 65-542-3333   Emp: N/A
Bus: *International air transport services.*   Fax:65-545-5034

   SINGAPORE AIRLINES LTD.
   333 Bush Street, San Francisco, CA   94104
   CEO: Steven Soh, VP   Tel: (415) 781-7304   Emp: 50
   Bus: *International air transport services.*   Fax:(415) 296-8080   %FO: 100

   SINGAPORE AIRLINES LTD.
   Delmonico Plaza, 55 East 59th St., Ste. 20B, New York, NY   10022-1112
   CEO: Sudneer Raghavan, VP   Tel: (212) 644-8801   Emp: 50
   Bus: *International air transport services.*   Fax: %FO: 100

   SINGAPORE AIRLINES LTD.
   5670 Wilshire Blvd, Ste. 1800, Los Angeles, CA   90036-3709
   CEO: Teoh Tee Hooi, Sr. VP   Tel: (213) 934-8833   Emp: 75
   Bus: *International air transport services.*   Fax:(213) 934-4482   %FO: 100

● **SINGAPORE TELECOMMUNICATIONS LTD.**
31 Exeter Road, Comcentre 239732, Singapore
CEO: BG Lee Hsien Yang, Pres.   Tel: 65-838-3388   Emp: 11000
Bus: *International telecommunications services &*   Fax:65-733-3008
   equipment.

   SINGAPORE TELECOM USA
   320 Post Road West, Suite 100, Westport, CT   06880
   CEO: J. Christopher Rudy, Mgr.   Tel: (203) 454-6800   Emp: 6
   Bus: *Representative office; service/sales*   Fax:(203) 454-1923   %FO: 100
       telecommunications services/equipment.

● **UNITED OVERSEAS BANK LTD.**
80 Raffles Place, UOB Plaza, Singapore 0104
CEO: Wee Cho Yaw, Chrm. & CEO   Tel: 65-533-9898   Emp: 6000
Bus: *Commercial banking and financial services*   Fax:65-534-2334

   UNITED OVERSEAS BANK LTD.
   529 Fifth Avenue, 10th Fl., New York, NY   10036
   CEO: Lye Soon Teo, Gen. Mgr.   Tel: (212) 382-0088   Emp: 25
   Bus: *Commercial banking & financial services.*   Fax:(212) 382-1881   %FO: 100

   UNITED OVERSEAS BANK LTD.
   911 Wilshire Boulevard, Los Angeles, CA   90017-3478
   CEO: Kang Ngoh Chew, Gen. Mgr.   Tel: (213) 623-8042   Emp: N/A
   Bus: *Commercial banking & financial services.*   Fax:(213) 623-3412   %FO: 100

UOB REALTY (USA) LTD PARTNERSHIP
592 Fifth Avenue, UOB Bldg., New York, NY   10036

CEO: Lye Soon Teo, Gen. Mgr.	Tel: (212) 382-0088	Emp: N/A
Bus: *Develops/manages real estate investment partnerships.*	Fax:(212) 382-1881	%FO: 100

Slovenia

- **NOVA LJANSKA BANCA, D.D.**
  Trg Republike 2, 1520 Ljublijana, Slovenia
  CEO: Marko Voljc, Chrm.   Tel: 386-611-250-155   Emp: NA
  Bus: *Banking services.*   Fax:N/A

  LBS BANK - NEW YORK
  12 East 52nd Street, New York, NY   10022
  CEO: Rudolf Gabrovec, Pres.   Tel: (212) 207-2200   Emp: 40
  Bus: *International banking services.*   Fax:(212) 593-1967   %FO: 100

South Africa

● **ANGLO AMERICAN CORP. OF SOUTH AFRICA LTD.**
44 Main Street, Johannesburg 2001, South Africa
CEO: Julian Ogilvie Thompson, Chrm.　　　　　Tel: 27-11-638-9111　　Emp: 86000
Bus: *Mining company; diamonds, gold, platinum, & coal.*　Fax:27-11-638-2445
Financial services. Mfr. steel, paper, timber &
chemicals.

　　MINOROCO (U.S.A.), INC.
　　30 Rockefeller Plaza, New York, NY　10112
　　CEO: H.R. Slack, Pres. & CEO　　　　　　Tel: (212) 332-3636　　Emp: N/A
　　Bus: *U.S. headquarters to supervise North*　　Fax:(212) 332-3647　　%FO: 100
　　　　American activities; Adobe Resources,
　　　　Inspiration Resources. (see Luxembourg).

● **NEDCOR BANK LIMITED**
100 Main Street, P.O. Box 1144, Johannesburg 2001, South Africa
CEO: Richard Laubscher　　　　　　　　Tel: 27-11-630-7111　　Emp: N/A
Bus: *Commercial banking services.*　　　　Fax:27-11-630-7891

　　NEDCOR BANK LIMITED
　　230 Park Avenue, Suite 1000, New York, NY　10169
　　CEO: Grant D. Tarr, Rep.　　　　　　　Tel: (212) 808-3011　　Emp: 2
　　Bus: *International banking services.*　　　Fax:(212) 808-4987　　%FO: 100

● **SOUTH AFRICAN AIRWAYS CORP.**
39 Wolmarans Street, Braamsontein P.O. Box 7778, Johannesburg 2000, South Africa
CEO: A.T. Moolman, Dir.　　　　　　　　Tel: 27-11-356-2035　　Emp: 11115
Bus: *Commercial air transport services.*　　Fax:27-11-356-2019

　　SOUTH AFRICAN AIRWAYS CORP.
　　515 East Las Olas Blvd., Suite 1600, Ft. Laudrdale, FL　33301
　　CEO: A.T. Moolman, Dir.　　　　　　　Tel: (954) 767-8722　　Emp: 100+
　　Bus: *Commercial air transport services.*　　Fax:(954) 522-1287　　%FO: 100

● **STANDARD BANK INVESTMENT OF SOUTH AFRICA LTD.**
P.O. Box 7725, 5 Simmonds Street, 9th Fl., Johannesburg 2001, South Africa
CEO: Dr. Conrad Strauss, Chrm.　　　　　　Tel: 27-11-636-9115　　Emp: 30000
Bus: *Commercial banking services.*　　　　Fax:N/A

　　THE STANDARD BANK OF SOUTH AFRICA LTD.
　　153 East 53rd Street, 38th Fl., New York, NY　10022
　　CEO: A.J. Strutt, SVP　　　　　　　　Tel: (212) 407-5020　　Emp: N/A
　　Bus: *International banking services.*　　　Fax:(212) 507-5027　　%FO: 100

STANDARD NEW YORK INC.
153 East 53rd Street, 38th Fl., New York, NY   10022
CEO: S.M.O' Connor, Mng.Dir.   Tel: (212) 407-5000   Emp: 45
Bus: *International banking services.*   Fax:(212) 407-5025   %FO: 100

Spain

- **ACERINOX SA**
Santiago de Compostela 100, 28035 Madrid, Spain
CEO: Victoriano Munoz, CEO   Tel: 34-1-398-5100   Emp: 2800
Bus: *Mfr. stainless steel.*   Fax:34-1-398-5101

> **ACERINOX CORPORATION**
> Two University Plaza, Hackensack, NJ   07601
> CEO: Leonard Arnold, EVP   Tel: (201) 489-6767   Emp: 14
> Bus: *Distributor stainless steel.*   Fax:(201) 489-7506   %FO: 100

- **AEI/IBERFREIGHT**
Avda de la Hispanidad 13, 28042 Madrid, Spain
CEO: Carlos Sevilla, Pres.   Tel: 34-1-301-9022   Emp: 200
Bus: *Freight forwarding (specialty: fashion footwear)*   Fax:34-1-320-1588

> **IBERFREIGHT**
> Bldg. 151, South Lobby, 2nd Fl., JFK International Airport, Jamaica, NY   11430
> CEO: Carlo Paravani, Pres.   Tel: (718) 244-6759   Emp: 10
> Bus: *Freight forwarding (specialty : footwear,* Fax:(718) 244-8972   %FO: 100
> *fashion goods).*

- **ARGENTARIA-CORPORATION BANCARIA DE ESPANA**
Paseo De Recoletos, 10, Madrid 28001, Spain
CEO: Francisco Gonzalez, CEO   Tel: 34-1-537-7000   Emp: 16500
Bus: *Commercial banking services.*   Fax:N/A

> **BEX AMERICA-BANCO EXTERIOR DE ESPANA**
> 320 Park Avenue, 20th Fl., New York, NY   10022
> CEO: Jose Ignacio Leyun, Gen. Mgr.   Tel: (212) 605-7400   Emp: 10
> Bus: *Commercial banking; regional office.*   Fax:(212) 754-9306   %FO: 100

- **BANCO ATLANTICO, S.A.**
Avenita Diagonal, E-28013 Barcelona, Spain
CEO: Jose Maria Chimeno   Tel: 34-1-538-9084   Emp: N/A
Bus: *Commercial banking services.*   Fax:34-1-538-9568

> **BANCO ATLANTICO, S.A.**
> 801 Brickell Avenue, Miami, FL   33131
> CEO: Emilio Martinez, Mgr.   Tel: (305) 374-7515   Emp: 35
> Bus: *International banking services.*   Fax:(305) 374-4076   %FO: 100

> **BANCO ATLANTICO, S.A.**
> 62 William Street, New York, NY   10005
> CEO: Jose M. Herendez-Font, EVP   Tel: (212) 422-3400   Emp: 45
> Bus: *International banking services.*   Fax:(212) 742-9438   %FO: 100

● BANCO CENTRAL HISPANOAMERICANO, S.A.
Calle de Alcala 49, 28014 Madrid, Spain
CEO: Jose Maria Amusategui, CEO   Tel: 34-1-532-8810   Emp: 35000
Bus: *Commercial banking services.*   Fax:34-1-532-7659

BANCO CENTRAL HISPANOAMERICANO, S.A.
245 Park Avenue, 16th Fl., New York, NY   10167
CEO: Francisco Alcon, EVP   Tel: (212) 557-8100   Emp: N/A
Bus: *International banking services.*   Fax:(212) 557-8349   %FO: 100

BANCO CENTRAL HISPANOAMERICANO, S.A.
505 Sansome Street, San Francisco, CA   94111
CEO: Jose Castello, Sr. VP   Tel: (415) 398-6333   Emp: N/A
Bus: *International banking services.*   Fax:(415) 398-3173   %FO: 100

● BANCO DE BILBAO VIZCAYA, S.A.
Plaza de San Nicolas, 4 Bilbao, 48005 Spain
CEO: Emilio de Ybara y Churruca, Chrm. & CEO   Tel: 34-4-487-6000   Emp: N/A
Bus: *International banking and financial services.*   Fax:34-4-487-6161

BANCO BILBAO VIZCAYA, S.A.
116 East 55th Street, New York, NY   10022
CEO: Raymond E.C. Surguy, EVP   Tel: (212) 826-1320   Emp: 80
Bus: *International banking*   Fax:(212) 755-9070   %FO: 100

● BANCO DE SANTANDER SA
Paseo de Pereda 11 y 12, E-39004 Santander, Spain
CEO: Rodrigo Echenique Gordillo, Mng. Dir.   Tel: 34-42-206100   Emp: N/A
Bus: *Commercial, investment and consumer banking services.*   Fax:34-42-206392

BANCO DE SANTANDER INTL
1000 Brickell Avenue, Miami, FL   33131
CEO: R. Lopez, Mgr.   Tel: (305) 358-1504   Emp: N/A
Bus: *International banking services.*   Fax:(305) 374-7807   %FO: 100

BANCO DE SANTANDER SA
45 East 53rd Street, New York, NY   10022
CEO: Antonio Garcia de Riego, SVP & Gen.Mgr.   Tel: (212) 350-3500   Emp: N/A
Bus: *International banking services.*   Fax:(212) 350-3535   %FO: 100

● BANCO ESPANOL DE CREDITO SA
Alcala 14, E-28014 Madrid, Spain
CEO: Alfredo Saenz, Chairman   Tel: 34-1-338-1000   Emp: N/A
Bus: *Commercial banking services.*   Fax:34-1-262-8410

BANCO ESPAÑOL DE CRÉDITO
730 Fifth Avenue, New York, NY   10019
CEO: Luis Basagoiti, EVP   Tel: (212) 835-5300   Emp: N/A
Bus: *International commercial banking services.*   Fax:(212) 262-8410   %FO: 100

● **BANCO EXTERIOR DE ESPAÑA**
Goya 14, E-28001 Madrid, Spain
CEO: Francisco Luzon, Pres.   Tel: 34-1-537-7000   Emp: 11000
Bus: *International commercial banking subsidiary of*   Fax:34-1-578-1047
     Argentaria.

    BANCO EXTERIOR DE ESPAÑA
    320 Park Avenue, 20th Floor, New York, NY   10022
    CEO: José Ignacio Leyun González, Gen. Mgr.   Tel: (212) 605-9800   Emp: 60
    Bus: *International banking services.*   Fax:(212) 755-4211   %FO: 100

    BANCO EXTERIOR DE ESPAÑA
    701 Brickell Avenue, Suite 1350, Miami, FL   33131
    CEO: Luis de Lara Fernández   Tel: (305) 371-5008   Emp: 22
    Bus: *International banking services.*   Fax:(305) 374-4452   %FO: 100

● **BANCO SANTANDER S.A.**
Paseo De La Castellana, 24, Madrid 28046, Spain
CEO: Emilio Botin-Sanz, Chrm.   Tel: 34-1-342-4884   Emp: 68000
Bus: *Banking and investment products.*   Fax:34-1-342-4880

    BANCO SANTANDER INTERNATIONAL
    1401 Brickell Avenue, Ste. 1500, Miami, FL   33131
    CEO: Raul Perex-Lopez, Mng. Dir.   Tel: (305) 539-5900   Emp: 130
    Bus: *Private banking.*   Fax:(305) 374-7807   %FO: 100

● **BERMARMOL SA**
Ledua 1, 03660 Novelda, Spain
CEO: Manuel Fernandez-Cachorro   Tel: 34-6-560-0512   Emp: 215
Bus: *Natural stone manufacturer.*   Fax:34-6-560-5817

    MB MARBLE & GRANITE CO., INC.
    20005 South Rancho Way, Rancho Dominguez, CA   90220
    CEO: Javier Alfaro, VP & Gen.Mgr..   Tel: (310) 886-1844   Emp: 6
    Bus: *Natural stone distribution.*   Fax:(310) 886-0004   %FO: 100

● **CARRERA Y CARRERA, S.A.**
A.P. Correos 1 km 31.5 NI, San Augustin de Guada, 28750, Spain
CEO: Manuel Carrera, CEO   Tel: 3-41-843-5193   Emp: N/A
Bus: *Manufacturer of gift items.*   Fax:3-41-843-5825

    CARRERA Y CARRERA, INC.
    1270 Avenue of the Americas, New York, NY   10036
    CEO: R. Cristobal, Pres.   Tel: (212) 332-3170   Emp: 5
    Bus: *Wholesale gift items.*   Fax:(212) 332-3179   %FO: 100

- **CHUPA CHUPS SA**
Avda Diagonal 660, 08016 Barcelona, Spain
CEO: Xavier Bernat, Pres.   Tel: 34-3-280-1414   Emp: 600
Bus: *Mfr. candy.*   Fax:34-3-280-4694

  CHUPA CHUPS, USA
  5901-C Peachtree Dunwoody Road, Atlanta, GA   30328
  CEO: Alejandro Siniawski, VP & Gen.Mgr.   Tel: (770) 481-0440   Emp: 20
  Bus: *Distributor candy, product development.*   Fax:(770) 481-0340   %FO: 100

- **CODORNIU, S.A.**
Gran Via 644, 08007 Barcelona, Spain
CEO: Jordi Raventos, Pres.   Tel: 34-3-301-4600   Emp: N/A
Bus: *Produces alcoholic beverages.*   Fax:34-3-317-9678

  CODORNIU NAPA INC.
  1345 Henry Road, Napa, CA   94558
  CEO: Michael Keaton, Pres.   Tel: (707) 224-1668   Emp: N/A
  Bus: *Production/bottling wines.*   Fax:(707) 224-1672   %FO: 100

- **CSI PLANOS, S.A.**
Paseo de la Castellana, 91, Madrid 28046, Spain
CEO: Francisco Prado Gayoso, Pres.   Tel: 34-1-596-9400   Emp: N/A
Bus: *Production of integrated steel.*   Fax:34-1-596-9510

  ENSISTEEL, INC.
  745 Fifth Avenue, Suite 1610, New York, NY   10151
  CEO: Eduardo Alvarez Lastra, Pres.   Tel: (212) 838-2431   Emp: 5
  Bus: *Mill agents.*   Fax:(212) 888-0546   %FO: 100

- **EMPRESA NACIONAL DE ELECTRICIDAD**
Principe de Vergara 187, E-28002 Madrid, Spain
CEO: Feliciano Fuster Jaume, Chrm.   Tel: 34-1-566-8800   Emp: N/A
Bus: *Mines/produces coal, generates energy/electricity.*   Fax:34-1-563-8181

  EMPRESA NACIONAL DE ELECTRICIDAD
  745 Fifth Avenue, New York, NY   10151-0061
  CEO: Fernando Lario, Dir.   Tel: (212) 750-7200   Emp: N/A
  Bus: *Mines/produces coal, generates*   Fax:(212) 750-7433   %FO: 100
      energy/electricity.

● **ESBELT SA**
Provenza 385, 08025 Barcelona, Spain
CEO: Enric Xargay, CEO   Tel: 34-3-2073311   Emp: N/A
Bus: *Mfr. thermoplastic conveyor belting.*   Fax:34-3-2071363

>   **ESBELT CORPORATION**
>   56 Ash Circle, Warminster, PA   18974
>   CEO: Xavier Xargay, Pres.   Tel: (215) 957-5473   Emp: 13
>   Bus: *Mfr. thermoplastic conveyor belting.* Fax:(215) 957-5390   %FO: 100

● **J & A GARRIGUES**
José Abascal, 45, 28003 Madrid, Spain
CEO: Jose Villar, Mng.. Ptnr.   Tel: 34-1-456-9800   Emp: N/A
Bus: *International law firm.*   Fax:34-1-399-2408

>   **J & A GARRIGUES**
>   115 East 57th Street, Ste.1230, New York, NY   10022
>   CEO: Ramon Llado, Mng. Ptnr.   Tel: (212) 751-9233   Emp: N/A
>   Bus: *International law firm.*   Fax:(212) 355-3594   %FO: 100

● **IBERIA AIRLINES (LINIAS AEREAS DE ESPANA)**
Velasquez 130, 28006 Madrid, Spain
CEO: Xabier de Irala, Pres.   Tel: 34-1-587-8787   Emp: N/A
Bus: *International air transport.*   Fax:34-1-587-6924

>   **IBERIA AIRLINES OF SPAIN**
>   6100 Blue Lagoon Dr, #200, Miami, FL   33126-2086
>   CEO: Salvatore Humbert, VP & Gen.Mgr.   Tel: (305) 267-7747   Emp: 20000
>   Bus: *International air transport.*   Fax:(305) 267-9401   %FO: 100

● **INDITEX, S.A.**
Polígono de Sabón 79-B Arteixo, LaCoruña 15142, Spain
CEO: Jose Maria Castellano, CEO   Tel: 34-81-185420   Emp: 8000
Bus: *Clothing (men/women/children) manufacture and*   Fax:34-81-185496
distribution to Inditex 600 worldwide stores.

>   **ZARA INTERNATIONAL, INC.**
>   750 Lexington Avenue, New York, NY   10022
>   CEO: Moises Costas, Mng. Dir.   Tel: (212) 355-1415   Emp: 100
>   Bus: *Zara chain of fashion stores.*   Fax:(212) 754-1128   %FO: 100

● **IVEX - INSTITUTO VALENCIANO DE LA EXPORTACIÓN**
Iplaza de America, 2, 46004 Valencia, Spain
CEO: Jose Maria, Dir.   Tel: 34-6-395-2001   Emp: N/A
Bus: *Government owned export services provider.*   Fax:34-6-395-2879

     IVEX - INSTITUTO VALENCIANO DE LA EXPORTACIÓN
     675 Third Avenue, New York, NY   10017
     CEO: Faustino Salcedo, Dir.   Tel: (212) 922-9000   Emp: N/A
     Bus: *Government owned export services provider.*   Fax:(212) 922-9012   %FO: 100

● **JUMBERCA SERVICE CORPORATION**
Jacinto Benavente 32, Badalona, Spain
CEO: Jose Delmau, Pres.   Tel: 34-3-389-1262   Emp: N/A
Bus: *Mfr. knitting machines and parts.*   Fax:34-3-3891612

     TEXTILES PARTS & SERVICE, INC.
     100 Summa Avenue, Westbury, NY   11590
     CEO: Andreu Valls, Pres.   Tel: (516) 338-4747   Emp: 9
     Bus: *Knitting machine parts, service & repair*   Fax:(516) 338-8811   %FO: 100

● **LLADRO COMERCIAL**
Crta. de Alboraya, s/n. Tavernes Blanques, Valencia 46016, Spain
CEO: Francisco Varea, Exec. Dir.   Tel: 34-6-185 01 77   Emp: 2000
Bus: *Mfr./sales/marketing of high quality, hand-crafted*   Fax:34-6-186 04 20
     porcelain figurines, vases, lamps and sculptures.

     LLADRO USA, INC.
     1, Lladro Drive, Moonachie, NJ   07074
     CEO: Jose Luis Perez-Herreo, Dir..   Tel: (201) 807-1177   Emp: 150
     Bus: *Sales/marketing of high quality, hand-crafted*   Fax:(201) 807-1089   %FO: 100
         porcelain figurines, vases, lamps and
         sculptures.

● **MESTRE INFANTIL, S.A.**
Alberdo 40-42, 28029 Madrid, Spain
CEO: Morris Hallak, Pres.   Tel: 34-1-315-9276   Emp: N/A
Bus: *Fine children's clothing and footwear.*   Fax:34-1-315-9276

     YES OUI SI, INC.
     131 West 33 Street, Ste. 904, New York, NY   10001
     CEO: Morris Hallak, Pres.   Tel: (212) 564-2620   Emp: N/A
     Bus: *Fine children's clothing and footwear.*   Fax:(212) 564-2450   %FO: 100

- **NATRA CACAO S.A.**
Autovia A-3, Salida 330-B Camino De Cos Hurnillos s/n, Quart De Poe, Valencia 46930, Spain
CEO: German Sanjuan, Pres.   Tel: 34-61-920764   Emp: 100
Bus: *Mfr. of cocoa derivatives.*   Fax:34-61-920453

> **NATRA US, INC.**
> 12801 Ponce DeLeon Blvd., Ste. 1070, Coral Gables, FL   33146
> CEO: German Sanjuan, Pres.   Tel: (305) 447-8999   Emp: 4
> Bus: *Cocoa derivatives.*   Fax:(305) 447-0885   %FO: 100

- **REYLAN, S.A.**
336 General Lugue, Inca, Mallorca 07300, Spain
CEO: Bartolome Piris, Pres.   Tel: 34-71-50-1358   Emp: 50
Bus: *Mfr. leather garments.*   Fax:34-71-50-1283

> **MARTIN G. PIRIS COMPANY**
> 200 East 32nd Street, Ste. 17-E, New York, NY   10016
> CEO: Martin Piris, Pres.   Tel: (212) 679-9710   Emp: 3
> Bus: *Wholesale of leather garments.*   Fax:(212) 679-9710   %FO: 100

- **RICHEL SA**
Aribau 185-187, 08021 Barcelona, Spain
CEO: Michel Catris, CEO   Tel: 34-3-2001333   Emp: 115
Bus: *Mfr. neckties and women's scarves.*   Fax:34-3-2002151

> **RICHEL USA, INC.**
> 730 Fifth Avenue, New York, NY   10019
> CEO: Stephen H. Turk, Sales Mgr.   Tel: (212) 315-0777   Emp: N/A
> Bus: *Sale/distribution neckties and scarves.*   Fax:(212) 315-0664   %FO: 100

- **SOCIEDAD GENERAL DE AUTORES Y EDITORES (SGAE)**
Fernando VI, 4, Madried 28004, Spain
CEO: Eduardo Bautista-Garcia, Pres.   Tel: 34-1-349-9550   Emp: N/A
Bus: *Music licensing organization.*   Fax:34-1-310-2120

> **SOCIEDAD GENERAL DE AUTORES Y EDITORES (SGAE)**
> 240 East 47th Street, Ste. 12B, New York, NY   10017
> CEO: Emilio Garcia, Director   Tel: (212) 752-7230   Emp: N/A
> Bus: *Music licensing organization.*   Fax:(212) 754-4378   %FO: 100

- **TECNICAS REUNIDAS, S.A.**
Arapiles, 14, Madrid 28015, Spain
CEO: Jose Llado, Pres.   Tel: 34-1-592-0300   Emp: 950
Bus: *Engineering/construction.*   Fax:34-1-592-0399

> **TECHICAS REUNIDAS INTERNATIONAL, INC.**
> 12012 Wickchester, Ste. 475, Houston, TX   77072
> CEO: Salvador Diaz, VP   Tel: (281) 679-7511   Emp: 3
> Bus: *Engineering services.*   Fax:(281) 679-7336   %FO: 100

● **TORRAS SA**
Via de Ronda S/N, Caldes de Montour, 08140 Barcelona, Spain
CEO: Juan Serra, Pres.   Tel: 34-3 8653636   Emp: 400
Bus: *Mfr. leather and knit jackets/ sweaters.*   Fax:34-3 8654442

    BCN FASHIONS, INC.
    P.O. Box 30, Suffern, NY   10901
    CEO: Mel Singer, Pres.   Tel: (914) 368-1775   Emp: N/A
    Bus: *Sales/distribution leather and knit*   Fax:(914) 357-6590   %FO: 100
       jackets/sweaters.

● **URÍA & MENÉDEZ**
Jorge Juan 6, 28001 Madrei, Spain
CEO: Rafael Sebastian, Mng. Ptnr.   Tel: 34-1-586-0400   Emp: N/A
Bus: *International law firm.*   Fax:34-1-586-0403

    URÍA & MENÉDEZ
    712 Fifth Avenue, 30th Fl., New York, NY   10019
    CEO: Carlos DeCalminis, Mng. Ptnr.   Tel: (212) 801-3460   Emp: N/A
    Bus: *International law firm.*   Fax:(212) 801-3465   %FO: 100

● **VIDRIO NATURAL, S.L.**
Pol. Ind. "La Cava", Montaverner 46892, Spain
CEO: Jose Diaz Patton   Tel: 34-6-229-7612   Emp: 200
Bus: *Mfr. bottles/jars and recycled glass.*   Fax:34-6-229-7611

    VIDRIO NATURAL USA, INC.
    640 Marine Pkwy., Ste. N., Chula Vista, CA   91910
    CEO: Martin Brabenec, Ptnr.   Tel: (619) 498-1884   Emp: 2
    Bus: *Glassware; sales support/customer service.*   Fax:(619) 498-1855   %FO: 100

Sweden

• ABA OF SWEDEN
Scheelegatan 28, S-112 28 Stockholm, Sweden
CEO: Lars Nordin, Mktg. Dir.   Tel: 46-8-654-1401   Emp: 250
Bus: *Mfr. hose clamps.*   Fax:46-8-653-3410

ABA OF AMERICA INC
4004 Auburn Street, Rockford, IL   61101
CEO: Arne Stegvik, Pres.   Tel: (815) 965-5170   Emp: 10
Bus: *Mfr. hose clamps.*   Fax:(815) 965-7559   %FO: JV

• ABS PUMP AB
Kroksiätts Parkgata 4, Box 2053, S-431 02 Moindal, Sweden
CEO: Hans Borneson, Pres.   Tel: 46-31-83 6300   Emp: 100+
Bus: *Mfr./import/distributor of pumps for municipal,*   Fax:46-31-18 4906
industrial and residential markets.

ABS PUMPS, INC.
140 Pond View Drive, Meriden, CT   06450
CEO: Gerald A. Assessor, Pres.   Tel: (203) 238-2700   Emp: N/A
Bus: *Sales/distribution of pumps and pumping*   Fax:(203) 238-0738   %FO: 100
equipment.

• AGA AB
S-181 81 Lidingö, Sweden
CEO: Lennart Selander, Pres.   Tel: 46-8-731-1000   Emp: 10521
Bus: *Industrial gas & gas equipment.*   Fax:46-8-767-6344

AGA GAS INC.
PO Box 94737, Cleveland, OH   44101-4737
CEO: Patrick F. Murphy, Pres. & CEO   Tel: (216) 642-6600   Emp: 1177
Bus: *Industrial gas & gas equipment.*   Fax:(216) 642-8516   %FO: 100

• AGEMA INFRARED SYSTEMS (Sub of Spectra-Physics AB)
Box 3, S-182 11 Dandered, Sweden
CEO: Arne Almerfors, Pres.   Tel: 46-8-753-3400   Emp: N/A
Bus: *Mfr. infrared systems.*   Fax:46-8-753-2364

AGEMA INFRARED SYSTEMS
550 County Avenue, Secaucus, NJ   07094
CEO: David Smith, Pres.   Tel: (201) 867-5390   Emp: 20
Bus: *Sale/service infrared systems.*   Fax:(201) 867-2191   %FO: 100

• AIMPOINT AB
Jagershillgatan 15, S-213 75 Malmo, Sweden
CEO: Gunnar Sandberg, Pres.   Tel: 46-40-671-5020   Emp: N/A
Bus: *Electronic gun sights mounting systems; red dot*   Fax:46-40-219238
     sights.

AIMPOINT INC
7700 Leesburg Pike, Suite 310A, Falls Church, VA 22043
CEO: Per-Anders Hallquist, Pres.   Tel: (703) 749-2320   Emp: 7
Bus: *Import electronic gun sights, mounting*   Fax:(703) 749-2323   %FO: 100
     systems; red dot sights.

• AKAB OF SWEDEN AB
Bussgatan 4, Viared, S-505 94 Borås, Sweden
CEO: Jan Karrman, Mgn. Dir.   Tel: 46-33-257030   Emp: 80
Bus: *Mfr. automatic sewing machines for home textile*   Fax:46-33-136867
     industry.

AKAB OF AMERICA INC.
4209 Pleasant Road, Fort Mill, SC 29715
CEO: Rolf Stridh, Pres.   Tel: (803) 548-6815   Emp: 6
Bus: *Automatic sewing machines for home textile*   Fax:(803) 548-6820   %FO: 100
     industry.

• ÅKERLUND & RAUSING, AB
S. Industriomradet, Box 22, S-221 00 Lund, Sweden
CEO: Staffan Erenmalm, Mgn.Dir.   Tel: 46-46-183000   Emp: 10
Bus: *Food packaging systems.*   Fax:46-46-113600

ÅKERLUND & RAUSING N.A., INC.
3450 Corporate Way, Ste. C, Duluth, GA 30136
CEO: Rita Kerlin, Controller   Tel: (770) 623-8235   Emp: 10
Bus: *Food packaging systems.*   Fax:(770) 623-8236   %FO: 100

• ÅKERS INTERNATIONAL AB
S-640 60 Åkers Styckebruk, Sweden
CEO: Ingvar Lundborg, Pres.   Tel: 46-159-32100   Emp: 300
Bus: *Mfr./marketing cast & forged steel rolls.*   Fax:46-159-32101

AKERS AMERICA INC
58 S Main Street, #14, Poland, OH 44514-1978
CEO: William D. Bigley, Pres.   Tel: (216) 757-4100   Emp: N/A
Bus: *Sale cast & forged steel rolls.*   Fax:(216) 757-4235   %FO: 100

• ALFA LAVAL AB
Borgen, Landerigrand, Ruben Rausings gata, S-221 86 Lund, Sweden
CEO: Leif Rogersson, Pres.   Tel: 46-46-36-7000   Emp: 11000
Bus: *Mfr./engineering/design services for diversified*   Fax: 46-46-36-4950
industrial systems.

ALFA LAVAL PUMPS INC.
9201 Wilmot Road, PO Box 1426, Kenosha, WI   53141-1426
CEO: John Pepper, Pres.   Tel: (414) 942-0166   Emp: N/A
Bus: *Sale/distribution pumps.*   Fax: (414) 942-0177   %FO: 100

ALFA LAVAL AUTOMATION INC.
PO Box 788, 9201 Wilmot Road, Kenosha, WI   53141-0788
CEO: Carl Larsson, Pres.   Tel: (414) 842-9310   Emp: N/A
Bus: *Mfr./engineering/design services for*   Fax: (414) 942-3777   %FO: 100
diversified industrial systems.

ALFA LAVAL CARDINAL SYSTEMS
25 Research Center, St. Louis, MO   63026
CEO: Thomas J. Winters, Pres.   Tel: (314) 447-1555   Emp: N/A
Bus: *Clean & electroplate stainless steel fittings &*   Fax: (314) 447-1653   %FO: 100
tubing.

ALFA LAVAL CELLECO INC.
1000 Laval Blvd., Lawrenceville, GA   30243
CEO: John Sams, Pres.   Tel: (770) 963-2100   Emp: N/A
Bus: *Sales, parts & systems, to paper pulp industry.*   Fax: (770) 339-6132   %FO: 100

ALFA LAVAL CONTHERM, INC.
111 Parker Street, Newburyport, MA   01950
CEO: Dinko Mutak, Pres.   Tel: (508) 465-5777   Emp: N/A
Bus: *Mfr./engineering/design services for*   Fax: (508) 465-6006   %FO: 100
diversified industrial systems; plate heat
exchangers.

ALFA LAVAL INC.
9201 Wilmot Road, P.O. Box 840, Kenosha, WI   53141-0840
CEO: Quintin T. Jackson, Pres.   Tel: (414) 942-9310   Emp: 1600
Bus: *Mfr./engineering/design services for*   Fax: (414) 942-3777   %FO: 100
diversified industrial systems.

ALFA LAVAL SAUNDERS INC.
16516 Air Center Blvd., Houston, TX   77032
CEO: Brian Tripoli, Pres.   Tel: (281) 443-0000   Emp: N/A
Bus: *Mfr. industrial diaphragm valves.*   Fax: (281) 230-2121   %FO: 100

ALFA LAVAL SEPARATION INC.
955 Mearns Road, Warminster, PA   18974-9998
CEO: Yannick Richomme, Pres.   Tel: (215) 443-4000   Emp: 516
Bus: *Mfr./marketing centrifuges.*   Fax: (215) 443-4205   %FO: 100

ALFA LAVAL THERMAL INC.
5400 International Trade Drive, Richmond, VA   23231
CEO: Kirk Spitzer, Pres.   Tel: (804) 222-5300   Emp: N/A
Bus: *Mfr./marketing plate heat exchangers.*   Fax:(804) 236-1333   %FO: 100

G&H PRODUCTS CORP.
PO Box 909, 8201-104th Street, Pleasant Prairie, WI   53158-0909
CEO: Keith Potts, Pres.   Tel: (414) 947-4700   Emp: N/A
Bus: *Marketing/distribution stainless steel*   Fax:(414) 947-4727   %FO: 100
processing equipment for food, beverage,
dairy, pharmaceutical & biotech industries.

TRI-CLOVER INC.
9201 Wilmot Road, Kenosha, WI   53141-1413
CEO: Ole Andersen, Pres.   Tel: (414) 694-5511   Emp: N/A
Bus: *Mfr. sanitary stainless steel pumps, valves,*   Fax:(414) 694-3173   %FO: 100
fittings for food, pharmaceutical & biotech
industries.

• **ALIMAK AB**
Box 30614, S-931 03 Skellefteå, Sweden
CEO: Krister Kempainen, Pres.   Tel: 46-910-8700   Emp: N/A
Bus: *Mfr. industrial & passenger service elevators.*   Fax:49-910-56690

ALIMAK ELEVATOR CO.
3040 Amwiler Road, Atlanta, GA   30360
CEO: Hans-Olof Lofstrand, Mgr.   Tel: (404) 441-9055   Emp: N/A
Bus: *Distribution/service industrial & passenger*   Fax:(404) 441-9095   %FO: 100
service elevators.

ALIMAK ELEVATOR CO.
1100 Boston Avenue, P O Box 1950, Bridgeport, CT   06601
CEO: Ulf Lundell, Pres.   Tel: (203) 367-7400   Emp: 80
Bus: *Distribution/service industrial & passenger*   Fax:(203) 367-9251   %FO: 100
service elevators.

• **ALTHIN MEDICAL AB**
St Gråbrödersgatan 17B, S-222 22 Lund, Sweden
CEO: Anders Althin, Chrm.   Tel: 46-46-150155   Emp: 1000
Bus: *Sale/distribution medical products, equipment, &*   Fax:46-46-137220
accessories.

ALTHIN MEDICAL INC.
14620 N.W. 60th Avenue, Miami Lakes, FL   33014
CEO: Anders Althin, Pres.   Tel: (305) 823-5240   Emp: 500
Bus: *Mfr./sale/distribution medical products,*   Fax:(305) 822-6217   %FO: 100
equipment, & accessories.

- **AMERICAN SCANDINAVIAN STUDENT EXCHANGE (ASSE)**
Kindstugatan 1, Box 2017, S-103, Stockholm, Sweden
CEO: Lena Bello, Mgr.   Tel: 46-8-230300   Emp: 200+
Bus: *Educational services.*   Fax:46-8-240543

> **ASPECT, INC.**
> 350 Samsone Street, San Francisco, CA   94103
> CEO: Håkan Bille, Pres.   Tel: (415) 228-8000   Emp: 100+
> Bus: *Worldwide educational organization providing*   Fax:(415) 228-8200   %FO: N/A
> *innovative, high-quality programs.*

- **AB ARITMOS**
Box 843, Helsingborgse 25108, Sweden
CEO: Thore Ohlsson   Tel: 46-42-197170   Emp: N/A
Bus: *Holding company.*   Fax:46-42-130683

> **TRETORN, INC.**
> 147 Center Street, Brockton, MA   02403
> CEO: Tim Bushell, Pres.   Tel: (508) 583-9100   Emp: N/A
> Bus: *Mfr./distribution athletic footwear.*   Fax:(508) 588-4919   %FO: 100

- **ARLA**
Torsgatan 14, S-10546 Stockholm, Sweden
CEO: Lars Lamberg, Chrm.   Tel: 46-8-789-5000   Emp: N/A
Bus: *Produces milk and milk products.*   Fax:46-8-209826

> **MEDIPHARM USA, INC.**
> 10215 Dennis Drive, Des Moines, IA   50322
> CEO: Mark Richards, Mng. Dir.   Tel: (515) 254-1280   Emp: N/A
> Bus: *Mfr. bacteria cultures for food and*   Fax:(515) 254-1356   %FO: 100
> *agricultural industry.*

- **ASKO CYLINDA AB**
(Jung) S-534 82 Vara, Sweden
CEO: Hans Linnarson, Pres.   Tel: 46-512-32000   Emp: 100+
Bus: *Household appliances.*   Fax:46-512-22303

> **ASKO INC.**
> 1161 Executive Drive West, PO Box 851805, Richardson, TX   75085
> CEO: Leon R. Bausch, Pres.   Tel: (972) 644-8595   Emp: 20+
> Bus: *Sales of dishwashers, washers/dryers.*   Fax:(972) 644-8593   %FO: 100

• **ASTRA AB**
Vastra Malarehamnen 9, S-151 36 Sodertalje, Sweden
CEO: Dr. Håkan Mogren, Pres. & CEO   Tel: 46-855-326000   Emp: 20000
Bus: *Mfr. pharmaceutical products.*   Fax:46-855-329000

    ASTRA MERCK INC.
    725 Chesterbrook Boulevard, Wayne, PA   19087-5677
    CEO: Matt Emmons, CEO   Tel: (610) 695-1000   Emp: N/A
    Bus: *Research product development and marketing*   Fax:(610) 695-1250   %FO: JV
        joint venture.

    ASTRA USA, INC.
    50 Otis Street, Westborough, MA   01581-4500
    CEO: Ivan Rowley, Pres. & CEO   Tel: (508) 366-1100   Emp: 1340
    Bus: *Product development/mfr./marketing*   Fax:(508) 366-7406   %FO: 100
        pharmaceuticals.

• **ATLAS COPCO AB**
S-105 23 Stocholm, Sweden
CEO: Anders Scharp, Chrm.   Tel: 46-8-743-8000   Emp: N/A
Bus: *Mfr. power tools, mining & construction equipment,*   Fax:46-8-644-9045
    pneumatic tools, assembly systems.

    ATLAS COPCO AFS, INC.
    5500 18th Mile Road, Sterling Heights, MI   48314
    CEO: Davis Johnson, Pres.   Tel: (810) 268-7400   Emp: N/A
    Bus: *Mfr. industrial machinery.*   Fax:(810) 268-5940   %FO: 100

    ATLAS COPCO NORTH AMERICA, INC.
    Hambaurg Turnpike, 2nd Fl., Wayne, NJ   07470
    CEO: Mark Cohen, EVP   Tel: (201) 633-8600   Emp: 2000
    Bus: *Mfr. compressors, mining construction*   Fax:(201) 633-9722   %FO: 100
        equipment, pneumatic tools, assembly systems.

    ATLAS COPCO RENTAL, INC.
    285 Eldridge Road, Fairfield, NJ   07004-2508
    CEO: Ernest Power, Pres.   Tel: (201) 227-2755   Emp: 90
    Bus: *Rental compressors.*   Fax:(201) 227-3755   %FO: 100

    ATLAS COPCO ROBBINS, INC.
    PO Box 97027, Kent, WA   98064-9722
    CEO: Lars de Verdier, Pres.   Tel: (206) 872-0500   Emp: N/A
    Bus: *Mfr./sale/service construction, mining &*   Fax:(206) 872-0199   %FO: 100
        materials handling equipment.

    ATLAS COPCO ROTOFLOW, INC.
    540 East Rosecrans Ave., Gardena, CA   90248
    CEO: Michael Allen, Pres.   Tel: (310) 329-8447   Emp: N/A
    Bus: *Mfr./sale/service construction, engines and*   Fax:(310) 329-3597   %FO: 100
        special industrial machinery.

ATLAS COPCO TOOLS, INC.
37735 Enterprise Court, Suite 300, Farmington Hills, MI 48331
CEO: Charles Robinson, Pres.　　　　　　　　Tel: (248) 489-1260　　Emp: 130
Bus: *Mfr./distribution pneumatic/electric industrial*　Fax:(248) 489-1260　%FO: 100
　　　power tools.

ATLAS COPCO WAGNER, INC.
P.O. Box 20307, Portland, OR 97220-0307
CEO: Jim Hendersen, Pres.　　　　　　　　　　Tel: (503) 255-2863　　Emp: N/A
Bus: *Mfr./sale heavy mining/construction equipment.*　Fax:(503) 255-7075　%FO: 100

CHICAGO PNEUMATIC TOOL CO.
2200 Bleeker Street, Utica, NY 13501
CEO: Necip Soyak, Pres.　　　　　　　　　　　Tel: (315) 792-2918　　Emp: 1700
Bus: *Pneumatic & electric power tools, light*　　Fax:(315) 792-2668　%FO: 100
　　　construction equipment.

• ATLET AB
S-435 82 Mölnlycke, Sweden
CEO: Knuit Jacobsson, Pres. & CEO　　　　　　Tel: 46-31-984000　　Emp: 775
Bus: *Mfr. lift trucks.*　　　　　　　　　　　　Fax:46-31-884686

ATLET USA
502 Pratt Ave. North, Schaumburg, IL 60193
CEO: Larry Couperthwaite, Pres.　　　　　　　Tel: (847) 352-7373　　Emp: 15
Bus: *Sale/service lift trucks.*　　　　　　　　Fax:(847) 352-8001　%FO: JV

• AXEL JOHNSON AB
BOX 26008, S-100 41 Stockholm, Sweden
CEO: Goran Ennerfelt, Pres.　　　　　　　　　Tel: 46-8-701-6100　　Emp: N/A
Bus: *Mfr. industrial machinery.*　　　　　　　Fax:46-8-213026

ADS ENVIRONMENTAL SERVICES INC.
5025 Bradford Blvd., Huntsville, AL 35805-7952
CEO: Thomas Neel, Pres.　　　　　　　　　　　Tel: (205) 430-3366　　Emp: N/A
Bus: *Environmental engineering services.*　　　Fax:(205) 430-3961　%FO: 100

AXEL JOHNSON AB
300 Atlantic Street, Stamford, CT 06901
CEO: Paul Graf, Pres.　　　　　　　　　　　　Tel: (203) 326-5200　　Emp: N/A
Bus: *Mfr./sales/service industrial machinery.*　Fax:(203) 326-5280　%FO: 100

BIRD-JOHNSON COMPANY
110 Norfolk Street, Walpole, MA 02081-1798
CEO: Peter Gwyn, Pres.　　　　　　　　　　　　Tel: (508) 668-9610　　Emp: N/A
Bus: *Mfr./sale/service industrial machinery.*　Fax:(508) 668-5638　%FO: 100

HEKIMIAN LABORATORIES, INC.
15200 Omega Drive, Rockville, MD   20850-3240

CEO: Robert Ginnings

Bus: *Mfr./sales/service industrial electronic machinery.*

Tel: (301) 590-3600
Fax:(310) 590-3599

Emp: N/A
%FO: 100

LARSCON INC.
4600 Patrick Henry Drive, Santa Clara, CA   95052

CEO: Deborah Soon

Bus: *Mfr./sales/service telecommunications equipment.*

Tel: (408) 988-6600
Fax:(408) 986-8626

Emp: N/A
%FO: 100

● **AXIS COMMUNICATIONS AB**
Scheelevägen 16, Ideon, S-223 70 Lund, Sweden

CEO: Mikael Karlsson, Pres.

Bus: *Mfr. computer and office equipment.*

Tel: 46-46-191800
Fax:46-46-136130

Emp: 100+

AXIS COMMUNICATIONS INC.
800 El Camino Real, Mountain View, CA   94040

CEO: Bengt Christensson, VP

Bus: *Computer and office equipment.*

Tel: (415) 903-2221
Fax:(415) 903-2224

Emp: 100+
%FO: 100

● **BESAM AB**
Lodjursgatan 10, Box 131, S-261 22 Landskrona, Sweden

CEO: Bertil Samuelsson, Pres.

Bus: *Mfr. metal products; doors.*

Tel: 46-418-51000
Fax:46-418-23800

Emp: N/A

BESAM INC.
171 Twin River Drive, East Windsor, NJ   08520

CEO: Joseph Loria, Pres.

Bus: *Automatic door systems.*

Tel: (609) 443-5800
Fax:(609) 443-3440

Emp: N/A
%FO: 100

● **BILSPEDITION TRANSPORT & LOGISTICS (BTL) AB**
S-412 97 Göteborg, Sweden

CEO: Håkan Larsson, Mgn. Dir.

Bus: *Land/sea/air logistics company and freight forwarder.*

Tel: 46-31-703-8000
Fax:46-31-407873

Emp: 12000

WILSON UTC INC.
750 Walnut Avenue, CN 1196, Cranford, NJ   07016

CEO: Stephen M. Gill, Mng. Dir.

Bus: *Customs broker, international freight forwarders.*

Tel: (908) 709-8700
Fax:(908) 709-0441

Emp: 230
%FO: 100

● **BINDOMATIC AB**
Vretenborgsvägen 9, Box 42101, S-126 12 Stockholm, Sweden
CEO: Sture Wiholm, Mgn. Dir.   Tel: 46-8-709-5800   Emp: N/A
Bus: *Mfr. binding systems.*   Fax:46-8-188652

     COVERBIND CORP
     3200 Corporate Drive, Wilmington, NC 28405
     CEO: Nick Downes, Dir.   Tel: (910) 799-4116   Emp: N/A
     Bus: *Mfr. binding systems.*   Fax:(910) 799-3935   %FO: 100

● **BODA NOVA INTL AB**
Box 23, S-263 21 Höganäs, Sweden
CEO: Olof Marköö, Pres.   Tel: 46-42-331100   Emp: N/A
Bus: *Design/mfr. dinnerware, flatware, glassware, wood*   Fax:46-42-349823
     items.

     BODA NOVA INC.
     406 North Clark Street, Chicago, IL 60610
     CEO: Charles I. Moore, Mktg. Dir.   Tel: (312) 321-1540   Emp: N/A
     Bus: *Dinnerware, flatware, glassware, wood items.*   Fax:(312) 321-9614   %FO: 100

● **BRIO AB**
Västra Järnvägsgatan 9, Box 3, S-283 00 Osby, Sweden
CEO: Bengt Ivarsson, Pres.   Tel: 46-479-19000   Emp: 825
Bus: *Mfr./marketing specialty toys.*   Fax:46-479-14124

     BRIO CORP
     N120 West 18485 Freistadt Road, Germantown, WI 53022
     CEO: Peter F. Reynolds, Pres.   Tel: (414) 250-3240   Emp: 30
     Bus: *Importer marketing/distribution toys.*   Fax:(414) 250-3255   %FO: 100

● **BROMMA CONQUIP AB**
Krossgatan 31-33, S-162 26 Vallingby, Sweden
CEO: Svante Lundbriank, Mgn. Dir.   Tel: 46-8-380030   Emp: 146
Bus: *Mfr. spreaders.*   Fax:46-8-739-3786

     BROMMA, INC.
     2285 Durham Road, P.O.Box 451, Roxboro, NC 27573
     CEO: Terry E. Howell, Pres.   Tel: (910) 599-3141   Emp: N/A
     Bus: *Mfr. container-handling equipment & related*   Fax:(910) 599-4499   %FO: 100
     attachments.

• BT INDUSTRIES AB

S-595 81 Mjolby, Sweden

CEO: Calle Ridderstrale, Pres.   Tel: 46-1-428-6000   Emp: 3245

Bus: *Mfr. material-handling trucks.*   Fax:46-1-428-6080

THE PRIME-MOVER CO

3305 North Highway 38, Muscatine, IA   52761-8800

CEO: Dave Freedman, Pres   Tel: (319) 262-7700   Emp: 300

Bus: *Mfr. material-handling equipment.*   Fax:(319) 262-7600   %FO: 100

• CAR-O-LINER AB

Box 7, S-736 00 Kungsör, Sweden

CEO: Björn Ramberg, Pres.   Tel: 46-227-12000   Emp: 200

Bus: *Mfr. collision repair equipment.*   Fax:46-227-13826

CAR-O-LINER CO.

29900 Anthony Drive, Wixom, MI   48393-3609

CEO: Larry J. Carter, Pres.   Tel: (810) 624-5900   Emp: 15

Bus: *Distribution collision repair equipment.*   Fax:(810) 624-9529   %FO: 100

• CARNEGIE HOLDING AB

Gustav Adolphstorg 18, S-103 38 Stockholm, Sweden

CEO: Lars Bertmar, Pres.   Tel: 46-8-676-8800   Emp: 300

Bus: *Stockbroker, asset management services.*   Fax:46-8-212840

CARNEGIE INC.

20 West 55th Street, New York, NY   10019

CEO: Mogens Vad, Pres.   Tel: (212) 262-5800   Emp: 10

Bus: *Stockbroker, investment management services.*   Fax:(212) 265-3946   %FO: 100

• CELSIUS AB

Box 7214 S-103 88 Stockholm, Sweden

CEO: Olof Lund, Chrm.   Tel: 46-8-463-0000   Emp: 15600

Bus: *Defense industry, non-military technology, real*   Fax:46-8-611-6894
     estate management, information technology.

AERO SYSTEMS ENGINEERING INC.

358 E. Filmore Avenue, St. Paul, MN   55107

CEO: Dr. Leon Ring, Pres.   Tel: (612) 227-7515   Emp: N/A

Bus: *Develop/mfr. test system for jet engines,*   Fax:(612) 227-0519   %FO: 100
     computerized measure & control systems,
     mechanical testing equipment.

AERO THRUST CORP.

P.O.Box 522236, Miami, FL   33152

CEO: James E. McMillen, Pres.   Tel: (305) 871-1790   Emp: N/A

Bus: *Jet engine maintenance.*   Fax:(305) 871-7967   %FO: 100

CELSIUS INC.
1800 Diagonal Road, #230, Alexandria, VA   22314
CEO: Christer Persson, Pres.   Tel: (703) 683-0007   Emp: N/A
Bus: *Holding company U.S. operating companies.*   Fax:(703) 549-8536   %FO: 100

CELSIUS TECH INC.
1800 Diagonal Road, #230, Alexandria, VA   22314
CEO: Per Hansson, Reg. Dir.   Tel: (703) 683-0007   Emp: N/A
Bus: *Marketing/sale/service defense systems.*   Fax:(703) 549-5028   %FO: 100

FFV AEROTECH INC.
10 Airways Blvd., Nashville, TN   37217
CEO: Robert A. Davis, Pres.   Tel: (615) 367-2100   Emp: N/A
Bus: *Component & hangar maintenance for aircraft.*   Fax:(615) 367-4327   %FO: 100

KOCKUMS COMPUTER SYSTEMS, INC.
900 Bestgate Road, Site 201, Annapolis, MD   21401
CEO: Bryan J. Miller, Pres.   Tel: (410) 224-4854   Emp: N/A
Bus: *Sales/service computer system design.*   Fax:(410) 224-8322   %FO: 100

● **CHRIS-MARINE AB**
Box 9025, S-200 39 Malmö, Sweden
CEO: C. Glyden, Mktg. Mgr.   Tel: 46-40-210320   Emp: N/A
Bus: *Sales/service engine repair tools & service.*   Fax:46-40-214068

CHRIS-MARINE USA, INC.
732 Parker Street, Jacksonville, FL   32202
CEO: Kent Ekenberg, VP   Tel: (904) 354-8784   Emp: N/A
Bus: *Diesel engine & turbocharger repairs.*   Fax:(904) 358-7862   %FO: 100

● **CHRISTOFFERSON & PARTNERS AB**
Arsenalsgatan 4, 6 tr, S-111 47 Stockholm, Sweden
CEO: N/A   Tel: 46-8-614-5262   Emp: 10
Bus: *Advertising, marketing and sales services.*   Fax:46-8-679-9909

CHRISTOFFERSON & ASSOCIATES, INC.
10866 Wilshire Blvd., Suite 1270, Los Angeles, CA   90024
CEO: Lennart Christofferson, Pres.   Tel: (310) 441-0639   Emp: 10
Bus: *Advertising, sales and marketing services.*   Fax:(310) 475-7330   %FO: 100

● **COMPONENTA INTERNATIONAL**
Box 621, S-151 27 Sodertalje, Sweden
CEO: P.G. Nilsson, Pres.   Tel: 46-8-498220   Emp: N/A
Bus: *Mfr. electric submersible pumps and swimming pool cleaners.*   Fax:N/A

SVEDALA PUMPS & PROCESS, INC.
621 South Sierra Madre, Colorodo Springs, CO   80903
CEO: Ron Robinson, Pres.   Tel: (719) 471-3443   Emp: N/A
Bus: *Sales/service pumps.*   Fax:(719) 471-4469   %FO: 100

• **COOL CARRIERS AB**
Berga Backe 2, S-182 85 Danderyd, Sweden
CEO: Matt Jansson, Chrm.   Tel: 46-8-753-9000   Emp: 10
Bus: *Water shipping/transportation.*   Fax:46-8-753-4423

    COOL CARRIERS, INC.
    PO Box 639, Port Hueneme, CA   93044
    CEO: Gerald A. Fountain, Pres.   Tel: (805) 488-1222   Emp: 10
    Bus: *Steamship agent for water transportation.*   Fax:(805) 986-8320   %FO: 100

• **DUNI AB**
Box 95, S-101 21 Stockholm, Sweden
CEO: Conny Karlsson, Pres.   Tel: 46-8-402-1300   Emp: N/A
Bus: *Food service and table products.*   Fax:46-8-206- 609

    DUNI US INC.
    W 165 N5830 Ridgewood Dr., Menomonee Falls, WI   53051-5655
    CEO: David Dooley, Pres.   Tel: (414) 252-7700   Emp: 200
    Bus: *Mfr. disposable food service and table*   Fax:(414) 252-7710   %FO: 100
        products.

• **DUX INDUSTRIER AB**
Strandridargatan 8, Box 1002, S-231 61 Trelleborg, Sweden
CEO: Claes Ljung, Pres.   Tel: 46-410-58700   Emp: N/A
Bus: *Mfr. furniture & mattresses.*   Fax:46-410-17615

    DUX INTERIORS, INC.
    305 East 63rd Street, New York, NY   10021
    CEO: Bo Gustafsson, Pres.   Tel: (212) 752-3897   Emp: N/A
    Bus: *Wholesale furniture and mattresses.*   Fax:(212) 319-9638   %FO: 100

• **EGE WESTIN AB**
Box 20, S-694 21 Hallsberg, Sweden
CEO: Jan-Erik Westin, Pres.   Tel: 46-583-613950   Emp: 25
Bus: *Mfr. blinds, awnings, sunscreens.*   Fax:46-582-511922

    EGE SYSTEM SUN CONTROL INC.
    15203 NE 95th Street, Redmond, WA   98052
    CEO: Wayne Sneva, Pres.   Tel: (206) 869-6575   Emp: 22
    Bus: *Mfr./retail sale awnings, sun screens.*   Fax:(206) 869-6581   %FO: JV

● **EISER TRIKÅ AB**
Planteringsgatan 36, Box 3, S-275 21, Sjöbo, Sweden
CEO: Per Höiby, Pres.   Tel: 46-416-188 15   Emp: 10+
Bus: *Children's clothing manufacturer.*   Fax:46-416-128 96

> **EISER INC.**
> 235 NW Park Street, Portland, OR   97209
> CEO: Per Höiby, Pres.   Tel: (503) 224-6218   Emp: 10+
> Bus: *Children's clothing manufacturer.*   Fax:(503) 224-8656   %FO: 100

● **EKA NOBEL AB**
Bohus, S-445 80 Bohus, Sweden
CEO: Dag Strömqvist, Pres.   Tel: 46-31-587000   Emp: 500+
Bus: *Mfr. chemicals and allied products.*   Fax:46-31-587400

> **EKA NOBEL INC.**
> 1519 Johnson Ferry Road, Ste. 200, Marietta, GA   30062
> CEO: Bo Welander, Pres.   Tel: (770) 578-0858   Emp: 100+
> Bus: *Mfr. chemicals and allied products.* Fax:(770) 578-1359   %FO: 100

● **ELECTROLUX ORIGO**
Box 9052, S-30009 Halmstad, Sweden
CEO: Anders Magnusson, Pres.   Tel: 46-35-218860   Emp: 20
Bus: *Mfr. stoves/heaters for mobile homes & boats.*   Fax:46-35-130238

> **ORIGO USA INC.**
> 1121 Lewis Avenue, Sarasota, FL   34237
> CEO: Anders Ebbeson, Pres.   Tel: (941) 365-3660   Emp: 4
> Bus: *Sale/service heaters, ventilation systems for*   Fax:(941) 955-2596   %FO: 100
>   *boats, mobile homes.*

● **AB ELECTROLUX**
Luxbacken 1, Lilla Essingen, S-105 45 Stockholm, Sweden
CEO: Michael Trescher, Pres.   Tel: 46-8-738-6000   Emp: 112140
Bus: *Mfr. household & commercial appliances &*   Fax:46-8-656-4478
      outdoor products.

> **AMERICOLD**
> 2340 Second Avenue, N.W., Cullman, AL   35057
> CEO: Reginald Carter, Exec.VP   Tel: (205) 734-9160   Emp: N/A
> Bus: *Mfr. compressors; refrigerators, freezers etc.*   Fax:(205) 739-0217   %FO: 100

> **BEAM INDUSTRIES**
> 1700 West Second St., PO Box 788, Webster City, IA   50595
> CEO: John Coghlan, Pres.   Tel: (515) 832-4626   Emp: N/A
> Bus: *Mfr. central vacuum systems.*   Fax:(515) 832-6659   %FO: 100

DOMETIC CORP
2320 Industry Parkway, Box 490, Elkhart, IN   46515
CEO: John Delaney, Pres.   Tel: (219) 294-2511   Emp: N/A
Bus: *Mfr. products for recreational vehicles.*   Fax:(219) 293-9686   %FO: 100

ELEX GROUP, The Washex Machine Company
5000 Central Freeway North, Wichita Falls, TX   76306
CEO: Larry Talkington, Pres.   Tel: (817) 855-3990   Emp: N/A
Bus: *Mfr. industrial laundry equipment.*   Fax:(817) 855-9349   %FO: 100

THE EUREKA COMPANY
1201 East Bell Street, Bloomington, IL   61701
CEO: Leo Cadello, Pres.   Tel: (309) 828-2367   Emp: N/A
Bus: *Mfr. floorcare products.*   Fax:(309) 823-5203   %FO: 100

FRIGIDAIRE COMMERCIAL PRODUCTS CO.
707 Robins Street, PO Box 4000, Conway, AR   72032
CEO: John Waters, Pres.   Tel: (501) 327-8945   Emp: N/A
Bus: *Mfr./sale commercial refrigeration equipment.*   Fax:(501) 450-3782   %FO: 100

FRIGIDAIRE HOME PRODUCTS
6000 Perimeter Drive, Dublin, OH   43017
CEO: Robert Cook, Pres.   Tel: (614) 792-4100   Emp: 1500
Bus: *Household appliances, outdoor products.*   Fax:(614) 792-4075   %FO: 100

FRIGIDAIRE HOME PRODUCTS
104 Warren Road, Augusta, GA   30907
CEO: Robert Cook, Pres.   Tel: (706) 860-2290   Emp: N/A
Bus: *Corporate headquarters for household*   Fax:(706) 860-2274   %FO: 100
      appliances lawn & garden equipment.

HUSQVARNA FOREST & GARDEN COMPANY
9006-J Perimeter Woods Drive, Charlotte, NC   28216
CEO: David Zerfoss, Pres.   Tel: (704) 597-5000   Emp: N/A
Bus: *Distributor/service chain saws; lawn & garden*   Fax:(704) 597-8802   %FO: 100
      equipment.

THE KENT COMPANY
2310 Industrial Parkway, Box 1665, Elkhart, IN   46515
CEO: Philip Hayes, Pres.   Tel: (219) 293-8661   Emp: N/A
Bus: *Mfr./sales vacuum cleaners.*   Fax:(219) 295-8610   %FO: 100

PARTNER INDUSTRIAL PRODUCTS
905 West Irving Park Road, Itasca, IL   60143
CEO: Stan Levy, Sales Mgr.   Tel: (630) 773-2801   Emp: N/A
Bus: *Import/sales heavy material handling*   Fax:(630) 773-6339   %FO: 100
      equipment.

POULAN/WEED EATER

5020 Flournoy-Lucas Road, P.O.Box 8, Shreveport, LA   71149-1329

CEO: John Waters, Pres.

Bus: *Mfr./sale lawn & garden equipment.*

Tel: (318) 687-0100   Emp: N/A

Fax:(318) 683-3567   %FO: 100

SCHROCK CABINET COMPANY

6000 Perimeter Drive, Dublin, OH   43017

CEO: Mervin W. Plank, Pres.

Bus: *Mfr./sale household cabinetry.*

Tel: (614) 792-4970   Emp: N/A

Fax:(614) 792-4979   %FO: 100

VIKING HUSQVARNA SEWING MACHINES

11760 Berea Road, Cleveland, OH   44111

CEO: Bengt Gerborg, Pres.

Bus: *Wholesale. household sewing machines.*

Tel: (216) 252-3300   Emp: N/A

Fax:(216) 252-3311   %FO: 100

WCI INTERNATIONAL CO.

10 Parkway Center, Pittsburgh, PA   15220

CEO: J.L. Rushworth, Pres.

Bus: *Exporter/marketer household appliances.*

Tel: (412) 928-3321   Emp: N/A

Fax:(412) 928-9407   %FO: 100

WHITE CONSOLIDATED INDUSTRIES INC.

11770 Berea Road, Cleveland, OH   44111

CEO: Michael Treschow, Pres.

Bus: *Holding company - US Operations..*

Tel: (216) 252-3700   Emp: 22316

Fax:(216) 252-8073   %FO: 100

● ELFA INTERNATIONAL AB

Elfagatan 5, S-593 87, Våstervik, Sweden

CEO: Stefan Ferm, Pres.

Bus: *Furniture, fixtures and home furnishings*

Tel: 46-490-36600   Emp: 10+

Fax:46-490-30025

ELFA CORPORATION OF AMERICA, INC.

980 North Michigan Avenue
Suite 1400, Chicago, IL   60611

CEO: Jan Söderberg, Pres.

Bus: *Furniture, home furnishings, and home storage organization systems.*

Tel: (312) 214-3988   Emp: 10+

Fax:(312) 214-3510   %FO: 100

ELFA CORPORATION OF AMERICA, INC.

300-3A Route 17 South, Lodi, NJ   07644

CEO: Michael Reiner, Pres.

Bus: *Furniture, home furnishings, and home storage organization systems.*

Tel: (201) 777-1554   Emp: 10+

Fax:(201) 777-1564   %FO: 100

● **ELMO CALF AB**
S-512 81, Svenljunga, Sweden
CEO: Goran Truedson, Mng. Dir. Tel: 46-325-10050 Emp: 369
Bus: *Design/mfr. high quality furniture & automotive* Fax:46-325-11004
leathers.

    ELMO LEATHER OF AMERICA
    2809 Earlham Place, High Point, NC 27263
    CEO: Evert Emauelsson, Exec.VP Tel: (910) 434-4071 Emp: 123
    Bus: *Design/mfr./marketing high quality furniture* Fax:(910) 434-5394 %FO: 100
    & automotive leathers.

    ELMO LEATHER OF AMERICA
    24 Kilmer Road, Edison, NJ 08817
    CEO: Gary R. Benson, Pres. Tel: (908) 777-7800 Emp: 50+
    Bus: *Design/mfr./marketing high quality furniture* Fax:(908) 777-7373 %FO: 100
    & automotive leathers.

● **ELOF HANSSON AB**
Första Långgatan 17, S-413 80 Göteborg, Sweden
CEO: Thomas Pettersson, Pres. Tel: 46-31-856000 Emp: N/A
Bus: *Mfr. pulp, paper & wood products.* Fax:46-31-126735

    ELOF HANSSON INC
    565 Taxter Road, Elmsford, NY 10523
    CEO: William P. MacDevette, Pres. Tel: (914) 345-8380 Emp: N/A
    Bus: *Importer; pulp, paper products.* Fax:(914) 345-8114 %FO: 100

● **ELTEX OF SWEDEN AB**
Box 608, S-343 24 Almhult, Sweden
CEO: Staffan Ferm, Mgr. Tel: 46-476-48800 Emp: 180
Bus: *Electronic yarn monitoring equipment; battery* Fax:46-476-13400
chargers; catalogers.

    ELTEX OF SWEDEN INC.
    P O Box 868, Greer, SC 29651
    CEO: Jonathan Bell, Pres. Tel: (864) 879-2131 Emp: 5
    Bus: *Sales/service electronic yarn monitoring* Fax:(864) 879-3734 %FO: 100
    equipment; battery chargers; dataloggers.

● **ERICSSON TELEFON AB**
Telefonplan, S-126 25 Stockholm, Sweden
CEO: Lars Ramqvist, Pres. Tel: 46-8-719-0000 Emp: 84513
Bus: *Telecommunications; electronic defense systems.* Fax:46-8-719-1976

    ERICSSON NORTH AMERICA INC.
    740 East Campbell Road, Richardson, TX 75081
    CEO: Bo Hedfors, Pres. Tel: (972) 583-8800 Emp: 1700
    Bus: *Mfr./distribution/service telecommunications,* Fax:(972) 437-6627 %FO: 100
    switching & cellular radio systems.

● **ESAB AB**
Herkulesgatan 72, Box 8004, S-402 77 Göteborg, Sweden
CEO: Bengt Eskilson, CEO   Tel: 46-31-509000   Emp: 6000
Bus: *Mfr. welding equipment, gas cutting machinery.*   Fax:46-31-230740

     THE ESAB GROUP INC
     P O Box 100545, Florence, SC   29501-0545
     CEO: Ray Hoglund, Pres.   Tel: (803) 669-4411   Emp: N/A
     Bus: *Mfr. welding products.*   Fax:(803) 664-4459   %FO: 100

● **ESSELTE AB**
Sundbybergsvägen 1, Box 1371, S-171 27 Solna, Sweden
CEO: Bo Lundquist, Pres.   Tel: 46-8-272760   Emp: 20000
Bus: *Office equipment & stationery, packaging, printing*   Fax:46-8-825632
     & bookbinding, cartography, school equipment,
     publishing, book shops.

     ESSELTE AMERICA CORP.
     71 Clinton Road, Garden City, NY   11530
     CEO: Robert K. Scribner, Pres.   Tel: (516) 741-3200   Emp: 1000
     Bus: *Mfr. bar coding systems, labeling systems,*   Fax:(516) 873-3320   %FO: 100
     labels & tags, printer supplies & consumables,
     imprinting services.

     ESSELTE METO USA
     1200 The American Road, Morris Plains, NJ   07950
     CEO: Travis Howe, Pres.   Tel: (201) 455-8100   Emp: 259
     Bus: *Mfr. bar coding systems, labeling systems*   Fax:(201) 455-7492   %FO: 100
     labels & tags, printer supplies & consumables,
     imprinting services.

● **ETAC AB**
Långgatan 4, Box 203, S-334 24, Anderstorp, Sweden
CEO: Kjell Karlsson, Pres.   Tel: 46-371-17790   Emp: 10+
Bus: *Surgical, medical equipment and supplies*   Fax:46-371-17310
     (wheelchairs, crutches, walking aids).

     ETAC USA INC.
     2315 Parklawn Drive, Suite J, Waukeshau, WI   53186
     CEO: Carola Öberg, Pres.   Tel: (414) 796-4600   Emp: 10+
     Bus: *Surgical and medical equipment and supplies*   Fax:(414) 796-4605   %FO: 100
     (wheelchairs, crutches and walking aids).

- **ETON SYSTEMS AB**
Djupdal, S-507 71, Gånghester, Sweden
CEO: Inge Davidson, Pres.　　　　　Tel: 46-33-24-90-65　　Emp: 10+
Bus: *Unit production systems for apparel and home*　Fax:46-33-24-91-67
　　fashion.

　　ETON SYSTEMS, INC.
　　4000 McGinnis Ferry Road, Alpharetta, GA　30202
　　CEO: Toivo Anttila, Pres.　　　　Tel: (770) 475-8022　　Emp: N/A
　　Bus: *Unit production systems for apparel and home*　Fax:(770) 442-0216　　%FO: 100
　　　　fashion.

- **FERMENTA AB**
Kungsgatan 4A, 2tr, S-111 43, Stockholm, Sweden
CEO: Kent Singhall, Pres.　　　　　Tel: 46-8-23-83-50　　Emp: 50+
Bus: *Mfr.. pharmaceuticals, antibiotics, insecticides for*　Fax:46-8-411-3124
　　the animal health industry.

　　FERMENTA ANIMAL HEALTH
　　10150 North Executive Hills Blvd., Kansas City, MO　64153
　　CEO: Henry D. Bobe, Pres. & CEO　　Tel: (816) 891-5500　　Emp: 50+
　　Bus: *Pharmaceuticals, antibiotics, insecticides for*　Fax:(816) 891-0663　　%FO: 100
　　　　the animal health industry.

- **FOLKSAM INTL**
Bohusgatan 14, S-106 60 Stockholm, Sweden
CEO: Anders Henricksson, Mng. Dir.　　Tel: 46-8-772-6000　　Emp: N/A
Bus: *Insurance services.*　　　　　Fax:46-8-702-9621

　　FOLKSAMERICA REINSURANCE CO
　　One Liberty Plaza, 19th Floor, New York, NY　10006
　　CEO: Steven E. Fass, Pres.　　　　Tel: (212) 312-2500　　Emp: 70
　　Bus: *Reinsurance services.*　　　Fax:(212) 385-2279　　%FO: 100

- **FORSHEDA AB**
Storgatan, S-330 12 Forsheda, Sweden
CEO: Sonny Lindquist, Pres.　　　　Tel: 46-370-81250　　Emp: 1200
Bus: *Mfr. pipe & shaft seals, industrial polymers,*　Fax:46-370-81872
　　automotive components.

　　FORSHEDA PIPE SEAL CORP.
　　2200 South McDuffie Street, Anderson, SC　29624
　　CEO: Steven Daukas, Pres.　　　　Tel: (861) 261-3445　　Emp: 100
　　Bus: *Mfr. pipe seals, custom rubber extrusions,*　Fax:(861) 226-9834　　%FO: 100
　　　　automotive components.

● **GAMBRO AG**
Magistratvägen 16, Box 10101, S-220 10 Lund, Sweden
CEO: Berthold Lindquist, Pres.   Tel: 46-46-169000   Emp: N/A
Bus: *Mfr. medical equipment.*   Fax:46-46-112939

    COBE BCT INC.
    1201 Oak Street, Lakewood, CO   80215-4407
    CEO: Ed Wood, Pres.   Tel: (303) 232-6800   Emp: 600
    Bus: *Mfr. medical specialties.*   Fax:(303) 232-4160   %FO: 100

    COBE CARDIOVASCULAR INC.
    14401 West 65th Way, Arvada, CO   80004-3599
    CEO: Edward J. Giachetti, Pres.   Tel: (303) 232-6800   Emp: N/A
    Bus: *Mfr. cardiovascular surgical products.* Fax:(303) 467-6525   %FO: 100

    COBE LABORATORIES INC.
    1185 Oak Street, Lakewood, CO   80215-4498
    CEO: Mats Wahlström, Pres.   Tel: (303) 232-6800   Emp: 5100
    Bus: *Mfr. medical specialties, US headquarters.* Fax:(303) 231-4615   %FO: 100

    GAMBRO HEALTHCARE PATIENT SERVICES, INC.
    1919 Charlotte Avenue, Nashville, TN   37203
    CEO: David Berry, Pres.   Tel: (615) 320-4200   Emp: N/A
    Bus: *Supplies kidney dialysis services.*   Fax:(615) 320-4205   %FO: 100

    GAMBRO HEALTHCARE, INC.
    1185 Oak Street, Lakewood, CO   80215-4915
    CEO: Mats Wahlström, Pres.   Tel: (303) 232-6800   Emp: N/A
    Bus: *Mfr. medical specialties; kidney dialysis* Fax:(303) 231-4915   %FO: 100
         products.

● **GEOTRONICS AB**
Rinkebyvägen, Box 64, S-182 11 Danderyd, Sweden
CEO: Karl Ramström, Pres.   Tel: 46-8-622-1000   Emp: 350
Bus: *Mfr. electronic total station survey instruments &* Fax:46-8-753-2464
    satellite positioning systems.

    GEOTRONICS OF NORTH AMERICA
    911 Hawthorn Drive, Itasca, IL   60143
    CEO: Frank T. Larsson, Pres.   Tel: (630) 285-1400   Emp: 30
    Bus: *Sales/service electronics total station survey* Fax:(630) 285-1410   %FO: 100
        instruments & satellite positioning systems.

● **GILLEBAGARN AB**
Näckrosvägen 19, Box 2114, S-286 72 Örkelljunga, Sweden

CEO: Lars Ekstöm, Pres.	Tel: 46-435-60320	Emp: 10
Bus: *Food products.*	Fax:46-435-60881	

    DANTRADE, INC.
    747 East Green Street, Ste. 307, Pasadena, CA   91101

CEO: Kirsten Wood, Mgr.	Tel: (818) 577-0414	Emp: N/A
Bus: *Importer of food products.*	Fax:(818) 577-5141	%FO: 100

● **GOTAVERKEN ENERGY AB**
Box 8734, S-402 75 Goteborg, Sweden

CEO: Gustav Stolk, Pres.	Tel: 46-31-501000	Emp: N/A
Bus: *Chemical & energy recovery systems.*	Fax:46-31-239864	

    KVAERNER INC.
    8008 Corporate Center Drive, Charlotte, NC   28226

CEO: Ernst Nygren, Pres.	Tel: (704) 541-1453	Emp: 50
Bus: *Recovery of chemicals & energy chemical pulping industry.*	Fax:(704) 542-5969	%FO: 100

● **GRÄNSFORS BRUKS AB**
Gränsfors Yxsmedja, S-820 70 Bergsjo, Sweden

CEO: Gabriel Bränby, Pres.	Tel: 46-652-14070	Emp: 75
Bus: *Mfr. axes, wrecking bars, protective material.*	Fax:46-652-14002	

    GRÄNSFORS BRUKS INC.
    821 W 5th N Street, P.O.Box 818, Summerville, SC 29484

CEO: Yvonne Caruso, Pres.	Tel: (803) 875-0240	Emp: 20
Bus: *Mfr./marketing safety apparel for forest industry.*	Fax:(803) 821-2285	%FO: 100

● **GRINDEX AB**
Hantverkarvägen 24, Box 538, S-136 25 Haninge, Sweden

CEO: Bjorn Callin, Mng.Dir.	Tel: 46-8-606-6600	Emp: 80
Bus: *Mfr. electronic submersible heavy duty drainage & sludge pumps.*	Fax:46-8-745-1606	

    GRINDEX PUMPS
    18524 South 81st Avenue, Tinley Park, IL   60477

CEO: Magnus Lundberg, Gen.Mgr.	Tel: (708) 532-9988	Emp: 8
Bus: *Sale/service drainage & sludge pumps.*	Fax:(708) 532-8767	%FO: 100

● **HÄGGLUND DRIVES AB**
S-890 42 Mellansel, Sweden
CEO: Anders Lindblad, Pres.   Tel: 46-660-87100   Emp: N/A
Bus: *Armored & all-terrain vehicles, marine transport*   Fax:46-660-87160
     equipment, hydraulic drives.

   HAGGLUNDS INC.
   35418 Mound Road, Sterling Heights, MI   48310
   CEO: Urban Lundberg, VP   Tel: (810) 264-8280   Emp: N/A
   Bus: *Representative office.*   Fax:(810) 268-9320   %FO: 100

● **HALDEX AB**
Instrumentgatan 15, Box 501, S-261 Landskrona, Sweden
CEO: Arthur Bowers, Pres.   Tel: 46-418-24435   Emp: N/A
Bus: *Mfr. automatic brake adjusters, air dryers, drain*   Fax:46-418-57700
     valves & air oil separators for commercial vehicle
     market.

   HALDEX CORP
   2400 Northeast Coronado Drive, Grain Valley, MO   64029
   CEO: Charles Kleinhagen, Pres.   Tel: (816) 229-7582   Emp: N/A
   Bus: *Automatic brake adjusters, air dryers,*   Fax:(816) 228-6524   %FO: 100
        automatic drain valves & air-oil separators for
        commercial vehicle industry.

● **HALLDE MASKINER AB**
Box 1165, S-164-22 Kista, Spanga, Sweden
CEO: Christer Lithander, Pres.   Tel: 46-8-7520400   Emp: 75
Bus: *Mfr. food process equipment.*   Fax:46-8-7504887

   PAXTON CORP.
   897 Bridgeport Avenue, Shelton, CT   06484
   CEO: Leif Jensen, Pres.   Tel: (203) 925-8720   Emp: 5
   Bus: *Distribution food process equipment.*   Fax:(203) 925-8722   %FO: 100

• HOERBIGER-ORIGA AB
P.O.Box 67, S-736 22 Kungsor, Sweden
CEO: Bo Granbom, Pres.   Tel: 42-227-41100   Emp: N/A
Bus: *Mfr. electrical linear actuators, band cylinders,*   Fax:42-227-41129
pneumatic valves & cylinders.

HOERBIGER-ORIGA CORP.
100 West Lake Drive, Glendale Heights, IL   60139
CEO: Joseph M. Hughes, Pres.   Tel: (630) 871-8300   Emp: N/A
Bus: *Mfr./sale/service electrical linear actuators,*   Fax:(630) 871-1515   %FO: 100
band cylinders, pneumatic valves & cylinders.

• HÖRNELL ELEKTROOPTIK AB
Ernst Hedlundsvågen 35, S-780 41, Gagnef, Sweden
CEO: Wille Lauren, Chrm.   Tel: 46-241-620-30   Emp: 10+
Bus: *Mfr.. of auto darkening welding lenses and air*   Fax:46-241-621-07
purifying systems.

HORNELL SPEEDGLAS, INC.
2374 Edison Boulevard, Twinsburg, OH   44087
CEO: Kenneth Palmman, VP   Tel: (216) 425-8880   Emp: 10+
Bus: *Auto darkening welding lenses and personal*   Fax:(216) 425-4576   %FO: 100
air purifying systems.

• INCENTIVE AB
Box 7373, S-103 91 Stockholm, Sweden
CEO: Lars Kylberg, Chrm.   Tel: 46-8-613-6500   Emp: N/A
Bus: *Engineering, industrial and professional equipment,*   Fax:46-8-611-2830
consumer housewares group.

DIAB GROUP
315 Seahawk Drive, DeSoto, TX   75115
CEO: Jeremy Caldwell, Pres.   Tel: (972) 224-8441   Emp: N/A
Bus: *Distribution rigid PVC structural foam.*   Fax:(972) 224-2667   %FO: 100

ENERGY CONSERVATION SERVICE
19 Mansfield Avenue, Shelby, OH   44875
CEO: Randolph Sampel, Pres.   Tel: (419) 347-2472   Emp: 15
Bus: *Distribution/sale energy conservation &*   Fax:(419) 347-1235   %FO: 100
comfort products & systems.

GARPHYTTAN, INC.
PO Box 4080, Blue Springs, MO   64014-4080
CEO: Lars Kylberg, Pres.   Tel: (816) 229-7585   Emp: N/A
Bus: *Mfr. components for auto & material-handling*   Fax:(816) 224-7085   %FO: 80
industry.

HAGGLUNDS DRIVES, INC.
2275 International Street, Columbus, OH 43228

CEO: Rolf Ericksson, Pres.　　　　　　　　　Tel: (614) 527-7400　　Emp: 43

Bus: *Sale hydraulic motors, spare parts, power*　Fax:(614) 527-7401　　%FO: 100
units.

HALDEX BARNES CORPORATION
PO Box 6166, Rockford, IL 61125-1166

CEO: John Pepe, Pres.　　　　　　　　　　　Tel: (815) 398-4400　　Emp: 325

Bus: *Mfr. hydraulic pumps, electro-hydraulic*　Fax:(815) 398-5977　　%FO: 100
powerpacks.

HALDEX CORP.
2400 Northeast Coronado Drive, Grain Valley, MO 64029

CEO: Charles Kleinhagen, Pres.　　　　　　　Tel: (816) 229-7582　　Emp: N/A

Bus: *Mfr. automatic brake adjusters for trucks,*　Fax:(816) 224-7090　　%FO: 100
trailers, etc.

VICTOR HASSELBLAD, INC.
10 Madison Road, Fairfield, NJ 07006

CEO: Steven B. Cohen, Pres　　　　　　　　　Tel: (201) 227-7320　　Emp: N/A

Bus: *Sale/service cameras.*　　　　　　　　　Fax:(201) 227-3249　　%FO: 100

INCENTIVE GROUP, INC.
50 Chestnut Ridge Rd, Montvale, NJ 07645

CEO: Gerald R. Cioci, CEO　　　　　　　　　Tel: (201) 476-0488　　Emp: N/A

Bus: *Holding company. Engineering industrial*　Fax:(201) 476-9044　　%FO: 100
group.

LORENTZEN & WETTRE USA, INC.
1055 Windward Drive, Suite160, Alpharetta, GA 30005

CEO: Bruce Kopkin, Pres.　　　　　　　　　　Tel: (770) 442-8015　　Emp: N/A

Bus: *Sale/service equipment for paper pulp industry.*　Fax:(770) 442-6792　　%FO: 100

MACGREGOR, INC.
PO Box 708, Pine Brook, NJ 07058

CEO: John Albino, Pres.　　　　　　　　　　Tel: (201) 244-4100　　Emp: N/A

Bus: *Sales/service cargo-handling equipment.*　Fax:(201) 244-4101　　%FO: 100

THE MUNTERS CORP.
PO Box 6428, Fort Myers, FL 33911

CEO: Sven Lundin, Pres.　　　　　　　　　　Tel: (941) 936-1555　　Emp: N/A

Bus: *Mfr. media for air & water treatment,*　　Fax:(941) 275-8790　　%FO: 100
dehumidifying equipment & services.

ORREFORS KOSTA BODA, INC.
140 Bradford Drive, Berlin, NJ 08009

CEO: Lyvind Satere, Pres.　　　　　　　　　Tel: (609) 768-5400　　Emp: N/A

Bus: *Sale crystal giftware & stemware.*　　　Fax:(609) 768-9726　　%FO: 80

● **INDUSTRI-MATEMATIK AB**
Kungsgatan 12-14, Box 7733, S-103, Stockholm, Sweden
CEO: Stig Durlow, CEO   Tel: 46-8-676 5000   Emp: 50+
Bus: *Computer and data processing services.*   Fax:46-8-676 5010

> **INDUSTRI-MATEMATIK INTERNATIONAL**
> 560 White Plains Road, Tarrytown, NY   10591
> CEO: David J. Simbari, Pres.   Tel: (914) 631-2700   Emp: 50+
> Bus: *Computer and data processing services.*   Fax:(914) 631-5111   %FO: 100

● **INTERSPIRO AB**
Box 10060, S-181 10 Lidingo, Sweden
CEO: Hans O. Almqvist, Pres.   Tel: 46-8-636-5110   Emp: 170
Bus: *Mfr. breathing apparatus.*   Fax:46-8-765-4853

> **INTERSPIRO INC.**
> 31 Business Park Drive, Branford, CT   06405
> CEO: Ken Warner, Gen. Mgr.   Tel: (203) 481-3899   Emp: 30
> Bus: *Mfr. breathing apparatus.*   Fax:(203) 483-1879   %FO: 100

● **ITT FLYGT AB**
Svetsarvagen 12, Box 1309, S-171 25 Solna, Sweden
CEO: Lief E. Carlsson, Pres.   Tel: 46-8-627-6500   Emp: N/A
Bus: *Mfr. pumps.*   Fax:46-8-627-6900

> **ITT FLYGT CORP.**
> 2400 Tarpley Road, Carrollton, TX   75006-2407
> CEO: John Friedl, Reg. Mgr.   Tel: (972) 418-2400   Emp: N/A
> Bus: *Regional sales office.*   Fax:(972) 416-9570   %FO: JV

> **ITT FLYGT CORP.**
> N27 W23291 Roundy Dr., Pewaukee, WI   53072
> CEO: Jim Randall, Reg. Mgr.   Tel: (414) 544-1922   Emp: N/A
> Bus: *Mfr./sales electric pumps, hydroturbines,*   Fax:(414) 544-1399   %FO: JV
>   *mixers.*

> **ITT FLYGT CORP.**
> 790-A Chadborne Road, Fairfield, CA   94533
> CEO: Darryl Smith, Reg. Mgr.   Tel: (707) 422-9894   Emp: N/A
> Bus: *Mfr./sales electric pumps, hydroturbines,*   Fax:(707) 422-9808   %FO: JV
>   *mixers.*

> **ITT FLYGT CORP.**
> 90 Horizon Drive, Suwanee, GA   30174
> CEO: John Adams, Reg. Mgr.   Tel: (770) 932-4320   Emp: N/A
> Bus: *Mfr./sales electric pumps, hydroturbines,*   Fax:(770) 932-4321   %FO: JV
>   *mixers.*

ITT FLYGT CORP.
P.O. Box 1004, Trumbull, CT   06611-0943
CEO: K.I.I Ericsson, Pres.   Tel: (203) 380-4700   Emp: 205
Bus: *Mfr./sales electric pumps, hydroturbines,*   Fax:(203) 380-4705   %FO: JV
mixers.

● **KANTHAL AB**
Box 502, S-734 27 Hallstahammar, Sweden
CEO: Ola Rollen, Pres.   Tel: 46-220-21600   Emp: N/A
Bus: *Mfr. resistance alloys, heating elements, bimetals.*   Fax:46-220-21154

THE KANTHAL CORP
119 Wooster Street, Bethel, CT   06801-0281
CEO: Jack Beagley, Pres.   Tel: (203) 744-1440   Emp: 107
Bus: *Mfr. resistance alloys, heating elements, hi-*   Fax:(203) 748-2229   %FO: 100
temp tubing.

● **KARLSHAMNS AB**
Vastra Kajen, S-374 82 Karlshamn, Sweden
CEO: Anders Traff, Pres.   Tel: 46-454-82000   Emp: 1300
Bus: *Mfr. edible vegetable oils.*   Fax:46-454-19692

KARLSHAMNS USA, INC.
525 West First Avenue, PO Box 569, Columbus, OH   43216-0569
CEO: Tommie Holmberg, Pres.   Tel: (614) 299-3131   Emp: 500
Bus: *Sales/distribution edible vegetable oils.*   Fax:(614) 299-2584   %FO: 100

● **KAROLIN MACHINE TOOL AB**
Box 2001, S-930 30 Ursviken, Sweden
CEO: Bjorn Kumlin, Chrm.   Tel: 46-910-51600   Emp: N/A
Bus: *Mfr. fabrication machinery & systems, punching &*   Fax:46-910-51680
beveling machinery, laser systems.

PULLMAX, INC.
1201 Lunt Avenue, Elk Grove Village, IL   60007
CEO: Johann Arnberg, Pres.   Tel: (847) 228-5600   Emp: 12
Bus: *Mfr. fabrication machinery & systems,*   Fax:(847) 228-5650   %FO: 100
punching & beveling machinery, laser systems.

● **KOCKUM SONICS AB**
Industrigatan 39, Box 1035, S-212 10 Malmö, Sweden
CEO: Lars Mattsson, Mng. Dir.   Tel: 46-40-671-8800   Emp: 100
Bus: *Mfr. marine signal & lighting, industrial sonic*   Fax:46-40-216513
cleaning, and civil alarm equipment.

    KOCKUM SONICS INC.
    819 Veterans Blvd, #201, Kenner, LA   70062
    CEO: W.C. Edwards, Gen. Mgr.   Tel: (504) 466-9740   Emp: 7
    Bus: *Sale/service marine signal light equipment.,*   Fax:(504) 466-9792   %FO: 100
    industrial sonic cleaning & civil alarm
    equipment.

● **LAGERLÖF & LEMAN**
Strandvägen 7A, PO Box 5402, S-114 84 Stockholm, Sweden
CEO: D. Wersén, Mng. Ptnr.   Tel: 46-8-665-6600   Emp: N/A
Bus: *International law firm.*   Fax:46-8-667-6883

    LAGERLÖF & LEMAN
    712 Fifth Avenue, 30th Fl., New York, NY   10019
    CEO: Magnus Andren, Mng. Ptnr.   Tel: (212) 801-3450   Emp: N/A
    Bus: *International law firm.*   Fax:(212) 801-3455   %FO: 100

● **MANNHEIMER SWARTLING**
Norrmalmstrong 4, Box 1711, S-111 87 Stockholm, Sweden
CEO: Magnus Wallander, Mng. Ptnr.   Tel: 46-8-613-5500   Emp: 200
Bus: *International law firm.*   Fax:46-8-613-5501

    MANNHEIMER SWARTLING
    101 Park Avenue, 43rd Fl., New York, NY   10178
    CEO: Maria Schuck, Mng. Ptnr.   Tel: (212) 682-0580   Emp: 9
    Bus: *International law firm.*   Fax:(212) 682-0982   %FO: 100

● **MASKIN AB RAPID**
Industrivagen 2, Box 9, S-330 10 Bredaryd, Sweden
CEO: Karl-Valter Fornell, Chrm.   Tel: 46-3-708-0340   Emp: N/A
Bus: *Mfr. granulators.*   Fax:46-3-708-0251

    RAPID GRANULATOR, INC.
    PO Box 5887, Rockford, IL   61125
    CEO: Carl Caldeira, Pres.   Tel: (815) 399-4605   Emp: 20
    Bus: *Mfr./distribute granulators.*   Fax:(815) 399-0419   %FO: 100

- **MoDo**

Hörneborgsvägen 6, S-891 80 Örnsköldsvik, Sweden

CEO: Bengt Petterson, Pres. & CEO   Tel: 46-660-75000   Emp: N/A

Bus: *Mfr. forestry products; wood, pulp, and paper.*   Fax:46-660-75970

IGGESUNG PAPERBOARD, INC.

107 John Street, Southport, CT   06490

CEO: Uno Lausen, Pres.   Tel: (203) 256-9064   Emp: N/A

Bus: *Mfr./distributor forestry products; wood, pulp,*   Fax:(203) 256-9097   %FO: 100
      and paper.

MEAD PULP SALES

Courthouse Plaza NE, Dayton, OH   45463

CEO: Bill Bloebaum, Pres.   Tel: (937) 495-3442   Emp: N/A

Bus: *Mfr./distributor forestry products; wood, pulp,*   Fax:(937) 461-0318   %FO: 100
      and paper.

- **MOLNLYCKE AB**

Wallinsgatan 6, S-405 03 Goteborg, Sweden

CEO: N/A   Tel: 46-31-678-0000   Emp: N/A

Bus: *Mfr. diversified products.*   Fax:46-31-746-1900

S. C. HYGIENE PAPER

2 Annabel Lane, Suite 220, P.O.Box 125, San Ramon, CA   94583-0125

CEO: Hakan Molin, Gen.Mgr.   Tel: (510) 830-2970   Emp: 95

Bus: *Sale of industrial wipes & other paper*   Fax:(510) 830-0628   %FO: 100
      products.

- **MORGARDSHAMMAR AB**

S-777 82 Smedjebacken, Sweden

CEO: Leif Almhed, Pres.   Tel: 46-240-668500   Emp: N/A

Bus: *Mfr. equipment for steel mills & mines.*   Fax:46-240-668501

MORGARDSHAMMAR INC.

9800-L Southern Pine Blvd., P.O. Box 240582, Charlotte, NC   28273

CEO: Grant Philip, Pres.   Tel: (704) 522-8024   Emp: 6

Bus: *Sales/service equipment for steel mills & mines.*   Fax:(704) 522-0264   %FO: 100

- **NEDERMAN & CO, AB**

Sydhamnsgatan 2, S-252 28, Helsingborg, Sweden

CEO: Per Yngve Larsson, Pres.   Tel: 46-41-188700   Emp: 10+

Bus: *Environmental pollution control for dust and fume.*   Fax:46-42-14-7971

NEDERMAN INC.

6100 Hix Road, Westland, MI   48185

CEO: B. V. Converse, Pres. & CEO   Tel: (313) 729-3344   Emp: 10+

Bus: *Environmental pollution control for dust and*   Fax:(313) 729-3358   %FO: 100
      fume.

● **NEFAB AB**
Box 2184, S-550 02, Jönköping, Sweden
CEO: Lasse Rydh, Pres.   Tel: 46-36-100521   Emp: 10+
Bus: *Mfr. of plywood packaging products.*   Fax:46-36-150444

    NEFAB, INC.
    815 West Van Buren Street, Ste. 330, Chicago, IL   60607
    CEO: Jan Sjöström, Pres.   Tel: (312) 733-2200   Emp: 25+
    Bus: *Plywood packaging products.*   Fax:(312) 733-7866   %FO: 100

● **NOBEL BIOCARE AB**
Bohusgatan 15, Box 5190, S-402 26, Göteborg, Sweden
CEO: Jack Forsgren, Pres.   Tel: 46-31-818800   Emp: 50+
Bus: *Surgical, medical and dental supplies.*   Fax:46-31-163152

    NOBEL BIOCARE INC. (Northeast Div.)
    366 Massachusetts Avenue, Suite 303, Arlington, MA   02174
    CEO: Ken Putney, VP   Tel: (617) 641-2032   Emp: 50+
    Bus: *Distributor of surgical/medical/dental*   Fax:(617) 641-0914   %FO: 100
        equipment.

    NOBEL BIOCARE USA INC.
    777 Oakmont Lane, Suite 100, Westmont, IL   60559
    CEO: James Derleth, Pres.   Tel: (630) 654-9100   Emp: 500+
    Bus: *Distributor of surgical/medical/dental*   Fax:(630) 654-1833   %FO: 100
        equipment.

● **NOLATO AB**
Box 66, S-260 93 Torekov, Sweden
CEO: Krister Jorlen, CEO   Tel: 46-431-63340   Emp: 570
Bus: *Molded rubber & plastic products.*   Fax:46-431-64497

    SUNNEX INC.
    3 Huron Drive, Natick, MA   01760
    CEO: Sven O. Emilsson, Pres.   Tel: (508) 651-0009   Emp: 24
    Bus: *Mfr./Distributor machine mounts, industrial* Fax:(508) 651-0099   %FO: 100
        work lights.

● **NORDBANKEN AB**
Smålandsgatan 17, S- 105 71 Stockholm, Sweden
CEO: Hans Dalborg, Pres.   Tel: 46-8-614-7000   Emp: 6290
Bus: *Banking services.*   Fax:46-8-614-9184

    NORDBANKEN - New York Representative Office
    450 Park Avenue, New York, NY   10022
    CEO: Anders Ingmarsson, Chief Rep.   Tel: (212) 755-3800   Emp: 2
    Bus: *Banking-Liaison office.*   Fax:(212) 755-1304   %FO: 100

● **ORREFORS KOSTA BODA AB**
Box 8, S-380 40 Orrefors, Sweden
CEO: Goran Bernhoff, Pres.   Tel: 46-481-34000   Emp: 200+
Bus: *Mfr. crystal products. (Sub of Incentive AB)* Fax:46-481-30400

    GALLERI ORREFORS KOSTA BODA
    58 East 57th Street, New York, NY   10022
    CEO: Jan Forbes, Mgr.   Tel: (212) 752-1095   Emp: 50
    Bus: *Sale/distribution crystal products.*   Fax:(212) 752-3705   %FO: 100

    GALLERI ORREFORS KOSTA BODA
    Crystal Court, 3333 Bear Street, Costa Mesa, CA   92626
    CEO: Annika Haghighi, Pres.   Tel: (714) 549-1959   Emp: 8
    Bus: *Sale/distribution crystal products.*   Fax:(714) 549-8247   %FO: 100

    GALLERI ORREFORS KOSTA BODA
    140 Bradford Drive, Berlin, NJ   08009
    CEO: Oyvind Saetre, Pres.   Tel: (609) 768-5400   Emp: 100
    Bus: *Sale/distribution crystal products. Sub of* Fax:(609) 768-9726   %FO: 100
        INCENTIVE AB.

● **PELTOR AB**
Malmstengatan 19, Box 2341, S-331 02 Värnamo, Sweden
CEO: Leif Palmaer, Mng. Dir.   Tel: 46-370 -64200   Emp: 247
Bus: *Mfr. personal hearing protectors & communications* Fax:46-370-15130
    headsets for high noise areas.

    PELTOR INC.
    41 Commercial Way, East Providence, RI   02914
    CEO: Ralph V. Miller Jr, Pres. & CEO   Tel: (401) 438-4800   Emp: 25
    Bus: *Personal hearing protectors & communication* Fax:(401) 434-1708   %FO: 85
        headsets for high noise areas.

● **PERSTORP AB**
S-284 80 Perstorp, Sweden
CEO: Åke Fredriksson, Pres.   Tel: 46-435-38000   Emp: 7300
Bus: *Mfr. specialty chemicals, analytic instruments,* Fax:46-435-38100
    decorative laminates, flooring, wood products..

    HYCLONE LABORATORIES INC
    1725 South Hyclone Road, Logan, UT   84321
    CEO: Leland Foster, Pres.   Tel: (801) 753-4584   Emp: 212
    Bus: *Mfr. cell culture serums.*   Fax:(801) 753-4589   %FO: 100

    NATIONAL PLASTICS CORP
    Industrial Avenue, Port Gibson, MS   39150
    CEO: Earl Moore, Pres.   Tel: (601) 437-4211   Emp: 145
    Bus: *Mfr. molded plastic dinnerware.*   Fax:(601) 437-3068   %FO: 100

PERNOVO INC.
P.O. Box 117, 3747 N. Meridian Rd., Rockford, IL   61105
CEO: Nils Lindeblad, Pres.	Tel: (815) 968-0747	Emp: N/A
Bus: *New business development.*	Fax:(815) 968-7316	%FO: 100

PERSTORP COMPOUNDS INC.
238 Nonotuck Street, Florence, MA   01060
CEO: Torsten Nilson, Pres.	Tel: (413) 584-2472	Emp: 55
Bus: *Mfr. melamine & urea molding compounds.*	Fax:(413) 586-4089	%FO: 100

PERSTORP FLOORING INC.
524 New Hope Road, Raleigh, NC   37610
CEO: Lars von Kantzow, Pres.	Tel: (919) 773-6000	Emp: N/A
Bus: *Mfr. laminate flooring.*	Fax:(919) 773-6004	%FO: 100

PERSTORP INC.
92 Main Street, Florence, MA   01060
CEO: Mats Turner, Pres.	Tel: (413) 584-9522	Emp: 4
Bus: *Holding company.*	Fax:(413) 587-3040	%FO: 100

PERSTORP PLASTIC SYSTEMS
4927 95th Street, PO Box 99057, Tacoma, WA   98499
CEO: Spencer Hoopes, Pres.	Tel: (253) 582-0644	Emp: N/A
Bus: *Mfr. plastic-based materials handling systems.*	Fax:(253) 588-5539	%FO: 100

PERSTORP POLYOLS INC.
600 Matzinger Road, Toledo, OH   43612-2695
CEO: David Wolf, Pres.	Tel: (419) 729-5448	Emp: 86
Bus: *Mfr. pentaerythritol, sodium formate, trimethylolpropane, specialty polyols, other chemicals.*	Fax:(419) 729-3291	%FO: 100

PERSTORP UNIDUR INC.
7343-L W. Friendly Avenue, Greensboro, NC   27410
CEO: Peter Sanders, Pres.	Tel: (910) 316-0166	Emp: N/A
Bus: *Sale decorative laminate.*	Fax:(910) 316-0139	%FO: 100

PIERCE CHEMICAL CO.
3747 N Meridian Road, P O Box 117, Rockford, IL   61105
CEO: Robb Anderson, Pres.	Tel: (815) 968-0747	Emp: N/A
Bus: *Mfr. analytical chemicals, separation products.*	Fax:(815) 968-7316	%FO: 100

R-CUBED COMPOSITES INC.
3392 West 8600 South, West Jordan, UT   84088-9706
CEO: Rick Gardiner, Pres.	Tel: (801) 569-0401	Emp: N/A
Bus: *Mfr. components in composite materials.*	Fax:(801) 569-0817	%FO: 51

YLA, INC.
2970 C Bay Vista Court, Benicia, CA   94510
CEO: Gary Patz, Pres.   Tel: (707) 747-2750   Emp: N/A
Bus: *Mfr. components in composite materials.*   Fax:(707) 747-2754   %FO: 61

• PHARMACIA & UPJOHN AB
67 Alma Road, Windsor, Berkshire SL4 3HD, United Kingdom
CEO: Fred Hassan, Pres.   Tel: 44-1753-74-4100   Emp: 35000
Bus: *Research/mfr./sales pharmaceutical &*   Fax:44-1753-74-4011
biotechnology products. ('95 merger of Pharmacia
AB/Sweden & The Upjohn Company/US.)

PHARMACIA & UPJOHN LABORATORIES INC.
7000 Portage Road, Kalamazoo, MI   49001
CEO: Ley S. Smith, Pres.   Tel: (616) 833-4000   Emp: N/A
Bus: *Research/mfr./sales pharmaceutical &*   Fax:(616) 833-4077   %FO: JV
biotechnology products. ('95 merger of
Pharmacia AB/Sweden & The Upjohn Co/US.)

PHARMACIA IOVISION INC.
15350 Barranca Parkway, Irvine, CA   92618
CEO: Håkan Edström, Pres.   Tel: (714) 753-8040   Emp: 100+
Bus: *Mfr./distributor ophthalmic products.*   Fax:(714) 753-8040   %FO: JV

PHARMACIA & UPJOHN INC.
8484 US 70 West, Clayton, NC   27520
CEO: Davis Abner, Plant Mgr.   Tel: (919) 553-3831   Emp: 165
Bus: *Mfr. pharmaceuticals; IV preparations.*   Fax:(919) 553-1403   %FO: JV

PHARMACIA ALLERGON
Highway 96 West, Carthage, MO   64836
CEO: Borje Hyllen, Mgr.   Tel: (417) 358-9710   Emp: 10
Bus: *Mfr. pharmaceuticals; pollen allergens.*   Fax:(417) 358-1754   %FO: JV

PHARMACIA BIOTECH INC
800 Centennial Avenue, P O Box 1327, Piscataway, NJ   08855-1327
CEO: Michael Woehler, CEO   Tel: (908) 457-8000   Emp: N/A
Bus: *Biotechnology research and development.*   Fax:(908) 457-0557   %FO: JV

PHARMACIA HEPAR INC.
160 Industrial Drive, Franklin, OH   45005-4428
CEO: Ola Andersson, Pres.   Tel: (513) 746-3603   Emp: 100+
Bus: *Mfr. bulk heparin.*   Fax:(513) 746-9855   %FO: JV

• POTTER & THORELLI OFFICES
Birger Jarlsgatan 73-75, S-113 56 Stockholm, Sweden

CEO: Thomas Thorelli, Ptnr. Tel: 46-8-143430 Emp: N/A
Bus: *International legal services.* Fax:46-8-100666

POTTER & THORELLI OFFICES
Sears Tower, 233 South Wacker Dr., #7100, Chicago, IL   60606

CEO: Thomas Thorelli, Ptnr. Tel: (312) 258-5820 Emp: N/A
Bus: *International legal services,* Fax:(312) 258-5828 %FO: 100

• MASKIN AB RAPID
Industrivägen 4, Box 9, S-330 10 Bredaryd, Sweden

CEO: Karl-Valter Fornell, Pres. Tel: 46-370-80340 Emp: N/A
Bus: *Mfr. granulators.* Fax:46-370-80251

RAPID GRANULATOR INC.
5217 28th Avenue, Box 5887, Rockford, IL   61125

CEO: Carl Caldeira, Pres. Tel: (815) 399-4605 Emp: 170
Bus: *Granulators, spare parts & service.* Fax:(815) 399-0419 %FO: 100

• ROTTNE INDUSTRI AB
S-360 40 Rottne, Sweden

CEO: Jarl Petersson, Pres. Tel: 46-470-91170 Emp: 175
Bus: *Mfr. forestry equipment.* Fax:46-470-92268

BLONDIN INC.
85 Cool Spring Road, P O Box 1287, Indiana, PA   15701

CEO: Rikard Olofsson, Pres. Tel: (412) 349-9240 Emp: 7
Bus: *Sales/distribution forestry equipment.* Fax:(412) 349-9242 %FO: JV

• SAAB AIRCRAFT AB
S-581 88 Linköping, Sweden

CEO: Hans Krüger, Pres. Tel: 46-13-180000 Emp: N/A
Bus: *Design/mfr. aircraft & parts.* Fax:46-13-181802

SAAB AIRCRAFT OF AMERICA INC.
21300 Ridgetop Circle, Sterling, VA   20166

CEO: Hendrik Schroder Tel: (703) 406-7200 Emp: N/A
Bus: *Design/mfr. aircraft & parts.* Fax:(703) 406-7224 %FO: 100

• SAAB AUTOMOBILE AB
S-461 80 Trollhättan, Sweden

CEO: Robert.W. Hendry, Pres. Tel: 46-52-085000 Emp: 8092
Bus: *Mfr. automobiles.* Fax:46-52-035016

SAAB CARS USA INC.
Gwinnett Summit 4405-A International Blvd., Norcross, GA   30093

CEO: Joel K. Manby, Pres. Tel: (770) 279-0100 Emp: 182
Bus: *Import/distribution/service automobiles.* Fax:(770) 279-6499 %FO: 100

● **SAAB COMBITECH AB**
P.O.Box 1017, S-551 11   Jönköping, Sweden
CEO: Per Risberg, Pres.   Tel: 46-36-194000   Emp: N/A
Bus: *Research/design/mfr. telecommunications software*   Fax:46-36-194510
tools.

  SAAB SYSTEMS, INC.
  10235 West Little York, Ste. 258, Houston, TX   77040
  CEO: Drake Turrentine, Pres.   Tel: (713) 849-2092   Emp: 10
  Bus: *Sales/technical support telecommunications*   Fax:(713) 896-6404   %FO: 100
  software tools.

● **SAAB ERICSSON SPACE AB**
Delsjömotet, S-405 15 Göteborg, Sweden
CEO: Ivan Öfverholm, Pres.   Tel: 46-31-350000   Emp: N/A
Bus: *Design/mfr. guided missiles, space vehicles and*   Fax:46-31-359520
parts.

  SAAB ERICSSON SPACE, INC.
  1634 I Street, N.W., Ste. 600, Washington, DC   20006-4083
  CEO: Ivan Öfverholm, Pres.   Tel: (202) 783-1700   Emp: N/A
  Bus: *Design/mfr. guided missiles, space vehicles*   Fax:(202) 783-2625   %FO: 100
  and parts.

● **AB SAJO MASKIN**
Mosslegatan 11 13, S-331 01 Varnamo, Sweden
CEO: N/A   Tel: N/A   Emp: N/A
Bus: *Mfr. milling machines*   Fax:N/A

  SWEDISH MACHINE GROUP
  696 Bonded Parkway, Streamwood, IL   60107
  CEO: Robert Scooley, Gen. Mgr.   Tel: (630) 372-8121   Emp: 5
  Bus: *Milling machines*   Fax:(630) 372-8121   %FO: 100

● **SANDVIK AB**
Mossvägen 10, S-811 81 Sandviken, Sweden
CEO: Claes Åke Hedström, Pres.   Tel: 46-26-260000   Emp: N/A
Bus: *Mfr. cemented carbide & steel products, tools,*   Fax:46-26-250340
specialty steels & alloys, conveyors & industrial
systems.

  SANDVIK COROMANT COMPANY
  PO Box 428, Fair Lawn, NJ   07410
  CEO: James T. Baker, Pres.   Tel: (201) 794-5000   Emp: 500+
  Bus: *Mfr./distribution/service cemented carbide*   Fax:(201) 794-5165   %FO: 100
  metalworking tools & systems.

SANDVIK HARD MATERIALS COMPANY
21551 Mullin Avenue, Warren, MI   48089
CEO: Garry Davies, Pres.   Tel: (810) 755-2000   Emp: 20+
Bus: *Mfr. metal products; cemented carbide.*   Fax:(810) 755-3106   %FO: 100

SANDVIK INC.
1702 Nevins Road, Fairlawn, NJ   07410
CEO: James T. Baker, Pres   Tel: (201) 794-5000   Emp: 25+
Bus: *Holding company.*   Fax:(201) 794-5165   %FO: 100

SANDVIK LATIN AMERICA INC
2801 Ponce de Leon Blvd., Coral Gables, FL   33134
CEO: David Levy, Pres.   Tel: (305) 444-5220   Emp: 10+
Bus: *Regional sales representative.* Fax:(305) 444-6052   %FO: 100

SANDVIK MILFORD CORP.
PO Box 817, Branford, CT   06405
CEO: Peter Renwick, Pres.   Tel: (203) 481-4281   Emp: N/A
Bus: *Mfr. cemented carbide & steel products, tools,*   Fax:(203) 483-1384   %FO: 100
specialty steels & alloys, conveyors &
industrial systems.

SANDVIK PROCESS SYSTEMS INC
21 Campus Road, Totowa, NJ   07512
CEO: Walter Maier, Pres.   Tel: (201) 790-1600   Emp: 100+
Bus: *Mfr./sale/service conveyors, handling &*   Fax:(201) 790-9247   %FO: 100
automatic sorting systems.

SANDVIK ROCK TOOLS INC
PO Box 40402, Houston, TX   77240-0402
CEO: Olof A. Lundblad, Gen. Mgr.   Tel: (713) 460-6200   Emp: 100+
Bus: *Mfr./distribution/service rockdrilling tools.*   Fax:(713) 460-6229   %FO: 100

SANDVIK SAWS & TOOLS CO
PO Box 2036, Scranton, PA   18501
CEO: William M. Lavelle, Gen. Mgr   Tel: (717) 341-9500   Emp: 100+
Bus: *Mfr./distribution saws, blades, hand tools.*   Fax:(717) 341-9294   %FO: 100

SANDVIK SORTING SYSTEMS, INC.
500 East Burnett Avenue, Louisville, KY   40217
CEO: Hermann Miedel, Pres.   Tel: (502) 636-1414   Emp: 100+
Bus: *Design/mfr./service industrial handling*   Fax:(502) 636-1491   %FO: 100
systems.

SANDVIK SPECIAL METALS CORP.
PO Box 6027, Kennewick, WA   99336
CEO: Kirk P. Galbraith, Pres.   Tel: (509) 586-4131   Emp: 50+
Bus: *Mfr./distribution tube products in titanium &*   Fax:(509) 582-3552   %FO: 100
zirconium alloys.

SANDVIK STEEL CO.
PO Box 1220, Scranton, PA   18501

CEO: Edward Nuzzaci, Pres.

Bus: *Mfr./distribution stainless, high alloy steel & specialty metal tubes, strip & wire, welding consumables*

Tel: (717) 587-5191   Emp: 500+
Fax:(717) 586-1722   %FO: 100

SANDVIK WINDSOR CORP
41 Windsor Road, Milan, TN   38358

CEO: Rob Payne, Pres.

Bus: *Mfr./distribution power-saw chains & guidebars.*

Tel: (901) 686-4000   Emp: N/A
Fax:(901) 686-1303   %FO: 100

• SCAN COIN AB
Jägershillgatan 26, S-213 75 Malmö, Sweden

CEO: Jack Karlsson, Pres.

Bus: *Mfr. coin counting sorting machinery, currency counters, coin wrappers.*

Tel: 46-40-220130   Emp: 400
Fax:46-40-946272

SCAN COIN INC
21580 Beaumeade Circle, Suite 150, Ashburn, VA   20147

CEO: Per Lundin, Pres.

Bus: *Currency handling equipment.*

Tel: (703) 729-8600   Emp: 5
Fax:(703) 729-8606   %FO: 100

• SCANCHEM AB
Anetorpsbagen 100, Box 60066, S-21610 Malmö, Sweden

CEO: Sven Ohlsson, Pres.

Bus: *Mfr. construction materials, cement, concrete, aggregates, brick & paperboard products.*

Tel: 46-40-165000   Emp: N/A
Fax:N/A

ALLENTOWN CEMENT
P.O. Box 619, Blandon, PA   19510-0619

CEO: Daniel Harrington, Pres.

Bus: *Mfr. construction materials, cement, concrete, aggregates, brick & paperboard products.*

Tel: (610) 926-1024   Emp: N/A
Fax:(610) 926-1906   %FO: 100

• SCANDECOR MARKETING AB
Box 656, S-751 27 Uppsala, Sweden

CEO: Goran W. Huldtgren, CEO

Bus: *Mfr. posters, greeting cards, art prints, etc.*

Tel: 46-18-549190   Emp: N/A
Fax:46-18-553244

SCANDECOR INC.
430 Pike Road, Southampton, PA   18966

CEO: R. Gary Beatty, Pres.

Bus: *Distribution posters, greeting cards, art prints.*

Tel: (215) 355-2410   Emp: 25
Fax:(215) 364-8737   %FO: 100

- **SCANDINAVIAN AIRLINES SYSTEM**
Frösundaviks allé 1, S-161 87 Stockholm, Sweden
CEO: Jan Stenberg, Pres.   Tel: 46-8-797-0000   Emp: 21000
Bus: *International air transport services.*   Fax: 46-8-797-1290

    SCANDINAVIAN AIRLINES OF NORTH AMERICA, INC.
    9 Polito Avenue, Lyndhurst, NJ   07071
    CEO: Jorgen Hoe-Knudsen, Gen.Mgr.   Tel: (201) 896-3600   Emp: 200
    Bus: *Commercial airline.*   Fax: (201) 896-3725   %FO: 100

    SCANDINAVIAN AIRLINES SYSTEM
    1301 Fifth Avenue, Ste. 2727, Seattle, WA   98101-2669
    CEO: Klavs Pedersen, Reg. Mgr.   Tel: (206) 682-5250   Emp: N/A
    Bus: *Commercial airline (Western regional sales*   Fax: (206) 625-9057   %FO: 100
    office).

- **SCANDINAVIAN NEWS AB**
P.O. Box 612, S-301 16 Halmstad, Sweden
CEO: Stefan Sardh, CEO   Tel: 46-40-104875   Emp: N/A
Bus: *Publishing services.*   Fax: 46-40-973589

    NORDSTJERNAN, SWEDISH NEWS INC.
    123 West 44th Street, Suite 12C, POB 2143, New York, NY   10185-0018
    CEO: Ulf Mårtensson, Publisher & Editor   Tel: (212) 944-0776   Emp: 5
    Bus: *Publishing services.*   Fax: (212) 944-0763   %FO: JV

- **SELCOM AB**
Ögärdesvägen 19 A, Box 250, S-433 25 Partille, Sweden
CEO: Claes-Göran Lomberg, Pres.   Tel: 46-31-362510   Emp: N/A
Bus: *Optoelectronic monitoring/measuring equipment.*   Fax: 46-31-446179

    SELCOM, INC.
    21654 Melrose Avenue, Southfield, MI   48075-7905
    CEO: Sven Johansson, VP & Gen.Mgr.   Tel: (248) 355-5900   Emp: 10+
    Bus: *Optoelectronic monitoring/measuring*   Fax: (248) 355-3283   %FO: 100
    equipment.

- **SIEMENS ELEMA AB**
Rontgenvagen 2, S-171 94 Solna, Sweden
CEO: Carl Goran Myrin, Pres.   Tel: 46-8-730-7541   Emp: N/A
Bus: *Hospital/medical equipment; mammography,*   Fax: N/A
imaging, mobile x-ray..

    ELEMA-SCHONANDER INC.
    2501 North Barrington Road, Hoffman Estates, IL   60195
    CEO: Russell Hall, Gen.Mgr.   Tel: (847) 842-2150   Emp: 23
    Bus: *Service medical imaging equipment;*   Fax: (847) 842-2195   %FO: 100
    mfr./sales/service film viewing equipment.

● **SIFO MANAGEMENT GROUP AB**
Klarabergsviadukten 70, Suite 500, Box 70408, S-107 25 Stockholm, Sweden
CEO: Robert Lundberg, Pres.   Tel: 46-8-698-9900   Emp: 175
Bus: *Market research, management consulting services.*   Fax:46-8-218002

    SMG NORTH AMERICA INC.
    160 Sansome Street, San Francisco, CA   94104-3703
    CEO: Bruce Carruthers, Pres.   Tel: (415) 434-5300   Emp: 12
    Bus: *Telecommunications management consulting.*   Fax:(415) 434-5301   %FO: 100

● **SKANDIA GROUP INSURANCE COMPANY LTD.**
Sveavägen 44, S-103 50 Stockholn, Sweden
CEO: Björn Wolrath, Pres.   Tel: 46-8-788-1000   Emp: N/A
Bus: *Insurance; property & casualty.*   Fax:46-8-788-3080

    AMERICAN SKANDIA LIFE ASSURANCE CORPORATION
    One Corporate Drive, 10th Floor, Shelton, CT   06484
    CEO: William Carlson, Pres.   Tel: (203) 926-1888   Emp: N/A
    Bus: *Financial services; annuities, mutual funds.*   Fax:(203) 929-8071   %FO: 100

    SKANDIA AMERICA REINSURANCE CORPORATION
    One Liberty Plaza, New York, NY   10007
    CEO: Johannes Norrby, Chrm.   Tel: (212) 978-4700   Emp: 10
    Bus: *Reinsurance services.*   Fax:(212) 385-2421   %FO: 100

    SKANDIA U.S. INSURANCE CO.
    55 Alahambra Plaza, Coral Gables, FL   33134
    CEO: Maria Rodriguez-Scott, Pres.   Tel: (305) 461-7400   Emp: 10
    Bus: *Insurance; property & casualty.*   Fax:(305) 461-4399   %FO: N/A

● **SKANDINAVISKA ENSKILDA BANKEN**
Kungsträdgårdsgatan 8, S-106 40 Stockholm, Sweden
CEO: Björn Svedberg, Pres.   Tel: 46-8-763-5000   Emp: N/A
Bus: *International banking services.*   Fax:46-8-763-7163

    SKANDINAVISKA ENSKILDA BANKEN - NY BRANCH
    245 Park Avenue, New York, NY   10167
    CEO: Claes von Post, Pres.   Tel: (212) 907-4700   Emp: 50+
    Bus: *International banking & financial services.*   Fax:(212) 370-1642   %FO: 100

● **SKANSKA AB**
Vendevägen 89, S-182 25 Danderyd, Sweden
CEO: Melker Schörling, Pres.   Tel: 46-8-753-8000   Emp: 37000
Bus: *Engineering, construction, development & rental of*   Fax:46-8-755-7126
real estate.

    BARNEY CONSTRUCTION
    360 Lexington Avenue, New York, NY   10017
    CEO: Willaim W. Scragg, Pres.   Tel: (212) 975-0720   Emp: 100+
    Bus: *General building contractors.*   Fax:(212) 953-6870   %FO: 100

BEERS CONSTRUCTION COMPANY
70 Ellis Street, Atlanta, GA   30303
CEO: Larry Gellerstedt, III   Tel: (404) 659-1970   Emp: 500+
Bus: *General contractor/construction services.*   Fax:(404) 656-1665   %FO: 100

KARL KOCH ERECTING CO., INC.
400 Roosevelt Avenue, Carteret, NJ   07008
CEO: Jack Daly, Pres.   Tel: (908) 969-1700   Emp: 50+
Bus: *General contractor; heavy construction, steel.*   Fax:(908) 969-0197   %FO: 100

SKANSKA (USA) INC.
60 Arch Street, Greenwich, CT   06830
CEO: Claes Bjork, Pres.   Tel: (203) 679-8840   Emp: 1300
Bus: *Heavy construction, construction management*   Fax:(203) 869-4313   %FO: 100
    & development, rental of real estate.

SKANSKA ENGINEERING & CONSTRUCTION, INC.
11590 North Meridian Street, Carmel, IN   46032
CEO: Henry Salzberg, Exec.VP   Tel: (317) 570-3290   Emp: 50+
Bus: *General building contractors.*   Fax:(317) 571-3292   %FO: 100

SLATTERY ASSOCIATES INC.
16-16 Whitestone Expressway, Whitestone, NY   11357
CEO: Stuart E. Graham, Pres.   Tel: (718) 767-2600   Emp: N/A
Bus: *Heavy construction, construction management*   Fax:(718) 767-2663   %FO: 100
    & development, rental of real estate.

SORDONI SKANSKA Construction Co.
Morris Corporate Center III, Bldg. C, 400 Interpace Pkwy, Parsippany, NJ   07054
CEO: Michael Healy, Pres.   Tel: (201) 334-5300   Emp: N/A
Bus: *Heavy construction, construction management*   Fax:(201) 334-5376   %FO: 100
    & development, rental of real estate.

VANCE CORPORATION
1809 7th Avenue, Ste. 300, Seattle, WA   98101
CEO: Mark Houtchens, Pres.   Tel: (206) 623-8030   Emp: N/A
Bus: *Real estate owners & operators.*   Fax:(206) 467-6809   %FO: 100

● **AB SKF**
Hornsgatan 1, S-415 50 Göteborg, Sweden
CEO: Peter Augustsson, Pres.   Tel: 46-31-371000   Emp: 42000
Bus: *Mfr. roller bearings, seals & special steels, and*   Fax:46-31-372832
    control measurement & testing equipment.

SKF CONDITION MONITERING, INC.
4141 Ruffin Road, San Diego, CA   92123-1841
CEO: Jan Brons, Pres.   Tel: (619) 496-3400   Emp: 100+
Bus: *Electronic measuring & control equipment.*   Fax:(619) 496-3531   %FO: 100

SKF SPECIALTY PRODUCTS CO.
1530 Valley Center Parkway, Corp. Center, Lehigh Valley, PA 18017
CEO: Jane Richmond, Gen. Mgr.   Tel: (610) 391-8000   Emp: 25+
Bus: *Mfr./import ball & roller bearings; actuation*   Fax:(610) 861-3737   %FO: 100
     systems.

SKF USA INC.
1100 First Avenue, King of Prussia, PA 19406-0907
CEO: Krister Peil, Pres.   Tel: (610) 962-4300   Emp: 6000
Bus: *Mfr./sale rolling bearings & seals.*   Fax:(610) 265-1457   %FO: 99.8

SKF USA INC.
5385 McEver Road, Box 545, Flowry Branch, GA 30542
CEO: Steve Stuart, Gen. Mgr.   Tel: (770) 967-3311   Emp: 100+
Bus: *Mfr. heat testing, surface finishing & assembly*   Fax:(404) 967-4258   %FO: 100
     machinery.

● SMEDBO AB
Grustagsgatan 1, Box 13063, S-250 13 Helsingborg, Sweden
CEO: Svante Andrae, Pres.   Tel: 46-42-151500   Emp: N/A
Bus: *Mfr. decorative hardware, bathroom accessories.*   Fax:46-42-155135

SMEDBO INC.
1001 Sherwood Drive, Lake Bluff, IL 60044
CEO: Börje S. Jemsten, Pres.   Tel: (847) 615-0000   Emp: 12
Bus: *Import/distribution decorative hardware,*   Fax:(847) 615-1001   %FO: 100
     bathroom accessories.

● SMG SWEDISH MACHINE GROUP, AB
S-721 22 Vasteras, Sweden
CEO: Ingemar Larsson, Mgn. Dir.   Tel: 46-21-48062880   Emp: 656
Bus: *Mfr. milling machines.*   Fax:N/A

SWEDISH MACHINE GROUP, INC.
696 Bonded Parkway, Streamwood, IL 60107
CEO: Robert W. Schooley, Pres.   Tel: (630) 372-8121   Emp: 44
Bus: *Sale milling machinery.*   Fax:(630) 766-6902   %FO: 100

● SMT MACHINE AB
P.O.Box 800, Vasterås S-72 122 Sweden
CEO: C.G. Johansson, CEO   Tel: 46-21-805100   Emp: 115
Bus: *Mfr. lathe equipment.*   Fax:46-21-805111

AMERICAN SMT INC.
613 Lunt Avenue, Schaumburg, IL 60193
CEO: Stig Schedin, CEO   Tel: (847) 352-0013   Emp: 3
Bus: *Sales lathe equipment.*   Fax:(847) 352-0388   %FO: N/A

- **SMZ INDUSTRIER AB**
Mossvagen 8, S-641 49 Katrineholm, Sweden
CEO: L. Bobman, Pres. Tel: 46-150-16220 Emp: 300
Bus: *Mfr. hydraulic liftgates.* Fax:46-150-10428

 WALTCO TRUCK EQUIPMENT CO
 285 Northeast Avenue, Tallmadge, OH 44278
 CEO: Rod Robinson, Pres. Tel: (330) 633-9191 Emp: 300
 Bus: *Mfr./distribution/sale hydraulic liftgates &* Fax:(330) 633-1418 %FO: 100
  cylinders.

- **STORA KOPPARBERGS BERGSLAGS GROUP**
Asgatan 22, S-791 80 Falun, Sweden
CEO: Lars-Ake Helgesson, Pres. Tel: 46-23-780000 Emp: 35000
Bus: *Mfr. forest products/paper.* Fax:46-23-13858

 STORA NORTH AMERICA CORPORATION
 Six Landmark Square, 4th Floor, Stamford, CT 06901-2792
 CEO: Leif Smedman, Pres. Tel: (203) 359-5630 Emp: 100+
 Bus: *Distribution forest products; pulp, papers,* Fax:(203) 359-5830 %FO: 100
  packaging paper & board, and building
  materials.

- **STUDSVIK AB**
S-611 82 Nyköping, Sweden
CEO: Töive Kivikas, Pres. Tel: 46-155-221000 Emp: 10+
Bus: *Computer research, development and testing* Fax:46-155-26300
 services.

 ALNOR INSTRUMENT COMPANY
 7555 North Linder Avenue, Skokie, IL 60077
 CEO: Alan Traylor, Mgr. Tel: (847) 677-3500 Emp: 80
 Bus: *Mfr. precision measurement & control devices.* Fax:(847) 677-3539 %FO: 100

 STUDSVIK OF AMERICA INC.
 1087 Beacon Street, Ste. 301, Newton, MA 02159
 CEO: Malte Edenius, Pres. Tel: (617) 965-7450 Emp: 15+
 Bus: *Mfr./distributor computer software.* Fax:(617) 965-7549 %FO: 100

- **SUNDS DEFIBRATOR AB**
S-851 94 Sundsvall, Sweden
CEO: Lars Näsman, Pres. Tel: 46-60-165000 Emp: N/A
Bus: *Mfr. machinery & equipment for pulp, paper &* Fax:46-60-165500
 viscose industry.

 SUNDS DEFIBRATOR INC.
 2900 Courtyard Drive, Norcross, GA 30071
 CEO: Bob Harrison, Pres. Tel: (770) 263-7863 Emp: 400
 Bus: *Sale/service machinery & equipment for pulp,* Fax:(770) 441-9652 %FO: 100
  paper & viscose industry.

- **SVEDALA INDUSTRI AB**
Kaptensgatan 1, Box 4004, S-203 11 Malmö, Sweden
CEO: Thomas Oldér, CEO　　　　　　　　　　　　Tel: 46-40-245800　　　Emp: 1000+
Bus: *Design/mfr./sales systems & equipment for mineral*　Fax:46-40-245876
　　processing, material handling, road construction,
　　and waste processing.

　　DYNAPAC (Div. of Svedala Industries, Inc.)
　　16435 IH-35 North, Selma, TX　78154
　　CEO: Art Kaplan, Pres.　　　　　　　　　　Tel: (210) 651-9700　　Emp: N/A
　　Bus: *Construction/mining/materials handling*　Fax:(210) 651-6784　　%FO: 100
　　　　equipment.

　　SVEDALA INDUSTRIES, INC.
　　PO Box 2219, Appleton, WI　54913-2219
　　CEO: R. Steve Morrison, VP & Gen. Mgr.　　Tel: (414) 734-9831　　Emp: 1000+
　　Bus: *Mfr. construction/mining & materials handling*　Fax:(414) 734-9756　　%FO: 100
　　　　equipment.

　　SVEDALA INDUSTRIES, INC.
　　20965 Crossroads Circle, PO Box 1655, Waukeshau, WI　53187-1655
　　CEO: Ron Robinson, Pres.　　　　　　　　　Tel: (414) 798-6200　　Emp: N/A
　　Bus: *Design/mfr./sales systems & equipment for*　Fax:(414) 798-6211　　%FO: 100
　　　　mineral processing, material handling, road
　　　　construction, and waste processing.

　　SVEDALA INDUSTRIES, INC., BULK MATERIALS HANDLING
　　4800 Grand Avenue, Neville Island, Pittsburgh, PA　15225-1599
　　CEO: R.M. Koper, Pres.　　　　　　　　　　Tel: (412) 269-5000　　Emp: 100+
　　Bus: *Mfr./sales bulk handling equipment.*　　Fax:(412) 269-5050　　%FO: 100

　　SVEDALA INDUSTRIES, INC., INSTRUMENTATION DIV.
　　6235 Lookout Road, Boulder, CO　80301
　　CEO: James D. Shotton, Gen. Mgr.　　　　　Tel: (303) 530-1600　　Emp: 10+
　　Bus: *Mfr. construction handling equipment.*　Fax:(303) 530-5210　　%FO: 100

　　SVEDALA INDUSTRIES, INC.,　Northwest Design & Equipment
　　North 2020 Dollar Road, Spokane, WA　99212
　　CEO: Tom Gilligan, Pres.　　　　　　　　　Tel:(509) 535-1044　　Emp:15+
　　Bus: *Mfr./sales construction/mining handling*　Fax:(509) 535-7164　　%FO:100
　　　　equipment.

　　SVEDALA INDUSTRIES, INC., SVEDALA TRELLEX
　　3588 Main Street, Keokuk, IA　52632
　　CEO: Bob Ridge, Gen. Mgr.　　　　　　　　Tel: (319) 524-8430　　Emp: 100+
　　Bus: *Mfr./sales rubber and plastic products.*　Fax:(319) 524-7290　　%FO: 100

SVEDALA INDUSTRIES, PUMPS & PROCESS
621 South Sierra Madre, Box 340, Colorado Springs, CO   80901

CEO: Wayne Troyer, Pres.   Tel: (719) 471-3443   Emp: 100+

Bus: *Design/mfr./sale of equipment; mineral &*   Fax:(719) 471-4469   %FO: 100
food processing; environmental controls.

SVEDALA, PACIFIC CRUSHING & SCREENING
311 Nevada Street, Auburn, CA   95603

CEO: Brad Critchfield, Gen. Mgr.   Tel: (916) 885-0204   Emp: 25+

Bus: *Import/distribution crusher & screening*   Fax:(916) 885-1715   %FO: 100
equipment.

SVEDALA, PYRO SYSTEMS DIVISION
1308 North Walnut, Drawer D, Pittsburg, KS   66762

CEO: Timothy F. McNally, Pres.   Tel: (316) 231-3000   Emp: 100+

Bus: *Mfr. industrial process equipment.*   Fax:(316) 231-0343   %FO: 100

UNIVERSAL ENGINEERING
800 First Avenue, N.W., Cedar Rapids, IA   52405

CEO: R.E.Spencer, Pres.   Tel: (319) 365-0441   Emp: 100+

Bus: *Mfr. construction/mining heavy materials*   Fax:(319) 369-5440   %FO: 100
handling equipment.

● **SVENSKA CELLULOSA AKTIEBOLSGET (SCA)**
Box 846, S-851 23 Sundsvall, Sweden

CEO: Bo Rydin, Chrm.   Tel: 46-60-194000   Emp: N/A

Bus: *Mfr. forestry and paper products.*   Fax:N/A

SCA GRAPHIC PAPER, INC.
220 East 42nd Street, Ste. 3010, New York, NY   10017

CEO: Robert Keppler, VP   Tel: (212) 953-3210   Emp: N/A

Bus: *Mfr. forestry and paper products.*   Fax:(212) 953-3211   %FO: 100

● **SVENSKA HANDELSBANKEN**
Kungsträdgårdsgatan 2, S-106 70 Stockholm, Sweden

CEO: Arne Mårtensson, Pres.   Tel: 46-8-701-1000   Emp: N/A

Bus: *Commercial banking services.*   Fax:46-8-611-5071

SVENSKA HANDELSBANKEN
153 East 53rd Street, New York, NY   10022

CEO: Stephan Oxenburg, Gen. Mgr.   Tel: (212) 326-5100   Emp: N/A

Bus: *Commercial banking services.*   Fax:(212) 326-5196   %FO: 100

● **SVENSKT STÅL AKTIEBOLAG**
Birger Jarlsgätan 58, P.O. Box 16344, S-103 26 Stockholm, Sweden
CEO: Leif Gustafsson, Pres.   Tel: 46-8-789-2500   Emp: N/A
Bus: *Mfr. steel.*   Fax:46-8-107974

    SWEDISH STEEL, INC.
    4700 Grand Avenue, Pittsburgh, PA   15225
    CEO: M. Hedin, CEO   Tel: (412) 269-2120   Emp: N/A
    Bus: *Mfr./sale steel & steel products.*   Fax:(412) 269-2124   %FO: 100

● **SVERIGES TELEVISION AB**
S-105 10 Stockholm, Sweden
CEO: Sam Nilsson, Mgn. Dir.   Tel: 46-8-784-8050   Emp: N/A
Bus: *Broadcasting, telecommunications.*   Fax:46-8-660-1498

    SWEDISH BROADCASTING CO.
    375 Greenwich Street, New York, NY   10013
    CEO: Ms. Elizabeth Johansson, Mgr.   Tel: (212) 644-1224   Emp: N/A
    Bus: *Broadcasting representative.*   Fax:(212) 644-1224   %FO: 100

● **SWEDBANK (SPARBANKEN SVERIGE AB)**
Brunkebergstorg 8, S-105 34 Stockholm, Sweden
CEO: Reinhold Geijer, Pres.   Tel: 46-8-790-1000   Emp: N/A
Bus: *Commercial banking services.*   Fax:46-8-796-8092

    SWEDBANK NEW YORK
    12 East 49th Street, 20th Floor, New York, NY   10017
    CEO: Lennart Lundberg, Gen. Mgr.   Tel: (212) 486-8400   Emp: 30
    Bus: *Commercial banking services.*   Fax:(212) 486-3220   %FO: 100

● **SWEDTEL AB**
Sankt Eriksgatan 117, Box 6296, S-102 35 Stockholm, Sweden
CEO: Lennart Ljunblad, Pres.   Tel: 46-8-690-2200   Emp: N/A
Bus: *Telecommunication products & services.*   Fax:46-8-318319

    SWEDTEL INC.
    3900 N.W. 79th Avenue, Suite 568, Miami, FL   33166
    CEO: Jan Carlsson, Pres.   Tel: (305) 593-9559   Emp: 10
    Bus: *Telecommunications products & services.*   Fax:(305) 593-8482   %FO: 100

● **TELIA AB**
Marbackagatan 11, S-123 86 Farsta, Sweden
CEO: Lars Berg, Pres. & CEO   Tel: 46-8-7131000   Emp: 35000
Bus: *Telecommunication services.*   Fax:46-8-7249029 .

    TELIA INTL NORTH AMERICA INC
    1270 Ave of the Americas, #2212, New York, NY   10020
    CEO: Magnus Kjell, Pres.   Tel: (212) 246-3609   Emp: N/A
    Bus: *Telecommunication services.*   Fax:(212) 246-3436   %FO: 100

• **TRELLEBORG INDUSTRI AB**
Nygatan 102 AS-231 81 Trelleborg, Sweden
CEO: Kjell Nilsson, Pres.   Tel: 46-410-51000   Emp: 2268
Bus: *Mfr. molded rubber products, wear resistant rubber,*   Fax:49-410-42763
industrial hoses, protective clothing, v-belt, motor
vehicle parts/equipment.

  BIT MANUFACTURING, INC.
  State Highway 68, Copperhill, TN 37317
  CEO: Wayne Pittman, Pres.   Tel: (615) 496-3331   Emp: 100+
  Bus: *Sulfur and copper derived industrial products.*   Fax:(615) 496-1329   %FO: 100

  TRELLEBORG BOLIDEN INC
  3 Landmark Square, Stamford, CT 06901
  CEO: Torgny U. Astrom, Pres.   Tel: (203) 325-8599   Emp: N/A
  Bus: *U.S. headquarters operations. Mfr. molded*   Fax:(203) 325-8605   %FO: 100
  rubber products, wear resistant rubber,
  industry hoses, protective clothing, v-belt,
  motor vehicle parts/equipment.

  TRELLEBORG BOLIDEN METECH INC.
  120 Mapleville Main Street, Mapleville, RI 02839
  CEO: John D. Koskinas, Pres.   Tel: (401) 568-0711   Emp: N/A
  Bus: *Metals recycling systems.*   Fax:(401) 568-6003   %FO: 100

  TRELLEBORG BOLIDEN SULEX INC.
  1237 Pier G Avenue, Berth 214, Long Beach, CA 90802
  CEO: Clinton Godown, Opers.   Tel: (310) 435-8950   Emp: N/A
  Bus: *Mfr./sale chemicals.*   Fax:(310) 435-4835   %FO: 100

  TRELLEBORG MONARCH INC.
  61 State Route 43 North, Box 430, Hartville, OH 44632-0430
  CEO: Timothy Ryan, Pres.   Tel: (216) 877-1211   Emp: N/A
  Bus: *Mfr./sale rubber motor vehicle products.*   Fax:(216) 877-2346   %FO: 100

  TRELLEBORG RUBORE INC.
  3000 Northwoods Parkway, Suite 350, Norcross, GA 30071
  CEO: Sven Olsson, Pres.   Tel: (770) 729-8030   Emp: N/A
  Bus: *Mfr./sale motor vehicle equipment.*   Fax:(770) 729-1820   %FO: 100

  TRELLEBORG VIKING INC.
  170 West Road, Portsmouth, NH 03801
  CEO: John Schramko, Pres.   Tel: (603) 436-1236   Emp: N/A
  Bus: *Mfr./sale protective textile products.*   Fax:(603) 436-1392   %FO: 100

- **TRYGG-HANSA SPP**
Fleminggatan 18, S-106 26 Stockholm, Sweden
CEO: Jan Bruneheim, Pres.   Tel: 46-8-6931000   Emp: N/A
Bus: *Insurance services.*   Fax:46-8-6509367

> **HANSA REINSURANCE CO. OF AMERICA**
> 220 White Plains Road, Tarrytown, NY   10591-9012
> CEO: Kenneth J. Bolen, Pres. & CEO   Tel: (914) 631-6011   Emp: 28
> Bus: *Reinsurance services.*   Fax:(914) 631-7402   %FO: 100

- **UNITED BARCODE INDUSTRIES AB**
Vandevagen 85-A, S-182 25 Danderyd, Sweden
CEO: Sven Skarendahl, Pres.   Tel: 46-8-753-3810   Emp: 350
Bus: *Mfr. bar code & magnetic stripe readers, thermal*   Fax:46-8-753-6099
transfer printers, bar code data collection networks.

> **UNITED BARCODE INDUSTRIES INC.**
> 12240 Indian Creek Court, Beltsville, MD   20705
> CEO: Jeremy Metz, Pres.   Tel: (301) 210-3000   Emp: 100+
> Bus: *Distribution/sale/service bar code, magnetic*   Fax:(301) 210-5498   %FO: 100
> *stripe readers, thermal transfer printers, bar*
> *code data collection networks.*

- **VACUUM-EXTRACTOR, AB**
Räntmästraeg 7, Box 6253, S-400 60 Goteborg, Sweden
CEO: Lasse Beijer, Mgn. Dir.   Tel: 46-31-848530   Emp: 20+
Bus: *Surgical/medical/dental instruments and supplies.*   Fax:46-31-196670

> **AMEDA-EGNELL CORPORATION**
> 755 Industrial Drive, Cary, IL   60013
> CEO: Roland Muller, VP   Tel: (847) 639-2900   Emp: 20+
> Bus: *Surgical/medical/dental instruments and*   Fax:(847) 639-7895   %FO: 100
> *supplies.*

- **VAVSTOLSFABRIKEN GLIMAKRA AB**
Box 125, S-280 64 Glimakra, Sweden
CEO: Jan Helmmbring, Pres.   Tel: 46-44-43000   Emp: N/A
Bus: *Mfr. loom & weaving accessories.*   Fax:N/A

> **GLIMAKRA LOOMS & YARNS INC.**
> 1338 Ross St, Petaluma, CA   94954-6502
> CEO: Lars Malmberg, Pres.   Tel: (707) 762-3362   Emp: N/A
> Bus: *Import/distribution looms, weaving*   Fax:(707) 762-0335   %FO: 100
> *accessories, yarns.*

● **VOAC HYDRAULICS INC**
Box 913, S-501 10 Boras, Sweden
CEO: Johan Halling, Pres.　　　　　　　　　　　Tel: 46-33-169100　　　Emp: 900
Bus: *Mfr. hydraulic valves, pumps, motors, cylinders.*　　Fax:46-33-121830

　　VOAC HYDRAULICS
　　409 W. Algonquin Road, Mt .Prospect, IL　60056
　　CEO: Kjell Jansson, Pres.　　　　　　　　Tel: (847) 437-8200　　Emp: 27
　　Bus: *Sale/service/assembly hydraulic valves, pumps,*　Fax:(847) 437-8272　%FO: 100
　　　　motors, cylinders.

● **AB VOLVO**
Torslandaverken, S-405 08 Göteborg, Sweden
CEO: Håkan Frisinger, Chrm.　　　　　　　　Tel: 46-31-590000　　Emp: 79050
Bus: *Mfr. cars & trucks, marine, industrial/aircraft*　Fax:46-31-532602
engines, aerospace components, hydraulic systems,
construction equipment.

　　VOLVO CAR FINANCE INC.
　　25 Philips Pkwy, Montvale, NJ　07645
　　CEO: Janes R. Ryan, Pres.　　　　　　　Tel: (201) 358-6600　　Emp: N/A
　　Bus: *Financial services.*　　　　　　　Fax:(201) 307-6749　%FO: 20

　　VOLVO CARS OF NORTH AMERICA
　　7 Volvo Drive, Box 913, Rockleigh, NJ　07647
　　CEO: Helge Alten, Pres.　　　　　　　　Tel: (201) 768-7300　　Emp: N/A
　　Bus: *Mfr./sale automobiles.*　　　　　　Fax:(201) 784-4535　%FO: 100

　　VOLVO CARS OF NORTH AMERICA
　　15340 Barrance Parkway, Irvine, CA　92718
　　CEO: Mitchell A. Duncan, VP　　　　　　Tel: (714) 753-9535　　Emp: 20+
　　Bus: *Sales/service motor vehicles/equipment.*　Fax:(714) 753-9540　%FO: 100

　　VOLVO CONSTRUCTION EQUIPMENT NORTH AMERICA
　　One West Park Square, Asheville, NC　28801
　　CEO: Helmut Peters, Pres.　　　　　　　Tel: (704) 257-2500　　Emp: N/A
　　Bus: *Mfr. construction & mining equipment.*　Fax:(704) 257-2590　%FO: 50

　　VOLVO GM HEAVY TRUCK CORP.
　　7900 National Service Road, Box 26115, Greensboro, NC　27402-6115
　　CEO: Per Lindquist, Pres.　　　　　　　Tel: (910) 279-2000　　Emp: N/A
　　Bus: *Mfr./sale trucks.*　　　　　　　Fax:(910) 279-2117　%FO: 87

　　VOLVO MONITORING & CONCEPT CENTER
　　700 Via Alondra, Camarillo, CA　93012
　　CEO: Sylvia Voegele, Gen. Mgr.　　　　　Tel: (805) 388-0399　　Emp: 20+
　　Bus: *Research/development motor vehicles.*　Fax:(805) 388-1403　%FO: 100

VOLVO NORTH AMERICA CORP
535 Madison Ave, New York, NY   10022
CEO: Albert R. Dowden, Pres.   Tel: (212) 754-3300   Emp: N/A
Bus: *Administers subsidiaries & investments.*   Fax:(212) 418-7437   %FO: 100

VOLVO PENTA OF THE AMERICAS
1300 Volvo Penta Drive, Chesapeake, VA   23320
CEO: Clint Moore, Pres.   Tel: (804) 436-2800   Emp: 100+
Bus: *Mfr./sale marine & industrial engines &*   Fax:(804) 436-5150   %FO: 100
  propulsion systems.

● **WALLAC AB**
Box 305, S-161 26 Bromma, Sweden
CEO: Nils I. Ollson, Pres.   Tel: 46-8-799-8000   Emp: N/A
Bus: *Mfr. chemical & biological instruments.*   Fax:46-8-988-6364

   WALLAC INC.
   9238 Gaither Road, Gaithersburg, MD   20877
   CEO: Gerard B. Buckley, Pres.   Tel: (301) 963-3200   Emp: N/A
   Bus: *Mfr./sale chemical & biological instruments.*   Fax:(301) 963-7780   %FO: 100

● **WALLENIUS LINEES AB**
Swedenborgsgatan 19, S-104 62 Stockholm, Sweden
CEO: Christer Olsson, Pres.   Tel: 46-8-772-0500   Emp: 800
Bus: *Specialized shipping for motor vehicle & heavy*   Fax:46-8-640-6854
  cargo industries.

   WALLENIUS HOLDING INCORPORATED
   188 Broadway, Box 1232, Woodcliff Lake, NJ   07675
   CEO: Raymond P. Ebeling, Pres.   Tel: (201) 307-1300   Emp: 165
   Bus: *Holding Company; for specialized shipping*   Fax:(201) 307-9740   %FO: 100
     firms for motor vehicle & heavy cargo
     industries.

   WALLENIUS LINES NA INC.
   5601 Edison Drive, Oxnard, CA   93033
   CEO: James J. Kirkpatrick, Gen. Mgr.   Tel: (805) 488-4000   Emp: 100+
   Bus: *Transportation automobiles/trucks & other*   Fax:(805) 488-4009   %FO: 100
     rolling cargo.

Switzerland

● **ABB ASEA BROWN BOVERI LTD.**
Affolternstrasse 44, P O Box 8131, CH-8050 Zurich Oerlikon, Switzerland

CEO: Percy Barnevik, Pres. Tel: 41-1-317-7111 Emp: 209600

Bus: *Engineering services for power, process, industrial* Fax:41-1-317-7321
automation, mass transit, environment control. (JV
of ASEA AB & BBC Brown Boveri).

ASEA BROWN BOVERI, INC. (US Headquarters)
501 Merritt Seven, Norwalk, CT 06851

CEO: Peter S. Janson, Pres. Tel: (203) 750-2200 Emp: 25000

Bus: *Products/services for power, process,* Fax:(203) 750-2283 %FO: 100
industrial automation, mass transit,
environmental control markets.

ABB AIR PREHEATER, INC.
Post Office Box 372, Wellsville, NY 14895

CEO: Edward Bysiek, Pres. Tel: (716) 593-2700 Emp: N/A

Bus: *Environmental control systems.* Fax:(716) 593-3829 %FO: 100

ABB ENVIRONMENTAL SERVICES, INC.
P.O.Box 7050, Portland, ME 04112

CEO: Robert Hemler, Pres. Tel: (207) 775-5401 Emp: N/A

Bus: *Environmental control systems and* Fax:(207) 772-4762 %FO: 100
engineering services.

ABB FLEXIBLE AUTOMATION, INC.
2487 South Commerce Drive, New Berlin, WI 53151

CEO: Sy Nichols, Pres. Tel: (414) 785-3400 Emp: N/A

Bus: *Industrial automation systems.* Fax:(414) 785-3466 %FO: 100

ABB INDUSTRIAL SYSTEMS, INC.
650 Ackerman, Columbus, OH 43202

CEO: Donald Aiken, Pres. Tel: (614) 261-2000 Emp: N/A

Bus: *Industrial automation systems.* Fax:(614) 261-2521 %FO: 100

ABB POWER GENERATION, INC.
5309 Commonwealth Center Pkwy., Midlothian, VA 23112

CEO: Alex Brnilovich, Pres. Tel: (804) 763-2000 Emp: N/A

Bus: *Power engineering services.* Fax:(804) 763-2019 %FO: 100

ABB POWER TRANSMISSION AND DISTRIBUTION COMPANY, INC.
201 South Rogers Lane, Raleigh, NC 27610

CEO: Åke Almgren, Pres. Tel: (919) 212-4700 Emp: N/A

Bus: *Power engineering services.* Fax:(919) 212-5045 %FO: 100

ABB VETRO GRAY, INC.
PO Box 2291, Houston, TX   77252
CEO: Donald Grierson, Pres.   Tel: (713) 681-4685   Emp: N/A
Bus: *U.S. sub. of ABB Asea Brown Boveri, Ltd.*   Fax:(713) 878-5155   %FO: 100

ABB, INC.
2000 Day Hill Road, P.O. Box 500, Winsdor, CT   06095
CEO: Fritz Gautschi, Pres.   Tel: (860) 688-1911   Emp: N/A
Bus: *Engineering services.*   Fax:(860) 285-3253   %FO: 100

● **ADIA SA**
Place Chauderon 4, PO Box 1003 Lausanne, Switzerland
CEO: Peter Pfister, CFO   Tel: 41-21-341-0200   Emp: 3500
Bus: *Temporary/permanent personnel placement service.*   Fax:41-21-323-4090

ADECCO/ADIA SERVICES INC.
100 Redwood Shores Parkway, Redwood City, CA   94065
CEO: Debbie Pond-Heide, Pres.   Tel: (415) 610-1000   Emp: 25+
Bus: *Personnel services.*   Fax:(415) 610-1076   %FO: JV

AJILON SERVICES, INC.
210 West Pennsylvania Avenue, Ste. 650, Towson, MD   21204
CEO: Roy Haggerty, Pres.   Tel: (410) 821-0435   Emp: N/A
Bus: *Personnel services.*   Fax:(410) 828-0106   %FO: 100

LEE HECHT HARRISON, INC.
200 Park Avenue, New York, NY   10166
CEO: Stephen G. Harrison, Pres.   Tel: (212) 557-0009   Emp: N/A
Bus: *Temporary/permanent personnel placement*   Fax:(212) 922-0838   %FO: 100
     service

● **AGIE HOLDINGS SA**
P.O.Box 1358, CH-6616 Losone, Switzerland
CEO: Leonard Gysin, Pres.   Tel: 41-91-806-9111   Emp: N/A
Bus: *Holding company/mfr. electrical discharge*   Fax:41-91-806-9202
     machinery.

AGIE USA LTD. - ELOX CORP.
Griffith St., P.O. Box 220, Davidson, NC   28036-1146
CEO: Gabriele G. Carinci, Pres.   Tel: (704) 892-8011   Emp: 5
Bus: *Industrial machinery & equipment, machine*   Fax:(704) 896-7512   %FO: 100
     tool accessories.

- **ALUSUISSE-LONZA GROUP**

Feldeggstrasse 4, Postfach 495, CH-8034 Zurich, Switzerland

CEO: Sergio Machionne, CEO   Tel: 41-1-386-2222   Emp: 30869

Bus: *Aluminum, chemicals, packaging.*   Fax:41-1-386-2585

ALUSUISSE COMPOSITES INC.

77 West Port Plaza, Ste. 421, St. Louis, MO   63146

CEO: J.J. Butler, Pres.   Tel: (314) 878-2303   Emp: 140

Bus: *Mfr./distributor composite materials.*   Fax:(314) 878-7596   %FO: 100

ALUSUISSE-LONZA AMERICA INC.

17-17 Route 208, Fair Lawn, NJ   07410

CEO: Hans Noetzli, Pres.   Tel: (201) 791-5200   Emp: 900

Bus: *Mfr./distributor chemicals, packaging, & aluminum.*   Fax:(201) 794-2597   %FO: 100

LAWSON MARDEN WHEATON, INC.

1101 Wheaton Avenue, Millville, NJ   08332

CEO: Hank Carter, Pres.   Tel: (609) 825-1400   Emp: N/A

Bus: *Mfr./distribution chemicals, packaging, & aluminum.*   Fax:(609) 327-5931   %FO: 100

LAWSON MARDON FLEXIBLE INC.

5303 Charles Road, Bellwood, IL   60104

CEO: Marcel J. Pilon, SVP   Tel: (708) 544-1600   Emp: 526

Bus: *Mfr. flexible packaging, aluminum foil.*   Fax:(708) 649-3887   %FO: 100

LAWSON MARDON PACKAGING INC.

8800 Sixty Road, P.O. Box 460, Baldwinsville, NY   13027

CEO: Marcel J. Pilon, Pres.   Tel: (315) 638-4355   Emp: 400

Bus: *Flexible packaging/cartons, labels.*   Fax:(315) 638-8421   %FO: 100

LAWSON MARDON THERMAPLATE INC.

200 Circle Drive North, Piscataway, NJ   08854

CEO: Rochard Strenkowski, Pres.   Tel: (908) 469-6300   Emp: 134

Bus: *Plastic packaging/food services.*   Fax:(908) 469-0167   %FO: 100

LONZA INC.

17-17 Route 208, Fair Lawn, NJ   07410

CEO: Hans Noetzli, Pres.   Tel: (201) 794-2400   Emp: 940

Bus: *Mfr./distribution chemicals, packaging, & aluminum..*   Fax:(201) 794-2597   %FO: 100

● **AMEDA AG**
Bosch 106, CH-6331 Hunenberg, Switzerland
CEO: Robert Riedweg, Chrm. & Pres.   Tel: 41-42-785-138   Emp: 120
Bus: *Mfr. neonatal products, breast pumps &*   Fax:41-42-785-5150
     breastfeeding accessories, medical suction pumps,
     bloodflow monitors.

   AMEDA/EGNELL CORP
   755 Industrial Drive, Cary, IL   60013
   CEO: Roland Müller, VP   Tel: (847) 639-2900   Emp: 45
   Bus: *Neonatal products, breast pumps,*   Fax:(847) 639-7895   %FO: 100
        breastfeeding accessories, medical suction
        pumps, bloodflow monitors.

● **THE ARES-SERONO GROUP SA**
Chemin des Mines 2, CH-1202 Geneva, Switzerland
CEO: Ernesto Bertarelli   Tel: 41-22-738-8000   Emp: 2500
Bus: *Development/marketing pharmaceutical &*   Fax:41-22-739-3040
     diagnostics products.

   ARES ADVANCED TECHNOLOGY, INC.
   280 Pond Street, Randolph, MA   02368
   CEO: Robert Campbell, Exec.Dir.   Tel: (617) 963-0894   Emp: 140
   Bus: *Research/development life sciences.*   Fax:(617) 963-6058   %FO: 100

   ARES-SERONO INC
   53 State St., Exchange Place 37th Fl, Boston, MA   02109
   CEO: Jack Barlow, Pres.   Tel: (617) 723-1300   Emp: N/A
   Bus: *Distributor/sale/marketing & developers* Fax:(617) 723-1319   %FO: 100
        pharmaceuticals & diagnostic products.

   SERONO LABORATORIES, INC.
   100 Longwater Circle, Norwell, MA   02061-1616
   CEO: Hisham Samra, Pres.   Tel: (617) 982-9000   Emp: 200
   Bus: *Mfr./research/marketing/distribution*   Fax:(617) 871-6754   %FO: 100
        pharmaceutical products.

● **BACHEM FEINCHEMIKALIEN AG**
Hauptstrasse 144, 4416 Bubendorf, Switzerland
CEO: Peter Grogg, Pres. & CEO   Tel: 41-61-931-2333   Emp: N/A
Bus: *Mfr. of bulk peptide pharmaceuticals and amino* Fax:41-61-9312549
     acid derivatives

   BACHEM BIOSCIENCE, INC.
   3700 Horizon Drive, King of Prussia, PA   19406
   CEO: Dr. José de Chastonay, EVP   Tel: (610) 239-0300   Emp: 25
   Bus: *Mfr. organic chemicals.*   Fax:(610) 239-0800   %FO: 100

BACHEM CALIFORNIA, INC.
6868 Nancy Ridge Drive, San Diego, CA   92121
CEO: R. Makineni, Pres.   Tel: (619) 455-7051   Emp: 10
Bus: *Mfr. organic chemicals.*   Fax:(619) 455-5741   %FO: 100

BACHEM CALIFORNIA, INC.
3132 Kashiwa Street, Torrance, CA   90505
CEO: R. Makineni, Pres.   Tel: (310) 539-4171   Emp: 75
Bus: *Mfr. organic chemicals.*   Fax:(310) 530-1571   %FO: 100

● **THE BALOISE INSURANCE GROUP**
Aeschengraben 21, CH-4002 Basel, Switzerland
CEO: Dr. Rolf Schauble, Chrm.   Tel: 41-61-285-8585   Emp: N/A
Bus: *Insurance services.*   Fax:41-61-285-7070

  THE BALOISE INSURANCE GROUP
  One Providence Washington Plaza, Providence, RI   02903
  CEO: Richard Hoag, Chrm.   Tel: (401) 453-7000   Emp: N/A
  Bus: *Insurance services.*   Fax: %FO: 100

● **BANK JULIUS BAER**
Bahnhofstrasse 36, P.O. Box 8010, Zurich, Switzerland
CEO: Rudolf E. Baer, Chrm.   Tel: 41-1-228-5111   Emp: N/A
Bus: *Banking, investment & securities services.*   Fax:41-1-211-2560

  BANK JULIUS BAER, NY BRANCH
  330 Madison Avenue, New York, NY   10017
  CEO: David E. Bodner, EVP   Tel: (212) 297-3600   Emp: 183
  Bus: *Commercial banking services.*   Fax:(212) 557-7839   %FO: 100

  JULIUS BAER INVESTMENT MANAGEMENT INC.
  330 Madison Avenue, New York, NY   10017
  CEO: Jay A. Dirnberger, Mng. Dir.   Tel: (212) 297-3850   Emp: 5
  Bus: *Investment advisory services.*   Fax:(212) 557-7839   %FO: 100

  JULIUS BAER SECURITIES
  330 Madison Avenue, New York, NY   10017
  CEO: Bernard Spilko, Mng. Dir.   Tel: (212) 297-3800   Emp: 14
  Bus: *Securities broker/dealer.*   Fax:(212) 557-7839   %FO: 100

● **BANQUE SCANDINAVE EN SUISSE**
Cours de Rive 11, CH-1211 Geneva, Switzerland
CEO: Harold Ehrenstrom, Dir.   Tel: 41-22-7873111   Emp: 275
Bus: *Asset management services.*   Fax:41-22-7353370

  BSS ASSET MANAGEMENT
  50 Main Street, White Plains, NY   10606
  CEO: Ulf Nofelt, Senior V.P.   Tel: (914) 328-6404   Emp: 3
  Bus: *Asset management services.*   Fax:(914) 328-6421   %FO: 100

● **BAUMANN + CIE AG**
8630 Rüti, Switzerland
CEO: Hans R. Rüegg, CEO   Tel: 41-55-286-8111   Emp: N/A
Bus: *Mfr.. of springs.*   Fax:41-55-286-8516

    BAUMANN SPRINGS USA INC.
    10710 Southern Loop Blvd., PO Box 410167, Charlotte, NC   28241
    CEO:Urs Schaffützel, Gen. Mgr.   Tel: (704) 588-2700   Emp: 50
    Bus: *Mfr. of springs/wire products.*   Fax:(704) 588-8354   %FO: 100

● **BERNA AG**
Industriestrasse 211, CH-4600 Olten, Switzerland
CEO: Thomas Weilenmann, Chrm.   Tel: 41-62-287-8787   Emp: N/A
Bus: *Mfr. bimetallic cylinders, coating equipment;*   Fax:41-62-287-8793
     coating service center.

    SYLVESTER & CO.
    24700 Highpoint Rd., Beachwood, OH   44122
    CEO:Mark K. Meyer, Pres.   Tel: (216) 831-0880   Emp: 10
    Bus: *CVD coating service center; sale CVD coating*   Fax:(216) 831-0852   %FO: 100
     equipment.

    XALOY, INC.
    101 Xaloy Way, Pulaski, VA   24301
    CEO:Walter Cox, Pres.   Tel: (540) 994-2229   Emp: 320
    Bus: *Mfr. bimetallic cylinders; coating equipment.;*   Fax:(540) 980-5670   %FO: 100
     service centers.

● **BOBST S.A.**
P.O. Box 1001, CH-1001 Lausanne, Switzerland
CEO: Hanspeter Möckli   Tel: 41-21-621-2111   Emp: N/A
Bus: *Mfr., distribution, & servicing printing & converting*   Fax:41-21-626-1270
    machines for paper and cardboard.

    BOBST GROUP
    140 Harrison Avenue, P.O.Box 2800, Roseland, NJ   07068
    CEO:Philippe Michel, EVP   Tel: (201) 226-8000   Emp: 464
    Bus: *Mfr., distribution, & servicing printing &*   Fax:(201) 226-8625   %FO: 100
     converting machines for paper and cardboard.

● **BRUDERER AG**
P.O.Box 9320 Frasnacht, Switzerland
CEO: Markus E. Bruderer, Pres.   Tel: 41/71-446-9146   Emp: N/A
Bus: *Mfr./sales high speed punching presses.*   Fax:41-71-447-7780

    BRUDERER INC.
    Highway 72, East, PO Box 208, Huntsville, AL   35804-0208
    CEO:Werner Vieh, VP   Tel: (205) 859-4050   Emp: 100
    Bus: *Mfr. high speed presses.*   Fax:(205) 859-0944   %FO: 100

BRUDERER MACHINERY INC.
1200 Hendricks Causeway, Ridgefield, NJ 07657

CEO: Alois Rupp, Pres.	Tel: (201) 941-2121	Emp: 40
Bus: *Sales high speed presses.*	Fax:(201) 886-2010	%FO: 100

• BSI - BANCA DELLA SVIZZERA ITALIANA
Via Magatti 2, P.O. Box 2833, CH-6901 Lugano, Switzerland

CEO: Alberto Togni, Chrm.	Tel: 41-91-809-3111	Emp: 20
Bus: *International commercial & private banking services.*	Fax:41-91-809-3678	

BSI - BANCA DELLA SVIZZERA ITALIANA
Park Avenue Tower, 65 East 55th Street, New York, NY 10022

CEO: Yves Gaden, SVP	Tel: (212) 326-3100	Emp: 20
Bus: *International commercial & private banking services.*	Fax:(212) 326-3105	%FO: 100

• BUHLER LTD.
CH-9240 Uzwil, Switzerland

CEO: Urs Bühler, Pres.	Tel: 41-71-955-1111	Emp: N/A
Bus: *Engineering/mfr. food processing & industrial machinery.*	Fax:41-71-955-3379	

BUHLER LTD.
1100 Xenium Lane North, PO Box 9497, Minneapolis, MN 55441-4499

CEO: Rudolf Gutmann, Pres.	Tel: (612) 545-1401	Emp: 272
Bus: *Mfr./sales food processing; industrial machinery.*	Fax:(612) 540-9296	%FO: 100

• BUSS AG
10 Hohenrainstrasse, CH-4133 Pratteln 1, Switzerland

CEO: Ranier Sigrest, Mng. Dir.	Tel: 41-61-8256-111	Emp: 700
Bus: *Mfr. compounding & bulk handling equipment, dryers, logistic systems.*	Fax:41-61-8256-699	

BUSS (AMERICA) INC.
303 Covington Drive, Bloomingdale, IL 60108

CEO: Claus Langgartner, Pres.	Tel: (630) 307-9900	Emp: 50
Bus: *Mfr. kneaders for plastic & chemical industries.*	Fax:(630) 307-9905	%FO: 100

• CHEMIE UETIKON AG
CH-8707, Vetikon am Zee, Switzerland

CEO: Dr. Mortiz Braun, CEO	Tel: 41-1-921-9111	Emp: N/A
Bus: *Fertilizers, chemicals, molecular sieves.*	Fax:41-1-920-2093	

ZEOCHEM
P.O. BOX 35940, Louisville, KY 40232

CEO: Kenneth J. Gustafson, Genl Mgr.	Tel: (502) 634-7600	Emp: 100
Bus: *Molecular sieve absorbents.*	Fax:(502) 634-8133	%FO: 50

● **CLAIRANT INTERNATIONAL LTD.**
Rothausstrasse 61, 4132 Muttenz, Switzerland
CEO: Rolf W. Schweizer, Chrm. & Pres.　　　Tel: 41-61-469-6195　　Emp: N/A
Bus: *Mfr./sales of dyes and related chemicals.*　Fax:41-61-469-6590

　　CLAIRANT CORPORATION
　　4000 Monroe Road, Charlotte, NC　28205
　　CEO: Cary W. Campbell, VP　　　　　　　Tel: (704) 331-7084　　Emp: 1200
　　Bus: *Mfr./sales of dyes and related chemicals*　Fax:(704) 377-1063　%FO: 100

● **CLARIANT INTERNATIONAL LTD.**
Rothausstrasse 61, 4132 Muttenz, Switzerland
CEO: Dr. Rolf W. Schweizer, Chrm. & Pres.　　Tel: 41-61-469-6195　　Emp: N/A
Bus: *Mfr../sales of dyes and specialty chemicals*　Fax:41-61-469-6590

　　CLARIANT CORPORATION
　　4000 Monroe Road, Charlotte, NC　28205
　　CEO: Kenneth Brewton, Pres.　　　　　　Tel: (704) 331-7084　　Emp: 1200
　　Bus: *Mfr./sales of dyes and specialty chemicals*　Fax:(704) 377-1063　%FO: 100

● **CORIM AG**
Dufourstrasse 65, 8702 Zolikon, Switzerland
CEO: B. H. Wililngham, Jr., Dir.　　　　　　Tel: 41-1-391-7123　　Emp: N/A
Bus: *Investment financing.*　　　　　　　　Fax:41-1-391-2726

　　CORIM TENNESSEE, INC.
　　172 Second Avenue North, Nashville, TN　37201
　　CEO: Vicki Saito, VP　　　　　　　　　　Tel: (615) 259-3200　　Emp: 5
　　Bus: *Real estate investment/property management.*　Fax:(615) 259-3210　%FO: 100

　　CORIM TERRATRADE, INC.
　　7 Drayton Street, Savannah, GA　31401
　　CEO: Sylvia King, Mgr.　　　　　　　　　Tel: (912) 233-5520　　Emp: 5
　　Bus: *Real estate investment/property management.*　Fax:(912) 233-9163　%FO: 100

　　CORIM, INC.
　　100 Laura Street, PO Box 359, Jacksonville, FL　32201
　　CEO: Bill Wellingham, Pres.　　　　　　　Tel: (904) 355-3500　　Emp: 25
　　Bus: *Real estate investment/property management.*　Fax:(904) 355-2099　%FO: 100

• CREDIT SUISSE GROUP

Nüschelerstrasse 1, P.O.Box 669, CH-8021 Zurich, Switzerland

CEO: Lukas Muhlemann Tel: 41-1-212-1616 Emp: 33527

Bus: *International banking; asset management; securities* Fax:41-1-212-0669
broker/dealer & underwriting services.

BEA ASSOCIATES, INC.

One Citicorp Center,
153 East 53rd Street, 57th Floor, New York, NY 10022

CEO: William W. Priest, Jr., Mng Dir. Tel: (212) 832-2626 Emp: 200

Bus: *Asset management/consulting, pension funds.* Fax:(212) 355-1662 %FO: 100

CREDIT SUISSE

12 East 49th Street, New York, NY 10017

CEO: Christopher W. Roberts, CEO Tel: (212) 238-2000 Emp: 627

Bus: *Commercial banking, North America Region.* Fax:(212) 238-2600 %FO: 100

CREDIT SUISSE FIRST BOSTON, INC.

55 East 52nd Street, New York, NY 10055

CEO: John Hennessy, Chmn. Tel: (212) 909-2000 Emp: 770

Bus: *Commercial & investment banking services.* Fax:(212) 753-2390 %FO: 100

CREDIT SUISSE ASSET MANAGEMENT

12 East 49th Street, 38th Fl., New York, NY 10017

CEO: Kenneth Tarr, Pres. Tel: (212) 238-5800 Emp: 30

Bus: *Investment management services.* Fax:(212) 238-5850 %FO: 100

CREDIT SUISSE FINANCIAL PRODUCTS

55 East 52nd Street, New York, NY 10055

CEO: Jim Healy, Mng. Dir. Tel: (212) 322-5900 Emp: 750

Bus: *Financial products & services.* Fax:(212) 308-2357 %FO: 100

CREDIT SUISSE- PRIVATE BANKING

12 East 49th Street, 40th Fl., New York, NY 10022

CEO: Ruedi Stalder, Chmn. Tel: (212) 238-5821 Emp: 500

Bus: *Commercial banking, asset management and* Fax:(212) 238-5814 %FO: 100
securities services.

SWISS AMERICAN SECURITIES, INC.

100 Wall Street, New York, NY 10005

CEO: George J. Helwig, Pres. Tel: (212) 612-8700 Emp: 140

Bus: *Securities broker/dealer* Fax:(212) 363-6884 %FO: 100

● **EBEL SA**
113, rue de la Paix, 2300 La Chaux-de-Fonds, Switzerland
CEO: Pierre-Alain Blum, CEO   Tel: 41-39-22-3123   Emp: N/A
Bus: *Mfr.. of watches.*   Fax:41-39-22-3124

    EBEL, INC.
    750 Lexington Avenue, New York, NY   10022
    CEO:Ronald L. Wolfgang, Pres. & CEO   Tel: (212) 888-3235   Emp: 50
    Bus: *Watch sales.*   Fax:(212) 888-6719   %FO: 100

● **ENDRESS + HAUSER INTL HOLDING AG**
Kägenstrasse 4, CH-4153 Reinach, Switzerland
CEO: Klaus Endress, Pres.   Tel: 41-61-715-6333   Emp: 3000
Bus: *Mfr./distribution level, pressure, flow and moisture*   Fax:41-61-711-0682
instrumentation and process recorders..

    ENDRESS & HAUSER INSTRUMENTS INC.
    2350 Endress Place, PO Box 246, Greenwood, IN   46143
    CEO:Joseph W. Schaffer, VP & Gen.Mgr.   Tel: (317) 535-7138   Emp: 180
    Bus: *Level, pressure, flow and moisture*   Fax:(317) 535-8498   %FO: 100
    instrumentation process recorders.

● **GEORG FISCHER LTD.**
Ebnat-Strasse 111, P.O. Box 671, CH-8201 Schaffhausen, Switzerland
CEO: Martin Huber, Pres.   Tel: 41-52-631-1111   Emp: 5378
Bus: *Mfr. automotive castings & products; piping*   Fax:41-52-631-2847
systems; machine tools, plant engineering &
construction.

    CHARMILLES TECHNOLOGIES CORP.
    560 Bond Street, Lincolnshire, IL   60069-4224
    CEO:Harry C. Moser, Pres.   Tel: (847) 913-5300   Emp: 120
    Bus: *Distributor/service electrical discharge*   Fax:(847) 913-5340   %FO: 100
    machines

    CHARMILLES TECHNOLOGIES MANUFACTURING CORP
    1550 East South Street, Owosso, MI   48867
    CEO:Dan Nierste, Pres.   Tel: (517) 725-2129   Emp: 140
    Bus: *Machining & assembly facility for electrical*   Fax:(517) 723-7266   %FO: 100
    discharge machines.

    GEORG FISCHER DISA INC.
    407 Hadley Street, PO 40, Holly, MI   48442-0040
    CEO:Norman Patterson, Pres.   Tel: (810) 634-8251   Emp: 100
    Bus: *Mfr./sales industrial machinery.*   Fax:(810) 634-2181   %FO: 100

    GEORG FISCHER DISA INC.
    One Pleasant Grove Road, PO. Box 1607, Seminole, OK   74868
    CEO:Charles A. Prucha, Pres.   Tel: (405) 382-6900   Emp: 80
    Bus: *Mfr./sales industrial machinery.*   Fax:(405) 382-7013   %FO: 100

GEORGE FISCHER CORP
230 Covington Drive, Bloomingdale, IL   60108-3106

CEO: J. Lou Pedicini, Pres.	Tel: (630) 351-5593	Emp: 46
Bus: *Holding company.*	Fax:(630) 307-9905	%FO: 100

GEORGE FISCHER INC
2882 Dow Avenue, Tustin, CA   92680-7285

CEO: Peter C. Georgi, Pres.	Tel: (714) 731-8800	Emp: 52
Bus: *Distribution plastic piping systems, plastic values, fluid sensor products.*	Fax:(714) 731-6201	%FO: 100

SIGNET SCIENTIFIC CO
3401 Aerojet Ave., PO Box 5770, El Monte, CA   91734-1770

CEO: John Nelson, Pres.	Tel: (818) 571-2770	Emp: 110
Bus: *Mfr. fluid sensor products.*	Fax:(818) 573-2057	%FO: 100

WAESCHLE INC.
230 Covington Drive, Bloomingdale, IL   60108

CEO: Heinz W. Schneider, Pres.	Tel: (630) 539-9100	Emp: 30
Bus: *Design/construction components, operating units & plans.*	Fax:(630) 539-9196	%FO: 100

● FORBO INTERNATIONAL SA
Bauelenzelgstrasse 20, CH-2311 Eglisau, Switzerland

CEO: Rene K. Ruepp, CEO	Tel: 41-1-868-2550	Emp: N/A
Bus: *Decorative building products, construction materials holding company.*	Fax:41-1-868-2526	

FORBO AMERICA, INC.
1105 North Market Street, Suite 1300, Wilmington, DE   19899

CEO: Eugene Chace, Pres.	Tel: (302) 427-2139	Emp: N/A
Bus: *Mfr. /sales building materials & home products.*	Fax:(302) 427-2139	%FO: 100

FORBO INDUSTRIES INC
Humbolt Industrial Park, P.O. Box 667, Hazelton, PA   18201

CEO: Dennis P. Darragh, Pres.	Tel: (717) 459-0771	Emp: 63
Bus: *Floor coverings.*	Fax:(717) 450-0258	%FO: 100

FORBO WALLCOVERINGS INC
3 Kildeer Court, P.O. Box 457, Bridgeport, NJ   08014-0457

CEO: Douglas H. Grimes, Pres	Tel: (609) 467-0200	Emp: 40
Bus: *Distribution wallcoverings.*	Fax:(609) 467-4880	%FO: 100

SIEGLING AMERICA, INC.
12201 Vanstory Road, Huntersville, NC   28078

CEO: Wayne E. Hoffman. Pres.	Tel: (704) 948-0800	Emp: 250
Bus: *Systems technology.*	Fax:(704) 948-0995	%FO: 100

● **FRANKE HOLDING AG**
CH-4663 Aarburg, Switzerland
CEO: Michaek Pieper, Pres.　　　　　　　　Tel: 41-62-787-3131　　Emp: 2600
Bus: *Kitchen sinks & accessories, food service*　　Fax:41-62-791-6761
　　　equipment, industrial & medical equipment.

　　FRANKE INC. CONTRACT GROUP WEST
　　685 Glendale Avenue, Sparks, NV　89321-5812
　　CEO: Willaim M. Cherkitz, Pres.　　　　　Tel: (702) 358-8484　　Emp: 40
　　Bus: *Mfr. food service equipment, kitchen sinks &*　Fax:(702) 359-1005　%FO: 100
　　　　accessories.

　　FRANKE, INC.
　　212 Church Road, North Wales, PA　19454-4140
　　CEO: Hans-Juerg Ott, Pres.　　　　　　　Tel: (215) 699-8761　　Emp: 170
　　Bus: *Mfr. food service equipment, kitchen sinks &*　Fax:(215) 699-7464　%FO: 100
　　　　accessories.

　　IRC PARTS & SUPPLIES INC.
　　310 Techpark Drive, La Verge, TN　37086
　　CEO: Hans-Juerg Ott, Pres.　　　　　　　Tel: (615) 793-5990　　Emp: 75
　　Bus: *Sales/distribution spare parts.*　　　Fax:(615) 793-5940　%FO: 100

● **FUCHS PETROLUB AG**
Algisserstrasse 10, CH-8500 Zurich, Switzerland
CEO: Manfred Fuchs, Pres.　　　　　　　　Tel: 41-52-728-0028　　Emp: N/A
Bus: *Mfr. industrial lubricants.*　　　　　　Fax:41-52-728-0029

　　FUCHS LUBRICANTS CO.
　　17050 Lathrop Avenue, Harvey, IL　60426
　　CEO: L. Frank Kleinman, Pres.　　　　　　Tel: (708) 333-8900　　Emp: 320
　　Bus: *Mfr. industrial lubricants.*　　　　　Fax:(708) 333-9180　%FO: 100

● **HANRO LTD.**
CH-4410 Liestal, Switzerland
CEO: Charles Handschin, Director　　　　　Tel: 41-61-921-0011　　Emp: 500
Bus: *Manufacturer of sleeper and underwear..*　Fax:41-61-921-4536

　　HANRO USA, INC.
　　40 E 34th Street, New York, NY　10016
　　CEO: Niki Sachs, Pres.　　　　　　　　　Tel: (212) 532-3320　　Emp: 10
　　Bus: *Distributor underwear, sleepwear.*　　Fax:(212) 685-4823　%FO: JV

● **HOLDERBANK FINANCIÈRE GLARIS LTD.**
Zurchenstrasse 156, CH-8745, Jona, Switzerland
CEO: Thomas Schmidheiny, Chrm.   Tel: 41-55-222-8620   Emp: N/A
Bus: *Mfr. cement & building materials.*   Fax:41-55-222-8629

    HOLNAM INC.
    6211 North Ann Arbor Road, Dundee, MI 48131
    CEO: Paul A. Yhouse, Pres.   Tel: (313) 529-2411   Emp: 2500
    Bus: *Mfr./supplier cement, aggregates & concrete.*   Fax:(313) 529-5512   %FO: 100

    INDEPENDENT CEMENT CORP., INC.
    3 Columbus Circle, Albany, NY 12203
    CEO: Dennis Skidmore, Mng. Dir.   Tel: (518) 459-3211   Emp: 300
    Bus: *Mfr./distribution cement.*   Fax:(518) 449-5525   %FO: 100

● **INFRANOR INTER AG**
Scharenmoosstrasse 117, CH-8052 Zurich, Switzerland
CEO: Nicholas Eichenberger   Tel: 41-1-302-2727   Emp: N/A
Bus: *Mfr./service systems, motors & industrial equipment.*   Fax:41-1-302-7189

    INFRANOR INC
    45 Great Hill Road, P.O.Box 1307, Naugatuck, CT 06770
    CEO: W. B. Spring, Pres.   Tel: (203) 729-8258   Emp: 20
    Bus: *Mfr./service systems, motors & industrial equipment.*   Fax:(203) 729-6969   %FO: 100

● **JELMOLI HOLDING AG**
St. Ahhagasse 18, Postfach 272, CH-8021, Zurich, Switzerland
CEO: Gaudenez Staehelin, CEO   Tel: 41-1-220-4411   Emp: N/A
Bus: *Operates retail chain stores, restaurants, and mail order facilities and specialty stores.*   Fax:41-1-211-0465

    JOHNNY APPLESEED'S
    30 Tozer Road, Beverly, MA 01915
    CEO: Hank Billeter, Pres.   Tel: (508) 922-2040   Emp: N/A
    Bus: *Mail order fashion and fashion store operator.*   Fax:(508) 922-7001   %FO: 100

● **LAMPRECHT TRANSPORT LTD.**
PO Box 194, 8058 Zurich Airport, Zurich, Switzerland
CEO: Richard P. Dünki, Mgr.   Tel: 41-1-816-2512   Emp: N/A
Bus: *International air cargo forwarding company.*   Fax:41-1-816-4212

    AMERICAN LAMPRECHT TRANSPORT INC.
    PO Box 4946, Spartanburg, SC 29305
    CEO: Jean Dill, EVP   Tel: (864) 433-8585   Emp: 5
    Bus: *Air/ocean, import/export forwarding and customhouse brokers.*   Fax:(864) 433-8555   %FO: 100

AMERICAN LAMPRECHT TRANSPORT INC.
700 Rockaway Turnpike, Lawrence, NY   11559

CEO: Alain Tiercy, EVP

Bus: *Air/ocean, import/export forwarding and customhouse brokers.*

Tel: (516) 239-6200   Emp: 5
Fax:(516) 239-0844   %FO: 100

AMERICAN LAMPRECHT TRANSPORT INC.
2218 Landmeier Road, Elk Grove Village, IL   60007

CEO: H. P. Widmer, EVP

Bus: *Air/ocean, import/export forwarding and customhouse brokers.*

Tel: (847) 364-0555   Emp: 5
Fax:(847) 364-9350   %FO: 100

● LANDIS & GYR AG
Gubelstrasse, CH-6301 Zug, Switzerland

CEO: Robert Bachmann, Pres.

Bus: *Mfr. building control systems, energy management equipment and systems, phone and money handling equipment.*

Tel: 41-42-729-1124   Emp: 18000
Fax:41-42-724-3522

LANDIS & GYR METERING, INC.
3601 Sagamore Parkway North, Lafayette, IN   47903

CEO: Phil Jackson, Pres.

Bus: *Mfr./sale building control systems, energy management equipment & systems.*

Tel: (765) 429-1200   Emp: 650
Fax:(765) 742-0936   %FO: 100

LANDIS & GYR SYSTEMS INC.
1730 Technology Drive, San Jose, CA   95110-1365

CEO: John Boucher, Gen.Mgr..

Bus: *Mfr./sale building control systems, energy management equipment & systems.*

Tel: (408) 453-5222   Emp: 200
Fax:(408) 452-5260   %FO: 100

LANDIS & STAEFA INC.
1000 Deerfield Parkway, Buffalo Grove, IL   60089

CEO: John J. Grad, Pres.

Bus: *Mfr./sale building control systems, energy management equipment & systems. (JV with Staefa Control Systems AG)*

Tel: (847) 215-1000   Emp: 900
Fax:(847) 215-1093   %FO: 100

• LEICA AG

9435 Heerbrugg, Switzerland
CEO: Jörg Wullschleger, Pres.   Tel: 41-71-727-3131   Emp: N/A
Bus: *Develop/mfr./sales of microscopes and*   Fax:41-71-727-4678
optoelectronic sensors, surveying instrument and
photogrammetic equipment.

LEICA INC.

3374 Walden Avenue, Depew, NY   14043
CEO: Martin Green, Pres.   Tel: (716) 864-5000   Emp: 130
Bus: *Ophthalmic instruments div.;*   Fax:(716) 686-4545   %FO: 100
development/mfr./sales of ophthalmic
instruments and equipment.

LEICA INC.

111 Deerlake Road, Deerfield, IL   60015
CEO: Hank Smith, Pres.   Tel: (847) 405-0123   Emp: 300
Bus: *US sales of products of the Leica Microscopy* Fax:(847) 405-0147   %FO: 100
and Scientific Instruments Group.

LEICA INC.

3362 Walden Avenue, Depew, NY   14043
CEO: Rudi Oertli, Pres.   Tel: (716) 686-3000   Emp: 200
Bus: *Optical products division;*   Fax:(716) 686-3085   %FO: 100
development/mfr./sales of ophthalmic
instruments and equipment.

LEICA INC.

23868 Hawthorne Blvd., Torrance, CA   90505
CEO: Neil VanCans, Pres.   Tel: (310) 791-5300   Emp: 85
Bus: *Development/mfr./sales of Global Positioning* Fax:(310) 378-6627   %FO: 100
Systems for navigation and surveying.

LEICA INC. (LSG Atlanta)

3155 Medlock Bridge Road, Norcross, GA   30071
CEO: Gregg Shull, Pres.   Tel: (770) 447-6361   Emp: 49
Bus: *Marketing., sales, support and software*   Fax:(770) 447-0710   %FO: 100
development of the Leica Surveying
Instruments Group.

LEICA TECHNOLOGIES INC.

107 North King Street, Leesburg, VA   22075
CEO: William Dunnell, Pres.   Tel: (703) 777-3900   Emp: 5
Bus: *Sales of optronics and special products*   Fax:(703) 777-3940   %FO: 100

● **LIEBHERR-INTERNATIONAL AG**
Rue de l'Industrie 19, CH-1630 Bulle, Swizerland
CEO: Paul Wagishauser, Mng. Dir.   Tel: 41-29-33111   Emp: N/A
Bus: *Mfr. industrial machinery, cranes, machine tools,* Fax:41-29-21240
     assembly lines, automation, and aviation machinery.

    LIEBHERR MINING TRUCK
    P.O. Box 269, Baxter Springs, KS 66713
    CEO:H. Peter Eller, Pres.   Tel: (316) 856-2309 Emp: 60
    Bus: *Mfr. Industrial machinery.*   Fax:(316) 856-2364 %FO: 100

    LIEBHERR SALINE
    1465 Woodland Drive, Saline, MI 48176
    CEO:Peter Kozma, VP   Tel: (313) 429-7225 Emp: N/A
    Bus: *Mfr. Industrial machinery.*   Fax:(313) 429-2294 %FO: 100

    LIEBHERR-AMERICA, INC.
    4100 Chestnut Avenue, Newport News, VA 23605
    CEO: Ronald Jacobson, Pres.   Tel: (757) 245-5251 Emp: 60
    Bus: *Mfr. Industrial machinery.*   Fax:(757) 928-8701 %FO: 100

● **LINDT & SPRÜNGLI INTERNATIONAL**
Seestrasse 204, 8802 Kitchberg, Switzerland
CEO: Hans Jürg Klingler, SVP   Tel: 41-01-716-2233 Emp: N/A
Bus: *Mfr./trading of chocolate products.*   Fax:41-01-716-2662

    LINDT & SPRUENGLI INC.
    One Fine Chocolate Place, Stratham, NH 03885
    CEO:Lee Mizusawa, Pres.   Tel: (603) 778-8100 Emp: 100
    Bus: *Mfr./sales of Swiss chocolates.*   Fax:(603) 778-3102 %FO: 100

● **MEDITERRANEAN SHIPPING COMPANY SA**
40, Avenue Eugene Pittard, CH-1206 Geneva, Switzerland
CEO: Gianluigi Aponte, Pres.   Tel: 41-22-703-8888 Emp: 6000
Bus: *Steamship company.*   Fax:41-22-703-8787

    MEDITERRANEAN SHIPPING COMPANY (USA) INC.
    420 Fifth Avenue, New York, NY 10018
    CEO:Nicola Arena, Pres.   Tel: (212) 764-4800 Emp: 250
    Bus: *Steamship agents.*   Fax:(212) 764-8592 %FO: 90

● **MERCK KGAA**
Frankfurter Strasse 250, Postfach 41 19, D-64271 Darmstadt, Germany
CEO: Hans Joachim Langmann, Pres.   Tel: 49-6151-720-000   Emp: 10000
Bus: *Mfr. pharmaceuticals, chemicals and laboratory*   Fax:49-6151-722-000
preparations.

    EM INDUSTRIES, INC.
    5 Skyline Drive, Hawthorne, NY   10566
    CEO: Walter Zywottek, Pres.   Tel: (914) 592-4660   Emp: 850
    Bus: *Mfr./wholesale of organic and inorganic*   Fax:(914) 592-9469   %FO: 100
    chemicals.

● **MONTRES ROLEX SA**
Rue Francois-Dussaud, PO Box 430, 1211 Geneva 24 Switzerland
CEO: A. J. Heiniger, Chrm.   Tel: 41-22-308-22 00   Emp: N/A
Bus: *Manufacturer of watches.*   Fax:41-22-300-22 55

    ROLEX WATCH, INC.
    665 Fifth Avenue, New York, NY   10022
    CEO: Roland Puton, Pres. & CEO   Tel: (212) 758-7700   Emp: 330
    Bus: *Import/sales/service of watches*   Fax:(212) 223-7443   %FO: 100

● **NESTLÉ SA**
Ave Nestle 55, CH-1800 Vevey, Switzerland
CEO: Helmut O. Maucher, Chrm.   Tel: 41-21-924-2111   Emp: 200000
Bus: *Develop/mfr. foods, beverages, and pharmaceuticals.* Fax:41-21-921-1885

    ALCON LABORATORIES INC
    6201 South Freeway, Ft. Worth, TX   76134
    CEO: Edgar H. Schollmaier, Pres.   Tel: (817) 293-0450   Emp: 4500
    Bus: *Mfr./sale pharmaceuticals products;*   Fax:(817) 551-4705   %FO: 100
    ophthalmic products.

    GALDERMA LABORATORIES, INC.
    3000 Alta Mesa Blvd., #300, Ft. Worth, TX   76133
    CEO: Stephen Clark, VP   Tel: (817) 263-2600   Emp: 150
    Bus: *Mfr./sales skin care products.*   Fax:(817) 263-2609   %FO: 100

    NESTLÉ BEVERAGE INC.
    345 Spear Street, San Francisco, CA   94105
    CEO: Ed Marra, President   Tel: (415) 546-4600   Emp: N/A
    Bus: *Mfr./sales beverages; coffee, chocolate, water.* Fax:(415) 896-1701   %FO: 100

    NESTLÉ CHOCOLATE & CONFECTIONS CO.
    637 South Pine Street, Burlington, WI   53105
    CEO: Peter Ferris, CEO   Tel: (414) 763-9111   Emp: 550
    Bus: *Mfr. foods, candies, and confections.*   Fax:(414) 763-5037   %FO: 100

NESTLÉ COFFEE SPECIALTIES INC.
214 east 52nd Street, New York, NY   10022
CEO: Daniel Lalonde, Pres.   Tel: (212) 755-0585   Emp: 100
Bus: *Mfr./sales specialty coffees/beverages.*   Fax:(212) 755-0043   %FO: 100

NESTLÉ FROZEN FOOD INC.
30000 B. Bainbridge Road, Solon, OH   44139
CEO: James Dintaman, Pres.   Tel: (216) 349-5757   Emp: 4500
Bus: *Mfr./sales frozen consumer foods.*   Fax:(216) 498-0830   %FO: 100

NESTLÉ HOLDINGS INC.
Five High Ridge Road, Stamford, CT   06905
CEO: Michael Davis, V.P.   Tel: (203) 322-4567   Emp: 28
Bus: *Commodities international trading.*   Fax:(203) 322-7756   %FO: 100

NESTLÉ USA INC.
1133 Connecticur Avenue, NW, Suite 310, Washington, DC   20036
CEO: Maxine C. Champion, VP   Tel: (202) 296-4100   Emp: N/A
Bus: *Government relations representative.*   Fax:(202) 296-8555   %FO: 100

NESTLÉ USA INC.
800 North Brand Blvd., Glendale, CA   91203
CEO: Joseph Weller, Chmn.   Tel: (818) 549-6000   Emp: 38500
Bus: *Food, beverages, pet food, hospitality.*   Fax:(818) 549-6952   %FO: 100

• NOKIA-MAILLEFER HOLDING SA
Route du Bois 37, CH-1024 Ecublens, Switzerland
CEO: Jaakko Asanti, Pres.   Tel: 41-21 6944111   Emp: N/A
Bus: *Equipment to produce telecommunications & power*   Fax:41-21 6912143
     cable, installation wire, optical fiber cable.

NOKIA-MAILLEFER INC
1856 Corporate Drive, #135, Norcross, GA   30093
CEO: Tim Donovan, Pres.   Tel: (770) 931-0051   Emp: 21
Bus: *Sale/service equipment to produce cable &*   Fax:(770) 931-0747   %FO: 100
     wire.

SYNCRO MACHINE COMPANY INC.
611 Syre Avenue, Perth Amboy, NJ   08861
CEO: David Johnson, VP Operations   Tel: (908) 442-5500   Emp: 30
Bus: *Mfr. wire drawing equipment.*   Fax:(908) 442-5500   %FO: 100

● **NOVARTIS AG (formally CIBA-GEIGY AG & SANDOZ AG)**
Lichstrasse 35, CH-4002 Basel, Switzerland
CEO: Dr. Daniel Vasella, Pres.   Tel: 41-61-324-1111   Emp: 134000
Bus: *Research/mfr./marketing of healthcare, agribusiness*   Fax:41-61-324-3300
    and nutritional products.

CHIRON/BIOCINE COMPANY
4560 Horton Street, Emeryville, CA   94608
CEO: Ed Penhoet, Pres.   Tel: (510) 655-8730   Emp: 2000
Bus: *Biotechnology research.*   Fax:(510) 655-9910   %FO: 100

CIBA SPECIALITY CHEMICALS CORP.
540 White Plains Road, P.O. Box 2005, Tarrytown, NY   10561-9005
CEO: Stanley Sherman, Pres. & CEO   Tel: (914) 785-2000   Emp: 15000
Bus: *Mfr./sale specialty chemicals.*   Fax:(914) 785-2227   %FO: 100

CIBA SPECIALTY CHEMICALS CORP., Performance Polymers Div.
281 Fields Lane, Brewster, NY   10509
CEO: Jim Uselton, Pres.   Tel: (914) 785-3000   Emp: 400
Bus: *Mfr. epoxy resins and formulated industrial*   Fax:(914) 785-3476   %FO: 100
    systems.

CIBA VISION CORP
11460 Johns Creek Parkway, Duluth, GA   30155
CEO: Dr. C. Glen Bradley, Pres.   Tel: (770) 448-1200   Emp: N/A
Bus: *Mfr./distribution soft contact lenses & lens*   Fax:(770) 418-4261   %FO: 100
    care products.

GENEVA PHARMACEUTICALS INC.
2655 West Midway Blvd., Broomfield, CO   80038-0469
CEO: Charles T. Lay, Pres.   Tel: (303) 466-2400   Emp: 1000
Bus: *Mfr./distribution generic pharmaceuticals.*   Fax:(303) 466-3717   %FO: 100

GERBER LIFE INSURANCE COMPANY
66 Church Street, White Plains, NY   10601
CEO: Ron Masiero, Pres.   Tel: (914) 761-4404   Emp: 230
Bus: *Life insurance services. Sub. of Gerger*   Fax:(914) 761-4772   %FO: 100
    products company.

GERBER PRODUCTS COMPANY
445 State Street, Fremont, MI   49413
CEO: Al Piergallini, Pres. & CEO   Tel: (616) 928-2000   Emp: 1200
Bus: *Mfr./markets baby/children's nutritional*   Fax:(616) 928-2723   %FO: 100
    products.

NOVARTIS
2001 Pennsylvania Avenue, NW, Suite 925, Washington, DC   20006
CEO: Michael Ailsworth, VP   Tel: (202) 293-3019   Emp: 11
Bus: *Industry government relations and public*   Fax:(202) 659-0249   %FO: 100
    affairs office.

NOVARTIS CONSUMER HEALTH CORP.
556 Morris Avenue, Summit, NJ   07901
CEO: Fred Huser, Pres.   Tel: (908) 598-7600   Emp: N/A
Bus: *Mfr./markets consumer over-the-counter*   Fax:(908) 273-2869   %FO: 100
  healthcare products.

NOVARTIS CORPORATION
5550 Morris Avenue, Summit, NJ   07901
CEO: Douglas G. Watson, Pres.   Tel: (908) 277-5000   Emp: N/A
Bus: *Research/mfr./marketing of healthcare,*   Fax:(908) 277-5752   %FO: 100
  agribusiness and nutritional products.

NOVARTIS CROP PROTECTION, INC.
410 Swing Road, P.O.Box 18300, Greensboro, NC   27419-8300
CEO: Emilio Bontempo, Pres.   Tel: (910) 632-6000   Emp: N/A
Bus: *Develops/mfr. agricultural products & services*   Fax:(910) 632-7353   %FO: 100
  for crop protection.

NOVARTIS FINANCE CORPORATION
608 Fifth Avenue, New York, NY   10024
CEO: Claude Dulex, Pres.   Tel: (212) 307-1122   Emp: N/A
Bus: *Corporate administrative & financial services.*   Fax:(212) 246-0185   %FO: 100

NOVARTIS NUTRITION CORP.
5100 Gamble Drive, PO Box 370, Minneapolis, MN   55440
CEO: David Pyott, Pres.   Tel: (612) 925-2100   Emp: 700
Bus: *Clinical enteral nutrition products, and food*   Fax:(612) 593-2087   %FO: 100
  services.

NOVARTIS PHARMACEUTICALS CORP.
Route 10, East Hanover, NJ   07936
CEO: Wayne P. Yetter, Pres.   Tel: (201) 503-7500   Emp: 7000
Bus: *Develop/mfr./market pharmaceuticals.*   Fax:(201) 503-8265   %FO: 100

NOVARTIS SEED'S, INC.
5300 Katrina Avenue, Downers Grove, IL   60515
CEO: Fred Fuller, Pres.   Tel: (630) 969-6300   Emp: 600
Bus: *Mfr./distribution flower seeds, plugs, plants &*   Fax:(630) 696-6373   %FO: 100
  other horticultural products.

NOVARTIS SEEDS, INC.
PO Box 4188, Boise, ID   83711-0727
CEO: John Sorenson, Pres.   Tel: (208) 322-7272   Emp: 700
Bus: *Research/mfr. vegetable seeds.*   Fax:(208) 322-1436   %FO: 100

NOVARTIS SEEDS, INC.

7500 Olson Memorial Highway, Golden Valley, MN 55427

CEO: Ed Shonsey, Pres.

Bus: *Research/mfr./market agricultural products &*
seeds: corn, wheat, soybean, alfalfa, sorghum
& sunflower.

Tel: (612) 593-7333   Emp: 2000
Fax:(612) 542-0194   %FO: 100

RED LINE HEALTHCARE CORP.

8121 10th Avenue North, Golden Valley, MN 55427

CEO: Robert Carr, Pres.

Bus: *Distribution of medical supplies.*

Tel: (612) 595-6000   Emp: 700
Fax:(612) 595-6677   %FO: 100

• OERLIKON-BÜHRLE HOLDING AG

Hofwiesenstrasse 135, P.O. Box 2409, CH-8021 Zürich, Switzerland

CEO: Dr. Hans Widmer, Pres.

Bus: *Mfr./distribution shoes & leather goods; vacuum*
technology; defense & space technology.

Tel: 41-1-363-4060   Emp: 15543
Fax:41-1-363-7260

BALLY, INC.

One Bally Place, New Rochelle, NY 10801

CEO: Dr. Richard Wycherley, CEO

Bus: *Markets shoes, accessories, leather goods &*
apparel.

Tel: (914) 632-4444   Emp: 507
Fax:(914) 632-8264   %FO: 100

BALZERS PROCESS SYSTEMS INC.

25 Sagamore Park Road, Hudson, NH 03051

CEO: Russ Buckley, Pres. & CEO

Bus: *Mfr./distribution precision & vacuum*
equipment, thin film coating systems.

Tel: (603) 889-6888   Emp: 1061
Fax:(603) 595-3250   %FO: 100

CONTRAVES, INC.

Keystone Commons
700 Braddock Avenue, East Pittsburgh, PA 15112

CEO: N/A

Bus: *Mfr./distribution/research aircraft/defense*
products.

Tel: (412) 829-4800   Emp: 250
Fax:(412) 829-4812   %FO: 100%

PFEIFFOR VACUUM TECHNOLOGY INC.

24 Trafalgar Square, Nashua, NH 03063-1988

CEO: George McGee, Mng. Dir.

Bus: *Mfr./sales agent; instruments, vacuum*
measurement and control devices; optics film
and coatings.

Tel: (603) 578-6500   Emp: N/A
Fax:(603) 578-6550   %FO: JV

• PANALPINA WORLD TRANSPORT LTD.
Hüebweg 25, 4102 Binningen, Basel, Switzerland
CEO: Gerhard Fischer, Pres.   Tel: 41-61-306-2222   Emp: N/A
Bus: *International forwarding agents.*   Fax:41-61-306-2333

HENSEL, BRUCKMAN & LORBACHER, INC.
500 Bi County Blvd., Farmingdale, NY   11735
CEO: Frederick E. Glasser, SVP   Tel: (516) 755-9100   Emp: 25
Bus: *International freight forwarder/customs house*   Fax:(516) 755-9141   %FO: 100
    broker.

PANALPINA INC.
67 Park Place, Morristown, NJ   07960
CEO: Rolf Altorfer, Pres.   Tel: (201) 683-9000   Emp: 1000
Bus: *International freight forwarder/custom house*   Fax:(201) 254-5799   %FO: 100
    broker.

• PRECIPART SA
Aebistrasse 75, PO Box 7008, 2500 Biel, Switzerland
CEO: Edouard O. Laubscher, Chrm.   Tel: 41-32-365-2883   Emp: N/A
Bus: *Mfr. steel, aluminum, metal high precision screw*   Fax:41-32-365-2885
    machine parts.

AMATRIX CORPORATION
88 Finn Court, Farmingdale, NY   11735
CEO: A. O. Welti, Pres.   Tel: (516) 694-5993   Emp: 5
Bus: *Selector boxes for knitting machines.*   Fax:(516) 293-0935   %FO: 100

AMERICAN LAUBSCHER HOLDINGS CORP.
80 Finn Court, Farmingdale, NY   11735
CEO: Lloyd W. Miller, Pres. & CEO   Tel: (516) 694-5900   Emp: 80
Bus: *Import/service steel, aluminum, metal high*   Fax:(516) 293-0935   %FO: 100
    precision screw machine parts & industrial
    jewels, ceramic, gear and turned parts.

PRECIPART CORP.
90 Finn Court, Farmingdale, NY   11735
CEO: John P. Walter, Pres. & CEO   Tel: (516) 694-3100   Emp: 40
Bus: *Mfr./develop mechanical counters for medical*   Fax:(516) 694-4016   %FO: 100
    instruments, precision gears/pinions/turned
    parts.

● **WALTER REIST HOLDING AG**
CH-8340 Hinwil/Zurich, Switzerland
CEO: Walter Reist, Pres.   Tel: 41-1-938-7000   Emp: 1700
Bus: *Mfr. conveying & processing system for printing*   Fax:41-1-938-7070
industry.

   FERAG INC.
   190 Rittenhouse Circle, P O Box 137, Bristol, PA   19007-0137
   CEO: Marty Roark, Pres.   Tel: (215) 788-0892   Emp: 150
   Bus: *Mfr. conveying & processing system for*   Fax:(215) 788-7597   %FO: 100
   printing industry

● **RICOLA AG**
Basselstrasse 31, PO Box 4242, Laufen, Switzerland
CEO: Felix Richterich, Pres.   Tel: 41-61-765-4121   Emp: N/A
Bus: *Manufacturer of confectionery.*   Fax:41-61-765-4122

   RICOLA USA, INC.
   51 Gibralter Drive, Morris Plains, NJ   07950
   CEO: Dan Thomas, Pres.   Tel: (201) 984-6811   Emp: 10
   Bus: *Distribution and marketing of Ricola*   Fax:(201) 984-6814   %FO: 100
   confectionery products

● **RIETER HOLDING AG**
Klosterstrasse 20, CH-8406 Winterthur, Switzerland
CEO: Kurt E. Feller, CEO   Tel: 41-52-208-7171   Emp: N/A
Bus: *Mfr. spinning systems.*   Fax:41-52-208-7060

   RIETER CORPORATION
   PO Box 4383, Spartenburg, SC   29305
   CEO: E. Stoller, Pres.   Tel: (864) 582-5468   Emp: N/A
   Bus: *Mfr./distribution/service spinning systems.*   Fax:(864) 585-1643   %FO: 100

● **ROCHE HOLDING AS**
Grenzacherstrasse 1 24, CH-4002 Basel, Switzerland
CEO: Fritz Gerber, Chrm.   Tel: 41-61-688-8888   Emp: 50497
Bus: *Research/mfr./marketing pharmaceuticals,*   Fax:41-61-691-0014
medicinals, botanicals, biological products, &
drugs, fragrance & flavors.

   GENENTECH INC.
   460 Point San Bruno Blvd., South San Francisco, CA   94080
   CEO: Arthur Levinson, Pres.   Tel: (415) 225-1000   Emp: 3000
   Bus: *Mfr. pharmaceuticals; biotech research.*   Fax:(415) 225-2739   %FO: 64

   GIVAUDAN-ROURE CORP.
   100 Delawanna Avenue, Clifton, NJ   07015
   CEO: Richard Carraher, Pres.   Tel: (201) 365-8000   Emp: 600
   Bus: *Mfr. flavors & fragrances*   Fax:(201) 365-1015   %FO: 100

HOFFMANN-LA ROCHE INC.
340 Kingsland Street, Nutley, NJ   07110-1199

CEO: Patrick J. Zenner, Pres.   Tel: (201) 235-5000   Emp: 17327

Bus: *Mfr./distribution/research pharmaceuticals,*   Fax:(201) 235-4264   %FO: 100
chemicals, diagnostics & lab services.

HOFFMANN-LA ROCHE INC.
1301 I Street, NW, Suite 520 West, Washington, DC   20005-3314

CEO: Rita Norton, VP   Tel: (202) 408-0090   Emp: N/A

Bus: *Corporate government relations.*   Fax:(202) 408-1750   %FO: 100

ROCHE BIOSCIENCE
3401 Hillview Avenue, Palo Alto, CA   94304-1320

CEO: Dr. James Woody   Tel: (415) 855-5050   Emp: 1100

Bus: *Mfr./distribution pharmaceuticals*   Fax:(415) 354-7646   %FO: 100

• ROULEMENTS MINIATURES SA
Eckweg 8, CH-2500 Bienne, Switzerland

CEO: R. Perrenoud, Dir.   Tel: 41-32-414721   Emp: 1600

Bus: *Mfr. miniature ball/rollerbearings.*   Fax:N/A

RMB MINIATURE BEARINGS INC.
800 Lel Camino Real West, Ste. 18, Mountainview, CA   94040

CEO: Jeff Perkins, Pres.   Tel: (415) 903-2220   Emp: 5

Bus: *Mfr. bearing & ballscrews.*   Fax:(415) 903-2220   %FO: 100

RMB MINIATURE BEARINGS INC.
29 Executive Pkwy, Ringwood, NJ   07456

CEO: J.C. Bieri, Pres.   Tel: (201) 962-1111   Emp: 12

Bus: *Mfr. bearing & ballscrews.*   Fax:(201) 962-1101   %FO: 100

• SANTEX LTD.
9555 Tobel, Switzerland

CEO: Christian Strahm, Pres.   Tel: 41-71-918-6666   Emp: N/A

Bus: *Mfr. textile machines.*   Fax:41-71-918-6600

AMERICAN SANTEX INC.
485 Simuel Road, P.O. Box 8648, Spartansburg, SC   29305-8648

CEO: Christain Strahm, Pres.   Tel: (864) 574-7222   Emp: 100

Bus: *Mfr., sales, service textile machines.*   Fax:(864) 574-0804   %FO: 100

● **SARNA POLYMER HOLDING INC.**
Industriestrasse Sarnen CH-6060, Switzerland
CEO: Hanspeter Kaser, Grp. CEO   Tel: 41-41-666-9966   Emp: 2046
Bus: *Processing and application of polymeric materials.*   Fax:41-41-660-4917

    SARNAFIL INC.
    100 Dan Road, Canton, MA   02021
    CEO: Richard K. Foley, Pres.   Tel: (617) 828-5400   Emp: 136
    Bus: *US Mfr. of reinforced single-ply thermoplastic*   Fax:(617) 8285365   %FO: 100
      roofing and waterproofing membranes.

● **SAURER GROUP**
Stelzenstrasse 6, CH-8152 Glattbrugg, Switzerland
CEO: Heinrich Fischer, CEO   Tel: 41-1-809-4111   Emp: 8000
Bus: *Mfr. textile machinery, textile system components.*   Fax:41-1-809-4110

    SCHLAFHORST INC
    8801 South Blvd, Charlotte, NC   28273
    CEO: Tracy E. Tindal, Pres. & CEO   Tel: (704) 554-0800   Emp: 188
    Bus: *Sale/service textile equipment, machinery &*   Fax:(704) 554-7350   %FO: 100
      parts.

● **SBC WARBURG DILLON READ, INC.**
Aeschenplatz 6, CH-4002 Basel, Switzerland
CEO: Marcel Ospel, CEO   Tel: 41-61-288-2020   Emp: 18000
Bus: *International banking and asset management*   Fax:41-61-288-9923
services.

    SBC WARBURG DILLON READ, INC.
    277 Park Avenue, New York, NY   10172
    CEO: Simon Canning, Pres.   Tel: (212) 224-7000   Emp: 2400
    Bus: *Investment banking and advisory services.*   Fax:(212) 224-7251   %FO: 100

    SWISS BANK CORP
    Swiss Bank Tower, 10 East 50th St., 32nd Fl., New York, NY   10022
    CEO: Simon Canning, Pres.   Tel: (212) 574-3000   Emp: N/A
    Bus: *International banking services. Relocating to*   Fax:(212) 574-5499   %FO: 100
      SBC Warburg Dillon Read Center 1, 677
      Washington Blvd., Stamford, CT 06912. (203)
      719-3000

- **SCHINDLER HOLDING AG**
Seestrasse 55, CH-6052 Hergiswil, Switzerland
CEO: Alfred N. Schindler, Vice Chrm.   Tel: 41-41-958550   Emp: N/A
Bus: *Elevators and escalators.*   Fax:41-41-393134

> **SCHINDLER ELEVATOR CORPORATION**
> 20 Whippany Road, Morristown, NJ   07962
> CEO: Erich Ammann, VP & CFO   Tel: (201) 397-6264   Emp: 5900
> Bus: *Manufacture/sales/service of elevators and* Fax:(201) 397-6142   %FO: 100
> *escalators*

> **SCHINDLER ELEVATOR CORPORATION**
> 1900 Center Prk Drive, Suite J, Charlotte, NC   28217
> CEO: Ray Falduti, District Mgr.   Tel: (704) 329-1471   Emp: N/A
> Bus: *Install and service/modernize elevators and* Fax:(704) 329-1478   %FO: 100
> *escalators*

- **SIEGFRIED LTD.**
CH-4800 Zofingen, Switzerland
CEO: B. Siegfried, Chrm.   Tel: 41-62-746-1111   Emp: N/A
Bus: *Mfr. pharmaceuticals, bulk medical chemicals.* Fax:41-62-746-1202

> **GANES CHEMICALS INC.**
> 630 Broad Street, Carlstadt, NJ   07072
> CEO: Rolf Reinstried, Pres.   Tel: (201) 507-4300   Emp: N/A
> Bus: *Mfr. bulk medical chemicals.*   Fax:(201) 507-1930   %FO: 100

- **SMH SWISS WATCHMAKING CORP.**
6, Faubourg du Lac, 2501 Bienne, Switzerland
CEO: Nicholas G. Hayek, Chrm.   Tel: 41-32-343-6811   Emp: N/A
Bus: *Mfr../marketing of major brand watches including* Fax:41-32-343-6911
Blancpain, Omega, Longines, Hamilton, Balmain,
Swatch.

> **SMH USA INC.**
> 1200 Harbor Boulevard, Weehawken, NJ   07087
> CEO: Roland Streule, Pres. & CEO   Tel: (201) 271-4680   Emp: 400
> Bus: *Assembly/repair/distribution of watches,*   Fax:(201) 271-4709   %FO: 100
> *clocks and movements.*

- **SNH FINANCE LTD. (SWISSÔTEL)**
PO Box 8058, Zurich Airport, Zurich, Switzerland
CEO: Bruno Niederer, SVP, Finance   Tel: 41-01-812-5451   Emp: N/A
Bus: *Hotel industry.*   Fax:41-01-812-9490

> **THE DRAKE SWISSÔTEL**
> 440 Park Avenue, New York, NY   10022
> CEO: J. Gerrese, Gen. Mgr.   Tel: (212) 421-0900   Emp: 270
> Bus: *International hotel.*   Fax:(212) 752-4593   %FO: 100

SWISSÔTEL ATLANTA
3391 Peachtree Road, Atlanta, GA   30326
CEO: Marvin Perez, Gen. Mgr.   Tel: (404) 365-0065   Emp: 275
Bus: *International hotel.*   Fax:(404) 365-8434   %FO: 100

SWISSÔTEL BOSTON
One Avenue de Lafayette, Boston, MA   02111
CEO: David Gibbons, Gen. Mgr.   Tel: (617) 745-1005   Emp: 240
Bus: *International hotel.*   Fax:(617) 451-0054   %FO: 100

SWISSÔTEL CHICAGO
323 Wacker Drive, Chicago, IL   60601
CEO: Carl Kortum, Gen. Mgr.   Tel: (312) 565-0565   Emp: 275
Bus: *International hotel.*   Fax:(312) 565-0540   %FO: 100

• STAEFA CONTROL SYSTEM AG
CH-8712 Stafa, Switzerland
CEO: Robert Bachmann, Pres.   Tel: 41-1-928-6111   Emp: 2495
Bus: *HVAC controls.*   Fax:N/A

LANDIS & STAEFA, INC.
1000 Deerfield Parkway, Buffalo Grove, IL   60089
CEO: John Grad, Pres.   Tel: (847) 215-1050   Emp: 900
Bus: *Manufacturer of heating and air conditioning*   Fax:(847) 215-1093   %FO: 100
     equipment. (JV with Landis & Gyr AG)

LANDIS & STAEFA, INC.
9835 Carroll Center Rd., Ste. 100, San Diego, CA   92126
CEO: Frank Shadpour, Gen.Mgr.   Tel: (619) 693-8711   Emp: 180
Bus: *Manufacturer of heating & air conditioning*   Fax:(619) 693-1896   %FO: 100
     equipment.

• STAEUBLI INTERNATIONAL AG
Poststrasse 5, 8808 Pfäffikon, Switzerland
CEO: Anthony O. Stäubli, Pres. & CEO   Tel: 41-55-410-8161   Emp: N/A
Bus: *Mfr.. textile machinery, robot systems, weaving* Fax:41-55-410-4626
     preparation systems and quick connect couplings.

STAEUBLI CORPORATION
201 Parkway West, PO Box 189, Duncan, SC   29334
CEO: Harald Behrend, VP   Tel: (864) 433-1980   Emp: 100
Bus: *Sales/service for textile machines, robot*   Fax:(864) 433-1988   %FO: 100
     systems, weaving preparation systems and
     quick safety couplings.

• SULZER AG

P.O.Box 414, Winterthur, CH-8401 Switzerland

CEO: Dr. Fritz Fahrni, Pres.	Tel: 41-52-262-1122	Emp: N/A
Bus: *Engineering systems: textile, energy, oil, gas &* *chemicals, mining, water technology, wood & food* *products industries.*	Fax:41-52-262-0101	

CALCITEK, INC.

2320 Faraday Avenue, Carlsbad, CA   92008

CEO: Steven Hanson, Pres.	Tel: (760) 431-9515	Emp: 125
Bus: *Design/mfr. dental implants.*	Fax:(760) 431-9753	%FO: 100

CARBOMEDICS, INC.

1300 East Anderson Lane, Austin, TX   78752

CEO: Terry L. Marlatt, Pres.	Tel: (512) 873-3200	Emp: 900
Bus: *Design/mfr. medical devices.*	Fax:(512) 873-3395	%FO: 100

ELMA ELECTRONICS INC.

44350 Grimmer Blvd., Fremont, CA   94538

CEO: Fred Ruegg, Pres.	Tel: (510) 656-3400	Emp: 100
Bus: *Design/mfr. electronics.*	Fax:(510) 656-3783	%FO: 100

HICKHAM INC.

11518 Old La Porte Road, La Porte, TX   77571

CEO: Donald E. Babb, Pres.	Tel: (713) 471-6540	Emp: 200
Bus: *Servicing industrial processing machinery.*	Fax:(713) 471-4821	%FO: 100

INTERMEDICS ORTHOPEDICS, INC.

1300 East Anderson Lane, Austin, TX   78752

CEO: Jerry L Marlar, Pres.	Tel: (512) 835-1970	Emp: 600
Bus: *Design/mfr. orthopedic medical devices.*	Fax:(512) 835-6014	%FO: 100

INTERMEDICS, INC.

4000 Technology Drive, Angleton, TX   77515

CEO: John E. Garcia, Pres.	Tel: (409) 848-4000	Emp: 1600
Bus: *Design/mfr. medical devices.*	Fax:(409) 848-4137	%FO: 100

SULZER (USA) INC.

200 Park Avenue, New York, NY   10022

CEO: José Galindéz, Pres.	Tel: (212) 949-0999	Emp: 36
Bus: *Import/sales/service of machinery and systems* *for process technology.*	Fax:(212) 370-1138	%FO: 100

SULZER BINGHAM PUMPS INC.

2800 Northwest Front Avenue, Portland, OR   97210

CEO: Robert L. Ayers, Pres.	Tel: (503) 226-5200	Emp: 850
Bus: *Design/sales/service pumps; energy industry .*	Fax:(503) 226-5286	%FO: 100

SULZER INC.

200 Park Avenue, 16th Fl., New York, NY   10166-0068

CEO: Alexander Bossard, Pres.	Tel: (212) 949-0999	Emp: 11
Bus: *US holding company.*	Fax:(212) 661-0533	%FO: 100

SULZER METCO (US) INC.

1101 Prospect Avenue, PO Box 1006, Westbury, NY   11590

CEO: Mario Kyd, Pres.	Tel: (516) 334-1300	Emp: 360
Bus: *Design/mfr. industrial spraying materials & systems.*	Fax:(516) 338-2488	%FO: 100

SULZER RUTI INC.

1-85 & Highway 9, P.O.Box 5332, Spartansburg, SC   29304

CEO: Peter Egloff, Pres.	Tel: (864) 585-5255	Emp: 75
Bus: *Sales/service textile machinery.*	Fax:(864) 585-5064	%FO: 100

• SWAROVSKI INTERNATIONAL HOLDING AG

General-Wille-Strasse 88, P.O. Box 163, CH-8706 Feldmeilen, Switzerland

CEO: Michael Gentes, CEO	Tel: 41-19-257-111	Emp: N/A
Bus: *Mfr./sales/service crystal objects & gifts.*	Fax:41-19-257-210	

SWAROVSKI AMERICA LTD.

2 Slater Road, Cranston, RI   02920

CEO: Michael Gentes, CEO	Tel: (401) 463-8848	Emp: 175
Bus: *Mfr./sales/service crystal objects & gifts.*	Fax:(401) 463-8459	%FO: 100

SWAROVSKI JEWELRY US LTD.

One Kenney Drive, Cranston, RI   02920-4400

CEO: Daniel Cohen, CEO	Tel: (401) 463-6400	Emp: 550
Bus: *Mfr. jewelry.*	Fax:(401) 463-5257	%FO: 100

• SWISS LIFE RENTENANSTALT

General Guisan Quai 40, CH-8022 Zurich, Switzerland

CEO: Dr. Carl Muhlebach, CEO	Tel: 41-1-284-3797	Emp: N/A
Bus: *Insurance services.*	Fax:41-1-202-1980	

ALLMERICA FINANCIAL

First Americas Financial, 440 Lincoln Street, Worcester, MA   01653

CEO: John O'Brien, Pres.	Tel: (508) 855-1000	Emp: N/A
Bus: *Employee benefit & insurance consultants.*	Fax:(508) 853-6332	%FO: 100

SWISS LIFE NORTH AMERICAN INTERNATIONAL SERVICES INC.

1200 E. Ridgwood Ave, Ridgwood, NJ   07450

CEO: Philipp A. Frei, Pres.	Tel: (201) 670-1515	Emp: 11
Bus: *International employee benefit, insurance & consulting services.*	Fax:(201) 670-0709	%FO: 100

● **SWISS REINSURANCE CO**
Mythenquai 50/60, CH-8022 Zurich, Switzerland
CEO: Walter Kielholz, Chrm.　　　　　　　Tel: 41-1-208-2929　　　Emp: N/A
Bus: *Insurance and reinsurance services.*　　Fax:41-1-285-2999

NORTH AMERICAN SPECIALTY INSURANCE CO.
650 Elm Street, 6th Fl., Manchester, NH　03101-2524
CEO: James P. Slattery, Pres.　　　　　　Tel: (603) 644-6600　　Emp: 100
Bus: *Insurance services.*　　　　　　　　Fax:(603) 644-6613　　%FO: 100

SWISS REINSURANCE ADVISERS INC.
200 Park Avenue, New York, NY　10166
CEO: Stanley Taben, Pres.　　　　　　　　Tel: (212) 973-5000　　Emp: 24
Bus: *International investment advisory services.*　Fax:(212) 297-3508　　%FO: 100

SWISS REINSURANCE AMERICAN CORP.
237 Park Avenue, New York, NY　10017
CEO: Heide E. Hutter, Chrm. & Pres.　　　Tel: (212) 907-8000　　Emp: 54
Bus: *Property and casualty reinsurance*　　Fax:(212) 907-8728　　%FO: 100
　　　underwriters

● **SWISSAIR**
P.O.Box 8058, Zurich-Airport, CH-8058 Zurich, Switzerland
CEO: Hannes Goetz, Chrm.　　　　　　　　Tel: 41-1-812-1212　　　Emp: N/A
Bus: *International air transport services.*　　Fax:41-1-810-8046

SWISSAIR N.A. - Headquarters
41 Pinelawn Road, Melville, NY　11747
CEO: Jean-Pierre Allemann, Pres.　　　　　Tel: (516) 844-4550　　Emp: 174
Bus: *International air transport services.*　　Fax:(516) 844-4559　　%FO: 100

SWISSAIR
3391 Peachtree Road, Ste. 210, Atlanta, GA　30326
CEO: E. Suhr, Gen. Mgr.　　　　　　　　　Tel: (404) 814-6300　　Emp: 20
Bus: *International air transport services.*　　Fax:(404) 814-6319　　%FO: 100

SWISSAIR
20 Park Plaza, Boston, MA　02116
CEO: Gerry Walther, Gen. Mgr.　　　　　　Tel: (617) 556-5000　　Emp: 50
Bus: *International air transport services.*　　Fax:(617) 556-5020　　%FO: 100

SWISSAIR
222 N. Sepulveda Blvd., 15th Fl., El Segundo, CA　90245
CEO: D. Luethi, Gen. Mgr.　　　　　　　　Tel: (310) 335-5900　　Emp: 25
Bus: *International air transport services.*　　Fax:(310) 335-5935　　%FO: 100

SWISSAIR
150 N. Michigan Ave., Ste. 2900, Chicago, IL　60601
CEO: J. Patrick O'Brien, Gen. Mgr.　　　　Tel: (312) 630-5820　　Emp: 100
Bus: *International air transport services.*　　Fax:(312) 630-5825　　%FO: 100

SWISSAIR
608 Fifth Avenue, New York, NY   10022
CEO: Mark Ellinger, Gen. Mgr. Tel: (212) 969-5760 Emp: 15
Bus: *International air transport services.* Fax:(212) 969-5746 %FO: 100

SWISSAIR
One Bala Plaza, Philadelphia, PA   19004
CEO: R. Zbinden, Mgr. Tel: (610) 660-5480 Emp: 15
Bus: *International air transport services.* Fax:(610) 660-5490 %FO: 100

SWISSAIR
1717 K Street, NE, Ste. 1100, Washington, DC   20006
CEO: P. Huber, Gen. Mgr. Tel: (202) 785-5500 Emp: 15
Bus: *International air transport services.* Fax:(202) 855-5510 %FO: 100

● **TEUSCHER CONFISERIE**
Storchengasse 9, 8001 Zurich, Switzerland
CEO: R. Teuscher, Pres. & CEO Tel: 41-01-211-5151 Emp: N/A
Bus: *Handmade Swiss chocolates.* Fax:41-01-212-2958

TEUSCHER CHOCOLATES OF SWITZERLAND
620 Fifth Avenue, New York, NY   10020
CEO: Brad Bloom, Mgr. Tel: (212) 246-4416 Emp: 18
Bus: *Sales of handmade Swiss chocolates.* Fax:(212) 765-8134 %FO: 100

● **COMPAGNIE FINANCIÈRE TRADITION**
11, rue de Langallerie, P.O.Box 2400, CH-1002 Lausanne, Switzerland
CEO: N/A Tel: 41-21-343-5252 Emp: N/A
Bus: *International securities broker.* Fax:41-21-3435500

TRADITION (GOVERNMENT SECURITIES) INC.
61 Broadway, 4th Fl., New York, NY   10006
CEO: Raymond Baccala, Mng. Dir. Tel: (212) 797-5300 Emp: 25
Bus: *International securities dealer.* Fax:(212) 797-7204 %FO: 100

TRADITION (NORTH AMERICAN) INC.
61 Broadway, 4th Fl., New York, NY   10006
CEO: Emil Assentato, Mng. Dir. Tel: (212) 797-5300 Emp: 175
Bus: *International securities dealer.* Fax:(212) 797-7207 %FO: 100

TRADITION DERIVATIVES CORP.
180 Maiden Lane, 20th Fl., New York, NY   10038
CEO: Jeff Mehan Tel: (212) 943-6916 Emp: 10
Bus: *International securities dealer.* Fax:(212) 943-8504 %FO: 100

TRADITION FINANCIAL SERVICES INC.
180 Maiden Lane, 1st Fl., New York, NY   10038
CEO: David Pinchin, Pres. Tel: (212) 943-6916 Emp: 50
Bus: *International securities dealer.* Fax:(212) 943-8504 %FO: 100

- **UNION BANCAIRE PRIVEE**
96-98 rue du Rhone, CH-1211 Geneva, Switzerland
CEO: N/A   Tel: 44-22-819-2111   Emp: N/A
Bus: *International private investment banking services.*   Fax:N/A

> **UNION BANCAIRE PRIVEE**
> 630 Fifth Avenue, Suite 1525, New York, NY   10111
> CEO: Maurice de Picciotto, Rep.   Tel: (212) 265-3320   Emp: N/A
> Bus: *International private investment baking*   Fax:(212) 247-4310   %FO: 100
>   *services.*

- **UNION BANK OF SWITZERLAND**
Bahnhofstrasse 45, CH-8021 Zurich, Switzerland
CEO: Robert Studer, Chrm.   Tel: 41-1-234-1111   Emp: 29000
Bus: *Banking, securities trading & underwriting, asset* Fax:41-1-236-5111
    management and corporate finance services.

> **UBS ASSET MANAGEMENT (NEW YORK) INC.**
> 1345 Avenue of the Americas, New York, NY   10105
> CEO: James McCoughan, Pres.   Tel: (212) 649-7100   Emp: N/A
> Bus: *Institutional asset management services.*   Fax:(212) 698-6565   %FO: 100

> **UBS ASSET MANAGEMENT INC**
> 555 California Street, Suite 4650, San Francisco, CA   94104
> CEO: Nance Tengler, Mng. Dir.   Tel: (415) 352-5555   Emp: N/A
> Bus: *Institutional asset management services.*   Fax:(415) 698-6521   %FO: 100

> **UBS SECURITIES LLC**
> 30 South Wacker Drive, Chicago, IL   60606
> CEO: Michael Reilly, VP   Tel: (312) 993-5630   Emp: N/A
> Bus: *Securities trading & underwriting services.*   Fax:(312) 993-5614   %FO: 100

> **UBS SECURITIES LLC**
> 299 Park Avenue, New York, NY   10171
> CEO: Richard C. Capone, Pres. & CEO   Tel: (212) 821-4000   Emp: 600
> Bus: *Securities trading & underwriting services.*   Fax:(212) 821-3285   %FO: 100

> **UBS SECURITIES LLC**
> 555 California Street, Ste. 4650, San Francisco, CA   94104
> CEO: Jim Fueille, Mng. Dir.   Tel: (415) 352-5650   Emp: N/A
> Bus: *Securities trading & underwriting services.*   Fax:(212) 352-5510   %FO: 100

> **UNION BANK OF SWITZERLAND - North America Region**
> 299 Park Avenue, New York, NY   10171-0026
> CEO: Richard C. Capone, Pres. & CEO   Tel: (212) 821-3000   Emp: 2200
> Bus: *Banking, securities trading & underwriting,*   Fax:(212) 715-3285   %FO: 100
>   *asset management and corporate finance*
>   *services.*

UNION BANK OF SWITZERLAND - Los Angeles Branch
444 South Flower Street, Los Angeles, CA 90071
CEO: Roger Wacker, Mgr. Tel: (213) 489-0600 Emp: N/A
Bus: *Banking, securities trading & underwriting,* Fax:(213) 489-0637 %FO: 100
asset management and corporate finance
services.

UNION BANK OF SWITZERLAND - San Francisco Branch
555 California Street, San Francisco, CA 94104
CEO: Robert G. Vanneman, Mgr. Tel: (415) 398-4411 Emp: N/A
Bus: *Banking, securities trading & underwriting,* Fax:(415) 433-3682 %FO: 100
asset management and corporate finance
services.

UNION BANK OF SWITZERLAND - Texas Agency
1100 Louisiana, Suite 4500, Houston, TX 77002
CEO: Evans Swann, Mgr. Tel: (713) 655-6500 Emp: N/A
Bus: *Banking, securities trading & underwriting,* Fax:(713) 655-6553 %FO: 100
asset management and corporate finance
services.

● **VIBRO-METER SA**
P.O.Box 1071, CH-1701 Fribourg, Switzerland
CEO: Dr. Richard W. Greaves, Pres. Tel: 41-26-407-1111 Emp: 500
Bus: *Design/mfr. transducers & electronic measuring* Fax:41-26-407-1731
instruments.

VIBRO-METER CORP
3995 Via Oro Avenue, Long Beach, CA 90810
CEO: Ronald Vadas, VP Tel: (310) 830-7778 Emp: 40
Bus: *Design/mfr. transducers & electronic* Fax:(310) 830-2300 %FO: 100
measuring instruments.

● **VOLKART BROTHERS HOLDING LTD.**
8401 Winterthur, Switzerland
CEO: Andreas Reinhart, Chrm. & Pres. Tel: 41-52-212-1212 Emp: N/A
Bus: *Holding company.* Fax:41-52-212-9444

ANDERSON CLAYTON CORPORATION
615 South 51st Avenue, Phoenix, AZ 85062
CEO: Walter Locher, CEO Tel: (602) 272-2641 Emp: 1300
Bus: *Processor of cotton and cotton seeds.* Fax:(602) 278-7456 %FO: 100

VOLKART INTERNATIONAL, INC.
PO Box 2988, Phoenix, AZ 85062
CEO: Walter Locher, Pres. Tel: (602) 447-4250 Emp: 15
Bus: *Cotton trading.* Fax:(602) 447-4269 %FO: 100

- **VON MOOS HOLDING AG**
Kasernen Platz 1, CH-6002 Lucerne, Switzerland
CEO: Dr. Peter Kratz, Pres.   Tel: 41-41-595111   Emp: 2200
Bus: *Mfr. steel products.*   Fax:41-41-595020

    COMMERCIAL PANTEX SIKA, INC.
    1032 East Chestnut, Louisville, KY   40204
    CEO: B. Hodgsen, Mgr.   Tel: (502) 473-1010   Emp: 40
    Bus: *Mfr. steel ribs/girders/plates for tunnel*   Fax:(502) 473-0707   %FO: 100
        construction.

    CONNECTICUT STEEL CORP
    30 Toelles Road, PO Box 928, Wallingford, CT   06492
    CEO: W. Fergus Porter, Pres.   Tel: (203) 265-0615   Emp: 185
    Bus: *Mfr. wire rod, mesh, rebar coils.*   Fax:(203) 284-8125   %FO: 100

- **VON ROLL HOLDING LTD.**
Bahnhofstrasse, Gerlafingen, CH-4563, Switzerland
CEO: Max D. Amstutz, CEO   Tel: 41-32-674-2234   Emp: 5700
Bus: *Environmental engineering & services, electrical*   Fax:41-32-674-2208
insulation, casting, pressure pipes & valves.

    IMI INSULATING MATERIALS INC.
    One Campbell Road, Schenectady, NY   12306
    CEO: Gary Bivona, Pres.   Tel: (518) 344-7200   Emp: 230
    Bus: *Mfr./sale insulation materials.*   Fax:(518) 344-7287   %FO: 100

    VON ROLL INC.
    3025 Breckinridge Blvd., Suite 170, Duluth, GA   30136
    CEO: Mitch Gorski, VP   Tel: (770) 925-9997   Emp: 10
    Bus: *Waste management, sewage treatment,*   Fax:(770) 925-9957   %FO: 100
        multiple hearth plants, recovery systems.

    WASTE TECHNOLOGIES INDUSTRIES
    1250 St. George Street, East Liverpool, OH   43920
    CEO: Fred Sigg, VP   Tel: (330) 385-7337   Emp: 170
    Bus: *Waste incineration, waste management,*   Fax:(330) 385-7813   %FO: 100
        remedial consulting.

- **VONTOBEL HOLDING LTD.**
Toedistrasse #27, CH-8022 Zurich, Switzerland
CEO: Dr. Hans Dieter, Chrm.   Tel: 41-1-283-5900   Emp: 558
Bus: *Banking & financial services holding company,*   Fax:41-1-283-7500
parent of Bank J. Vontobel & Co. Ltd.

    VONTOBEL USA INC.
    450 Park Avnue, New York, NY   10022
    CEO: Henry Schlegel, Pres.   Tel: (212) 415-7000   Emp: 20
    Bus: *Investment advisory.*   Fax:(212) 750-7853   %FO: 100

- **WAGNER INTERNATIONAL AG**
Industriestrasse 22, Altstaetten, Switzerland
CEO: Tel:41-71-757-2268   Emp:
Bus: *Mfr. Paint spray equipment.*   Fax:41-71-757-2268:

   WAGNER SPRAY TECH CORPORATION
   1770 Fernbrook Lane, Plymouth, MN   55447
   CEO: Sean C. James, Pres.   Tel: (612) 553-7000   Emp: 300
   Bus: *Mfr. paint spray equipment.*   Fax:(612) 553-7288   %FO: 100

- **WEITNAUER TRADING COMPANY LTD.**
Petersgasse 36-38, 4001 Basel, Switzerland
CEO: N/A   Tel: N/A   Emp: N/A
Bus: *Watchmakers.*   Fax:N/A

   DUTREPEX
   Newark International Airport, Bldg. C, Newark, NJ   07114
   CEO: N/A   Tel: (201) 623-6761   Emp: 25
   Bus: *Operation of airport duty free shops.*   Fax:(201) 623-8654   %FO: 100

   WEITNAUER AMERICA TRADING SERVICES INC.
   2335 N.W. 107th Avenue, Miami, FL   33172

   CEO: Manuel Sosa, Gen. Mgr.   Tel: (305) 591-1763   Emp: 40
   Bus: *Supplier of duty free merchandise to   Fax:(305) 593-9893   %FO: 100
        cruise/cargo ships, duty free retailers,
        airliners, military/diplomatic corps.*

   WEITNAUER AMERICA, INC.
   200 East Robinson Street, Suite 500, Orlando, FL   32801
   CEO: Robert Hendry, Chrm.   Tel: (407) 843-5850   Emp: N/A
   Bus: *U.S. headquarters. Holding company.*   Fax:(407) 425-7905   %FO: 100

   WEITNAUER GROUP OF COMPANIES
   11420 Kendall Drive, Ste. 202, Miami, FL   33178
   CEO: J. Gonzales, Reg. Dir.   Tel: (305) 595-7907   Emp: N/A
   Bus: *Regional headquarters.*   Fax:(305) 595-1388   %FO: 100

   WEITNAUER HOUSTON, INC.
   PO Box 279, Humble, TX   77347
   CEO: Daniel Abitbol, Gen. Mgr.   Tel: (713) 233-7380   Emp: 40
   Bus: *Operation of airport duty free shops.*   Fax:(713) 233-7385   %FO: 100

   WEITNAUER ORLANDO DUTY FREE & RETAIL LTD.
   9649 Tradeport Drive, Zone Nr. 42, Orlando, FL   32827

   CEO: R. Janmohamed, Mgr.   Tel: (407) 859-7530   Emp: 75
   Bus: *Operation of duty free shops.*   Fax:(407) 851-6383   %FO: 100

• WINTERTHUR SWISS INSURANCE CO.
Gen Guisanstrasse 40, CH-8400 Zurich, Switzerland
CEO: Peter Späiti, Pres.   Tel: 41-52-261-1111   Emp: N/A
Bus: *General insurance services.*   Fax:41-52-261-3083

BLUE RIDGE INSURANCE COMPANIES
86 Hopmeadow Street, Simsbury, CT   06070
CEO: Peter Christen, Pres.   Tel: (860) 651-1065   Emp: N/A
Bus: *General insurance services.*   Fax:(860) 408-3266   %FO: 100

GENERAL CASUALTY INSURANCE
One General Drive, Sun Prairie, WI   53596
CEO: John R. Pollock, Pres.   Tel: (608) 837-4440   Emp: N/A
Bus: *General insurance services.*   Fax:(608) 837-0583   %FO: 100

REPUBLIC FINANCIAL SERVICES, INC.
2727 Turtle Creek Boulevard, Dallas, TX   75219
CEO: W. C. Hassard, Pres.   Tel: (214) 559-1222   Emp: N/A
Bus: *Holding company: finance, general insurance*   Fax:(214) 748-9590   %FO: 100
    services.

SOUTHERN GUARANTY INSURANCE COMPANIES
2545 Taylor Road, Montgomery, AL   36117
CEO: James L. Riding, Pres.   Tel: (334) 270-6000   Emp: N/A
Bus: *General insurance services.*   Fax:(334) 270-6198   %FO: 100

UNIGARD INSURANCE GROUP
15805 NE 24th Street, Bellevue, WA   98008
CEO: Laurence P. O'Connor, Pres.   Tel: (425) 641-4321   Emp: N/A
Bus: *General insurance services.*   Fax:(425) 562-5256   %FO: 100

WINTERTHUR LIFE RE
2727 Turtle Creek Boulevard, Dallas, TX   75265-0391
CEO: Gordon Jardin, Pres.   Tel: (214) 559-1800   Emp: N/A
Bus: *General insurance and reinsurance services.*   Fax:(214) 522-8417   %FO: 100

WINTERTHUR REINSURANCE CORP. OF AMERICA
2 World Financial, 225 Liberty St., 42nd. Fl., New York, NY   10281-1076
CEO: John G. Bidell, Pres.   Tel: (212) 416-5700   Emp: N/A
Bus: *General insurance and reinsurance services.*   Fax:(212) 524-6839   %FO: 100

WINTERTHUR U.S. HOLDINGS, INC.
902 Market Street, 13th Floor, Wilmington, DE   19899-5130
CEO: Dr. Hans-Rudolf Stücki, Pres.   Tel: (302) 655-2875   Emp: N/A
Bus: *Holding company: finance, general insurance*   Fax:(302) 655-2875   %FO: 100
    services.

● **WOODTEC FANKHAUSER**
Oberdorfstrasse 21, Reiden, CH-6260, Switzerland
CEO: Thomas Fankhauser, Pres. Tel: 41-62-7583170 Emp: N/A
Bus: *Mfr. vacuum gluing systems.* Fax:41-62-7583966

    E & R SYSTEM TECHNIK INC.
    85 St. George Road, Springfield, MA 01104
    CEO: Robert G. Weithofer, Pres. Tel: (413) 827-7600 Emp: 10
    Bus: *Imports/distributes specialty woodworking* Fax:(413) 827-0696 %FO: 100
    machinery & vacuum coaters.

● **ZEHNDER HOLDING LTD.**
Moortalstrasse 1, 5722 Gränichen, Switzerland
CEO: Paul Aeschimann, VP Tel: 41-62-855-1500 Emp: N/A
Bus: *Holding company.* Fax:41-62-855-1515

    HAENNI INSTRUMENTS, INC.
    1107 Wright Avenue, Gretna, LA 70056
    CEO: David Morgan, Gen. Mgr. Tel: (504) 392-3344 Emp: 5
    Bus: *Sales of pressure gauges.* Fax:(504) 392-6500 %FO: 100

    RUNTAL NORTH AMERICA, INC.
    187 Neck Road, PO Box 8278, Ward Hill, MA 01835
    CEO: Wesley Owens, EVP Tel: (508) 373-1666 Emp: 35
    Bus: *Mfr./sales of special radiators.* Fax:(508) 372-7140 %FO: 100

    VIATRAN CORPORATION
    300 Industrial Drive, Grand Island, NY 14072
    CEO: Donald Joslyn, CEO Tel: (716) 773-1700 Emp: 125
    Bus: *Pressure transducers and transmitters;* Fax:(716) 773-2488 %FO: 100
    measuring systems.

● **EGON ZEHNDER INTERNATIONAL, INC.**
Toblerstrasse 80, P.O. 231, CH-8044 Zurich, Switzerland
CEO: Dr. Mark R. Hoenig, Managing Partner Tel: 41-1-267-6969 Emp: N/A
Bus: *Executive & board search; management consulting.* Fax:41-1-267-6967

    EGON ZEHNDER INTERNATIONAL, INC.
    One Atlantic Center, Suite 3000, Atlanta, GA 30306
    CEO: Joel M. Koblentz, Managing Partner Tel: (404) 875-3000 Emp: 9
    Bus: *Executive & board search, management* Fax:(404) 876-4578 %FO: 100
    consulting.

    EGON ZEHNDER INTERNATIONAL, INC.
    100 Spear Street, Suite 1135, San Francisco, CA 90071
    CEO: S. Ross Brown, Mg Ptnr. Tel: (415) 904-7800 Emp: 7
    Bus: *Executive & board search, management* Fax:(415) 904-7801 %FO: 100
    consulting.

EGON ZEHNDER INTERNATIONAL, INC.
One First National Plaza, Suite 3300, Chicago, IL   60603

CEO: Kai Lindholst, Mg Ptnr.	Tel: (312) 782-4500	Emp: 20
Bus: *Executive & board search, management consulting.*	Fax:(312) 782-2846	%FO: 100

EGON ZEHNDER INTERNATIONAL, INC.
55 East 59th Street, 14th Fl., New York, NY   10022

CEO: Fortunat Mueller-Maerki, Mng. Ptnr.	Tel: (212) 838-9199	Emp: 25
Bus: *Executive & board search, management consulting.*	Fax:(212) 750-0574	%FO: 100

● **ZUELLIG GROUP OF COMPANIES**
P O Box 1049, CH-8640 Rapperswil, Switzerland

CEO: Oscar Hoehn, Director	Tel: 41-55-278200	Emp: N/A
Bus: *Holding company.*	Fax:41-55-274473	

WILCOX NATURAL PRODUCTS
P O Box 391, Boone, NC   28607

CEO: Chuck Wanzer, Pres.	Tel: (704) 264-3615	Emp: 43
Bus: *Wholesale botanicals.*	Fax:(704) 264-2831	%FO: 80

ZETAPHARM, INC.
70 West 36th Street, New York, NY   10018

CEO: D. Luelsdorf, Pres	Tel: (212) 643-2310	Emp: 20
Bus: *Import distribution pharmaceuticals & food additives, generic pharmaceuticals*	Fax:(212) 643-2316	%FO: 100

ZUELLIG BOTANICALS INC
2550 El Presidio St, Long Beach, CA   90810

CEO: Volker Wypyfzyk, Pres	Tel: (310) 637-9566	Emp: 50
Bus: *Botanicals.*	Fax:(310) 637-3644	%FO: 100

● **ZURICH INSURANCE CO**
Mythenquai 2, CH-8022 Zurich, Switzerland

CEO: Rolf F. Hüppi, Pres.	Tel: 41-1-205-2121	Emp: 36000
Bus: *Insurance, risk management products, investment advisory services.*	Fax:41-1-201-3397	

EMPIRE FIRE AND MARINE INSURANCE COMPANY
1624 Douglas Street, Omaha, NE   68102

CEO: John J. McCartney, Pres.	Tel: (402) 341-0135	Emp: N/A
Bus: *Property and casualty insurance.*	Fax:(402) 271-2509	%FO: 100

FIDELITY AND DEPOSIT COMPANY OF MARYLAND
300 Saint Paul Place, PO Box 1227, Baltimore, MD   21203

CEO: Richard F. Williams, Chrm. & Pres.	Tel: (410) 539-0800	Emp: N/A
Bus: *Surety bonding services.*	Fax:(410) 539-7002	%FO: 100

MARYLAND PERSONAL INSURANCE GROUP
3910 Keswick Road, 4 NE, Baltimore, MD   21211
CEO: John A. Karanik, Pres.   Tel: (410) 366-1000   Emp: N/A
Bus: *Insurance services.*   Fax:(410) 338-9526   %FO: 100

UNIVERSAL UNDERWRITERS INSURANCE CO.
6363 College Blvd., Overland Park, KS   66211
CEO: Kenneth F. Goldstein, Pres.   Tel: (913) 339-1000   Emp: N/A
Bus: *Property & casualty insurance underwriting*   Fax:(913) 469-3727   %FO: 100
    services.

ZURICH INSURANCE GROUP - U.S.
325 Seventh Street, NW, Ste.1225, Washington, DC   20004-2801
CEO: Sean Cassidy, VP   Tel: (202) 628-7065   Emp: 9800
Bus: *Government affairs representative office.*   Fax: %FO: 100

ZURICH KEMPER INVESTMENTS INC.
222 South Riverside Plaza, Chicago, IL   60606
CEO: Steven B. Timbers, Pres.   Tel: (312) 537-7000   Emp: N/A
Bus: *Institutional and mutual fund asset*   Fax:(312) 537-5609   %FO: 100
    management.

ZURICH KEMPER LIFE ASSURANCE CO
One Kemper Drive, Long Grove, IL   60049
CEO: John B. Scott, Pres.   Tel: (847) 320-4500   Emp: N/A
Bus: *Insurance services.*   Fax:(847) 550-5530   %FO: 100

ZURICH LIFE INSURANCE COMPANY OF AMERICA
Zurich Towers, 1400 American Lane, Schaumburg, IL   60173-4987
CEO: John B. Scott, Pres.   Tel: (847) 517-7900   Emp: N/A
Bus: *Life insurance.*   Fax:(847) 517-8397   %FO: 100

ZURICH REINSURANCE CENTRE INC.
One Chase Manhattan Plaza, New York, NY   10005
CEO: Steven M. Gluckstern, Pres.   Tel: (212) 898-5300   Emp: N/A
Bus: *Reinsurance and insurance services.*   Fax:(212) 898-5400   %FO: 100

ZURICH-AMERICAN INSURANCE COMPANIES
Zurich Towers, 1400 American Lane, Schaumburg, IL   60196-1056
CEO: Constantine Iordanou, Pres.   Tel: (847) 605-6000   Emp: 9800
Bus: *Insurance, risk management products &*   Fax:(847) 605-6011   %FO: 100
    services.

- **ZUST & BACHMEIER AG**
Palazzo Zuest & Bachmeier, CH-6830 Chiasso, Switzerland
CEO: E Scherer, Chrm.   Tel: 91-44-6942-4344   Emp: N/A
Bus: *International shipping & forwarding.*   Fax:91-44-6942-4377

    ZUST BACHMEIER OF SWITZERLAND, INC.
    14 East 4th Street, Ste. 607, New York, NY   10012
    CEO: Thomas Graefe, Pres.   Tel: (212) 388-1815   Emp: 35
    Bus: *International freight forwarding.*   Fax:(212) 388-1908   %FO: 100

Taiwan

● **ACER INC.**
156 Min Sheng East Road, Sec.3, 6F, Taipei 105, Taiwan
CEO: Stan Shih, Chrm.   Tel: 866-2-545-5288   Emp: 11000
Bus: *Computers & peripheries.*   Fax:866-2-545-5308

    ACER AMERICA CORP.
    2641 Orchard Parkway, San Jose, CA   95134
    CEO: Max Wu, Pres.   Tel: (408) 432-6200   Emp: N/A
    Bus: *Mfr./sales computers & peripherals.*   Fax:(408) 922-2933   %FO: 100

● **ADI CORP.**
14F No. 1, Section 4, Nan King Road 10569, Taipei, Taiwan, ROC
CEO: James Laio, Pres.   Tel: 886-2-713-3337   Emp: N/A
Bus: *Computer peripherals.*   Fax:886-2-713-6555

    ADI SYSTEMS INC.
    2115 Ringwood Avenue, San Jose, CA   95131
    CEO: Steven Liu, Pres.   Tel: (408) 944-0100   Emp: 60
    Bus: *Mfr./sales display monitors.*   Fax:(408) 944-0300   %FO: 100

● **BANK OF TAIWAN**
120 Chungking South Road Section I, P.O. Box 305, Taipei 1100, Taiwan
CEO: C.T. Lo, Chrm.   Tel: 886-2-349-3456   Emp: N/A
Bus: *Commercial banking services.*   Fax:886-2-381-4139

    BANK OF TAIWAN
    1 World Trade Center, Ste.5323, New York, NY   10048
    CEO: K.C. Wang, Gen. Mgr.   Tel: (212) 938-3470   Emp: N/A
    Bus: *International banking services.*   Fax:(212) 775-9026   %FO: 100

● **CHANG HWA COMMERCIAL BANK, LTD.**
38 Tsu Yu Road, Sec.2, Taichung, Taiwan
CEO: Mou Hsing Tsai, Chrm.   Tel: 886-4-222-2001   Emp: 6356
Bus: *Commercial, savings, trust & international banking*   Fax:N/A
    services.

    CHANG HWA COMMERCIAL BANK - L. A. Branch
    Wells Fargo Ctr. 1, 6th Fl.,
    333 S. Grand Ave., Los Angeles, CA   90071
    CEO: Hao-Yung Cheng, SVP & Gen. Mgr.   Tel: (213) 620-7200   Emp: 26
    Bus: *Bank branch operations, lending & treasury*   Fax:(213) 620-7227   %FO: 100
    services.

CHANG HWA COMMERCIAL BANK - N. Y. Branch
1 World Trade Center, Suite 3211, New York, NY   10048
CEO: Wan Tu Yeh, VP & Gen. Mgr.   Tel: (212) 390-7040   Emp: 21
Bus: *Bank branch operations, lending & treasury*   Fax:(212) 390-0120   %FO: 100
services.

● **CHINA AIRLINES**
131 Nanking Road East, Sec 3, Taipei, Taiwan, ROC
CEO: C.F.Fu, Pres.   Tel: 886-2-715-2626   Emp: 8152
Bus: *Commercial air transport services.*   Fax:N/A

CHINA AIRLINES
6053 West Century Blvd, Ste. 800, Los Angeles, CA   90045
CEO: T.S.Chang, CEO   Tel: (310) 641-8888   Emp: 30
Bus: *Commercial airline services.*   Fax:(310) 641-0864   %FO: 100

CHINA AIRLINES
630 Fifth Ave., #1468, New York, NY   10111
CEO: Jerry Chou, Pres   Tel: (212) 399-7870   Emp: 32
Bus: *Commercial airline services.*   Fax:(212) 399-7873   %FO: 100

● **CHINA STEEL CORPORATION**
Lin Hai Industrial District, Taipei, Taiwan, ROC
CEO: T.H. Fu, Pres.   Tel: 886-7-802-1111   Emp: N/A
Bus: *Scrap metal, mfr. steel bars.*   Fax:886-7-802-2511

CHINA STEEL CORP
1 World Trade Center, #2273, New York, NY   10048
CEO: Peter Pan, CEO   Tel: (212) 775-1088   Emp: N/A
Bus: *Mfr./sale steel bars & scrap.*   Fax: %FO: 100

● **CHINESE PETROLEUM CORP.**
83 Chung Hwa Road, Section 1, Taipei 10031, Taiwan
CEO: W.Y. Pan, CEO   Tel: 886-2-361-0221   Emp: N/A
Bus: *Petroleum exploration & refining.*   Fax:886-2-331-9645

OPICOIL SERVICE INC.
1 World Trade Center, Suite 3861, New York, NY   10048-0279
CEO: E. L. Chen   Tel: (212) 755-1098   Emp: N/A
Bus: *Petroleum marketing services.*   Fax:(212) 775-7272   %FO: 100

- **EVERGREEN MARINE CORPORATION (TAIWAN) LTD.**

166 Minsheng East Road, Sec 2, Taipei 10444, Taiwan

CEO: Sun-san Lin, Chrm.   Tel: 886-2-505-7766   Emp: 1300

Bus: *International shipping, air cargo,*   Fax:886-2-505-5255

> **EVERGREEN AMERICA CORP. (EVA)**
>
> One Evertrust Plaza, Jersey City, NJ 07302
>
> CEO: Maecel Chang, Pres.   Tel: (201) 915-3200   Emp: N/A
>
> Bus: *International commercial shipping & air cargo* Fax:(201) 915-3898   %FO: 100
> *and transport - US, Canada & Caribbean*
> *operations..*

- **FIRST COMMERCIAL BANK**

30 Chungking Road, Section #1, Taipei, Taiwan

CEO: Vincent Tzu-Chain Chen, Gen. Mgr.   Tel: 886-2-311-1111   Emp: N/A

Bus: *General banking services.*   Fax:886-2-331-6962

> **FIRST COMMERCIAL BANK - New York Branch**
>
> 2 World Trade Center, Ste. 7868, New York, NY 10048
>
> CEO: Vincent Tzu-Chain Chen, Gen. Mgr.   Tel: (212) 432-6590   Emp: 25
>
> Bus: *General banking services.*   Fax:(212) 432-7250   %FO: 100
>
> **FIRST COMMERCIAL BANK - Los Angeles Branch**
>
> 515 South Flower Street, Los Angeles, CA 90071
>
> CEO: Mr. Lu   Tel: (213) 362-0200   Emp: 20
>
> Bus: *General banking services.*   Fax:(213) 362-0244   %FO: 100

- **FORMOSA PLASTICS CORPORATION**

201 Tun Hwa North Road, Taipei, Taiwan

CEO: Chinshu Wang, Pres.   Tel: 886-2-712-2211   Emp: 3585

Bus: *Mfr. PVC leather, sheeting, polyester fiber, copper* Fax:886-2-717-5287
clad laminates, PVC pipe fitting, plate, engineering
plastics.

> **FORMOSA PLASTICS CORP. U.S.A.**
>
> 9 Peach Tree Hill Road, Livingston, NJ 07039
>
> CEO: Susan Wang, Pres.   Tel: (201) 992-2090   Emp: 700
>
> Bus: *Mfr. PVC rigid & flexible sheeting, polyester* Fax:(201) 992-9627   %FO: 100
> *fiber, ethylene glycol.*

- **HUA NAN COMMERCIAL BANK LTD.**

#38 Section One, Chung King South Road, Taipei, Taiwan

CEO: N/A   Tel: 886-2-371-3111   Emp: N/A

Bus: *Commercial banking services.*   Fax:886-2-382-1060

> **HUA NAN COMMERCIAL BANK LTD.**
>
> 2 World Trade Center, New York, NY 10048
>
> CEO: Cheng Fu Lee, Gen.Mgr.   Tel: (212) 488-2330   Emp: 14
>
> Bus: *Commercial banking services.*   Fax:(212) 912-1050   %FO: 100

- **THE INTERNATIONAL COMMERCIAL BANK OF CHINA**
100 Chi-Lin Road, Taipei, Taiwan
CEO: P.Y. Pai, Chrm.   Tel: 886-2-563-3156   Emp: 2500
Bus: *Commercial banking services.*   Fax:886-2-563-2614

    THE INTERNATIONAL COMMERCIAL BANK OF CHINA
    445 S. Figueroa Street, Ste. 1900, Los Angeles, CA   90071
    CEO: N/A   Tel: (213) 489-3000   Emp: 25
    Bus: *Commercial banking services.*   Fax:(213) 489-1183   %FO: 100

    THE INTERNATIONAL COMMERCIAL BANK OF CHINA
    65 Liberty Street, New York, NY   10005
    CEO: Wen Long Lin, SVP Gen.Mgr.   Tel: (212) 608-4222   Emp: 60+
    Bus: *Commercial banking services.*   Fax:(212) 608-4943   %FO: 100

    THE INTERNATIONAL COMMERCIAL BANK OF CHINA
    2 North Lasalle Street, Ste 1803, Chicago, IL   60602
    CEO: N/A   Tel: (312) 782-8035   Emp: 25
    Bus: *Commercial banking services.*   Fax:(312) 782-2402   %FO: 100

- **NAN YA PLASTICS CORPORATION**
201 Tun Hwa North Road, Taipei, Taiwan
CEO: Y.C. Wang, Chrm.   Tel: 886-2-712-2211   Emp: N/A
Bus: *Mfr. plastics, PVC leather, sheeting, & pipe;*   Fax:886-2-717-8533
polyester fibers, laminates, plate & engineering
plastics. (Sub of Formosa Plastics Corp.)

    NAY YA PLASTICS CORP., AMERICA
    Nine Peachtree Hill Road, Livingston, NJ   07039
    CEO: C.J. Wu, Pres.   Tel: (201) 716-7488   Emp: N/A
    Bus: *Mfr. plastics; PVC sheeting, polyester fibers.*   Fax:(201) 716-7470   %FO: 100

- **RET-SER ENGINEERING AGENCY**
207 Sung Chiang Road, Taipei, Taiwan, ROC
CEO: Y.Y. Tseng, Pres.   Tel: 886-2-503-2233   Emp: 13440
Bus: *Construction.*   Fax:886-2-5032068

    RSEA INTERNATIONAL (USA) INC.
    3490 Shallowford Road, Suite 301, Chamblee, GA   300341
    CEO: Yu Chang An, VP   Tel: (404) 452-7899   Emp: N/A
    Bus: *Procurement services.*   Fax:(404) 452-7998   %FO: 100

    RSEA INTERNATIONAL (USA) INC.
    509 Madison Ave, #806, New York, NY   10022
    CEO: Yu Chang An, VP   Tel: (212) 980-8800   Emp: 5
    Bus: *Procurement services.*   Fax:(212) 223-5185   %FO: 100

● **UNITED WORLD CHINESE COMMERCIAL BANK**
65 Kuan-Chien Road, Taipei, Taiwan
CEO: N/A   Tel: 886-2-312-5555   Emp: N/A
Bus: *Commercial banking services.*   Fax:886-2-21378

UNITED WORLD CHINESE COMMERCIAL BANK
555 West Fifth Street, Suite 3850, Los Angeles, CA   90013
CEO: Shihchen Joseph Jao, Gen. Mgr.   Tel: (213) 243-1234   Emp: 18
Bus: *International banking services.*   Fax:(213) 627-6817   %FO: 100

Thailand

- **BANGKOK BANK PUBLIC COMPANY**
  333 Silom Road, Bangkok 10500, Thailand
  CEO: Chartsiri Sophonpanich, Pres.   Tel: 66-2-231-4333   Emp: N/A
  Bus: *Banking services.*   Fax:66-2-231-4742

  > **BANGKOK BANK PUBLIC COMPANY**
  > 801 Figueroa Street, Suite 1600, Los Angeles, CA   90017
  > CEO: Piyaratana Condron, AVP & Mgr.   Tel: (213) 488-9170   Emp: N/A
  > Bus: *General banking services.*   Fax:(213) 629-1863   %FO: 100

  > **BANGKOK BANK PUBLIC COMPANY**
  > 29 Broadway, 20th Floor, New York, NY   10006
  > CEO: Chalit Phaphan, VP & Mgr.   Tel: (212) 422-8200   Emp: 40
  > Bus: *General banking services.*   Fax:(212) 422-0728   %FO: 100

- **BANK OF THAILAND**
  273 Samsen Road, Bankhunprom, P.O. Box 154, 10200 Bangkok, Thailand
  CEO: Rerngchai Marakanond, Governor   Tel: 66-2-283-5353   Emp: N/A
  Bus: *Government, Central Bank of Thailand.*   Fax:66-2-280-0449

  > **BANK OF THAILAND**
  > 40 East 52nd Street, New York, NY   10017
  > CEO: Aroonsri Tivakul, CEO   Tel: (212) 750-0310   Emp: 10
  > Bus: *Central Bank of Thailand.*   Fax:(212) 223-7454   %FO: 100

- **KRUNG THAI BANK**
  35 Sukhumvit Road, Bangkok 10110, Thailand
  CEO: Sirin Nimmanachaeminda, Pres.   Tel: 66-2-255-2222   Emp: NA
  Bus: *Commercial banking services.*   Fax:66-2-253-2940

  > **KRUNG THAI BANK - Los Angeles Branch**
  > 707 Wilshire Boulevard, Ste. 3150, Los Angeles, CA   90017
  > CEO: Viruch Wongnirung, SVP   Tel: (212) 488-9897   Emp: 15
  > Bus: *International commercial banking.*   Fax:(213) 891-0734   %FO: 100

  > **KRUNG THAI BANK - New York Branch**
  > 415 Madison Avenue, 8th Fl., New York, NY   10017
  > CEO: Pannipa Apichatabutra, SVP & Gen. Mgr.   Tel: (212) 832-5600   Emp: 10
  > Bus: *International commercial banking.*   Fax:(212) 832-5993   %FO: 100

● **SAHA-UNION CORP. LTD.**
1828 Sukhumvit Rd, Soi 58, 10250 Bangkok, Thailand
CEO: Damri Darakananda, Exec.Chrm.　　Tel: 66-2-3115111　　Emp: 20000
Bus: *Distributor textile products, exploration fabrics,*　　Fax:66-2-3315668
garment accessories, footwear, plastics, etc.

　　SAHA-UNION INTL (USA) INC
　　419 Allan St, Daly City, CA　94014
　　CEO: Ong-Arj Kriengkripetch, Pres　　Tel: (415) 467-5330　　Emp: N/A
　　Bus: *Mfr. textiles, sewing threads.*　　Fax:(415) 239-2625　　%FO: 100

● **SIAM CEMENT GROUP**
1 Siam Cement Road, Bangkok, 10800, Thailand
CEO: Chumpol NaLamlieng, Pres.　　Tel: 66-2-586-3333　　Emp: 35000
Bus: *Commercial & industrial conglomerate:*　　Fax:66-2-587-2199
cement/construction materials.; iron/steel;
ceramics; metal/electric; tire/auto access

　　TILECERA, INC.
　　300 Arcata Boulevard, Clarksville, TN　37040
　　CEO: Prayong Hirunyawanich, Pres.　　Tel: (615) 645-5100　　Emp: 450
　　Bus: *Manufacturer of ceramic tile.*　　Fax:(615) 647-9934　　%FO: 100

● **SIAM COMMERCIAL BANK PLC**
9 Rutchadatick Road, Ladyao, Jatujak 10900, Thailand
CEO: Olarn Chaipravat, Pres.　　Tel: 66-544-1111　　Emp: N/A
Bus: *Commercial banking services.*　　Fax:66-937-7777

　　SIAM COMMERCIAL BANK PLC- New York Agency
　　One Exchange Place - 8th Floor, New York, NY　10006
　　CEO: Chulatip Nitibhon, Mgr.　　Tel: (212) 344-4101　　Emp: 25
　　Bus: *International banking services.*　　Fax:(212) 747-0106　　%FO: 100

　　SIAM COMMERCIAL BANK PLC
　　601 S. Figueroa Street, Ste.3575, Los Angeles, CA　90017
　　CEO: Ms.Paspun Suwanchinda, Mgr.　　Tel: (213) 614-1805　　Emp: 20
　　Bus: *International banking services.*　　Fax:(213) 622-0049　　%FO: 100

● **THAI AIRWAYS INTERNATIONAL**
89 Vibhavadi Rangsit Road, Bangkok 10900, Thailand
CEO: Thamnoon Wanglee, CEO　　Tel: 66-2-513-0120　　Emp: N/A
Bus: *Commercial air transport services.*　　Fax:66-2-513-3398

　　THAI AIRWAYS INTERNATIONAL
　　630 Fifth Avenue, Suite 351, New York, NY　10111
　　CEO: Prin Yooprasert, Gen.Mgr.　　Tel: (212) 265-6021　　Emp: 150
　　Bus: *International commercial air transport.*　　Fax:(212) 644-9351　　%FO: 100

- **THAI FARMERS BANK LTD.**
400 Phahon Yothin Avenue, Bangkok, Thailand
CEO: Banyong Lamsam, Chrm.   Tel: 66-2-273-1199   Emp: N/A
Bus: *Commercial banking services.*   Fax:66-2-470-1144-5

 THAI FARMERS BANK LTD.
 333 South South Grand Avenue
 Suite 3570, Los Angeles, CA   90070
 CEO: Vichai Luengluepunya, Gen.Mgr.   Tel: (213) 680-9331   Emp: 17
 Bus: *International banking services.*   Fax:(213) 620-9362   %FO: 100

 THAI FARMERS BANK LTD.
 1 World Trade Center, Ste. 8373, New York, NY   10048
 CEO: Vasant Charlyatantiwate, VP & Mgr.   Tel: (212) 432-0890   Emp: 17
 Bus: *International banking services.*   Fax:(212) 524-0494   %FO: 100

- **TOUR ROYALE AIR CARGO CO LTD.**
1561-7 New Letchbuir Rd, Bangkok, Thailand
CEO: S Chatapasorn, Pres.   Tel: N/A   Emp: N/A
Bus: *Freight forwarding services.*   Fax:N/A

 AIRTRADE EXPRESS INC
 8939 South Sepulveda, Los Angeles, CA   90045
 CEO: Boon Keerikoolparn, Pres.   Tel: (310) 670-8141   Emp: N/A
 Bus: *Freight forwarding services.*   Fax:(310) 337-0066   %FO: 100

Turkey

- **HACI ÖMER SABANCI HOLDING A.S.**
  Sabanci Center, 80745 Istanbul, Turkey
  CEO: Sakip Sabanci, Chrm.   Tel: 90-212-281-6600   Emp: N/A
  Bus: *Financial services; banking, insurance.*   Fax:90-212-281-0272

  ### HOLSA INC.
  650 Fifth Avenue, 16th Floor, New York, NY   10019
  CEO: Halit Ozbelli, Gen. Mgr.   Tel: (212) 307-6522   Emp: 4
  Bus: *Financial services; banking, insurance.*   Fax:(212) 307-6710   %FO: 100

- **KOÇ HOLDING A.S.**
  Nakkastepe, Azizbey Sokak No.1, 81207 Istanbul, Turkey
  CEO: Inan Kirac, CEO   Tel: 90-216-341-4650   Emp: N/A
  Bus: *Holding company; automotive, consumer goods,*   Fax:90-216-343-1944
  financial, tourism and energy industry services.

  ### RAMERICA INTERNATIONAL, INC.
  Empire State Bldg., 350 5th Ave., #4721, New York, NY   10118
  CEO: Feyzi Celik, Gen. Mgr.   Tel: (212) 971-9100   Emp: 6
  Bus: *US representative: automotive & consumer*   Fax:(212) 736-4958   %FO: 100
  goods, financial, tourism and energy industry
  services.

- **T.C. ZIRAAT BANKASI**
  Ankara, Turkey
  CEO: Sait Sozen, Pres.   Tel: 90-312-557-5612   Emp: N/A
  Bus: *General banking services.*   Fax:90-312-490-8076

  ### T.C. ZIRAAT BANKASI
  330 Madison Avenue, 32nd Floor, New York, NY   10017
  CEO: Sail Sozen, Senior Officer   Tel: (212) 557-5612   Emp: 4
  Bus: *International banking services.*   Fax:(212) 491-8076   %FO: 100

- **TURK HAVA YOLLARI AO**
  Ataturk Intl Airport, Yesilkoy, 34834 Istanbul, Turkey
  CEO: Raha Pakkan, Dir.   Tel: 90-212-663-6300   Emp: 10000
  Bus: *International commercial air transport services.*   Fax:90-212-663-4744

  ### TURKISH AIRLINES
  437 Madison Ave, #17B, New York, NY   10022
  CEO: Raha Pakkan, Dir   Tel: (212) 339-9650   Emp: 35
  Bus: *International commercial air transport*   Fax:(212) 339-9683   %FO: 99
  services.

- **TURKIYE CUMHURIYET MERKEZ BANKASI**
Istiklal Caddeis, NO.10, 06100 Ankara, Turkey
CEO: Gazi Ercel, Governor   Tel: 90-312-310-3646   Emp: N/A
Bus: *Central banking institution of Turkey; issues*   Fax:90-312-310-7434
       currency, sets monetary policy.

CENTRAL BANK OF TURKEY
821 United Nations Plaza, 7th Fl., New York, NY   10017
CEO: Ms. Perihan Ucer, Chief Rep.   Tel: (212) 682-8717   Emp: 4
Bus: *Central banking institution of Turkey.*   Fax:(212) 867-1958   %FO: 100

United Arab Emirates

● **EMIRATES AIR**
Dubai International Airport, Dubai, United Arab Emirates
CEO: H.H. Sheikh Ahmed Bin Saeed Al Maktoum, CEO   Tel: 97-1-421-5544   Emp: 3400
Bus: *Commercial air transport services.*   Fax:97-1-423-9817

    EMIRATES AIR
    405 Park Avenue, Suite 403, New York, NY   10022
    CEO: James Baxter, VP North America   Tel: (212) 758-4252   Emp: 26
    Bus: *International commercial air transport*   Fax:(212) 758-4434   %FO: 100
       services.

● **MASHREQ BANK PSC**
P.O.Box 1250, Deira, Dubai, United Arab Emirates
CEO: Mr. Azhar   Tel: 97-4-229131   Emp: N/A
Bus: *Commercial banking services.*   Fax:N/A

    MASHREQ BANK PSC.
    255 Fifth Avenue, First Floor, New York, NY   10016
    CEO: Shariq Azhar, Gen.Mgr.   Tel: (212) 545-8200   Emp: 32
    Bus: *Commercial banking services.*   Fax:(212) 545-0919   %FO: 100

● **NATIONAL BANK OF ABU DHABI**
Khalidiya Office Bldg., P.O. Box 4, Abu Dhabi, United Arab Emirates
CEO: John Symonds, CEO   Tel: 97-1-345-777   Emp: N/A
Bus: *Commercial banking services.*   Fax:97-1-336-078

    ABU DHABI INTERNATIONAL BANK INC.
    1020 19th Street NW, Suite 500, Washington, DC   20036
    CEO: Michael L. Young, Mng. Dir. & EVP   Tel: (202) 842-7900   Emp: 22
    Bus: *International commercial banking services.*   Fax:(202) 842-7955   %FO: 100

Uruguay

- **BANCO DE LA REPUBLICA ORIENTAL DEL URUGUAY**
Cerrito Ye Zabala, Montevideo, Uruguay
CEO: Cesar Batlle, Chrm. & CEO   Tel: 598-2-95-0205   Emp: N/A
Bus: *General banking services.*   Fax:598-2-95-1522

  ### BANCO DE LA REPUBLICA ORIENTAL DEL URUGUAY
  1270 Avenue of the Americas, Suite 3001, New York, NY   10020
  CEO: Walter Calcagno, SVP & Gen. Mgr.   Tel: (212) 307-9600   Emp: 25
  Bus: *International commercial banking services.*   Fax:(212) 307-6786   %FO: 100

757

Venezuela

- **AEROVIAS VENEZOLANAS SA**
Torre Humbolt, Av. Rio Cacro, Caracas, Venezuela
CEO: Henry Lord Boulton, Pres   Tel: 58-2-907-82-000   Emp: 2700
Bus: *Commercial air transport carrier.*   Fax:58-2-907-8027

  AVENSA AIRLINES
  645 Fifth Avenue, East Wing, New York, NY   10022
  CEO: Tony Lutz, Gen.Mgr.   Tel: (212) 644-0455   Emp: N/A
  Bus: *International commercial air transport carrier.*   Fax:(212) 644-4931   %FO: 100

  AVENSA AIRLINES
  JFK International Airport, West Wing, Building #52,, Jamaica, NY   11430
  CEO: Irene Sanchez, Mgr.   Tel: (718) 244-6857   Emp: N/A
  Bus: *International commercial air transport carrier.*   Fax: %FO: 100

- **BANCO CONSOLIDADO CA**
Torre Consolidada, Avda Principal la Castellana, Plaza La Castellana, Caracas, Venezuela
CEO: Jose Alvarez Stelling, Pres.   Tel: 58-2-206-3124   Emp: 4500
Bus: *Commercial banking services.*   Fax:N/A

  BANCO CONSOLIDADO
  845 Third Avenue, 5th Fl., New York, NY   10022
  CEO: Carlos A. Romero, Gen. Mgr.   Tel: (212) 980-1770   Emp: 45
  Bus: *International commercial banking services.*   Fax:(212) 644-9809   %FO: 100

- **BANCO DE VENEZUELA SA**
Edif Banco de Venezuela, Avda Universidad, Esq Sociedad, Caracas, Venezuela
CEO: Enrique Neira, Mgr.   Tel: 58-2-501-3333   Emp: N/A
Bus: *Commercial banking services.*   Fax:58-2-501-2546

  BANCO DE VENEZUELA
  450 Park Ave., New York, NY   10022
  CEO: Marinita Riviera, Mgr   Tel: (212) 980-0350   Emp: N/A
  Bus: *International commercial banking services.*   Fax:(212) 793-3948   %FO: 100

  BANCO DE VENEZUELA INTL
  800 Brickell Ave., Miami, FL   33131
  CEO: Santos Coello, Pres.   Tel: (305) 374-0999   Emp: N/A
  Bus: *International commercial banking services.*   Fax:(305) 374-3387   %FO: 100

● **BANCO INDUSTRIAL DE VENEZUELA**
Edif Maio P B, Avda Prin de Sabana Grande, Caracas, Venezuela
CEO: N/A   Tel: N/A   Emp: N/A
Bus: *Commercial banking services.*   Fax:58-2-952-7048

> **BANCO INDUSTRIAL DE VENEZUELA**
> 900 Third Avenue, Suite 1400, New York, NY   10022
> CEO: Mario Caires, Gen.Mgr.   Tel: (212) 688-2200   Emp: N/A
> Bus: *International banking services.*   Fax:(212) 888-4921   %FO: 100

● **BANCO MERCANTIL CA, SACA**
P.O.Box 789, Avda. Andres Bello 1, Caracas, Venezuela
CEO: Gustavo A. Marturet, Chrm.   Tel: 58-2-503-1204   Emp: N/A
Bus: *Commercial banking services.*   Fax:58-2-503-1391

> **BANCO MERCANTIL**
> 2199 Ponce de Leon Boulevard, Coral Gables, FL   33134
> CEO: Alberto Gonzalez, Gen. Mgr.   Tel: (305) 460-8500   Emp: N/A
> Bus: *Banking agency.*   Fax:(305) 460-8595   %FO: 100

> **BANCO MERCANTIL**
> 11 East 51st Street, New York, NY   10022
> CEO: Fabio R. Fernandez, Gen. Mgr.   Tel: (212) 891-7400   Emp: 19
> Bus: *Bank agency.*   Fax:(212) 891-7411   %FO: 100

● **BANCO UNION SACA**
Aptdo Postal 2044, Torre Banco Union, Caracas 1010, Venezuela
CEO: Ignacio Salvatiera, Pres.   Tel: 58-2-501-7111   Emp: N/A
Bus: *International banking services.*   Fax:N/A

> **BANCO UNION DE VENEZUELA**
> 1000 Brickell Avenue, Suite 1100, Miami, FL   33131
> CEO: Jose D. Carrillo, Reg. VP   Tel: (305) 374-6611   Emp: N/A
> Bus: *International banking services.*   Fax:(305) 358-2144   %FO: 100

> **BANCO UNION DE VENEZUELA**
> 609 Fifth Avenue, New York, NY   10017
> CEO: Alfredo Gonzalez-Rubio, Reg. VP   Tel: (212) 735-1500   Emp: N/A
> Bus: *International banking services.*   Fax:(212) 735-1528   %FO: 100

● **COMPANIA DE ELECTRICIDAD DE CARACAS**
Aptdo Postal 2299, Caracas, Venezuela
CEO: Francisco Aguerreberi, Pres.   Tel: 58-2-574 9111   Emp: N/A
Bus: *Energy industry machinery & services.*   Fax:58-2-576 4330

> **TRANSAMERICAN TRADING CORP.**
> 3 School Street, Glen Cove, NY   11542
> CEO: Franf Storment, Pres.   Tel: (516) 676-3250   Emp: N/A
> Bus: *Energy industry machinery & services.* Fax:(516) 676-4919   %FO: 100

● **PETRÓLEOS DE VENEZUELA SA (PDVSA)**

Edif Petróleos de Venezuela, Avda Libertador   Apartado #169, La Campina, Caracas 1010-A,
Venezuela

CEO: Luis E. Giusti, Pres.   Tel: 58-2-7084111   Emp: 45000

Bus: *Exploration, production, distribution oil,*   Fax: N/A
petrochemicals & coal.

BITOR AMERICA, INC.

5100 Town Center Circle, Suite. 450, Boca Raton, FL   33486

CEO: Juan J. Pulgar, Pres.   Tel: (561) 392-0026   Emp: 8

Bus: *US sub of PETRÓLEOS DE VENEZUELA SA.*   Fax: (561) 392-0490   %FO: 100

CITGO PETROLEUM CORP

P. O. Box 3758, One Warren Place, Tulsa, OK   74102

CEO: David Tippeconnic, Pres. & CEO   Tel: (918) 495-4000   Emp: 1500

Bus: *Oil refining & marketing.*   Fax: (918) 495-4511   %FO: 100

PDVSA SERVICES, INC.

11490 Westheimer, Ste. 1000, Houston, TX   77077

CEO: Johann Litwinenko, Gen. Mgr.   Tel: (281) 531-0004   Emp: N/A

Bus: *Petroleum information systems & services.*   Fax: (281) 588-6290   %FO: 100

PETROLEOS DE VENEZUELA (PDV) AMERICA INC.

750 Lexington Avenue, New York, NY   10022

CEO: Alonso Velasco, Pres.   Tel: (212) 339-7770   Emp: 8

Bus: *US headquarters. Petroleum information*   Fax: (212) 339-7727   %FO: 100
systems & services.

ALPHABETICAL
LISTING
OF FOREIGN FIRMS

Part Two is an alphabetical listing of all the foreign firms in Part One, giving the name and country in which it is located, and the number of the page where the complete listing can be found in Part One.

BANQUE SCANDINAVE EN SUISSE (Switzerland) 709

BANQUE SUDAMERIS (sub of Banca Commerciale Italiana Group) (France) 230

BANQUE WORMS (France) 230

BARALAN INTL S.p.A. (Italy) 399

BARCLAYS BANK PLC (England) 123

BARCO INDUSTRIES, NV. (Belgium) 23

BARMAG AG (Germany) 277

BARRICK GOLD CORPORATION (Canada) 54

BASF AG (Germany) 277

BASS PLC (England) 124

BATTENFELD MASCHINEN-FABRIKEN GMBH (Germany) 278

CHRISTIAN BAUER GMBH & CO. (Germany) 279

BAUMANN + CIE AG (Switzerland) 710

BAYER AG (Germany) 279

BAYERISCHE LANDESBANK GIROZENTRALE (Germany) 281

BAYERISCHE MOTOREN WERKE AG (BMW AG) (Germany) 281

BAYERISCHE VEREINSBANK AG (Germany) 281

BBA GROUP, PLC. (England) 124

BCD HOLDINGS N.V. (Netherlands) 576

BDDP GROUPE (France) 230

BECKER GMBH (Germany) 282

BEHR GMBH & CO. (Germany) 282

BEIERSDORF AG (Germany) 282

BEITEN BURKHARDT MITTL & WEGENER (Germany) 283

NV BEKAERT SA (Belgium) 23

BELGACOM (Belgium) 24

BENETEAU SA (France) 231

BENETTON GROUP, S.p.A. (Italy) 399

BENTALL DEVELOPMENT COMPANY INC. (Canada) 54

BENTELER AG (Germany) 283

BERGEN DIESEL AS (Norway) 618

BERGES ANGRIEBSTECHNIK GMBH & CO. FG (Germany) 283

THE BERISFORD GROUP (England) 125

BERLINER HANDELS-UND FRANKFURTER BANK (BHF BANK) (Germany) 283

BERMANS (England) 125

BERMARMOL SA (Spain) 652

BERMUDA DEPARTMENT OF TOURISM (Bermuda) 32

BERNA AG (Switzerland) 710

BERNDORF BAND G.m.b.H. (Austria) 17

BERTELSMANN AG (Germany) 284

BESAM AB (Sweden) 665

BESNIER SA (France) 231

BESPAK PLC (England) 125

BEVAN FUNNELL, LTD. (England) 126

BFII, SUDAMERIS (Brazil) 41

BHARAT ELECTRONICS LTD. (India) 374

BHK-HOLZU KUNSTSTOFF KG (Germany) 285

SOCIÉTÉ BIC S.A. (France) 231

BICC PLC (England) 126

BIESSE S.p.A. (Italy) 399

BILFINGER + BERGER (Germany) 285

BILSPEDITION TRANSPORT & LOGISTICS (BTL) AB (Sweden) 665

BINDOMATIC AB (Sweden) 666

BLUE CIRCLE INDUSTRIES PLC (England) 126

BLYDENSTEIN-WILLINK N.V. (Netherlands) 576

BM & F - BOLSA DE MERCADORIAS E FUTUROS (Brazil) 42

BOBST S.A. (Switzerland) 710

THE BOC GROUP INC (England) 126

BODA NOVA INTL AB (Sweden) 666

THE BODY SHOP INTERNATIONAL PLC (England) 127

BOIRON (France) 231

BOMBARDIER INC. (Canada) 54

BONDIOLI & PAVESI S.p.A. (Italy) 400

BONEHAM & TURNER LTD. (England) 127

THE BOOTS COMPANY PLC. (England) 127

BORAL LIMITED (Australia) 7

C

D

E

G

I

J

L

M

N

O

P

S

U

V

ALPHABETICAL
LISTING
OF AMERICAN
AFFILIATES

Part Three is an alphabetical listing of all the American affiliates in Part One, giving the name, and the country where its foreign parent or investor is located, and the number of the page where the complete listing can be found in Part One.

B

C

E

FERAG INC. (Switzerland) 727

FERMENTA ANIMAL HEALTH (Sweden) 675

FERMER INTERNATIONAL FINANCE
CORPORATION (Brazil) 43

FERODO AMERICA, INC. (England) 194

FERRARI NORTH AMERICA, INC. (Italy) 404

FERRERO USA INC. (Italy) 403

FFV AEROTECH INC. (Sweden) 668

FGH REALTY CREDIT CORP. (Netherlands) 583

FGH USA INC. (Netherlands) 583

FIAT AUTO R&D U.S.A., INC. (Italy) 404

FIAT AVIO, INC. (Italy) 404

FIAT U.S.A, INC. (Italy) 404

FIATALLIS NORTH AMERICA, INC. (Italy) 405

FIBRA SECURITIES INC. (Brazil) 39

FIBRES INTL INC. (Canada) 72

FICHTEL & SACHS INDUSTRIES INC. (Germany) 327

FIDELITY AND DEPOSIT COMPANY OF
MARYLAND (Switzerland) 742

FILA FOOTWEAR U.S.A., INC. (Italy) 406

FIMAT FUTURES USA INC (France) 264

FINA INC. (Belgium) 28

FINCKH MACHINERY CORPORATION (Germany)
311

FINDLEY ADHESIVES, INC. (France) 244

FINNAIR (Finland) 212

FIORUCCI FOODS INC (Italy) 406

FIREMAN'S FUND INSURANCE COMPANY
(Germany) 275

FIREMAN'S FUND INSURANCE (Germany) 276

FIRESTONE BUILDING PRODUCTS CO. (Japan) 422

FIREYE, INC. (England) 206

FIRST BANK OF THE AMERICAS (Colombia) 98

FIRST COMMERCIAL BANK - Los Angeles Branch
(Taiwan) 747

FIRST COMMERCIAL BANK - New York Branch
(Taiwan) 747

FIRST FORTIS LIFE INSURANCE CO (Belgium) 26

FIRST FORTIS LIFE INSURANCE COMPANY
(Netherlands) 584

FIRST MARYLAND BANKCORP. (Ireland) 382

FIRST MARYLAND LEASE CORP. (Ireland) 382

FIRST MARYLAND LIFE INSURANCE &
MARKETING CO. (Ireland) 382

FIRST MARYLAND MORTGAGE CORP. (Ireland) 382

FIRST MARYLAND NATIONAL BANK (Ireland) 382

FIRST NATIONAL SUPERMARKETS INC.
(Netherlands) 602

FIRST NATIONAL TRADING, CO., INC. (Hong Kong)
366

FIRST OMNI BANK, N.A. (Ireland) 383

FISHERY PRODUCTS INTERNATIONAL
CLOUSTIN, INC. (Canada) 65

FISKARS MANUFACTURING (Finland) 212

FLEISSNER INC. (Germany) 301

FLETCHER PACIFIC CONSTRUCTION (New
Zealand) 615

FLEXIBLE TECHNOLOGIES INC. (England) 189

FLOMATIC CORP. (France) 265

FLOMATIC CORPORATION (Denmark) 103

FLUID SYSTEMS HI INC. (France) 261

FLUX PUMPS CORP. (Germany) 302

FOKKER SERVICES, INC. (Netherlands) 583

FOLKSAMERICA REINSURANCE CO (Sweden) 675

FOMO PRODUCTS, INC. (Germany) 302

FOOD LION INC. (Belgium) 25

FORBO AMERICA, INC. (Switzerland) 715

FORBO INDUSTRIES INC (Switzerland) 715

FORBO WALLCOVERINGS INC (Switzerland) 715

FORTIS SALES (Belgium) 26

BUCK FORKARDT, INC. (Germany) 302

FORMOSA PLASTICS CORP. U.S.A. (Taiwan) 747

FORSHEDA PIPE SEAL CORP. (Sweden) 675

FORSTER, INC. (Germany) 315

FORTAFIL FIBERS INC (Netherlands) 574

FORTE AND LE MERIDIEN HOTELS & RESORTS
(France) 255

FORTIS ADVISERS INC (Belgium) 26

FORTIS ADVISERS, INC. (Netherlands) 584

FORTIS BENEFITS INSURANCE CO. (Belgium) 26

H

I

M

N

O

Q

R

S

U

W

PART FOUR

PUBLISHER'S NOTES

Related publications

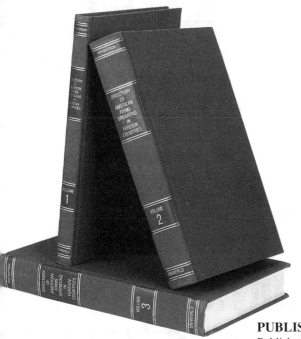

14ᵗʰ Edition

DIRECTORY OF
AMERICAN FIRMS
OPERATING IN
FOREIGN COUNTRIES

PUBLISHED BY UNIWORLD BUSINESS PUBLICATIONS, INC.

Published July 1996 - 15th Edition scheduled Summer/Fall 1998

THREE VOLUMES   PRICE: $220.00
1750 PAGES   ISBN: 0-8360-0041-2

COMPREHENSIVE LISTINGS

- Over **2,500** American Firms
- **18,500** Foreign subsidiaries, affiliates or branches
- **132** Countries

EASY AND FLEXIBLE ACCESS

The firm(s) you are looking for can be found:

- **by name** — US companies listed alphabetically (Volume I)
- **by country** — US companies and their affiliates and branches by foreign country (Volumes II & III)

KEY CONTACT AND LOCATION INFORMATION

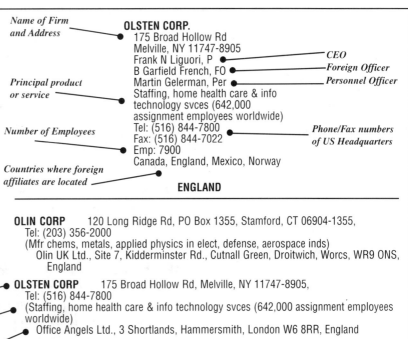

Name of Firm and Address

OLSTEN CORP.
175 Broad Hollow Rd
Melville, NY 11747-8905
Frank N Liguori, P — *CEO*
B Garfield French, FO — *Foreign Officer*
Martin Gelerman, Per — *Personnel Officer*

Principal product or service
Staffing, home health care & info technology svces (642,000 assignment employees worldwide)

Number of Employees
Tel: (516) 844-7800 — *Phone/Fax numbers of US Headquarters*
Fax: (516) 844-7022
Emp: 7900

Countries where foreign affiliates are located
Canada, England, Mexico, Norway

ENGLAND

OLIN CORP   120 Long Ridge Rd, PO Box 1355, Stamford, CT 06904-1355,
Tel: (203) 356-2000
(Mfr chems, metals, applied physics in elect, defense, aerospace inds)
Olin UK Ltd., Site 7, Kidderminster Rd., Cutnall Green, Droitwich, Worcs, WR9 ONS, England

Name of firm and address in US
OLSTEN CORP   175 Broad Hollow Rd, Melville, NY 11747-8905,
Tel: (516) 844-7800
Principal product or service
(Staffing, home health care & info technology svces (642,000 assignment employees worldwide)
Name and address of subsidiary, affiliate or branch
Office Angels Ltd., 3 Shortlands, Hammersmith, London W6 8RR, England

ON-LINE SOFTWARE INTL INC   2 Executive Dr, Fort Lee, NJ 07024,
Tel: (201) 592-0009
(Software & related servs; consult & educ servs)
On-Line Software (UK) Ltd., Tenterden House, 3 Tenterden St., Hanover Square, London W1R 9AH, England

9th Edition Directory of
Foreign Firms Operating in the United States

14th Edition Directory of
American Firms Operating in Foreign Countries

Now Available

COUNTRY, REGIONAL, STATE EDITIONS & MAILING LISTS—LABELS

The 9th Edition of the *Directory of Foreign Firms Operating in the United States* and the 14th Edition of *Directory of American Firms Operating in Foreign Countries* now in **Country**, **Regional** or **State** editions. (Softbound)

- **Country and Regional Editions**
  - ~ list the companies alphabetically within each country.

- **State Editions**
  - ~ *Directory of Foreign Firms Operating in the United States*, lists by State the Foreign Firms (alphabetically), at each American Affiliate headquarters location within the state.
  - ~ *Directory of American Firms Operating in Foreign Countries*, lists by State the American firms (alphabetically), at the headquarters location within the state.

- **Mail Lists–Labels**
  - ~ available for all directories, **Country**, **Regional** or the complete **World List:** *Name and American Address of the Parent Company* with a corporate officer: *CEO, International Operations Officer or Human Resources Director* (where available), with telemarketing list.

- **Custom orders**
  - ~ Create your own regions or country groupings to suit your project needs.

  To place an order, please call (212) 496-2448 or send the attached **Order Form** by FAX (212) 769-0413. Orders for Country, Regional, State editions and Mailing lists require pre-payment by credit card, check or money order in U.S. dollars, from a U.S. Bank. All sales are final. Please see reverse side for title and pricing information.

Directory of American Firms Operating in Foreign Countries, 14ᵗʰ Edition Country/Regional Editions Softbound

AFRICA $59.00
Algeria, Angola, Benin, Botswana, Burkina Faso, Burundi, Cameroon, Cent. African Rep., Chad, Congo, Dem. Republic of Congo, Djibouti, Egypt, Ethiopia, Gabon, Gambia, Ghana, Guinea, Ivory Coast, Kenya, Lesotho, Liberia, Libya, Madagascar, Malawi, Mali, Mauritius, Morocco, Mozambique, Namibia, Nigeria, Reunion, Senegal, Seychelles, Sierra Leone, South Africa, Sudan, Swaziland, Tanzania, Tunisia, Uganda, Zambia, Zimbabwe

ASIA $119.00
Bangladesh, Brunei, Cambodia, China, Hong Kong, India, Indonesia, Japan, Korea, Laos, Macau, Malaysia, Mongolia, Myanmar, Nepal, Pakistan, Philippines, Singapore, Sri Lanka, Taiwan, Thailand, Vietnam

South Asia $39.00
Bangladesh, India, Myanmar, Nepal, Pakistan, Sri Lanka

South East Asia $69.00
Brunei, Cambodia, Indonesia, Laos, Malaysia, Philippines, Singapore, Thailand, Vietnam

Japan & Korea $59.00

China Group $79.00
China, Hong Kong, Singapore, Taiwan, Macau

Near & Middle East $49.00
Bahrain, Cyprus, Israel, Jordan, Kuwait, Lebanon, Oman, Qatar, Saudi Arabia, Syria, Turkey, United Arab Emirates, West Bank, Yemen

The Arabic Countries $49.00
Algeria, Bahrain, Egypt, Jordan, Kuwait, Lebanon, Morocco, Oman, Qatar, Saudi Arabia, Sudan, Syria, Tunisia, United Arab Emirates, West Bank, Yemen

Near & Middle East & Arabic Countries Combined $59.00

AUSTRALIA GROUP $59.00
Australia, New Zealand, Fiji, French Polynesia, Guam, New Caledonia, New Guinea, No. Mariana Is., Palau, Papua, Polynesia.

EUROPE Western $159.00
Austria, Belgium, Channel Is., Denmark, England, Finland, France, Germany, Gibraltar, Greece, Iceland, Isle of Man, Ireland, Italy, Liechtenstein, Luxembourg, Madeira, Malta, Monaco, Netherlands, No. Ireland, Norway, Portugal, San Marino, Scotland, Spain, Sweden, Switzerland, Wales

Europe All $169.00

British Isles $89.00
Channel Is. , England, Gibraltar, Ireland, Isle of Man, No. Ireland, Scotland, Wales

EUROPE West. excl. British Is. $139.00
France $59.00
Germany $59.00
Italy $49.00
Netherlands $49.00
Spain $39.00
Sweden $39.00
Switzerland $39.00
Scandinavia (Denmark, Finland, $59.00
Iceland, Norway, Sweden)

EUROPE Eastern $49.00
Albania, Armenia, Azerbaijan, Belarus, Bulgaria, Croatia, Czech Rep., Estonia, Hungary, Kazakhstan, Latvia, Lithuania, Macedonia, Poland, Romania, Russia, Slovakia, Slovenia, Turkmenistan Ukraine, Uzbekistan, Yugoslavia

NORTH AMERICA
Canada $69.00
Mexico $49.00

Caribbean Islands $39.00
Anguilla, Antigua, Aruba, Bahamas, Barbados, Bermuda, Brit. W. Indies, Cayman Is. Dominican Rep., Grenada, Haiti, Jamaica, Neth. Antilles, Trinidad & Tobago, Turks & Caicos

SOUTH AMERICA
Argentina, Bolivia, Brazil, Chile, $79.00
Colombia, Ecuador, Guyana, Paraguay, Peru, Surinam, Uruguay, Venezuela
Argentina $29.00
Brazil $39.00
Argentina, Brazil, Chile $59.00
Venezuela $29.00

CENTRAL AMERICA
Belize, Costa Rica, El Salvador, $39.00
Guatemala, Honduras, Nicaragua, Panama

Directory of Foreign Firms Operating in the United States, 9ᵗʰ Edition Country/Regional Edition Softbound

AFRICA $29.00
Egypt, Ivory Coast, Morocco, Nigeria, South Africa

ASIA $79.00
China, Hong Kong, India, Indonesia, Japan, Korea, Malaysia, Pakistan, Philippines, Singapore, Taiwan, Thailand

Japan & Korea $69.00

China Group $29.00
China, Hong Kong, Singapore, Taiwan

Near & Middle East $39.00
Bahrain, Cyprus, Egypt, Iran, Israel, Jordan, Kuwait, Lebanon, Morocco, Saudi Arabia, Turkey, United Arab Emirates

AUSTRALIA GROUP
Australia, New Zealand $29.00

NORTH AMERICA
Canada, Mexico $39.00

LATIN AMERICA
South/Central America & the Caribbean $39.00
Argentina, Bermuda, Bolivia, Brazil, Chile, Colombia, Costa Rica, Dominican Republic, Guatemala, Mexico, Panama, Paraguay, Peru, Uruguay, Venezuela

EUROPE All $119.00
Austria, Belgium, Czech Republic, Denmark, England, Finland, France, Germany, Greece, Iceland, Ireland, Italy, Luxembourg, Netherlands, Norway, Poland, Portugal, Romania, Russian, Scotland, Slovenia, Spain, Sweden, Switzerland

British Isles $59.00
England, Ireland, Scotland

Europe - excluding the British Isles $109.00
France $39.00
Germany $59.00
Italy $29.00
Scandinavia $49.00
Sweden $39.00
Switzerland $39.00

Uniworld Business Publications, Inc.
257 Central Park West, Suite 10A
New York, New York 10024
Tel: (212) 496-2448
Fax: (212) 769-0413
E-mail: uniworldbp@aol.com
WEBsite: http://www.uniworldbp.com

October 31, 1997
Prices subject to change without notice.